PROTESTANT CHURCH MUSIC
A HISTORY

Also by Friedrich Blume

Classic and Romantic Music
Renaissance and Baroque Music

PROTESTANT CHURCH MUSIC

A HISTORY

by *Friedrich* *Blume*

in collaboration with Ludwig Finscher, Georg Feder,

Adam Adrio, Walter Blankenburg, Torben Schousboe,

Robert Stevenson, and Watkins Shaw

Foreword by Paul Henry Lang

LONDON
VICTOR GOLLANCZ LTD
1975

FIRST EDITION
The major portion originally published in Germany as
GESCHICHTE DER EVANGELISCHEN KIRCHENMUSIK by Friedrich Blume,
© by Bärenreiter-Verlag Karl Vötterle KG 1964
ISBN 0 575 01996 4

Printed in the United States of America

Contents

Foreword

Fanny Burney charmingly remarks in her diary that her aged father, the great music historian, is always "full of spirits, full of manuscripts, and full of proof sheets." The remark is singularly appropriate for another great music historian, Friedrich Blume, the dean of German and international musicology. For the last half century there has scarcely been an important musicological project in which he did not take a leading part, often as its initiator. All the while, he tended his own garden with books and articles, the latter recently gathered into two impressive volumes entitled *Syntagma Musicologicum*. His writings are based on sound scholarship, an unfailing eye for essentials, a great respect for reason, and an attractive turn of mind that can hold together apparently conflicting elements in a strong and subtle design. Every sentence is factual and positive, but the facts notwithstanding, we always see the writer. He is inexorable toward illusions, peels off prejudices, discusses the realities, and all this in a clear and readable style.

Professor Blume's original work, *Die Evangelische Kirchenmusik,* in Bücken's *Handbuch der Musikwissenschaft* (1931), was a pathbreaker in dealing with the history of religious music. But now, with the vast extension of the Lutheran core of the work and the inclusion of the music of other denominations to encompass the entire domain of Protestant church music, no single mind, however well equipped, could cope with the multiplicity of materials. The present greatly enlarged and revised study calls on the collaboration of several outstanding scholars, some of them once Professor Blume's own students, all of them kindred spirits familiar with his principles and beliefs.

There are questions the historian must pose right at the outset, precise, vital, and perplexing questions as to the very nature of sacred music. Distinctions, if indeed they exist, must be drawn between sacred and profane music, and further differences made between sacred and church music, liturgic and non-liturgic music, and so forth. We know that in primitive societies, music is cult; but even in certain stages of our Western history the entire musical life was dominated by cultic considerations. Then again, confession, cult, and rite divide church music into various categories. But wherever we look we see the eventual intrusion of "secular" elements, raising doubt about the specifically "sacred" quality of a texture which can hardly be distinguished from music known as "secular."

The liturgy is both discipline and poesy; it imposes upon the composer certain forms and attitudes. One composition will be liturgic while another will be dramatic-theatrical as each responds to the exigencies of either the church *or* the theater. But what if the composer uses dramatic means to arrive at liturgic ends? We must realize that the liturgy, or even the simple order of service in the low churches, is also a *mise en scène,* and that the Gospel as drama, stark drama, has been an artistic force from the medieval liturgic and mystery plays to the Lutheran Passion oratorio and beyond. For the musician the liturgy provides the destination. He is, however, free—as an artist even compelled—to speak a musical language that is his own and that may carry the originally sacred genre from the church to the secular world, even to the "play-house" so abhorrent to the moral scruples of certain segments of the Protestant world. Neither Catholic nor Protestant composers could escape the urge to do *artistic* justice to these dramatic texts, good examples being oratorio and Passion. The spiritual exercises in St. Philip Neri's oratory were invaded by elements coming from opera. Aria and recitative appeared, as well as an orchestra that constantly grew in size and importance; soon the oratorio left the church for the concert hall. The same is true of the German motet, which developed into the Protestant "sacred concerto" and the church cantata, the transplanted oratorio following suit. Here too we encounter schisms, for there are both sacred and secular cantatas and oratorios. The historian discovers, however, that the work of art can still be great and significant even if it misses its churchly function or category: neither Bach's B-minor, nor Beethoven's D-major Mass is satisfactory—even usable—liturgically, and most of Handel's great "sacred oratorios" turn out to be English secular music dramas despite their biblical texts.

The historian of church music must also cope with the particular problem of settings by composers for liturgies not their own, and with religious music by unbelievers. Lacking faith in the Nativity and the Resurrection as dogma, a composer can still cherish them as subjects for art. Treating such subjects is not a game for him; he loves what they represent to others, he admires them in his own way. If this admiration of the artist does not possess theological virtues, it is still love and worship, the love and worship of the creative poet. On the other hand, we have the legions of devout believers who considered it their duty to give the church their best as composers, again proving that sacred music is often the art of an epoch applied to religious purposes.

These and other wayward ideas prompted Professor Blume and the other distinguished scholars to approach the vast body of Protestant church music first of all as music. The historical, liturgic, theological, and socio-cultural aspects are described and discussed with hitherto unknown thoroughness and detail, but it is precisely because of the prominence accorded to music itself that the picture so gained has become rich and effective. History is elevated in this fine book to a new present.

Washington, Connecticut, 1974   *Paul Henry Lang*

Preface

About three decades after its first appearance this book is presented for a second time. The first edition bore the title *Die Evangelische Kirchenmusik* (Evangelical-Lutheran Church Music) and was the counterpart to Otto Ursprung's *Die Katholische Kirchenmusik* in the *Handbuch der Musikwissenschaft* series edited by Ernst Bücken and published by Athenaion-Verlag, Potsdam. The somewhat more ambitious title of *History of Protestant Church Music* for the new edition may be justified by the fact that it attempts to reach farther and to deal with larger complexes of what may constitute the category "Protestant Church Music," much larger complexes, in any case, than could be dealt with in the first version. It is still, of course, far from absolutely comprehensive. Indeed, what is "Protestant church music"?

The contract for the first version, which I received almost thirty-five years ago, stipulated 160 pages. This was so little that if the 16th and 17th centuries were to be dealt with at all adequately, strict observation of that limitation would leave little space for the 18th century and practically none for more recent history. Since all my protests were in vain, I had to treat the age of J. S. Bach very cursorily and limit myself to a few indications about the rest. The loss of the later 18th century and the whole 19th century did not seem too serious at that time, for those were considered the periods of decline and downfall. The new creativity of the 20th century was still in its infancy. Thus, the truncated condition of the book could be tolerated. Yet, it was already clear then that if and when a new edition materialized, these gaps would have to be filled in.

Political conditions in the 1930s and 1940s rendered any thought of a revision illusory. In the mid–1950s, however, the publisher Karl Vötterle very kindly pushed forward the plan for a thoroughly improved and extended new edition. If publication had to be postponed from year to year, it was for good reasons, resulting especially from the state and progress of research. Knowledge of the history of music was growing rapidly; it was becoming specialized to a degree hitherto unknown. Knowledge of the 16th century and research on Bach in particular developed so quickly that it seemed unwise to assess prematurely the contribution of Lutheran church music in these fields. When the first edition of this book was written, the music of the Calvinist and Reformed denominations was known only in its most general outlines, and the little that was known could easily be subsumed in the context of Lutheran music. But now a number of studies were made public that revealed for the first time the importance of those areas for Protestant church music as a whole; to deal with these properly required a special chapter. It was the same with research on music of the Bohemian Brethren, which brought an increasing body of material to light that did not fit into the history of either Lutheran or Calvinist Reformed music; it, too, required a special chapter. The history of Anglican church music, recognizable only in misty outline thirty years ago, had also come forward as a result of recent investigations, revealing a historical field of considerable magnitude. Although it is not represented in the German edition of this book, a special chapter is devoted to it in the English edition, as is another on the music of the American denominations, and a third on Protestant music in Scandinavia.

With continuing research, the attitude toward the entire course of Lutheran church music changed, and the phenomena it produced in the second half of the 18th century and in the 19th century were placed in a new light. What was formerly castigated as an era of indifference, of decadence and decline, began to acquire a value of its own, and a path was broken for a new understanding of the hitherto disparaged era from J. A. Hiller to Max Reger. There was sufficient material to form a special chapter for this period also. Finally, what was only the first groping toward a new life in 1920 has developed in recent decades into a large and respectable output, Lutheran in character, and requiring special treatment.

Such an increase in the quantity of the material and in the knowledge of the material led me to keep postponing the idea of a second edition. It also gave me the notion of dividing this material, too abundant to be encompassed by one specialist, among several scholars. I am greatly indebted to my friends and colleagues who undertook these tasks; without their collaboration this new edition would probably never have materialized. Professor Ludwig Finscher, formerly of Kiel, has critically revised the chapter on the *Period of the Reformation* from the first edition and brought it up to date. Dr. Georg Feder of Cologne has taken care of the late 18th and entire 19th centuries under the title *Decline and Restoration,* and the late Professor Adam Adrio did the same for the new creations in church music of the 20th century, under the title *Renewal and Rejuvination.* Church music in the Reformed areas of Europe and the music of the Bohemian Brethren have been dealt with in two special chapters by Dr. Walter Blankenburg of Schlüchtern. I myself have revised and extended the chapter on *The Age of Confessionalism* to close the gaps. Yet, increases in quantity of material and scope of knowledge, and the separation of individual areas brought with it doubts and difficulties. What is "Protestant church music"? The question has a quantitative aspect and a qualitative one.

Quantitatively, the greatest obstacle lies in the worldwide spread, the vast fragmentation, and the varied abundance of denominations that should or must be regarded as "Protestant." Only in their hymn singing do the Church of England and the Scottish churches resemble German Lutheranism and French Calvinism, the historic starting points of all "Protestant church music"; with regard to art music, they are more remote from those starting points than is Roman Catholic church music. The Scandinavian countries have developed their own forms. It is not yet possible to assess the position of the numerous American sects and the "young churches" of other regions of the world within the totality of a history of church music. There can be no question, therefore, of any claim to absolute completeness, and any choice must be arbitrary.

The qualitative aspect of "Protestant church music" raises even more doubts. I shall not venture upon thin ice by attempting definitions, and shall confine myself to indicating how ambiguous is the division of music into "sacred," "religious," and "secular" (or half-religious and half-secular). Are Leonhard Lechner's *Sprüche von Leben und Tod,* or Buxtehude's *Rhythmica Oratio ad unum quodlibet membrorum Christi,* or Johann Rist's songs sacred or "only" religious music? Are Lasso's *Penitential Psalms,* which circulated widely among court and church choirs of the waning 16th century, church music? What is K. H. Graun's *Tod Jesu,* for a century the Passion music sung most often in Protestant regions? What about Handel's *Messiah,* which the 19th century regarded as sacred along with his Old Testament oratorios? And Hasse's *Pellegrini,* a favorite with concert societies everywhere? Is all this church music or is it not? How are we to regard organ music from Scheidt to Reger that is not connected with a cantus firmus, or even the organ chorale arrangement from Praetorius to Reda? Is it music for the service? Music for private devotions? Music for concert performance? Have Willi Burkhard's *Das Gesicht des Jesajas* or Ernst Krenek's *Lamentationes Jeremiae* anything to do with the service, or are they spiritual concert music? What about Brahms's *Deutsches Requiem* or Verdi's Requiem for Manzoni? What about Bruckner's Te Deum? Consider the religious *Singspiele* that J. Theile composed for the house in the Hamburg Goose Market and the music for evening concerts that Buxtehude, organist of the *Marienkirche* at Lübeck, wrote for his audience of wealthy merchants. The former was intended for the opera stage, and the latter for the church gallery, yet they are as close to each other as were Bach's sacred and secular cantatas (a number of which were, in fact, identical in musical substance). Neither the contrafacta of the 16th century nor the parodies of the 18th century recognized any boundary lines of a musical nature, and in the oratories of the 19th and 20th centuries the distinctions between "sacred" and "secular" were completely erased.

For this reason, too, it is clear that any delimitation of the material must be an arbitrary one. We must cast the net far in determining what to deal with in a history of Protestant church music, for otherwise works of great artistic merit will be left on the periphery and works of more historical than musical importance will dominate the scene. The net must not be cast too far, however, lest it be lost in the boundless void. Anyone who understands by "church music" only what is based on texts and melodies required by the liturgy relegates nine-tenths of our most valuable musical inheritance to the vague sector of "religious music." Anyone who anxiously excludes everything even vaguely related to "secular music" forgets that the arias of *Die Zauberflöte* have been used now and then as church songs and that the masters of the Bach period were thoroughly aware how dangerously close to opera their cantata compositions were.

One could avoid the dreaded consequences of discussing a "decline and fall" by keeping within the safe harbor of the original concepts of orders of service. However, in so doing, one would have to toss overboard the most devout creations of some of the most earnest Protestants. The fact is that some church musicians hesitate to acknowledge as church music those deepest and most honest avowals of the words of Scripture, the *Vier ernste Gesänge* by Brahms, a Protestant and a firm believer in the Bible. And it was only recently that a controversy arose over recognizing the deeply Protestant music of Max Reger, a quarrel that was both dismaying and amusing to historians.

The boundaries are not permanent, nor can one expect them to be more sharply drawn. In the older periods no fundamental differences of this sort were recognized, and in more recent times the religious has often been equated with the churchly, whether justifiably or not. Moreover, the border between Protestant and Catholic has been established only in limited areas of history. In those areas in which both denominations used the same texts, a common literary tie lasted for centuries, and anyone who would exclude music composed by non-Protestants would arrive at a very incomplete picture of Protestant church music. In all periods musicians have crossed the line between the denominations, consciously or not. The Catholic Lasso wrote settings of Lutheran church songs, the Catholic Reger composed Protestant organ chorales and chorale motets; the Lutheran Bach and his compatriot Buttstett wrote Masses for the Roman Catholic service, and the confirmed Protestant Mendelssohn created Anglican services and also set Psalm 100 for use in the synagogue.

Two conclusions may be drawn from all this. One is that a history of Protestant church music must concern itself with a wide marginal territory, including or excluding whatever is not music for the Protestant service of worship, in the strict liturgical sense. In the present book, we have included everything that could fit in the Protestant service, everything that does not have a definitely Catholic or secular, concert-like, or operatic character—everything that goes back to a Protestant base. This includes not only service music in the strict sense but also everything that, although passing beyond liturgical requirements, has at one time or another been regarded as suitable for the service. This includes also music intended for the service, whether or not it was actually used.

Only by drawing the boundary lines this broadly was it possible to unite within the same frame Schütz's religious chamber music for the court with the middle-class natural-religious song of the Gellert period, Reger's virtuoso and expressive organ works with Ahle's unpretentious and provincial arias, the historicizing attempts to the "true church music" with the primal freshness of Walter's cantus-firmus settings, and, not least, the dramatic sermon of Bach's cantatas with the simple confession of the congregational song.

The other conclusion, however, is that a history of Protestant church music must be approached from the standpoint of music and can only be understood from such a standpoint. This may not be entirely self-evident, even though it is obvious that a comprehensive picture of the historical events, including all their abundance and all their contradictions, can be drawn only be means of such an approach.

Church music can quite properly be examined from theological points of view, too. These, however, must necessarily always be selective or normative. In the face of the abundance and contradictions of historical materials, theological points can only be directed toward specific phenomena or specific phases of individual phenomena. It is the historian's task to do justice, to the extent to which he is capable, to all this abundance with all its inner contradictions. The new edition of this book is consequently based on the proposition that church music is first of all music. That is the basic principle from which it is to be understood.

Schlüchtern, February, 1964   *Friedrich Blume*

PART I

The Period of the Reformation

BY FRIEDRICH BLUME
REVISED BY LUDWIG FINSCHER

Translated by F. Ellsworth Peterson

Just as the Reformation, by its protest, reflected in many ways the intellectual currents of its age, so also did its music arise from the contemporary stylistic surroundings. Protestant church music was never an independent musical genre in the sense that out of the essential nature of the Reformation it developed its own musical principles, its own world of musical language and form, and protected them from outside musical influences. On the contrary, it accepted, assimilated, and developed substances of all spheres of pre-Reformation music culture—the German folk song and folk dance, the highly developed German art song, just beginning to flourish, and the great supranational sacred and secular art of the Netherlanders. On one hand, it unconsciously utilized elements of tradition as a technical and stylistic substratum for an assertion of thought activated by new impulses; on the other hand, it consciously, even calculatingly, transformed the existing traditions. This could be done more safely and effectively to the degree that those features already in existence could be taken over and placed in the service of the new idea; the more this was possible, the more clearly could something new be expressed with the vocabulary of an established and commonly intelligible language.

From these beginnings it is possible to understand whence this music has taken its strength throughout the centuries. Such an attitude presupposes a relationship to the present, a liveliness, and an actual "modernity," an undogmatic grasp of the continuing elements of the past and the good qualities of the present without sterile limitations, an openness to all possibilities of future development as well as to the diversities of the present, all of which for a long time assured for Protestant church music a timeliness in any age.

This attitude further led to the absorption of all levels of traditional music culture into Protestant church music. The most important of the components, corresponding to the significance of vernacular language for the Reformation, was the national: the German folk song as expression of the broadest social strata, whose revolutionary mood was to be caught up and made fruitful. Further determining elements were the German art song, greatly nourished by the folk song and forming the center of pre-Reformation music culture as expression of the town burghers, and the supranational art music of the Netherlanders, above all that of the Latin-Catholic sphere, as the realm of the educated patrician, of the clergy, and of the flourishing humanistic town culture.

Such a conscious attachment to tradition is also shown by the third root of Protestant church music, the reformation in the content of the Catholic liturgy and the preservation as far as possible of the liturgical forms, in patent rejection of every proletarian radicalism as well as every dogmatic impoverishment. Concerning this aspect, we notice a flexible policy and worldly wisdom which were to make possible, almost imperceptibly, extensive results penetrating all areas of musical and intellectual life.

This starting position left open two possibilities: a quick flowering of Protestant musical culture or an equally fast decline. Its complete openness attracted the best minds of even the opposing camp and made Protestant church music into a reservoir for all the artistic currents of the period. But this very same openness also proved to be a weakness. Its weakening influence was manifest in the disintegration of liturgical ties, since Luther's dislike of regulations that were binding for all led to the formation of countless separate ordinances, state churches, and special local rules, all of which varied greatly among each other. This process went hand in hand with the dissolution of the Reich, with the strivings for independence of the separate peoples of the Reich who had first attained their majority in the arts at the time of the Reformation, and with the consolidation and institutionalization of the smaller sovereignties and city states. This development could be felt even in the middle of the 16th century. The complete openness of Protestant church music became a weakness again as the national sources of strength disintegrated, the peasants became impoverished, the urban bourgeoisie lost its power, and German art in general became Italianized in consequence of the growing early absolutism, a development to which Protestant church music did not close itself. In this manner the wider influence of this music was lost. It became a thing for the educated class and the institutionalized new church, whose Reformational enthusiasm slowly evaporated as the 16th century progressed.

The tie of Protestant church music to the present, its constantly renewed modernity, remained intact the longest. Even as an educating art and as the "official," supervised music of a church that was becoming rigid, an institution, it always stayed in close touch with the currents of the general history of music, even playing a determining role in its progress. By the 16th century, however, there had appeared, as countercurrent, a conservatism that is the hallmark of sacred institutions and that gave rise to the danger of music being solidified in dogmatized traditions. Only with the arrival of the Enlightenment and rational theology did art in the church decline into casual adornment, severing the development of ecclesiastic music from the progress of ecclesiastic ideas, thereby banishing all "modern" music to the secular sphere. What did continue were cantorial traditions, whose outlook stirred only lesser minds and whose narrowness could be transcended by the strength of a great personality but not that of ideas. It is also from this background that we must look at the "cantor" Bach.

In the historical reality these basic tendencies of development are widely differentiated, especially because of the divergence of regional and local directions. This was characteristic even of the early development of Protestant church music.

The freedom from an all-embracing and thoroughly organized liturgical regimentation belongs to the most basic elements of Reformational thought, despite all opposing ideas and corrections. It proved to be a strength, since, in backing away from liturgy as pure ritual, it forced a concentration on the liturgical spirit. On the other hand, the freedom was a weakness, since flexibility and adaptability to the ever changing present, ecclesiastical and intellectual, carried in them the seeds of particularistic and subjective arbitrary action. Even in the time of the Reformation, accordingly, there developed many varying views on the nature of the liturgy and, therefore, varying forms of liturgy: for edification of the congregation, as a necessary ritual for praise and thanksgiving, or as a religious-pedagogical exercise in the "education in the Word of God," centered around the sermon. As a result there were irreconcilable conflicts: the pedagogical worship service could not be combined with the idea of a general priesthood in any comprehensive and logical fashion, nor could the service in which there was a sermon be linked to a ritual congregational offering. The power of the concept of preaching led rapidly, and consistently, to a dissolution of the rituals of the celebration of Mass, to a liturgy that was to be a "frame" for the sermon, to an optional celebration of the Last Supper, and to the optional inclusion of other parts of the Mass. This "practical" tendency toward compromise and inconsistency appears in the argument over language, too. Pragmatic action based on a will to accomplishment could not be reconciled with basic ideas. Thus the history of the Lutheran service is justly called a history of its decline (Graff).

Weakness and strength appear simultaneously again in the conscious structuring of Protestant church music, in its ties to supranational and national, art and folk musical forces, and the resulting effect these forces had on all strata of the nation. As long as these ties remained intact, they brought about a continuous rejuvenation in the currency of categories, forms, styles, and idioms of musical expression. As soon as they were lost, there was necessarily a rapid and fundamental decline. As long as the lied maintained its central position, the national character of the church was assured, as was the activity of the congregation through song, with its deep, far-reaching influence. This position made certain that the immediateness and intensity of that influence was disproportionately greater than in the supranational Catholic church, which was liturgically more strictly regimented and in which this effect was only indirectly expressed. As soon as this source of strength dried up, Protestant church music became nonproductive in the area most particularly its own. A continuation in the manner of the subordinated structure of the dogmatized "church style" of Catholic church music was impossible for the very lack of a liturgical basis for such dogmatization. Because it has lacked the structural artificiality of Catholic church music since the Counter-Reformation—or since, at the latest, the beginning of the 18th century—Protestant church music has paid dearly with a sharp rate of decline from the 18th century to the present.

Just as the Reformation was set in motion by a great individual who, as an individual, visibly crossed the threshold from the Middle Ages to the modern period, Protestant church music in the actual age of the Reformation was decisively shaped by this Reformer. Therefore, at the beginning of any history of Protestant church music we must place the figure of Martin Luther.

MARTIN LUTHER

Luther received the normal musical education of a clergyman of the late Middle Ages, a basic and comprehensive education which, together with his extraordinary hunger for cultural development and his strong drive for knowledge, made it possible for him to bring to fruition his obviously superior musical talent. For Luther, as for every medieval man, music was not just a beautiful ornament for church festivals; it was an essential ingredient of the life of the spirit and soul. His relationship to music was not incidental but part of his very existence, and since he was a clergyman, the relationship was that of an expert, not of a layman. In Luther's age music belonged to everyday life—at least for the townspeople and the clergy; it was part of both daily experience and festivities in the church, of secular celebrations and the dance, of instruction in school and life at home. In its hierarchical organization, in its functional relation to the secular and, more especially, to the sacred and liturgical occasions of life, it was a power for order simultaneously reflecting and buttressing the routine customs of life in general. It shaped and penetrated the life of the lay performer scarcely less than it did that of the clergyman educated in theoretical and practical music. Luther also experienced music as a power for life and order.

A profile of the Reformer's knowledge of music and music theory and the degree to which he was a practical musician can be inferred from his biography and his writings. As a pupil in the Magdeburg cathedral school (1497), he probably sang in the cathedral worship services as a member of the school choir; as a pupil in the *Trivial* and Latin schools in Mansfeld and Eisenach he became acquainted with the principal features of medieval musical theory and sang as a *Kurrende-Knabe* (a schoolboy who sang along with others in the streets for money and food). In his period of study in Erfurt he received the basic university instruction of the time in *musica theorica* (perhaps after the writings of Johannes de Muris, more probably after those of Johannes Tinctoris) and in *musica speculativa* (Aristotelian concepts of music); like every music student of the late Middle Ages, he sang diligently and played the lute, evidently with superior aptitude. According to his own testimony, he not only improvised lute accompaniments to his own voice or for group singing but also mastered the art of transcribing polyphonic vocal compositions for the lute. After he had broken off his juristic studies and turned to theology, he evidently deepened in particular his knowledge of the musical concepts of Augustine and Thomas Aquinas (and, naturally, his practical knowledge of the Catholic liturgy). When the thirty-four-year-old Luther publicly began his work of reformation, he apparently already had a comprehensive musical and liturgical education, comparable to that of the most significant intellectual figures of the time. In his relations with Johann Walter, the first Protestant cantor, and Georg Rhau, the first and greatest music publisher of the Reformation, he broadened both his knowledge of composition, unison and polyphonic, and his overall concept of music.

Luther's use and knowledge of *musica practica* was many-sided, intensive, and theoretically well founded. He had "always loved music"; after his student days he did not neglect his lute playing, and in his music making at home he cultivated sacred polyphony with an ironic insight into the limitations of his "small, stupid tenor voice" and into the quality of the performance: "We sing as well as we can here at table and afterward. If we make a few blunders, it is really not your fault but our ability, which is still very slight even if we have sung [the piece] over two or three times. . . . Therefore you composers must pardon us if we make blunders in your songs, for we would much rather do them well than badly." The fact that he was familiar with the rules of polyphonic composition and that he could apply them creatively and correctly within modest limits is shown by the four-voice psalm motet *Non moriar sed vivam* (Psalm 118:17), which has been handed down in Joachim Greff's humanistic school-drama *Lazarus* of 1545 as a work of Luther, and very probably is genuine. The concise, full-sounding, triadic setting has somewhat awkward part writing and shows little rational organization; it more closely resembles the older German tenor lied than the psalm motets and motets on scriptural texts of the Josquin era. There is little to be seen of the rationalized, intensive word-tone relationship which Josquin and his predecessors and students employed in new textures; what is represented here is rather the somewhat conservative art of the lied of the time of Adam von Fulda. This is probably the result of Luther's lack of mastery of the new techniques rather than a conscious stylistic aim. The tenor cantus firmus Tone 8 of Introit psalmody, *tonus major*, which was also used by Senfl and Walter for their motets to this text, is presented one time, slightly ornamented; the alto is clearly conceived as a "filler" part; soprano and bass move frequently in parallel tenths. There is a great distance between Luther's modest piece and the broadly planned compositions of Walter and Senfl.

On the other hand, a four-voice model setting of the first psalm tone is attributed to Luther in a broadside print of Klug in 1546, but is very probably by Johann Walter. Only indirect information concerning other compositions of the Reformer has been handed down. Matthias Ratzeberger reports that *Didonis novissima verba,* Vergil's lament of Dido, frequently set to music in the early 16th century, was sung in Luther's home music circle in his own setting (this fact may imply a more than sporadic relation to humanistic thought and music); moreover, Luther himself is said to have taken faulty compositions on occasion and corrected them. In a letter to Johann Agricola (May 15, 1530) the Reformer reported that he had supplied an additional voice, with text, to a three-part composition found "in cloaca." His judgment of a work of Senfl shows that he considered himself a modest dilettante in spite of the fact that his knowledge in this field was above average: "I would not be able to write such a motet even if I should tear myself apart; on the other hand, he could not read a psalm as I can" (*Tischreden* 6247).

His unbiased assessment of the disparity between his own polyphonic compositions and the works of the great German-speaking composers of his time, and even more his oft-declared preference for Josquin des Prez, indicate that Luther had a comprehensive knowledge of the music of his time, that he knew how to evaluate correctly its stylistic development, and that he thoroughly understood the difference between locally composed lieder and motets and the greatest creations of the period. According to Ratzeberger's report, Latin responsories and hymns in cantus-firmus settings from Luther's own *partes* predominated in the household music after the evening meal. (Unfortunately, a catalogue of his collection of printed and manuscript partbooks has not survived; it appears that he performed from Johann Ott's *Novum et insigne opus musicum* I, 1537.) Similarly conservative but of high quality, as it is reflected in the Jena choirbooks, was the figural repertory of the palace church at Wittenberg. This repertory was certainly known by Luther. Senfl is not included at all, and Josquin is represented merely by older, stylistically conservative Masses. Luther's preference for Senfl, which led to their contact through letters, is therefore all the more striking. His expertness and clear-sightedness are revealed in his emphasis on the special position of Josquin, whose music (whether older or more recent is not known) elicited the following statement: "Josquin is the master of the notes: they must do as he wishes; the other masters of song must do what the notes wish. Certainly, the composer had good judgment . . . especially when he combined the *Haec dicit Dominus* and the *Circumdederunt me gemitus mortis* in an effective and lovely manner" (according to the report of Johannes Mathesius, 1566). And in another place: "For God also proclaimed the Gospel through music, as it appears in Josquin, whose composition flows out joyfully, willingly, tenderly, like the song of the finch, and is not forced or restrained by rules" (*Tischreden* 1258; Luther speaks of the bird but may intend an allusion to the composer Heinrich Finck). One cannot deduce from this quotation an affirmation of the later art of Josquin, which is characterized by a new kind of textual representation and word expression; but it is clear that here Luther is judging as a musician would in matters of craftsmanship and aesthetic effectiveness, and that he recognizes the special character of Josquin's art in its individuality and "naturalness."

Spontaneous judgments of this kind are characteristic not only of Luther's relation to the musical art of his time but also of his concept of music—not carefully pondered and therefore often inconsistent—in which traditionally theological, subjectively musical, humanistic, and practical liturgical processes of thought interpenetrate and often contradict one another. The principal source for a study of Luther's concept of music is his foreword to Georg Rhau's *Symphoniae jucundae* of 1538, which Johann Walter translated into German and placed before his poem *Lob und Preis der himmlischen Kunst Musica* in 1564, although he differed with many of Luther's ideas. Luther's view originated in Augustinian thought: music is a "Donum . . . divinum et excellentissimum" which rules the entire creation and was given to man "ab initio mundi"—thus, before the Fall. "Primum, si rem ipsam spectes, invenies Musicam esse ab initio mundi indictam seu concreatam creaturis universis, singulis et omnibus. Nihil enim est sine sono, seu numero sonoro" (Foreword, 1538).[1] Man was the only living thing of creation to which voice and word were given; therefore he is obliged to praise the Creator with word and tone: "Denique homini soli prae ceteris, sermo voci copulatus, donatus est, ut sciret, se Deum laudare oportere verbo et Musica, scilicet sonora praedicatione et mixtis verbis suavi melodiae" (ibid.).[2] At the same time, however, Luther the musician judged pragmatically, pointing to the amazing diversity in the apportionment of musical gifts, "quantum differat homo ab homine in voce et verbo, ut alius alium mirabiliter excellat," and it is also Luther the musician who included the famous section concerning the special place of "musica artificialis": "Ubi autem tandem accesserit studium et Musica artificialis, quae naturalem corrigat, excolat et explicit. Hic tandem gustare cum stupore licet (sed non comprehendere) absolutam et perfectam sapientiam Dei in opere suo mirabili Musica, in quo genere hoc excellit, quod una et eadem voce canitur suo tenore pergente, pluribus interim vocibus circum circa mirabiliter ludentibus, exultantibus et iucundissimis gestibus laudem ornantibus, et velut iuxta eam divinam quandam choream ducentibus, ut iis, qui saltem modico afficiuntur, nihil mirabilius hoc saeculo exstare videatur. Qui vero non afficiuntur, ne illi vere amusi et digni sunt, qui aliquem Merdipoetam interim audiant vel porcorum Musicam"[3] (ibid.; in his translation Walter added at the end of this section an invective against the "vulgar, savage braying of the chorale," a statement that would scarcely have come to Luther's mind, at least in this connection).

In this same foreword the catalogue of the effects of music often follows medieval tradition, Tinctoris almost literally and at times other authors: "Musicam esse unam, quae post verbum Dei merito celebrari debeat, domina et gubernatrix affectuum humanorum (de bestiis nunc tacendum est) quibus tamen ipsi

---

1"First then, looking at music itself, you will find that from the beginning of the world it has been instilled and implanted in all creatures, individually and collectively. For nothing is without sound or harmony." (This and the following translations are by Ulrich S. Leupold, *Luther's Works,* LIII:321–24, Philadelphia, 1965.

2"After all, the gift of language combined with the gift of song was only given to man to let him know that he should praise God with both word and music, namely, by proclaiming [the Word of God] through music and by providing sweet melodies with words."

3"But when [musical] learning is added to all this and artistic music which corrects, develops, and refines the natural music, then at last it is possible to taste with wonder (yet not to comprehend) God's absolute and perfect wisdom in his wondrous work of music. Here it is most remarkable that one single voice continues to sing the tenor, while at the same time many other voices play around it, exulting and adorning it in exuberant strains and, as it were, leading it forth in a divine roundelay, so that those who are the least bit moved know nothing more amazing in this world. But any who remain unaffected are unmusical indeed and deserve to hear a certain filthy poet or the music of the pigs."

homines, ceu a suis dominis, gubernantur et saepius rapiuntur. Hac laude Musicae nulla maior potest (a nobis quidem) concipi. Sive enim velis tristes erigere, sive laetos terrere, desperantes animare, superbos frangere, amantes sedare, odientes mitigare, et quis omnes illos numeret dominos cordis humani, scilicet affectus et impetus seu spiritus, impulsores omnium vel virtutum vel vitiorum? Quid invenias efficacius quam ipsam Musicam?"[4] At the conclusion, it became pedagogical: "Tu iuvenis optime commendatam hanc nobilem, salutarem et laetam creaturam tibi habeas, qua et tuis affectibus interim medearis contra turpes libidines et pravas societates. Deinde assuescas in hac creatura Creatorem agnoscere et laudare. Et depravatos animos, qui hac pulcherrima et natura et arte abutuntur, ceu impudici poetae ad suos insanos amores, et summo studio caveto et vitato, certus quod Diabolus eos rapiat contra naturam, ut quae in hoc dono vult et debet Deum solum laudare auctorem, isti adulterini filii, rapina ex dono Dei facto, colunt eodem hostem Dei et adversarium naturae et artis huius iucundissimae."[5] That these views were not simply repetitions of traditional educational ideas but were inwardly experienced is shown by a report of Ratzeberger concerning a fainting spell of Luther's (evidently a light epileptic attack) that was cured with music: "Then he found that as soon as he heard music, his weakness and depression were ended."

More important for the work of the Reformation and more clearly stamped with Luther's personality than the above concepts (which are a blend of traditional education and musical experience) is his uniting of theology and music: "After theology I give music the highest place and highest honor" (*Tischreden* 7304; similarly 968, 3815, and in a letter to Senfl of October 4, 1530). On the one hand, it is the constantly resounding praise of God and His creation; on the other, it leads the man who practices it to God, teaches him to understand better God's Word (it is primarily sacred vocal music that Luther had in mind), and prepares him for the reception of divine grace, while making him a better man and a happy Christian and driving out the devil and all vices. Luther was not consciously aware of the difference between this concept of music (as an "ancilla theologiae") and his developing "aesthetic" views—those determined by subjective and purely musical considerations. The former concept led to a high evaluation of *musica practica* (related to the Trivium of medieval studies) as the "optima ars"—in

---

4"Next to the Word of God, music deserves the highest praise. She is a mistress and governess of those human emotions—to pass over the animals—which govern men as masters or, more often, overwhelm them. No greater commendation than this can be found—at least, not by us. For whether you wish to comfort the sad, to terrify the happy, to encourage the despairing, to humble the proud, to calm the passionate, or to appease those full of hate—and who could number all these masters of the human heart, namely, the emotions, inclinations, and affections that impel men to evil or good? —what more effective means than music could you find?"

5"And you, my young friend, let this noble, wholesome, and cheerful creation of God be commended to you. By it you may escape shameful desires and bad company. At the same time you may by this creation accustom yourself to recognize and praise the Creator. Take special care to shun perverted minds who prostitute this lovely gift of nature and of art with their erotic rantings; and be quite assured that none but the devil goads them on to defy their very nature, which would and should praise God its Maker with this gift, so that these bastards purloin the gift of God and use it to worship the foe of God, the enemy of nature and of this lovely art."

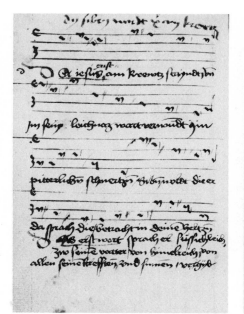

1. *Da Jesus an dem Kreuze stund.* The oldest source of a German setting of the hymn *Christe, qui lux es et dies.* Vienna, Österreichische Nationalbibliothek, Cod. Vind 30207, fols. 295b–296a.

2. *Christ der du bist des Licht und Tag,* Protestant translation into German of the same hymn by Urbanus Regius. Broadside, 1523.

3. Title page and page C 1 r of *Ach Gott vom Himmel siehe darein* from the *Achtliederbuch*. Nuremburg, 1523–24, Jobst Gutknecht.

contrast to *musica speculativa* of the Quadrivium as the "optima scientia"; the true reformative nature of Luther's concept of music lay precisely in this shifting of value from *scientia* to *ars,* the giving of the central place to performed music. True music is that which praises God, Christ, and the Gospel; it is produced indirectly in the "music" of the speechless creature, but directly only by singing, music-making man, whose "cantus ex abundantia gaudentis cordis oritur" (Weimar Luther Edition, III, 253). Thus, man is at the center of this concept of music, which, because of its reformative nature, begins to bring about the "desymbolizing of the real world of tone" (Birtner); the concept was also espoused by the humanist Erasmus of Rotterdam.

Luther's ideas concerning the liturgical function of music developed out of the basic tenets that practical music was first of all praise of God and worship per se; secondly, an aid to the exercise of devotion and piety for the faithful Christian; and, finally, an educational tool for the spreading of the Gospel. Half naïvely, half charismatically, he identified his own deeply sensitive, discriminating, and trained response to music with the slowly developing musical understanding of the congregation. He emphatically demanded that the "musica artificialis" of "fine musicians" and "learned people" (i.e., Latin polyphonic music; *Tischreden* 3516) be used for the worship service in a church building as well as in the private practice of music, and that it be used regardless of the religious confession to which its composer belonged. On pedagogical grounds, both musical and linguistic, he not only allowed its use for the school choir but even recommended it: "I will in no way allow the Latin language to be removed completely from the worship service, for young people mean everything to me. And if I were able, and if Greek and Hebrew were as familiar to us as Latin and had as much fine music and as many fine songs, we would hold Mass, sing, and read one Sunday after the other in all four languages—German, Latin, Greek, and Hebrew" (*Deutsche Messe,* 1526). Perhaps as a result of this statement by Luther, the change of languages "one Sunday after the other" was realized in some church regulations, and services were performed by turn in Latin, German, and in a mixture of the two (church regulations of Halle-Neumarkt at the end of the 16th century).

However, for the Eucharistic service of an active "congregation of priests" (a situation aspired to if not consistently realized), this devotional art was not fitting. In its place appeared the congregational lied, which was intended to serve at the same time for the active participation of all in the Eucharist, for the Christian improvement of man (in its effect as performed music), and for the musical and evangelical education of the youth. "I also want us to have many German songs which the people can sing during the celebration of Mass or along with the Gradual and along with the Sanctus and Agnus Dei," he wrote in the *Formula Missae* of 1523; and a year later, in the foreword to the first edition of Johann Walter's *Geistliches Gesangbüchlein:* "Therefore, I too, with the help of others, have brought together some sacred songs, in order to make a good beginning and to give an incentive to those who can better carry on the Gospel and bring it to the people. In so doing, we may boast, as Moses does in his song in Exodus 15, that Christ is our praise and our song and that we should know nothing to sing or say but Jesus Christ our Savior, as Paul says in I Corinthians 2. And these

songs were arranged in four parts for no other reason than that I wanted to attract
the youth (who should and must be trained in music and other fine arts) away
from love songs and carnal pieces and to give them something wholesome to learn
instead, so that they can enter with pleasure into that which is good, as is befitting
to youth. Nor am I of the opinion that through the Gospel all arts should be cast
to the ground and should perish, as some misled religious people claim. But I
want to see all the arts, especially music, used in the service of Him who has given
and created them. I therefore pray that every pious Christian will agree with this,
and if God has given him equal or greater gifts, will lend his aid. It is unfortunate
that everyone else forgets to teach and train the poor young people; we must not
be responsible for this too."

Luther's reforms of liturgy and practice grew from the triple root of these views
of church music: as a praise of God, as an offering by the congregation, and as
a means for the Christian education of man in a comprehensive sense. They grew
into their characteristic combination of basic principles and pragmatic decisions,
basing the organization of a Protestant church music on liturgical unison singing
in the tradition of Gregorian chant, German songs of a primarily monophonic
nature, and polyphony. From this combination of insights into the special possibilities of music—that "the notes bring the text to life" (*Tischreden* 2545)—with
the basic theological tenet "that everything should contribute to the bringing of
the Word to the people" (Weimar Edition, III, 37), the special significance of the
lied developed for Protestant church music and Luther came to play a commanding role as a creator, arranger, and promoter of the genre. Even his most prominent colleagues and successors (among whom were Paul Eber, Justus Jonas, and
Conrad Hubert in Luther's immediate vicinity, Lazarus Spengler in Nuremberg,
Duke Albrecht of Prussia and Paulus Speratus in Königsberg and Pomerania,
Nikolaus Herman in Joachimsthal, and Wolfgang Dachstein in Strasbourg) could
not compete with him for this role.

SOURCES OF THE LUTHERAN CHURCH LIEDER

As they had done in all other musical and liturgical spheres, Luther and his
co-workers consciously made use of pre-Reformation traditions in their creation
of a repertory of German lieder for church, home, and school. Liturgical chants
of the Catholic church, pre-Reformation German sacred lieder, and German folk
and fraternal songs were the sources of the largest number of texts and melodies;
they were assimilated in extremely diversified ways. Both text and melody might
be used, in which case the text was merely "improved in a Christian manner" (i.e.,
a manner suitable to the Reformation) or simply translated from Latin into the
vernacular; or new texts might be written for melodies whose special popularity
made their fullest use desirable; or—vice versa—texts that had been taken over
or translated might be supplied with new melodies or melodies originally associated with other texts; or, finally, texts and melodies could pass through several
of these methods of revision and combination one after another. The supply of
lieder newly composed or only loosely based upon older examples, though signifi-

cant in quality, was small in number. Taking all this together, the history of the early Reformation lied presents a confusingly multiform overall picture, further complicated by the juxtaposition of purely mechanical adaptations and arrangements with those of textual, musical, and liturgical significance.

The most important pieces of the abundant Catholic repertory of hymns were taken over with their melodies and left in their customary *de tempore* place:

Veni redemptor gentium	*Nun komm, der Heiden Heiland* (Luther, published in 1524. Advent. A translation by Thomas Müntzer appeared in the same year; pre-Reformation translations are traceable from the 14th century on and are probably very much older.)
A solis ortus cardine	*Christum wir sollen loben schon* (Luther, 1524. Christmas.)
Veni creator spiritus	*Komm Gott Schöpfer, heiliger Geist* (Luther, 1524. Pentecost. A translation by Müntzer also appeared in 1524; pre-Reformation German versions are documented from the 12th century on and are probably older.)
Pange lingua	*Mein Zung erkling* (pre-Reformation, 1525. Pentecost.)
Te Deum laudamus	*Herr Gott, dich loben wir* (Luther, 1529. Hymn, particularly a lied for Matins, Vespers, and different occasions. Luther's text in the Strasbourg hymnals of 1541 and 1545 with a melismatic setting of the melody. Other translations by Michael Weisse [*hymnal* of the Bohemian Brethren, 1531] and Valentin Triller [*Schlesisch Singebüchlein,* 1555] were not successful. A translation by Müntzer appeared in 1524; pre-Reformation translations are certified from the 9th century on.)
Christe qui lux es et dies	*Christe, der du bist Tag und Licht* (pre-Reformation, documented 1526, probably taken from a Low German translation. Vesper hymn, Vesper and evening song, also a Passion lied. There have been other German settings since the 8th century. A later Protestant translation by Erasmus Alber, *Christe du bist der helle Tag,* appeared in 1556 and again in Spangenberg in 1568 with a folk melody, the *Berghäuerton.*)
O lux beata Trinitas	*Der du bist drei in Einigkeit* (Luther, 1543; in Lossius, 1553, again in Latin but with the melody edited in the way that has been most customary since that time. Vesper hymn, Vesper and evening song. Another translation by Michael Weisse in the Brethren hymnal of 1531.)

A different melody was applied to:

Hostis Herodes impie	*Was fürchtst du Feind Herodes sehr* (Luther, 1541. The melody of *A solis ortus cardine* was used; it had not

been customary for *Hostis Herodes impie* in pre-Reformation times.)

Finally, many new hymn translations with their melodies made their way into the repertory from Weisse's hymnal of the Bohemian Brethren, 1531; their significance remained limited in geographical area and in duration of time, however. The more widely circulated were:

Veni redemptor gentium	*Von Adam her so lange Zeit* (hardly a translation, but a contrafactum in contrast to Luther's version.)
Rex Christe factor omnium	*Sündiger Mensch, schau wer du bist* (contrafactum, not a translation. Protestant translations appeared in Königsberg, 1527 [*Kön'g Christe, Gott des Vaters Wort*], in Triller, 1555 [*Herr Christe, Schöpfer aller Welt*], in Spangenberg, 1568 [*O Christe, Schöpfer aller Ding*], and more often.)

From different sources come:

Corde natus ex parentis	*Aus des Vaters Herz ist gboren* (Johann Zwick, Zurich, c. 1537.)
Jam lucis orto sidere	*Die Nacht ist hin, der Tag bricht an* (Wolfgang Köpfel, Zurich, c. 1550 with the hymn melody.)
Jesu dulcis memoria	*O wie süss ist dein Gedächtnis* (Petrus Herbert, Brethren hymnal, 1566.)

This incomplete list shows the essential facts. Those hymn translations belonging to the basic repertory, which spread quickly and survived, were the hymns central to the most important celebrations of the liturgical year. They were conservative works, preponderantly Ambrosian or in Ambrosian style, whose simple verse meters made translation easy and whose correspondingly simple melodies could be conveniently cast into a song-like mold. Primarily hymns such as these, moreover, had already enjoyed an honorable tradition of German translation and were partially familiar to the people as congregational song. Here, as in all other cases, the Reformation did not hesitate to use elements already in existence. On the other hand, the striking parallel between these lieder and a whole group of translations by Müntzer suggests (as do other connections) that Luther was trying to counteract Müntzer's attempts with his own versions.

Traditional sequences were used in Protestant church music to a much smaller degree than the hymns, mainly because of their florid melodies and their generally very complicated textual structure, far removed from the lied. Another reason for this neglect was the Lutheran hostility toward the entire genre, an opposition grown up as a reaction to the excessive production in the late Middle Ages of sequences and sequence-like pieces for Marian and saints' feasts.

Notker's Christmas and New Year's sequence *Grates nunc omnes* appeared in pre-Reformation translations and as Müntzer's *Lasst uns nu alle Dank sagen,* and later in Michael Weisse's translation in the Brethren hymnal (1531) as *Lobet Gott, o* (later *ihr*) *lieben Christen;* in this version it was taken over into many Protestant hymnals after 1560. The generally widespread translation *Dank sagen wir alle Gott unserm Herrn Christo* followed in 1538 (Strasbourg) and 1545 (Spangenberg); *Nun danksaget Gott dem Vater* in 1555 (Triller); and *Danket dem Herrn Christo* in 1561 (Nikolaus Herman; also used in Catholic areas). An excerpt from Notker's sequence *Natus ante saecula* appeared in Spangenberg in 1545, rewritten as the lied *O Christe Gottes einiger Sohn* (it was referred to by Spangenberg as "hymnus"). Notker's *Petre summe Christi pastor* appeared in the hymnal of the Bohemian Brethren in 1566 as *Alsbald Christus geboren war,* a contrafactum text rather than a pure translation; it was therefore reinterpreted liturgically for use on December 28 rather than on the Day of Peter and Paul. Neither this piece nor Spangenberg's baptism lied *Da Christ dreissig Jahr vollendet hat,* based upon parts of the sequence *Festa Christi omnis christianitas celebrat,* enjoyed great popularity. However, translations of Wipo's (?) Easter sequence *Victimae paschali laudes* were, like their Latin model, widely disseminated: Müntzer's *Heut solln alle Christen loben* (1524), Weisse's *Singen wir fröhlich allesamt* (1531) and *Preisen wir allzeit mit Freuden* (1544); also Weisse's translation of the (probably German) sequence *Summi triumphum regis* as *Nun loben wir heut allesamt* (1544). The Pentecost sequence *Veni Sancte Spiritus* was very widely dispersed in Müntzer's translation, *Komm du Tröster, Heiliger Geist* (1524); Weisse's version of *Heiliger Geist, Herre Gott* (1544) was significant most of all for the Bohemian Brethren. Petrus Herbert provided the Bohemian Brethren with a second Pentecost sequence, Notker's *Spiritus Sancti adsit nobis gratia,* translated as *O Heiliger Geist, sei heut und allzeit mit uns* (1566). The beautiful Marian sequence *Mittit ad Virginem,* especially beloved in the Middle Ages, Thomas Aquinas's *Lauda Sion Salvatorem,* and a few sequences associated with apostles and saints were found partly in translation and partly as contrafacta; they were restricted, however, to the repertory of the Bohemian Brethren and the hymnal (1555) of Valentin Triller, a man especially enthusiastic about sequences (traditions peculiar to Bohemia and Silesia obviously played a role here). Finally, Luther's two magnificent sequence compositions occupy a special place on formal grounds and, because of their power of language and depth of thought, for reasons of quality as well. The Pentecost lied *Komm, Heiliger Geist, Herre Gott* is a free imitation and amplification of *Veni, Sancte Spiritus, reple tuorum corda fidelium,* which had also been translated in pre-Reformation times; it is associated with a hymn-like melody which perhaps can be traced to the hymn *Adesto, Sancte Spiritus. Mitten wir im Leben sind* is derived by the same technique of translation and expansion from the pseudo-Notker sequence *Media vita in morte sumus* and is also associated with a new melody. In this case, as in *Komm, Heiliger Geist, Herre Gott,* Luther appears to have been thinking of a pre-Reformation translation handed down in a Basel book of Gospels of 1480.

This survey of sequence settings, like that of the hymn translations, indicates that the young church primarily used examples which had already been adopted to a certain extent in pre-Reformation German versions and which were quite familiar to the congregation as standard items of extraliturgical church life. The striking preference for sequences originating in German church provinces and for those composed by Notker or ascribed to him offers still another example of establishing a prudent connection to tradition.

A second source for the Protestant church lied occupies a place between the more or less song-like hymns and sequences and the sacred and secular German lieder. This group of Latin or macaronic Latin-German *cantiones* and songs had generally enjoyed a long medieval tradition and had frequently been used by the people in pre-Reformation worship. In the 15th century they had experienced a rich flowering as congregational songs, as household devotional lieder, as processional and pilgrimage *cantiones,* and probably also as school songs. They were especially welcomed by the Reformation because they were closely related to the people, useful in congregational singing, and extremely popular. As school and *Kurrende* songs, and even as children's songs, they were quickly and widely disseminated, and they appeared in countless polyphonic settings, especially in the 16th century. Since they were firmly rooted in the people, a translation was not absolutely necessary (in the case of German-Latin macaronic lieder, translations were really not appropriate, though they appeared anyway). German translations were frequently provided along with the Latin texts. Their traditional and continuing popularity and vigor are finally documented by countless local variants, by new compositions using the beginnings of the old lieder, by German-Latin macaronic settings of songs originally wholly in Latin, and also by retranslations of German lieder back into Latin. The latter practice began in the second half of the 16th century, probably in relation to the growing popularity of the songs as school lieder and to the rising interest of the period in the Latin language. In accordance with the popular support of this type of lied, most of these pieces were associated with the popular seasons of the church year—Advent and Christmas, Passiontide and Easter.

The most famous of these lieder are Advent and Christmas songs:

Dies est laetitiae	*Der Tag der ist so freudenreich* (Latin since the early 15th or late 14th century; German since the 15th century with an added verse, "Ein Kindelein so löbelich," which in the Reformation period became the beginning verse of a new lied with the same melody.)
Puer natus in Bethlehem	*Ein Kind geborn zu Bethlehem* (Latin since the 13th century; German since the translation of Heinrich von Laufenberg, 1439. As with *Dies est laetitiae,* both versions appear in the Protestant church.)
In natali Domini	*Da Christus geboren war* (Latin since the 15th century; Low German, 1571, High German, 1573; only the German versions were used by the Protestants.)
Resonet in laudibus	*Joseph, lieber Joseph mein* (Latin since the 14th century; German perhaps even older, as a congregational lied in Christmas Matins and Vespers to a pantomimed cradle-rocking. The Reformation took over both versions but made additional translations of the Latin, *Singet frisch und wohlgemut, O Jesu liebes Herrlein mein* [Matthesius], and others.)
Quem pastores laudavere	*Den die Hirten lobeten sehre* (the famous *Quempas,* a pre-Reformation line-by-line alternation song, usually sung by four choirs on Christmas Eve. The custom is apparently of Bohemian origin and was observed in Protestant school choirs into the 19th century. The

usual Protestant version is put together out of three *cantiones* of the 14th century, the third of which also serves as a refrain for *Resonet in laudibus.* The traditional Protestant version is correspondingly motley.)

To Passiontide belongs *Patris sapientia,* in German as *Christus wahrer Gottessohn* or *Christus der uns selig macht* (Latin since the 14th century as a prayer for the canonical hours, the worship services which follow the hours of the Passion on Good Friday; the German translations in the Brethren hymnal of 1531 are by Michael Weisse; there are also pre-Reformation translations and French, Czech, and Netherlandish versions).

Easter lieder are:

Surgit in hac die	*Christus ist erstanden* (Latin in the 15th century in Bohemia; German after a Czech model by Michael Weisse, 1531.)
En trinitatis speculum	*Der Spiegel der Dreifaltigkeit,* also *Der eingeborne Gottessohn* (neither was widely disseminated; both were used as Easter or Trinity lieder.)

A great number of other lieder in translations by Michael Weisse came into early Protestant sources from the rich Bohemian *cantio* literature (especially the Hussite) of the 14th and 15th centuries via the hymnal of the Bohemian Brethren: *Mortis en cum gloria* as *Freuet euch heut, o ihr Christen, Hoc festum venerantes* as *Die Zeit die ist itzt freudenreich, Gaudeamus pariter* as *Nun lasst uns zu dieser Frist, Ave gratiosa* as *Hochgelobet seist du, Ave hierarchia* as *Menschenkind merk eben, Jesus Christus nostra salus* as *Jesus Christus Gottes Sohn, Surrexit Christus hodie* as *Gelobet sei Gott im höchsten Thron, Cedit hiems eminus* as *Weltlich Ehr und zeitlich Gut,* and others.

In this group the macaronic lieder recede in importance. A few examples are macaronic versions of lieder traditionally either in Latin or in German *(In natali Domini, Puer natus in Bethlehem);* others are genuine macaronic lieder, among which *In dulci jubilo, nun singet und seid froh* occupies first place. (This was handed down from the 14th century apparently as a one-stanza dance song; in the 15th century it had four stanzas in different dialect versions, Low German and Dutch. It appeared as a Protestant piece in Klug, 1533; in Bapst, 1545, with the order of stanzas changed and "improved in a Christian manner," i.e., the last stanza cleansed of its praise of Mary; and in pure German translations by Weisse, 1531, and Triller, 1555. Like the *Quempas,* the lied was used by school choirs into the 19th century.)

The third extensive source of the Protestant church lied was the group of pre-Reformation German sacred lieder, pilgrim songs and *Leisen,* sacred songs of the Minnesinger and Meistersinger, songs of penitence (*Geisslerlieder*—songs of the flagellants), Crusade songs, and sacred folk songs, for which the Germans had long been famous; they were taken over unchanged by the new church or were merely improved in small details "in a Christian manner." Beginning in the 14th century at the latest, especially with the growth of religious lay movements since the time of the penitents (1349), many of these lieder had penetrated the

Catholic liturgy from their original sphere of life, partly against the express resistance of the church. Like the Latin *cantiones* and the macaronic lieder, they adorned the popular principal feasts of the church year as well as the Marian feasts, which grew ever more important with the enthusiastic Marian cult of the 15th century. Though they were not really liturgical interpolations, many provincial church regulations gave them a strictly liturgical place. The derivation of the texts and melodies was of less significance than the inner folk piety with which the lieder were sung and passed down in liturgical and extraliturgical life. Differences in their social origins seem to have meant little: precisely the simplest and probably the oldest lieder, dear to the laity because of their venerability, remained intensively alive the longest and were most quickly taken over by the Protestant church. In contrast, complicated Minnesinger and Meistersinger "craftwork" generally had a shorter life-span.

The young Protestant church, in its striving after extensive and abundant congregational song, naturally did not neglect this treasure of musical lay piety. Most of the songs taken over belonged to the oldest stock of German lieder. The Easter lied *Christ ist erstanden* (sung in the Mass and apparently also in sacred dramas, and widespread since the 12th century) had by the 15th century become a strong standard item in the Roman Easter liturgy in German-speaking provinces. In the Protestant church it occupied a firm place as the nucleus around which the repertory grew, and Luther placed it above all others: "In time we sing all lieder to the point of weariness, but *Christ ist erstanden* must be sung again and again." The Reformer "improved" the lied in his own *Christ lag in Todesbanden;* he rewrote it exegetically after the model of the sequence *Victimae paschali laudes,* seeing Christ's death and resurrection as one event. The fact that Luther also used the melody of the sequence as a pattern for his lied is very likely connected with the close relationship (probably not genetic, but explainable as a widespread melody type) of the melodies of *Christ ist erstanden* and *Victimae paschali laudes.* Also accepted unchanged by the new church were the Easter lied *Erstanden ist der heilig Christ* (apparently of 14th-century origin), the Ascension lied *Christ fuhr gen Himmel* (also from the 14th century, after the model *Christ ist erstanden*), and the Pentecost lied *Nun bitten wir den Heiligen Geist* (possibly roughly contemporary with the *Christ ist erstanden* and equal to it in popularity). To the traditional stanzas of the latter piece Luther added three new ones, which fit the original melody with magnificent exactitude and grace. The rapid dissemination of this Protestant setting was due to its use during and after Communion, between the Epistle and Gospel, as an Introit lied for Advent and Pentecost, as a funeral song, and before and after the sermon.

The very old pilgrim song *In Gottes Namen fahren wir,* mentioned in Gottfried von Strasbourg's *Tristan und Isolt,* came into the Protestant lied repertory relatively late. It found entrance via the Bonn hymnal of 1550 and via Nikolaus Herman's book of 1562, where it was described as a "sacred lied for Christian wanderers." Its late acceptance was perhaps due to the indifference, or even hostility, of the Reformation to pilgrimages. (Luther realized the fame of the melody and used this to his advantage for his Ten Commandments lied.) The

Passion lied on the seven last words of Christ, *Da Jesus an dem Kreuze stund,* is very much earlier. It has been passed down in written form only since 1494 and has appeared in Protestant hymnals since the late 1530s. The lied stanza "O du falscher Judas" has a tradition going back to the late 14th century; it was removed from its original associations (as the final stanza of *Eia der grossen Liebe*) and was rewritten on different occasions primarily as a song of political slander. In his controversial treatise *Wider Hans Worst,* Luther made a contrafactum version of it to the text *Ach du arger Heintze.* The sacred recasting of the text as *Unsre grosse Sünde und schwere Missetat* is apparently of pre-Reformation origin; the Protestant church rewrote it as *Ach wir armen Menschen* (Königsberg, 1527) and also used the melody for *Lob und Dank wir sagen* (Triller, 1555). Hermann Bonn (Bonnus) supplied a version in Low German which soon found general use (Magdeburg, 1542); its High German translation, *O wir armen Sünder,* appeared first in Lossius, 1550. The Corpus Christi lied *Gott sei gelobet und gebenedeiet,* which played a role in Luther's argument for the offering of the Sacrament in both forms (*Von der Winkelmesse und Pfaffenweihe,* 1533), probably originated in the 15th century. The Reformer preserved and rewrote it as a Protestant Communion lied, although he turned against the Corpus Christi feast with special vehemence.

A new version by Luther also introduced into the Protestant church the Christmas lied *Gelobet seist du, Jesu Christ,* of 14th-century origin. This lied's significance to the congregation as an expression of heartfelt Christmas joy is shown by the fact that it finally appeared in Luther's version even in Catholic songbooks, although Catholic versions by Michael Vehe (1537) and Leisentritt (1567) were available.

Gott der Vater wohn uns bei, traditional since the early 15th century, was originally a litany and processional song; it was customary to insert the names of various saints into its first line. Luther rewrote it as an invocation to the Trinity; Michael Weisse departed from the original text to an even greater extent in his version, *Vater der Barmherzigkeit* (Brethren hymnal, 1531).

The lieder of known pre-Reformation poets and composers that have gone into the Protestant repertory are much less numerous and in general have not survived as well. Johann Tauler's magnificent visionary *Uns kommt ein Schiff gefahren* was used for a time; soon, however, it was given up, probably because of its undertone of mysticism. *Du Lenze gut, des Jahres teuerste Quarte,* by Konrad von Queinfurt, lasted only a little longer. Heinrich von Laufenberg's *Ach lieber Herre Jesu Christ* lived on primarily in the Low German version of Johannes Freder (which appeared posthumously in 1565); as a baptism lied and sacred cradlesong it made use of only the first two lines of its model. Only Nikolaus von Kosel's Credo lied, *Wir glauben all an einen Gott* (recorded in 1417), found comprehensive and extensive use. Luther added stanzas to it, intending it as a Trinity lied; in general practice, however, and later also by Luther himself, it was again used as a Credo lied, as it had been in pre-Reformation times. This lied was also taken over into Catholic hymnals, partly in new imitations following the Reformation example, partly in Luther's version. Adam von Fulda's *Ach hülf mich Leid* had

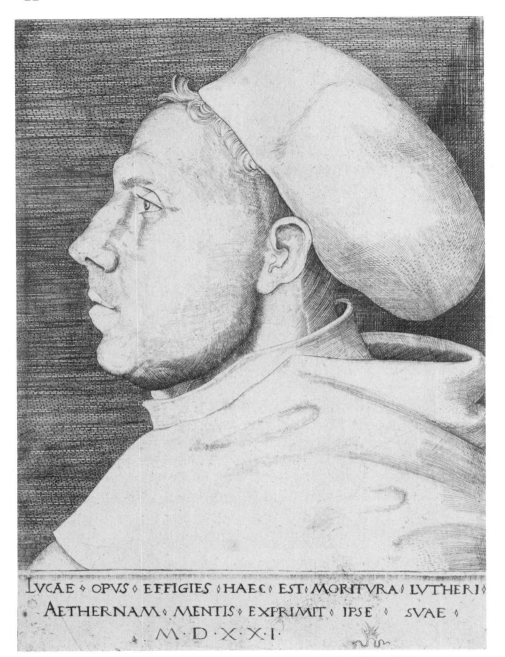

4. Martin Luther, engraving by Lucas Cranach the Elder, 1521.

5. The interior of the palace church at Wittenberg, after an ink drawing by Michael Adolph Siebenhaar, c. 1730. Wittenberg, Lutherhalle.

6. Address and text of the letter from Martin Luther to Johann Walter, December 21, 1527. Private collection.

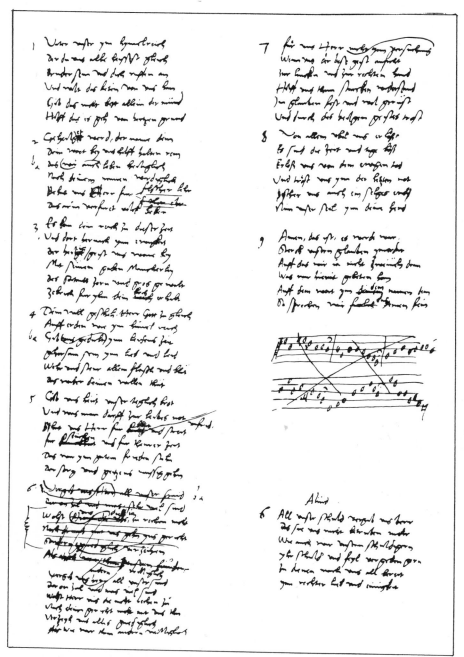

7. Martin Luther's notes on the lied *Vater unser im Himmelreich,* with the original melody, later rejected. Wittenberg, Lutherhalle.

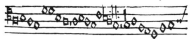
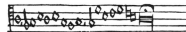

Der.xi.Psalm. Saluum me fac.

Ch got võ hymel sihe dareyn/vnd las
dich das erbarmen. Wie wenig sind ð
heyligẽ dein/verlassen synd wir armẽ
Dein wort man lest nit haben war/ð
glaub ist auch verloschen gar.
Bey allen menschen kyndern
Sie leren eyttel falsche lyst/was eygen witz erfyn
det. Jr hertz nicht eines sinnes ist yn Gottis wort
gegrundet. Der welet dys der ander das/sie treñ
nen vns on alle mas.
Vnd gleyssen schon von aussen.
Gott wolt ausrotten alle lar die falschen scheyn
vnns leren. Da zu yhr jung stoltz offenbar/spricht
trotz wer wils vnns weren? Wir haben recht vnd
macht allein/was wir setzen das gylt gemeyn.
wer ist der vns solt meystern?
Darumb spricht Got ich muß auff seyn/die armen

seint verstöret. Jhr sufftzen dringt zu mir ereyn/ich
hab yhr klag erhöret. Mein heylsam wort soll auff
den plan/getrost vnd frisch sie greyffen an.
vnd seyn die krafft der armen.
Das silber durchs feur sybenmall bewert/wird
lautter funden. Ain Gottis wort man warten sall/
des gleichen alle stunde. Es wil durchs Creutz be
weret seyn/da wirt seyn krafft erkant vñ scheyn.
vnd leucht starck ynn die lande.
Das wolstu Got bewaren reyn/für dysem argem
gschlechte. Vnnd las vns dir befolhen seyn/das
sichs ynn vns nicht flechte. Der gotlos hauff sich
vmbher syndt/wo dyse losse leute seyn.
yn deinem volck erhaben.
Eer sey Gott vatter alle zeyt/auch Christ dem eyn
geboren. Vnd dem tröster heyligen geist/gar hoch
yn hymel erkoren. Wie es ym anfang vñ auch ytzt/
gewesen yst vnd bleibet stetz.
yn der wellt der welt Amen.

Psalmus. cxxiiij. Nisi quia dñs erat in rc.
auff dẽ thon/so man syngt dẽ.xi.Psalm.
Wo Gott der herr nicht bey vns helt/wen vnser
feynde tobenn. Vnnd er vnnser sach nicht zufelt/
ym hymel hoch dort oben. Wo er Jsrahel schutz
nicht yst/vnd selber bricht der feynde lyst.
So yst mit vns verloren.

8. Martin Luther's lied *Ach Gott vom Himmel siehe darein* from *Ein Enchiridion oder Handbüchlein,* Erfurt, 1524, "Zum Färbefass."

Enchiridion
Oder eyn Handbuchlein/
eynem yetzlichen Christen fast nutzlich
bey sich zuhaben/zur stetter vbung
vnnd trachtung geystlicher ge
senge/ vnd Psalmen/ Recht/
schaffen vnnd kunstlich
vertheutscht.

M. CCCCC. XXIIII.

¶ Ain ende dyses buchleins wyrstu fin/
den eyn Register/in welchẽ klerlich
angezeygt ist was vnd wie viell
Gesenge hieryn begriffen
sindt.

¶ Mit dysen vnd dergleychen Gesenge
solle mann byllich die inngenn
iugendt aufferzyhen.

worht die huet vnnd weyde ist/die alles volck
erhalten. Jn rechter ban zu wallen.
Es dancke Got vnd lobe dich/das volck in
gutten thatten. Das lande bryngt frucht vñ
bessert sich/dein wordt ist wol geratten. Vns
segen vater vñ der son/vns segẽ vnser der heylig
geyst. Dem alle welt die ehre thun/fur ym sich
furcht allermeyst. Nu spricht võ hertzen Amẽ

Das lyed Christ ist erstandẽ Gebessert.

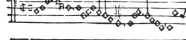
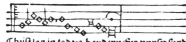

Christ lag in todtes bandenn/fur vnnser sund
gegeben. Der ist wider erstanden/vñ hat vns
bracht das leben. Des wir sollenn frölich sein.
Got loben vnd danckbar sein vñ singen/Alle.
Den todt nyemand zwingen kundt/bey al en
menschen kinden. Das macht alles vnser sund
keyn vnnschulde war zu finden. Daruon kam
der todt so bald/vnd nam vber vns gewalt.

9. Title page and the lied *Christ lag in Todesbanden* from *Enchiridion oder
ein Handbüchlein,* Erfurt, 1524, "Zum schwarzen Horn."

10. Johann Walter, *Geistliches Gesangbüchlein,* Worms, 1525, Peter Schöffer. Title page of the tenor partbook and tenor of the setting of the lied *Fröhlich wollen wir Halleluja singen.*

been transformed before the Reformation (perhaps by the composer himself) from a secular love song to a sacred piece. Though this setting was still "improved" by the Protestants, it could not hold its ground, probably because of the extraordinary artfulness of text and setting.

The creations of the Meistersinger had an even smaller but historically quite relevant influence on the Protestant lied repertory of the Reformation period. In 1525 Hans Sachs made the most important contribution with three lieder, all of which were contrafacta of secular models: *Wach auf, meins Herzens Schöne, du christenliche Schar*, after the secular *Wach auf, meins Herzen ein' Schöne, zart Allerliebste mein; O Christe, wo war dein Gestalt*, after *Rosina, wo war dein Gestalt;* and *O Gott Vater, du hast Gewalt*, after Adam von Fulda's humanistically tinged *Ach Jupiter, hättst du Gewalt*. Interestingly, it is the simplest of these lieder —*Wach auf, meins Herzens Schöne*, which has the least trace of erudition, the fewest abstract concepts in the text, and the smallest number of Meistersinger-like flourishes in the melody—that has thrived. Even it, however, did not by any means find the same dissemination as its contrafactum by Bartholomaus Ringwaldt, with the new text *Es ist gewisslich an der Zeit* (after the *Dies irae* sequence) and with a simplified folk-like melody. At the extreme edge of the development period stands Hans Sachs's combination of his *Silberweise* with his own Protestant contrafactum of the Salve Regina text (based upon a Salve Regina translation by Heinrich von Laufenberg), *Salve, ich gruss dich schone, Rex Christe in dem Throne*. Finally, scarcely more than an academic curiosity from the period of decline of the Meistersinger and of the Protestant liturgy, is the Gospel cycle for the entire church year (including a Passion in twenty-one lieder) composed in 1602 after traditional Meistersinger melodies on biblical texts by Benedikt von Watt, the collector and preserver of late Nuremberg Meistergesang.

Luther wanted only to limit, not to abolish entirely, the musical-liturgical worship of Mary flourishing especially in the 15th century. Marian themes were still very widely used (to a degree greater than Luther wished to concede), particularly in Protestant compositions based on Latin hymns. Nevertheless, no German Marian lieder were accepted into the Protestant repertory unchanged. Even the number and dissemination of the Marian songs rewritten with a focus around Christ were kept within modest limits. The most famous of these lieder is *Es ist ein Ros' entsprungen*, based upon a four-stanza Marian version traced back no earlier than 1599; the Protestant abridgment and "improvement" appear to have come from Michael Praetorius. *Maria zart von edler Art* was rather mechanically "improved' by Hans Sachs (in a broadside of 1524) and more carefully adapted by Erasmus Alber (1544?); the melody was given new texts by Michael Weisse (Brethren hymnal, 1531) and in anonymous arrangements. The pilgrims' lied *Die [dich] Frau vom Himmel ruf ich an*, probably from the end of the 15th century, appeared also in a mechanical recasting by Hans Sachs, *Christum vom Himmel ruf ich an* (1524). The melody to *Maria du bist Gnaden voll* was passed on only in a contrafactum, as a second melody to Luther's psalm-lied text *Es woll uns Gott genädig sein*.

THE CONTRAFACTA

The portions of the Protestant lied repertory discussed above were made up of examples accepted without textual and melodic change, or at most translated, expanded by the addition of new stanzas of text, "improved" in small details of content, or simplified musically into forms more closely resembling the lied. Another group of lieder, as extensive as it was important, was procured through the contrafactum technique—i.e., through the provision of a new text, usually completely independent from the original—for a melody already popular with its own text and whose popularity was useful in disseminating new doctrine and activating congregational prticipation in the musical service of worship. In view of this, it was not important, at least in the first half of the 16th century, whether the text generally associated with the music was sacred or secular. In contrast to the humanistic thought affecting the educated classes ever more strongly in the course of the 16th century, Protestantism preserved the medieval classification of the world, with secular art subjected to an intellectual discipline characterized by piety and churchliness. Under these conditions the disparity between sacred and secular music could at first hardly become a problem. Therefore, accepting secular lied melodies into the sacred Protestant repertory was as unobjectionable as using secular lied melodies or phrases for cantus firmi or parody models in the Mass compositions of the 15th and 16th centuries. This practice was probably also a labor-saving device, since the use of a liturgical cantus firmus generally related a Mass to one specific feast of the church year. Parody was also used in the Protestant figural Mass. In the second half of the 16th century, however, humanistic thought and the ideas of the Italian Renaissance had loosened the ties binding the individual to the ecclesiastic community. A contrast had developed between the sacred and secular spheres of life, between intellectual outlooks, thus creating a problem. This process, as well as the religious wars, had forced an intellectual clarification of even the bases of artistic creation. It led to a rejection, at least theoretically, of the artistic rapproachment—by the Catholics through the Council of Trent, and by the Protestants through the orthodoxy which arose with the weakening of the original ardor of the Reformation and the institutionalizing of the church. In addition, the use of pre-exsistent melodies for new texts had been sanctioned and aesthetically justified through the craft traditions of the musical guilds. Composing poems to traditional melodies according to poetic-musical schemes and models had been customary in Germany from the time of the Minnesinger and had been turned into a learnable craft particularly by the Meistersinger. A relatively undistinguished melody (thus multivalent in its expressive possibilities) could be made to take on any specific expressive character through its text of the moment; different texts could therefore reveal different sides (also relatively undistinguished) of its essential nature. Luther's statement that "the notes bring the text to life" was thus also inversely true in this sense.

The Protestant lied contrafacta must be viewed and evaluated with this understanding. Since ancient times, contrafacta had existed as a weapon in intellectual disputes, as well as a means of practice in an unfamiliar style and of assembling a musical repertory quickly. However, the intensity and degree to which this intellectual weapon—the use of commonly known melodies—served the Reformation and widened its repertory was new. Luther initiated and established the practice, for he felt that it was not necessary for the devil to usurp all the beautiful melodies. It was not important whether these melodies seized from the devil had sacred or secular texts (Luther's vehement attacks on "love songs and carnal pieces," from which the youth were to be especially protected, were always directed against the obscene texts of the uncouth German folk songs, not against secular lieder in general). It was much more important to preserve the "beautiful melodies" so that the people could more easily be brought "to the apprehension of [Protestant] truth through familiar sound," as was stated in 1574 in a letter of the Bohemian Brethren to the Saxon Elector Friedrich III.

The techniques of Protestant lied contrafacta were graduated in a diversified manner. They ranged from the "Christian improvement" of single words (which may be considered contrafacta in the broadest sense of the term), through the new sacred interpretation of secular texts and the Protestant rewriting of Catholic texts (as has been mentioned above), to the supplying of a completely new text for a melody without regard to the emotional content and subject of the original verse; finally, several different new texts could be written for one and the same melody, older melodies could be furnished with texts belonging to other tunes, and whole groups of poetic lied texts could be organized more or less mechanically around a single melody, in reliance upon its musical popularity. The details of all of these contrafactum procedures have scarcely been investigated today; the total number of Protestant contrafactum lieder with long or short life-spans has not yet even been surveyed. More than 170 examples in Lutheran spheres and more than 100 in Reformed areas have been verified as 16th-century contrafacta at least loosely related to the content and wording of their poetic models; these numbers give an impression of the order of magnitude of the body under consideration. By contrast, the contrafacta in Catholic areas before the Reformation were insignificant, since the lied played a subordinate role in their worship services and was officially only tolerated. In the age of confessional arguments they were occasionally used, especially the polemic lieder, as intellectual weapons. The number was held within modest limits: altogether, scarcely more than 40 contrafactum lieder have so far been discovered for the entire 16th century.

The significance of the contrafacta for the early Protestant church lied is evidenced by Luther's statement concerning the "beautiful melodies" and by the participation of the most important poets of the young church even more clearly than by the relatively large number of contrafacta which can be traced from the beginning. Luther wrote *Vom Himmel hoch, da komm ich her* using the "Ton" (i.e., the style and poetic and musical form) of "singing at [the presentation of] a ceremonial wreath"; for this purpose he also based his poetry on an actual old village song, *Ich komm aus fremden Landen her.*

He consciously preserved the traditional quasi-dramatic element of the lied, obviously intending it as a round dance for the Christmas manger play (which was very popular in Catholic spheres and which Protestantism had no desire to discontinue). *Vom Himmel hoch* offers an especially instructive example of the often complicated paths followed by the texts and melodies of the contrafactum lieder. At first Luther's text appeared with the original tune of the wreath song (in a Nuremberg print of four lieder, c. 1530, and Klug's hymnbook, 1535), then with the tune still in use today, perhaps by Luther himself (Schumann hymnbook, 1539), then with the tune now belonging to *All Morgen ist ganz frisch und neu* (Petreius, 1541); both the original folk tune and Luther's new melody were associated with his text *Vom Himmel kam der Engel Schar,* for which the Reformer indicated a chorale could be made from three tunes: *A solis ortus cardine, Vom Himmel hoch,* and *Ein Kind geborn zu Bethlehem.*

The three Meistersinger contrafactum lieder of Hans Sachs have already been mentioned. From Paulus Speratus comes *Es ist das Heil uns kommen her,* based on the melody of a pre-Reformation Easter lied, *Freut euch, ihr Frauen und ihr Mann;* in the first source of the Protestant version, the Nuremberg *Achtliederbuch* (1523–24), the melody is also prescribed for no fewer than three Lutheran psalm lieder, *Ach Gott vom Himmel sieh darein, Es spricht der Unweisen Mund wohl,* and *Aus tiefer Not*—a fact probably to be explained by the editor's momentary difficulty in obtaining other melodies. (Similarly, five psalm lieder in the Leipzig *Enchiridion* of 1530 are to be sung "Im thon: Aus tieffer not": *Ich will dem Herren sagen Dank, Herr, wer wird wohnen in deiner Hütt, Mein Seel lobe den Herren mein, Singet dem Herrn ein neues Lied,* and *Wollt ihr denn nicht reden einmal;* there is clearly no concern in achieving an exact correspondence of accent in the combination of words and melody as long as the music is in accordance with the verse structure and linear patterns.) Also from Speratus comes *Ich armer Sünder klag mein Leid* to the melody *Ich armes maidlein klag mich sehr.* Lazarus Spengler wrote *Durch Adams Fall ist ganz verderbt* on the *Pavier-Ton,* the melody of the broadside lied *Was wölln wir aber heben an* about the German mercenaries in the battle of Pavia in 1525 (Klug, 1529). Spengler's text was combined in the 16th century with no fewer than four other melodies after the broadside lied had lost its short-lived popularity; on the other hand, its melody was used by the Catholics as late as the 17th century with the text *Der grimmig Tod mit seinem Pfeil.* From a somewhat later period comes Johann Walter's rewriting of the lied on the seasons of the year, *Herzlich tut mich erfreuen die schöne Sommerszeit;* neither Walter's own melody nor one published in 1628 by Johann Staden could compete in popularity with the original melody. *Ich dank dir, lieber Herre* by Johannes Kolros (broadside, c. 1535) is associated with the melody *Entlaubet ist der Walde,* which was used by the Bohemian Brethren (Michael Weisse or Johannes Horn) for *Lob Gott getrost mit Singen* (1544). From the Tyrolean branch of the Baptist movement comes Georg Grünwald's *Kommt her zu mir, spricht Gottes Sohn* (found in Protestant songbooks since 1539, and in earlier broadsides since 1530, the year the Baptist martyr was burned to death in Kufstein); it was sung to the *Lindenschmiedton,* a very old folk tune associated around the turn of the century primarily with the broadside lied about the *Lindenschmied,* a robber-knight executed in 1478. The psalm lieder *In dich hab ich gehoffet, Herr* and *Ewiger Gott im Himmelreich* come from Adam Reusner. The first goes back to a pre-Reformation melody which was most frequently associated with an Easter *cantio, Christus jam surrexit* (traceable from the 14th century on, more frequently with the melody of *Christ ist erstanden*); it was also, however, associated with the melody of *Da Jesus an dem Kreuze stund.* The second of the texts mentioned above uses the very old melody to the epic poems of Duke Ernst and Dietrich von Bern. Ambrosius Blarer's deeply moving lament on the death of his sister, *Mag ich dem Tod nicht widerstan,* which soon traveled from private domain into Protestant hymnals, offers the rare case of a contrafactum on the lied melody of a composer known by name. This was Ludwig Senfl's music to the lied text "Mag ich Unglück nicht widerstan," which was probably written in 1522 or 1523 (to an unknown melody) by Duke Albrecht of Prussia for Maria of Hungary; Duke Albrecht himself had "improved" it after his conversion to the Protestant faith c. 1525 (since 1529 it has appeared in Protestant songbooks with Senfl's melody and with further Protestant alterations). Duke Albrecht's *Was mein Gott will, das g'scheh allzeit* was nourished from a completely different source. Its melody is taken from Claudin de Sermisy's chanson printed in 1529, *Il me suffit,* which was widely disseminated in Germany and found its way to Königsberg probably through the ducal musician Paul Kugelmann.

It is scarcely possible to survey the number of contrafactum lieder which come from anonymous or minor poets; the amount grew constantly from the time of the first hymnals of the Reformation. Many examples from this repertory did not survive the 16th century or even one or two editions of a local songbook; some remain immortally fresh even today. *Herr Christ, der einig Gotts Sohn,* by Elisabeth Kreutziger (Cruciger), is set to the folk tune *Mein Freud möcht sich wohl mehren* from the *Lochamer Liederbuch.* The folk melody *Weiss mir ein Blümlein blaue* served for both *O Herre Gott, dein göttlichs Wort* by Count Anarg von Wildenfels (?) and Johann Agricola's *Ach Herre Gott, wie haben sie sich wider dich so hart gesetzet,* as well as a model for Hans Kugelmann's composition to Johann Gramann's text *Nun lob, mein Seel, den Herren. Lieblich hat sich gesellet* by the young Johann Walter, the son of Luther's cantor, goes back to a secular melody with the same beginning; Nikolaus Selnecker's lieder *Ich stund an einem Morgen* and *Der Maie, der Maie bringt uns der Blümlein viel* and Philipp Nicolai's *So wünsch ich ihr ein gute Nacht* also make use of corresponding secular lied melodies and texts. Johann Witzstat's *Nun höret zu, ihr Christenleut* can be recognized from its stereotyped beginning as a contrafactum of a broadside lied ("im Ton des Buchsbaums"). Nikolaus Herman's *Heut singt die liebe Christenheit* goes back to the tune of the anonymous *Ich hab mein Sach zu Gott gestellt,* which was itself written to a folk tune (as was the closely related *Ich hab mein Sach Gott heimgestellt*); the melody was later handed down with different texts. Michael Weisse's *Lob sei dem allmächtigen Gott* very probably follows a lied or *cantio* melody going back to Herman's *Steht auf, ihr lieben Kinderlein.* The origin of a melody to which Herman set *Erschienen ist der herrlich Tag, Am Sabbath früh Marien drei,* and *Als vierzig Tag nach Ostern war* in his rhymed *Sonntagsevangelia* (1560) is not completely clear; in spite of its similarity to the Easter and Easterdrama antiphon *Ad monumentum venimus gementes,* it probably goes back directly to a representative of the song type traceable in a broadside lied *Ich sing euch hie ohn all Gefähr,* apparently related to the tunes of miners' songs. The melody to which Ludwig Helmboldt wrote the text *Von Gott will ich nicht lassen,* traceable to France in its pre-Protestant version, is similarly unclear in origin, though it probably also stems from popular sources. A ballad melody brought to Germany by English actors at the end of the 16th century, and very likely of English origin, has been combined with sacred texts many times since David Spaiser's *O Gott, ich tu dir's klagen* (1609). (The association with Paul Gerhardt's *Ist Gott für mich* appears for the first time in the *Deutsches Evangelisches Gesangbuch* of 1950 and is one of the most recent examples of Protestant lied contrafacta.) Christoph Knoll's *Herzlich tut mich verlangen* also comes from the late period of lied contrafacta; it was perhaps written to go with Hans Leo Hassler's *Mein Gmüt ist mir verwirret* (1601); in any case, it was set to that five-voice composition in 1613. Johann Crüger later used the melody in his *Praxis pietatis melica* (edition of 1656) for Paul Gerhardt's text *O Haupt voll Blut und Wunden.* Gerhardt's version of St. Bernard's hymn *Salve, caput cruentatum* thus offers one of the few examples in which a lied new in content was definitely not written for the melody with which it was later associated, but only followed a widely used strophic scheme which could be combined with a current melody. In most cases, however, in which text quotations or paraphrases do not point directly to a secular model, the relationship between the origin of the new text and the traditional melody is unclear and must be determined on an individual basis. Heinrich Isaac's famous discant melody *Innsbruck, ich muss dich lassen* has enjoyed perhaps the longest history as a contrafactum in Protestant church music; it was associated in the 16th century with *O Welt, ich muss dich lassen* (perhaps by Johann Hess), in the 17th century with Paul Gerhardt's *Nun ruhen alle Wälder* (which was again contrafacted at the end of the 19th century by Otto Julius Bierbaum), and in the 18th century with Matthias Claudius's *Der Mond ist aufgegangen.* It is the most vivid example of the vigor, fertility, and expressive versatility of a great lied melody perfect in itself, and therefore an example of the basic characteristics which made possible the enormous effectiveness and dissemination of the contrafactum lied.

In view of the general popularity and dissemination of the contrafactum lied, it is no wonder that whole songbooks made up of contrafacta were put together or that secular songbooks were contrafacted in their entirety. Wachter's Nuremberg *Liederbuch* (1535) was a beginning in this direction; the Magdeburg *Geistliche Ringeltänze* (1550) followed it, as did the Low German *Neue christliche Gesänge und Lieder* of the pastor Hermann Vespasius (Wespe) from Stade (Lübeck, 1571). The most important collection, also of 1571, was that of the contrafacta of four-voice *Gassenhauer, Reuter- und Jägerliedlein* (Egenolff, Frankfurt, 1535) and other models by Heinrich Knaust. It appeared, again published by Egenolff, as *Gassenhauer, Reiter- und Bergliedlein, christlich, moraliter und sittlich verändert, damit die bösen ärgerlichen Weisen, unnützen und schandbaren Liedlein auf der Gassen, Feldern, Häusern und anderswo zu singen, mit der Zeit abgehen möchten, wenn man christliche, gute, nützliche Texte und Worte darunter haben könnte.* [6] Most of these lieder found no further dissemination. From Wach-

---

[6]"Street songs, knightly and miners' songs, changed in a Christian, moral, and ethical manner, in order that the evil, vexatious melodies, the useless and shameful songs to be sung in the streets, fields, houses, and elsewhere, may lose their bad effects if they can have good, useful Christian texts and words."

ter's publication, *Lobt Gott, ihr frommen Christen* (sung to a mercenaries' tune by Brother Veit) spread to southern Germany. A High German version of *War'n meiner Sünd' auch noch so viel* (after *Und wär der Neider noch so viel*) from Vespasius's lieder is still preserved in today's *Evangelisches Kirchengesangbuch.*

The *Schlesisch Singbüchlein aus göttlicher Schrift* of the Panthenau pastor Valentin Triller (1555) falls outside the bounds of the ordinary songbooks in that it ignored the central group of lieder associated with Luther and Wittenberg (perhaps under the influence of Caspar von Schwenckfeld and his adherents). Instead, with the interest in folklore and "history" reviving at this time (probably under the influence of humanism), Triller collected and made contrafacta of folk-song melodies. In addition, his collection contained numerous "secondary" contrafacta of sacred songs which were themselves already contrafacta.

The life of the Protestant contrafactum lied depended upon the vigor and popularity of its melodies and the modernity of its new texts. Since, according to Luther's statement, most of the melodies were overworked and not very many texts had enough substance to survive, and since the often mechanical application of a single melody to whole groups of songs led to the rapid exhaustion of both melody and text, most contrafacta did not enjoy long life. Moreover, many of them never penetrated beyond local use or even beyond a single songbook. Those with the shortest life-span were naturally the songs of dispute and ridicule concerned with church politics and quarrels between the confessions. Such lieder were not to be despised, however, as sharp weapons in the battles of opinion. They used the best-loved tunes of ever popular jesting songs or of much older songs touching on customs deeply rooted in the people. For example, the comic lied *Der Kuckuck hat sich zu Tode gefallen,* apparently fashionable at that time (at any rate, widely disseminated), was used as *Der Papst hat sich zu Tode gefallen* by the *Neue Zeitung von dem Papst zu Rom, wie er sich zu Tode hat gefallen von seinem hohen Stuhl* (1535). The song "for children to use to drive out the Pope in mid-Lent," *Nun treiben wir den Papst hinaus* (printed in 1541, probably with Luther's approval), made use of the archaic custom of exorcising the seasons *(Nun treiben wir den Winter aus).* Thus, its appeal, which seems to us today to have been quite unscrupulous, was to the most primitive layers of the childlike mind. There were also insulting lieder, less harmful in spite of their occasionally dirty allusions, such as *Calvin, du und dein Kind* (after *Venus, du und dein Kind*) or the Catholic song of ridicule concerning Luther's marriage, *Wat han ick dummer Monnich gedaan?*

The great period of Protestant lied contrafacta ended with the 16th century. The exchange of one sacred text for another for use with accepted lied melodies was continued more or less mechanically by compilers of songbooks into the 18th century, partly without the knowledge of the lied poets. However, the emphasis in lied production shifted more and more toward genuinely new creation—"free" poetry (based, of course, on accepted stanza patterns but without direct lied models) and melodies composed *ad hoc* to these new texts. Among the factors contributing to this development were the loss of energetic desire to disseminate doctrine, the loss of awareness of the effectiveness of the contrafactum lied as an intellectual weapon, the decline of the function of the congregational lied in the worship service and the growth of private devotional songs, the growing consciousness of the inviolable individuality of the creative achievement and, with it, the tendency (then becoming normal) for the poet and composer to step out of anonymity. The climax of this development is the Protestant church lied of the 17th and 18th centuries, composed by the most significant musical figures of the age and written by poets usually very conscious of their creative ability, well educated in theology and in general subjects, and dedicated to the pretentious poetic theory of Opitz and his successors. The relation of the lied to the folk song, one of the essential sources of its power, was confined from this time forth to special moments of poetic-musical inspiration.

Apart from the above-mentioned lieder of ridicule and confessional strife, the contrafactum lied had an extraordinarily large share in the quick creation and dissemination of a Protestant song repertory. Together with the translations or "improvements" of Latin or pre-Reformation German sacred models discussed above, it was responsible for the fact that songs which were not original in the modern sense were more numerous in the 16th-century Protestant lied repertory than songs with new texts or melodies. Such a relationship corresponds thoroughly with the situation of the age and the contemporary interpretation of the nature and technique of lied production. The usefulness of a song, measured by the intensity and geographical area of its effect, was more vital than poetic-musical originality, which lost its effectiveness to the degree that it moved away from the easily comprehended general repertory of the period. Poetic-musical craftsmanship was understandably trained to imitate tested examples. Poet and musician worked with a supply of formulas that was rich enough, and whose elements appeared diverse enough, to allow the construction of perfectly convincing poetic-musical works of art with complete textual-musical unity. It was precisely this relation to tradition and this aim of serviceability that made possible the personal union of poet and composer, largely preserved in the Protestant church lied of the 16th century. Here, as in other branches of the musical and artistic production of the time that followed similar laws, the tradition of pure craftsmanship finally prevailed. Between the sense of obligation and the sense of personal responsibility, between the medieval spirit and the modern, sufficient freedom was guaranteed for the genius of a great creative personality to unfold. In other words, Luther and Thomas Stoltzer, Nikolaus Herman and Ambrosius Blarer, Zwingli and Michael Weisse, Dürer and Riemenschneider could become what they were and are.

LUTHER'S LIEDER

The question of the originality of a lied was as unimportant for the age of the Reformation as it would become essential for the 17th century. For this reason the question of quality moves all the more into the foreground. Its answer indicates that songs of the new church based on borrowed material were noteworthy only for their quantity, while the relatively few newly created texts and melodies were the more noteworthy in quality, especially those songs written by "poet musicians," with text and music conceived as a unit. This is true even if such lieder were modeled in some way after traditional melodies and forms—in other words, less "original." Luther's own songs are at the center of this fourth, and most important, source of the Protestant church lied during the Reformation. With a few examples by others, all with texts that followed Luther's doctrines, some with newly composed melodies and others contrafacta, they formed the nucleus of the Protestant lied repertory. In these lieder, almost all of which are still in use, Luther's teachings are represented in their purest form. Their rapid dissemination (often in association with only one melody which, unlike so many others, was not exposed to migration from text to text) and their vigor, still effective today, prove that these lieder came from the center of faith and affected the center of faith, and that from the beginning they possessed the greatest degree of usefulness, so essential to the age. Their unforced, "natural," expressive, and binding connection between word and tone is proof of their high aesthetic rank, far above so many songs of the period which were fitted together more or less mechanically.

Many questions concerning the melodies of these central lieder have long been unresolved and will remain so until a systematic investigation of the lied is begun on the broadest basis, with strict methods of comparative melodic study. Which were newly composed? How many were created according to models and formulas? How many were taken over directly from other sources? Individual investigations have already shown that direct melodic borrowing was much less common in this lied repertory than the use of techniques corresponding to the above-mentioned artisan tradition of writing poetry and music according to models and formulas. The similarity of many songs with one another, as well as with the secular lied repertory of the age, is explained by the application of such techniques: the use of a regular melodic framework and the typical turns of expression associated with specific modes, the spinning out of traditional formulas, and the taking over of typical melody beginnings and endings. Thus, a repertory came into existence that remained within the framework of tradition but allowed for independence in melodic creation. This repertory frequently sounded familiar because of the materials it borrowed and the typical manner in which they were used. Yet what emerged had musical coherence and a well-shaped character. The fact that this manner of composition was applied with ease and subtlety—and that the composition of text and melody was a unified process —makes the analytical comprehension of its elements even more difficult.

The principles mentioned are valid not only for the central lieder of the Reformation era but also, in a modified way, for the Catholic hymn melodies taken over into the Protestant repertory with translated texts or new, more or less independent ones. The hymn melodies were rarely preserved note for note. Most often their general character, already resembling that of the secular lied, was solidified, thoroughly organized, and simplified in a song-like manner—all of which illustrates their many-sided and symbiotic relationship with the sound and style of the secular lied. They approached so closely a straightforward song-like realm of expression that differences between the free lied melodies of the early Protestant repertory and those based upon Latin hymns are often scarcely discernible. A comparison of the German melody of *Veni redemptor gentium* with the lieder based on the hymn (in text and melody or only in melody) shows the flexible manner in which the hymn melody was transformed into a lied and how suitable this transformation was for the text.

In Müntzer's translation of the text the words correspond exactly to the notes of the melody. It was not a congregational lied that carries within itself, in its song-like qualities, the seed for wider dissemination, but a piece of "German Gregorian chant" (similar to some German versions of traditional examples used by the Bohemian Brethren). At most it would be useful for the group singing of a small, rigidly organized sect (the melodic divergencies are variants found in the Catholic examples which have been handed down; they are not infringements by Müntzer). Luther's translation, on the other hand, in its identity of the first and last lines and in its marked rhythmic treatment, which gives each line an unalterable musical shape, is a complete recasting of the model in the direction of the lied; at the same time, its careful and "natural" synchronization of word, meaning, and melodic accents ("Heiden," "wunder," "Geburt") makes it a perfect consolidation of word and tone. By contrast, *Erhalt uns, Herr, bei deinem Wort* is related more freely to the musical model, in correspondence with the new text;

it goes its own way from the third line on, with the stress on "Christum"; in the last line, in which the melodic frames of the third and fourth lines of the model are consolidated, a small, picturesque pre-madrigalism appears with "stürzen von deinem Thron" (the second note of the first line could be a variant of the Gregorian model). *Verleih uns Frieden gnädiglich* is a transition into the area of free, original creation based upon typical formulas and the combination of different melodic patterns; the first line, probably directly from the model for the text, takes over the antiphon *Da pacem;* then, however, presumably inspired by the identity of the beginnings of *Da pacem* and *Veni redemptor,* it goes over into the melody of the hymn and only at the end adds a line, characterized by the use of formulas, to support the text.

Although there is no evidence of direct borrowing, a group of Ionian melodies (strongly major-oriented) are associated with a distinct, very old lied type (*Vom Himmel hoch, Ein feste Burg, Ein neues Lied wir heben an,* and Luther's first melody to *Vater unser im Himmelreich,* later discarded and not admitted to the songbooks). They are characterized by the steady pursuit of a descending melodic idea within the span of an octave (usually traversing stepwise the entire octave during the first two lines, with an intermediate cadence on the "dominant"), by a triadic melody along with the stepwise movement, and by an emphatic rhythm at the beginning, often intensified through repetitions of tones. This latter characteristic appears surprisingly often in the early Protestant lied and is derived less from the German folk song than from the French chanson; or perhaps it developed independently from the heightened impulse toward proclamation and confession shown by many texts of this group.

Martin Luther

Vom Himmel hoch, da komm ich her, ich bring euch gu-te neu-e Mär, der gu-ten Mär bring ich so-viel, da-von ich sing'n und sa-gen will.

Apparently the roots of this melody type reach back to the early period of the Eurasian population migrations. One of Luther's greatest melody creations, the German Sanctus, is also related, indirectly, to the type. It seems to show a direct correspondence with the Sanctus of the Gregorian Mass *in Dominicis Adventus et Quadragesimae* from the 11th century; at the same time it is clearly reminiscent of some of the monophonic German Ordinary compositions of the late 15th and early 16th centuries, which in turn are based partly upon secular lied melodies.

San - ctus, San - ctus, San - ctus Do-mi-nus De - us Sa - ba - oth.

Luther (Deutsche Messe 1526)

Je - sa - ia dem Pro-phe-ten das ge-schah, daß er im Geist den Her-ren sitzen sah, auf ei-nem hohen Thron in hellem Glanz,

Ple-ni sunt cal - li et ter - ra glo-ri - a tu - a. Ho - san - na in ex-cel - sis.

sci nes Kleides Saum den Chor füllet ganz. Es stunden zween Seraph bei ihm daran, sechs Flü-gel sah er einen jeden han,...

Finally, a third and more extensive lied group also goes back to secular song types and in certain cases to individual melodies. The principal characteristics of

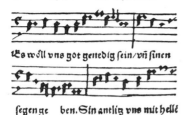

11. *Deutsches Kirchenamt*, Strasbourg, 1525, Wolf Köpphel. Title page and the lieder *Aus tiefer Not schrei ich zu dir* (with the Ionian melody) and *Es woll uns Gott genädig sein.*

12. *Kirchenamt zu deutsche,* Erfurt, 1526, Thomas Müntzer. Title page and
the first lines of the sequence for Pentecost *Komm du Tröster heiliger Geist.*

this group are seven- and eight-line *Bar* and *Reprisenbar* forms,[7] which predominated especially in the contemporary social songs of town and court. The use of particular melodies, or the construction according to melodic formulas within this structural framework, changes from case to case; the more formula-like the melodic materials, the more difficult it is to trace the sources in individual cases. The most famous example of specific similarities either as conscious "compositional props" or unconscious reminiscences is the beginning of Luther's Phrygian melody to *Aus tiefer Not;* the melodic sequence B-E-B-(C-B) appears on the one hand to be a turn of phrase basic to Phrygian melodic formation; on the other hand, it is also found in a Marian lied of Frauenlob, the beginning of the French chanson *Petite camusette* (and the *Mi-Mi* Masses related to it by Ockeghem and others), the Josquin motet *Petre tu pastor,* the German tenor lied *Meins Traurens ist* (Hofhaimer), the Huguenot psalm *Tes jugements, Dieu véritable* (Clément Marot), the chanson *Au bois, au bois, ma dame* of Pierre Moulu, and in other contexts. It cannot actually be proved that Luther set up the combination of the descending leap of a fifth and the "threnodic" second *b-c-b* with the intention of melodic symbolism; but such an intention can scarcely be ruled out, in view of similar very clear affective gestures in many of his lied melodies and in view of his conjectured knowledge of similar gestures of expression in the German tenor lied and in his favorite composer, Josquin (the "threnodic" second in *Miserere mei Deus*).

Luther's own lieder, which originated partly as contrafacta with a more or less song-like recasting of the parent examples, partly as melodies patterned after models and formulas as described above, form the center of the core repertory of early Protestant lieder. Luther's share in the creation of the melodies of his songs is therefore difficult to determine in detail and has long been passionately disputed. Altogether 36 songs have been ascribed with certainty to the Reformer. They can be organized textually into poetic works based upon Latin hymns and other traditional liturgical pieces, upon psalms or other passages in the Old and New Testament, upon pre-Reformation German sacred and secular lieder, and upon a few examples still unknown. They can be organized according to melodic formulation into more or less note-for-note contrafacta and new creations characterized to some degree by the use of formulas and patterns. Luther wrote no fewer than 23 of these lieder in an incomparable exercise of creative power during the short time between 1523 (the Brussels martyr song *Ein neues Lied wir heben an* probably marks the beginning of this activity) and the appearance of Walter's songbook of 1524; a few of his greatest creations can be found among them. Twelve of the early works are translations, contrafacta, paraphrases, or expansions of one-stanza pre-Reformation songs: *Mitten wir im Leben sind, Jesus Christus unser Heiland, Gelobet seist du, Jesu Christ, Nun komm, der Heiden Heiland, Christum wir sollen loben schon, Christ lag in Todesbanden, Komm, Gott Schöpfer, Heiliger Geist, Nun bitten wir den Heiligen Geist, Komm, Heiliger Geist, Wir glauben all an einen Gott, Gott der Vater wohn uns bei,* and *Gott sei gelobet*

---

[7]The *Bar* form is *A-A-B,* or *Stollen, Stollen, Abgesang.* If a part of *A* returns in *B,* the pattern is called a *Reprisenbar.*

und gebenedeiet. Most of them retained the melodies of their pre-Reformation models. A few appeared even in the first songbooks with different melodies; in later use, those songs in which words and melody were most closely bound together were generally the most successful, one of the many signs that current practice was indeed conscious of quality, a consciousness unimpeded by the use of the contrafactum technique. The remaining eleven lieder of this group are free poems, among which are found the six great psalm lieder: *Aus tiefer Not, Ach Gott vom Himmel sieh darein, Es spricht der Unweisen Mund wohl, Es woll uns Gott genädig sein, Wär Gott nicht mit uns diese Zeit,* and *Wohl dem, der in Gottes Furcht steht.* Direct musical models for the melodies of these particular psalm lieder cannot be traced. Apparently, Luther's share in the shaping of the melodies was very great. On the other hand, it is striking that precisely the psalm lieder were handed down from the beginning with quite a diversity of melodies and that some songbooks prescribed the same melody for a whole group of psalm lieder (either as a matter of convenience or because of a dissatisfaction with the melodies originally associated with the lieder). The melody assignments in the early sources for *Dies sind die heiligen zehn Gebot* and *Jesus Christus, unser Heiland* are similarly flexible. *Nun freut euch lieben Christen gmein,* which probably belongs with the first lieder of the year 1523, appears with three melodies: one that probably belonged originally to Speratus's *Est ist das Heil uns kommen her* (the two Erfurt *Enchiridia*); one that first appeared in Klug, 1535, and was for a long time the favorite; and one from the *Achtliederbuch,* 1523–24, which follows a widely disseminated incipit formula from secular song with the characteristic leaps of a fourth in its first line, and which probably was written by Luther himself (at any rate, of all three melodies it is the one best fitted to the text).

Mit Fried und Freud ich fahr dahin was apparently not quite so fortunate in its word-tone relationship, its song-like form and expression; it is tempting to believe that it is a German arrangement of a (Gregorian?) model rather than a freely composed melody of Luther. Neither is the melody of the martyr song *Ein neues Lied wir heben an,* probably composed by Luther himself, equal to his greatest lieder. Moreover, after its opening lines—reminiscent of the characteristic beginning of the lied type which includes *Vom Himmel hoch* and *Ein feste Burg*—it is put together from artful transpositions of motifs. On the face of it this confirms the admiring statement of Cyriakus Spangenberg (1569) that Luther has been "the greatest Meistersinger," referring, of course, to his craftsmanship rather than to the quality of his work (which was the original meaning).

Luther's remaining lieder all come from the years after 1524. *Sie ist mir lieb, die werte Magd,* resembling the Meistersinger type in text and melody, was probably not written without a direct model; it stands in complete isolation among Luther's lieder. *Vom Himmel hoch, Vom Himmel kam der Engel Schar,* and *Was fürchtst du Feind Herodes sehr* have already been considered. The baptism song *Christ unser Herr zum Jordan kam,* first published in 1541, has been since 1543 connected to the melody that appeared in 1524 with the psalm lied *Es woll uns Gott genädig sein.* It was perhaps written by Johann Walter, originating therefore in Luther's immediate surroundings. *Verleih uns Frieden* and *Vater unser im Himmelreich,* with its first melody rejected by Luther, have already been mentioned; the final *Vater unser* tune was probably also written by Luther himself. Confirmation that both text and melody are by Luther is strongest with regard to the German Sanctus *Jesaja dem Propheten das geschah* (because of information in Johann Walter's memoirs as handed down by Michael Praetorius); the tune, however (see above), is based on a model, which it followed relatively closely. Finally, the melody to the psalm lied *Ein feste Burg,* written probably between 1526 and 1528, was certainly composed by Luther, and in spite of all individual borrowings of turns of phrase from melody types or from direct models, it is one of the most magnificent examples of the perfect unity of word and tone and of compactness, achievement of an affect, and significance of melodic form—qualities that made Luther's greatest lieder the mightiest source of strength for the Reformation and raised them into the immortality of great works of art.

Luther's lieder rapidly formed the basis of the central Protestant song repertory. For the songbooks of the 16th and 17th centuries they were the indispensable core of an otherwise very changeable repertory, which was formed around them. They were regarded as stimuli, not necessarily as examples, for those who could "do it better"; the latter were not found, however, in the expected quality and number. While the creative eruption of the "lieder year" 1523–24 quite obviously overstepped the aim of mere utility, Luther's song output after 1524, not very abundant, may have sprung from the desire—indeed the compulsion—to close the gaps himself in the repertory being built up. To be sure, some of his contemporaries attained the level of Luther as a lied composer, but they could not surpass him. The songs flowed in a strong stream from his inspired heart, proclaiming Protestant truth and making a breach for the doctrine as did no sermon or writing. From the Jesuitic point of view it has justly been said that Luther's lieder "destroyed more souls than his writings and speeches."

The inner significance of the lieder cannot be valued highly enough. They were poetic words of Scripture, not merely devotional thoughts and prayers like the German song in the Catholic church. They not only possessed a general religious content, but in them the layman was given the biblical word itself and the extrabiblical liturgical text as his own property, not easily lost. The psalm lieder are not just borrowings and paraphrases but really the psalms themselves: they can justly be called "German psalms"; *Jesaja dem Propheten das geschah* is not the reflection of the Sanctus in the congregation but the Sanctus itself in a Protestant interpretation. That is precisely the decisive basic idea of the Protestant lied: it is the biblical word itself, not its substitute; it is an essential part of the liturgy, not its appendage. This fundamental fact was musically significant insofar as the melodies became liturgical along with the lied texts, and therefore sacrosanct. Like the ritual chant of the Catholic church, which raised the Gregorian melodies to essential parts of the liturgy equal in worth to their texts, the Protestant lied melodies very quickly won the rank of liturgical, secure, inviolable heirlooms withdrawn from the grasp of the individual, a fact of basic significance for the history of Protestant polyphonic music.

LIEDER OF OTHER COMPOSERS

THE OLDEST HYMNBOOKS AND POLYPHONIC LIEDER COLLECTIONS

The corpus of Reformation lieder developed slowly from its basic repertory (which, along with Luther's songs, consisted primarily of hymn translations and pre-Reformation sacred lieder) and changed constantly, insuring the currency and stylistic modernity of the material. On the other hand, the entire repertory contained a relatively small proportion of lieder which were generally accepted and appropriate at any time. The change especially affected the contrafacta of secular songs, which rarely attained the timeless greatness of Luther's lieder, and which could not share the advantage enjoyed by the hymns of being liturgically sacrosanct from the beginning. Thus the early Protestant repertory grew primarily through new creations, deeply rooted in faith, by a few of the more significant poets from Luther's immediate and more distant surroundings.

Luther's earliest lied was preceded in the south by Ambrosius Blarer's *Wie's Gott gefällt, so g'fällts auch mir* and in the north by Nikolaus Decius's Low German songs *Alle in Gott in der Höh' sei Ehr, Heilig ist Gott der Vater,* and *O Lamm Gottes unschuldig,* the melodies of which anticipated astonishingly Luther's principle of recasting Gregorian models in a song-like mold; the pieces also anticipated Luther's principle of inserting lieder as substitutes for the corresponding portions of the traditional liturgy. In Luther's closest environs, Justus Jonas followed with *Wo Gott der Herr nicht bei uns hält,* Elisabeth Kreutziger (Cruciger) with *Herr Christ, der einig Gotts Sohn,* and Paul Eber with *Herr Jesu Christ, wahr'r Mensch und Gott* and *Wenn wir in höchsten Nöten sein,* two songs in which the weaker, sentimental tone of the first generation after the Reformation is already apparent. In the wider circle of followers of the Reformation, Paulus Speratus contributed *Es ist das Heil uns kommen her,* perhaps the most beautiful example in lied form of the Protestant doctrine of justification, magnificently simple and folk-like; Lazarus Spengler followed with the artful Meistersinger-like *Durch Adams Fall ist ganz verderbt,* Erasmus Alber with *Ihr lieben Christen, freut euch nun, Steht auf, ihr lieben Kinderlein, Christe, du bist der helle Tag,* and *Wir danken Gott für seine Gab'n,* Johann Gramann in Königsberg with *Nun lob, mein Seel, den Herren,* and Duke Albrecht of Prussia with *Was mein Gott will, das g'scheh allzeit.* In the course of time a whole group of lieder by Michael Weisse were taken over from the song supply of the Bohemian Brethren: *Gottes Sohn ist kommen, O süsser Herre Jesu Christ, Christus, der uns selig macht, Gelobt sei Gott im höchsten Thron, Nun lasst uns den Leib begraben, Es geht daher des Tages Schein,* and others that generally did not become popular. From the Strasbourg songbooks, in which a few very prolific lied poets and composers built up a repertory with an individual stamp, came Konrad Hubert's *Allein zu dir, Herr Jesu Christ* and *O Gott, du höchster Gnadenhort* and Wolfgang Meuslin's

Mein Hirt ist Gott, der Herre mein. From the Zurich songbooks came Ambrosius Blarer's *Wach auf, wach auf, 's ist hohe Zeit* and *Wie's Gott gefällt, so g'fällts auch mir* and Johann Zwick's *Nun wolle Gott, dass unser G'sang, Auf diesen Tag bedenken wir, O Gott und Vater gnadenvoll, All Morgen ist ganz frisch und neu, Du höchstes Licht, ewiger Schein,* and *Herr Gott, dein Treu mit Gnaden leist.* Two songs by Johann Kolros of Basel came into general use: *Wo Gott zum Haus nicht gibt sein' Gunst* and *Ich dank dir, lieber Herre.*

Finally, at the border of the age of the Reformation are the lieder of the Joachimsthal cantor Nikolaus Herman from his *Sonntagsevangelien über das ganze Jahr, in Gesang verfasset für die Kinder und christlichen Hausväter* (1560, and ten new editions up to 1607) and the *Historia von der Sintflut . . . samt etlichen Historien aus den Evangelisten, auch etlichen Psalmen und geistlichen Liedern* (1562, and seven further editions up to 1607), creations tender and fanciful in inflection, subjective and sentimental in content, compositions with a markedly simple, folk-like strophic form and correspondingly simple melodies, apparently influenced primarily by the miners' songs of his German-Bohemian sphere of activity. *Lobt Gott, ihr Christen allzugleich, Erschienen ist der herrlich Tag, Wenn mein Stündlein vorhanden ist, Die helle Sonn' leucht' jetzt herfür,* and *Hinunter ist der Sonnen Schein* are in general church use. With their introverted tone and their special designation as devotional songs for the worship hours of children and household, they announced a new age. They divided the intellectual and stylistic unity of the original Reformation church lied into special categories such as educational songs, songs of edification, rhymed songs based upon the Gospels and Histories, household devotional songs, and others, all of which were cultivated with an encyclopedic thoroughness and completeness (Martin Agricola's *Sangbüchlein aller Sonntagsevangelien* of 1541 was a forerunner of these tendencies). For the time being, however, the lied supply maintained its original unity, in which Luther's entire world of thought and feeling stood behind each individual lied, and in which each lied was still sung by and written for the total congregation. Just as the tradition of the craft guilds can be explained by external reasons, the magnificent inner compactness of the entire stock of early Protestant lieder and the similarity of so many lieder to one another can be explained by the spiritual unity arising from the heart of the Reformation. Because of this unity of the repertory, together with the fact that the lied creation of the time still depended completely on one overwhelming personality, many anonymous songs were attributed to Luther without further thought. The Gloria lied *All Ehr' und Lob soll Gottes sein* may really be by Luther, but the versification of the 127th Psalm, *Vergebens ist all Müh und Kost,* often ascribed to the Reformer, was written by Jörg von Frundsperg. The attributing of anonymous songs to Luther (which also reflected a veneration of him that was becoming almost mythical) finally reached its climax in Seth Calvisius, whose song book presented no fewer than 137 texts and melodies as genuine works of Luther.

The quick rise and decline of contrafacta, especially of secular songs, led to a constant fluctuation in the Protestant stock of lieder, but it allowed the size of the total repertory to grow only relatively slowly; moreover, this development did not by any means proceed in a straight line. Johann Walter's songbook contained only 30 German lieder (a few in multiple settings) in the first edition of 1524, among them 23 by Luther. The Erfurt *Enchiridion* from the printing press "Zum schwarzen Horn" offered 26 songs in the first edition of 1524, 38 songs in the second edition a year later; the first (lost, but reconstructable) Klug songbook (1529) contained 50 lieder. The Bapst songbook (1545) contained 128 pieces; the songbook of Keuchenthal (1573) almost thirty years later, however, had only 192 lieder with 155 melodies—not a very great increase for a period so important and decisive for Reformation music.

Because of the constant change of repertory, these figures are not quite a true representation of the fertility of this lied-created epoch: rather, they represent the development of songbook production. This, however, clearly reflects the history of the Protestant church song, since the goal of general congregational singing could not well be reached through the traditional unwritten or manuscript dissemination of lieder. (On the other hand, it is evident, from the high cost of printing and the limited editions that were brought out, that not every member of the congregation had a songbook in his hand during the service; moreover, such a dissemination of songbooks was not Luther's intention.) The reciprocal effect between the Reformation and the trade of book publishing, just beginning to flourish, is confirmed in the field of music printing; the centers of the printing trade, promoted by humanism and favored by the early capitalistic administrative structure of large cities, were also the centers of songbook production.

The period from the posting of the theses (1517) to the first Luther lied (1523) and the first lieder book (1523–24) was the "songless period" of the Protestant church. The idea of a special Protestant worship service and of a corresponding lied art seems to have developed only gradually. It was prepared by the breaking away from musical-liturgical traditions of the old church, and resulted in the first liturgical writings of Luther and the first hymnals, which appeared, not by coincidence, almost at the same time.

The history of the Protestant songbook begins with the *Achtliederbuch* of the Nuremberg printer Jobst Gutknecht (1523–24); half of it was put togecher from slightly older broadsides, mostly from Magdeburg. It contained four Luther lieder, three songs of Speratus, and one anonymous two-voice setting for *In Jesus Namen heben wir an,* not poorly planned but executed in an extremely dilettantish manner and full of errors. It was followed in 1524 by the two Erfurt *Enchiridia,* which were almost identical in content, enterprises of the printing firms "Zum schwarzen Horn" (Maler) and "Zum Färbefass" (Loersfeld). The first systematically planned collection, authorized and given an introduction by Luther, also appeared that year—Johann Walter's *Wittenberger Geystliche gesangk Buchleyn.* This contained 38 German and 5 Latin compositions for three to five voices and became the model for all later choral songbooks of the young church. The fact that Luther brought out his own first songbook not with monophonic melodies but with polyphonic settings by the most famous composer available to him may be an indication that Walter had an important share in the creation of the unison repertory. It can also mean, however, that Luther was at first even more concerned with artistic polyphonic performance for church use than with the dissemination of monophonic melodies for congregational singing; this would not have been the only inconsistency in his development of reforms.

In 1525 new editions of the Erfurt *Enchiridia* appeared, as well as a Nuremberg *Enchiridion*, a Breslau songbook, and one from Zwickau. They were all only extracts from or slight additions to the repertory contained in sources of the previous year. There also appeared an unchanged new edition of Walter's songbook published by Peter Schöffer, probably in Worms; it was followed by essentially larger new editions in 1534 and 1537, published by Schöffer & Apiarius in Strasbourg, and in 1544 and 1551 published by Georg Rhau and his heirs in Wittenberg respectively. The most significant new publication of 1525, however, was Wolf Köpphel's Strasbourg *Deutsch Kirchenamt,* in which the lied repertory was increased and enriched by some important new melodies, such as those for Luther's *Ach Gott vom Himmel sieh darein* and *Es woll uns Gott genädig sein* and the Ionian melody to *Aus tiefer Not.* In 1526 this source was followed by the *Psalmen, Gebett und Kirchenübung,* which went through many editions and whose importance extended beyond the local environs of Strasbourg; in 1537–43 the four editions of *Psalmen und Geystliche Lieder;* and in 1541 the first "official" *Gesangbuch für Stett und Dorf Kirchen, Lateinische und Deudsche Schulen* (Songbook for Town and Village Churches, Latin and German Schools), with a preface by Martin Bucer. The productive period of hymnals in Strasbourg came to an end in 1545 with the *Neu Auserlesene Gesangbüchlin* (except for the 1541 volume, all published by Köpphel).

A similar independent development, which had less effect beyond its immediate area, however, is shown by the Augsburg songbooks brought out between 1529 and 1539 by various publishers. Of greater importance were the Constance songbook (1533–34, printed in Zurich by Froschauer, with new editions in 1536–37, 1540, and later) and the Zurich songbooks following it (published by Froschauer since 1536–37 with changing titles). A further special tradition began in Nuremberg in 1525. In 1526 there appeared, as the first Wittenberg congregational songbook, the *Enchiridion* of Hans Lufft, in 1528 a (lost) second Wittenberg songbook published by Hans Weiss, and—probably dependent upon that—the Leipzig *Enchiridion,* published by Michael Blum (1528 or 1529), and the Zwickau *Enchiridion.*

Not until the Wittenberg songbook published by Joseph Klug in 1529 was something essentially new presented again; the collection is lost but reconstructable through its reprints by Rauscher (Erfurt, 1531) and Gutknecht (Nuremberg, 1531) and through the altered new editions of 1533, 1535, and 1543 (with only the title page changed, 1543–45). Luther authorized it and wrote a foreword. Its organization into sections of Luther lieder, lieder "from others of us," "sacred lieder composed by pious Christians that lived before our time," and "Varia" was a prototype for a long time and was partly copied in the Bapst songbook. In 1531 the Bohemian Brethren hymnal edited by Michael Weisse appeared in Jungenbunzlau; it was an essential source from which countless new texts and melodies came into the Protestant lied repertory. It was newly edited and partially expanded in Nuremberg in 1544, 1564, and even as late as 1596; moreover, it was taken over in 1534–36 by Strasbourg and in 1539 by Ulm. In 1537 the songbook of Michael Vehe appeared as the first Catholic collection to make use of a large number of Protestant lieder.

Most of the large songbooks of the next few years were dependent upon Klug in content as well as organization; among them are the Erfurt songbook, c. 1539 (Wolfgang Stürmer), the Leipzig songbook of Valentin Schumann, 1539, and the Magdeburg songbook of Michael Lotter (1540, 1542–43). The series of songbooks edited by Luther or in direct relationship to him was closed by the Bapst songbook in Leipzig in 1545. To a still relatively strictly organized "stock" of 80 lieder and a few Latin songs, an appendix was added as a second part, *Psalmen und geistliche Lieder, welche von frommen Christen gemacht und zusammen gelesen sind* (Psalms and religious songs, which are made and read together by devout Christians). At first it contained 40 non-"canonical" songs; by the edition of 1551 this number had increased to 70. From that time on, changes in the lied stock took place primarily in such regional and quite varied appendices (which were not necessarily isolated as such in the publication); only rarely did individual songs among them push their way into the "canon" of basic lieder.

Luther began the Bapst songbook with a warning:

> Many false masters now hymns indite,
> Be on your guard and judge them aright.
> Where God is building his church and word,
> There comes the devil with lie and sword.[8]

This warning was not unjustified. The vigorous lied production of the time, soon regionally splintered, could easily have led in some publications to a neglect of the spirit of the Reformation and of the meaningful organization of materials in Klug and Bapst. Soon after Luther's death there appeared not only new types of songbooks, such as those limited to Psalter and Gospel versifications, but also some planned along traditional lines that the Reformer certainly would not have approved.

Finally, a change in the development is also indicated by the appearance of the first comprehensive collections of the entire body of German and Latin pieces sung in the church. The overlapping tendencies to institutionalize and formalize all sung portions of the Protestant service and the beginning of a decline in the liturgy both show up in the new hymnals, which soon came to resemble each other even less than had previous collections. Johann Spangenberg organized his encyclopedic songbook (Magdeburg, 1545) into *Cantiones ecclesiasticae* (Latin liturgical prose compositions and songs) and *Kirchengesänge deutsch* (German liturgical prose pieces and lieder). Johannes Keuchenthal (*Kirchengesänge lateinisch und deutsch*, Wittenberg, 1573) brought together the entire repertory in a liturgical manner; he included 192 lieder. Nikolaus Selnecker (*Christliche Psalmen . . .* Leipzig, 1587) organized basically the same material, this time according to genre. On the other hand, specialized songbooks originated in quick succession and some had great success. Thus, the entire Psalter appeared in 1553, after the example of the Reformed church, in verses and melodies by Burkhard Waldis. In 1573 there followed the German Psalter of Ambrosius Lobwasser, a translation, with the melodies, of the French Reformed Psalter of Marot and Beza (this was the greatest music publishing success of the century). The Sunday Gospels

---

8Transl. P. Z. Strodach, *Luther's Works,* LIII: 332, Philadelphia, 1965.

of Nikolaus Herman appeared in 1560, the Histories in 1562, and the *Schlesisch Singebüchlein* of Valentin Triller in 1555. At the same time the traditional type of songbook, more varied in content and made up of a basic group of lieder and individual appendices, swelled to a gigantic size, which was to be further increased around the turn of the century. In 1566 there appeared a very greatly expanded edition of the Bohemian Brethren hymnal, which was reprinted in Nuremberg in 1580. It had a strong influence upon the Protestant songbooks of the 17th century, affected the Moravian songbooks of the 18th century, and still exerts its influence today. The final songbooks of the epoch, which brought the stocks of old and new lieder together in comprehensive collections, were those of Spangenberg in Eisleben, 1568 (137 lieder), Johann Wolff in Frankfurt, 1569 (380 lieder), and Valentin Fuhrmann in Nuremberg, 1569 (213 lieder).

With a few exceptions these songbooks of the Reformation period were concerned only with monophonic lieder. To them can be added a small group of collections of polyphonic lied compositions, at first anthologies put together at a publisher's initiative, later mostly individual prints of the works of single composers. Manuscript collections limited to lieder have hardly ever been found. Most of them are more broadly planned and include Latin polyphonic music along with German lied settings. Examples of this type are provided especially by the group of so-called Walter manuscripts between 1540 and 1560 and by countless manuscript choirbooks and partbooks scattered over the entire German-speaking area. They are mostly nonliturgical, sometimes arranged according to musical forms but often without any organization of the contents at all. They took their supply of polyphonic sacred lied compositions in part directly from the printed collections and added only insignificantly to the total repertory, generally with local compositions of no consequence.

Most of the printed sources had little influence even when they served as models in the limited transmission of manuscripts. Two of the earliest collections, however, authorized by Luther or originating in his circle, had greater impact: the songbook of Johann Walter (1524), the first and decisive source of Protestant lied polyphony, and the *Neue deutsche geistliche Gesänge* from the most important publisher for the young church, Georg Rhau (1544) The countless secular lied prints of the time—which, like those of Ott and Forster, generally include a few sacred songs—are less significant. Alongside these prints stands the *Melodiae Prudentianae,* with four-voice compositions of Sebastian Forster and Lukas Hordisch on hymn texts of Prudentius and Sedulius (Leipzig, 1533), a few of which were taken into the Protestant church. The *Concentus novi trium vocum* by Johann Kugelmann of Königsberg, published in 1540 by Kriesstein in Augsburg, was meaningful in content but completely limited in effect to a peripheral local area; it contained not only three-voice compositions, some of high quality, but also a number of new lied melodies.

Even after Rhau's *Neue deutsche geistliche Gesänge* the number of Protestant polyphonic lied publications remained extraordinarily small. In 1551 Rothenbucher in Nuremberg published the *Bergreihen auf zwo Stimmen componirt* as a specialty of "folklore." Triller's *Schlesisch Singebüchlein* followed in 1555 (reprinted in 1559 with an altered title) with three-voice compositions; it is important mainly as a source of melodies. In 1561 and 1566 Walter brought out a few smaller works *(Ein neues christliches Lied, Ein gar schöner christlicher Bergreihen,* and *Das christlich Kinderlied D. Martini Lutheri "Erhalt uns Herr" mit etlichen lateinischen und deutschen Gesängen vermehrt).* Another collection appearing in 1566 was outstanding in quality: the four- and five-voice *Geistliche und weltliche deutsche Gesang* by Matthäus Le Maistre, Johann Walter's successor as *Kapellmeister* in Electoral Saxony (70 of the 92 compositions are based upon Protestant lieder). In 1568 came the collection *Schöner ausserlessner deutscher Psalm und andere künstliche Moteten und geistliche Lieder XX* by Clemens Stephani, with works of Benedictus Ducis, Johannes Hagius, Caspar Othmayr, Valentin Rabe, and others. At the end of the Reformation period proper are the collections restricted to special categories of the church lied or to complete Psalters. Thus, in 1569 we have Sigmund Hemmel's posthumous work *Der gantz Psalter Davids* in four-voice compositions, edited by Lukas Osiander and Balthasar Bidenbach, a counterpart to the unpublished German Psalter of the Hessian *Kapellmeister* Johann Heugel after the versified Psalter of Burkhard Waldis. In addition there were Joachim Magdeburg's *Christliche und Trostliche Tischgesange,* 1572; Wolfgang Figulus's *Zwantzig artige und kurtze Waynacht Liedlein, alt und new,* with settings by Martin Agricola, Johannes Galliculus, Clemens non Papa, Ludwig Senfl, Figulus himself, and others (1575); and the ode and lied compositions on poems of Ludwig Helmboldt by Joachim a Burck and Johannes Eccard (1574), Joachim a Burck alone (1575), and Johannes Steuerlein (1575).

In a final group of sources are some isolated lieder handed down in connection with the far-reaching tradition of the Latin liturgical chants which in the beginning formed the basis of the Protestant liturgy and which the church lied slowly supplemented and gradually displaced altogether. These sources consist mainly of the countless regional and local *Kirchenordnungen*—i.e., regulations for services of worship and affairs of the church—which in the Reformation era appeared everywhere in manuscript and print. This group of sources further includes the encyclopedic songbooks from the end of the epoch which aimed at a comprehensive collection and preservation of the Latin and German monophonic repertory (Keuchenthal, Spangenberg) or expressly at an obligatory organization and clarification of the liturgy itself. Of basic importance to this last-named endeavor was the *Psalmodia, hoc est Cantica sacra veteris ecclesiae selecta* of Lucas Lossius (1553, 1561, 1569, 1579, and at other times), which, as its title declared, desired to present exclusively a selection of the liturgical chants of the old church for use in the new. It organized into three comprehensive divisions all of the Latin items useful and necessary for the Protestant church; it included very few lieder. Originally planned as an agenda only for the Lüneburg churches, the work became centrally important in all of northern Germany. As Lossius himself stated in the foreword, it attempted to counteract musically the quick decline of the Protestant liturgy. The book received the stamp of highest authority through a foreword by Melanchthon, a friend and teacher of the collector. In relation to the *Psalmodia,* the remaining sources for liturgical song step into the background. Beginning with Luther's own writings of 1523 and 1526 concerning the order of services of worship through the Bugenhagen church regulations (Brunswick, 1531, and others), on to the orders of Kalenberg, 1542, and Erfurt, 1541, there were countless orders of service containing texts and melodies to Latin songs and German lieder. They all were absorbed into the above-named later collections of Keuchenthal, Spangenberg, and Lossius.

LATIN AND GERMAN LITURGY

It is not the tradition of Latin liturgical chant in Luther's day that will be considered here, but the use of this tradition. The Protestant church did not bring any new material to this field; Luther's new specifications for the psalm tones of the recitations (Tone 8 for the Epistle and Tone 6 for the Gospel) and the notes provided for the Words of Institution (set by Luther himself, according to Johann Walter's testimony) were only simplifications and limitations compared to the wealth of recitation tones of the Catholic church. The examples of liturgical chants (i.e., pieces for the Ordinary and Proper of the Mass, antiphons, hymns, tracts, and other types) contained in the above-named collections and orders of worship were nothing other than those also found in the Roman Graduals and Antiphonals; they were only limited to pieces usable in the Protestant service. Such limitations followed for two reasons: first, the changes gradually coming into the liturgical structure of the service itself, which in contrast to the Roman tradition necessitated abbreviations, omissions, and substitutions, and second, the changes that Luther made in the liturgical year. Because many feasts of Mary, of the saints, and of the martyrs were omitted and because the Protestant church, since Luther's *Ordnung des Gottesdiensts* of 1523, took over only Matins, Mass, and Vespers from the large number of Roman services (Vigils were added only on the evening preceding the three high feasts), many pieces of the traditional liturgy were discontinued. The core remaining after those items consisted of exactly the same textual and musical material as that required by the Roman church, with one basic difference: the Roman church strictly prescribed the liturgy for a specific day of the church year, for the rank of a particular feast or service; this was never the case in the Protestant church. The Protestant order was frequently upset by special regional and local regulations—some of which went back to local pre-Reformation traditions only tolerated by the Catholic church—and finally completely forgotten. The provincial variants of the traditional Gregorian melodies, especially those from central Germany, explain to a large degree the melodic deviations of the Protestant settings from the versions of the Catholic church in use today, as they are codified in the *Editio Vaticana*.

Since Luther essentially retained the Roman service for Mass, Matins, and Vespers, the Latin liturgical chants remained unchanged as basic material for the Protestant service. The Mass was and remained the principal service. The Roman church had created for it a formula that had gone almost unchanged for centuries; old melodies might occasionally be replaced by new ones, but the repertory of texts was inviolable. It did not occur to either Luther or other, more radical reformers to undermine this foundation. The celebration of the Lord's Supper is the content around which the total ceremony of the Mass forms the vestment. Only those portions of it had to be omitted that ran contrary to Luther's altered interpretation of the Lord's Supper. Even though he preserved the doctrine of the Real Presence, the mystical presence of the body and blood of Christ in the bread and wine, he decidedly rejected the central doctrine of the transubstantiation, which formed the main support of the Catholic interpretation of the Lord's Supper and to which all ceremonies of the Mass were related. In consequence, the portion containing the transubstantiation with all its preparations and especially the many prayers accompanying it, the *Canon Missae,* had to be taken out of its liturgical association and everything related to it removed from the other parts of the Mass ceremony. Through Luther's views concerning the ceremonies (they do not grow out of faith, but they do no harm to faith; they are valuable for the weak, but can never be ends in themselves and thus become rules), the way was paved for a further breaking up of the ritual and even for the introduction of arbitrary acts. Luther rejected the Mass as a symbol, as a "thing done," and filled it with a "pneumatic" (Fendt) content through the ideas of constantly operative grace and the everlasting assurance of this grace. Through his doctrine of justification, he removed from the Mass the character of *opus operatum,* of a good work pleasing to God, substituted the concept of divine influence imparting itself to the penitent congregation celebrating the Lord's Supper, without their having to deserve it by special merit. Finally, he took from it the rank of a sacrosanct rite and made it instead a celebration that depended less on the form than on the spirit. From all this there resulted changes in the external form of the Mass that were insignificant in relation to the fundamental change in content, but those alterations opened the door to freedom in all ceremonies. This led to the further diminishing of liturgical form and, finally, to an almost complete loss of it. In this apparently unimportant step, however, lay a wise restraint: if Luther had created a new form of worship, it would have remained a sectarian service, ineffectual for the whole body. Because he kept the Roman Mass with only slight alterations, however, and filled it with a new spirit, he must have had an uncommonly strong influence upon the Catholic men of his time (Fendt).

Luther's *Formula Missae et Communionis* of 1523 provided for an entirely Latin celebration of a Protestant Mass order for "monasteries and cathedrals." The Roman as well as the Protestant Mass makes a distinction between parts with unchanging texts (the Ordinary—Kyrie, Gloria, Credo, Sanctus with Hosanna and Benedictus, Agnus Dei) and parts with texts that change according to the day of the liturgical year (the Proper *de tempore*) and according to the feasts of the saints, apostles, and martyrs (the Proper *de sanctis*—Introit, Gradual with Alleluia or Tract, Offertory, Communion). The Proper *de sanctis* played a small role in the Protestant church, however; only a few Marian feasts and the Evangelists' and apostles' days were generally retained (in addition, individual territories and congregations observed other special saints' days according to their tradition). The basis of the Proper in the Roman church—the order of which was soon entirely neglected in the Protestant church—was formed by the pericopes, i.e., the order of the changing Epistle and Gospel excerpts to be read on each day. All other changing texts are meaningfully related to them.

13. Martin Luther, *Deudsche Messe und Ordnung Gottisdienst,* Wittenberg, 1526, M. Lotter. Title page.

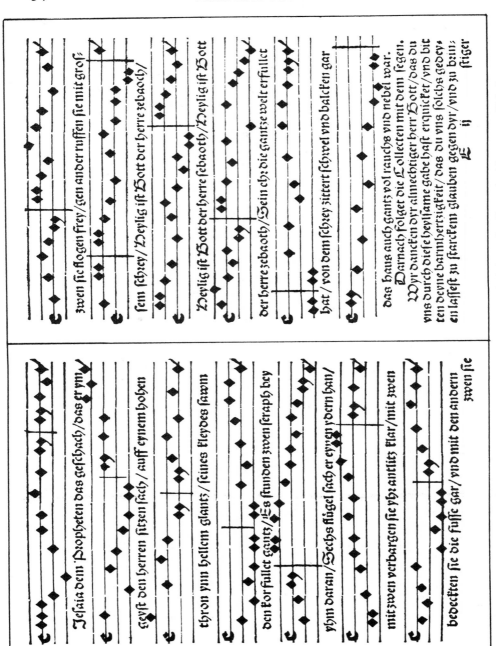

14. Martin Luther, Sanctus lied *Jesaja dem Propheten das geschah* from the *Deutsche Messe*, page E 1–2.

15. From Johannes Bugenhagen, *Der Kaiserlichen Stadt Lübeck christliche Ordnung*, Lübeck, 1531, Johann Balhorn.

16. Illustration and the lied *Christum wir sollen loben schon* from the Klug
songbook, Wittenberg, 1533.

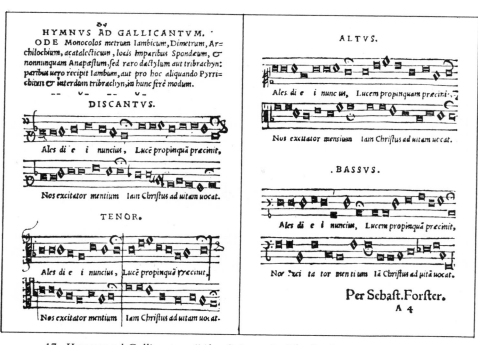

17. *Hymnus ad Gallicantum "Ales diei nuncius"* in the four-voice setting of
Sebastian Forster from *Melodiae Prudentianae*, Leipzig, 1533, N. Faber.

The Introit, generally a psalm verse followed by a doxology after which the verse is repeated, was in both churches the act of preparation for the Mass. The choir performed this Latin text as a polyphonic composition only at High Mass in the Roman church, but probably always in the Protestant. During the singing of the Introit the priest stepped up to the altar with the ministrants and prepared himself for the action by silently confessing his sin. Then followed the *Kyrie eleison—Christ eleison—Kyrie eleison* three times, preferably in the troped settings that were banned in the Catholic church by the Council of Trent; then the *Gloria in excelsis,* occasionally also troped and in settings resembling the lied (after the example of pre-Reformation original compositions perhaps intended for congregational singing). Kyrie and Gloria were normally presented by the choir polyphonically (in the Roman liturgy this portion, as well as all choral pieces to be mentioned below, were performed, in a *Missa lecta,* monophonically in Gregorian chant or responsorially in alternation between priest and choir; they were sung polyphonically only in High Masses, *Missae solemnes*).

The section of preparation was followed by a spoken portion, i.e., Salutation ("Dominus vobiscum," etc.), Collect (a *de tempore* prayer for parts of which Luther had developed new formulas), and the reading of the Epistle by the priest in a simple recitation tone. Then followed the Gradual, again one or more psalm verses in a polyphonic setting, and the Alleluia with verse (psalm verse) and repetition of the Alleluia, also polyphonic. At this point the Roman church included a sequence, also sung, with a nonbiblical text of a contemplative nature in poetic form. The Protestant church from the beginning rejected the sequence, with the exception of those for Christmas; it occasionally kept sequences for Good Friday, Easter, Pentecost, and a few other feast days (since the Council of Trent the Catholic church was limited to five). In contrast, it frequently kept the Tract, which took the place of the Alleluia in Advent and Lent. This entire group of pieces (beginning with the Gradual and ending with the sequence) maintained a very unsteady position in the Protestant service of the 16th century, and correspondingly few polyphonic Gradual compositions are represented in the main sources. The real Gradual was soon discontinued, leaving only the Alleluia with its verse or the Tract—if, indeed, the whole section was not replaced by a German congregational lied. This was followed again by a salutation and the announcement of the Gospel, then the reading of it in a simple recitation tone. The Latin Credo followed as a confession of faith, at first generally sung polyphonically by the choir in the Protestant church (as may be concluded from the polyphonic Masses that have been handed down); later it was more frequently sung monophonically by the priest if not omitted altogether, as often happened. Finally, in the Latin celebration of the Mass it could also be replaced by Luther's German Credo lied, a practice made easier because the composition of new monophonic Latin Credo and Sanctus melodies resembling the lied and patterned after folksong melodies (a process especially vigorous around 1500) had played a leading role in German-speaking areas.

Thus was the first portion of the Latin Mass treated; the sermon now followed in German. The Roman church in German-speaking countries frequently put it here, too, but with them it had only a subordinate position. In Protestant worship, where its contents were adjusted to interpret the previously read Gospel, it became a controlling force and tore apart the formal coherence of the action of the Mass. For spiritual reasons, too, its place was badly chosen, for, according to Luther's wishes, it was to be the decisive implement in shaking up the unbelievers, in calling them to faith, and in preparing them for the Gospel. Actually, the consummation of the Mass presupposed this faith, and therefore the correct place for the sermon would have been at the beginning of the service. Its assigned place was the result of careful compromise with tradition rather than of consistent reform in the celebration of the Mass.

After the sermon the real Communion ceremony began, at which time bread and wine were placed upon the altar. In the Roman church it was begun with the Offertory (a psalm verse sung by the choir or the priest). This part, as an introduction to the *Canon Missae*—the prayers accompanying the transubstantiation, always surrounded by special mystery—was completely omitted together with this canon in the Lutheran church from the very beginning. Only the Preface remained, a short introductory prayer formula; it was followed with the Sanctus sung by the choir, with Hosanna and Benedictus; during the latter the much debated elevation of the bread and the cup took place, which Luther wanted to preserve "because of the weak." More prayers followed, then the proclamation of peace and forgiveness, then the distribution of the elements in both kinds while the choir sang the tripartite Agnus Dei. After the distribution came the Communion, the last of the *de tempore* portions (again a polyphonically sung psalm antiphon); like the Gradual, the Communion was not used for long in the Protestant church. The conclusion was formed by the Post-Communion: prayers, salutation, and blessing. If no communicants were present, the entire portion after the sermon was essentially abbreviated, and it more or less lost its liturgical form.

The Mass order created by Luther's *Formula Missae* was very close to the Roman tradition, even in details. The Latin language, the use of Eucharistic vestments and candles, the sign of the cross, and the elevation were kept. There was really no place in this form for German lieder. Luther, however, wanted the congregation to sing German lieder after the Gradual, Sanctus, and Agnus Dei; the idea appeared for the first time in the year of the *Formula Missae, 1523.* Few lieder were as yet available; new ones had to be written, especially since it was necessary to have German versions either of the Ordinary pieces in question or the psalm text of the respective *de tempore* piece. Men of this period, for whom the liturgy of each Sunday or feast embodied a specific idea belonging only to that day, felt that it destroyed both the content and the form of the Mass to insert lieder of just any kind, as was later the custom. Thus the liturgical order, especially the *de tempore,* indicated specific assignments for the poets; it is understandable why Luther, in a letter of December 21, 1527, asked Spalatin and Electoral Councillor von Dolzigk for poems on certain texts—namely, Psalms 6, 143, 119, and also 33, 34, and 103; these psalms had specific places in the liturgy that were to be filled through lieder.

The ever more strongly advancing idea of a priesthood of all believers, along with political considerations grounded in the revolutionary activities of a radical group of preachers led by Thomas Müntzer, the tendency toward liberty in observance of ceremonies, and probably also the desire to present his own solutions in contrast with the older German Masses: these forces impelled Luther forward from the *Formula Missae* of 1523 to the *Deutsche Messe und Ordnung des Gottesdiensts* of 1526. This does not mean that he later completely discarded the Latin Mass. In addition to the passages above concerning Luther's concept of music, countless further proofs can be adduced that throughout his life the Mass always seemed to him a higher, more festive form when it was performed completely or at least partially in Latin; in 1536, in Luther's own vicinity of Wittenberg, pure Latin Masses were still being held, along with pure German ones.

It is absolutely certain that older attempts to create a German Mass had made a strong impression on Luther without affecting the independence of his decisions. The Protestant Mass of Kaspar Kantz, the Reformer from Nördlingen, had appeared in 1522. From 1523 on, Thomas Müntzer, whose dangerous radicalism pulled Karlstadt into his sway and caused Luther to give up his safe asylum in the Wartburg and come forward against him in Wittenberg, produced his German Mass orders (*Deutsch Evangelische Messe* and *Deutsch Kirchen Ampt;* both Alstedt, 1524). In the unchanged reprints of the Erfurt *Kirchenämter* (1525, 1526, 1527, and expanded and altered to conform more with Luther in 1541, 1543, 1550), with Müntzer's name very wisely omitted, they penetrated even Luther's immediate neighborhood. If the Mass of Kantz was basically only a German version of the Roman order without significant inner changes, Müntzer's order anticipated much of Luther's in content (the displacing of the priest by the congregation, the elimination of un-Protestant pieces) as well as in its form and its relationship to music. With Müntzer—a revolutionary extremist, to be sure, but a deeply religious man unjustly reproached by Luther—there already appeared hymns in the form of German lieder, some of which were taken over into the Lutheran songbooks: *Der Heiligen Leben tut stets nach Gott streben (Vita sanctorum)*, a rewriting of the Christmas sequence *Grates nunc omnes* as *Lasst uns nun alle danksagen,* and others. Some of Müntzer's German versions, such as that of *Veni redemptor gentium* (see page 37), are comparable to Luther's *lied* creations, although they lack the structural strength and oral appeal of the German *lied* needed for widespread effectiveness. Others, especially the prose pieces, in spite of an earnest dignity in the fundamental attitude, suffer from a word-tone relationship sometimes no more than formal, from false accentuation and meaningless diastematicism. In this case Luther could be critical with justification in accordance with his principles of a meaningful German translation, wholly apart from the deep aversion he had for the anarchistic "Alstedter Geist" for political reasons. His sharp rejection of Müntzer and the Müntzer Masses do not, however, alter the fact that many direct influences from Müntzer are found in his own German Mass, as well as indirect influences from the Erfurt orders. Although the orders from Strasbourg and Basel (essentially from Karlstadt) of the same years point in the same direction, the Müntzer Mass is musically closest to Luther's. Luther's work has given the most decisive and most fruitful impulses to the development of Protestant church music; in originality, consistency, and liturgical significance, however, as an expression of a thought and will radically determined to do something new, it was surpassed by its predecessors. Luther's German Mass was the most successful and the most decisive for the future because it was by Luther, but there is no question that it gave the impulse to the countless compromise forms following it and thereby led to the later dissolution of the Mass form.

On October 29, 1525, the twentieth Sunday after Trinity, Luther held the first German Mass in the palace church at Wittenberg. The music as well as the text had presented him with many difficulties. "I would like very much to have a German Mass, and I am preoccupied with the idea. But I want it to have a real German quality. If the Latin text is translated and the Latin tones or notes are preserved, I do not object, but it sounds neither agreeable nor correct. Text and notes, accent, melody, and movement must come out of the correct mother tongue and voice. Otherwise everything is a monkey-like imitation." (*Wider die himmlischen Propheten,* 1524; similarly also in the correspondence with Hausmann, who made an attempt in 1525 to set the German Mass to music but did not gain Luther's approval). In fact, here lay the central musical problem. Luther's artistic sense protected him from the superficiality of merely placing the German text under the customary melody of the Latin piece; the music did not have to be entirely rewritten, but it still had to be carefully adapted if it were to be sung in German. For this purpose Luther called to Wittenberg two of his compatriots, the *Kapellmeister* Konrad Rupsch and the bass Johann Walter, still young at the time, who a year earlier had brought out Luther's Wittenberg songbook with his polyphonic compositions; Luther wanted the help of the two men in the musical execution (the report by Walter handed down by Michael Praetorius and two letters of Luther to the composer provide testimony of this cooperation). The order of the Collects (performed without a rich musical dress), of the prayers, Prefaces, Salutations, Words of Institution and Distribution remained principally the same as in the Latin Mass, except that all parts were presented in German and sung to correspondingly modified recitation tones. In the vocal pieces that may also be performed by the choir, however, much was changed. A psalm verse in prose remained for the Introit; it is not clear who was intended to sing it. It is unlikely that the choir would have performed it as a motet, since the sources from this period contain almost no psalm motets in the German language and since settings of a later date were of entire psalms (which would have been too long for the Introit) rather than of psalm verses (which would have been more useful from the liturgical point of view). Perhaps the pastor performed the Introit monophonically. The Kyrie remained as in the Latin Mass, but was reduced to a three-fold instead of a nine-fold execution (Luther's proposal found little support in the church orders, however). The Gloria was completely omitted, but in most Protestant Mass orders of the time it was fitted in following the example of Bugenhagen (Brunswick, 1528) as a translation of the Latin text or as a German lied. The German lied *Nun bitten wir den Heiligen Geist* or another *de tempore* lied was to be sung after the Epistle. After the Gospel the entire congregation sang the German affirmation of faith: *Wir glauben all an einen Gott.* The sermon was followed by the exhortation to Communion, the Words of

Institution, and Luther's German Sanctus lied *Jesaja dem Propheten das geschah* (this "narrative" lied was liturgically an unhappy choice as a substitute for the Sanctus, in spite of its visionary grandeur). During the Distribution this lied was continued; if there were many communicants, further lieder were added, *Jesus Christus unser Heiland* or others. After Communion there followed a German Agnus Dei, *Christe, du Lamm Gottes* or another lied. The Communion and the Offertory disappeared completely; the Gradual was reduced to one lied, as it was later in the Latin Protestant Mass.

Luther's essay on the German Mass shows how hard he had struggled with all the details of the musical formulation. New forms of recitation tones were developed for the German Introit, stylistically dependent upon the Gregorian tradition but regulated by the rules of the German language. Three or four of the Kyrie melodies of the old liturgy were preserved with few alterations; the substitution of the Credo and Sanctus by German lieder had been somewhat anticipated by the new song-like Latin compositions in the German-speaking area. For Collect, Epistle, and Gospel the traditional recitation tones were again reorganized (the fact that they were not replaced everywhere is shown by special local solutions, such as the Gospel and Epistle tones of the cantor David Ciceler for the Magdeburg churches). Luther's improving hand can be seen throughout; at the end he even added an "exercise of the melodies."

The performance rested principally in the hands of the priest. Nothing special was said of the choir, and there are, as has already been said, almost no motet compositions of the respective prose texts from this period. General practices of the time and numerous reports and orders of worship make clear that if a choir was available it always participated, even if at first only in the singing of polyphonic lieder in the German Mass. Johann Walter's songbook, which could offer material for at least the lied portion of the German Mass, might also have been commissioned and executed with this situation in mind.

Luther's Latin and German Masses form the poles between which lie all the Mass orders used in subsequent practice. In no case was one of the two formulas simply taken over in its entirety; everywhere they incorporated changes stemming from local custom or reformative zeal, encouraged by the flexibility of Luther's prescriptions. Johannes Brenz followed first with an order for Schwäbisch-Hall, then for a large part of the southwest. Bugenhagen organized great parts of north Germany. His orders clearly show attempts at mixed-language versions of the Mass. Thus, his Brunswick order of 1528 calls for a German Introit verse but a Latin Kyrie and Gloria (perhaps to preserve the tradition of the polyphonic Latin Mass); later, a Latin Alleluia with psalm verse, but not the real Gradual; the confession of faith in German prose by the whole congregation; then the Credo lied, Sanctus in Latin, and between them German lieder. Instead of an enumeration of the countless alterations, a later example will suffice. In 1553, Lossius prescribed the following order, obligatory in the second half of the century at least for wide regions of north Germany (all Latin): Introit *de tempore*; Kyrie (according to season and rank of the service); Gloria, in place of which *Allein Gott in der Höh sei Ehr* could "sometimes" also be sung; Epistle; Alleluia with sequence for feasts, on other days a German psalm lied; sermon with an annexed Litany;

Credo or *Wir glauben all* (consequently the affirmation of faith after the serman, an order not widely used); Exhortation and Preface; Sanctus or *Jesaja dem Propheten;* altar prayers, Institution, and Distribution, during which lieder were sung, such as *Jesus Christus unser Heiland, Gott sei gelobet,* and others; Agnus Dei or *O Lamm Gottes unschuldig;* prayer of thanksgiving, prayer for the church, and benediction; closing lied, *Erhalt uns, Herr, bei deinem Wort.* In this order Latin pieces were preferred and in the majority. A closing lied, as was later always the case, was substituted for the Communion; and in later use the Introit was normally replaced by an opening lied. Lossius did not yet indicate the interpolation of the sermon song as a new permanent section immediately before the sermon, a custom already widespread about this time (additional strophes were also frequently sung after the sermon). The Offertory was missing, as always later on; only the Alleluia with verse remained of the Gradual pieces, but even here it could be replaced by a lied (as it usually was from this time forth). In the main, however, Lossius preserved the five Ordinary movements.

It is not necessary for an understanding of music history to follow all the countless variations to which the Protestant Mass formulas were subject from the time of the Reformation on through the centuries; it is sufficient to know the extreme possibilities and an average solution of the problem such as that of Lossius. There are no combinations that did not appear in some church regulations; from the end of the 16th century through the following centuries the Mass became more and more abbreviated, disarranged, and curtailed. In some regions of south Germany the Latin order had been completely suppressed by the end of the 16th century; in others, especially in Leipzig and Nuremberg, it was preserved into the beginning of the 18th century.

Matins and Vespers were subject to even greater alterations than the Mass; Lossius's order can serve here also as an example of the average structure of these services toward the end of the Reformation period. Matins began with an antiphon, which might be a motet by the choir or a chant by the pastor; on the highest feasts it was preceded by an Invitatory, a verse of invitation "quod sui est festi proprium." Three psalm readings followed ("Beatus vir," "Quare fremuerunt gentes," "Domine, quid multiplicati sunt," or others); then the antiphon was repeated. This was followed by the Gospel "latine in choro," which a boy then repeated in German "ante chorum"; for the highest feasts it was sung in Latin by the cantor and a short responsory was added to it. (Lossius does not mention the sermon, but probably one was given most of the time.) After this came the Te Deum in Latin and, as a standard conclusion, the *Benedicamus Domino,* sung again by the pastor or the choir.

Vespers began with an antiphon, which was to be sung by boys "specially chosen and trained to do it"; there followed a psalm and the repetition of the antiphon. As in Matins a boy sang the Gospel of the next Sunday or feast, to which a short responsory was again added. Then came one or more hymns, Latin or German, the antiphon to the Magnificat, and, as the standard principal musical item of Vespers, the Magnificat itself. The choir repeated the Magnificat antiphon (it could also be played by the organ at this time); the *Benedicamus,* again sung by "selecti pueri," formed the conclusion, as in Matins. On the eve of the highest feasts Compline was also observed. It consisted of four psalm readings ("Cum invocarem," "In te, Domine, speravi," "Qui habitat in adjutorio," and "Ecce nunc benedicite"), the canticle of Simeon, Nunc Dimittis, and the *Benedicamus*. All of these—the psalms, antiphons, responsories, and even the *Benedicamus*—are obviously *de tempore* pieces, changing according to the rank of the service. On particular feasts this formula underwent certain changes, the most important of which were the Passion readings according to the four Gospels in Matins, one each on certain days of Holy Week (the specific days varied greatly). Here the figural setting of the Passion—i.e., the polyphonic through-composed Passion text—could be used either in place of the reading or in addition to it. On Good Friday the Lamentations of Jeremiah were sung, first of all in unison and perhaps then, optionally, also through-composed in the manner of a motet. All of these stipulations were varied in many ways in the orders of worship.

THE LIED IN THE LITURGY. THE SINGING OF LIEDER

Much of the interest music historians have shown in these orders of worship is based on the principle of substitution and addition peculiar to the Protestant liturgy. The new arrangements in German in no way immediately displaced the Latin Mass; on the contrary, in many regions there was an attempt to keep the Latin form pure, partly for political reasons (to parry the opposition of Charles V). Thus, Melanchthon in the 24th article of the Augsburg Confession expressly attested the strong preservation in the Protestant church of the traditional Mass orders and ceremonies and their equivalence with those of the Catholics; the difference lay only in the fact that "here and there German songs were added to the Latin" (as had definitely been customary and permissible in the pre-Reformation period). The flexibility which characterized the Protestant arrangements from the outset, which was definitely not a matter of indifference to Luther but a matter of principle, was probably intentionally passed over in silence by Melanchthon; still, his declaration doubtlessly originated in an existent tendency which, strengthened through the Augsburg interim, became more perceptible in certain state churches as the Reformation neared its end. In reality, however, the flexibility of the Protestant liturgy admitted in practice any theoretically imaginable combination. The most important of these combinations from the standpoint of music history are shown in the following: 1) any service could be held completely in Latin; 2) any service could be held completely in German; 3) for any Latin portion of text a German lied could be substituted; 4) for any Latin or German prose text a German lied could be substituted; 5) to any Latin or German prose text a German lied could be added; 6) in certain places (before and after the sermon, during Communion) German lieder could be freely added.

Such is the outline of the entire, infinitely variable system of the liturgical functions of Protestant church music. Of course, the substituted or added German lieder had to "fit"; only in the period of decline of the liturgy were favorite lieder substituted with no considerations other than their popularity and the congregation's wish to sing them. The sections of the Mass Ordinary could be replaced or duplicated by only a small number of corresponding lieder (Kyrie: *Kyrie, Gott Vater in Ewigkeit,* for the first time in the Naumburg church order of 1537, although the untroped or translated troped Kyrie pieces of the Roman liturgy remained at least as popular; Gloria: *All Ehr und Lob soll Gottes sein* or *Allein Gott in der Höh sei Ehr;* Credo: always Luther's *Wir glauben;* Sanctus: always Luther's *Jesaja dem Propheten;* Agnus: *O Lamm Gottes unschuldig* or *Christe, du Lamm Gottes*). All other lieder—those replacing or duplicating the Proper as well as the freely inserted pieces—had to be *de tempore.* Lieder which replaced or duplicated psalms or psalm verses had to be either translations of the psalms in question or related to them in meaning, appropriate to the character of the day; they could also be general lieder of faith. The apparent variability of the system was limited through the *de tempore* principle: it was necessary to preserve the basic character of the day as well as the content of the individual portions of the service. This principle was steadily adhered to, at least during the Reformation period, in spite of all the "liberty in the ceremonies"; herein lay the unshakable foundation of the Protestant service despite the elasticity of the liturgy. From this principle the sermon also acquired its true central importance; among the many interpretations of the individual parts of the service, it was, as the exegesis of the Gospel, the controlling nucleus. Everything else came more and more to relate to the sermon as the celebration of the Lord's Supper became more an independent portion, or merely an appendage of the principal service, and also as the remaining standard liturgical portions gravitating around the sermon fluctuated between devotional and educational ideas.

It has already been mentioned that certain songs, such as the Ordinary lieder and the closing lied, were established as fixed standard portions in specific places within the liturgy. In place of the pronouncement of peace, *Verleih uns Frieden gnädiglich* was soon regularly used; *Komm Heiliger Geist,* or another song entreating the divine Presence, was frequently found as an opening lied along with the Introit or in place of it. With such a penetration and establishment of lieder at certain places within the service, an ever greater opportunity was given for congregational participation. This was true mainly for village churches and smaller congregations; where choirs were available in larger churches, they soon claimed the principal share even in the singing of the lieder, a fact that led to embarrassing conditions and complaints toward the end of the Reformation era. Under the principle of substitution and addition, other musical forms were given great opportunity for development along with the lied. In the first place, the use of Latin Mass compositions, greatly flourishing at this period, was unhindered. In the second place, Latin motets could be used ad libitum as long as they were textually suitable; a sister genre in the German language gradually came into being. Finally, the practice of the time allowed the organ many opportunities for participation. It is true that Luther himself mentioned it only seldom, and the orders of Bugenhagen and Jonas even expressly forbade its use for Wittenberg; still, Musculus reported its use in Wittenberg as well as in Eisenach, and many other sources, primarily church regulations and later agendas, such as that of Lossius, confirm its use (this topic will be considered below in detail).

In any case the lied was, at least in theory, primarily the concern of the congregation. How the congregation actually carried out the assignment intended for it is even today not completely clear. People accustomed to singing only in secular surroundings and to remaining silent in the traditional church (if the few admitted lieder are excepted) now had to learn how to sing in church. The texts of the songs were new and so were the melodies, especially those of the core lieder, even when they resembled familiar prototypes. Luther's admonition to his indolent fellow citizens of Wittenberg that they apply more industry to memorizing the new songs shows that there was opposition to be overcome. Soon there were abundant songbooks, but they were intended for the pastor and the cantor, not for the people. Their costliness and the small size of the editions limited their dissemination even among the wealthy citizenry; moreover, Luther expressly refused to let the congregation use them (Gebhardt). The use of well-known melodies in contrafacta could not solve the problem; at most that merely reduced it (and this only for those in the congregation familiar with the lied model in a secular context). Nevertheless, this primary difficulty was overcome in other ways, particularly with the help of the school. The children learned the lieder and led the singing in the service; thus the repertory penetrated the heart and soul of the young generation. There is much evidence, too, that boys were placed among the adults, that the cantor stood in the middle of the nave of the church to lead the singing, and that the youth of the congregation were summoned to church on Sunday afternoons to rehearse the lieder (there were even specialists who were called into the congregation for this work). *Kantoreien* and *Kaland-Bruderschaften,* societies in which adults from educated circles came together for the cultivation of choral music, were formed everywhere for this purpose. Along with the school choirs, these organizations were soon the strongest supports of Protestant choral music. (At the same time, they acted as burial organizations, taking care of the dignified ceremony and music for the funerals of their members, and also sang for weddings, and so on.) They enjoyed the special protection of the religious and secular authorities or, as in the case of the famous Torgau *Kantorei* founded and led by Walter, of the princes. In addition, the *Kantorei* members, as experienced singers, naturally helped facilitate the singing of the congregation. In spite of all of this assistance, however, the congregation still had to learn the words and melody at some time, even more so since in this period "trailing along" after an organ accompaniment was not yet possible (organ accompaniment for congregational song first appeared in the 17th century). The singing of a congregation was always "choral," i.e., in unison and unaccompanied (from which—completely misleading but customary even today—the word "chorale" later came to mean the lied itself. From the very beginning the "chorale" was the Gregorian chant, or its respective Protestant recasting, and "choral" or "choraliter" designated monophonic singing in contrast to "figural," i.e., polyphonic singing, not the piece itself). And here the second difficulty arises: if the congregation learned text and melody, it also had to sing the lied together rhythmically.

The actual treatment of this rhythm is still largely unclear, and even by exact methodical procedures part of it can be inferred only hypothetically. In any case, it is certain that the real performance was not just the simple isometric presentation of the melody that has become generally customary since the middle of the 17th century—in equal note values in 4/4 time or in a uniform 3/4 rhythm with fermatas at the ends of lines.

The lied poet working in the manner of the Meistersinger composed his own melodies. These may have been written down at first in a predominantly non-rhythmic chant notation or in equal mensural note values without rhythmic significance. In any case, Luther apparently worked in this manner. Melodies borrowed from secular lieder were naturally taken over with their freer and normally more diversified rhythms or, if they came from polyphonic compositions, in the rhythmic form of the models. New melodies composed "nonrhythmically" also must have passed through intermediate stages on their way into the songbooks. There they appear in the most varied rhythmic forms, which only in individual cases can be explained by printing convenience or local tradition: in Gothic *Hufnagel* notation with rhythms suggested or differentiated by dotting and ligatures; in cantus-fractus notation combining *Hufnagel* neumes and mensural notes; in forms almost rhythmless but nevertheless mensurally notated, with semibreves as a basic value, breves for the stereotyped extension of line beginnings and endings, and fermatas for the ends of lines (thus forming an isometric rhythmic pattern that later became the customary congregational pattern); and finally in a rhythmic mensural notation differentiated throughout like the tenor voice of the complicated polyphonic lied compositions of the time. In fact, many melodies may have been taken over into the songbooks rhythmically unchanged from polyphonic compositions. This practice is strongly indicated not only by the impractical ranges for congregational singing but also by the notating of mensural rests at the beginning of the melody; the rests would be meaningless in a unison performance. On the other hand, cases may be found in which such a melody has a beginning notated mensurally with rests but uses in the course of the piece a mensural isometric notation; thus in this respect the sources offer no clear complete picture. Moreover, we must take into consideration the fact that in many songbooks there is often a demonstrably careless treatment of the rhythmic details in the melody. A good example of the complexity of the situation is offered by the melody to *Ein feste Burg*, which was first published in Klug's songbook of 1529 and subsequently appeared always in the same rhythmic form. Because of the meaningless opening rests (semibreve and minim) and the stereotyped syncopations of the musical cadences, the melody gives the unequivocal impression of having been taken over unchanged from the tenor of a polyphonic setting. It does, in fact, appear in exactly the same form, although not until 1544, in two four-voice settings by Johann Walter; moreover, the settings begin with all voices together in the same rhythm, so that here too the first of the introductory rests is unnecessary. Thus either Luther, as the composer of the melody, gave it its rhythmic pattern (which is very unlikely in view of his normal use of isometric notation, as shown in the first melody to *Vater unser im Himmelreich*), or Walter had worked over the melody rhythmically before writing the two settings in his

18. *Initio cuiusque Misse* "*Veni sancte Spiritus*" from Johann Spangenberg's *Cantiones ecclesiasticae latinae . . . Kirchengesänge deutsch*, Magdeburg, 1545, M. Lotther.

Kirchen Gesenge

Latinisch vnd Deudsch / sampt

allen Euangelien / Episteln / vnd Collecten / auff die
Sontage vnd Feste / nach Ordnung der zeit /
durchs gantze Jhar /

Zum Ampt / so man das Hoch=

wirdige Sacrament des Abendmals vnsers HERRN
IHESV CHRISTI handelt / oder sonst Gottes wort prediget /
Inden Euangelischen Kirchen breuchlich / Aus den besten Ge=
sangbüchern vnd Agenden / so fur die Euangelischen Kir=
chen in Deudscher sprach gestellet vnd verordnet
sind / zusamen gebracht.

Vnd itzund erstlich auff diese Form im
Druck ausgegangen.

Witteberg.   M. D. LXXIII.

19. Johann Keuchenthal, *Kirchengesänge lateinisch und deutsch*, Wittenberg,
1573, Lorentz Schwenck. Title page.

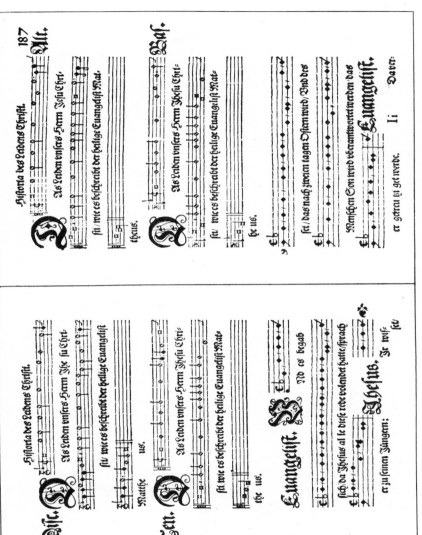

20. Opening of the St. Matthew Passion (by Johann Walter?) with the introductory formula for four-voice chorus (above) and the parts for the Evangelist and Jesus in the recitation tone (below) from Johann Keuchenthal, *Kirchengesänge lateinisch und deutsch*, Wittenberg, 1573, Lorentz Schwenk.

ORDO CANTIONVM IN MISSA SEV sacro.

1. Introitus, quem cuiusq; Dominicæ & diei Festi proprium, Vide supra.
2. Kyrie, cum, Et in terra, vel Canticum, Allein Gott in der Höge sey ehr.
3. Halleluia, & sequentia seu profa diei Festi, quæ interdum omittuntur, & canitur eorum loco aliquod canticum seu Psalm, Germanicè:
4. Wy geloben/ Lutheri, & Symbolum Athanafii, alternatim.
5. Sanctus.
6. Jhesus Christus unser Heiland/ sub communicatione.
7. Agnus Dei.
8. Erhalt uns HERR by dinem Wordt/ etc.

KYRIE.

Est hæc Orientalis Ecclesiæ verus precatio, qua Trinitatem agnoscit & invocat. Testatur igitur duo: Primò distinctionem personarum in diuinitate Patriæ, Filij, & Spiritus sancti, qui vnus est verus, omnipotens & æternus Deus, qui se Ecclesiæ suæ, dato verbo & misso Filio, patefecit. Deinde, cùm ad Christum, & Spiritum sanctum inuocationem Ecclesia dirigit, agnoscit verumq; esse distinctam personam à Patre, & coæternam, æquipotentem cum Patre: quia tribuit eis infinitam potentiam, inuenendi motus cordium, quos creatura non intelligunt.

IN

IN SVMMIS FESTI-VITATIBVS, ET DOMI-nica Trinitatis, cum textu.

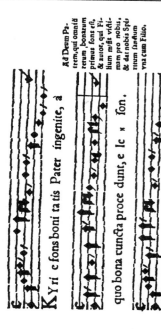

KYri e fons boni ta tis Pater ingenite, à

quo bona cuncta proce dunt, e le i son.

Kyrie, qui pati Natum mundi pro crimine,

ipfum vt faluaret, mififti, e lei fon, Kys

ri e, qui feptiformis das dona Pneumatis,

à quo coelum, terra replentur, e le i fon.

Ad Deum Patrem, qui omniũ rerum, bonarum primus fons est, & autor, qui Filium mifit victimam pro nobis, & dat nobis Spiritum fanctum vna cum Filio.

Ddd 3   Christe

21. *Ordo Cantionum in Missa seu sacro* and *Kyrie fons bonitatis* from Lucas Lossius, Psalmodia, third edition, Wittenberg, 1579, Anton Schön

songbook (which might be proved by an anecdote similar to the one furnished by the very unreliable Torgau chronicler Michael Boehme), or Walter had composed his settings before 1529 and then for unknown reasons did not publish them in his songbook in 1537 but waited until 1544 (which would be very curious). None of these hypotheses, moreover, can explain the superfluous beginning rests; an explanation would be possible only if one would be willing to admit the unlikely existence of another polyphonic setting of the melody written before 1529 and now lost. This one example thus suffices to undermine the frequently encountered thesis that all melodies with superfluous beginning rests were taken over ipso facto into the songbooks from polyphonic settings. Finally, it should be mentioned that sometimes the same melody appeared in contemporary songbooks in rhythmic versions differing greatly from one another, perhaps an indication that local peculiarities of singing were here more faithfully preserved than one is generally inclined to admit.

From this abundance of notational procedures, as well as from the exceedingly complicated rhythmic structure of many of the lied melodies, it can be seen that what has come down to us in written form can be only a limited reflection of actual practices of congregational singing. It is improbable that congregations using the Bapst songbook to support congregational singing followed its notation. To do so they would have had to memorize and sing *Christum wir sollen loben schon* isometrically with extensions of line beginnings and endings, *Herr Christ der einig Gotts Sohn* or *Vom Himmel hoch* in a simple songlike style with the same rhythmic structure for each line with short upbeats, *Ein feste Burg* or *Sie ist mir lieb, die werte Magd* with all of their complicated melismas, syncopations, rests, and extensions, and *Nun lasst uns den Leib begraben* with all of its declamatory vigor.

Certainly distinctions were made that might have corresponded approximately to the easily recognized groups of typical rhythmic forms (triple-meter songs in iambic or trochaic rhythm throughout; melodies belonging to the rhythmic type of *Vom Himmel hoch,* either newly composed or simplified from models and organized in an ordinary way; secular lied melodies in which at least stereotyped extensions of periods or syncopations—though not, perhaps, extensive melismas —were easy to master). Basically, however, we have to assume that the congregation sang complicated rhythmic forms in a simplified manner and, on the other hand, enlivened isometric examples according to the rhythm of the text, as it was accustomed to do in the secular lied. The fact that the lieder had to be learned by rote and then remembered only abetted this process. The invention of a special notation for Protestant congregational singing was superfluous under such conditions, and using mensural notation to record the versions as sung by the people would only have impaired the vitality of the lieder and hampered their constant re-creation in the act of singing. Thus, too, from this point of view the strength of living secular folk song flowed fruitfully into the congregational song of the early church. The later transformation of all differentiated rhythms, full of life, into an isometric-lied pattern may have been done for convenience, or because of the growing formal inflexibility and dogmatization of a monotonous "solemnity," or because of the decline of the secular folk song.

The small notes inserted give variations from Erfurt, 1524; the example itself is taken from Babst, 1545.

The translations and melodic recastings of Latin prose models intended only in part or not at all for congregational singing were in Protestant sources noted down uniformly either in simple *Hufnagel* notation or in an isometric mensural representation. This fact may serve as indirect evidence that the Gregorian models were also sung isometrically at this time. However, discussion of this possibility does not belong here, and the idea is mentioned only to prevent misunderstanding.

THE POLYPHONIC LIED SETTING

These reflections show how intimately the problems of the monophonic Lutheran church lied were bound up with the polyphony of the Reformation. The Protestant church did not create a new style of art music for itself. It made use of the existing practice, which at that time cultivated, in the polyphonic lied setting, a specifically German form of secular art music adopted by townsfolk and nobility and in which resided a refined popular element with a characteristic national and contemporary stamp. The polyphonic German lied setting of this period reached back repeatedly, it is true, to western traditions; however, because of the general lag of about one generation in adaptations of style, it is essentially different from the contemporary Netherlandish and French secular and sacred art, as well as from the Italian music of this period, also nationally tinged. It is also clearly different from the later German lied setting, which controlled the following epoch of Protestant church music.

The German art song of the Reformation era was based upon the tenor practice taken over from Netherlandish tradition; it was in large measure obsolete, at least compared to the secular Netherlandish music of Luther's time and more especially to the French music then beginning to flourish. The traditional melody was placed with its text in the tenor part of a composition for four or more voices, in the middle or lower part of two- or three-voice pieces, and, more rarely, in the upper part (in this case "tenor" designates less the voice range than the principle of "holding fast" to one voice as a foundation, as the primary element of the piece, in relation to which the added voices play subordinate roles). The free voices surrounded it and played around it in the type of active polyphony described in Luther's vividly picturesque statement quoted above concerning the polyphonic lied. Imitative interweaving of motifs freely invented or derived from the cantus firmus was customary only at the beginning of compositions, and rare for extended sections; it was of only incidental rather than basic significance. The lied here develops symbolically the full magnitude of its religious potential and its social mission: it becomes the scaffolding and the axis of the composition, the constructive basis and primary point of reference, and therefore stands in contrast to the other voices. This contrast in coexistence is manifest in every relationship: the tenor is an entity in itself; the other voices interweave among one another to create a union also complete within itself. The tenor moves in quiet, broad, basic rhythmic values which fall into a certain motion only through consideration of the polyphony; the other voices move in a lively rhythm. The tenor is fixed in the strict traditional manner required by its liturgical significance as bearer of the divine Word; the other voices are completely dependent upon the discretion of the composer—Protestant truth enhanced by art. The composer is only the "setter"; proclaimer instead of interpreter; the representative of the congregation, not its leader responsible only to himself; a worshiper among many, not an individual exegete; an ornamenter, like a graphic artist who illustrates holy books, not the shaper of the contents; servant, not master. In this apparent limitation lies the greatness of this art: the art itself is worship in its association with the Word and its obligation to the Word; the Word receives form in the lied; the music serves the divine Word with unmistakable symbolic power.

This art found its classic characterization for Protestant church music through Johann Walter. In view of the statements made above concerning the traits of the Protestant lied melody, it is uncertain whether and to what degree Walter was an inventor of melodies. As a "setter" he must have fulfilled Luther's demands in full measure; otherwise the Reformer would probably not have entrusted the musical arrangement of his basic songbook to a twenty-eight-year-old. Walter did not create a new form, but he changed the character of the traditional one, making it essentially simpler; this is not a stylistic peculiarity of the Walter generation as opposed to the older masters, but rather a characteristic—if there is one—of the Protestant polyphonic lied setting. Walter plainly belongs to the same generation as the principal master of the genre, Ludwig Senfl, and as the majority of leading Protestant lied composers born between c. 1480 and 1500: Sixtus Dietrich, Benedictus Ducis, Balthasar Resinarius, Stephan Mahu, Johannes Stahl, Johann Kugelmann, and others. He constantly changed, improved, and above all expanded his Wittenberg songbook in every one of its six editions; in the last one he smoothed out the movement of the voices and the sonority in an effort to bring the pieces more in line with contemporary style (which had changed in twenty-seven years). A few statistics are significant: the first edition of 1524 contained 38 German lieder and 5 Latin motets; the sixth in 1551, 78 German lieder, an increase to twice the original number, and 47 Latin motets, an increase of about nine times the original. This corresponds to a tendency that constantly became stronger toward the end of the Reformation period, a tendency which was mentioned above in connection with the order of the Mass and which will be considered again in other contexts. Similarly, the relationship between tenor and discant lied was changed: the first edition contained, among 38 lieder, 36 with cantus firmus in the tenor, 2 (i.e., one-nineteenth) with the melody in the upper voice; the last edition, however, among 78 lieder, contained 15 (i.e., one-fifth) of the latter type. Thus a generally valid tendency can also be seen in this case.

The basic form of Walter's lied settings remained that described above. The often very perceptible harmonic foundation of a simple, relatively quiet bass movement by fifths and fourths shows a tendency to simplification and to adaptation of the modern style of the Netherlandish and French music of the time; sonorities of open fifths and inversions of triads were in general avoided on strong beats. The most frequently encountered type maintains a large degree of independence in the free voices; the contrast between them and the tenor is evident. Imitation appears irregularly at the beginnings of lines, but with no inherent structural power; on the contrary, it is frequently found only at the beginning and forms a broadly conceived, almost prelude-like introduction in the style of the older Netherlandish cantus-firmus motet; it then disappears either completely or for the remainder of the *Stollen* and enters again only at the beginning of the *Abgesang*. In this type of lied there is no thoroughgoing rationalization and unification of the free voices in the sense of pervasive imitation with one another or with the tenor; the cantus firmus always remains the clearly isolated axis of the composition, the inflexible framework around which the free, ornamental linear movement of the other voices, whose treatment of the text is far removed from declamatory, unfolds with a large measure of independence. No aspect of this relationship is changed by the occasional doubling of the cantus firmus by a voice in canon, increasing the composition to five voices; in such cases there are two voices instead of one that form the scaffolding around which the remaining voices freely move.

Johann Walter

The opening section of *Nun komm, der Heiden Heiland* shows an example of beginning, anticipatory imitation giving way, upon the entrance of the parts in canon, to a free treatment of the other voices. The beginning of the second line, "der Jungfrauen Kind erkannt," occasions neither a unified caesura in the structure for all voices nor a resumption of the imitation. By the beginning of the third line, "dass sich wundert," it becomes clearly apparent that the composer is deliberately avoiding form-defining rests: the cadence on the F-major triad, care-

fully prepared up to the last moment, is not effective since at the decisive place
the tenor enters with D' and the beginning of a new line, and the two lower voices
immediately carry the new movement further. From this point on, the other
voices remain independent of the two canonic parts. The conclusion shows another peculiarity. In the large majority of lieder the tenor remains the bearer of
the pure cantus firmus, as up to this point in the present example (together with
the voice in canon). As the piece goes on, however, this strictness is forsaken; the
two canonic voices only suggest the principal notes of the melody and decorate
them in rich melismatic splendor (in the concluding line the pure cantus-firmus
technique is resumed). This procedure, not very frequent with Walter, signifies
a breaking away from the compositional principle of the German lied schematically represented above, to the extent that the contrast in movement, if not in
melodic substance, between the tenor and the other voices is suspended and there
is achieved a temporary coalescence of all voices into a quiet and continuously
flowing melismatic stream. From the viewpoint of the history of style, Walter's
lied shows how the old tenor practice, characterized by freedom, independence,
and lively motion in the non-cantus-firmus voices, is broken up by the attempt
at a unified organization throughout all the parts—with respect at least to motion,
not yet to motivic imitation. This attempt was brought about by Netherlandish
influences and prepared by the lied compositions of Heinrich Finck, Heinrich
Isaac, and others. Walter's pieces of this type (the canonically organized *Christ
lag in Todesbanden,* or *Komm, Gott Schöpfer, Heiliger Geist,* in which a similar
breaking away from the principle allows the cantus firmus to wander from the
tenor into the upper voices) show the relative modernity of his treatment of
sonority, which is responsible for the striking, melodious, and full sound of his
lieder as well as his motets; they also show, however, that he adhered to a specific
German "late Gothic" style developed in its essential qualities in the 15th century: the principal voice was enveloped in the unceasing, almost unarticulated
stream of movement in the other voices, giving the impression of a basic design
of incessant motion; the influence of Netherlandish music can be recognized only
in the occasional examples of imitation and in the occasional breaking away from
the principle (almost never for the sake of textual declamation, however). How
much depended on achieving this effect of unceasing movement is evidenced by
the scarcity of rests in the setting, the ornamental melismatic quality of the
non-cantus-firmus voices, and the complete lack of textual declamation, either
emphatic or merely representative; it is further shown by the contrasts in texture
and degree of motion, in the effacement and bridging of cadences, the avoidance
of line-by-line imitation, and the relative agility and melismatic textual treatment
of the bass in spite of its supporting harmonic function. This is indeed a specifically German art, but one of a cultured circle of composers, not at all folk-like,
bound by tradition, and highly cultivated. Walter, still very young at that time,
did not forsake the path of tradition; on the contrary, like most of the lied masters
of the age, he was, from the viewpoint of historical development, more conservative in this type of setting than the considerably older Heinrich Isaac and infinitely
more so than the contemporary secular lied composers of France and the Netherlands. This type of lied setting, which made up almost exactly one-half of Walter's

songbook of 1524, showed no significant increase in the later editions, while the contrasting type, which formed the other half in 1524, predominated by far in his later publications.

The second type is based upon a kind of polyphonic lied setting frequently cultivated by older masters such as Isaac, Stoltzer, Finck, and Hofhaimer. Walter's principal significance for Protestant church music lies in his ever increasing interest in this type. The beginning of *Aus tiefer Not* shows strikingly the completely different stylistic design: the other voices are added to the cantus firmus in a quite concise treatment, with few melismas and no imitation. Each line is sharply concluded with a rest in all voices and a harmonic cadence. The harmonic skeleton is revealed in the fundamental intervals of the bass voice and the full triads, generally equal in rhythm and progressing according to a basically syllabic declamation of the text, scarcely disturbed by suspensions or passing notes. The composer's intention to emphasize the sonority at the expense of all other compositional factors becomes evident. The tenor is the axis of composition in these settings also, but it is no longer the scaffolding for the flourishing development of linear independence of the polyphonic, heterorhythmic, quasi-centrifugal, non-cantus-firmus voices; instead it absorbs the other voices, which now seem laden with centripetal force, so that the final impression is one of an almost complete homorhythm and homophony. With these settings by Walter two new elements enter Protestant lied composition: emphasized artlessness, which obviously strives toward a folk-like expression, and Renaissance style. The cantus firmus, no longer treated as an abstract axis of construction, can now be heard as a lied melody. The simplicity and conciseness achieved by this type of composition presents the lied melody in a much more easily comprehensible form, clearly perceptible in melody and rhythm, understandable in articulation, and therefore

Johann Walter

better suited than the older type to the folk-like texts. The composer's goal is no longer to release an unceasing flow of movement contrasting with the inflexible quietness of the tenor, but rather to strive after groups that correspond metrically and harmonically and are balanced side by side (in this example, even organized in four-beat units and almost modern dominant-tonic relationships). In addition, the composer henceforth shows a concern for the closest coordination of voices in an emphatically vertical rather than a horizontal arrangement. Thus, these compositions reveal the Renaissance impulse that had already played so significant a role with Isaac and now, its force renewed by the late motets of Josquin, crossed over with strong effectiveness into Germany. The Netherlandish and Italian influences (especially of the frottola) which first penetrated into Germany about this time were met by Walter's efforts to find the one form of composition most suitable for the mission of the Protestant church lied. Without such an effort (even if not expressly announced in words), the coexistence of two so essentially different types of lied setting in the same collection—moreover, one with a specific program—is scarcely explainable unless one assumes a stylistic uncertainty on Walter's part; and of this the masterfully organized compositions offer not the slightest indication. It is only a small step from this point to the shifting of the melody from the tenor into the discant; Walter did this only twice in 1524 but fifteen times in 1551. Thus that type of four-voice Protestant lied which has been maintained from the end of the 16th century to the present as the standard "cantional" style is here achieved in its basic features.

As is stated in Luther's foreword, Walter's collection was primarily intended as a school songbook for Protestant youth: "And these songs were arranged in four parts for no other reason than that I wanted to attract the youth (who should and must be trained in music and other fine arts) away from love songs and carnal pieces and to give them something wholesome to learn instead, so that they can enter with pleasure into that which is good, as is befitting to youth." The fact that Walter's songbook also made its way into the worship service is shown by the inclusion of a considerable portion of the lieder and Latin pieces in the manuscript collections of the time intended for liturgical use, especially, of course, in the so-called Walter manuscripts (insofar as they were applied to the liturgy) but also in south- and east-German, north-German, and Danish sources. The performance of both types of lied setting generally must be thought of as basically vocal; according to given local conditions and traditions, however, instruments could have been added to strengthen all the voices, the cantus firmus, or only the non-cantus-firmus parts; they could also have taken over by themselves the non-cantus-firmus voices of the melismatic pieces, a practice corresponding to the traditional multiplicity of performance practices in German, Netherlandish, French, and Italian sacred and secular music of the time. Finally, the lieder could also have been transcribed for organ or sung to a lute. (The latter method of performance was especially applicable to the second type of lied because of its similarity to the frottola, which was frequently performed that way.)

In Walter's two types of lied settings, two artistic worlds collided: in the first is found a sense of form that reflects the hierarchical organization of the departing Middle Ages, constructive and irrational at the same time in its inflexible tenor-axis organization and in its treatment of the other voices, secondary in importance and hardly related to the text, with their free linear play following melodic dynamics; the second shows a Renaissance sense of form on a German foundation but with a supranational covering, the characteristics of which are simplicity and audibility of construction, clear textual representation, rational conciseness of the musical language, and plastic objectivity. Humanism undoubtedly had a major share in the realization of the latter type. Stimulated by Konrad Celtis and his sodalities, there had appeared in German prints from 1507 on four-voice compositions based upon ancient meters, Latin poems of Horace, Vergil, Catullus, Ovid, and others in the barest *contrapunctus simplex,* strictly chordal compositions in a note-against-note style, declaimed in breves and semibreves exactly according to the verse measure; they were written by Tritonius, Murmelius, Cochläus, the Transylvanian Reformer Johannes Honterus, and other learned dilettantes who followed masters of rank such as Martin Agricola (the very widely disseminated *Melodiae scholasticae,* with school odes and *de tempore* hymns and lieder for school, 1557), Paul Hofhaimer, Benedictus Ducis, and Ludwig Senfl. Similarly directed attempts followed with sacred poetry, such as the above-mentioned compositions of Hordisch and Forster to the hymns of Prudentius. They had been preceded in 1513 by Wolfgang Grefinger, the pupil of Hofhaimer, and later by Senfl with texts of Prudentius; they too were followed by lesser masters with sacred odes newly written by humanistic pedagogues. Melodies to poems of Melanchthon appeared in ode collections; ode melodies were taken over into church lieder; Latin hymns were sung in the Latin school daily at the beginning of classes in compositions declaimed in an ode-like manner *(Hymni aliquot sacri,* Zwickau, 1552, with pieces by Martin Agricola and Paul Schalreuter). The relationship between the Protestant circles around Walter and the school and university circles interested in such ode compositions is shown by the manuscript appendix to a partbook of a Walter print that came from such a circle and in which two sacred ode compositions are copied down; the print is in the possession of the Lutherhalle in Wittenberg. In addition, the strict ode composition and the freer setting of the second Walter type played a leading role in the choruses of humanistic school-dramas (Hans Ackermann, Joachim Greff, Paul Rebhun, Georg Rollenhagen), to which such important masters as Gallus Dressler made contributions. Humanistic Italy gave the impulse to ode composition: the pieces in ancient meters contained in Italian manuscripts of the late 15th century and in the frottola prints of Petrucci had served as examples for the Germans. Whether the relatively rare homorhythmic declamatory pre-Reformation German lied settings originated independently is still an open question. A segment of the history of ideas here becomes directly visible in a chain of characteristic musical productions, easily traceable into the 17th century, which have had a fruitful effect upon the most diversified areas of music. The coordination of voices, the similarity of their modal conduct, the homorhythm, the frequent shifting of the principal part into the discant, and the strong harmonic foundation are characteristics also found in Walter's second type; there, however, they are applied to the requirements of German poetry and well-established melodies. The designation "auf Bergreihenweis," frequently appearing in Walter, probably does not point to a homophonic composition based on a secular example but to the organization of either polyphonic-melismatic or homophonic-syllabic compositions by fermatas at the end of every line, a practice apparently taken over from the improvised polyphony of *Bergreihen* (miners' songs) presumably in the manner cultivated by the miner population of upper Saxony, Silesia, and Bohemia.

Walter's two basic types as they have here been represented are only rarely encountered in a pure form, of course; on the contrary, transitional steps of all degrees predominate. However, there is significance in the intermediate position of the Walter compositions between two diametrically opposed artistic conceptions. On the one hand, it shows the lied in a polyphonic cantus-firmus setting typical of the age; on the other, it shows Walter's constantly increasing preference for the second type as a conscious striving to create an adequate form for the Protestant lied based upon its specific requirements.

In view of this endeavor it astonishes us today to observe no decisive progress along this line in the second basic collection of the epoch, Georg Rhau's *Neue deutsche geistliche Gesänge für die gemeinen Schulen* of 1544. The reason lies in the inherent overall tendency of Protestant church music to absorb contemporary, living musical expression and to create for itself no special doctrinaire schemes. Generally speaking, the German lied setting underwent no thoroughgoing change in the period between 1524 and 1544; only an increase in the number of types within the old basic principle is discernible. This is not surprising in view of the fact that Walter's songbook contains only his own compositions, while Rhau's work is an anthology embracing works of nineteen different masters (excluding the twelve anonymous pieces), among them a piece by Johann Walter listed as anonymous and a composition by Cosmas Alder ascribed to Senfl. The largest and most important group of composers are Rhau's contemporaries, belonging to the second generation, the most fertile composers of the epoch (a few lesser masters are considerably younger, however).

Balthasar Resinarius, Isaac's pupil from the musical establishment of Maximilian's court and later "bishop" (pastor) of Bohemian Leipa, is the composer most generously represented; there are thirty of his works. Arnold von Bruck, court *Kapellmeister* to Emperor Ferdinand I in Vienna from 1527 on, is represented by seventeen; Ludwig Senfl by eleven (among them a false attribution); Benedictus Ducis—presumably a Finck pupil, who lost his position due to his conversion to Protestantism and ended his life in a small pastorate near Ulm— by ten; Sixtus Dietrich by only eight, although he was one of the leading masters of Protestant church music. Those with fewer pieces are Stephan Mahu, who probably belongs with the youngest masters of the collection (five compositions), the Magdeburg cantor Martin Agricola, otherwise known principally as a writer about music and a composer of odes (three pieces), the physician, composer, and music publisher Georg Forster, perhaps the youngest composer of the collection (two compositions), the Magdeburg or Halle organist Wolff Heintz (two pieces), Virgilius Hauck (one piece), Nikolaus Piltz (one piece), Huldreich Brätel (one piece), Johannes Stahl (two pieces), Thomas Stoltzer (five pieces, of which one was wrongly attributed), Georg Vogelhuber (one piece), and the Nuremberg and Wittenberg organist Johann Weinmann, apparently the oldest master of the

22. The victorious Reformation. Woodcut by the Master of the Michelfeld tapestry (?), c. 1530. Dresden, Kupferstichkabinett.

23. Contemporary caricature of the Augsburg Interim of 1548. *Beatus vir qui non abiit in consilio impiorum* (Psalm 1). *Selig ist der Mann, der Gott vertrauen kann und williget nicht ins Interim, dan es hat den Schalk hinterim.* Four-voice setting.

24. Hans Kugelmann, *Concentus novi trium vocum,* Augsburg, 1540, Melchior Kriesstein. Printer's colophon and title page of the tenor partbook.

25. *Magnificat octo modorum seu tonorum,* Wittenberg, 1544, Georg Rhau. Title page of the tenor partbook.

26. *Neue deutsche geistliche Gesänge CXXIII,* Wittenberg, 1544, Georg Rhau. Title page.

27. *Neue deutsche geistliche Gesänge CXXIII.* Title page of the discant part-book.

28. Discant voice for the antiphon *Domine, ad adiuvandum me festina* and Psalm 116, *Dilexi quoniam exaudiet Dominus,* for Easter Monday. *Vesperarum precum officia,* Wittenberg, 1540, Georg Rhau.

collection (one composition). It is still not clear why Lupus Hellinck is represented in the Rhau anthology with the considerable number of eleven compositions. Active in Bruges and an indirect follower of Josquin, he is the only Netherlander in the publication; moreover, these compositions form a considerable part of his total known output. Neither is it clear whether he had a close relationship to the Reformers' circle or only sympathized with the German Protestants indirectly through the crypto-Protestant movement in the Netherlands.

It is remarkable, at any rate, that among the principal masters of this significant collection no fewer than five were definitely or probably members of the Catholic church: Stoltzer, Senfl, Arnold von Bruck, Mahu, and Hellinck. It is true that Stoltzer had composed German psalms in Luther's translation for Maria of Hungary and Duke Albrecht of Prussia, one of which (Psalm 13) appeared in Rhau and even earlier in Kugelmann. His lied settings in Rhau's collection, however, were based throughout upon pre-Reformation lieder, and he never made the step to a public confession of Protestant tendencies. It is possible that he experienced the power of the words of Luther's German psalms only as a "pure musician," without taking into account their close association with the new doctrine. It is also possible, in view of the intellectual ties between Wittenberg and the Hungarian court, that his compositions indeed implied a confession of faith. This still remains an open question.

The Swiss Ludwig Senfl, Isaac's most important pupil and successor as court composer to Maximilian I, later "musicus intonator" (thus probably also court composer) of the Bavarian duke Wilhelm IV in Munich, had secret communications with Luther, as is well known. Deeply depressed over the outcome of the Augsburg Imperial Diet and filled with the passionate wish to die, Luther wrote to him from the Veste Coburg the famous letter of October 4, 1530, in which he begged the master for a polyphonic setting of *In pace in idipsum* ("I lie down and sleep completely in peace, for Thou alone, Lord, helpest me to dwell in safety"), which he had never found composed (this is remarkable in the light of Luther's acquaintance with contemporary music) and whose melody he loved greatly (he had even written it on the wall of his room); he hoped to create no difficulties for Senfl through the exchange of letters. Whether Luther knew Senfl personally is uncertain; it is not improbable that they met on Luther's Rome journey in 1510 in Innsbruck or at the trial before Cajetan in Augsburg in 1518. In any case, it appears not to have been the first exchange of letters between the two. Instead of fulfilling Luther's wish immediately, Senfl answered relevantly with a composition to the text "Non moriar, sed vivam" ("I shall not die, but live and proclaim the work of the Lord"—an exceptionally heretical choice of text for a Catholic in view of Luther's beliefs); he later sent Luther the desired motet *In pace*. On January 1, 1531, Luther thanked him by sending him some books and a letter. Senfl's position in Munich was very difficult, however. He was suspected, and his correspondence with Luther could be carried on only through an intermediary, like his correspondence with the music collector Duke Albrecht of Prussia (in whose Königsberg music library Senfl's *Non moriar* was found); Senfl continued this, however, until the end of the 1530s. On the other hand, Senfl's importance for Protestant church music as a whole must not be overestimated on the basis of his correspondence with Luther; in spite of everything else, it is significant that among his eleven compositions (including the one really by Cosmas Alder) not one has an out-and-out Reformation lied as a basis. His *Seven Last Words,* a cyclical through-composed work on the nine stanzas of the Passion lied *Da Jesus an dem Kreuze stund,* also made use of a pre-Reformation song. And yet the master who so magnificently further developed the Latin psalm compositions of Josquin apparently never availed himself, in contrast to Stoltzer, of the power of Luther's psalms for composing; this fact is perhaps more illuminating than the correspondence between the two great spirits so congenial in musical matters. Senfl's sacred lieder, which appeared with works of Protestant and Catholic composers in different collections, also treated only pre-Reformation texts and melodies. Thus, his connection to the Reformation can be assessed no higher than that of the many Germans of high intellectual standing of the time who felt sympathy for the spirit of Wittenberg and looked forward to its effects, but because of political or personal reasons found no closer contact.

Apart from his compositions there is nothing to prove an association of Arnold von Bruck with Protestantism. To relate these works closely to his life seems questionable, since similar attempts with other musicians of the time also lead to very doubtful results. On the contrary, it is highly improbable that precisely this court *Kapellmeister* of Ferdinand I (he was a priest at the same time) did have a significant relationship to the Reformation. Nevertheless, he set polyphonically a group of Luther's own lieder, such as *Komm, Heiliger Geist, Herre Gott, Gott der Vater wohn uns bei,* and *Mitten wir im Leben sind,* which were published by Ott in 1534 and by Rhau in 1544; a contemporary historical source reports that Arnold had written them in connection with the presentation of the Augsburg Confession. Moreover, Rhau included further Luther lieder by him: *Aus tiefer Not, Christ lag in Todesbanden, Vater unser im Himmelreich, Wir glauben all an einen Gott,* and still other Protestant lied compositions. The lied *O allmächtiger Gott* (a setting by Senfl is also included in Rhau's collection) has a political character, with a plea for terminating the strife tearing Christendom apart. It is difficult to imagine that a man who wrote compositions on all of these lieder, and also on Speratus's song of faith *Es ist das Heil uns kommen her,* should not have sympathized with Protestantism, but it cannot be proved that his associations with it went further than Senfl's. The idea that music bridges over all dividing lines of nationality and confession lay deeply grounded in the contemporary concepts of art; rarely has music history gone through a period of such far-reaching internationalism and such complete interconfessionalism. Luther asked the Catholic Senfl to compose his funeral motet because Senfl was then the most famous composer in Germany, at the same time, apart from all confessional convictions, expressly praising the artistic taste of the Bavarian dukes. Why should Rhau, with equal confessional broad-mindedness, not have commissioned a number of compositions for his collection from the leading figure of the imperial musical establishment, the most representative musical organization of the realm? The strikingly large portion of south German and Austrian contributions and the inclusion of the internationally known Lupus Hellinck indicate, moreover, that in this respect too Rhau tried to plan his collection to be as all-embracing, as full of quality, and as nonprovincial as possible.

Nothing is known of Stephan Mahu's relationship to Protestantism; since he was a trombonist for and, from 1532 on, the vice-*Kapellmeister* of Ferdinand I, he cannot have been Protestant. It is true, however, that the share of his works included by Rhau and his setting of a polemic text in Ott, 1544, seem to place him close to Protestantism. Lupus Hellinck's relationship to the Reformation is equally unknown. Since he occupied a church position in Bruges, and since Charles V and Margaret of Austria, then Maria of Hungary used the power of the Inquisition to suppress the dissemination of the new doctrine in the Netherlands during Hellinck's time, he can hardly have had more than an inner sympathy for the Reformation, perhaps through connections with the crypto-Protestant currents in his homeland.

In contrast to these Catholic composers, Rhau's anthology also includes masters who were the real leaders of early Protestant music, along with Walter: Sixtus Dietrich, Benedictus Ducis, and Balthasar Resinarius. That Ducis was Protestant is seen from his later close relationship to Protestant circles in Ulm and Constance, which provided for him, the "propter veritatem exsul," a modest position for the last years of his life. His compositions in Rhau's collection were perhaps written on order for the printer, since to judge from his remaining attested works he appears to have been more a specialist in *tricinia* and humanistic odes than in German lieder of the type presented by Rhau. Ducis was of about the same age as Balthasar Resinarius, who grew up as a choirboy and pupil of Isaac in Maximilian's musical establishment and was probably identical with Balthasar Harzer, who is known to have been a student in Leipzig in 1515 and a Catholic clergyman in 1522. As a Lutheran "bishop" of Bohemian Leipa, he showed an exceedingly rich and systematic compositional activity in the last years of his life, apparently in close association with Wittenberg. His output has made him the third "archcantor" of early Protestant church music, along with Dietrich (whose humanistic education and familiarity with worldly matters he lacked, however) and Walter. Sixtus Dietrich, finally, is the south German counterpart of Johann Walter, whom he at least equaled in education and universality and surpassed in creative ability. He appears to have been a Protestant artist in the ideal sense of the term. Born in Augsburg between 1490 and 1495, he received his education in the choir school of the Constance cathedral (thus also in the sphere of Isaac) and at the universities of Freiburg and Strasbourg. He had close friendships with the most important learned men of southwest Germany, such as Johann Rudolfinger and Bonifacius Amerbach, later with Grynäus and Glarean. From 1517 on he was active in a clerical-musical position at the Constance cathedral. Dietrich personally experienced all phases of the heroic battle of the city against Charles V because of its attachment to a Protestantism strongly influenced by Zwingli. Only after the imperial troops had stormed a suburb of Constance was the sick master brought to safety in St. Gallen, where he died in the same year (1548). Through Dietrich's personality runs a tendency to Lutheranism: obstinate uprightness and unshakable strength of faith. His direct association with the

Luther's circle can also be traced: from 1540 on he came to Wittenberg several times, probably primarily to prepare and supervise Rhau's printing of a series of his compositions directly at the place of publication. This practice was at that time customary in the printing of works of distinguished scholars (one thinks of Erasmus and the publisher Froben in Basel) but apparently rare for musicians. Another distinction accorded Dietrich was especially rare: Rhau's printing of two equally large publications devoted to his works (see below). Dietrich was also directly associated with Ducis. All of these connections indicate that he was closely involved with the people active in early Protestant church music.

Georg Forster had been acquainted with Luther and Melanchthon in his Wittenberg student years (1534–39); knowing his interest in music publishing, we can be practically certain that he was also already associated with Rhau at this time. Wolff Heintz, organist in Magdeburg and Halle and one of the leaders of the Halle townspeople in the Schmalkaldic War, must have had a close personal association with Luther; in a beautiful letter of 1543 the Reformer comforted him upon the loss of his wife. In 1537 he collaborated on Michael Vehe's Catholic songbook. In 1541, after the departure from Halle of his master, Cardinal Albrecht of Brandenburg, he joined Protestantism and became organist of the Protestant *Marktkirche*. Only Luther's words of praise bear witness to his instrumental performance; very few of his vocal works have been preserved.

Little is known of the remaining minor figures and their relation to Luther. Huldreich (Ulrich) Brätel, who worked in Stuttgart as court composer and law secretary and possessed a basic humanistic education, had apparently had associations earlier with Hofhaimer in Vienna; there are stylistic traces of Hofhaimer in his work. The number of his preserved compositions is small; their dissemination, predominantly in Protestant areas and in those anthologies which served both confessions, is uncommonly large. Latin sacred works predominate; Brätel's contribution to Rhau's collection is his only verifiable sacred lied (thus the conjecture that it was commissioned by the publisher is also possible in this case).

Apparently, Virgilius Hauck (Haugk) was also in direct contact with Rhau. In any case, a few of his Latin compositions are to be found in Protestant manuscripts, along with his contributions to the *Neue deutsche geistliche Gesänge* and the *Sacrorum hymnorum liber primus* (four hymns). As with Brätel, his only known German sacred lied is included in Rhau's collection. His musical tract, *Erotemata musicae practicae ad captum puerilem formata*, went through two editions in 1541 and 1545.

Johann Weinmann, like Wolff Heintz, was one of the Protestant organists whose instrumental works were probably never written down and are therefore completely lost, and whose vocal works were not numerous. After studies at the universities in Leipzig and Erfurt, and after service as organist in Nuremberg, he came to Wittenberg in 1506 as organist of the palace church and in 1519 also became organist of the municipal church. He probably went over to the new faith in 1521. An association between him and Rhau must be taken for granted, if only because the two men worked in the same circle.

Johannes Stahl must also have had a close association with his printer. Nothing biographical is known about him, but he is represented not only in the *Neue deutsche geistliche Gesänge* but also in Rhau's *Bicinia,* the *Opus decem missarum* (a Mass), and definitely in the *Vesperarum precum officia.* The compositions in the last-named collection are not very good testimony to his ability as a craftsman. It is quite possible that he was a personal friend of the printer and, where it was necessary, was appointed to fill the musical gaps.

The same can be said for Vogelhuber and Piltz, as well as for the other minor composers of the collection, also without biographical verification. Precisely because they were lesser masters, little known in their time, and because their works were isolated, their inclusion in a representative print was hardly possible without some direct contact with Rhau (which may have been the result of the printer's initiative).

How many anonymous compositions in the collection stem from Rhau himself has often been discussed but can scarcely be determined from a style-critical study. It is interesting to note that half of these works are found among the first twenty lieder (organized according to *de tempore* usage): possibly the printer himself took up the pen here to fill the gaps in his collection. The only verifiable contribution of Johann Walter, *In dulci jubilo,* is also found among these anonymous lieder, however; perhaps it was already so famous that it was neither necessary nor of interest to give the composer's name. The question of Rhau's share in the compositions (as well as that of further contributions of Walter) must thus remain unanswered.

The publisher undoubtedly brought with him the craftmanship necessary for worthy contributions to his own anthology. He was born in 1488 in Eisfeld on the Werra and studied at the universities of Erfurt and Wittenberg. In 1518, in Leipzig, he became an *Assessor*—i.e., teacher at the university—and cantor at St. Thomas's as well; in this latter capacity he wrote a twelve-voice *Missa de Sancto Spiritu* for Luther's disputation with Eck in 1519. As a disciple of Luther he had to give up his Leipzig posts in 1520 and retreat to modest positions in his home town, where he wrote elementary instruction books in music theory. In 1524 he began his work as a publisher in Wittenberg; in this capacity he is revealed not only as energetic and highly educated but also as one of the very few greatly talented men among the book and music printers of his time. His activity as a publisher will be considered further below. At his death in 1548 he was mourned by the city and university of Wittenberg and especially by Melanchthon.

Rhau's comprehensive collection shows the stability of the German lied style to as great a degree as it does the revolutionizing foreign influences to which he was exposed in the second quarter of the 16th century. A composition such as Stoltzer's old-fashioned *O Gott Vater* remains completely within the polyphonic type of lied, with tenor cantus firmus and relatively freer, flowing linear movement in the contrasting voices. The same master's textless *In Gottes Namen fahren wir,* with the melody in the alto, is arranged more loosely, supplied with more pauses, and articulated more sharply by cadences. *Christ ist erstanden,* also attributed to Stoltzer, but actually the work of Heinrich Isaac, proves to be completely progressive. The composition is almost continuously imitative throughout; the interplay of motifs and rhythmic movement results from the essential equality of voices; it is only occasionally interrupted by freely flowing counter motifs; and it has an astonishingly precise, compact diction that is reminiscent of Josquin. In Stoltzer's setting of the 13th Psalm, *Herr, wie lang wilt du mein so gar vergessen?*, one of the few pieces in Rhau's collection that is not a lied setting, the influence of Josquin and especially of his psalm motets appears to have been assimilated quite independently in the dense, sound-saturated imitation technique and in the passionate excitement of the diction.

Senfl contributed to the old polyphonic linear lied type with settings such as *O allmächtiger Gott* and *Ewiger Gott, aus des Gebot.* The picture is only slightly supplemented by such half-secular pieces as his famous *Der ehlich Stand* and *Mein freundlichs B;* and his *Also heilig ist der Tag,* for six voices over a quasi-ostinato tenor, certainly intended as an instrumental *carmen* (the text is only intimated), also retains the old style. To this style also belongs the chorale quodlibet *Christ ist erstanden* for six voices, in which the three middle voices treat three different melodies with three text variants of the lied; the piece is held together by the relatively independent movement of the three other voices. A setting of the pure cantional type, like his *Mag ich Unglück nicht widerstahn* in Forster in 1549, is not among Senfl's contributions to Rhau's collection. His most significant contributions lay in another area: through the contact of the traditional lied setting with the Netherlandish motet (especially that of Josquin), a hybrid developed. Its characteristics included a relatively freely treated chorale motet of imitative texture and a pithy word-tone relationship in short declamatory motifs. The five-voice composition *Gelobet seist du, Christe* clearly shows the meeting of the two styles. The lied melody is presented intact as a cantus firmus in the tenor; it is always enveloped and accompanied, however, by the strongly imitative texture of the two lower voices, so that the three parts form a cantus-firmus complex that moves in contrast to the two freely flowing top voices. And since the lines of the lied are separated by ample rests, the total impression given is of an architecture constructed from groups of pillars over which flows the free play of lines—the impression of a conscious, individual organization. There is an evident desire for a form that creates by choir division and combinations of voice pairs (motet techniques) a static counterweight against the dynamism of the upper voices flowing unceasingly as if they had no goal. *O Herre Gott, begnade mich,* with its discant melody, also falls into this stylistic contest.

The tendency toward the chorale motet becomes completely clear, however, in the splendid composition *Da Jakob nun das Kleid ansah,* which Rhau with some stylistic justification ascribed to Senfl, but which in truth had been written by the Bern town clerk and composer Cosmas Alder in 1538 as an interpolation for a sacred folk play. The minor Swiss master created his masterpiece in closest dependence upon the late psalm motets of Josquin (Rhau presumably took the work over from German sources, in which it often appeared as a composition of Senfl). Here the cantus firmus has lost its constructive tenor significance and forms only the general melodic scheme, the reservoir of motivic formation. The lied melody completely evaporates in the free-form structure of the piece. All the devices of the Netherlandish motet are brought over into the lied—construction in sections, contrasts, division into duets that contrast with the following four-voice texture, wide-spanned symmetries (three-section structure), alternation between moving lines, short declamatory motifs and chord columns, and formations of cadences and caesuras. Another decisive tendency, also completely Netherlandish and formerly foriegn to the lied, was to use these devices unmistakably to serve enunciation of the text. Single words or phrases are significantly declaimed and underlined: "Schmerzen," "Leide," "fahren von dieser Erden"; cries are expressed in chords and set off with rests in all voices: "O weh!" "O Joseph!"; important words ("Mein lieber Sohn," "und sein Kleid") are brought to the fore in a type of syllabic motif developed completely out of the word in emphatic declamation.

Such a form planned consciously to achieve a definite artistic expression and impression became a historic starting point and decisively characteristic for the entire chorale motet. This construction should not be thought of as a "breakthrough of personality"; it is rather an individualization, an accenting of uniqueness in subject through a unique, self-justified formulation. The loosening of the

constructivism and ornamental character of the older lied composition resulted in the favoring of an individualized structure, significant in itself, arising from requirements peculiar to the material. The Renaissance aesthetic principle of autonomy of form in musical work of art, in contrast to the dependence of musical form upon extramusical factors in the older epoch, had already manifested itself fifty years earlier in the motets of Josquin's middle period. The breakthrough of something similar finally occurred in the works of Senfl and Alder. Up to that point, the conservatism of lied compositions and the national peculiarities of German style joined with the kind of clumsy imitativeness frequently found on the peripheries of a stylistic center to prevent any such developments.

Like all German music of that time, Rhau's collection treated the question of traditional construction versus individuality in several ways. Balthasar Resinarius leans most strongly toward the conservative style and toward Walter's first type. A few of his pieces *(Nun komm, der Heiden Heiland, Komm, Gott Schöpfer, heiliger Geist)* show the old linear style with tenor cantus firmus in a relatively compact form approaching the cantional setting; there is a pure example of the latter *(Jesus Christus, unser Heiland, der von uns)*. Resinarius prefers to give the traditional type special charm by allowing only alto and bass to move freely, putting the lied melody in the tenor somewhat broken up by quite modest melismas, and setting the discant in a loosely imitative relationship to the tenor; the voices thus relate to one another crosswise *(Christ lag in Todesbanden, Christum wir sollen loben schon)*. The approximate co-ordination of the two voices originating thereby leads on one hand to a migrating cantus firmus, as in *Es woll uns Gott genädig sein,* and on the other to broadly worked-out settings like *Komm heiliger Geist, Herre Gott,* which, with the cantus firmus dissolved in figuration and imitation, produces a general co-ordination of voices almost approximating the chorale motet. Resinarius comes closest to the chorale motet in his beautifully articulated and intensive setting *Mitten wir im Leben sind;* with its parallel voices, its textural contrast, and its pervasive imitation of voices, it reaches the limits of the German lied style. He does not, however—and this points up his conservatism as well as, in the final analysis, his limited talent—move away from a generally conventional, formula-filled melodic style toward an intensive textual declamation in individually characterized motifs, as in Senfl or Alder. Therefore the master's strength does not lie here, but rather in those places where he can unfold his polyphonic fantasy unhindered in a free play of lines: in his four-section setting of *Erhalt uns, Herr, bei deinem Wort* he allows the lied melody to wander with each stanza from tenor to discant, then to the bass, and finally again to the discant, while the remaining voices, in bold streams of melody rarely connected to one another through imitation, "play with joy around one another, wonderfully decorating the melody and embracing each other heartily and lovingly" (Luther). Even the boundaries set by the stanzas are occasionally overstepped by the flowing element, and only one time, significantly, does a chordal concentration appear: "Gib deim Volk einerlei Sinn" (Give thy people one mind). The stylistic proximity of Resinarius to Walter's greater lied compositions is nowhere clearer than here, although his tendencies to rhythmic monotony and to a sluggish, melismatic, homorhythmic movement of the free voices still indicate which of the two men is the lesser talent. The setting of a prose text, the Lutheran Psalm 111, "Ich dank dem Herrn von ganzem Herzen," shows in comparison to Stoltzer's visionary psalm motets the limitations of the Leipa composer, his unbroken alliance with tradition in spite of all the modern tendencies, and his reserve in remaining within the boundaries of a solid, craftsman-like representation of the text, still on this side of the threshold which leads to a passionate confession and a visionary proclamation of the Word, a threshold over which Stoltzer had already stepped. The composition, a cantus-firmus work on the *tonus peregrinus* (similar to the chorale version in Klug, 1533) shows most of the characteristics of the new style—clear arrangement into small sections, motivic parallel voices, a syllabic homorhythmic distribution of declamation, text-inspired contrasts and declamatory motifs. All of these characteristics, however, are used only formally, and the motifs remain stereotyped. The decisive factors, individualization and emphasis, are completely lacking.

Ducis, too, has his roots in the older German style, connecting him closely to Resinarius, and the discant-tenor orientation mentioned for the Bohemian master appears with him as well *(Erbarm dich mein, o Herre Gott)*. An important peculiarity emerges in his music: in pieces of the linear-polyphonic type he breaks up the tenor melody melismatically, thus creating what is almost a special form, one that achieves an equality of voices with respect to figuration, while maintaining the old technique and the old constructivist principle of form *(Wohl dem, der in Gottes Furchte steht)*. This tendency goes so far that completely free melodic groups can be inserted into the cantus firmus *(Erbarm dich mein, o Herre Gott)*. An approximation of Senfl's chorale motet type arises out of this desire to assimilate the voices with one another, although the approach is made from a different direction. Here, the coordination of voices is achieved not by a melismatic breaking up and elongation of the cantus firmus, but rather by rests in the other parts *(Aus tiefer Not, Ich gläub und darum rede ich)*. These are pseudo-motet-like settings on a constructivist basis, pseudo-individual forms in traditional spirit. Departing completely from the type, however, is the setting *Nun freut euch, lieben Christen gmein,* in which each line of the lied is first sung by the tenor and then repeated chordally by the choir with a varied repetition of the melody. Rhau's collection contains no other example of this practice, which is borrowed from folk singing and was probably suggested by the secular origin of the melody (see above).

In contrast to these masters, Dietrich shows a tendency toward a compact, modern, less fanciful style. His settings of *Es ist das Heil* and *Aus tiefer Not* are of the purest cantional type. Settings with moving non-cantus-firmus voices, such as *Ach höchster Gott, O barmherziger Gott,* or his German Sanctus and Benedictus *Heilig ist Gott der Vater,* in spite of—or precisely because of—their external similarity to the linear type, make this disparity evident. They are basically conceived as compact chordal, static cantional compositions; they depart from their immobility only in the pseudo-polyphonic movement of the non-cantus-firmus voices, wherewith they anticipate a practice later elevated to something of a principle by Johannes Eccard (who transformed it by placing the melody in the discant and sharpening the contrasts technically and expressively between the melody and the other voices). Dietrich's lied-based compositions also show other astonishing "anticipations": his *Vater unser im Himmelreich,* in six sections for from three to five voices, treats the complete melody as a tenor cantus firmus in each section; in addition, one line of the six-line first stanza is put each time in the bass as the foundation, so that during the entire first section the bass constantly repeats the first line, "Vater unser im Himmelreich," in the second section the second line, "der du uns alle heissest gleich," and so on. Here Dietrich anticipates a technique that Michael Praetorius confidently proclaimed as his own invention in the ninth part of the *Musae Sioniae* (similar devices in pre-Reformation German hymn compositions point, in fact, to a tradition beginning before Dietrich). This six-section work is also of importance in many other respects: it clearly shows how close at hand organ music is and hints at the practice of alternation performance, about which more will be said below.

If the German Dietrich can be distinctly characterized as a representative of a new direction, the contributions of Arnold von Bruck lead one step further. Considered stylistically, they stand completely in the Netherlandish motet tradition. To be sure, the master often writes settings that embellish the cantus firmus profusely and permeate it with interpolations; the manner in which it is assimilated by the other voices is reminiscent of Ducis. Yet the pervading imitation technique of these pieces points in another direction *(Christ lag in Todesbanden, Komm, heiliger Geist, Mitten wir im Leben sind).* It is remarkable that the works belonging to this classification had for the most part already appeared in Ott in 1534; perhaps Rhau took them over from that print. A whole group of Arnold's settings in the *Neue deutsche geistliche Lieder,* however, belong unequivocally to the form of the chorale motet in which the lied melody is dissolved into a cantus-firmus-free pervading imitation (at most, a migrating cantus firmus appears here and there), and the formal individuality of the Netherlandish motet style gives the composition its structural principle *(Christ ist erstanden,* both settings of *Christ, der ist erstanden).* It is most fortunate that for these compositions the connection can easily be made evident: with his three Latin motets for four high voices *(Pater noster, Ave Maria, Da pacem)* Arnold stands completely on the stylistic level of the followers of Josquin.

Lupus Hellinck, the master of the Rhau collection who stands even personally the furthest apart, takes the last step in this direction by a complete eradication of the traditionalist-constructive style: the lied is treated in exactly the same manner as Gregorian chant in Latin church music; the melody becomes an object to be freely treated according to the personal laws of the individual artist *(Christ lag in Todesbanden, Mit Fried und Freud, Durch Adams Fall,* the especially characteristic *Mensch, willtu leben seliglich* and *An Wasserflüssen Babylon).* How completely self-imposed is the law of construction, in the overall handling as well as in the treatment of organizational details, is shown by the many repetitions of parts of the melody and also by the purposeful abundance of contrasts, both of which induce a balance of structure and act as a rhetorical support of the text. This style is still very far removed from personal expression of feeling, but the individual autonomy can no longer be mistaken; in this case it signifies the end of a specific style of setting for the German lied. Not all of Hellinck's pieces are of this type, but most of them are. Sometimes influences of the German lied are unmistakable *(Wohl dem, der in Gottes Furchten steht, Aus tiefer Not),* but in every case Hellinck reverts to his typical style. The smooth, carefully balanced melodic line and the technique of strengthening the conclusion through longer repetitions of a section lend his style a great similarity to the Netherlandish motets of Clemens non Papa and his circle.

The lesser composers do not add much to the picture provided by the works of the great masters. Mahu's pieces oscillate in style somewhere between Resinarius and Arnold von Bruck; his *Christ ist erstanden* for five low voices is an especially happy inspiration. Vogelhuber *(Aus tiefer Not)* and Wolff Heintz

(Nun bitten wir den heiligen Geist) are distinguished by their "organ-like passage work," i.e., by the instrumental scale figures in the non-cantus-firmus voices; with his *Christ unser Herr,* however, Heintz also contributes a composition of the second Walter type, lightly modified. Brätel represents the linear German type with tenor melody in a model example *(Der höchste Schatz);* Johannes Stahl similarly offers a five-voice setting with cantus firmus in canon between the two middle voices, *Nun lasst uns den Leib begraben,* in which the lied appears for the first time with what became its standard melody, perhaps composed by Stahl himself. Virgilius Hauck also remains completely within the old style in his chorale quodlibet, which couples *Vater unser* with *Wir glauben* in the two middle voices. It is remarkable that Georg Forster, presumably the youngest man in the print, scarcely distinguishes himself in his compositions from the older masters and yet keeps himself so far from them in his own famous lieder collection. Martin Agricola contributed a few simple but insignificant compositions; Johann Weinmann's *Vater unser im Himmelreich,* with its discant melody, is a relatively progressive piece.

The anonymous settings in Rhau's collection pose a particularly interesting problem, already touched upon, because a group of anonymous Christmas songs are the only representatives of the type otherwise lacking in the collection—the simplest cantional setting with discant melody. This type corresponds to a formal style which had apparently developed before the Reformation (and not only in Germany) out of the triadic melodies and the dance-like rhythms of most of these cantus firmi; this style may have contributed to the eventual decline of Christmas lieder into a children's genre. In Germany the style was preserved uninterrupted throughout the entire 16th century. A few of the other anonymous compositions clearly resemble Hellinck closely in style, however, such as the anonymous paraphrase of the Lord's Prayer (the same text in Hellinck's setting immediately precedes it) or the *Jesaja dem Propheten.* From the viewpoint of historical development, almost all of the anonymous compositions belong to the most progressive of the collection.

In dedicating his work to the burgomaster and council of his home town, Eisfeld, Rhau emphasized the phrase in the title "für die gemeinen Schulen" (i.e., for the citizen-supported Latin schools of the larger cities). Naturally, his collection was also intended for the service and it was used in church; moreover, a connection between school and church always existed through the school choir and the *Kurrende.* In the organization of the compositions, the collection follows the Klug songbook (1533) in its principal parts, although favorite pre-Reformation pieces are inserted right at the beginning between the Luther lieder arranged *de tempore* (they are similarly included in the corresponding lied groups later in the collection). After the *de tempore* lieder through *Gott der Vater wohn uns bei* (Trinity) follow the two Ten Commandments lieder of Luther, the German Credo, the Lord's Prayer with *Pater noster* and Lord's Prayer lieder, Luther's baptism lied and Communion songs (reversed in comparison to Klug), Luther's psalm lieder, Sanctus lieder, *Da pacem* in Latin, and *Da pacem* lieder. After that the arrangement becomes looser; another group of psalm lieder follows between other songs, and the *Te Deum* lieder, *Herr Gott, dich loben wir* (Luther), and *O Gott, wir loben dich* are at the end. A collection arranged in this way, from which selections could be made, was equally suited to the worship service and the school choir for the exercise of a proper faith and for distraction from "love songs and carnal pieces." Settings from this publication did not find their way into Protestant manuscripts for liturgical use to the same degree as many Latin compositions from Rhau's other published works. This fact is related to the increasingly modest role played by the polyphonic lied setting in the Protestant service, in contrast to the unison congregational lied.

This limitation does not detract from the main historical importance of Rhau's great collection of lieder, for herein is offered the principal supply of Protestant lieder at that time, in the most varied settings by the best masters of the age; the settings are so far removed from routine patterns and experiments that the collection becomes an excellent mirror of the German lied style in its most critical period. The different currents which here influenced traditional styles, transforming them or finally completely dissolving them, are the same moving forces which affected the music of all Europe during this active era, so rich in basic changes. All the driving forces of the style of the age are at work in these lied settings, from the rationalistic, formally limited ode compositions of the humanists, through the autonomous rhetorical-architectural art of Josquin, to the echoes of a late Gothic fanciful mysticism. What is important is that no one of them dominates, no form becomes conclusively obligatory; instead, the colorfulness of contemporary musical life uninterruptedly lends its brilliance to this church collection.

The *Concentus novi* of Johann Kugelmann (1540), a collection published by Melchoir Kriesstein in Augsburg four years before Rhau's work, was much less significant, in spite of the high quality of some of its compositions. It is dedicated to Duke Albrecht of Prussia, who decisively influenced the publication and helped finance it by ordering no fewer than three hundred copies. This Renaissance prince, statesman, and humanistically educated man, creatively active as a lied poet and perhaps as a melody composer, was one of the most interesting of the great personalities of the 16th century. His enthusiastic participation in the genesis of Kugelmann's work and his generous support of the printing are good indications of the wholeheartedness with which he pursued his aspirations and with which he made his Königsberg residence into a flourishing music center, universal but at the same time markedly Protestant, competing with Augsburg, Munich, and Krakow.

In contrast to Rhau's lied collection, Kugelmann's work is expressly intended for church use in East Prussia and only secondarily "for the use of schools"— "Ecclesiarum usui in Prussia praecipue accommodati"; it is therefore a mixed collection of 39 liturgical Latin compositions, German sacred lieder and German liturgical prose pieces, German prose psalms and psalm lieder, in the arrangement and the loose liturgical order characteristic of the manuscripts in use at that time. The nucleus of the collection is formed by 26 three-voice Latin and German settings by Kugelmann, to which is added an appendix of four- to eight-voice pieces. In the print, the compilation of which was done by the Augsburg citizens

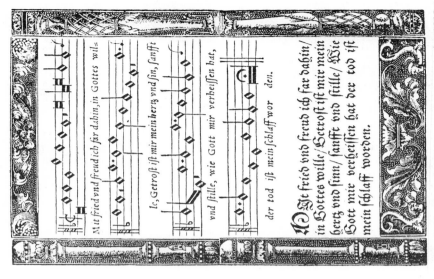

29. Illustration page and the chorale *Mit Fried und Freud ich fahr dahin* from the Babst songbook, Leipzig, 1545.

Jr gelb krauß har gespzenget / jr mündlin wie ein Ru=
bin/Sie krencket mich von hertzē seer/in allem meinem
sinn/die schönste Keyserinn.
  Sie frewt mir all mein gmüte/die aller schönst vnnd
reyn :|: Darzů all mein geblüte/jr eygen wil ich sein/Jr
steter dienet ich wil sein/mit wesen gantz vnderthan/die
weil ichs leben han.
                        VII.   M. G.

net jm vff der beyden/drei frewlin hübsch vnd stoltz.
  Das ein das hieß Margretlin/das ander Vrsele/das
dritt das hat keyn namen/des Jägers wil es sein.
  Er nam sie beider mitte da sie am schwänckisten was
Schwangs hinder sich zu rucke wol auff sein hohes roß.
  Er fürt sie gar behende durch das grüne graß / der
grünen beyd ein ende ghen Wirtzburg auff das schloß.
                        VIII.   Balthasar Arthopius.

E S wolt ein Jäger jagē vor jenem holtz/Was begeg

D Je brünkln die da fliessen.

30. Matthäus Greitter, cantus firmus of the four-voice setting *Es wollt ein Jäger jagen* from *Gassenhauer und Reiterliedlein,* Frankfurt on the Main, 1535, Christian Egenolff.

---

27   Gassenhawer/rc.
Es wolt ein Jäger jagen / vō dem
Glauben/ hoffnung/ vnd liebe/
Christlich verendert.
          D. H. K

E S wolt ein Jäger jagen/ der wol vor jenem
 holtz/ was begegnet ihm auff der heiden/ drei
frewlin hüpsch vnd stoltz.
  Das ein das hieß fraw glaube / das ander
fraw liebe/ hoffnung des dritten Name / des jä=
gers wölt es sein.
  Er nam sie in der mitte / sprach hoffnung nit
von mir laß / schwenckts hinder sich zurücke/ wol
auff sein hohes roß.
  Er fürt sie gar behende/ wol durch das grüne
graß/ behielts biß an sein ende/ nicht hat jn gere=
wet das.
  Hoffnung mache niche zuschanden im glau=
ben rest an Gott/ dem nechsten geht zuhanden/
die liebe in der not.
  Hoffnung/lieb/vn glaube/die schönen schwe
stern drei/ wenn ich die lieb anschawe / die gröst/
sag ich/ sie sei.
              X X X.
Lieblich hat sich gesellet/von Got
tes wort/Christlich veren=
dert. D. H. K.
                            Getrost

31. *Es wollt ein Jäger jagen, von dem Glauben, Hoffnung und Liebe christlich verändert* from *Gassenhauer und Reiterliedlein, christlich, moraliter und sittlich verändert* by Heinrich Knaust, 1571. Contrafactum of the work of Egenolff.

Sigmund Salminger and Sylvester Raid, appear, along with four additional lieder by Kugelmann, works by Stoltzer (the 13th Psalm, mentioned above), Heugel, Planckenmüller, Schnellinger, and a few anonymous pieces. Kugelmann's contrafactum melody to Johann Gramann's psalm lied *Nun lob mein Seel den Herren* is represented by no fewer than four settings, all by Kugelmann himself.

The limiting of most of the collection to three-voice writing, which at this time was preserved almost solely in school compositions, is certainly an expression of the enforced adaptation to a provincial and technically limited church musical life, no matter how lively, in the outermost periphery of the area. On the other hand, the three-voice works of this Augsburg-born composer, former trumpeter of Emperor Maximilian I and later *Kapellmeister* of Albrecht of Prussia, show a quite progressive style: the voices blend in concise imitations quickly following one another; almost all of the pieces are treated syllabically with effectively placed contrasts, rests in all voices, and examples of homorhythmic chordal declamation; the melodies often lie in the upper voice. Kugelmann is very far from the linear German lied style characteristically circulated in the *bicinia* and *tricinia* of the time (as in Rhau's entire *bicinia* collection of 1545). A composition, however, such as the five-voice setting of *Nun lob mein Seel den Herren* remains in the category of the first Walter type, although without approaching Walter's quality; one has the feeling that this is not Kugelmann's real sphere. He exhausts himself in standard formulas, and the simple transparency of his three-voice compositions contrasts with a confusing lack of clarity. A special characteristic appears, however: a tendency to move the voices pseudo-polyphonically over a strongly chordal foundation in a short span of time. It is not difficult to accept the idea that Kugelmann's greater, if much later, successor in office in Königsberg, Johannes Eccard, found inspiration here.

Besides Kugelmann himself there are only two other significant masters represented in the *Concentus:* Stoltzer with the 13th Psalm, also found in Rhau's collection, and the Kassel court *Kapellmeister* Johann Heugel with an important, very "Stoltzerish" six-voice psalm and a four-voice lied setting. The lesser masters from south Germany, Valentin Schnellinger and Jörg Planckenmüller, contributed motet-like, freer lied settings of little significance and a chordal, syllabically declaimed table blessing. Among the anonymous compositions, a Mass for three low voices stands out at the conclusion of the first part. It is a fine work, combining traces of Netherlandish cantus-firmus technique with free, beautifully sonorous passages in pervasive imitation; like Heinrich Finck's three-voice Mass, it could belong, in a relationship as yet unexplored, to the tradition of German three-voice Mass compositions around 1500. Kugelmann himself also contributed two Masses in addition to a Magnificat and other liturgical pieces; they correspond stylistically to his German lied settings.

The two German prose psalms in Kugelmann's collection are among the most important examples of what is perhaps, along with the Protestant lied, the only specifically Protestant form of church music in the age of the Reformation: the German psalm motet. Its creator, according to his own testimony, was the Catholic Thomas Stoltzer, who at the end of 1525 or the beginning of 1526, as *Kapellmeister* in Ofen, set for Maria of Hungary "in the manner of a motet"

Luther's translation of the 37th Psalm, *Erzürne dich nicht;* a little later he wrote three more German psalms, among them those handed down by Kugelmann and Rhau. Their powerful dimensions and their five- and six-voice writing (only the 13th Psalm has five-voices, and in the 37th Psalm a seventh voice is added ad libitum at the end) show the four motets to be exceptional works. In their masterful development of all compositional techniques of the late Josquin Latin psalm motets, their very personal expressive intensity passionately conjured up in emphatic textual declamation, and their visionary greatness, they tower over all comparable contemporary works, Senfl's Latin psalms not excepted.

Thomas Stoltzer: *Herr, neige deine Ohren* (Psalm 86) beginning of the second part.

Stoltzer's compositions, completely isolated in Catholic church music by their use of Luther's texts, are handed down only in Protestant sources. They stimulated a group of minor Protestant composers, mostly from central Germany, to their own attempts at German psalm motets. A few of these composers also produced Latin psalms, as Stoltzer had done; others are primarily known only for their few German psalm motets (Johann Reusch, Johann Burgstaller, Gallus Dressler, Hans Heugel, Valentin Rabe, Thomas Pöpel, Nikolaus Kropstein, David Köler, and others): altogether more than a hundred German psalm motets have been found from the period up to 1570. Even the most important composers —Hans Heugel, David Köler, and, somewhat later, Gallus Dressler—were not able to achieve the greatness of Stoltzer. Their contribution, and that of their lesser contemporaries, is more meaningful in other ways: they attempted to insure that the seed of Stoltzer's work of genius would bear fruit; they created a tradition of a Protestant psalm motet (since Dressler's 14th and 128th Psalms, preferably with German church lied melodies as cantus firmi); they transmitted the idea to Lasso's generation and, finally, to the Schütz period. The few simple German psalms based on *falsobordone* settings handed down in manuscript, some with a monophonic liturgical intonation, are in comparison to the broadly planned motet-like German psalms aesthetically and probably also historically insignificant.

The liturgical applicability of the German psalms, as of the Latin ones, was actually restricted in Protestant and Catholic church music—limits were set even by the scope and personal mode of expression of most of these works—and perhaps there is a relation between this condition and the fact that very few of the so-called specialists could publish collections of German psalm motets (Köler, 1554; Dressler, 1562). The most likely possibility is that such works were used in the Mass (in the Gradual, after the Gospel reading, and during Communion) and as representative and confessional festival music for the most varied occasions. They were certainly sung in school, as is shown by Dressler's remark that he had written his German psalms to be sung "in churches and schools" and "for our dear youth for Christian usage." It also must be assumed, however, that many were written not as real church music but out of a personal impulse, "out of a special pleasure in the very beautiful words" (Stoltzer on the composition of Latin psalms). In that capacity, standing at the brink of the development of early Protestant church music, they form the bridge to the personal expressive art of a later era, an art not primarily bound to the liturgy or intended for it.

If the *Concentus* of Johann Kugelmann is not as towering a document as Rhau's collection, it still reveals the prevailing practice of the time and for that reason is historically instructive. The remaining lied collections, as well as the individual songs and lied groups scattered around in manuscripts of collected pieces, generally contribute nothing essentially new in content and style to the picture of the contemporary Protestant lied settings as it has been so far presented. Like Rhau's work, the collections emphasize Luther's pedagogical thought; they are intended primarily for the "gemeinen Schulen" and only secondarily for the service. There are few of these, however. The repertory handed down in manuscript is always to be found in the larger, usually multilingual collections or in the many manuscript appendices to the widespread Rhau prints. This repertory was nourished by local creations that aimed at little more than workman-like solidity and attained no further dissemination. The printed collections containing both sacred and secular lieder—such as those of Johann Ott, 1534 and 1544, Paul Kugelmann, 1558, and even of Scandellus (whose other work is entirely in another direction) in his songbooks of 1568, 1570, and 1575, which in part already belong to a new epoch in music history—are shown to be very retrospective in their sacred lied settings. Lasso's first German lieder of 1567 already belonged to a new era of lied style. A year earlier Matthäus Le Maistre had appeared as an especially strong advocate of the Protestant lied setting in the Reformation period. He was the Netherlandish successor to Walter in the position of Saxon Court *Kapellmeister*. Le Maistre probably came from the Bavarian court *Kapelle* and took over the position of *Kapellmeister* in Dresden after his conversion to Protestantism in 1554; he remained there until his pensioning in 1568. In 1566 Le Maistre published his *Geistliche und weltliche teutsche Gesänge zu 4–5 Stimmen* (in reality up to seven voices) and in the year of his death, 1577, a second lied work, *Schöne und auserlesene teutsche und lateinische geistliche Gesänge zu 3 Stimmen;* the first work contains no fewer than 70 sacred compositions along with 22 secular ones; the last, 70 German and 4 Latin sacred pieces. Obviously dependent upon Walter, Le Maistre used the entire available Protestant lied repertory, to which were added lieder by Selnecker (who at that time was court preacher in Dresden and was later driven out as a "crypto-Calvinist"), Paul Eber, Wolfgang Dachstein, songs of the Bohemian Brethren, and others. In the 1566 print there is an especially remarkable setting of the psalm *Herr, du bist unsere Zuflucht* for five to six voices; it combines the psalm text with a lied and thus represents an early example of the familiar form of the chorale motet with combined texts, which was to become standard from the late 17th century on. Two other motet-like psalms and one through-composed setting of the Decalogue with the lied intonation *Dies sind die heiligen zehen Gebot* also have great individuality.

In view of his probable age, Le Maistre's style is relatively conservative for the time at which the compositions appeared. The cantus-firmus setting predominates in the collection of 1566. To be sure, there is a group of pieces in a very simple, somewhat free cantional style, such as the two settings of *Allmächtiger, gütiger Gott* (one with the cantus firmus in the discant, the other with the cantus firmus in the bass), *Aus tiefer Not, Allein zu dir, Herr Jesu Christ, Hör, Menschenkind;* in the remaining pieces, however, Le Maistre prefers the old type of German lied setting with a contrast between cantus firmus and the other, freely moving voices, which imitate one another only occasionally. The style is close to that of Walter, Senfl, and Resinarius; Le Maistre could certainly have known Rhau's collection of 1544. Sometimes he even uses the old technique of doubling the cantus firmus canonically, as in *Mensch, willtu leben seliglich* or *Herr Jesu Christe, Gottes Sohn,* in which the free voices are partly dependent upon the chorale melody and partly independent of it. A bridge position between the contrasting types is taken by *Ein feste Burg,* which is not a completely pure cantus-firmus composition; the melody is presented fragmentarily in the discant in free canonic imitation with the *quinta vox,* a style somewhat comparable to the settings by Resinarius in Rhau's collection. The independent, motet-like chorale setting in the style of Hellinck or of the type represented by Alder's *Da Jakob nun das Kleid ansah* is completely lacking in Le Maistre's 1566 print. This omission could indicate either the avoidance of an extreme text interpretation in the Josquin style as developed by contemporary Netherlandish and French composers, or a central German Protestant conservatism determined by the almost canonic significance of the collections of Walter and Rhau. The three-voice settings of 1577, however, tend toward an essentially modern treatment resembling the style of the Heidelberg leider school (Lorenz Lemlin, Jobst vom Brandt, Georg Forster, Stephan Zirler, Caspar Othmayr) and Lasso. Two basic methods can be seen in these settings: they may break up the chorale melody thematically and present it in concisely articulated, largely syllabic motifs that are imitated throughout all voices with little use of stereotyped figures but completely equal in importance *(Aus tiefer Not, o treuer Gott);* or they may present the cantus firmus intact in one voice, while the other two play around the chorale melody with much use of figuration and line-by-line imitation *(Ein feste Burg).* Both kinds show Le Maistre's style during a time that was transitional for the German lied in general. It still partially follows the old specifically German lied principles; it is in part already affected by the late Netherlandish techniques flourishing in the circle around Lasso, which in the following epoch of Protestant church music were to lead to an entirely new lied type. Le Maistre, however, was always a thoroughly individual musician with his roots deep in tradition, a composer who knew how to solve each task in a different and always independent manner. Stylistically, he occupied a middle ground between Stoltzer and Lasso, and in a few works (perhaps in the motet *Herr Gott, du bist unsre Zuflucht für und für*) he equaled both of these masters.

Le Maistre's work from 1577 on is, like so many of the above-mentioned prints (especially almost all of the *tricinia* publications), directed toward the young. This explains the presence of a Latin text; it also explains what is probably the first appearance of a peculiarity that subsequently became widespread. Here is the the text of the closing piece:

Si mundus hic daemonibus   Princeps mundi superbiat,
Scateret sicut vermibus   Ringatur ac insaniat,
Nil timeremus anxie,   Nocere nescit nebulo
Vincemus tandem strenue.   Cum victus sit ve! verbulo.

This is nothing other than a Latin translation of the third stanza of Luther's *Ein feste Burg:*

And though this world, with devils filled,
Should threaten to undo us;
We will not fear, for God hath willed
His truth to triumph through us:
The prince of darkness grim,
We tremble not for him;
His rage we can endure,
For lo! his doom is sure,
One little word shall fell him.

(Transl. Frederick H. Hedge, 1805–90)

More will be said later about such retranslations into Latin. They point in the same direction as the penetration of the Latin motet into Protestant church music; they belong in the same category as the complaints loudly voiced in the 1560s and '70s concerning the waning of congregational song and the preponderance of art music, especially the Latin motet. Le Maistre set the text as a free motet-like composition, as if he knew absolutely nothing of its relation to the Luther lied. This stylistic malformation in the manner of a humanistic schoolmaster is typical of the character of those years in which the musical expression of the Reformation period came to an end and was replaced by new tendencies.

Although it does not really belong to the lied category, another work of Le Maistre may be mentioned here, his *Catechesis numeris musicis inclusa et ad puerorum captum accommodata,* i.e., catechism in musical settings suitable for the understanding of children (Nuremberg, 1559). As a representative of the concept of school music, the work is close to the collections of lieder; like the composition mentioned above, it is a retranslation into Latin, this time of the Lutheran catechism. The five principal pieces appear as extremely simple three-voice compositions, note against note; in addition, there are two settings of "table talks" *(Tischreden)* in which two voices move in strict canon, while the third is independent. The little work is characteristic because it attempts to serve the pedagogical views of Luther and toward that end employs a speech-bound, simple homorhythmic-homophonic ode style, consequently a specifically humanistic style, and the canon, a device of style from the oldest Netherlandish tradition. Le Maistre's position in music history could not be characterized more concisely.

Thus is completed the circle of polyphonic lied settings which, according to their style and the attitude toward the doctrine expressed in them, the Word enclosed within the song, can be considered the lied settings of the age of the Reformation. The innermost essence of this style is the position of the musician toward his assignment as servant of the text. The lied is liturgical property in text and melody and therefore sacrosanct. The musician treats the lied melody, which for him is the bearer of the divine content, either as a permanent scaffolding to be ornamented (as in the case of the late Gothic German lied principle) or as substance inviolable in itself to be arranged and shaped according to autonomous aesthetic laws as a work of art complete in itself (a Renaissance principle influenced by the Netherlandish motet style). In both cases, however (and this is important), the lied remains untouched in its basic state. The musician is not allowed to interpret subjectively the content laid down in word and melody; he is allowed only to represent this content by artistic means. He is not a preacher, but a worshiper among many; his work represents the ideal relation of the congregation to the Word.

The basic relationship of the poets to their assignment, like that of the musicians, underwent a change around 1570: slowly there appeared a personalization that allowed the chorale to become the vehicle of a desire for spontaneous expression. Lasso, whose first lieder were written before this change, was at first the strongest bearer of personalization; Le Maistre, in his first collection, was still essentially a representative of the Reformation period. He still thought from the viewpoint of the congregation and met the demands of the Lutheran lied text accordingly. What was said above about the lieder and lied settings of the time applies to Le Maistre: the whole is perceptible in every example, the entirety of the faith and doctrine rooted in the totality of the congregation. It is significant that in the following period this character of totality is stripped off and the unity of the lied repertory and of the polyphonic style of composition breaks up. The new period is thus differentiated from the age of the Reformation and, moreover, justifies the drawing of a line of separation around 1570. More will be said below of the characteristics of this new historical epoch.

THE PRACTICE OF ALTERNATION AND ORGAN MUSIC

The number of polyphonic lied settings remained relatively small, their dissemination in prints and manuscripts was slight, and monophonic congregational singing of lieder was common practice. Why polyphonic lied settings were really needed other than for school and private devotional societies can be explained by the multiplicity of church music practices during the Reformation and by a special feature of the church lied, its many stanzas. The bad custom later in vogue of tearing single stanzas out of a lied was not yet known in the Reformation period or even in the entire 17th century. A Lutheran lied represented a unified thought; it was an entire psalm, an entire catechism piece, or a portion of the Mass text, no second-rate substitute or extract. This unity of thought could not be torn apart: the meaning of the lied lay in its totality. Therefore it was always sung complete, *per omnes versus*. However, the congregation was rarely required to sing by itself all the stanzas of a lied. Instead, a method of performance was used that had already been well developed in the Roman church and to an even higher degree in the Lutheran church—the performance of music in a system of alternation. According to this practice, traditional pre-Reformation lieder with one stanza (which could, of course, easily be sung by the people themselves) were expanded to structures with many stanzas; these were portioned out among congregation, choir, and organ. The congregation always sang in unison and unaccompanied; the support of congregational singing by organ or other instruments was unknown in the Reformation period. The polyphonic lied settings were sung by the choir; it performed single stanzas of the lied in alternation with the congregation and the organ. (Above all, the fact that the polyphonic setting is always provided only with the text of the opening stanza proves nothing; any other stanza of the text might just as well have been sung. On the other hand, according to the freedom of choice in performance practices, the entire lied might have been performed alone by choir or organ.) The choir either could have sung a cappella or, as already suggested, could have been supported or replaced in individual voices by instruments (lutes, fiddles, recorders, crumhorns, bass shawms, and dolcians; cornetts, trumpets, and trombones were probably used principally for cantus-firmus voices). It is doubtful whether the rare purely instrumental settings (like Senfl's *Also heilig ist der Tag* in Rhau's lieder collection) or compositions which, though vocal, could also have been performed instrumentally (like Stoltzer's 37th Psalm) were actually played instrumentally in the service. Still, a psalm composition might have been used as an as especially festive Introit. At any rate, the performance practices of the time, as in the secular sphere, probably made practical use of all types of musical presentation that were theoretically possible. In the face of this basic multiplicity of performance possibilities, the question of how a work was realized in detail is of minor importance; moreover, the process was subject to constant change.

In this conception of performance practice the organ apparently played a large role, not only as a soloist but also in vocal-instrumental combinations. Wolfgang Musculus, who makes an exact distinction between mixed vocal-instrumental and alternation music (*vicissim* and *alternatim*) in his precise description of services in Eisenach and Wittenberg, 1535, reports that the Credo lied *Wir glauben* and the lied taking the place of the Gradual, *Gott der Vater wohn uns bei,* were performed by choir and organ together, not in alternation. Musculus and other sources also give information about another practice taken over from the pre-Reformation church and traceable until the end of the 16th century: when the choir performed Latin hymns, sequences, or canticles in polyphony, the congregation sang in unison the stanzas of the corresponding German lied translation or a related song in alternation with those of the Latin piece. Thus, according to Musculus, the congregation intoned the stanzas of *Christ ist erstanden* between the verses of the Easter sequence *Victimae paschali laudes* performed by choir and organ; according to other sources, the lied *Nun bitten wir den heiligen Geist* was inserted stanza by stanza into the Christmas sequence *Grates nunc omnes.* Finally, to this practice also belongs the custom of inserting corresponding *de tempore* songs *choraliter* or *figuraliter* between the verses of the Magnificat or into the Ordinary compositions of the Easter Mass, or of making the lied melodies into cantus firmi in the polyphonic section of the composition (or, at least, of quoting them there). The custom was of pre-Reformation origin and, like hymn and sequence performances, limited almost always to Christmas and Easter—in other words, to the feasts for which German lieder were especially reverent and abundant.

A very colorful picture of the practical performance of church music arises from the alternation between unison and polyphonic singing and, within the latter, the different possibilities of presentation, as well as from the practice of inserting different texts into one another. If the full richness is to be recognized, however, a third sound factor in the practice of alternation must be taken into account, that of independent organ playing. The place of the organ in the Protestant church of the Reformation was, to be sure, very much assailed in theory. Independent organ playing was frequently considered (in a close analogy to the thought processes of Calvinism and, a little later, to those of the Counter-Reformation) a far too secular element; reports that love songs, street songs, and noisy program pieces in the style of instrumentally intabulated battle compositions were played on the organ were hardly calculated to establish the instrument's authority in the church. Iconoclasm was always directed against the "papist devil's work" of the organ. Karlstadt flew into a passion against it orally and in writing; the organ in the Zurich *Grossmünster* was pulled down in 1527 while Zwingli stood by. Luther rarely mentioned organ playing, but occasionally he did express an opinion against it, reckoning it among the externals of the Roman service; on the other hand, he was also musician enough in this area to appreciate and praise the art of a Protestant organist like Wolff Heintz (see above). Most Lutheran church regulations, at least in the Reformation period, paid no attention to the organ; a few left it as "adiaphorous" (neither forbidden nor approved) as long as "psalms and sacred songs" rather than "love songs" were played upon it, and as long as the organ playing did not, through its length or autocracy, encroach upon the principal parts of the service. The latter danger existed because of the characteristic use to which the organ was put in this period: it was granted an equal place with singing by pastor, congregation, and choir with instruments. The organ could participate as an essential element in the practice of alternation because it could completely take over individual stanzas of a lied, a hymn, a sequence, or entire parts of other vocal pieces. The purely instrumental performances of the respective text excerpts served as well as the vocal and were interpreted as if the text had really been sung. The conditions for such an understanding of liturgical organ music existed in the Catholic as well as in the Protestant church; the congregation was so thoroughly familiar with the text in its meaning and liturgical place that the instrumental playing could in fact take the place of the sung word.

It appears to have been essentially the extensive substitution of organ music for portions of text that the Protestant church regulations and doctrinal writings rejected as unchristian. A virtuoso or soloistic performance by the organists was also regarded as an objectionable assertion of individuality, inappropriate to the ideas of the priesthood of all believers and of the congregationally centered lay service. Finally, the third element to give offense (and here a specifically Protestant moral philosophy is shown as well as the general musical change of taste and interpretation of the period) was the use of secular melodic material for organ

32. Philipp Nicolai, *Wachet auf, ruft uns die Stimme* from the *Freudenspiegel des ewigen Lebens,* Frankfurt on the Main, 1599.

33. Martin Luther's lied *Ein feste Burg ist unser Gott* in Wolfgang Ammon, *Neues Gesangbuch, deutsch und lateinisch,* Frankfurt on the Main, 1581.

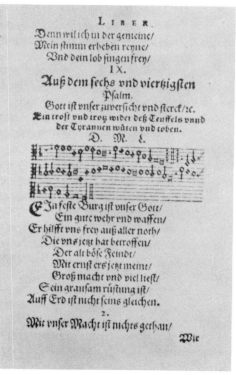

34. Leonhard Lechner, two sections from the four-voice St. John Passion (1593) in the handwriting of Heinrich Leitgeb (1593). Kassel, Murhardsche Bibliothek der Stadt Kassel und Landesbibliothek, MS 2o Mus. fol. 15.

pieces in the service. The relationship here between sacred and secular must be considered from a different viewpoint than in modern interpretations. The Protestant church admitted a large amount of secular lied material and raised it to liturgical rank. Certain forms of secular music, however, were deliberately not admitted, and it was precisely these against which the opposition to organ music was directed. The age of Josquin and even the generation of Lasso had made abundant use of French chanson melodies, as well as Netherlandish and Italian secular songs, as foundations for sacred musical composition, against which practice the Council of Trent raised energetic protest (even if the results were limited). Compositions of the type that could be given equally-effective purely vocal, purely instrumental, or mixed performances were taken over in great number into German organ tablatures; they were probably played fairly often by the Protestant organists. Moreover, primarily in the second half of the 16th century, dances were widely disseminated in organ settings; they also penetrated into the church. More than half of the organ literature of the century, moreover, was made up of secular lied compositions in organ settings which really had nothing to do with church music. For a proper understanding of this fact, it must be realized that in the literature for organ and other keyboard instruments there was as little differentiation between sacred and secular at this time as there was in the instrumental ensemble literature, that the organ in the 16th century was by no means exclusively a church instrument but at least equally an instrument for chamber music of town and court, and that finally, in the instrumental field (more strongly, of course, than in the vocal), there continued to be a literature almost completely common to both confessions. Compositions sacred and secular, of the court and the town, of the church and the home, Catholic and Protestant, flowed completely together in this area. This explains how things were probably often performed in church that were really detrimental to the service. Since as a rule the organist himself compiled his repertory from printed vocal collections, he often did not have in his possession a composition that was particularly required or suitable and would then help himself to nonsacred pieces. This situation was compounded by the fact that there was not yet a printed repertory specifically for the organist and, with the obstinately defended craft tradition of intabulation, there could not be; thus he was to a great extent removed from churchly control and on his own. Moreover, the musician, whose social position was relatively low and who also performed in secular spheres to improve his income, did not have the same close connection to his church as did the members of the vocal *Kantorei.* Countless documents confirm that the organists of both confessions were, at least in the early 16th century, for the most part coarse and often obstinate fellows. Church regulations and complaints such as those mentioned above bear eloquent witness that really embarrassing conditions often prevailed and that the controversial place of organ playing in the Protestant church was due to something more than theological narrow-mindedness.

Despite all theoretical wrangling, however, the functional use of the organ was very large during the Reformation. In addition to the practice of alternation between congregation and choir (the latter again supported by the organ) in lieder singing, there was a similar practice of alternation between pastor and choir in the performance of noncongregational liturgical texts of the service. In both Catholic and Protestant churches, the organ could take over the principal parts of the Mass itself until into the 17th century. It was customary (especially in nonfestal Masses and in those places where there was no polyphonic choir) to treat the Kyrie so that the *Kyrie eleison* was performed by the priest or choir, the *Christe eleison* by the organ, and the second *Kyrie eleison* like the first; the Agnus Dei, also in three parts, was similarly performed. The Gloria and the Credo were correspondingly divided: the priest intoned; the choir joined in and performed the extended text in alternation with the organ (as Musculus attested for Eisenach and Wittenberg). All these practices were of pre-Reformation origin; this is shown by, among other things, the anecdote that Luther himself told about the time he was still a monk and had to go out from Erfurt into the villages to hold services. Wearing vestments, he had stepped up to the altar of a village church. Unexpectedly, the sexton had begun to play the Kyrie and later the Credo on the lute, and Luther had to fit his Gloria in. That was certainly not what Luther had in mind, and the Protestant church sought to prohibit as many of the excesses in deep-rooted traditions as it could. Thus the Wittenberg church regulations of 1525 state that if there is already an organ, it shall only play the Te Deum (in Matins) and *germanica carmina* (which obviously refers to the German lieder and specifically to the alternation and co-operation of organ and choir). The Mecklenburg church regulations of 1540–45 prescribe organ preludes and interludes to the stanzas of the sequence *Grates nunc omnes*. For the rest, organ playing was limited and as a matter of principle excluded from certain parts of the service, especially the Credo. Soon, however, the trend apparently reversed itself; organ playing again gained a foothold in the second half of the 16th century to the degree that the service was enriched with art music and congregational song subordinated. As a reciprocal effect of this, the social position of the organists improved. Soon important composers worked in this area and raised the standard of organ music to the heights of vocal art music, thus eliminating some of the grounds for the church's objections. At the end of this development came the statement in 1597 by the Wittenberg theological faculty that organ music was unobjectionable (see below); this is perhaps reflected practically in the extraordinarily large share given to the organ in the order of worship of the *Laurentiuskirche* in Halle-Neumarkt at the end of the 16th century.

Eventually, organists were given additional assignments: the improvisation of preludes, the independent insertion of a short, quiet organ piece during the Elevation, or free playing during the Communion if lieder were not sung. All in all, in view of the fact that the Protestant church had no special organ literature in this epoch, so much activity seems astonishing. It can be explained first of all by a literature common to both organ and clavier, sacred and secular, Protestant and Catholic, but there is a second, deeper reason: a completely common literature also existed between vocal and instrumental music; everything that was contained in the polyphonic lied collections, even the enormous host of polyphonic Latin Masses, motets, hymns, and canticles, served for organ music as well as for material for the combination or alternation of vocal and instrumental masses of sound described above. Thus, if the organist needed a middle part for the Agnus Dei, one or two stanzas to a *lied* or hymn, a few Magnificat versets for pure organ playing, he transcribed them from the supply of polyphonic compositions on hand, adapting the piece as far as was necessary to organ techniques; he also applied grace notes, coloraturas, runs, and ornamentation (i.e., he "colored" the piece at the same time) but left the basic substance of the composition untouched. There was no special organ literature at this time because there was no demand for it; the frequently stressed unity of all church-music compositions of the epoch also included organ literature. As was the case in many other areas of Protestant church music, a division and specialization took place here only in the following period. The more the craft of intabulation sank in esteem and the more the composer stepped into the foreground as a musical interpreter and an important personality, the more value was placed upon the composer, creative and self-assured, the less upon the subservient craftsman.

The organists of the Reformation period were in large part identical with the composers and lied arrangers. The low theoretical and liturgical value placed upon the organ throughout early Protestantism probably explains why there are only a few significant names among organists. Related to this (but also qualified by tradition) was the low social position of organists in the church hierarchy. A person who felt called to greatness and wanted to reap fame as a composer did not become an organist (Hofhaimer and his circle in the Catholic south are, in many respects, exceptions, not the rule). Information about Protestant organists of the Reformation period is up to the present time correspondingly slight, and what has survived of their vocal works is correspondingly sparse. There apparently was no independent, characteristically Protestant group of organists. In view of Paul Hofhaimer's commanding importance in German organ music, it must be supposed that most of the Protestant organists known at least by name, or even the artistically ambitious among them, had been directly or indirectly "Paulomimes," disciples of the great organist of Maximilian's court and the Salzburg cathedral. The decisive influence of the south-German-Austrian musical culture around Maximilian upon Protestant church music in its early stages could also have had its effect in this area. A somewhat younger generation of primarily north-German organists probably grew up independently; their compositions are just as elusive (the Mors brothers from Antwerp in Schwerin and Dresden, the Koch brothers in Zwickau, and others).

Of the significant south German organ masters, Leonhard Kleber was probably Protestant; there is documentary evidence that Johann (Hans) Kotter was a Protestant from 1520 on. Kotter had had to pay for his confession of faith, like Benedictus Ducis, by being driven from his position, even suffering imprisonment and torture; an organ piece of his on the Ionian melody of *Aus tiefer Not* (the choice of this particular lied was probably not coincidental) is preserved in his sizable tablature planned for Bonifacius Amerbach and probably intended for clavichord also. Like all German organ tablatures that have survived, it contains scarcely any Protestant lied material, but rather many French and Netherlandish lied setting, dances, and also a *Salve Regina*. Hans Buchner, Wolfgang Gräfinger, Othmar Luscinius, Vogelmeier, and Conrad Brumann were and remained Catholic like their master Hofhaimer; also the Buchner pupil Fridolin Sicher in St.

Gallen, and presumably the Hofhaimer pupil Hans Oyart. Compared to these, the middle- and north-German organists hardly count at all. Nothing of their work has been preserved. Wolff Heintz and Johann Weinmann, already mentioned, are known by name and represented in Rhau by vocal compositions. The first real preserved intabulation of a Lutheran church lied after Kotter seems to be the setting of Stephan Zirler's widely disseminated *Bewahr mich, Herr, und sei nicht fern* in lute tablature in a 1562 manuscript appendix to Ochsenkhun's tablature book of 1558 (*Staatsbibliothek,* Berlin). The Breslau organ tablatures of the 1560s already belong to a new era.

LATIN ART MUSIC

The picture of church music in the Reformation period would be incomplete if, in addition to liturgical chant, congregational song, lied polyphony with all of its practical performance possibilities, and organ playing, there were no consideration of the superabundance of Latin art music. There was more production in this area than in any other of Protestant church music, and because of its liturgical significance, its predominance even over polyphonic lied composition was fitting. In spite of all attempts to establish a German service of worship, in practice Latin played the greater part by far. Within the usual mixed-language service, Latin was as a rule retained at least for the most important pieces—the Ordinary settings of the Mass, and the hymns and Magnificats of the Offices. Since all of the pieces could be performed not only as monophonic chant but also wholly or in part (through the practice of alternation) as polyphonic choral compositions, it is quite evident that the Protestant church had a great demand for such works. On the other hand, it is difficult to determine in the majority of cases whether pieces of this type were written for the Protestant or the Catholic church, since the textual foundation was the same for both. With the wide international and interconfessional orientation of the music of this epoch, as mentioned above, a Mass of Morales could be used in Protestant as well as in Catholic worship, in Spain as well as in Germany. Since in those areas where Luther's proposals were taken seriously, the Protestant church did not require all the Mass movements, there was nothing to hinder the use of only the necessary items. Because the Roman church during the Reformation period already had a strong tradition and an immensely large repertory of church compositions, and because these works could be used by the Protestants without change, it is evident why, in spite of the great demands of their church, Protestant composers were relatively inactive in that area. Here the boundaries truly disappeared completely: there was, to be sure, a rather large body of Latin church music specifically for the Protestant church; but, on the other hand, some things that had come from Protestant pens had more value for the Catholic church, and many things from Catholic pens had more value for the Protestants. Thus a large number of printed anthologies with a predominantly Catholic content that had found strong Protestant approval appeared between 1537 and 1559 in Nuremberg, a center of early Protestantism. Finally, a clear picture is provided by the Protestant manuscripts for liturgical use, in which a German and Latin repertory made up of material of both Catholic and Protestant origin is all mixed up together.

Out of the extensive material handed down from this period one large-scale project stands out, testifying to a farsighted, idealistic, and enterprising spirit: the church music publications of Georg Rhau. His intention was nothing less than to give the early Lutheran church a comprehensive repertory for all of its liturgical requirements. The importance attached to Luther's concept of educating youth through music (expressly indicated by titles and forewords) resulted in the assigning of Latin church music performances in the service primarily to the Latin pupils. The strong preference for the Latin language in Rhau's repertory thus had not only liturgical but also pedagogical causes: "habetis hic, optimi viri, cantiones simplicissimas, quae juventutis exercendae causa diebus sacris in Templo cani solent" (Rhau's foreword addressed to schoolteachers in the *Vesperarum precum officia,* 1540). The degree to which this basic consideration went hand in hand with the encyclopedic collection and arrangement is also shown by the detailed forewords of Luther, Melanchthon, Bugenhagen, and Rhau himself that accompany the prints, reviewing and interpreting them (and at the same time recommending them); they constitute some of the most instructive material on early Protestant concepts of music in Luther's immediate surroundings. In elegant Latin, free from the affected similes and metaphors of humanists' forewords, the basic idea is presented (varied again and again in a solemn manner penetrated with religious conviction) that music is of divine origin, given naturally to men, that it is indissolubly bound with the words of Scripture, and that it is itself divine service in its function as a principal means of disseminating the doctrine. In addition, the forewords offer information concerning Rhau's plans and give some account of the cultivation of practical church music. Their contents were confirmed and extended through the publication of musical textbooks, which modestly began with Rhau's own small treatises on elementary theory (*Enchiridion utriusque musicae practicae,* 1517; *Enchiridion musicae mensuralis,* 1520); later, however, with the consideration of all aspects of contemporary musical theory in the writings of Martin Agricola, Johannes Galliculus, Nicolaus Listenius, Wenzeslaus Philomates, Johann Spangenberg, and Johann Walter, there was an apparent aspiration to encyclopedic thoroughness and canonical significance.

Rhau's music printing began in 1538 with the *Selectae harmoniae de Passione Domini* and the *Symphoniae jucundae atque adeo breves.* These were followed in 1539 by the *Officia Paschalia de Resurrectione et Ascensione Domini;* in 1540 by the *Vesperarum precum officia;* in 1541 by the *Opus decem missarum* and the print devoted to a single composer, the *Novum et insigne opus musicum triginta sex antiphonarium* of Sixtus Dietrich (Rhau expressly stated that he considered the single-author prints, at least in part, an element of his total plan); in 1542 the *Tricinia* and the *Sacrorum hymnorum liber primus;* in 1543 another single-author print, Resinarius's *Responsoriorum . . . libri duo;* in 1544 the *Postremum vespertini officii opus,* the *Neue deutsche geistliche Gesänge,* and the penultimate edition of Johann Walter's *Geistliches Gesangbüchlein* (not previously published by Rhau). The imposing series ended in 1545 with the *Officiorum . . . de Nativitate, Circum-*

cisione, Epiphania Domini . . . tomus primus, both parts of the *Bicinia,* Sixtus Dietrich's *Novum opus musicum tres tomos sacrorum hymnorum continens,* and in 1551 with the last edition of Walter's *Gesangbüchlein.*

This huge output, for which in Rhau's immediate surroundings there was a more modest Catholic model in a few of the Jena choirbooks (Isaac's *Choralis Constantinus* could have been known to him at most through hearsay) and a counterpart of which did not appear in the Protestant church until Michael Praetorius supplied it, can be divided basically into three groups of publications: for Vespers, for the Mass, and for diverse liturgical and nonliturgical purposes. The Vespers music group is the most strictly organized (it scarcely corresponds with Luther's liturgical intentions, but it does show once again how essential the pedagogical viewpoint was to Rhau). It embraces all of the pieces that the Latin pupils had to sing in the daily Vespers service: psalms, antiphons, hymns, responsories, and Magnificats, organized either for the seven days of the week (*Vesperarum precum officia* and Dietrich's antiphons) or according to the *de tempore* of the year (both of the hymn publications and the responsories of Resinarius); the Magnificat collection is, as usual, arranged only according to the succession of church modes. The group of prints for the Mass includes Ordinary compositions *(Opus decem missarum)* and Proper cycles, or complete Masses for the principal feasts of the year *(Officia de Nativitate, Selectae harmoniae de Passione, Officia Paschalia).* Finally, the third group offers different collections for liturgical, pedagogical, and domestic purposes *(Symphoniae jucundae, Neue deutsche geistliche Gesänge,* Walter's songbook) or probably exclusively for pedagogical and social use *(Bicinia* and *Tricinia,* both prints multilingual—German, French, Netherlandish, and Latin).

The series of prints for the Mass began in 1538 with the *Selectae harmoniae de Passione,* which, in contrast to the later publications of the group, is loosely organized. Protestant and Catholic composers are about equally balanced here; one side is represented by pseudo-Obrecht (Longaval), Isaac, Compère, and Senfl (three masters very old-fashioned at this time and only one that was "modern"), and the other by Walter, Galliculus, Ducis, Lemlin, and the lesser masters Cellarius, Eckel, and Stahl. The repertory includes the two motet-like Passions which were everywhere compulsory for the use of *Kantorei* until the end of the century (Galliculus and the Passion almost always ascribed in Germany to Obrecht, actually by Petrus Longaval; both works will be discussed below in connection with the history of the genre), Lamentations and an *Oratio Jeremiae,* a Passion motet cycle, and single Passion motets. The succession of systematically organized prints for the Mass was begun with the *Officia Paschalia,* 1539; the second volume including the remaining feasts *(Officia de Nativitate . . .)* appeared in 1543. Because they contain complete services with all of the polyphonic pieces belonging to them, Rhau's *Officia* are of priceless value for a knowledge of the history of practices of worship. Thus the print of 1539 offers a completely through-composed Protestant Easter Mass by Johannes Galliculus, consisting of an Introit with verse, Kyrie, Gloria, Alleluia with verse, the three-part Easter sequence *Agnus redemit oves,* Gospel with salutation, Sanctus with *Pleni* and *Benedictus,* Agnus Dei, and Communion. In spite of the succession of texts entirely in Latin, allowance was made for Protestant requirements not only by the omitting the Gradual, the Credo (which was to be sung as a congregational lied), and the Offertory, and by abbreviating the Gloria text, but also by setting the Gospel with its salutations, not customarily done in Catholic areas, and especially by including a German lied in the Mass text itself, a practice also found in Catholic Easter and Christmas compositions. In the first part of the sequence the three free voices sing the Latin text, while the tenor presents complete, as a cantus firmus, the lied stanza "Christ ist erstanden von der Marter alle," the Easter lied par excellence; in the second section, "Dic nobis, Maria," the three upper voices have the Latin text, while the bass cries three times "Christ ist erstanden!" to the beginning of the lied melody; only in the third section do all the voices unite in Latin on the words "Credendum est magis." That is not enough, however; as the Agnus Dei the following text appears: "Agnus Dei, qui tollis peccata mundi, miserere nobis. Des sollen wir alle froh sein. Christ soll unser Trost sein, Kyrie eleison"—a combination of the Agnus Dei with the lied stanza. The text and melody of the Easter lied sung in unison by the congregation itself during Mass are therefore presented as a leading idea in the last piece before the Gospel as well as in the concluding piece of the Mass. The same print contains still another, incomplete Easter Mass by Johannes Alectorius (identical with Galliculus), a third complete one, put together from compositions by Konrad Rein and Adam Rener, and, finally, a succession of Introit, Gradual verse, Alleluia with verse, and a sequence in three sections by Thomas Stoltzer. Then follow Easter motets, among them one again combining the Latin text with "Christ ist erstanden" (probably also by Galliculus), an Easter psalm by Senfl, and others. In the second part of the volume there are similar Masses for Ascension; they are shorter, however, corresponding to the lesser significance of the feast in the church year. The *Officia de Nativitate* of 1545 is similarly planned. Both *Officia* prints together impart an excellent and comprehensive insight into the problems presented by Latin polyphonic music in the principal Protestant service. The *Missa quodlibetica* type (i.e., a Mass in which German lieder are inserted into the Latin liturgical text) found here actually later became a favorite kind of Protestant Mass.

Rhau's *Opus decem missarum* of 1541 contains ten four-voice Masses not associated with special feasts but intended for Sunday and ferial worship. Even though the concern of the *Officia* is primarily with music written for specific Protestant purposes, the Catholic tradition dominates this publication. Probably the only Protestant composer of the collection is Johannes Stahl, and his composition, like five others, is worked out over a secular cantus firmus and thus does not correspond to the type of Mass the Reformation theoretically required. Apparently Rhau found no composers who could create a Protestant repertory for the collection; or perhaps he did not want to lose time by conferring commissions. In any case, he kept to the tradition, and to a large degree the repertory, of the old Saxon Court *Kapelle* as contained in the Jena choirbooks—that is, to works that had long been outmoded. Accordingly, he offers three Masses of Rener based upon secular lieder, Isaac's Mass *Une musque de Biscaye* and *Missa Carminum,* and one Mass each by Pipelare, the younger Petrus Roselli (based upon

Baisez-moi), and Sampson (on *Es sollt ein Mägdlein holen Wein*). All in all, it offers an old-fashioned repertory; only Senfl's parody Mass on his own psalm motet *Nisi Dominus aedificaverit domum* belongs with the most modern compositions of the period. Since Rhau's work was generally accepted as exemplary, he presumably encouraged the latent tendency of Protestant church music toward conservatism with this selection of Mass compositions and also in part with his motet offerings.

In 1540, Rhau began a new series within his total plan for church music with the *Vesperarum precum officia* (probably after the example of the Jena choirbook 34), which, in contrast to the Mass collections, brought together material for Vespers. As in the Mass prints, the works are arranged not according to type but in the form of a complete service; thus these prints too impart a living impression of the practice of that time. For Vespers of each weekday there appears an antiphon with five psalms in four-voice chordal settings based upon the psalm tones, not mensural but in chant notation, in the kind of purely liturgical *falsobordone* presentation then customary in polyphonic psalmody; they are followed by a responsory with verse, one or more hymns, versicle, Magnificat with Proper antiphon, all like the introductory antiphon of the *falsobordone* psalms in very simple chordal settings. Rhau himself states that these "cantiones simplicissimae" were published for school use (see above); it would have pleased him more if he could have presented "excellentes harmonias et mutetas" instead of such simple things, which cause musicians more boredom than pleasure; young people, however, had to have the material to progress from the simple to the difficult. Among the simple compositions designed for that purpose, however, are some by the finest masters: Walter (21 compositions), Stoltzer, Isaac, Rener, Ducis, Georg Forster (9 compositions), and Johannes Galliculus, along with the minor composers Johannes Stahl (37 pieces), Johann Cellarius, and Andreas Cappellus. There is also a Magnificat cycle by Walter on all eight modes in simple *falsobordone* settings; the composer followed it in 1557 with a cycle of large polyphonic Magnificats.

Rhau continued the series of Vespers publications in 1541 with the 36 antiphons by Dietrich, who lived in Wittenberg at that time and who sent the work into the world with a strong confession of the new doctrine. As a third part of the *Vesperarium* there followed in 1542 the famous collection of 134 hymns, primarily including contributions by Stoltzer, Finck, and Arnold von Bruck, along with the Netherlanders Isaac, Josquin, and Rener, and the German masters Walter, Senfl, Resinarius (under the name Harzer), Breitengraser, and many others. Since the publication also contained several hymn texts rejected by the Protestant church, Rhau believed that he would have to defend himself especially against the charge that he was deviating from the Lutheran doctrine, and made the characteristic statement that he had included the pieces only because of the beautiful music, not the texts—an idea that in later decades often served as a bridge to the use of Catholic music in Protestantism. It seems doubtful that the hymns in question were really used in the service; essentially Rhau's *Hymnarium* provided musical material for household meditations. As a fourth part of the *Vesperarium* the 80 responsories of Resinarius appeared in 1544. In the same year

Rhau concluded the series with the Magnificat collection, the *Postremum Vesper-tini officii opus*. The great publisher and printer, afflicted with severe illness and feeling the end near, considered himself fortunate to have been able to conclude the Vespers series, upon which he placed very special value. The repertory of the Magnificat print is just as "un-Protestant" and almost as old-fashioned as that of the *Opus decem missarum;* the Jena choirbooks appear to have been godfather to both publications. Again there is only one Protestant master (Galliculus) as compared to an overwhelming majority of Catholic Netherlandish and French composers, of whom Rener, La Rue, Divitis, and Pipelare embody the oldest layer of tradition (that of the Jena choirbooks), while Fevin, Richafort, and Verdelot belong to the first generation after Josquin. Again, the really contemporary state of development is represented by a single master, Morales.

In the publications for Mass and Vespers, a large role is played, in spite of the widest possible preference for Protestant masters, by the oldest available layer of the Netherlandish repertory. In the collections without a strictly liturgical aim there is also a vast Netherlandish selection, but one essentially more modern. The *Symphoniae jucundae* offers 52 Latin motets, among them a few secular ones, which are ascribed to 21 anonymous, 24 Catholic, and only 7 Protestant composers. Among the Catholic masters the oldest are in the majority: Josquin, Brumel, Crispin van Stappen, La Rue, Mouton, and Lapicida. Along with Senfl are included the younger Verdelot, Claudin de Sermisy, Lafaghe, Richafort, Hellinck, and Johannes Lupi (one of whose works is erroneously ascribed to Verdelot). The Protestant share in the collection is represented by Georg Forster, Walter, Ducis, and Matthias Eckel. The *Symphoniae jucundae* were intended, as Luther's famous foreword states, primarily for "studiosi musicae"; in practice the motets could, of course, be used on occasion in the service, in school, and for household music. Rhau's *Bicinia* and *Tricinia* collections of 1542 and 1545 are very similar to them in this versatility, as well as in the nationalities, age groups, and confessions of the composers represented.

In Rhau's publications a body of material not only liturgically complete but also extremely rich artistically was made available for Protestant worship. Rhau remained the only printer who undertook to provide the Lutheran church with entire musical services and who, at the same time, gave preference to the German Protestant musician, as far as it was possible to do so. If to the large body of Latin compositions the multilingual works are added—the *Bicinia* and *Tricinia* with their supply of sacred and secular pieces (the sacred ones are probably to a considerable degree contrafacta of secular works)—it becomes very clear that the *Neue deutsche geistliche Gesänge* of 1544, though significant in itself, is only a single part of Rhau's giant *opus summum* of early Protestant church music, and that its function is understandable only in connection with the total work. Rhau's lieder collection, as mentioned above, appears to have had relatively slight dissemination. His *Bicinia* and *Tricinia* were only single collections in a whole group of similar prints of other publishers. The Latin anthologies of Rhau's total plan, however, because of their peculiar liturgical significance and the towering importance of the Latin sphere in Protestant polyphonic music, apparently had an influence approaching canonical significance and were accepted throughout Protestant Germany. Partial copies are found in manuscripts from Rostock and Stuttgart, Bartfeld in Hungary, Augsburg, Dresden, and from the region of Berg in the Rhineland. Numerous manuscripts of services of worship, principally from central and eastern Germany, contain collections of liturgical *falsobordone* settings after the example of the *Vesperarum precum officia* (they had been individually anticipated in the early songbooks and were found on German soil from pre-Reformation times in the *falsobordone* psalms of the Leipzig Apel codex). The whole rich and ramified complex that has been handed down remains even today largely uninvestigated.

The desire of the young church for energetic further cultivation of its music for worship on the basis of that already in existence but consistently carrying out its own principles attained its most beautiful and imposing expression in Rhau's total work. A critical stylistic evaluation of the Latin Masses, hymns, antiphons, Magnificats, psalms, and motets of all kinds contained therein need not be undertaken here; the musical style of those types of compositions does not represent something peculiarly Protestant, but is part of the general stylistic history of the time, modified by the retarding effects of a latent conservatism, often mentioned, and by the lag in development in comparison with the musical centers of Italy and France. The explanation for the broad musical-stylistic union of the Protestant repertory with the Catholic lies in the constantly renewed striving after modernity, in the desire not to become isolated. These factors also explain why, with the exception of the Rhau publications, German masters played a far from leading role in the formation of the repertory. Protestant Latin church music was also dominated by the contemporary direction of fashion, which led over an Italian-Spanish-Netherlandish stylistic orientation to a French-Netherlandish and, toward the end of the century, finally to an Italian one. In the prints of the great publishing firms of the 16th century (especially Petreius, Formschneider, Berg & Neuber, and Gerlach in Nuremberg, Kriesstein and Ulhard in Augsburg), fewer and fewer German masters appeared as time went on, and Protestant composers in still smaller number. Most of the works in those publications were certainly as useful for the Protestant as for the Catholic church and were probably intended for both. Some could have come about only as the result of Protestant stimulation, especially the flood of psalm compositions and the related Josquin renaissance in Germany around the middle of the century. Some collections can be claimed as predominantly Protestant, such as the anthologies edited by Clemens Stephani of Buchau in 1567 and later and Erasmus Rothenbucher's *Diphona amoena et florida,* 1549, with an introduction by Johann Spangenberg; it gives space, however, almost entirely to Catholic authors, with only a few Protestants (Martin Agricola, Resinarius, Stahl, Lampadius). How little concern there was anywhere, however, about a specifically Protestant music, with regard to the composers and the style, is shown by the Mass collection published in 1568 by Michael Voctus in the very citadel of Protestantism, Wittenberg. Of the five composers, four were Netherlanders and one a Frenchman, four Catholics and one a Protestant (Le Maistre).

The situation is the same in the manuscript tradition of the heartlands of the Reformation and also in the manuscripts undoubtedly used for the Protestant service. From this point on, the Mass compositions were dominated by the international repertory—Josquin, Morales, Moulu, Crecquillon, Clemens non Papa, Lupus Hellinck, Mouton, Claudin de Sermisy, and others. Compromises were made in the Protestant liturgy through the omission of the Agnus Dei, and sometimes of all the pieces after the Gloria. From this practice the way was slowly prepared for the Protestant *Missa brevis* (Kyrie and Gloria, the remaining pieces replaced by the corresponding lieder). In spite of the scruples of the church, new Protestant compositions followed the international prototypes in setting all the movements as well as in the use of secular cantus firmi or models. Very rare are works based upon Protestant lied melodies, or compositions such as the anonymous parody Mass on Stephan Zirler's *Bewahr mich, Herr* and the cantus-firmus Masses of Paminger and Johannes (Josquin) Baston on the same lied melody; Protestant Masses for special services, such as the memorial Mass by Scandellus for Elector Moritz of Saxony (1553), are also rare.

A similar situation exists in the motet portions of the manuscript collections and in the pure motet sources. Certain works such as Josquin's *Praeter rerum seriem* or the motet Passion of pseudo-Obrecht (Longaval) were passed on throughout the entire century as almost canonical pieces. How close a connection with the international motet art of the Netherlanders, French, and Italians was made, beyond the conservative repertory of Rhau, depended primarily upon local conditions. The steady tendency toward modernity in this area is as distinct as the cross-tendency toward the canonization of a conservative repertory. The Protestant supply of motets in manuscripts (including the *falsobordone* psalm settings) was nourished primarily by Rhau's collections or by the individual prints of a few single composers. It profited little from such local talents as Joseph Schegel, Paul Russmann, Hans and Paul Kugelmann, Georg Hemmerley, Martin Könner, Thomas Kellner, Johannes Buchmayer, Nikolaus Puls, the more important Jörgen Presten in Copenhagen, and many others, or through the Netherlanders close to Protestantism, such as Baston (of whom a whole body of motets is preserved in a Rostock manuscript). Individual types of compositions began to flourish toward the end of the period in both confessions at the same time. This was especially true of the Latin Gospel motets, the repertory of which was made available in the Gospel settings for the whole church year, printed in five volumes by Berg & Neuber (1554–55); for that reason the material scarcely needed to be circulated in manuscripts too. A similar situation existed for the Latin psalm motets after the example of Josquin, the supraconfessional stock of which (especially gathered together in Nuremberg prints) was apparently increased essentially only by specialists like Johann Heugel. More will be said in detail about this development in the second chapter.

Only the publications devoted to single Protestant masters stand out clearly among the almost identical literature of the two confessions. That the number of such prints is very small is due to the basic condition of contemporary music publication. The market was controlled by the anthologies put together by the publishers themselves or by their musician friends. The supraconfessional quality of the anthologies also offered better possibilities for sale. It was rare for a single composer to succeed in getting his works published individually, possibly by one of the great Nuremberg printers. To such publications belong the responsories of Resinarius already mentioned and the antiphons and hymns of Dietrich that Rhau had included in his *Vesperarium*. In 1535, Dietrich's *Magnificat octo tonorum* had been printed by Schöffer & Apiarius. Reference should also be made here again to the *Melodiae Prudentianae* of Lukas Hordisch and Sebastian Forster (published in 1553 by Nikolaus Faber in Leipzig). The leading master of the Heidelberg lieder school, Caspar Othmayr, brought out one volume each of *bicinia* and *tricinia*, a collection of humanistic *symbola* (motets based on mottoes), and an *Epitaphium D. Martini Lutheri*, but scarcely any larger Latin motets; the focus of his work is humanism rather than Protestant church music. Le Maistre's Latin pieces have already been mentioned in part; to them can be added at this point his *Sacrae cantiones* of 1570, dedicated to the Elector August of Saxony. While the early (Munich) Masses of this composer belong completely to the old Netherlandish cantus-firmus Mass type, Le Maistre wrote in Dresden a Protestant Mass on *Ich weiss mir ein fest gebauets Haus*, in the *Qui tollis* of which he placed as a cantus firmus the lied *O du Lamm Gottes, das der Welt Sünde trägt*. Though they originated in the age of the Reformation, the works of Leonhard Paminger were published only posthumously, from 1573 to 1582; in the incomplete collected edition prepared by Paminger's son Sophonias, there are more than six hundred Latin psalms and psalm verses, Gospels, antiphons, responsories, hymns, and sacred lieder. Paminger is a typical Protestant composer of his time in his combination of retrospective and progressive style characteristics. While his psalms completely follow the example of Josquin, the remaining Latin works adhere to canon techniques, use of a cantus firmus, and comparatively indifferent textual treatment. In the association of a Latin Christmas Gospel with inserted German Christmas lieder, Paminger provides a new variant of the tradition of quodlibet macaronic compositions for the principal feasts of the year, abundant with lieder. The concord of the composers despite differing confessions is indirectly seen once again in the fact that no less a composer than Jacobus Gallus studied Paminger's work and perhaps received inspiration for his encyclopedic *Opus musicum* from the arrangement of Paminger's posthumous print. Finally, Wolfgang Figulus is at the end of the period, with two motet publications in 1553 and 1575, a *tricinia* volume "ad voces pueriles in usum scholarum" (1559), and a collection of Latin and German Christmas lieder (not all of which were composed by him) in 1575.

The preceding survey of Protestant creative activity in the Reformation period in areas lying outside the lied shows clearly that such music was produced in much greater quantity than the lied and that it took precedence in practical use (as is proved by contemporary reports, the Rhau publications, and the manuscript sources). The course of history confirms this observation: as time passed Latin art music more and more took the upper hand in relation not only to the polyphonic lied setting but also to the congregational song. Reference has already been made to the significant changes in the numerical proportions in the editions of Walter's songbook (see above); this is symptomatic. In the 1550s and '60s there were more and more complaints that interest in lied singing was constantly decreasing, that the congregation was tired of singing, that Latin choral and organ music was overrunning the service and competing with the spoken word, the sermon, and the liturgical chant for a place in the proceedings. It is significant that even in Rhau's publications the introductory formulas of the Gospel motet, not belonging to the Bible text, were also set to music, a fact clearly proving that the Gospel motet was not sung in addition to the reading but rather in place of it. Similarly, the Cologne provincial synod complained in 1536 that choral singing and organ playing were pushing aside even the Epistle, Credo, Preface, Lord's Prayer, and so on. Admonitions that the congregation itself should sing and that art music should be subordinate to congregational singing were contained to an increasing degree in almost every church regulation of the time. Even those parts of the Mass rejected by Lutheran doctrine from the very beginning, the Offertory and Communion, forced their way again into the service in the guise of the Latin motet. The basic ideas of Lutheran church music were increasingly forgotten; the congregation became tired of singing; laziness in matters of church music became widespread. An energetic reorganization of congregational singing and a deliberate suppression of the Latin in favor of the German language was therefore necessary in the following period.

The result of this development is easily perceptible: an uprooting of Luther's basic idea of the priesthood of all believers, a dissolution of the unified service understandable to all, a renewed division of the religious community. The result was not, however, as in the Catholic church, the hierarchical separation into priesthood and laity, but rather the division, by the humanistic order of precedence of the intellectual aristocracy, into the educated and the noneducated. With the predominance of Latin and the preponderance of art music, the service of worship became an affair of the educated classes. The people lost the direct relation to the Word that had been given them in the congregational lied. Aesthetic contemplation threatened to enter in place of the inner penetration of the service by Scripture, the longing for beautiful form as fulfillment of religious need in place of an ecstatic, though formless, impulse for Christian truth and freedom. Luther himself had opened the door to this development by not rejecting and condemning churchly ceremonies, traditional art, and secular life, desiring instead a "piety of the world" (F. Strich), a "spiritualization and transfiguration" of secular life, of art, and of ceremonies through his teachings. In placing the experience of God within the individual, freeing it from the cultic form, Luther opened to the individual the way to formation of a service of worship based upon his own needs and his educational level. Luther had desired, however, that every man in his station in life be a spiritual human being and that he unite with others in religious experience to form a community. The result of the development as reflected in church music, however, was a fateful division of the congregation according to station and education, according to city and country. Herein Lutheranism offered Calvinism the broadest field of attack; to that division the Reformed church owed its increasing success in Germany. The tremendous exertion of will that had forged the unity of the Protestant congregation in the Reformation period abated. Melanchthon stepped into Luther's place. From the new demand of a uniform congregational service on the one hand, and from the progression of the division that had begun on the other, there developed the forces which in the following period flowed through Protestant church music and transformed it.

PART II

The Age of Confessionalism

BY FRIEDRICH BLUME

Translated by Theodore Hoelty-Nickel

The Period of the Counter-Reformation

Protestantism had continued to gain ground in the first four decades after the Reformation. By 1560, nine-tenths of the German Empire professed adherence to Lutheranism or to some other Protestant faith. The religious movement was allied with the newly awakened national consciousness, struggling in equal measure against Spanish and papal "servitude."

Political complications had prevented the Schmalkaldic War from crippling the young Protestant movement. The Interim of 1548, which suspiciously resembled an attempt at re-Catholicization, had awakened the people's resistance to an unprecedented extent. In 1555, the same year the Imperial Diet at Augsburg agreed upon a religious and political peace based on parity, Cardinal Carafa became Pope Paul IV: the fanatic of church reform and the reviver of the Inquisition had become the head of the Catholic church.

Lutheranism was no closely knit church organization, but rather a doctrine represented by a totality of state churches. Divided by differing doctrinal positions (Philippist, Gnesio-Lutheran), it had a difficult time in the face of Catholic reform and the consistent political organization of the Calvinistic church. One territory after another was lost. Johann Casimir of the Palatinate was one of the first rulers to "reform" his territory. Anhalt followed in 1596, Moritz of Hesse in 1605, and Johann Sigismund of Brandenburg in 1613. Party strife reigned in place of badly needed political unity and religious tolerance. Peace attempts were unsuccessful. The battle between the confessions was made permanent when the various Lutheran denominations and state churches rallied around Jakob Andreä's Formula of Concord of 1577, the intent of which was to "express openly the separation of the adherents of the Augsburg Confession from the other communions" (Leube). For almost two hundred years the Formula also bound musicians to the confession of Lutheran orthodoxy. Teachers, cantors, and students still subscribed to it by oath in the 18th century. After the Synod of Dordrecht of 1618–19, when the strictest form of Calvinism had won out in the Reformed church, leading theologians like Polykarp Leiser and Matthias Hoë of Hohenegg (both in Dresden and both exerting strong influence on church music) began to consider seriously whether it might be better for Lutherans to join with Catholics against Calvinism rather than the reverse. The unleashed "madness of the theologians" (Melanchthon), unfruitful and disintegrating, survived the Thirty Years' War. It determined the course of Paul Gerhardt's life, and was the root of the later conflicts between orthodoxy and Pietism, which so profoundly disturbed music too. Protestantism was to feel its destructive effect into the 19th century.

The bitter enmity of the confessions caused Protestantism to split apart internally and caused it to lose impetus externally. The Society of Jesus swiftly asserted itself in Germany, finding in Elector Maximilian I of Bavaria its base of political power. Very soon the schools of the Jesuits constituted a force in the intellectual, and thereby the musical, life of the nation. The Protestant *Gymnasia* and universities proudly arrayed themselves as a counterforce, becoming centers for the new natural sciences, humanistic-philosophical studies, and music. Institutions such as the Johanneum in Hamburg, the Katharineum in Lübeck, the *Thomasschule* in Leipzig, the *Kreuzschule* in Dresden, and the princely schools in Grimma and Schulpforta (to name only a few from a huge number) openly became the upholders of the tradition of Protestant church music and a training ground for the rising generation. Supports for the intellectual struggle of Protestantism continued to come from the cities, above all the free cities, whose decline was still hidden by an aura of outward splendor. The actual leadership of Germany's cultural life, however, passed to the courts of the princes and the nobility. Like the great merchant princes of Catholic southern Germany, they opened their doors wide to the art of Italy and the Low Countries. Princely absolutism adopted a framework of Baroque art.

These changes directly affected Protestant church music, in which essentially all elements—north and south, city and country, court society and middle class—had participated equally during the Reformation. There was, to be sure, music meant for simple and for more pretentious occasions in chapel, but no church music had been earmarked for the courts or for the cities, just as there had been almost no difference between north and south. Now, however, divisive impulses became apparent. South Germany, especially Württemberg, continued for a while to play a positive, though hardly decisive, role in Protestant church music, but the leadership soon passed to Franconia, Saxony-Thuringia, and north Germany. South of the Main, Nuremberg remained creative for a long while, increasingly expressive of strict orthodox Lutheran tradition, yet at the same time remaining receptive to newer Italian music and taking the lead in religious poetry. In these areas the city's influence radiated to the smaller Franconian cities, such as Rothenburg on the Tauber. The simplest kind of song became the sole type of music in the rural churches until the 17th century, when even rural congregations participated to an amazing degree in the cultivation of church music. During the Counter-Reformation, however, music as an art was mainly restricted to the large cities and princely seats. The courts of Dresden-Torgau, Wolfenbüttel, and, for a time, the Brandenburg residences of Ansbach, Königsberg, and Berlin were in the vanguard until well into the Thirty Years' War—in some cases even after it. For a while, small residential towns such as Heidelberg, Neuburg in the Palatinate (still Protestant then), Sigmaringen, and others shone in splendor. From the Peace of Westphalia (1648) on into the middle of the 18th century, Protestant church music again found its strongest support in the cities. Among many others, Hamburg, Leipzig, Nuremberg, and the small Thuringian towns such as Weimar, Gotha, Arnstadt, and Mühlhausen may be mentioned. These remained the real upholders of Protestant musical culture into the days of Bach—that is, until dissolution of the burghers' traditional guild-based way of life and the rising of a new, emancipated bourgeoisie, which shifted its interest primarily to secular music.

Taken as an intellectual and cultural movement, the Counter-Reformation

35. Chorale fantasia *Nun lobe meine Seele den Herren auf 2 Clavier* by D. H. Lübbenau organ tablature, MS Ly B 1.

36. Johannes Eccard (1553–1611) in an engraving by Johann Herman (1642) in *Erster Teil der Preussischen Festlieder* by Johannes Eccard and Johann Stobäus, Elbing, 1642, Bodenhausen.

37. Johannes Eccard and Johann Stobäus, *Erster Teil der Preussischen Fest-lieder,* Elbing, 1642. Bodenhausen. Title page of the tenor partbook.

channeled immeasurable currents of strength into music as a whole. If Palestrina and the Roman school and, in more modest measure, Jacob de Kerle and his circle may stand as the specific expression of the Catholic reform spirit in music, then many decisive stimuli that have endured to the present time had their origin in the spirit of the Counter-Reformation and in the art of the Baroque emerging from it. Just as the Catholic Reformation gave new blood to the life and piety of the old church, altering these to their very core, it also had an indirect effect on Protestantism. Despite inner conflicts—but also because of them—Protestant music profited from the music of the Counter-Reformation. Marked simplification, contraction, and recognition of the need to make texts understandable, which characterized post-Tridentine Catholic music, also corresponded to Protestant wishes. The style of the Roman school or of its south German equivalent, the Lasso-Gallus group, could simply be taken over. An almost classic example is that a simple piece like the *Ecce quomodo moritur justus* of Jacobus Gallus remained alive in Protestant church music for four centuries without interruption. The literary community between the confessions that had existed during the age of the Reformation thus found its unbroken and natural continuation. This explains why such huge quantities of Catholic and Latin Masses, motets, Magnificats, and so on, found their way into Protestant music down to the time of Bach (and, in the face of altered cultural needs, again from the late 18th century on). In a sense, Protestant music participated as *tertius gaudens* in the split that began in Italy around 1600 between *prima pratica* and *seconda pratica,* benefiting from both by taking over their literature and continuing in its own way the small and large concertos, the religious monodies and madrigals from Viadana, G. Gabrieli, and Monteverdi on. Protestant church music from the close of the 16th century to Bach could never have become what it was without the developments in Catholic Italian church music: adherence to the Roman style *(prima pratica— stylus antiquus)* and the revolutionary thrust toward the Baroque *(seconda pratica —stylus modernus).* While bringing to this union its own heritage, the church song and the cantus-firmus setting, Protestant church music indulged without reservation in the shared literary heritage. But as this happened, it impressed its own stamp with surprising rapidity and clarity on what it took over. Alongside the borrowed musical materials used in the Lutheran church from the time of Lasso to Bach without restraint or inhibition, there arose for the first time, through adaptation of the Italian Baroque, a church music that had a Protestant spirit and a Protestant physiognomy. There are many formal resemblances between Michael Praetorius and Giovanni Pierluigi Palestrina, more still between Praetorius and men like Viadana, Gabrieli, Agazzari, Fattorini, and so on. Schein's *Israelsbrünnlein* can be traced back to Monteverdi's madrigals, as can Schütz's *Kleine geistliche Konzerte* to Monteverdi's monodies. But no difference in attitude and expression is sharper than that between Praetorius and Palestrina, between Schein or Schütz and Monteverdi. While the literary community signified a unity of style during the age of the Reformation, the picture now changed and became richer—from literary community through adaptation of style to genuine acceptance and self-expression. Protestant church music had entered its maturity.

The struggle with the forces of re-Catholicization pressed another, hitherto latent, problem into the foreground, that of language. Luther and the whole circle of Reformers had taken for granted that while the vernacular was appropriate to the participating congregation in church services, Latin was the proper medium for the priest or the liturgical, florid counterpoint of the choir. Now, however, stimulated by the Interim and then strongly emphasized through the Counter-Reformation, the conflict simultaneously became also a contest between the languages. Entirely in accord with churchly tendencies and teachings, Latin remained longest in use beside German in the citadels of strictly observed Lutheranism (in Saxony, especially in Leipzig, into the 18th century; in Franconia, especially in Nuremberg, even longer). Calvinism, by contrast, from the very beginning suppressed Latin in favor of the vernacular. A great variety of intermediated compromises remained possible in practice, but in principle the contest may be regarded as having been settled around 1600. Since the beginning of the 17th century, there has been a preponderance of the national language in art music and to a large extent also in liturgical altar chant. But for a long time to come, Latin would find a safe retreat in the Ordinary of the Mass (rarely in the Proper), the Magnificat, Vesper hymns, the Te Deum, occasional Marian antiphons, Communion songs, and so forth.

The Reformed church played the most important role in the development of the language question. It undertook, in any case, the "purification" of divine services from all other remnants. Calvinism's sober, puritanical conception of divine worship as unadorned teaching and preaching, its sharp rejection of the miracles of the Mass, its leaning toward the ethical and pedagogical, like its aggressive, anti-Catholic, even anti-Lutheran attitude, drove it to extinguish all "papistic abominations." This meant organ music as well as candles on the altar, the Latin language as well as the trappings of the priest, florid counterpoint as well as pictures in the church—indeed, the whole ceremonial cult and the form of the Mass above all. Johann Scultetus, the court preacher of Elector Johann Sigismund, was even allowed to attack the Mass and the singing of Latin in church with great vehemence in Lutheran Brandenburg. Hoë, the arch-Lutheran in Dresden, still (like Luther) declared ceremonies, altars, pictures, and art music in the church to be adiaphora, tolerated rather than encouraged. Georg Calixt, however, though a Lutheran, declared his outright opposition to the celebration of the Mass. Even the Great Elector, Friedrich Wilhelm of Brandenburg, still felt it necessary in his will to recommend to his son that he should "do away with the Lutheran customs in a polite way" (Leube). The consequence of these undertakings and attitudes was in fact that the celebration of the Mass was more and more simplified and an impoverishment set in; of the whole ceremonial that had been so fruitful for music, only the Kyrie and Gloria (the so-called *Missa brevis* —at that time usually called *Missa*) were left. Consequently, the demand became so small that it could be filled from the common musical literature, and the stimulus for Protestant composers to write *Missae* declined greatly.

BEGINNINGS OF THE REFORMED PSALM LIED AND THE ORIGINS

OF THE LUTHERAN CANTIONAL SETTINGS. THE CANTIONALES

As a result of the attitude of the Reformed confessions toward music and liturgical form, all but the simplest types of art music were drawn more and more into the orbit of Lutheranism. As far as the general history of music is concerned, the Reformed churches were productive only in the field of the hymn and, for a time, that of hymn settings. Only hymns were acknowledged, and then only in their simplest form, as choral congregational song. Indeed, even Zwingli, though himself the poet and perhaps composer of the melodies of several songs, and to a greater degree Calvin, had consciously eliminated the associations with the musical tradition of the old church and with contemporary art music which Luther had been at pains to preserve. Furthermore, the sharp emphasis on morality had severed the connection with secular folk song that had been so fruitful in the Lutheran church. Thus, only one path for the creation of a body of songs for congregational singing remained open: new settings of the contemporary literary material following the trends at court.

The artistic genesis of a Calvinistic treasury of songs had its own historic background. The Strasbourg songbooks of the 1520s and '30s (see p. 46 f.), which show an affinity to the Zwinglian position, already reveal a strong tendency to utilize the content of the Psalms for congregational singing. In 1538 Jakob Dachser at Strasbourg and in 1542 Hans Gamersfelder at Nuremberg had each published a complete rhyming Psalter with tunes. In 1540 the *Souterliedekens*, Flemish psalm lieder with secular tunes, had appeared in Antwerp. These were revised and published (1556–57) for three voices by Jakob Clemens non Papa. The Ulhart Psalter and the significant, complete psalm composition of Burkhard Waldis (see p. 48) also belong to this series. For southern Germany, the Zurich songbook of Froschauer (1540, 2nd or 3rd edition; see pp. 47 and 513) had already represented a decisive step in the direction of the Zwinglian position. Its authors, the Constance Reformers Johann Zwick and Ambrosius Blaurer, aided by the poets Matthäus Greitter, Heinrich Vogther, Ludwig Öler, and others, are known in music history for their connections with Ducis and Dietrich. Zwick's musical limitations are very clear: he relegates countless hymns to a few known melodies that recur again and again—the number of new tunes is extremely small. In the important preface he expresses the conviction that although precedence might readily be given to psalm singing, the other kinds of religious song must not be neglected in its favor; still, in church, music should be restricted exclusively to congregational song. But Zwick did not have his way. Soon the only material for congregational singing in the Reformed church was the Psalter. When, doubtless in response to a direct suggestion from Calvin, Clément Marot began writing the "official" rhyming Psalter, propagandist motives must have played a part too. The French court, whose favorite poet was Marot, received the Psalter with enthusiasm. King Francis I had the poet send a copy to Emperor Charles V, who in turn spoke of it with praise. Catherine de' Medici, Marguerite of Navarre, King Henry

II, and Diane de Poitiers all outdid themselves in the use of the Marot psalm lieder. This was apparently one of the many subtle attempts of Calvinism to penetrate the leading circles and gain a footing there, but Catholic reaction would not permit it. It was not until after many struggles, and long after Marot's death, that a complete rhyming Psalter could be published for the first time (1562). (For the further history of the Reformed hymn and of the so-called Huguenot Psalter, see chap. V, p. 507 ff.)

Within German Lutheran church music, the Reformed psalm lied achieved only secondary importance, and this not until after the translation of the Marot Psalter into German (1565) by the Königsberg law professor Ambrosius Lobwasser (incidentally, a Lutheran) and its publication in 1573 (see p. 546). Thereafter it was disseminated in countless editions, well into the 19th century. In France the Marot Psalter appeared in various arrangements for several voices, among others in three different versions by Claude Goudimel. The last of these (1565; see p. 535) offered the Psalter in an unpretentious four-voice form, in *contrapunctus simplex*—that is, homophonic, with the cantus firmus in the tenor. (Earlier arrangements by Bourgeois [1547, 1554, and 1561], as well as those by Goudimel of 1551–66 and 1564, had no significant place in Lutheran music.) Lobwasser's Psalter now appeared with the settings of Goudimel's last version (1565), achieving through this an amazingly wide distribution. Thus, the historically important factor for Lutheran church music was not Lobwasser's texts or the French melodies introduced with them, but the presentation in simple, four-voice, note-against-note cantional settings at such a relatively early time. Previously, settings of this type had scarcely appeared at all in German secular songs. In the area of religious song they turned up only in a few works by Johann Walter (Walter's so-called second lied type), and otherwise only in the humanistic ode. What significance the different compositions and types or styles of settings of the Huguenot Psalter had for the Reformed church and how they were employed there (within or outside the church service) will not be discussed here (see chap. V). But for Lutheran church music the appearance of a German-language rhyming Psalter in pure cantional setting was an event of far-reaching significance. It does not matter whether the melody lay in the tenor or, as later became the rule, the soprano. It was, in any case, the only part actually sung. As the evidence shows, men and women could sing it in octaves, and the other parts, it must be supposed, were instrumental. Indeed, it is quite possible that organ accompaniment to congregational singing came about in this way. The organist could intabulate the more complicated, polyphonic settings usual in the Reformation period, and use them to alternate with the congregation but not to accompany it, whereas the simple cantional settings were almost ideal for accompanying. As a matter of fact, the latter seem to have been used in this manner in the Reformed church too. The Zwinglians had dismantled the organs in their churches, but it is reported from Bern as early as 1581 that the congregation sang with the help of a cornett (obviously the soprano part is meant here) and three trombones or, for the sake of students, with an organ. The Hamburg *Melodeien Gesangbuch* (1604) speaks expressly of the organ accompaniment to hymn singing. The complicated and metrically involved settings of the Reformation period were probably also often presented so that only the cantus firmus was sung, while the other parts were played on instruments or pulled together on the organ. In any case, they remained art music and did not lend themselves structurally to congregational singing. Now, however, the polyphonic settings were arranged so that the congregation could sing the melody to the accompaniment of a simple, four-voice setting. The concept of "choral singing" (see p. 63 ff.) changed from one of absolute unison singing to one of accompanied unison singing. The word "chorale," originally designating liturgical altar chant and its monodic presentation, gradually came to mean the congregational song; this was, to be sure, monodic, but now it could be sung with accompaniment. From now on one finds this provided for in songbook titles, like that of Lukas Osiander: "So arranged that an entire Christian congregation can easily sing along." The Huguenot Psalter therewith provided the impetus for a practice that has remained to the present day one of the foundations of all Protestant church music.

Johann Walter (see p. 73 ff.) had approached the practice very closely in his "second type" of lied setting, which, incidentally, was even then sung chiefly in unison with instrumental accompaniment. But for the most part, composers followed him along this path only hesitantly. Indeed, the younger ones held rigidly to the old type, the genuine polyphonic lied setting. Yet it is significant that precisely in those Lutheran districts bordering on Calvinistic or Reformed areas, the pure cantional type had already evolved around the middle of the 16th century and many hymnbooks employed it consistently. The 156 settings for the German rhyming Psalter of Burkhard Waldis (the verses first printed in 1553) that J. Heugel of Kassel composed in four and five voices (between 1555 and 1570, according to W. Brennecke; *MGG* VI, 342) extend from the pure homophonic cantional settings to the richer, more contrapuntal type (still extant in manuscript). At about the same time, however, *Der ganze Psalter Davids* appeared in Stuttgart and Tübingen, which also bordered on Calvinist territory. This was composed by Sigmund Hemmel, choir director of Duke Ulrich, and was published posthumously in 1569; according to Brennecke, it was written between about 1561 and 1564 (see *MGG* VI, 140). Hemmel collected the texts of his psalm lieder from Strasbourg, Augsburg, Constance, and Basel songbooks, especially from the Bonn songbook (edition of 1561)—in other words, from the greatest variety of poets. Similarly, his melodies stemmed from the greatest variety of sources (*MGG* VI, 141). His settings were in a predominantly cantional style— here and there perhaps a bit livelier, though hardly any longer polyphonic—with the tenor carrying the melody (see Ex. *a*). The Breslauer David Wolkenstein should be mentioned in this connection; he published his *Psalmen für Kirchen und Schulen, auf die gemeinen Melodien syllabenweise zu vier Stimmen* at Strasbourg in 1577 and 1583. The editors of Hemmel's Psalter, which subsequently enjoyed a broad dissemination beyond confessional lines, were the two Stuttgart court preachers Balthasar Bidenbach and Lukas Osiander. Their preface states that in hymn singing, too, "such language should be used as may be understood by the entire Christian congregation." Like Marot's Psalter in the French court,

Hemmel's Psalter delighted the Württemberg court. It was bestowed upon the schools and came to be used throughout southwestern Germany. With these models as a basis, the same Lukas Osiander took the decisive and permanently effective step in 1586 when he published his *Fünfzig geistliche Lieder und Psalmen mit vier Stimmen auf Kontrapunktsweise*. These were rendered in the simplest cantional settings, the melody in the upper voice (see Ex. *b*), homorhythmically but not isometrically: the original rhythm of the song remains, though it is bestowed simultaneously upon all four voices. Osiander's book, containing the principal Lutheran lieder "so arranged that an entire Christian congregation can sing along," became the prototype of all future congregational hymnbooks. With that, the extended influence of the Huguenot Psalter on Lutheran hymn setting practically came to an end. The model for the future was complete; musicians had only to make use of it. Osiander, who was related to Jakob Andreä and participated in the drafting of the Formula of Concord, was a Lutheran of the strictest observance, and commanded the sort of influence to promote his work in the broadest Lutheran circles. It has not unjustly been called a "musical Formula of Concord" (see U. Siegele in *MGG* X, 429). Osiander concluded for the Lutherans what the Calvinist Psalter had begun: he distinguished between the Lutheran cantional lied setting and its origins and established a model for the future, the Protestant archetype containing all its inner musical conviction and limitation. Artistically, Osiander's work should not be overestimated. It represents that point of development at which the practical needs of the church and artistic values separated decisively for the first time. The Cantionales (songbooks for congregational use) that appeared in a long series after Osiander sought to present practical music for congregational worship. They did not impinge upon art music, but stood independently beside it, raising no claim to exclusivity (on this section, cf. p. 47 ff.).

Openings of Cantionale settings of *Ein feste Burg* (Psalm 46), transposed to the same tonality.

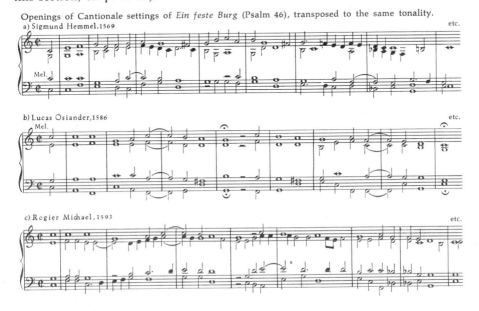

d) Seth Calvisius, 1597

e) Barth. Gesius, 1601

f) David Scheidemann, 1604

g) Melchior Vulpius, 1604

h) Hans Leo Hassler, 1608

i) Michael Praetorius, 1610

The Protestant Cantionale underwent no basic change in the following centuries, and the kind of accompaniment to congregational singing on which it settled has in principle remained the same to this day. The most important later Cantionales are: Andreas Raselius, Regensburg, 1588; Rogier Michael, Dresden, 1593; Seth Calvisius, Leipzig, 1597; the Eisleben hymnbook, 1598; Melchior Franck, Coburg, 1602; Bartholomäus Gesius, Frankfurt on the Oder, 1594, 1601, 1605; Melchior Vulpius, Weimar, 1604; Johann Jeep, Weikersheim, 1607; Martin

Zeuner, Ansbach, 1616; Gotthard Erythräus, Altdorf, 1608. The first comprehensive Cantionale of northern Germany is the Hamburg *Melodeien Gesangbuch* of 1604. Among the composers of its lied settings were David Scheidemann, uncle of the later famous Hamburg organist Heinrich Scheidemann; Joachim Decker; Hieronymus Praetorius, famous composer and organist at St. Jacob's in Hamburg; and Jakob Praetorius, his son, later organist at St. Peter's in Hamburg (see Ex. *c–g*).

The group of south German Cantionales finds its climax in Hans Leo Hassler, who published his *Kirchengesänge, Psalmen und geistliche Lieder, auf die gemeinen Melodien mit vier Stimmen simpliciter gesetzt* in Nuremberg in 1608, a year after his *Psalmen und christliche Gesänge mit vier Stimmen, auf die Melodeien fugweis Komponiert* had appeared. It contains the established festival and Sunday lieder of the old Lutheran church, as well as catechismal and psalm lieder and a few of general content. There are only sixty-eight, all told, but they are masterful, even in their simplicity: "the best Lutheran chorale book in this style" (Teschner). The book was reissued in 1637 in Nuremberg by S.G. Staden, with the addition of several settings by himself and his father Johann. Since the republication by Teschner (Berlin, 1865), it has gone through a series of reprintings within the past hundred years. The north German counterpart to Hassler's *Kirchengesänge simpliciter* may be found in parts VI–VIII of the *Musae Sioniae* of Michael Praetorius, Wolfenbüttel, 1609–10. Part VI contains the festival songs, part VII the catechismal, Communion, thanksgiving, and other hymns, while part VIII embraces songs about the cross, the church, death, and judgment, for morning and evening, and for the home, as they were "commonly used in churches and homes" and "as sung . . . in different localities and lands." But while Hassler's *Psalmen simpliciter* is restricted to the old repertory of lieder, *Musae* VI–VIII comprises a great amount of new material in addition, such as just then began to appear in great abundance (see below). It includes over four hundred and fifty songs in about seven hundred and fifty settings. The inventiveness of the settings—simple, note against note, loosened up only rarely—is inexhaustible. This Cantionale is of the greatest hymnological interest, because it is the only source for the texts of many hymns, and because Praetorius here systematically employed the melodies in the various versions in which they were used at the time in the different state territorial churches. Melodic imprints from Brunswick, Mark (Brandenburg), Meissen, Thuringia, the coastal towns, Franconia, and so on, appeared regularly. Thus the powerful Cantionale of Praetorius represents an unparalleled source for the entire stock of Lutheran-Protestant hymns around 1600. At the same time, it brings to a close the first phase of the history of the Cantionale. Schein's *Leipziger Kantional* (1627) occupies an intermediate position between these older groups and the characteristic hymnbooks of the 17th century.

NEW LUTHERAN SONG PRODUCTION. SCHOOL ODE, SCHOOL
HYMNBOOK, AND CONGREGATIONAL HYMNBOOK

The more or less strict application of the four-voice cantional setting was a common feature of the older Cantionales; the texture may have been expanded here and there into a loose pseudo-polyphony, but it never lost its basic nature. Another common feature was the faithful retention of the basic lieder of the Reformation period. The collections were enriched by the adoption of some of the lieder from the later hymnbooks of the Bohemian Brethren (see chap. VI, p. 591 ff.) rather than those newly composed. Only Michael Praetorius surmounted these limitations. Taking his entire work into account, he wrote about seven hundred different melodies and well over a thousand texts—this in contrast to the roughly eighty songs constituting the narrower "stock." The figures make clear how rapidly production rose in the Counter-Reformation. Here, too, one notices the impetus stemming from the dissemination of the Lobwasser Psalter and stimulating Lutheran poets and musicians to new creativity.

But the area within which this new production of hymns could take place was restricted, and the reverse side of the lively quantitative revival was a rapid decline in creative intensity. Neither the texts nor the melodies of the Counter-Reformation can compare in force and directness with those of the Reformation. Songs for the Ordinary of Sunday services were fixed. There was an adequate repertory of festival songs. Most of the catechismal, funeral, and other lieder of the Reformation period mantained their position. There was no shortage of any of these. To be sure, psalm, Gospel, cathechismal, funeral lieder, and the like, continued to be composed according to the old pattern, but often the result was only a watering-down of the older compositions, the strength of which could not be equaled. The change and decline can be traced in the case of the psalm lied, which suffered as a result of the Reformed model. In Luther's time, the psalm was looked upon as a textual source for content, imagery, and so on, which poets interpreted in reference to Christ. But now they clung with a certain timid pedantry to the very words of the Bible. Consequently, the force of fervent conviction disappeared and the songs assumed a didactic, preaching tone. Courageous confession was replaced by edifying contemplation, which easily carried a trace of permissiveness. This tendency encouraged the appearance of whole categories of new hymns, especially for the household. All members of the entire family circle and all the little cares and joys of everyday existence were brought into a relationship with God that was sometimes crudely picturesque but more often dryly enumerative and moralizing. Georg Niege of Herford (1585) commended everything to God—his possessions, his wife, his children, his relatives, down to mere acquaintances. "The home atmosphere not infrequently becomes a home-baked atmosphere" (Nelle). Children's songs such as those composed by Nikolaus Herman constituted an entire literature of their own, especially cultivated by Kaspar Stolshagen (Kinderspiegel, Eisleben, 1591). Joachim Magdeburg's Tischgesänge (Erfurt, 1571) were widely used. His hymn Wer Gott vertraut, hat wohl gebaut was included in many collections. The inclination toward a sort of private devotional song, which at times could be quite intimate but which at other times also plaintively made connection with the horrors that war and pestilence let loose upon mankind, caused the blossoming of an abundance of hymns devoted to death. Valerius Herberger of Fraustadt near Posen wrote his *Valet will ich dir geben* (1613) and Bartholomäus Ringwaldt his *Es ist gewisslich an der Zeit.* Christoph Knoll of Sprottau (1599) wrote *Herzlich tut mich verlangen* (see p. 33), which subsequently rose to fame, indeed attained universality, through Bach's cantatas, especially No. 161, *Komm, du süsse Todesstunde.* Johann Leon in Wölfis (Thuringia) wrote burial songs exclusively; from him stems one of the period's most beautiful compositions on death, *Ich hab mein Sach Gott heimgestellt,* which similarly attained universality through Bach in Cantata No. 106, the *Actus Tragicus (Gottes Zeit).* Two hymns on death among those sung most frequently for a century and a half are anonymous: *Christus, der ist mein Leben* (1609) and *Freu dich sehr, o meine Seele* (1620).

The specialization of hymns within well-defined subject groups was accompanied by prominent references to one's own self. Nelle had already correctly observed that the poetry of the Moravians may be found in embryo in Martin Behm's *O Jesu Christ, meins Lebens Licht.* The poetry of the time follows this direction not only in content but also in language. Its mawkishness often contrasts curiously with the timid cleaving to inherited imagery and conceptions. Christ's sufferings are eagerly painted, with gruesomely realistic touches. The overwhelming contrition of the sinner is also graphically expressed. Redemption is sought through an absorption in Christ that is carried to the point of self-surrender. The sensuous and at the same time transcendental mysticism of nuptial love establishes itself and, with it, an entire literature of "Jesus songs." At the head of the list are two masterful achievements of Philipp Nicolai (see p. 32), *Wie schön leuchtet der Morgenstern* and *Wachet auf, ruft uns die Stimme (Freudenspiegel des ewigen Lebens,* Unna, 1598), which, characteristically enough, occasioned two of the grandest of Bach's cantatas (Nos. 1 and 140). With their allegorical, fiery profession of love for the "King and Bridegroom," Nicolai's hymns have assured themselves their place in Protestant mysticism and Pietism. They still live today and have earned immortality for their creator. Following the path pioneered by Nicolai, Martin Moller of Görlitz freely rendered the pseudo-Augustinian *Jesu dulcis memoria* into *Ach Gott, wie manches Herzeleid.* The anonymous *Jesu Kreuz, Leiden und Pein,* with its rapturous seventeen verses, and *In dir ist Freude* also appeared around 1600. Earlier, Martin Schalling had already written *Herzlich lieb hab ich dich, o Herr* (Nuremberg, 1571). This song too gained a permanent place in the hymnbooks and Bach used one stanza from it to conclude his *St. John Passion.*

Alongside such new paths, a certain tradition was preserved, maintaining contact with the thought and emphasis of Luther's world. Nikolaus Selnecker (see pp. 32 and 48), like Joachim Magdeburg, Martin Moller, and many others, had to pay for his strict Lutheran conviction with persecution, loss of position, and much suffering. Suspected of being a crypto-Calvinist, he was removed from his post as court preacher in Electoral Saxony in 1561. In him is least noticeable the anxious concern over purity of doctrine that characterizes so many songs of that period and so clearly illustrates the hard-pressed position of Lutheranism between

38. Ludwig Senfl (c. 1486–c. 1543) in a medal by Hans Schwarz, Augsburg, c. 1519–20.

39. Contemporary woodcut of Georg Rhau (1488–1548) in his later years.

40. Woodcut of Michael Praetorius (1571?–1621). Title page of *Musae Sioniae*, Regensburg, 1605, B. Gräf.

41. Hans Leo Hassler (1564–1612) as organist of the house of Fugger in an engraving by Dominicus Custos, Augsburg, 1593.

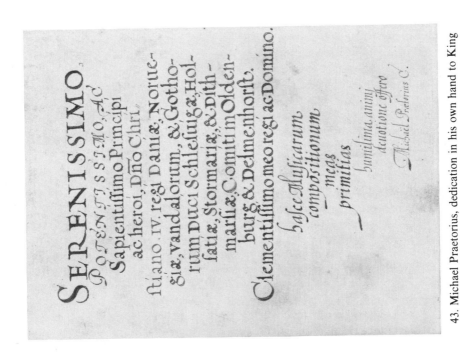

43. Michael Praetorius, dedication in his own hand to King Christian IV of Denmark of the *Musarum Sioniarum Motectae et Psalmi latini* (Nuremberg, 1607, A. Wagenmann). Copenhagen, Det Kongelige Bibliotek.

42. Michael Praetorius, *Musae Sioniae*, part V, Wolfenbüttel, 1607, court printer. Title page of the *quinta vox.*

Reformed Catholicism and Calvinism. To be sure, his *Herr Jesu, hilf, dein Kirch erhalt,* later altered to *Ach, bleib bei uns, Herr Jesu Christ, weil es nun Abend worden ist,* gives some intimation of the fear of the time and the need for security. But the language is hard and vigorous; flowing through the few lines is a strong awareness that he is pleading for the religious unity of the congregation to be given precedence over private needs. The tender, trusting tone of his *Lass mich dein sein und bleiben* proves, however, that the sentimental world of contemporary poets was not foreign to him. Selnecker published his own songs, combined with related ones by Luther, Lobwasser, the Bohemian Brethren, and so on, in a large collection, *Christliche Psalmen, Lieder und Kirchengesänge, in welchen die christliche Lehre zusammengefasst und erkläret wird* (. . . in which the Christian Faith is Summarized and Explained; 1587). At the same time, with this publication he entered the ranks of those who wrote hymn settings; along with Matthäus Le Maistre, Antonius Scandellus, and a certain Baccusius of Gotha, Selnecker himself contributed a number of four-voice cantional settings. Whether he may be considered an inventor of melodies as well is not certain (though Winterfeld ascribes twenty-eight to him). His settings are still to be found, among others, in the hymnbook of Vopelius (1682) and in Georg Ebeling's collection *Geistliche Andachten* of Paul Gerhardt (1667). Wolfgang Ammon included odes by Selnecker in the third book of his *Libri tres odarum* (1579) and his rhyming didactic dialogue on the Last Judgment may perhaps be the earliest example of that category in Protestant hymnbooks.

Cornelius Becker occupies a special position. A university professor in Leipzig, he was forced to leave his post in 1601 because of his Lutheranism, but he was soon reinstated. In 1602 he published the entire Psalter with new texts, "to which the melodies usual in Lutheran churches are adapted." Although it may be said that this publication merely placed him in the ranks of the composers of rhyming Psalters, in one respect the work should be given greater credit. It was a deliberate, if ineffectual, attempt to displace the Lobwasser Psalter, which had gradually penetrated the Lutheran hymnbooks too. Precisely for this reason Becker had linked his texts with known church melodies. Their failure was probably caused by their emphasis on learning and their lack of popular appeal. Seth Calvisius of Leipzig published Becker's Psalter with the melodies in four-voice cantional settings (1605) and was successful, as can be seen from the series of new editions which rapidly followed. The Salza schoolmaster Valentin Cremcovius and the Magdeburg cantor Heinrich Grimm, a student of Michael Praetorius, published a Latin version of the Becker Psalter. It was a peculiar enterprise, bearing the title *Cithara Davidica Luthero-Becceriana . . . ex Musis Cremcovianis errantibus instructa* (4th ed., 1624; preface, 1609); including forty-two settings by Grimm, it was intended for the Magdeburg school choir. Despite these musical efforts, the Becker Psalter would presumably have left no deeper traces if Heinrich Schütz had not devoted an entirely independent composition ("not of great art or labor") to it, supplying primarily his own tunes (only eleven of the older ones are included). Schütz's work appeared in 1628, with an enlarged second edition in 1640, and until 1712 it reappeared frequently. Becker's version of the 23rd Psalm, *Der Herr ist mein getreuer Hirt,* later became known through one of Bach's cantatas (No. 112). It is probably his only psalm lied to remain in use for a long period of time. The texts were anemic and the powerful Heinrich Schütz was no inventor of melodies. By and large, this undertaking remained a failure.

A growing number of poets allied themselves with reputable musicians in order to promote the success of their new texts: Selnecker with Le Maistre and Scandellus, Becker with Calvisius, and later Gerhardt with Crüger, Elmenhorst with Franck, Wockenfuss, and Böhm, and Rist with a whole flock of well-known composers. It was in this way that Ludwig Helmboldt of Mühlhausen (Thuringia) became famous, chiefly through his connection with Joachim a Burck and Johannes Eccard, who set his verses to music (see p. 50). The texts are light and fresh in tone and display an elegant polish in form and language, unusual among hymn writers of the time. They were influenced by French and Italian literature —the poetry of the Pléiade in *vers mesurés* and the Italian villanella. As Burck himself says, he set the texts to music "with sweet harmony in the manner of Italian villanellas" *(XX Odae sacrae Ludovici Helmboldi Mulhusini,* Erfurt, 1572). In 1574, Burck and Eccard together published new odes of Helmboldt. Burck followed this with German hymns by Helmboldt in 1575; the series of German and Latin compositions with Burck's music extends to 1604. A sort of complete edition of all odes and German songs by Burck and Helmboldt was published by the town council of Mühlhausen in 1626. Burck's works mark a step of far-reaching importance in Protestant hymn and ode composition. The composer invented the melodies himself, but did not treat them as a continuous cantus firmus. Instead (following late Netherlands models, among whom he himself cites Lasso, Vaet, Utendal, and Werth), he broke them up in a loose, pseudo-polyphonic setting, often strongly emphasizing the harmony. Even when he permitted the melody to run on in a continuous line, it no longer dominated as in the older cantus-firmus setting or in the *contrapunctus simplex* of the cantional setting. The whole compositional structure was drenched with melody and yet it was not always possible to reconstruct a *cantus prius factus.* It is this villanella-motet style that distinguished Burck as well as his friend and pupil, the Mühlhausener Johannes Eccard (later a student of Lasso in Munich). The late Netherlands

Joachim a Burck, 1599. Text by L. Helmbold

group surrounding Lasso became the arbiters of style in Protestant church music with the arrival of Burck, one of the earliest exponents of lied and ode motets, on the scene.

Poems like the innumerable Latin odes of Helmboldt, in musical settings by Burck, Eccard, Leonhard Schröter, and others, were the principal religious song literature for Latin schools. The increase in their number was a result of the steady growth of Protestant secondary schools and universities during the Counter-Reformation. They were a continuation of the humanistic, secular ode so much cultivated by the generation of Senfl, Ducis, Hofhaimer, and so on. Musically, Burck was a pioneer in this area also, for he freed the ode from the inflexible bonds of strict meter and treated it "in villanella style" like a song.

Following the precedent of the *Melodiae Prudentianae* by Hordisch and Forster (see above, pp. 49, 79, 121), Martin Agricola (1557) and Bartholomäus Gesius (1597 and 1609) had published their *Melodiae scholasticae*. The most important work in this field, however, was the *Paraphrasis psalmorum poetica,* a translation of the Psalms into Horatian meter by the Scottish scholar George Buchanan (1566). Nathan Chyträus published it for the first time in 1585 (with additions, 1619), with simple settings by Statius Olthof. It remained in circulation in various new editions until at least 1664. The melodies are taken partly from older ode compositions; the settings show how the style of the humanistic period merged into the cantional type, to which it was related. In the Latin schools, this collection became the strongest competitor of the Lobwasser Psalter and its compositions by Goudimel. It was Lutheranism's conscious self-defense against the infiltration of Calvinist ideas, similar to what Cornelius Becker, for example, had attempted to do for the German psalm lied. Several of the Buchanan-Chyträus texts with melodies by Olthof even found their way into Lutheran hymnbooks and remained in occasional use into the 18th century.

Obviously there must have been a great demand for this kind of Latin school song. Here a curious literary category comes into the picture, the re-Latinized German hymn (see p. 104), which helped to lead Protestantism, with its tendency to educate, into an apparent repudiation of Lutheran congregational singing. Indeed, it was difficult to reconcile neo-humanistic secondary education with popular Lutheran congregational singing. As a rule, the presentation of these re-Latinized songs was such that the four-voice setting appeared on two facing pages, with two voices in German text on the one page and two in Latin on the other. In 1578, at Frankfurt on the Main, Wolfgang Ammon first published his *Libri tres odarum,* which was reprinted countless times. Sylvester Steier of Nuremberg in 1583 brought out two volumes entitled *Christliche Haushymnen.* Each volume was divided into eight "classes" (morning blessing, evening blessing, table prayers, and so on), with seven hymns in each class. *Cithara Christiana* by Christian Lauterbach (Leipzig, 1585; new edition in 1586) contained no less than 175 such hymns, with 92 melodies, mostly old. A similar edition appeared anonymously in Hamburg in 1592, with only melody beginnings provided. It is strikingly paradoxical that even the Psalter of the Reformed church, which fought Latin so fiercely, was rendered into Latin for school purposes, with the Huguenot melodies in four-voice settings (Andreas Speth, *Psalmorum Paraphrasis metro-*

rhythmica, ad melodias gallicas et rhythmos germanicos . . . Lobwasseri . . . scholasticae juventuti, Heidelberg, 1596). This branch of literature was called forth by a particular pedagogical objective, and it lasted far into the 17th century. As late as 1648, Georg Leuchner of Colditz in Saxony rendered Lutheran hymns metrically into Latin and even into Greek (Moser). In the same year there appeared a collection of no less than 267 odes by Hauschkonius and others. There was even a hybrid type of school songbook that combined Latin odes with German and re-Latinized hymns in four-voice cantional settings. An example is the Görlitz collection, *Harmoniae hymnorum* (1587; 2nd ed., enlarged, 1599; 3rd ed., further enlarged, 1613). Its repertory extends from Martin Agricola, Hofhaimer, Schalreuter, Tritonius, and Senfl through Calvisius and Sylvester Steier to Joachim a Burck, Michael Praetorius, and others. Naturally, this special brand of literature, although voluminous and widely disseminated, had only a negligible influence on the broader course of Protestant church music (see also p. 79).

The later composers for the Huguenot Psalter also failed to achieve anything like Goudimel's influence. Samuel Mareschall of Basel revised the Goudimel settings of 1565 to the Lobwasser texts, shifting the melody to the top voice. He published this version as *Der ganz Psalter . . . aus der französischen Komposition mit gleicher Melodei und Zahl der Syllaben in teutsche Reimen gebracht* (1606, perhaps as early as 1594; later editions to 1743). But the same Mareschall published a Cantionale with Lutheran hymns, too, indicating (at least in the area of school music) how little the Reformed and Lutheran hymnological heritages were felt to be mutually exclusive. Finally, it should be noted that Mareschall made a contribution to the Latinized category with his *Melodiae suaves et concinnae psalmorum . . . in usum classis octavae et nonae gymnasii Basiliensis* (1622). Here it becomes obvious that trends which appear to the historian to be separate may actually intersect, indeed depend on one another. Even Landgrave Moritz of Hesse published in 1601 a *Gesangbuch von allerhand geistlichen Psalmen und Liedern,* with twenty-four monophonic melodies by himself, and in 1612 his four-voice settings of these. His *Psalmen Davids nach französischer Melodei* (1607) contains the entire Huguenot Psalter, in part with his own melodies and settings. Indirectly, he too contributed to religious school literature with a commission entrusted to his court musician, Valentin Geuck. This appeared as *Novum et insigne opus continens textus metricos sacros* (3 volumes, 1603–04). Geuck had the task of composing motet settings in five, six, and eight voices for versions of the Gospel lessons in contemplative distichal form for the entire church year. The number of voices was determined by the ecclesiastical significance of the particular Sunday. The portion of the work not completed by Geuck was finished by the "scholarly" Landgrave himself; indeed, quite possibly the texts were his also. Whatever the circumstances surrounding this entire literature may have been—competition incited by the success of the Huguenot Psalter, a simple intermixing of currents, or just a taking over in what were in any case Reformed territories (as in Hesse)—it is certain that Marot, Goudimel, Lobwasser, and Osiander left behind a highly fruitful stimulus to new creativity.

The inclination to include home, family, and private life within the scope of the church hymn was a new tendency of this period. At the same time, the old Lutheran hymn of the Reformation period, with its presentation or proclamation of the word of God and of doctrine, continued to maintain itself. Also new was the inclination toward a mystic Jesus cult and the cultivation of numerous sub-categories which in their colorful variety enliven the hitherto rather uniform Reformation picture. The years between about 1570 and 1620 witnessed a note-worthy productivity in all of these directions and fields. If one considers the large number of collections of new hymns, and adds those collections repeatedly repro-ducing the old favorites interspersed more or less abundantly with new ones, the result is a large number of hymns and hymnbooks, and there is little wonder that these hymnbooks grew in size. In 1599 a hymnal appeared in Nuremberg contain-ing 525 hymns, one in Frankfurt on the Main in 1600 with 535. The Görlitz hymnal of 1611 increased the figure to about 700, the Fuhrmann hymnbook, appearing in Nuremberg in the same year, to 748, while a hymnal of 1626 even reached a total of 836. (All these figures, it is important to note, refer only to texts.) Despite this swelling number, the great day of the hymnals was already past. Despite the high figures, what was produced did not usually achieve more than local importance. The effect of the new production on the basic stock of congregational hymns should not be overestimated. It is true that the direction was not yet exclusively or predominantly toward private household devotions (as later in the 17th century). Writers still composed with church and home equally in mind, but popular recognition was limited, as was the use of their hymns in congregational singing. Exceptions like Philipp Nicolai prove the rule. To be sure, Selnecker, Ringwaldt, and others, for a while, found their way into congrega-tional hymnbooks, but they did so slowly and were able to maintain themselves only within limited areas of time and place. There now appeared a hymnbook tailored to fit the needs of a particular congregation or state church. While the earlier hymnals had been the work of individual authors or printers, from now on "leadership in this matter" moved "more strongly than before into the hands of 'privileged' publishers and those officially commissioned" (Mahrenholz in *MGG* IV, 1881). The cantional setting, performed by the organ, by instruments, or by a students' choir, often made the printing of tunes in the hymnbook unnecessary. Many hymnbooks dispensed with them entirely, while others gave only the beginnings. In comparison with the rapidly growing number of new hymn texts, the number of new melodies was rather sparse. The Fuhrmann hymnal mentioned above offered few melodies with its 748 texts, that of 1626 only ten for its 836, not one of them new. As has been said, the new poetry preferred to restrict itself to old and proved verse and strophe patterns for the sake of easier dissemination and employed old, known melodies. Writers like Selnecker, who offered his own (or if not his own, at least new) melodies and settings, or Helm-boldt, who made his appearance clothed in the compositions of Burck and Ec-card, were rare. New melodies in larger numbers appeared only with Michael Praetorius, Melchior Vulpius, Bartholomäus Gesius, or in the *Threnodiae* of Christoph Demantius (1620; see also below). A collection like that of Georg Österreicher for Windsheim (Rothenburg on the Tauber, 1614, as *Geistliche Lieder aus dem Catechismo;* 2nd ed., 1623, as *Ein recht Christlich Gesangbüch-lein*) with its own 24 melodies, as well as numerous older ones to hymns by both older and newer writers (among them Helmboldt, Melchior Franck, Michael Altenburg), was by then exceptional.

The beginning of the Thirty Years' War (1618) and several publications appearing about the same time date the end of the Counter-Reformation both politically and musically. In a way, the long series of arrangements of the Reformed Psalter found its termination in the polyphonic arrangements by Landgrave Moritz (1607 and 1612), while the long history of the Lutheran psalm lied ends with the Psalter by Heinrich Schütz after Cornelius Becker (1628). In 1626 the collected works of Burck and Helmboldt appeared. In 1627 the almost unimaginably large series of Lutheran Cantionales was concluded with a work that must be regarded as the final and most significant contribution to this field but that simultaneously marked the beginning of a new development. This was the Leipzig Cantionale by Johann Hermann Schein, the second in the great line of cantors at St. Thomas's Church extending from Calvisius to J. S. Bach. The significance of the book, for which Polykarp Leiser provided a preface, is threefold. First, in addition to the old melodies it added many excellent, often multiple settings (four to six parts), usually in cantional style, often also in free arrangement. Second, of the 313 hymns in 235 settings (in the second edition), no fewer than 62 in text, melody, and setting were by Schein himself, as were 21 melodies and 2 texts. Third, in his own creative contribution, visibly reflecting private experience and personal commitment, many of Schein's own verses and melodies foreshadowed the age of the self-oriented, emotional, and affective lied. Schein's *Kantional oder Augsburgisches Gesangbuch* had superseded the earlier Leipzig hymnbook, the *Harmonia cantionum ecclesiasticarum* of Seth Calvisius (1597; 5th ed., 1622). Partly from the latter and partly from other sources it adopted 13 settings by Calvisius and other masters. In 1627 it contained 286 songs, to which apparently Schein's successor, Tobias Michael, added "27 lovely songs" in the second edition (1645). Many of the settings found their way into later hymnals, such as the Gotha Cantionale (1646) and the hymnbook of Vopelius (1682). Of those with text and music by Schein himself, a Ten Commandments' hymn, 22 "meditations" on psalms, and 18 songs on death stand out. The last-named were in part occasioned by the deaths of his wife and children, all of whom he saw die as a result of pestilence brought by the war. Few of Schein's tunes remain in use now.

CONGREGATIONAL SONG AND ART MUSIC

THE LIED MOTET

Schein's Cantionale also marks a dividing line in that it shows how thoroughly the original unity of the Lutheran congregational song had been shattered. The influence of the Huguenot Psalter, the defensive creativity of Lutheran poets and musicians, the humanistic aspirations, the rise of whole categories of songs for special occasions and in areas of religious life that hitherto had not appeared in the Protestant literature—all this led to a diversity not known in the Reformation. Further on in the course of development, the result was a more decisive separation between the body of tradition and the new creativity. While songs produced in the late 16th and early 17th centuries may have been intended for both church and home, or at least made no clear distinction between them, as time progressed writers and musicians tended more and more toward the private, devotional song.

The writers preferred to publish their work in small, handy, and often elegantly printed little books to be held by ladies or by the pious, thus creating a form that later helped to further the fondness for Pietistic songs.

Luther had weighted the individual with the burden of responsibility and had placed him face to face with the Divine. However, the individual is part of the whole: only within the churchly community does he completely fulfill the purpose of his existence. It had been the conviction of the Reformation that the individualistic character of responsibility, guilt, and atonement had to find a balance through union with the Christian congregation. But toward the end of the period there was again an increasing individualization. From responsible member of the congregation and participant in the service, the individual proceeded to entertained listener and private worshiper, from "doer of the word" to "hearer alone" —beyond that, to contemplating observer. The new kind of song arose for and from this new attitude. Looked at in this way, the introduction of the cantional setting and the slow advance toward accompaniment of congregational singing may be seen as a sort of counteroffensive of the church, attempting to oppose individualization with congregational activity. Now another rift opened that proved to be serious in the later 17th century—the rift between congregational music and art music.

These two types of music did not conflict during the Reformation. Both proclaimed the Word, only in different forms. Both were bound to the cantus firmus of the inherited (and, through Luther, reformed) liturgical chant or song. The German lied setting in particular held firmly to the practice of a "scaffolding of voices" above the cantus firmus in the tenor. The melodies of the songs were common property and familiar to all. Whether the congregation sang them in unison or with a precentor or with chordal accompaniment, or whether the *Kantorei* used them polyphonically with instruments, or the organ employed them as cantus-firmus foundation for its contrapuntal playing—these were just different ways of presenting one and the same melody that represented one and the same text and thought. It was congregational music in the most comprehensive sense. Now there arose, as early as Joachim a Burck, an art song of a quite new sort that either dissolved—shattered—the cantus firmus of the chorale or introduced entirely new and unfamiliar melodies, woven into an indissoluble setting, thus making the whole into a vessel with a new content and purpose.

Like the poets, the musicians strove toward a new world of contemplation, of emotion-suffused observation, of devotional piety. In the age of the Reformation the arrangement of songs had been a purely expository art. The given content was placed within a beautiful ornamental framework, just as painters, following the traditional pattern, would set their altar panels in a rich Gothic background. But during the Counter-Reformation, song arrangement became an interpretative art, directing attention to the word of revelation and explaining it. It engaged in homiletics, just as Netherlands painters of the late 16th century underscored the meaning of their themes with the animated features and declarative gestures of the figures. Still, this was not yet an expressive style of the sort that arose later in the 17th century. First the Baroque set itself to reproducing the individual word with pathos, to depicting action in detail, to conveying feeling with fervor through the medium of music. The point of departure for such a relationship of word and tone lay in the Counter-Reformation, which exerted itself to produce in the hearer a reaction to words and events. For an expository art such as had existed in the Reformation, the primary concern was that the subject be treated as the given, the unchangeable, the untouchable; the creative artist merely provided the framework and ornamentation. Interpretative art, on the other hand, consciously sought to illuminate its subject, to put it in a particular perspective, to place it intimately before the observer or hearer and awaken in him an emotional response. The musicians of Luther's day were servants of the Word; to them, artistic arrangement of songs was a craft, an *ancilla theologiae* of the church. The type of song composed by a Finck, a Hofhaimer, a Senfl, above all by a Johann Walter, illustrates this. The style of the High Renaissance of Italy and the Netherlands played only a subordinate role in Lutheran song arrangement. As the history of German architecture in many respects displays a leap without transition from late Gothic to Baroque, so the history of Protestant hymn arrangement moves from Kugelmann and Le Maistre via Scandellus and Schröter, Dressler and Burck directly to Eccard and Lechner, from a late Gothic rather than a Renaissance-like style to a sort of manneristic or pre-Baroque style. It was the aspiration of composers of this period to clarify the material, to realize its potential through its own special qualities and nuances. This was an expression of the will to interpret. For Johann Walter, the song melody was the bearer of the Word of God, as unchangeable and as exempt from arbitrary tampering as the Word itself. His task was to embellish that melody with the richest devices of his craftmanship. But for Leonhard Lechner the same melody became material to which its arranger was to give shape and form, to endow it with meaning and the power to stir human feelings. Ultimately, a generation later, Schütz was able to deny the sanctity of the melody entirely and to alter the text according to his own lights, to treat it like prose, to transform, interpret, dramatize, and to fill it with pathos. No longer inhibited, he felt free to make the hymn into a vehicle of his personal expression. Obviously the course of this development caused a deepening gulf between congregational singing and congregational understanding, between the hearers passive surrender and the connoisseur's demands.

Though not active in the field of Protestant church music, Orlando di Lasso figured largely in the background of this development, affecting the course of all German music in the late 16th and early 17th centuries. As yet, it is hardly possible to measure the full breadth of Lasso's effect on Lutheran music through his pupils or followers. This is true, above all, of music for the Mass and for Vespers, insofar as these categories were maintained in Latin in Protestant services. But it is also true of lied settings. It cannot be supposed that Lasso himself consciously or deliberately made arrangements of Protestant hymns. For related types of settings he took words and melodies from secondary, Catholic sources. Precisely in his case, however, one can trace step by step the transition from older German techniques of hymn arrangement to the newer ones. The three hymnbooks of 1567, 1572, and 1576 (each appearing in three or four editions and consequently widely disseminated) still held basically, like the lied settings of the Protestant masters, to the old practice of scaffolding. But with the four- and five-voice songs of 1583 interest shifted to interpretation of the text. There was a distinct trend toward symbolism and musical imagery (so-called rhetorical figures); the compositional technique, the declamation, indeed the structuring as a whole—all were adapted to the goal of interpretation. That densely woven network of eloquent motifs characterizing Lasso's later madrigals is evident in his six-voice *Neue teutsche und etliche französische Gesänge* of 1590. One can no longer speak of song-like melody in these later arrangements; "madrigal-like" would be a more fitting description.

The type of lied motet that was evolved in this way found in Lasso its chief master and in Joachim a Burck a productive and versatile, if somewhat limited, Protestant representative. It was of the greatest significance for all future treatment of songs, insofar as it was not restricted to the cantional setting. Lasso's model long remained alive in all fields, especially in that of the Latin motet. His works were widely disseminated through countless anthologies, new editions of his own prints, and manuscript copies. In 17th-century Germany there was probably no other 16th-century master who for so long was regarded as the authoritative example. His influence extended from his direct and personal pupils like Johannes Eccard and Leonhard Lechner, beyond the Kassel School of Georg Otto, Valentin Geuck, and Landgrave Moritz and the indirect or following generation of students such as Dressler, Burck, Schröter, Meiland, Gregor Lange, Hieronymus Praetorius, Philipp Dulichius, Andreas Raselius, and many others, all the way to Melchior Franck, Hans Leo Hassler, and Michael Praetorius. Lasso's cosmopolitan status should not lead us to overlook the fact that for a good half century he was also a real "praeceptor Germaniae."

Johannes Eccard was involved through Joachim a Burck of Mühlhausen in the composition of Ludwig Helmboldt's odes and hymns. He grew up under the influence of Burck and Helmboldt, was later chapel singer and pupil of the "world-renowned Orlando" in Munich, then in the service of the Catholic house of Fugger in Augsburg, and afterward Prussian *Kapellmeister* in Königsberg and Berlin. In 1574 he published his own compositions in *Zwanzig neue christliche Gesänge Ludovici Helmboldi*. In 1578 there followed a collection of songs almost entirely secular and in 1589 another collection, half secular and half religious. A connection with the older song style is still traceable through their use of older texts, but the freer inventiveness and looser technique show the orientation toward Lasso. Eccard's famous five-voice *Geistliche Lieder auf den Choral oder gemeine Kirchenmelodei*, all arrangements of standard Lutheran songs, followed in 1597. An extract from this work, supplemented with arrangements of his own, was published in 1634 by Eccard's Königsberg student, Johann Stobäus. Eccard's final work, the *Preussiche Festlieder*, for five to eight voices, was not published by Stobäus until long after Eccard's death (1642 and 1644). Eccard, who had begun early with Masses in the style of Lasso and who in all of his works moved "in the narrow border zone between motet-like and song-like construction" (Adrio), achieved an important success with his *Lieder auf den Choral* of 1597. The settings are basically chordal, with the chorale in the top voice; the accompanying voices, rhythmically lively, appear to have an independent polyphonic existence of their own. With the *Lieder* of 1597, Eccard broke through the homorhythmic inflexibility of most of the Cantionales up to his time and created something he had found wanting—a "Cantionale . . . containing something musically pleasant and artistically worthy." Eccard's manner of setting became a model that served for centuries. Bach's chorales are unthinkable without it. Winterfeld discovered in it the ideal of "true church music," such as that sought by the early Romantics. In comparison with these masterful settings, Eccard's earlier ones can only be called average. They are clearly dependent upon Burck. The song form is abandoned in favor of a freer treatment, more in the manner of a motet, with emphasis on vividness and forcefulness of expression. A continuous melody is not present. There is already a strong inclination to contrast the individual images and words of the text and to organize the setting out of the antitheses of the motifs so created. Expression is sometimes vehement. The lied motets of Eccard, paralleling Burck's and reaching beyond them, represent a Protestant church music that foreshadowed the pathos of the high Baroque. Tormented by the afflictions of the world and of sin, the soul cries out in anguish or triumphs in the certainty of salvation. The contrast of these early lied motets with the chorale settings of 1597 shows distinctly how the split between congregational music and art music was initiated: in *Lieder auf den Choral,* the musician is servant of the word; in the lied motets he is its interpreter. In the one there is exposition, in the other interpretation; in the one, music that is understandable by all for general use, in the other, artistic expression for the connoisseur.

If Eccard's *Lieder auf den Choral* may be regarded as occupying a middle position between cantional setting and lied motet, then the twenty-seven settings of the *Preussische Festlieder* stand midway between the lied motet in its freer form and the cantional-bound form of the *Lieder auf den Choral* (the path Eccard always followed was very narrow). The texts stem partly from Ludwig Helmboldt and Cornelius Becker, partly from the circle of Königsberg poets like Simon Dach, Sebastian Artomedes, Georg Reimann, and Peter Hagen. Sometimes the compositions contain portions of the melody, line by line, in the top voice, only

Johann Eccard: *Preussische Festlieder,* 1644. From *Ubers Gebirg Maria geht.* Text by L. Helmbold.
(From the Teschner edition. Original inaccessible.)

to have it dissolve again in an agitated polyphonic or pseudo-polyphonic texture; the interplay of parts in itself is expressive and animated. Thus, the impression of tunefulness and general intelligibility is achieved simultaneously with the impression of artistic setting and varied feeling. The expressive force of the early lied motet is not attempted. Instead, every song gains something like a character- istic basic color through the treatment of the accompanying voices. In a setting such as *Übers Gebirg Maria geht* the long line of the top voice is paralyzed by the constant stepping of the lower voices, contributing to an impression of walk- ing. There are only a few indications of a relationship to individual words of the text. A setting of unusual expressive power is *Im Garten leidet Christus Not,* a special case because of its resemblance to the melody *Da Jesus an dem Kreuze stund.* Eccard liked to exploit the double-choir aspect of eight-voice settings for the contrasting of content and the strengthening of formal structure.

Johann Eccard: *Preussische Festlieder,* 1642. Text by L. Helmbold. (From the Teschner edition. Original inaccessible.)

Romanticism, following Winterfeld, may have esteemed Eccard too highly, but no one can deny the masterfulness and precision of his settings or the intimacy of his penetration into the spiritual content of the texts. His *Festlieder* had surprisingly long-lasting effects. The whole "Prussian School" (Winterfeld) used them as a point of departure, at first for choral, then for solo songs: Johann Stobäus, Johann Weidmann, Konrad Matthäi, Christoph Kaldenbach, Georg Weber, and others. Eccard's influence on Heinrich Albert's "arias" was more intensive than Italian monody or any other song model (see also p. 93).

An incomparably stronger creative force than Eccard was his fellow student under Lasso, the South Tyrolean Leonhard Lechner. School assistant, "com- poser," and "arch-musician" *(Archimusicus)* of the city of Nuremberg, born of a Catholic family but converted at the age of eighteen and thereafter all the more fervent a Protestant, Lechner was *Kapellmeister* at the court of Hohenzollern- Hechingen, whence he fled (on confessional grounds?), finally to serve as *Ka- pellmeister* to the Duke of Württemberg in Stuttgart. In all, Lechner gives the impression of being extremely versatile. He was a visionary, deeply moved and

impelled by strong passions. Seen in perspective, he was the most significant
German musician of his generation. It is true that his Latin Masses, Magnificats,
and motets remain within the framework of the Lasso tradition and that his
choice of outstanding Italian masters for his anthology, *Harmoniae miscellae*
(1583), proves him an adherent of the *prima pratica*. Despite this, his settings of
religious songs of 1577 and 1582, and even more so those in his *Neue geistliche
und weltliche deutsche Lieder* (1589), far overshadow anything from lied setting
to motet setting written in the German language in those decades. There are no
closed strophic constructions; he uses through-composition of several strophes.
Straightforward adaptation of the flow of the upper voice to the line structure of
the texts (which are of unusually high literary quality) gives the impression of
song-like simplicity, without, as in Eccard's *Festlieder,* actually arriving at song-
like constructions. Settings such as *Allein zu dir, Herr Jesu Christ, Nun schein,
du Glanz der Herrlichkeit,* but especially that magnificent song *O Tod, du bist ein
bittre Gallen* are without parallel in their time. They show, as in the following
example, how what had been primarily technique with Burck and Eccard turned
into a language of experience; how everything grows out of graphic imaginings
of urgent immediacy, out of the contrast between cruel shock and blissful surrender. In the history of the lied and of the lied motet, these settings go far beyond

Lasso. The quality in Lasso's hymns suggesting a cosmopolitan mixture of
Flemish succulence, French clarity of form, Italian pathos, and German de-
termination appears in Lechner with stronger inwardness, more deeply inspired and more intensely experienced. Compositional technique, use of disso-
mnances, adaptation of rhythm to text—all are close to the Italian madrigal,
which in any case was then beginning to influence Protestant church music. It
is not known whether Lechner knew the madrigals of Marenzio written at about
the same time, but his are an equivalent German accomplishment. Since his own
Italian madrigals of 1579 and 1585 are now known (Konrad Ameln, prepublica-

Thomas Man-
cinus.

M. Prætorius.
F.B.Capelmeister.

Esaias Korner.

44. Michael Praetorius with Thomas Mancinus, the son of his predecessor in office, and the tenor Esajas Körner in the funeral procession of Prince Heinrich Julius of Brunswick and Lüneburg, October 6, 1613. Wolfenbüttel, Braunschweigisches Landeshauptarchiv.

46. Hans Leo Hassler, *Kirchengesänge, Psalmen und geistliche Lieder . . . mit vier Stimmen simpliciter gesetzt,* Nuremberg, 1608, Paul Kauffmann. Title page of the bass partbook.

45. Hans Leo Hassler, *Psalmen und christliche Gesänge, mit vier Stimmen . . . fugweis componiert,* Nuremberg, 1607, Paul Kauffmann. Title page of the tenor partbook.

tion from *Works,* vol. V), the sources from which he drew are obvious. From Lechner's later settings a bridge reaches to Schein's *Fontana d'Israel.*

In the field of the lied motet, Lechner achieved his finest and most original success in what is presumably his last work, *Neue geistliche und weltliche Gesänge,* for four and five voices. The Landgrave Moritz of Hesse must be commended for preserving for posterity the original manuscript (1606), of which the *quinta vox* has disappeared. The four-voice settings fall into two groups and are available as such in new editions: *Das Hohelied Salomonis* and *Deutsche Sprüche von Leben und Tod.* The settings from the Song of Solomon are highly emotional, vivid German madrigals based on biblical texts. In his treatment of the short, rhymed proverbs on death, distinguished by their unusually high literary quality, Lechner composed a dance of death without parallel in the entire history of German music; in intent and effect it is prophetic. While it is obvious in previous works that the Italian madrigal, more or less of Marenzio's type, was a model for the German lied motet, here it is plain that the master's late work underwent a sort of transfiguration. The Marenzian style became Lechnerian; all models and originals were fused into one. Strangely enough, the romantic movement, which prized Eccard so highly, seems to have overlooked Lechner (although Walther's *Lexicon* of 1732 preserved his memory). Had Brahms known these works, he would have been overwhelmed with admiration.

Leonhard Lechner: *Sprüche von Leben und Tod* (c. 1606)

LIED MOTET AND CHORALE MOTET

HASSLER, PRAETORIUS, AND FRANCK

As the 16th century turned into the 17th, the lied motet was an arena for the activities of countless minor masters; Eccard and Lechner, however, remained at the peak of this activity. The lied motet became fruitful for subsequent history in that it entered into a new relationship to the cantus-firmus setting. Its loose compositional arrangement, its free motivic treatment, its suggestions of villanella or madrigal, and its occasional expressive qualities—all contributed to the creation of a new type, either as a result of the hymn being treated as cantus firmus, or through the dissolution of traditional melodies into contrapuntal motifs, or by completely free invention, as in the case of the older masters. Where there was a linking up with the cantus firmus of the chorale, there arose a structure midway between genuine chorale motet and loose, motet-like cantional setting (similar to Eccard's hymns of 1597). This mixture is significant and historically important because it led to the specifically Protestant church-music style of the 17th century, so thoroughly characteristic and often beyond definition. This style eventually displayed elements of strict counterpoint, the madrigal, the villanella, the Lasso type of setting, the Eccard and Lechner lied motet, and the cantional setting. At the same time it opened the door to the spreading Italian concerto style for large and small ensembles. Only in some exceptional cases will it be possible to categorize the types distinctly. This is the beginning of the road which later leads as much to Schütz's *Geistliche Chormusik* as to Hammerschmidt's *Andachten,* as much to the "arias" of Ahle as to the chorale motets of the minor Thuringian masters.

Hans Leo Hassler and Michael Praetorius were the leading masters of this transitional situation at the beginning of the 17th century. Hassler, himself a Protestant, spent many years in the service of the Catholic house of the Augsburg Fuggers and of Emperor Rudolf II. During that time, commissioned by the imperial free city of Nuremberg and by the strict Lutheran Elector Christian II in Dresden, he wrote only two works designed specifically for Lutheran use: the *Psalmen simpliciter* (1608; see p. 133 f.), dedicated to the city of Nuremberg, and the *Psalmen und christliche Gesänge, mit vier Stimmen auf die Melodeien fugweis komponiert* (1607), dedicated to Elector Christian II of Saxony. The latter collection contains strictly polyphonic chorale motets based on chorale motifs, many of which are developed throughout all the stanzas in a sort of chain of variations. Only rarely is the chorale melody used as cantus firmus (e.g., *Vater unser im Himmelreich*). It is as if a kind of chorale arrangement that had declined in the previous generation had received a new lease on life by returning to strict polyphony. Here there is no trace of Hassler's Italianate *prima pratica*. Rather, the impression is one of strictness, even hardness, and the technique is similar to the chorale motets in part V of Praetorius's *Musae Sioniae.*

While Hassler was only occasionally active in the field of Protestant church music, Praetorius devoted almost his whole life to it. He is figuratively and in some respects even literally the successor of Johann Walter, the most vigorous representative of Lutheran orthodoxy in the whole history of church music. Like none other, he established this heritage and its meaning for all time. In his youth he experienced denominational conflicts in his own family. As *Kapellmeister* at the court of Duke Heinrich Julius of Brunswick-Wolfenbüttel, he became the highest musical authority in Germany during the period between Lasso and Schütz. Like Hassler, Praetorius built his career on the Lasso tradition. Unlike Hassler, who was presumably a pupil of Lechner and through him acquainted with Italian music, and who, according to Praetorius, "laid his foundations" in Venice (where Zarlino, Donato, and the two Gabrielis were active), Praetorius never saw Italy. In Prague he became acquainted with the Netherlandish circle that included Charles Luyton, Gedeon Lebon, and the De Sayves. He was inspired by Gregor Aichinger and perhaps by Andreas Raselius, whom he never met. Later on he studied the Italians of the *prima* and *seconda pratica* intensively and became an impassioned autodidact. He never made Hassler's acquaintance, as the latter died in Dresden in 1612, but Praetorius became active in that city in 1613 as *Kapellmeister*. He was in charge of music at the festival sponsored by the Naumburg principality in 1614; there or in Dresden he met the young Heinrich Schütz, who had just entered the services of Elector Johann Georg I. In the totality of his creativeness, Hassler was a preserver of tradition, breaking with it and renewing it only in the realm of secular social and dancing songs. Praetorius assiduously followed all the tendencies and movements of his period (with the single exception of Italian monody), concentrating on the lied motet and chorale motet, which comprise about two-thirds of his enormous output. For the remainder of his compositions he followed the newer concerted styles.

Parts VI–VIII of his *Musae Sioniae* (1609–10) belong to the history of the Cantionale (see p. 138). Part IX (1610), two- and three-voice settings, are on the borderline between the old *bicinia* and *tricinia* and the new small "concerto" (see below). Parts I–IV (1605–07), however, consist of eight- to twelve-voice, two- and three-choir chorale motets. Part V (1607–08) is a separate collection of two- to seven-voice chorale arrangements. It begins with the simplest cantional settings —*bicinia* and *tricinia* with or without cantus firmus, cantus-firmus settings in the style of Senfl (Praetorius printed several settings by Johann Walter here)—and progresses toward totally free chorale motets, without cantus firmus and even through-composed *(Herr Gott, dich loben wir)*. The collection is truly a historical compendium of chorale arrangements from Johann Walter to the threshold of later "concerto" settings. It is also a veritable textbook of composition and performance practice, exposing all the possibilities of choral, solo, vocal, and instrumental combinations, even the idea of divided groupings. Though still not making use of thoroughbass, it definitely points in performance practice to the large "concerto." The *Musae Sioniae* exhibits Praetorius's versatility, but the two remaining blocks of works—the *Leiturgodia* (Latin liturgical works) and the *Polyhymnien* (later choral concertos)—show even more the sharp profile of his personality and the comprehensiveness of his appeal. Parts I–IV of the *Musae* carry a relatively retrospective imprint (connecting particularly part V with Hassler's *Psalmen fugweis*). They resemble a woodcut, strong and severe, yet maintain a beauty of sound. They are not without some elements of personal interpretation, but these elements are always subordinated to an objective presentation of the chorale, whether it appears as a simple cantus firmus or as a web of contrapuntal motifs derived from the chorale. One could no more picture the first five parts of the *Musae* without the hundred-year-old tradition of German polyphonic lied settings than without the prior appearance of the lied motets of Burck and Eccard. With these motets the history of Protestant lied and chorale motets reached its absolute climax, and with them Praetorius overshadowed all his contemporaries. Even so prominent a contrapuntist as Seth Calvisius could not approach him in this respect. The overall conception emphasizes two features: lively interweaving of middle voices, continually using chorale motifs, which the listener can follow in the absence of a cantus firmus, and monumental contrasts in sound, which result from clearly articulated sectional construction. Like Eccard, Praetorius favors an accessible, objective treatment of the chorale—he does not use the whole complex of voice parts to provide a general characterization of the chorale—and achieves a unique combination of popular Lutheran idioms and Baroque pathos. There is no basic difference between these early "chorale motets" (so named only with many reservations) and the later types of chorale concertos for small or large ensembles. The enormous dimensions of *Polyhymnia caduceatrix* display a spirit and at times a technique similar to settings in *Musae Sioniae* I–V.

Melchior Franck of Coburg, a pupil of Hassler, ranks next to Hassler and Praetorius as a master of lied and chorale motets. He was about the same age as Praetorius, whom he resembled both in productivity and in the systematic nature of his output. Like Praetorius and Hassler, he began under the influence of Lasso. His *Sacrae melodiae* (1601–07), Latin motets principally on scriptural texts, still belong to the Lasso tradition, and the chorale motets of his *Contrapuncti compositi* (1602) are closely related to Hassler's *Psalmen fugweis* and to part V of Praetorius's *Musae*. He and Praetorius were among the oldest composers to contribute Psalm 116 to the *Angst der Höllen* of Burckhard Grossmann (1623); their psalms were in the style of a sacred madrigal similar to that of Schein. How closely Franck approached the Hassler-Lechner group can be seen from his *Geistliche Gesänge und Melodeien . . . aus dem Hohen Lied Salomonis* for five to eight voices, apparently influenced by Lechner's Song of Solomon compositions (1606) (see p. 157). Like most other major and minor figures of this circle, Franck also published a Cantionale, *Psalmodia sacra* (1631). The Latin motets of his *Viridarium musicum continens . . . ex Sacra Scriptura decerptos flosculos* for five to ten voices (1613), and the six-voice German penitential psalms of the *Threnodiae Davidicae* (1615), comparable to Schein's early work *Cymbalum Sionium* (also 1615), were still in the polyphonic style of the Lasso school. The Passion hymns and motets of the *Geistliche musikalische Lustgarten* for four to nine voices (1616) began to show an inclination toward the simplification of form and language. Franck published thirty-three German Magnificat compositions in the four sections of his *Laudes Dei vespertinae* (following the order used by Lasso: four, five, six, and eight voices). Through their use of a German text, they were supposedly intelligible to the general public and their "graceful, simple musical style" supposedly also opened them to the *Kantoreien* (Gudewill in *H. Albrecht in memoriam,* Kassel, 1962, 88–100). Moreover, this publication contains important information about the practice of alternation in the German Magnificat. While Melchior Franck, undoubtedly under the pressure of a deteriorating choral situation, found it necessary to simplify the polyphonic settings of his lied motets, adopting the cantional style, he made a belated attempt around 1620 to solve the problem by turning to the small sacred concerto. This resulted in a work like the *Cythara ecclesiastica et scholastica . . . in leichte vierstimmige Compositiones übersetzet* (1628), its subtitle (simple four-voice compositions) making clear the purpose and unpretentious nature of the collection. A similar work was the *Neues musikalisches Rosengärtlein . . . neben etlichen neuen Konzerten und Generalbass* for four to eight voices (1627–28). In addition to short and easy concertos, the latter included songs for which Franck himself provided texts and melodies, again following the example of Schein and Johann Staden. In his inclination to follow the new Italian style somewhat (but only as far as the concerto), Franck again reminds one of Praetorius. Only in his last sacred work did Franck use solo voices in imitation of Italian monody, thereby pointing to Johann Rosenmüller's similarly contructed compositions based on texts by the prophets. This work was the *Paradisus musicus . . . geistliches Lustgärtlein* (1636) in two parts, for two to four voices, composed on texts based on Isaiah. Franck produced many other printed works, often voluminous, as well as an immense number of single manuscript compositions. His creative accomplishments call for thorough investigation and a new edition. Research would show that Franck has a place with Hassler and Praetorius among the great masters of his period.

During the period beginning with the Counter-Reformation and ending with the outbreak of the Thirty Years' War, there was an immense increase in the production of Lutheran church music. Whereas most of the production up to the 1560s can be surveyed and described, the material during the following period increased to such an extent that it can be surveyed only cursorily. So large is the inventory of polyphonic compositions that it must be divided into more or less definite groups, though in reality many of these groups are overlapping rather than clearly separated. One such group comprises lied and chorale motets with all the nuances and ramifications already pointed out (see pp. 148 ff. and 158 ff.). A second group is the Latin biblical motets, and a third, the German biblical motets. Finally, there is a fourth group, comprising Latin liturgical texts of every kind, which is rather clearly separated from the others. Concerted works need not be classified separately, since the style did not generally appear in Lutheran church music until about 1620.

SUBSEQUENT HISTORY OF THE LIED MOTET AND CHORALE MOTET

THE LATIN PROVERB MOTET

The pre-eminent position of the song exercised the greatest influence in Protestant church music during the Counter-Reformation. The literature included lieder for various functions and of all musical types—from the Ordinary lieder of the Mass to school and household songs, from psalm and Gospel paraphrases to songs for special occasions, from unison (or cantional-style accompanied) congregational hymns to polyphonic lied and chorale motets. The predominance of the song grew out of the church's need for active congregational participation in the service and out of the emphasis on piety in Christian life. No wonder, therefore, that musicians paid special attention to this field (although they did not neglect the others).

With the lied motet at the center, the many printed works range from the Cantionale, on the one side, to the contrapuntal cantus-firmus motet based on a chorale, on the other. These works are often hard to define because the categories as such lack definite shapes and boundaries. Besides, at this time sacred and secular Latin and German songs and odes were often included in the same printed volume. As a rule, individual composers produced only one distinct Cantionale apiece; however, some musicians (e.g., Bartholomäus Gesius) published numerous Cantionales, or numerous versions of one Cantionale, all differing in content and size. It also seems to have been a friendly practice among colleagues to insert compositions of some other musician into one's own printed collection; there is hardly a publication which does not contain works by at least three composers. In actuality, the class of lied and chorale motets comprises many different things, even though they are all bound up with the concept of "song." In Saxony-Thuringia a large number of native and immigrant musicians were at work in addition to Burck and Eccard. Gallus Dressler (Magdeburg) published collections of songs—for instance, *Das schöne Gebet* (1569), other songs (1570), *Auserlesene Lieder* (1575). Leonhard Schröter, who grew up in Torgau, still in Johann Walter's circle, lived and worked in Magdeburg and published *Geistliche Lieder* (1562) and *Cantiones suavissimae,* (1576 and 1580; containing also school odes by Helmboldt). He has become particularly well known for his four- and eight-voice Christmas songs (1586–87); his excellent Latin hymns (1587) will be dealt with later. Wolfgang Figulus, cantor of St. Thomas's in Leipzig and later cantor of the princely school at Meissen, issued an anthology titled *Vetera nova carmina . . . de natali Domini* (1575) and its sequel *Amorum filii Dei hymni sacri de natali Domini* (1587), which contain settings of German and Latin Christmas songs composed by himself and others. His didactic work *Melodiae in Prudentium* (before 1594) is lost; a second one, *Hymni sacri et scholastici* (1604), probably a new edition of the first work, has been preserved. Seth Calvisius, St. Thomas cantor and predecessor of Schein, became well known through his Cantionale of 1597 (see p. 148 regarding Schein's Cantionale). His activities at the Meissen princely school included publication of *Hymni sacri latini et germanici* (based on Horace and Buchanan, 1594). His *Tricinia* based on German psalm lieder (1603) were widely circulated; in general, the *bicinium* and *tricinium,* particularly when based on hymns, enjoyed widespread popularity (see p. 143 regarding Calvisius's Psalter in the manner of Cornelius Becker). Cornelius Freundt, native of Plauen in Saxony, became known especially for his Christmas songs, collected and published by his chancellor, Jakob Fuhrmann (1591). Melchoir Vulpius published Cantionales in Weimar in 1604 and 1609. Johann Steuerlein's (Meiningen) *Geist-*

liche Lieder (1575) and *Neue Geistliche Gesänge* (1588), along with other works, evidently had wide circulation. Antonius Scandellus, the Dresden court *Kapellmeister*, was an eminent musician. A native of Bergamo and a Catholic, he was assigned in 1566 to the aging Le Maistre as deputy ducal *Kapellmeister;* he became *Kapellmeister* and a convert in 1568, and from then on composed some of the most important Lutheran works of his time; in 1574 he wrote the wedding music for Johann Walter's son. Particularly noteworthy among his songs are *Schöne weltiche und geistliche deutsche Liedlein* for four to six voices (1579), which, by the way, should be re-edited. Other works of Scandellus will be dealt with later on. Besides him, there was another foreigner as court *Kapellmeister* in Dresden (his third successor after two short-term interim office-holders), a Netherlander named Rogier Michael, who published excellent chorale settings, comparable to those of Eccard, in the second part of the Dresden songbook (1593). He also worked in other musical fields and, like Scandellus, composed *historiae* (see below). Georg Otto of Torgau followed in Johann Walter's and Leonhard Schröter's footsteps, later becoming a personal student of Le Maistre. He was in close contact with Selnecker in Leipzig and, as *Kapellmeister* of Landgraves Wilhelm and Moritz of Hesse in Kassel, taught the young Heinrich Schütz. With him came into being a small Kassel School, which accomplished a great deal and counted among its adherents Landgrave Moritz himself (see p. 146), Valentin Geuck (ibid.), and Christoph Cornet. Otto became known by his *Geistliche deutsche Gesänge . . . Lutheri* for five or six voices (1588). In eastern Germany, Eccard and Stobäus were active (for new source material concerning them, see H. Haase in the Blume *Festschrift*, 1963, pp. 176–88). In addition, there was Bartholomäus Gesius in Frankfurt on the Oder; besides his Cantionales (*Kirchen . . . Schulen . . . Hausvätern . . . Liebhabern;* see p. 137), he wrote many song settings, among them Latin *Hymni scholastici* (1597), which later appeared under the title *Melodiae scholasticae*. Nikolaus Zangius (Berlin) brought out three volumes of lied motets for three voices beginning in 1594 and later on many other compositions based on songs. Gregor Lange (Frankfurt on the Oder and Breslau) wrote distinguished Latin motets. A small group of composers, centering around Michael Praetorius, was active in Brunswick, Wolfenbüttel, and Celle. Thomas Mancinus, Praetorius's predecessor, is best known for his Latin motets and *historiae*. Otto Siegfried Harnisch, active in Helmstedt, Wolfenbüttel, and Göttingen, has left us a Cantionale named *Psalmodia sacra* (1621) and school songs, e.g., *Cantiones Gregorianae* (1624) and *Fasciculus novus* (1592; containing odes and motets). Johann Jeep (Celle, Altdorf, Weikersheim, later Frankfurt on the Main and Hanau) published a Cantionale (1607; see p. 137), *Geistliche Psalmen* (1629), *Weihnachtsgesänge* (1637), *Andächtiges Betbüchlein* (1631), and others. Adam Gumpelzhaimer, cantor of St. Anne's in Augsburg, was an excellent representative of Protestant church music in that city; even now his songs and motets are not known well enough. Clearly paralleling Hassler, Gumpelzhaimer composed and published the three-voice *Neue geistliche Lieder nach Art der welschen Villanellen* (1591; enlarged in 1619 under the title *Lustgärtlein*) and the four-voice *Neue deutsche geistliche Lieder nach Art der welschen Canzonen* (1594; enlarged

in 1619 under the title *Würzgärtlein*). His other works included strictly contrapuntal chorale motets with cantus firmus in the bass: *Contrapunctus* (1595),
Weihnachtslieder (1618), and others. Many of these works were intended for
school use; the musical quality was on a par with Hassler. Thomas Walliser of
Strasbourg composed and published chorale motets under the title of *Ecclesiodiae*
(1614) and *Ecclesiodiae novae* (1625). In the same age group, Hieronymus Praetorius (Hamburg) initiated the Hamburg and Schleswig-Holstein School, which
came to have great significance in Lutheran church music during the following
generations up to Buxtehude and Bruhns. His father Jakob (I) was known as a
collector of church-music manuscripts (*Opus excellens et novum, four to eight
voices, 1566*). Hieronymus distinguished himself primarily as a composer of Latin
church music; these compositions were given the title *Opus musicum* and were
published in five volumes (1616–25). Together with his son Jakob (II), an organist
of renown, in whose school there originated among other works the *Wisbyer
Tabulatur* (see p. 246), he contributed to the Hamburg *Melodeien-Gesangbuch*
(1604; see pp. 138 and 245).

While it is difficult to separate clearly the groups of lied and chorale motets,
Cantionales, collections of odes, and so on, the motet as a musical category is
patently definable. It must be understood as a work for many voices, more
polyphonic than homophonic, possibly even a polychoral setting. It could take
its motivic material from a chorale, or it could be freely invented. It was set to
prose texts, primarily of biblical origin; however, prayer texts, devotional texts,
and the like, and even texts from liturgical orders of worship were also used. In
the latter case, the motet was close to the Proper of the Mass, to the scriptural
lessons of the Vespers, and so on. Whereas the song setting on the one hand and
liturgical music on the other had been foremost during the Reformation, the main
interest during the Counter-Reformation was in the direction of biblical proverb
compositions, still preponderantly in Latin. They could take the form of single,
selected proverbs consisting of a few verses only, as well as continuous pericopal
texts, whole psalms, and so on. So much emphasis was placed on the motet based
on biblical or other prose texts that during the next historical period the predominance of song compositions was widely questioned. The Gospels, Psalms, and
Song of Songs stepped into the foreground as greatly favored textual material;
other Old or New Testament texts were not excluded but were seldom used—e.g.,
the Prophetical books, the Epistles, the Book of Job, and others.

A specifically Protestant motet based on biblical proverbs was almost entirely
unknown to the Reformation; even where Protestant composers predominated,
a literary communion remained between the two confessions. The liturgical placement of the music and its texts was one and the same, nor was there any difference
in styles. As for the numerous anthologies of Petreius, Formschneider, Kriesstein,
Ulhard, and others (see p. 119), it cannot be clearly determined for which of the
two churches they are intended; that is, in actuality they were destined for both.
For some time even during the Counter-Reformation, this practice prevailed
under the Pan-European influence of Orlando di Lasso. His motets, as well as his
Masses, Magnificats, hymns, and so on, were used without discrimination. Only
gradually did the situation change. Composers of the Roman school preferred the

old stock of liturgical texts, many of which went out of use in Lutheran worship, becoming more and more expendable. Protestant composers fell back increasingly on biblical quotations and on devotional and prayer texts, especially in the 17th century. The texts themselves had little or no place in the liturgy. The territorial disorganization in Germany and the liturgical indifference displayed in Protestant worship allowed any new texts to be introduced and to form the basis for musical works. The Protestant motet was largely characterized by Gospel excerpts or even entire Gospel lessons chosen according to the church calendar for Sundays and holidays (as early as the end of the 16th and definitely in the 17th century they developed into complete Gospel cycles for the year). Frequently, whole psalms were adopted, replacing the psalm lessons in Matins and Vespers; in like manner, Gospel motets were used in the Mass in place of the Gospel lesson. The text of the Gospel lesson was then read before the sermon in German for the better congregational understanding. In the case of many or even most texts, however, the question of liturgical placement cannot be answered satisfactorily.

It can be assumed that printed anthologies, such as the four-volume psalm settings published by Berg & Neuber in Nuremberg (1553–54) or the Gospel compilations in six volumes (1554–56) by the same publisher, were meant for use by both churches; there is, however, lack of proof that such Gospel motets were used in the Catholic liturgy, and, therefore, Moser's assumption that these publications are "a Protestant collection living on Catholic composers" may be correct. This opinion is backed by the large anthologies compiled by Lindner, Kaspar Hassler, Lechner, Schadaeus, and others, which doubtlessly drew from Catholic sources for Protestant purposes. The printed anthologies by Berg & Neuber, their *Magnum opus* (three volumes, 1558–59), their *Tricinia* (two volumes, 1559), their *Thesaurus* (five volumes, 1564); the collections of Formschneider and those published by Clemens Stephani of Buchau (beginning in 1567); those of Lindner, Kaspar Hassler, Schadaeus, Calvisius, and Bodenschatz; and Lindner's gigantic posthumous manuscript of the Nuremberg repertory (W. Rubsamen, *The International "Catholic" Repertoire* in *Annales Musicologiques* V, 1957, 229–327): all "live on" Netherlanders, Frenchmen, and the more recent ones on Italians— hence predominantly Catholics. German masters have a modest role only, although each of these collections was made for Protestant use. How intensive was the interest in psalm compositions is shown by Clemens Stephani's collection *Psalmus CXXVIII Davidis* for six, five, and four voices (1569). It contained seventeen settings of the Psalm *Beati omnes* by sixteen composers, making it the precursor of Burckhard Grossmann's *Angst der Höllen* (1623), which contained sixteen settings of Psalm 116 by sixteen composers (see below). In the case of composers who stood between the two denominations (e.g., Hans Leo Hassler), it is impossible to decide whether a composition was intended for Catholic or Protestant use. In reverse order, the arch Lutheran Michael Praetorius, in his earliest work *Musarum Sioniarum Motectae et Psalmi* (1607 or earlier), did not hesitate to insert works by Costanzo Porta, even by Palestrina and other Catholic composers, in spite of his wholly Protestant purpose. Looking at these copious and numerous collections it can be safely assumed that they were regarded purely and solely as "music per se"—music at everyone's disposal—and that the

European-oriented style of Lasso or the Italian *prima pratica* was valued more than confessional wrangling.

Aside from that, indigenous Protestant production of Latin motets greatly increased. Joachim a Burck brought out motets for school pupils in the form of a catechism in his *Sacrae cantiones plane novae ex veteri et novo Testamento* (1573). Gallus Dressler (between 1565 and 1585) presented numerous prints with *cantiones sacrae* (which now became the generic term for motets with a Latin text), based on psalms, Gospel, but also Epistle verses. Lechner published a whole series of works in motet style (1575–87), among them (in imitation of Lasso) *Sieben Busspsalmen*. Friedrich Weissensee, in his *Opus melicum, methodicum et plane novum* for four to twelve voices (1602) brought out seventy-two Latin and German motets. Wolfgang Figulus offered single Latin psalms, together with *Precationes aliquot* (1553), *Cantiones sacrae* (1575), and a compilation of *tricinia* "for boys to sing at school" (1559). Besides his German *tricinia*, Calvisius brought out a Latin Gospel series for the whole church year, entitled *Bicinia septuaginta ad sententias Evangeliorum . . . viginti canones* (1599), which later on was enlarged with compositions of other masters and repeatedly published. Handed down to us, but by no means carefully sifted through, are compositions of Latin *cantiones sacrae,* whole psalms, psalm parts, Gospel quotations, and so on, by composers such as Cornelius Freundt, Melchior Vulpius (1602, 1603, 1610), Johann Steuerlein (1588, 1589), Jakob Meiland (Hechingen, Ansbach, and Frankfurt), a latter-day member of the Walter-Le Maistre School (1569, 1572, and so on, in manuscript), Nikolaus Gastritz (Amberg, 1569), Gregor Lange (1580, 1584), Otto Siegfried Harnisch (1592), Andreas Raselius (1589), Johann Knöfel (Breslau, 1571, 1580, 1592), Thomas Elsbeth (Coburg, Liegnitz, and Jawor, 1599, 1610), Nikolaus Zangius (1612), Thomas Mancinus (1608 and in manuscript; a planned collection of 67 motets for four to eight voices was never published), and many others. Single scattered Latin motets by Scandellus and Rogier Michael have been preserved. In northern Germany the two most important composers in this category are Hieronymus Praetorius (Hamburg, beginning in 1559) and Philipp Dulichius (Stettin), whose numerous Latin motets were published from 1589 to 1612, among them the widely distributed *Centuriae* (four parts; 1607–12). Whole Latin Gospel series were published by Johann Wanning (Danzig, 1584), Ph. Dulichius (1599–1600), Leonhard Päminger (Passau), Nikolaus Rosthius, Adam Gumpelzhaimer, and others. We have Gospel series in *bicinium* form from Georg Otto (1601), Seth Calvisius (1599, see above), and Erhard Bodenschatz (1615). At the behest of Landgrave Moritz, Georg Otto composed a complete, large-scale Gospel series, *Opus musicum novum continens textus evangelicos* (1604), distributed between eight, six, and five voices, according to the ecclesiastical significance of the day. Valentin Geuck, also at the behest of Landgrave Moritz, composed a parallel work, *Novum opus continens textus metricos* (1604) in Latin distichs; it was completed by the Landgrave himself (see p. 146). Such learned poetical transcriptions of the Gospels frequently appeared in musical works; we find them in works by Lasso, Michael Praetorius, and, according to Moser, also in works by Daniel Friderici, Euricius Dedekind (about 1590), Wendelin Kessler (1582), and others. They are analogous to the re-

Latinizing of German hymns (see above) and shed light on the division between the Reformation requirement of general intelligibility in the service, pedagogical need, and the humanistic-aesthetic tendencies of the time.

THE GERMAN BIBLICAL PROVERB MOTET

The texts and musical style of Latin motets of these decades followed the general course of music history. As far as the texts are concerned, the confession to which they belonged can be determined only for those having no place in Catholic liturgy or for those which had already been superseded in Lutheran liturgy. On the other hand, a specifically Lutheran motet in the German language did come into being in this period. At first, German was used in the Lutheran service only for songs. For the more strictly liturgical texts of the Mass, Vespers, and so on, the transition to German came about very slowly and unevenly; Latin still held its place beside German far into the 18th century. In the case of biblical but not strictly liturgical texts, Latin predominated to the end of the 16th century; however, German was accepted more and more widely, and from the beginning of the 17th century on, German-language compositions were preferred. Praetorius, Scheidt, and Schein composed approximately as many Latin biblical texts as German, but Schütz was already using German for motets and the "concertos." Devotional texts remained predominantly in Latin with Schütz, Buxtehude, Geist, Bruhns, and others. In the Counter-Reformation there was a conspicuous preference for a specific text category in German—the Psalms. The biblical proverb motet, and by preference the psalm motet, became the characteristic domain of Protestant motet composition. As early as Thomas Stoltzer (see pp. 80 and 99 ff.) the composition of entire psalms had been attempted, though it was still infrequent at that time. From the middle of the 16th century on, a continuous line of lesser and greater composers joined the movement. This cultivation of composition of entire psalms, however, led in subsequent decades to the practice of setting other entire German text categories; thus, there was again a German-language bridge from psalm to Gospel composition.

In his *Zehn deutsche Psalmen* (1551), Johann Reusch (Meissen) followed Stoltzer's style (see p. 101). David Köler also published (in Schönfeld, Bohemia) *Zehn Psalmen Davids* and dedicated them to the city council of Zwickau (1554). Manuscripts of two German psalms by Lukas Bergholz have come down to us. Johann Purkstaller, Nikolaus Copus, Valentin Rabe, and others composed German psalms around 1560. Gallus Dressler left manuscripts of Latin psalm compositions, but with them and his numerous other Latin motets, he also published *Zehn deutsche Psalmen* (1562). Leonhard Schröter composed German psalms together with *Erhalt uns Herr bei deinem Wort* (1576) and a German Te Deum (1571, 1576). His Magdeburg successor, Friedrich Weissensee, left single manuscripts of German motets. With a large number of extant German motets by Cornelius Freundt in Zwickau (probably 1570s and '80s), with Psalm 111 by Wolfgang Figulus in Meissen (1586), and others, the setting of German psalms exhausted itself toward the end of the 16th century; at the same time it prepared the way for a singular rebirth during the 17th century. Seth Calvisius with Psalm 111 for twelve voices (1615), Georg Otto with several polychoral German psalms (1602–07), and Landgrave Moritz with a considerable number of similar compositions (most of which have disappeared) initiated the new development, forming a gradual transition from the older polychoral texture to the full-fledged style of the polychoral concerto. Before that, the modest Meiningen master Johann Steuerlein made a few unusual contributions to the German motet: *Deutsches Benedicite und Gratias* (1575) and *CXVII. Psalm Davids auf dreierlei Weise oder unterschiedliche Tonos* (1599). In 1616, the Saxon councillor in Jena, Burckhard Grossmann, commissioned sixteen composers to set to music Psalm 116; he published the collection (1623) under the title *Angst der Höllen und Friede der Seelen;* later it became very famous. Among the composers who contributed to the collection were Chr. Demantius, Nikolaus Erich, Melchior Franck, M. Praetorius, J. H. Schein, H. Schütz, and no less than four members of the Michael family. Dressler, Schröter, Weissensee, Melchior Vulpius, Meiland, Calvisius, H. Praetorius, M. Franck, and many others, continued to make use of German and Latin side by side in many different kinds of Bible texts. The basic annual series of German-language Gospel compositions around 1600 were those of Andreas Raselius in Regensburg, *Deutsche Sprüche aus den sonntäglichen Evangeliis* (1594) and *Deutsche Sprüche auf die fürnehmsten jährlichen Feste und Aposteltage* (1595, requiring up to nine voices), and by Christoph Demantius in Freiberg, *Corona harmonica, auserlesene Sprüche aus den Evangelien auf alle Sonntage und Feste durch das ganze Jahr* (1610, for six voices). Subsequently, there was Melchior Vulpius's *Evangelische Sprüche* (1612 and 1614; a third section added to these by Johann Christenius, 1625), also numerous single German motets, among them Thomas Elsbeth's (Breslau) *Sonntägliche Evangelien auf die fürnehmsten Feste,* (two parts, 1616 and 1621). The most splendid contributions to the German motet around 1600 were made by Leonhard Lechner (see pp. 153).

FROM THE SCHOOL OF LASSO TO THE CONCERTED MOTET

In the history of Lutheran church music, the last three decades of the 16th and the first two of the 17th century were the golden age, not only for the song motet in its various forms but also for the cantus-firmus-free verse or proverb motet based on the most diversified but predominantly biblical texts, Latin as well as German. Before then, a motet which could be distinctly characterized as Lutheran was manifest in rare instances only (e.g., Stoltzer's Psalms), and later on, around 1620, the species degenerated rapidly as a result of the massive invasion of the Italian concerted style. To some extent, there were liturgical reasons for the rise of the Protestant motet in the Counter-Reformation: the declining adherence to orders of worship increasingly offered an opportunity to replace the choral lection—the Psalms or the Gospels (in certain cases, the Passion History as well) —by art music. But the artistic reason was probably stronger: Lasso's overwhelming influence effected a turning point in motet composition. As a rule, the older

Netherlandish motet of the Josquin-Obrecht stratum had remained aloof from the text; the same was true of the Gombert-Willaert stratum, which in the printed anthologies of Berg & Neuber, Formschneider, and so on, enjoyed wide distribution in Germany. It treated the text as if it were the revealed Word of God, comprehensible to man only through music, but not susceptible to tampering. If the musician elucidates the revealed Word by the use of careful rhetorical-declamatory devices, rarely using the symbolic-tonal devices that would emphasize and clarify the text individualistically, the text remains transcendent and unapproachable. Lasso's motets, however, especially his later ones, took firm hold of the Word with an impassioned soul, revealing thereby—and differing from the Roman School of Palestrina and his successors—a new, immediate, and heartfelt attitude of the musician to the text. In a realistic manner, details were descriptively sketched; changing images and contents contrasted with one another. No longer was the musical setting exclusively dictated by an autonomous musical law, but rather by the desire to interpret. Such personal relationship to the text greatly encouraged a tendency rooted in Lutheran Protestantism, the individual's attempt to achieve a closer relationship to Holy Scriptures, his need for insight and illumination. That may be the reason why Protestant composers, beginning with Burck and Eccard, profited so much from Lasso's school, and why the influence of this school persevered as long as the Protestant motet continued to flower. From the point of view of the general history of music, one may look upon Lasso's motets as the first stage of the "madrigalization" of the motet. It still lacked the expressiveness of the personal, the personally experienced, the true "pathos of the Baroque." It obtains its historic-stylistic effect in Protestant vocal composition only beginning with Schein and Schütz, i.e., with the intrusion of the concerto, the monody, and hence, with a second stage of madrigalization. This subsequent stage was substantially prepared during the earlier stage by its mode of realistic pictorialization and interpretation: sleeping and waking, death and resurrection, light and darkness, rise and fall, hastening and lingering—all placed into contrast; sensuous sound combinations and rhythmic patterns were invented to depict the voice of God, the cry of pain, rejoicing and despairing. This all originated with Lasso, and from him it infiltrated the Protestant motet between 1570 and 1630 (see p. 101). Meiland, Gesius, Eccard, Dressler, Schröter, Otto, Vulpius, and numerous others, up to Michael and Hieronymus Praetorius, Hassler, Melchior Frank, and so on, were swayed by him. Occasionally, some of the masters went beyond the Lasso School, pressing forward toward an objectivity and emotionalism perhaps influenced by the recent Italian madrigal, especially that of Marenzio. In their Gospel motets, Demantius and Raselius had already chosen this path, as also did Melchior Franck in his early works. The pioneer Lechner led the way with his powerful later works. However, a complete breakthrough of the baroque pathos came only in the generation of Schein and Schütz.

The motet of Lasso and his school was founded on the strength and terseness of individual motif formation, which differed basically from the older Netherlandish manner of composition. Vicentino and Zarlino had established the theoretical foundations of a new word-sound relationship; no composer other than Lasso was able (at least in the motet) so effectively to unlock the text through the strength of word-created motifs. In a polyphonic setting, the motif construction resulted in short, concise single formations which, all depending on the text, contrasted to new configurations and thus gave plastic shape to the setting as it progressed. The characteristic imprint of this style resulted from several technical features, among them carefully differentiated sound groupings, exploitation of contrasts in register, harmonic effects, and novel color schemes, economic and effective uses of dissonance, alternation of dense and sparse textures, salient rhythms, and a wide scale of part writing, embracing patterns from homorhythm to involved complementary rhythms. The setting vacillated between two or three voices and the obligatory seven, eight, or nine voices, and made use of the contrast created by two or three four-voice choirs (also three- against five-voice, and the like). This "older" use of multiple choirs was by no means indigenous to Venice. It had already existed in other Italian localities even before the noted Vesper Psalms of Willaert (1550), and as early in various parts of Germany as in Rome or Venice. It ultimately grew out of the need for greater sonority, from effects created by contrast and dialogue, from the gradation of color that could be produced by ensembles the complements of which were varied rather than constant. The works of Praetorius are veritable collections of examples illustrating the practice of using more than one choir (which he also often described). One is justified in assuming a direct relationship with the Venetian polychoral practice only when this ensemble arrangement takes on the character of the *concerto per choros,* i.e., in the later works of Michael Praetorius and in those of Scheidt, Schein, and Schütz. The "older" polychoral practice clung tenaciously to the euphony of the single choir and the "ad libitum" ensemble that could use many or few instruments, or omit them entirely. Opposed to this, the polychoral concerto usually followed stringent rules concerning the composition of the ensemble (which, however, could be varied to a large extent). Sound masses of the most varied colors were contrasted with one another; they ranged from a trombone choir to solo soprano with thoroughbass, from the homophonic complementary choir to the intricate duet and trio setting for solo voices, from coloratura singing with lute accompaniment to the massive *ripieno* of all vocal and instrumental choirs. Each choir formed an autonomous sonority, and the number of these choirs, depending on place and circumstance, could be increased or reduced at will. A six-choir concerto consisting of twenty-four voices might be reduced to a two-voice choir with thoroughbass. All of it rested on a fundamental bass, which, distributed among the single choirs, was realized by the various thoroughbass instruments. Hand in hand with the polychoral concerto went the acceptance of new forms. As a rule, the older polychoral practice had adhered to the principle of joining individual developments of single motifs. The new concerto style preferred to use closed or ritornello forms, solo episodes suspended like arcs between projecting structures, as well as a consciously manipulated recurrence of groups of motifs, sections, and color effects. The structure of a Renaissance facade, its several parts aligned to each other, was changed into baroque structure, with its symmetrically aligned light and shadow effects distributed in depth. This transition from the older multiple-choir practice to the multiple-choir concerto was gradual in Lutheran church music, promoted partly by German musicians who pursued their studies in Italy, partly by the influx of printed music from Italy (which had been increasing since 1600). Only from 1620, however, did this new practice really assert itself and surmount the continuing influence of the late Lasso School.

Viewed as part of the general history of music, Lutheran church music in the Counter-Reformation proved to be an interim stage between the Netherlandish period ending with Lasso and the Italian period beginning with Palestrina and Marenzio, whose full impact was felt in Germany only around the beginning of the Thirty Years' War. In order to understand this church music completely, it is important to realize that during this very period a specifically German and specifically Protestant music issued from the two epochal waves of general music history. What had its beginning, especially in the field of the motet with Burck, Dressler, Schröter, and others, and what culminated toward the end of that era in the late works of Praetorius, was not lost again in subsequent times in spite of all the Neo-Italian inundation. However closely connected the old masters of the Lasso School may have been, and however conscientiously Praetorius had to study the Italian masters of the Gabrieli group in order to be able to write his later *concerti per choros*, a musical language was created by them all which possessed something peculiarly German and peculiarly Lutheran. This is true not only of song and chorale arrangements, but also (and especially) of free motet-like compositions. Lechner's *Sprüche vom Leben und Tod* can be traced back to the Lasso School and Marenzio's madrigals; Praetorius's *Polyhymnia caduceatrix* could not have come into existence without the precedence of Gabrieli, Viadana, and Agazzari; Schütz's *Symphoniae sacrae* and *Kleine geistliche Konzerte* show unmistakable acquaintance with Viadana, Monteverdi, Grandi, and later on perhaps with Ferrari and Carissimi—yet not a single piece of these works could be confused with its prototype. They all speak the language of an introverted piety stemming from the Lutheran spirit, a language whose passionate seriousness lends expression to German character in the guise of adapted foreign prototypes. This language, notwithstanding its erosion and the popularization of later decades, survived into the 18th century. Without it the works of J. S. Bach would be unthinkable.

LATIN LITURGICAL MUSIC

Concurrently with the impressive rise of lied and chorale motets and the free biblical proverb motet, Lutheran composition of Latin liturgical texts declined as the significance of these texts themselves diminished in public worship. To be sure, many, if not most, Lutheran composers set the Ordinary of the Mass *(Missa brevis)* and single Mass movements, like the Kyrie, Gloria, or Sanctus. They also set parts of the Proper of the Mass (mostly Introit, Vesper hymns, Magnificat, or Te Deum), seldom cycles of the *proprium*. However, they made these settings only for special occasions such as consecrations, student assignments, and so forth. Because of the relaxing of the liturgy and the swift decrease in the use of

Latin, the churchly need for such compositions declined in many places. In addition, the fact that the old literary sources were common to both denominations and could be retained without adaptation had a restraining effect on new composition. No one cared whether the Kyrie or the hymn to be performed was by a Catholic or a Protestant (see also p. 113).

Common literary sources were adhered to by the two confessions for Latin liturgical church music well into the era of J. S. Bach, and it is astonishing to note to what extent composers of definitely post-Tridentine tendencies were accepted before and after 1600. Lasso, Gallus, Hans Leo and Kaspar Hassler, all of whose Masses were certainly meant for Catholic usage (the latter two having been commissioned in part by the House of Fugger), were prominent in Protestant collections. As early as 1590, the collection of Masses of Friedrich Lindner, cantor of the Ägidienkirche in Nuremberg *(Missae quinque),* contained works by G. Florio, G. Guami, Ph. de Monte, and Palestrina. His collection of motets of the same years *(Corollarium),* besides Lasso, Palestrina, and De Monte, also contained works by A. Gabrieli, M. A. Ingegneri, Claudio Merulo, Annibale Stabile, and A. Scandellus; the only Germans were Aichinger and Klingenstein. Lindner's anthology of Magnificats (1591) contained, among others, works by M. Asolo, T. Riccio, V. Ruffo, and even by the Spaniard F. Guerrero. Nor does the assortment of composers look any different in Kaspar Hassler's large collection of motets entitled *Sacrae symphoniae* (three parts, 1598, 1601, and 1613), for five to sixteen voices. While this flood of motet collections of mainly Netherlandish-Italian character did not diminish the creative urge of Protestant masters during these decades, it apparently had a severely hampering effect in the field of Latin liturgical music. Compositions of that kind were generally few and far between. Only one Mass, for example, is known from Jakob Meiland's otherwise copious work (printed by Hieronymus Praetorius, 1622). The still more copious output of Melchior Vulpius contains only two Masses (according to Eitner, *Quellenlexikon).* Michael Praetorius published single Masses (1607, 1617). There are six Masses (1576) by A. Scandellus; in addition, his six-voice *super Epitaphium Mauritii*—that is, the Funeral Mass, composed for and used at the obsequies of Elector Moritz of Saxony, contains a masterful seven-voice Agnus Dei (1553; preserved in manuscript; the printed work is lost). There is also a Mass by Cornelius Freundt, and an uncertain number of Masses by Johannes Eccard. Whole volumes of Masses were published by Leonhard Lechner (1584), Michael Praetorius *(Missodia,* 1611), Hieronymus Praetorius *(Opus musicum III,* 1619, six Masses), and Bartholomäus Gesius *(Missae ad imitationem cantionum Orlandi et aliorum,* 1611, ten Masses and single compositions; *Opus plane novum . . . Missae ad imitationem cantionum Orlandi, Marentii et aliorum . . . Introitus, Kyrie, Sequentia . . . I,* 1613). Beginning with Michael Praetorius (1617) and Christian Demantius (*Triades Sioniae,* 1619; this work, like the one previously mentioned by Gesius, contains, besides four Masses, Introit, prose texts, and other Mass settings), the thoroughbass also entered into Protestant Mass composition. Eitner knew of a seven-voice Mass by N. Zangius. W. Senn (in *MGG* IX, 206) mentions Masses by D. Friderici and S. Besler; according to him, some extant Masses by H. Dedekind and J. Schedlich (1613) are said to be composed "in pronounced polyphonic style." All these compositions (a very modest number compared with the uncounted production of lied and proverb motets) differ in no way from those of Catholic composers. In fact, like the Catholic works, they are predominantly parody Masses—adaptations to the text of the Mass of existing motets, songs, madrigals, or choruses. The Protestant Mass received its own particular imprint only with the appearance of a "German Mass," that is, with the thrust of songs into this area; the songs making up the Ordinary of the Mass were put into the form of chorale motets and combined as "lied Masses" as, for instance, in the two German Masses by Praetorius in his *Polyhymnia caduceatrix* (1619). A German Mass was ascribed to Rogier Michael in 1601, but it is lost. This species continued to exist (also with Gesius, 1613) in isolated works throughout the 17th century, but was never extensively cultivated.

The Proper of the Mass in Latin was already disintegrating. Apparently its individual parts were being quickly replaced by songs, particularly during the Counter-Reformation, perhaps because of the impact of Calvinistic antipapal tendencies. Of the Latin parts, only the Introit kept its place somewhat regularly, and that only in the larger churches and court chapels; otherwise it could also be replaced by a song or an organ piece, as seen in a Liegnitz source dating from the first half of the 17th century (Liliencron). Insofar as Protestant composers dealt with the Proper at all, they sometimes inserted different portions of the Mass into a printed work (settings from the Proper and Ordinary, versicles, and so on). A few examples follow: Joachim a Burck published in 1569 *Symbolum apostolicum Nicenum et canticum Symbolum Sanctorum Augustini et Ambrosii, ac verba institutionis coenae Domini.* Bartholomäus Gesius published *Cantiones sacrae chorales: Introitus, ut vocantur, Kyrie, Sequentia et plures aliae de praecipuis diebus festis anniversariis* (1610) and part I of his *Opus plane novum* (1613; see above), the main contents of which dealt with the Ordinary; it was followed in the same year by *Pars posterior continens Introitus, Kyrie, Sequentia . . . ad melodias chorales . . . quibus praemissa est Historia Passionis . . . ex Evangelista Matthaeo.* Hymns, sequences, and "other Latin songs" are also contained in his German song collection *Concentus ecclesiasticus* (1607). However, the mixed-repertory type of collection for use at Mass appeared as early as 1575 when Johann Knöfel, then living in Liegnitz, issued his *Cantus choralis,* containing songs for both the Ordinary and Proper, as well as hymns, sequences, versicles, and so on, most of them in concise homophonic settings over a chorale cantus firmus; they were probably meant to be used in alternation with the organ. Side by side with the mixed repertory were isolated cycles uniform in content. Georg Otto of Kassel published as early as 1574 *Melodiae continentes Introitus totius anni* and Rogier Michael of Dresden brought out *Introitus Dominicorum dierum . . . festorum* (1603). Mixed repertories, however, were again contained in two publications of Gregor Aichinger in Augsburg, *Liturgica sive sacra officia* (1603) and *Fasciculus sacrarum harmoniarum* (1606). No musician endeavored to deal with the sum total of all sections pertaining to the Latin Mass as systematically and comprehensively as did Michael Praetorius, whose *Leiturgodia,* as a section of his work is known, includes, among others, a *Missodia Sionia* and an *Eulogodia Sionia* (both 1611). The first one begins with an entire section of the Kyrie, Gloria, and *Et in terra*, arranged, according to their settings, "in contrapuncto simplici" or "in contrapuncto colorato." There follows a section called *Mystochorodia*, which contains a number of versicles, collects, and the like (*Et cum Spiritu tuo, Domine, non secundum, Confitemini, Dominus vobiscum, Amen*, etc.), a *Symbolodia* with two Credo settings, a *Hierodipnodia* with Prefaces, Sanctus, Benedictus, and Agnus (movements which differ widely from each other). They relate strictly to particular feasts, some of which have special additions. Further parts contain a section called *Sub communione*, with the responsory *Discubuit Jesus* and finally two closing parts, the *Amen diversa*, ten Glorias, one Introit, and so on. At the close of the *Hierodipnodia* is a complete Ordinary composed by Praetorius for eight voices. That was by no means all he had planned to compose for the services of the complete church year; after the Introit, and after *Gradualia, Halleluja et Sequentiae*, he made the notation "quos (quas) vide in peculiari classe" (which see in their proper class). They never appeared in print, however. The immense undertaking published by Praetorius (*Syntagma musicum* III, 1619; see p. 204) far exceeded his powers and the span of his life. He subsequently supplied the missing Hallelujahs in *Polyhymnia exercitatrix* (1620), suggesting that a number of psalm compositions could be going to the *Alleluja*. The *Eulogodia Sionia* included the thanksgiving formulas *Benedicamus* and *Deo dicamus* in numerous settings, arranged again according to the order of Sundays and holidays. It is also evident from the *Catalogus* that Praetorius earmarked quite a number of other Latin liturgical texts for composition. Aside from that, there are twelve settings of *Benedicamus Domino* already composed by Thomas Mancinus, who was Praetorius's predecessor in Wolfenbüttel. From a historical point of view, the entire Protestant practice of composing Latin Masses and Mass sections in this period shows a strong tendency to cling to tradition. Both tone and murmur hold fast to Lasso's model; no tendency to switch to the concerted style can be observed. In even larger measure this holds true with regard to the period's Latin Vesper composition, particularly its hymns. The hymn, always adhering tenaciously to a cantus firmus, also preferred an archaic-sounding polyphonic setting. This was certainly the case with the hymns contained in the first three parts of Leonhard Päminger's *Cantiones ecclesiasticae* (1573–76); it is also true, perhaps in even stricter form, of Leonhard Schröter's *Hymni sacri* (1587) and of those composed by Bartholomäus Gesius (1595), Melchior Vulpius, and Samuel Besler. The conservative character retained by this genre is also clearly shown by its unwillingness to participate in the transition to the free-style hymns —i.e., solo voice with thoroughbass—which had become fashionable in Italy since G. Valentini (1618) and P. Agostini (1619). Only around 1630 do we find concerted hymn settings by Thomas Selle. In line with decreasing demand, Protestant hymn composition became almost extinct. The last comprehensive and substantial contribution in this area was made by Michael Praetorius, whose *Hymnodia Sionia* (1611) still comprised twenty-four hymns in 145 different two- to eight-voice settings, among them six organ settings. Other types of Latin liturgical music, e.g., the Te Deum, were always composed with comparate

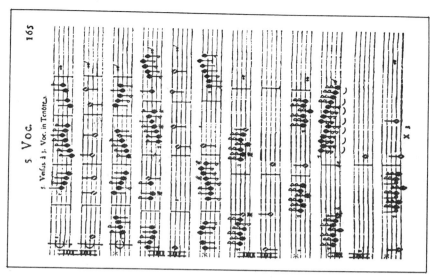

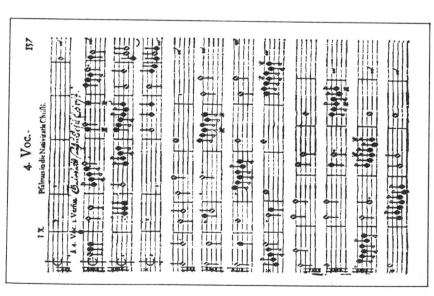

47. Samuel Scheidt, first Versus, four-voice setting, and fifth Versus, three-voice setting, of the chorale variation on *Gelobet seist du, Jesu Christ* in the *Tabulatura nova*, part II, Hamburg, 1624, Michael Hering.

48. Johann Hermann Schein, *Opella nova*, Leipzig, 1627, Lorenz Kober. Title page of the partbook for the first soprano.

49. Samuel Scheidt, *Tabulatura nova*, part I, Hamburg 1624, Michael Hering. Title page.

infrequency, and in many cases they evidently have not come down to us. A Latin Te Deum by Schröter and one by Rogier Michael appeared in 1584 and 1595 respectively. A notable Te Deum in German can be found in part III of the *Musae Sioniae* by Praetorius (1607).

The only Latin liturgical type continuously held in high esteem and widely distributed was the Magnificat. Stylistically, Lasso became the authoritative figure in this field too with his collection *Magnificat octo tonorum* (1567). As a rule, the first verse was intoned to a psalm tone; this was followed by an alternation of verses in plainsong and polyphony, with either even-numbered or odd-numbered verses set. Just as often, however, there were through-composed settings of the whole Magnificat text, including even the introduction and the concluding Doxology. Always, or almost always, the formulas of one of the eight psalm tones formed the foundation; completely "free" composition of the Magnificat seems to have come into use only with the concerted style, i.e., about 1620. Even though Protestant creativeness in this field was much less extensive than the Catholic, the number of Protestant Magnificat prints (generally *Magnificat octo tonorum*, i.e., with one composition for each psalm tone) by far exceeds that of all other Latin categories. From the large number we will mention only Gallus Dressler (1571), L. Lechner (1578), V. Haussmann of Königsberg (1588), manuscript compositions by J. Knöfel, Andreas Ostermaier, and Andreas Raselius (c. 1594), G. Aichinger (1595), E. Bodenschatz (1599), Landgrave Moritz of Hesse (c. 1600), Jakob Hassler (1601), Chr. Demantius (1602), Hieronymus Praetorius (1602), Melchior Vulpius (1605), B. Gesius (1607), G. Otto (1607), M. Praetorius (a single Latin Magnificat in *Musarum Sioniarum Motectae et Psalmi,* 1607), Nikolaus Zangius (1609), J. D. Schedlich (1613), and Gesius (1621, with an insertion of Christmas carols). In this area it is again Michael Praetorius who made the most important contribution; his *Megalynodia Sionia* (1611) contains fourteen Magnificats, eleven of which are motet, madrigal, and chanson parodies, and three of which are evidently original compositions, among them a *super chorale melos Germanicum,* i.e., on a German psalm formula, a composition already found in a German version in *Musae Sioniae I* (1605). Inserted into the first two Magnificats are German Christmas carols and into the third one German Easter songs—a custom that prevailed until the first setting of J. S. Bach's *Magnificat*. Besides the Latin, the German Magnificat gained favor beginning about 1600 without the one supplanting the other; it received a particularly masterful treatment in Melchior Franck's *Laudes Dei vespertinae* (1622). Simultaneously, from about 1620 onward the Magnificat accepted the form of the new concerto for small or large ensemble, thereby preserving its existence and its continued cultivation in Protestant church music. Indeed, it remained a favorite species until the time of J. S. Bach.

HISTORY AND PASSION

The need for insight into the divine Word and of illustrative textual interpretation in music brought about a change of style, largely the work of Lasso and his school. It led to the upsurge in Protestant motet composition during the Counter-Reformation and may well have been responsible for the surprisingly rapid and independent development of biblical Histories *(historiae)* and Passions, the most original and historically the most significant creations of Protestant music. Protestant Passions can be divided into five groups, forming no chronological sequence but partly overlapping for long periods of time: the responsorial Passion *(Choralpassion,* formerly "plainsong Passion"; for terminology, cf. K. von Fischer in *Archiv für Musikwissenschaft* X, 1954, 189, and in *MGG* X, 1963, 887); the through-composed Passion *(Figuralpassion,* formerly "motet Passion"); a group made up of a mixed style between the first two types; the oratorical (or *lektion)* Passion; and the Passion oratorio (the Passion cantata should be listed as a separate kind of cantata rather than as a Passion, and in like manner the Passion lied of the Reformation [see p. 86] should be classified with song settings rather than with the Passion in its narrower sense). The most active compositional period for responsorial Passions was during the Reformation and the Counter-Reformation, even though composition continued to take place long after that. The through-composed Passion and the mixed type were cultivated almost exclusively during the Counter-Reformation. The oratorical Passion belongs to the era of orthodoxy and mysticism, extending even into the era of Pietism; the Passion oratorio came into being in the last-named period only. Moreover, as we have remarked, the boundaries fluctuated; there were many border and transitional works.

The reading of the Passion History according to the four Gospels during Holy Week was an unvarying ritual in the Roman church (Palm Sunday according to St. Matthew, Tuesday according to St. Mark, Wednesday according to St. Luke, and Good Friday according to St. John). The custom was adopted by Luther but not without hesitation, perhaps because too much music might attach to it. As a rule, three clergymen took part in the presentation: Christ's words were sung by a deep voice, the narration of the Evangelist by a voice of middle range, and the words of all other persons—soloists and the choruses of the disciples, Jews, high priests, soldiers, and so on *(turbae)*—by a high voice. The musical formulas in these presentations were determined by a solemn Gospel tone, the so-called Passion tone; single parts (continuous recitation tone or *tuba,* formulas for beginnings and endings of sentences, for commas, colons, question marks, and so forth) were predetermined as in the "tones" allotted to ordinary psalm and Gospel lessons. However, as early as pre-Reformation times, extensions and enrichments were added to this purely liturgical concept, perhaps for the sake of satisfying an artistic urge, or as a result of the influence of music used for liturgical plays. Obviously the voices of the *turbae* had to be distinguished from individual persons through the use of a multiple-voice presentation; to this end, the voices of the three performing clergymen were combined by using the intervals of the fifth and fourth until, a little later, there came into use the *turba,* a plain, four-voice *falsobordone* setting above the tenor cantus firmus of the Passion tone. Inartistic, crude chords furnished the only contrast in the reading of the text, which, otherwise, was chanted in three registers:

Johann Walther: *St. Matthew Passion* (c. 1550)

It was this form of the responsorial Passion History with multiple-voice *turbae* that Luther knew. Aside from reducing the number of Gospels used from all four to one or two, he did not change that practice. In pre-Reformation times, the presentation of the Passion according to single Gospels (also in abbreviated form, less frequently in the form of the so-called *Evangelienharmonie,*) had been in use. Protestant composers in many cases gave preference to a *Passionsharmonie,* as published by Johann Bugenhagen in 1526; in it the accounts of the single Gospels were combined, being joined to the Seven Words on the Cross. This "harmony," or similar ones akin to it, was the basis of the text even when the Passion in question contained such words as "according to St. Matthew the Evangelist" in its title. The basic Passion models according to the four Evangelists were probably prepared in the middle of the 16th century by Johann Walter at Luther's request, perhaps even with his collaboration. In accordance with Luther's demand that church melodies be not haphazardly adapted to the German language but individually created so as to fit it, Walter transformed the old Passion tone, adding simple *turba* pieces of his own (see example above). What was intended was not a new composition but merely a transformation of the old Latin Passion into German. Quite correctly, therefore, it was considered a kind of model throughout the 16th and 17th centuries and well into the 18th, this model being available when transformation and adaptation to modern needs were planned. For that very reason, it found wide distribution throughout Germany in numerous manuscript copies, prints, imitations, and variants. "With his Passion according to St. Matthew, Walter created the prototype of the Protestant responsorial Passion. His successors in this field did not merely follow him, but in many cases they took over the choruses here, the essential parts of the recitatives there" (Gerber).

The material handed down to us starts with the Gotha Choirbook (1539) and a Grimma manuscript (c. 1550). From the beginning, there were differences in the tradition. In a widely distributed version in Keuchenthal's *Kirchengesänge* (1573; see plate 19), the *turbae* are noted down only now and then, and some of the solo parts have been changed. In a version by Selnecker (1587) the *Exordium* and *Conclusio* are added for the first time. Beginning with the *Missale* by Matthias Ludecus (1589), and leading up to Heinrich Grimm (1629, 1636), Christoph Schultze in Delitzsch (1636), and Gottfried Vopelius (Leipzig song-book, 1682), numerous printed editions included Walter's various Passions more or less accurately. From these sources they were handed down and can be found in the hymnbooks of the 18th century, where they have their place among the Passion hymns or in the appendices. In addition, Ludecus also wrote two Latin St. Matthew Passions which, following the one composed by Lukas Lossius (*Psalmodia,* 1553), closely resembled the Catholic version. A series of revised compositions, at first primarily the *turbae* but increasingly the solo parts as well, began with an edition of the St. Matthew Passion by Clemens Stephani (1570). Jakob Meiland brought out (1567, 1568, 1570) the choruses of three Walter Passions in a new, revised version; Samuel Besler edited the choruses of all four Passions (1612). Some versions were subsequently published by Melchior Vulpius (1613), Otto Siegfried Harnisch (1621), and Christoph Schultze (1653). This series also included the St. Mark Passion—contained in the Grundig manuscript (1665) and formerly ascribed to Heinrich Schütz—as well as the so-called Glas-hütter Passion of 1680. Beginning with Meiland and leading to Vulpius and Schultze, the *turbae* now became increasingly more flexible—in the style of the motet—and were dramatized (in the case of the latter two, expanded to six voices); also, the solo parts were more and more modernized, approaching monody. In this manner, the original Walter models were gradually changed into compositions of decided individuality. Looked at from this angle, the three late Passions of Heinrich Schütz must likewise be regarded as being closely connected with this species, although they have nothing more than this in common with the initial model.

Side by side with the responsorial Passion came the development of the through-composed Passion. The entire text of the Passion was composed from beginning to end in several voices, approximately in the manner of motets, differentiating only between the number and grouping of singers, the Evangelist, Jesus, and the *turbae*. In Lutheran church music it was linked with the motet-like through-composition of a *Passionsharmonie* which, at that time, was generally ascribed to Jakob Obrecht (G. Rhau first printed it under that name in 1538, and numerous other German reprints adhered to it); in older Italian manuscripts, however, it is ascribed to a certain Longueval (Longaval?). It must be classed with the oldest extant four-voice arrangements of a *Passionsharmonie;* it closely ad-heres to the Passion tone. It may perhaps have been a typical model composition which, similar to the many versions of Walter's Passions, cannot be ascribed with absolute certainty to any one particular master (see p. 115). But whoever its author may be, it laid the groundwork for the Protestant type of through-com-posed Latin Passion. As late as 1528 Joachim a Burck remarked in the preface of his own Passion "that the Latin Passion of the famous musician Jakob Obrecht was composed by a splendid mind, and was being sung everywhere" (J. Robijns in *MGG* VIII, 1960, 1190). However, it soon emancipated itself from the proto- type, placing all resources of the free motet-like art of interpretation at the service of the text. In later compositions, particularly those in German, it became an especially characteristic species of Lutheran church music, producing unparal- leled achievements in dramatization and descriptive illustration.

For a while, along with the prototype, the through-composed Passion entered Protestant music in Latin. The compositions of Galliculus (1538) and Resinarius (1543), still closely bound to the Passion tone and closely related to the "Obrecht" Passion, belonged to the era of Reformation. Strangely, only three Protestant through-composed Latin Passions, originating in the late 16th and early 17th century, are known: that of Ludwig Daser in Stuttgart (1578), that of Paulus Bucenus in Riga (Stettin, 1578), and that of Bartholomäus Gesius (1613, his last work). The latter two are for six voices; Daser's is the most individual and dramatic, and should probably be regarded as Lechner's prototype. All continued to follow the Passion tone. The German-language species, however, was remarka- ble in quantity as well as quality. In the lead was a masterwork, the four-voice Passion according to St. John by Joachim a Burck (1568), taking its stylistic pattern from Lasso. Burck's *Passion, im 22. Psalm beschrieben* (1574), however, is not a Passion but rather a psalm composition, and a third work of Burck, *Das 53. Kapitel Jesajae. Von dem Leiden und Auferstehen Jesu Christi* (*"Höret die Weissagung"*; 1573) has come down to us incomplete and is nothing but a contemplation on the Passion. There followed Passions by J. Steuerlein (1576) and J. Machold (1593); a work of the Dresden composer Georg Forster (1586–87) is known only by hearsay. About this time, the most outstanding work in the history of the German through-composed Passion came into being: Leonhard Lechner's Passion according to St. John (in manuscript, 1593; the printed edition of 1594 is lost); it also includes the Seven Words in its text. Together with the *Deutsche Sprüche* and the motets based on the Song of Songs, it forms a cycle of late Lechner works; the master poured his genius for dramatic characterization

Leonhard Lechner: *St. John Passion*, 1594

into the Passion, thereby creating the absolute climax of this species. After Lechner it quickly declined, but not before two more extremely expressive and dramatic masterworks were produced, the six-voice Passions by J. Herold in Graz (1594) and Christoph Demantius in Freiberg (1631).

The through-composed Passion flourished for only a brief time. The only explanation for this is that its development depended on the increasing possibility of emancipation from the pseudo-Obrecht prototype and on enrichment of the descriptive and emotional content. These motivations were actually more compatible with dramatic monody. The sequence of Passion scenes could be much more easily presented in many small contrasting movements of different styles than in an unbroken motet-like composition, even when motet-like compositions (like those Demantius) were thoroughly permeated with characterization and emotion. All the fervor in works of the greatest masters could not prevent the species from arriving at an insurmountable boundary. On the other hand, the mixed type, which was adopted in the meantime, was better able to adapt itself to the needs of the new era and to propagate itself. However small the extant number of these Passions may be, they nevertheless pointed to the future.

A. Scandellus in his five-voice St. John Passion (1561 or earlier; printed in 1568) seems to have been the first composer to imitate the north Italian models by using the recitation tone only for the Evangelist in the Protestant Passion and composing freely for the other participants. The ensembles varied: Jesus's music is in four parts, the servant girl's, Peter's, Pilate's, and others' in three; the soldier's, and occasionally also Pilate's, in two; the *turbae* in five. The stimulus

A. Scandellus: *St. John Passion* (c. 1560)

came from V. Ruffo, J. Nasco, and C. de Rore; Lasso's four Passions were also influenced by them (1575, 1580, 1582) and may, in turn, have influenced Daser's and Lechner's Passions. The work of Scandellus must have had a strong effect. Gesius shows a marked affinity with him in his first work, a Passion according to St. John (1588). As early as 1593 Johannes Gengenbach united Scandellus's St. John Passion with his Resurrection *historia* in one edition, while in 1621 Samuel Besler brought out a new edition with an added choral part. A Passion according to St. Mark by A. Beber in Naumburg (around 1610) resembles Scandellus and already strongly dramatizes the solo part of the Evangelist. Two of Rogier Michael's Passions, belonging definitely to the mixed type, are lost, an especially painful fact considering the excellent quality of his works and the small number of this type of Passion. From here too a path leads to Heinrich Schütz: his three late Passions are based the model of on Scandellus and Beber as well as on the dramatized arrangements by Vulpius or Besler of Walter's responsorial models. It is certain from his *Auferstehungshistorie* that Schütz knew the works of Scandellus, his predecessor in office, and of Rogier Michael. From them came the monodic turn, the depicting of emotions of the Evangelist, Christ, and other soloists in his Passions, and the pronounced dramatization of the *turbae*.

The reason Protestant composers did not contribute more extensively to all the Passion types is probably that Walter's Passions, in their many arrangements and revisions, were in use in congregational worship during the 16th and 17th centuries (partly even in the 18th). Because of their length, voluminous motet Passions by masters like Joachim a Burck, Gesius, Lechner, or Demantius could hardly have been used during the Mass. At most, they could have appeared in Vespers or other supplementary services. Furthermore, their technical demands were too high for school choruses. They were intended for private purposes or for court chapels (Scandellus and R. Michael wrote for the Electoral Chapel in Dresden). The responsorial Passions made no great demand on the performers and could even be abbreviated if necessary. They did not claim to be artistic but were rather a constituent part of the liturgy. If this opinion is correct, it is understandable that Protestant composers would have had little interest in Passions. During the following period, the number of compositions increased because of the rise of the oratorical Passion, a species that was easy to perform, could be utilized for congregational purposes, and was musically interesting, having monodic, concerted, and instrumental elements, ad libitum insertions, and the like.

It was probably for similar reasons that other biblical *historiae* were even less cultivated by Protestants than the Passion. The demand was considerably smaller and the performance requirements were necessarily modest; at best, they could be geared to court chapels. Even though we frequently find a notice in orders of worship that "Histories" were performed, they were usually of the simplest responsorial kind. The musical-historical meaning of *"historia"* (as opposed to the theological meaning) is a composition with a large and coherent biblical narrative, including the Passion; style and form are not part of the definition. The term came into use only near the end of the 16th century and has been used principally in Protestant circles. The Easter story, which was far removed from the Passion, was the only other "History" in this definition to become significant. The Christmas story, too, was used for musical composition, but only in a limited way. Other "Histories" were merely sporadic, isolated cases.

As in the case of the Passion, the story of the Resurrection had as its textual basis Johann Bugenhagen's *Historia des Leidens und der Auferstehung* (1526), a compilation from the four Gospels. This text appears in an anonymous Easter History that originated c. 1550, parallel to Walter's Passions, and came down to us in manuscript. It is based on a specific "Easter tone" and is monodic throughout; only the *turbae* are simple *falsobordone* settings above a cantus firmus in the tenor. Whether or not it was composed by Walter is debatable. Linked with it and next to it in time is the most important Resurrection History produced during the 16th century: the *Österliche Freude der siegreichen und triumphierenden Auferstehung* (Easterly Joy of the Jubilant and Triumphant Resurrection) by Antonius Scandellus (c. 1561? 1568? 1573?). It bears the same relation to the older, anonymous Easter History as Scandellus's Passion according to St. John (1561) bears to Walter's Passions. The recitation tone is retained for the Evangelist exclusively; all other persons are dealt with freely and with varying numbers and combinations of voices. The framing choruses are in five voices. It is of the same mixed type, following the north Italian model, that Scandellus introduced in the Passion. The work must have had a striking success: Johannes Gengenbach printed it in 1591 together with the Passion by Scandellus (no copy is known); Samuel Besler (1612) and O. S. Harnisch (1621) reprinted it. At the close of the 18th century, it was still being sung in St. John's Church in Zittau, and it was the only work of its kind to be translated into Czech (according to D. Haertwig in *MGG* XI, 1963; 1476). The conclusion of Scandellus's Easter History repeatedly includes the exclamation "Victoria!," proclaiming the victory of Christ. This subsequently occurred in Rosthius and later in Heinrich Schütz's Resurrection History, while other Easter Histories used it even in their titles—e.g., the *Triumphus musicus in victoriam resurrectionis* by Benedikt Faber (Coburg, 1621), which has been lost. As with his Passion, Scandellus established a tradition with his Resurrection History. *Die trostreiche Historie von der fröhlichen Auferstehung* by Nikolaus Rosthius (1598, in manuscript) is based on Scandellus, showing in its *turbae* the beginning of the same dramatization that can be observed in the History of the Passion. Easter Histories by A. Finold (Erfurt, 1611), D. Reinisch, and B. Faber have been lost; they probably followed the same trend. With his *Historia der fröhlichen und siegreichen Auferstehung* (1623), Heinrich Schütz adopted the Saxon chapel tradition founded by Scandellus, merely modernizing it to conform with the style of his time. After Schütz, the only Resurrection Histories to come down to us are those by Thomas Selle (*a 8 et 14;* c. 1660) and Christian Andreas Schulze (1686). The first-named work is a freely composed "oratorical" History, leaning closely on Schütz; the second one (according to P. Krause in *MGG* XII, chapter on Chr. A. Schulze) makes use of the Bugenhagen text, avoiding all insertions. Later Resurrection Histories (e.g., by J. Ph. Krieger) are known only from surviving references.

The development of Christmas Histories begins with Rogier Michael; his two closely connected Histories, *Die Empfängnis unseres Herrn . . .* and *Die Geburt unseres Herrn,* both for one to six voices and both composed in 1602, used Scandellus's model, once more for purposes of the Electoral Chapel in Dresden. The first Christmas History with musical instruments (i.e., in concerted style) is in a Breslau manuscript *Historia Nativitatis* (c. 1638); it was a product of the Dresden tradition and anticipated Schütz's *Auferstehungshistorie.* In addition, Tobias Zeutzschner of Breslau composed a Christmas History *a 18* (1649). This series concluded with the *Historia der freuden- und gnadenreichen Geburt Gottes* by Heinrich Schütz (1664), composed again for the Dresden chapel. Here, in a certain sense, the composition of Christmas Histories came to an end; later on its place was taken by Christmas "oratorios."

In relation to other Histories, only widely scattered material exists, e.g., a *Historia de navicula vehente Christum* by Paul Schede (1565) and two Histories dealing with St. John the Baptist by Elias Gerlach (1632) and Ambrosius Beber (beginning of the 17th century). The latter is lost, as is a Pentecost History by Sebastian Knüpfer, *Historia de Missione Spiritus Sancti "a 18,"* which is mentioned in the literature. (For more on this topic, particularly the dissemination of the Histories, their place in church worship, and their relation to the spiritual play, see *Historia* by W. Blankenburg, *MGG* VI, 1957, 465–89).

In the latter third of the 17th century, the composition of all types of *historiae,* like that of the Passion, underwent a transition to the "oratorical History," going beyond the mixed genre which had been created by Scandellus and brought to a kind of conclusion by Schütz. However, as far as is known, this development did not parallel the voluminous creation of Passions. Only when the composition of Histories ceased (c. 1700) and the genre was absorbed into the more comprehensive oratorio (in other words, when action turned into contemplation and the whole complex of biblical narrative composition withdrew from the sphere of the church, finding its way into the concert hall), only then did the most varied Old and New Testament narratives generate renewed interest among Protestant composers. The mixed type of the late 16th and early 17th centuries was the fruit of an endeavor to reconcile liturgical constraint with the drama of changing scenes, and the inviolability of the biblical narrative with the acknowledgment of reality. Here we find the seed of the development of Protestant *historia* and Passion composition up to Bach's St. John and St. Matthew Passions and his Christmas Oratorio, all of which, as it were, stand on the border between *historia* and oratorio. Indeed, the whole history of Protestant church music moved in one direction during the next decades, i.e., in the direction of bringing to life the Word in the reality of this world, in the direction of fusing emotional human personality with divine revelation, in the direction of a passionate reconciliation of the self-conscious ego with the transcendent inaccessibility of God.

The Period of Orthodoxy and Mysticism

Lutheran church music has undergone swift and obvious changes since the 17th century. It has absorbed and utilized the general movements of European music. Even though this took place unevenly, now faster, now slower, now penetratingly, now superficially, it is apparent that Lutheran church music on the whole went along with the times unhesitatingly, never trying to seclude itself from new currents, never becoming dogmatic or restrictive or standardized. The Reformed confessions, being completely devoted to congregational singing, gradually lost their importance in the development of ecclesiastical art music. Only Anglican church music still enjoyed a period of grandeur during the 17th century. The picture presented by Catholic church music is not so uniform. Torn by the split between *prima pratica* and *seconda pratica* that began shortly before 1600, it was inclined, on one hand, to assimilate all methods of secular, theatrical, courtly, and emotional music, resulting in music of breathtaking splendor at the close of the 17th century and in the 18th. On the other hand, it was able to remain in the proven world of the "Palestrina style" and to cultivate a distinct and specifically churchly practice. This practice has never died out, although it leads a more or less epigonous existence. However, the spiritual movements dominating Lutheran faith in the 17th century and the first half of the 18th (i.e., the firm establishment of doctrine in orthodoxy and the vigorous development of a deep piety based on mysticism) gave new incentives to Lutheran music and pointed toward future directions.

The surprising novelties in Lutheran church music from the beginning of the Thirty Years' War are only seemingly the result of a sudden change. The captivating qualities of magnificent euphony, vocal virtuosity, and instrumental effects are only the ripened fruit of a process of growth that began concurrently with the Counter-Reformation and the baroque era. For some decades, the outer veil of older forms covered up what was already in a stage of preparation; as the veil fell around 1620, it became apparent that something new had developed. No spiritual break affected Protestant church music at that time, and nothing took place that had not been prepared long before.

As early as the beginning of the baroque era, but very definitely since the appearance of the high baroque phase around 1620, chorale arrangements recede in favor of free composition. Only in the late baroque era did they again come into prominence (with the exception of organ music). Biblical texts, prayer and devotional texts of all kinds, as well as religious lyrics in ever increasing measure (a few of the latter appeared as hymns in congregational songbooks) were composed freely in huge quantities for all imaginable combinations of parts. This opened the way for a cleavage between congregational singing and art music. The new techniques of composition—the recitative and arioso solo strongly accentuated by emotionalism, the concerted style contrasting with traditional counterpoint, the colorful sensuality of sound, and the pathos-laden expressive gestures —all contributed increasingly to an estrangement between contemporary art music and congregational experience. It cannot be denied that a certain demand for culture and representation entered Lutheran music. Just how many of the compositions of that era could be regarded as strictly churchly in the congregational sense, and how many as more or less informal devotional music, must remain an open question. The richness of color, the new compositional techniques, and the freedom of artistic shaping affected the music of the period. Everything was designed to display sensuous abundance, thrilling expression, dramatic power, graphic images. High baroque Italy supplied the means, Lutheranism the ideas. And thus the captivating drama was unfolded: Protestant musicians, standing firmly in their own tradition, reforged the formal tools of secular and sacred Italian music and created out of the Lutheran spirit music that became the sound of the Lutheran faith.

The period appears to be contradictory and confused, for in sharp contrast to the splendor of royal courts there was the misery of universal decline. Only for a short time could the princes maintain adequate chapel forces; soon they too were drawn into the whirlpool of the depression. The expense of maintaining musical forces had increased considerably since the last decades of the 16th century, and only a few courts were able to pay for professionally trained singers, instrumentalists, and the necessary equipment. At the same time, the old organization of church music deteriorated more and more. By the late 16th century there were unending complaints about the decline of Latin-school choirs, the *Kantoreien,* and all the other institutions promoting church music. War quickly destroyed whatever remained. The increasing demand for small vocal ensembles and for solo performances is striking proof of the decline within the organization. Following the years after 1630, foreign control of court orchestras by Italian virtuosi rapidly increased. Thus, a dissension grew regarding performance technique; foreign professional musicians were performing refined art music at the courts, while the congregation had to be satisfied in most cases with what school choirs were still able to offer—for the most part, music in the *stylus antiquus* (see below). About 1615 Praetorius and Schütz, in Kassel, Dresden, and Wolfenbüttel, were writing ambitious works for large ensembles, but in the twenties these three court chapels were already rapidly declining. From 1633 to 1645, Schütz was more active in Copenhagen than in Germany. In 1640 the court chaplain in Dresden, Hoë von Hohenegg, made this bitter complaint: "Almost nothing can be presented polyphonically since no good alto is available and there is only one discant." About 1620 Johann Hermann Schein, Michael Altenburg, Michael Praetorius, Johann Staden, and many other composers could still declare that music had reached such heights that on earth it prepared the way for the choirs of heaven: one doubted whether it could climb any higher. This optimism was quickly followed by a setback. War, pestilence, plundering, conflagrations, and universal impoverishment caused the destruction of chapels, libraries, and musical centers. What is remarkable is that the creative work of musicians and the distribution of their printed works continued unabated. The 17th century was the grand period of printed Protestant church music. It is no less remarkable that new life soon blossomed on the ruins. Wherever destruction ceased and prosperity grew again, church musicians immediately displayed intense activity. The Westphalian Peace Treaty, enthusiastically greeted by the composers with *Fried-, Freud- und Jubelgeschrei* (J. R. Ahle, 1650, for fifteen, twenty, and twenty-four voices, and more) stabilized to some degree at least the Protestant territories and an equality of rights, although re-Catholicization was carried out with cruel force in Hapsburg-dominated countries, in some parts of Silesia, and in many smaller areas. From 1653, a Corpus Evangelicorum, recognized by statute, represented the interests of Protestantism in the Imperial Diets.

The situation within the inner confines of the church was as contradictory as the musical picture. Although the great war centered on the "to be or not to be" of Protestantism, it was not able to overcome the quarrels of different theological factions. Differences between Lutheranism and Calvinism became more aggravated. "Life and doctrine are falling apart; a vacuum of piety becomes noticeable" (Zeller). Those interested in theological reform aimed at compromise. Rupertus Meldenius, about 1626, coined the formula: "In essentials, unity; in nonessentials, liberty; in both of them, charity." A short time later, Nicolaus Hunnius of Lübeck submitted his paper on reconciliation to King Gustavus Adolphus and to Elector Johann Georg I of Saxony. The learned bishop of the Bohemian church Johann Amos Comenius, the powerful preacher and "founder" of Pietism Philipp Jakob Spener, Elector Friedrich Wilhelm of Brandenburg, and others carried on their attempts at settlement. But even a peace-loving man like Paul Gerhardt was too deeply involved in orthodox thinking to submit to the irenic aspirations of the Great Elector, and he accepted the dismissal from his Berlin position in 1666 rather than bow to the Tolerance Edict of 1663. Georg Calixt, the Helmstedt scholar, had to yield to the attack of orthodox theologians; Abraham Calov of Wittenberg, Johann Hülsemann, and Georg Quenstedt led the subsequent syncretism dispute. "Lutheranism has reached the lowest level of its development" (Karl Müller). At the same time that polemics reached their lowest level, a tendency arose in Lutheran orthodoxy, partly fostered by the same men and based on strong convictions, to strengthen anew the old fundamental doctrines: the doctrine of justification and the principle of adherence to Scripture. Some scholars like Calixt were prepared to negotiate and make concessions to Catholicism and to ecclesiastic opposition. They would have approved at least partially the doctrine of justification through works alongside that of justification by faith alone, and would have confined their idea of scriptural principle to certain basic biblical writings. However, orthodoxy moved toward an uncompromising and extremist interpretation of doctrine, conferring "on Lutheran dogma a degree of self-containment it had never known before" (Holl).

Alongside their newly established doctrine, soon driven to the rigidity of mere formulas, these very same men (e.g., Spener and Paul Gerhardt) often developed a new sense of piety, a feeling of deepened personal contact between God and man. These trends were obviously contradictory, but nevertheless the newly felt piety permeated all life; Johann Arnd's *Wahres Christentum* (True Christianity; first published in 1605) became the most popular book of the century. There was no attempt to upset the sacramental foundation, and the acts and forms of worship remained unchanged. But private devotions and pious contemplations were held in ever increasing esteem. In the case of Spener, "the absolute priority of personal piety could lead to a disregard, and even rejection, of the churchly concept of piety" (Zeller). In keeping with Luther's attitude, orthodoxy firmly adhered to the canon that preaching was the only legitimate agency of the divine Word, and that the rites of the church were the only authentic preparation for justification. Conversely, however, the doors were opened again, especially by Arnd, to ancient motifs of a mystical nature, and the feeling asserted itself that the individual could attain union with God also by means of active piety, devotional contemplation, and immersion in prayer. Even orthodoxy conceded the ancient doctrine of *unio mystica*—the mysterious, almost corporeal union of the person "reborn" in Christ through the experience of justification, giving it the new name "doctrine of indwelling." The deluge of prayer books, devotional tracts, and hymnals seem to indicate the great need for literature of spiritual edification and contemplation. The "consciousness of personal Christianity" and the "challenge of a cognizant conversion" (Holl) formed the foundation of a new tender, loving relation of the ego to God. The "close attention to one's own self" led to a new frame of mind, to a novel encounter with God and the universe. The self-conscious ego, responsible only to itself, sought its own concept of God and the universe, thereby seceding from the community to which, in Luther's opinion, the individual must always feel himself bound; it even became antagonistic to it. The individual's own will determined his relation to God and community. Never in the history of Lutheranism has there been so much talk about the ego and its inwardness as in this century of orthodoxy and mysticism. Here were the roots of the rich religious lyricism of the age and its new music. What really mattered was the personal experience, and it was this attitude, as in the case of Jakob Böhme, that grew into a conscious renunciation of one's own will so that it could undergo a transformation into the divine will. It is with these "initial attempts to bring about a more effective development of personal life and a community depending mainly on it," that the remoteness to Calvinism was mitigated: "It seems that the gulf should be overcome by beginning with the practical reshaping of everyday life" (Karl Müller). The *praxis pietatis* became a fundamental demand of human life. The inner contrasts remained unchanged: even at the close of the century, the most inveterate orthodox preachers such as Neumeister or Elmenhorst were the most tenderhearted poets of exuberant lyrics; the Rostock professor Heinrich Müller wrote belligerent homiletic tracts and, at the same time, *Hours of Spiritual Relaxation; Celestial Flame of Love, or Ten Spiritual Love Songs;* and *Spiritual Soul Music, consisting of ten homilies* (1659–73). It was precisely this inner conflict that became decisive in the realm of music.

The coexistence of orthodoxy and mysticism had in its wake a coexistence of congregational faith in the church and in the piety of the individual soul. Both could be found in one and the same person, the contrasts being overcome by the *praxis pietatis* of daily life. The contrast resulted in strong inner tensions discharging themselves in lyrical poetry and music, but it did not affect fundaments, nor did it yet lead to indifference or emancipation. At the time, however, the ideal of an all-embracing congregation, linked exclusively to the means of grace proffered by the church (the only prerequisites of justification), gradually receded. Preparatory steps were taken to establish smaller religious communities which, later on, were founded by Spener and by A. H. Francke, and received their final and characteristic expression in Zinzendorf's "Brotherhoods" *(Unitates fratrum).* Also contributing to the slow disintegration of congregational unity were the differentiation and isolation of the classes, the increasing separation of nobility and middle class, of clergy and laity. The church itself, acquiring the status of a state church and being subjected especially after the Thirty Years' War to a strong-willed princely absolutism, became frozen in its traditional doctrines and ceremonies; it lacked the will to satisfy the longing for active piety and a deepening of individual life in a Christian spirit. Although it still ruled over the believer, it had lost his soul. The second attempt to reshape Lutheran piety must be viewed from this background. It was put into action when Philipp Jakob Spener founded the "Collegia pietatis" (1670) and wrote his *Pia desideria* (Pious Desires; 1675). It is significant that these *Pia desideria* were originally designed as a preface to a new edition of Johann Arnd's *Wahres Christentum.*

Medieval mysticism poured in a broad stream over devotional literature even before the end of the 16th century. Much of the Lutheran religious movement can be traced back to it. A different approach, led by Paracelsus and his "nature mysticism," had some influence and found its extreme formulation in Jakob Böhme's spiritualism. Protestant devotional mysticism rotated mainly around the theme of a "bridal union" with Christ, which became a "Sabbath of the soul" after death. To strive for this "bridal union" was the highest goal of the Christian. The concept gave rise to the death-wish mood that pervaded the whole literature of the period and found its most forceful expression in Bach's cantatas. The basic publication was Arnd's *Wahres Christentum,* which was reprinted innumerable times from 1605 to the beginning of the 20th century. Johann Gerhard followed in Arnd's footsteps with his *Schola pietatis* (1622–23). Rather than a lively devotional book, it is a strict dogmatic guide to "devotional contemplation"; a copy of it was found in J. S. Bach's library. The church produced preachers like Gerhard and the orthodox theologians Johann Valentin Andreae in Württemberg, Tarnow, Quistorp, and Grossgebauer in Rostock, and many others who already were imbued with the spirit of the new piety and who, beginning from there, aspired to a reform of the entire life of the church. Hymn writing, already abounding in "love of Jesus" themes during the preceding period, received another strong impetus. Following the example of Philipp Nicolai—who, even before Arnd, must be regarded as a forerunner of the new piety during the time of Opitz—the poetry of the Fruit-bearing Society and the Society of Pegnitz Shepherds soon turned to the Arcadian, coquettish, languishingly tender, and dolorously sentimental songs of such poets as Johann Heermann, Valerius Herberger, Johann Rist, and Heinrich Müller. Their contemporary Paul Fleming, in contrast, was a much stronger personality. The classic hymn writer of the period was Paul Gerhardt, in whom "orthodoxy and the church life of his time became life in its true fulfillment and strength" (Müller), but who was nevertheless able to feel and describe the enchantment of the *unio mystica.*

The well-established forms of church discipline, doctrine, and traditional liturgy, all of them permeated by overwhelming piety and an intoxicating immersion in the *unio mystica*—these were the spiritual conditions under which musicians of the period worked. Political conditions could not have been more insecure. War and confessional disputes disorganized all civic order. The church was torn up into many territorially separated shreds, each of which had its own church administration, its own liturgy, its own hymnbook, and even its own confessional writing. Spiritual and political tensions increased and ties of custom and convention dissolved as the chronological distance from Luther grew, and as the new century became more imbued with the new piety, its individual perception of God, its ecstatic self-consciousness, and its increasing assertion of the personality. The unity of the Lutheran church became more and more a thing of the past; not all the severity of orthodox dogmas and church discipline could prevent the musicians from saturating themselves and their music with the spirit of an individualistic perception of God. Their compositions now became chiefly an expression of their creeds and their innermost feelings. Regulations had only local validity, calling for restraint in the use of "songs imported from Italy, in which the biblical texts are torn and hacked up into small pieces by fast runs through the gullet," as well as restraint in the all-too-frequent displays of virtuosity on the part of the organists. These attempts at restriction met with little success. When rulers intervened, they were content to incorporate the church organization into the framework of the state; they hardly ever paid any attention to liturgy and music. From around 1630, official hymnbooks came into use (Hesse-Darmstadt, Saxony, Württemberg, Brunswick-Calenberg); very slowly it became the custom, prohibited heretofore, to permit the congregational use of hymnbooks in the service. On the whole, neither secular nor church authorities hampered or fostered the activity of church musicians to any extent worth mentioning.

Orthodoxy and mysticism are the keys for understanding music of that era. With the revived and intensified emphasis on the scriptural principle, biblical texts necessarily became increasingly the subjects for composition. Taking for granted that every word, even every letter of Holy Writ, was "inspired," the duty devolved upon the composer to mold each word in his composition according to the proper form and conceptual meaning. By the same token, textual emphasis had to be apportioned meaningfully between words and sentences; a uniform through-composed text, as was customary in the 16th century, would have been regarded as obsolete. Special emphasis had to be placed on the facts of salvation and their annunciation, as well as on the tenets of belief and justification. These new needs were met at the right time by the influx of Italian concerted and emotion-laden music. It is instructive to note in Burckhard Grossmann's collection *Angst der Höllen und Friede der Seelen* (1623) how Psalm 116 was dealt with by sixteen composers; each made use in an individual way of a strongly emotional *stile madrigalesco,* yet each had similar intentions and used similar accents. Their common confessional medium was the biblical saying "I believe, therefore I speak." In the era of the Counter-Reformation descriptive music had already, at least in part, become an elucidative, interpretative art. Now it frequently became exegesis, even sermon. The musician faced the congregation not as one from their midst but rather as an independent herald and biblical interpreter, a personality as opposed to the masses. Music forgot to say "we"; it said "I," preaching by virtue of its own power. The orthodox clergy again emphasized that the sermon was the focal point of the service; Michael Praetorius, filled with self-confident pride, placed *cantio* (song) and *contio* (sermon) side by side as having equal status. In music, dogmatic rigidity in the orthodox doctrines joined with ego-conscious piety, and the individual soul emerged as the moving force. It proclaimed its experience of God. The soul (palpably represented as an allegorical figure, from Hammerschmidt to Bach) sang forth its lament and its jubilation in tones of fervent passion, in gestures of heavy pathos. Its pangs of death, the sweetness of its love for Jesus, the agony of its consciousness of guilt, and the heavenly bliss of the *unio mystica:* all these emotions were translated into gripping tones. Whenever other words were added to the biblical text, they were preferably poems expressing these very sentiments with an increased intensity, or else they were mystical and ecstatic "devotional texts" from the devotional literature of the latter part of the 16th century. The *Manuale Divi Augustini,* originating in Counter-Reformation circles, was also widely used by Protestant musicians like Schütz and Buxtehude. Such texts found a place in Lutheran worship—for example, as music for Holy Communion. People of this high Baroque era, buffeted by the most extreme contrasts, shaken by all the fevers of passionate sensuality and painful self-torture, found an elemental outlet for their inner tensions in church music much more than in secular music. To be sure, this high degree of tension already contained the germ of abatement. Emotional art, driven to extremes, quickly deteriorated with many musicians into virtuoso superficiality, into formalistic mannerism, even into shaky schematism. It stands to reason that the more subjective the music became, the more its leading representatives divorced themselves from the mere imitators and epigones. Only the greatest among them had the ability to manipulate the newly acquired style media for accomplishing an important task. The minor masters often carried equipment which was overwhelming in its impressive splendor. However, one must not overlook the fact that at the end of the 17th century the eruptive power of the Baroque outlook on life had already faded away. Pendantry and circumspection had taken the place of elemental experience. According to Augustin Pfeiffer, whose *Antimelancholicus* (1683) was part of J. S. Bach's library, edification was the "expeller of melancholy" (Zeller).

THE LATIN MOTET AND THE PRINTED COLLECTIONS:

STYLISTIC DIVISIONS

Lasso had paved the way in Germany for a music of personal expression. An extensive Lasso School came into being, its activities including Swabia and Prussia, Silesia and Schleswig-Holstein. Its adherents, in both a narrower and wider sense, included Joachim a Burck, Gallus Dressler, Jakob Meiland, Leonhard Schröter, Johann Steuerlein, Georg Otto and other Kassel composers, Gregor Lange, Hieronymus Praetorius, Philipp Dulichius, Bartholomäus Gesius,

Rogier Michael, Adam Gumpelzhaimer, Gregor Aichinger (originally Protestant, later a convert), Andreas Raselius, Johannes Eccard, and many others. Also under the spell of the Lasso School were masters like Hans Leo Hassler, Melchior Franck, and the "conquerors of Lasso followers" (A. A. Abert): Leonhard Lechner and Michael Praetorius. Although motets (especially Latin motets) and the related types of church or sacred music were produced in great number, the highly individual stamp given them by Lasso gradually leveled off. The history of the Protestant motet from about 1570 to 1630 is still unwritten. It would show how both the immediate and later Lasso schools affiliated themselves with a second trend, resulting in an increasingly shallow stream of motets, predominantly Latin.

After the 1580s Italian elements found their way into Germany in ever increasing measure. On the secular plane this came about mainly through the cultivation of music by the courts and upper-class citizens. Next to the Hapsburg courts and the smaller German free cities, Munich, Augsburg, and Nuremberg had an especially large part in this trend. In the case of church music, Augsburg and Nuremberg again, along with the Schulpforta princely school (Thuringia), were entrance points. A close musical connection existed between Schulpforta and the Leipzig *Thomasschule.* Somewhat later, other schools encouraged the more recent styles of Italian music: in the Catholic realm, especially southern German Jesuit institutions, and in Protestant territories the Lutheran Latin school. However, even before these schools and the language of the *affetti* (the art of individual and symbolic expression) became influential, an astonishingly wide stream of motets and related compositions poured out over Germany from Italy. In the last decade of the 16th century, a separation of style occurred in Italy between *prima pratica* and *seconda pratica* (Claudio Monteverdi's expressions). The traditional *stylus antiquus* (the older style of polyphonic motets and Masses) was superseded by the *stylus modernus* manifested in the "concerto," in the madrigal for solo voice, in solo recitative and arioso, and finally in all musical species stressing emotion. It was at this time that Protestant Germany began to take over the enormous heritage of such Italian *prima pratica* music: motets and, to a smaller degree, Masses, Magnificats, hymns, and so forth, including many, usually large, printed collections. Friedrich Lindner's many printed collections (Nuremberg, 1585–91) continued to offer indiscriminately works by Netherlanders, Romans, Venetians, Germans, older and younger masters, giving preference to large ensembles (six to twelve voices). Lindner followed the Dresden, Schulpforta, and Leipzig tradition and put together in seventeen manuscript choirbooks (Nuremberg, 1574–97) what is probably the most comprehensive German collection of Masses, motets, hymns, Mass selections, and so on, in the *prima pratica* style. The choirbooks contain compositions from Isaac and Walter to Aichinger and Hans Leo Hassler (cf. W. H. Rubsamen, *The International "Catholic" Repertoire* in *Annales musicologiques* V, 1957, 229–327). Similar works are the *Harmoniae miscellae,* a printed collection edited by Leonhard Lechner in Nuremberg (1583) and the three volumes of *Symphoniae sacrae* (1598–1613) by Kaspar Hassler, the brother of Hans Leo Hassler. In 1603, the Schulpforta cantor, Erhard Bodenschatz, published a collection entitled *Florilegium selectissimarum cantionum,* which seems in general to contain the repertory used by his predecessor and teacher, Calvisius. A revised edition appeared with the date 1618 and the title *Florilegium Portense;* together with the second part (1621), it has had a permanent place in Protestant churches and schools. Between 1720 and 1740, J. S. Bach, then in Leipzig, requisitioned new copies of this work several times. The last edition probably dates back to 1747. Another *Florilegium selectissimorum hymnorum,* also edited by Bodenschatz, is a revision of the 1594 hymn settings by Seth Calvisius; there were innumerable editions of this publication between 1606 and 1777. It contains 271 compositions by 89 composers (and a few of unknown origin) among whom are Lasso, Gallus, Hassler, H. Praetorius, Calvisius, and Bodenschatz; the Italians are in the majority: Viadana, Agazzari, the two Gabrielis, T. Massaini, older masters like Costanzo Porta and Orfeo Vecchi, and many others (the second part contains many works by Martin Roth, the Schulpforta cantor). *Florilegium Portense* has, for one-and-a-half centuries, furnished most of the musical material used by large churches in their minor services. The ensemble, in most cases, consists of eight voices, and the character of the collection is generally conservative, even retrospective. Evidently, there was no interest as yet for the polychoral concerto in the style of Giovanni Gabrieli or for the smaller concerted ensemble in the style of Viadana or his followers (such as Agazzari, Naldi, and O. Durante), although compositions of that kind had been available in large editions since 1600. G. Gabrieli, Marenzio, and Ingegneri are represented, but only with compositions in the old style; Monteverdi and Grandi do not appear. The voluminous *Promptuarium* of Abraham Schadaeus (Leipzig, Torgau), comprising four volumes (1611–17), also contains five- to eight-voice motets with a large array of Italians in addition to a limited number of Germans. Stylistically, this work is still entirely committed to the 16th century. Both the *Florilegium* and the *Promptuarium* were later provided with a thoroughbass, the latter with one by Kaspar Vincentius.

The Lasso School and the Italian *prima pratica* entered into a close union in Protestant Germany. The aftereffects of this music are clearly noticeable in the motet compositions of the great masters—for instance, in Hassler's *Cantiones sacrae* (1601), Schein's *Cymbalum Sionium* (1615), Scheidt's *Cantiones sacrae* (1620), and even in the compositions of Schütz and Hammerschmidt; nor should it be overlooked that this motet literature remained in constant use until the middle of the 18th century, along with "modern" music. That holds true of Leipzig, as well as of Nuremberg, Lübeck, Hamburg, and other cities. The consequential division in style did not originate with Protestant church music, but was taken over from Italy; the effects, however, were the same in both countries.

Knowledge of Italian music in the *stylus antiquus* grew in Germany through numerous printed collections and through trips for study in Italy by many German composers, who undertook these more frequently after the Italian journeys of Meiland and the two Hassler brothers. As in Italy, this style was used simultaneously with the *stylus modernus*. As quickly and extensively as the Germans became acquainted with the *stylus antiquus,* so reluctant were they to accept species and forms in the new style, and even more reluctant to face the problems presented by recent Italian music. Although Victorinus and Donfried in Catholic southern Germany began to publish collections of music for small performing groups and although many of Viadana's works were published from 1609 to 1626 in Germany (Frankfurt on the Main), Protestant collections still adhered to the old line. Georg Vintzius (Naumburg) published a large collection of Masses (Erfurt, 1630), one-third of which consisted of Italian compositions for Protestant usage; in spite of the use of thoroughbass throughout, these Masses adhered more to the *stile antico* than to the *stile nuovo.*

The reluctance of German Protestant composers can be explained partly by the technical demands of performance, without which the new species could not be mastered and the prerequisites of which were not everywhere available. There were also textual difficulties and a certain inertia. The new species required well-prepared solos and soloistic performances, a mastery of the art of improvised embellishment, instrumental obbligatos and at times truly virtuoso playing, a thoroughbass, and frequently very large ensembles. Already at this point, the possibilities for performance created divisions. Apparently, exacting concerted works could be performed during the whole Baroque era only by court orchestras and large city churches; more modest groups had to restrict themselves to those works in the new *stile moderno* written for small ensembles or to motet compositions in the *stile antico,* all of which were within the grasp of average Latin-school choirs. Textual difficulties arose from the fact that the Italian art song (recitative or arioso) had developed from "poesia per musica." There was no equivalent in Protestant poetry of the early 17th century, at least not within the framework of divine worship. Hence, soloistic vocal music of a religious nature could be introduced easily as sacred chamber music but only with great difficulty as music for congregational worship. A special problem in regard to the use of new Italian music was the hymn: the texts were closely connected with their traditional melodies, and a technique of composition based on a cantus firmus was diametrically opposed to concerted or melodically emotional music. How slowly the German composers adopted the thoroughbass is quite evident from the instructions of M. Praetorius, G. Aichinger, Chr. Demantius, J. Staden, H. Albert, and so on, about its requirements. First, treble-singers had to be trained in the new technique of ornamentation. As with numerous Italian teachers, this was the first concern of M. Praetorius (in his writings and in his last musical works; his projected treatise on the subject was never published), A. Herbst, Chr. Bernhard, and others. From Schein to Bach the required instrumental apparatus could not be fully supplied by the municipal bands; pupils and students had to be commandeered as assistants, and this created endless complications. Only the court orchestras were properly qualified to meet all demands. Not without reason did J. S. Bach, in his memorandum of August 23, 1730, on conditions in Leipzig, cite the Electoral orchestra of Dresden as exemplary. Finally, from the beginning the Protestant German thought it unbefitting worship and doctrine to express one's innermost feelings in musical language. Controversies about the place of "operatic" music in church were rampant from the early 17th century to Bach's time and beyond. Even in Bach's own time and environment, this kind of music met with strong opposition.

With such difficulties, it was only with great effort that German composers

50. Johann Hermann Schein, five-voice dirge *Seligkeit, Fried, Freud und Ruh* on the death of his daughter Susanna-Sidonia (August 21, 1623) in the *Cantional oder Gesangbuch Augsburgischer Konfession,* Leipzig, 1627. Published by the composer.

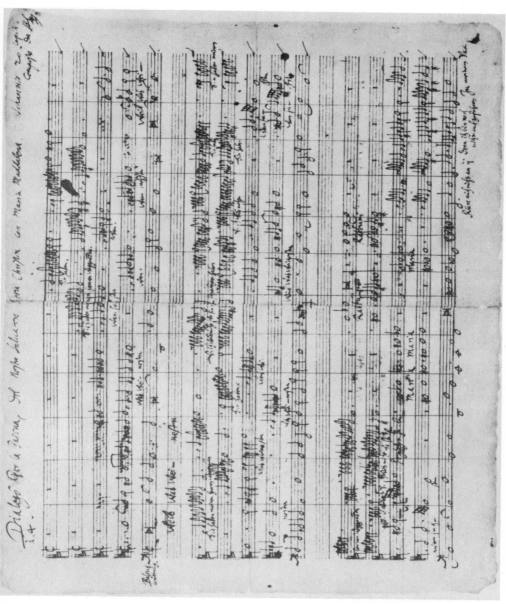

51. Heinrich Schütz, first page of the dialogue for Easter *Weib, was weinest du?* SWV 443, autograph. Kassel, Murhardsche Bibliothek der Stadt Kassel und Landesbibliothek, Mus. MS fol. 49 x [2].

opened the way to acceptance of the new Italian style. They accomplished it partly by compromise (as often with M. Praetorius), partly by spirited aggressiveness (Schein on certain occasions), until the genius of Heinrich Schütz found a way to the perfect union of foreign and native developments. The easiest breakthrough came with music for small ensemble, the so-called *Kleine geistliche Konzert* (two, three, rarely four voices with thoroughbass). It followed the style of the pure Italian model, and was usually interspersed with some degree of counterpoint. Later on it also displayed signs of "affected" monody, particularly with Schütz and his disciples. It became the most popular species of the 17th century; no other could compare with it in quantity. Where extensive musical facilities were available, the concerto for large ensemble was quickly adopted at the beginning of the century (two, three, four, and more instrumental and vocal choruses with solo voices and thoroughbass). It used a polychoral setting, following the *concerto per choros* of Giovanni Gabrieli; however, it never reached the gigantic dimensions of the "colossal Roman style" of Mazzochi, Agostini, Benevoli, and so on. With the hardships brought on by the Thirty Years' War, it finally yielded before the universally reduced personnel of the chapels, although remnants were in evidence up to the time of Knüpfer, Herbst, Buxtehude, and even Bach. "Affected" monody in the style of Monteverdi, which was adopted most slowly, found full expression first in Schein's later works (*Opella nova* II, 1627) and then with Schütz only after he had passed the height of his creativity (*Kleine geistliche Konzerte* I, 1636). In other words, it found expression in Germany when it had already reached its second stage in Italy, where a distinction between recitative and arioso singing was being made, and the bel canto style was beginning to be cultivated. These three newly accepted Italian styles were never clearly differentiated in Germany. Michael Praetorius and others show in many examples (Praetorius, for instance, in his *Polyhymnia caduceatrix*, 1619, and *Urania*, 1613) that small and polychoral concertos could be identical and that the one might be developed from the other. The *concerto per choros* was frequently stirred up with emotion, leaning at times toward dramatic vocal solos (as early as 1619 in the *Psalmen Davids* of Schütz and later in his early Dresden concertos for more than one choir). In the solo concerto for small ensemble, however, the concerted and monodic emotional styles merged (see Schein, *Opella nova* I, 1618). A comparatively unadulterated, affect-laden monody appeared for the first time at a very late date (see above). In German church music, all three species were merged with remnants of the *stylus antiquus*. Counterpoint was in the German blood (even Mattheson called Germany "the true land of the fugue") and the mentality steeped in counterpoint disliked the new style, which it found too theatrical or emotional. Nowhere in Germany during that period was there the wholesale discard of counterpoint that took place in *seconda pratica* Italy. The terminology of the period was unstable: "concerto," "motetto," "sinfonia," "cantio sacra," "concentus," "Gesänglein," and other such expressions did not indicate specific species; clearly defined types—the vocal solo, for example—were rarely called by their simple name. As a rule, they appeared under splendorous, allegorical-symbolic titles: *Lyra Davidica, Specchio d'amore, Confect der Liebe, Kreuzrute* (all of these appeared in Schein's works). Often the ornate, flowery titles of printed works from the first half of the 17th century even indicated the intermingling of species: *Fontana d'Israel, Israelsbrünnlein auserlesener Kraftsprüche alten und neuen Testaments. Auf eine sonderbar anmutige italianmadrigalische Manier* (Fountain of Israel: The Little Spring of Israel Chosen from Mighty Proverbs in the Old and New Testaments. In a Strange and Curious Italian-Madrigal Style; Schein, 1623); *Kronenkrönlein oder musikalischer Vorläufer, auf geistliche Concert-, Madrigal-, Dialog-, Melod-, Symphon-Motettische Manier* (The Kingdom's Crown or Musical Harbinger: Sacred Motets in the Style of Concertos, Madrigals, Dialogues, Monodies, and Symphonies; Stephan Otto, 1648); *Himmelsüsse Jesusfreude . . . durch schöne Konzertlein und Arien* (The Heaven-sweet Joy of Jesus . . . in Lovely Little Concertos and Arias; J.R. Ahle, 1648; these are two-voice settings with the text below a thoroughbass, hence performable as a *tricinium* but "auch nach Belieben ohne Fundament," i.e., also as an old-style *bicinium*). Hammerschmidt still called the five parts of his *Musikalische Andachten* (1639–53) partly concertos, partly madrigals, symphonies, or motets. On the other hand, one cannot tell by the title that *Symphonien auf Concertenmanier* (Scheidt, 1644) means instrumental works to be played "as a prelude before concertos, motets, or sacred madrigals with instruments."

Taking into account all factors that acted on Lutheran composers of the period, we can see that they were open to new trends without breaking ties with the old. Thus, they avoided isolating their art from developments in Europe. They also avoided the enormous division into *stylus antiquus* and *stylus modernus* which was leaving its imprint on Italian music and would later affect German Catholic church music. In 1648, Heinrich Schütz made the following statement: "It is true that the concerted style of composing on a basso continuo came to us in Germany from Italy, that we appreciated it very much, and that it attracted more followers than had anything else in the past." But "the indispensable prerequisite to a well-constructed composition, without which not a single composition of an experienced composer can exist," is to hold strictly to Roman rules of counterpoint and style (Schütz, without mentioning the name, was referring to Marco Scacchi). These must be learned under "similarly trained Italian, and other, older and newer classic authors." In effect, this meant to hold to a tradition that could be relaxed and enriched through the use of the new Italian musical devices—thoroughbass, concerted textures, and obbligato instruments—but that must remain the "foundation," the "hard nut" that budding German composers should "crack." (Indeed, the tradition was revived by no other than Schütz, who made use of all these devices, and remarked, "This style of church music without basso continuo is not always even.") His "well-meant admonition" lay at the basis of a whole system of thought. It explains why Lutheran church music of the 17th century clung so long to tradition, progressively rejuvenating it and adapting it to the changing styles of the times. It is this "foundation" that was the basis of J.S. Bach's development.

MICHAEL PRAETORIUS, J. HERMANN SCHEIN, SAMUEL SCHEIDT, AND HEINRICH SCHÜTZ

Whereas Hans Leo Hassler usually adhered to the Italian (especially the Venetian) *prima pratica* in his religious works, Michael Praetorius was already modifying the polychoral setting of the old style to conform with the *variatio per choros* in his early work, the *Musarum Sioniarum Motectae et Psalmi* (1607; first edition 1606 or perhaps 1603). The tendency is apparent to a surprisingly high degree in the modern style of his late works. Concerted elements appear in the earlier two- and three-voice settings of volume IX of his *Musae Sioniae* (1610); there are also some isolated uses of thoroughbass, an initial attempt that seems peculiarly primitive. He deviated from the genuine polyphony of the motet to the more porous texture interspersed with rests that Viadana used in his *Concerti ecclesiasti* (first edition, 1602). The chorale in Praetorius is treated less as a cantus firmus and more as a group of motifs to be tossed about in a "concerted" play of voices. This was a deliberate innovation. Praetorius himself clearly differentiated between "Muteten-Art," "madrigalischer Art," and a third sort invented by himself permitting the chorale to run through the whole passage in one voice as cantus firmus, with the other two voices treating a single line (and always the same one) of the chorale in counterpoint. This third type anticipated a technique of chorale treatment use by organists and later on by all masters of the 17th century. As for the "madrigal" variety, the concerted technique as developed by the north Italian school of Viadana (cf. R.

Michael Praetorius: *Musae Sioniae* IX,1610.3 Choraltricinien
a) "motettisch"

b) "madrigalisch" (concerted)

c) Tenor with cantus firmus, the other two voices with the same motif throughout the whole piece

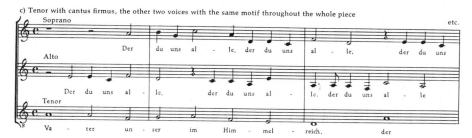

Haas, *Barock,* pp. 38 ff. and 75 ff.) was merged with the German *tricinium* style as represented by George Rhau's collection of 1542. In his late works Praetorius increased the dimensions of concerted writing, particularly in his *Polyhymnia caduceatrix* (1617), a collection of mostly choral concertos for large ensembles in which every imaginable choral, solo, and instrumental effect appears. There is a surprising abundance of contrasting sounds between instrumental and vocal choirs, including instrumental ritornellos with vocal passages, virtuoso vocal solos, idiomatic use of instruments, thoroughbass—all this combined with a variability of setting adapted as the occasion demands and a fertile imagination can supply. The *Polyhymnia* was contemporary with Schütz's *Psalmen Davids,* with which it is closely related; both probably are indebted to the same raison d'être. Arno Forchert has pointed out that Praetorius, who was never in Italy, must have studied the concertos of Fattorini (1602), Giacobbi (1609), Viadana (1612), and Agazzari (1613), perhaps also Monteverdi's Vespers (1610). The whole brilliant apparatus of Giovanni Gabrieli's late concertos was transplanted here to the Protestant realm. Yet the spirit of the music remained as before. The musical framework was still the chorale, the representative of Scripture. Parts of the edifice and their decoration were changed, but the concerted technique did not change the basic structure of the lied motets of the Counter-Reformation. This explains why the new stylistic devices for text expression were given such gingerly treatment in spite of all other modernizations. Expressive elements appropriate to Italian music were pushed to the background by Praetorius; the chorale dominated, intelligible to all in spite of its high Baroque accouterments. There were only differences of degree, not of character, between his chorale motets, the three-voice settings from *Musae* IX, and the pomp of the *Polyhymnia.* In spite of his acceptance of new Italian styles (he himself gave an explicit account of all he knew and studied), Praetorius nevertheless remained a representative of old Lutheran convictions to the end of his career. To be sure, he initiated a new stylistic phase in Protestant church music; yet he held himself entirely aloof from the mystical currents of the new century. His last two printed works (*Polyhymnia exercitatrix,* 1619; *Puericinium,* 1621) did not follow the new currents either; they were written for school choirs and are textbooks dealing with Italian vocal virtuosity as adapted to Lutheran chorale settings. Only once, in his setting of Psalm 116 for Burckhard Grossmann's *Angst der Höllen* (printed posthumously in 1623), did Praetorius make use of the expressive mannerisms of the *seconda pratica.* It was probably his last work; it has completely independent instrumental voices but no vocal solos in monodic style. He far surpassed his contemporaries—Christoph Demantius, Otto

Siegfried Harnisch, Melchior Vulpius, and many others—not only in volume but also in the versatility and originality with which he used the various stylistic resources.

The new Italian concerted style entered Protestant church music without directing musical expression to new ends or altering the functional concept of music. These fundamental changes were first felt in the activities of three masters to whom W. K. Printz referred in his *Historische Beschreibung* (1690) as the three big S's of his century: Johann Hermann Schein, Samuel Scheidt, and Heinrich Schütz. Like the huge number of lesser composers of the period, they were fully conscious of the stylistic schisms, which they tried to overcome through the synthesis recommended by Schütz; however, they were not aware of the other discrepancy, which resulted from their unchanging, orthodox way of thinking and their immersion in the mysticism of their time. What poets from Fleming to Tersteegen were saying in their ecstatic verses was as little contrary to inherited Christian convictions as was this new musical language.

Schein, who was molded under Rogier Michael in Dresden and Bodenschatz in Schulpforta, followed Calvisius in 1616 as cantor of St. Thomas's in Leipzig. From about 1614 he and Scheidt were close friends, and a little later he and Schütz as well; the latter composed a funeral motet for him when he died in 1630 at the age of forty-three (*Das ist je gewisslich wahr,* six voice parts separately printed in Dresden, 1631; included in the *Geistliche Chormusik,* 1648; concerning the connection between Schein's Cantionale of 1627 and his family, see p. 148). Like Praetorius and Scheidt, he began as a devout adherent of the *prima pratica.* His first printed work, *Cymbalum Sionium* (1615) for five to twelve voices, contains fifteen German and fifteen Latin texts (Gospels, psalms, Song of Solomon) with Lasso, Gallus, and Calvisius, among others, as the models. Perhaps even more than in Scheidt's first opus, there is a trend toward contrasting effects and highly emotional text declamation. His *Opella nova* (I, 1618, in three to five voices; II, 1626, from solo settings up to large ensembles) was Schein's first concerted work, composed, he said, "according to Italian invention currently in vogue." Even in volume I, his use of the Italian style went far beyond Praetorius. The volume contains only small-ensemble chorale settings for one or two voices and one or two obbligato instruments with thoroughbass. It shows how Schein, through gradual compromises, solved the problem of combining the chorale and concerto. In the first pieces, two voices "concertize" freely together; during the rests between lines, the tenor sings the chorale intact in cantus-firmus style:

Johann Hermann Schein: *Opella nova I,* 1618. Chorale concerto
a) 2 sopranos, tenor, thoroughbass. Chorale concerto with cantus firmus

Later on, concessions to the cantus firmus are omitted; two or three voices, "concertizing," toss the broken and ornamented chorale lines to each other. More important than the chorale melody itself is what happens to it; artistic considerations override doctrinal content. This type can be called "chorale concerto":

b) 2 sopranos, thoroughbass. Pure chorale concerto

In a third stage, the composer is no longer obligated to use the melody; in its place a free monodic setting of the text is used in the manner of the Italian "aria" of Caccini, Peri, and so on. This type, which conveys a personal interpretation of the text, can be called "chorale monody":

c) Solo violin, solo soprano, thoroughbass. Chorale monody

This kind of chorale treatment was kept up during the entire 17th century and still occurred in Bach's cantatas. From here it is only a step to part II of Schein's *Opella*. Like part I, it contains chorale concertos and a number of free monodic settings of Bible verses (Latin and German). The emotional content of single words is now the controlling factor in melody formation, rhythm, declamation, and the structure of the whole work. The composer took his cue from the solo madrigal of the Italians (closely related to the form used by Monteverdi, Grandi, and others) and emphasized whatever the text contained in the way of contrast, tension, and excitement. Out of all this he created a kind of dramatic scene, alternating between recitative-like and arioso forms with accompanying instruments and occasionally a chorus. A significant example of this, and one which was ahead of its time in Germany, is the Annunciation dialogue.

Johann Hermann Schein: *Opella nova II,* 1626. From the Annunciation dialogue for soprano, tenor, 4 trombones, and gambas.

Although there is no display of brilliance, this is the first sign of operatic influences, which became so significant later on. The Lord's Prayer and the Beatitudes were among the texts treated in this manner in part II of the *Opella.* The monodic style and the dramatic character of the settings, along with their choral insertions, anticipated the style of Schütz's dialogues. Schein would not have had to mention Viadana in his preface for us to recognize his source.

With these compositions, Schein reached a level of emotional expression never surpassed in the dramatic monody of Protestant church music; later on it was curbed rather than expanded. Works requiring large ensembles—e.g., the Te Deum (1618) or Psalm 150 (1620)—contain all the brilliance of the large Italian concerto but none of its emotional impact, not to mention its personal interpretation of the text. In the five-voice sacred madrigals of the *Fontana d'Israel* (see p. 199 for complete title and translation), Schein achieved the same height of lofty emotion using a related species, i.e., the expressive madrigal. This work was patterned after Italian madrigals from Marenzio to Monteverdi. The connection with Lasso's last disciples, such as Lechner, or with Hassler's motets (1601) is noticeable, but the language is much sharper, the richness of contrasts greater. The style is more like the Monteverdi arioso with recitative, more colorful, and filled with more dramatic effects. Schein's artistry in manipulating contrasting contrapuntal themes is unsurpassed. In fact, no other Protestant church music of the period can compare with the *Israelsbrünnlein* for dramatic power combined with perfection of musical form. Furthermore, its settings can be performed by five vocalists without thoroughbass or any other accompaniment. Taken from the Psalms, Gospels, and Prophets, these *Kraftsprüche* closely approximate

Johann Hermann Schein: *Israelsbrünnlein,1623*

Contrasting themes from a five-voice motet

Schütz. Compared to Schein, Samuel Scheidt on the whole seems more conservative and moderate. A pupil of Sweelinck, he became organist and orchestra leader
of the Halle municipal administration and temporarily the city's musical director.
He had ties with Michael Praetorius from 1614, and (as Halle's "Kapellmeister
von Haus aus") worked with him to institute the *Konzertmusik* in the Magdeburg
cathedral (1618). He and Praetorius also shared a penchant for composing large
cycles. His first printed opus, *Cantiones sacrae* (1620), mostly in eight voices,
contains miscellaneous Bible, hymn, and lied texts in Latin and German, in
settings that adhere, like the *Musae* of Praetorius, to the essentials of the older
polychoral style. His second opus, however, the *Concertus sacri* (1622), is closely
related to the *Polyhymnia caduceatrix* of Praetorius and resembles the *Psalmen
Davids* of Schütz in its use of monodic vocal solos. Its settings are two- to
twelve-voice "adjectis symphoniis et choris instrumentalibus." The affect-laden
melodies and pathos-laden declamation reach beyond Praetorius, but go nowhere
near the intensive energy of Schein's textual interpretation. In an old-fashioned
touch, an eight-voice setting of Psalm 8 in German is immediately followed by
a parody Mass on the piece. Sacred concertos in German for small ensembles were
published by Scheidt under the title *Neue geistliche Konzerte* in four parts (1634–
40; parts V and VI must have been published before 1634, but they are lost). The
settings are for two or three, occasionally four or six, vocal parts together with
thoroughbass. They were not originally in this form. Rather, they were "reduced
forms of polychoral works for large ensembles" (Adrio); this agrees with Praetorius's remarks in the prefaces to part III of his *Syntagma* and, in particular, to his
Urania (1613). Scheidt himself, in part II, expressly offered these concertos in
their polychoral form, but conditions during the Thirty Years' War prevented
him from getting them printed. They deal alternately with texts from the Psalms
and Gospels and texts of old and new songs. Scheidt's chorale concertos avoided
the occasionally oversubtle artistry of Schein; affected passages are frequent.

Samuel Scheidt: *Geistliche Konzerte II,* 1634. Openings of two chorale concertos
a) "pure" concerto

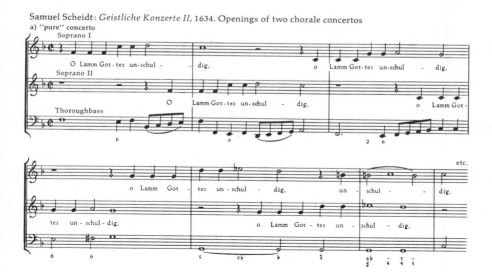

b) concerto with expressive elements

Although Scheidt retained the chorale intact in his concertos more often than did Schein, this predilection was frequently superseded by an easygoing "concertato" treatment that soon infused all of his music. Scheidt later confessed (in a letter to H. Baryphonus, January 26, 1651): "I stick to the pure old compositions and standards." The remark, which is comparable to the foreword of Schütz's *Geistliche Chormusik,* is not always compatible with the noisy mechanism of some of his concertos. His Bible-verse settings often reveal more clearly his remoteness from Schein, for in spite of his apparent knowledge of Italian models, he accepted only the outward appearance of monody and not its expressive power. In three of his Magnificats, German songs are inserted between the verses, an old custom that continued to the time of Bach.

It is significant that Scheidt's interest in concertos was in their structure, not their capacity for emotional expression. This can be seen in his *Dialog Christi mit den Gottseligen und Verdammten* as well as in his last concerted work based mostly on the Psalms, *Liebliche Kraftblümlein, aus des H[eiligen] Geistes Lustgarten abgebrochen und zum Vorschmack des ewigen Lebens in zweistimmigen Himmelschor versetzet* (Lovely, Fragrant Little Flowers from the Pleasure Garden of the Holy Spirit, Set for a Two-Part Heavenly Choir as a Foretaste of Eternal Life; 1635). Fully as pretentious as its title, its style abounds in superficial musical effects and concerted trifling:

Samuel Scheidt: *Liebliche Kraftblümlein,1635*

It is unfortunate that more than a hundred five-part sacred madrigals, which Scheidt promised to deliver to the Duke of Brunswick in 1642, have been lost. They probably constituted a counterpart to Schein's *Israelsbrünnlein*. An instrumental work, *Siebzig Sinfonien auf Konzertenmanier* (1644) contains seventy preludes, ten in each of the seven keys, which were intended as concerto introductions; each could be used with any of the beloved text settings, provided the key of both was the same.

Scheidt's moderate and somewhat conventional vocal style duplicated that of most of his contemporaries; it contrasts with the dramatic, affect-laden monody of Schein as well as his type of sacred madrigal, both of which found acceptance only with difficulty. Schein must have been a highly gifted and highly cultivated but fiery, emotional man. He gave expression to the mysticism of his day while Schütz, as he grew older, developed his own personal style. His expression grew more detached, more general, less personal. Schein seems, during the short span of his life, to have experienced a Jacobean struggle that kept growing more intense and passionate. In Scheidt arose the type of Lutheran church musician who endeavored with sound, traditional craftsmanship to unite the new and the old, thereby supplying models that easily became stereotyped in the hands of a wider circle of followers. The concerto as he used it enjoyed wide circulation and became a cozy medium for all composers. In the case of the motet, remnants of the Lasso School merged with monody and the madrigal. Here, even though composers remained in tune with changes in contemporary styles, something like an indigenous Protestant style came into being. It met the needs of the worship service, whereas music of a more intense emotional content and stronger individual tone was presumably intended for private devotions.

Far above his contemporaries, Henrich Schütz stood in solitary greatness, acclaimed and adored by everyone. From 1599 he was engaged as a choirboy under Moritz in Kassel; he studied under Georg Otto, and later under Giovanni Gabrieli in Venice. After the latter's death (1612), he became court organist in Kassel. From 1613 on he was several times released to Dresden, and in 1617 he became court *Kapellmeister* there—a position held by Michael Praetorius intermittently for four years—remaining the chief *Kapellmeister* of the Saxony Electors for fifty-four years, until his death in 1672. He made a second trip to Venice for study in 1628–29. After 1633, in addition to his Dresden activities, he was active as court *Kapellmeister* in Copenhagen; then from 1644 on he was once more engaged in that capacity in Dresden. In his declining years he spent more and more time in his native town, Weissenfels, his duties in Dresden being assigned to Vincenzo Albrici and Andrea Bontempi. He had close and more or less friendly relations with the courts of Hannover, Weimar, Gera, Zeitz, and especially Wolfenbüttel; his correspondence with Duchess Sophie Elisabeth of

Wolfenbüttel has been preserved. The Dresden orchestra became increasingly Italianized; Marco Giuseppe Peranda and Carlo Pallavicini were engaged as conductors, and Schütz's pupil, Christoph Bernhard, had to content himself with the status of assistant conductor. Because demands and styles changed quickly, even in church music, the lifework of the "saeculi sui musicus excellentissimus" (the most excellent musician of the century) did not outlast that century.

Schütz was a master in all fields; for more than half a century he was *Kapellmeister* to exacting courts. However, the small amount of his extant secular music does not permit an adequate evaluation of his whole output. Evidently he did not compose any instrumental music. What has been preserved is, for the most part, sacred music, of which only one composition can be classified as congregational music, his *Geistliche Chormusik,* dedicated to the burgomaster and city council of Leipzig (1648, with reference to the choir of St. Thomas's). According to Cornelius Becker, the Psalter was devotional music for the home. All other sacred music was written for the worship services of the court, whether it was large and showy or scaled down to chamber proportions for a smaller audience. Schütz's texts, as compared with those of Praetorius, Schein, and Scheidt, show the same rapid decline in the use of chorales that can be observed in the work of his contemporaries and somewhat younger composers. Plainly conspicuous are texts from both the Old and New Testaments, at first frequently in Latin, in later years almost exclusively in German. The proportion of pericope texts is small. In many instances there seems to have been a free selection of texts, at first of Latin devotional literature *(Cantiones sacrae)* and later on of rhymed Psalter texts (*Psalmen Davids . . . durch Cornelium Beckern,* 1628). Frequently, compilations were made from more than one source, although a continuity of meaning was always maintained. Schütz avoided the tendency toward cantata-like agglomerations that arose during the later years of his life. His *historiae,* dialogues, and Passions show that he regarded Biblical stories more as dramatic scenes than as liturgical subjects.

Musical development began, of course, as the Lasso School declined. The new trend was represented by the Kassel composers Otto, Geuck, and the Elector himself; Praetorius with his close Kassel affiliations was influential; Lechner and Hassler, whose compositions were well known in Kassel and who were in touch with the Elector (he asked Hassler to join his court), probably influenced the young Schütz. While in Venice, Schütz soon became acquainted with the concerto for small and large ensembles, with monody, and probably also with opera; Monteverdi's *Orfeo* and *Arianna* were five and four years old, respectively, when Schütz went to Venice, while his madrigals (1587 f.; the first five books had already appeared) were widely circulated. It must be assumed that Giovanni Gabrieli's large concertos, as well as the sacred and secular works of Donati, Croce, Merulo, Viadana, Grandi, Rovetta, Turini, and others, did not escape his notice.

His first printed work, the *Psalmen Davids* (1619), appearing in the same year as the *Polyhymnia caduceatrix* of Praetorius, shows how strongly Schütz was influenced by his Italian predecessors and how different he was from them in age. The large ensemble (more than twenty voices and up to six choirs in Schütz), the obbligato instruments, the ritornellos, the alternation between *soli* and *tutti,* techniques of contrast—all are the same; however, in using true monodic solo singing, Schütz went far beyond Praetorius. While Praetorius wrote settings mostly of chorales, Schütz used psalm, Gospel, and other Bible texts (all in German); whereas Praetorius, although using a large ensemble, preferred a bare presentation of the chorale, Schütz preferred to illustrate text segments, to express emotions, to interpret. It does not matter that many of the techniques Schütz used for his exegetical and emotional treatment were based on formulas from a current catalogue of technical expressions borrowed from rhetoric. Power and terseness depend on the assertiveness of an individual personality and not on the mechanical use of fixed and teachable formulas. Most of the concertos in the *Psalmen Davids* were probably composed at an earlier date, perhaps from his years in Kassel after 1612. A great number of single works, e.g., Psalms 24 and 133 (SWV 476 and 48; cf. SWV 412), and the grandiose Latin Magnificat for five choirs (SWV 468), which almost certainly belongs to an earlier period, demonstrate the love of display and the need for self-assertion that Schütz shared with many other composers. However, hardly anyone else could bind his artistic needs so intimately with the sincere fervor of a Baroque *grand seigneur.*

More impressive, perhaps, than the brilliance of his settings is the force of Schütz's personal expression and his freedom from mechanical formulas. These features are particularly evident in the small-ensemble works which, considering their nature, should be classed as sacred madrigals. Consider, for instance, Psalm 116 (SWV 51), which Schütz (and fifteen other composers, among them Praetorius and Schein) composed, presumably in 1616 or a little later, for Burckhard Grossmann's collection, *Angst der Höllen* (1623). Here, Schütz's personal reflection on the text is poured into the forging of motifs and the phrase structure intensifies changing images with flashing contrasts:

Heinrich Schütz: *Psalm 116* (SWV 51), after 1616

This psalm also illustrates Schütz's interest in formal design. He arranged the text so that the relationship of the parts to the whole creates a rationalized, symmetrical form. The piece begins leisurely, intensifies slowly, climaxes in the middle (part 4), calmly fades away, and finishes with an elegant, virtuoso concerted finale (the latter gesture is reminiscent of Gabrieli). Like many parts of the *Psalmen Davids,* the central section, the axis of a symmetry achieved through precise wing structures, also consists of carefully planned entrances, gradations, climaxes, and endings.

An intermediate stage between madrigal, motet, and (in a few pieces) concerto for small ensemble is occupied by the *Cantiones sacrae* (1625); their texts are taken from devotional literature (see p. 190; in this case from A. Musculus, a theologian). Their textual and musical structure was so interdenominational that Schütz could safely dedicate them to the imperial prince, Johann Ulrich zu Eggenberg. They were probably begun in 1617. Both texts and music reflect the mysticism that prevailed during the whole era. The *Cantiones* are the most expressive of Schütz's sacred chamber music, more delicate and not as outspoken as Psalm 116, leaner, more precise, and even more forceful. Thematic outlines and groupings, phrase structure, harmony—all are adapted to the necessity of expounding the text; affective declamation, tone painting, and symbolic paraphrases of the text (which can again be defined with technical terms from rhetoric) produce the impression of a deep religious experience:

Heinrich Schütz: *Cantiones sacrae,* 1625

The *Cantiones* represent an extreme in Schütz's output; they stand close to Monteverdi's madrigals, and parallel Schein's *Israelsbrünnlein;* yet behind them one can feel the personalities of Lechner, Hassler, perhaps also Praetorius.

Close in point of origin are the chorale variations, *Aria de vitae fugacitate* (1625, SWV 94), an unsurpassed work in the genre and also an exceptional part of Schütz's output—like the Becker Psalter (see p. 143). The second Italian journey inaugurated a second phase in his music, characterized by the predominance of monody and concertos for small ensembles. Undoubtedly he met Monteverdi, Grandi, and other leading Italians of the same bent. The experience came to fruition in the *Symphoniae sacrae* (I, Venice, 1629; II and III, Dresden, 1647 and 1650 respectively) and the *Kleine geistliche Konzerte* (I, Leipzig, 1636; II, Dresden, 1639). Both collections were composed over a period of many years. Inasmuch as long periods apparently elapsed between the writing of single compositions and their publication, and since Schütz arranged his compositions according to setting rather than chronology, several styles are intermingled. Only one very general trend of development is recognizable. The first part of the *Symphoniae* contains Latin pieces for one to three voices and obbligato instruments. The second and third parts contain German texts in increasingly larger ensembles. The *Kleine geistliche Konzerte,* mostly on German texts, are composed for only few voices, without obbligato instruments but with thoroughbass. The first parts of both works still reveal in many cases Schütz's willingness to subordinate musical diction to individual images; they (e.g., the *Cantiones*) follow strict laws of motivic construction. Vivid motifs depict the "sweetness" of Jesus, the cry for salvation, the actions of hurrying, getting up, fighting, sleeping, and waking. The motifs are subjected to intensified repetitions and contrasts, and the music grows into a living experience:

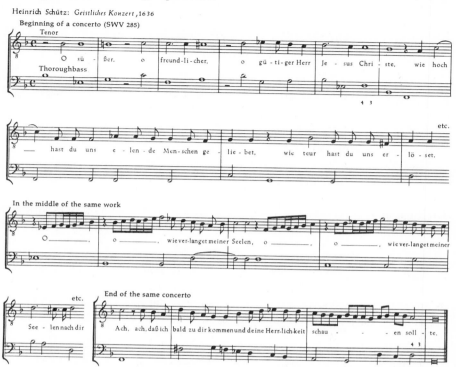

Here, too, there is a close resemblance to Schein. The expressiveness of the monodic-concerted style could hardly be greater. One need not be surprised, therefore, that a turning back is apparent in the later parts of the *Symphoniae*. There is a broadening of motifs and forms; the abrupt gesture spreads out in lyric fullness. Monody and concerto now join in a new alliance, a calm musical development rather than the ecstasy of the *stile oratorio*. The texts are frequently fragmented, so that the composition becomes multisectional. Each section takes on the character of an autonomous musical structure, and instrumental "symphonies" or ritornellos separate them:

The emotional impetus is by no means lessened, for it is emotionalism that holds the form together; Schütz never retreats into a convenient model. Yet the climaxes are calmer, and a unified thematic concept often counterbalances all the contrasts (as in the previous example). The incomparable emotional experiences that infuse the earlier monodies, and often the *Cantiones* as well, give way to a more reserved approach. The Word of God, once clothed in completely personal feelings, is again perceived as divine revelation or authoritative doctrine, and its presentation eschews emotion and ecstasy in favor of an interpretation with more general validity. There is no reason to speak of a "theological turnabout" on Schütz's part, nor is there any need to revert to the impersonal explanation that even a Schütz composed differently in old age than during his youth. Nor is it a matter of "overcoming" his earlier style. Nothing was forfeited. Rather, Holy Scripture was released from the overly subjective, affect-laden interpretations into which it had fallen, and was gradually raised to the sphere of revelation. The change resulted in greater strength and moderation, in a stricter perception of God's Word, in more musical formal designs, rather than in a rejection of earlier achievements. Future research should seek to determine whether the outside stimulus of recent styles in Italian chamber cantatas and oratorios (e.g., Ferrari, Manelli, Frescobaldi, Luigi Rossi, or Carissimi) had a part in the process. It seems to have begun in part II of the *Geistliche Konzerte,* and it became clear in parts II and III of the *Symphoniae.* It should be remembered, however, that works of different periods and style classifications are evidently intermixed.

The same holds true of the *Geistliche Chormusik* (1648), with its programmatic preface by Schütz (see p. 208), which was the absolute climax of Protestant motet composition in the 17th century. The five- to seven-voice compositions are based solely on Bible texts in German; part of them are pericope texts (established lessons for the church year). The intention, as already mentioned, was to provide congregational music. The composition probably extended over a thirty-year period; it is not certain whether two style classifications (1615–30 and 1630–48; J. Heinrich, 1956) can be distinguished. As for forms used, remnants of the Lasso motet style (or perhaps revivals of the Roman style) are mixed with traits of the madrigal, the concerto (small and large), and a new lyrical style combining the older techniques of declamation, varied contrasts, and a striving for unification (both a proclamation and an interpretation of the divine Word). Traces of older compositions, such as *Die Himmel erzählen die Ehre Gottes* and *Das ist je gewisslich wahr,* mingle with the calm unfolding of pieces like *Ein Kind ist uns geboren:*

Motets like *Ich weiss, dass mein Erlöser lebt* or the lament of Rachel in the Appendix (SWV 396) seem to be closely related to the Saul scene in part III of the *Symphoniae;* indeed, all the vocal-instrumental works that were gathered together at the end give the impression of being late works. Yet the stylistic resources of the time were so thoroughly integrated in the *Geistliche Chormusik* that it is risky to deduce a history of composition on the basis of these resources. With this landmark work, Schütz gave new life to the Protestant motet, which already was at the point of deterioration. Andreas Hammerschmidt, Christoph Bernhard, Dietrich Buxtehude, and Johann Theile all gave it close attention.

The late phase in Schütz's work began with his *Zwölf geistliche Gesänge* (1657) for four voices, published by his student Christoph Kittel. An incidental remark of Spitta has lent strength to the erroneous idea that they were a compilation of early works. This is completely improbable. In these compositions, the element of personal interpretation lies far in the background; rather, the impression of a liturgical statement predominates. Counterpoint replaces both uninhibited declamation and the lively play of concerted voices. Contrasts have almost disappeared. The terse structures in his earlier compositions—e.g., the *Cantiones* or the first parts of the *Symphoniae* and the *Kleine geistliche Konzerte*—give way to genuine polyphony, which bridges individual sections and ties the whole musical span into a cohesive unit. The style is directly linked to the motet technique of Lasso and Palestrina:

In no other work does Schütz appear more retrospective; nowhere else is there such dogmatic severity and orthodox submission to the divine Word. The *Zwölf geistliche Gesänge* can be regarded as the antithesis of the *Cantiones,* as a conservative confession to the "true nucleus and foundation of good contrapuntal writing" (preface to the *Geistliche Chormusik*) and, hence, to a personal but orthodox Lutheranism.

Schütz's late motet-like music has come down to us in fragments only, but his eight-voice *Deutsches Magnificat* (SWV 494) is a jewel, demonstrating in the power of its strict contrapuntal designs that the old fire had not been extinguished. A refined, monodic-concerto style of declamation is combined with the severity of an age-old ritual; mystic images and orthodox dogma merge to form a work that is perhaps without equal in the whole of Protestant church music.

With his *Historia der . . . Auferstehung . . . Jesu Christi* (1623), Schütz moved into the realm of Protestant *historia* compositions, continuing the tradition of his predecessor, Scandellus (see p. 184 f.). Aside from the introduction and the finale, the chorus is used only as *turba* and only once. All else is allotted to solo voices. Accompanied by four gambas, the Evangelist sings in a recitation tone, to which are added interpolations where the text called for musical imagery or symbolism. The characters of the *historia* itself, with the exception of a Cleophas passage, are set for two voices, one of which may be omitted or played on an instrument. Historically, this is an intermediate form between the old polyphonic treatment of soliloquies and Schütz's solo settings for the individual characters, which he was then using in dialogues and later used throughout his *historiae.* According to Schmitz, this reflected the Passion style of northern Italy. The ensemble was divided into three choruses, one for the Evangelist, one for the interlocutors, and a *plenus chorus.* Only the Evangelist was to be visible, with the other persons hidden from view. Although the composer stated that this work should be performed "in court chapels or halls," it was evidently widely distributed. The Halle church orders (1640–60) definitely prescribed its performance at Easter Vespers (H.J. Moser, *Schütz,* p. 326). The most impressive parts of the work are its dramatic scenes, such as the conversation between Christ and Mary Magdalene (also handed down separately); the walk of the disciples to Emmaus, with Cleophas saying, "Did not our heart burn within us?"; and the freely composed narratives of the Evangelist:

Heinrich Schütz: *Auferstehungshistorie,* 1623 (SWV 50)

The "Victoria" of the finale section, in anticipation of Monteverdi's *Madrigali guerrieri*, goes back to Scandellus and beyond him to an even older tradition.

Closely affiliated with the Easter *historia* are a number of dialogues by Schütz, e.g., the Annunciation dialogue in *Kleine geistliche Konzerte* I and the Easter dialogue (SWV 443) that survives in only one copy. They are unexcelled in their realistic portrayal of personality, which indicates that Schütz undoubtedly knew Monteverdian monody. The dialogue of the Pharisee and the Publican is instructive in this regard because of its consistent use of two evocative musical figures:

Heinrich Schütz: *Dialog Pharisäer und Zöllner* (SWV 444)

Consistent themes of the two characters

The lyric style of the choral dialogue *Ich beschwöre euch* (1641; SWV 339) and in the dialogue of the twelve-year-old Jesus in the temple (first printed in 1650 in part III of the *Symphoniae sacrae*) may disclose a later stage. The *Vater Abraham* dialogue (SWV 477) should probably be assigned to a much earlier period, preceding the Easter History.

The *historia* type next appeared in the *Sieben Worte am Kreuz* (if this work may be called a *historia;* 1645?); it contrasts greatly with his 1623 Resurrection History. The unconnected scenes are held together by strictly symmetrical structure: the work is framed by two pillars consisting of a choral setting of *Da Jesus an dem Kreuze stund* and an instrumental piece based on it; both are repeated toward the end but in reverse order. The main body of the work gradually builds to the climactic *Eli lama* and then dies down again. The realism of the older *historia* and the dialogues is replaced by a conception of the text as divine revelation. The words of Christ are not those of a dying man but those of

52. Heinrich Schütz (1585–1672) at the age of 85. Oil miniature on wood by
an unknown painter (1670). Berlin, Deutsche Staatsbibliothek.

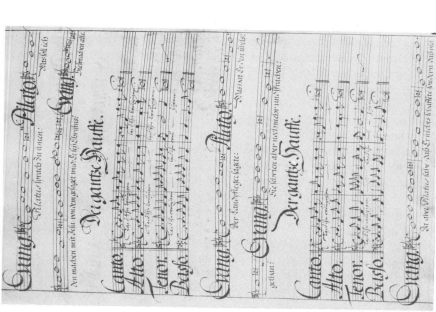

53. Heinrich Schütz, two pages from the St. Matthew Passion, SWV 47 (1666) according to the only preserved source, the manuscript of Johann Zacharias Grundig (c. 1692). Leipzig, Stadtbibliothek, Mus. MS II, 2.

salvation; they are set apart with ariosos and obbligato instruments, whereas the parts of the tormentors and the Evangelist (the latter presented by two to four voices) are mere background.

The *Historia* . . . *von der* . . . *Geburt* . . . *Jesu Christi* (printed in Dresden, 1664) must be a very late work. It was intended "for court chapels" and goes back to a special tradition within this genre, one that was never much utilized. Its line of descent includes a Breslau Christmas *historia* manuscript (c. 1638; cf. H. J. Moser, *Schütz*, p. 619 ff.) and another Breslau *historia* by Tobias Zeutzschner (after 1649); the line was continued later on with the lost Christmas *historae* of Peranda, Johann Philipp Krieger, and (probably) Erlebach (1698), and finally Bach's Christmas Oratorio. The eight "Intermedien" or "Konzerte" are all self-contained settings of the various words of the Evangelist, which Schütz stated could be performed in the unorthodox manner of old-style choral recitation ("alten choraliter redenden stylus"). He characterized individuals by means of soloistic ensembles (e.g., the high priests and scribes in a setting for four basses, two trombones, and thoroughbass) or solos that sound almost operatic (Herod, for example). Rather rigorous demands were made of the instruments. "With the separation from liturgical tradition that was attained here, and the emphasis on emotion, all types of *historia* composition were standing on the borderline of the oratorio" (W. Blankenburg in *MGG* VI, 479).

Three Passions according to Luke, John, and Matthew form the keystone of Schütz's "oratorical" work (1665–66; the Passion according to Mark was apparently not by Schütz). With these compositions the venerable master set himself somewhat apart from historical connections. Together with the old responsorial Passions, they made use exclusively of biblical texts without insertion of hymns or sacred lyrics. However, Schütz's Passions abandon the recitation tone in recitative passages for soloists and the Evangelist in favor of a rather monodic style; they also dramatize the *turbae*. Instruments and even thoroughbass are missing. The recitatives of the Evangelist and soloists include all styles from recitation tone in the narratives, with only slight musical allusions to situations and occurrences, to highly emotional portrayals. No other Passion music is so heart-stirring as *Und um die neunte Stunde* or *Eli lama* in Schütz's Passion according to St. Matthew. It is a thoroughly personal, thoroughly contemporary, thoroughly dramatic style which nevertheless produces a liturgical feeling as well, and even adapts itself to the individual character of each Gospel (St. John and St. Matthew especially). The *turbae*, brief and concise with their striking dramatic quality, provide effective contrasts. With the sparsest of means (precisely for this reason calling to mind the entire rich development of earlier pieces), Schütz constructed a type of liturgical drama that mirrored the soul's agitation but remained always submissive to the revealed Word. Thus he came close to the new type of Passion that was then developing and leading to the Passion oratorio —not in text and style but in purpose—bridging the gap between a mere presentation of the Passion story and its reflection in the compassion of a Christian soul. These Passions are not congregational music, but rather the almost unapproachable, solitary, and grandiose art of a man who had outlived his time; they had no imitators.

It is remarkable that Schütz's sacred works are based almost exclusively on biblical texts. Although he made use of secular lyrics (Italian and German; M. Opitz), he never turned to sacred poetry, which played a major role in the Protestant church music of other composers, at least after 1660. Chorale texts, too, are almost entirely absent. The few chorale settings use hymn texts freely to give the monody greater expressiveness *(Wenn unsre Augen schlafen ein)* or their expressive interpretation of the text forces the remniscences of a chorale melody into the background *(O hilf, Christe, Herzlich lieb hab ich dich, So fahr ich hin).* The free ostinato variations on the hymn *Ich hab mein Sach Gott heimgestellt* (*De vitae fugacitate,* 1625) are an isolated example, perhaps occasioned by a need for funeral music. There are also some scattered cantional settings (the Becker Psalter is in a class by itself), e.g., in the *Exequien* (1636), and a few chorale arrangements in the *Kleine geistliche Konzerte,* as well as two chorale concertos for large ensembles. All of these are exceptions, considering the gigantic output of Schütz. Hardly any other master of the same generation, or younger, followed the literal text of the Bible so consistently and still gave it so sincere and subjective a stamp. As with style and form, his choice of texts reflected the great change that the Baroque era meant for Protestant music; he still stood squarely on Lutheran tradition, yet he also freed himself to be an interpreter of it.

The works of Heinrich Schütz were the pinnacle of 17th-century German Protestant church music. He combined a complete mastery of older traditional forms and new Italian art styles, which were fast gaining acceptance. He merged both with the most heartfelt fervor, and spoke at last in his late works with a timeless wisdom, excelling by far anything that existed around him. While the separation into *prima* and *seconda pratica* is always discernible in others, with Schütz, at least from the *Geistliche Chormusik* on, the two styles blended into a unique and matchless personal language, forming a supreme unity of the controlling spiritual currents of the time—orthodoxy and mysticism. If there is such a thing as a historical mission, it was fulfilled here as a truly artistic style evolved from opposites, as Lutheranism found expression in the ecstasy of the 17th century. Although the opposing currents affecting theologians, poets, and musicians were frequently embodied in the same person, rarely has the embodiment resulted in such balance, to say nothing of such an artful style. This, surely, was Schütz's highest attainment in the field of Protestant church music. It was a natural historical development that his achievement disintegrated at the hands of his students, imitators, and followers. With the majority of later composers, the two musical tendencies were again separated; the wave of mysticism and rationalism, increasing during the era of Pietism, generally found its musical expression in a mystical, overly emotional language that approached a secular syntax, or in dull and rationalistic music lacking any piety or ecstasy. Only Johann Sebastian Bach arrived at a comparable balance and integration; he based his music on new premises and new stylistic resources, but he reached, as had Schütz, the highest summit of his century.

PASSION MUSIC IN THE LATTER 17TH CENTURY

There is nothing during this period that would stand comparison, either in quality or in style, with the *historiae* and Passions of Schütz. The German Passion according to St. John for six voices by Christoph Demantius (1631), the work of a sixty-four-year-old man, was one of the last through-composed motet Passions. It approached Schütz only in its personal and dramatic character. The Delitzsch Passion by Christoph Schultze, a sort of precursor of Schütz's St. Luke Passion, was still largely bound to the chorale recitation tone, and completely free only in the choral settings (Epstein). The St. Mark Passion ascribed to Schütz by tradition has not yet been identified; it lies between the old responsorial Passion and the three late Passions of Schütz. There was an intermediate stage between the responsorial and the through-composed Passion, represented by the Passions of Ambrosius Beber in Naumburg (1610) and probably by the two lost Passions of Rogier Michael in Dresden. Here, the Evangelist is treated in single voice, the other characters in two or three voices, the *turbae* in five, and the recitation tone is increasingly supplanted by a more or less unrestricted monodic style.

Historically speaking, these intermediary forms may be regarded as an expansion of the responsorial Passion, which by nature was conservative and incapable of expansion; it was supplanted by the through-composed motet Passion. However, from about the middle of the 17th century, a new Passion species appeared on the musical horizon which enjoyed a wide following through the first half of the 18th century and was still popular in the second half. This was the oratorical Passion, which in turn developed into the Passion oratorio proper around 1700. In accordance with current requirements, the oratorical Passion broke up the biblical Passion story by inserting contemplative passages and intermingling the Gospel text (either single or composite versions) with verses from other books of the Bible, with hymns, and, increasingly, even with sacred lyrics. Consequently, composers began to use cantional lied settings, chorale settings in various styles, and solo songs in the style of popular airs and Italian arias. Polyphonic settings often contained concerted features, and the *Exordium* (Introit) and *Conclusio* were written in the manner of a motet. Thoroughbass became obligatory, and concerting instruments were used more and more. The main emphasis was still on the *historia,* on settings of the biblical text of the Passion story, delivered by the Evangelist in a recitation tone or in a more recitative-like manner. Genuine recitatives were first used at the end of the century. Oratorical Passions of this kind were composed by many masters, although most of the works are lost. Frequently the texts have come down to us, but the composers cannot be identified. In Hamburg for the period 1676–1721 there are no less than 46 librettos of 18 different oratorical Passions, all by unknown composers; in Gotha there are five librettos for unknown works dating back to 1699–1720 (W. Blankenburg).

From the beginning, the oratorical Passion flourished mainly in northern and eastern Germany. The oldest identifiable oratorical Passions are those of Thomas Selle in Hamburg (first described by H. J. Moser, 1920). Between the three parts of a St. John Passion (1643), Selle inserted two verses taken from Isaiah and Psalm 22. These verses and the final chorale, *O Lamm Gottes unschuldig,* are a prophetical or contemplative paraphrase of the Passion story. These three "interludes" use a five-part chorus, three solo voices, a five-part orchestra, a solo violin, and thoroughbass. The Evangelist sings in a recitation tone and is accompanied by two bassoons; the soloists employ a somewhat monodic style accompanied by various instruments (two violins for Jesus, two cornets and a trombone for Pilate). The *Exordium* and the *turbae* are set for six-part chorus and orchestra. The style is fairly plain, occasionally reminiscent of Schütz and through him of Monteverdi (i.e., in the *Errette mich* at the end of the second interlude). Still plainer are Selle's miniature St. John Passion (1641?) and St. Matthew Passion (1642); these borrow their *turbae* from Heinrich Grimm's Passion (1629) and his Resurrection *historia* (c. 1660), which leans toward a somewhat more affected style.

Among the first representatives of this type were Thomas Strutius of Danzig and Christian Flor. Strutius inserted sacred lyrics and chorales of a contemplative character, divided the whole work into acts as in a play, and thereby brought the oratorical Passion to its definitive form (1664; only the text has been preserved, Lott). Flor wrote a Lüneburg St. Matthew Passion (1667), fragments of which have been preserved. The best known Passions of this type, but not the best artistically, are those of Johann Sebastiani in Königsberg and Johann Theile in Lübeck. Sebastiani's was "set in a recitation-like harmony for five voices and five instruments" (1663, printed in 1672) and performed for a long time. It goes only so far as to include the insertion of chorales for one voice with instrumental accompaniment. Johann Theile's Passion (1673) contains a long series of "arias" —song-like texts for solo voices with instrumental parts (ritornellos). Hidden behind the Hamburg librettos may be Christoph Bernhard, Dietrich Becker, and Joachim Gerstenbüttel, who is reported to have written a St. Matthew Passion *a 26.* An anonymous Riga Passion (1695) and a St. Matthew Passion by Valentin Meder of Riga (c. 1700) also belong in the Hamburg category. The existence of a St. Matthew Passion *a 16* by Friedrich Funcke of Lüneburg has been substantiated (J. Birke in *Archiv für Musikwissenschaft* XV, 1958). The Resurrection *historia* (1665) by the same composer has been preserved; of his St. Luke Passion "with intervening movements" only the text is known (1683). In the Halberstadt Passion by Christoph Clajus (1693), and in a Berlin version of Melchior Vulpius's Passion, characters of the Bible are introduced as allegorical figures. The northern German group is represented by J. G. Kühnhausen in Celle, the composer of a St. Matthew Passion (c. 1700) which was sent to Bremen by Vincent Lübeck in 1701 and has been lost; G. F. Handel's Hamburg St. John Passion (with aria texts by Postel, 1704; its authenticity is disputed); a Lüneburg Passion by Georg Böhm (1711?), of which only the text has been preserved; and others (according to the W. Blankenburg Catalogue in *MGG* X, 920 ff.). There is also a Saxon group of whose creative output almost nothing is known. It is claimed that J. Philipp Krieger composed no less than thirteen Passions between 1685 and 1722. Sebastian Knüpfer of Leipzig, his successor J. Schelle (Passion *a 19,* c. 1700), J. C. Rothe of Sondershausen (1697), Tobias Zeutzschner of Breslau (1697), Ph. H. Erlebach of Rudolstadt (Passion "in six acts," c. 1688; another, "divided into six acts and interspersed with fitting arias and songs," 1707), along with others, are known mostly from reports; occasional librettos have been preserved. Kuhnau's St. Matthew Passion (1721) is probably of a similar type, as are also the Passions of his contemporaries, the students and imitators of Bach. Their influence was noticeable in Bach's own Passions, although long before the new style of Passion oratorio had been combined with the older style. It dispensed partly or completely with Biblical texts and chorales, turned the Passion story into pure meditation on the subject, and thus eliminated it from church performance.

CONCERTO AND CONCERTED MOTET IN NORTH GERMANY,

FRANCONIA, AND SAXONY-THURINGIA

In other species of vocal church music (as with organ music), Schütz's contemporaries and successors increasingly reinforced the regional divisions that had begun in the early Baroque. The north German group showed distinct characteristics. The leading composer during this period was Thomas Selle of Hamburg, who was closely related to Samuel Scheidt in origin and style. His numerous sacred concertos for small ensembles began with *Hagio-Deca-Melydrion* (1627), "now with Italian innovations used here and there," and extended to the *Vierstimmiges Konzertlein* (1652). The superficiality that had begun with Scheidt degenerated here into indolence. A motet for six voices by Selle (1655), a few polychoral concertos, and above all an abundance of sacred lieder (among them Johann Rist's *Sabbathische Seelenlust,* 1651, and *Neue musikalische Festandachten,* 1655) round out the picture. It was an extremely fertile production, though not a profound one. Concerted works on biblical texts, chorale conertos in Scheidt's style, and above all sacred songs were intensely cultivated by the north German group. There is an urgent need for new editions of these works. In 1643, Johann Schop brought out in Hamburg a "First Part" of sacred concertos for one to eight voices and also numerous hymns, some of them published in Rist's *Himmlische Lieder* (1641) and *Frommer Christen . . . Hausmusik oder musikalische Andachten* (1654) and in other hymnals. He must be regarded primarily as a composer of hymns. There were two printed collections of concertos by Johann Vierdanck of Stralsund (1642 and 1643) other concertos are preserved in manuscript. Kaspar Förster, Jr., of Danzig, Copenhagen, and Hamburg, studied with Marco Scacchi in Warsaw; he left many works for solo voice, concertos, dialogues, and three Latin oratorios (which follow Carissimi) for the most varied ensembles. J. Adam Reinken, who lived until the time of Bach, also wrote concertos. Printed collections of concertos, hymns, and so on, were written by Martin Rubert of Stralsund, including a *Musikalische Seelenerquickung, aus hochgelahrter Männer Predigten entlehnet und . . . auf besondere Dialogen-Art gesetzet* (1664). Augustin Pfleger, temporarily working in Gottorf, wrote *Psalmi, Dialogi et Motettae* (printed 1661); his Gospel series for the church year (about 1670?) is preserved in manuscript, and there is a series of single compositions by him. Daniel Selich, successor to Michael Praetorius in Wolfenbüttel, is known for his sacred concertos (written from 1624 on). In addition to these there were many works by minor composers, for the concerto technique was easily mastered by lesser talents.

During the transition from Schütz to Buxtehude, three names stand out in north Germany: Matthias Weckmann, a pupil of Schütz who lived in Hamburg from 1637 and worked temporarily in Copenhagen and Dresden; Christoph Bernhard, also a pupil of Schütz who lived in Hamburg from 1664 to 1674 and worked in Dresden before and after this period; Franz Tunder, who was not (contrary to earlier assumptions) a pupil of Frescobaldi, but was organist of St. Mary's in Lübeck from 1641 and both the predecessor and father-in-law of Dietrich Buxtehude. Weckmann's monodic works obviously belong to the same tradition as the *Symphoniae sacrae* of his master. They go beyond these works, though, being broad and aria-like and giving a larger role to instruments. A dialogue like his Annunciation scene shows the characteristics of Schütz's dramatic dialogue, despite the instrumental usage. Concertos for vocal ensembles were Weckmann's forte. His Psalm 126 *(Wenn der Herr die Gefangenen zu Zion erlösen wird)* is a large-scale work full of beautiful sound and strong emotion. It is a very personal work in spite of all the virtuosity of the vocal parts. Although it presents the Bible texts pure and unbroken, its division into several sections shows the preference of the younger generation for segmented formal structures. Bernhard is close to Weckmann. His German sacred concertos were published in 1665 under the title of *Geistlicher Harmonien I. Teil . . . opus primum.* His German and Latin concertos and dialogues, mostly in small but sometimes in large settings, are preserved in manuscript. Both urgently need a new edition. His expressive force equals Weckmann's even if it does not surpass it. He is closer than Weckmann to the younger generation in compiling texts from different Bible passages and intermixing them with stanzas from solo songs and chorales. Like many of his works, the concerto *Ich sahe an alles Tun* was a forerunner of the cantata. In his early period Bernhard was probably influenced by Scacchi, and later taught by Schütz along the same lines; still later he wrote the most important German treatise of the time on polyphonic style and compositon, the *Tractatus compositionis.* He is one of the few masters of the period who wrote contrapuntal Masses. Among his motets only one title is known—the funeral motet *Cantabiles mihi erant justificationes tuae,* composed at the request of Schütz for his own burial service. Bernhard strictly followed the Roman School in his funeral music in four-part counterpoint, *Prudentia prudentiana* (printed 1669). It became the model for Buxtehude's *Mit Fried und Freud.* On the other hand, Bernhard's vocal style was strongly influenced by Carissimi, whom he met during two trips to Italy. This influence may be felt in the third part of Schütz's *Symphoniae sacrae.* The new Roman cantabile vocal style was happily blended in Bernhard with the old Roman "praenestine" style, which he had diligently studied with Schütz. Franz Tunder was the most striking musical personality after the two students of Schütz. His monodies on biblical proverbs are closer to Schütz than those of any of his contemporaries. His arioso vocal style shows an indirect Roman influence, although the passionate and dramatic impulse of Schütz is obvious in these pieces. He was one of the few composers of his time to write chorale monody in which the melody is completely dissolved *(Ach Herr, lass dein lieb Engelein).* Other chorale settings *(An Wasserflüssen Babylon)* are an extension of a type found only once in Schütz *(Erbarm dich mein)*. They use a continuous five-part instrumental accompaniment for lightly concerted solo presentations of chorale melody, in addition to the usual instrumental ritornellos. The chorale here remains intact, and the instruments "interpret" it ("chorale aria"). Michael Altenburg, Johann Crüger, and others also used this technique, which subsequently became very popular. It may be considered a forerunner of the aria-like chorale treatment with obligato instruments as used by Bach and his contemporaries. With Weckmann and Bernhard, the chorale receded entirely into the background, but Tunder seems to have been deeply interested in it (perhaps under the influence of organ music). He wrote a number of variations on chorales and sacred songs *per omnes versus*. In these he alternated between solo settings, choral settings, and concertos for small ensembles both with instruments and without them. Further alternations occurred between the greater or lesser extent to which melodies were ornamented. Such constant alternation of settings was similar to Schütz's *Aria de vitae fugacitate,* but much more diversified. In going through the whole sequence of stanzas, Tunder established a vocal parallel to the organ chorale variations of his time. As with Bernhard's multisectional concertos on texts compiled from many sources, Tunder's vocal chorale variations *per omnes versus* were a forerunner of the cantata. Bach's early cantata No. 4, *Christ lag in Todesbanden,* had its origins here, as did the whole species of chorale cantata.

Among Franconian composers, the style of the Hassler generation was continued by a group with Johann Staden of Nuremberg at its center. In his music, as was frequently the case in the Franconian circle, emotional and dramatizing monody in the style of Monteverdi and Schütz was on the decline. His output (large, in spite of an early death) emphasized the (slowly changing) motet, the concerto for small or large ensemble, and the sacred song. Staden himself was an early master in the field of the solo song (the "aria") with thoroughbass and instrumental ritornello. His motet modeled after Hassler, his polychoral psalm composition, and his concertos for large vocal and orchestral ensembles place him close to Schein. He did not, however, share Schein's fancy for experimentation or his radical acceptance of new Italian music. His printed sacred music (1616–33) included chiefly motets but also concertos for small ensembles (e.g., the four-part *Hausmusik,* 1623–28; the two-part *Kirchenmusik* for one to fourteen voices, 1625–26). *Herzenstrost Musica, geistliche Meditationen* was composed for only one voice with thoroughbass, *Geistlicher Musikklang* for one voice with two to three viols. Many of his works are preserved in fragments only, and new editions are urgently needed. Most of the extensive output of Melchior Franck of Coburg is lost; it belonged to the latter part of this whole development. His 116th Psalm, composed for Burckhard Grossmann's collection (1623), is close to the madrigal style of Schütz and Schein. *Neues musikalisches Rosengärtlein . . . neue Konzerte* for four to eight voices (1627–28) and other works show him as a poet and melodist of church lieder. *Gemmulae evangeliorum . . . Sprüche aus den Evangeliis . . . durchs ganze Jahr* (1623) were intended "for the most modest choirs." *Sacri convivii musica sacra* (1628) contains simple Eucharist songs in motet form; the composer himself calls them "easy compositions." The creative efforts of Franck and of many other composers of his group reflect the needs of modest *Kantoreien* and therefore point in the direction of song-like, simplified motets or simple concertos for small ensembles. Three late printed works contain sacred concertos for one to eight voices: *Votiva columbae sionea suspiria* (1629), *Dulces mundani exilii deliciae* (1631), and the two-part *Paradisus musicus* (1636). *Laudes Dei vespertinae* (1622) is an unusually large collection of thirty-three German Magnificats (K. Gudewill in the Hans Albrecht memorial volume, Kassel, 1962). Andreas Herbst, originally from Nuremberg and active in Frankfurt, performed concertos for large ensembles by Giovanni Gabrieli, Michael Praetorius, and Heinrich Schütz; he also composed many concertos (e.g., *Lob- und Danklied aus dem 34. Psalm samt einem Ritornello aus dem 92. Psalm,* thirteen voices for three choruses, 1637). His *Meletemata* (1619) for three and six voices are small sacred concertos similar to his *Suspiria cordis* (1646) for four voices. In his *Cantica sacra* (1653) he published concertos for one to three voices and for three instruments by different Italian composers. His *Harmonisches Choral- und Figural-Gesangbuch* (1659) contains twenty-nine chorales in settings for four to five voices. The important Erasmus Kindermann of Nuremberg was in Italy in 1635, where he may have met Carissimi or Frescobaldi. He especially cultivated the sacred concerto for small ensemble with obbligato instruments on biblical texts, chorales, and new religious poetry (*Cantiones pathetikai,* Passion songs for three to four voices, 1639; *Musikalischer Friedensseufzer,* three to four voices, 1642; and many other works). His *Concentus Salomonis* for two voices (1642) on Opitz's paraphrase of the Song of Songs is historically important. The dialogue *Mosis Plag* for three voices (1642) stands between Schütz and Hammerschmidt. Like Franck, Kindermann turned in his late period to a simplified motet style (*Musica catechetica* for five voices, 1643, "for churches, schools, and private music making"). Strophic songs are frequent in his *Musikalische Friedensfreud, welche mit 1 und 2 singenden Stimmen beneben 3 Violinen in Ritornello kann musizieret werden* (1650) and in the anthologies of Nuremberg poets whom he knew personally: Michael Dilherr, Johann Klaj, Johannes Vogel, and Georg Philipp Harsdörffer. The composers Paul Hainlein, Heinrich Schwemmer, and Georg Kaspar Wecker obviously favored concertos for large ensembles (the latter two were students of Kindermann and teachers of Johann Krieger and Johann Pachelbel). Among Wecker's works a through-composed hymn, *Allein Gott in der Höh sei Ehr,* is noteworthy; some of his other concertos come close to the development of the cantata. Wolfgang Karl Briegel of Nuremberg, working in Gotha and Darmstadt, definitely followed the line leading from the sacred concerto to the cantata and from the motet to the choral aria. His printed sacred works range from the *Geistliche Arien und Konzerte* (1652) to the *Apostolische Chormusik* (1697). They include a number of Gospel-cycle series in various forms; most of them are part of the "prehistory" of the cantata, i.e., the history of the earlier church cantata. In his *Evangelische Gespräche in Konzertenart,* two parts (1660–61), biblical texts set in concerto or dialogue form are interspersed with contemplative poetry in "aria" form, ending in appropriate chorale stanzas. In his *Evangelischer Blumengarten . . . auf leichte madrigalische Art* (four parts, 1666–68), the Gospel motet and the choral hymn are united. The *Geistliche Arien* (two parts, 1660–61) contain songs for one to two voices with orchestral ritornellos, among them lied dialogues, the *Oden* (1670), and songs on texts by Andreas Gryphius. Briegel compiled a type of dialogue based on the Psalms, other Bible passages, and chorale stanzas in his *Geistliche Gespräche . . . auf Konzertenmanier, sowohl vocaliter als instrumentaliter* (1674). His *Evangelisches Hosianna* contains odes by Samuel Kriegsmann "in easy compositions"; it is an early example of the "ode cantata." The *Musikalische Trostquelle* (1679), likewise a Gospel cycle, contains true cantatas based on many different text sources "set in an easy and simple way so that they can also be performed in small places (such as small towns and villages)." It is significant that the restricted resources of contemporary orchestras and choirs were taken into account and frankly discussed by composers everywhere. In another Gospel cycle, *Musikalischer Lebensbrunn* (1680), different Bible passages are mixed with contemporary song stanzas and chorales. They are based on the dialogue principle, but now their character is predominantly that of a meditation on a revealed text. The titles of two later prints characterize their contents: *Christian Rehefelds evangelischer Palmenzweig, bestehend in biblischen Kernsprüchen und darauf gesetzten Oden über die . . . Evangelia* (Christian Rehefeld's Protestant Psalms, Consisting of Choice Biblical Sayings and Followed by Odes on the Gospels; 1684) and *Davidische evangelische Harpfen* [of the Hanau cantor J. Georg Braun] *aus prophetischen Psalmsprüchen über die . . . Evangelia, in kurze heutiger Singart übliche Verse gebracht, nun in leichter Komposition . . . in grossen und kleinen Stadt- und Landkirchen* (from the Prophetic Psalm Passages about the . . . Gospels Arranged in Short Verses According to Modern Usage and Now in Easy Settings [for] Large and Small City and Country Churches; 1685); the latter contains true ode cantatas. Briegel's *Darmstadt Cantionale* (1687) contains 417 hymns with 291 melodies without thoroughbass. The *Sieben Busspsalmen* (1692) are "the best concertos . . . from Briegel's pen" (E. Noack). A cycle for the church year based on the Epistles (in contrast to the many Gospel cycles) is found in the *Apostolische Chormusik über die . . . Episteln* (1697), "more demanding than any earlier cycles" (ibid.; all references on Briegel are taken from E. Noack, *W. C. Briegel,* Berlin, 1963). Briegel was one of the most prolific composers of sacred works in an era noted for its extensive production. His output encompassed the progressive tendencies toward simplification and toward the infusion of orthodox tradition with Pietistic devoutness (in effect, Briegel was close to Spener). His last work was a collection of funeral songs for four to five voices, *Letzter Schwanengesang* (1709).

   The tendencies toward profundity and simplification so clearly visible in the Franconian group are present in music by three composers of the Saxon-Thuringian group: Michael Altenburg, J. Rudolph Ahle, and Andreas Hammerschmidt. Altenburg still belonged to the generation of the three great S's. His *Gaudium christianum* (1617) contains concertos for large ensembles with trumpets and bass drums—up to eighteen voices in the manner of Praetorius. In his four-part collection *Christliche Kirchen- und Hausgesänge* (1620–21) and in many other works he yielded to the tendency toward simplification. He could be called the first "popularizer" of Protestant church music in his time. As late as 1649 the

54. Heinrich Scheidemann (c. 1596–1663) in an engraving by J. F. Fleischberger, 1652.

55. Thomas Selle (1599–1663) in an engraving by D. Dircksen, Hamburg, 1653.

56. Johann Rist (1607–67) in a contemporary engraving.

57. Wolfgang Carl Briegel (1626–1712). Engraving by Elias Nessenthaler after a painting by Johann Heinrich Leuchter.

58. Andreas Hammerschmidt, opening of the five-voice motet *O Domine Jesu Christe*. Berlin, Deutsche Staatsbibliothek, Mus. MS 30210.

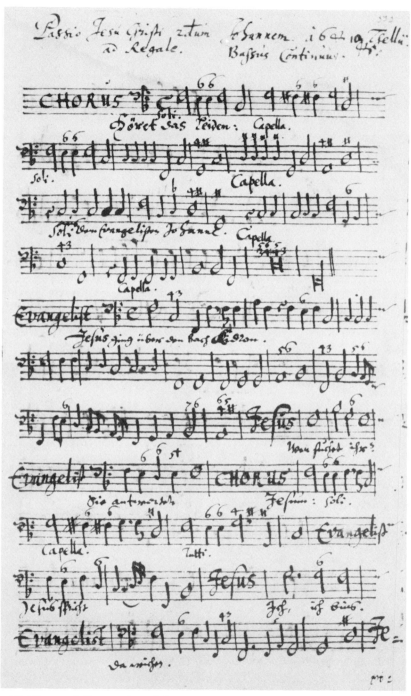

59. Thomas Selle, opening of the basso continuo of the St. John Passion for six solo voices, five-part chorus, six instruments, and continuo (1643). Hamburg, Staats- und Universitätsbibliothek, Cod. 251 in scrinio.

60. Andreas Hammerschmidt (1611 [1612?]–75) in an engraving by Samuel Weishun, 1646.

61. Adam Krieger (1634–66) in an engraving by Johann Caspar Höckner and Christian Romstet.

62. Paul Gerhardt (1607–76) in an engraving by Ludwig Buchhorn.

63. Vincent Lübeck in a pastel drawing, c. 1710. Hamburg, Altonaer Museum.

tremendously prolific Hammerschmidt wrote an almost purely monodic work, mostly on Latin texts. Like many other Hammerschmidt works, it leaned heavily on Schütz but captured only the manner, not the expressive essence, of his style. His *Kirchen- und Tafelmusik* (1622) contains twenty-two chorale monodies with instruments. The fact that only four of these monodies follow the chorale melody proves their closeness to Schütz. As a song composer he is represented in the collections of Christian Keimann (1646), in Rist's *Neue himmlische Lieder* (1651), and *Neue Katechismus-Andachten* (1656). His *Fest-, Buss- und Danklieder* (1658) are in the form of five-voice arias on texts by Johann Franck, Rist, Keimann, Harsdörffer, and others. Generally, "all of Hammerschmidt's church music belongs to the fascinating half-world between motet and concerto" (Adrio in *MGG* V, 1431), which was characteristic of this period, especially in Saxony. The *Musikalische Andachten* (five parts, 1639–53) contains concertos for small ensembles on biblical proverbs and song texts, sacred madrigals, motets, and concertos for larger ensembles; the fifth part approaches Schütz's *Geistliche Chormusik* and Schütz himself wrote a dedicatory poem for it. At the end of his life, Hammerschmidt went back to this style in his *Fest- und Zeitandachten für das Chor* (1671) for six voices. His *Motettae unius et duarum vocum* (1649) contains Latin concertos for very small ensembles in the manner of Schütz. Hammerschmidt gave Schütz's dramatic dialogue a most characteristic turn, already indicated by the title: *Dialogi oder Gespräche zwischen Gott und einer gläubigen Seele* (Dialogues or Conversations Between God and a Believing Soul; two parts, 1645). For the most part, they are allegorical dialogues in which Christian truths are discussed. There are two types. In the first, the two voices simultaneously deliver a dialogue on dogma. There is no attempt to be dramatic. The voices merely present a uniform, conversational text, frequently repeating themselves. In the second, God and the sinful soul engage in an allegorical, didactic dialogue, singing texts that do not really belong together. The same motifs are used in both voices, and the illusion of true dialogue is discarded. Part II of the *Dialogi* is based on Opitz's 1627 arrangement of the Song of Songs (as was Kindermann's *Concentus Salomonis* of the previous year). Hammerschmidt's subsequent *Evangelische Gespräche* (two parts, 1655–56) belongs to the early history of the cantata; insertions of other Bible passages, devotional poetry, and allegorical dialogues bring in a contemplative element. It is worth noting that Hammerschmidt also added to a vanishing genre by publishing a volume of *Missae* (1663), for five to twelve and more voices. His often simple, folkish style, ridiculed as the "Hammerschmiedischer Fuss" (the blacksmith's foot), was in accord with a popular trend of his time. Johann Beer, in his *Musikalische Diskurse* (1719), commented with justification that Hammerschmidt's popular style "had kept music in use in almost every village parish up to this day." His music, easy to understand and to perform, succeeded much more readily than did that of Schütz, who avoided all folk appeal.

In quantity, Rudolph Ahle's output may have surpassed even Hammerschmidt's; it was of inferior quality, however, and gave great impetus to the process of popularization. His forms ranged from the concerto for one voice (*Harmonias protopaideumata . . . Monadum seu uniciniorum . . . decas prima,*

1647) to concertos for small ensembles on various texts (*Himmelsüsse Jesusfreude
. . . Concertlein und Arien,* for two voices, 1648) to polychoral concertos for
twenty-four voices. He contributed to the dialogue genre, in a manner similar to
Hammerschmidt, with his *Geistliche Dialoge aus Sonn- und Festtags-Evangelien*
(1648) for two to four voices. In his *Neugepflanzter Thüringischer Lustgartens
Nebengang* (1663), Ahle paid tribute to the simple concerto for small ensemble.
His numerous songs seem to have been especially popular. They could be performed as "arias" by a choir of four voices or by a solo voice with thoroughbass.
He published many of these in various collections, e.g., in his *Arien* (1660) for
one to four voices with ritornellos for four viols, in his *Neue Andachten* (1662)
for one to four and eight voices "with or without basso continuo and including
optional ritornellos for four viols," and in his *Neue geistliche Chorstücke* (1663–
64) for five to eight voices, "in which even the thoroughbass is not necessary but
can be used if customary . . . in an easy style." The style aimed increasingly at

Johann Rudolf Ahle: Aria for four voices, or soprano solo with thoroughbass

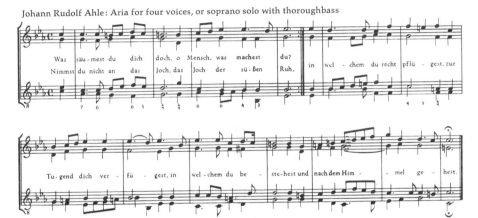

"sweetness" and avoided "heaviness." There is no doubt that in such popularization was the beginning of a Philistine laziness, even though Protestantism took
over many of Ahle's easily understood and popular songs. Ahle's expertness is
shown in his dialogues. The dialogue of the Pharisee and Publican, for example,
is still partly dramatic but entirely in Hammerschmidt's allegorical manner; the
text *Ich will singen von der Gnade* is combined with a *Misericordias Domini.*
Isolated monodies of high quality in the manner of Schütz's *Symphoniae* and
motets in the style of the *Geistliche Chormusik* leave no doubt concerning Ahle's
model. He was no great mind, but he had a workman-like skill perhaps closer to
Hassler, Eccard, and Praetorius than to Hammerschmidt's ingenuous style. His
humorous scene depicting the proclamation to the shepherds, in which four
bassoons represent the grumbling, tenderhearted, jovial peasants, is a masterful
realization in spite of its narrow confines.

Tobias Michael, Sebastian Knüpfer, and Johann Schelle, cantors of St.
Thomas's in Leipzig, exemplify the trend of the times. Michael was one of the
youngest composers to contribute a Psalm 116 to Burckhard Grossmann's collec-

tion (1623). In his *Musikalische Seelenlust* for one to six voices "with alternating instruments, symphonies, and choirs" (two parts, 1634 and 1637), he went back to Schein's sacred madrigal style *(Israelsbrünnlein)*. In his sacred concertos for small ensembles, he adopted Hieronymus Kapsberger's coloratura style (preface to part II). Like all composers of this time, he wrote numerous occasional compositions in a mixed genre that contained elements of the concerto, the madrigal, the motet, and the simple aria movement. Knüpfer wrote multisectional concertos for large ensembles on Bible passages with and without paraphrased chorale stanzas. The first and last movements were written for chorus and instruments, the middle movements for solo voices. In the 1650s and '60s, his noble, elevated style was already somewhat archaic—contrasting with Buxtehude's intimacy and delicacy and Geist's preciosity. Schelle inserted a series of stanzas (chorale variations or contemporary song stanzas) between the outer movements. These psalm or Gospel concertos are part of the early history of the cantata (see below). From 1689, he also wrote chorale cantatas on the basic Lutheran hymns. Despite the fact that the Reverend Carpzow returned orthodoxy to predominance in Leipzig, Schelle still set to music the *Andächtige Studenten* by the Leipzig professor Joachim Feller (1682), who was reprimanded for his Pietism. The strongly orthodox, conservative attitude in Leipzig might explain why the cantors of St. Thomas's did not set any more contemporary religious poetry.

Johann Rosenmüller, who substituted for Tobias Michael in Leipzig and later worked in Venice and Wolfenbüttel, was probably, after Hammerschmidt, the most popular and widely copied composer of this group. The appeal of his music, however, lay not so much in its unpretentiousness as in its expressiveness and beauty of sound. His dramatic Latin monodies on the Lamentations of Jeremiah, obviously relying on Italian models, rank among the best works of this genre. His only published sacred work, *Kernsprüche, mehrenteils aus Hl. Schrift* (two parts, 1648 and 1652–53), concertos for three to seven voices, is one of the foremost of this genre, although it was intended more for congregational use than for individual devotions. Most of his many concertos are preserved in manuscript only (besides the *Kernsprüche* about 175 church compositions survive; M. Geck in *MGG* XI, 1963, 917). In his twelve dialogues from the 1650s chorale or hymn stanzas are frequently added to the Bible text (ibid.). Rosenmüller's Latin concertos for large ensembles contain solo passages. His excellent songs place him beside the best song composers of the time (in 1726 J. S. Bach used, unchanged, Rosenmüller's funeral song *Welt, ade, ich bin dein müde* in his cantata No. 27, *Wer weiss, wie nahe mir mein Ende*). Adam Krieger, the great master of German secular song of the 17th century, was Rosenmüller's successor as organist of St. Nicholas's in Leipzig and Knüpfer's fellow applicant for the position as cantor of St. Thomas's. Only two of his sacred concertos are preserved; their intensity of expression places them close to Schütz. Other members of the Leipzig group were Werner Fabricius, pupil of Selle and Scheidemann in Hamburg, the *Stadtmusikus* Johann Pezel, and the lawyer J. Kaspar Horn, who wrote sacred hymns, vocal concertos, and other religious works. Horn's annual Gospel series (1680), like the one by Wolfgang Brückner of Rastenberg in Thuringia (1656), once again followed a pure Bible text (Moser); perhaps it stimulated Schelle to write his Gospel cycle, which has been lost.

LATIN LITURGICAL MUSIC

Liturgical music in the strict sense, especially on Latin texts, was increasingly pushed into the background by the abundance of vocal Protestant church music: biblical proverb compositions (in German or Latin) in motet form, concertos (for small or large ensembles), dialogues, sacred madrigals, solo songs with or without instrumental ritornellos, choral arias and other kinds of song, choral compositions extending from the chorale aria for one voice accompanied by instruments to the (rare) chorale motet and chorale concerto or chorale *variatio per choros* or variation *per omnes versus*. There were compositions in which traditional texts were interspersed with free additions, sacred poetry, chorale stanzas, or various text compilations—all leading eventually to the cantata. The Kyrie, the Gloria, sometimes the Credo and the Sanctus, the Magnificat, some sporadic Vesper hymns, occasionally even an Introit in Latin, continued to be composed into the 18th century—here and there even into the 19th. By and large, however, an interest in compositions on German texts of all sorts and combinations was increasing and interest in Latin texts was decreasing. Protestant composers preferred more and more to set pericopes and freely chosen texts rather than to cultivate the traditional liturgical genres, which were rarely used and could easily be borrowed from the Catholic repertory.

The return to Italian music on Latin texts seems to have been common in Protestant circles. Like the Stockholm Düben collection, the inventories of large city curches or active royal chapels (Lübeck, Lüneburg, Rudolstadt, Erfurt, and numerous others) offer striking evidence that this music was in abundant use. The only question is whether it was used in congregational worship or mainly in court and for private devotions. In 1683 the burgomaster of Leipzig expressly prohibited Johann Schelle from performing German compositions in the service after the Gospel lesson in place of the customary Latin selections of Italian origin. Obviously, this prohibition supported the continuation of a practice common with Lindner, Kaspar Hassler, Lechner, Schadaeus, Bodenschatz, and so on (see pp. 172 and 193) of importing new styles. There was, however, one difference: before the Thirty Years' War this imported material was gathered together in compendious volumes; now it was circulated in original prints or copies and collected by the larger churches in archives or libraries. The spreading of Italian music on Latin texts (and not only on liturgical texts in the restricted sense) within the contemporary German Lutheran church was connected with traditional irenics, whereby a far greater tolerance was extended toward Roman Catholicism than toward the Reformed or Calvinist denominations. It may also have been connected with the Jesuit Mission, which seems to have been very active musically in Germany. This development has yet to be recognized, let alone studied as a historical process. Research in this field could probably shed new light on some still unknown aspects of 17th-century Protestant usage, e.g., on the question of much devotional music and the like. Among other sources of information, the Dresden court orchestra at the end of Schutz's life—and after him with Peranda, Bontempi, Pallavicini, Albrici, etc.—could provide substantial documentary material.

The spread of Latin Masses and Magnificats from German or Italian Roman Catholic regions to the realm of Protestant church music may be traced in an abundance of preserved manuscripts. J. S. Bach still copied or arranged Masses and Mass settings by Palestrina, Kerll, Zelenka, and Lotti; he and Buttstett composed Latin Masses for Catholic church services. Copies of J. J. Fux's Masses were widely distributed. Many Italians worked and composed at German courts; there seems to have been little difference whether they worked for Roman Catholic or Protestant churches. In the late 17th century Ruggero Fedeli, and in the first decades of the 18th century Fortunato Chelleri, worked in Kassel and both composed Masses for the Reformed court. In no other place were the lines between the denominations obliterated to such an extent. As early as 1607 (perhaps even earlier), Michael Praetorius included a complete *Missa quodlibetica* and a Magnificat, both for eight voices, in his *Musarum Sioniarum Motectae*. The first reappeared, slightly revised, in his *Missodia* (1611), which, by the way, contains all parts of the Mass, the Ordinary as well as the collect and versicles, prefaces, Amen, and so on, "chorali cumprimis observata," using common choral cantus firmi. The Introits announced here failed to materialize. *Eulogodia* (1611), however, contains the Latin closing songs used in the service, the *Benedicamus, Deo dicamus* (during Christmastime with the songs *Puer natus* and *Resonet in laudibus*), and songs of the Completorium. *Megalynodia* (1611) is a collection of Latin Magnificats, nearly all of them parodies on chansons, madrigals, or motets. The *Polyhymnia caduceatrix* (1619) contains a setting of the German Magnificat in the style of a concerto for large ensemble, a *Missa ganz deutsch*—i.e., a short Mass, with a second Gloria "in echo"—and a German Mass on *O Vater, allmächtiger Gott* and *Allein Gott in der Höh sei Ehr*. Praetorius contributed more richly to the repertory using Latin texts than almost anyone else in the field. The lost parts of Scheidt's *Geistliche Konzerte* contained more Masses and Magnificats. There is hardly any one among the later Lutheran musicians of the 17th century who did not occasionally write a Latin Mass, a Magnificat, or a couple of Latin songs, hymns, or responsories, but very few were productive to any considerable extent. So-called *Missae*—short two-movement Masses consisting of Kyrie and Gloria, seldom with Credo or Sanctus—were written either in a concerto style or in the "Praenestine" counterpoint of T. Selle, C. Demantius, Hieronymus Praetorius, Henning Dedekind, D. Friderici, S. Besler, H. Grimm, J. Weichmann, and others. Twenty parody Masses for five to eight voices collected by Georg Vintzius of Naumburg (in about 1630) have been handed down in manuscript. In the 1650s, Masses were written by Capricornus, Stephan Otto, and J. R. Ahle; the German lied Mass by H. Schütz, in his *Zwölf geistliche Gesänge* (1657), belongs with this group. A. Hammerschmidt (1663), J. Theile (1673, 1686), and J. Buttstett (1720) were rather isolated figures with their whole volumes of Masses. Rosenmüller, Theile, Christoph Bernhard, and others occasionally took up composing in the *stylus antiquus,* but they also wrote in the widely disseminated concerto style; the short Mass attributed to Buxtehude (nowadays doubtful) is also in the *stylus antiquus*. The fate of Magnificat compositions is similar to that of Masses; until the time of Bach, sporadic Latin Magnificats were written by many composers—among them Ahle and Theile—none of whom devoted himself to this genre on a larger scale. In the worship service the Magnificat was performed more and more in alternation between sung (chorale) and instrumental (organ) verses. The Introit, Te Deum, and so on, had been treated by Praetorius as fixed parts of the liturgy; these sections did not entirely disappear but were rarely still composed, and then only for festive occasions. The Mass alone enjoyed a wider dissemination. In the larger churches Masses in the old contrapuntal style were performed along with those in the brilliant style of the concerto for large ensemble, e.g., by Knüpfer and Schelle at St. Thomas's in Leipzig. J. Philipp Krieger seems to have been an exception among the Lutheran composers of that period, for he is said to have composed more than a hundred Masses and Mass settings of all kinds and dimensions, culminating in his festive Mass for fifty-eight voices in a pompous Roman style, written for the dedication of the chapel in the castle of Weissenfels (1682). Nothing of this extensive production survives; it would have formed a Protestant equivalent to J. J. Fux.

CONGREGATIONAL SONG AND ART MUSIC

WORDS AND MUSIC FOR NEW HYMNS

THE HYMNBOOKS

The split between congregational song and art music, which began during the Counter-Reformation, opened wider during the 17th century as the turbulent musical developments toward new forms and styles took their natural course. The higher forms of music, whether sermon-like in their orthodoxy or edifyingly mystical, were to become more and more alien to the majority of churchgoers. Only the connoisseur and music lover appreciated them. Since these forms conformed increasingly to types of secular music, taking over stylistic elements from chamber music and opera, their secularization was inevitable. The intellectual and social separation was drastically revealed when a recommendation was made to the congregation to read their prayerbooks at the times they could not follow the music and when other church administrations expressly revoked such recommendations (Synod of Gotha, 1645; Graff). For a long time congregational song seems to have had no connection with art music. With Praetorius, even the most demanding compositions were interspersed with hymns and liturgical chorales. The decrease in chorale arrangements that can be observed in the works of most composers from about 1620 to 1670 was symptomatic of how wide the break with tradition had become. To the simple Christian, art music in the churches must have become as strange and almost as unintelligible as the bombastic 17th-century style of sermon that used an artificial language overloaded with pompous learned quotations. Even the tendency toward popularization on the part of Hammerschmidt, Ahle, Briegel, and others did not result in true congregational music, although their works were undoubtedly often used in services. Like everything else, most of the new hymn poetry was not intended for the congregation, although some of it may have found its way slowly into congregational use. The development of cantatas and cantata librettos merely reflected the process taking place with all types of church music. It is hard to tell how much the organ chorale affected the situation, because it is still uncertain how much the large-scale chorale arrangement for organ was accepted as church music in the restricted sense. Certainly the little chorale prelude was accepted (this developed only in the last third of the century), and the settings of alternate movements from Masses, hymns, Magnificats, and so on. The estrangement reached its peak in about 1700 (as testified to by the "Neumeister Reform" and similar signs). Only thereafter did congregational song and art music draw closer together and achieve a certain integration, especially in the work of Bach (see pp. 105 f. and 121 f.).

The estrangement did not mean, however, that hymns and hymn poetry did not develop further during the 17th century. On the contrary, the trend begun by Christoph Knoll and Bartholomäus Ringwaldt, Philipp Nicolai and Nikolaus Selnecker, was rapidly continued. Almost no other period produced as much new hymn poetry (but not music). However, the line bisecting other genres also bisected the creation of hymns: most new hymns were art music rather than congregational song. In addition, the two basic trends of the period—mysticism and orthodoxy—were set against each other. They were represented by two men of the same age, Johann Rist and Paul Gerhardt, until the one was absorbed by Pietism and the other was paralyzed by the sterility of late orthodoxy. As long as Rist's nature and education followed the mystical trend, and Gerhardt's the orthodox, they were both moved by a similar piety, deeply introverted and emotional. Both were prone to the same remorse, the same sacrifice of self, the same devotedness of the heart; a similar taste for poetic and emotional expression impelled them both. (Nothing could have been more characteristic of the atmosphere of the time.) At the same time, Rist represented the artistic aspect of contemporary hymn poetry, Gerhardt the popular.

During the Counter-Reformation, the number of hymns had greatly increased; now it grew immeasurably. In the late 17th century (counting the contents of hymnbooks as well as new hymns) there were about ten thousand. The quantity of texts grew much faster than the number of melodies, since most hymn texts were written for already existing melodies. Melodies increased again in number when the new type of "aria" became fashionable as a hymn type. This was the solo song accompanied by thoroughbass with or without instrumental ritornellos (which was identical to the homophonically set choral lied, the chords of which were sung by the lower voices instead of being played on accompanying instruments). Rist and Gerhardt played an important role in this development; both collaborated with musicians and stimulated them to compose hymns, as did Elmenhorst at the end of the century.

There was a great increase in Jesus songs, private devotional and vocational hymns, hymns about the cross, hymns for periods of stress, for dying and confessing. They began with Philipp Nicolai and Valerius Herberger, were altered in form under the influence of Opitz, and were spread by the poetic academies (the

Fruit-bearing Society in Weimar, the Society of Pegnitz Shepherds in Nuremberg, and the Order of Elbe Swans founded by Rist in Hamburg, and many others). Mystical devotion was already evident in the titles of collections by the Silesian Johann Heermann (*Andächtige Kirch-Seufzer . . . in welche den Saft und Kern aller . . . Evangelien reimweis gegossen* [The Pious Churchly Sigh . . . in which the juice and core of the entire Gospel are poured out in rhyme], 1616; *Exercitium pietatis* and *Devoti musica cordis,* 1630, etc.) and of individual hymns: *O Jesu Christe, wahres Licht, Herzliebster Jesu, was hast du verbrochen, Wo soll ich fliehen hin, O Gott, du frommer Gott.* The step from Arnd and Johann Gerhard to Heermann is as small as the one from Heermann to Pietism. In 1626, Matthäus Meyfarth of Coburg wrote the words to *Jerusalem, du hochgebaute Stadt,* and Martin Rinckart of Eilenburg, *Nun danket alle Gott.* Musicians, too, joined in. Michael Altenburg wrote *Gustav Adolfs Feldlied "Verzage nicht, du Häuflein klein,"* J. H. Schein wrote *Mach's mit mir, Gott, nach deiner Güt.* H. Schütz's cousin, Heinrich Albert of Königsberg, whose eight-part *Arien* (1638–50) made him the most important representative of the early solo lied, wrote *Gott des Himmels und der Erden* and *Einen guten Kampf hab ich auf der Welt gekämpfet.* There was a whole group of Königsberg poets: Simon Dach *(Ich bin ja, Herr, in deiner Macht),* Georg Weissel *(Macht hoch die Tür),* Valentin Thilo *(Mit Ernst, ihr Menschenkinder).* Paul Fleming, a student of J. H. Schein, was perhaps the most distinctive poet among them, especially with his highly emotional but well-structured hymn *In allen meinen Taten* and with his Eucharist hymns (which were not taken into the hymnbooks); all secular and religious poetry of the late 17th century was deeply influenced by him. David Pohle and Christian Dedekind set his verses to music. Johann Rist, pastor in Wedel near Hamburg, was the climax of this development. Rist, called the "grosse Cimberschwan" and the "nordische Apoll," edited numerous collections of sacred and secular songs and was acquainted with many musicians; Heinrich Schütz visited him in Wedel, and Christoph Bernhard wrote a funeral motet for him. His *Himmlische Lieder* (1641–43) were set to music by J. Schop, his *Neue Himmlische Lieder* (1651) composed by S. G. Staden, Hammerschmidt, H. Pape, H. Kortkamp, Jakob Praetorius, H. Scheidemann, and others. His *Sabbathische Seelenlust* (1651) and his *Neue musikalische Festandachten* (1655) were set by Thomas Selle; Schop and M. Jacobi wrote music for his *Alltägliche Hausmusik* (1654), Hammerschmidt and Jacobi for his *Katechismus-Andachten* (1656). His *Passionsandachten* were composed by M. Coler. All songbooks appeared with melodies and thoroughbass. Hidden behind Rist's sometimes affected language and seemingly hollow bombast was an ecstatic excitement. In the elegance of his verses and the self-indulgence of his verbosity, he is revealed as a "virtuoso of individuality" (Nelle). Rist's style is characterized by an emphasis on the ego, a celebration of the self through an expression of the emotions, an amplification of the soul's misery, a depiction of the torments of Hell or the torture of the Crucified—all presented with the polish and versatility of a man of the world. His collaboration with the composers of his songs became significant for the course of music history. As much as he insisted on simplicity and popular appeal, and as much as he instructed his composers in this regard, even he could not prevent the melodies from becoming artistic arias instead of folk- or chorale-like. Therefore, only a few of his hymns gradually made their way into the hymnbooks, e.g., *Ermuntre dich, mein schwacher Geist, O Traurigkeit, O Herzeleid,* and *O Ewigkeit, du Donnerwort,* which became widely known through Bach's cantatas Nos. 20 and 60. In general, the Italian "aria" governed the song writing of the period, whether this was in simple arioso style or embellished with coloraturas and supported by a bass (the dividing line was always vague). Composers of secular songs tended to change the simple melodic-metric form into a fully articulated, aria-like, coloratura style; the song was turned into a "solo aria" in the sense of a solo cantata. Representative composers include Nauwach, Kaspar Kittel, J. J. Löwe, J. Weiland, Friedrich Böddecker, Christian Dedekind, H. Albert, Adam Krieger (the great song master of the period), and especially late composers like Ph. Krieger, J. W. Franck, Buxtehude, and Erlebach. Even Rist's circle could not entirely avoid the tendency. A whole Hamburg School of secular as well as sacred songs followed the same tendency, which was later continued by the poet Heinrich Elmenhorst and his trio of composers, J. W. Franck, P. L. Wockenfuss, and G. Böhm.

Rist made it clear that he would have signed the Great Elector's Declaration of Tolerance, for opposition to which Paul Gerhardt was dismissed as provost of St. Nicholas's Church in Berlin (1666; temporarily reappointed in 1667, definitely dismissed in 1668). Rist came from the Rostock alignment with Lutheranism, which favored reforms. Gerhardt, coming from the strictest Wittenberg orthodoxy, was unpolemical in manner, the soul of resistance against his sovereign's irenic tendencies, his emotions receptive to mystical ideas, his professional concerns deeply committed to the purity of doctrine, his poetry reflecting the central doctrine of the Lutheran church, justification by faith. He was opposed to any kind of *Synkretismus,* saying that he "could not consider Calvinists as Christians." Once again the Lutheran model of the congregational hymn reveals itself in his songs. Once again the "love of Jesus" songs and hymns of private devotion declined somewhat in favor of delineations of personal salvation and faith. Yet often Gerhardt's expression was extremely emotional and frequently sentimental. Childlike trust in God and innocence of heart are frequently connected with stilted rhetoric and an exhibition of private feeling that is not always convincing. His songs popularized orthodox theology (Petrich). Emotion, piety, and elegance of form were characteristic of his period; "figurae Gerhardtianae" (Petrich) show the poet's relationship to musical rhetoric. Johann Arnd influenced him as much as did the style of orthodox preaching (Aullen). Many of his 133 songs that are known today were taken into the permanent congregational repertory, though slowly and, for the most part, not until the 18th century: *Ist Gott für mich, so trete gleich alles wider mich, Wie soll ich dich empfangen, Ich steh an deiner Krippe hier, O Haupt voll Blut und Wunden, Befiehl du deine Wege, Die güldne Sonne, Fröhlich soll mein Herze springen,* and many others. Like all religious verse of the period, Gerhardt's poems were written primarily for private devotions and to be set as art music, as "poesia per musica," meaning the "aria." No less than 53 of Gerhardt's songs, with melodies by Nikolaus Hasse in the style of the solo aria, were published in Heinrich Müller's *Himmlische Liebesflammen* (Rostock, 1659). However, Gerhardt's regular composer (until 1662) was Johann Crüger,

64. Johann Rosenmüller, opening of the motet *Miserere mei Deus,* Psalm 51, for alto, tenor, bass, two violins, and continuo. Dresden, Sächsische Landesbibliothek.

65. Dietrich Buxtehude, *Wachet auf, ruft uns die Stimme*, opening of the *Corale Concertato* for alto, tenor, bass, two violins, and continuo. From the collection of the Staatsbibliothek der Stiftung Preussischer Kulturbesitz (formerly Preussische Staatsbibliothek Berlin), temporarily at Marburg/Lahn, Mus. MS 2680.

his cantor at St. Nicholas's, and later (until 1668) Crüger's successor, Georg Ebeling. In 1640, Crüger edited the first Lutheran hymnal *(Neues volkömmliches Gesangbuch)*, closely following J. H. Schein's Cantoniale of 1627 (Fischer-Krückeberg). In 1647 the second edition appeared under the significant title *Praxis pietatis melica (Übung der Gottseligkeit in Gesängen)*, thus anticipating the rising slogan of the time. It contained 15 lyrics by Gerhardt, together with numerous others by Heermann, Ringwaldt, M. Schirmer, Rist (with melodies by Schop), and the Königsberg poets. In the fifth edition (1653), Gerhardt's songs increased to 81, in the tenth (1661) to 88. The *Praxis pietatis melica* became the most influential hymnbook of the 17th century (45 editions were issued in Berlin up to 1736, with numerous reprints; in 1647 it contained 387 hymns, since 1736, 1,316 hymns). An omnibus edition of Gerhardt's songs was published by G. Ebeling under the title *Pauli Gerhardi geistliche Andachten* (1666–67); it contains 120 hymns. From 1653 Gerhardt's poems slowly entered the hymnals with melodies by Crüger and later by Ebeling; spurred on by Pietism, they were firmly established by the 18th century. Bach's cantatas are interspersed with hymn stanzas by Gerhardt. Tersteegen's Rhenish songbook (1739; see below) contains ten hymns by Gerhardt with only two by Luther, but 50 by Scheffler.

Most of the melodies Crüger wrote for Gerhardt's texts were later replaced by other melodies; others were used for different texts. The Gerhardt-Crüger hymns were used in the Reformed Runge songbook of 1653 and from there taken into many other hymnals. In 1649 the first polyphonic arrangement of the *Praxis pietatis* appeared as *Geistliche Kirchenmelodien*. It was in four voices, with two parts freely concerted and with optional parts for high instruments and thoroughbass—in other words, in the "chorale aria" form. In 1657–58 the Great Elector, who regarded Crüger as the best church musician in Berlin, had him publish similar settings of the Lobwasser Psalter and a freely compiled song collection; they were obviously intended for private devotions. The important step Crüger took here was to reshape the old cantional style, continued straight into the *Praxis pietatis* and similar collections, and to modernize it with the addition of thoroughbass and instruments. (As early as 1622, Crüger was publishing concertos of his own.) Georg Ebeling's Gerhardt collection (1666–67), enlarged to include his own compositions, was similar in nature. After Crüger's death, Jakob Hintze of Berlin published subsequent editions of the *Praxis pietatis;* only in 1695 did he continue with the similar but more concerto-like settings of *Opitzens Epistolische Lieder,* which he had been announcing since 1666 (Fischer-Krückeberg). Song, aria, and concerted styles cannot be separated in this group. Johann Sebastiani of Königsberg composed arias with five-voice ritornellos, and he printed many sacred songs in the two parts of his *Parnassblumen* (Hamburg, 1672 and 1675).

The number of poets and melodists was immense; only a few can be mentioned here. In Silesia, Matthäus Apelles von Löwenstern wrote some 30 lyrics in classical meter and strophic form; he himself set them to music and published them in his *Frühlings-Maien* and again in his *Geistliche Kirchen- und Hausmusik* (1644). He called them "flowers grown near the house but plucked a little too early." His hymns *Christe, du Beistand deiner Kreuzgemeine* and *Nun preiset alle Gottes Barmherzigkeit* have had a permanent place in hymnbooks for a long time.

Löwenstern also composed motets and sacred concertos for various instruments. Andreas Gryphius, the Silesian playwright and maker of epigrams, was also a distinguished religious poet. Johann Franck wrote *Jesu, meine Freude, Schmücke dich, o liebe Seele,* and many others. Sigismund von Birken's *Jesu, deine Passion* and Christoph Tietze's *Alles ist an Gottes Segen,* among others, stem from the group called the Nuremberg Order of the Flower.

Roman Catholic poetry, closely related to the Lutheran mystical trend, established itself with the outstanding poets Johann Scheffler (Angelus Silesius) and Friedrich von Spee. Von Spee's *Trutznachtigall* (posthumous, 1649) was widely circulated; *Bei stiller Nacht zur ersten Wacht* and others of his were close to becoming religious folk songs. Such Scheffler songs as *Mir nach, spricht Christus unser Held, Jesus ist der schönste Nam,* and *Ich will dich lieben, meine Stärke* found a permanent place in Protestant hymnals. Scheffler's lyrics were published by Georg Joseph in Breslau in *Heilige Seelenlust oder geistliche Hirtenlieder der in ihren Jesum verliebten Psyche,* "graced with exceedingly beautiful melodies" (1657 and later, four volumes with 155 hymns). Martin Schneider of Liegnitz published 40 poems by Scheffler as "Arietten" for solo voice "cum Sonatella a 5 Violin" (that is, solo arias with ritornellos). They bore the title *Erster Teil neuer geistlicher Lieder.* Buxtehude was deeply influenced by Scheffler. Erdmann Neumeister, in his history of literature (1695) gave Scheffler a very high rating. Gottfried Arnold published the third edition of the *Cherubinischer Wandersmann* (1701). In his *Geistliches Blumengärtlein* (1729), Tersteegen printed poems by Scheffler and included no less than 50 of Scheffler's lyrics in his songbook (1739). Zinzendorf is unthinkable without him. The Silesian Christian Knorr von Rosenroth belonged to the group of Roman Catholic poets who found a place in Protestant hymnals; he published a *Neues Helicon . . . Geistliche Sittenlieder . . . von einem Liebhaber christlicher Übungen,* which included 76 arias with thoroughbass. There is reason to doubt whether he also wrote the melodies (Ameln). His hymn *Morgenglanz der Ewigkeit* remained in use for a long time.

Saxon-Thuringian poets included Christian Keimann *(Meinen Jesum lass ich nicht),* Georg Neumark *(Wer nur den lieben Gott lässt walten),* Samuel Rodigast *(Was Gott tut, das ist wohlgetan),* and Michael Franck *(Ach wie flüchtig, ach wie nichtig).* In Jena, Ahasverus Fritzsch published a collection called *Himmelslust und Weltunlust* (1679, perhaps even earlier), the second part containing 52 "beautiful songs of heaven," among which were a number of arias with thoroughbass. The many anonymous hymns included the well-known *Jesus, meine Zuversicht.*

Song production was endless and any survey can select only a few of the most prominent musical characteristics. All these songs shared to some extent the common aim of self-expression, of submersion in Christ, of dissolving temporality into eternity. They are mostly personal songs in the form of "aria" with thoroughbass, at times with instruments and ritornellos. Compared with these, the increase in liturgical (i.e., true congregational) hymns was insignificant. Nelle calls Johann Olearius of Halle "the true liturgical poet of Gerhardt's day." The poetry of Tobias Clausnitzer and Hartmann Schenk is also closely related to Gerhardt's.

Because of this flood of songs for private devotions, official hymnbooks had no choice but to reissue the old Lutheran hymns and add some of the new songs. The poets usually published new lyrics in anthologies of their own, often with melodies. The usual route from words to music began with the poetry collection, led to the solo song for private use, and finally (usually only after a long time) to the congregational hymnbook. Significantly, it was the hymnbooks of the Pietistic period that first paved the way for the creation of large numbers of new poems and settings. Besides Johann Crüger's *Praxis pietatis melica* (1644 and later; see above), the most important hymnbooks between Schein's Cantionale (1627) and Freylinghausen's *Geistreiches Gesangbuch* (1707–14) were the Gotha Cantionale, three parts (1648 and later) with 329 settings for two to six voices, the Erfurt hymnbook of 1663, a new Gotha hymnbook (1666) with many new editions (in 1725, 1,276 hymns), the Nuremberg hymnbook (1676–77; 1,160 hymns, but only 177 melodies with thoroughbass), the *Neues Leipziger Gesangbuch* of Gottfried Vopelius (1682; a revision of Schein's Cantionale containing Passions and liturgical pieces), the Lüneburg (1686; 2,002 hymns, but only 110 melodies), the Darmstadt of W.K. Briegel (1687), the Stuttgart (1691), and the Celle hymnbook (1696). A Leipzig hymnbook (1697) contained as many as 5,000 hymns. Many composers from this period, important and not, are represented in these collections. The increasing number of hymnbooks can be explained by the numerous territorial states that arose after the Thirty Years' War, each of which counted it as sovereign privilege to have its own hymnbook. The number of songs in each of the various books increased as a result of the need to provide churchgoers with a large repertory of new hymns in addition to the old stock. From a musical point of view, the hymnbooks changed considerably. Some still followed the Schein Cantionale type with settings for many voices (sometimes as many as eight); some presented the melodies in the traditional manner for one voice, others for one voice with thoroughbass, others with accompanying instruments. In all this, the boundary between hymnbooks for congregational and private use ceased to exist. Many books dispensed entirely with printed melodies. However, the most important development affecting "older" melodies was a gradual transition from polymetric (see p. 66 ff.) to isometric structures. Briegel's Darmstadt Cantionale (1687) is usually considered to be the decisive document, but the process had started earlier and spread very slowly (cf. especially W. Blankenburg, *Geschichte der Melodien des evangelischen Kirchengesangbuches*, Göttingen, 1957). With Crüger it was already far advanced. With Briegel, the melodies were reduced to metrical schemes that came into use mostly in the 18th and 19th centuries. The simplification of melodies and the "improvement" of texts also began in this period (Christian von Stöcken, 1680–81; H. A. Stockfleth, 1690; the Plön hymnbook, 1674; the Lübeck hymnbook, 1699, and so on). The spirit of rationalistic enlightenment became apparent. Admonitions on simplified singing by the orthodox clergy (justified in regard to the growing mass of lieder and "arias") contributed to the emasculation of the great Lutheran hymn tradition during the following period. There was still one other element behind these developments: congregations gradually came to enjoy the older hymns less and less, and new ones became increasingly necessary. The assimilation of new works therefore continued unceasingly from the middle of the 17th century until the middle of the 20th.

ORGAN MUSIC

There is still a need to clarify the duties of the organist during church services as well as the question of whether organ music had a liturgical or paraliturgical function between the times of Michael Praetorius and Dietrich Buxtehude. In the course of the century, organ accompaniments to congregational hymns gradually came into use, but they were not completely established before the beginning of the 18th century. Schein's Cantionale (1627) added a thoroughbass to the melodies, and many hymnbooks followed his lead; however, this accompaniment may have been intended for singing at home rather than in church. If an organist had to accompany congregational singing, he would not have needed printed or written parts. In the Hamburg *Melodeien-Gesangbuch* (1604) the accompaniment was an established practice; in Danzig it became common in 1633. If organ accompaniment (according to Graff) was reported to be still rejected here and there in the 18th century, it was either an exceptional case or else a reference to the practice of leaving out the organ for some stanzas of the hymn—a remnant of the practice of alternation customary in Berlin around 1750. Special chorale books with accompanying parts for the organist were not necessary. Every organist could improvise chords in the usual cantional style for the known hymns; only with new hymns would he have needed a thoroughbass. Samuel Scheidt's *Tabulaturbuch hundert geistlicher Gesänge* (the so-called Görlitz tabulature; 1650) and Daniel Vetter's *Musikalische Kirch- und Haus-Ergötzlichkeit* (1709–13) were a kind of manual for organ accompaniment to the chorale. Surprisingly, however, there are many simple four-part hymn settings without texts in German organ tabulatures.

It is difficult to decide the extent to which the contents of German organ tabulatures were "church music" in the restricted sense. During the entire century the tabulatures remained notations for any kind of keyboard instrument; they did not differentiate between organ and harpsichord. For most of the century the repertories mixed secular and sacred pieces, works with and without cantus firmus, simple tabulature settings or arrangements of vocal works and original keyboard compositions, works of German and foreign composers, Roman Catholic and Protestant composers. A mixture was the rule; specialization into one or a few species was exceptional. The tabulatures do not reveal to what extent pieces in strict style (such as ricercars, fugues), stylized dances (such as passacaglias, chaconnes, *passamezzi*), or pieces in free style (such as preludes and toccatas) were used in the church service. In addition it is uncertain to what extent larger compositions with cantus firmus (chorale fantasies, chorale variations) were used in the service. In fact, there is a question whether this whole literature should be regarded as didactic or practical. Orders for the service left little room for it. Provided they were still in use, parts of the Ordinary (Kyrie, Gloria) or of the Proper of the Mass (Introit, Gradual) could be replaced by organ music; more frequently, the organ followed the practice of alternation during the Mass as well as during the Magnificat of the Vespers. Protestant Mass versicles occur in part III of Scheidt's *Tabulatura nova* (1624) and in Johann Bähr's *Wisbyer Tabulatur* (1611). Beginning with Praetorius's *Hymnodia* and Bähr's tabulature (both 1611), many hymn versicles were written; they are to be found in the Vienna Minorite tabulature 714 (Riedel), in Scheidt's *Tabulatura nova,* and so on. They gradually became rarer and changed with Weckmann, Buxtehude, Pachelbel, and others into a form of hymn prelude or hymn variation. Magnificat versicles were greater in number, but they abandoned the realm of cantus-firmus composition and took the form of a sequence of small movements held together only by a common key. There were a few isolated organ settings for Marian antiphons or for the Te Deum (for example, by Tunder and Buxtehude). Generally in Protestant organ music of this period, compositions on a liturgical cantus firmus receded in favor of compositions on a hymn cantus firmus or on none at all.

Probably very few of the many and often copious German tabulatures were used in the service. It is more likely that the organist was limited to four functions: accompanying congregational singing (wherever it was customary); performing short preludes and interludes to congregational singing and to liturgical altar chants (apparently customary everywhere); performing alternate verses of the liturgy and congregational hymns (customary until the time of Bach); and inserting single selections, perhaps at the beginning or end of the service, in place of a Kyrie or Gradual, during Holy Communion, or the like. Undoubtedly the first two functions were performed extempore. The fourth cannot be placed in any category, since during Communion an organ piece could be played, a congregational hymn sung, or a sacred concerto or motet performed. (Investigation has not yet been undertaken to determine whether instrumental pieces were commonly inserted in Protestant services, as they were in the Roman Catholic.) The old practice of alternation (see p. 105 ff.) flourished throughout the 17th century. Michael Praetorius described it in his general foreword to *Musae Sioniae* (1606) exactly as it functioned later too. The congregation sang to organ accompaniment or was led only by a precentor or supported by a school choir in cantional style. The precentor or school choir might be accompanied by instruments in either concerto or motet style. Alternate verses could be sung by a soloist with instruments ("chorale aria") or played as an organ solo with variations on the hymn melody. Thus, a series of verses would call forth shifting masses of sound. The fact that the organ also had an independent role in the liturgy through its use in solo versicles in the Mass, in hymns, in the Magnificat, and so on, gave its antiphonal role a characteristic significance during the 17th century. As early as 1597, through a recommendation of the Wittenberg theological faculty, the organ was given great freedom (see p. 111) but with the understanding that it would be played in a genuine Protestant spirit, that no "genres" would be used ("only the genre of . . . sacred lieder . . . for the glory of God"), and that secular music would be avoided. The Calvinists, on the other hand, condemned organ music until the Synod of Delft (1638), and even destroyed organs. If sacred art music, including organ music, glorified God and moved the congregation, and if the organist observed the liturgical requirements appropriate to each day, everything remained strictly in accordance with Luther's ideas. If subsequent church orders sometimes mentioned that the organ must not impede congregational singing, this was perhaps directed against an overly elaborate practice of alternation or an egocentric accompaniment and embellishment of the chorale (Bach was reprimanded for this in Arnstadt).

There are few surviving sources of German organ music from the late 15th century, and a specifically Protestant tradition cannot be designated. The tabulature books by Elias Nikolaus Ammerbach, organist of St. Thomas's in Leipzig (1571 and 1575), by Bernhard Schmid the Elder, organist of the Strasbourg cathedral (1577), by Jakob Paix in Lauingen (1583), and by August Nörmiger in Dresden (1598) contain Lutheran hymns, mostly in simple four-voice cantional settings (the first part of Nörmiger's book contains 77 such pieces). Because they were written partly with a coloratura upper voice, partly also in the form of lied motets, it is apparent that they are intabulations of works that were originally vocal pieces. The so-called Wisbyer tabulature was named after Johann Bähr, although the copyist's name was Berendt Petri, who said he copied the book from Jakob Praetorius in Hamburg (1611). It contains an extensive Latin repertory, consisting of Magnificats (some of them by Jakob and Hieronymus Praetorius), hymns, Mass versicles, and sequences; it was written for Protestant use but does not contain specifically Protestant material. A similar Liegnitz tabulature from the first half of the 17th century (Liliencron) seems to have been lost. The Celle tabulature by Johann Stephani (1601), which was described by A. G. Ritter (1884), was lost for some time but was found again in 1940; today it is available only in photostat. It contains, in addition to a few settings of Masses, hymns, and Magnificats, many Lutheran hymns in a form approaching the chorale fantasy. The Danzig tabulature, MS 300 H, which dates from the same time, contains fantasies and intabulated motets. The so-called Plötz tabulature from Brieg (about 1600; formerly *Preussische Staatsbibliothek* Berlin, MS 40056) is lost. The tabulature book by J. Woltz of Heilbronn (1617), the title of which extolls its mixed contents *(Latin and German Motets and Sacred Songs . . . Fugues . . . Canzoni alla francese),* contains arrangements of works by Michael Praetorius, organ chorales by Simon Lohet, and so on. With the Celle tabulature and the few preserved organ settings by Michael Praetorius (large chorale fantasies, chorale variations, hymn versicles), our knowledge of a specifically Protestant organ music in the sense of the Wittenberg recommendation becomes more precise: it was music bound to a hymn-tune cantus firmus.

It may be assumed that the organ chorale up to Praetorius consisted usually either of free improvisations or of organ arrangements of cantional settings and lied motets. This can still be traced in Praetorius, who clearly differentiated between the chorale fantasy and chorale variation, the two genres that later became models for the 17th century. Praetorius may be called the father of these two genres; both developed from older models and became the nucleus of all Protestant organ music. The chorale variation

primarily follows the well-known and widespread technique of variation on liturgical melodies; in the setting of hymns, Magnificats, psalm verses, Te Deums, and Protestant songs, it had developed into a style that was sometimes contrapuntal, sometimes homophonic, or highly ornamented. In addition to this, chorale variations were influenced by 16th-century variations on secular songs and dances, especially from England (K. von Fischer in the Blume *Festschrift*, 1963, p. 145; a variation of a sentence from the first edition of this book).

The fantasy seems to have been an organic enlargement of the lied motet; it used the same technical means: imitations at the beginnings of lines alternating with contrasting homophonic sections, the connections between the various sections accomplished by no other means than an ongoing cantus firmus. In both genres the song melody stood out clearly. They differed in that the variation stanzas were shorter and the fantasy form was broader.

Scheidt's *Tabulatura nova* (1624; three parts) stood far above the few German organ-music prints of the 17th century. Copies prove that its influence reached Vienna, Hungary, and even further north. The first two parts contain a mixture of secular and sacred repertory, partly in strict style, partly in fantasy style, and partly in dance style for organ or clavier. Similar to the Visby tabulature, part III is a collection of organ arrangements of the Latin liturgy: versicles for Masses and Magnificats, hymn settings, and so on; they are all strictly composed on a cantus firmus, "pure and without any color." In addition to a *Ricercar Tabulatur* (1624), which is not specifically Protestant, the Stuttgart court organist Ulrich Steigleder published an important set of variations: *Tabulaturbuch, darinnen das Vaterunser auf zwei, drei und vier Stimmen komponiert und vierzigmal variert wird* (Tabulature Book, Wherein the Lord's Prayer is Composed for Two, Three, and Four Voices with Forty Variations; 1626–27). Scheidt's chorale variations, which followed the variations on *Vater unser im Himmelreich* by Sweelinck (lost) and Steigleder (in the form of a toccata), are the high point of the Protestant chorale variation: the cantus firmus may be taken by any voice, the number of voices may change from two to four, canons and fugues may be used, the organist's part may sometimes be very demanding; the cantus-firmus voices (as Steigleder expressly stated) may be supported by a "Geigelein" (fiddle) or a bassoon. Obviously, this is still close to the vocal chorale setting. A late counterpart to Steigleder is lost: the *Musikalische Sterbensgedanken* by Johann Pachelbel (1683; variations on four different songs of death); other variation cycles of his on hymn tunes are preserved. Besides pieces without cantus firmus, Johann Kindermann's *Harmonia organica* (1645) contains Magnificat and chorale settings. Generally, however, organ music was handed down in manuscript; prints played only a secondary role. A few prints continued to appear until the end of the century, when Johann Speth published a collection in Augsburg, *Organisch-Instrumentaler Kunst-, Zier- und Lustgarten* (1693). It was still a mixture of sacred and secular content, including compositions of Italian and German masters and "eight Magnificats together with preludes, verses, and interludes appropriate to each"; is also contained arias, variations, "and other short, entertaining pieces." The boundary between organ and clavier, between the church and the world, had not yet been drawn.

The most important organ manuscripts, which contain chorale fantasies and chorale variations or liturgical pieces, are the so-called Lübbenau and Lüneburg tabulatures. (For the following, see L. Schierning, *Die Überlieferung der deutschen Orgel- und Klaviermusik aus der 1. Hälfte des 17. Jahrhunderts,* Kassel, 1961; for the tradition of the late 17th century, see F. W. Riedel, *Quellenkundliche Beiträge zur Geschichte der Musik für Tasten-instrumente in der 2. Hälfte des 17. Jahrhunderts,* Kassel, 1960.) Of north German origin, the Lübbenau tabulatures (c. 1620–40), contain for the most part chorale settings and preludes, mostly anonymous, with the rest by Heinrich Scheidemann, Jakob Praetorius, Andreas Düben, and J. Pieterszon Sweelinck. Some settings are attributed to Melchoir Schildt, Gottfried and Samuel Scheidt, Peter Hasse the Elder, Paul Siefert, and others (Schierning). The Lüneburg tabulatures (c. 1640–60) also contain many chorale arrangements, preludes, fantasies, and hymns; one of them (KN 208, 2),[1] contains a Te Deum and two Kyries, one (209) is composed almost exclusively of intabulations of vocal works. The contents are completely mixed. Some of the masters in the Lüneburg manuscript belonged to the generation of Scheidt: Scheidt himself, Scheidemann, Jakob Praetorius, Schildt. The younger generation of organists was also represented: Weckmann, Strunck, Tunder, Flor (see below). It was natural that in these north German sources Protestant organists should be the most prominent (though not always with specifically Protestant compositions). On the other hand, it is remarkable that now and then there appeared in south German manuscripts the same composers, the same pieces, and naturally the same repertory that was used by Protestants. For example, this is true of Munich MS 1581 (perhaps as early as 1650), which contains numerous Mass, Magnificat, and hymn versicles, used Woltz's print (1617) as a source, and contains, for example, works by Simon Lohet and Johann Stephani. It is also true for the Vienna Minorite Convent MS 714 (see F. W. Riedel, *Das Musikarchiv im Minoritenkonvent zu Wien,* Kassel, 1963), which contains copies from Scheidt's *Tabulatura nova,* Steigleder's variations, some works by N. Zangius, P. Siefert, M. Praetorius, J. Knöfel, and other Protestant composers. Organ compositions of the same Protestant masters also entered Dutch tabulatures, e.g., Lübbenau MS Ly A 1, which Matthias Weckmann (according to Schierning, p. 66 f.) is said to have written in the school of Jakob Praetorius (also the origin of the Wisbyer tabulature). Uppsala MS 408, written by Gustav Düben in 1641, contains pieces by Scheidemann; Berlin, Graues Kloster MS 52 includes works by Steigleder and Kaspar Hass. Neither one contains specifically Protestant compositions. Thus the tradition remains confused and obscure, even for the entire second half of the 17th century. For example, at Yale University the so-called Lowell Mason Codex LM 5056 (from the 1680s), one of the main sources for Buxtehude's organ compositions, shows that in this period the most diverse Roman Catholic and Protestant masters, the most varied secular and religious or neutral genres were still being

---

1Cf. Friedrich Welter, *Katalog der Musikalien der Ratsbücherei Lüneburg,* Lippstadt, 1950.

mixed. The codex includes names like Jakob Bölsche, Martin Radeck, Peter Heidorn, Johann Krieger, Nikolaus Adam Strunck, etc. (Riedel, *Beiträge,* p. 99 f.), a group of composers who worked during the subsequent period (see below). A special family of manuscripts containing exclusively or predominantly Protestant organ music did not begin until about 1700, e.g., with collections by J. G. Walther.

Protestant church music offers a colorful picture from the death of Praetorius to the end of the century, and much in it is confusing. Border lines cannot be drawn. Praetorius was entirely a child of the Lasso-Gallus generation, although he fully advocated the Italian, high baroque ideas of Viadana and Giovanni Gabrieli. At the end of the century the same lines of development were continued without interruption by Buxtehude, Pachelbel, Kuhnau, and many other composers, who transmitted the entire tradition to Bach and his circle. The full spiritual range of this music, which grew from the antithesis of mysticism and orthodoxy, can scarcely be shown. It found its direct continuation during the following period when mysticism was fully transformed into Pietism, when both penetrated orthodoxy, and when the Enlightenment infiltrated and renewed the entire structure of Christian tradition and Christian life in a specifically German and characteristically Protestant way. This spiritual tension on the one hand, and the general development of style on the other, gave the Protestant church music of the period its characteristic stamp. If there is a feature that distinguishes the church music of this period from that of the Counter-Reformation, then it is this spiritual tension and the impulse toward the formation of a style with a Protestant individuality unknown before. Michael Praetorius initiated an epoch in which traditional forms and styles were "used" for Lutheran purposes to make a Lutheran music sui generis. The Protestant spirit was evident in the large chorale concerto of Praetorius, in the sacred madrigal of Schein, in the solo monody of Schütz, in the chorale variation of Scheidt, as well as in the cantata or organ chorale of Bach. Open to its environment (as it is still today), alert to everything new, true to its tradition, Lutheran music for the first time took on unmistakably Protestant features. This was one of the conditions without which a J. S. Bach could not have arisen.

The Era of Pietism and Rationalism

In German Protestantism of the 17th century, the attachment to traditional dogmas and forms hardened more and more. The result was an orthodoxy based on strict observance, looking for salvation only in the Sacraments, Holy Scripture, and the sermon. The reaction to this formal severity was an increasing trend toward an intensified and personal piety. The last third of the century and the first half of the 18th were marked by a sharpening of a battle that aligned itself with the opposition between orthodoxy and Pietism. Even though the battle grew wilder and sometimes degenerated into rage on the pulpits, both currents affected each other through interpenetration. The music of this era cannot be understood without an appreciation of this combination of opposition and amalgamation. Orthodoxy was self-contained in those days and could not be seriously prejudiced by the fanaticism of Pietism (though the more orthodox theologians were in need of the spiritual warmth of Pietism). While these patterns of acceptance and rejection were in process, French-inspired rationalism, the evolution of which can clearly be retraced from Descartes to Leibniz, Wolff, and Gottsched, subverted Lutheran doctrine by substituting reason based on experience for faith in a divine revelation of world order. As it asserted itself among the emancipated bourgeoisie, it dislodged the church from its position of leadership in national, social, intellectual, and individual life. The process was slow, but gradually the forces of tradition were weakened. Participation in church life decreased. Together with rationalistic philosophy and "natural theology," secular forms of art, poetry, and music began to penetrate the church. Orthodoxy was itself divided, for the very nature of Pietism gave rise to the most varied tendencies, groups, and sects. The picture is contradictory, for the same personalities, the same churches, and the same groups were set against one another. It was not until the middle of the 18th century that peace came to the fighting powers. The new era of Protestantism was neither orthodox nor Pietistic but tolerant. It was an era filled with humanitarian and philanthropic ideas, ready to give priority to science and art instead of to religion; an era when church tradition meant basically no more than the preservation of revered forms. It was a time in which church music meant very little compared to music in other areas.

Philipp Jakob Spener began work about 1670, following a theology that was friendly toward reform (see p. 188 ff.) and preceded by the Christian public instruction that had spread everywhere since the Thirty Years' War, especially in Thuringia, Bavaria, Württemberg, Brunswick, and Mecklenburg. He did not consider sermons and Sacraments to be sufficient to obtain divine grace. Instead, the wide dissemination of the Word of God, the deepening of personal piety, and the practice of the doctrine of the priesthood of all believers were necessary for salvation. A Christianity of experience, without disregarding sacred doctrine and authority, needed to be supplemented by a Christianity of action, the goal of

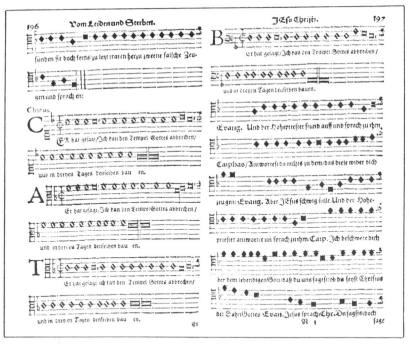

66. Johann Walter, excerpt with four-voice *turba*, Evangelist, Caiphas, and Jesus, from the St. Matthew Passion, in a late print in Gottfried Vopelius, *Neues Leipziger Gesangbuch,* Leipzig, 1682.

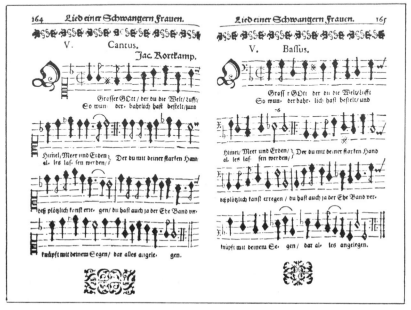

67. Jakob Kortkamp's lied *Grosser Gott, der du die Welt* for soprano and bass from Johann Rist, *Neue himmlische Lieder,* Lüneburg, 1651, Johann and Heinrich Stern.

68. Ambrosius Lobwasser, *Der Psalter Davids*. Title page of the late edition, Berlin, 1700, illustrating the streams of glory that flow out through all lands from the Psalter.

69. Hieronymus Kradenthaler, *Kommt, jauchzet alle Gott* for soprano and bass, with the accompanying allegoric flower and aphorism in the *Lust- und Arzenei-Garten*, Regensburg, 1671, Christoph Fischer.

which was to intensify and enlighten the piety of the individual and to enlarge his conception of Christianity. Small groups of worshipers supported this *praxis pietatis*. After the publication of Spener's *Pia desideria* (1657), the new doctrine spread quickly throughout Germany. Since it was accessible to every Lutheran Christian regardless of his social standing, Pietism became a popular movement. By reshaping daily life through the concept of tolerance and by emphasizing ethical values, it achieved results on the most basic level.

Orthodoxy could not have come to terms easily with this new concept. G. K. Dilfeld of Nordhausen began the fight in 1679, attacking Spener's orthodoxy; Spener in turn could point to the pure Lutheranism in the basic doctrines of justification, original sin, and the Trinity. When Spener differentiated in his writings between higher and lower revelation, when he differentiated between the essential dogmas of faith and mere questions of theology, when he made sanctification largely dependent on moral will and individual responsibility, then his rationalistic, enlightened point of view became readily apparent. Pietism and rationalism were originally a joint reform movement (according to B. Becker), and nothing would be more wrong than to equate Spener's concept of Pietism with the sentimental dallying of quietistic, mystical poetry. His search for inner holiness, uniting the individual in a bridal union with Christ, linked him rather with the mysticism of Johann Arnd and Johann Gerhard. And all these features were held together by absolute loyalty to the dogmas of Lutheran orthodoxy.

Contrary to Spener's clearheaded, tolerant approach, August Hermann Francke's "Halle Pietism" unleashed another side of the movement. Intolerance, aggressiveness, and obstinacy were its characteristics, along with an unusually sweet, overemotional bliss that dwelt inexhaustibly on a mysticism of ardent pain and ecstasy. Here began the irreconcilable struggle with orthodoxy. Francke's disputes with Christian Thomasius in Leipzig, the struggle against the philosopher Christian Wolff which led to his expulsion from Halle by King Friedrich Wilhelm I (1723), and the controversy with Valentin Ernst Loescher (1718) all opened up a deep gulf. The arrogance of those "enlightened" by the breakthrough of grace, the distinction between the "converted" and the "unconverted," which led to the withholding of Holy Communion from the latter, and the mystic interpretation of faith as experience and feeling resulted in Loescher's rebuke that Halle Pietism was nothing more than seemingly pious indifference. These controversies caused Pietism, at least in northern Germany, to change from a folk movement into a movement for a learned coterie. Only in Württemberg, under J. Albrecht Bengel, did it keep its popular character, even though it was suspected of being a kind of emancipation of the peasant class. According to Bengel, about 1740 Halle Pietism became "too abrupt" for the development of the period. It had removed Spener's spirit without providing a substitute. Its main potential had been exhausted by those years.

The church music of this period must also be understood in the light of these events. The mission of music to proclaim the revealed Word was not changed; it was included among the scriptural principles defended by orthodoxy. The music had to be based on a biblical text and a chorale, to support these or translate them into the language and understanding of the congregation. It was a vital necessity of music; in this concept was one of its strongest roots. It did not enter the minds of musicians, however, to stay aloof from the swelling need to express with passion the piety of their time, or to resist the trends toward suffusing God's Word with emotion, toward personal expression, or even toward the increasing use of secular art forms in church life. It was not part of their nature and would, moreover, have meant self-isolation. This explains the influence of the Pietistic movement on musical productivity. Its inherent mysticism inspired the composers, as in the preceding period, even though its purism, sobriety, and rationality led the most prominent musicians to a theoretical rejection of all higher art music. Spener, Francke, Zinzendorf, and others were agreed that only plain hymns with simple organ accompaniment were right for the pious Christian. At least, however, the theoretical limitation resulted in a tremendous upsurge of poetry writing and song composition, for there was now a correspondingly wider acceptance of secular art forms, i.e., the solo song styles of opera and chamber music; in a roundabout way, it renewed and broadened the foundation for the art music so opposed by the church.

It would therefore be a tremendous misunderstanding of historical truth to suppose that music collapsed under the impact of the battles between orthodoxy and Pietism. In their interpenetration, the two trends of the epoch actually encouraged productivity. The effect of Pietism was felt even in circles that strongly opposed it. This resulted partly from its far-reaching activities in youth education. Spener said, "Youth is the hope of the future," and Zinzendorf called children "little majesties." Singing lessons for children disseminated the new lieder. The effect of Pietism was also felt through household devotions and catechisms, from which even orthodox clergymen like Loescher could not fully exclude themselves. We must not be misled by the tumult of the theological quarrel, or forget that Pietists considered themselves to be members of the orthodox church and that orthodoxy unconsciously took over a great deal of the sanctimony and emotional approach of the Pietists. One cannot be considered without the other. Enemies of the Pietists, such as Loescher, Elmenhorst, or Neumeister, spoke in a language of mystical, sentimental exultation or sober reason differing in no way from that of Francke, Neander, Arnold, or Rambach; these, in turn, placed great value on their orthodoxy and avoided anything that might seem to be in conflict with it. The crucial point for music, however, lies not in the theological polemics but in the psychological penetration of orthodoxy and Pietism in the sacred poetry of that time.

"In spite of the outward assertions of materialistic orthodoxy and in spite of the religious character of the states" (Troeltsch), there was a force at work within rationalism that increasingly undermined the structure of the church's doctrine and soon imposed its power over intellectual and material life. In the conflict between reason and revelation, reason took over. In the relations between church and state, sovereign rationality triumphed over theocratic supranaturalism. The practical results of the new spirit were a submission of the church to the secular government, a tolerance for all confessions (which Leibniz had influenced with his *Systema theologicum,* and which Locke had demanded in his conception of a "free church in a free state"), a rational order of life, and a "reform-happy utilitarianism" (Troeltsch). Neither irreligiousness nor atheism was a necessary consequence of rationalism, but rather an alienation of the church, the dominance of secular interests over spiritual ones, and the removal of church and religion from their age-old position of dominance over the human spirit. Church doctrine was slowly replaced by a "natural theology," a "natural religion," which demanded, as in Leibniz, Locke, and Wolff, agreement between revelation and reason, or, as in Socinianism, that revelation be submitted to the judgment of reason.

A parallel process within music had long since begun. The gradual, perhaps almost unnoticed, change in musical points of view did not alienate musicians from the Augustine Lutheran tradition, but combined it with a firm belief in the rational progress, in the validity of irrefutable natural laws, and in artistic autonomy. From Descartes *Compendium musicae* (1618) and *Traité des passions de l'âme* (1649) to Leibniz's *Von der Weisheit,* F.E. Niedt's *Musikalische Handleitung* (1700), W.K. Printz's *Historische Beschreibung* (1690), and the numerous writings of A. Werckmeister (1686–1707) and others, German musicians were inundated with a flood of rationalistic professional writings. They relaxed the traditional theocentric view of music and led musicians of the Kuhnau-Bach generations to a kind of "believing rationalism" that did not bring them into conflict with orthodox church doctrine because it made the seemingly incompatible into an "unproblematic possession of the inner self" (W. Blankenburg, *Bach und die Aufklärung,* 1950). Traditional species and forms of Protestant church music fused readily with the new efforts toward an affect-laden humanism and with the adoption of the "theatrical style." The music of masters such as Buxtehude and Bach did not recognize any conflict between orthodoxy and Pietism, but only an interpenetration of the two (perhaps they had also become an "unproblematic possession of the inner self"). Without these presuppositions, Bach could not have become Bach. He could not have synthesized the forces of a tradition of two centuries old (and stretching back to medieval times) with the demands and needs of his own generation; he could not have paved the way with this synthesis for the future of Protestant church music. If church musicians had clung only to tradition during the period of orthodoxy and Pietism, their works would have been doomed to a traditionalistic sterility. If they had thrown themselves one-sidedly into the currents of Italianized opera and instrumental music, they would have quickly arrived at a secularized art, and their music would have degenerated into a mere ornament in the worship service. It was the great accomplishment of musicians during these seven or eight decades that this did not happen, but rather that an independent "new" form of Protestant church music was shaped by the fusion of tradition-bound faith, heartfelt piety, and logical order.

One after another of the original basic forces in Protestant music died out. The liturgical forms had been disintegrating since the time of Reformation. Now Pietism and rationalism brought them to a point of total decay. The service, which had already concentrated more and more on the sermon, neglected liturgical formulas and merely preserved their remnants. Thus, possibly the Kyrie and Gloria of the Mass, isolated hymns, and the Magnificat of the Vespers survived.

Concurrently, the Latin language was used less and less. In large churches, such as in Lübeck, Hamburg, Leipzig, and Nuremberg, a few remainders of liturgical practice were kept alive. The popularity that the Protestant hymn had enjoyed during the 16th century was not completely lost in the 17th, but because the official hymnbooks (and consequently the services) restricted themselves to traditional material, the treasury of hymns became outdated. Verse and word construction, rhythms and melodies became obscure, and at the end of the 17th century adaptations and simplifications, "embellishments," and "improvements" finally destroyed their true nature. Few songs the Pietistic era produced were accepted to any degree in the hymnbooks and worship services; and even less did they achieve popularity. Poetry and melody were overcultivated and from the outset had little prospect of becoming truly popular, as was the case with so many songs from Luther to Philipp Nicolai (cf. p. 37 f.).

Not only did the song become an edifying object of art, but all artistic music for the Protestant church in this era had to cope increasingly with a lack of comprehension among the parishioners. This raises the question of the extent to which sacred concertos of Schein, Schütz, and other masters of their time found a place in the service, and of how understandable these were to the average churchgoer. How much more doubtful must the role of Buxtehude's organ chorales and Bach's cantatas appear! Was not the price for fashioning Protestant church music to the prevailing taste, and for accepting inevitable trends in church music, the understanding of the congregation? Here the dilemma of the era becomes visible. The volumes of hymns and cantata-text cycles, written by theologians and set to music by musicians who agreed with the authors, were addressed to the educated, the exacting, the connoisseurs; thus, the rift became wider between the unenlightened churchgoer and the music imposed upon him. It is the same dilemma that attended the revival of the reform movement in the 20th century after the quietism of church music during the late 18th and 19th centuries. The cantatas of Buxtehude and Bach, as well as their organ music, must have remained incomprehensible to the average churchgoer. Like the hymns of their time, they were art of a truly refined nature.

The positive results of these processes should not be overlooked. Musicians effected a fusion of contrasting tendencies; untroubled, they went along with the times, without denying tradition. They maintained one of the basic heritages in Protestant church music, its ties between past and present. As long as it independently maintained this union, it preserved its status as an equal member of musical life in general. But when religion, politics, philosophy, and art were pushed out of the church, when the music no longer served for "praise of God" and for "re-creation of the soul," but focused on beauty and human ecstasy for their own sake, then the accord between Protestant church music and overall musical development was disturbed. The standstill that it suffered in the middle of the 18th century thrust it into the background of musical life. Natural religion together with "true Christianity" could not but drive creative musicians from the Church. Handel, Graun, Telemann, and many others went this way. We can now see all the more clearly to what extent Bach's works were "out of date" (a final product of a two-hundred-year heritage of the Protestant spirit) and to what extent they were "up to date" (a fusion of this heritage with the forward-looking trends of the time).

THE PIETISTIC SONG

THE HYMNBOOKS

The Pietistic movement gave new impetus to song composition. Poems increasingly emphasized self-contemplation and sentimental rapture. The melodies, in conforming with Pietistic devoutness by stressing subjective enthusiasm, gradually became independent creations, and thereby contributed to the secularization distinguishing all music of the period (cf. W. Blankenburg, *Geschichte der Melodien des evangelischen Kirchen gesangbuchs,* Göttingen, 1957, 103). On the one hand, melodies tended toward the isometric settings of secular and folk music; on the other, they leaned on the art song and an aria-like style. Of necessity, these conflicting models led to a split between congregational and private devotional songs.

The poetry began with Spener himself (*Es sei, Herr, deine Gütigkeit, So bleibet's denn also;* 1676?) and J. Jakob Schütz, who in Frankfurt on the Main belonged to Spener's circle (*Sei Lob und Ehr dem höchsten Gut;* 1673). Joachim Neander was one of the leading song writers of his time. His songs frequently entered the hymnbooks, although the collection he assembled (1679) was meant for private circles. His poems are closely related to those in the Calvinistic Psalter, and sometimes borrowed their melodies from there. Others were composed by Neander himself, who once used a melody by Adam Krieger. His best known are: *Lobe den Herren, den mächtigen König der Ehren, Wunderbarer König,* and *Der Tag ist hin.* No true festival or congregational humns are to be found in his work; they are all intended for home devotions, journeys, or "Christian enjoyment out of doors." Their subjects are characteristic for the period: repentance, sanctification, love of Jesus, and so on. Laurentius Laurenti wrote *Ermuntert euch, ihr Frommen* and *Wach auf, mein Herz, die Nacht ist hin* (1700). Christian Scriver, editor of *Seelenschatz,* the most popular devotional book next to Johannes Arnd's, wrote *Jesus, meiner Seele Leben;* Adam Drese, who in Bach's early years was *Kapellmeister* in Arnstadt, wrote *Jesu, ruf mich von der Welt, Seelenweide, meine Freude,* and *Seelenbräutigam, Jesu, Gottes Lamm* (which Nelle has called "a prospectus of Pietism"). Bartholomäus Crasselius was the author of *Dir, dir, Jehova, will ich singen* (1697). Johann Kaspar Schade in Berlin wrote quietistic texts such as *Ruhe ist das beste Gut* and *Meine Seel ist stille* (1699). J. Heinrich Schröder is still known today for *Eins ist not* (1697), written to a melody from Adam Krieger's *Arien* (1675). To the tradition of Gottfried Arnold's "uprooted spiritualism," which extended "from J. Böhme to Klopstock" (Günther Müller, *Deutsche Dichtung von der Renaissance zum Barock,* Potsdam, 1927, 256), came songs like *O Durchbrecher aller Bande* and *Herzog unsrer Seligkeiten.* They represent the most beautiful aspects of Pietistic poetry, while others, such as *Verliebtes Lustspiel reiner Seelen,* reveal the secular, seemingly frivolous tone of the 18th century.

The Halle School was especially productive. August Hermann Francke in Halle (according to W. Blankenburg, one of the "three great Pietists of Germany") wrote *Gottlob, ein Schritt zur Ewigkeit,* while Christian Friedrich Richter wrote *Es kostet viel, ein Christ zu sein* and *Hüter, wird die Nacht der Sünden* (1697 and 1698). The names of J. Anastasius Freylinghausen, Joachim Lange, J. Friedrich Ruopp, J. Justus Breithaupt, J. Daniel Herrnschmidt, Justus Henning Böhmer, and many others, have survived in hymnals to the present day. From Saxony and Thuringia came J. Joseph Winkler, Ludwig Andreas Gotter, J. Eusebius Schmidt *(Fahre fort, fahre fort),* and many more. Among the best poets of the early 18th century were Ernst Lange in Danzig (whose hymn *O Gott, du Tiefe sonder Grund,* 1714, was especially praised by Schleiermacher) and Adolf Lampe (*Mein Leben ist ein Pilgrimsstand* and *O, wer gibt mir Adlerflügel,* 1726).

The late period of Pietistic poetry was initiated by J. Jakob Rambach. While Francke had an indirect influence on the early church cantata, Rambach exerted a very direct one by publishing a collection of cantata texts in 1720 which were later frequently used by composers. In his songs the new century's rationalistic restraint and occasional banal shallowness became evident: *Ermuntre dich, mein blöder Geist* (Cheer up, my stupid spirit), *Dein Mittler kommt, auf, blöde Seele, Erwürgtes Lamm* (1720, 1723, etc.). Karl Heinrich von Bogatzky wrote *Hosianna, Davids Sohn,* Philip Balthasar Sinold, a contemporary of Schütz, wrote *Ich will mich mit dir verloben.* A separate group was formed in Cöthen by Konrad Allendorf, Leopold Friedrich Lehr, and J. Sigismund Kunth; in Silesia, Ernst Gottlieb Woltersdorf wrote markedly rationalistic hymns, among them one with 263 stanzas (Nelle). Pietist poetry in Württemberg was represented by its leader, J. August Bengel, by Philipp Friedrich Hiller, Johann Pöschel, J. Jakob, and Friedrich Karl Moser, as well as by Karl Ludwig von Pfeil.

The "Herrnhut Circle" (see chap. VI, *The Music of the Bohemian Brethren*) carried rationalistic superficiality, banality, and mystical ecstasy to an extreme. Its overproduction brought about a depreciation of the new song literature and, indirectly, a further secularization of it. Zinzendorf himself is said to have written approximately 2,000 song texts, reaching from Paul Gerhardt's simplicity to an almost psychopathic eccentricity. Only a few of these continued in use, and most of them were modified. Christian Gregor rewrote the poems for the Brethren hymnal (1788)—for instance, *Jesu, geh voran,* which was shortened from two very long poems to four stanzas, and *Herr, dein Wort, die edle Gabe,* which was reduced from the 320 stanzas by Zinzendorf to only two. From this circle, J. Andreas Rothe could still be found in later hymnbooks with his *Ich habe nun den Grund gefunden.*

The only truly great poet in this period was Gerhard Tersteegen. Like Paul Gerhardt, he combined the rapturous subjectivity of Pietistic devotion with traditional dogma. Extreme rationalism and sentimentality are absent from his work. Günther Müller attributed to him "a quiet, disciplined thought, more meditation than contemplation, a balance between opposing currents . . . similar to what Paul Gerhardt achieved." His *O Jesu Christ, meins Lebens Licht, Nun sich der Tag geendet hat, Jauchzet, ihr Himmel,* and so on, survive in the hymnbooks of modern times. J. Scheffler (Angelus Silesius) shared much of Tersteegen's mystic spiritualism. He was a Catholic whose poems, with the melodies of Georg Joseph (*Heilige Seelenlust,* 1657 f.), penetrated deeply into Protestant circles. Tersteegen did as much as anyone to promote his work, and in his hymn collections (1729 ff.), which contained 672 items, he printed two by Luther, ten by Paul Gerhardt, and 50 by Scheffler (G. Müller).

The production of religious lyrics was extremely abundant in the late 17th and early 18th centuries. However, the borderline is especially hazy between "sacred" and "churchly" (what was used or intended for use in the church), between what was intended for private circles and what, in spite of being subjective, aspired to the worship service (as, for example, the lyrics of Rist, Gerhardt, Tersteegen, and so on). Most of it was indeed religious devotional literature. Only a little of it found its way into the worship service and the hymnals (still less as time went on). This was because of the relationship between orthodoxy and Pietism, and because of the rigid adherence of hymnbook editors to the old stock of Lutheran congregational hymns. Like the hymnbooks of the early 17th century, the new ones reprinted the stock, adding varying selections of new hymns. The hymnbooks of the late 17th century, however, provide significant testimony to the effect of antihistorical and rationalistic Pietism on even the most loyal adherents to Lutheran orthodoxy. The more Pietistic a hymnbook was, the more its traditional stock of hymns was crushed, modernized, and rationalized, and the more traditional hymns were discarded. This process continued until the second half of the 18th century and even into the 19th. Irreverently and with no feeling for historical values, hymnbooks such as the one by Porst in Berlin (1708, often reprinted; revised edition published in 1905), the one by Rambach in Giessen (1735), and the one from Hannover (1740) continued to "improve" the old texts, just as the late 17th century had begun to do. In collections of the second half of the 18th century (Diterich, 1765, etc.) the foundations of Protestant hymn writing were systematically undermined.

The hymnbook of Daniel Speer (Stuttgart, 1692; 316 hymns with melody and thoroughbass) "inaugurates the series of chorale books of the 18th and 19th centuries" (Zahn) with its notation (melody and bass) and its selection of tunes, which many later hymnals took over. The contemporary hymnbook for Wolfenbüttel by H. G. Neuss (1692) shows the influence of French opera airs. A Bohemian Brethren hymnal (Lissa, 1694) was basically a republication of the one edited by J. A. Comenius in 1661; it shows the temporary conservatism of the Brethren, who did not accept Pietistic hymns (cf. Brethren hymnals, chap. VI). The first distinguishably Pietistic hymnbook appeared in 1692, published in Wesel by Andreas Luppius. It was followed by J. G. Hassel's *Geistreiches Gesangbuch* (1697), first published in Halle and republished in Darmstadt in 1698. It was the direct forerunner of a book that was influential throughout the 18th century, the *Geistreiches Gesangbuch* by J. Anastasius Freylinghausen. It was issued in two parts, 1704 and 1714, by the Halle orphanage (19 editions of part I by 1759); both parts together, greatly augmented, were published by Gotthilf August Francke (1741; 2nd ed., 1771). It spurred the Wittenberg theological faculty to issue a judgment (1716; printed by W. Serauky, *Musikgeschichte der Stadt Halle II,* 1, Halle, 1939, 464 f.) roundly criticizing the "pompous, superficial, and almost licentious manner of the secular songs" that had now generally and specifically with Freylinghausen's hymnbook appeared in churches. It also condemned the "many hopping, jumping, dactylic" songs in this collection. Feelings about the secular nature of this new song style were obviously sensitive.

The hymnbook by Johann Porst mentioned above became the authorized one for Berlin and for wide areas of Prussia. In Daniel Vetter's *Kirchen- und Hausergötzlichkeit* (Leipzig, 1709 and 1713) each hymn is notated in a simple setting for organ to which a "broken variation" for harpsichord was added, proving (along with the title) that chorale variations for keyboard instruments were at least partly intended for home music making. The prevailing type of "official" hymnbook for individual cities or territories followed the old custom of adding a selection of new hymns to an older stock. Of the vast number of hymnals (Zahn mentions more than 150 from Speer, 1692, to the odes of Gellert and Doles, 1758; a newer bibliography of the Lutheran or Protestant hymnals does not exist), one can mention only those of Gotha (Christian Friedrich Witt, 1699, 1715), Darmstadt (Christoph Graupner, 1728), Nuremberg-Bayreuth-Onolzbach (Cornelius Heinrich Dretzel, 1731; abridged edition, 1748; used in an edition of 1773 until the 19th century and thus a south-German counterpart of Porst's hymnal), Hesse-Homburg (1734), Frankfurt on the Main (J. Balthasar König, 1738), and the Palitinate (J. Martin Spiess, Heidelberg, 1745). (See chap. V for Swiss and Reformed hymnals.) The Naumburg-Zeitzsche hymnbook (Georg Christian Schemelli, 1736) acquired renown through its musical adaptor, Johann Sebastian Bach. Bach himself, however, contributed and signed only one melody *(Vergiss mein nicht, du allerliebster Gott)*. Among the many hymns ascribed to him by various authors, possibly two more are indeed his *(Komm, süsser Tod* and *Dir, dir, Jehova, will ich singen)*. But most probably his contribution is restricted to the one melody and, for the rest, to the figured basses.

All in all, it was a massive production, and the musical gain was in inverse proportion to the quantity. Monotonous tunes like *Seelenbräutigam* and *Wunderbarer König*, still widely used, were the rule rather than the exception. The rapid decline in quality resulted in the generally low level of German songs (both sacred and secular) at the end of the 17th century and in the first half of the 18th century. The period of Adam Krieger had long passed, and in the sacred domain the high point had been the songs of Rist, Buxtehude, and their followers (see p. 238). The secularization of the sacred hymn went hand in hand with the foreign influences on all song writing. Under the influence of the French opera, Germany was flooded with the melodies of fashionable dances and airs, against which the church authorities struggled in vain (cf. the Wittenberg judgment against Freylinghausen, mentioned above). The clergy's complaints against the secularization of church music were continued from Quistorp and Grossgebauer (see p. 190), to Spener and Muscovius and to the cantata battles of Schiff, Buttstett, Meyer, Guden, and so forth (see below). Georg Bronner (Hamburg, 1715) added French tempo markings to melodies. Georg Philipp Telemann (Hamburg, 1730) considered it necessary to disassociate his melodies from the types then prevalent. He was justified. For the "improvement" of old texts was linked to an "improvement" in the melodies; they were mutilated, made isometric, pressed into measured patterns, refined, distorted, and in many cases forcefully adapted to the major-minor system. In addition, there was the widespread and almost devastating parody practice by which popular operatic arias, dances, and so on, were fitted out with hymn texts; the practice remained popular into the 19th century. (Hymnbooks with melodies from *The Magic Flute, Der Freischütz,* and so on, are not rare.) The Hannover hymnbook of 1740–41 adorned the melodies with embellishments, probably for home clavier practice.

In general, the more Pietistic a hymnbook's origin and author, the less noteworthy was the music. On the other hand, the relative high point of the period was reached by music written to texts of Heinrich Elmenhorst, the orthodox Hamburg theologian. Even though his poems were among the most banal products of orthodox literature under the influence of Pietism, they were valuable for the history of music because Elmenhorst followed Rist's example and collaborated with good musicians: the Hamburg opera composer J. Wolfgang Franck, the Kiel Cantor Peter Laurentius Wockenfuss, and the Lüneburg organist Georg Böhm. The first editions of Elmenhorst's *Geistliche Lieder* (1681 ff.) contain melodies by Franck only, while Wockenfuss and Böhm contributed much to the last edition (1700). Franck's tunes reveal a change from the rather affected folk style of Rist to an aria style, frequently virtuoso. Altogether, the melodies of the three masters, out of the "poorest products of the church song in the 17th century" (G. Müller, *Geschichte des deutschen Liedes,* 1925), developed into the last flowering of the art of sacred song. Of course, the success of C. Böhm's *Bringet meinen Herrn zur Ruh,* which anticipated Bach's St. Matthew Passion by thirty years, was never matched by his two contemporaries.

ORGAN MUSIC. J. S. BACH'S ORGAN WORKS

The functions of the organ changed little during the late Baroque period. Organ music was still produced in large quantities in the Protestant (especially Lutheran) areas, even though organists improvised most of their own music for the service. Preludes to hymns, interludes between stanzas, and postludes were usually improvised. The practice of alternation continued for congregational songs as well as for the Mass, the Magnificat, and traditional hymns; however, it was gradually dropped as the use of Latin hymns and Mass texts diminished and organ accompaniments to congregational hymns (not common until the early 18th century) became the rule. The practice was most commonly maintained during Vespers for the Magnificat. It has frequently been confirmed that there was organ music at the beginning and end of the service, but this was usually improvised too. As a result, there is a certain gap between the organ literature handed down to us and the music actually heard during the service. To what extent can chorale fantasies or large-scale chorale variations or the "free" forms of the toccata, the fantasia, the chaconne, the capriccio *(stylus phantasticus)* be regarded as church music in the strict sense? The question has not yet been resolved. But it seems certain that the larger forms were not used during the service except, perhaps, *sub communione.* They were probably considered to be either demon-

70. Johann Sebastian Bach (1685–1750) in the oil painting of Elias Gottlieb Haussmann, 1748. Princeton, New Jersey, William H. Scheide.

strations of contrapuntal skill and teaching aids, or else the virtuoso pieces one played at church concerts, which spread from Holland to Germany between 1670 and 1680, especially to the Hanseatic towns of northern Germany. Reinken, Scheidemann, Buxtehude, and Bach surely did not write their great organ works for the service; they were for concert use or they were free improvisations later recorded for purposes of instruction.

The leading group of German composers for organ in the 17th century lived in northern Germany: Heinrich Scheidemann, Johann Adam Reinken, and Vincent Lübeck in Hamburg; Melchior Schildt in Hannover; Franz Tunder in Lübeck; Matthias Weckmann in Hamburg, partly in Copenhagen; Delphin and Nikolaus Adam Strunck together with Georg Bölsche and Georg Leyding in Brunswick; Nikolaus Bruhns in Husum; Melchior Brunckhorst in Celle; Peter Morhardt and Georg Böhm in Lüneburg. They all regarded Dietrich Buxtehude of Lübeck as their outstanding master. The larger forms of the chorale fantasy, the toccata, the capriccio, and the ricercar were cultivated by this group; here, too, the fugue was gradually transformed. All musical species inclined more or less toward virtuosity. The pedal began to be used for solo effects, for which the north-German organ-building school of Arp Schnitger (with deliveries from Holland to Russia, from England to Portugal) provided the suitable instruments. Nevertheless, the larger forms and virtuoso playing were pushed out of the service and replaced by one-stanza chorale preludes (represented well by Nikolaus Hanff in Schleswig and Daniel Erich, but conceived best by Buxtehude), short, free preludes, and smaller fugal works. Perhaps the most important new development was the short chorale prelude, with a single statement of the cantus firmus in a simple setting. This became the vehicle for personal interpretations of the chorale (not part of organ music until then) and was thus the organist's counterpart to the Pietistic hymn. In most cases the composition dates of organ works by all these masters are not certain. Scheidemann's and Schildt's works belong to the years 1630–50. Those of Buxtehude can be dated around 1670 (the fact that their most important sources date from the middle of the 18th century is evidence that they were still being used by the generation of Bach's students). On the other hand, Böhm and Lübeck were composing until Bach reached middle age. Altogether, the activity of the north-German organ school may have extended over more than a century.

Older species such as Mass versicles, hymn stanzas, and hymn variations were cultivated sporadically in the later 17th century. Magnificat versicles (often without a cantus firmus and bound together only by their common tonality) remained in use to the middle of the 18th century. To keep up appearances, a few chorale settings in the strict style—i.e., according to the rules of Roman counterpoint—were composed (Buxtehude, 1674; J. Ph. Förtsch, 1680; N. A. Strunck, 1684; Chr. Flor, 1692; see F. W. Riedel in *MGG* X, 352, and *Quellenkundliche Beiträge*, 1960, 82).

In addition to the north German circle, a smaller Franconian one was established; it soon merged with a central German group. Besides Kindermann the composers who worked in Nuremberg were Georg Kaspar Wecker, Heinrich Schwemmer, and Johann Pachelbel, the most prominent master. In contrast to north German virtuosity, this school emphasized a new simplicity and singable melodies, and cultivated the chorale partita, the chorale fugue, and the little chorale prelude. Pachelbel was a master in all three. He combined the chorale fugue (in the form of a broadly executed quasi-*Vorimitation* of the first chorale line) with cantus-firmus settings (in the form of a single variation on the chorale melody with simple accompanying voices). The resulting form seems to have become known to Bach, either because of the close relationship of Pachelbel to the Bach family or through Pachelbel's teaching activities in Erfurt; at any rate, he adopted the idea. The chorale partita took over some aspects of the song variations for clavier and the dance-like models frequently used for the chorale. In this form it was cultivated not only by Pachelbel but also by Johann Krieger in Greiz and Zittau, Johann Michael Bach in Gehren, J. Heinrich Buttstett in Erfurt, Andreas Nikolaus Vetter in Erfurt, Rudolstadt, etc., J. Friedrich Alberti in Merseburg, F. W. Zachow in Halle, Andreas Armsdorf in Erfurt, and others. The style of the little chorale prelude was widely accepted and was skillfully cultivated by J. Gottfried Walther in Erfurt, a relative and contemporary of Bach, and perhaps the only organ composer of the time who could compare with Bach, at least in this one area.

Bach's *Orgelbüchlein* was written in Weimar as an "introduction to the various ways of setting a chorale" and as instruction in the use of the pedal (see the article by G. von Dadelsen, *Zur Entstehung des Bachschen Orgelbüchleins,* in the Blume *Festschrift,* 1963, pp. 74–79). In this work Bach created a type of little chorale prelude, borrowing from the chorale partita (Dietrich), employing the most varied types and models (as he did later in the *Goldberg Variations*), and following somewhat the short chorale preludes of Buxtehude and other composers. His type has retained its quality of timeliness. In a style pithy and concise, he placed the chorale melody most often in treble, frequently set it in canon with another voice, and accompanied it with obbligato voices (usually three), to each of which he assigned independent motifs repeated in quasi-ostinato fashion. He infused strict counterpoint into the freer forms of Pachelbel and Buxtehude. But at the same time—and this is the most important element—he subordinated strict forms to his interpretation of the text. The countermotifs, rather than stemming from the cantus firmus, were determined by the chorale text, as were the harmony, the rhythm, and the technical construction. This conception often resulted in a highly exciting interpretation of the chorale, now jubilant, now deeply moving, which reached a climax in a piece like *O Mensch, bewein dein Sünde gross.* The extent to which Bach's countermotifs were conceived under the influence of the doctrine of figures is irrelevant; nor is an interpretation by means of symbolic numbers and proportions convincing.

Bach's chorale partitas, which probably belong to his earliest period, follow the line of Georg Böhm; his chorale fugues stem from Pachelbel and must also be very early. The manner of his organ settings, the frequent coloration of the chorale, and other features were derived from northern models, especially from Buxtehude and Böhm. His large chorale settings in particular point in that direction. These latter were affected by the same process of secularization that can be observed in all church music of the era; in addition, they reveal the same synthesis of styles characteristic of late Baroque music. In the great organ works, especially Bach's chorale settings, not only did the boundaries dissolve between free types, and secular dance and song styles, but the types interpenetrated each other and were further influenced by styles outside the organ literature. The *stylus antiquus* penetrated the free forms of toccata, prelude, passacaglia, and chorale arrangement formerly reserved for the *stylus phantasticus*. On the other hand, the ricercar and fugue were infused with free-style characteristics. Dance models underlie many chorale partitas as well as some movements of Bach's *Orgelbüchlein*. The tone color and idiomatic features of clavier and lute music, of the instrumental concerto, even of the solo song, penetrated organ music. "One finds a supreme blending of all elements in the works of J. S. Bach" (F. W. Riedel, in *MGG* X, 358). In addition, the remnants of older styles remained in use, and the works of former masters continued to be performed. The organ works of Buxtehude, Pachelbel, and Kuhnau, among others, were copied again and again and widely diffused up to the middle of the 18th century. Several masters of the old generation, such as Reinken, Lübeck, and Böhm, lived far into the 18th century. The chorale fantasy was considered obsolete even at the time Bach visited Reinken in Hamburg (1720), as can be seen from the well-known anecdote.[2] A few organists of the 18th century still wrote chorale works in a strict style; of these Bach's canonical variations *Vom Himmel hoch* (printed 1748) is the most convincing example, if not the latest.

Even now Bach's organ works cannot be dated with certainty, but there is much evidence that they belong mainly to the Weimar period (1708–16), though they were only later gathered together and revised. The great chorale settings which form the third part of the *Klavierübung* (printed 1739) are not, as often maintained, a "chorale Mass"; Bach merely placed the chorales in their usual hymnbook sequence.

Even though some of the settings were late works, it is probable that Bach composed them to fill out an incomplete series of earlier compositions (as was the case with the chorale cantatas, a series begun in 1724–25 and completed in later years by the addition of single compositions in the same form and style as the earlier ones); this would support the assumption that most settings were earlier creations. Moreover, the *Sechs Choräle von verschiedener Art* (printed 1747), the so-called Schübler chorales, are adaptations of vocal chorale trios from cantatas, four of which belong to the years 1724–25; perhaps they, too, date back to earlier models. The *Achtzehn Choräle* that Bach collected and prepared for publication during his last years might also have been composed before Leipzig, probably at Weimar. Only the chorale variations *Vom Himmel hoch* (printed 1748) belong together with the *Musikalisches Opfer,* the canons, and the *Kunst der Fuge* to the great, spectacular works representative of his later years. The characteristic feature of the large chorale settings is the juxtaposition of the chorale and a web of independent voices that are freely invented. The compositions are broad hymn settings, periodically ostinato, in which single chorale lines, separated by rests, are imbedded. This is the same procedure Bach used in the introductory fantasies

---

2For an account of this episode see Karl Geiringer, *Johann Sebastian Bach,* New York, 1966, p. 48.

in the second cycle of chorale cantatas (1724–25). The difference between vocal and organ chorale settings had ended.

The organ works of Bach's contemporaries and pupils were far simpler in compositional technique and spiritual concept, and they were also easier to perform. The slightly older masters, such as Zachow, Buttstett, A.N. Vetter, and so on, have already been mentioned. Other contemporaries included Telemann, J. Gottfried Walther, the younger Pachelbel (Wilhelm Hieronymus), Georg Friedrich Kauffmann, and J. Christoph Vogler. In the next generation, the Berlin circle around J. Philipp Kirnberger, Friedrich Wilhelm Marpurg, J. Friedrich Agricola, and C. Philipp Emanuel Bach was closely associated with Sebastian Bach. In central Germany an entire group of Bach pupils carried on his tradition: J. Ludwig Krebs, Gottfried August Homilius, J. Christian Kittel, J. Peter Kellner, and, last but not least, W. Friedemann Bach. This gave rise to the less distinguished music of Christoph Oley, Christian Gotthilf Tag, Christoph Kühnau, and many more (see chap. III).

Bach's organ works in their entirety are the apex in the history of organ music, equaled neither before nor after him, just as his cantatas and Passions are certainly the apex of Protestant church music. It must be left for future research to determine how much of his organ music was actually church music. However this is decided, the music itself (so far as chorale settings in any one form are concerned) became the foundation, the historical precedent, the raison d'être of Protestant church music. Bach's organ chorales (in all forms) were a true image of Protestantism in his time: still within a strict orthodox tradition, they were open to Pietistic attempts at contemplation and personal expression, emotional piety, and an enthusiastic uplifting of the soul. They were submerged in their texts, preaching, interpreting, illustrating the pain of the Passion and the sweetness of Christ's love. They were a consummation (like many of Bach's cantatas in the same style) of the *unio mystica,* the bridal union of the soul with Christ. No other master was able to make the organ speak in this way. The vocal music of Bach's time can be understood in terms of the basic element of tension in his organ music—the tension between the revealed Word (for which the chorale, in a certain sense, substituted) and the emotional setting that expressed the relationship of the ego to the Word. The basic contrast between the melody and an independent, song-like, seemingly unrelated complex of contrapuntal textures that yet interpret the chorale—this contrast is also the basis of numerous cantata choruses and arias on chorales by Bach and his predecessors and contemporaries. Bach was in the deepest sense the formative power of his age. Texts and compositions were pressing toward rational exegesis and emotional interpretation. The union of proclamation with exegesis was becoming more and more clearly the goal of organ as well as vocal music. In the opposition of Bible text to interpretative poetry, the chorale could be a third contrasting element, or a substitute for Scripture in opposition to poetry, or an interpretation of Scripture substituting for poetry. How these alternatives could be resolved by poetry and music had increasingly occupied the minds of musicians and librettists since the 1660s; with the Bach era, a new phase of development was reached. Organ music reflected efforts to solve the problem in its development from a restricted older art form to the free and interpretative style of Bach. Vocal music reflected these efforts in its slow transition from the concerto to the cantata.

THE MOTET TO J. S. BACH

Around the turn of the century, the church cantata developed into a species that attracted, as no other had, the productive forces of the day. The hymn had sunk to the lowest level in its history. The older "figural History" had died out; the "responsorial History" (especially the Passion) would continue to live into the 19th century, but its life would be sterile. The vocal concerto, based on the Psalms, Gospels, or other biblical texts, slowly lost its independence and joined in the development toward the cantata. The motet fell into complete decline from the days of Hammerschmidt, Tunder, Ahle, and so on. Its strength had been its ability to proclaim a biblical text; it was not suited to interpretative texts. It was used for processions at Christmas and New Year's, as incidental music for weddings and other festivities, and at funerals, where it retained a permanent place —not in the church service but at the open grave. The setback of the motet was caused partly by the decline in school choirs, which was the complaint in Lübeck, Hamburg, Leipzig, Nuremberg, and all other Protestant cities; in 1730, Bach himself made some devastating remarks about the qualifications of his fifty-four boarding students. In addition to this, there was an increasing interest on the part of music lovers, and thus of churchgoers as well, in instrumental music. Instrumental ensemble music and mixed vocal-instrumental chamber music penetrated the service in spite of strong protests by church authorities. With this the fate of the motet was sealed. It became an obsolete, mechanically constructed miniature art form, falling into the workaday hands of local choirmasters.

Saxony-Thuringia remained the center of motet composition. All through the 18th century and far into the 19th, the motet tradition was continued there by men of little or no importance. Its best representatives were the Eisenach composer J. Christoph Bach and his brother Michael in Gehren, Philipp Heinrich Erlebach of Rudolstadt (whose songs, instrumental music, and cantatas were better than his motets), and finally Georg Böhm of Lüneburg. Like the rest of his music, Bach's motets towered above all others, which is the more remarkable since he considered them incidental to his other work. Among his contemporaries, Telemann was one of the best composers of the motet. A long line of lesser composers followed him rather than Bach: Johann Topf, Friedrich Erhard Niedt, Nikolaus Niedt, Georg Theodor Reineccius, the uneven but prolific Liebhold (first name unknown), Christoph Lausch, J. Philipp Käfer, Gottfried Vockerodt, Konrad Wagner, and many others. To serve the special purposes of funeral music, a new type of text and music was developed for the motet. The word setting, already simplified by Hammerschmidt and Ahle in comparison to Schütz, became more and more homophonic and melodious, often entirely chordal. Appended to it, or (more frequently) woven contrapuntally into its last section, was a chorale melody stated by the soprano. In this modest form the basic motif of Protestant church music of the period—the antithesis of proclamation and exegesis—manifested itself. Even the best representatives of the motet, such as Telemann *(Selig sind die Toten)* and J. Christoph Bach *(Herr, wenn ich nur dich habe)*, show how little the composers valued the species. Bach's motets, at least the few that have survived, were all funeral motets adhering to the prevailing style. However, they developed out of the underlying antithesis of scriptural text and chorale to become immense creations of the boldest conception, unequaled by any other composer of the time. This is apparent in the earliest motet, handed down as a single work, the five-part *Jesu, meine Freude* (before 1723). The six stanzas of the funeral chorale alternate with verses 1, 2, 9, 10, and 11 of St. Paul's Letter to the Romans, chapter 8. A contrast between flesh and spirit thus becomes the framework for both form and content in the motet. The musical structure is symmetrical (somewhat reminiscent of the *Actus tragicus* and certainly an early version of this type): in terms of matching texts, part 1 equals 11, part 2 basically equals 10, part 3 corresponds to 9, part 8 is analogous to 4; the whole is built around a central section that presents the most succinct version of the underlying thought ("Not flesh but spirit am I") in the most concentrated form, a fugue. Such a unique conception could be found only in Bach. Much of the same can be said of his other motets. Of the four eight-voice motets *(Singet dem Herrn,* c. 1723; *Fürchte dich nicht,* c. 1726; *Der Geist hilft unsrer Schwachheit auf,* before 1729; *Komm, Jesu, komm,* c. 1723) the first three have the same basic structure as the five-voice motet just discussed, even though they differ completely from it in detail and far surpass it structurally. The fourth should more properly be called a large-scale funeral hymn: the first stanza is a monumental, overextended, contrapuntally treated song form; the second stanza is a simple "aria." The four-voice motet *Lobet den Herrn, alle Heiden* may be an earlier work, if authentic. A large number of motets formerly ascribed to J. S. Bach are not his. The four-voice *Sei Lob und Preis mit Ehren* is one of the motet settings that appear in Bach's cantatas, part of No. 28 (1725). It also appears as part of another, larger motet, *Jauchzet dem Herren alle Welt,* which is probably by Telemann. An eight-voice funeral motet, definitely by Bach, *O Jesu Christ, meins Lebens Licht,* has mistakenly been catalogued with the cantatas as No. 118. Apart from this, there are many motet settings within Bach's cantatas: *Nun komm, der Heiden Heiland* in No. 61, *O ewiges Feuer* in No. 34, the eight-voice single movement *Nun ist das Heil und die Kraft,* which is perhaps a fragment of a cantata (No. 50), *Nun danket alle Gott* (No. 192), and many more. These, however, are merely settings in motet style; they could hardly have been used as single motets, since there was so little opportunity for performance.

THE OLDER CHURCH CANTATA

The motet reached its last flowering about the middle of the 17th century and then gradually disappeared. Limited to use at funerals and special occasions, it lost additional ground as a result of the increasing interest in vocal music with obbligato instruments, and in the trends toward pious contemplation and operatic dramatization. The old songs were preferred for congregational worship, while modern sacred lyrics and melodies (especially those under the emotional influence of Pietism) were used increasingly for private devotions and by "enlightened" circles. The motet, to the extent it was still being composed, was more and more intended for private devotions or family celebrations, while the need for motets for public worship continued to be met by old collections from the end of the 16th and the beginning of the 17th centuries (such as those by Lindner, Hassler, Calvisius, Bodenschatz, Schadaeus, and so on). For the choir at St. Thomas's, Bach ordered new copies of the old *Florilegium Portense* of 1618, the final edition of which was printed in 1747. Because it kept up with the times and satisfied the needs for all occasions in and out of the worship service, the cantata was the most active species of Protestant church music. Indeed, the cantata has flourished from the 1660s right up to the present day. It combined in form and content what previously had been separated. For Michael Praetorius the correct form of the worship service was still based on the equal status of *contio* and *cantio* (see p. 192). The later 17th century strove for a musical equivalent of preaching and exegesis. The Word of God as proclaimed in the liturgy and interpreted in the rhetoric of a sermon was now proclaimed and interpreted musically in the cantata (especially by Bach). This musical dress (with some more or less important restrictions) was tailored from remnants of an older German tradition and from contemporary secular chamber cantatas and *opera seria*. The new development satisfied the sophisticated listener, although, as contemporary reports tell us, it remained incomprehensible to the average churchgoer, who was sometimes advised to study his hymnbook during the music. Here we can see that the cantata lived up to the original goal of Protestant church music: to keep pace with the general development of musical style. It cannot be considered apart from opera of the time. Erdmann Neumeister, who created the standard form of 18th-century cantata poetry, said in the preface to his first cantata cycle (1700; 2nd. ed. 1704) that a church cantata was about the same "as a piece from an opera made up of the recitative style and arias." He was not inaccurate. He also added a theological justification: "Even though this kind of poetry borrows its model from theatrical verse, is it not sanctified by being dedicated to the honor of God?" This was considered a progressive argument completely in the spirit of Luther, but the new form found numerous opponents nevertheless.

The term "cantata" is not clear cut. In the early 18th century the text and music of the cantata were of the most flexible and diverse construction and the names used for it were equally varied: "Kirchenmusik," "Kirchenstück," "Stück," "Concerto," "Motetto," "Motetto concertato," "Dialogo," "Actus," "Musikalische Andacht," and many more. The texts were put together from many sources: *de tempore* Bible verses (so-called dicta) or related texts, biblical quotations and analogies, hymns (chorales) or selected hymn stanzas, quotations from chorales, and freely written poetry. The latter might consist of sacred lyrics in several stanzas with a unified verse-and-refrain scheme (odes) or of one-stanza poems in freely devised verse and rhyme schemes (madrigals), within which classification the most colorful mixtures were possible. A similar variety characterized the combinations of musical style set forth by Johann Mattheson (1739): motet-like elements as used in chorale settings (either contrapuntal or monophonic textures), chorales or other liturgical melodies in cantus-firmus settings, solo or choral settings, simple cantional settings, duos, arias, recitative *(secco* or *accompagnato),* ariosos, and independent instrumental or vocal settings with concerted instruments. For purposes of historical perspective, it is useful to distinguish between "cantata" and "concerto," the former consisting principally of a series of independent movements based on a variety of texts, and the latter consisting basically of one or more movements composed to a single, unified text, with only occasional interludes. Thus, the cantata reaches its boundary in a through-composed work on a unified "ode" text, while the pure chorale cantata *per omnes versus* is closer to the concerto. On the basis of its religious purpose, the following subdivisions may be made: if the work is prefaced by a dictum, it is a "biblical proverb cantata" (Gospel cantata, psalm cantata); if it is opened by an elaborate chorale movement or a chorale dominates the work, it is a "chorale cantata." Interpretive subdivisions may also be made: "edification cantata," "sermon cantata," "contemplative pericope cantata," "lyric chorale cantata," and "dramatized biblical proverb cantata." According to setting, one can differentiate between cantatas for chorus (with or without soloists) and cantatas for one or more soloists (without choir; simple chorale settings were sung by all the soloists together). Like the concerto, the cantata was performed before the sermon; cantatas in two sections were performed with the sermon between (the second part sometimes occurring simultaneously with Communion). This practice varied according to local conditions.

The compilations of texts or poetry, often chaotic mixtures, were furnished to composers by poetically inclined theologians or amateurs; in rare cases authorship by the composer can be verified (for example, occasionally with Kuhnau). Three precedents for the "older cantata" can be distinguished. One is the biblical concerto in the manner of Heinrich Schütz. Here, a once unified text became increasingly interwoven with quotations and parallels from the Bible, and with stanzas from chorales, odes, and madrigals. The musical segments become more and more independent, as can be observed from Schütz's *Symphoniae sacrae* III (1650) to J. Ph. Krieger, J. N. Hanff, D. Buxtehude, N. Bruhns, A. Pfleger, J. Gerstenbüttel, and J. Kuhnau, and finally to Bach's early works. It became the mode to "frame" compositions: opening movements were frequently repeated at the end, or (as often with Buxtehude) choral fugues on "Hallelujah" or "Amen" (rarely chorale settings) were put at the end. At the same time, solo vocal forms became differentiated: there were strophic song types, some with the melody repeated in each stanza and some varied throughout (ostinato variations were common); there were also ariosos, bits of quasi-recitative, and so on. The second precedent was the type of chorale variation in which individual stanzas were self-sufficient musical settings, each with a distinctive overall sound, instrumentation, or vocal-instrumental combination. This was particularly common when the sequence of chorale stanzas did not adhere strictly to the cantus firmus and freely composed solo sections could be contrasted with cantus-firmus settings for chorus. In some cases the chorale comprised only the basic material and this was enriched by unrelated texts and musical forms (for instance, Buxtehude's *O Gott, wir danken deiner Güt, Wo soll ich fliehen hin?, Ihr lieben Christen, freut euch nun,* and *Erbarm dich mein, o Herre Gott).* The strictest form of a chorale variation *per omnes versus* always bordered on the concerto, but in freer forms the chorale cantata developed as a new genre, bountifully cultivated by masters such as Tunder, Buxtehude, Knüpfer, Schelle, Pachelbel, J. Ph. Krieger, Chr. A. Schulze, J. Ph. Förtsch, Zachow, and many others. The third precedent for the church cantata was the ode, the sacred lyric poem. The same structure was used for all stanzas, which were set as strophic songs (the music either repeated or varied) or through-composed (following the model of the more recent Italian chamber cantata). In the later 17th century odes were apt to have an opening biblical dictum (perhaps in verse) mixed in various ways with other texts. Genuine church music for use in the service included, in addition to the biblical proverb cantata (with its predecessor, the biblical concerto) and the chorale cantata (with the chorale concerto or chorale variation), the ode cantata (and the true ode without interludes). This is shown by the first works in the genre by Thomas Strutius of Danzig (1656) and Tobias Ennicelius of Tönning and Flensburg (1667), which are early evidence of the penetration of art music into the Protestant service through settings of nonbiblical or chorale-bound texts. The genre was also enriched with various kinds of ode cantatas by C. Chr. Dedekind (1672), W. K. Briegel (1680), J. Ph. Krieger (1688), Förtsch, Lübeck, Erlebach (1704), and many others, particularly Buxtehude. One of the most important steps toward the "Neumeister Reform" and the earlier church cantata was the later form of the biblical proverb cantata, with its introductory biblical or poetic motto; since Briegel (1660) it had become popular with composers such as Pachelbel, J. Ph. Krieger, Kuhnau, Böhm, Erlebach, and others. Finally, dialogues, which had been popular since the days of Kindermann and Hammerschmidt, survived to a great extent in Schelle, Briegel, Pfleger, Förtsch, J. Ph. Krieger, and above all in Buxtehude. They were carried over into the 18th century, when they figured prominently in Bach's cantatas (i.e., No. 140, *Wachet auf, ruft uns die Stimme*). From the beginning two kinds of dialogue had existed, and they maintained themselves in the 18th century: the dialogue between actual biblical characters and the instructional dialogue between allegorical figures.

The production of these various kinds of church cantata must have been tremendous from the 1660s to the beginning of the 18th century (and even far beyond). Many composers produced cantata cycles for several church years, often as many as 60 to 70 pieces annually. What is preserved is but a fraction of what once existed. In many cases we have only the printed yearly cycle of texts with the names of the authors and perhaps the composers; the music itself is not included. Nevertheless, we still have a sizable complex of "older church cantatas," which have been only partially investigated and in only a few cases made available in modern editions. Present-day knowledge permits a classification according to type (cf. the excellent *Systematik der Protestantischen Kirchenkantate* of G. Feder in *MGG* VII, 581–607). According to this, the repertory can be subdivided into biblical proverb cantatas, chorale cantatas, ode cantatas, proverb-ode cantatas, and dialogue cantatas. Even if such a breakdown is only a method of order, it does permit one to survey the surviving repertory. It is not chronological, for all the existing types originated shortly after the mid-17th century and were used simultaneously and arbitrarily. They overlapped in their historical development and formed the most diverse mixtures. Precisely this tremendous variety in textual and musical forms (reminiscent of opera) was characteristic of the second half of the 17th century. Musical structures exhibited constant modifications and surprises. In the choral realm there were endless possibilities, from the fugue to the simple cantional setting to the most varied cantus-firmus settings; there were also concerted chorale settings with obbligato instruments or orchestra (rarely without instruments). In the solo realm there was every conceivable form —free, recitative-like ariosos, the aria in its various guises (the da capo aria appeared about 1700 in the works of Erlebach and Kuhnau, but without the four-line strophic texts that were common later on; Erlebach and Kuhnau even used prose texts), duets, and strophic or varied or through-composed songs. All the solos usually had instrumental accompaniments but seldom the free, contrapuntal, dazzling virtuoso parts so common in Bach. The placement of ritornellos, sonatas, or symphonies created "frames" and ritornello forms and contributed to the conception of the cantata as a unified whole with symmetrical repetitions. Regularity and symmetry in the overall structure of a cantata was not atypical.

Many composers wrote "older church cantatas"; only the most important can be listed here. The printed compositions of Christoph Bernhard (1665) belong mostly to the concerto type. In addition, his church pieces surviving in manuscript include ode cantatas (with and without an introductory verse), dialogues, and Gospel concertos with stanzas of some hymns or lyric poems inserted. Much of this music is excellent, and far too little of it is available in modern editions. His south-German contemporary, W. K. Briegel, was extremely productive, publishing between 1652 and 1709 a large number of works more or less in the manner of the cantata. Compared to Bernhard, they are frequently tuneful and of great simplicity and popular appeal. His best works seem to have been ode cantatas (for instance, *Musikalischer Lebensbrunnen,* 1680) and proverb-ode cantatas (*Evangelischer Blumengarten,* four parts, 1666–69; *Musikalische Trostquelle,* 1679; *Evangelischer Palmenzweig,* 1685). He also wrote numerous dialogue cantatas in various styles (*Evangelische Gespräche,* three parts, 1660, 1662, 1681; *Musikalische Trostquelle,* 1679; *Musikalischer Lebensbrunnen,* 1680; *Concentus Apostolico-Musicus,* 1697, etc.). Other works of his are true odes. Closely related to Bernhard is Constantin Christian Dedekind of Dresden, with many prints from the 1660s and '70s, and especially with the diversified ode cantatas of his *Seelenfreude* (1672). The extensive cantata output of the Görlitz composer Christian Ludwig Boxberg belongs to this group and has only recently received a thoroughgoing assessment (S. Sørensen in *Natalicia,* K. Jeppesen *Festschrift,* Copenhagen, 1962, 217–42). In the preface to his Passion (1672), J. Sebastiani of Königsberg offered a whole Gospel cycle for publication; the offer was in vain.

Cantata compositions had once been widespread in northern Germany. Tobias Ennicelius, Friedrich Meister, and J. Nikolaus Hanff were active in Schleswig, Flensburg, and Hamburg. Ennicelius published *Melismata epistolica* (based on M. Opitz) in 1667; from the other two, only manuscripts of cantatas have been handed down. They cover the whole range of biblical cantatas and chorale cantatas; Ennicelius's print belongs to the ode-cantata genre. Christian Geist, who should be mentioned here, was active in Copenhagen; as Buxtehude's "predecessor," he furnished Gustav Düben in Stockholm with concertos in Latin and German for one to six voices with instruments. They include multisectional concertos, biblical proverb compositions with arias added, and through-composed odes; the texts are not yet of diversified origin, structure, and content. Düben's somewhat precious style, especially in the Latin pieces, approaches Bruhns and Buxtehude; K. Förster may have been his model. A chorale aria, *Wie schön leuchtet der Morgenstern,* comes close to early Bach; a five-voice concerto, *Die mit Tränen säen,* with three gambas, compares favorably with Buxtehude's best works; another displays a remarkable virtuoso solo for violone. There are also concertos for large ensembles. The frequently mentioned manuscript cycle of Gospel cantatas by A. Pfleger, dedicated to the city council of Flensburg (1670), is an instructive example of the mixture of various texts and musical styles (though it is certainly inferior in quality). A counterpart to this is the sometimes admirable Gospel cycle of the Dresden composer J. Kaspar Horn (1680–81). It was printed in two parts, for summer and winter. The texts were taken complete and unaltered from the biblical pericopes, and because there are no additional text sources, the cycle remains within the province of the concerto. Joachim Gerstenbüttel of Hamburg left thirty-one manuscripts (1690–1700); forty more, inventoried in Lüneburg, are lost. Those preserved are of the older biblical cantata type (among which are Epistle cantatas such as *Dazu ist erschienen*), or the chorale cantata and the ode cantata; stylistically, however, they are very conservative for their period.

Dietrich Buxtehude, the greatest master in northern Germany, occupies a central position (chronologically as well as artistically). His more than 120 cantatas all date from about 1680–85 and include all types and styles, from the simplest chorale setting to the most elaborate solo aria with accompanying instruments. Ostinato variations, instrumental movements, ode stanzas, and cantus-firmus settings are all of the highest quality, while the arioso solo pieces in a manner of *stile oratorio* (for example, the bass cantata *Mein Herz ist bereit*) are among the outstanding achievements in German music of this era. Buxtehude aligned himself with the chorale variation of Tunder *(Wachet auf, ruft uns die Stimme)* and with the dialogue concerto of Schütz and Hammerschmidt (*Herr, ich lasse dich nicht* and many more), but he also knew the vocal concerto for large ensemble (as evidenced by his motet *Laudate pueri* for six choirs). The resplendent Roman style of Mazzochi and Agostini found followers in the Baltic School, as did the new bel canto of the Carissimi-Rossi group. The connection, however, has not been clarified. Of great importance in Buxtehude's style, next to the recitative-like or monodic arioso style and the concerted elements, were the expansive forms he used for setting long lines in stanzas of sacred texts (odes). He gave new weight to the content of the "edification cantata," now and then paraphrasing the biblical text and interpreting it by means of chorale stanzas in which the cantus firmus, as later with Bach, was occasionally given to instruments *(Gott, hilf mir).* The organ chorale became identical in style to the vocal chorale, the organ registration being equivalent to the relationship between voices and instruments. None of his contemporaries could rival the penetration of Buxtehude's expressiveness or the richness of his methods of text interpretation or his romantic lyricism. At the same time, he was the most advanced musician in respect to style. His lyricism, both brilliant and melancholy—especially in his Latin cantatas—followed in the path of late Schütz and Carissimi. He was the only composer of his time who could rival in forcefulness J. S. Bach, younger by almost fifty years. In addition to the more concerted or arioso-like forms he produced genuine da capo arias (though on biblical prose texts). The arioso forms included some that closely approached recitative. Buxtehude's chorale cantatas are distinguished partly by the strictness of the cantus-firmus technique, partly —quite the reverse—by the freedom of their language, and especially by their tone color, with stanzas distributed among the most varied ensembles. The "symphonies" and stanza ritornellos are among the best 17th-century German achievements in the field. Buxtehude's special forte was the ode cantata; with amazing inventiveness he modified the forms of the strophic, varied, and through-composed types *(Jesulein, du Tausendschön, Was frag ich nach der Welt?, Jesu, komm, mein Freud und Lachen)*. He even treated the chorale as an ode without cantus firmus *(Wie soll ich dich empfangen?)*. Buxtehude's masterpieces include on the one hand biblical cantatas of often breathtaking vitality *(Gott fähret auf mit Jauchzen* with poem by R. Rist inserted; *Ich suchte des Nachts in meinem Bette);* on the other hand, there are dialogue cantatas with striking characterization *(Wo soll ich fliehen hin?, Gott, hilf mir, Ihr lieben Christen, freut euch nun)*. Here, the points of contact with Bach become apparent *(Actus tragicus,* No. 106). A type that Buxtehude cultivated with the deepest feeling was the Latin devotional text with or without insertions; his *Rhythmica Oratio* (1680) is a masterpiece of the style and time.

Among younger composers in northern Germany, Buxtehude's pupil Nikolaus Bruhns, of Husum, stands out because of the vigorous, concise, and at the same time poetic tenderness. Of his few extant cantatas there are twelve; two others are erroneously ascribed to him. They fall in all the various text categories, including some in Latin (as with his teacher). Closely linked with him is J. Philipp Förtsch, who was active in Husum, Schleswig, and Eutin. Eighty-two cantatas in manuscript, most likely produced in Gottorf (1686–88), have been handed down. They include chorale cantatas, ode cantatas, and dialogues; a new edition of them is urgently needed. Georg Österreich, a pupil of Förtsch and Johann Schelle in Leipzig but twenty years older than J. S. Bach, worked in Gottorf. His fifty to sixty extant works of the present type date from before 1695; they waver between concerto and cantata. His biblical cantatas adhere to older models, but include also some recitative-like settings; the Latin devotional cantatas are similar to those of Buxtehude and Bruhns.

In Saxony, three of Bach's predecessors in the cantorate of St. Thomas's, Sebastian Knüpfer, Johann Schelle, and Johann Kuhnau, wrote many cantatas in the older style and completed the transition from concerto to cantata. All three composers wrote chorale cantatas. Sebastian Knüpfer, teacher of Weckmann and Johannes Kaspar Horn, wrote much church music, most of which has disappeared. Among the preserved works, the concerted type of the Schütz circle predominates; arioso solo parts closely approach the style of recitative. The style of his solo songs resembles that of Buxtehude. His biblical proverb cantatas date from before 1676. The richness of instrumentation is striking. A piece like *Machet die Tore weit* (1692) has an archaic quality resulting from its massive density. The advent of the Protestant cantata in Leipzig dates back to Schelle, who probably followed in Horn's path (see above); his lyrics were provided by Paul Thymich, from whose works Bach took the text for his motet *Komm, Jesu, komm.* The biblical proverb cantata, often richly "orchestrated," was outstanding in Schelle's work; he, too, occasionally used polychoral textures. Like Buxtehude, Schelle provided lyrical texts with animated melodies and composed ode cantatas beginning with proverb mottoes (the earliest was 1682–83). Again like Buxtehude, he advanced to a type of cantata with mixed texts *(Also hat Gott die Welt geliebet, Und da die Tage ihrer Reinigung).* Kuhnau's extensive church music at one time probably embraced several cycles of church cantatas; except for a few works, it has disappeared. The preface to a printed cycle of cantata texts (1709–10) reveals that he strove for a definitive compilation of his librettos and for a correct application of musical styles. His psalm cantata *Gott, sei mir gnädig* and the Isaiah cantata *Ich freue mich im Herren* are concertos in several movements with solos. *Wenn ihr fröhlich seid* contains da capo arias and a kind of *secco* recitative in addition to older elements of style. The cantata *Wie schön leuchtet der Morgenstern* paraphrases the chorale text and approaches the "sermon cantata" with its strong emphasis on contemplation. The pull toward a unified form is clearly perceptible: a frame is established by enclosing the entire work between artistic settings of the first and last stanzas; intensely emotional solo parts contrast strongly with the congregational hymn and utilize *secco* and *accompagnato* recitative, ariosos, and da capo arias. The old-style "aria" had been dropped, and the composition of odes was also declining. The instrumental introductory movement (still preferred by Bach in his Weimar days) was rarely used, and the old variety of forms gave way to a growing feeling for regularity. Even greater value was attached to the unifying of all elements through the use of a frame or some other symmetrical construction.

The composers most closely related to the cantors of St. Thomas's were Friedrich Wilhelm Zachow of Halle (Handel's teacher); Johann Philipp Krieger of Weissenfels (a master of great renown and far-reaching influence in his day); Christian Ritter of Halle, Dresden, and Stockholm; Philipp Heinrich Erlebach of Rudolstadt; and Georg Böhm of Lüneburg. All of them lived well into the period of Bach's cantata. With his cantata *Das ist das ewige Leben,* Zachow established a type often used by Bach: a Gospel verse followed by three movements in different verse forms containing a highly rationalistic interpretation of the Gospel; the latter movements consisted of recitatives, arias, and a closing chorale stanza. The biblical movement with its multiple sections (and fugue) and the da capo arias with obligato instruments are both like Bach. A chorale cantata *Vom Himmel kam der Engel Schar* is a variation *per omnes versus* in which the solo stanzas partly dispense with the chorale melody; later on, Bach often did the same. The old cantata type is represented by *Ruhe, Friede, Freud und Wonne.* In the *Deutsches Magnificat,* a aria-stanza follows and paraphrases each verse of the Gospel text. With the cantatas for Christmas, Easter, and Pentecost (the latter, 1712) *Es wird eine Rute aufgehen, Dies ist der Tag,* and *Nun aber gibst du, Gott,* the contents of the "edification cantata" were established in rough outline; Bach used this model in his early days. Of Krieger's original two thousand cantatas, barely sixty have been preserved. Judging by these few samples, Krieger may be looked upon as an especially progressive cantata composer. As early as 1696–99, he composed parts of Erdmann Neumeister's *Poetische Oden* (Neumeister was, like Krieger, active at the Weissenfels court); these were published in 1726 in the second part of the preacher-poet's *Fortgesetzte Fünffache Kirchenandachten.* Krieger also set in total Neumeister's first and fifth cycles of cantata poems (see below) and the two complete cycles of his *Fortgesetzte Fünffache Kirchenandachten.* Texts by Johann Olearius and Johann Schieferdecker have also been identified among Krieger's works. Like Buxtehude, he followed in the path of the older concerto, the dialogue, and the chorale variation; like Kuhnau, his later works included two large "edification cantatas," which, as in early Bach, used all kinds of text combinations together with richly varied musical forms. Italian recitative and aria forms were characteristic of Krieger's style. By now a transitional stage had been reached wherein the older forms of text and music were mixed with those of more recent date, i.e., the Neumeister cantata type. Christian Ritter's output of church music seems to have been voluminous. Of the few works preserved, the major portion, in manuscript (like that of Buxtehude), is in Uppsala. The types Ritter used, including his Latin devotional cantatas, are similar to Buxtehude in instrumentation, structure, melodic delicacy, and inventiveness. This is also true of his ode cantatas which begin with proverb mottoes (1704 and 1706). Compared with Ritter, Erlebach seems colorless and also more retrospective. His *Gottgeheiligte Singstunde* (printed 1704) was devoted to the dying style of the ode cantata; it lacks the melodic intimacy of Buxtehude, Schelle, or Ritter. Erlebach also set the complete second cycle of Neumeister's cantata poems. Georg Böhm wrote a chorale cantata in strict style; it stands midway between Buxtehude and Bach *(Nun komm, der Heiden Heiland).* Generally speaking, his cantatas were retrospective, harking back to the days of Knüpfer and Weckmann. *Der Himmelreich ist gleich einem König* points to the multifarious concerto type: solo arias and concerted chorale settings on biblical texts contrast with several chorale stanzas of an exegetic nature. *Jauchzet Gott* is merely a psalm concerto. Only the Song of Solomon cantata *Mein Freund ist mein* and the psalm cantata *Wie lieblich sind deine Wohnungen* contain contemplative insertions; the latter is a series of uniformly constructed ode stanzas, a schoolbook example of the biblical proverb motet.

In southern Germany the composition of cantatas seems to have been of little consequence during these decades. The only true master was Johann Pachelbel of Nuremberg, who also excelled in the field of vocal music. Kaspar Wecker of Nuremberg may possibly approach him. His published *Geistliche Konzerte* (1695) continued at a comparatively late date the biblical proverb cantata; however, he modernized it by ending on an "Amen" or "Hallelujah" fugue. Pachelbel's cantata with chorale variations, *Was Gott tut, das ist wohlgetan,* is outstanding. Remnants of many of his vocal compositions, which had disappeared, have recently come to light (see H.H. Eggebrecht in *AfMw* XI, 1954). The types he used included proverb cantatas and dialogues. His works include several motets on psalm texts (some with concerting instruments), Masses, and so on; these are but fragments of what was once a much larger collection.

Although he was a contemporary of J.S. Bach, J. Friedrich Fasch belongs with the present group. He was a pupil of Johann Philipp Krieger in Weissenfels and of Kuhnau in Leipzig. In his youth he composed cantatas on texts by Hunold; from 1722–23 to 1755 (according to B. Engelke), after some eventful years as court *Kapellmeister* in Zerbst, he wrote a Passion and other types of church music. He produced at least five double and six single cycles of church cantatas, a few on texts of his own and others on poems by Benjamin Schmolck. In addition, he set to music Neumeister's second and third cycles of cantata texts. A detailed historical analysis of his works from the standpoint of his cantatas is still lacking, and only one cantata is available in modern edition (*Sieh zu, dass deine Gottesfurcht nicht Heuchelei sei,* 1930). Despite the texts, which place him with Bach, and despite his philanthropical and Pietistic tendencies (correspondence with Count Zinzendorf), it would seem that in the form of his cantatas Fasch remained in the transitional stage represented by Zachow and Kuhnau.

THE NEWER CHURCH CANTATA

J.S. BACH'S CANTATAS AND ORATORIOS

The Protestant church cantata, in its older form, remained exuberant and imaginative, like many other vocal genres of the time. Its texts culled from liturgical and biblical sources, from chorales, hymns, and odes, its music drawing on madrigalesque techniques, changing "aria" forms, and a maze of diverse styles, species, and forms, the church cantata stood apart from the course of music history, which in the late Baroque period was leading to a uniformity of style. It obviously fulfilled the Pietistic needs of violent emotion, fervent excitement, and rhetorical interpretation of the Word; it allowed music to lead to a *compunctio cordis* (warming of the heart), to edification, and indoctrination. The massive production speaks for itself. However, it lacked everything that makes a homogeneous work of art. The checkered patterns within which textual and musical elements were indiscriminately mingled needed a discriminating hand. The chaos resulting from so many components had to be systematized if the church cantata (like secular music of the time) was to satisfy the highly developed taste of an 18th-century artist, connoisseur, or amateur.

Parallel developments occurred everywhere in music as the accumulated freight of late Baroque fancy and sentimentality was cleared away and replaced with a well-reasoned and sober uniformity of ideas clothed in stylized affects and images. It was Apostolo Zeno (1696 ff.) who did this for the *opera seria,* Arcangelo Spagna (1706) who did it for the Italian oratorio, Christian Friedrich Hunold who did it for German opera and the Protestant oratorio (Menantes; 1707), and Erdmann Neumeister who did it for the cantata (1700; manuscripts even earlier). The history of the "newer church cantata" began with the "Neumeister Reform" and continued through Bach's lifetime. It was superseded in the second half of the 18th century by a late phase of the movement, in which a natural religious philanthropism prevailed.

The forms that became characteristic of the newer cantata gradually entered the older type as well; the transition can be seen in the works of Kuhnau and Zachow, to a degree in J. Ph. Krieger, and also in Erlebach and Fasch. These forms included *secchi* recitatives on Italian models—strongly emotional, however, and frequently changing into ariosos; sometimes they developed into polyphonic settings, occasionally interwoven with chorales but mostly in a madrigal-like style (i.e., irregularly constructed texts in a free rhyme scheme with more animated verses used in the accompaniment). Another form used in the newer cantata was the da capo aria. No longer composed to prose or arbitrarily constructed texts, it was now used for setting stanzas of four to six lines patterned on Italian opera librettos. The aria itself was usually accompanied by string instruments; the solo voice was no longer surrounded by concerting instruments, but often provided with contrapuntal, and sometimes virtuoso, obbligato instrumental decoration. The ode form gradually declined and was replaced by a series of different one-stanza arias—such as those written by Salomo Franck (1710 ff.) and set to music by Bach (1714–16), partly modernized with insertions of recitative. The one-stanza aria text gradually became the rule. The text of the chorale, and thus of the newer chorale cantata, still consisted of several stanzas; strict settings, however, were more or less abandoned in favor of freer ode-like compositions in which the stanzas were set partly in a simple choral style and partly as solo arias on the chorale text with the melody either free or imitating that of the chorale. Bach also used a cantus firmus or added an extraneous cantus firmus in one of the contrapuntal voices. This special manner of paraphrasing a chorale cantata (see below) seems to have been utilized in Bach's time only by him. All these new forms came into use in the course of time and were not "inventions" of Neumeister. It was Neumeister's contribution that he rejected outright the old forms and systematically introduced the new ones, applying them in the most varied combinations. He thus probably "saved" the cantata as a genre for a later period when the confusion of the older textual and musical forms would have been intolerable, just as a century later the rationalistic soberness and the stylized affectations of Bach's texts became intolerable to the beginning of Romanticism. In his poetic treatise *Allerneueste Art zur reinen und galanten Poesie zu gelangen* (Hamburg, 1707), based on Neumeister's models and lectures, Hunold provided theoretical justification for the reform of opera, oratorio, and cantata.

It has not yet been determined when Neumeister's activity began. The three text cycles printed in his *Fortgesetzte fünffache Kirchenandachten* (1726) were known at least in part in the 1690s in Weissenfels, because Johann Philipp Krieger composed some of them. The first text cycle that Neumeister himself had printed bore the characteristic title *Geistliche Kantaten statt einer Kirchenmusik* (Spiritual Cantatas Instead of a Church Music); it was published in Weissenfels, singly in 1700 and collectively in 1704. The texts included freely rhymed poems (in madrigal style) for recitatives, alternating with rhymed stanzas for arias. They were modeled after the newer Italian chamber cantata (represented by Stradella,

Legrenzi, Scarlatti, or Gasparini), which was then being adopted at German courts. As indicated by its title, the artistic needs of the time were fulfilled by letting the fashionable "cantata" take the place of the older "church music." These texts were principally intended for solo cantatas, although individual arias could also be set as choruses (Bach, too, used stanzas as chorus texts which his librettists had intended for solo arias.) In Neumeister's second cycle, written for Rudolstadt, printed in 1708, and set to music by Erlebach, the title sounds a little more cautious: *Cantaten über alle Evangelien*. Like the first, it included poetry for recitatives and arias, including the choir. The third cycle, written for Eisenach, and performed there by Telemann (as stated on the title page) appeared in 1711 (there are different editions with altered titles, some referring to Frankfurt on the Main). The fourth cycle appeared under the title *Geistliche Poesien mit untermischten biblischen Sprüchen und Chorälen* (1714). These last two settled matters in that they replaced the texts for choir with biblical quotations or hymn stanzas; thus, they went far beyond the ultimate objective of the "Reform." The compromise between the newer and older text designs became the basis for the "newer church cantata." A fifth cycle, however, consisted again of strophic odes; it was published by Gottfried Tilgner, together with the first four cycles, as *Fünffache Kirchenandachten* (1716–17). Up to his last years Neumeister, who died in 1756, was active as an author of cantata texts. At first he had avoided any formalism in the arrangements of texts, but later on he changed this as schematic groupings of whole cycles became fashionable. Entire cycles of Telemann and Graupner were arranged according to uniform patterns, and Neumeister himself set up a whole year's cycle for Telemann in Hamburg (1752) in the following order: dictum, chorale, recitative, aria, chorale; he then repeated the dictum at the end, an old-fashioned idea (G. Feder in *MGG* VII, 600).

The "Neumeister Reform" was tremendously successful. It attracted countless poets, among them Christian Postel, Nikolaus König, Benjamin Neukirch, Burkhard Menke (1710), Gottlieb Siegmund Corvinus (1710), Christoph Woltereck (1712), Christian Günther, Michael Richey, J. J. Rambach, and Benjamin Schmolck. Some became Bach's librettists: Salomo Franck, Christian Friedrich Henrici (Picander), Mariane von Ziegler, Neumeister and Gottsched at times, perhaps Christian Weise the Older or the Younger, and probably many others. While the representatives of Pietism had always protested against "operatic" church music in the older cantata, now an extensive literary dispute broke out. As early as 1694 the feud began between Christian Schiff and Johann Muscovius. Polemic treatises of Christian Gerber were published in 1703, 1704, and 1711. Johann Buttstett, in 1716, fought against "dissolute trash in the church that has come in with the theatrical recitative style" (the latter half of the remark probably aimed at his neighbor, J.S. Bach). Similar polemics were still being written in 1726 and 1728 by Joachim Meyer. Publications in defense of the cantata began with Hunold, Neumeister and Tilgner themselves, and Georg Motz (1703, 1708), and extended to the writings of the Lübeck cantor Kaspar Ruetz (c. 1750). Joachim Meyer challenged Martin Heinrich Fuhrmann with two publications (1728 and 1729); Fuhrmann bolstered his argument with Spener, stating that the latter by no means wanted to ban new-style music from the church but had only opposed the "wild, luxurious theatrical style." Meyer was sharply criticized by Mattheson (*Der neue Göttingische Ephorus,* 1727; *Der musikalische Patriot,* 1728), who declared that he did saw no reason for church music not to be "theatrical or operatic" because on the opera stage itself "many serious things do happen."

Since about 1710, musicians had made their choice in favor of the newer cantata, although the various older styles were kept alive through the 1720s and '30s. When it became customary for librettists to write and publish complete yearly cycles of texts, composers began to produce in huge quantities, creating in the first half of the 18th century a superabundance of "theatrical" church music, little of which has been investigated. Authenticity has been established for 1,518 church cantatas by Telemann, 1,418 by Graupner, and 235 by Johann Theodor Römhild (the remnants of at least twelve cycles). No one has yet attempted to calculate how many Stölzel wrote. The number by Bach is still disputed (hardly more than 200–250); J.F. Fasch's production is estimated at about 700. The use of a well-organized church music extended even to small towns and villages, where every organist or choirmaster, no matter how undistinguished, had an accumulation of his own cantatas. The new style made it possible to dispense with a choir almost completely and to rely on the modest vocal-instrumental components of solo settings. Consequently, every form of dilettantism entered the door and contributed to the general decline of Protestant church music.

The way had been prepared for all the media and styles used by J.S. Bach in his cantatas. Bach himself did not invent any new types; he took the older ones and combined them with the newer. At times he favored types which had been used infrequently by the older masters or in a different manner. The first method is perceptible in his chorale cantatas, which are based on liturgical congregational hymns and follow the manner and style of a sacred ode; they approach the traditional cantata in their paraphrasing of madrigal or arioso styles. The second method can be seen in Bach's occasional preference for the solo cantata. However, none of the types he used was new; one should speak rather of a renewal of older types. The fact that renewal was what Bach strove for may be one reason for his frequent change of librettists. Neumeister's poems, which were otherwise much in vogue and often set to music, were used by Bach in only a few cases; there are no more than five complete librettos by Neumeister in all of his cantatas. Whereas other cantata composers of his generation, like Telemann or Graupner, composed complete cycles with each cantata following the same pattern, only once did Bach hold to one type—in his chorale cantatas (1724–25)—and then only for about six months. Other than this, he often changed direction without any discernible reason. There is no overriding form that could be taken as characteristic for Bach's cantatas as a whole. As in many other fields, Bach appropriated from tradition whatever suited him, and did not attach himself to the specific tradition of any one school. The *Actus tragicus,* No. 106, in which the biblical dialogue of the 17th century was resuscitated, is among his earliest cantatas. Another, *Christ lag in Todesbanden,* No. 4, followed strictly the old practice of the chorale variation *per omnes versus.* Still another, the election *(Ratswahl)* cantata *Gott ist mein König,* No. 71, follows the line of the biblical proverb cantata. In his early days, Bach followed the older German tradition in methods of musical expression as well. He used neither recitatives nor da capo arias, but motet-like movements, song-like ariosos, and chorale cantus-firmus settings with and without concerted instruments. It was not until he began composing cantatas in Weimar (1714) on texts of Salomo Franck, which follow the model of Neumeister's third and fourth cycles (1711 and 1714), that Bach began to fuse the new Italian style with the old German tradition. From then on, he was the sovereign who could create his own world.

Bach's cantatas arrived late on the scene and concluded the development from concerto to cantata with the greatest achievements ever realized in this sphere. It would be a mistake, however, to maintain the previous historical view that Bach was the end of the species. Composers of the following generations—his two oldest sons, his pupils Goldberg, Doles, Scheibe, Kellner, Homilius, G. Benda, and others—were not mere imitators; they successfully maintained the cantata through the style changes of their own time, though they imbued it with their new understanding of Christianity as an enlightened, natural religion.

What makes the Bach cantatas stand out from those of all others is not so much their novelty, their versatility, their superior workmanship, or the vitality of their inspiration. Rather, it is their intellectual penetration, the facility of their word interpretation, and (despite Bach's love for detail) the breadth of their vision, which never loses sight of the totality of the text and its connotations. The conception is one of all-inclusive plasticity and exegetic pictorialization. It aims at complete realization of the emotional potential and at mystic-symbolic inter-pretations of ideas, which are often placed in such mysterious, obscure relation-ships that even the text does not clarify them. Bach's best cantatas are musical sermons, with a profundity and richness of ideas greater than words could have expressed or than any other musician could have achieved in them. He often changed librettists and may have influenced some of them, such as Henrici or Mariane von Ziegler (or even modified their texts); in his compositions the raw materials of the librettos were sublimated and brought to a higher unity of form and content. This, finally, is what distinguishes his cantatas from all the other great and important ones by J. Ph. Krieger, Buxtehude, Bruhns, Pachelbel, and others.

It is not entirely certain which are Bach's oldest extant church cantatas. *Denn du wirst meine Seele,* No. 15, formerly thought to be one of his earliest cantatas (Jauernig: 1704; Dürr: 1703 in Weimar), does not belong to Johann Sebastian but to Johann Ludwig Bach of Meiningen (W. H. Scheide in the *Bach-Jahrbuch,* 1959). Its similarity with the Buxtehude style made for some confusion in regard to Bach's early works in the field. No cantata can be dated with certainty prior to his stay in Mühlhausen (1707–08). It is certain that two election cantatas originated in Mühlhausen: No. 71, *Gott ist mein König,* for 1708, and a second one for 1709, which has been lost; both were printed and were the only cantatas of Bach to be published during his lifetime. To his Mühlhausen period we can ascribe with certainty the cantata No. 131, *Aus der Tiefe rufe ich,* and probably also the *Actus tragicus,* No. 106, *Gottes Zeit,* the chorale setting No. 4, *Christ lag in Todesbanden,* and the wedding cantata No. 196, *Der Herr denket an uns.* This small inventory is probably all that has been preserved of Bach's pre-Weimar cantatas. Nos. 71 and 106 are closely connected. Both of their texts probably come from Bach's friend Eilmar, the orthodox pastor; both are combinations of psalm verses, other Old Testament texts, chorale stanzas, and an occasional freely written text. In Cantata No. 71 Bach began his task of depicting the pageant of human life. A loosely connected sequence of texts refers on a superficial plane to the outgoing and incoming city councils; old age and youth become a balanced contrast determining the two-part form. The first part opens with a concerto-like movement related to the occasion. This is followed by a duet in which the bass text *Ich bin nun achtzig Jahr* (I am now eighty years old) is stated simultaneously with a chorale in the soprano; here the bottom voice becomes a symbolic representation of the burdens of old age. In the second part, by contrast, the solos come first to portray youthful strength, and then the choir, indicative of the occasion, again in concerto style. Between these two parts, exactly in the middle and in a contrasting key, stands the one a capella section—a fugue, *Dein Alter sei wie deine Jugend* (May thy age be as thy youth); the two basic concepts are intertwined in the polyphony of the setting, symbolizing the coexistence and the confrontation of the generations. The formal symmetry of the entire work is a symbol of the antithetical tensions within and obviously corresponds with the concept of form that determined so much of the young Bach's vocal music (cf. the analogous structure of the motet *Jesu meine Freude,* p. 269). From the point of view of form and the exploitation of stylistic resources, this cantata (contrary to Spitta) lacks the skill of a Buxtehude or Böhm. It sounds archaic. Although inventiveness is indeed present, it seems daredevil and ungainly rather than mature and well developed. However, the essential point—the skillful selection of a principal idea, and the shaping of an amorphous substance to give that idea musical form—he did accomplish. The same holds for the other early works, especially the so-called *Actus tragicus,* No. 106. This piece cannot be dated with certainty, but 1707 is generally assumed to be the year of its completion. Here, too, the text is colorful, almost amorphous, having been pieced together from various proverbs, chorales, and other quotations. Here, too, an antithesis is set up—old ties against new—which gives the cantata its form. The nucleus of the work is based on a unique combination: a fugue acting as a symbol for the old, and a soprano solo symbolizing the new; the whole is interwoven with a third component, a chorale. On either side of this nucleus the opposing ideas are developed in free, arioso-like, contemplative sections; these, too, compete with the simultaneously sounding, interpretative chorale. The relationship of keys underlines the structure. However simple the work may appear, it is a masterpiece of hidden meanings and interrelationships expressed through the resources of the composer, not the librettist. This pervasive connection between the biblical and the archaic gave Bach a special priority in the Romantic period. The cantata *Aus der Tiefe,* No. 131, with its perfectly symmetrical design, its archaic elements, and once again its predominantly biblical orientation (Psalm 130, with only two chorale stanzas inserted) closely resembles the two works already mentioned. Cantata No. 196, *Der Herr denket an uns,* is basically the same. The only work completely different from this Mühlhausen model (if one may call it that) is the

71. Johann Sebastian Bach, opening of the motet *Der Geist hilft unserer Schwachheit auf,* BWV 226 (1729), autograph. From the collection of the Staatsbibliothek der Stiftung Preussischer Kulturbesitz (formerly the Preussische Staatsbibliothek Berlin), temporarily at Marburg/Lahn, Mus. MS. autogr. Bach P 36 (No. 1).

72. Johann Sebastian Bach, opening of the cantata *Ein Herz, das seinen Jesum lebend weiss,* BWV 134 (1724), autograph. Berlin, Deutsche Staatsbibliothek, Mus. MS autogr. Bach P 1138.

chorale cantata No. 4, *Christ lag in Todesbanden,* a kind of variation *per omnes versus,* completely in the 17th-century style of Tunder, Buxtehude, Pachelbel, Knüpfer, Kuhnau, and so on. If it was actually composed in 1707–08, it is evidence of Bach's retrospective attitude, for this type had already become old-fashioned then. The complete absence of Italian forms and stylistic resources of recitatives, arias, and obbligato and concerted instruments (which connect it with the cantatas mentioned above) indicates an early date of composition.

These earliest cantatas of Bach can be grouped under the heading "edification cantata." We cannot determine with certainty when and how he changed to Neumeister's type of "sermon cantata," because (according to Dürr) no exact chronology between 1708 and 1714 is possible. Cantata No. 18, *Gleich wie der Regen und Schnee,* formerly misplaced in this interim period, probably belongs to the post-Weimar period, specifically to the year 1715. It is not certain if the cantata that (according to his own testimony) Bach composed in 1713 during his stay in Halle was the Christmas cantata No. 63, *Christen, ätzet diesen Tag,* or another one. With his appointment as *Konzertmeister* to the court of Weimar (March 2, 1714), he was required to compose one cantata a month. He met this requirement conscientiously until he withdrew from the position at the end of 1716 (not all the cantatas of these years have been preserved or identified as such). From this time on, Bach's cantata composition (at least in the narrower sense of the church cantata) was interrupted for a long period. It was not resumed until his move to Leipzig (installation, June 1, 1723).

Eighteen or twenty of Bach's extant cantatas can be assigned with some degree of certainty to his Weimar period, and four or six others probably belong there, too (see Dürr, *Studien über die frühen Kantaten Bachs,* p. 54 f.). A number of cantatas, once thought to date from this period or considered "comparatively early," must with more or less certainty be eliminated from Bach's list of works: Nos. 53, 141, 142, 150, 156, 160, and 189 are spurious, according to the latest findings; Nos. 141, 156, and 160 are completely Telemann's work, as is one movement from No. 145. The texts of Bach's Weimar cantatas are for the major part ascribed to the court preacher Salomo Franck (see F. L. Tagliavini, *Studi sui testi,* pp. 59–76), who might also have been the author of some of the unidentifiable librettos; some others stem from Erdmann Neumeister (ibid., pp. 41–58). Bach's Weimar period produced such important compositions as No. 182, *Himmelskönig, sei willkommen* (Franck, 1714); No. 12, *Weinen, Klagen, Sorgen, Zagen* (Franck?, 1714); No. 172, *Erschallet, ihr Lieder* (Franck?, 1714); No. 199, *Mein Herze schwimmt im Blut* (?, 1714); the famous Advent cantata No. 61, *Nun komm, der Heiden Heiland* (Neumeister, 1714); the original version of the Reformation cantata *Ein feste Burg,* No. 80a, *Alles, was von Gott geboren* (Franck, 1715); the Easter cantata, No. 31, *Der Himmel lacht* (Franck, 1715); and the cantata for the sixteenth Sunday after Trinity, the tender, intense No. 161, *Komm, du süsse Todesstunde* (Franck, 1715).

Cantata No. 182, *Himmelskönig, sei willkommen,* seems to be characteristic of the new type. The poem is a contemplation on the theme of the text and, apart from the final chorale, contains only one short psalm verse in its original wording (arranged by Bach as a recitative). Thus, the idea of an antithesis is not emphasized. The Palm Sunday motif, the entry of Christ into Jerusalem and the people's reception of him, is given a new allegorical interpretation: it is the sinful heart opening to accept.the love of Christ. The artistic solution is striking, and it is no longer the work of the composer alone, but of the librettist as well. Three separate arias form a middle group symbolizing divine love, the opening heart, and the union of both under the sign of the cross. The choral movements contain symmetrically placed images of the entry into Jerusalem and of the entry of the "enlightened" (the Pietistic expression fits perfectly here) into the celestial "Salem of happiness." The da capo-like arrangements of the two chorale settings and the three central arias produce a striking regularity of form which may have been deliberate but may also only show how much Bach was attracted by the new Italian styles coming his way. The chorale fantasy *Jesu, deine Passion* was obviously a later insertion (Schering); it disturbs the relationship between content and form, and may owe its existence to a later performance in Leipzig. Cantata No. 161, *Komm, du süsse Todesstunde,* is in a similar vein, although reminiscent of its Mühlhausen forerunners. The basic idea, a longing for death and for union with Christ *(Ich habe Lust, bei Christo bald zu weiden, ich habe Lust, von dieser Welt zu scheiden),* is wrapped in free, contemplative "poetry"; only one chorale stanza at the end harks back to older conceptions of what a text should be. Here, the composer no longer wanted only to give shape to an idea. Rather, he wanted to express emotions and to preach heartrendingly with arias and dramatic, moving, colorful recitatives (among which *Der Schluss ist schon gemacht* is a masterpiece). Cantata No. 31, *Der Himmel lacht,* on the other hand, shows important innovations in the interpretative use of the text as well as in form. The text consists entirely of poetry on a motif of death and resurrection, but the emphasis is no longer on the antithesis itself. Instead, the cantata develops the motif in two ways: in the first part it is applied to Christ, and in the second part to the believer. The impression of symmetry remains, for opening and closing choruses are strongly stressed, even though they are no longer equally balanced columns (at the beginning there is a free chorus tied to the essential idea of the work; a chorale is at the end). In the middle there is a definite break; the core movement, which the Mühlhausen cantatas had, might be thought to be missing if one did not know that the sermon took its place (before the recitative *So stehe denn).* The preacher's role was to shed new light on the theme of death and life taken from nature and symbolized in Christ, interpreting it to include mankind. Following the preacher's exegesis, the musician would join in with his own. Thus, the highest degree of unity was established between the sermon and the music, based on the *de tempore* motif, and the "sermon cantata" came into being. Cantata No. 31 also shows Bach to have been in full control of the new Italian styles. The introductory "sonata" is one of those magnificent concerted settings for large orchestra that he frequently composed later on. The first chorus, which combines this concerted orchestral style with an ingenious choral fugue, is interrupted by a contrasting, highly emotional Adagio. The recitatives display Bach's entire expressive range from simple parlando to dramatic pathos. The arias exploit all possible combinations of voice and different instruments; one aria is combined with a simultaneously performed chorale, the only archaic element in the work. As in many of

Bach's early cantatas, the final chorale is crowned with an orchestral superstructure. It is an early example of the excellent festival cantatas that compare with the architectural embellishments reminiscent of a flourish of trumpets utilized by Balthasar Neumann or Dominikus Zimmermann, who placed late Baroque splendor at the service of the church, thus helping it to achieve once again a grandiose representation of its power.

The Cöthen court, where Bach served from 1717 to 1723, did not require cantatas at its Reformed services. It is uncertain whether the cantata No. 47, *Wer sich selbst erhöhet,* was written in 1720 or whether it was written for Hamburg, as was thought earlier, or whether it is even Bach's. As F. Smend proved in great detail (*Bach in Köthen,* 1950), Bach composed a number of congratulatory cantatas during his Cöthen years for the birthday of Prince Leopold, for the New Year, and perhaps for other occasions as well; with one exception (*Lobet den Herrn, alle seine Heerscharen,* 1718), they follow a practice then common of paying homage to the prince and dispensing with references to the church. In three cases only the texts survive (by Christian Friedrich Hunold); three others (among which are two more by Hunold) were rearranged by Bach in Leipzig as church cantatas (*Durchlauchtster Leopold,* undated, became No. 173, *Erhöhtes Fleisch und Blut,* 1724; *Der Himmel dacht auf Anhalts Ruhm und Glück,* 1719, became No. 66, *Erfreut euch, ihr Herzen,* 1724; *Die Zeit, die Tag und Jahre macht,* 1719, became No. 134, *Ein Herz, das seinen Jesum lebend weiss,* 1724). Moreover, Smend discovered with more or less certainty that several other Leipzig cantatas were parodies whose models (probably belonging to the Cöthen years) have not yet been identified (No. 84, *Erwünschtes Freudenlicht,* 1724; No. 145, *Auf, mein Herz, des Herren Tag,* date uncertain, of which the second chorus, *So du mit deinem Munde bekennest,* stems from Telemann; No. 190, *Singet dem Herrn,* 1724; No. 193, *Ihr Tore zu Zion,* 1726, fragment; No. 32, *Liebster Jesu, mein Verlangen,* 1725; the wedding cantata No. 202, *Weichet nur, betrübte Schatten,* date uncertain). There were probably additional Leipzig parodies of Cöthen works—if not of entire cantatas, at least of a large number of as yet unidentified arias, duos, choruses, etc., especially from the chorale cantatas (for instance, No. 144, *Nimm, was dein ist,* 1724, arias 2 and 5; No. 2, *Ach Gott, vom Himmel sieh darein,* 1724, aria 5; No. 38, *Aus tiefer Not,* aria 3). Much that seems to be parody cannot be authenticated because of the lack of models. In any event, as far as we know today, Bach did not compose vocal church music during his Cöthen years (unless one counts *Lobet den Herrn,* 1718, of which only the Hunold text survives); assuredly, he wrote none to be used in Cöthen. If the Magnificat or the St. John Passion were composed here, they were actually intended for use in Bach's new position as cantor of St. Thomas's; this is also true of the trial cantata No. 22, *Jesus nahm zu sich die Zwölfe,* 1723.

With his call to Leipzing (1723), Bach entered a third period of cantata writing, strenuous and productive. The investigations of G. von Dadelsen and A. Dürr (1958 and 1957, respectively; see Bibliography) on the chronology of the Leipzig vocal works have shown that Philipp Spitta's conclusions, accepted for more than seventy years, were not accurate. We may conclude that the bulk of Bach's Leipzig cantatas belong to the first three, perhaps five, years of his tenure as

"Cantor zu St. Thomae" and "Director Chori Musici Lipsiensis." At the beginning Bach exerted himself to compose complete cycles of cantatas, and in later years he even filled in any gaps that remained. The cycles can be almost completely reconstructed for the first two years, but from the third year on the certainty and completeness of the reconstruction process rapidly diminish. In each case, the cycles begin with the first Sunday after Trinity and end with Pentecost or Trinity Sunday.

Bach's tremendous productivity during his first Leipzig years is shown by the performance schedules prepared by A. Dürr and G. von Dadelsen. In cycle I, 1723–24, Bach actually composed a new cantata for almost every Sunday. Only for church festivals, when he was pressed for time, did he use cantatas of his Weimar period and occasionally (as mentioned above) write parodies based on secular works of his Cöthen period. Cycle II (1724–25) contains almost all of Bach's extant chorale cantatas. Cantata No. 177, *Ich ruf zu dir, Herr Jesu Christ*, 1732, belongs among these; it was composed later to complete the cycle. Here, too, is the series of more than forty so-called late chorale cantatas, wrongly placed by Spitta in the years 1735–44. This cycle was also a gigantic undertaking, even though at Easter, 1725, Bach stopped composing chorale cantatas for unknown reasons. Only for the period between Quasimodogeniti and Trinity, 1725, was there a complete series of new compositions, an especially uniform series because their texts were written by one poet, Mariane von Ziegler, the "learned" Leipzig lady (see F. L. Tagliavini, pp. 104–17), who published some of these texts in 1728 in her collection of poems. They are the cantatas Nos. 42, 85, 103, 108, 87, 128, 183, 74, 68, 175, and 176 (for the first two, the authorship of the texts is not certain; Bach seems to have used her texts again for Nos. 39 and 43, both 1726, if these were indeed her poems; regarding the texts to Nos. 166, 86, 37, and 44, see p. 292).

From cycle III on (1725–26), the extant materials are neither complete nor reliable. No new cantatas can be assigned with certainty to the 1725 Trinity season (with the exception of the Reformation cantata No. 79, *Gott der Herr ist Sonn und Schild*). From the second day of Christmas, 1725, to the third Sunday after Epiphany, 1726, there is once again a small series of significant new works (Nos. 57, 151, 28, 16, 13, 72). In the long series of Sundays from the Purification to the third day of Pentecost, Bach performed cantatas composed by his cousin, Johann Ludwig Bach, manuscripts of which were found in Sebastian's estate. Only for Ascension is there a new composition, No. 43, *Gott fähret auf mit Jauchzen.*

With the beginning of cycle IV, from the first to the twenty-third Sunday after Trinity (1726), there is an almost complete series of newly composed cantatas (Nos. 39, 88, 170, 187, 45, 102, 35, 17, 19, 27, 47, 169, 56, 49, 98, 55, 52). One of these is a chorale cantata, No. 98, *Was Gott tut, das ist wohlgetan* (1st version). Cantatas by Johann Ludwig appear four more times in this Trinity season. Then the source materials for 1726 break off, and for the second half of the cycle only a few cantatas can be dated with any certainty. After this cycle, Bach's cantata composition slackened considerably. During his remaining twenty-three or -four years in Leipzig, he seems to have written church cantatas very rarely; most were parodies and repetitions. Reconstruction of the fourth cycle can be only approximate, and it is utterly impossible for the fifth cycle, which was mentioned in the Obituary prepared by C. Ph. E. Bach and Friedrich Agricola (Mizler's *Musikalische Bibliothek* III, 1754). The existence of the last two cycles has recently been contested (W. H. Scheide against A. Dürr). From 1729 on, Bach's activity as a composer for the church seems to have become secondary to his secular committments (Collegium Musicum with open concerts). Requirements for church services were presumably covered in the main by repetitions and also by the adaptation of older compositions. New compositions were confined to special occasions. The store of compositions Bach produced during his first Leipzig years obviously satisfied him, and in his later years he found it unnecessary to enlarge it substantially or even to expand it systematically.

Among the 1727 cantatas are nine with texts taken from a cantata cycle that Christian Friedrich Henrici (Picander; see F. L. Tagliavini, pp. 77–103) presumably wrote for Bach and then published in 1728 (Nos. 84, 145, 149, 156, 159, 171, 174, 188, and 197a). Cantata No. 197a, in the form of a church cantata, exists only as a fragment; Nos. 149 and 171 are partly parodies, and No. 145 only fills out a work by Telemann to make it a complete cantata. It is noteworthy that Bach composed such a small selection from this particular cycle of a close collaborator. Henrici wrote many secular cantata librettos for Bach. He probably parodied many secular cantata texts for him, turning them into sacred texts. He put together the whole Christmas Oratorio libretto, the major part again consisting of parodies on secular models, and he may have provided the Easter Oratorio with its sacred text. Finally, he compiled, partly with parodies, the librettos of the St. Mark and St. Matthew Passions as well as the funeral music for Prince Leopold. The nine excerpts from Henrici's cycle mentioned above are all that exist of it, and it is unlikely that major portions of Bach's complete works have been lost. The few cantatas produced after 1727, according to present-day knowledge, consist of a small group of solo cantatas, which are among the best known today. There are also four major chorale cantatas: from 1731 (according to Dürr's convincing evidence), No. 140, *Wachet auf, ruft uns die Stimme;* from 1732 (autograph date), the cantata written to complete the second cycle, No. 177, *Ich ruf zu dir, Herr Jesu Christ;* from 1734 (autograph date), No. 97, *In allen meinen Taten;* and from 1735 (also an autograph date), No. 14, *Wär Gott nicht mit uns diese Zeit,* which may be the last original cantata of Bach that survives. Later works include single compositions for special occasions—changes of city council, funerals, weddings, and so on—and adaptations of earlier works or parodies, such as No. 30, *Freue dich, erlöste Schar* (1738–39) parodied after No. 30a, *Angenehmes Wiederau,* or No. 34, *O ewiges Feuer,* parodied after No. 34a, which has the same text beginning and may date from 1742. A few works can be dated with less certainty but probably belong to the early 1730s: No. 100, *Was Gott tut, das ist wohlgetan* (3rd version), and No. 112, *Der Herr ist mein getreuer Hirt,* among others. Compared to Bach's production of cantatas in Weimar or in his first Leipzig years, this is a very modest output.

It is striking that Bach was so little inclined toward a systematic approach in the composition of his cantatas. There was no pattern of development or use of certain types one by one throughout his career (as was characteristic of Telemann's cantatas), nor did he compose complete cycles to the texts of a single poet (about types and use patterns cf. F. L. Tagliavini, *Studi sui testi,* 1956, and K. Gudewill, *Über Formen und Texte* in the Blume *Festschrift,* 1963, p. 162 ff.). There were tendencies in these two directions, but Bach rarely followed the same pattern for very long. Thus, among his earliest Weimar cantatas, there sometimes appears a formal scheme that Bach found in the texts of Salomo Franck (in conjunction with Erdmann Neumeister): an opening chorus in freely rhymed poetry followed by a biblical text set as a recitative, then several arias in a row without connecting recitatives, and finally a chorale stanza. The first three Weimar cantatas of 1714 (Nos. 182, 12, and 172) are constructed in this manner, their texts presumably originating with Franck.

The first Leipzig cycle initiated a turn toward the special type previously referred to as "contemplative pericope cantata." Simultaneously, Bach turned toward a completely modern, highly emotional style often operatic in character, devoid of any archaic traits, and even anticipating a kind of pre-Romantic sensitivity and expressiveness. Many of his most important vocal creations in Leipzig can be characterized as "Romanticism in Baroque dress." This style became one of the cornerstones of the Bach renaissance in the 19th century, especially for the outburst of Bach enthusiasm on the part of the Mendelssohn generation; it permitted Bach to be classified as a "Romantic artist." Cantata No. 104, *Du Hirte Israel* (Misericordias, 1724), is a good example. The quotation from Psalm 80, which opens the cantata, brings to mind both pericopes for this Sunday: the Epistle, I Peter 2:21–25, with Christ portrayed as a shepherd of the lost sheep; and the Gospel, St. John 10:12–16, describing the Good Shepherd who gives his life for his sheep. Neither the idea of stresses simultaneously developed nor the idea of forms built around a central core (as pursued in the earlier cantatas) is present here. Instead, the thought of the libretto—Christ, the Shepherd, leading his sheep after a life of anguish through easy death to heavenly salvation—is expressed in a sequence of images. The unity of the work derives from the overall pastoral, idyllic, romantic atmosphere rather than from the earlier concept of building outward from a central core and suffusing all movements with the same central thought. The opening chorus with its forceful entreaties interrupted by fugatos is both graphic and sonorous, and it establishes the main idea of the work. The contemplative solo sections, which elaborate on the thoughts of the pericopes, are loosely joined to it. In part the music refers to it directly, as in the profound and deeply moving bass aria; in part it contrasts, as in the tenor aria. At the end, the simple chorale stanza once again reflects the basic thought.

This type of treatment extended all through the first cycle and even beyond it. Among the cantatas of 1724 it is evident in No. 65, *Sie werden aus Saba alle kommen,* based on the text of the Epistle for Epiphany, Isaiah 60: 1–6. No. 104, *Du Hirte Israel,* contains a similarly image-evoking chorus and has a similarly romantic atmosphere. Here, too, the contemplative sections are loosely joined recitatives and arias, in part musically connected to the opening movement, in part contrasting with it. Here, too, the "form" consists of a freely constructed sequence of images neither concentrated on a single image nor part of a philosophical antithesis. *Sie werden aus Saba* contains as a special feature a short chorale movement which is not part of the closing chorale, and is therefore more closely connected with two cantatas Bach composed for the second and third days of Christmas, 1723: No. 40, *Dazu ist erschienen,* and No. 64, *Sehet, welch eine Liebe.* Both are similar to the Epiphany cantata, lofty, sweeping, vivid, even dramatic in their imagery. The only difference is that each of them contains two stanzas from two different hymns, to which a third hymn is added as a closing chorale. Thus, in the first cycle a kind of sequence is evident; a certain type is used, or varied, in a number of compositions. Were the librettos of these cantatas not so mediocre, one might assume that Bach had commissioned one (unknown) poet to write the texts following a single pattern.

A few cantatas that preceded this series are closely related, having been written for the ninth, tenth, and fourteenth Sundays after Trinity, 1723: No. 105, *Herr, gehe nicht ins Gericht;* No. 46, *Schauet doch und sehet;* and No. 25, *Es ist nichts Gesundes an meinem Leibe.* They follow the pattern of the "contemplative pericope cantata" mentioned above, drawing on a biblical verse taken from the pericopes, or closely related to them, and developing it into a broad and evocative chorus, a series of contemplative recitatives and arias, often again of similar bearing and often quite dramatic (cf. the examples above), and a chorale having the general character of the opening movement. (In Nos. 46 and 105 the chorale is reinforced with obbligato instruments.) These three cantatas also form a closely knit group because of their multisectional and artistic chorale settings; in the case of No. 25 there is even a double fugue with intricate chorale quotations.

At the beginning of this cycle are two kindred works, No. 75, *Die Elenden sollen essen,* and No. 76, *Die Himmel erzählen die Ehre Gottes,* composed for the first and second Sundays after Trinity, 1723. These deviate completely from the type described above. They are in two parts, are very long, and are obviously planned to accommodate the custom of inserting the sermon in the middle with its change of subject. In the second half of the cycle, there is another group of cantatas similar to each other and different from the type described above. They were written for Cantate, Rogate, Ascension, and Exaudi, 1724: No. 166, *Wo gehest du hin;* No. 86, *Wahrlich, ich sage euch;* No. 37, *Wer da glaubet;* and No. 44, *Sie werden euch in den Bann tun.* The similarity of their verbal style indicates that they are probably by the same librettist (F.L. Tagliavini, following P. Brausch, ascribes them to Mariane von Ziegler). The brief introductory verse in each is treated as an aria, an arioso, a chorus, or a duet with chorus. In each case an aria follows and then a stanza from a chorale that is different from the closing chorale (in this there is a resemblance with the group Nos. 40, 64, and 65). The interior chorale is treated as an aria (either solo or duet) with obbligato instruments. A recitative, another aria, and a closing chorale follow. The organization is slack, without the precision found in the cantatas mentioned earlier, and the musical imagery is less striking. These works, with two exceptions, dispensed with a choir, even though the texts could easily have permitted choral settings in the first movements or in the chorale interludes. Since the solo voices could perform the four-part closing chorale, a sort of "fortuitous" solo cantata resulted. Two genuine solo cantatas directly preceded this group, and their texts were intended from the outset to be set for solo voices: No. 81, *Jesus schläft,* and No. 83, *Erfreute Zeit.* They were both written in 1724 for the fourth Sunday after Epiphany or for the feast of the Purification of the Virgin Mary and are interchangeable liturgically. In the first one, the voice of Christ is heard in an arioso and in an aria for bass, both highly dramatic and almost operatic; the latter contains the Nunc Dimittis of Simeon, chanted by the bass on a *choralton,* accompanied by instruments and intermittently interrupted by a recitative. It is a strange and singular composition.

There is no explanation for the rapid change of types in this first cycle. If Bach had not come to Leipzig as an experienced composer of cantatas, we might assume that he was experimenting in order to find a style of his own. But his already perfect mastery in both the use of forms and the handling of texts excludes any such thought. Instead, one can assume that the librettists he needed for such rapid production were not always on hand. Who they were during his early years in Leipzig is a much debated question, and only in isolated cases can they be identified. His collaboration with Henrici (Picander) probably did not begin until early in 1725—with a secular piece, the pastoral cantata *Entfliehet, verschwindet,* which became the parody model for the Easter Oratorio. It is not certain whether there were prior contacts. It is possible that one librettist wrote all the texts of the many chorale cantatas Bach composed from the first Sunday after Trinity, 1724, to Palm Sunday, 1725 (the so-called second cycle). If so, the versatility of this author's diction, the facility of his versification, and his vivid use of metaphors would all point to Henrici.

It is not known who wrote the texts of these "lyrical chorale cantatas." Most of them are typical examples of their genre, and following their outlines during his second year of composing cantatas in Leipzig, Bach created a model to which he still had recourse from time to time in later years. His use of this type unexpectedly ended with Easter, 1725. It was followed by a series of ten cantatas with texts (presumably all of them) by Mariane von Ziegler.

The structure of this type of chorale cantata, which Bach often used and modified, is simple. The original first and last stanzas of a hymn were used for the beginning and closing movements. The first was usually set as an extensive chorale fantasy, the latter as a simple four-part hymn accompanied by instruments *colle parti.* The stanzas in between were cast as recitatives and arias (duets, trios) depending on the length of the hymn. If it was very long, several stanzas were drawn together into a recitative or an aria (as in No. 78); if short, independently written recitatives and arias were inserted as connecting links (as in No. 140) to increase the work to the normal length of a church cantata. There were usually six or seven movements. The paraphrases gave the librettist considerable opportunity to prove his skill. The inner continuity of the hymn had to be maintained, and the individual thoughts interpreted, embellished, and elucidated. Here the author could show his erudition by frequently intermingling quotations from widely scattered Bible passages, allusions to well-known Gospel stories, and so on. He could also take single lines from the underlying hymn and work them into the arias and recitatives, subdivide a stanza into its component parts, use verses or groups of verses literally or interweave them with recitatives. Recitatives with quotations from chorales or chorale settings with inserted recitatives were not uncommon ("Recitativo e Corale"; for example, Nos. 91, 101, 115, etc.). He could also leave a central stanza unchanged, which the composer could then treat as a solo piece with thoroughbass or obbligato instruments (for example, Nos. 114, 140). Such a richness of alternatives permitted the hymn to be forcefully interpreted for the congregation; at the same time the musician had the means to depict images and emotions, to unfold contrasts and dramatic pathos, and to engage in thunderous rhetoric and the most delicate, lyrical spirituality.

The examples are numerous. Almost each cantata from the second half of the year 1724 (that is, from the beginning of the second cycle) embodies this type (Nos. 20, 7, 10, 107, 178, 101, 78, 8, 114, 116, 91, 125, 1, etc.). Two musical features are noteworthy: the introductory movements take the form of extended chorale fantasies for choir and orchestra, and there are equally extended arias, duos, and vocal trios. The recitatives occurring in these chorale cantatas (*secchi* recitatives that convey many contrasting tensions, and accompanied recitatives whose mystical fervor stirs the emotions) are not distinguishing features, for they can be found throughout Bach's cantatas, from the earliest ones to the latest. Likewise, a simple four-part chorale at the end, without orchestral support, is something that Bach used in every period of his career. The extended chorale fantasy, however, is a distinctive mark of the present period (one that was repeated in some of the later chorale cantatas). The orchestra produces masses of sound in these settings; it acts as an independent body weaving a concerted, symphonic fabric that is usually unrelated, melodically, to the chorale tune. The orchestral accompaniment depicts the underlying images and ideas of the chorale and produces a self-contained movement that in some instances could function as an instrumental composition without chorus. Cantatas such as Nos. 116, 140, 1, 8, and 10 contain typical examples of the chorale fantasy. The choir performs the tune line by line, usually with the cantus firmus in the soprano and with a loosely woven polyphony in the lower voices; the lines are separated by longer or shorter interludes in the orchestra. Thus, the chorale itself sounds like a later insertion. This impression is reinforced if the orchestra (as it usually does) closes the movement with a repetition of the opening ritornello. The derivation from the 17th-century chorale concerto is as unmistakable as is the pull toward the 18th-century instrumental concerto.

Only rarely does Bach's handling of opening movements deviate from this pattern. In No. 2, *Ach Gott vom Himmel, sieh darein,* he wrote a motet-like movement with the chorale cantus firmus in the alto and no obbligato orchestra. In No. 14, *Wär Gott nicht mit uns diese Zeit* (autograph manuscript dated 1735), the cantus firmus is performed with intermittent pauses by a group of instruments while the four chorus parts weave an unbroken, closely knit, fugue-like fabric made up of motifs of the chorale tune—a most singular case. Closely related to this is the opening movement of the psalm cantata No. 25, *Es ist nichts Gesundes an meinem Leibe* (cycle I), with quotations from the chorale in the strings and a complete presentation of it, interrupted only occasionally, by a five-part brass ensemble—all set against a double fugue in the chorus. A unique conception is the canon-like opening movement of No. 80, the chorale cantata *Ein Feste Burg* (which is partly a parody on a Weimar cantata; it cannot be dated with certainty). This movement is, however, related to the highly artistic chorale canons in No. 77, the Gospel cantata *Du sollst Gott, deinen Herrn, lieben,* from the first cycle, 1723. The last examples illustrate 1) how the introductory chorale-fantasy type could be modified or replaced by other types; 2) how these types could appear in other categories, and thereby create connections between the various cantata types; and 3) how these variations could become reconcilable, harmonious interpretations. In the settings mentioned, there are many conceptual links of a symbolic nature in addition to the presence of emotion and imagery; this is perhaps the highest degree of exegetic interpretation ever achieved in choral compositions.

The large and expressive arias, duets, and vocal trios that follow these opening movements in the chorale cantata also distinguish the type; they make great technical demands on both voices and concertizing instruments, which are often given unbroken, independent, and virtuoso parts. Some of the most typical arias are: *Herr, der du stark und mächtig bist,* from No. 10, for soprano, two oboes, and strings; *Gleich wie die wilden Meereswellen,* from No. 178, for bass and strings; *Doch weichet, ihr tollen, vergeblichen Sorgen,* from No. 8, for bass, solo flute, and strings; *Bete aber auch dabei,* from No. 115, for soprano, flute, and violoncello piccolo; *Gott ist mein Freund,* from No. 139, for tenor and violino concertante; *So schnell ein rauschend Wasser schiesst,* from No. 26, for tenor, solo flute, and solo violin; *Ach, unaussprechlich ist die Not,* from No. 116, for alto and oboe d'amore solo; and *Erfüllet, ihr himmlischen, göttlichen Flammen,* from No. 1, for soprano and oboe da caccia. The list could be extended still further. Some noteworthy duets are: *Er denket der Barmherzigkeit,* from No. 10, for alto, tenor, trumpet, and two oboes; *Wir eilen mit schwachen, doch emsigen Schritten,* from No. 78, for soprano, alto, obbligato organ and violoncello accompaniment, and pizzicato contrabass; *Ein unbegreiflich Licht,* from No. 125, for tenor, bass, and strings; and the two soprano-bass duets in No. 140, *Wann kommst du, mein Heil?* and *Mein Freund ist mein* (the one with violino piccolo, the other with oboe solo). Among the most magnificent of Bach's vocal settings are the vocal trios in the chorale cantatas: *Wenn meine Trübsal als mit Ketten,* from No. 38, for soprano, alto, and bass, and *Ach, wir bekennen unsre Schuld,* from No. 116, for soprano, tenor, and bass. Comparison of solo sections in the Weimar cantatas with those in the first Leipzig cycle shows that in Leipzig, Bach reached the pinnacle of formal ingenuity and expressiveness, not only in the choruses of the chorale fantasies but in the solos as well. It is understandable that the musical maturity of these works should have led earlier Bach scholars to place them at the end of his career.

Next to the long line of chorale cantatas that are based on paraphrased texts, are musically homogeneous, and comprise, chronologically, the first half of cycle II (along with a few later examples), there is a small group of nine chorale cantatas using pure chorale texts. With the one exception, No. 4, *Christ lag in Todesbanden* (probably 1707–08), these belong musically with the chorale cantatas of cycle II. For the most part they were produced comparatively late. Without having them rephrased by a librettist and without regard to the original texts, Bach set the "interlude" stanzas of these hymns as recitatives and arias, with the first stanza a chorale fantasy and the last a cantional setting as usual. According to A. Dürr, one of these cantatas on an unaltered chorale text can be attributed to cycle II: No. 107, *Was willst du dich betrüben;* others may belong to the late 1720s and early '30s: No. 137, *Lobet den Herren, den mächtigen,* perhaps 1725; No. 129, *Gelobet sei der Herr, mein Gott,* 1726 or 1727; No. 112, *Der Herr ist mein getreuer Hirt,* 1731; No. 117, *Sei Lob und Ehr dem höchsten Gut,* date uncertain, probably about 1731; No. 177, *Ich ruf zu dir, Herr Jesu Christ,* autograph dated 1732; No. 97, *In allen meinen Taten,* autograph dated 1734; No. 100, *Was Gott tut, das ist wohlgetan,* between 1732 and 1735? (Dürr). Also, the fragmentary cantata No. 192, *Nun danket alle Gott* (1732), must be considered; it is one of the cantatas composed on a pure chorale text. If, as with No. 177 (see p. 289), Bach composed these cantatas as a supplement to cycle II, the assumption could follow that the librettist who wrote all the paraphrased texts was no longer available. This may have been the case as early as Easter, 1725, and was perhaps the reason that Bach discontinued the second cycle and turned to the poetry of Mariane von Ziegler. The only chorale cantatas that Bach wrote after 1726–27 were the six composed on an unaltered chorale text (Nos. 97, 100, 112, 117 [?], and 177) and the three others (No. 14, *Wär Gott nicht mit uns diese Zeit,* 1735; No. 9, *Es ist das Heil uns Kommen her,* 1732–35; and No. 140, *Wachet auf, ruft uns die Stimme*) he wrote on chorale paraphrases.

The group of cantatas based on texts by Mariane von Ziegler (eleven, if Nos. 42 and 85 are ascribed to her) was begun after Bach stopped writing chorale cantatas and extended without interruption from Quasimodogeniti until Trinity, 1725. In textual layout, this group is not uniform, and Bach's various ways of handling the text show that he himself was not interested in developing a uniform type. The picture becomes even less clear if one assumes that the texts for Ascension and the first Sunday after Trinity in 1726, Nos. 43, *Gott fähret auf,* and 39, *Brich dem Hungrigen dein Brot,* were von Ziegler's. Each of the first two texts of the 1725 series, Nos. 42 and 85, contains an inserted chorale stanza, which causes them to resemble Nos. 40, 64, and 65 from cycle I. This further obscures the intended plan, which included: No. 42, *Am Abend aber desselbigen Sabbaths;* No. 85, *Ich bin ein guter Hirt;* No. 103, *Ihr werdet weinen und heulen;* No. 108, *Es est euch gut, dass ich hingehe;* No. 87, *Bisher habt ihr nichts gebeten;* No. 128, *Auf Christi Himmelfahrt allein;* No. 183, *Sie werden euch in den Bann tun;* No. 74, *Wer mich liebet, der wird mein Wort halten;* No. 68, *Also hat Gott die Welt geliebt;* No. 175, *Er rufet seinen Schafen;* and No. 176, *Es ist ein trotzig und verzagt Ding.* Eight of the eleven texts begin with *de tempore* quotations from the Gospel according to St. John, two begin with chorale stanzas, and one begins with a quotation from Jeremiah. Bach set three of the opening passages as recitatives (one of which is accompanied by wind instruments), two as ariosos or arias, and six as choruses (among which is one adapted from the Weimar cantata No. 59, 1716). After the opening chorus the poet provided, somewhat irregularly, a recitative, aria, recitative, aria, and closing chorale; however, in the first two texts an aria appears first, then an inserted chorale, and then a recitative, aria, and closing chorale. In one example (No. 74), there are eight sections, the fourth an arioso on a verse from St. John and the sixth a recitative on a verse from St. Paul's letter to the Romans. In another example (No. 87) the fourth section is a recitative linked to an arioso on a verse from the book of John. An understanding of these more or less arbitrary arrangements is further complicated by the circumstances that Bach did not always use the same version of the text published by Mariane von Ziegler in 1728 and that a number of texts were parodies or adaptations of other Bach works. The opening chorus of No. 74 is an adaptation of the opening movement of Weimar cantata No. 59; the first aria contains a new text but the same music as the corresponding aria in the Weimar source. In No. 68 two arias (one of which is the famous *Mein gläubiges Herze*) are parodies on secular models; the closing chorus, which does the unusual in quoting a verse from John, gives the impression of being a parody (the poet's closing hymn was dropped). No. 175 contains a parody aria; the introductory *recitativo accompagnato* may be a parody, and the closing chorale was borrowed from Weimar cantata No. 59 and also used for No. 74. The series of Ziegler cantatas cannot be called homogeneous; on the contrary, it reflects the dissolution of prevailing types, and those cantatas from the second half of the series that are definitely parodies suggest that some paraphrases of Bach's older compositions exist in the first half as well. This group still contains many puzzles to intrigue the scholar.

If the texts of Mariane von Ziegler share a common element, it is the tone of tender sincerity, often of heartfelt emotion, that infuses many of them and that distinguishes them from the sturdy, dramatic texts of the chorale cantatas. Bach could not remain unaffected. *Am Abend aber,* No. 42, is one of his most profound cantatas; especially noteworthy are the opening recitative and the subsequent aria for alto, *Wo zwei und drei versammelt sind.* In the following cantatas, arias such as *Seht, was die Liebe tut* (from No. 85), *Ich will leiden* (No. 87), and *Komm, leite mich* (No. 175; possibly a parody), or the orchestral recitative *Ich bin bereit* (No. 183) express a gentle fervor not often found in Bach. On the other hand, a chorus such as *Ihr werdet weinen und heulen* (No. 103) is one of Bach's most stirring works. The beauty and individuality in these cantatas cannot be systematized, for there is even less of a pattern here than in the early Leipzig cantatas; indeed, the former "contemplative pericope cantata" almost dissolves in romantic lyricism.

In line with this trend, Bach dispensed with the choir for six of the eleven Ziegler texts and composed them as solo cantatas (the texts themselves do not demand this treatment). The verses from the Gospel according to St. John, with which Nos. 42, 85, 87, 108, 183, and 175 begin, could have been composed for chorus. They are no different from the Jeremiah verse with which No. 176 begins, or the verses from St. John at the opening of Nos. 103 and 74 (the latter was a duet in the Weimar version), all of which were set for chorus. Instead of this, Bach arranged them as recitatives, ariosos, or arias. Of the two cantatas that begin with choral arrangements of a hymn, only No. 128 is based on a real congregational hymn (which may be why the setting is choral), while No. 68 begins with a lied that could equally well have been set for a soloist. Bach's predilection for individual, atypical treatment and even his antipathy for developing a new cantata type are apparent in this group.

Because of the greater uncertainty in both chronology and sources (see p. 288

f.), Bach's later cantata production, beginning with the second half of the 1726 cycle, is less clear. Certain later chorale cantatas, as mentioned above, hark back to older types or modifications of them. Some compositions, principally those with opening verses from the Prophets or the Psalms (from the first Sunday after Trinity to the fourteenth) again use the old Weimar bipartite scheme with the sermon in the middle (No. 39, *Brich dem Hungrigen;* No. 187, *Es wartet alles auf dich;* No. 45, *Es ist dir gesagt, Mensch, was gut ist;* No. 102, *Herr, deine, Augen sehen nach dem Glauben;* No. 35, *Geist und Seele wird verwirret;* No. 17, *Wer Dank opfert*). However, this scheme was not maintained throughout the cycle. Some cantatas take over movements from instrumental concertos for their introductions or use them as models for vocal parodies (No. 35, *Geist und Seele wird verwirret;* No. 169, *Gott soll allein mein Herze haben;* No. 49, *Ich geh und suche mit Verlangen;* No. 52, *Falsche Welt, dir trau ich nicht;* twelfth to twenty-third Sunday after Trinity; later isolated examples are No. 174, *Ich liebe den Höchsten,* and No. 51, *Jauchzet Gott in allen Landen,* both 1729). Finally, beginning in 1726, Bach wrote a series of solo cantatas that became his most famous in the medium (No. 56, *Ich will den Kreuzstab gerne tragen;* No. 49, *Ich geh und suche mit Verlangen;* No. 52, *Falsche Welt, dir trau ich nicht;* No. 55, *Ich armer Mensch, ich Sündenknecht;* nineteenth to twenty-third Sunday after Trinity, 1726). In later years Bach continued to write solo cantatas, producing his most mature works: No. 82, *Ich habe genug;* No. 84, *Ich bin vergnügt;* No. 157, *Ich lasse dich nicht;* the concerto in dialogue, No. 58, *Ach Gott, wie manches Herzeleid,* which is not a chorale cantata either in terms of its text or its music (all four 1727); No. 51, *Jauchzet Gott in allen Landen;* No. 156, *Ich steh mit einem Fuss im Grabe;* No. 159, *Sehet, wir gehn hinauf gen Jerusalem;* No. 174, *Ich liebe den Höchsten* (these four 1729); No. 188, *Ich habe meine Zuversicht;* and No. 197a, *Ehre sei Gott in der Höhe,* only a fragment of which survives (both probably 1728–29). The series of solo cantatas is in part identical with the nine cantatas Bach composed to texts from Henrici's cycle of 1728–29 (see p. 290).

Bach selected texts for his later cantatas, which were composed more and more sporadically, in an arbitrary and seemingly haphazard manner. He seems to have made no effort to establish a definitive form. Comparison with the systematic arrangement that prevails, for example, in Telemann's cantata cycles for 1715–16 to about 1750 (only after that, according to Menke, did Telemann adopt less rigid formal schemes) leads to the conclusion that Bach apparently dispensed with any set plan. Bach's recourse to movements from instrumental concertos can only be regarded as a kind of emergency measure. The few chorale cantatas of his late years maintained all the essentials of his former style. With regard to text, the Henrici cantatas make no attempt at uniformity, and are, moreover, in part parodies. A late predilection of Bach seems to be revealed in the long series of solo cantatas, the texts of which (partly by Henrici, partly by unknown persons) were obviously intended for solo settings. They speak in the first person, express a childlike acquiescence, a pious devotion, a modesty, a blessed hopefulness *(Ich will den Kreuzstab gerne tragen, Ich geh und suche mit Verlangen, Ich armer Mensch, ich Sündenknecht, Falsche Welt, dir trau ich nicht, Ich habe genug, Ich bin vergnügt, Ich liebe den Höchsten, Ich habe meine Zuversicht).* Rarely do they reach the grand pathos of many of Bach's earlier texts. The prevailing tone of festive jubilation in No. 51, *Jauchzet Gott,* is an exception. Liturgical connections in the texts are scanty; most of them could be used for almost any occasion. Some of them are like prayers. Their structure is simple, being determined by the requirements of a setting for one or more soloists. As a rule they follow the pattern of aria, recitative, aria, chorale—or something similar. Two (Nos. 49 and 58) close with a chorale duet, one (No. 51) with a chorale worked into a borrowed concerto setting. An introductory sinfonia appears in four (Nos. 49, 52, 156, and 174). Special forms, such as arias with a chorale (Nos. 156 and 159), are rare. Everything follows a simple construction and a simple form. By contrast, the emotional content is overwhelming, and some of Bach's most stirring and most frequently performed arias are found in his later solo cantatas: *Ich will den Kreuzstab* (No. 56) for bass and strings; *Erbarme dich* (No. 55) for alto with flute solo; *Schlummert ein, ihr matten Augen* (No. 82) for bass and strings; *Ich esse mit Freuden* (No. 84) for soprano with oboe and solo violin; *Jauchzet Gott* and *Sei Lob und Preis* with *Hallelujah* (No. 51) for soprano with trumpet solo and strings; *Es ist vollbracht* (No. 159) for bass, oboe, and strings; *Greifet zu* (No. 174) for bass and strings; and many more. A new aspect of Bach's pre-Romanticism appears in these cantatas: the stress on emotional intensity and the not infrequent simplicity of diction. They make great demands on the singer, less in terms of glamour and virtuosity than in expressiveness and sensitivity.

Bach's cantata output took a last major turn (if it may be considered a general development) in the six dramatic Gospel cantatas for the three days of Christmas, for New Year, and the two following Sundays in 1733–34. Together they form the Christmas Oratorio (with texts almost certainly by Henrici-Picander). The drama is provided here by the Evangelist, who presents the Christmas story in recitative and often in dialogues with somewhat misty allegorical figures (such as the daughter of Zion, representative of the Christian congregation) or with the dramatis personae of the story (Shepherd, Herod). Subsidiary persons like the wandering shepherds and the Magi are introduced as choral groups *(turbae).* Contemplative elements are related in various ways to other parts of the text (chorale interwoven with recitatives; dramatic chorus of the Magi with recitative-like answers by an allegoric figure; the Herod scene; dramatic shepherds' chorus followed by a chorale; the use of transitions between narrative or contemplative recitative and an emotional aria to develop a kind of scenic imagery). Finally, the contemplative sections are made dramatic by the involvement of the allegorical figures with each other; the believing soul is answered with an aria by the Echo, representing the Heavenly Voice, while other arias closely approach the outlines of certain *opera seria* arias. Two lamenting voices are joined in a trio by the voice of Promise, creating the effect of a stage ensemble. Thus, the pericope cantata reached a stage on the way toward dramatic realism that was close to the boundaries of sacred music and that was to lead to the nonliturgical oratorio. All of the Evangelist's recitatives are unaccompanied, the contemplative recitatives (with one exception) accompanied. Thus, the handling of recitatives here approaches that of the St. Matthew Passion, where a third manner of treatment (with strings) is added for the voice of Jesus. Of the six large opening choruses of the six sections, five are parodies on secular models (the origin of the opening chorus of part V is not yet clarified), and almost all arias, along with the duet and the vocal trio, are also parodies. The sixth section, including even the recitatives and the closing chorale, is a parody on a church cantata that has been lost (Blankenburg and Dürr, *Kritischer Bericht* to *Neue Bach Ausgabe* II, 1). Moreover, the models of these parodies were for the most part parodies from still older models. The historical importance and the artistic merit of Bach's Christmas Oratorio are in no way lessened by this fact. Knowledge of historical origins is important, however, because it reveals so clearly Bach's attitude toward the composition of cantatas in this comparatively late period. In the main, only the recitatives of the Evangelist, the contemplative recitatives, the chorale settings, and the pastoral sinfonia at the beginning of part III, possibly also the opening chorus of part V, were composed specifically for this work.

Taken in its entirely, the Christmas Oratorio is the climax of the 18th-century Protestant oratorio. It stands on the border between *historia,* oratorio, and cantata, and contains textual elements of all three categories. Its formal pattern is that of a cantata complex, with the performance distributed over six days (thus reminiscent of Buxtehude's Vesper concerts in oratorio style). In compositional style, it stands between the church cantata and the sacred drama. If J. F. Reichardt was correct in calling C. Ph. E. Bach's *Israeliten in der Wüste* (1775) "church music," even though it contains no oratorio-like contemplative elements and is rather more like a sacred drama in the style of Handel, we may consider Bach's Christmas Oratorio as church music. The individual cantatas are models of the type of "dramatic Gospel cantata."

Bach's Easter Oratorio is, as shown by F. Smend in 1942, a parody on a secular birthday cantata of the year 1725. The biblical account was freely set in verse, and the text, whose author is unknown, is not fully convincing. The Ascension Oratorio (Bach explicitly called it *Oratorium Festo Ascensionis Christi*) is only a somewhat enlarged cantata (No. 11, *Lobet Gott in seinen Reichen,* eleven movements). The librettist is unknown; the work could hardly have originated before the 1730s. As a "dramatic Gospel cantata," the work is closely related to individual cantatas in the Christmas Oratorio. The story is presented by an Evangelist using the biblical text (according to the books of Luke, Mark, and Acts); two contemplative recitatives, two arias, and a chorale are inserted. The introduction is a magnificent chorale setting with a large orchestra, while the ending is a chorale fantasy in the style of the chorale cantatas of 1724–25. It has been partly ascertained that parody was used here, and once again the recitatives of the Evangelist, the contemplative recitatives, and the opening choral movement may have been composed specifically for the oratorio. The closing chorale fantasy may have had a somewhat earlier origin.

Bach's cantata composition in Leipzig extended mainly from 1723 to 1726–27, slowed down for a while, then, except for a few latecomers in the 1730s, ceased altogether. The oratorios of the 1730s, so closely associated with the cantata genre, were mostly parodies, i.e., works put together for church use by reusing older material of a different origin. If one includes the wedding and funeral music, as well as the cantatas for council elections and other occasions, Bach's extant cantatas number almost two hundred. The question whether this output reveals a historical development in the relationship between the musician and liturgical obligations must be approached with more caution than ever because of the new chronological evidence. Such subdivisions as "edification cantata," "sermon cantata," "contemplative pericope cantata," "lyrical chorale cantata," and "dramatic biblical proverb cantata" can certainly be retained; these distinctions, derived from the cantata text and from the circumstances of composition, are still valid for Bach as well as for his immediate forerunners (less so for his contemporaries). It is still an open question, however, if (or to what extent) they may have followed in a chronological order or reflected Bach's inner development. Certainly the "dramatic biblical proverb cantata" appeared only in the later period, and there essentially only as a parody; certainly the "edification cantata" marks an earlier period dating back to Bach's youth. Yet the "sermon cantata" is not restricted to his early period; the "lyrical chorale cantata" is no late product, but appears at the height of Bach's cantata production; and the "contemplative pericope cantata" spans most of the years he wrote cantatas. The basic outlines were established when he began, and their further development, as shown by the more recent chronology, was not a matter of a lifetime but was accomplished in two well-defined periods of three and five years respectively (not counting the early period in Mühlhausen and the later works after 1727–28). In view of these conditions, a fundamental development in the relationship of the music to church needs can hardly be expected. As in other areas, Bach took up previously established media and potentialities, styles and settings, musical and textual categories, and fused them with late Venetian opera forms and modes of expression (often closely connected with A. Scarlatti). The result was that Bach brought all elements into line with the stylistic needs of his own era. At the same time he brought the church cantata back in line with the established use of pericopes and *de tempore* chorales in the service. In all of this he fulfilled each assignment exhaustively, thinking of every aspect. To summarize, he combined the tendencies of Lutheran orthodoxy and mysticism, of Pietism and rationalism, and gave them a musical form, thus once more realizing the Lutheran objective of a congregational, *de tempore* service.

Furthermore, there is no lack in Bach's cantatas of traits pointing to the future. Among them is a pronounced realism (especially in his early works) that sometimes becomes an almost bizarre, naturalistic portrayal. Like the single affect dominating a movement, this feature is a manifestation of the aesthetic outlook that considered "imitation" and "true emotion" to be the composer's mission. The tendency toward a dramatic allegorical dialogue is closely connected with the illusory painted ceilings of the late Baroque and the personal characterization of the *opera seria*. In Bach's Leipzig cantatas of whatever category, but especially in the late solo cantatas, a simplification of form evolves and gradually takes on a classical appearance. There is an increasing preference for melody and often an almost visionary tone that indicates things to come. The door is opened on a new world. The next generation was to pass through it, as did the children of rationalism, who left the home of church dogma and replaced Protestant thought with a sentimental natural religion based on human emotions. With his intuitive coalescence of past and present, of the archaic and the living, Bach in his cantatas revived one of the original qualities of Lutheran church music. He represented its entire history, and he laid the foundation with this "coincidentia oppositorum" (coincidence of the opposites)[3] for the Bach renaissance of the next century.

J. S. BACH'S PASSIONS

Like the Christmas Oratorio cantatas, Bach's two preserved Passions border on the church Passion History. Out of the "oratorical Passion" of the 1600s, the "Passion oratorio" emerged around the turn of the century. According to the custom of those days, there was no need to adhere to conventional church styles. Reintroducing Bible passages and chorale texts among the freely written "madrigal" texts (as J. Mattheson reported about Hamburg in 1739), it became transformed into a type somewhere between the oratorio-like Passion, the History, and the Passion oratorio—in other words, a type closely akin to the Christmas Oratorio. Practical considerations placed this type of Passion between music for the church service and music for concert performance. For Bach, the narrative of Christ's suffering remained the central feature despite all contemplation, dramatization, allegory, or symbolic congregational participation; thus, his Passions retained some of the characteristics of the History. He was willing to accept elements from opera in his cantatas and cantata-like oratorios, but he always subordinated them to the needs of the whole work. In contrast to the Italian Passion oratorios of the same period (especially since Metastasio's *Passione di Gesù Cristo,* 1730) there is no series of operatic solo songs, but rather a larger, interdependent complex. In most cases they make use of a narrator (the recitative of the Evangelist), biblical characters (sung by soloists or *turba* choirs), allegorical characters, such as the daughters of Zion, Mary, and the believing soul (who take part in solo songs, recitatives, arias, or even contemplative choruses), and the Christian congregation (which participates in the chorale stanzas). Each character has a style of his own and combinations of them produce multifaceted groups, each of which carries some part of the story forward. The large dimensions cause problems in regard to the total work. These are not solved consistently: symmetry of tonality and design may result in a self-contained structure (St. Matthew Passion, part I) or, just as easily, a loose sequence of scenes (St. Matthew Passion, part II).

The textual requirements of Bach's Passions were similar to those of his cantatas. Evolved from the History on the one hand and the responsorial Passion on the other, the oratorical Passion had grown into long, freely written, allegorical dialogues (similar to Buxtehude's music for Vespers). Around 1700 a text reform took place that coincided with the reform in Neumeister's cantatas; it was initiated by Christian Friedrich Hunold (Menantes) of Hamburg. With the exclusion of biblical texts, including Gospel narratives and chorales, the Gospel was completely rewritten in verse form, and allegorical figures were introduced as part of

---

3A philosophical theory, espoused by Nikolaus of Cusa, according to which two things in opposition to one another in the world of experience are one in a reality which transcends that experience.

the lyric elements of meditation. Hunold's *Der blutende und sterbende Jesus,* performed in Hamburg in 1704 in a setting by Reinhard Keiser, is a typical example—grossly sensual, indulging in gruesome as well as in mawkish images and thoughts, and "wavering between crude realism and truly religious symbolism" (Schering). It was a vivid and popular work, dealing with matters of eschatology in a way that was deeply moving to listeners of that time. Closely related were C. H. Postel's aria texts for Handel's St. John Passion (also Hamburg, 1704). The model was quickly imitated: in Hamburg by Ulrich König's *Tränen unter dem Kreuz Christi* (music by Keiser, Hamburg, 1711) and in other works by Keiser; also in Thuringia and in southern Germany (see W. Blankenburg in *MGG* X, 1962, 1928). The second step taken in accordance with the reforms Neumeister instituted in his cantata poetry (beginning with his third cycle, 1708–09) was made by B. H. Brockes of Hamburg in his famous Passion poem *Der für die Sünde der Welt gemarterte und sterbende Jesus* (1712). He reintroduced the Evangelist, having him paraphrase in poetry, rather than merely relate, the biblical narrative; following Hunold's example with no substantial differences, he added allegorical figures. His text met with the greatest approval. As early as 1712 it was used by Keiser, in 1716 by both Telemann and Handel, in 1718 by Mattheson (who performed all four works in Hamburg in 1719), and in 1727 by G. H. Stölzel. About 1750 the text was set to music again by Jakob Schuback, J. Friedrich Fasch, Paul Steiniger, J. B. C. Freislich (Lott), and even by the Swiss-Reform composer J. C. Bachofen (Blankenburg, based on K. Nef). Only one other text later on, C. W. Ramler's *Der Tod Jesu,* was so widely used. Soon it became popular to combine single parts from the texts of Brockes with Gospel texts and chorales. In this way Bach pieced together the text of his St. John Passion, although not without thoroughly revising the original material.

The custom of performing oratorio-like Passion music first came into use in Leipzig in 1721; prior to this (and after) responsorial Passions in the old style, following Johann Walter and Gottfried Vopelius, were used. The *Neukirche* took the first step in 1717; in 1721 and 1722, Johann Kuhnau offered his St. Mark Passion for the Good Friday Vespers service at St. Thomas's; it must have been a very modest piece, and it has disappeared. The Passions usually consisted of two parts, with the sermon between. Bach probably composed four Passions altogether, among which was a work for one choir based on Matthew, probably composed in Weimar. Only the one based on John and the one for double choir based on Matthew have been preserved. The former was performed in 1723 or 1724 in St. Thomas's, and in 1724 or 1725 in St. Nicholas's (performances of oratorical Passions, or Passion oratorios, have alternated since then between these two main churches). The St. Matthew Passion was first performed in 1729 in St. Thomas's, where Bach's St. Mark Passion, with a text by Henrici, was first performed in 1731. Much of it was a parody on the funeral music to a text by Gottsched that Bach had composed in 1727 for the deceased Electoress Christiane Eberhardine; other parts were perhaps parodies of unknown models. One was an aria from cantata No. 54, and one chorus was used in the Christmas Oratorio. It can be assumed that Bach took the arias and contemplative choruses in this work from earlier pieces and composed new music only for the Evangelist's narrative, the *turba* choruses, and the chorales; contemplative recitatives were not called for in the text. The controversial St. Luke Passion, which was included in the old Bach Complete Edition at the instigation of Philipp Spitta, is preserved in Bach's holograph, but is undoubtedly a copy of an unknown work from about 1700. Many such copies exist in Bach's hand, among them a St. Mark Passion by Keiser. According to the Obituary of C. Ph. E. Bach and J. F. Agricola, Bach composed a fifth Passion, but nothing more is known of it. An earlier supposition that it was based on Henrici's *Erbauliche Gedanken* of 1725 cannot be proved and is unlikely. Texts from this libretto were used in the St. Matthew Passion, but it is not known whether they had already been set to music by Bach, although it is conceivable that they were indeed parodies of earlier works.

The history of the St. John Passion is being re-examined (especially by A. Mendel). It seems certain that the work in its present form was not composed uninterruptedly and not according to a plan prepared in advance; rather, in the course of repeated performances it was subjected to numerous transformations of overall structure and revisions of individual parts. As far as we know today (A. Mendel), it seems that the number of movements was the same in the first version as in the last. In an interim stage, the chorale fantasy *O Mensch, bewein dein Sünde gross* was placed at the beginning as a majestic introduction; it was later placed at the end of the first part of the St. Matthew Passion. Similarly, the chorale fantasy *Christe, du Lamm Gottes,* which had earlier been used in an intermediate version of the Leipzig cantata No. 23, *Du wahrer Gott und Davidssohn,* was used in an equivalent stage of the Passion and then discarded in favor of the simple chorale setting, *Ach Herr, lass dein lieb Engelein.* In addition to these settings for chorus, three arias belonged temporarily to the St. John Passion (Schmieder, BWV 245a-c). Whether they originally belonged to the lost "fourth" Passion (Schmieder) cannot be ascertained. Over a period of time Bach made many revisions, such as transpositions, new instrumentations, and so on, in addition to these structural modifications. Since different versions of the Passion probably existed up to the 1740s, the variant versions present a confused picture. Its generally accepted design, according to W. Rust in vol. XII, 1, of the Bach Complete Edition, conforms to the latest surviving sources from which, however, a "final intention" on Bach's part cannot be assumed. Clearly organized within complex tonalities, the work is built from a series of sharply contrasted scenes. It follows the objective, sober account in John, in which the quiet majesty of God's Son confronts the senselessness of a raging mob. A realistic report of the events in the tragedy outweighs the contemplative passages, which are restricted to two ariosos, seven arias, and one aria with choir (among which one arioso and one aria belong to the pieces substituted for earlier arias). The only contemplative choruses are the opening movement and the setting of *Ruht wohl;* other than this, the choir participates only in the *turba* settings, the chorales, and once in an allegorical dialogue, *Eilt, ihr angefochtnen Seelen.* There are no contemplative recitatives. Like their key centers, the contemplative recitatives and the *turbae* clash against each other. In their unsparing realism, reminiscent of medieval German Crucifixion scenes, the choirs of Jews, the high priests, the mercenaries, and so on, dominate the overall conception. The chorales function mostly as connecting and concluding elements in the various scenes. More strongly than its sister work of 1729, the St. John Passion emphasizes its connection with the History and the 17th-century Passion from which it stemmed.

In comparison, the St. Matthew Passion (text by Henrici) is much richer in choral settings. They are either of a lyrical character (*O Schmerz, Ich will bei meinem Jesu wachen, Ach, nun ist mein Jesus hin, Nun ist der Herr zur Ruh gebracht,* etc.) or of a contemplative and sometimes also a descriptive nature *(So ist mein Jesus, Sind Blitze, sind Donner).* There is almost always an element of pious devotion in the foreground. There is a stronger pull toward the oratorio, and the Passion story, following Matthew's account, is quieter and more epic in character. *Turbae* are used less extensively and not in the overly realistic manner found in the St. John Passion. Symbolism outweighs the dramatic elements. The construction of the work reaches beyond a mere sequence of scenes and probably conceals deeper, more meaningful connections. Dramatic elements abound in the narrative recitatives and *turbae* (in fact, the drama of the Christmas Oratorio, which is surprisingly strong in comparison with Bach's cantatas, seems only moderate when compared with the Passions). The contemplative recitatives in the St. Matthew Passion are accompanied, with illustrative and affecting embellishments by wind or stringed instruments; they are among its most expressive sections and were unparalleled in the music of around 1730. They contribute much to the lyrical, descriptive character of the whole work. Pieces such as *Wiewohl mein Herz in Tränen schwimmt* (with two oboes), *Der Heiland fällt vor seinem Vater nieder* (with strings), *Mein Jesus schweigt* (with two oboes and gamba), *Ach Golgatha* (with two oboi da caccia) and the deeply moving arioso *Am Abend, da es kühle war* (with strings) are crowning musical achievements. The accompanied recitatives contrast strongly with the dramatically animated unaccompanied recitatives of the Evangelist and the simple words of Christ, which are supported by strings in a choral style and gradually develop (as in the Words of Institution) into ariosos. Compared with the earlier Passion, the arias are distinguished by their great feeling and imagery; their spaciousness calls to mind corresponding movements in the chorale cantatas. It is not certain to what extent the arias are original settings of the Passion texts or parodies of the funeral music for Prince Leopold of Cöthen (1729; text also by Henrici). Even though it does not seem convincing at first glance, such expressive pieces as *Buss und Reu, Erbarme dich,* and *Aus Liebe will mein Heiland sterben* may have been composed originally to other texts. The fact that aria texts like the last two mentioned, as well as a recitative text like *Erbarm es Gott,* are found in Henrici's *Erbauliche Gedanken* (1725) may imply that the Passion goes back to older works which have been parodied or that it belongs in part to one of Bach's earlier creative periods.

Another distinguishing feature not found in the St. John Passion is the frequent use of the choir—not only for the *turbae* and chorale insertions but also, extensively, for the freely written poetic contemplations. For the most part the *turbae* are sung by two choirs, occasionally by one. The inserted chorale stanzas Bach set in a simple four-voice cantional style, as usual. The contemplative texts gave rise to more varied forms. The combination of recitative plus chorale or aria plus chorale *(O Schmerz* and *Ich will bei meinem Jesu wachen)* each appears once. These forms were common in the chorale cantata series of 1724–25; it is perhaps significant that the text of the recitative comes from Henrici, 1725, and that the aria was taken over from the funeral music for Prince Leopold. Bach used only one choir in these settings and in the chorale fantasy *(O Mensch, bewein dein Sünde gross)* that was temporarily used in the St. John Passion and now closes part I of the St. Matthew Passion. The "Aria a doi Cori" *So ist mein Jesus nun gefangen* is set for two choirs and has a distinctly contemplative chai. ter; in the connecting choral fugue, *Sind Blitze, sind Donner,* the choirs are combined into one. The two alto arias with choir are of a similar contemplative nature. One *(Ach, nun ist mein Jesus hin)* is accompanied by flute, oboe d'amore, and strings, and has a choral response from the Song of Solomon; the other is accompanied by two oboi da caccia and has brief choral insertions *(Sehet, Jesus hat die Hand).* The monumental closing group of the entire work consists of a recitative in which the four soloists and the choir participate, and a concluding setting for double choir; the latter thus takes the place of the aria after a recitative *(Nun ist der Herr zur Ruh gebracht, Wir setzen uns mit Tränen nieder).* The closing chorus was also taken over from the funeral music for Prince Leopold. Perhaps the most magnificent passage in this Passion is the Introit for two choirs, *Kommt ihr Töchter, helft mir klagen* with a cantus firmus on *O Lamm Gottes unschuldig* for soprano *ripieno,* which has the effect of a high arch above the orchestra and the choirs; in its way it is unique in Bach's entire output. This text, too, appeared in Henrici's *Erbauliche Gedanken,* and the music was probably produced before 1728–29.

The profundity of its accompanied recitatives, its arias, its recitatives and arias with chorus, and its contemplative settings for double choir place the St. Matthew Passion closer to the Passion oratorio than was the St. John Passion. While in the St. John Passion the biblical story formed the basic fabric into which single contemplative selections were woven, the scenes of the story here seem to be imbedded in a meditation on Christ's suffering. At the same time the Passions are similar in that the Evangelist in both relates the biblical text in *secco* recitative, and the dramatis personae speak the language of the Gospel in the most varied styles of recitative and choral *turbae.* It is not likely that the two Passions were composed concurrently. A number of settings seem to go back to the hypothetical St. Matthew Passion of Weimar (A. Mendel). The definitive text was printed in 1729 in the second volume of Henrici's poems. Bach's autograph score probably dates from no earlier than the 1740s. It is not certain what the musical version of 1729 looked like or how much of the music was composed before 1729. The history of the work is obscure and probably will never be fully known. One discovery has proved that the aria *Mache dich, mein Herze, rein,* which appears in the Passion as well as in the funeral music for Prince Leopold, must have existed prior to 1726 (von Dadelsen). Both works have eight arias and the closing chorus in common, but it is debatable which of these were original and which were parodies. The Passion was further modified for performances after 1729, as was the rule with Bach, and the known version of the opening prelude was apparently a late development. Moreover, as is the case with many other works of Bach, it is hardly possible to speak of a "definitive" version of the St. Matthew

Passion, for its history probably covers as many years as its creator performed it. Since mankind has been aware of its existence—i.e., since Mendelssohn's rediscovery and performance in Berlin in 1829,—it has become one of the fundamental works of Protestantism. From the viewpoint of music history, it is the most important musical Passion of all time.

The treatment of the Passion story in 18th-century Protestant music changed considerably. Generally speaking, the Passion-oratorio type predominated. This reached its first peak with the *Tod Jesu* of Ramler and Graun (1755) and continued to prevail, influenced in central Germany by J. A. Hasse's oratorios of Catholic and Italian origin (*I pellegrini al sepolcro,* 1742; *La deposizione della croce,* 1744; *Sant'Elena al Calvario,* 1746; and others). It speaks well for its endurance that it was kept alive in spite of more fashionable trends and the general development of style. Musicians like G. H. Stölzel returned to it, and in some places annual performances of oratorical Passions are recorded for long periods (Hamburg, 1675–1765, and Gotha, 1699–1770; W. Blankenburg, *Die Aufführungen von Passionen... in Gotha*). The old responsorial Passion survived in many places to the end of the 18th and even into the 19th century (W. Braun, *Mitteldeutsche Choralpassion*). By the same token, however, the Passion became an isolated genre, undermining more and more one of the strongest roots of Protestant church music, its active ties with ongoing history. The uncertain attitude of composers toward their assignment, and thus toward the selection of texts, may have been the result of the uncertain position of the Passion in church life. As long as it had some function in the service (which obviously was true in the 18th century, although Luther and Bugenhagen had already been "at least temporarily distrustful of its usefulness"; W. Braun) it could be considered church music—not only in its old form of responsorial chorale Passion, but later on in the form of a oratorical Passion, and finally in Bach's time in the form of a Passion oratorio. On the other hand, a Passion-oratorio performance was from the beginning looked upon as a church concert (G. Bronner's oratorio *Seelenwallfahrt zum Kreuz und Grab Christi* in the Hamburg *Heiliggeistkirche,* 1710; the Telemann-Brockes Passion in the Frankfurt *Barfüsserkirche,* 1716) or as a public concert, completely outside the realm of the church—for example, Telemann's *Seliges Erwägen* in Hamburg, 1740, which became the "favorite fashionable devotional piece in Hamburg" (K. Stephenson in *MGG* V, 1397) and the Hamburg concert performances of Mattheson's oratorios beginning in 1717 (cf. H. Becker, *Die frühe Hamburger Tagespresse,* etc., in *Beiträge zur Hamburgischen Musikgeschichte,* ed. H. Husmann, 1956, 22). As early as 1704, Handel's St. John Passion and Keiser's *Blutiger und sterbender Jesus* were performed in concerts in Hamburg, and B. H. Brockes had Passion music (cantata or oratorio?) produced in his home in 1712. In 1735 J. Mattheson mockingly called the Hamburg concert hall *(Drillhaus)* "the undisputed training ground for fancy churches" *(Kleine Generalbass-Schule).*

The performance practice of the Passion oratorio has by no means been thoroughly explored. No doubt it was subject to far-reaching local deviations. In Hamburg between 1719 and 1724 the Passion oratorios of Mattheson, Keiser, Handel, and some unknown composers were still performed at times in church (but in concert form), at times in the refectory of the cathedral, and at times in the *Drillhaus;* since the 1730s, in Hamburg and other places, this kind of music has been performed mostly in the concert hall. In the Leipzig of Bach it had a definite place in the church service, i.e., as a Passion Vesper. This might be why the St. Matthew Passion preserved the core of the *historia* in spite of its strong trend toward the oratorio. Not only is the use of the Passion oratorio in the 18th century still largely unknown but so is the history of the genre. Still less clearly defined is the so-called Passion cantata, which combines meditations on the Passion story with selected verses but avoids the actual narrative (cf. W. Blankenburg in the Blume *Festschrift,* 50 ff., and in *MGG* X, 911 ff.). Neither species reached full bloom until about 1740, the beginning of the early classical period.

J. S. BACH'S LATIN LITURGICAL MUSIC

The order of worship as laid down in the Pontifical State of Leipzig of 1710 was comparatively conservative; it still used Latin texts for the liturgy on many Sundays and holidays of the church year. The Mass—Introit, Kyrie, Gloria, Credo, Sanctus, and other texts—could be celebrated in Latin, alternately in Latin and German, or in German with Latin intonations. At Vespers, especially during Christmas time, the Magnificat, for which the Protestant liturgies always had shown a certain fondness, was sung in Latin. To a limited extent, the old textual similarity between the confessions came back to life. Telemann composed Latin Masses for Eisenach between 1708 and 1712; the Catholic Chelleri composed them for Kassel between 1725 and 1730. Buttstett, equally active in the service of a Protestant and a Catholic church in Erfurt, published four Masses in 1720 and composed at least three more. Other Protestant composers like Kuhnau and Pachelbel wrote Latin church music. J. Ph. Krieger is said to have composed more than one hundred Masses and Mass settings, among them one for fifty-eight voices (Senn in *MGG* IX, 208). This practice remained widespread. Bach, and later Harrer, copied Masses and Mass settings of Catholic composers and adapted and performed them in Leipzig. Protestants like Heinichen, J. F. Fasch, and, not least, J. S. Bach himself provided compositions for services in the royal Catholic chapel in Dresden. Bach copied and adapted Masses or Mass settings by Palestrina, Bassani, Kerll, and Zelenka (for the Leipzig repertory of Catholic compositions, cf. F. W. Riedel, *Musikgeschichtliche Beziehungen zwischen J. J. Fux und J. S. Bach* in the Blume *Festschrift,* 1963, p. 290 ff.). Apparently the faithful preservation of Latin texts helped to maintain a sentimental attachment to the old confessional community in music.

Even though the cantors may have borrowed most of the music for the Latin sections of the service from older sources (as was the custom with the Latin motet), later generations are indebted to the conservatism of the liturgy for some of Bach's Latin church music. According to Spitta, the Magnificat in D major was first performed in 1723 at Christmas in St. Thomas's; it was, however, probably given in the still older setting in E-flat major which, according to an old popular custom, was interwoven with four Christmas carols (see M. Geck, *Bachs*

73. Johann Sebastian Bach, gamba part for the bass aria *Komm, süsses Kreuz* from part II of the St. Matthew Passion, BWV 244 (between 1738 and 1746), autograph. Stiftung Preussischer Kulturbesitz, Depot der Staatsbibliothek, Tübingen, Mus. MS autogr. Bach St. 110.

74. Johann Sebastian Bach, *Nun komm der Heiden Heiland*, BWV 599, from the *Orgelbüchlein* (c. 1714–16), autograph. Berlin, Deutsche Staatsbibliothek, Mus. MS autogr. Bach P 283.

Weihnachts-Magnificat und sein Traditionszusammenhang, in *Musik und Kirche* XXXI, 1961, 257 ff.). The version in D major may not have been produced until some years later. Its tone is extremely festive, clear, and bright. Nevertheless, a thought-provoking interpretation of the Gospel text appears in contrasting movements *(Quia respexit—Omnes generationes).* In the background is a magnificent contrast: the burden of original sin, carried by all mankind, against the promise of redemption by the Virgin Mother and her Son. Not without reason does the *Sicut locutus est ad patres nostros* use a concentrated fugato (this movement solely a capella) to combine the antithetical elements and to lead into a grandiose Doxology where the entire concerted splendor is again displayed, thus forming a ritornello-like link with the opening verse. The form of the entire work is strictly symmetrical, and the style corresponds to the "cantata-like" compositions on sacred texts that evolved from Neapolitan practice and were in use everywhere. In this, Bach and his Catholic contemporaries were alike.

Probably none of the five individual Sancti handed down in Bach's name are really his, although all are preserved in his autograph (cf. Dadelsen, *Beiträge,* pp. 89, 113; BWV 237 and 238 date from 1723, and 239 and 240 from later years). The one for eight voices (BWV 241) is a free adaptation by Bach of Johann Kaspar Kerll's *Missa "Superba"* (H. T. David, *A Lesser Secret,* 1961). The origin of the four *Missae breves* has not yet come to light; none is an original composition. Parody models are known for all but one aria and for most of the choral movements (i.e., for twenty out of twenty-five). It is not clear why Bach preferred to use material from the cantatas Nos. 79, 102, 179, and 187, and only supplemented his choices with material from such others as Nos. 17, 40, 67, 72, and 138. Perhaps the *Missae breves* did not result from demands in Leipzig but were commissioned by the Bohemian Count Franz Anton Sporck, who moved in the social circle of Bach's aristocratic patrons in Dresden. It is uncertain whether the commonly used date, 1737–38, is correct; there are parts for the Mass in A major that stem from Bach's latest period (Dadelsen, *Beiträge,* p. 117). Their parody-like style tends to connect them with the other large works of the 1730s.

To a great extent, Bach's most voluminous Latin church work, the Mass in B minor, belongs to the parody classification. It was praised by C. F. Zelter as "the greatest work of art that the world has ever seen" (1811). It was studied by Haydn and Beethoven. G. Spontini paid "homage" to it with a Berlin performance of the first Credo movement in 1818. More than any other of Bach's large vocal creations, it has carried the master's fame throughout the world from the days of romanticism to the present. Yet, it is the most controversial composition in Bach's entire vocal output. This is not the place to retrace the controversy over its origin (cf. especially C. F. Smend, *Bachs H-Moll Messe,* in the *Bach-Jahrbuch,* 1937; his *Kritischer Bericht* to *Neue Bach-Ausgabe* II/1, 1956; G. von Dadelsen, *Beiträge zur Chronologie,* etc., Trossingen, 1958; his *Zum Problem der H-Moll-Messe* in the program of the 35th German *Bachfest,* Stuttgart, 1958, p. 77 ff.). According to present information, it seems certain that Bach (as with his other four Masses) originally composed the first two movements as a *Missa brevis,* presenting them to Elector Friedrich August II of Saxony with a petition to be awarded a "Praedicat von Dero Hoff-Capelle" (July 27, 1733); in so doing he obligated himself to compose at any time church music, or music of any other kind, upon command of the Elector. The Sanctus (1724, according to von Dadelsen) was written much earlier. It was an independent composition and had nothing to do with the *Missa*. It was not until the end of his life that Bach completed the Mass. He then composed the Credo, added the already existing Sanctus, and reworked the remaining movements from the Hosanna to the *Dona nobis pacem*—the latter all parodies of older compositions. Some of the choruses and solos of the Credo stem from earlier models (among which is the much disputed *Et in unum*), and at least three movements of the Gloria are adaptations or parodies of existing pieces. Apparently only the Kyrie was newly composed specifically for this purpose. Bach may have composed new sections to add to the existing material of the Gloria and Credo. It is likely that the entire work contains more parodies than is generally known, and that the Mass in B minor thus fits in completely with the great vocal works of the 1730s. Otherwise, there would hardly be adequate reason to include it in the history of Protestant church music. It is not certain that the four *Missae breves* were composed for Count Sporck, and thus for use in the Catholic liturgy, but Bach clearly dedicated the *Missa*, i.e., Kyrie and Gloria, to the Elector of Saxony and King of Poland for worship services in the Catholic court in Dresden. None of the many attempts to make a performance of the Mass seem more appropriate in either a Catholic or a Protestant service (for instance, by Schering), or to attribute specifically Lutheran content to it (Gerber, Smend), has proved convincing. Almost sixty years after the first two movements were created, C. Ph. E. Bach's posthumous index (1790) designated the work as "the great Catholic Mass." Its style is closely related to that of the Magnificat. Both belong in that narrow border area of interconfessional creativity, as mentioned above (see p. 308). It is questionable whether the Mass in B minor or only the *Missa brevis* was produced in Bach's lifetime, either in Dresden or elsewhere. Later generations can be grateful that the aging Bach felt the need to round out his lifework with a complete Mass (which, incidentally was not performed in its entirety until the middle of the 19th century), and that he was unaffected by confessional idiosyncrasy. Romanticism took this "greatest work of art of all times and nations" (H.G. Nägeli, 1818) as an all-embracing proclamation of the humanitarian spirit. The testimonial can well stand today.

From the stylistic point of view, the Mass in B minor is a genuine "cantata Mass." It reveals the "Neapolitan" style that was well known in Austria and south Germany through the printed Masses of G. Bassani (1709) and G. A. Bernabei (1710), and still more through the circulation of manuscripts of Masses and other church music by Italian composers. Bach's knowledge of works by Kerll, Zelenka, and Caldara indicates that he may have known the large body of church music of Viennese provenance in Dresden. Whereas musical settings of the Passion had tended in Bach's time either to stagnate in an adherence to tradition or to lose contact with the church in the pursuit of newer methods, Latin church music was free to follow modern trends and to keep up with the general development of style. Obviously, such music could not exhibit a specifically Protestant character, and this is true of Bach's Mass in B minor. It is one of the most impressive testimonies in history for the supraconfessional, totally European spirit that enveloped music at the end of the Baroque period. For this reason, since its revival in the 19th century, it has justifiably maintained its reputation as one of the greatest works of art "of all times and nations."

Bach's vocal church music, at least as far as cantatas and passions are concerned, was already out of date in his lifetime. Some contemporary composers—Telemann, Mattheson, Graupner, or Bach's rival in Leipzig, J. Gottlieb Görner—turned in the 1720s to the gallant style of church music, with its languishing melodies and unpretentious techniques, avoiding the cantorial erudition of artistic fugues and canons, and the emotional drama of Bach's musical language. A few lesser contemporaries—G. Kirchhoff of Halle or pupils like J. G. Goldberg of Dresden (church cantatas of both in *Erbe deutscher Musik* 35, 1957, ed. A. Dürr; those of Goldberg presumably composed for Leipzig)—preserved the style of Bach and his circle. Here and there a few musicians like H. G. Stölzel, J. F. Fasch, J. D. Heinichen, or even later ones such as J. F. Doles, maintained some of this tradition. But on the whole the generation of Bach's sons brought about the change to a new era, which J. A. Scheibe's *Critischer Musicus* had declared in 1737 with his attack on Bach, and which, half a century later, with Bach's third successor in Leipzig, J. A. Hiller as spokesman, censured the "crudities" in his music. The new era did not lack for religious feeling or intensity of conviction, even though F. Rochlitz not without justification reproved Hiller for his "weak, fickle philanthropism from Basedow's school" (Schering, *Musikgeschichte Leipzigs* III, 657). What it lacked was the undergirding of irrefutable tenets and regulations from the church, and a steadfast conviction that church music served no purpose other than "honoring God and uplifting the soul" (Bach's definition). With the commitment to liturgy and to *de tempore* music, the commitment of musicians to the "Office" (in the Lutheran sense of a God-given burden) fell apart; the original purpose of all church music as praise and proclamation was lost, and with it the devotion to the Word of the Bible and to the chorale. In the maudlin emotions engendered by natural religion, where the glory of God in nature meant more to people than the worship of God in church, Bach's vocal music declined rapidly. J. N. Forkel's booklet of 1802 mentions his church music only in passing. When at the beginning of the 19th century Bach's work was revived—which is one of the strangest events in the entire history of church music—it did not come about through any stimulation by the church, nor was it for the most part on the strength of his vocal compositions. It resulted from the efforts of civic concert associations and choral societies and an interest in his instrumental works. His vocal compositions were re-established very slowly and only over a great deal of opposition; this was true especially of his German cantatas and Passions. The Latin church works were more readily accepted for the reasons mentioned above; for other reasons, the motets were accepted. It took a long time—until Mendelssohn's generation—before a larger public could spontaneously experience Bach's music and understand it; only then was the groundwork laid for the worldwide Bach renaissance that has continued to the present day. Even beyond the mid-20th century, the Bach movement seems not to have reached its apex. It is not just that Bach has enjoyed undisputed esteem for 150 years as one of the world's greatest masters of music, but it is a *consensus omnium* that he and his work were the culmination of Protestant church music.

In fact, the forces from which this period in history drew its individuality and its greatness were nowhere so completely and so convincingly synthesized as in Johann Sebastian Bach. In Baroque music, Lutheranism found its most personal and most denominational expression. Moreover, under the influence of Pietism, it also found its deepest emotional imprint—in form and language, in style and spirit. The music of the Baroque unequivocally reached its climax in Bach. The Bach renaissance was necessary, for it enabled other and older masters of Protestant church music to come to life again—chiefly those of the Baroque era, from Michael Praetorius to Scheidt, Schein, Schütz, Buxtehude, Pachelbel, Weckmann, and so on, all the way to the one in whom resided the quintessence of all past ages, J. S. Bach. The results and the skills of all older musical traditions were carried up to his day, where they revealed for the last time their powerful magic. Since the days of Luther, what had revealed itself in music by way of liturgical conviction, proclamation of the Gospel, scriptural exegesis, and adherence to the basic elements of biblical word and the chorale—all this was given vitality once again. The conservative or even retrospective character of Protestant church music (already established by Luther, Johann Walther, and Georg Rhau) and its adaptability to contemporary trends—these tendencies, too, were realized by Bach; this interaction produced some of Bach's most telling compositions. In Bach's work, historical Lutheranism became altogether synonymous with music, and Bach, standing at the close of a historically burdened tradition, was able to awaken the power of "mystic sounds," which, though hidden under a false sense of tradition, were yet still "miraculously slumbering." Bach was the last one who could reactivate the spring of creative life from weather-beaten rocks at a time of stagnant orthodoxy and shallow Pietism, a time of decaying liturgical forms and growing religious disintegration brought about by the advance of enlightened rationalism, a time when the institutions of church music approached a standstill, when the self-awareness of Protestant church musicians was degenerating into secular modes of thought, when even the cantors of St. Thomas's were fighting a hopeless battle for the maintenance of medieval privileges and a theocentric view of music that could not possibly stand up against the natural sciences and the new humanism. Scripture, the chorale, allegory, exegesis, cantus-firmus settings, fugue and canon, the art of expressing oneself rhetorically and weaving mysterious numerical symbolism into the score—all the traditional arts were deeply penetrated in Bach by the beguiling sensuality of sound and by the ardor of a pre-Romantic perception, anticipating the progress of history far into the future. Dogmatic sternness and overriding serenity, liturgical drama and emotional idyll, the mysticism of pious devotion and the trumpet blast of radiating heavenly glory: such synthesis has been accomplished only once in history—in the work of Bach.

It is immaterial whether Bach, the man behind the work, considered himself originally or later a church musician, or whether he was aware of his mission. Nor does it matter by which intricate path his work reached the high regard in which it is held today, backed up by so much historical evidence. It was still a long time after Mendelssohn's famous performance of the St. Matthew Passion (1829) until Bach's vocal works, especially his cantatas and Passions, slowly came into their own, and it took even more time until they were accepted in their original form, without alterations and modernizations. In other words, it was a long time before the historical Bach was understood on the basis of the original design of his work. His music was not revived because it was churchly; rather, its connection to the church made it foreign to the Romantic era both textually and musically. Bach's vocal church music was revived by a process of secularization (which cannot be discussed here), and it is only in the 20th century that the church (with varying success) has tried to reintroduce this music into the service. The Bach renaissance was a result of the everlasting greatness of his music and of an autonomous event in the history of music, to which extramusical impulses made few, if any, significant contributions. Its importance in the performance practice of church music was not understood until the revival had already become an accomplished fact.

PART III

Decline and Restoration

BY GEORG FEDER

Translated by Reinhard G. Pauly

Decline

There is unanimity of opinion that Protestant church music after Bach declined in comparison to the achievements of earlier days. The essential truth of this statement cannot be doubted. As early as the second half of the 18th century, voices began to be heard deploring the low level of church music and its steady decline: Adlung in 1758, Albrecht in 1764, Steinberg in 1766, Knecht in 1783, Türk in 1787, Spazier in 1788, Hiller in 1791, and many others. Complaints became more numerous soon after 1800; they did not cease throughout the century. Nevertheless, we must distinguish between real deterioration and what was merely a change in taste; between a decline of the level of performance and a decline in composing; between a decline in the musical aspects of the art and the ecclesiastical ones. The picture is complicated; it would be oversimplification to say that Protestant church music underwent a steady and equal deterioration in all spheres. In the field of the church cantata, for instance, the late Baroque works of Seibert, Glaser, Wirbach, and Wundsch show clearer signs of decay than do later cantatas of composers such as Vierling. Nor can one state simply that an absolute low point was reached in the 19th century and that after this a gradual, steady improvement took place. The year 1817, the 300th anniversary of the Reformation, does represent a turning point, the most suitable date to mark the beginning of the restoration. But 1817 did not witness a new flowering of Protestant church music. The first signs were not visible before the end of the 19th century, the end of the period discussed in this chapter. Viewed as a whole, the period of "decline" shows even more originality than the period of restoration, not only in the music but also in the way it dealt with the ideas and problems of church music. Close scrutiny will show that the restoration failed to create a prominent place for Protestant church music in the general consciousness. Only the Bach revival, which did not come from within the church, accomplished this. During the period of "decline," however, church music continued to have a function in public life, though this function steadily diminished in importance.

Finally, regional differences must be considered. In 1790 Pastor S. Ch. Fiedler expressed the opinion that church music "had now reached a summit, especially in Saxony." In making this statement he seems to have been thinking of Dresden, where Homilius had been active for some time and where Ch.E. Weinlig was then the conductor of the excellent *Kreuzchor;* he was impressed by Graun's *Tod Jesu,* Homilius's motets, Weinlig's *Christ am Grabe Jesu,* and by the compositions of J.H. Rolle, J.A. Hiller, J.G. Naumann, Bach (undoubtedly not J.S. Bach), J.A.P. Schulz, J.F. Reichardt, Agricola, Tag, J.A. Hasse, and others. Indeed, the practice of sacred music in Saxony and Thuringia never really deteriorated, as later evidence also shows. Spazier already had exempted these provinces from his general censure. Kretzschmar wrote in 1894 that "the parishes of Saxony . . . continued to use the so-called *Kirchenmusik* [i.e., church music in the narrower

sense of cantatas] even during the time when the liturgy was at its most impoverished." In 1899 Vollhardt described church music in Saxony as "very vigorous
and well developed" right up to his own time.

The death of J.S. Bach did not result in an interruption of the course of music
history. The period between Bach and the age of Viennese classicism has been
labeled the Hasse-Graun period by some of the older music historians. At the time
of Bach's death, Johann Adolf Hasse and Carl Heinrich Graun had already
composed the majority of their works, and Reinhard Keiser had preceded them.
In Germany, the concept of music that is oriented toward melody and away from
counterpoint goes back in essence to Keiser. After Bach this concept set the trend
in church music as well. Although Hasse became converted to Catholicism early
in life and wrote no specifically Protestant church music, he and Graun exerted
a strong influence on Protestant sacred music, especially in the second half of the
18th century. In contrast to Handel, Bach exerted practically no influence
through his vocal works: they were the exact opposite of what was in vogue at
the time. Almost nowhere except in the field of organ composition, especially in
the works of J.L. Krebs, is anything of his spirit revealed. His other pupils did
not write in the style of their great teacher but showed more affinity to Hasse and
Graun, following their manner quite expressly in some instances. If one measures
church music from the second half of the 18th century with J.S. Bach as the
yardstick, a steep decline is indeed apparent. But if the comparison is made to
Bach's contemporaries—Telemann, Stölzel, Römhild, Graupner, J.F. Fasch,
and so on—then the change appears to be more gradual. By the end of the century
it becomes evident that few works reach what used to be an average level of
quality, while secular music is reaching its culmination in the Viennese Classical
School.

The same sources that contaminated the musical life of the Protestant church
nourished the blooming concert and theater music: basically, the Enlightenment,
the principal intellectual development of the age. From about 1740 (the accession
of Frederick the Great) or 1750, it became the ruling influence upon the educated
middle class in Germany, a class that became more and more estranged from the
church. "In vain do words of eternal truth resound in our temples; devout
listeners there are none, and the holy places are empty," as it is put in the
recitative of a cantata for Reformation Day (Flensburg, 1817; music by Demuth,
text by A.P. Andresen). In the name of Deism "unnatural" dogmas were refused;
instead, one practiced a "natural" religion. The dogmatic foundations of theology
itself were softened by "neology" and by its offspring, rationalism, which had
replaced Pietism since about 1770. "*Sapere aude!* Have the courage to use your
own intellect! This is the motto of the Enlightenment," Kant wrote in 1784. And:
"Our age is the true age of criticism, to which all must be subjected" (1781). The
critics of the Enlightenment did not exclude the traditions of Protestant church
music from their scrutiny. They shook them to their foundations, they severed
their ties with the liturgy, and they supplied new goals. Only later did it become
evident that the rational, reformatory zeal of the Enlightenment was not the right
leader, that it led church music astray to its eventual destruction.

DISSOLUTION OF THE INSTITUTIONAL FOUNDATIONS

Practically speaking, Protestant church music meant music for services on Sundays and holidays, for weddings, funerals, and other special occasions. Its existence depended on the institutions of the school choir, the cantorate, the town and court musicians who were obliged to participate in church music, and also on voluntary assistance from citizens and students. To these can be added the *Kantoreien* (adult singing societies) in the towns and the rural *Adjuvantenvereine,* especially in Saxony and Thuringia. The most important among these institutions, the trained choir of students, could exist only in the Latin schools, where music formed an important part of the instruction. So much time was devoted to choral obligations that academic training inevitably suffered. Disagreements between the headmaster and cantor were the result. When neo-humanism invaded the old Latin schools of Melanchthon stamp, they became academically oriented and lost their ecclesiastical character. Music, as a result, did not retain its former importance, its place in the curriculum, and was only reluctantly tolerated. Choirs now came to be regarded as bothersome appendages to the "institutions of learning"; they therefore existed on shaky foundations. They derived their support from what endowments were left to them, and from singing processions through the town, though these increasingly came to be considered mere begging. It became the task of the lower school classes to make the ordinary rounds *(Kurrende),* to sing at funeral processions, and to provide music for the ordinary church services. In their black or gray choir robes, with wig or pigtail, three-cornered hat or top hat, the choristers became the butt of many jokes in a secularized environment. They soon felt out of place themselves in their old-fashioned role as they walked through the streets of an "enlightened" world, singing chorales, motets, or spiritual songs. They frequently turned to secular songs and were then censured, perhaps with justification, for their dissoluteness. For humanitarian reasons alone, the abolition of these choral practices was demanded. It now was considered inhuman that these boys should make their rounds in all kinds of weather, and it seemed brutal that they should sing not only at funerals but (according to testimony from many places) at executions. Nor did it seem proper to have them do all this for money. Furthermore, the artistic level, not only of the *Kurrende* but of choirs in general, was lowering. Statements by Mattheson (1755), Reichardt (1782), Spazier (1788), Zelter (1803–04), and others testify to this. Friends of church music such as Rellstab (1789), Forkel (1797), K.W. Frantz (1802), Zelter (1803–04), and J.F.S. Döring (1806) felt called upon to make suggestions for reform, but these were essentially fruitless. Sooner or later the institutions, once so splendid, perished, and by the early 19th century those that managed to survive played a very subordinate role in musical life, with the exception of the *Thomasschule* chorus in Leipzig and the *Kreuzschule* chorus in Dresden. To the regret of some of the neo-humanistic pedagogues, school choruses elsewhere in Saxony also continued to cultivate church music (in Halberstadt, Magdeburg, Merseburg, Naumburg, Quedlinburg, Schulpforta, and Torgau, according to A. Werner). Some of the *Kurrenden* remained alive and even survived the second blow, which was administered to the remaining traditions by the revolution of 1848. But they were of no great importance any more. The new *Singakademien* took over the artistic function of the school choirs. They began to flourish early in the 19th century when the practice of church music had reached a low ebb. The Berlin *Singakademie* was the model for all later ones. The statutes define its tasks as follows (1816): "The *Singakademie* is an artistic society for the cultivation of serious and sacred music, especially for music in contrapuntal style [*im gebundenen Stil*]." To the cultivation of "ecclesiastical or sacred music," it added in 1821 the cultivation of "the most closely related serious vocal music." The cultivation of this music, however, was an end in itself; it did not serve the church. A. Werner rightly said that it hardly advanced the cause of liturgical music.

In earlier days the cantor had often also been the town's musical director and the leading figure in its musical life. Now, his venerable position, too, suffered a gradual artistic and social depreciation. New concepts of creative genius rendered the connection of art and office suspect. The new ideal was a composition "written for eternity" (Preussner), an ideal which C.P.E. Bach had in mind when he wrote his famous *Heilig* for double choir. Against such concepts the dignity of official composing could not maintain itself. In the Prussian Code of 1794 neither cantors nor organists (which latter had always had less security in the social order) are listed as professionals in their own right; they are listed on a level with custodians, as "lower church employees" (Söhngen). The better musicians among them were anxious to find work in secular musical life, and the cantors themselves esteemed their secular compositions more than their sacred ones, for to be known as a church composer was no longer a recommendation. Thus, the word "cantor" became "almost an invective" (Schlimbach, 1805). By 1800 the position of cantor had lost most of its earlier artistic and social prestige. Organists fared no better; if their profession was not considered attractive, this was due only in part to the poor pay.

As time went on, the quality of work of the town musicians, whose duties included sacred music, compared less and less favorably with that of independent musicians. In earlier days privileges had protected the town musicians from this competition, but now free musicians reached the leading positions in amateur and professional concerts. In the early 19th century in Prussia, all town musicians were recruited from the ranks of retired army musicians (see Schlimbach, 1805, and others); they were not likely to raise the standards of church music. Thus, Zelter could complain in 1804 that the town musicians *(Stadtpfeifer)* knew how to play neither dance music nor church music properly. The decline of the towns' *Kantoreien* began to be noticeable in the first half of the 18th century. Many were dissolved at the end of the century. The others lost some of their best voices to the patriotic male choruses which began to flourish early in the 19th century. Those that did not disappear altogether were transformed into male choruses, mixed choruses, or singing societies; some degenerated into purely social groups or pallbearer societies. Others, organizing themselves along entirely different lines, became professional, paid church choirs. The lay choruses from the country

(Adjuvantenchöre), unlike the *Kantoreien* of the burghers, lasted well into the 19th century, reflecting the slower pace of change typical for rural areas. Later on they, too, declined.

Public concert life tended to draw musicians away from the church as well as listeners. Since the citizens' need for serious music could now be satisfied outside of the church, it was inevitable that interest in church music of high quality should diminish. This is what Preussner describes as the replacement of church music by public concerts during the age of Bach's sons. The repertory of public concerts included works that earlier would have been heard in church. Musical settings of the Passion thus moved from church to concert hall, to the *concert spirituel* and similar institutions, many of which grew up everywhere during the second half of the 18th century. Soon works of an oratorio character were given in church (in concert form) only in order to accommodate large orchestral forces or for better financial gain (Triest, 1801). In Prussia it was eventually decreed that admission could not be charged at church concerts except for charitable purposes (see G. Krause and others). Naturally, this worked to the advantage of public concerts rather than church concerts. In general, the clergy made no attempt to prevent the exodus of music from the church.

IDEAS ON THE NATURE OF "TRUE" CHURCH MUSIC

The Enlightenment brought about the decline of those institutions which had previously supported Protestant church music. It also was to affect opinions on the music itself—on the purpose of liturgical music, congregational singing, organ playing, and sacred polyphony, and on the "usefulness" of traditional forms. The Enlightenment held that the chief function of all church music was "edification." Everything that seemed to be edifying was to be kept; everything else was either to be abolished or to be revised. To "edify" meant to induce feelings of reverence, whether they were only sentimental or more elevating in nature. To attribute such one-sidedness of purpose to church music contained a danger which is best described in J.A. Hiller's words (after 1793): "To induce feelings of reverence, music may not be superfluous, but neither is it indispensable." The older belief —that church music was an indispensable part of an immutable tradition, instituted by God for His praise—was voiced, probably for the last time, by J.L. Albrecht in 1764. The same theocentric view was expressed in 1762 by the Weida cantor Ch.E. Martius, although with less convincing reasons. Later still, the church fathers of St. Bartholomew's in Danzig objected to plans for abolishing church music by pointing out that "church music has been instituted by the Lord Himself in order to lend greater splendor to the divine service." (see Rauschning, p. 382). But these are exceptions. In 1766, Ch.G. Steinberg had already answered Albrecht that church music was by no means necessary but only "commendable and proper." If church music were to be "useful," this implied a further condition: it had to be edifying for *all* members of the congregation. It was not enough for the connoisseur of Latin to understand the liturgy or for the connoisseur of music to understand polyphony and organ preludes: everyone should understand everything. Only through simplicity could this be brought about, and simplicity was one of the requirements of contemporary aesthetics. Gottsched (1736) had demanded "noble simplicity" of the orator; Mattheson (1737) had applied this term to melody. In 1755, Winckelmann had written the famous sentence: "The noble simplicity and silent grandeur of Greek sculpture also distinguish Greek writing of the greatest period." Thus he defined classicism for the period to follow. This concept of classicism applied to music as well. It is part of practically all contemporary definitions of what specifically constitutes church style and continued to exert its influence throughout the 19th century. "Noble simplicity and dignity" and similar wordings—these slogans were used to define the nature of church music during the second half of the 18th century and far beyond. They were applied to all kinds of music in the church: to the liturgy, to the chorales and their accompaniment, to organ playing in general, and, not least, to polyphonic music. It is evident from numerous statements, from 1750 into the early 19th century, about specific works—even by Telemann and Handel and especially by Hasse, C.P.E. Bach, Doles, J.H. Rolle, J.B. Kehl, the Bückeburg Bach, J.G. Naumann, F.W. Rust, J.A.P. Schulz, Reichardt, Kittel, J.Ch. Kühnau, Karl Fasch, F. Schneider, B. Klein, Ch.H. Rinck, A.F. Hesse, and others—that the ideal of noble simplicity and dignity was not merely a dream, or something to be found only in ancient music. It was seen in some contemporary church music as well: one is tempted to speak of classicism in church music. "Noble simplicity" does not always refer to the same qualities, but the principal concern always is the creation of a devotional mood through simple, intelligible means. Its original meaning was usually that melody should dominate. Along with this, the notion became increasingly popular that simplicity and dignity were best expressed through a simple chordal style. A third view, that a strict contrapuntal style represented the ideal, was voiced less often and less loudly. The first and second views agree in their condemnation of all artfulness for its own sake; the second and third, in their renunciation of everything secular. The music of J. S. Bach in particular was deemed to be only artful or artificial.

Nichelmann expressed agreement (1755) with Scheibe's well-known criticism of Bach's works as being "confused." An opinion by C. P. E. Bach has been preserved in which he refers to the useless contrapuntal artifices of his father. Türk (1787) described Bach's canonic variations on *Vom Himmel hoch* as "Augenmusik." The Abbé Vogler believed that Bach did not heed the maxim "Artis est celare artem." According to the *Musikalische Korrespondenz* (Speyer, 1792, p. 41f.), the opinion had been widespread for some time that Bach's four-part chorales were "too learned"; the writer did not agree with this opinion, though other authors did. In 1803, Kittel wrote about his teacher that his intention had been "to elicit, according to the spirit of his age, admiration for his great erudition rather than to move through the grace and expressiveness of his melodies"; that his free compositions were too closely modeled on fugues and therefore resulted in "learned chaos." During the period of restoration, Bach's vocal and organ compositions were considered unsuitable for the church, due to excessive artificiality and a lack of edifying quality (Kessler, Rohleder, Winterfeld, Schoeberlein, etc.)

Views about what was too worldly and hence inappropriate differed widely and were narrowed down by the Romantics. Naturally enough, some individuals held eclectic points of view; some theorists and many practical musicians avoided going on record as favoring either one or another viewpoint, but this did not change the situation as such. The first view, emphasizing melody, can best be considered as an expression of the Enlightenment; the second, priority of chordal writing, of Romanticism; the third, favoring a contrapuntal style, was traditional but not typical of the age.

Doles, cantor of St. Thomas's Church, is a typical representative of the "modern," popular, and melodious style in church music in the spirit of the Enlightenment. In his Gellert songs (1758) his intention was, according to the preface, to present "easy" melodies, "without artificiality." In his quasi-autobiography he discusses having been instructed by J.S. Bach "in the contrapuntal style," but he adds that he had not "carried this to excess," and that he did not forget to write in the "gentle and touching melodious style" for which Hasse and Graun had been his models. His preface to his cantata *Ich komme vor dein Angesicht* (1790) has often been quoted; in it he demands that church music should contain "rhythms that are easily understood, simple and forceful harmonies, and melodies that will go to the heart," qualities found in operas, especially in recent ones (here he may have thought of Naumann and Mozart, to both of whom his cantata is dedicated). Fugal style, on the other hand, is considered unintelligible for the churchgoer; it serves to "amuse the intellect" rather than to "touch the heart" and therefore is inappropriate for church music. In the preface to his *Singbare und leichte Choralvorspiele* (Singable and Easy Chorale Preludes), he assures the reader that these compositions were written "in the style of ariettas, not in the strict and confining church style which cannot be grasped, let alone comprehended, by most listeners, and which does not induce a devotional frame of mind." Doles's successor, J.A. Hiller, subscribed to similar beliefs, if in a less one-sided manner. In 1787 he voiced criticism of the Baroque "mania to overburden all music with harmony and many voices, or to force it into stiff, canonic imitation." In 1791 he published as *Beyträge zu wahrer Kirchenmusik* (Contributions to True Church Music) six arias, one duet, and one chorus from operas and oratorios by Hasse, in score, in some cases with additional instruments, with German sacred texts written by him—examples of the "true church style". His favoring of a melodious style is also apparent in other editions of adaptations for use as Protestant church music: the *Stabat Maters* of Pergolesi and Haydn as Passion music, Mozart's *Davidde Penitente* as an Easter cantata. Still, he took pains to disassociate himself from the decidedly fashionable style of Doles (by 1790 Hasse no longer was fashionable), but he admitted that church music might, "without detriment to its dignity, well lose some of its severity and seek to come a little closer to the current taste" (1789). Occasionally he stressed the primary importance of choral music (1789). In the long run Hiller's attitude—hostile to tradition and always ready for experimentation—did not exert a beneficial influence. A certain Schulze arranged Haydn symphony movements as church cantatas; they were published in Leipzig about 1810–11. Another contemporary demanded that serious operatic choruses by Gluck and Mozart should be allowed in church (see Graff). Still another, in 1805, cautioned country organists not to play "artful fugues or difficult, frequently unmelodious compositions" (*Leipziger AmZ* VIII, 189). G. W. Fink (1827) also showed his dislike of fugues in church. In 1829 one author stated that secular music might be used in the Protestant church as long as it was not the work of charlatans. In 1831 J.Ch. Lobe, in agreement with Doles, wanted to ban fugues from the church as being incomprehensible and preventing devotional feelings; in 1852 he recommended Méhul's opera *Joseph in Egypt* as suitable music for the church but expressed opposition to J.S. Bach. G. Nauenburg (1845) was also a decided though late representative of the Enlightenment when he demanded that vocal church music must be "above all truly popular." He deplored choruses and organ fugues "that are full of contrapuntal technique and artifice, cold and rational but void of any holy sentiments."

The Romantic movement was not strongly in evidence until the 1780s, the period during which Handel's monumental works came into Germany and Palestrina became known. A different point of view gradually established itself during these years, decisive for the future: to look to purely choral music for representation of the true church style. For a time, Handel's choral style was considered ideal for church music—not its Baroque characteristics but the qualities that appealed to the new way of feeling. This predilection for Handel, however, was only a preliminary step for the Palestrina cult. At first Palestrina's music was cultivated only in private circles and choral societies; later on it made its way into the church service as well.

It is significant that Kittel (1808) finds in Handel's choruses the beginnings of the new style in which the strict and free manners of writing are mixed, as in works by Mozart (finale of the *Jupiter Symphony*) and Haydn. According to Schering, certain compositions by Handel found their way into church services in Leipzig under J. A. Hiller. In 1780 Hiller also published the Utrecht Te Deum, adding the Latin text that was still usual in the Protestant church for important feasts. In 1805 a certain Schaum published (in Reichardt's *Berlinische Musikalische Zeitung*) an invitation to subscribe to an edition of Handel's oratorios in which texts suitable for church use were to be substituted, as a "replacement for the old, completely unsuitable *Jahrgänge*" (i.e., cycles of cantatas for the whole year). The edition did not materialize; nevertheless, individual movements found their way into the service—for instance, through Sander's *Heilige Cäcilia* III (Berlin, 1819). C.F.G. Schwencke, music director in Hamburg, arranged an Easter cantata from the *Messiah*. A Good Friday cantata based on *Saul* also appeared.

Reichardt's writings show best the emergence of early Romantic views. In 1774 and 1776 he saw the simplicity and dignity of church music fully realized in the works of Graun, C.P.E. Bach, Karl Fasch, Homilius, and J.H. Rolle. His statement of 1782 about the value of contemporary music is more critical. That his concept of the ideal is now somewhat narrower is shown by his examples of "true, noble character in church music" a bold choral composition by Leonardo Leo; a through-composed choral song by J.A.P. Schulz (homophonic, with occasional unison passages and solos, interspersed with imitative entries, pathetic modula-

tions and emphatically rising melodic lines, "slow and solemn"); a duet with
figured bass from a psalm setting by Kirnberger; and Handel's aria *Er weidet seine
Herde* (He shall feed his flock). When they are song-like, pieces such as this duet
and aria are suitable for the church, but not with recitative or instrumental
accompaniment. Choral writing that is "pure and simple," arising from well-
ordered harmony—this is the true music of the church. It is significant that the
purely chordal passages in Schulz's chorus impressed him as the most suitable
for the church. Reichardt's own sacred compositions, published in the *Musikalisches Kunstmagazin* of 1782, clearly exemplify the new concept of church music.
He composed two odes by Klopstock, for four-part chorus with organ continuo,
in a chordal, metrical, declamatory style, "solemn" and "noble" *(erhaben)*. Klopstock's *Messiah* represented Reichardt's ideal of musical poetry; he reprinted an
abbreviated version suitable for composing, which was set by A. Romberg. Several other choral works by Reichardt (strophic, without figured bass) also achieve
their effects entirely through chordal writing and dynamics. He went to Italy in
1783 and again in 1790. After this, quite predictably, he regarded Palestrina as
"the greatest known composer of works in the noble, solemn church style" (1791)
—meaning, of course, Palestrina the composer of successions of consonant chords
in a slow tempo. Reichardt brought back from Italy a Mass by Orazio Benevoli
for four choirs. He showed it to Karl Fasch, who, as a result, broke completely
with his earlier style of composition and henceforth considered it his only aim
to create similar a cappella works—not for the church but for the Berlin *Singakademie,* which he had founded in 1791. But neither Reichardt nor Fasch
insisted on a Palestrina style in the narrower sense of the term. Reichardt thought
primarily of a solemn choral style, as is shown by his laudatory remarks about
C.P.E. Bach's *Heilig,* which, except for the opening arietta, consists of antiphonal, hymn-like choral singing, in the manner predicted by Klopstock (see
below). What constituted ideal choral writing remained so loosely defined that
even choruses in the *Liedertafel* (19th-century male choral society) style were
considered dignified church music.

Herder went through a development similar to Reichardt's. Both men knew
and probably influenced each other. Herder's hierarchy of poetic categories
(1766) showed the cantata in third place from the top. A cantata from this time,
Die Ausgiessung des Geistes, contains long recitatives and da capo arias. His
Auferstehung des Lazarus (1773) is dramatically conceived. Thus his early texts
for sacred music do not conform to the essential points of his later theories; the
later texts (up to 1783) come somewhat closer. He had intended to complete a
cycle of cantata texts for one year in 1780; it remained a fragment. In 1781,
impressed by Handel's *Messiah,* he accorded a higher place to scriptural texts
than to "a beautifully rhymed cantata," and he aligned himself with Klopstock's
ideal of church music (see below). In 1783 he viewed the Psalms of the Old
Testament as music primarily for enthusiastic choral singing, and he reprinted
an article by M. Claudius, first published in 1771, which praises Palestrina's
music: "Its pace is slow and full of devotion, lacking capriciousness; eyes are
steadfastly directed toward heaven; every step goes to the heart." After his stay
in Italy in 1793, Herder's views were solidified. Antiphonal "hymns of praise"

were to be the essence of church music, the foundation of which was to be choral singing of all gradations, "from the softest solo to the fullest choir, interrupted or, as it were, received, pacified, or inspired by hymns and songs." Arias, duets, and trios were secondary in importance and should not force themselves into the limelight. Recitatives must be extremely simple, short, and forceful. Church music, unlike opera, must not be dramatic, for which reason dramatized Bible stories (such as oratorical or responsorial Passions) do not belong in the church. The purpose of church music was not to be artful for its own sake or to be different, but "to move the hearts of all mankind." This did not prevent Herder, however, from considering as models not only the older Italian composers but also Handel and Bach, though he hardly could have known any of Bach's sacred music other than the published collections of four-part chorales. At any rate, Herder gradually favored church music that was predominantly choral, solemn, and based on Bible texts (especially psalm texts)—an ideal quite opposite to the concerted cantata and to the dramatic oratorio.

This view of church music in essence goes back to Klopstock, who in his ode *Die Chöre* (1767) had announced the ideal of a hymn-like choral music that does not exclude instruments but does include congregational participation through antiphonal singing. He had already said the same thing in more prosaic language in 1758, in the preface to part I of his *Geistliche Lieder*.

The third of the directions outlined above stands out less clearly; perhaps it cannot be considered as strong a movement as the two others. It is characterized only by stressing the value of fugue in sacred music.

In 1783, J.H. Knecht, who represented the chorus-oriented point of view, spoke out for contrapuntal writing, fugues and canons, in which the instruments were to be subordinate to the voices. His setting of Psalm 1 (1791) shows that he knew how to write polyphony, and the fact that he completed Bach's *Art of Fugue* (1804) also fits into this picture. However, his organ compositions (see below) do not, so that in practice his position seems to be ambiguous. Christmann, with whom he edited a chorale book (hymnbook for organists), had planned to write a dissertation against Doles on "the aesthetic value of fugal writing in church music" (1791). In 1806 Michaelis also expressed the opinion that choral writing gained in effectiveness through contrapuntal and fugal treatment. E.T.A. Hoffman (1814) likewise demanded contrapuntal work, though in the music of his idol Palestrina he found nothing but chords. Thibaut (1826) tolerated both fugal and nonfugal writing, but for him, too, Palestrina was "the master of writing in pure triads." But there also are advocates of choral style who completely reject the fugue, among them J.A.P. Schulz (see Loewe's autobiography, p. 154), Kocher (1823), Rohleder (1833), and Häuser (1834). On the other hand, Agricola (1771), a proponent of melodious style, permits fugal writing depending on the text. Kittel, too, wants to serve both: the connoisseur with fugues and double counterpoint, "untrained ears" with "pleasant and expressive melodies," which nevertheless must be written in "a true church style." In general, Kittel seems to favor "noble popularity." Against Lobe, D.K. Stein, in defending the fugue, resorted in 1831 to an argument which opposed the theory that remained current for some time: that church music should "not stoop to the masses, but rather should lift

75. Johann Adolf Hasse (1699–1783). Engraving by Lorenzo Zucchi, Dresden, after a painting by Pietro Antonio Conte Rotari.

76. Carl Heinrich Graun (1703 [1704?]–59) in an oil painting by Andreas Möller, 1752. Formerly in the Singakademie, Berlin.

77. Carl Philipp Emanuel Bach (1714–88) in a copy of the engraving by J. C. Krüger.

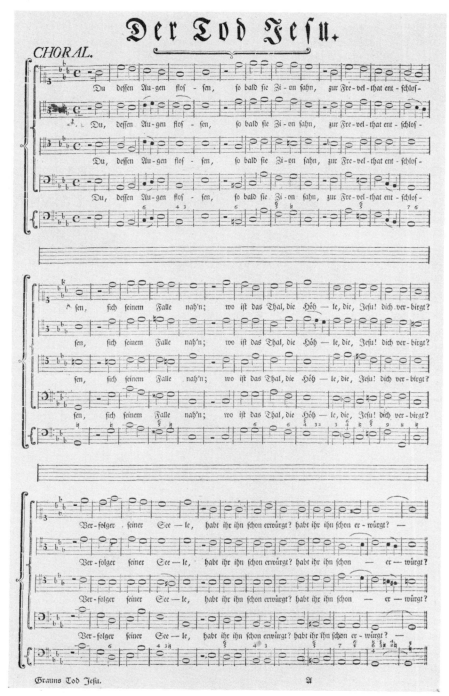

78. Carl Heinrich Graun, chorale *Du dessen Augen flossen* for four-voice chorus and basso continuo from *Der Tod Jesu,* Leipzig, 1760, Breitkopf & Härtel.

them up to its own level," thereby "making them receptive to a higher comprehension and contemplation of the divine." In this he agreed with the Hamburg musician C. G. P. Grädener, who in 1856 expressed similar views on J. S. Bach's works. The fugue was expressly tolerated by authors such as J. A. Gleichmann (1831) and Anthes (1846), who did not commit themselves to any one form of church music. Thus, among the discussions of "true" church music in the post-Bach period the concept of fugal writing does not occupy a central place, but it does maintain itself. This is in accordance with the facts: practical church composers at no time completely frowned on contrapuntal writing, though it often was merely a conventional device.

The idea of "true church music" imposed limitations of both form and content; however, the latter first became apparent only in the early Romantic period, and eventually amounted to a veritable quietism. While the broad scale of expression of the Baroque (as reflected in Telemann's church cantatas by the extraordinary variety of expression marks) had been reduced by the Enlightenment to feelings of optimism, ranging from naïve mirth to gentle melancholy, the Romantics stressed a lofty idealism in which there was a place for little else but solemn or devout attitudes of adoration.

M. Claudius believed (1771) that church music should be a "humble servant," and all possible variations on this theme were sounded in the early 19th century (especially by Michaelis in 1806, Kocher in 1823, and Thibaut in 1826, and also in some respects by Kittel in 1808, W. A. Müller in 1822, Rinck in 1824, Natorp and Häuser in 1834, and Anthes in 1846). The restoration movement adopted it sight unseen. Slow tempo, 4/4 time, uniform sonorities, reduction of the affective language to a contemplative mediocrity, an undefined generality of sentiment—these became the chief requirements. "Dignity" turned into "calmness." No wonder that Thibaut did not like Bach's St. Matthew Passion. C. P. E. Bach, Zelter, and J. N. Schelble, true children of an age that liked to criticize, did not hesitate to polish and retouch passages in Bach's vocal works. In line with Winckelmann's "silent grandeur," the Romantics rejected loud instruments. In 1834 Häuser remarked derisively that "trumpets, timpani, and fiddles could not induce feelings of devotion." Lobe (1852) inveighed against the sacred music of Bach and his time, saying that all he heard in it was "the rigid puritan, the cold Protestant, fighting for his sect with fanaticism." The more the influence of the a cappella ideal increased, the more instrumental accompaniment was curtailed (see above, concerning Reichardt). Schaum (1805) wanted to abolish it altogether; to him vocal music with organ accompaniment was the "most effective and most moving" kind of church music. A. J. Rambach (1815) likewise was satisfied with a choir of forty voices and the organ. Natorp (1817) considered wind instruments also suitable for the church, as well as the organ, as did Kocher (1823) who, along with Thibaut (1826) and others, was partial to trombones.

The one-sided views of the Romantics were challenged only in exceptional issues. In 1825 W. Ch. Müller, cathedral cantor in Bremen, wrote in the Mainz *Cäcilia* that Kocher sought "sanctity in music in what was musically naïve and limited," and that dissonance was the salt of music. "Should one wear a nightcap to listen to music?" (*Cäcilia* II, p. 141 ff.). Incited by Thibaut's book, Gottfried

Weber reinforced this criticism soon thereafter (*Cäcilia* III, p. 173 ff.), although his remarks dealt with Catholic church music.

All these movements had one thing in common: they rejected the realistic text interpretation so popular in vocal church music of the first half of the 18th century.

The anti-Baroque attitude of the generation after Bach is well characterized by C.H. Graun's statement (1752) addressed to the aged Telemann: he (Graun) sought only "to express the essential meaning of the entire passage, totally disregarding the *Expressiones* of individual words (unless this happens naturally), in order not to fall into the ridiculous" (*ZfMw* IX, 402). J. Brown (1763) found that Handel too often engaged in word painting instead of "expressing the basic affection" (Schering). Reichardt in particular advocated subjective expression in church music, as opposed to the objective tone painting of the Baroque: Handel's "brushwork", Telemann's and Mattheson's "descriptions," Keiser's "paintings," and J.S. Bach's "hunting for striking ways of expressing single words." Herder, too, demanded (1802) that church music should not provide "description" but "feeling." Following Türk (1787), organists were continually admonished to avoid the "most ridiculous allusions to the text" when accompanying chorales, especially in the interludes between the lines.

In spite of objections by the leading critics, many church cantatas and motets by lesser masters, in the 1760s and later, continued to display this kind of realistic tone painting, along with other late Baroque features, at times grotesquely exaggerated. But it was the trend of the times to turn away from this aspect of the older sermonizing church music. In the mid-19th century the opposite orientation frequently prevailed, and even correct declamation was sacrificed for purely musical expression.

In addition to the attempts toward general musical reform, there were similar efforts to reform the texts. Here also, two tendencies can be distinguished, which frequently went hand in hand: a favoring of purely lyrical poetry, and a return to scriptural or hymn texts. Both were characterized by a dislike of sermonizing cantata texts, which had set the style in the first half of the 18th century and continued in use after that time.

These, it was said, contained nothing but "run-of-the-mill thoughts, weak and unsuitable for music"; they were "frosty" (Hiller, 1768), mostly "mediocre or miserable" (Herder, 1781); they offered nothing but "dry stories, boring moral lectures, learned demonstrations" (Türk, 1787). The flood of derogatory adjectives continued, directed especially against recitatives, which were "unmusical" (1793), "didactic" (Michaelis, 1804–05), "ridiculous" (Schlimbach, 1805), "miserable, weak doggerel" (Rohleder, 1833), "cold, dogmatic preachments" (Häuser, 1834; Nauenburg, 1845). This point of view, too, the restoration movement took over unchanged from the Enlightenment. Instead, texts were to be "poetic," full of "sentiment," "pathetic," "lyric," "touching," "truly edifying," "emanating from an inspired and enthusiastic soul."

One lost sight of the *de tempore* concept and instead desired an expression of general religious thoughts and sentiments. These demands were fully realized in hymnic texts of the decades around 1800. Bible texts, especially psalm texts, were favored, though not exclusively, by Hiller (in 1767 and at other times; in 1791 he favored groupings of psalm verses), Fiedler (1790), Rambach (1815), Häuser (1834), and others. A few late adherents of rationalism very pointedly indicated their preference for poetry (Gleichmann, 1831; Nauenburg, 1845). Hiller advocated newly written song texts (1766) along with new or old hymns (1791) as textual foundations.

Along with the general ideas about musical reforms, criticism of the texts concentrated itself upon a devastating condemnation of the madrigalesque pericope cantatas (cantatas on the Scripture readings for the day), which had been in vogue up to this time. A genre that had been controversial throughout its existence was thus attacked although this existence heretofore had not been seriously threatened. But around the middle of the century many musicians also voiced their scruples concerning "theatrical style" (Mizler, 1740), Italian "lavishness" (Scheibe, 1745), and the operatic (Marpurg, 1750) in church music, thereby paving the way for disintegration of the church cantata in the second half of the century. Hiller had rejected it as early as 1769. Later (1791) he praised in its stead his own Hasse cantrafacta; if someone was not satisfied with an aria, let him add a chorale, even perhaps find some suitable (introductory) chorus. Wherever the new concept of choral style had not yet established itself, and wherever no other solutions were found, arias and fragments of oratorios now could be interpolated in the service. There was much experimentation, and the integration of church music with the rest of the service disappeared. Hiller and others were happy to welcome the *Odenmusiken* by Gräfe and J.H. Hesse (see below), along with the ornamented *(figurierte)* chorale in the manner of Doles (see below). From this, only one small step led to simple congregational singing accompanied only by wind instruments; in many churches this soon took the place of all other, more artful music (Leupold, Graff, Vieweg). By 1785 a writer could state that many cities had already done away with operatic church music (i.e., in cantata style), and that the choirs sang at most only four-part chorales, motets, hymns, and arias, to the accompaniment of organ and wind instruments (see Lott in *AfMw* III).

What the post-Bach era thought about "true" church music does not always correspond with musical reality, but it forms a useful key to its understanding. The actual developments—the suppression of the cantata, the growing vogue of the homophonic motet (in song-like or in chordal style), the estrangement of the art of organ playing from polyphony, the rise of a cappella singing, even the origin of trombone choirs—these were largely determined by the new ideas of "true" church music. To the extent that it did not attempt through historical research to revive discontinued Protestant traditions, the 19th-century restoration movement added little that was essentially new to those ideas. In this sense the restoration was a direct continuation of the period of "decline," forming an integral part of it.

THE LITURGY

In the eyes of the Enlightenment, the value of a church service depended wholly on the degree to which it was edifying. The sermon was of central importance, a fact occasionally reflected architecturally in the location of the pulpit directly above the altar. Rather than dogma, sermons laid stress on simple faith in divine guidance and on morality, occasionally indulging in sentimental sermonizing about nature, or degenerating into sober homilies on everyday, practical matters (Heussi). The liturgy was considered a concession to man's sensual, i.e., nonintellectual, nature. Klopstock, on the other hand, considered adoration and, as part of it, singing to be the essential part of the service, more so than the sermon (introduction to part I of his sacred songs, 1758); he thus anticipated a point of view that was to gain currency only later. In general, traditional liturgies decreased in importance and the service became correspondingly simpler. By the same token, the church interior no longer was to be Gothic and dark or Baroque and ornate, but light and simple, lacking "foolish frills"; walls were therefore whitewashed, in order to induce the serene, calm frame of mind expressed in the prayers of the age of Enlightenment: grateful, optimistic, full of faith in Providence. The reduction of liturgy resulted from the express desire to set aside, in the spirit of the Reformation, the veneration of liturgical or other sacred forms or traditions (Leupold). But developments were not the same everywhere; if some provinces remained conservative, others moved in all the more radical ways, especially if individual clergymen were given a free hand in liturgical matters. Often all parts of the liturgy other than the sermon were abolished, at least in theory. In practice, what frequently remained, following the example of the Reformed church, were the sermon, prayers, and hymns. In general, chanting was greatly reduced, and the chanting of pericopes was altogether abolished. At most, at the beginning of the 19th century, the Collect with versicle and salutation, only rarely the Preface, and also the Lord's Prayer and Words of Institution, were still sung. Altogether, the liturgy for Communion—now completely separated from the service with sermon—was best preserved. The lesser liturgical services, on the other hand, were abolished completely. It was one of the psychological maxims of the Enlightenment to avoid monotony, which might interfere with edification; in conformity with this belief, the singing of the Ordinary was dispensed with and hymns were substituted at the discretion of the minister. The fixed Bible readings likewise largely disappeared, thus removing the foundation for the *de tempore* cantata. The holidays of the church year, which had once provided such rich opportunities for the display of polyphonic music, were gradually abolished after 1770 or reduced in significance. A new holiday was introduced, not specifically Christian but rather appealing to general humanitarian feelings: Memorial Day *(Totenfest),* made official in 1816 by Friedrich Wilhelm III. Thus were broken up, in the liturgical as well as the social sphere, the firm foundations to which church music had previously been anchored. This was a result of a conscious use of freedom rather than of neglect. After the Seven Years' War much was written about liturgical matters, causing Graff to speak of a first liturgical movement within the Protestant church. But the force to create something new did not equal the eagerness with which old bonds were broken. Attempts to realize fully the liturgical ideal of the Enlightenment, the ideal of a stylistically unified order of service (Leupold), succeeded only outside of the state churches *(Landeskirchen)*.

The *Liturgie* of the Herrnhut Brethren amalgamated chorale verses, sung by the congregation divided into choirs, with Bible verses read by the leader of the gathering, to which the congregation occasionally made responses. With the addition of songs, arias, or motets by the choir, variety within a unified whole was achieved. Basedow adopted this liturgical plan for his *Philanthropin,* which he founded at Dessau in 1774 as a model institution for enlightened and natural education. In his *Allgemeine Gottesverehrung* (1776) hymns alternate with prayers by the leader of the service and with responsorial singing by the choir. In 1781–82 his successor, Salzmann, published his own *Gottesverehrungen;* to this was added in 1785 the *20 vierstimmigen Chöre im philanthropinischen Betsaale gesungen* of Karl Spazier, consisting of simple song-like settings, including arrangements based on models by Graun and Rolle (see Graff). "If they are sung well and at the right place in relation to the [minister's] address, and preferably accompanied by the organ only, these could be most effective," said Spazier in his *Freymüthige Gedanken* (1788) of such choruses, among which are works by Handel, Graun, C. P. E. Bach, Kirnberger, Homilius, Hiller, Wolf, Rolle, Weimar, and Neefe. Old and new Masses and old motets could also be used for this purpose, if appropriate German texts were supplied, as was done on numerous occasions in the 19th century.

In the state churches such innovations could only be realized through compromises. Nevertheless, antiphonal singing of several kinds gained a foothold there, too. Leupold credits the Enlightenment with this renaissance. He distinguishes between "hymn antiphons," "hymn responsories," and "hymn chants." The first kind, going back to Klopstock's sacred songs (1758), were still to be found in numerous 19th-century hymnals, less often in the form of new hymns written for this purpose (e.g., Christmann's *Antiphonen,* J. A. Hiller's Communion hymn in Münter's first collection; see below) than by applying this way of singing already existing hymns. Such antiphonal singing, in this instance consisting of children's choirs alternating with congregational singing, is said to have been the only kind of sacred music cultivated in Frankfurt on the Main since 1830. More elaborate forms are occasionally encountered, as in J.G. Vierling's Communion service, which combines choruses, chorales sung by the congregation, and solos. The second kind is that practiced by Salzmann, in which addresses by the minister alternate with congregational and choral singing. In the third type the minister either has the traditional intonations, to which the congregation responds with hymns, or he sings newly composed melodies with organ accompaniment, which, together with the hymn-like responses of the congregation, create the effect of an opera scene. All these seem to have been isolated experiments. A theologian of the time found the right words to describe these contradictory efforts: "It seems that our churches waver between two purposes: to be temples of aesthetic and religious edification, or to be elementary schools teaching morality to adults" (see Graff).

Insofar as the chanting of the liturgy maintained itself at all (primarily with the Lord's Prayer and the Words of Institution), it could not remain unchanged when exposed to the "enlightened" criticism of men such as Spazier. He ridiculed the manner in which the words of institution were sung, "like a monkish melody —if such dragging around of the notes within a minor third can be called melody" (1788). Some changes were gradually effected: the Lord's Prayer and the Words of Institution were modernized, following contemporary taste, often with the addition of organ accompaniment as in the Catholic church; or completely new compositions with organ accompaniment were substituted. In the first case, sentimental embellishments were introduced and, if organ accompaniment was added, the entire work was treated merely as a special form of hymn, even to the addition of interludes between lines. The first newly composed example was published in 1796. Carl Loewe and J. G. Schicht also devoted themselves to this category, in which, however, nothing of significance was produced. The earlier, recitative-like style (as in Passion settings) led to works completely in the style of hymns or songs, often extremely sentimental. Thus, this genre too had become "touching," the quality sought above all others in church music.

HYMN, SACRED SONG, CONGREGATIONAL SINGING

Church music was to edify the congregation: this point of view worked against polyphonic music and in favor of chorale singing by the congregation. To the extent that the actual state of congregational singing gave cause for complaint, its importance was stressed all the more. Many musicians (Doles, Reichardt, Türk, Hiller) now regarded the chorale as the best kind of church music; Graun's four-part settings in his *Tod Jesu* were considered models. While the aesthetes favored the chorale, congregational singing tended to be extremely poor. E.T.A. Hoffmann (1812) tried to solve this dilemma by the romantic suggestion that the choir should sing in four parts by itself and the congregation should merely read along in the hymnal. Unfortunately, the general concern for the chorale went hand in hand with an equally strong desire to reform it, so that the end result of all this was again nothing more than the notorious deterioration.

Three factors have a bearing on the fate of hymn texts during the Enlightenment: many of the old hymns were crowded out, fashionable modern poetry gained ground, and the hymns that were retained underwent modifications. There always had been some change, but rewriting of texts on a large scale was characteristic of the second half of the 18th century. In earlier times there had been effective protests also from theological quarters, but now there was agreement among those whose opinions counted, with some exceptions such as Herder and a few nontheologians like Claudius and Schubart. Congregations that had been but slightly affected by the Enlightenment frequently turned against the new hymnals—for example, the best-known *Gesangbuch zum gottesdienstlichen Gebrauch in den Königlich-Preussischen Landen* (Berlin, 1780), whose chief editor had acquired a reputation of making the most ruthless changes (see p. 258 ff.). But generally speaking, the protests were unsuccessful.

The most effective advocacy of thorough rewriting of the old hymns was presented by Klopstock, in the appendix to part I of his sacred songs (1758); many others followed his example, and such changes became the rule. As P. Sturm shows, people objected to the irregular metric structure of the old hymns, to the impure rhymes, to the liberties taken with word order, to the partial unintelligibility, to certain expressions felt to be uncouth or ambiguous, to a typical early Protestant mood of belligerence, and, in Pietistic hymns, to the spiritual eroticism. Instead, they sought clarity of expression and pious, devotional sentiment. The newly written texts, too, were for the most part unimaginative and didactic; some of them were full of tearful sentiment, "easily grasped and touching." From the theological viewpoint it is worth noting that there were more songs about a merciful God, about a humanized Jesus; that the world no longer was represented as a vale of tears nor man as a clod of earth. An optimistic view of man and the world gained ground, in which belief in original sin and the devil no longer had a place. The hope for resurrection, for meeting again in the hereafter, became prominent, but otherwise, denominational dogma was avoided; in its place, hymns about general human virtue and about nature were given more space. The chief writer of hymns during the Enlightenment was Gellert, whose poetry represents a decisive break with Baroque style. His *Geistliche Oden und Lieder* (1757), divided into moralizing "Lehroden" and *empfindsam* lieder, were enthusiastically accepted at the time. In Gellert's poetry a rational tone is prevalent, whereas in Klopstock the sentimental and the sublime are much in evidence.

Of Gellert's 54 sacred songs, 33 were written to be sung with already existing hymn tunes, but melodies had to be created for the meters of the remaining 21. Composers tackled this task at once. C.P.E. Bach was the first to set Gellert's songs, and in their entirety (1758), not as church hymns but as art songs with piano accompaniment, for devotional use in the home. His compositions were already admired by his contemporaries and, in the opinion of later critics as well, they surpass all others of his age. The Berlin Bach indeed created models of lyricism, *empfindsam* without being tearful.

Only a little later (but still in 1758) Gellert's friend Doles composed music for the 21 texts in unusual meters. These were intended for use in both church and home, and were printed in two versions: one for four-part chorus, the other for solo voice with figured bass. But his melodies, somewhat arioso-like and with too many sentimental embellishments, did not remain in favor. Johann Joachim Quantz, who otherwise did not concern himself with church music, supplied these texts with *Neue Kirchen-Melodien* in 1760, in four-part harmony, with hardly more success. His style is simpler than that of Doles, but melodically and rhythmically not as ascetic as that of C.P.E. Bach, who in 1787 once more set ten of the Gellert song texts, included in the *14 Neue Melodien zu einigen Liedern des neuen Hamburgischen Gesangbuchs*. They were now treated as sacred melodies with figured bass and were also included in some chorale books. Despite their almost monotonous simplicity, C.P.E. Bach's chorale melodies are gentle yet intense, testifying to true devotion. In 1761 there appeared settings by J.A. Hiller, who in his autobiography (1784) reports that Gellert assured him they were "just as he would have set them if he had known how to compose." His *25 neue Choralmelodien zu Liedern von Gellert* (simple four-part writing, in score) appeared in 1792. Hiller's melodies were favorably received. They display a simple, chorale-like style—tuneful, somewhat melancholy, and gentle. There are many other settings of Gellert, up to the time of Carl Loewe (1831), most of which were for home devotions rather than for church use. Among them we may mention J. Haydn's polyphonic *Du bist's, dem Ruhm und Ehre* and *Herr, der du mir das Leben*, which have often been heard in Protestant churches; also Beethoven's *Sechs Lieder von Gellert am Klavier zu singen* (1803); these, in the form of arrangements, have also been used as church music *(Die Himmel rühmen des Ewigen Ehre)*.

Among other poets whose sacred songs were repeatedly set to music, Johann Andreas Cramer, Christoph Christian Sturm, and Lavater belonged to Klopstock's school; Balthasar Münter and Uz to Gellert's.

C.P.E. Bach set *Herrn Doctor Cramers übersetzte Psalmen mit Melodien zum Singen bey dem Claviere* (1774) and *Herrn Christoph Christian Sturms . . . geistliche Gesänge mit Melodien zum Singen bey dem Claviere* (1780–81). J.Ch. Friedrich Bach from Bückeburg composed the *Zweyte Sammlung geistlicher Lieder* by Münter (1774), with melodies that are graceful and lively, though occasionally with aria-like beginnings. Earlier he had contributed to the first collection (1773), along with his brother C.P.E. Bach, J.A. Scheibe, J.H. Rolle, J.A. Hiller, E.W. Wolf, A.K. Kuntzen, G. Benda, and J.W. Hertel. He did not, however, reach the depth of expression of his brother or the well-rounded quality of Hiller. This first collection also contained new "chorale melodies." Rolle composed *Sechzig auserlesene Gesänge über die Werke Gottes in der Natur* (1775), based on a collection edited by Sturm, and in the same year published a *Sammlung Geistlicher Lieder für Liebhaber eines ungekünstelten Gesangs und leichter Clavierbegleitung* (Gellert, Funck, Sturm, Klopstock, Zachariä), in which the *empfindsam* and embellished melodies are not as popular in style as the title might lead one to expect. *Johann Peter Uzens* [and others] *lyrische Gedichte religiösen Innhalts* [sic] . . . *mit Melodien zum Singen bey dem Claviere*, composed by J.A.P. Schulz, appeared in 1784; its contents all show his great melodic talent, some resembling arias, others folk songs; only rarely are they given chorale-like treatment. His *Religiöse Oden und Lieder aus den besten deutschen Dichtern mit Melodien zum Singen bey dem Claviere* followed in 1786. Later, many of Schulz's songs appeared in Sander's *Heilige Cäcilia* (1818–19), in arrangements for four-part choice suitable for church use. The procedure had been advocated by Spazier as early as 1788. Lavater's sacred songs were also composed, chiefly by Reichardt (published 1790), either with piano accompaniment or as choruses. *Gottes Nähe* (*Musikalisches Kunstmagazin*, 1782) is an especially beautiful example.

Among Klopstock's songs, *Auferstehn, ja auferstehn wirst du* acquired the greatest fame. Set to music by Carl Heinrich Graun (1758, in the *Geistliche Oden, in Melodien gesetzt von einigen Tonkünstlern in Berlin*), it remained a beloved funeral song for a long time, and it marked a high point in the history of the sacred choral song: a noble expression of exalted *Empfindsamkeit* in a well-integrated form. Piety of this kind came closer to the spirit of the time than the congregation-oriented sentiment of the real chorale. If arranged for chorus, songs of this kind border on the choral aria (see below, *The Motet*, p. 367 ff.).

In the same way that the sacred art song made inroads into congregational singing from one direction, the spiritual folk song did so from another. According to Petrich, the latter blossomed from about 1770 to 1820, with a late flowering until 1850. The most characteristic of these songs (many of which owed their popularity chiefly to the melody) include those listed below; not all the dates are certain.

Der Mond ist aufgegangen (M. Claudius, 1779; melody by J.A.P. Schulz, 1790); *Wie sie so sanft ruhn, alle die Seligen* (A.C. Stockmann, 1780; the best-known melody is that by F.B. Beneken, 1787); *Lobt froh den Herrn, ihr jugendlichen Chöre!* (G. Gessner, 1795; melody by H.G. Nägeli, 1815); *Wenn ich ihn nur habe* (Novalis, 1799; the best known melody by K. Breidenstein, 1825); *Ihr Kinderlein kommet, o kommet doch all* (Ch.v. Schmid, 1811; melody by J.A.P. Schulz, 1794); *Du lieber, heilger, frommer Christ* (E.M. Arndt, 1811; melody by G. Siegert, 1821?); *O du fröhliche, o du selige* (J.D. Falk, 1816; arranged c.1850 to fit the melody of a Sicilian *Marienlied* that Herder had brought back from Italy); *Nach dem Sturme fahren wir (Wie mit grimmgem Unverstand;* poetry by J.D. Falk, 1816; appeared in 1822 with an allegedly ancient melody; textual and musical revision by Luise Reichardt, 1823–26; sung to other melodies as well); *Stille Nacht, heilige Nacht,* originally Catholic (J.F. Mohr, 1818; melody by F.X. Gruber, 1818); *Ich bete an die Macht der Liebe* (J. Gossner, 1825 or earlier, after G. Tersteegen; melody from a Mass by Bortnjansky, 1822); *Wo findet die Seele die Heimat der Ruh?* (L. Jörgens, 1827, after an English song; the much abused melody also of English origin); *Weisst du, wieviel Sternlein stehen?* (J.W. Hey, 1837; composer unknown, c. 1818); *Alle Jahre wieder kommt das Christuskind* (J.W. Hey, 1837; melody F. Silcher); *Harre, meine Seele* (F. Räder, 1845; melody after César Malan, 1827?); *Lasst mich gehn* (G. Knak, 1846; the melody that used to be most popular by K.F. Voigtländer, 1853); *So nimm denn meine Hände* (J.v. Hausmann, 1862; melody by F. Silcher, 1842).

These and similar songs vary greatly in value, both textually and melodically. *Der Mond ist aufgegangen,* for instance, was accepted into the new *Evangelisches Gesangbuch* (1950). On the other hand, the text of *Wie sie so sanft ruhn,* extremely lugubrious and sentimental, had already been suppressed by the Breslau Consistory in 1864 because of its unchristian content; to save the melody, which is strongly reminiscent of Graun, the text was rewritten a number of times.

Sacred folk songs generally were not concerned with matters of dogma. They served as devotional songs for the home, as Christmas or children's songs, and during the 19th century they were much in use in missionary circles and in religious societies in general. They also found their way into hymnals, at least into the appendices.

It is true that during the Enlightenment chorale melodies for the church were also written, "with true enthusiasm or at least with a purpose" (Knecht), not only by the above-mentioned composers of sacred art songs but also, in great numbers, by Knecht, Christmann, Schicht, and other authors of chorale books. Even then, some of the more perceptive critics doubted that their age was still capable of producing any melodies truly suitable for the church. Thus, it is all the stranger that the old hymns were rejected, that a need was seen for tampering with the old melodies, and that they were actually replaced with new ones. However, the changing of basic melodies was only partly due to subjective impulse; indeed, some even spoke up for the beauty of the old, unfortunately disfigured melodies. Much of the deterioration was doubtless the natural result of careless congregational singing; insofar as it resulted from modernization, it was actually furthered by musicians such as J. A. Hiller, Knecht, and Kocher. Also, the *Singechöre* and *Kurrenden,* by adding coloraturas and embellishments, hardly contributed to the preservation of the chorale's purity. Only bad things about congregational singing are reported by most sources. Most of all, the constant dragging of tempo is deplored, though originally such slow tempo seems to have been intentional (Herder, 1781; Cramer's *Mag. d. Mus.* II, 1784, p. 223; Türk, 1787; Knecht, 1799).

How slow the tempos had become during the first half of the 19th century, before the introduction of the "rhythmical" chorale, can be gathered from Häuser's recommendation (1834) to increase the tempo to ♩ = M.M. 30 (the chorale being notated in half notes). Ebhardt (1828) agrees (two pulses for one syllable; see H.J. Wagner), as does K.W. Frantz, who demands in 1848 that the half note of the chorale melody should last two seconds (see Petzold); faster singing would not have been considered sufficiently "dignified." Actually, some of the singing was even slower. A report from Baden in 1847 states that each syllable was held for approximately four pulse beats, fermatas being held 8–12 pulse beats (see von der Heydt).

Such creeping tempos were an invitation to the congregation to enliven the melody by adding ornamentation, of which Natorp (1817), Kessler (1830), and Häuser (1834) provide drastic musical examples. As late as 1859, Schoeberlein found it necessary to censure this practice. Added to this was the widespread practice of *Sekundieren,* in which the men of the congregation sang an accompanying part below the melody. Because of this, organists were urged—by Adlung, as early as 1758, J. S. Petri (1767), Ch. Gregor in the preface to his chorale collection for the Brethren churches (1784), and Türk (1787)—to use the most obvious harmonization in the accompaniment, in order to avoid harmonic conflicts. Gregor states that this practice of improvisation had existed in the Brethren churches "for a long time"; however, unlike 19th-century authors, he does not condemn it. Other 18th-century writers also tolerated it.

Attempts were made around 1820 in Württemberg to follow the Swiss example of four-part singing by the congregation. This was widely discussed and received official encouragement, but failed to take root, despite the efforts of Kocher (Stuttgart), Silcher (Tübingen), and Frech (Esslingen). An important reason for the poor congregational singing was the fact that, since the Enlightenment, the hymnals no longer contained music; thus, even musical members of the congregation were able to sing neither the correct melody nor an accepted version of it. Only the organist, with the help of his chorale book, could do this. The organists, on the other hand, were reproached for contributing to distortion of the singing by introducing arbitrary variations into their accompaniments, a practice already common throughout the 18th century (see Winterfeld and Blindow). These reproaches were also addressed to the precentors, who led the singing either by themselves or with the organist; moving on from the fermata at the end of one line to the first tone of the next, they added "a shorter or longer passage, along with mordents, turns, and other unsuitable embellishments" (Natorp and others).

Such additions apparently were in imitation of the interludes between lines that were generally inserted by organists in the 18th and 19th centuries, particularly between 1750 and 1850. The fact that chorale books from the Baroque era, and later, may not have contained interludes in no way excluded the use of improvisations. J. S. Bach supplied the first written examples. Many arguments were cited to justify this practice: that during the interludes the congregation members could read the text of the next line; that they were more likely thus to find the first note of the following line; and so on. Actually, as A. G. Ritter (1857) states, these interludes probably resulted less from congregational needs than from the organists' eagerness to play, as a relief from the boredom induced by the fermatas in melodies that moved throughout in equal note values. Well into the 19th century these interludes therefore contained traits of improvisation in toccata style. In the 18th century they were sometimes called "Passagien" or "Läufer." Not until their late stage of development did the interludes wholly assume a "dignified," chordal style conforming to the chorale itself, thereby rendering congregational singing even more monotonous. Because of the strong opposition to interludes that arose during the first half of the 19th century, they were bound to disappear in the second half—not the least reason for this being the return to favor of the rhythmically animated chorale, which was a musical entity and hence no longer in need of being patched up by organ passages; all that remained were the interludes between stanzas. Only very few of the interludes had any artistic value; usually "they were reeled off, trivial and empty, a long stretch of so-called organists' yarn" (Petzold).

"Snail-like" tempo and uniform rhythm blurred the characteristic expressive differences among melodies so that "each song of praise or thanksgiving in performance became a hymn of penitence and death" (Häuser, 1834). In vain did Knecht and Rinck try to clarify the basic mood of a song with words such as "penitent and thirsting after mercy" (Knecht-Christmann *Choralbuch,* 1799) or "with an agreeable sense of duty" (Knecht); in vain did Vierling (1789) and others demand that in general every stanza should be sung with different expression or, in the early 19th century, that congregational singing should observe dynamic shadings. It was customary to sing a great variety of texts to the same melody: in one Leipzig hymnal from around 1800, ninety-one texts are said to have been sung to the melody *Wer nur den lieben Gott lässt walten,* and in a Dresden hymnal from the early 19th century, forty used the tune *Herzliebster Jesu, was hast du verbrochen.* Such conditions reduced the number of melodies that the congregation knew; it also inevitably reduced their sensitivity to expressive differences. Yet a certain uniformity was part of the devotional concept of an age during which the "almost creeping" (Zelter) and soft singing of the Herrnhut congregation was considered an excellent model by Reichardt (1774), Kessler (1830), Häuser (1834), and Freudenberg (1851; *Aus dem Leben eines alten Organisten*).

There may be truth in the contention that a connection exists between the deterioration of congregational singing and the introduction, about the middle of

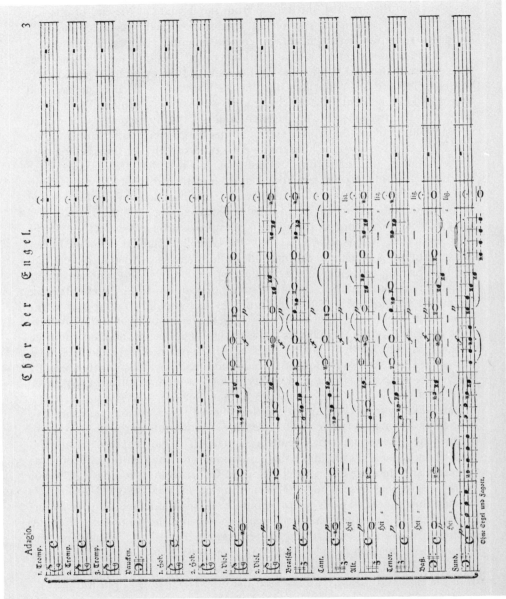

79. Carl Philipp Emanuel Bach, chorus of angels from *Heilig mit zwei Chören*, Hamburg, 1779. Published by the composer.

80. Christian Fürchtegott Gellert (1715–69). Engraving by Johann Elias Haid, c. 1780.

81. Karl Wilhelm Ramler (1725–98). Drawing in red chalk by Daniel Nikolaus Chodowiecki.

KLOPSTOCK

82. Johann Gottlieb Herder (1744–1803). Etching by Carl Pfeiffer after a painting by Friedrich Tischbein.

83. Friedrich Gottlieb Klopstock (1724–1803). Engraving by Amadeus Wenzel Böhm after a painting by Jens Juel, 1780.

84. Typical sermon church of the 18th century, the Johannis-kirche in Göttingen after its reconstruction, 1792.

85. *Kurrende-Knaben* in Hamburg at the end of the 18th century. Engraving by Frédéric Hillemacher, 1875.

86. Johann Heinrich Rolle (1716–85). Engraving by Christian Gottlieb Geyser after a painting by Jacob Adolph Fischer.

87. Gottfried August Homilius (1714–85). Engraving by Christian Ludwig Seehas, 1782.

88. Johann Philipp Kirnberger (1714–83). Oil painting by Schaupp after Christian Friedrich Reinhold (?) Lisiewski. Berlin, Deutsche Staatsbibliothek.

89. Johann Adam Hiller (1728–1804). Engraving by Christian Gottlieb Geyser after a painting by Friedrich Heinrich Füger.

the 17th century, of organ accompaniment as such. Although organ accompaniment was omitted during certain periods of the church year and at certain points in the service even until the end of the 18th century, from then on it became obligatory. This development reached its end about the middle of the 19th century. During this period organs were installed in many smaller churches that previously had been without them (though not in all churches; see Katterfeld, 1845, p. 12).

The introduction of organ accompaniment evoked the appearance of an enormous number of chorale books, to be used with the many new hymnals; this destroyed the homogeneous character of the hymn repertory. Chorale books at first contained only melody and figured bass, but with the decline of the age of continuo, and to make the books more useful for choirs, four-part settings gradually became the norm. (Some collections with figured basses lasted into the mid-19th century, but these served mostly pedagogical purposes.) Some chorale books were published for private use; others were officially introduced. G.A. Homilius, in 1767, made the first attempt to bring out an official chorale book with four-part settings, for use in the state church of Saxony, but his effort had no success with the Saxon administration. As the name of Homilius indicates, during this first period some important musicians devoted themselves to the editing of chorale books—Doles, Hiller, Schicht, and Rinck among them—whereas later on chorale books became primarily the concern of seminary teachers. The first fairly well known chorale book to appear in print was not Doles's collection (1785) but—and this is generally overlooked—a collection of four-part chorales by J.S. Bach. It was published in four sections, from 1784 to 1787, by Breitkopf in Leipzig, at Kirnberger's initiative and with a preface by C.P.E. Bach; a shorter edition had already been published by Birnstiel in Berlin, 1765–69, rather inconsistently edited by Marpurg, Agricola, and C.P.E. Bach. The chorales were taken from Bach's vocal works. Corresponding to their function in a chorale book, they were printed on two staves, but it is doubtful that they were ever used as intended. Kühnau, in the preface (1784) of his chorale book of 1786, acknowledges them to be masterpieces but considers them much too difficult. The Abbé Vogler and C.M. von Weber deplored their lack of the "noble simplicity" and even "dignity" that should characterize the chorale. During the age of restoration, early 17th-century settings were preferred to the Bach versions, so rich in dissonances. But the chorale books mentioned above enjoyed great popularity, especially J.A. Hiller's (1793) and, in southern Germany, those by Knecht and Christmann (1799), and, somewhat later, also those by Rinck (1814 and 1829). Kühnau's chorale book (1786–90), for which Kirnberger had been godfather, had gone through ten printings by 1885. Schicht's formidable collection (1819), consisting of 1285 melodies, also was highly esteemed. Hiller's chorale book most clearly reveals the enlightened taste of the time, opposed in certain respects to J.S. Bach. Eager to keep up with other reformers of the hymnals, Hiller believed that the melodies themselves also needed re-examination. He eliminated (as Kühnau had begun to do) "useless repetitions of single words or entire lines" and "unsuitable melismatic extensions of unimportant syllables." In other places, however, he added slurred passing notes. (A.C.G. Blüher's chorale book, Görlitz, 1825, also does away with "unnatural extensions.") Modal melodies are, for the most part, notated in major or minor by Hiller; of the modal characteristics he preserves only the Phrygian cadence. In this he differs from Kühnau and Doles, who preserve the old modes in at least some settings. In his harmonizations he stands for moderate progress, uses the six-four chord, and, in contrast to the "rigid" ancient masters, dotes on fluent and supple voice leading. With regard to triple time, seldom used in his chorale book or in others, he advises not to accentuate it too much in singing, since triple and dotted rhythms remind one too much of the dance. This kind of aesthetic quietism is in line with the slow manner of singing chorales. Triple time was all but eliminated, thus bringing about complete uniformity in the chorale rhythms. Major tonalities were often preferred; "the less minor the better" was the typical "enlightened" view of one contemporary.

THE CANTATA

Cantatas written by the post-Bach generations at first represented a direct continuation of tradition. Around 1750, other forms came into fashion as well, and the traditional cantata gradually disappeared. No clear distinction can therefore be made between the cantata style of the late Baroque and that of the Enlightenment. The following discussion is limited to cantata composers born after 1700.

The earliest group of composers (born 1700–06) centers around C.H. Graun: J.G. Hoffmann, J.G. Graun, G.A. Sorge, J.P. Kellner, J.K. Wagner, J.K. Simon. According to his own testimony, the Breslau organist J. Georg Hoffmann had composed several yearly cycles before 1740; these were still offered in Breitkopf's music catalogues of 1761–70 but, except for relatively few works (preserved chiefly in Frankfurt on the Main), these have now disappeared. As an admirer of Keiser, he admitted in Mattheson's *Ehrenpforte* that he had become fond of "reasonable melody" and that he let others create compositions with "harmonic difficulties," i.e., contrapuntal writing. To judge by some of his cantatas, he indeed avoids counterpoint, but without otherwise dissociating himself from Baroque conventions, including the less desirable ones. He loves noisy homophony with bustling passage work and broken chords (reminiscent of certain opera intradas by Keiser), empty figuration, and painting with strongly contrasting colors. Syncopated rhythm begins to permeate the melodic lines, and gallant triplets are much in evidence, as is the repetition of short phrases, and some characteristics of the *empfindsam* style. However, the basic Baroque orientation is sufficiently attested by the texts (by J. J. Rambach, among others) alone. According to Steinberg (1766, p. 95), Hoffmann also composed psalms.

Carl Heinrich Graun, *Kapellmeister* at the royal Prussian court, made more significant contributions in fields of church music other than the cantata. Two yearly cycles of cantatas, composed in his Dresden period (before 1725), do not, according to Hiller's biography (1784), contain the "elegant, singable, and pleasant melodies which lend such distinction to the later compositions of our Graun." Some single works which are preserved still show the Baroque style.

Among members of the next group (born 1708–11) J. A. Scheibe, G. Gebel the Younger, W. F. Bach, J. G. Röllig, and J. C. Seibert should be mentioned. J. S. Bach's oldest son, Wilhelm Friedemann, wrote cantatas while he held the position of *director musices* in Halle, 1746–64. Approximately twenty of these have been preserved, including some solo cantatas. In these works Baroque traits, sometimes strongly reminiscent of his father—polyphonic part writing with much figuration, skillful fugal writing, and realistic word painting—are mixed rather incongruously among arias with thematic material in the Neapolitan manner and songs with *empfindsam* melodic lines. The forty-seven cantatas ascribable to Johann Conrad Seibert, *Kapellmeister* of the principal churches in Frankfurt on the Main, are set to texts containing typical Baroque sentiment, which, like others of the period, are a gold mine of unintentional humor. All opportunities for the most superficial word painting are exploited to the hilt; for example, "So tröpfelte ein Gnadensegen" (The blessing of mercy dripping down) is set to an indescribable coloratura on the word "tröpfelte" (dripping). With Tag (see below) and others he shares the idiosyncrasy of ritornellos and accompaniments that strongly suggest violin concertos of the early Classic period. Seibert stands between Hoffmann and Glaser, on a line that sinks further with Wirbach and Wundsch (see below).

The nucleus of the first post-Bach generation (born 1713–17) is formed by J. W. Glaser, C. P. E. Bach, G. A. Homilius, J. F. Doles, G. G. Petri, G. S. Gebel, J. Trier, J. G. Quiel, J. H. Rolle, and J. Ch. Fischer. Johann Wendelin Glaser was cantor in Wertheim on the Main; more than 300 of his cantatas from 1744–55 have been preserved, including a few solo cantatas. According to Treiber, they are strongly rooted in Telemann-oriented Baroque traditions and as yet reveal hardly anything of the spirit of *Empfindsamkeit*. One yearly cycle, on texts of J. F. v. Holten, had appeared in Lübeck as early as 1725; another one, by J. F. v. Uffenbach, appeared the following year. Glaser's quality as a composer has, with reason, been considered quite inferior; his cantatas—to judge by a few works—must be numbered among the late Baroque's symptoms of decay.

As music director of Hamburg's principal churches (beginning in 1768), C.P.E. Bach was not as industrious as his predecessor Telemann. He wrote only a few cantatas for Sundays, apparently preferring to use cycles by the older masters—J.S. Bach, G.H. Stölzel, Fasch the Elder, and (Christoph) Förster—and also single cantatas by C.H. Graun, Homilius, and others. Compositions for Easter, St. Michael's Day, and Christmas are more numerous, especially the extensive works for the installation of a new preacher (see Miesner). His style is preponderantly *empfindsam*, with concise melodies, in a Neapolitan or popular manner, predominating. In his setting of Klopstock's *Morgengesang am Schöpfungsfeste* (1783; published 1784), a hymn about the first sunrise after the creation of the world, he rose above routine and created a model for the new type of cantata, idealistic but no longer liturgically constrained. Instead of *secco* recitative and da capo arias, there are fluid transitions, surprising modulations, and choruses that are intensified echoes of the solos. The work has a unified character that goes well with Klopstock's free rhythms.

Gottfried August Homilius, since 1755 *Kreuzkantor* and director of music at the three principal churches in Dresden, is known to have written approximately 160 church cantatas, most of which are preserved; however, a detailed study is so far lacking, although he was considered one of the best church composers of his time. His style ranges all the way from substantial choral fugues to simple, song-like duets, and he was fond of da capo arias with many coloraturas and syncopations in the reigning style. In spite of the gallant influences, Homilius's manner is noble and *empfindsam;* his part writing is clean and his declamation careful. Homilius and his Leipzig colleague, Johann Friedrich Doles (cantor at St. Thomas's since 1755, the second successor to J.S. Bach) both wrote almost exclusively for the church, and can be considered the foremost representatives of Protestant church music of their time. Homilius may have been the more profoundly talented and may have had stronger ties to tradition; Doles's cantatas (which have been investigated) are historically more interesting because of the variety of forms they employ. There are the traditional madrigalesque pericope cantatas—an almost complete yearly cycle, with the stereotyped structure: chorus (verse)—chorale—recitative—aria—chorale—aria—repetition of the opening chorus; this cycle was written during his days as cantor in Freiberg. With his 46th Psalm (published 1758) he turned to the German psalm cantata, where the text is set essentially as in an ordinary cantata, with choruses, solos (predominantly in da capo form), and recitatives. A chorale cantus firmus is usually woven into the texture, and there are some aria stanzas with freely composed texts. As a result, these works do not yet show the overall arrangement of a choral hymn. In 1766 (according to E.L. Gerber), he resumed the composition of chorale cantatas as cultivated by J.S. Bach and Telemann, with choruses, arias or duets, and accompanied recitatives. As in Bach, the movements that do not introduce the cantus firmus in its entirety will at least suggest it through motivic work. Unlike Bach, Doles does not attempt profound textual interpretation. From the late 1760s on, Doles cultivated "a new kind of church music" (Hiller), the ornamented chorale, for which, because of their instrumental accompaniment, the sacred songs by J.F. Gräfe (1760) and J.H. Hesse (I, 1766) form a point of departure. According to Hiller (1769), Doles's "chorale . . . is sung by the choir with the usual melody in four parts; the composer uses a trombone choir to reinforce it. The rest of the orchestra plays opening and closing ritornellos, and between the lines it plays several bars taken from these ritornellos, to effect the harmonic transition from one line to the next; it also fills in the harmony during the vocal portions, using only eighth-note motion." All stanzas are treated this way, without any profound text interpretation. "It was a great joy to hear the entire congregation join in the singing. Indeed, never has any piece of church music touched us so much as this one." As Doles's successor, Hiller occasionally performed chorales of this kind instead of the usual church compositions. Doles made almost two dozen chorale settings of this type. According to Schering and Banning, Doles's more than 160 cantatas (the last one, based on Gellert's song *Ich komme vor dein Angesicht,* was published in 1790) generally reflect the optimism of the Enlightenment and make use of the most accessible techniques; in the choruses the texture is homophonic (although not excluding contrapuntal devices), often relieved by solo passages; solos have short melodic phrases, but are copiously embellished; rhythms do not stray far from the basic meter but are lively, as are the tempos in general; harmony is diatonic, with many six-four chords; forms are symmetrical; texts of praise and thanksgiving are preferred.

Johann Heinrich Rolle, director of music and cantor in Magdeburg from 1752 on, also belongs to this generation. However, his reputation does not rest primarily on his works for the church but on his "Musikalische Dramen" (oratorios), written for the *Magdeburgische Concert,* which he had founded in 1764. According to E. Valentin, only thirty-seven of his cantatas are preserved, most of them for the major feast days.

The nucleus of the post-Bach generation leads into the group of those born 1718–28, with G. Benda at its center: F. Ch. Morheim, J. Ch. Altnikol, J. F. Agricola, A. C. Kunzen, J. E. Bach, Ch. G. Scheinpflug, J. K. Wiedner, F. H. Graf, J. W. Hertel, J. A. Hiller. Of the three yearly cycles (1751, 1754, 1761) that Georg Benda wrote while he was *Kapellmeister* in Gotha, a considerable number still exists, although no study of them has yet been made. The following scheme occurs frequently: choral aria—*secco* or accompanied recitative—aria—chorale —aria—repetition of the choral aria (of the scheme of Doles). Benda makes use of a great variety of stylistic devices. Along with examples of highly ornate *galanterie* (e.g., in *Vertrauet ihm,* for the fifth Sunday after Trinity), there are expressive traits of *Sturm und Drang* (e.g., in *Im Grabe wohnt ein sanfter Schlummer,* for the twenty-fourth Sunday after Trinity), and there still are many Baroque traits. Noteworthy among the works of Friedrich Hartmann Graf is a "Cantata," also labeled "Psalm," for a service commemorating the Peace of Westphalia; despite the title, it is neither a traditional cantata nor an actual psalm. Rather, it is based on a hymn-like poem and set to music without recitatives; it is predominantly choral, with solo episodes and ensembles, uniformly lyrical, and rather in the style of a lied. Individual sections offer little contrast. Johann Wilhelm Hertel also seems to look to the future rather than to the past, as his only known works in this genre are psalm cantatas (probably beginning in 1756) and cantatas on lyrical texts by J.H. Tode (1770s and 80s), written for the court at Ludwigslust (Schwerin), a center of progressive church music. Johann Adam Hiller wrote a few church cantatas prior to 1754; because of his point of view (see above, p. 323 ff.), it would have been inconsistent for him to continue to do so.

The following composers, birth dates unknown, cannot be placed more precisely: J.J. Du Grain from Danzig, in whose cantatas (some said to be dated 1737 and 1740) Rauschning finds the nobility and clarity of Gluck announced, although the examples he quotes do not quite confirm this; two other Danzig composers, J.B. Ch. Freislich and J.D. Pucklitz; the Breslau cantor Martin Wirbach; Heinrich Wundsch, music director in Blankenhahn; and also a certain Cantor Geere. With Wirbach and Wundsch the late Baroque church cantata reached its lowest ebb. In the work of Wirbach (approximately one year's cycle of cantatas has been preserved) whom Steinberg (1766, p. 95) describes as a "felicitous imitator of Herr Graun," texts such as "Es knallet der Donner der göttlichen Rache" (The thunder of divine vengeance is banging) and "Die triefenden Spuren der göttlichen Güte" (The dripping traces of divine mercy) enter into a congenial marriage with music that is utterly trivial and superficial. Wundsch's cantatas, of which about fifty are extant, are even slighter and more banal than Wirbach's, if that is possible.

A second, somewhat less substantial group consists of musicians born around 1735 (1731–38): J.G. Seifert, J.Ch.F. Bach, N.G. Gruner, E.W. Wolf, F.V. Buttstett, J.G. Kirsten, Ch.G. Tag, K. Fasch, J.Ch. Kellner, J.S. Petri. The few cantatas (from the 1770s and '80s) by the Bückeburg concertmaster J. Christoph Friedrich Bach deserve attention, since some of them are based on texts by Herder. According to Schünemann, he follows the style of his brother Emanuel. Nathanael Gottfried Gruner, cantor in Gera, chiefly wrote psalm cantatas. Franz Vollrath Buttstett, organist and cantor in Rothenburg on the Tauber beginning in 1767, composed a year's cycle in 1773, of which most of the extant cantatas show, according to H. Kern, the condensed form: chorus or solo (Bible verse)— accompanied recitative and da capo aria on Baroque poetry—final chorale. They are shallow works, lacking in counterpoint; with their obvious tone painting, the coloraturas are belated Baroque mannerisms. Christian Gotthilf Tag, cantor in Hohenstein, Saxony, stands on a somewhat higher level. Over a hundred of his cantatas are known, probably written during the 1760s and '70s. To judge by some examples, they display a somewhat superficial brilliance; perhaps for this very reason, they were much in demand at the time. Alongside the truncated form just mentioned, the normal arrangement (according to Vieweg) includes: chorus on a scriptural text—aria or duet—recitative (often accompanied)—aria—recitative *(secco)*—chorale, and there also are chorale cantatas in Doles's manner. Extreme but conventional tone painting illustrates the flowery Baroque texts as in Buttstett's cantatas. Tag's choral fugues, like Glaser's, are based on insignificant themes. Rochlitz describes Tag's cantatas as "simplified and somewhat modernized imitations of Hasse and Homilius." Among the works of Ernst Wilhelm Wolf, *Kapellmeister* in Weimar, an Easter cantata (1781) on a text by Herder was celebrated. Quite in contrast to his earlier cantatas are some later works, such as his *Der Sieg des Erlösers* (1788, text by Ch. A. Oberbeck), which in its amalgamation of soloistic (arioso and recitative) and choral sections is an example of the dissolution of the earlier "number cantata." Some cantatas by the Kassel organist Johann Christoph Kellner exist in Frankfurt on the Main, listed there under the name of his father, Johann Peter; a clear distinction between the works of the two men has not yet been made. The cantatas are simple, small, pleasant "number cantatas," displaying no profundity but also not without taste.

Any grouping of the younger composers by generations would be forced. The following composers (with birth dates given) are among those who wrote cantatas: J.G. Schwanenberger (1740), J.W.C.v. Königslöw (1745), J.G. Weiske (1746), F.L. Benda (1746), J.G. Schicht (1753), L.Ch. Dieter (1757), J.Ch.G. Eidenbenz (1761), F.H. Himmel (1765), G.B. Bierey (1772), J.I. Müller (1774), J.G. Lägel (1777), G.A. Krille (1779), Ch.Th. Weinlig (1780), C. Eberwein (1786), J.L. Böhner (1787), J.G. Meister (1793), K. Mosche (1796), C.E. Bräuer (1796), T.E. Pachaly (1797), E. Köhler (1799), H.W. Stolze (1801), E.J. Otto (1804), E.F. Gäbler (1807?), A.F. Hesse (1809?). There is disagreement about the birth date of G.P. Weimar. The dates of birth for Ch.G. Krille, W.G. Rebentisch,

J.G. Berge, Ch.F. Herrmann and N. Stössel are unknown, as are the birth and death dates for C.F. Beck (music director in Kirchheim/Teck from 1791) and C.E. Reichert.

Friedrich Wilhelm Rust, also active as music teacher at the *Philanthropin* in Dessau, devoted himself chiefly to church works after 1784. Aside from a psalm cantata, he wrote several festive cantatas for special occasions. These are progressive in style; according to Czach, they are characterized by a good sense of lied-like melody, simple harmonies, basically homophonic texture, and effective dynamics. His cantata *Herr Gott, dich loben wir* (text by Basedow), written no later than 1784, blends choruses of many kinds with solos in the manner of arias or recitatives, into a freely flowing whole, without division into "numbers." The Dresden court *Kapellmeister* Johann Gottlieb Naumann wrote much Catholic church music, but also psalm cantatas and others (with texts by H. J. Tode), for the Herrnhut Brethren church and for the court at Schwerin. In these, too (according to Leupold) the individual movements are run together, without clear boundaries. His setting of Klopstock's paraphrase of the Lord's Prayer (most of it written in 1798; performed in 1799) became famous. Each petition of the original prayer is set in a cappella style, with or without instruments, to which the second choir each time adds a chorale-like motif, sung in unison, in a different key for each petition, rising from C, by way of D, E, F, G, A, and B, to C, the key of the final fugue, *Denn dein ist das Reich* (For Thine is the kingdom). The paraphrasing interludes are both choral and soloistic, corresponding in form to the text, without da capos or recitatives, and are set in cantabile style, with many coloraturas, falling somewhere between Graun and J. Haydn; the effect, however, is somewhat pallid. The movements are all more or less run together. About a hundred cantatas by Johann Gottfried Krebs, organist and cantor in Altenburg, have been preserved (of some, only the text survives); their design is mostly conventional. Some contain attractive examples of the early Classic *empfindsam* style as applied to the Protestant Enlightenment. Of the Silesian cantor Friedrich Gottlieb Stark, who was still working on a year's cycle of church cantatas in 1793, Eitner reports that at Waldenburg (Stark's place of employment) one or the other of Stark's sacred works for soloists, chorus, and orchestra was still performed in the 1840s, before the sermon on alternate Sundays. Christian Ehregott Weinlig succeeded Homilius as *Kreuzkantor* in Dresden in 1785, and in this capacity wrote some thirty cantatas with *de tempore* indications, which already give evidence of a restriction to the major feasts of the church year. Weinlig also wrote about a dozen others without *de tempore* indications as well as psalm cantatas. His contemporaries praised him as "one of the greatest composers for the heart," but censured his later works on the ground that he "eventually fell too much in love with theatrical style," which he cultivated with bravura arias. Johann Matthäus (Matthias) Rempt was cantor in Suhl and later in Weimar; his preserved works include *18 figural- oder kantatenmässig bearbeitete Choräle mit Singstimmen und Instrumenten für verschiedene Feste und Gelegenheiten,* which seem to be imitations or developments of comparable works by his teacher, Doles. Aside from a few *concertante* cantatas in the old manner and a small psalm cantata, Daniel Gottlob Türk of Halle also wrote *Chorale für vier Solostimmen mit ab-*

wechselndem Chor, mit figurirter Instrumentalbegleitung, which are, with minor variations in pattern, similar to Doles's ornamented chorales (cf. p. 349); they comprise, all told, a round dozen unassuming, melodious works, written during the 1780s and '90s. Johann Gottfried Vierling, an exact contemporary of Türk and cantor-organist in Schmalkalden, still wrote complete yearly cycles, from which about 150 cantatas survive (35 of them in the *Stadt- und Universitätsbibliothek* in Frankfurt on the Main). They are easy to sing and could still be heard in many Thuringian village churches through much of the 19th century. The following familiar arrangement can be found, among others: chorus (hymn stanza or Bible verse)—recitative—aria or duet—chorale. Vierling's gentleness of expression relates these works to the style of Homilius, but they have a stronger tendency to simple, song-like expression. In the duets can still be found the traditional dialogues between Jesus and the Soul, which in Homilius's texts had already come close to being a secular dialogue between the Soul and Religion in one specific case. According to Kümmerle, the Nuremberg *Kapellmeister* and organist Johann Karl Mainberger wrote almost two complete Sunday cycles, but no details about them are known. In his *Wechselgesang zwischen Mirjam und Deborah* (1781; intended for the church?), based on a text from Klopstock's *Messias,* the Swabian Justin Heinrich Knecht, music director in Biberach, produced a work of progressive tendencies which used no recitatives or strict da capo forms and runs some of the movements together. In 1783 he composed a *Neue Kirchenmusik,* based on Cramer's paraphrase of the 23rd Psalm, for four voices, organ, and instruments ad libitum. The novelty here is clearly the setting of the psalm in the manner of a motet rather than cantata, and the use of a new translation. His 1st Psalm (1791), for the same scoring, also makes use of a rhymed paraphrase, probably also by Cramer. This, too, is a large motet of several sections, in a solidly contrapuntal style; the four voices are supported by an independent instrumental bass line, and tonal variety is provided by the mixture of *tutti* and solo passages. Knecht also experimented in other ways. In 1784, Cramer's *Magazin der Musik* announced (on p. 679 ff.) his year's cycle entitled *Heilige Gesänge aus den besten geistlichen Dichtern* [Cramer, Gellert, Klopstock, Schlegel, Uz, and others], *vorzüglich der Sonn- und Festtäglichen Erbauung gewidmet, und zwar auf eine vielfach brauchbare ganz neue Art, sowohl zur besonderen Unterhaltung für Liebhaber des Alleingesanges am Clavier . . . als auch für die öffentliche Kirchenmusic, mit vier Singstimmen und einer willkührlichen Instrumentalbegleitung* (two violins, instrumental bass; for the major feasts trumpets and timpani as well); these works, it was said, were suitable for both Protestants and Catholics. These may have been lied cantatas, similar to those published in the appendix of his chorale book of 1799, in which stanzas for the congregation (chorale melody) and for the choir (free composition) were alternated. Or perhaps they resembled the *ganz neue, populär gesetzte geistliche Kantaten, zur Beförderung der Kirchenmusik, vornehmlich in kleinen Orten* (1805), of which about a dozen have been preserved. (According to E. Kauffmann these latter have the following structure: solo, based on motifs of an original hymn, with chorus— short chorus—aria or duet—recitative—closing chorale.) Johann Friedrich Reichardt, court *Kapellmeister* in Berlin, turned in the 1780s to the setting of psalm texts (mostly in M. Mendelssohn's translation). Basically homophonic, with broad masses of sound, full harmonies, and expressive unison passages, these works show him to be a progressive composer. From cantatas of the older type (a *Weihnachts-Cantilene* of 1785, to a text by M. Claudius, with choruses, recitatives, arias, and chorales, seems to belong in this category), he moved on to the choral hymn as exemplified by his 65th Psalm of 1784: a succession of choral movements in which the orchestral accompaniment is for the most part not obbligato, with short solo sections in the second chorus and brief duet passages in the fifth chorus. In his almost entirely choral setting of Klopstock's ode *Dem Unendlichen* with wind accompaniment (performed in Berlin in 1807), the almost Beethovenian pathos makes one forget the feeble counterpoint. Johann Abraham Peter Schulz, as court *Kapellmeister* in Copenhagen, followed the same path with his hymns and similar works for chorus, solos (duets and trios, more than arias), and orchestra, dating from the 1790s. Thus, the hymn *Gott, Jehova, sei hoch gepreist* (text by J. H. Voss, translated from the Danish of Thaarup) has choruses in a chordal style, occasionally reduced to unisons or opened up by brief imitative passages. Between the choruses there are ensembles in the style of lied or aria and solos without a da capo section; there are no recitatives, and some movements are run together. Nineteen madrigalesque *de tempore* cantatas by Christoph Friedrich Wilhelm Nopitsch, organist and cantor in Nördlingen, are known. Probably written during the 1780s and '90s, they are based on familiar texts from the first half of the century (some of which can be dated 1738), and consist of: chorus on a Scripture text—aria—recitative *(secco)*—aria—chorale. However, the musical idiom is not at all Baroque. All polyphonic ballast has been thrown overboard, and sentimental dynamic shadings take the place of more substantial tensions. The choruses foreshadow the style of the *Liedertafel* (male choral society), with unison passages, strongly rhythmical triadic fanfares, and a popular quality in the melodic lines of the upper voices; the arias, often with abbreviated da capo, are lied-like and lack coloratura.

The change from the *de tempore* cantata, for specific occasions, to the hymn and the psalm cantata (using recent, classicistic translations) is well demonstrated by the writing of Johann Rudolf Zumsteeg, court *Kapellmeister* in Stuttgart. Fourteen cantatas of his, composed for the Stuttgart *Schlosskirche* and originally intended as part of an entire year's cycle, were published in 1801–05, along with four parodies (older works with new texts), and were widely disseminated. The psalm text usually serves for three musical numbers, which may be connected to form a simple, larger form, or through-composed in many sections. The texts, normally general expressions of praise, nondenominational and sometimes not even specifically Christian, are treated in the same way; thus, if there are distinct musical numbers the result is a strophic lied cantata, while the simplest arrangement produces a choral song. In the preferred arrangement there is a chorus (a cappella in exceptional cases)—which may be interrupted by ensembles or solos —along with arias (without da capo), duets, and trios. Recitatives appear as rarely as do the old chorales. The style is homophonic (except for an occasional dry-as-dust fugue) and ranges from choral movements in the manner of Schulz to arias in a more or less Classic melodic style while the orchestra ranges from the string orchestra to the smaller Classic orchestra. Friedrich Ludwig Aemilius Kunzen deserves mention for his great cantata *Das Hallelujah der Schöpfung* (Danish text by Baggesen, German translation by C.F. Schmidt von Phiseldeck), first performed in Copenhagen in 1796 and long popular in Germany, though primarily in the concert hall. The text is vague, ecstatic and laudatory, based on some episodes from the story of the Creation. There are solos, duets, and choruses, some of them connected, with an Alleluia ritornello and a closing fugue. Kunzen's *Hymne auf Gott* (text by Schmidt von Phiseldeck) is through-composed in a lyrical arioso style, with no clear distinction between recitative and aria. The text, not unexpectedly, is noble, optimistic, and idealistic. Ernst Häusler was cantor in Augsburg from 1800; in his *Kirchengesänge* (listed by Bopp; probably lied cantatas) the accompaniment is restricted to wind instruments, but he also wrote occasional cantatas for larger forces. In 1801 J. Ch. Ludwig Abeille, having accepted the position of *Stiftsmusikdirektor* in Stuttgart, offered to compose, over a period of time, an entire year's cycle of works for sixty-four Sundays and holidays, based on the Gospel (and thus probably traditional in form); it is not known whether he realized this plan (see Haering). Johann Friedrich Samuel Döring, a pupil of Doles and cantor in Görlitz and Altenburg, wrote chorale settings for church performances that took place every Sunday, using each of the three kinds in vogue during the second half of the 18th century. Döring describes them (1827) in the preface to his edition of four-part chorales drawn from these settings. In the first kind "the choir students sang all verses, using the sheets usually printed for this purpose. Organ and wind instruments alternated in furnishing the accompaniment, the former without the so-called interludes, the latter using now trombones, now woodwinds. . . . One or several [verses] were sung by the students alone." Certain verses called for "voices, organ, and winds, especially the first and last verses." In the second kind "orchestral music was provided in the manner of Doles's chorales—thus, in Doles's words, the treatment was *figuraliter*. But they are and remain chorales, even if there are instrumental interludes and if the singers, where possible, conclude with a coda." The listeners may sing along. The third kind is found in "actual church compositions—i.e., those which are treated in cantata style with recitatives, arias, duets, choruses, etc.—with the chorale appearing only in the first or last stanza." According to Rohleder, yearly cycles were still composed by Heinrich Agatius Gottlob Tuch, a pupil of Gruner and Doles.

In general, however, cantatas now were limited to the holidays of the church year and to special occasions, as in the case of Christian Heinrich Rinck, master organist in Darmstadt. His three *Kleine Kirchenmusiken* of 1836, for the first and fourth Sundays in Advent and for Christmas Day, are small lied cantatas for four male voices and organ obbligato, culminating in the settings of chorale melodies. In the work for the fourth Sunday in Advent the first stanza is treated as a free choral song, the second is sung to the melody *Wachet auf, ruft uns die Stimme,* with congregational participation. In his music for the first Sunday in Advent, two stanzas are free compositions in the homophonic motet style of the time, with occasional bits of imitation, and harmonized in the Romantic fashion; the third stanza is a simple setting of *Nun danket alle Gott*. The Christmas piece, smacking slightly of the *Liedertafel* style, has the same construction except that at the end is added a dictum (Bible verse), treated as a fugato but ending homophonically (a common procedure of this time). A *Kirchenmusik für das Reformationsfest* (1831), for mixed voices and organ accompaniment, might be described as chorale cantata from the end of the age of rationalism. Its central movement, the first stanza of *Ein feste Burg,* is sung in three parts, with the congregation joining in. It is preceded by a pair of newly written stanzas, the first treated as a chorale, set like the central movement, the second a free, lied-like "Chor der Kinder" (set, in the fashion of the time, for two children's voices supported by a male voice) that leads without interruption into the central movement. A different type of stanza follows, which is set as a lied-like solo, leading into the concluding chorale stanza, again with the congregation. The organ comes to the fore with preludes and interludes. The work corresponds perfectly with the ideas harbored by the Enlightenment about church music: simple and devotional, based on alternating (antiphonal) singing, with no instruments other than the organ. This ideal is reflected with similar clarity in a *Cantate zur Einweihung einer neuen Kirche* of the same year, for four mixed voices and organ. A text suitable for the consecration of a church is set as duet and solo; the first (modified) part of the German Te Deum, in a free chordal setting for the choir, serves as introduction, recurs in several places, and concludes the work. The entire piece is held together by a flowing organ accompaniment. The hymnic character is in accordance with music deriving from Mozart's "humanitarian style." In larger works, such as the cantata for the wedding anniversary of the Grand Duke of Hesse in 1827 *(Vater, wir danken dir),* Rinck uses an orchestra as well and stays closer to the traditional cantata form, although avoiding the *secco* type of recitative (in line with a demand frequently voiced at the time) and the da capo type of aria. Christian Gottlob August Bergt, organist and music teacher at the seminary in Bautzen, wrote (in the late 1830s?) his "leicht ausführbare Kantaten für die christlichen Feste"; these do call for an orchestra. He also composed two works designated as "Hymnus," and a few other published cantatas, as well as many unpublished works, including hymns, psalms, and cantatas. In his *Briefwechsel eines alten und jungen Schulmeisters* (published posthumously in 1838), Berg strongly recommends that performances of sacred music should take place "only on the major holidays, for the harvest thanksgiving, and for the church dedication festival." Forkel, let it be remembered, considered too frequent performances be among the reasons for the decline of church music. The large cantatas by Friedrich Wilhelm Berner, heard until the middle of the 19th century, represented a high point in the history of church music in Breslau, according to his biographer Eschenbach. During the first quarter of the century Berner wrote a variety of sacred works, in which the male chorus is already prominent; alongside works designated as cantatas, there are cantata-like choruses and hymns that, insofar as they have orchestral accompaniment, may be considered in the category of the "cantata"—a term that by then had undergone a change of meaning. Carl Maria von Weber's hymn *In seiner Ordnung schafft der Herr* (1812; text by Rochlitz) might also have been called a cantata by the composer. By this time, indeed, most cantatas were basically hymns; the presence or absence of independent solo sections was no longer of great consequence, since the choruses themselves often incorporated solo passages. Friedrich Schneider, composer of the *Weltgericht,* wrote real cantatas beginning in 1800, when he was a *Gymnasium* student in Zittau, but later on gave preference to psalms and hymns. Johann Friedrich Schwencke, organist in Hamburg during the second quarter of the century, wrote church cantatas with organ accompaniment. Moritz Hauptmann, cantor at St. Thomas's, composed a cantata with trombones and organ as well as *Drei Kirchenstücke für Chor und Orchester* without solos. The first of these pieces, on a prose text, contains a da capo that is freely constructed; the second is a through-composed choral song with rondo traits; the third, also based on a poem, is a fugue, framed by two essentially similar song-like structures. The poorly declaimed text serves Hauptmann merely as a foundation for the expression of musical sentiment, and the rounded form accentuates the basically lyrical character of the whole. Cantatas by Wilhelm Adolf Müller, cantor in Borna near Leipzig, are more numerous, some calling for an accompaniment by wind instruments.

As a choir pupil, Carl Loewe, the son of a small-town cantor who taught school in the morning, took care of his fields in the afternoon, and performed a work from a yearly cycle every other Sunday, had grown up in the old tradition; later, as music director and cantor in Stettin, he, too, composed cantatas. In 1837 he assembled a cycle of sacred works for all the feasts of the year (which had been composed and performed at services from 1825 to 1836) into an oratorio, *Die Festzeiten.* Conforming to conditions of his time, he indicates that accompaniment by organ alone is possible. The seven cantatas (for Advent, Christmas, Good Friday, Easter, Ascension, Pentecost, and Trinity Sunday) comprising the work give rise to the question of whether their form is the product of an uninterrupted tradition or the result of historical studies. The former was probably the basic factor, and the study of the music of Bach (some of whose works Loewe had already encountered through his teacher Türk, and whose St. Matthew Passion he had performed in Stettin in 1831) probably gave rise to a historically oriented stylization. In Loewe's works we can see especially clearly the cantata's eventual return to its first stage of development. As in the period before Neumeister, all recitatives are biblical, not madrigalesque. Those parts of cantatas based on new texts have stanzas of like form, as in the 17th century, rather than sections with varying verse schemes as found in the 18th century. Reminiscent of the early cantata types, whose nucleus was an ode of several verses set as an aria sung by the solo voices in alternation, is the form of Loewe's Advent cantata, in which the instrumental introduction is followed by song strophes presented alternately by the solo voices and finally by the solo quartet; these are separated by verses from the Prophets sung by the chorus, and followed by a series of scriptural quotations and a closing chorale. Loewe's practice in this work and in the others (especially the Good Friday cantata) of connecting most of the sections (some of which are quite short) is in line with historical development, but also points back to the earlier church cantata. Some of these latter types restricted themselves to settings of biblical texts exclusively (Gospel, Epistle, the Psalms, verses from the Prophets), or of biblical texts in connection with chorales. Such treatment, as well as the frequently motley and formless mixture found in can-

90. Johann Abraham Peter Schulz, opening of the four-voice motet *Vor dir, o Ewiger.* In J. F. Reichardt, *Musikalisches Kunstmagazin*, Berlin, 1782. Published at composer's expense.

91. *Wir glauben all' an einen Gott* from Johann Adam Hiller, *Allgemeines Choral-Melodien-Buch.* Leipzig, 1793. Published by the composer.

92. Johann Philipp Kirnberger, *Wer nur den lieben Gott lässt walten* from the collection of varied chorales on two and three systems, autograph. Berlin, Deutsche Staatsbibliothek, Amalienbibliothek 396.

93. Gottfried August Homilius, opening of the four-voice motet *So gehst du nun, mein Jesu, hin* (November 29, 1762), autograph. Berlin, Deutsche Staatsbibliothek.

94. Johann Ludwig Krebs, opening of the chorale arrangement *Was Gott tut, das ist wohlgetan,* autograph. Berlin, Deutsche Staatsbibliothek.

95. Johann Friedrich Reichardt (1752–1814). Engraving by Johann Anton Riedel (1814) after a painting by Anton Graff (1794).

96. Johann Gottlieb Naumann (1741–1801). Engraving by Gottlieb Wilhelm Hüllmann after a painting by Crescentius Seydelmann.

97. Carl von Winterfeld (1784–1852) in a contemporary lithograph.

98. Philipp Spitta (1841–94) in a photograph c. 1875.

tatas around 1700, also can be found in the cantatas of the *Festzeiten*. Nevertheless, in those frequent instances where the biblical text is molded into rhymed or
unrhymed verses and drastically shortened, primarily in order to permit a lied-
like treatment, the spirit of rationalism is felt more strongly than that of the 17th
century. The only da capo aria (its first part containing a da capo of its own) is
an inheritance from the 18th century, to which Loewe is indebted in other ways
as well: in his counterpoint, which is typical for the organ writing of Bach
followers; in his "bassus continuus" (the term used by Loewe: a bass line consisting of running eighth notes); in his settings of choral arias (one of them even in
da capo form); and in his Classicist fugal technique (with occasional Baroque
flourishes). Other elements belong to the late 17th century as well as the 18th:
the combination of verse and chorale (the verses assuming the function of interludes between lines); the line-by-line imitation found, for instance, in the *turba*
choruses, declamatory rather than melismatic in the older Italian manner; the
oratorio-like style of the recitatives. The accompaniment, if considered as organ
accompaniment, fits in with the general picture of early 19th-century organ
music, and that period's chorale-prelude style is reflected in the chorale arrangements using only fragments of the cantus firmus. The choir of angels from the
Ascension music (solo quartet for high voices, without instruments, Grave, "to
be sung from a distance") is clearly indebted to the a cappella ideal of Romanticism, while in the Easter music, epic style and direct discourse are mixed and
combined into a lyric unity, recalling the style of Loewe the composer of ballads
(whereas in the other cantatas we are more aware of Loewe the cantor). In spite
of much counterpoint, the general tone of the *Festzeiten* is popular, relating it as
much to similar trends in the 17th century as to the Enlightenment. Some other
cantatas by Loewe deserve mention; a short Christmas cantata (1826) and several
others preserved in manuscript, among them some fragments. Among his oratorio-like works, parts of the biblical scene *Die Heilung des Blindgeborenen*
(organ or piano accompaniment only; published in 1860) were intended for the
service as well. Karl Ludwig Drobisch, like Loewe, wrote a *Sammlung von
[5] Kirchenkantaten nach Worten der heiligen Schrift* (1844 ff.) entitled *Die
Festzeiten* (see also above, concerning Bergt). Though Drobisch wrote primarily
for the Catholic church, he was for a time director of Protestant church music
in Augsburg.

With Felix Mendelssohn-Bartholdy's cantatas, the history of the post-Bach
cantata reaches a kind of conclusion. Three of his five psalm cantatas (written
between 1830 and 1843) and the vocal parts of his symphony-cantata *Lobgesang*
(1840) are among the best achievements of the time, both in musical form and
in the exploration of the possibilities of timbre. Many of the movements are
connected and there is little recitative; two of the cantatas are entirely choral.
While Berner, Lägel, and others had used free poetry and an occasional chorale
for such hymnic works, and while Loewe had mixed three types of textual
material, Mendelssohn used pure psalm texts in Luther's translations. Only for
the 115th Psalm, set originally to the Vulgate text, did Mendelssohn make his
own translation; the *Lobgesang,* based on freely chosen Bible passages, contains
one chorale. Mendelssohn scorned the da capo aria in favor of lied-like construc-

tions. These works are resplendent, though occasionally they also depict God's wrath (final portion of the 95th Psalm) and His fearful might (the wondrous deeds of the 114th Psalm). There are some fugues. Mendelssohn also wrote five chorale cantatas (unpublished, between 1827 and 1832) to which R. Werner called attention in his monograph. The hymn forms the sole textual foundation (in one instance there is also a connecting Bible verse, set as recitative). With the exception of one purely choral work, however, the stanzas do not always adhere closely to the chorale, being sometimes only loosely related to the melody, and more often freely composed in the traditional manner. Choruses (cantus-firmus settings, chorale fugatos, simple chorale settings, and free movements) alternate with lied-like solos. In the movements with more complex cantus-firmus treatment, there is a conscious reaching-back to J. S. Bach, and hence a clean deviation from the traditional style. At times this historical orientation is a bit too obvious; for example, the chromatically rising tetrachord in the second stanza of *Ach Gott vom Himmel sieh darein* could just as well occur in Scheidt or J. S. Bach. The historicism that can only be presumed in Loewe's *Festzeiten* is a certainty in the chorale cantatas of Mendelssohn, who, as a product of the Berlin *Singakademie,* had originally been exposed to church music through learning rather than through practical experience.

With Mendelssohn's works we may conclude our attempt to survey the cantata literature after Bach. It is true that in the later 19th century some further cantata-like works were written to maintain the tradition, but they played a subordinate role. The needs of those congregations in Saxony and Thuringia that continued to demand, at least on holidays, a cantata, a *Kirchenmusik,* or a *Kirchenstück* were met with limited means, since cantors frequently had at their disposal only the "most curious combinations of instruments"—more usually a wind accompaniment consisting of one flute, two clarinets, two horns, one or two trumpets, one tenor horn, and one trombone (according to Frankenberger, 1854). Larger works resembling cantatas were also written, especially the many psalm cantatas following Mendelssohn's, but as a rule these were not intended for the service. Mendelssohn's historically oriented attempt to bring back the chorale cantata was not taken up by others until the end of the century, when the reformation of church music "on a historical foundation" was attempted. (See p. 376 ff., *Restoration.*)

PASSION, ORATORIO, MASS, TE DEUM, MAGNIFICAT

The Passion oratorio and the oratorio in general occupied a lesser place in church music than the cantata. Their cultivation is not a precise indicator of the vigor of church music activity, for while they formed the high points, they were also the exceptions among musical events of the church year. The oratorio, furthermore, represents sacred concert music more than liturgical music.

Generally significant for the development of Passion music after Bach was the fact that a reading of the Passion text by the minister, interrupted by the congregation's singing of chorale verses, often replaced the dramatic responsorial Passion, and also supplanted the oratorical Passion (the form of Bach's Passions). The responsorial Passion was felt to be unedifying; in those places where it had been maintained, it was now abolished, sometimes even forbidden. It remained alive in only a few villages, although it was performed in these places even in the 19th century. The central position was now held by the lyrical Passion oratorio, especially its smaller variant, the Passion cantata. A principal reason for the decline of the oratorical Passion was the dislike for the realism of the biblical account of the Passion. Rather vague paraphrases were preferred, in which the story of Christ's suffering was presented only indirectly, through its effect on the "weichgeschaffnen Seelen" (text of an aria in Ramler's *Tod Jesu*) of an *empfindsam* age. This was considered more edifying than a direct, "theatrical" representation of events and persons. Sentimentality is the outstanding trait of those Passion cantatas, of which K. W. Ramler's text, *Der Tod Jesu,* is the best known example. The text was composed repeatedly; C. H. Graun's version (1755) is the most convincing one. At the time Mendelssohn presented Bach's St. Matthew Passion to an astonished public in 1829, the setting by Graun, the "favorite singer of his nation" (Reichardt, 1774), enjoyed the position later taken over by Bach's work. The popularity of Graun's Passion faded gradually, to the point where today it is considered—wrongly—the prime example of the deterioration of church music after Bach. A work that delighted connoisseurs and amateurs for almost a century cannot be that bad, and it is not. The choruses are often strongly expressive, and all are extremely well written; it is understandable that they were considered models of fugal writing in the second half of the 18th century and even later. The arias display florid, sometimes (as in *Singt dem göttlichen Propheten*) sumptuous bel canto writing, but also genuine sentiment. Only the occasionally stilted text detracts from the work's longest admired feature, the recitatives interspersed with arioso passages. Despite Graun's motto, "No unnatural difficulties should be introduced except for very good reasons," the display of craftsmanship is considerable.

There are many other Passion oratorios (or Passion cantatas), since most cantata composers interested themselves in these genres as well; among these the following are best known: *Die letzten Leiden des Erlösers* (text by Luise Karsch) by C.P.E. Bach (written 1770); *Die letzten Stunden des leidenden Erlösers am Kreuze* by E.W. Wolf (written before 1783); *Die Feyer des Todes Jesu* (Niemeyer) by J.H. Rolle (1783); Rosetti's *Der sterbende Jesus* (1785–86, text by Zinkernagel); *Christus durch Leiden verherrlicht* by Ch.G.A. Bergt (reviewed in 1814 by E.T.A. Hoffmann); and *Das Ende des Gerechten* (Rochlitz) by J.G. Schicht. According to Kretzschmar, Beethoven's *Christus am Ölberg* (1803) also was frequently performed in the Protestant parts of Germany. As late as the first half of the 19th century, in some of the bastions of church music such as Leipzig, Passion oratorios were still performed in the service as well as in concert (see F. Schmidt). The growing familiarity with J.S. Bach's St. Matthew Passion (the score was published in 1830, edited by A. B. Marx) inhibited the writing of new Passion settings and influenced the form of many new works, either directly or indirectly (through Mendelssohn's *Paulus*). Slowly but surely the St. Matthew Passion became the absolute ruler of the field, even though performed only on the concert stage. Next to it only a few new compositions entered the repertory, for varying lengths of time: *Des Heilands letzte Stunden* (Rochlitz; the same text as for Schicht's *Das Ende des Gerechten*) by L. Spohr (1835); *Gethsemane und Golgatha* by F. Schneider (1838); F. Kiel's *Christus: Oratorium aus Worten der heiligen Schrift zusammengestellt* (1871–72, published 1874), which deals primarily with the Passion; the *Passions-Oratorium nach Worten der heiligen Schrift*, Op. 45 (with *testo*), by F. Woyrsch (vocal score published 1899). Ferdinand von Roda's *Das Leiden und Sterben Jesu Christi: Ein Passionsoratorium in zwei Teilen, nach Worten der heiligen Schrift zusammengestellt* (performed in 1865) shows the influence of the St. Matthew Passion especially clearly, in specific ways such as the chorale treatment as well as in the overall form.

Next to Passion oratorios, Resurrection oratorios and Christmas cantatas enjoyed special popularity because the subjects lent themselves to hymnic or pastoral treatment. For these, too, Ramler was one of the principal poets. Among the settings of his *Auferstehung und Himmelfahrt Jesu,* the one by C.P.E. Bach deserves mention (1777–78, published 1787). It strives for gripping dramatic effects reminiscent of Handel, but is—in contrast to his *Israeliten in der Wüste* —melodically weak, and most of its choruses do not measure up to Graun's *Tod Jesu*. Of the numerous settings of Ramler's Christmas idyll *Die Hirten bei der Krippe zu Bethlehem,* the most noteworthy was the one by Carl Westenholz (published 1774; said to have been performed as early as 1765); Türk's composition (published 1782) was also popular. The chorales found in these indicate loose ties to the church which were severed during the 19th century, though chorales continued to be included in oratorios for concert purposes, to create a churchly atmosphere.

After coming to a standstill at the beginning of the 19th century, the oratorio changed from the idyll of the sentimental second half of the 18th century to follow new paths in the works of B. Klein, F. Schneider, Spohr, Loewe, and especially Mendelssohn. By the late 19th century, the sacred oratorio had been superseded by the secular oratorio and cantata. However, this development need not be discussed here, for it was primarily related to the musical festivals of the middle class.

The Protestant *Missa brevis* (Kyrie and Gloria), used on high feasts, all but lost its reason for existing with the curtailment of the liturgy; its use of Latin was a further handicap. As a result, the writing of Masses was substantially reduced in the second half of the 18th century.

The following composers should be mentioned: J.G. Harrer, C.H. Graun, W.F. Bach, J.F. Doles (in some of whose Masses chorales appear as cantus firmi), Georg Benda, J.E. Bach (who contributed a *Missa super cantilenam "Es woll uns Gott genädig sein"*), J.A. Hiller (who wrote single Mass movements), Ch.G. Tag (seven of his eleven short Masses have been preserved), and J.G. Krebs (Masses in which the Gloria is abbreviated or omitted). The German Sanctus was composed more frequently, and its liturgical melody is also found occasionally in cantatas (e.g., Homilius). C. P. E. Bach's *Heilig, mit zwey Chören und einer Ariette zur Einleitung* (1776, published 1779) has already been mentioned as one of the most significant works of its time. It is a free setting of the German Sanctus, coupled with the first two lines (text and melody) of Luther's German Te Deum, which makes an effective appearance in the long and dashing final fugue. The work begins with an arietta to a free prose text with an obbligato by the first violin, after which the entrance of the "chorus of angels," mysterious and modulating through remote keys, and the "chorus of the people," loud and tonally clear, creates all the more magnificent an effect. Karl Fasch's previously mentioned *Missa brevis* for four choirs and continuo (1783–88) also enjoyed deserved fame. It mixed features of the old Italian and of the *empfindsam*-melodic style into a work whose texture is varied by numerous changes from *tutti* to solo; this work, however, was not composed for liturgical use. Paraphrases of a German Kyrie and a Sanctus taken from Zumsteeg's earlier Latin Masses eventually appeared as cantatas. Until the mid-19th century (according to Kretzschmar, F. Schmidt, and Rohleder) and even later (see *MfGkK* II, 282), Mass movements were performed liturgically on major feasts in Saxony, Thuringia, and Silesia. These works were not only taken over from the Catholic repertory but also newly composed (nine Masses by Bergt). Nevertheless, Protestant composers of the 19th century (L. Spohr, F. Schneider, M. Hauptmann, A.E. Grell, E.F. Richter, Schumann, R. Volkmann, F. Kiel, F. Draeseke) usually wrote complete concert Masses (instrumentally accompanied or a cappella, including some for male voices) and concert Requiems (R. Schumann, F. Kiel, and others), which no longer have anything to do with Protestant tradition. This fact is not altered by F. Draeseke's use of a Protestant chorale cantus firmus in his skillfully written but not very rewarding Requiem in B minor, Op. 22 (written 1865–80). A unique interpretation of the Requiem concept, later imitated, exists in Brahms's *Deutsches Requiem nach Worten der hl. Schrift* (written 1861–68), whose textual content, according to Schering, had been anticipated in Hermann Küster's oratorio *Die ewige Heimat* (1861) and (with less formal similarity) even earlier in F.W. Markull's oratorio *Das Gedächtnis der Entschlafenen* (1848). Without any ties to dogma and without any Protestant chorales it expresses in most general form the thoughts of the *Totenfest* (Memorial Day) which had been introduced during the Enlightenment. It is a sublime work of art within the Christian realm of experience, but it is not church music. During the 19th century its performance in the Bremen cathedral was allowed only with a specifically Christian interpolation— usually Handel's *I know that my Redeemer liveth* (see Hernried).

The Te Deum was cultivated in two musical forms, either as a festive instrumental addition (brass and timpani) to the Lutheran *Herr Gott, dich loben wir* or as a polyphonic setting of the Latin text with orchestral accompaniment. Settings by J.L. Albrecht (Berlin, 1768) and J.Ch. Kuhnau (c. 1784) represent the first type; the second is shown by Hasse's compositions (best known is the Te Deum in D major of 1751, which was also used in Protestant churches) and those of Graun, whose Te Deum (1757) for the victory of Frederick the Great at Prague became justly famous. The chorus *Tu ad dexteram Dei sedes* resembles the *Hallelujah* from Handel's *Messiah*. A duet in E major, *Te ergo quaesumus,* stands out, with its noble, cantabile quality, from among other solo movements of unequal merit. C.P.E. Bach added trumpets and timpani to the orchestra. Hasse's Te Deum is lighter and has more fire. With its three-movement arrangement in the manner of an Italian sinfonia, its fugue-like ending, and a beautiful repeat of the beginning, it achieves great effects with modest means. Many 19th-century composers continued to occupy themselves with the writing of Te Deums.

Among Magnificat settings with orchestra special mention must be made of one by C.P.E. Bach (1749). The style of this noble work is closer to Hasse than to J.S. Bach. It achieves its effect mainly through a magnificent "Amen" fugue and through a second version, harmonically bold, of the *Et misericordias* (found in the appendix of the Simrock edition, publisher's no. 2758), as well as through the beautiful duet *Deposuit potentes*. During the 1780s Homilius wrote numerous a cappella Magnificat settings of a liturgical nature. This text was still set occasionally in the 19th century.

THE MOTET

As instrumentally accompanied church music declined, in accordance with changing views, there was a corresponding increase in the writing of motets and choral songs. Literally countless motets were written in the course of the 19th century. Except for those of Brahms, hardly any are sung today, certainly not by leading choirs. The same applies to works from the second half of the 18th century, though some of them deserve a better fate.

A representative sample of motet writing after Bach is offered in the collection *Vierstimmige Motetten und Arien in Partitur, von verschiedenen Componisten, zum Gebrauche der Schulen und anderer Gesangsliebhaber gesammelt und herausgegeben von Johann Adam Hiller* (six parts, Leipzig, 1776–91; the sixth part is entitled *Vierstimmige lateinische und deutsche Chorgesänge, zum Gebrauch der Singchöre in Kirchen und Schulen*). By and large the quality of the music grows less from the older to the more recent composers included. The highest level is represented by C.H. Graun and Homilius. Also included are Harrer, Fehre, Ch. Wolf, J.F. Doles, J.H. Rolle, J.A. Hiller, Ch.G. Tag, Ch. F. Penzel, J.G. Weiske, a certain "Häsler" (J.W. Hässler?), Ch.G. Neefe, and "Kaiser," said to be the Kayser with whom Goethe was acquainted. Among older masters we find Gallus (*Ecce quomodo moritur justus,* a piece traditionally sung at services for the dead; here with many changes by Hiller), Caldara, and Th.Ch. Reinhold. Graun's motets are based on biblical texts; one of them *(Lasset uns aufsehen auf Jesum)* is a movement from a Passion without the original instrumental accompaniment. The three others may also be arrangements. Such motet arrangements are occasionally found at this time—for example, by Homilius and Rolle. In some cases the arrangement may have been by the composer, in others not—a factor to be considered in evaluating these works. All four pieces by Graun are distinguished by the combination of solid contrapuntal work with good vocal writing; there are some substantial fugues.

Almost 60 motets written after 1755 can be attributed to Homilius, including several choral arias; most of them are extant. Characteristic of him are motets in one movement, based on Bible verses (so-called biblical proverb motets), with a suitable chorale cantus firmus (not always in the soprano) sung simultaneously, line by line. This technique had already been employed in motets from Thuringia in the second half of the 17th century and the first half of the 18th. With Homilius these movements take on an expressive, homophonic style, sometimes interspersed with imitation, at other times reduced to a parlando. Thus the three lower voices might sing, "Herr, lehre uns bedenken, dass wir sterben müssen," while the discant presents the lines of the chorale verse "Wer weiss, wie nahe mir mein Ende" in even note values with pauses between the lines. The *Unser Vater,* one of the motets without chorale, was written before 1770. With its final fugue it is a remarkably expressive work. The spirit of *Empfindsamkeit* also dominates Homilius's choral arias (a category that enjoyed great popularity in the second half of the 18th century), though in his case the sentiment is noble. His successor, Christian Ehregott Weinlig, it was said (by a contemporary who knew both composers), "turned the familiar choral airs into street ditties."

In contrast to the mild and intimate manner of Homilius, J.F. Doles and J.H. Rolle were more concerned with effects. This manifests itself in the constant changes between solo and *tutti* sections, through which Doles at times achieves startling results. His 35 motets (including 15 for double choir) are characterized by Schering as being for the most part "light and bright, like the whitewashed rooms in churches of the Enlightenment." Most of them contain a chorale either interpolated between biblical or free texts, or appended to them. When using Bible verse and chorale simultaneously, Doles's procedure is opposite to that of Homilius: the chorale is sung polyphonically, in even notes and with caesuras between lines, while an ornamental solo voice, singing a biblical text, embroiders the lines of the chorale. He first used this effect in his psalm cantata printed in 1758, and then he continued to use it ad nauseam. He also made use of another technique: the lines of the chorale are sung in four parts and interrupted by a Bible verse also set in four parts. This procedure had occurred in the works of Harrer, his predecessor as cantor at St. Thomas's. Sectional motets for double choir frequently end with a fugue. Doles's only pure chorale motet, *Ein feste Burg,* enjoyed the greatest popularity and was still reprinted in the 20th century.

Sixty motets by J.H. Rolle are known. They were widely used in their day; in Magdeburg, the scene of his activity, they still were sung in the last third of the 19th century. Many use psalm texts, and a few, like those of Homilius, have a chorale cantus firmus. Mostly owing to a lack of figuration, his fugues break down into chordal sections with a penetrating, sustained six-four chord in major usually in the final cadence. Generally speaking, his writing is skillful but also, in spite of a few fascinating passages, coated with a glossy superficiality.

A funeral motet, *Alles Fleisch ist wie Gras,* is outstanding among J. A. Hiller's motets. Two contrasting sections are followed by a simple chorale setting. The polished writing that anticipates Mendelssohn, frequently with homophony in gallant style, characterizes his Latin responsories for the Vesper Psalm *Deus in adjutorium* and his choral arias, which consist of several stanzas. Among these, aside from funeral songs, exists a German *Stabat Mater (Hymnus),* "to be sung by the choir during Communion, with feeling." Fugal writing does not seem to have been Hiller's forte, to judge by some crude attempts in one of the biblical proverb motets. Most of Ch. G. Tag's motets are lost, though one well-written proverb motet in contrapuntal style is known. Nevertheless, with his choral writing we enter the age of the *Liedertafel* style, if such a term may be used for mixed choruses, and before the vogue of the *Liedertafel*. Extreme sentimentality is coupled with the pathos of unison writing and solo entrances by bass or tenor, whose long sustained tone may elicit a forte entrance by the other voices. The beginnings of this *Liedertafel* style are already found in a *Geistliche Ode* for three voices (1768, in Hiller's *Wöchentliche Nachrichten* . . . II, 374) by the young Christian Gottlob Neefe, the teacher of Beethoven. Later on, Neefe continued to develop this style. Rolle sometimes writes in a similar vein. Because of its style, a chorale motet in one movement on Gellert's *Wenn Christus seine Kirche schützt* holds a place of distinction in Hiller's collection (II, 1777). Christian Friedrich Penzel, the composer, had acquired a thorough understanding of Bach's style: while he was prefect of St. Thomas's choir in Leipzig, he devoted much time and effort to making scores of Bach cantatas. What he had learned in the process he put to use more faithfully than had Bach's actual pupils. The cantus firmus *(Ein feste Burg)* is introduced polyphonically, in anticipatory imitation; it moves, line by line, through the four voices until near the end of the piece, where the procedure is discarded. Schering has already pointed out that the initial motif is borrowed from the fifth movement of Bach's cantata BWV 80. The principal Bach traits are the dissonant, contrapuntal writing and the forceful manner that is neither gallant nor *empfindsam,* both of which set the motet apart from other numbers in the collection and from Penzel's own choral arias on Cramer's psalm lieder.

A manuscript anthology (*Stadtbibliothek* Lübeck, A 327), probably used for special occasions and singing processions, holds some insights into the singing of motets and choral arias in Lübeck at the end of the 18th century. The names of Neefe, Weimar, Graun, Tag, Rolle, Gebel, Reichardt, J. G. Krebs, and others appear; most of the pieces are anonymous. They consist of several types: biblical proverb motets in one movement with added chorale cantus firmus in the Homilius style, some with choral arias added; motets in several sections on texts from the Psalms and Song of Songs in which one section may be combined with a chorale cantus firmus as before; choral aria combined with chorale cantus firmus; biblical proverb motets combined with chorales in the Doles style; a psalm motet in several sections with a final chorale; a pure biblical proverb motet; motets based on two Bible verses with an aria between; a choral aria in rondo form; and, especially, simple choral arias on texts suitable for funerals, for occasions of praise and thanksgiving, on moral questions, on nature, or other subjects, some of them completely secular. The substantial number of cantus-firmus motets confirms a remark by Doles in 1790 that pieces of this kind were much in demand. There is frequent change from *tutti* to solo sections. The general level is considerably below that of Hiller's collection.

A similar manuscript collection of motets and choral arias was compiled in Berlin, probably between 1790 and 1810 (*Westdeutsche Bibliothek* Marburg, Mus. MS 30153). As usual, some of the arias have a da capo, others do not; some have several stanzas, and some have the following sequence: aria 1—aria 2—aria 1 da capo. Many of the motets combine Bible verses and chorales in Homilius's manner (but some of them with the cantus firmus in two voices); in one motet by Rolle (J. H.?) the Bible verse is treated in an exceptional manner, as a fugue. In a few motets the lines of a chorale alternate with a Bible verse, resembling Harrer's technique. The following other forms occur: Bible verse—aria—verse da capo; Homilius's combination—aria with da capo—Harrer's combination; a purely scriptural text (a Latin psalm in one case), either in several sections or as an introduction and fugue; a simple chorale setting—Bible verse—aria with da capo—verse da capo. Composers listed by name include a certain Ulich, a certain Schweinitz, Tag, Reichardt, and, principally, Rolle. Many works are anonymous.

Vier Motetten und vier Arien für Singechöre by "A.G." Fischer (said to be Michael Gotthard Fischer) date from about the same time, published about 1808. The arias are short strophic songs expressing no specifically Christian content. Characteristically enough, the only religious concept is that of resurrection. In spite of the indication that they are "especially suitable at times of death" the musical style is serene, even cheerful in a secular way. The motets contain rhymed poetry or Bible verses in two sections, the first chordal and arioso, and the second fugal. There are also settings of hymnic prose texts dressed up with bombastic homophony, and a piece using Homilius's typical combination with a short fugal ending.

Hiller's collection was representative chiefly of the Saxon school, to which one might add J.L. Krebs (two large motets in conservative style) and composers from Thuringia such as Johann Ernst Bach of Eisenach, and the Erfurt cantor Georg Peter Weimar. The collection *Die Heilige Cäcilia. Lieder, Motetten, Chöre und andere Musikstücke religiösen Inhalts. Herausgegeben . . . von J.D. Sander* (Berlin, 1818–19), on the other hand, clearly reflects the Berlin environment. Most of the composers included were no longer living then: C.H. Graun, Ch.F. Schale, Kirnberger, Karl Fasch, J.A.P. Schulz, J.F. Reichardt. Among living composers we find M.S.D. Gattermann, K.F. Zelter, J.D. Sander, F.L. Seidel, B.A. Weber, K.F. Rungenhagen, and J.Ph.S. Schmidt. Johann Philipp Kirnberger, who in theory advocated the cause of his teacher J.S. Bach, in practice stands closer to C.P.E. Bach and Graun, as is shown by his few but remarkable psalm motets. (However, his Latin motet on the 122nd Psalm is written in the Palestrina style of continuous imitation, which is not typical for the Protestant motet of this period.) By adhering to the continuo, which by this time had been generally discarded, Kirnberger shows himself to be conservative. The motet *Erbarm dich unser Gott!* (in the *Kunst des reinen Satzes* II/3, 1779) is based on M. Mendelssohn's watered-down translation, mostly of the 51st Psalm. Its several short sections contain solos and a lied-like duet, thus approaching cantata form. Karl Fasch attempted a development of the chorale motet in his ornamented chorales (cf. p. 353); the term refers to variations of the cantus firmus and the accompanying voices that become increasingly free from one stanza to the next. There is also constant change in texture and timbre from solo to *tutti* writing. This applies as well to Fasch's other melodious a cappella works (among them psalm and other motets) which combine Homilius's gentleness with Reichardt's pathos. Fasch's ornamented chorales were imitated by his pupil Karl Friedrich Zelter. D.G. Türk of Halle also wrote a cappella chorales with *Figuralsolos.* (Concerning the motets of Schulz and Reichardt see p. 326.) Reichardt's simple harmonies are both noble and well conceived, as shown by his motets on poems by M. Claudius. The younger Berlin composers, on the other hand (especially Gattermann, B.A. Weber, and J.Ph.S. Schmidt), seem to have equated simplicity and dignity with banality. Their settings sound either like harmony exercises (cadences; exercises in modulation) or like typical organ phrases to which texts have been added. Others pay homage to the sentimental *Liedertafel* style. Karl Friedrich Rungenhagen writes on a higher level. The "Bückeburg Bach," J. Ch. Friedrich, is represented in this collection by choral songs, probably arrangements. His large motet *Ich liege und schlafe* (1780) uses the Homilius combination of verse and chorale, followed by a fugue and a simple concluding setting of the chorale. The entire work is well proportioned. This work and another large motet, *Wachet auf, ruft uns die Stimme,* show the proximity to J.S. Bach, although in other ways both motets are typical products of their time. *Wachet auf* is a pure chorale motet. Its first stanza is a free introduction and cantus-firmus setting; the second is in free motet style; the third has a free introduction followed by a simple chorale setting and a final fugato. It even includes a chorale setting by J. S. Bach (BWV 140.7), one of his most polished.

ORGAN COMPOSITIONS FOR THE CHURCH

The post-Bach era, especially the 19th century, produced a wealth of organ music, particularly for church use. Yet the "decline" of church music is perhaps more apparent in this field than in any other. The causes were sociological (lessened prestige of the organist's profession) and ideological (an anti-art emphasis on edification and on emotionalism rather than craftsmanship), as well as compositional style (the favoring of a melodically oriented chordal homophony), instrumental style (intrusion of heterogeneous style traits borrowed from pianistic, orchestral, vocal, or string writing), and instrumental technology (influence of the Classic orchestra on organ construction). All these factors acting together brought about a radical change in the composition of sacred organ works—a turning away from the foundations of J. S. Bach's organ music. It was a gradual rather than a sudden change, and the old style continued to exist in the background, influenced by the new style. The change also affected Bach's pupils, among whom the following deserve mention for their organ compositions: W. Friedemann Bach (better known for the many legendary details of his life than for his few organ works), Johann Ludwig Krebs, G.A. Homilius, Johann Christian Kittel, Johann Gottfried Müthel, Johann Schneider, and, indirectly, J.S. Bach's friend Johann Peter Kellner. Around the middle of the 18th century at the latest, a general turning away from the old and strict polyphonic organ style and a gradual intrusion of a gallant manner of playing set in. Inspired by the new *Empfindsamkeit,* the old art of organ composition still produced some works of singular beauty, especially by J.L. Krebs and Homilius. The trend was toward the melodic, character piece, for which piano music had already supplied the precedent. Where counterpoint continued to be an essential ingredient, it tended to be pretentious and learned, of the kind found in works by J.F. Agricola, J. Ph. Kirnberger, F.W. Marpurg, and J. Ch. Oley.

Bach's youngest pupil, J. Ch. Kittel, wrote in a predominantly melodious and gallant style, tending partly toward Graun-Hasse, partly toward Haydn-Mozart (most of his preserved organ compositions appear to be late works), and less toward the contrapuntal writing of his teacher. Yet Kittel appears conservative when compared with Justin Heinrich Knecht, his contemporary from southern Germany, who was less influenced by Bach than by the Catholic Abbé G. J. Vogler. Vogler rebuilt many organs according to his own simplified system and thereby laid the foundation for the Romantic orchestral organ. His organ playing ranged from notorious improvisations (in which he is said to have represented thunder by using his elbow on the manual) to nondescript sacred works. Like Kittel, Knecht distinguished between the gallant and strict styles. In the former his standards were even lower, so that some of his organ settings look like cantabile movements from contemporary piano or chamber music. Gallant elements are more noticeable in his strict works than in Kittel's. Christian Heinrich Rinck also began in the gallant idiom, but then turned to an equally nondescript ecclesiastical manner. Aside from this he showed increasing interest in florid counterpoint.

This middle-of-the-road, neutral style is the basis for most sacred organ music from the first half of the 19th century; purely applied, it resulted in the most uninteresting music: homophonic, sustained movements made up of harmonic cadences, modulations, and sequences; lifeless part writing; and rhythm in a respectable 4/4 meter, the tempo being moderato, andante, or adagio. Apparently the intention was to have the mere sound of the organ induce a devotional mood, without communicating anything of musical significance. Artistically speaking, organ music had reached the lowest level in history, but from a certain liturgical point of view it was better than the melodious piano pieces Knecht and others passed off as organ music. A better result was obtained when chordal, "a cappella" writing was paired with a top line of some melodic distinction, forming a "song without words" for organ.

Lively polyphonic movements using traditional Baroque formulas formed the opposite extreme. Kittel's pupil Michael Gotthardt Fischer is an important representative of this latter style. Though his solid technique has often been praised, his frequently stereotyped sequences cannot be overlooked. His Thuringian colleague, K. G. Umbreit, came from the same school, as did J.G. Vierling, who, like Kittel, wrote in both the gallant and strict styles.

By whatever name they are called, the different varieties of "character piece" (Fellerer) also influenced cantus-firmus settings. At first these settings gave way to a trio-like arrangement of the initial motif or to an older treatment, a fughetta on the opening of a chorale melody; eventually they were pushed into the background by cantus-firmus-free chorale preludes. This type is represented by the anonymous *Präludium zu einem Lob- und Dankliede* in Hiller's *Wöchentliche Nachrichten* (II, 94 ff.). Türk had already referred to it in 1787 as the "gemeine

99. The Bach memorial, donated by Felix Mendelssohn-Bartholdy and dedicated in 1843, in front of St. Thomas's Church, Leipzig.

100. The court cathedral of Berlin in a watercolor by F. A. Calau, beginning of the 19th century.

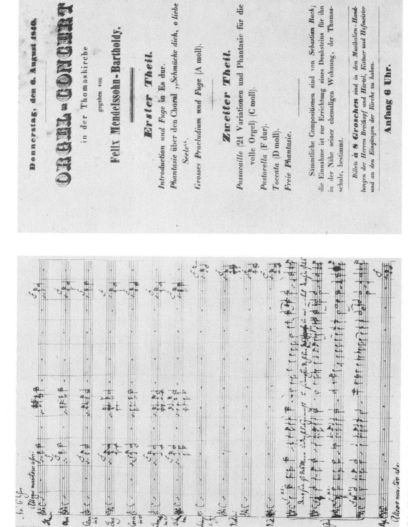

101. Felix Mendelssohn-Bartholdy, from his Psalm 95 for mixed chorus, soloists, orchestra, and organ (April 11, 1839), Op. 46, autograph. Berlin, Deutsche Staatsbibliothek.

102. Program of the organ concert given by Felix Mendelssohn-Bartholdy on August 6, 1840, in St. Thomas's Church in Leipzig, with works of J. S. Bach.

Vorspiel oder die freye Fantasie." It did not altogether replace the older cantus-firmus treatment (or the ornamented chorale), but the vigor of true contrapuntal creativity was gone. Most of the pieces published by Hiller in his *Wöchentliche Nachrichten* (late 1760s) show this. The trend of the time was toward free preludes, in which the composer had complete liberty to express to the fullest the "mood" of the chorale and could choose whether or not to weave chorale motifs into the prelude. The chorale preludes also reflect the trend away from occasional music to the generally devotional—a trend that caused the *de tempore* hymn to be replaced by a hymn chosen at random and pericope cantatas by psalms, hymns, and motets expressive of the unchanging aspects of the service. Simplicity and simplification were the keywords which, in the case of organ technique, led to lowered standards, to purely functional music for "teachers and organists in town and country." Little organ pieces "for use in the public worship service" could be heard everywhere in the early 19th century. In line with the limited concepts of what was suitable for the church, such a title eliminated any high artistic standards. What the theoreticians of sacred music were never tired of preaching was put fully into practice. The old, artistic forms of organ music, still represented by works of J. L. Krebs, were despised and eventually became extinct. Only the fugue survived, but written in a manner that was dry and antiquarian, with easygoing themes lacking in profile and built up by equal periods; there was little or no cohesion or tension in the construction and the voice leading was lifeless.

The trend to works of small dimensions is shown by the fughetta. Johann Ernst Rembt was considered its master; his 50 four-part fughettas based on verset themes by Gottlieb Muffat were first published in 1791. A "Postludium" had been in use earlier (see Mattheson's *Vollkommener Kapellmeister*, 1739, p. 473), but it was not considered a special type of composition until the early 19th century. Played at the end of the service or after the principal hymn while the minister entered the pulpit (for which reason it was jestingly referred to as a "pulpit march"), it could be written in any number of styles and lacked a distinctive form. The reigning type was a vaguely "expressive" organ composition (with or without any reminiscence of a chorale), appropriate at any time during the service.

Restoration

The decline of church music stemmed from two concurrent phenomena: a lessening interest in the church itself and the systematic estrangement of church music from the essentials of both art and church. The deplorable results of this twofold condition were manifest in the early 19th century: congregational singing that dragged along laboriously; an impoverished liturgy in which music filled a role of questionable value; organ music and organ playing which either cultivated a gallant, pianistic style or was stiff and pompous; cantatas of slight musical substance and choral music that was sentimental or bombastic. This was the situation at the time the restoration set in. It was part of a general religious reaction to the dissolution of Christian beliefs during the Enlightenment. This reaction coincided with the awakening of national sentiment during the Wars of Liberation following Napoleon; it fits into the general restorative policies during the age of the Holy Alliance, an age that tried to undo the consequences of the French Revolution.

The 95 Theses against rationalism by the Kiel pastor Klaus Harms appeared in 1817, the 300th anniversary of the Reformation. This was the beginning of a rejuvenation of orthodox Lutheranism which, after about 1830, again reached a position of superiority over the theology of rationalism. From the 1820s on, modern Pietism developed concurrently, picking up considerable momentum. But these changes took place within a limited area: the circles still professing active church membership. A general consequence of the Enlightenment was the overthrow of the church as the life-regulating power and the center of intellectual activity. In the rapid growth of population during the age of industrialization, there was less and less contact with the church, a development that has continued down to the mid–20th century along with the general secularization of social life. Under these circumstances even the most perfect church music could not retain its importance. Church music was at the periphery of musical life; it no longer formed the center. The writers of the restoration age contributed substantially to this artistic degradation. Events of real importance to the world of music, to the "musical public," took place in the concert hall, in the opera house, in the homes of music lovers, possibly in sacred concerts.

A number of essays on Luther's views of music appeared in 1817; they were preceded in 1813 by A.J. Rambach's treatise *Über Dr. M. Luthers Verdienste um den Kirchengesang.* . . . An awareness of historical origins thus appears to have been the point of departure for the restoration movement. As a result, historical studies of all branches of Protestant church music now made their appearance: hymnology, liturgy, and the history of polyphonic music and organ music. The knowledge gained was applied to contemporary musical practices, to varying extent and degree of success but never to the exclusion of the ideas of the Enlightenment and of early Romanticism, which continued to exert their influence. This combination of historical awareness with immediate tradition produced a dualistic result. On the one hand, the rhythmical chorale of the 16th century was studied and gradually revived, and the Lutheran liturgy was widely reintroduced; on the other hand, the demands of the Enlightenment for polyphonic music in a popular and devotional style were not rescinded. The a cappella concept of early Romanticism continued to set the standard. In fact, only now did it become fully operative.

LITURGICAL EFFORTS

The first steps to bring about a restoration were taken in the liturgical field. J.F.W. Naue's *Versuch einer musikalischen Agende* appeared in 1818, preparing the ground for the restoration of chant. Naue's interpretation of historical sources was not entirely accurate, nor did he give up organ accompaniment with modern harmonization; yet it is to his credit that he advocated chanting as indispensable. With his help the view prevailed that the chant should not follow a metrical rhythm but be freely declaimed. The musical part of the Prussian liturgy used to be attributed to Naue, but wrongly (see Leupold). The liturgy of the Prussian church is essentially the personal achievement of King Friedrich Wilhelm III. The intention behind it had been to secure once more room for prayer and singing, near the sermon (*Publicandum* of September 17, 1814). The plans were realized in 1816, when a number of different orders of service were printed in succession, each one coming closer to the model of the old Lutheran order. From these developed the *Kirchenagende für die Königlich-preussische Armee* (1821), the *Kirchenagende für die Hof- und Domkirche in Berlin* (1822), and, to the accompaniment of heated literary discussions (called the *Agendenstreit*), the *Agende für die evangelische Kirche in den Königlich Preussischen Landen* (1829). Bavaria followed in 1856 with a specifically Lutheran liturgy, which met considerable opposition from many segments of the middle class, still imbued with the spirit of rationalism (see Kressel).

Musically speaking, the Prussian liturgy was far from a return to the liturgical singing of the Reformation; rather it represented a mixture of a great variety of ingredients: Lutheran intonation formulas, Gregorian chant, and elements of Russian church music. With these ingredients, a cappella arrangements were made by Berlin musicians (B.A. Weber, L. Hellwig, G.A. Schneider, A.E. Grell, and Zelter, and by the director of the Russian court chapel, D. St. Bortnjansky); responsorial singing by the congregation was intentionally slighted. These arrangements were officially sanctioned—canonized, so to speak. They constituted a victory for the a cappella ideal (to which the king had been converted by the imperial church music of Russia) and for uniformity, but they were by no means a victory for church music. Special permission had to be obtained for any other kind of polyphonic music. But there were insurmountable obstacles to compliance with the edict, for some churches had no choirs. As early as 1823 the king granted permission to have the responses read by the cantor, sexton, or teacher; to have them sung by the congregation, with organ accompaniment, was considered desirable after 1843. Simplified editions of the parts of the liturgy appeared, for various combinations of voices. The original strict rules were thus more and more relaxed, especially after the appearance, in 1834, of an "abbreviated liturgy." King Friedrich Wilhelm IV also permitted new settings of the liturgy, to which his predecessor had been generally opposed, and he invited Grell and Mendelssohn (1846), and Nicolai and Loewe (1847), to write such compositions. There were numerous contributions by other composers as well, but nothing of lasting value was created.

After the middle of the century the liturgically informed felt that the musical foundations of the Prussian liturgy were out of date. Loud voices were now heard clamoring for a thorough restoration of Gregorian music. Since it was considered necessary to replace the Latin texts with Luther's German Bible texts, difficulties inevitably arose. Friedrich Riegel, music editor of Ludwig Schoeberlein's *Schatz des liturgischen Chor- und Gemeindegesangs nebst den Altarweisen in der deutschen evangelischen Kirche aus den Quellen vornehmlich des 16. und 17. Jahrhunderts geschöpft* (Göttingen, 1865–72), treated the Gregorian melodies rather freely, while Otto Kade, music editor of the *Cantionale für die evangelisch-lutherischen Kirchen im Grossherzogtum Mecklenburg-Schwerin* (published 1867–80, with T. Kliefoth), used an equally free approach to the Bible texts. The 1895 revision of the Prussian liturgy did not satisfy those who were intent on bringing about a return to earlier practices. Compared to the conditions existing in 1829, participation of the choir (which had lost its liturgical function) had even been reduced. As a result, Rochus von Liliencron drew up a unified Protestant liturgy (*Chorordnung* [Order of Choral Worship] *für die Sonn- und Festtage des evangelischen Kirchenjahrs,* Gütersloh, 1900). Its purpose was to provide a secure place in the liturgy for choral singing, based on *de tempore* texts and Gregorian style. In this it followed the lines of the liturgy of the Old Prussian Union, and it stayed close to the north German Lutheran service of the 16th century. Liliencron's conceptions were filled out with new compositions or arrangements of older works by Heinrich van Eyken (1902–06).

RESTORATION OF THE CHORALE

At the same time these liturgical efforts took place, the hymns of the Reformation (at first the texts, later also the music) were studied and put back into practical use. This development began in 1817; it continued with some interruptions until the appearance of the *Evangelisches Kirchengesangbuch* of 1950. The principal task with regard to the texts was to return the old hymns to a position of central importance. Distortions had to be removed from these while the many inferior hymns of the Enlightenment had to be eliminated.

Ernst Moritz Arndt was the first to issue a plea for restoration (*Von dem Wort und dem Kirchenliede,* 1819); he was followed by K. v. Raumer, Ch. K. J. v. Bunsen, R. Stier (whose watchword was *Gesangbuchsnoth* [hymnal crisis], 1838), A. Vilmar, and others, who published stirring appeals. Hymnological studies for thorough and practical restorative work were undertaken by A. J. Rambach

(*Anthologie christlicher Gesänge,* 1817–32, continued as *Der heilige Gesang der Deutschen . . . seit Gellert und Klopstock,* 1832–33); by, especially, Philipp Wackernagel (*Das deutsche Kirchenlied von Martin Luther bis auf Nicolaus Herman und Ambrosius Blaurer,* 1841; *Bibliographie zur Geschichte des deutschen Kirchenlieds im XVI. Jahrhundert,* 1855; *Das deutsche Kirchenlied von der ältesten Zeit bis zu Anfang des XVII. Jahrhunderts,* 1864–77); and later by Albert Fischer and W. Tümpel (*Das deutsche evangelische Kirchenlied des 17. Jahrhunderts,* 1904–16). Private hymn collections, intended for immediate practical use, soon appeared along with the above. Though they represented more or less of a compromise, they brought the new orientation to the people (J.A. Kanne, 1818; K. v. Raumer, 1831; *Geistlicher Liederschatz,* Berlin, 1832; v. Bunsen, *Versuch eines allgemeinen evangelischen Gesang- und Gebetbuchs zum Kirchen- und Hausgebrauche,* 1833; R. Stier, 1835; and others). Their tendency to compromise shows up in the still extensive textual liberties; whether or not these were admissible in principle became the subject of a controversy between R. Stier and his purist adversary, H. Scholz. Some official hymnals, it should be noted, also reflected the efforts at restoration, among them the *Evangelisches Gesangbuch zum kirchlichen Gebrauche* (Elberfeld, 1824) and (with many compromises) the more widely used *Gesangbuch zum gottesdienstlichen Gebrauch für evangelische Gemeinen* (Berlin, 1829). Up to the middle of the century an increasing number of hymnals showed evidence of attempts to restore the chorale. Some hymnals published after 1851 achieved complete success.

Along with the desire to restore the old hymns, there developed another movement, partly induced by the rising national consciousness: the desire for one common hymnal. While E.M. Arndt had made the romantic suggestion to create a common hymnal for all German Christians regardless of creed, others, especially Karl von Raumer (1829) and August Vilmar (1843), advocated uniformity in a more specifically Protestant sense. At the German Protestant congress in Elberfeld in 1851 it was resolved (following the Prussian General Synod of 1846) "to compile a list of hymns from the time of the Reformation, in use in all Protestant churches, with the same text, to serve as a nucleus to which every state church [*Landeskirche*] might add its own hymns." An investigation undertaken by E.E. Koch showed how small this common body of hymns had become: in all the hymnals in use at the time he found only six hymns that were included in all of them (*Allein Gott in der Höh sei Ehr, Befiehl du deine Wege, Ein feste Burg, Jesus, meine Zuversicht, O Gott, du frommer Gott, Wer nur den lieben Gott lässt walten*). A "conference of delegates of the highest German Protestant church authorities" had convened in 1852 in Eisenach; in the following year it submitted a *Deutsches Evangelisches Kirchen-Gesangbuch. In 150 Kernliedern.* It was incorporated in the Bavarian hymnal of 1854 and in the hymnals of a few small state churches; elsewhere it ran into strong opposition. But even though a uniform hymnal for all of Germany did not materialize for some time, at least the countless hymnals of individual towns and small territories were replaced by regional hymnals.

The Eisenach "basic hymnal" (i.e., exactly as it was originally translated) is significant not only textually but also musically because the melodies, too, are in their original form—both the notes and the rhythm. The movement for restoration of the chorale rallied to its own slogan: "Back to the original melody, to the oldest sources." Not the least important result was a return to the church modes and to the unequal rhythms, which in turn led to faster tempos in singing.

The question of the church modes had first been taken up by Peter Mortimer (*Der Choral-Gesang zur Zeit der Reformation . . .* , Berlin, 1821). Chorales from the time of the Reformation became known through several collections: C.F. Becker and G. Billroth's *Sammlung von Chorälen aus dem XVI. und XVII. Jahrhundert, der Melodie und Harmonie nach aus den Quellen herausgegeben* (Leipzig, 1831); Carl von Winterfeld's *Dr. Martin Luthers deutsche geistliche Lieder nebst den während seines Lebens dazu gebräuchlichen Singweisen und einigen mehrstimmigen Tonsätzen über dieselben von Meistern des 16. Jahrhunderts* (Leipzig, 1840); L. Ch. Erk and F. Filitz's *Vierstimmige Choräle der vornehmsten Meister des 16. und 17. Jahrhunderts* (Essen, 1845); Gottlieb von Tucher's *Schatz des evangelischen Kirchengesangs im ersten Jahrhundert der Reformation* (Leipzig, 1848; an earlier printing, Stuttgart, 1840); Friedrich Layriz's school hymnal of 1839, and especially his *Kern des deutschen Kirchengesangs . . .* (1844); later, Schoeberlein's *Schatz des liturgischen Chor- und Gemeindegesangs . . .* (1865–72); and, finally, Johannes Zahn's *Die Melodien der deutschen evangelischen Kirchenlieder, aus den Quellen geschöpft und mitgeteilt* (1889–93). Winterfeld's *Der evangelische Kirchengesang und sein Verhältniss zur Kunst des Tonsatzes* (Leipzig, 1843–47) also provided the basis for research in the field of Protestant church music in general, though in practice he had some reservations about the rhythmical singing of chorales (*Über Herstellung des Gemeine- und Chorgesanges in der evangelischen Kirche,* 1848). "Rhythmical" chorales in their original form were first introduced in Bavaria through the so-called Munich Chorale Book (W. Ortloph, J. Zahn, G. Herzog, F. Güll) of 1844. There followed the official *Vierstimmiges Melodienbuch zum Gesangbuch der evangelisch-lutherischen Kirche in Bayern* (Erlangen, 1854), edited by Zahn with the advice of Tucher, Layriz, and Winterfeld. The settings are in early 17th-century style. The *Melodien der deutschen evangelischen Kirchen-Gesangbuchs in vierstimmigem Satz für Orgel und Chorgesang* appeared at the same time (Stuttgart, 1854), commissioned by the Eisenach conference and edited by Tucher, Faisst, and Zahn. Outside of Bavaria the rhythmical chorale succeeded only in a few provinces such as East Frisia (through the efforts of Eduard Krüger) and Hannover. For the time being the rest of Germany followed the chorale restoration to one degree or another: sometimes compromising with alternate versions, sometimes taking over individual improvements and sometimes rejecting it completely. Moritz Hauppmann, cantor at St. Thomas's, thought the even-note chorale to be more "dignified"; the Thuringian organist F. Kühmstedt opposed the restoration efforts in the 1850s with the syllogism that "rhythm is essentially nothing but organized time," while the chorale and the church were to lead man to eternity and to God. Friedrich Schneider (1852) went so far as to call rhythmical singing "a deplorable desecration and profanation of the sacred." Musicians who took such a negative view expressed the classic concept of the "dignity" of church music—a concept that was to make room for a less stodgy one, at least with regard to the chorale. Zahn (1854) suggested a tempo of one second per chorale note (M.M. $\downarrow$ = 60) for singing; Eduard Krüger (1855) suggested one pulse beat (at a pulse of 70 beats per minute this amounts to M.M. $\downarrow$ = 70—more than twice as fast as the tempo advocated for the even-note chorale in the first half of the century); Oesterley (1863) asked for M.M. $\downarrow$ = 45–75 for a chorale moving in half notes. The reformers completely rejected organ interludes between lines of the chorale.

The realization of all these aims progressed slowly and sporadically. Even in some parts of Bavaria the rhythmical manner of singing existed on paper only. If, in 1887, the *Evangelischer Kirchengesangverein für Deutschland* had voted on the issue of the rhythmical chorale the idea would have been defeated. For this reason the question was avoided at the time. No more than about a dozen of the rhythmical melodies found their way into hymnals, often next to alternate versions in even note values. Only in the first decade of the 20th century did the rhythmical chorale succeed more widely. Later on the so-called song weeks and the publications of the so-called singing movement contributed to its understanding and dissemination. Theoretical discussions of details such as problems of rhythm, bar lines, fermatas, etc., continued and reached a provisional solution in the *Evangelisches Kirchengesangbuch* of 1950.

This volume was a culmination of the efforts to create a common hymnal. Such efforts had died down during the second half of the 19th century (the *Melodienbuch zu dem Evangelischen Militär-Gesang- und Gebetbuch*, 1892, and the *Festbüchlein* issued in 1898 by the *Evangelischer Kirchengesangverein* had been compromises), but had gained momentum after the First World War through the *Deutsches Evangelisches Gesangbuch* of 1926 (melodies published in 1927, chorale book by Arnold Mendelssohn in 1928), which textually is identical with the *Deutsches Evangelisches Gesangbuch für die Schutzgebiete und das Ausland* (1915). The 1926 hymnal had more success than its predecessor of 1853; it formed the nucleus of the hymnals of many state churches up to 1931. The *Verband evangelischer Kirchenchöre Deutschlands* (formerly *Evangelischer Kirchengesangverein für Deutschland*) then led the efforts for creation of a new hymnal. In 1939 it appointed a hymnal committee under the chairmanship of Chr. Mahrenholz. Basing its work on recent hymnals and hymnological research, it prepared a draft for a *Gesangbuch für die evangelische Christenheit* and submitted it in 1947. In the Old Prussian Union the work of revising the *Deutsches Evangelisches Gesangbuch* and its regional appendices had begun in 1940, under the direction of O. Söhngen. This led to the establishment in 1947 of a separate hymnal committee of the churches in the Russian-occupied zone of Germany, the region in which the *Deutsches Evangelisches Gesangbuch* was most widely used. In 1948 joint discussions between East and West eventuated in an agreement and finally in the *Evangelisches Kirchengesangbuch*, which in 1949 the General Synod of the United Protestant-Lutheran Church in Germany acknowledged as the common Lutheran hymnal. By 1956 it formed the nucleus of the hymnals of almost all the state churches. Improvements also were made in the actual congregational singing. "If one examines congregational singing in Protestant churches soberly, from a historical point of view, one must admit that today it is better than ever, though it still is not ideal" (Blankenburg).

Few hymns composed during the 19th century have survived. Subjective, devotional songs were more in vogue than hymns for congregational singing. Philipp Spitta the Elder (*Psalter und Harfe,* 1833) and Albert Knapp (hymn texts published after 1829) were the principal hymn writers; both are represented in the new *Evangelisches Kirchengesangbuch,* along with Ernst Moritz Arndt and others. Of the 19th-century melodies, however, hardly any survived as hymns. Not intended for the church, the spiritual song was nevertheless widely used to "embellish" the service, though in a manner that seems trivial if compared with its use in the second half of the 18th century.

Only the minister Friedrich Mergner seems to have had real concern for the specifically Protestant hymn. His main contribution was setting to music all the hymns not of a contemporary poet but of Paul Gerhardt (composed from 1859; the collection appeared in 1876, second ed., 1918). Many of his melodies and settings were rays of light among the sacred works of the time. They have a forceful rhythm and display either a chorale-like or an arioso style. Most of them are for four-part choir, some for solo voice and piano.

In the 19th century the spiritual "folk song" steadily grew in significance. Though it no longer flourished after 1850, it was cultivated increasingly in the circles of the growing domestic and foreign missions and other church-related organizations. A large number of song collections testify to this, outstanding among them Heinrich Volkening's *Kleine Missionsharfe* (after 1852) and *Frohe Botschaft in Liedern* by the Methodist preacher Ernst Gebhardt (since 1875). The latter collection belonged to the category known variously as English songs, communal songs, sanctification songs, Gospel songs, or songs of the kingdom *(Englische, Gemeinschafts-, Heiligungs-, Evangeliums-, Reichslieder),* which now started on their road to victory. According to Petrich, Gebhardt first sang them in 1875 at a revival meeting in Zurich, accompanying himself at the harmonium, the typical instrument of revival circles (Ehmann). Their popularity was remarkable and they have not yet died out. In an edition for brass choir of the *Reichslieder: Deutsches Gemeinschafts-Liederbuch* (second edition, Neumünster i. H. 1923; first ed., 1909) we find a motley mixture of old Protestant chorales, German spiritual songs of the 18th and 19th centuries, and especially hymns translated from the English, the original texts (according to Petrich) coming from Methodist Episcopal churches in America. The melodies present a large selection from which the popular hits of the middle and late 19th century could be chosen. The "singing movement" of the 20th century was a much needed reaction to this kind of spiritual community singing.

RESTRUCTURING THE BASIC FOUNDATIONS

To make choral liturgical singing possible, and to raise the level of congregational singing through examples of excellence, restoration was needed in the early 19th century in another area: the new foundation of church choirs. Attempts to maintain the old school choirs as church choirs had largely failed. In Saxony, around 1830, there were unsuccessful efforts to revive the old *Kantoreien,* in order to counteract the influence of the male choruses, which were considered politically dangerous. The problem of reorganization on new foundations was solved by a decision to bring in children from elementary schools to sing in church. With this in mind, singing instruction was introduced, for which M.T. Pfeiffer and Nägeli had paved the way with a method of voice training (1809–10). Instructions were issued from Berlin for pupils to form choirs for liturgical and chorale singing under the direction of their teachers. These plans were realized in Brandenburg, Westphalia (due to the initiative of Natorp), and elsewhere, with varying success. In Westphalia, around the middle of the century, the undertaking was considered a failure. Elsewhere the institution of children's choirs managed to survive, though by no means destined to produce artistic results. Suitably arranged liturgical and smaller choral pieces were sung during the service; Eduard Grell was the chief composer. In Lübeck children (especially girls) made up the only official church choirs, even in the 20th century (see Stahl). Attempts were soon made to enlarge the children's choirs by enlisting girls and boys beyond elementary school age—a "selected group of the most serious-minded young people from the congregation"—in order to develop a church choir of higher ability. The idealism inspiring these efforts contrasted greatly with the essentially financial orientation of the older kinds of school choirs, now defunct: remuneration was now frowned upon. In 1815 attempts were made in Berlin to form a choir from young people of the congregation whose remuneration was to consist of voice lessons. They were to dedicate themselves only to sacred music, shunning participation in all secular musical activities, and expenses were to be defrayed through voluntary contributions from the congregation. Such romantic attempts clearly were not destined to be very successful. As a rule, things probably worked out as described by August Bergt in his (fictitious) *Briefwechsel eines alten und jungen Schulmeisters über allerhand Musikalisches* (Correspondence Between an Old and a Young Schoolteacher on Things Musical; 1838): "My pupils sing in tune in two parts; I supply the bass."

Seeing the need for measures more in keeping with reality, King Friedrich Wilhelm IV reorganized the Berlin cathedral choir in 1843 (whose origins went back to the era of liturgical efforts under Friedrich Wilhelm III) into a salaried group with a yearly budget of 33,288 marks. It became probably the best German a cappella choir of the mid-19th century. The court chapel at St. Petersburg served as model, and the choir consisted of boys and men only (a total of sixty to eighty singers) under the direction of a conductor and a voice teacher. The choir was invisible to the congregation, thus conforming to the most romantic aspect of the a cappella concept. Other paid choirs were formed following the Berlin model, among them the *Schlosschor* in Schwerin (founded in 1857; conducted by Otto Kade), the *Schlosskirchenchor* (cathedral choir) in Hannover (formally organized in 1852; actually founded in 1857 by King George V), and the Salzungen church choir (sixty singers; founded in 1860 by Bernhard Müller under the patronage of the heir apparent to the throne of Meiningen), which gained a fine reputation. However, the willingness or means to form a choir even moderately well paid did not exist everywhere.

The founding of church singing societies, which began during the 1870s, brought better results. This was a product of the lay movement in music which got off to a vigorous start early in the 19th century with male choruses and oratorio societies, and was a direct outgrowth of the Catholic St. Cecilia Society (1868), though not sworn, like that society, to the Palestrina cult. In some places, especially in Württemberg, volunteer church choral groups had formed earlier, since about 1820. These were mixed choruses (women's and men's voices), with no pretension, however, to a place in the worship service. Some men's choruses did take part in the service, occasionally or on a regular basis, but many so-called choral societies for church music (such as the famous Society for Classical Church Music in Stuttgart) did not devote themselves at all to liturgical music. With the consolidation of several choral groups in southwestern Germany, and through the initiative of H.A. Köstlin (soon vigorously supported by Ludwig Hallwachs), a strong movement now came into being which attracted public attention through "church singing festivals" *(Kirchengesangfeste),* the first of which took place in 1875. The liturgical uncertainty of the early stages of the movement manifested itself in the unusual nature of some of the festive services: Christmas music might be heard in midsummer, or a "journey through the church year" might be undertaken (this custom lasted until after 1900). The movement gave rise to the *Evangelischer Kirchengesangverein für Südwest-deutschland* (1881) and the *Evangelischer Kirchengesangverein für Deutschland* (1883), and gradually extended to all of Germany.

Support from church authorities soon materialized, advancing the movement by putting existing choirs on a firmer basis and by encouraging the founding of a growing number of new ones. It is no accident that the movement originated in Württemberg (Hesse and Baden also were in on its beginnings). Württemberg had next to no liturgy. After Kocher's futile attempts to introduce congregational singing in four-part harmony (see above), a desire to beautify the service in other ways was bound to arise; accordingly, amateur groups were formed to present musical interludes. The movement included not only volunteer mixed choirs but also school choirs and paid church choirs, which existed especially in the king-dom of Saxony, where they had developed out of the old *Kantoreien.* In the 19th century, Saxony, the cradle of Protestant church music, was still the region in which church music was most vigorous. Traditions that had practically disap-peared from the rest of Germany had maintained themselves here. Vollhardt's statistics throw light on the conditions of Saxon church choirs in the later 19th century. Aside from the traditional choirs at a few *Gymnasia,* such as at the princely schools of Grimma and Meissen, there were choirs at the new teacher training institutions. Most important were the choirs of boys who were paid (poorly) and sometimes had tuition scholarships, and of men *(Adjuvanten, Kanto-risten),* often augmented with women volunteers, schoolgirls, or additional men. Some paid choirs consisted of boys only, frequently joined by volunteers—teach-ers, schoolgirls, a mixed choir, or a male choral society. Other types included new mixed choirs consisting either of volunteers or, as was the case in Augsburg's Protestant church choir after 1858 and in the *Kirchengesang-Chor* of Reutlingen, of paid singers (men and women). Such a group often called itself *Kirchengesang-verein;* boys' or children's choirs may have joined it at times. Finally, exclusively male singing societies also served the church, along with such rarely encountered groups as ladies' singing societies. If a church maintained choirs of several kinds —as a rule a paid choir of boys and men and a mixed or male choir—they would alternate or, for the performances of larger works, join forces.

The *Evangelischer Kirchengesangverein für Deutschland* took an interest in paid choirs (though it continued to consider volunteer mixed choirs to be its primary concern). It also continued to engage in other valuable work, showing strong interest in all matters pertaining to the musical life of the Protestant church, above all in liturgy and the chorale. The topics of lectures and papers given at its congresses and meetings give an idea of the scope of its activities (see the *Festschrift* of 1933). In 1933 the organization acquired the new name *Verband evangelischer Kirchenchöre Deutschlands*.

The institution of "trombone choirs" followed that of church choirs. Isolated instances of these had occurred slightly earlier, but an extensive movement did not arise until the revival movement spread from the Ravensberg region of Westphalia, led by Heinrich Volkening. The first of the trombone choirs was formed in 1842 or 1843 by a young men's religious group in Jöllenbeck near Bielefeld, where Volkening was pastor; the idea soon spread to neighboring localities. In Westphalia the movement was organized by the "father of trombone choirs," Eduard Kuhlo, and later by his son Johannes Kuhlo, in northern Germany by Fritz Fliedner, and in Saxony by Gottfried Müller. It took root and flourished less within the strict confines of church life than as part of group activities outside the church—as a "trombone mission" in the service of the home mission. The first trombone choirs were in fact made up of trombones; later that instrument was replaced by the flügelhorn (or tenorhorn), so that since then the term "flügelhorn choir" would be more accurate. French horns were more often used than trombones, which rarely appeared.

The formation, early in the 19th century, of children's and other choirs to take part in the liturgy raised the problem of the musical training of teachers, meaning the elementary school teacher who also officiated as organist and/or cantor, and who at the same time usually was the conductor of the local singing society. For the 19th century he was the typical church musician. Natorp saw a solution in the founding of teacher's singing societies, developing out of the teachers' professional meetings. But the most important thing had to be to give musical training to the future teacher while he was receiving his professional education. State teacher colleges and their preparatory institutions took cognizance of this and offered training by college music instructors, who included many of the best and best known organists of the 19th century. Arno Werner acknowledged the competence of the elementary school teacher who had had this kind of training, and who, since the early 19th century, had begun to replace the traditional schoolmaster with no specialized music training. According to Werner, a great improvement of church music resulted from these changes after 1830. This view stands in strong contrast to that of Karl Straube, who claimed that the 19th-century cantor and organist contributed next to nothing to the national musical life, because his talent, knowledge, and ability were insufficient, some exceptions notwithstanding. To this one should add that the many exceptions did affect the total picture. Johann Schneider, G.A. Merkel, F.W. Berner, Adolf Hesse, J.G.

104. Felix Mendelssohn-Bartholdy (1809–47) in a sketch by Johann Peter Lyser, 1835. Frankfurt on the Main, private collection.

103. Karl Loewe (1796–1869) in a contemporary lithograph.

106. Johannes Brahms (1833–97) in a pastel drawing by Olga von Miller.

105. Max Reger (1873–1916) in a photograph of 1913.

Töpfer, A.G. Ritter, A.W. Bach, Louis Thiele, August Haupt, Otto Dienel, Immanuel Faisst, and J.G. Herzog were all able organists who set high standards. Donat even believed that standards they established for church organ playing were maintained at the same high level up to his own time (1931). Able organists other than those mentioned were active in many cities, and the only criticism one can level against them is that they played works which today are no longer considered appropriate organ music, in a style that is now considered outdated. Yet they developed a growing appreciation of J.S. Bach's works during the 19th century. Johann Schneider in particular was admired as a Bach player; he is said to have played after each lesson any Bach organ composition requested. Felix Mendelssohn should be named here as an organ player of the highest caliber, though he held no organist's appointment. Generally speaking, however, the caliber of organists and the esteem of organ playing was lower in the first half of the 19th century than after the time of Straube and Reger. Numerous contemporary complaints testify to this, especially those by Alberti (1843) and Altmann (1853), who speaks of "general indifference to matters concerning the organ."

However one might evaluate the actual significance of musical training in the 19th-century seminaries, there is no doubt that it was of relatively considerable importance. It was, therefore, a setback when, in 1872, Prussia repressed the study of music in the seminaries in favor of science. In 1924 the seminaries were dissolved and church music academies founded for training in that field. A few such schools already existed in the early 19th century; among these the *Königliches Akademisches Institut für Kirchenmusik* (its official name after 1875) in Berlin was outstanding. At the instigation of Zelter, it had been founded in 1822 as part of the Prussian restoration movement, with the composer Bernhard Klein and the organist A.W. Bach as the first teachers. Many of the leading church musicians of the second half of the century received at least some of their training there.

Church musicians (who had achieved a modest amount of professional status) formed professional organizations in some places, e.g., the *Orgelverein* in Thuringia (1843) and the Berlin *Organistenverein* (1873). According to Nelle, such organizations existed in the early 20th century in practically every state or provincial church. Greatly to its credit, the Berlin *Organistenverein* protested, in 1876, against the legal classification of Prussian church musicians among the "lower church employees" and brought about a partial rectification of this state of affairs. Yet the general picture drawn in 1885 by the theologian Friedrich Zimmer shows the rather deplorable condition of church music in Prussia, about which there seems to have been no official concern.

Most clergymen lacked any understanding of church music, and few church musicians understood liturgical requirements. In general, the the church required no higher accomplishment of musicians than being able to beat time for the liturgical choral singing and to start or accompany the singing of the chorale. Pay was correspondingly low. A reorganization of the profession of church music, demanded periodically during the entire 19th century, never took place.

The efforts of Friedrich Wilhelm IV in Prussia and of Georg V in Hannover were thus all the more valuable. In the choral organizations they founded, consideration was given to both liturgical and musical requirements. Also praiseworthy was the idealism of those church musicians who, in spite of all obstacles, exerted every effort to bring about "a well-regulated church music." Generally speaking, however, this goal was still far in the future, and it would be wrong to speak of a new flourishing of Protestant church music in the 19th century.

In 1881 Schoeberlein complained that choral singing "had practically disappeared from our services (unless one considers the singing of untrained young people worthy of that name), except for a few remnants from the old days and a few recently formed groups." In 1899 Bachmann still speaks of the "deterioration of our church music" and of the "low level of any true musical life in the church." Once more Saxony was an exception. For better or worse, cantatas there were an essential part of the service even in the late 19th century (see the resolution adopted by the plenary session of the *Kirchenchor-Verband,* Protestant-Lutheran State Church of Saxony, 1892). According to an official report covering the years 1896–1900, there was so much artistic church music in some of the larger cities that it was considered excessive (see *Blätter für Haus- und Kirchenmusik* V, 90 f.).

For the church musician who wished to develop and display his musical ability, the sacred concert was the best outlet. To be sure, organ recitals by traveling virtuosos already existed in the 18th century, exemplified primarily by Abbé Vogler. Other organists soon imitated his thunderstorms and doomsdays. There had probably never been a complete lack of organ recitals and choral society concerts in church. But now, under pressure of demands such as those of Rohleder (1833), Alberti (1843), and Katterfeld (1845), the church concert was to become once again a permanent institution, similar to earlier organ recitals by Sweelinck in Amsterdam or the evening concerts at the *Marienkirche* in Lübeck.

They were realized primarily in Berlin. Periodic organ recitals had been given before invited guests by A.W. Bach. In 1864 Otto Dienel began his free public organ recitals, which became a weekly event in 1895. A growing number of organ recitals and evening concerts took place in the churches of Berlin until the First World War. The situation was similar in Lübeck, where several organ recitals were held at the end of the century. *Volkskirchenkonzerte* and *liturgische andachten* (devotional services) were given in Eisleben beginning in the 1890s by Otto Richter, later cantor at the *Kreuzkirche*. Other cities may have seen similar developments. The devotional services were particularly successful; they had existed for a long time in Leipzig, where the St. Thomas's choir had sung a "motet" every week (on Saturdays and on the evenings before holidays). Similar evening services were customary in Dresden (Vespers of the *Kruzianer*), Dessau (Saturday Vespers at the palace church, after 1822 directed by Friedrich Schneider), and Berlin (evening devotional services of the cathedral choir, instituted in 1849). As a consequence of the liturgical efforts of the restoration movement (especially by Max Herold) these gained new life, receiving special encouragement after 1890. These two institutions—the sacred concert and the special musical service—offered ample opportunity for the cultivation of sacred music, making up for the continued lack of opportunity in the formal service.

THE QUESTION OF CHURCH STYLE

What kind of music should those in charge of Protestant church music now cultivate? The reply most frequently heard in the 19th century was choral music, sung a cappella. The Prussian church orders had already given official sanction to the a cappella concept; now the specific content was to be determined as well. Winterfeld played the leading part in this, studying the history of Protestant church music to find an a cappella choral style in which the chorale was treated in a predominantly homophonic manner, interspersed with a bit of polyphony. His answer lay in the works of Eccard, whom he consequently raised to the stature of a German Palestrina. Eccard's *Festlieder* received his highest recommendation for the service; his second choice was not Schütz or even Bach, but "the magnificent creations of Catholic masters of sacred music in the later 16th century." Without questioning, Winterfeld had adoped the views of quietism; their meaning for him and for like-minded persons has been ably summarized by J. Smend: "Protestant church music must take care to remain within the venerable bounds of a distinctly prayerful mood. Under no circumstances should it express passion; it must exude divine calmness and peaceful consecration." The Baroque tensions in the music of the two Protestant masters Schütz and Bach could not be reconciled with such views. Winterfeld's ideas were no more novel than his arguments against solo singing and instrumental music. Yet he approached the study of Protestant church music with these standards in mind, thereby channeling the taste of Protestants in one specified direction and providing them with a narrow historical view of their own sacred music. These factors give added significance to Winterfeld's views. Men in influential positions followed him, among them Gottlieb von Tucher, who had been a member of Thibaut's a cappella singing group in Heidelberg and who in 1827 had dedicated to Beethoven a collection of old Italian a cappella music. Another follower was the hymnologist Philipp Wackernagel at the fifth German Protestant Church Congress in Bremen (1852). The expert on liturgy, Schoeberlein, took up Winterfeld's ideas extensively in 1859 and 1865. He stated that the 16th century and first half of the 17th century represented the classic period of the church style; that solo singing should be eliminated; that choral music, as the voice of the ideal church, should be restricted to antiphonal singing (with the congregation) or responsorial singing (with the minister) during holiday services, should be popular (i.e., easily understandable), and should move within the expressive boundaries "of chaste moderation." He felt that Bach's works were artful rather than edifying or, as he said in 1881, were concert music rather than church music; besides, they were too subjective. In this later essay, Schoeberlein once more repeated the old slogan about "noble simplicity"; he also warmly advocated Palestrina's music. He rejected all instruments for the service except the organ and perhaps the trombone. In 1863 Oesterlein, another expert on liturgical matters, generally endorsed Schoeberlein's views. He was more open-minded in some details: he tolerated men's and women's choirs and to a small extent instrumental music; he admitted crescendo and decrescendo as well as organ fugues by Bach. In other ways he showed himself to be more narrow-minded: he rejected the works of Schütz as "opera arias with sacred texts," and he demanded that chorale settings of all kinds be syllabic, chordal, and have equal note values. Similar views were voiced by Mergner (1884), who did, however, point out that an a cappella style did not necessarily mean Palestrina style, and by Rietschel (1884), who still expressed a wish for more independent organ music in the service. Friedrich Riegel, Schoeberlein's musical collaborator, imposed a further restriction on Protestant church music: compositions should always be based on a Gregorian cantus firmus, just as sermons should be based on the Bible. Rochus von Liliencron likewise revealed strong leanings to Catholicism by at first (1880) opposing cantatas in favor of Mass settings by Palestrina (Kyrie, Gloria, Credo, with Sanctus and Agnus added at Communion). Nor did he wish to neglect instrumentally accompanied Masses by Mozart and by Michael and Joseph Haydn. Polyphonic chorale settings, cantatas, and so on, concerned him far less. His order of choral worship (1900) represents a wholehearted return to Winterfeld's a cappella requirements. In his outline for the *Tagamt* (main service), following Winterfeld, he attributed the greatest importance to Protestant chorale settings. Other choral compositions should be based on Gregorian melodies, as had already been demanded by Riegel. For the time being he advocated compositions by Palestrina, Lasso, and others, in German translations. These had been customary in Protestant services for some time. They had first been introduced in the services of religious circles outside the state churches, as in Johannes Falk's Weimar Sunday school in 1822 (see Leupold). After 1820 a growing number of collections of old Italian a cappella music appeared, largely for instructional purposes. Individual pieces from these also found their way into collections for use in the service. Volumes of this kind continued to be published even in the 20th century. Friedrich Spitta criticized them rather sharply as "undiscriminating hodgepodge, containing old Italian church music [i.e., by Palestina and his contemparies] with poor translations of the original Latin texts, and a few examples of German a cappella writing from the 16th to 18th centuries. To these some Bach chorales have recently been added, along with some works of questionable value by conductors and schoolmasters [of the 19th century]."

The growing appeal of the a cappella ideal is reflected in the founding of paid choirs made up of boys' and men's voices. Their stated purpose was the cultivation of a cappella music, primarily in the spirit of the restoration movement (as evidenced by the instructions to the choir of the Hannover palace church). As Ehmann shows, even trombone choirs came under the spell of these ideas. They were equipped with flügelhorns because the timbre of that instrument is fuller, mellower, closer to the human voice, and more likely to blend well than trombone or trumpet. Ehmann speaks of the devotional tone quality of the flügelhorn. From the beginning, the trombone-choir repertory consisted of vocal music only, especially of works by Eccard and his contemporaries. Bach chorales were added later, along with *Reichslieder* (see above). Special occasions called for Handel choruses, 19th-century motets, and similar works. A need for original works for wind instruments never arose. The a cappella concept affected even organ music.

The officially endorsed aesthetic of a cappella music came to be opposed by those who saw in the works of J.S. Bach the essence of Protestant church music. This was possible only for those who had completely renounced the quietistic or, in a popular sense, devotional view of church music, thus breaking with the Enlightenment. The first steps to bring Bach closer to the present had been taken in the concert hall beginning in 1829. J. Theodor Mosewius, director of the Breslau *Singakademie,* one of the first to program Bach's music in concert, was the first to claim Bach's cantatas for the service as well (in his book *J.S. Bach in seinen Kirchen-Cantaten und Choralgesängen,* Berlin, 1845). A.E. Müller, cantor of St. Thomas's in Leipzig, had already attempted it early in the 19th century, but only in passing and without finding others to follow his example. After 1842, Bach's cantatas gradually found their way back into the service of St. Thomas's under the cantor Moritz Hauptmann even though he, as a classicist, continued to have strong reservations about Bach on ecclesiastical as well as musical grounds. In his small book *Johann Sebastian Bach in seiner Bedeutung für Cantoren, Organisten und Schullehrer* (Bleicherode, 1865), C.A. Ludwig, cantor in Niedergebra (Thuringia), admits that Bach's vocal music is characteristically Protestant, yet he fails to recommend it for the service and speaks only of the educational value of his works, especially those for clavier and organ. It was left for the Bach biographer Philipp Spitta (*Die Wiederbelebung protestantischer Kirchenmusik auf geschichtlicher Grundlage,* 1882) to declare Bach the Protestant church composer absolute and his music *the* Protestant church music, the foundation of which was, and should be, congregational singing and the organ chorale. It was wrong, he said, to sing Bach's cantatas in the concert hall and Catholic a cappella music during the service. "Let us, for once, turn things around —give Protestant church music its rightful place in the house of God and cultivate a cappella music in concerts." In their own way, Spitta's views were no less doctrinaire than Winterfeld's. S. Kümmerle, particularly, propagated them in his *Encyclopedia of Protestant Church Music* (1888 ff.). The *Neue Bachgesellschaft* was founded in 1900; its aim was to make the Complete Edition issued by the old *Bachgesellschaft* (1850–1900) available for practical use. Only now did theologians take notice of Bach and claim him for their own—to the irritation of liberal musicians such as Max Reger. Soon Bach was canonized, so to speak, as "the fifth Evangelist." Bach cantatas were now heard in the service often—even regularly—though in recent times their liturgical use has again been discouraged. Another rediscovery was to become even more important for the service, introducing a kind of music that in every respect stands between Eccard and Bach and, therefore, appeared to be especially useful: the music of Heinrich Schütz. There had been occasional earlier performances of Schütz; the Frankfurt St. Cecilia Society had performed, among other works, *Saul, Saul, was verfolgst du mich?* in 1835. Karl Riedel's badly mutilated versions of the Passions had been performed at least since 1858. In somewhat modified form they were published in 1870–72. Arnold Mendelssohn and Friedrich Spitta had performed the St. Matthew Passion in 1881 and the St. John Passion the following year. In 1885 Philipp Spitta tackled the Schütz Complete Edition. Since then the works of this master have established themselves more and more solidly in the repertory of church choirs.

The various (i.e., these attempts described above) and partly contradictory attempts to revive Protestant church music "on a historical basis" (Ph. Spitta) eventually led to the realization, late in the 19th century, that there was no such thing as one style of Protestant church music. Kümmerle wrote in 1888: "It is impossible to establish a priori rules and definitions about what constitutes church music," though in practice he sided with Ph. Spitta and emphasized the central importance of chorale settings. In the following year Friedrich Spitta recommended Bach's organ works, among others, for the service. He also rectified the Romantic notion of the church choir by stating that the choir simply consisted of those members of the congregation with musical ability. The choir should participate in every service, with or without instruments, and it should by no means sing only "older classical," i.e., Renaissance, music. It might also include soloists, as long as they considered themselves members of the choir. He opposed pure solo singing. In 1897 Heinrich von Herzogenberg assailed any veneration of old music per se and especially of Catholic sacred music of the 16th and 17th centuries. Instead, he championed the works of Eccard as well as Schütz and Bach—both vocal and instrumental. F. Bachmann expressed similar views in 1899, though less clearly, calling for a cappella but not Catholic music. The old "noble simplicity" still crops up in the views of Köstlin (1901), but it no longer excludes any styles and now tolerates instrumental participation and solo singing. In the same year F. Spitta reaffirmed with certain modifications his earlier opinion that solo singing was valid if it was not only "of concert caliber" but represented a "testimony of faith."

As he says, it was against Lutheran principles to declare one certain style to be the only true one. J. Smend (1904) supported both of Spitta's points: he considered it an aberration to sanction one style; to ban solo singing was an encroachment on Protestant liberties. F. Sannemann presented a summary of these and similar views to the Vienna meeting of the *Internationale Musikgesellschaft* in 1909; they were agreed upon by that body.

This does not mean that tolerance at any price was the objective of these men. They wanted to prove first of all that the 16th-century a cappella style was not the only road to salvation. In doing so, they did not set out to defend mainstream 19th-century musical practice, which was an uncritical continuation of what the Enlightenment, through Doles and J.A. Hiller, had established, and which still found advocates in G. Nauenburg and J. Ch. Lobe. J. Smend summarized the attitudes behind this practice: "Whatever is performed in Protestant churches anywhere is church music. It sounds holy and familiar; the Good Lord is mentioned in the text; the church authorities approve." The repertory, he stated, consists of such indestructible pieces as Handel's *Largo,* Gounod's *Ave Maria* based on Bach's C-major Prelude, Rinck's *Preis und Anbetung* (sturdy, overflowing with typical male-chorus sentiment, and with poor declamation), and the Great Doxology by Bortnjanski (somewhat too pleasantly homophonic). Many similar examples could be quoted, among them Mendelssohn's *Es ist bestimmt in Gottes Rat* (for funerals), *Schäfers Sonntagslied* by Konradin Kreutzer, and Nägeli's *Der Herr ist mein getreuer Hirt* (choral arrangement by Th. Rückert; the favorite composition of Emperor Wilhelm II). Some discriminating choice was, of course, possible, even on such a basis. In 1901 Arnold Schering tried to make a place in the service for "outstanding solo performance." His recommendations, other than organ compositions, included adagios for violin by Tartini, arias by Mendelssohn, Beethoven's *Busslied,* and sacred songs by Brahms. To this, one pastor replied that one should not try to wish back the old days when young ladies regaled the congregation with lengthy arias between liturgy and sermon. Choral music no longer was considered the only kind of church music; yet it has retained a dominant position to the present day, though its character may have changed.

NEW DIRECTIONS IN MUSIC

Although even Winterfeld had issued warnings (1848), the danger continued to exist that composers would lapse into copying the style of glorified historical examples, and it is true that composers did not always escape this danger. Generally speaking, however, modern elements entered into the imitations of historical models. Some composers applied their knowledge of history to their own musical idiom, resulting in an amalgamation of old and new, with varying degrees of success. There is a basic difference between these works and others in which there is no recognizable borrowing from outdated historical models. The mere occurrence of a fugue, for instance, is no proof of such historical consciousness, for the tradition of fugal writing had never become completely extinct. Nor should Palestrina's influence be exaggerated. Many Protestant composers did visit the papal chapel in Rome (Mendelssohn, Nicolai, Kocher, Reinthaler, Neithardt, and others), some at the behest of the Prussian government, but they appeared to be concerned merely with the a cappella sound. For the same reason, journeys to the imperial court chapel in St. Petersburg were also undertaken. Compositions with a superficial resemblance to Palestrina were rare, for the chief characteristic of late Renaissance vocal polyphony of Flemish provenance was generally missing: strict imitation, carried through line by line. "Palestrina's influence" usually meant no more than successions of triads, including some secondary triads, certain cadential formulas, and drawn-out plagal cadences.

Sacred vocal music in the 19th century meant principally a cappella music. Among the many composers active in this field, representatives of the Leipzig and the Berlin schools should be singled out: in Berlin, Bernhard Klein and Eduard Grell; in Leipzig, Schicht and Moritz Hauptmann. Mendelssohn stands between these two schools. The high point was reached in the motets of Brahms.

Johann Gottfried Schicht, who became cantor of St. Thomas's in 1810, linked himself directly with tradition. Some of his motets were published in 1818–19, most of them posthumously in 1832; they were held in high regard for some time. They range from the simple choral song in several stanzas to the large chorale or psalm motet in many sections, from chordal chorale settings and melodically oriented homophony with some imitation (a mixture considered in the early and later 19th century to be appropriate for the motet) to florid contrapuntal writing and, frequently, fugue. The combination of chorale and Bible verse in Harrer's manner also occurs. Schicht had undertaken the first edition of J.S. Bach's motets (1802–03), which were apparently the models for his own motets, in regard both to technical difficulty (to a degree seldom found in works since Bach) and to their often vigorous polyphony and subtle treatment of dissonance. The melodic construction, on the other hand, shows the influence of Viennese Classicism, so that there is no unity of style; one feels suddenly transplanted from the church to the finale of a Mozart opera. Schicht is no stranger to certain effective devices already found in the works of Doles and other composers of the older school of Saxony and Thuringia. Thus an aria-like, melismatic soprano solo may float over sustained pianissimo chords by the whole choir. Similar effects can also be found in the *Motetten ohne Fugen* by the Magdeburg organist August Mühling. Though they ostentatiously avoid fugues, there is a general resemblance to Schicht's manner. Even Grell uses such effects.

The St. Thomas cantor Moritz Hauptmann strove for greater unity and simplicity in the "church style." Too often, however, he sacrificed intelligible declamation in favor of purely musical considerations. Hauptmann was at his best when writing in a cantabile style with expressive harmony; he was less successful in movements with march rhythms, which at times veer toward the popular and trivial. The best known of his motets, which were praised by Kretzschmar and Leichtentritt, is a *Salve Regina* (Op. 13, published in 1822). It displays a Catholic spirit and an extraordinary beauty of sonority, though its melody does not reach the level of its supposed model, Mozart's *Ave verum*. The frequent use of solo passages represents Hauptmann's inheritance from the age of Doles—an inheritance maintained in general use during the 19th century. After Hauptmann the chief representatives of the Leipzig motet school were his successors at St. Thomas's, Ernst Friedrich Richter and Gustav Schreck.

The restoration movement had a stronger influence on the Berlin school, though this was not apparent until the time of Grell. Bernhard Klein, a Catholic, had come to Berlin in 1818 and was active there at the Institute for Church Music. He had taken part in Thibaut's *Singverein* and was a friend of Tucher; both had high hopes for him. In 1824–25 he had established contact in Italy with Baini and Santini, the connoisseurs of old music. His eight books of *Religiöse Gesänge für Männerstimmen* (1828–31, and later), which became extremely popular during the heyday of male choral societies, were no Palestrina copies. Consisting of German and Latin psalm motets, lied motets, chorales, etc., with piano accompaniment that is usually optional, they are stylistically close to the traditional German motet, with fugues in the classic manner, and sometimes with line-by-line imitation. Some are in the tradition of the lied or the simple chorale harmonization. No. 5 in book III combines Klopstock's *Auferstehn* with the German Te Deum. In general, Klein makes a more serious impression than Schicht. Gallant and *empfindsam* elements have disappeared, to be replaced at times by a march-like quality. The Te Deum in book VI appears to be the best piece.

The restoration movement had its most devoted practical adherent in August Eduard Grell, who was deeply involved with church music in Berlin and the

Singakademie there. In spite of his notorious tendencies he wrote many completely traditional motets. His historical bent is apparently revealed only in his strictly liturgical works, which display a style reminiscent of the older Italian style and, just as often, of German motets from the age of Praetorius and Schütz. His occasional use of church modes is striking. Although Grell's style is correct, it lacks originality. It is generally festive and dignified but in the end has a tiring sameness about it, except for a few lively works from his early days. Through Grell's pupils J. G. Heinrich Bellermann and Martin Blumner—Reinhold Succo also should be mentioned here—and Bellermann's pupil Martin Grabert, the Grell style was maintained into the 20th century, although not without some modifications.

The foundation for Mendelssohn's motet writing lay in the tutelage of Zelter, under whom the twelve-year-old boy wrote choral fugues and also participated in the rehearsals of the Berlin *Singakademie.* There he became acquainted with the music of Bach, Handel, Karl Fasch, and Mozart, as well as with older Roman, Venetian, and Neapolitan church music. Contact with Thibaut in Heidelberg provided stimuli that are reflected in Mendelssohn's motet *Tu es Petrus* (1827), a work which follows in the style of Palestrina—really the contrapuntal style rather than the homophonic. Other works show that Mendelssohn amalgamated inspiration from history and from more immediate tradition, resulting in unaffected yet frequently artful compositions. These display a consistent texture—melodious, chordal and declamatory, or contrapuntal—varied by contrasting antiphonal and solo passages. All bear his personal stamp, though they differ from his secular vocal works. Romantic traits are more evident in Mendelssohn than in Protestant motets by other composers of the time. Classic clarity (or "rationalistic" triteness) is replaced by a more irrational melodic polyphony with emphasis on legato writing (frequently including "pedal" effects) and a pervasive lyricism which before Mendelssohn and Hauptmann was found only in small, *empfindsam* choral arias. Gentle ecstasy and moderate pathos are the prevailing moods. The phrase-by-phrase imitative writing in the *Deutsches Magnificat* (Op. 63, no. 3) impresses us as a personal expression of genuine feeling rather than as a stylistic statement. The same applies to the double fugue contained in this work, so very different from the fugues of Schicht and Klein, which are also well written but dry in comparison. Other motet writers followed in Mendelssohn's footsteps, among them Immanuel Faisst, whose writing was less subtle and skillful. R. Werner denies that Mendelssohn was in any way tied to the restoration movement except, superficially, by his compositions for the Berlin cathedral choir (including *Drei Psalmen,* Op. 78; *Sechs Sprüche,* Op. 79; and the *Deutsche Liturgie*). When this choir was founded in 1843, Friedrich Wilhelm IV entrusted Mendelssohn with its general direction (which did not prevent him from composing works for the Catholic and Anglican liturgy as well). In spite of his a cappella works, Werner says, he was more strongly attracted to instrumentally accompanied vocal music. Along with most 19th-century composers, Mendelssohn was surely more concerned with music that was freely religious than with church music in the stricter sense. He saw no possibility for the latter to flourish within the Prussian liturgy (letter to Pastor Bauer, 1835). Mendelssohn's Berlin appointment had raised many hopes for a fundamental revival of Protestant church music; these hopes were not to be fulfilled.

A stylistic cross-section of mid-19th-century a cappella writing is provided by the *Psalmen auf alle Sonn- und Festtage des evangelischen Kirchenjahres. Auf Allerhöchsten Befehl Sr. Majestät des Königs Friedrich Wilhelm IV. von Preussen componirt . . . und zum Gebrauche des Königlichen Domchores sowie aller evangelischen Kirchenchöre, herausgegeben von Emil Naumann* (Musica Sacra VIII–X, Bote & Bock). These psalms, insofar as they closed with the Lesser Doxology, could take the place of the Introit in accordance with the Prussian church orders, thus offering musical possibilities that went beyond the short "liturgical choruses." The works of August Heinrich Neithardt, conductor of the Berlin cathedral choir, represent the average. They range from chordal writing for double choirs in the 17th-century manner, with some "Palestrina" features, to the opposite extreme: the pure *Liedertafel* style. In between are compositions reminiscent of the rudimentary homophony found in Sander's *Heilige Cäcilia* (see above). Emil Naumann's *Psalmodien* should be mentioned since they show a tendency that became increasingly strong in the restoration movement in the 1850s. The model was Allegri's famous *Miserere,* to which Naumann specifically called attention in his essay *Über Einführung des Psalmengesanges in die evangelische Kirche* (1856). Verses set polyphonically or in a homorhythmic, *falsobordone* manner alternate with others employing free recitation on one tone, in which the congregation was to join. Mendelssohn's 22nd Psalm, with its juxtaposition of unaccompanied solo recitatives and full choir, is a revelation of how the concept of psalmody (in this case responsorial psalmody) could be raised to an artistic level. Nor are there any stylistic cracks in Mendelssohn's other a cappella psalms, even though the contours of 17th-century works for double choir are noticeable. Similar approaches are used by Ferdinand Hiller (whose 119th Psalm ends with an extensive fugue in the 18th-century manner) and Carl Reinthaler, whose works more strongly suggest the 17th century. Double-choir writing (often varied by solo passages) and homophonic declamatory sections dominate the entire collection, probably as a result of Mendelssohn's example.

Some composers are completely unaffected by the older historical models and follow, untroubled, the German motet tradition. This applies to Otto Nicolai, who, in his 97th Psalm, writes an effusive soprano *Aria* (with sustained chord accompaniment provided by the other voices, in the manner of Schicht mentioned above) followed by a conventional fugato. The height of modernity is reached in Meyerbeer's 91st Psalm. Without inhibition, he utilizes all the expressive devices of choral and ensemble writing found in contemporary opera and concludes with a lively double fugue for eight voices. It is an ingenious work (i.e., the whole, not the fugue only), though it runs counter to many views—held then as now—concerning what is suitable for the church. Isolated examples of the opposite extreme are Eduard Grell's Psalms, euphonious and rather melancholy, flawless copies of an older style, and with the appearance of being two to three hundred years older than they actually are.

Mendelssohn's attitude, though tinged by Romanticism, had been generally optimistic—an inheritance from the Enlightenment. Johannes Brahms stood at

107. Johannes Brahms, *Selig sind, die da Leid tragen* from the *Deutsches Requiem* Op. 45 (1867), autograph. Vienna, Gesellschaft der Musikfreunde.

108. Max Reger, opening of the organ fantasia on the chorale *Wachet auf, ruft uns die Stimme,* Op. 52, No. 2 (1900), autograph. Bonn, Max Reger-Institut.

some distance from this attitude. He showed a preference for texts that were serious, suggesting moods of longing and *Weltschmerz*. (It is no accident that Brahms wrote a *Deutsches Requiem* while Mendelssohn wrote a *Lobgesang* [Hymn of Praise].) Their basic sentiment is hope rather than faith. In his motets as in his Requiem he avoids Bible verses and hymn verses that express specifically Christian dogma (see Köser). He was not a church composer and did not consider himself one. Nevertheless, certain compositions have frequently been used in the service.

Brahms's earliest sacred works (around 1860) also include *Marienlieder* (Op. 22) and Latin texts of Catholic provenance (Op. 37), although Latin texts were not customary in 19th-century Protestant motets. (The *Salvum fac regem,* composed so often, is an exception, and Latin compositions by Klein, Hauptmann, and others cannot be counted here.) Beginning with the simple choral songs, Op. 22, he continued with the historically oriented motets of Op. 29, rich in learned counterpoint (one chorale motet, one psalm motet), and the women's choruses of Op. 37, some of which show strong Palestrina traits. These led to two motets of Op. 74, dedicated to Ph. Spitta, in which the imitation of 16th- and 17th-century style still seems somewhat artificial, and finally to the two mature sacred a cappella works: the *Fest- und Gedenksprüche,* Op. 109, and the *Drei Motetten,* Op. 110.

The large, biblical *Fest- und Gedenksprüche* were written 1886–88 and display a devout patriotism. Brahms handles the really eight-part double choir with a musical imagination exceeding Mendelssohn's. Lively declamation and other traits evoke Schütz—the colorful secondary chords, affective dissonances, and forceful modulations, the lyricism devoid of sentimentality, the dynamism in the polyphony. Although a more subjective spirit—admittedly hard to define—pervades the whole work, there is a feeling that Schütz has come back to life. Opus 110 also reveals Brahms's development. The earlier motets had been based on historical studies, and were strongly influenced by the older manner of chorale treatment; they had shown an indebtedness to Bach's spirit (rare up to this time), and they had avoided all sentimentality. Opus 110 shows that these features were now part of the composer's personal style. The *Begräbnisgesang,* Op. 13 (1858), is in a category of its own: a through-composed choral song with an obbligato accompaniment by wind instruments, i.e., a kind of lied cantata. The archaic element here is not found in the technique of composition but in the austere mood, medieval in a romantic way—the mood of a pilgrims' procession.

Herzogenberg said in 1898 that Brahms's virile and serious approach to texts was bound to enrich Protestant church music. It must be noted, however, that Brahms declined to contribute music for the "academic worship services" instituted by Friedrich Spitta, professor of theology. The latter had received an appointment in Strasbourg in 1887 and had organized the services in question during the following year. Liturgical music was to be provided by a choir under his direction.

Among the composers who complied with F. Spitta's request (others included A. Becker, M. Bruch, A. Mendelssohn, Herzog, Wolfrum, and Richard Bartmuss; later also Reger) was Heinrich [Freiherr] von Herzogenberg, who, as a result of Brahms's influence, had devoted himself to Protestant church music during the last years of his life, although he was a Catholic. His *Liturgische Gesänge für Chor a cappella für die akademischen Gottesdienste zu Strassburg i. E. componirt*, Op. 81, date from 1893–94. A later installment (Op. 99, 1897) contains an antiphonal work, based on a chorale, for choir and congregation with organ accompaniment. This indicates one of the two principal objectives aimed at by various groups in the late 19th century—to liberate the service from the more or less haphazard singing of motets. (The other objective, not attained, is characterized by Liliencron's order of choral worship; see p. 378.) Congregational singing was to alternate with choral polyphonic singing and thereby strengthen the choir's ties with the liturgy. In its essentials this had been an idea of the Enlightenment. It was again advocated with some force after about 1890, especially by the theologian Julius Smend. It is reflected in compositions such as the *Passionsgesang für Gemeinde und Chor* by Heinrich XXIV, Prince Reuss (1903, with organ; the choral verses are large chorale variation motets in a Bach-Brahms style) and Arnold Mendelssohn's *15 Choräle zum Wechselgesang für gemischten Chor*, 1912.

Spitta's plan included active congregational participation in church concerts, musical meditations, and the like, which would give them the character of a service attended by a congregation. "Church oratorios," originally suggested by the theologian Friedrich Zimmer, were to serve this purpose.

Zimmer had written in 1885 a *Denkschrift über die Einführung von Oratorien mit Gemeindebeteiligung* [Statement on the Introduction of Oratorios with Congregational Participation]. Having arranged a Christmas Oratorio text in this manner, he had it set to music by a composer from Königsberg. During the following years Breitkopf & Härtel published fourteen volumes of his *Sammlung von Kirchenoratorien und Kantaten*. They include singing for choir, solos, and congregation; most of the accompaniments are for organ only. Aside from older works (Schütz) there are compositions by L. Meinardus, R. Schwalm, H. Franke, K. Berneker, and others. In addition to a church oratorio *Selig aus Gnade* (1890), Albert Becker contributed a Mass in B-flat minor (first performed in 1879), which is significant because of its use of Protestant chorale cantus firmi.

Herzogenberg's works written for the same purpose were more successful. They had been suggested by Friedrich Spitta, who compiled the texts, and include the church oratorios *Die Geburt Christi* (1895), *Die Passion* (1896), and *Erntefeier* (1899). *Die Geburt Christi* is a good sample. It calls for solo voices, mixed choir, and children's choir accompanied by harmonium, strings, and oboe; there is also congregational singing with organ accompaniment. The work consists of a series of biblical recitatives, set in a manner frequently reminiscent of Schütz, together with polyphonic chorales (cantus firmus in soprano, bass, or tenor) in 16th-century style, biblical motets in the spirit of the 17th century, aria-like choruses in the 18th-century manner, orchestral interludes inherited from Romanticism, and the immortal congregational chorales. Frequently the models are copied all too faithfully. The striving for popularity is apparent in the simple overall arrangement and in the large number of Christmas carols and chorales. The general concept, relatively sober and pure (in spite of the harmonium), points to the future, as do the rich and substantial counterpoint and the harmony, which, in places, represents a continuation of Schütz. To base the recitatives of his Passion on Protestant chorales represented an original touch.

Philipp Wolfrum in Heidelberg also aimed at a popular style in his *Weihnachts-mysterium nach Worten der Bibel und Spielen des Volkes* (1898), an attempt to continue the tradition of medieval Christmas plays; the work is intended for scenic presentation in church. Richard Strauss characterized the work as representing "the skill of Bach, the ecstasy of Liszt," although his opinion is debatable. Wolfrum's concept of sound was formed by the orchestral writing of Liszt and Wagner. His sacred semiopera was not transformed into church music simply through the insertion of liturgical intonations and chorale melodies. Also, the orchestral accompaniments he added to vocal works by Bach show him to be completely wrapped up in the world of late Romanticism. Herzogenberg, on the other hand, associated himself with the Leipzig *Bachverein,* which was at first historically oriented and a pacesetter for neo-Baroque performance practices.

Like Herzogenberg, the Catholic Max Reger had been encouraged by Friedrich Spitta to write sacred vocal works with congregational participation. His *Choralkantaten zu den Hauptfesten des evangelischen Kirchenjahres* (composed 1903–05) were the result. Herzogenberg had paved the way for this genre with his chorale cantata *Gott ist gegenwärtig,* Op. 106 (1901), for congregation, choir, and orchestra.

One of Reger's first cantatas was *Vom Himmel hoch da komm ich her,* in which all fifteen verses are set without pause. The cantus firmus, continuously repeated, occurs mostly in one of the simply treated voice parts. Great care is lavished on the vigorous accompaniment (organ and two solo violins) with strongly chromatic voice leading. There is little that reminds one of the chorale; instead the Christmas carol *Stille Nacht, heilige Nacht* is occasionally quoted in the counterpoint. The general effect is of nervous motion. In most stanzas one voice has the cantus firmus with an instrumental accompaniment, suggesting the organ chorale as a model. The participation of the congregation in the sixth and last stanzas contributes to the dynamic resources of the work and helps to achieve the final climax, "sempre con tutta forza al Fine." The remaining three cantatas are on the whole similar. One has the impression that Reger's interpretation of congregational participation differed from that of the liturgists. At any rate, the strict adherence to a cantus firmus represents a liturgical element, while the general musical treatment shows more subjective artistry. In addition, Reger wrote simple four-part settings of Protestant chorales, clearly influenced by Bach's works in that category, and his motets should also not be overlooked. Greater significance should be attached, however, to his organ music.

Though several scholars have investigated the immense organ repertory of the 19th century, the picture today is neither clear nor without contradictions. The prevailing opinion is that there are no outstanding Protestant organ works before Reger, with the possible exception of Mendelssohn's organ sonatas. Even Brahms's chorale preludes (1896), in spite of the expressive qualities of some of them, are of little significance if compared with his masterworks in the fields of symphony, lieder, chamber music, and so on.

Nevertheless, some substantial and even interesting chorale preludes were written, especially in the later 19th century. Composers of note were Gustav Flügel of Stettin; J.G. Herzog, who was active in Munich and Erlangen; Karl Piutti, who was organist at St. Thomas's in Leipzig; and Theophil Forchhammer, who was cathedral organist in Magdeburg. To these should be added Reger, whose chorale preludes were written after his great chorale fantasies and partly for the *Monatsschrift für Gottesdienst und kirchliche Kunst,* the periodical of the liturgical movement that was led, around 1900, by Friedrich Spitta and Julius Smend. R. Walter sees in them a change in Reger's inner makeup. But Reger's importance as an organ composer lies not in his liturgical music but in his works for concert use. In this he followed in the 19th-century tradition of a clearly divided repertory: largely insignificant music for the service, written and published in large quantities (the chief publisher of organ music since 1838 had been G.W. Körner in Erfurt), and more taxing sonatas, variations, fantasies, concert fugues, and so on, for concert performance. Concert works were written chiefly by Louis Thiele, A.F. Hesse, Mendelssohn, J.G. Töpfer, F. Kühmstedt, A.G. Ritter, G.A. Merkel, F.W. Markull, and others, with a few contributions by Schumann and Brahms. Transcriptions and works for two players were also written. Often, as in the case of W. Volckmar, the music indulged in a superficial striving for effect. Innovations occurred in the field of concert music only. Works for church use (meaning especially the free, impressionistic pieces but also chorale preludes based on cantus firmi) continued to follow the road which had been charted in the early 19th century. Others, under the influence of the Bach renaissance, returned to the type represented in Bach's *Orgelbüchlein.* Throughout the 19th century one notices a general dualism of style: the "song without words" and "character piece" for organ on one side, cantus-firmus settings and fugues in the traditional contrapuntal style on the other.

Chief among the innovations are Mendelssohn's chorale sonatas, exemplified by three of his six organ sonatas. The organ sonata without chorale, which had reached a high point in the works of Rheinberger, may be omitted here. The Mendelssohn sonata with chorale quotation resulted in a long line of successors. The Sixth Sonata, a particular indication of future trends, is based, in turn, on the Baroque chorale partita, which had been revived here and there in the early 19th century as the chorale variation (by Rinck, Kittel, and others). Mendelssohn harmonizes the chorale in a simple manner, continues with several settings of the cantus firmus, and ends with a fugue on the first line of the chorale. A tender "Song Without Words" serves as an epilogue.

Töpfer's chorale fantasies (1859) follow this model; in general and in certain specific traits they already point to Reger. This observation applies even more to K. Müller-Hartung's Third Organ Sonata (1861) and to Gustav Flügel's fantasy *Wachet auf, ruft uns die Stimme,* both written under Liszt's influence. Heinrich Reimann's chorale fantasy *Wie schön leuchtet der Morgenstern* was the immediate model for Reger's chorale fantasies (1898–1900). According to H.E. Rahner's perceptive interpretation, these major works by Reger are a combination of chorale variation and symphonic poem (first found in organ music in Liszt's *Weinen-Klagen Variationen* of 1862), a combination that points toward a Romantic apotheosis, a climax of 19th-century technical and expressive advances fused with discoveries arising from the study of Bach.

According to his own declaration, the instrument in which Reger believed was the late Romantic (c. 1900) organ, capable of "orgies of sound" (Quoika). This sort of instrument had emerged around the middle of the 19th century, foreshadowed by Abbé Vogler's "simplification system." It had high wind pressure and a correspondingly high volume of sound. Tubular or electric pneumatic action resulted in greater facility of execution, while the crescendo pedal made gradual dynamic changes possible. Such an instrument had the largest possible number of registers, manuals, and couplers, and could move from a whispering pianissimo to a tumultuous fortissimo. Its heavy sound lacked the transparency and distinct colorings of the Baroque organ. The Thuringian cantor C. A. Ludwig had pointed out as early as 1865 that the character of the instrument had been distorted: "The organ tone can be compared with dogma. . . . A character pliant enough to adapt itself to another character will lose its individuality. If an organ stop is to have definite character it must not blend or adapt itself. Operating in collaboration with a variety of others, it should produce its own perfect tone rather than orchestral effects." The "organ movement" back to the Baroque organ did not begin until the early 20th century, with Albert Schweitzer and the *Internationales Regulativ für Orgelbau* (1909). It gained considerable momentum in the following decades. Reger's organ music is in every respect the crowning synthesis of the partly historical, partly modern trends of the 19th century, though (especially in his early works) it relies heavily on contrapuntal and formal devices of Baroque organ music (passacaglia). In the eyes of some (especially Söhngen and Kalkoff) he appears as the pioneer of the new Protestant church music, but while it is true that around 1900 he served the cause of restoration, the pertinent works are relatively unimportant. Reger's most characteristic qualities, his expressionism and his waste of compositional technique, do not yet contain the seeds of the development which began after him. These matters are discussed in the periodicals *Musik und Kirche* and *Das Musikleben,* 1952. The discussion was occasioned by the criticism which Helmut Walcha, among other things, had directed against the "painful formlessness" of the inner voices and against other idiosyncrasies of Reger's organ style—a style in which all compositional devices exist only as means to an end, not as being of value in themselves. The discussion clarifies the high degree to which Reger was a child of his time. This does not detract from his historical or absolute significance. He influenced the new church music in an indirect manner. Through his nonliturgical works he led German organ music in general to a higher level than had been attained since the time of Bach, providing encouragement and fresh momentum to later organ composition. His influence on organ playing was primarily felt through his pioneering interpreter Karl Straube, the "maker of organists" in the first half of the 20th century.

PART IV

Renewal and Rejuvenation

BY ADAM ADRIO

Translated by Leland R. Giles

TRANSITIONS AND HISTORICAL DETERMINANTS

This description of the revitalization of church music in the 20th century, which has occurred primarily in Germany since the 1920s, is merely an attempt to trace the outlines of an era that has justifiably been called "the renaissance of church music" (O. Söhngen). Like other epochs of Protestant church music, this most recent one stands on the shoulders of its predecessors. Consequently, it is necessary to show the main lines of development of the many different historical determinants of this renaissance, whose influence extends to the present and perhaps even into the future. It is a rebirth, moreover, that owes a great deal more to hymnologists and liturgists, to the church-music restorers and the liturgical reformers, to musicological research, as well as to several 19th-century creative musicians, than was immediately apparent to the new generation about 1930.

The enormous heritage of Protestant church music, which liturgical and musicological research and the "restoration" uncovered in almost endless quantities of historical material, not only bridged the arid period brought on by the Enlightenment but also brought about the growth of the new forces responsible for the current renaissance. It would be an injustice to the men of "historicism" to regard as their only purpose the revival of historical heritage. Indeed, Rochus von Liliencron, one of the leading figures of historicism, said that "the new [in liturgy and music] can be discovered only through reverent contact with the Catholic art of the 16th century and the Protestant art of the 18th, but the aim should be to permeate the music of today with the exalted, genuinely religious spirit of the old art, not to copy it insensitively; this would be, to quote Luther's famous comment on the church song: *'ein Nachahmen, wie die Affen thun'*" (a monkey-like imitation). In 1900, with modernization of sacred "music for the living" as his goal, von Liliencron proposed a *Chorordnung für die Sonnund Festtage des evangelischen Kirchenjahres,* based on his researches in liturgical history. Its purpose was to "restore to music its long-lost function as an organic element in the Protestant service." Quite logically, he entrusted the musical arrangements of the order of choral worship to a contemporary composer, the

H. van Eyken: Psalm for the second Sunday after Epiphany: *Prologue*

von Herzogenberg student Heinrich van Eyken, who provided the choral sections of the liturgy with settings by the old masters and with compositions of his own (1902–06).

Not only von Liliencron but also many of his theological and musical colleagues were convinced that historicism would ultimately prevail. For example, the Lutheran theologian Max Herold, founder and editor of *Siona, Monatsschrift für Liturgie und Kirchenmusik* (1876 ff.), anticipated, "in cooperation with the other restorationists, . . . contemporary church musicians will produce a new, liturgically related music out of the spirit of the old, but always new, faith."

Nineteenth-century hymnological, liturgical, and musicological researches continue to affect current church music, and some musical trends of the 19th and early 20th centuries reflect the influence of historicism. Philipp Spitta made accessible to no less a person than Johannes Brahms not only the works of Bach but also the contrapuntal organ music of Samuel Scheidt and the sacred vocal music of Heinrich Schütz. Brahms was one of the first great musicians of the 19th century to draw upon the historical tradition in a creative way. He added substantially to his instrumental and vocal output, with sacred and secular choral works as well as with the posthumously published organ pieces, by incorporating Christian themes into his works through the use of Protestant chorales and biblical texts. Brahms's younger friend and spiritual disciple Heinrich Freiherr von Herzogenberg, although Catholic by birth, emulated Brahms in his own later choral works, above all in his *Liturgische Gesänge* for a cappella chorus (Opp. 81, 92, 99; 1894–97), which were suggested by the theologian and musician Friedrich Spitta and written "for the academic worship services at Strasbourg." Together with his *Vier Choralmotetten* for four-part chorus a cappella (Op. 102), they testify to his conception of sacred music: "that the work of art be written specifically for a worship service in a specified form or, at least, so that it can be inserted without difficulty" (from *Johannes Brahms in seinem Verhältnis zur evangelischen Kirchenmusik* [The Relationship of Johannes Brahms to Protestant Church Music]). In the same essay von Herzogenberg also indicated meaningful goals for the younger generation: "From now on, may every superficial choice of material, every sentimental interpretation of the Scriptures, every feeble, saccharine harmony and melody be excluded; may the relationship of the composer to the church and to the parish become and remain manly, serious, and warmhearted! An age that has so successfully understood Heinrich Schütz and has experienced at first hand the expressive intensity of a Brahms can no longer content itself with Philistine hypocrisy; it can and must bring forth from its bosom works that in seriousness and magnitude of expression reflect the great figures of the past." Here, all the essential prerequisites for a revitalization of church music are already clearly spelled out: the necessary purging of every "superficial choice of material," the overcoming of any "sentimental interpretation of the Scriptures," the regeneration of "harmony and melody," and the clarification of the composer's relationship to the congregation and the church.

H. von Herzogenberg: *Zum Totensonntag (Schluss des Kirchenjahres)*, Op. 92

At the same time, however, the works of J. S. Bach are no longer considered the only historical standard. Rather, there is a new awareness of Heinrich Schütz, and Johannes Brahms is looked upon as a pioneer. Brahms had directed his attention toward the field of a cappella music, which had been almost completely banished in an age dominated by instrumental music. Von Herzogenberg had tried to promote an understanding of the function of music in the worship service, and it was to the undeniable credit of the younger Max Reger that he joined with Brahms in regarding the physical properties of the church and the music written specifically for the organ as legitimate problems to be dealt with seriously by the creative musician.

With his chorale-based organ works and a series of a cappella and accompanied choral pieces, Reger became one of the first musicians of the new age to make extensive use of the organ, the chorus, and—with both these "instruments"— Christian subject matter. Problems of style in the organ and choral works and questions concerning the compromise instrument of his period, for which Reger wrote his organ compositions, will not be discussed in this context (see p. 402 f.). The fact that the polyphony in Reger's relevant works is rooted in the harmony of late Romanticism does not alter his achievements from the standpoint of music history: that he readopted creatively the stylistic idea of polyphony, that he realized this ideal convincingly, within the limitations imposed upon his dynamic personal style by his own era, and that by so doing he opened doors to the future. The historical influence of Reger's music was not interrupted by the First World War, nor was it effaced by the ensuing change in taste from the late Romantic expressivity of his style, the dynamic music of a waning epoch.

It must not be overlooked that this reversal of stylistic trends was evident quite early, particularly in the field of church music. Among the musicians of the transitional period whose artistic goals led to the ideals of the style change about 1930, one of the first was Arnold Mendelssohn. Eighteen years older than Reger and outliving him by almost as many years, he was "a sensitive and highly polished neo-Romanticist" (*Riemann-Lexicon* 11, 1929). To a large extent he incorporated "Christian material" into his output, writing mostly cantata-like works for solo voices, chorus, and orchestra on biblical texts and with Protestant chorales. These include *Das Leiden des Herrn* (1900), and the chorale cantatas *Aus tiefer Not* and *Auf meinen lieben Gott* (1912), Psalm 125 and Psalm 137 (1913).

Mendelssohn was especially interested, however, in the problem of a cappella music for the worship service. After the early four-part *Chorsätze nach Spruchdichtungen des Angelus Silesius,* Op. 14, he composed his first chorale settings, the five four-part *Geistliche Tonsätze,* Op. 32. The *16 kirchliche Lieder und Motetten* for three-part boys' or women's chorus are polyphonic chorale settings that follow the sequence of the church calendar. In large a cappella works such as the *Reformationskantate,* Op. 87, the *Deutsche Messe,* Op. 89, Psalm 100 (without opus number), as well as in other works, the influence of Heinrich Schütz is evident, most of all in the *14 Motetten für das Kirchenjahr,* Op. 90 (1924), inspired by the St. Thomas choir in Leipzig and related to Bach's motet *Singet dem Herrn.* With a dedication addressed to the Leipzig City Council, Mendelssohn was imitating Heinrich Schütz in his *Geistliche Chormusik* (1648). Although his composing model was Schütz's *Psalmen Davids* (1619)—settings mostly for double chorus, occasionally including solo voices—his use of a *de tempore* principle recalled Schütz's later works. The *14 Motetten,* with appropriate scriptural texts or chorales, embrace the principal feasts of the church calendar (e.g., the advent motet *Träufelt ihr Himmel von oben,* which appears in Liliencron's order of choral worship as "Eingang zum 3. Advent"; *Ach wie flüchtig, ach wie nichtig,* which is a chorale motet). Arnold Mendelssohn was one of the first post-Herzogenberg composers to oppose seriously and creatively the historical models of Bach and Schütz; going even further than von Herzogenberg, he was critically at odds with Brahms in regard to the essence of genuinely liturgical music.

Arnold Mendelssohn: *Advent Motet,* Op. 90, V

In his *Aufzeichnungen*, Mendelssohn says: "Where his [Brahms's] religious music is genuine, it sings only of his longing for the freedom of Heaven, but this itself we never see." Mendelssohn's writings reveal how thoroughly he involved himself with the problems of historicism, of the archaic style (in church music), of polyphony, and of a cappella writing. His insight into the necessity of following the old masters of Protestant church music was revealed by the seventy-four-year-old composer in 1929: "Today, of course, because newly awakened religious feeling is seeking an outlet, artists find themselves temporarily obliged to emulate the old religious music (which undoubtedly is more substantial than the insincere music currently popular), in order to find a way to that point where an original style of religious music will again be possible" (*Aufzeichnungen*, p. 67). In full knowledge of the problems of 19th-century church music, he demanded above all the revival of an a cappella art devoted to the worship service: "If it is to be revived, this style of composition, which has become stunted and deplorably banal since its golden age, will at first require emulation of the old masterworks." Mendelssohn considered neither the "somewhat Philistine motets of Grell" nor the "sleek, elegant ones of Felix Mendelssohn" to be suitable models; his own "large a cappella works" he described only "as stages in the development of the completely free, original art work . . . that the future will bring" (ibid., p. 68). The following words were written during the years in which the stirring of a new spirit was already being felt (c. 1930): "In church music, hitherto despised by our educated classes (and also by the dilettante youth movement in music) as being second- or third-rate art, the wave of the future appears to be cresting" (ibid., p. 73). In 1931 or 1932 the venerable old master could, in regard to his own sacred compositions, express the hope that "in time, the church may perhaps evolve in such a way that my works will find their proper place." Here he had in mind primarily the *de tempore* motets of Opus 90, which are "highly rated, indeed, but seldom sung." Today these pieces still deserve respect for the honest effort and superb compositional skill directed toward the creation of a polyphonic vocal style modeled on the old masters. They are noteworthy for their superior manipulation of polyphonic textures such as the canon, the fugue (Op. 90, No. 12, a chorale fugue), the double fugue (Op. 90, No. 11), the triple fugue (Op. 90, Nos. 13 and 14), and the quadruple fugue (Op. 84), as well as for the straightforward yet individual way in which the composer has mastered "archaism" in psalmody and recitative, and for the masterful treatment, based on Bach and Schütz, of the double chorus.

Arnold Mendelssohn: *Advent Motet*, Op. 90, V; opening of the sixth movement

In addition to his use of the chorale (in Op. 90, Nos. 3 to 11), which is always determined by its content, Mendelssohn's interpretation of texts reveals his desire to develop polyphonic structures out of the symbolic content of the text, to confer an adequate musical form upon the spiritual substance (the religious subject matter). Thus, it was not merely as a philosopher that he called for the return to a cappella choral music, the unification of the Word and the chorale, and the liturgical function serving as the fundamental prerequisite of genuine church music; it was also as a musician who created a series of works intended for the worship service, who should not be underestimated as a pioneer in the renewal of Protestant church music, and who ushered in the triumph of historicism in the field. Not surprisingly, several younger composers (such as P. Hindemith, H. Spitta, G. Raphael, and K. Thomas) absorbed the teachings of this master, applying his ideas to modern music and thereby to the new church music as well.

Arnold Mendelssohn's ideas and accomplishments were so much in advance of his time that only in the last decade of his life could he see the long-awaited breakthrough of a new Protestant church music. Heinrich Kaminski, a generation younger, belonged to a somewhat peripheral group of personalities in modern German music who followed and promoted the new church music with a host of important works, even though they were not connected to the church in the strictest sense. As the son of an Old Catholic rector, Kaminski was concerned with the problems of liturgical Protestant church music but only insofar as they related to his own creative efforts. Like Reger (who was thirteen years older), he felt close to the expressivity of the late Romantic musical spirit. He had struggled passionately all his life to escape the limitations of his own musical background and to develop out of the spirit of genuine polyphony a musical style of his own. For the time being it must be left to posterity to pass final judgment upon whether this honest struggle achieved enduring results, but it cannot be overlooked that Kaminski provided an essential impetus to the incipient new Protestant church music through his entirely personal conquest of a linear polyphonic style.

Kaminski's first compositions evince a strong relationship to the works of Bach. This is clearly discernible in his Psalm 130, which had already appeared in 1912; a motet for four-part mixed chorus a cappella (Op. 1a), which shows his concern for a genuine polyphonic choral style; and in the *Sechs Choräle* for four-part mixed chorus a cappella (1915), presumably inspired by Wilhelm Klatte, Kaminski's teacher in Berlin. The last-named six chorales contain several melodies taken from Schemelli's *Musikalisches Gesangbuch* of 1736 and therefore attributed to J. S. Bach. Three of these cantus-firmus settings, fundamentally oriented toward Bach's "cantional settings," also utilize the basso continuo of their prototypes.

Heinrich Kaminski: *Psalm 130,* Op.1a; opening of the first movement

The strength of Kaminski's bond to the late Romantic ideal of sonority is demonstrated primarily in the sacred concert piece that established his reputation, Psalm 69, for eight-part chorus, four-part boys' choir, tenor solo, and orchestra (1913–14); the B-A-C-H quotation in the bass voice (measure 4) pays its respects, stylistically, to the Bach ideal as well. The subjective choice of the psalm verse and the composer's alterations of its text are appropriate to the equally subjective orchestral texture, which, in striving for "romantic" expression, often obscures the linear structure. However, the polyphonic goal is achieved with élan in the quadruple fugue of part I and the double fugue of part II. In the 1918 motet *O Herre Gott* for eight-part mixed chorus and organ ad libitum, based upon the three mystic couplets from Will Vesper's collection *Der deutsche Psalter* (which Reger set as a sacred solo song; Op. 137, No. 5), Kaminski was relatively successful in breaking away from his models. Consequently, several characteristic traits of his personal style already begin to emerge more clearly: the use of unison chorus and pedal point; the "flowing motion" achieved by triplet figurations, polyrhythms, and tempo changes; and, not least, a new expressive power in the polyphony that is implied by the detailed specifications for phrasing and execution. In two further works he strove toward a new a cappella style: the 1926 motet *Der Mensch,* for alto and six-part mixed chorus on texts by Matthias Claudius *(Motet* and *Der Mensch),* and the motet *Die Erde* (*Zarathustra: Yasna 19,* in the translation of Paul Eberhardt), for six-part mixed chorus a cappella (1928). These works testify to the composer's mature personal choral style and are significant landmarks on the path toward a new choral music. However, they are not church music even though, by their use of philosophical and religious material in the choral statement, they do stand relatively close to the essence of genuine church music as so clearly defined by von Herzogenberg or Mendelssohn. The same applies to both of the larger sacred concert works: *Introitus und Hymnus* and the mature Magnificat. In the *Introitus und Hymnus,* for soprano, alto, baritone, violin, viola, cello, orchestra, and small mixed choir (1918–19), Kaminski the "mystic" is unmistakable in the highly subjective alliance of heterogeneous texts: to the *Nachtlied* from Nietzsche's *Zarathustra* in the *Introitus,* he juxtaposed his own ecstatic verses and I Corinthians 13 (verses 1–3, 8–10, 13) in the *Hymnus,* set for "Chorus mysticus in the distance." Coming after the motet *O Herre Gott,* this work, which is suitable for the concert hall, represents a further step in the development of Kaminski's own style and his search for an "earlier" (pre-Bach) polyphonic ideal. His personal style reached its artistic culmination in the formal clarity of his Magnificat for soprano, viola, orchestra, and small offstage choir (1925). In accordance with his conception of the Magnificat "as Mary's hymn of praise in the brilliant light of the prophecy, and thus as the rejoicing of every soul struck by that light" (see Bibliography, section VI, F. Stein, 1930–31), Kaminski placed selected verses of the "angel's prophecy" (Luke 1) ahead of a partially adapted Magnificat text (Luke 1:46b–49). Additional texts are assigned to the "small offstage choir" (Alleluja, Sanctus, and *Osianna in excelsis Deo*), and a solo soprano is used with the choir in an abbreviated Doxology. The concentration on one textual source, the biblical word, matches the formal clarity and greater transparency of the orchestral accompaniment in this mature work. It is not a setting of the Magnificat that would be suitable for a liturgically oriented worship service, for it is a highly personal interpretation of Mary's (liturgical) hymn of praise, both in its subjective profession of faith and in the way in which its linear, objective quality evokes the secular atmosphere of a concert hall.

As a member of the Old Catholic sect standing above narrow denominational thinking, Kaminski influenced the course of Protestant church music between the two world wars. In the conviction that the concept of *Kunst* [art] derives from that of *künden* [announce], that "the ultimate, most essential sense of a work of art" is "to bring tidings of the Light" ("Einiges über 'alte und neue Musik,' über Sinn"; see Bibliography, section II) he brought a singularly intense feeling of mission to his artistic task. The essence of genuine polyphony for which he strove in his vocal and instrumental works was not counterpoint, not merely musical craftsmanship, but rather, as he put it, "eternal laws of life becoming sound— simply, the 'living Being' becoming evident; polyphony is prophecy 'speaking in tongues'; its mouth, the abundance and extravagant profusion of its 'many voices' " (*Über polyphone Musik;* see Bibliography, section II). Written after June 30, 1934, and released by his estate after the last war, the *Messe deutsch,* for five-part choir a capella, is a moving testimony to Kaminski's personal conception of music. The work consists almost exclusively of meditations on his own experiences translated into musical terms. It refers to the text of the Mass only with the words "Kyrieleis" in the first movement, "Christe eleison" in the second, and "Gloria patri, gloria filio, gloria in excelsis deo" in the last. It is probably not by chance that the text for the third movement was never set to music; yet what was completed of this personal avowal of faith will forever command respect.

Kaminski's few compositions for organ include the *Choralsonate* (1926), which is a setting of four chorales, *Drei Choralvorspiele für Orgel* (1928), *Toccata und Fuge für Orgel* (1939), an early *Canzona* (1917), and a later *Canon für Violine und Orgel* (1934). Only the toccata on the chorale *Wie schön leuchtet der Morgenstern* (1923) has historical as well as artistic significance: it was one of the first works to come near the objectives of the new organ movement, to the extent that it makes fundamental use of terraced dynamics. This fact is pointed up in the foreword: "The composer urgently requests that . . . manual changes be restricted to those indicated at any given time, and that any swell or 'tone coloring' effects be dispensed with completely, since these are absolutely contrary to the spirit of the work." But the "spirit of the work" is really determined by the individually contrasting facets of all the movements, derived from the substance of the chorale tune, as well as by the decided inclination toward a new organ style based on a linear polyphonic texture.

The new music and the new Protestant church music of the 20th century are not separate phenomena in the history of either music or style. The church music that emerged with increasing prominence after the First World War belongs in a larger sense with the new music resulting from a fundamental change in style. In the twenties, when many "churchly" choral and organ works, Masses, motets, cantatas, etc., first became objects of discussion at the most diverse "secular" music festivals, it was not because of their ultimate potentiality as church music. Rather, it was because they, too, were part of a struggle for a new style free from the expressive excesses of late Romantic music; in this way, they were one with secular concert or chamber music. It would be a misrepresentation of the facts to regard the regeneration of church music as a result of events within the church, or to view it as an accomplishment solely of the church and its musical servants, isolated from the development of secular music. Indeed, other musicians, not only those in the service of the church, had turned to Christian subject matter, to the Bible, to the textual and musical wealth of the Protestant chorale, and to the Latin texts of the Mass or the Te Deum. A renewal of a cappella music—and this was among the goals of new music—could be achieved only by assimilating more substantial texts, newer and weightier spiritual materials. If we believe that the religious—specifically Christian—"theme" was this influential in the development of modern music, for purely artistic reasons, then we must recognize that the new religious consciousness, the prevailingly spiritual orientation of large segments of the populace following the catastrophe of the First World War, was behind the artistic events.

Within the Protestant church a subdual of 19th-century liberalistic theology became the theological goal. This led to a renewed consciousness that one of the foundations of the Protestant church is the concept of reformation, an eternally changing process that may be traced to the present and one whose incredibly entwined course cannot be projected further at this time. With the return to Lutheran fundamentals, the forms of worship at the time of the Reformation won renewed consideration and esteem. Thus, the historically oriented liturgical efforts of the 19th century merged with the active work of the "liturgical movement" of the 20th. Based on the theology of Karl Barth and through the musical initiative of the cantor Friedrich Buchholz, the "Religious Movement at Alpirsbach" aspired primarily to achieve a "German Gregorianism." The *Berneuchener Arbeit,* created principally by Wilhelm Stählin, Karl Bernhard Ritter, and Wilhelm Thomas and supported by the *Evangelische Michaelsbruderschaft* (Protestant Brethren of St. Michael), which was founded in 1931, was bent on an "inner renewal of the church" and was particularly concerned with the "creative reorganization" of the liturgy, using liturgical tradition as a point of departure. Finally, the Lutheran Liturgical Conference, headed by Christhard Mahrenholz, prepared over a period of years a new order of worship for the United Protestant-Lutheran Church of Germany. In 1951 it submitted an *Agenda* for Lutheran "churches and communities," as well as other pertinent publications. The present liturgical situation may be characterized here in the words with which Rudolph Stählin summarized his review of *Die Wiedergewinnung der Liturgie in der evangelischen Kirche* (*Leiturgia* I, p. 74 ff.) in 1954: "In spite of minor differences, a common cause is emerging that disregards political and denominational boundaries: the overthrow of subjectivism, an orientation to the early church, the reinstatement of the total worship service, a renewal of the evangelical proclamation of the Gospel, and the re-establishment of the Eucharistic purpose of the altar sacraments." These maxims may serve as fundaments in the regaining of the liturgy. In the knowledge that "liturgy is the Mother Earth of church music" (O. Söhngen), basic decisions were reached about the essence of genuine church music, the various forms of worship service were opened up to receive new church compositions, and goals were established to which young composers could dedicate themselves if they were in spiritual readiness.

Of great significance for the acceptance of new church music in the twenties was the understanding of "old music" gained through active singing and playing by the "musical youth movement." Rooted in the folk-song romanticism of the prewar *Wandervogels,* this movement embraced the great a cappella art of the 16th and 17th centuries in the choral societies and numerous "festivals" that arose after the First World War. In dealing practically with the heritage of "classical" choral literature—with the song-oriented style of the 16th century and the text-oriented "polyphony" of the 17th century—the young generation discovered an entirely new dimension of music. They achieved a deep understanding of the creative mystery of this music, which always has a purpose, an external and internal message. They gained an understanding of the cantus-firmus techniques of polyphonic composition as revealed in the lied settings of Johann Walter, Ludwig Senfl, and all the masters of the century of the Reformation. They also recognized the fundamental ingredients of this great music—the exalted spiritual motifs of the chorale and the Scriptures (the latter, mostly through the textual art of Heinrich Schütz) and its functional basis in the service. But above all, in cultivating the "old," they attained an understanding of the "new polyphonists"; indeed, they realized the intrinsic necessity of providing "new" music for the church and the worship service.

In addition to the theological-liturgical movement and the choral movement, the organ movement emerged as a third source of the regeneration of church music, thanks to the initiative of such men as Wilibald Gurlitt, Christhard Mahrenholz, and Hans Henny Jahnn. Founded upon the musicologically established fact that every historical epoch has produced instruments corresponding to its ideals of sound, the "old" organ, primarily the more or less authentic Baroque instrument, became popular with organists, organ builders, musicians, and composers. The historical model led to a reassessment of the modern organ, which had increasingly incorporated all technical advances. This, along with the return to the sound-ideal of the old organ, led to a recognition of the "law of the organ," thus establishing a fundament prerequisite to the emergence of a new polyphonic organ style appropriate to the newly acknowledged original essence of the instrument.

In addition to internal prerequisites, there was an improvement in external conditions: the social elevation and security of the church musician (initiated by church authorities) and his spiritual and artistic promotion through the founding of new training centers at a series of state church-music schools, new regulations in the training and certification of organists and cantors, and so forth.

The revival as briefly sketched above often derived its energy from the momentum of history; it would not have led to a "renaissance of church music" in the creative sense, however, had it not been accompanied by the fundamental change in musical style often somewhat summarily characterized as the reconquest of polyphony. The return to the ideal of polyphonic linearity indicated the only stylistic path along which genuine church music could again become possible; this had already been recognized by such men as von Herzogenberg and A. Mendelssohn. In the old polyphonic art of the 16th century, in the *contrapunctus gravis* of the *stile antico*, Heinrich Schütz (and his contemporaries) had already perceived the essence of sacred music, had recognized the criterion of the *stylus antiquus . . . auch wohl a cappella, ecclesiasticus genennet*. Thus, with the impending triumph of traditional music, the way opened out of the spirit of polyphony to produce church music within the stylistic sphere of present-day music. After approximately 150 years of stagnation, Protestant church music again entered into current musical development, into that *Aktualität* (F. Blume) so fundamentally significant to its story, with which it embarked on its historical journey in the time of the Reformation.

RESTORATION OF THE VOCAL CHORALE SETTING

Since the mid-twenties the new emphasis upon Christian repertory, internally connected with the change in musical style, has led to a significant revitalization of choral music and organ composition. One of the first exciting choral events in the more recent history of music was the 1925 Leipzig premiere of the Latin *Messe in A* for soloists and two choruses, Op. 1, by Kurt Thomas. The enormous success of the work, confirmed in Kiel the same year, was symptomatic in two respects. For the first time in a long while a young composer had, with an unaccompanied choral work, successfully participated in the genesis of new music and at the same time established his artistic reputation. Furthermore, Thomas's Opus 1 was the first work of a dawning musical epoch that restored a cappella music within the complex of living musical developments, thereby placing it on a par with great instrumental music.

Kurt Thomas gained further experience in a cappella composition the same year with his Psalm 137 for two choruses a cappella, Op. 4, dedicated to "Master Arnold Mendelssohn in gratitude and respect." In 1926 the St. Thomas choir performed his *Passionsmusik nach dem Evangelisten Markus,* for mixed chorus a cappella, Op. 6, dedicated to Karl Straube. So far, however, relatively few of the composer's vocal works are "chorale settings." In addition to the large chorale cantata *Jerusalem, du hochgebaute Stadt,* for four soloists, chorus, large orchestra, and organ (1928–29) from *Sechs kleine Choralmotetten,* Op. 46b (1929) and several pieces from the *Kleine geistliche Chormusik, Werk 25* (1934– 36), are works in which a chorale is occasionally utilized within the larger context of a motet.

The use of the Protestant "chorale setting" was spotlighted at the 1929 Duisburg Music Festival of the Association of German Composers, where several movements of Ernst Pepping's 1928 *Choralsuite* for large and small chorus were premiered. Here is another case of a young composer who succeeded in impressing the musical world with a religious a cappella choral work. Except for a previous *Suite* comprised of *6 Choralvorspiele für Orgel,* the monumental *Choralsuite* marks the beginning of Pepping's involvement with the musical and spiritual-religious substance of the Protestant congregational hymn, an involvement that fundamentally affected not only a considerable number of his choral and organ works but his entire vocal and instrumental output as well. At first an older compositional technique was used for cantus-firmus settings, but at the same time a new principle was established, one of significance for all of modern composition and especially for church music.

In this three-part *Choralsuite* the composer employs all the contrapuntal skill at his command to set the chosen chorale melodies, the three-strophe *Wir glauben all an einen Gott* of Martin Luther in part I, the three hymns encompassing Christmas, Good Friday, and Easter in part II, and the three hymns in celebration of mortality, morning, and evening in part III. The order of the seven chorale motets obeys artistic laws of contrast, e.g., by varying the number of choral parts from three to twelve, and by distinguishing between "small" and "large" chorus. In the uncompromising polyphonic technique of these cantus-firmus settings, the composer clearly established his attitude toward musical material: a free tonality developed from the church modes and a richly creative melodic variation technique in a primarily linear a cappella style, derived from the shape and substance of the chorale melody. The basis of his personal attitude toward music was seen to be deeply rooted in tradition and filled with that consciousness of mission required of his generation.

The perceptible spirit of genuine church music in this *Choralsuite* arises from the composer's strict adherence to the cantus firmus of the chorale melody and from the linear movement of the individual voices, which obey the laws of counterpoint and rise above subjectivity; it is realized in the austere, masculine sonorities of the pure a cappella chorus, excluding "every feeble saccharine harmony and melody" (von Herzogenberg). In the same year (1928), the small *Kanonische Suite in drei Chorälen* for three-part male chorus appeared, also a free suite that became a liturgical cycle, the *Deutsche Choralmesse* for seven-part chorus (premiered in 1931 at the Bremen Music Festival of the Association of German Composers). In addition to the customary Gloria and Credo (*Allein Gott*

Ernst Pepping: *Deutsche Messe: Kyrie Gott Vater in Ewigkeit.* Third movement, from the second strophe
(pages 16 and 17 of the score)

in der Höh, Wir glauben all an einen Gott in the single-strophe setting), the Kyrie
utilizes the old *Nun bitten wir den heiligen Geist* and the Sanctus draws from the
melodic store of the Bohemian Brethren in *Kommt her, ihr Elenden;* in addition
to the fifth movement, *O Lamm Gottes, Verleih uns Frieden gnädiglich* (for the
Dona nobis pacem), generally attributed to Luther, is used as the sixth movement.
The six-movement work is not a mass in the sense of the Latin Ordinary, nor is
it a Protestant lied mass or chorale Mass; however, the order of the six chorale
motets clearly points up their intended connection with the liturgy. There is a
definite liturgical relationship in the *Deutsche Messe, Kyrie Gott Vater in Ewigkeit,*
for four- to six-part mixed chorus a cappella (1938); following the titular Kyrie
is a prose setting of the Gloria, *Lob, Ehr, und Preis sei Gott;* and following
Luther's three-strophe *Wir glauben all,* again in prose, is the *Heilig ist Gott der
Vater;* the finale is based on *Christe, du Lamm Gottes.* The maturity of the vocal
style is in keeping with the liturgical atmosphere of the work, attained through

adherence to the chorale and the liturgical order of the "Protestant" Mass.

The *Choralbuch* of 1930–31, dedicated to Friedrich Blume, marks the close of Pepping's early "chorale period"; its *30 kanonische Choräle* for mixed chorus a cappella have been edited and arranged according to the church calendar by Chr. Mahrenholz. Because of the composer's effort to come to terms with the repertory of Protestant church songs, these tend to predominate. In the transformation of the chorale tune into a canonic voice the listener recognizes, in addition to the ever present chorale, the composer's unique melodic skill in the contrapuntal treatment of a chorale melody.

Ernst Pepping: *Choralbuch/ 30 Canonic Chorales;* opening of *Aus tiefer Not*

A few years later Hugo Distler, who was trained primarily in Leipzig under Hermann Grabner, began his vocal writing with chorale-based compositions. He presented his first choral work in 1931, the motet on the chorale *Herzlich lieb hab' ich Dich, o Herr,* for two mixed choruses a cappella, Op. 2 (1931); in its overall form and polyphonic structure it was an imposing test of the young musician's talent. Martin Schalling's three-strophe song determines the organization. Set for double chorus, the outer movements embrace the middle strophe (arranged in five parts); single, freely selected verses of the 18th Psalm are contrapuntally organized against a psalmodizing solo soprano voice, thus indicating an attempt to unite the polyphonic cantus-firmus movement with a personal interpretation of the song text. Contributing to this end are precise interpretative markings and characteristic, strongly contrasting tempo indications. As organist at St. Jacob's in Lübeck (from 1931), Distler rapidly matured to the specific task of his office —writing church music. In 1931 he composed *Eine deutsche Choralmesse* for six-part mixed chorus a cappella, Op. 3 (published 1932). It was performed in October 1931, by Bruno Grusnick's Choral Society of Lübeck at the Nordic-German Organ Conference, even though the work was intended not to serve a liturgical function, but rather (composer's afterword) "to meet the increasingly urgent needs of our newly oriented choral societies, which either emerged from the choral movement or have accepted its standards and leadership." This goal also determined the more transparent contrapuntal structure of the work: "From the concern for practical performance stemmed the idea of choral division into large chorus and small chorus" (afterword), as well as the "latent double-chorus character" of the six-part setting, visibly influenced by early classical choral music. Only the first three movements correspond to the liturgical cycle of the

Ordinary: 1. *Die Fürbitte;* 2. *Der Lobgesang;* 3. *Der Glaube.* The cantus-firmus foundation of the first movement consists of a troped Kyrie handed down by Spangenberg (*Kirchengesänge deutsch,* Magdeburg, 1545); in movements 2 and 3 a one-strophe Gloria and a three-strophe Credo of the Bohemian Brethren (1566) are used. Movement 4 consists of *Die Stiftungsworte* (in place of the Sanctus). Here, in addition to the *Verba testamenti aus Luther's Deutscher Messe 1526,* for solo soprano, a three- to five-part treatment of the song setting of the sacramental words "aus Veit Dietrichs Agendbüchlein 1548" is combined with the melody *Es sind doch selig alle die* (by Matthias Greitter, 1525; better known as the melody of *O Mensch, bewein dein Sünde gross.*) The chorale strophe *Wir*

Hugo Distler: *Eine deutsche Choralmesse,* Op. 3; opening of the fourth movement, *Die Stiftungsworte*

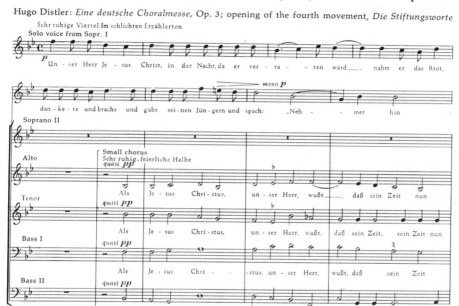

danken deiner Wohltat Gross (1570) takes the place of the Agnus as the closing prayer of thanksgiving of this "German chorale Mass."

Other composers also took up the cycle of the German chorale Mass after Pepping and Distler. While on the faculty of the Institute of Protestant Church Music in Heidelberg, Wolfgang Fortner, from the Leipzig school of Hermann Grabner (as were Thomas and Distler), wrote *Eine deutsche Liedmesse* for mixed voices a cappella (1934, published 1935). It was "intended primarily for the celebration of the worship service, that is, for the collective worship service embracing Holy Communion, as in the German Mass of Martin Luther" (composer's foreword). Fortner utilized as cantus firmi the melodies from the Ordinary of the German Mass: *Kyrie, Gott Vater in Ewigkeit, Allein Gott in der Höh sei Ehr, Wir glauben all an einen Gott, Jesaja, dem Propheten das geschah, Christe, du Lamm Gottes.* In line with the revival of alternation, the executants have the option of allowing the congregation to perform single strophes of the Gloria and

Credo in unison ("with the usual organ accompaniment"); the demanding *Jesaja, dem Propheten,* notated in part without bar lines, can "be omitted entirely, for which the 'Holy, Holy' of the congregation may be substituted." The *Deutsche Liedmesse,* for three-part mixed voices and three instruments ad libitum (two violins and violoncello), written by Karl Marx in 1950, is also "primarily intended for the worship service" (composer's foreword). It utilizes the same cantus firmi except for the Sanctus, where the song of Isaiah is replaced by the liturgical-prosodic *Heilig ist Gott der Vater* (as in Pepping's *Deutsche Messe Kyrie Gott Vater*). In these polyphonically relaxed chorale settings, consciously treated in a straightforward manner, the composer offers smaller church choirs "more challenging music for their liturgical service" (ibid.). A more recent composition in this category is Johann Nepomuk David's *Deutsche Messe* for mixed chorus, Op. 42 (1952), whose cantus firmi are the same as those in Fortner's Mass. Each of the five chorale motets is different stylistically. In some sections of the work, particularly in the Amen of the Credo or in the Holy of the Sanctus movement, the strict contrapuntal writing is juxtaposed with colorful chordal sonorities, testifying to David's concern for finding a new and individual solution to the relationship between text and music.

There can be no doubt that the active resumption of the cyclic form of the German Mass or the German chorale Mass was stimulated by a practical edition of the first five settings from Heinrich Schütz's *Zwölf geistliche Gesänge* (1657), which were published by H. Holle in 1925 under the title *Die Deutsche Messe.* Composers began gradually to use hymns (and their cantus firmi) from the German Ordinary, in order to arrive at a cyclic form that could justifiably be called a German Mass or German chorale Mass. In every case, the first, third, and fifth movements of these Masses are cantus-firmus-based chorale motets. The choice of texts for the Gloria and Sanctus varies. If the Gloria *Allein Gott in der Höh sei Ehr* is utilized for the second movement, and Luther's Sanctus melody *Jesaja dem Propheten* for the fourth movement (with their cantus firmi), then all five movements belong to the category of the cantus-firmus-based chorale motet. Only then is the title "German chorale mass" appropriate for the cycle.

Hans Friedrich Micheelsen's *Deutsche Messe* for five-part chorus a cappella (1953) ought to be mentioned here only because of its title; none of the movements except the last is based upon a chorale melody, and the cycle is not cantus-firmus-based. The Kyrie and Gloria use texts from the so-called *Deutsche Messe* of Heinrich Schütz; the Credo is based on R. A. Schröder's Credo poem *Wir glauben Gott im höchsten Thron* (1937), the Sanctus on an early orthodox version of *Heilig ist der Herr Zebaoth,* and the Agnus Dei on the German Agnus hymn *Christe, du Lamm Gottes* (only the last one appears with the corresponding melody).

In addition to its function within the cyclic form of the "Mass," the chorale motet also became increasingly important as an independent genre. From the outset Distler's vocal chorale treatments closely resembled the simple chorale setting, particularly in the *Drei kleine Choralmotetten,* Op. 6, No. 2, of 1933. The strophic variation form he uses here is the same as that of the four larger chorale motets (Nos. 3–6) in the *Geistliche Chormusik,* Op. 12 (nine compositions altogether), written after 1934.

In the "small" chorale motet *Es ist das Heil uns kommen her* the two four-part outer strophes enclose the two-part setting of the middle strophe; the cantus firmus is more or less freely varied according to the content of each strophe of text. The same design is evident in the larger-structured four-part *Motette auf die Weihnacht* from the *Geistliche Chormusik* (Op. 12, No. 4), *Singet frisch und wohlgemut*. In the next section of the four-part first strophe, the cantus firmus migrates from the soprano to the alto; the model for this Reformation-based (Walterian) note-against-note cantus-firmus setting is just as clear as is Distler's attempt, through his own stylistic means, to bring the simple chorale setting closer to the shape of a motet (which may be seen, among other places, in the melismatic extensions at the ends of lines; cf. *Auf Erden*).

In the larger chorale motets, as they emerged in the course of the thirties, the polyphonically structured chorale setting of Johann Walter (Walter's second type, according to F. Blume) became more or less consciously established as the point of departure. For example, the penetration through imitative technique of the chorale's substance into all voices characterizes the polyphonic structure of

Hugo Distler: *Singet frisch und wohlgemut*, motet No. 4 from the *Geistlichen Chormusik*, Op. 12. Measure 13 ff. of the first part

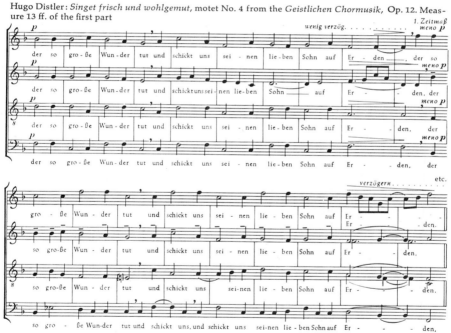

Günter Raphael's chorale motet *Erhalt uns, Herr, bei deinem Wort*, for five-part mixed chorus a cappella, Op. 30, No. 2 (published 1932). The unison statement of the first strophe is followed by its polyphonic restatement with the cantus firmus descending, one line at a time, from the upper voice into the bass. The second strophe is similarly handled, its cantus firmus appearing each time with the closing line "dass sie dich lob in Ewigkeit" in the uppermost voice of each part of the divided chorus. In the third strophe, the cantus firmus remains entirely in the second soprano.

Günter Raphael: Chorale motet *Erhalt uns Herr bei deinem Wort*, Op. 30, No. 2; end of the second chorale strophe

The first chorale settings of the Upper Austrian composer Johann Nepomuk David (who was born Catholic) were written under the influence of the active a cappella tradition in Leipzig. In 1936 he dedicated to Karl Straube and the St. Thomas choir a tripartite motet of monumental Baroque proportions: *Ex Deo nascimur—in Christo morimur—ex spiritu sancto reviviscimus*, for eight-part mixed chorus. The Latin motto opens part I, the first strophe of Luther's devotional hymn *Wir glauben all*. In part II the chorus is divided into two three-part groups; the motto *In Christo morimur* is sung by the lower chorus, and the first and third strophes of the Requiem hymn *Wenn mein Stündlein vorhanden ist*, with its melody, by the higher chorus. Part III, set for eight-part double chorus, has as its basis the third strophe of Luther's Credo which appears at the end in fourths with the theme of the first movement in the Latin summary *De spiritu sancto reviviscimus*. The work is indicative of David's ideal of a consistent, uncompromising polyphonic style. Supreme mastery of musical-contrapuntal craftsmanship, occasionally approaching "contrapuntal wizardry," is at the root of the harmonic severity and the austere sonority of this a cappella work. Four additional, more concisely structured, four-part chorale motets belong to the same period (1935–36): *Nun bitten wir den Heiligen Geist* (in which the first strophe of the chorale appears in strict canon against an ostinato bass); *Ein Lämmlein geht und trägt die Schuld; Herr, nun selbst den Wagen halt* (four to five voices); and *Ich wollt, dass ich daheime wär*. In his organ works David dealt much more comprehensively with the problems of the cantus-firmus setting.

It is not feasible at this point to trace *in extenso* the subsequent path of the chorale-motet genre. Apart from the composers already mentioned, substantial contributions were made by J. N. David's pupil Helmut Bräutigam, also Hans Friedrich Micheelsen, Hans Chemin-Petit, Eberhard Wenzel, and many others. However, the direction was not simply toward greater precision in the outlines of the genre, but rather toward a multiplicity of types, embracing everything from "small" chorale motets, much like chorale strophe settings, to the larger forms of the artistically structured chorale motet. In spite of stylistic variance, efforts devoted to this genre have been united by a common sense of responsibility toward the text and melody of the chorale, a recognizable desire to re-create the traditional "romantic" a cappella ideal, and a common goal: the creation of vital vocal music out of the stylistic strength of polyphony.

Before turning to the chorale cantata, a genre which has become popular again since about 1930, it seems advisable to look at the most modest form of chorale setting, strophe by strophe. Hugo Distler was the first among the young musicians of the time to regard as necessary the revival of this form and to undertake the task. In 1933 he published as *Der Jahrkreis,* Op. 5, "a collection of 52 two- and three-part sacred choral works for use by church, school, and amateur choirs." According to Distler's foreword, the collection "ensues from church-music practice and aspires to meet the general need for simple *de tempore* music in the worship service."

Apart from several liturgical compositions and settings of biblical proverbs, the collection, arranged according to the church calendar, contains about 40 three-part chorale settings, significant in their fundamental rejection of the epigonic four-part chorale setting. Each of the independent voices in these two- and three-part settings obeys the law of its own linear progress. For the most part, the upper voice carries the chorale cantus firmus, occasionally slightly altered.

Hugo Distler: Chorale setting *Mit Freuden zart,* No. 18 from *Der Jahrkreis,* Op. 5

In contrast to Distler's new beginning stands Ernst Pepping's *Spandauer Chorbuch* (published 1934–41), which is given over entirely to sacred songs related to the music in the worship service at the Berlin School of Church Music. With its 271 chorale settings of 250 melodies, the collection represents a definitive document of modern Protestant church music. Indeed, there has been no comparable work since the Cantionales of Praetorius and Schein.

Liturgical function determines the order. Books I to XIV contain settings of *de tempore* hymns from Advent to the end of the church year *(Tod und Ewigkeit);*

books XV to XIX contain additional settings of hymns grouped by subject: *Kampf und Not, Anbetung, Gottesdienst und Sakrament, Morgen,* and *Abend;* as a "short cycle for like voices," book XX offers 25 more settings for the period from Advent to the end of the church year. All the settings are based on the melodic versions of the *Evangelisches Gesangbuch,* adopted in 1931; the keys of those versions are retained so that there can be antiphonal participation by the congregation. In most (161) of the settings the cantus firmus is in the upper voice; in the three-part settings the cantus-firmus melody appears in the middle voice in 71 cases, in the lower voice in 30 cases; in 9 instances the cantus firmus is canonically doubled. About half the settings are for three voices, scarcely a third for four; a smaller group of five-part settings (20) compares with an almost equal number (18) of two-part settings and a group of three pieces for six voices. In 34 settings there exists "the possibility of exchange of parts between the upper and middle voices"; however, according to the composer's remarks on performance of the settings, the exchange "should be made only in performances of more than one strophe" and then "only in such a way that the altered version is clearly secondary to the original version." Like Distler *(Jahrkreis),* Pepping was aiming "toward the possibility of a vocal-instrumental performance . . . in which, through strophic variation, an often cantata-like expansion . . . can be realized. In this regard the choice of an instrumental complement has few limitations. In any given instance . . . it should be determined by instrumental resources available at the moment. The more colorful it is, the better. In most cases the inclusion of wind instruments is desirable." The composer offers (book XX, appendix) several possibilities for instrumental combinations.

As a genuine Cantionale, the *Spandauer Chorbuch* includes all the melodies that are used by, and antiphonally with, the congregation in the service. It is based on the *Evangelisches Gesangbuch* of 1931. In accord with newly initiated efforts to augment the traditional stock of melodies, 26 hymns of the Bohemian Brethren (1531, 1544, and 1566) were incorporated. If the settings of these particular examples are "exquisite in text, melody, and compositional skill," then clearly the quality of the chorale settings corresponds in large measure to the quality of the hymns. Here, too, Pepping's linear technique and melodic skill serve to enhance the dominating, always audible cantus firmus. The form of the hymn tune determines the form of the setting. In the three-part settings, which outnumber the others, the linear principle is especially prominent, making it easy to follow the progress of each of the independent voices. The polyphonic energy of individual

Ernst Pepping: Chorale setting *Wie soll ich dich empfangen, Spandauer Chorbuch,* No. 5

voices is also effective in settings for four and more voices, for even in thick chordal sections the independent lines are subject only to their own peculiar melodic laws. With the relaxation of polyphonic texture and the enrichment of a more simplified chorale setting, the problem of relating text and music was posed in a new way. Pepping's soaring melodic phrases reflect vocal movements; they are indebted in large measure to the text and melody of the hymn.

A performance practice coming from the Reformation allows for the possibility of instrumental support for one or another of the vocal parts, or permits instruments to play the entire piece. Moreover, this attests to a movement away from the traditional, exclusively a cappella performance of chorale settings. The attempt to revive the chorale setting on the basis of the spirit of the Protestant chorale and the strengths of polyphony could have resulted in stylistic plagiarism. Contemporary musicians have overcome this danger by synthesizing the artistic-polyphonic principles of Reformation song settings with the simplicity required for congregational singing and the often modest capabilities of church choirs. Such a solution is similar to what was realized toward the end of the 16th century in the so-called cantional setting. That kind of setting had been forced to surrender a good deal of its artistic quality; the extent to which that quality can be restored will determine whether the chorale setting can be taken seriously in contemporary music and also whether it will lead to future developments.

"The insight and experience of the collaborators made it possible to meet the demand for a simple, technically clean, artistic body of vocal chorale music, as stylistically unified as possible. Thus, in these books we encounter for the first time contemporary collections of chorale settings appropriate to the present circumstances of our choirs. Moreover, in presenting singers with a unity of style as well as musical and choral problems, they prepare them for richer and more challenging tasks by their demands." With these words (foreword) Christhard Mahrenholz defined in 1940 the temporal limitations and the practical and pedagogical significance of two collections of "new" chorale settings based on melodies in the *Evangelisches-lutherisches Gesangbuch der Hannoverschen Landeskirche:* the *Choralsingbuch für 3 gemischte Stimmen,* one male and two female voices (ed. by Ferdinand Schmidt), and the *Choralsingbuch für 3 gleiche Stimmen* (ed. by Chr. Mahrenholz). The melodic versions of the *Evangelisches Kirchengesangbuch (EKG),* adopted in 1951, greatly stimulated publication of chorale collections whose settings have attempted similarly to unite the principles of simplicity and craftsmanship: *Das Wochenlied* for mixed or like voices, edited by K. Ameln, G. Schwarz, Ph. Reich; the chorale books *Die helle Sonn* (two- to three-part settings), *O gläubig Herz* (two- to three-part women's or children's chorus), *Komm Gott Schöpfer* (three- to four-part mixed chorus), edited by A. Strube in his *Sammlungen leichter Choralmusik;* and many others. The innumerable practicing church musicians and composers who began to produce such sacred collections for church use became, in the words of Carl von Winterfeld, "setters" of given melodies (of the Christian community) and have left their mark on a diversified stylistic picture (included among them are Bornefeld, Baur, Bender, Beyer, Brod, Degen, Dietrich, Distler, Driessler, Fiebig, C. Gerhardt, Gottschick, Hessenberg, Kiefner, Knab, Kraft, Neumeyer, Petzold, Rahner, Raphael, Reda, Ruppel, F. Schmidt, W. Schmidt, G. Schwarz, H. Stern, Stier, Thate, Voppel, A. Wagner, Walcha, E. Weiss, E. Wenzel, and Zipp).

Collections of chorale settings by contemporary composers appeared simultaneously with a number of more recent chorale collections by the early masters. All of them follow the order used in the Protestant congregational hymnals (since 1951: *EKG*). The third edition of Hans Michael Schletter's *Musica sacra* (vol. I), edited by Ralf von Saalfeld in 1927, assured the propagation of the tradition and at the same time its use in the musical reconquest of the Protestant hymn in the thirties. Along with more recent, scientifically based source works (for example, *Luthers Kirchenlieder in Tonsätzen seiner Zeit,* ed. by K. Ameln, 1934; *Handbuch der deutschen evangelischen Kirchenmusik,* ed. by K. Ameln, Chr. Mahrenholz, W. Thomas, C. Gerhardt, vol. III: *Das Gemeindelied,* 1935 ff.), there emerged the *Chorgesangbuch,* published in 1934–35 by Richard Gölz. The latter offered music for church performance, consisting mostly of cantional hymn settings from the "time of Martin Luther to Sebastian Bach" (preface). Fifteen years later G. Grote published his *Geistliches Chorlied* (1949), containing new two- to six-part settings and intended primarily for choral rather than congregational singing. The timely juxtaposition of these publications of "old" and "new" hymn settings in that fourth decade testifies to the increasingly fruitful interrelation of the force of history and contemporary efforts. Important support came from the initiative and professional interest of the publishers involved.

Among many other simple chorale settings are the three-part *Lieder für das Jahr der Kirche* of Gerhard Schwarz, in which the cantus firmus is always in the middle voice. Another collection is the *Kanonische Choralmotetten für alle Kirchenzeiten und kirchlichen Feste* of Walter Kraft, which contains 24 settings in motet style "for two to four cantus-firmus voices and one free voice." According to Kraft's foreword, his arrangements stem "from the necessity . . . of creating absolutely valid polyphonic . . . chorale settings for choruses of every description and stage of development, but especially for children's church choirs with modest, almost 'monophonic' resources."

In a basic and far more comprehensive way, Helmut Bornefeld dedicated his musical output to an educational goal, particularly in his *Choralwerk,* a series consisting of eight different categories. The preface to the *Kantoreisätze zu zwei bis fünf Stimmen mit Instrumenten* (six sections in *de tempore* order) clarifies their pedagogical purpose: "The *Kantoreisätze* are devised to introduce the resources of sound. They may be played by any ensemble from small to large, and should be combined into cantata-like forms with other chorale pieces (accompanied settings, organ chorale settings, etc.). . . . All ranges of the voice, recorders, strings and woodwinds, some brass and keyboard instruments (organ, positive, harpsichord, piano) should be considered as possible sound resources." Thus Bornefeld follows the practice of vocal and instrumental participation that prevailed into the early 17th century (M. Praetorius). In addition, he reckons with a far more demanding improvisatory style of performance, for the realization of which a number of "rules" are proposed, such as: "2. All voices can be put an octave above and often an octave below, but always striving for a unified whole. If instruments double the voices, then they must conform [in their phrasing, etc.] precisely to the text underlay. With instrumentation on a larger scale, fifths also may be added. 3. When there is a bass voice, it should not be obscured by doubling the upper voices at the lower octave. On the other hand, exchange and deletion is desirable and often quite exciting. Keyboard instruments may play two voices that are suited to them. Many settings may also be underscored with fifths or chords in *bourdon* style, played by the left hand (on the organ, with pedals)." As is apparent from these instructions and "rules," and from the detailed introduction to the *Kantoreisätze,* 1949 (*Musik und Kirche* XIX, 8–16), Bornefeld was attempting to provide more than a pedagogical tool. He was trying to replace the traditional a cappella principle of the simple chorale setting with the principle of a mixed vocal-instrumental complement. Using the sound of the (organ-derived) "Baroque" concerto as his historical ideal, he tried to link it creatively with contemporary musical tendencies.

In the composer's view, performances of unadorned chorale settings, which depend on the presence of musicians who can improvise, require careful preparation and meticulous rehearsal. Only through the realization in sound of the composer's notated "res facta" will performers and listeners become conscious of the degree to which it can musically enhance a given hymn tune in terms of a progression and development of sonorities embellishing a cantus firmus.

The attempt to combine vocal and instrumental resources in chorale treatments was already becoming evident in efforts directed toward the "new" chorale setting. In the same way, the first example of the more recent (vocal-instrumental) chorale cantata was dedicated not to the limited uses and possibilities of liturgical music but rather to the spirit of the concert hall: *Jerusalem, du hochgebaute Stadt,* for four solo voices, mixed chorus, orchestra, and organ, Op. 12 (1929), by Kurt Thomas, dedicated to Fritz Stein and the Oratorio Society of Kiel. This composition, much like an oratorio in form and sound resources, is one of the first of the newer choral works with orchestra to be based on a hymn text: the eight strophes written by J. M. Meyfarth in 1626, with the corresponding melody of 1663. Because of its commitment to a large orchestra, however, the work scarcely could serve as a model chorale cantata for contemporary church music.

Since the thirties, the task of creating chorale cantatas for the worship service has been undertaken principally by church musicians, among whom were Fritz Werner, Carl Gerhardt, Kurt Fiebig, Gerhard Schwarz, Hans Friedrich Micheelsen, Walter Kraft, and Kurt Hessenberg. These practical musicians were guided by the principle of performance in alternation, the distribution of all possible strophes of a "congregational hymn" among congregation, chorus, and soloists with organ or obbligato instruments (ad lib.), with contrasts between monophonic and polyphonic strophes and between purely vocal and vocal-instrumental (organ) ones. The composers' pride in making the most skillful use of the text and melody of the hymns what distinguishes the genre, for artistic quality is dependent in large measure upon the substance of the chorale tune. After the last war, this unpretentious genre, frequently called the "small" chorale cantata, was cultivated by H. Chemin-Petit, Friedrich Högner, Helmut Bornefeld, Friedrich Zipp, and many others.

Bornefeld's chorale works, consisting of several series (see p. 428 f.: *Kantoreisätze*; also *Choralmotetten, Orgelchoralsätze, Begleitsätze, Choralpartiten, Choralvorspiele, Choralsonaten*), includes a succession of eleven chorale cantatas. Like the *Kantoreisätze*, they provide for additional vocal parts (in chorale cantatas Nos. 1 and 5) or ad libitum instrumental parts (in No. 1, 2, 3, 6, and 8), and combine their liturgical function as music for the worship service with the pedagogical goal of developing the improvisational skills of singers and instrumentalists and stimulating them to serve the spirit and content of the chorale.

In addition to four solo cantatas for soprano—Nos. 1, 5, 9, and 11 (with the addition of a five-part chorus)—there are six cantatas for one to three like or mixed voices (Nos. 2, 3, 6, 7, 8, and 10) and one for five mixed voices (No. 4). In the preface to chorale cantata No. 8, *O Traurigkeit, o Herzeleid,* the composer states that the "simple appearance of the notes" is not an indication of "plain *Gebrauchsmusik*"; even if the work "is not technically difficult to perform, it is conceived 'expressively' from beginning to end." The conductor "must take great pains to regulate tone color in order to reconstruct the painful, ominous atmosphere of the Entombment, which I have tried to realize in this music." Of significance in Bornefeld's chorale cantatas is the definite turn toward an expressive style and, linked to this, toward the solo cantata; inventiveness, style, and

Helmut Bornefeld: *Kantoreisätze II*

a) No. 53, *Jesus Christus, unser Heiland, der den Tod . . .*

b) No. 66, *Gott, der Vater wohn uns bei*

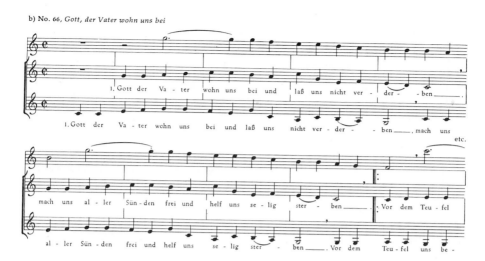

structure, however, even in these chorale settings with higher artistic aims, are fundamentally directed toward the sound-ideal of the organ. It is not coincidental that in the composer's written instructions the concept of "regulated tone color" plays such an important role. The filling-out of sonorities by ad libitum instruments (in cantatas Nos. 1, 2, 3, 5, 6, and 8) is as characteristic of this concept as his choice of obbligato instruments (in Nos. 2, 3, 5, 7, 8, and 11), and his choice of organ as the foundation for the sound of all the cantatas (with registration indicated as unambiguously as possible). In three cantatas, the formal structure includes strophes to be sung by the congregation (Nos. 4, 6, and 7).

Cantata No. 8, also called a "small" chorale cantata, is based on the six-strophe Passion song *O Traurigkeit, o Herzeleid:* the same setting is used for strophes 1 and 6, for 2 and 5, and for 3 and 4. Strophes 2 and 5, which are sung by the congregation, have an instrumentally accompanied cantus firmus. The desired "painful, ominous atmosphere" is produced by a cantus-firmus-carrying background played by the organ and two obbligato violins (with cello ad lib.) and containing the chorale motifs. In this simple three-part chorale setting, articulated (in strophes 1 and 6) one line at a time or (in strophe 4) half a line at a time, contrasts with the third strophe, which is presented "forcibly" in a declamatory style using seventh and ninth chords. It clearly reveals the composer's own interpretation of the text and hence the controlling relationship between word and sound in this music.

The chorale cantatas published since 1953 in the *Werkreihe für Bläser und Sänger* owe much to the stimulus of Wilhelm Ehmann, "to encourage once again the musical union of vocal and brass choirs." The cantatas include two each by Johannes H. E. Koch, Walter Rein, and Karl Marx, and one each by H. F. Micheelsen, Jan Bender, Hermann Stern, and Friedrich Zipp. According to the editor, "these publications transcend the *Kantoreisätz*. They emerged after long years of effort and extensive experimentation among composers, music historians,

and practicing musicians"; here, too, an educational ideal with a sense of history
is at the root of music that strives "for the utmost simplicity, however decisively
it makes its way."

The creative involvement with the Protestant congregational hymn that was
taken up between the wars was not halted with the catastrophe of the Second
World War. However, the enormous number of vocal chorale settings written
since 1945 can neither be examined here nor properly introduced. A number of
younger composers followed those already mentioned. The three principal types
(chorale setting, chorale motet, and chorale cantata) still constitute the nucleus
of vocal chorale settings. The artistic gains have included a large body of independent a cappella music (the chorale motet), a structurally transformed chorale
setting, and (emanating from the old *per omnes versus* practice) the revival of
chorale cantatas using diversified resources—vocal and instrumental, soloistic
and choral.

Among the more recent chorale settings are those of Siegfried Reda, who has
said that he used the organ as his point of departure and found, as did his teachers
Pepping and Distler, the intellectual base of his creativity in the Protestant hymn.
His *Zwölf kanonische Choräle,* for two like voices, were modeled after Pepping.
Following the composition of this work, he remained continuously involved, like
Bornefeld, with the problems of cantus-firmus settings, and his *Chormusik für das
Jahr der Kirche* contains several series of the genre. Its contents include the
Psalmsprüche und -lieder for two to eight voices from the collection *Das Psalm-
buch* (1951) and the collection *Das Graduallied* (1953). The former, apart from
free compositions based on biblical psalm verses (and several complete psalms),
includes 13 settings of sacred texts (primarily of psalms); the latter contains only
chorale settings for two to eight voices (primarily four voices, although not
entirely in the traditional arrangement of two male and two female); so far, part
I, with 39 settings of texts embracing 36 weeks, has been completed. Formally
and structurally, Reda's chorale arrangements occupy a middle ground between
the chorale setting and the chorale motet, alternating between simple and more
richly structured motet-like types. Reda adheres to the melodic versions of the
EKG, and his rhythmically and harmonically free idiom follows strictly linear
principles of movement. In his introduction to the *Graduallied* he recommends
some "possibilities for instrumental or combined vocal-instrumental arrange-

Siegfried Reda: „O Mensch, bewein dein Sünde groß"

On the repeat of the first two lines, the lower voices retain the underlying text

ments of a hymn setting based on available instrumentation." He also expresses the ideal to which his chorale settings are dedicated:

> The cantus is always the axis of the setting. Its shape must be firmly secured in taut but spacious progressions of sound. In their . . . relationship to the syllabic shape of the cantus all linear events should be conceived as temporary "digressions." The resounding shape of the cantus, its inherent forms of movement, and its declamatory independence should be a corrective force in the movement of every other voice. It is only the capacity to maintain this relationship that will give the setting internal vitality and a resilient tension, and, through the . . . aural enhancement of space, make the cantus-firmus setting a mediator to the understanding of its immortal content.

During the last decade, a series of chorale motets *(de tempore)* for three- to six-part mixed chorus has appeared as part of H. Bornefeld's *Choralwerk.* Having already expressed his very personal ideas of reform in his teaching and writing, the composer abandoned the improvisatory ad libitum practice (of the *Kantoreisätze* and the chorale cantatas) and strove in this series to realize an individual, exacting a cappella style. His musical imagination, obviously based on strong constructivist tendencies, produced a series of form-building elements: organum-like parallel movement of free voices accompanying the cantus firmus, ostinato and the canon, the strict imitation (with reference to the three-movement chorale motet No. 7, *Mit Freuden zart,* for five-part choir a cappella), and a consistently realized polyphonic technique that nevertheless observes the critical limits of "artistic counterpoint." All of these elements serve the compositional goal of mastering as a musical form the cantus-firmus setting in the manner of a motet.

Helmut Bornefeld: Close of the four-voice chorale motet IX, *Heilger Geist, du Tröster mein*

As may be observed in the chorale-based vocal works of Bornefeld, Reda, and others, the distinction between types is not always clear, and the particular form of a chorale setting is not always accurately described in the composer's title. This is often the case with the smaller forms as well; for example, the third part of H. F. Micheelsen's *Hamburger Motettenbuch* contains three "chorale motets" for three like voices, in which the three single strophic movements are connected, and in which the overall form is no different, fundamentally, from that of his earlier *Kleine Kantate* for three- to four-part chorus on the lied *Wir wollen alle frölich sein.* (They do differ in that two of the chorale motets incorporate settings of biblical texts without cantus firmi.) Nor are motets of the larger format to be found in the *Fünf kleine Festmotetten* for three mixed voices with instruments ad libitum; rather, these are simple, strophically varied chorale settings in the form of "small" chorale cantatas with instrumental preludes and interludes and an ad libitum instrumental accompaniment.

In addition to simple works written to accommodate modest performance situations, considerably more demanding chorale settings have appeared recently. Günther Raphael, who had already published thirty chorale motets for three and four like voices under the title *Das Kirchenjahr,* produced three chorale partitas, Op. 84, for mixed chorus and organ (composed in 1952 and 1957). Another young composer who has emerged since 1950 is Heinrich Poos, a pupil of Pepping. Since 1956 he has published cantus-firmus-based liturgical chorale motets and partitas (three of each) for small vocal and instrumental ensembles (organ; some with one or two obbligato instruments). He has written other vocal and instrumental compositions as well and contributed a four-part cantus-firmus motet setting of the Pentecost sequence *Veni sancte spiritus* to G. Grote's series, *Geistliches Chorlied II.*

This survey of chorale settings during the last four decades (those for organ will be discussed below) will close with the last three cantus-firmus-based works of Ernst Pepping, published between 1950 and 1960. Pepping was one of the first composers of the late 1920s to take up the tradition of the Lutheran hymn, and in these cantus-firmus works he remained dedicated to the tonal ideal generally postulated at the time, the a cappella chorus.

In the *14 Liedmotetten nach Weisen der Böhmischen Brüder,* for four- to six-part chorus a cappella (1951–52), he used the rough, powerful poetry of the hymns and the free melodic-rhythmic shape of their modal melodies as his point of departure. He developed a through-composed lied-motet form that treats the many strophes of the hymn as a single entity. Without regard for the internal organization of individual verses as they were set out in the cantus firmus—departing from it in some strophes and returning to it in others—he maintained

Ernst Pepping: From the lied motet, *Komm, Gott Schöpfer, Heiliger Geist,* measure 45ff.: transition from the second to the third strophe (cantus firmus—freely handled) of *Erleucht das Gmüt* (first cantus firmus line in the bass, second cantus firmus line in the soprano)

a polyphonic flow, in which the "simplicity and devotion," the "introspection and brotherhood" (as Herder characterized the particular essence of songs handed down by the Bohemian Brethren) were absorbed and re-created in the vocal lines and sonorities of a contemporary musical language. These motets stem from the opinion that "the way to free form" lies in the direction of the cantus-firmus composition, which promotes and demands "faithful craftsmanship, self-expression, and creative discipline." The cantus-firmus treatment of the lied motets—strict and at the same time free, neither schematic nor constructivist—illustrates the idea of "submission to obligation" as well as the artistic fertility of the "polyphonic form-idea" (Pepping) through a rich musical reflection and interpretation of the complex unity of song.

In contrast to this magnificent realization of the a cappella ideal are thirty-four chorales arranged according to the church calendar, which appeared in 1954 as part I of the *Bicinien für gleiche Stimmen*. They follow the 16th-century tradition of *bicinium* composition and have been justifiably praised as "parables of a spiritual order" (G. Witte).

Pepping's *Neues Choralbuch* for three- and four-part chorus (1959) contains seventy-six settings of twenty-four melodies from the *EKG* in *de tempore* order. There are eleven melodies each with two settings, four melodies with three settings, four with four, four with five, and one, *O Haupt voll Blut und Wunden*, with six settings. These simple chorale settings are the product of an autonomous polyphonic art, an intensive, almost forty-year association with the spiritual, religious, and musical vigor of the Protestant chorale heritage. Above and beyond all questions of style connected to an era, singers and listeners alike perceive in these strophic chorale settings the greatness of a simplicity acquired through complete subordination to the cantus-firmus principle.

The chorale settings written since the revival of the old cantus-firmus practice up to the present (and, from all appearances, those of the future as well) manifest anew the vitality of their source: the centuries-old tradition of Protestant hymns and melodies. New works based on hymns evince an enormous diversity of form, although they center around three principal historical types: the chorale setting, the chorale motet, and the chorale cantata. We have shown that, primarily for artistic reasons, musicians were initially concerned with the more challenging form of the chorale motet (Pepping, Distler, and so on). Later they turned to simple chorale settings for the worship service and to the more complex chorale cantatas, or even those that were more simply constructed and easier to perform. As relatively unpretentious *Gebrauchsmusik* for use in the service, some of these works remained a matter of experiment or speculation and some merely followed fashion. But this situation seems insignificant in the face of their broad musical involvement with the Protestant chorale, which in its organic relationship to the cantus-firmus principle has had a lasting influence on the compositional and stylistic development of contemporary music and on church music in particular. The results of the involvement with problems of the chorale setting may be summarized as follows: 1) a concern for economy and craftsmanship in the treatment of a given melody; 2) restoration of traditional forms and types of chorale setting; 3) increased understanding of the *de tempore* and liturgical ties of music intended for the service; 4) mastery of the a cappella style, to which the polyphonic ideal of the age was dedicated; 5) resumption of mixed vocal and instrumental settings in the form of the chorale cantata, along with "cantorial practices" connected with the revival of performing in alternation; 6) the development of a new relationship between text and music based on cantus-firmus compositions.

BIBLICAL TEXTS IN CONTEMPORARY CHURCH MUSIC

PSALM, PROVERB, GOSPEL, AND EPISTLE MOTETS

The stylistic development of modern choral music and the return to "Christian materials" as subjects of musical treatment are internally related phenomena conditioned by the historical and stylistic dictates of the new age. The revival of the chorale setting discussed above is proof enough that the emergence of genuinely new choral music, corresponding to the stylistic ideals of the 1920s and '30s, is dependent upon the use of substantially weightier, more demanding spiritual texts. Until now no one has undertaken the stimulating, essential task of investigating the process of choral text selection in recent decades. Even a cursory survey would reveal the predominance of religious or religiously colored texts. (In the field of secular choral music, efforts to overcome the thematic narrowness of the 19th century may also be observed.) In all likelihood it would clearly demonstrate that the return to biblical texts, so important to modern church music, was the result of a gradual development leading from the choice of purely religious texts to a progressively closer adherence to the Scriptures. In naming a series of characteristic contributors along this path to the biblical text, at least two names must be mentioned: Angelus Silesius, the 17th-century Silesian mystic, and Matthias Claudius, a simple, pious poet of the "enlightened" 18th century. Only through intense devotion to the biblical word did composers of our own time gain the right to place their creative resources at the service of the church, writing music to serve the liturgy of the Christian community.

The first of the more recent choral works to turn to biblical texts can only be interpreted as documents of the religious yearning of their time. The extent of their technical demands for performance shows that they were directed at the concert audience, not primarily at the congregation gathered to worship. In 1923, after a period of study in Leipzig, the Swiss composer Willy Burkhard wrote as the first of a large series of vocal works a cantata (for solo tenor, mixed chorus, and orchestra) on biblical texts (Op. 3), in which, along with the scriptural texts, are featured the words and melody of the chorale *Aus tiefer Not schrei ich zu dir.* Two years later in Germany, following the enormous success of his a cappella Mass, Op. 1, Kurt Thomas published his musical representation of the Scriptures, Psalm 137 *(An den Wassern zu Babel)* for two choruses a cappella, Op. 4. In 1930 G. Raphael brought out Psalm 104 *(Lobe den Herrn, meine Seele)* for twelve-part mixed chorus (two six-part choruses) a cappella, Op. 29, and in the same year, Kurt Thomas's Psalm 90 for solo baritone, six-part chorus, and orchestra, Op. 15, was published. In 1925, W. Burkhard set the psalm text *Ich hebe meine Augen auf zu den Bergen* in his motet for men's and boys' choir a cappella (Op. 10). In 1927 he set Angelus Silesius's *Acht Sprüche aus dem Cherubinischen Wandersmann* for three like voices and for mixed chorus (Op. 17, Nos. 1 and 2) and composed a four- to eight-part motet for mixed choir a cappella (Op. 19), based on the 11th-century *Ezzolied.* In 1932, under the title *Neue Kraft,* he published his suite for mixed choir, in which Eichendorff's verse *Wir wandern nun schon viel hundert Jahr* (No. 1) is followed by the psalm verse *Aus der Tiefe ruf ich* (No. 2), two verses of Tersteegen's poem *Gott ist gegenwärtig* (No. 3), and finally the psalm verses *Lobe den Herrn, meine Seele* (No. 4) and *Jauchzet dem Herrn, alle Welt* (No. 5). Burkhard's early cantata calls for a large orchestra, as does Thomas's Psalm 90, although the latter, in reaching back to the choral principle of the Baroque orchestra (woodwind choir: 3 oboes, 3 bassoons; brass choir: 3 trumpets, 3 trombones; 3 timpani, and string choir), is clearly concerned with freeing itself of late Romantic sonority, and with achieving an objective tone color.

Also intended more for the concert-goer than the congregational worshiper are the two long, double-chorus, a cappella works of Thomas (Psalm 137) and Raphael (Psalm 104), suggested and inspired by the richness of allusion and feeling in the Psalms. (Raphael's does allow for the possibility of extracting five larger, or even smaller, sections of his [669-measure] through-composed work.) In form and layout these works show clear signs of having been inspired by Leipzig motet composition. But more, they are an expression of the religious longing of a dynamic decade; the composers are obviously dedicated to the task of developing a choral music in the great tradition, of receiving the torch ignited by Brahms and Reger and passing it on to their contemporaries.

These and similar works, historically indicative of the future, have made creative musicians aware of biblical texts as a subject for artistic treatment. Through texts taken mainly from the Psalter, the relationship of word and music, demanding new solutions, forced its way into contemporary creative thought. The demands of the church, concerning the nature of liturgical music, led to a necessary reduction in performance resources and to the creation of vocal music with a message, or restricted to a scriptural text. These demands doubtlessly contributed to the stylistic clarification of contemporary music.

The large number of a cappella works without cantus firmi that have appeared in the last four decades may be only briefly surveyed here. It must also be noted that the religious and historical factors responsible for this biblical-musical crescendo have primarily been of German origin. These factors, operating within sacred art-music circles and largely uninfluenced by politico-cultural principles of the time, facilitated the organic evolution of a musical ideal based on style changes of the twenties. The often surprising immediacy of scriptural texts chosen by composers sheds considerable light on the creator's situation and thus on the creative stimulus behind so many of the works, bound as they frequently are to the personal and universal destiny of the age.

A set of biblical compositions by Günther Raphael, written with a creative vehemence which Karl Straube compared to that of Max Reger, uses texts that are presumably deeply connected to the personal destiny of the composer. In 1927, at the age of twenty-four, he wrote a Requiem for four solo voices, two mixed choirs, large orchestra, and organ (Op. 20), and in 1930, a Te Deum for three solo voices, eight-part mixed chorus, orchestra, and organ (Op. 26); in 1931 he continued his series of unaccompanied choral works (begun with the 104th Psalm) with the four- to eight-part composition *Vom jüngsten Gericht* (Op. 30, No. 1; Matthew 25:31–46), and in 1934 with *Die Versuchung Jesu* (Op. 35; Matthew 4:1–11). In the motet *Vom jüngsten Gericht,* Raphael had already established an a cappella style flowing out of strong tradition. As Otto Riemer has pointed out, Raphael's creative powers were stimulated above all by the dramatic content of "biblical scenes and allusions," less by the "charming, egalitarian, conciliatory, hope-instilling features" than by the "terrifying, unsettling, apocalyptic words of the Scriptures." In providing sermon-like illumination for a "scene," in creating a vivid musical portrayal of a biblical event, Raphael displays the superior ability of a craftsman. Every polyphonic detail is incorporated into a quasi-homophonic, all-embracing sound picture. There are passages of word-bound syllabic declamation within a melodic style stamped with madrigalist impulses. There is a varied rhythmic style often accompanied by tempo changes, there are appropriately applied unisons, and there are recitative sections adhering closely to the original text. At least one aspect of the music reveals how intensely the composer has involved himself with the musical heritage of the 19th century (M. Mezger): the juxtaposition of canonic or imitative passages with columnar chords that unfold in broad masses of sound often utilizing antiphonal, double-chorus contrasts.

Raphael's wholly unpretentious choral output fits effortlessly into its historical context. It bears no characteristics of the style change, either in the experimental or the speculative sense. Only future generations will be able to determine the extent to which this music, with its strongly personal choral language and its invariably restrained mastery of form, should be regarded as a significant factor in contemporary developments in spite of all its traditional ties.

Apart from the three lied motets of Opus 39, the chorale motets of 1938 and 1941, and the *Sechs kleine Motetten* (with obbligato flute) of 1945, Raphael worked hardly at all within the modest choral possibilities of ordinary sacred music. Still, he remained dedicated to biblical texts throughout his life. In 1945 he composed two richly evocative works, the 126th Psalm and the *Klagelieder Jeremiae.* There are also the chorale cantata for four-part chorus, orchestra, and organ, Op. 58, written before 1937 and based on Luther's *Vaterunser* lied, and the biblical *Vaterunser* text setting of 1945, written for a sixteen-part a cappella chorus. His Opus 63, for a cappella chorus, was begun in 1935 and completed in 1946; intended for use in the worship service, it consists of four settings from the Gospels and Epistles: 1) *Christus, der Sohn Gottes* (Matthew 14:22–33) for seven-part chorus; 2) *Im Anfang war das Wort* for two five-part choruses; 3) *Hebräer-Brief* (Hebrews 10:32–39); 4) *Die Aufterstehung Jesu* (Matthew 28). Parts 3 and 4 are basically four-part compositions, texturally varied by division of the chorus into as many as twelve parts. The Epistle from Hebrews, which Raphael set "In memoriam Johann Albrecht Bard," is based not on Luther's version but on Bard's freely interpreted transcription, a highly subjective version reflecting experiences conditioned by the times and written to serve an exclusively liturgical function.

In 1930 Kurt Thomas prepared a performing edition of the *Geistliche Chormusik* (1648) of Heinrich Schütz, based on Spitta's Complete Edition. The effect of this project is clearly manifest in Thomas's seventeen motet settings of Proverbs, written from 1934 to 1936, the *Kleine geistliche Chormusik, Werk 25,* the liturgical purpose of which is indicated by its arrangement in *de tempore* order.

The basically four-part a cappella pieces are settings of single proverbs or, even more frequently, combinations of two or more proverbs. In four of the pieces (Nos. 9, 10, 11, and 13), the biblical verses are set to chorale melodies. Occasionally the a cappella sound is enriched by the addition of solos and instruments (Nos. 2, 5, and 9). These motets, specifically liturgical, disclose the fundamentally traditional attitude of the composer perhaps more clearly than the earlier, larger compositions. The influence of Schütz may be seen in the musicality of the diction, which always springs from the declamatory possibilities of the text, and in the relaxed polyphonic texture of the primarily sonorous, harmonically conceived motet constructions. In much of this *Gebrauchsmusik*—for example, in the Passion motet (No. 6) *Fürwahr, er trug unsere Krankheit*—Thomas probes far below the surface of the text in his highly convincing musical interpretation.

Kurt Thomas: *Fürwahr, er trug unsre Krankheit (Kleine geistliche Chormusik, Op. 25, No. 6)*; opening of the Passion motet

From the historical point of view, these accessible and simple *de tempore* motets deserve credit for reminding musicians of their obligation to sacred music, and for having stimulated the revival of biblical text settings for use in the church.

Hugo Distler leaned consciously on Schütz in a series of nine motets that were begun in 1934 under the collective title *Geistliche Chormusik,* Op. 12. The four chorale motets of this series (Nos. 3–6) have already been mentioned in another context (p. 422 f.).

In the *Motette zum Totensonntag* (No. 2), a spoken text reconstructed by Johannes Klöcking *(Alte niederdeutsche Strophen des Lübecker Totentanzes)* is combined with 14 four-part settings of verses from the *Cherubinischer Wandersmann* of Angelus Silesius. (The choral movements may be performed without the spoken text.) In the foreword to this *Totentanz,* the composer acknowledges his debt to the "powerful example provided by Leonhard Lechner's *Sprüche von Leben und Tod,*" which had been reprinted for the first time in 1929 (edited by W. Lipphardt and K. Ameln under the same title). The composer characterized his "artistic structural principle" as derived largely from Lechner's *Sprüche*— from their "urgency and aphoristic conciseness," their "sharp contrasts," their "precise depiction of momentary moods," as well as their "diversity of inventive imagination." The work resulting from identification with a revered historical model merits great admiration: overcoming the danger of self-effacement, the individual style of an imitative composer was allowed to emerge unimpaired.

Distler followed his great spiritual mentor, Heinrich Schütz, most slavishly in the four motets on biblical texts (Nos. 1, 7, 8, and 9). The texts of Nos. 1 and 8 point to two works of the early master that were favored early in the recent Schütz movement: Op. 12, No. 1, on Psalm 98 for double chorus (1619), and No. 8, on the six-part funeral motet of 1630 for J. H. Schein (No. 20 of the *Geistliche Chormusik,* 1648). Distler's three-part motet (No. 1) *Singet dem Herrn ein neues*

Hugo Distler: *Singet dem Herrn ein neues Lied:* Motet No. 1 from the *Geistliche Chormusik,* Op. 12; end of the second part

Lied departs from Schütz in the treatment of several selected verses from the 98th Psalm (part I: verse 1a; II: 1b, 4; III: 5, 6a, 7, 8, and 1a). It is typical of Distler's vocal output, particularly in its text-dominated a cappella style and the intense dedication of the composer's expressive power to the textural content—in the opening unison melisma, which is rhythmically enhanced by dotted and triplet figuration; in the *Singet* exultations of the finales to parts I and II, where parallel fifths revolve around an imaginary focal point; in the frequent repetitions of sharply declaimed motifs; and in the shimmering, almost impressionistic coloring of the harmony.

The terseness of the burial motet, *In der Welt habt ihr Angst* (No. 7), provides a forceful setting for the consoling words of Christ (John 16:33); this contrasts with a closing personal prayer, the chorale verse *Wenn mein Stündlein vorhanden ist,* which is set straightforwardly with the cantus firmus in the upper voice. Motet No. 8, on I Timothy 1:15–16, *Das ist je gewisslich wahr,* clearly shows the powerful influence of the Schütz experience, as well as the essential features of Distler's own style. A through-composed biblical motet, it uses the hymn verse *Ehre sei dir, Christe* (widely known as the final chorus of Schütz's St. Matthew Passion) and, in a separate closing section, the traditional Passion melody *O wir armen Sünder,* which is set in simple cantional style and ends with a unison *Kyrie eleison.* No. 9, *Fürwahr, er trug unsere Krankheit,* is divided into three sections; it clothes the prophecy of the Passion in gripping music containing expressive word repetitions, chromaticism, and experimental harmonies. A chorale setting of *Ein Lämmlein geht und trägt die Schuld* concludes the work with a simplicity that leads the congregation to meditate upon its meaning. If one surveys the motets of Distler's *Geistliche Chormusik,* one finds an array of texts that turn more and more from the youthful, stormy beginnings of *Singet dem Herrn ein neues Lied* to thoughts of mortality and death, texts which take into account only two events of the church year (the Passion and All Souls' Day) and which correspond in only a few instances to Scriptures heard in the worship service.

We are left with the painful conclusion that Distler's output of sacred vocal music, begun "with his personal kind of 'triumph over historicism' " (H. Bornefeld's article, *Distler,* in *MGG* III, 1954, 582 ff.), did not attain a mature stylistic perfection. The composer carried to his early grave whatever potential lay behind a promising beginning. He might have proved a valuable force for the development of the new church music, especially in view of the music he wrote for liturgical use—for example, the 1936 *Liturgische Sätze über altevangelische Kyrie- und Gloriaweisen.* We will never know if this early promise could have also found fulfillment later on in sacred choral music not based on cantus firmi.

Ernst Pepping's choral works based on original melodies date from 1929 with five (Latin) *Hymnen für 4stimmigen Chor.* These were followed in 1930 by the secular cycle *Sprüche und Lieder* (on poems by Goethe, Rilke, and Eichendorff), and then by a significant landmark in the development of Pepping's own style as well as that of contemporary a cappella music: a setting of the 90th Psalm, *Herr Gott, du bist unsere Zuflucht für und für* (1934). This was Pepping's first work on a biblical text. Set for six-part chorus, it meets head on the problem of doing justice to a rich, contrasting, comprehensive text with choral resources only (there are no solo voices or instruments) and of achieving a contemporary, vocal-polyphonic treatment of texts.

This through-composed composition develops out of a germinal motif in which the interval of a fourth is prominent. The musical unity of the composition rests on this motif, and the polyphonic treatment of it leads to an ever increasing illumination of the fundamental thoughts of the text and to musical relationships that correspond to the substance of the text. The declamation of the text is

Ernst Pepping: From Psalm 90

subordinate to the musical phrasing, to the flowing diatonic vocal lines, which strongly support the thoughts behind the text or, in the sense of madrigalistic realism, paint a picture of the text. The composer's devotion to the biblical text and identification with its spirit and content led him to create a work with far-reaching implications.

Based on a text as it is, and with its stylistic equality between linear and harmonic elements, the 90th Psalm proves that even a text-based composition can be musically autonomous and that the goal of a vocal composition is to express in its own musical "language" the spiritual content of the text. Regarded in the light of the history of musical style, this work is the first sign of a newly won a cappella art independent of the symbolic power of a *cantus prius factus.* As such it compares favorably with the formal magnitude of both older and more recent symphonic instrumental music.

The 90th Psalm was followed in 1937 by a three-part motet based on Ecclesiastes *(Prediger-Motette)—Ein jegliches hat seine Zeit,* for four-voice mixed chorus a cappella (I, Ecclesiastes 3:1–15; II, 9:3–6; III, 12:1–7).

This "magnificent motet," according to Hans Hoffmann's assessment, "is an absolutely ideal choral setting . . . in which all the voices actively participate . . . , full of ingenious melodic ideas resulting from the transformation of every word into music . . . , into melody. . . . It is not slavishly bound to a major or minor diatonic formula, but takes advantage of the unique character of particular intervals and thus always achieves striking and characteristic turns of phrases. It is constantly in motion, shaping the textual thought entirely from within, not presenting the listener with puzzles to solve; nor does it confuse him. . . . Here, with enormous concentration on the most modest resources, the essence of these profound words is realized and impressed upon the consciousness and understanding of the listener, as was once the case with Schütz."

The 90th Psalm and the *Prediger-Motette* are autonomous musical creations that make great technical and stylistic demands and can therefore be used in the worship service only in exceptional cases. However, through the power of their spiritual-religious affirmation, these works exude the spirit and dignity of the liturgy. They will be able to fulfill their function primarily in the context of those church concerts in which the spiritual and artistic order is closely bound to the essence, dignity, and proclamation of the Christian Word.

With characteristic caution Pepping also addressed himself to the composition of liturgical settings of biblical texts. In 1936 he wrote the four-voice Christmas motet *Uns ist ein Kind geboren,* and in 1937, *Sechs kleine Motetten* for four-part choir. They were a reaction to stimuli from theological sources. In addition to these tersely constructed compositions (dedicated to Confirmation Day, Cantata Day, Reformation Day, etc.), he wrote in the same year three four-voice Gospel motets for the sacred musical services of the Berlin School of Church Music: the *Gleichnis vom Unkraut zwischen dem Weizen* (Gospel for the fifth Sunday after Epiphany, Matthew 13:24–30), *Jesus und Nikodemus* (Gospel for Trinity Sunday, John 3:1–15), and the four- to six-part *Gleichnis von der königlichen Hochzeit* (Gospel for the twentieth Sunday after Trinity, Matthew 22:1–14). The exegetical clarity of the musical language in these compositions is appropriate to their function in the worship service. The *Gleichnis vom Unkraut* and the conversation between *Jesus und Nikodemus* are through-composed; the greater part of the parable of the *Königliche Hochzeit* is "recited" (ideally on the tone recitation of the liturgy); direct utterances of the king are represented in four choral settings, of which the last, in six voice parts, contains only the final words of the king: *Denn viele sind berufen, aber wenige sind auserwählt* (For many are called, but few are chosen). In the motet *Jesus und Nikodemus,* the narrative verses of the Evangelist are reproduced in quasi-recitative by the bass, the words of Nicodemus by the tenors and basses, and the words of Jesus, which comprise the main portion of the text, by the entire chorus in four parts. The composer's wish to make clear the background "conversation," wherein the text is interpreted, is realized in the tonal attributes given the three speaking characters by the instrumentation. These liturgical compositions are remarkable for the realism of their text declamation, which reflects the essential character of the speakers, and for the exaltation of the

Ernst Pepping: From the Gospel motet, *Jesus und Nikodemus* (mm. 99–106)

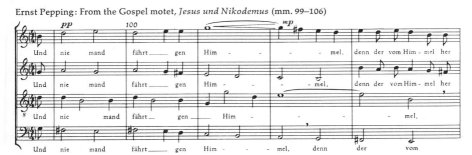

words of Jesus as he is inflamed by the secret of his holy mission. This is equally true of the Christian promise made to the congregation in a powerful chordal setting, "So must the Son of man be lifted up . . . that whoever believes in him should not perish," and of the magnificent, quietly proclaimed assertion of faith, "but have eternal life."

With the exception of the *Passionsbericht des Matthäus* of 1950, to be discussed below, Pepping did not return to motet settings of biblical texts until a decade and a half later. The second part of the *Bicinien für gleiche Stimmen* (1954) contains eleven settings of complete psalms (Nos. 1, 8, 23, 46, 70, 100, 121, 126, 133, 137, and 139); part III (1955) contains five Gospel and four Epistle settings: one Epistle and four Gospels for Epiphany, one Gospel for Invocavit, one Epistle each for Palm Sunday, Trinity, and St. John's Day. In addition to the chorales in part I, G. Witte has paid instructive homage to the psalm settings (see Bibliography, section VI) as well. His conclusions might well apply to the whole of Pepping's vocal compositions, particularly those relating to his "treatment of the text as doctrine" and his resultant "reverent adherence to the Word." Limited to two equal voices, these compelling *bicinia* use the stylistic materials at the composer's command with the utmost economy. They demonstrate Pepping's artistic aims in concentrated form, rendering "not only the Word but the context in which it stands . . . luminous and transparent"; they convey the "sense of the text in musical logic." Recognition of the stylistic traits discussed by Witte can contribute to an understanding of Pepping's most recent composition intended for the service, a four-voice Gospel motet for chorus, *Das Weltgericht.* It was written in 1958 for the centennial celebration of St. John's Seminary in Spandau.

Ernst Pepping: *Das Weltgericht,* Gospel motet (opening)

Its opening measures exemplify the liturgical spirit of the composition and the plastic rendering of its text ("Herrlichkeit").

Up to now, Johann Nepomuk David's choral output has included only a few settings of biblical texts, but even in the case of so strictly disciplined a contrapuntalist, the influence of the text on vocal line must be considered. In 1939 he wrote the four-voice motet *Wer Ohren hat zu höre*, based upon verses 6 and 20 from the 21st chapter of the Revelation of John, and the four- to five-voice motet *Und ich sah einen neuen Himmel*, based on freely selected verses from the same chapter (Op. 23 a/b). The extent to which pictorial elements of the text are fused with the polyphonic structure may be examined in the first motet, and even more clearly in the three-section second motet, the words of which are treated almost programmatically: "Brunnen des lebendigen Wassers" in part I, "Feuer, Schwefel! Der Greulichen und Totschläger und Zauberer" in part II; or "Klar wie ein Kristall" (in contrast to the preceding "lauteren Strom des lebendigen Wassers") in part III. These compositions, presumably not intended for use in the worship service, seem to be marked by a stylistic conflict between a madrigal-like treatment of the text and a contrapuntal musical technique. In contrast, David's six four-voice motet settings of Gospel texts published in 1958, which are clearly intended for the service, are written in a terse, chiseled style in which every attempt is made to avoid euphony: 1) *Der Pharisäer und der Zöllner;* 2) *Lasset die Kindlein zu mir kommen;* 3) *Die Ehebrecherin;* 4) *Das Scherflein der Witwe;* 5) *Der Barmherziger Samariter;* 6) *Die zwei Blinden.* The individual voice parts, intimately related to the text, are frequently combined through octave doublings into two parts or sometimes only one. A plastic, distinctly declaimed presentation of the Gospel text is achieved. On the whole, however, the motets rarely display independent musical structures that are convincing to the listener and do justice to the overall design.

Of the almost limitless quantity of choral settings based upon biblical texts that have been published since the 1930s, a considerable number are based on texts from the Gospels and the Epistles, in many cases upon only a single verse. Among those composers who contributed to this category—strictly speaking the liturgical motet—are H. Simon, H. F. Micheelsen, Eberhard Wenzel, Fritz Werner, Adolf Brunner, and K. Fiebig.

About 1948, as part of his comprehensive project *Chormusik für das Jahr der Kirche,* Siegfried Reda began to publish one cycle each of Epistle and Gospel settings (to date there are forty-one compositions based on *Die alten Epistellesungen* and five *Evangelienmusiken*). In these choral works, which are fashioned in a more concentrated style than the usual polyphonic motet, Reda unites Distler-like principles of declamation with his own very personal "affect-laden treatment of the language." This is "counterbalanced by the developmental, almost instrumentally conceived melismas," which, according to Reda himself, "serve to 'intensify expression of the irrational' " (*MGG* XI, 1963, 92 f.).

The strict, declamatory relationship of the music to the text makes one more aware of Reda's use of harsher sounds and a richer variety of dissonances to

Siegfried Reda: *Danksaget dem Vater,* from *Chormusik für das Jahr der Kirche. Die alten Epistellesungen,* Part IV

reflect textual content. This practice is connected to others—the use of ostinato repetitions of words and motifs, of canonic formations and other contrapuntal techniques of compression (cf. a composition devoted to the *Evangelium auf den vierten Advent* [John 1:15–18] for five-part mixed chorus a cappella, in which a one- to two-voice [tenor and bass] introduction is followed by a five-voice passacaglia with sixteen variations on the passacaglia theme). In addition, the juxtaposition of solo voice and chorus is occasionally employed in the predominantly four-voice choral compositions. In the *Evangelienmusik auf den Karfreitag: Die beiden Schächer* (1948), the solo role of the Evangelist is sung over a four-voice setting of the chorale verse *Christe, du Lamm Gottes;* at the same time, the words of the evildoer are also being sung by the chorus. In 1960 Reda rewrote the work for soloists with large and small chorus. In the *Evangelienmusik zu Estomihi: Leidensverkündigung und Heilung eines Blinden* (Luke 18:31–43), a monophonic recitative setting of the Evangelist's narrative and a choral version of the direct discourse in part I is contrasted with a setting which combines the two elements in part II. For all these compositions, revealing as they do a sound-oriented means of expression, the manner of performance is crucial. This is expressly illustrated in the composer's detailed performance instructions (given in the score and in supplementary footnotes). Stylistically related to Reda is his pupil Wolfgang Hufschmid, who published a series of eight Epistle motets for four-part chorus.

Johannes Driessler's Passion motet for five-part choir and baritone solo, Op. 9 (1950) combines Passion melodies with texts from the Old and New Testaments. In 1955 he wrote a complete series of verse settings from the four Gospels (Op. 37). In addition to works already mentioned, numerous individual contributions were made by U. Baudach, H. Chemin-Petit, K. Hessenberg, H. Peter, J. Petzold, P. E. Ruppel, and others.

Except for the Gospels and Epistles, the Psalter has thus far been the favorite source of biblical texts. Parts VII–IX of H. F. Micheelsen's *Hamburger Motettenbuch* contain individual psalm settings for six-part a cappella chorus; part II contains two- to six-part settings. Ernst Lothar von Knorr combines psalm texts with Gospel texts in the motet *Suchet Gott, so werdet ihr leben* (1948). In 1950, W. Burkhard published six simple four-part polyphonic psalm settings (*Kleiner Psalter*, Op. 82). Dietrich Manicke composed two inspired eight-part polyphonic works on the 90th and 23rd Psalms (1954); J. Driessler, too, wrote a 90th Psalm for five-part choir and baritone solo (Op. 25, No. 1), and F. Gottschick composed a 30th Psalm for five-voice chorus a cappella.

The extent to which Igor Stravinsky's *Symphony of Psalms* (for large orchestra and chorus, 1930; revised 1948) has influenced numerous instrumentally accompanied psalm compositions of the present is a question that cannot be taken up at this time. W. Burkhard has used psalm texts in a very personal way, as exemplified by his 1937 Psalm 93 for mixed unison chorus and organ (Op. 49), which Ernst Mohr characterized (see Bibliography) as follows: "The vocal line, almost chorale-like and absolutely monophonic, soars . . . far out and, in the manner of a cantus firmus, is firmly embedded in the organ accompaniment, where strict polyphonic elements appear alongside programmatic elements." The composer's solemn *Cantate Domino* for three-part mixed chorus and soprano solo with string orchestra and timpani (organ and winds ad lib.; Op. 61, No. 2), based on verses from Psalms 96, 149, 150, and 98, was dedicated to the Bern Conservatory at the ceremonial opening of its new building. Burkhard's 149th Psalm for unison chorus and instruments, Op. 96, was also written for a special occasion —the centennial celebration of the Muristalden Seminary. The work allows for a freedom of instrumentation, about which the composer states in the foreword: "In principle, the most diverse instrumentation is permissible, from full orchestra to only a few instruments (e.g., winds). Organ alone is also possible. . . . In no case may the timpani be omitted, even when the organ is used alone." As is the case with Burkhard's works for special occasions, many other psalm-based compositions are intended more for concert use than for the service. Examples include the three psalm settings (Psalms 130, 121, and 126) for soprano, tenor, four-part chorus, and orchestra (1947) by the Swiss Robert Oboussier; the compositions based on Psalms 143, 13, and 146 for four-part chorus and organ by Hans Studer; the 70th Psalm for the same complement of performers by Lukas Wieser; and the 124th Psalm, also for four-part chorus and organ, Op. 25, No. 2, by J. Driessler, which, more than any of the others, is suited to the worship service.

Werner Zimmermann goes his own way in an *Introitus-Motette* for five-part mixed chorus and double bass: *Lobet, ihr Knechte des Herrn* (Psalm 113) of 1956, explaining in his foreword:

Obviously unusual in this motet is the use of the double bass. Its even pizzicato must provide a strong rhythmic foundation for the five heavily syncopated choral voices above. At first glance the syncopation appears arbitrary and difficult; however, upon closer inspection and in performance, it will prove to be effortless and right because it is based entirely on the natural, logical declamation of the text. I am conscious of the fact that this rhythm . . . has parallels in the dance music of our day—as does the harmony. This is not necessarily unfortunate. I am hoping that a new vitality, which is so essential at present, may thus be injected into our church music. The knowledgeable observer will not overlook the fact that these motets . . . are rooted firmly in the tradition of Protestant church music and are concerned with the advancement of that tradition through new expressive means.

The characteristics of this motet, apart from its "dance" rhythms, are the absence of melismas, owing to the strictly syllabic treatment of the text, and the use of cantus-firmus technique in a free biblical setting.

In the four motets for four-part mixed chorus and double bass, which bear the composite title *Weihnacht,* verses 4, 3, 2, and 1 of the Christmas song *Gelobet seist du, Jesu Christ* provide the textual and musical cantus firmi aligned with four biblical texts. In this confrontation between scriptural and chorale texts (as well as in a larger work, his *Vater Unser* for seven-part mixed chorus and double bass, in which a motet-like setting of the Lord's Prayer is juxtaposed with an interpretative cantus firmus taken from the Passion chorale *Christe, du Lamm Gottes),* the composer convincingly demonstrates his "Christian" desire to clarify.

Zimmermann set a course for himself in these motets that he continued to follow in two other large works. Because of their instrumentation and form they more properly belong in the next section, but they should be mentioned here because of their scriptural texts. Both compositions may be called cantatas, although here the "concept of the cantata," according to Zimmermann's fore-word, "appears to embrace two works in distinct contrast to each other." The *Geistliches Konzert* of 1954 is a three-movement solo cantata for bass-baritone and eleven jazz soloists that "belongs in the concert hall because of its instrumentation" (foreword). It was followed in 1956–57 by the *Psalmkonzert* (for bass-baritone, five-part mixed chorus, unison boys' choir, three trumpets, vibraphone, and double bass), a "five-movement choral cantata . . . designed for the church." It shares with the *Geistliches Konzert* the common goal of "imparting the musical breath of life to the biblical word. . . . The two works also share a common involvement with the heritage of musical form, and are concerned with carrying that great tradition into a transformed present." The five movements of the *Psalmkonzert* are based on selected verses from Psalms 96, 40, 103, 107, and again 96 (a repetition of movement I). In Zimmermann's vocal works, elements of the polyphonic motet and jazz are juxtaposed without connection. The composer himself seems to have been aware of the irreconcilable gulf between religious and secular forces. His use of the cantus-firmus principle was obviously intended to bridge the stylistic differences by calling on the symbolic power of the chorale (which at the same time serves to interpret the Scriptures).

Among scriptural texts connected with the liturgy, the Magnificat (Luke 1: 46–55) has received scant attention from contemporary composers. W. Burkhard's Magnificat for soprano and organ, Op. 64 (1942; also arranged by the composer for soprano and string orchestra [Op. 64a]) is a concert cantata without cantus firmus that confines itself to the first three verses of the Latin Magnificat and the Gloria Patri, which is also abbreviated. This extraordinary composition may be compared with several works intended for the worship service. For his Magnificat *peregrini toni* for solo voice, chorus, and organ concertante (1948), S. Reda has taken the liturgical melody named in the title as his basis, but has treated only a portion of the text (Luke 1:46–50).

Among the less demanding choral works are Ulrich Grunmach's Magnificat for three like voices, *Meine Seele erhebt den Herrn;* H. F. Micheelsen's Magnificat for three-part womens' or boys' chorus; and Karl Marx's *Magnificat deutsch* for two three-part choirs (1955). H. F. Micheelsen's *Lobgesang der Maria,* for six-part chorus and solo soprano (*Hamburger Motettenbuch* V, 1957), is of a considerably more demanding motet-like character. Micheelsen uses an early Magnificat antiphon (Soest, 1532) as his textual and melodic point of departure; the closing Gloria Patri refers back to the music of the antiphon, which is not repeated after the Magnificat. Bernard Reichel's Magnificat for two four-part choirs presumably has its inspiration in Schütz's Magnificat of 1671 for double chorus. The complete *Vespern* (1954–55) of Jan Bender are settings specifically written to meet liturgical requirements: *Vesper I,* for chorus, *Liturg,*[1] organ and congregation, goes from an organ prelude into an *Eingangslied,* Psalm 121, Responsorium, Hymnus, and Magnificat, with a closing *Abendlied.* The organ postlude is a four-section partita on the chorale *Nun ruhen alle Wälder* (fughetta, *bicinium,* passacaglia, and aria). Bender wrote his *Vesper II, O wie selig seid ihr doch, ihr Frommen,* for *Liturg,* congregation, chorus, and organ to be used in "liturgical service in memory of the deceased" or "in any memorial service for the dead." Its focal point is an instrumentally accompanied chorus on the canticle Nunc Dimittis (Simeon's hymn of praise, *Herr, nun lässest Du Deinen Diener im Frieden fahren,* Luke 2:29–32) and its antiphon. Bender's compositional style, which he is at pains to keep simple and accessible, is subordinated to pedagogical objectives—for example, that of reaffirming a stronger liturgical influence in the writing of music for the service. In 1961, on commission from the Loccum Monastery, E. Pepping wrote a four-part Latin a cappella Vespers service for the liturgy to St. John's Day, *Johannis der Täufer: Ecce mitto angelum meum.* The antiphon *Ecce mitto angelum meum* precedes part I, the 92nd Psalm, *Bonum est confiteri Domino.* Part II (called *Motette 1* and *2*) consists of responds to the Gospel readings, *Fuit homo missus a Deo* (John 1:6–8). Part III is *Facta est autem quaestio ex discipulis Joannis* (John 3:25–31a). After a congregational hymn sung in German and a versicle, *Siehe, ich sende meinen Engel,* part IV follows, consisting of Zachary's canticle, *Benedictus dominus deus Israel.* Its preceding antiphon, *Puer, qui natus est nobis,* uses as cantus firmus the melody given in the *Antiphonale monasticum.* The high point of the canticle is the Doxology fugue. At the end of the movement the antiphon is taken up again by the two upper voices, while simultaneously the male voices bring the *Sicut erat* to a close; it is an impressive demonstration of the polyphonic skill in the work, in which liturgical function and treatment of musical form are factors in the free but cohesive artistic structure. In 1962, H. W. Zimmermann wrote a complete Vesper for five mixed voices, vibraphone, harpsichord, and double bass, which was not intended for any

---

[1] The priest who sings the liturgy in the worship service.

specific occasion in the church year. His choice of obbligato instruments in this liturgical composition introduces elements of jazz into the musical treatment of the *Ingressus* (part I), of Psalms 118 and 46 (parts II and III), of the *Hymnus* (part IV), and the closing Magnificat (part V).

HISTORIES AND PASSIONS

As was the case in earlier eras, the forms and categories into which Protestant church music divides itself today are not always clearly differentiated. For this reason, some of the works mentioned above are motets only in a limited sense, whether because of their instrumentation, the use of solo voices and chorus, the addition of an organ and/or other instruments, or because of the title the composer used. Some works already mentioned in the context of motet composition could be classified as cantatas or oratorios, just as some of the compositions discussed below could equally well have been presented in connection with the motet, either because of their texts (Histories, etc.), instrumentation, structure, or form. Histories and Passions (and a number of recent oratorios) are musical forms dealing with a broader biblical context. (The music-historical development of these biblical narratives, or *historiae,* is discussed elsewhere in this book.) The works produced since the 1920s that are based on biblical themes of large scope clearly bear the marks of an artistic struggle to master the elements of contemporary style and remain within the bounds of the new a cappella ideal. The cantata-like forms, especially, have lent themselves to a wide variety of musical treatment.

From the beginning, two biblical motifs have been of primary interest: the dramatic event of the Passion and the story of Christmas. Because the Christmas story satisfied the musical tastes of youth groups, it was quick to become a favored theme; beyond doubt, it was a secularized version, overriding strong denominational ties. However, as one of the most universal and directly accessible religious subjects, it was promoted as a basis for musical fellowship among young people.

This was the case with the small Christmas cantata of Walther Hensel, initiator of the "Finkenstein Singing Movement"; the cantata was published in 1925 under the Lutheran title *Susaninne* (affectionate name for the Christ-child) and based on the *Weihnachts-Cantilene* of Matthias Claudius. In the same year, and in a similar vein, Ludwig Weber published under the title *Christgeburt* (listed as Kallmeyer Edition No. 1) a "chamber piece on a text of Oberufer, with music based on old melodies, for acting, singing, and dancing. In 1928 Hans Mersmann saw this as a new "genre of ritual drama . . . which brings together the two elements of choral music and representational dance," and went on to say:

> [It] is dependent on the power of the chorale. . . . Its strength lies in the vitality it imports to old materials. This strength manifests itself in the simplest of formulas. No complication, no unique colors, no special aural or harmonic effects. Male and female voices stand as great choral entities in contrast to one another as in the congregational hymn. A third part is added for (unison) instruments. Thus, a three-part texture emerges from the massive, sculpted cornerstone. Two chorales stand in contrast to one another. What may appear arbitrary to the eye coalesces perfectly upon hearing.

Weber's work provided impetus primarily to musicians connected in some way with youth music programs or music education. One such was Eugen Bieder, who published his *Christvesper* in 1931 as *Weihnachtsmusik in fünf Teilen zum Singen und Spielen* for solo voices, chorus, and small orchestra; it has little to do with the liturgy for Vespers, although (according to the composer's preface) "the pieces" should "provide the background for, as well as intermittently interrupt, the Christmas story and selections from the Bible, perhaps also a brief address." An instrumental "sinfonia" introduces the sequence of vocal and instrumental song arrangements; two settings designated as "chorale cantata" (on *Vom Himmel hoch* and *Gelobet seist du, Jesu Christ*) constitute the outside movements. The strong emphasis on instruments in Walter Rein's *Dreikönigsmusik zum Spielen und Singen in der Weihnachtszeit* (1932) makes it "predominantly instrumental music." The sequence of movements follows "historical" models: Preamble, Chorale (vocal), Concerto, Dialogue (vocal), Sarabande, Aria (vocal-instrumental), March, Intermezzo, Chorale (vocal or vocal-instrumental), and *Ballo*. In 1932, Joseph Haas dedicated to his "dear friend, Dr. Karl Laux" *Ein deutsches Weihnachtsliederspiel nach oberbayerischen und tiroler Weisen mit verbindenden Worten von Wilhelm Dauffenbach* (A German Christmas Carol Play Based on Melodies from Upper Bavaria and the Tyrol with Connecting Narrative by Wilhelm Dauffenbach) for solo voices, narrator, mixed chorus (or women's or children's chorus) and small orchestra. In the directions for performance, "the utmost simplicity" is requested. Kaspar Roeseling's *Kreis-Spiel von der Geburt Christi, von Kindern zu singen und darzustellen* of 1934 belongs to the same Catholic "tradition."

These works portray the events of Christmas primarily with arrangements of carols. They are related to both the smaller and the more extensive Christmas cantatas, which invariably involve vocal or vocal-instrumental Christmas-carol settings. Some examples are those published by Heinrich Spitta, Karl Marx, Arnim Knab, Paul Höffer (*Weihnachtskantate nach Worten der frühmittelalterlichen Christmette* for lay and school choirs with instruments, Op. 38), Gerhard Schwarz (*Kleine Weihnachtskantate nach Worten von Kurt Müller-Osten*), and Cesar Bresgen (*Es ist ein Ros' entsprungen: Eine Weihnachtskantate* for mixed voices, three violins, flutes, and double bass, 1938). As indicated by publishers' notices, these works are, as a rule, intended for congregational participation. The composers draw on Christmas materials with the interests of laymen or the musical education of young people in mind; thus, they look for inspiration in Christmas chorales and folk songs. The Christian message in the biblical Christmas story is always discernible in the background, but it does not become the creative focal point.

Kurt Thomas was among the first of this generation's young composers to take a strictly scriptural point of departure. Directly following the enormous success of his a cappella Mass, Op. 1, the composer (then 22) directed his energies toward the monumental Passion theme. In 1921, Fritz Stein had already made reference to Leonhard Lechner's four-part St. John Passion of 1594 (see Bibliography). This multisectional, polyphonic, through-composed motet Passion was the historical model for Thomas's *Passionsmusik nach dem Evangelisten Markus* for mixed chorus a cappella (Op. 6), which was composed in 1926 and premiered in

1927 by the Berlin State and Cathedral Choir under Hugo Rüdel.

The work is in four to eight voice parts and contains five movements. Except for the introductory chorale strophe, *Jesu, deine Passion,* and the concluding *Wir danken dir, Herr Jesu Christ,* it is similar to older forms of the dramatic Passion in that it is based exclusively on chapters 14 and 15 (slightly abbreviated) of Mark. It dispenses with reflective interludes, soloists, and instruments in order to represent the Passion drama solely through the homogeneous medium of the mixed chorus; it illustrates the Passion events within the manifold possibilities of a vivid polyphonic vocal setting. The composer was concerned above all with providing a passionate representation of the story that would engage the spiritual empathy of the listener. At the end, the listener should feel the same emotion experienced by the Roman centurion who exclaimed, "Truly, this man was the Son of God!" (Mark 15:39). Changing combinations of voices add vividness to the work: the Evangelist's narrative is sung by one of the two four-part choruses, but the texture is often reduced to a monophonic quasi-recitative before the beginning of the direct utterances of Christ; these are usually sung by the double chorus.

Kurt Thomas: *Passionsmusik nach dem Evangelisten Markus,* Op. 6; from the first part, m. 25 ff.

The high priest is represented by male voices, Pilate by the four inner parts (tenors and altos), and the handmaidens by female voices; for the most part, the utterances of Christ, raised to solemn and exalted euphony, are set homophonically for double chorus. The truly vocal nature of the choral language is bound to traditional tonality and derives its fundamental inspiration from the dramatic emotionalism of the text. The work is seeded with madrigalistic, pictorial elements, is passionately filled with the "human characteristics" (F. Stein) of the suffering Son of Man, and has a stamp of stark realism in the dramatic accents of the choral crowd scenes.

The young composer's ability to assimilate the essence of a historic model and endow it with the qualities of his own unique style has made the 1926 *Passionsmusik* worthy of our admiration even today. This was one of the first works of the twenties to achieve the contemporary a cappella ideal and to lead the field of unaccompanied choral music back into the mainstream of musical development. The historical significance of the work is closely related to the spiritual foundation on which it rests: its vocal part has a fundamentally polyphonic orientation and serves demanding biblical materials; as it unfolds musically it remains bound to the religious content of its exalted subject; it faces the problem imposed on a choral composer, the relationship between word and sound. It follows tendencies of the period of Praetorius, Schein, and Schütz, but maintains the objective to which the style change of the present is dedicated: to master anew the magnificent themes of the Scriptures and to bring them closer to modern man in a musical language appropriate to our time.

Kurt Thomas was also quick to turn to purely choral settings of the Christmas story, as witnessed by his 1931 *Weihnachts-Oratorium nach den Worten der Evangelisten* for six-part chorus a cappella, Op. 17. Apparently, he called it an oratorio in the context of Leipzig usage; the designation is appropriate neither to the text nor to the musical form of this four-movement work.

The motet-like first and last movements, *Einleitung* and *Beschluss,* are based on the Gospel according to John; *Im Anfang war das Wort* and *Das Wort ward Fleisch* (John 1:1 and 14) comprise the opening, and *Also hat Gott die Welt geliebt* (John 3:16) the close. Like the musical declamation, the choice of texts in these two motets reveals the deep effect on Thomas of Schütz's *Geistliche Chormusik.* These works obviously served the composer well in his choral motet settings of the four biblical scenes that lead the listener from the story of the Annunciation and the Nativity (I: Luke 1:26–33 and 38; Luke 2:4–7), to the shepherds in the fields (II: Luke 2:8–20), to the wise men from the Orient (III: Matthew 2:1–12), to the presentation of Christ in the temple and the aged Simeon's blessing (IV: Luke 2:25–32), and finally to the closing verse (Luke 2:40, "and the child grew . . ."). Thomas himself presumably regarded the multiverse chorale settings that conclude each of the four sections as the oratorio element in the work (which concentrates on the biblical Christmas story). These settings are used to draw the listening congregation into the biblical event.

The vocal style of the composition seems to stem largely from the lyric character of the biblical materials. The polyphonic details in the biblical portions, as in the cantus-firmus settings of the chorale motets, appear to derive their inspiration from the mood and programmatic elements of the text. Certain stylistic mannerisms may have their basis here, for the mannerisms are more prominent in this composition than in the *Passionsmusik,* which was designed to communicate the essence of a historical event. However, this hardly diminishes the historical significance of the oratorio. The young composer, in genuine dedication to the enormity of his subject, was able to master the task of representing the story of Christmas in a vital, artistic way, using only the resources of an a cappella chorus.

In 1932 Hugo Distler's involvement with the Christmas and Passion stories began in a work similar in instrumentation, form, and style to the Christmas music mentioned at the outset of this discussion: *Kleine Adventsmusik,* Op. 4, for flute, oboe, violins, chamber chorus, organ (harpsichord or piano), cello (ad lib.), and narrator. "Between the 7 movements of the *Adventsmusik,* a narrator (from the chorus) reads from the Gospel" (composer's footnote, page 5 of the score). The Gospel reading for Advent (narrator) is commented on by seven one- to three-part instrumentally accompanied chorale settings of the early melody *Veni redemptor gentium;* four verses of Luther's *Nun komm der Heiden Heiland* and three verses of the Advent hymn *Gott sei Dank durch alle Welt* are also used here. An instrumental sonata opens and closes this unassuming chorale cantata. The sequence of its movements provides ample evidence of the intent to master a biblical narrative of large scope: I. The Prophecy; II. The Annunciation; III. The Visitation; IV. Mary's Hymn of Praise; V. The Road to Bethlehem; VI. The Fulfillment. But the biblical materials are only a backdrop for the settings of old Advent melodies. Here, too, Distler attempted to serve the contemporary interest in choral and instrumental music with a cyclic, cantata-like form of music derived from the essence of the hymn. Because of the particular creative stimulus from which this modest composition springs, it is nonliturgical music in much the same sense as the bulk of the secularized Christmas music mentioned above.

In the same year the twenty-four-year-old composer took up the theme of the Passion; in Lübeck "in December of 1932" he signed the epilogue of his *Choralpassion,* Op. 7 (for five-part mixed chorus a cappella and two solists—Evangelist and Jesus), *nach den vier Evangelien der Heiligen Schrift.* Distler refers (epilogue) to the "gripping impression" made on him when he "experienced for the first time the annual Good Friday performance of Schütz's St. Matthew Passion in Lübeck," and says that he was moved to compose a "representation of the Passion story . . . in raiment appropriate to the times . . . but in the spirit of the early a cappella Passion as it culminated in Schütz, a form which uses to advantage every means to speak a folk-like, universally comprehensible, concise, and primitive as well as penetrating language." Distler thoroughly understood and enthusiastically revered this historical example. He departed from Schütz in regard to his text, which is presumably based on his own selections from the four Gospels. However, he went beyond a mere biblical narrative in his seven-part story of the Passion by combining it with "eight chorale variations on . . . *Jesu deine Passion.* " (It is this fact to which the composer's title, "Choralpassion," refers.) The hymn verses of the chorale variations, which open the work and close each of its sections, are derived from various Passion melodies; the chorale tune *Christus, der uns selig macht* serves as cantus firmus for all eight reflective chorale motets, thus unifying the composition both internally and externally. The recitatives are not confined to any specific church mode. They are rhythmically declaimed and metrically well defined, always in the manner of speech, and they make use of the traditional registers (Evangelist: tenor; Christ: bass; high priest: high tenor; the voices of Judas, Pilate, and the thief: a bass from the chorus).

Hugo Distler: *Choralpassion*, Op. 7. Recitative from the third part: *Das Abendmahl*

The artistic significance of this responsorial Passion rests in its primarily five-part chorale motets and in the terse and powerful effect of the people's choruses, which seek to emulate Schütz and are as resolute as they are bold in their search for hard, dramatic realism through the use of clashing seconds and passages in fourths and fifths.

Distler's *Weihnachtsgeschichte*, Op. 10, for four-part mixed chamber chorus a cappella and four soloists (1933), received its inspiration from the same source as the *Choralpassion* and has much the same overall form. It traces the story of Christmas through the Annunciation, the Magnificat, the Nativity, the shepherd scene, the wise men, and Simeon's blessing; the foregoing scenes are introduced by cantus-firmus settings of all six verses of the Christmas melody *Es ist ein Ros' entsprungen*, and the biblical narrative is concluded with the closing verse, *So singen wir all Amen*. The introduction consists of the prophecy, *Das Volk, so im Finstern wandelt, siehet ein Licht*, and the finale is based on the words of John, *Also hat Gott die Welt geliebet*. Both motets lead from A minor to E major, the characteristic key of Christmas in this solo-choral depiction of the Christmas story and in the seven four-voice chorale variations.

Hugo Distler: *Choralpassion*, Op. 7. From Chorus No. 20 in the last part of the Passion: *Golgatha*

In contrast to the *Choralpassion,* the recitative portions of Op. 10 are notated in unmeasured Gregorian rhythm. They are in the key of A minor so that a return to E major in the closing Simeon scene can be made after the modulations in other scenes. With regard to key, the four *turba* choruses (the choir of angels, the shepherds, the three wise men, and the chief priests and scribes) stand apart from the rest of the work. Unity of form and mood is achieved by means of the cantus-firmus melody, *Es ist ein Ros' entsprungen.* In Distler's opinion (foreword), "the recitatives [may be inserted] into the liturgical order of worship more easily than the corresponding 'Passion' soliloquies." Although the goal of music for the service is not yet precisely defined at this point, there are clear indications of what is to come. There is a presentation of the Gospel in a recitation tone, out of which the voices of the angels, shepherds, and so on, emerge in vivid polyphonic motet structures; there are opening and closing motets based on Scripture and polyphonic variations on the universally understandable cantus-firmus chorale verses. The inspirational background of this musical construction is the work of the great composer of the *Geistliche Chormusik* and the Passions: Heinrich Schütz. Distler attempted not only to emulate this master of declamation but even to surpass him if possible. For the sake of "comprehension and construction of the linear thematic essence" (foreword), he has "consistently maintained in all four voices the principle of polyrhythmic notation derived from the natural declamation of the text." Thus the bar lines are so arranged that each individual voice is permitted to run its given thematic course, a strong indication of the experimental phase to which the young Distler was still strongly bound.

Hugo Distler: *Die Weihnachtsgeschichte,* Op. 10; opening of the shepherds' chorus

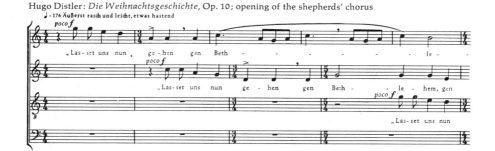

Distler's unaccompanied recitative, intended for liturgical use and performed in a recitation tone, was taken up by others, primarily in liturgical works of smaller scope—for example, Fritz Dietrich's *Kleine Weihnachtskantate nach dem Evangelisten Lukas,* which was intended to serve modest musical requirements. The recitation of the Gospel (Luke 2:1–20) is executed without accompaniment on a (rhythmically unmeasured) "plainsong tone" of quite individual character. In addition to the biblical text, "four verses from *Gelobet seist du, Jesu Christ* are used as meditations, each of which is inserted at the most appropriate place" (foreword). Flutes, violins, and gamba or violoncello are prominent in the prelude, postlude, and shepherd music; these instruments also accompany the modest two-part chorale settings. Dietrich used similar procedures in his *Dreikönigskantate,* his *Kleine Osterkantate,* and his *Kleine Passionsmusik.* In 1949, as part of the *Evangelienmusiken* series in his *Chormusik für das Jahr der Kirche,* S. Reda wrote *Die Weihnachtsgeschichte* for precentor [*Vorsänger*] and a cappella choir in which (at the suggestion of O. Brodde) the precentor's execution of the Gospel text is based on the slightly varied Gospel tone formula of Luther. The polyphonic choral settings of the title *(Die Geburt . . .),* of portions of the Gospel text, and of the *Danksagung* "are derived from the melodic substance of the recitation formulas and cadences" (foreword). In his *Weihnachtsgeschichte* for solo voice and choir (1952), Jan Bender combined the Gospel narrative of Christmas with those for Epiphany and the Massacre of the Innocents (Matthew 2:1–12 and 13–18). Johannes Petzold's *Kleine Kantate* for women's or children's voices, one or more men's voices, piano, and soprano recorder (1939) was written "for Christmas celebrations or small services in the family." Christian Lahusen's *Weihnachtsgeschichte,* a "cantata for home use" on a text by R. A. Schröder, has the same pedagogical objectives as the Christmas music mentioned above. Similar works by Carl Gerhardt, Ina Lohr, Heinz Wunderlich, among others, have more modest musical possibilities.

H. F. Micheelsen, in addition to a *Weihnachtsevangelium* for five-part chorus a cappella (1940), also produced a Passion according to John (for four mixed voices), one according to Mark (for tenor, bass, four mixed voices, and one solo voice from the chorus), and a third according to Matthew (for two to seven mixed voices). The Passion according to Mark follows the example of Schütz's "oratorio-like responsorial Passion," whereas those according to John and Matthew belong to the category of the dramatic or motet Passion. The choral style of these Passions, largely characterized by a doubling of parts at the octave and the use of fauxbourdon technique, may be considered representative of the composer's structural procedures. He once indicated that he composes "four different versions of the melody to some texts" before he finally achieves "the kind of 'melodic objectivity' which, in compelling simplicity and cool detachment, is appropriate to the power and severity of the underlying biblical text."

Ernst Pepping's *Passionsbericht des Matthäus* for a cappella chorus (1949–50) occupies a significant position in the more recent history of the Passion. Since its first performance (1950) by the St. Thomas choir in Leipzig, with G. Ramin conducting, and its almost simultaneous Berlin premiere by the *Spandauer Kantorei*, with G. Grote conducting, the work has become well known outside Germany. Beginning early in his career, the composer was involved with the Passion theme in numerous chorale settings for organ or chorus as well as in vocal Mass compositions; only later did he turn to the awesome task of setting the entire Passion story to music. Pepping's choral *Passionsbericht* is a resumption of the polyphonic motet Passion resurrected by Kurt Thomas. In style and form it surpasses any of its historical prototypes and achieves a completely independent shape conforming to contemporary musical tastes. Its artistic objective is clearly evident even in the title: to bring closer to us all, via a cappella choral resources, the "Passion Narrative of Matthew the Evangelist," the human drama of the Son of God, the immediacy of events on Golgotha, to portray the historical account in the musical language of our time and interpret it through that musical portrayal.

The *Passionsbericht* traces the account of Christ's sufferings from the betrayal by Judas to the Crucifixion (Matthew 26:14 to 27:50). The *Bericht* (Account) is preceded by an *Einleitung* (Introduction), closes with a *Schluss* (Finale), and is divided into two scenes by an *Intermedium;* the first five scenes lead up to the *Gefangennahme* (Arrest), the seven ensuing scenes to the death of Jesus on *Golgatha.* Two choruses stand in opposition: chorus I delivers the *Bericht,* whose outstanding stylistic characteristic is its epic realism; chorus II offers reflection, depth, meaning, and participation, joining with chorus I in the double choruses of the Introduction, *Intermedium,* and Finale motets, and at important points in the Passion narrative where choruses I and II are combined to intensify the interpretation.

With the Introduction, *Fürwahr, er trug unsere Krankheit* ("Surely he has borne our sicknesses"; Isaiah 53:4–5, chorus II) and the summons, *Höre die Passion unseres Herrn Jesu Christi . . .* ("Hear the Passion of our Lord Jesus Christ, who was born, suffered, and died for you—as it stands written by Matthew the Evangelist"; chorus I), the listener is prepared for the Passion events, which are delineated *für dich!* ("for you!"). The *Gefangennahme* is followed (*attacca*) by the *Intermedium,* which reflects on the meaning of Easter and Christ's sufferings and in which the cry "Save us, Lord; we are perishing!" (Matthew 8:25) is joined with the request "Abide with us, for it is toward evening and the day is now far spent" (chorus II), from the story of the Resurrection (Luke 24:29). Chorus I answers with the promise of the resurrected Lord, "Lo, I am with you always, to the close of the age" (Matthew 28:20). Chorus II transforms the passage "with you always" into the assurance of the faithful, "with us always, to the close of the age." This is followed directly by the beginning of the second part, *Die aber Jesum gegriffen hatten* ("Then those who had seized Jesus"). The finale motet begins with the entreaty *Herr Christe, erbarme dich unser . . .* ("Christ our

Lord, have mercy upon us, you who suffered for us, you who were crucified for our sake"; choruses I and II) and proceeds to the crucial verses in the prologue of John (John 1:1, 3–5, 14, and 16): "In the beginning was the Word," "And the Word was made flesh," "And from his fullness have we all received, grace upon grace." This reinforces the view of the Passion in the context of the Gospel narrative and reclarifies the incarnation of Christ between Good Friday and Easter.

Through the three additional text complexes, the listener is drawn into the Passion drama, with chorus II intervening at crucial points in the narrative. In the scene of the Last Supper, the text of the Evangelist ("Now as they were eating, Jesus took Bread") is heard together with the sacramental words from I Corinthians (11:23–25: "The Lord Jesus on the night . . ."). The simultaneous appearance of these two texts for ten-part double chorus constitutes the first musical climax of the work. In the *Jesus und Petrus* portion of the narrative (Matthew 26:30–35), Christ's sorrowful prophecy, "Before the cock crows . . . ," is emphasized by chorus II; Christ's spiritual struggle in *Gethsemane* (Matthew 26:36–46) is portrayed with impressive musical depth as chorus II takes up verses 38–42 ("My soul is very sorrowful, even to death"). In the second part of the *Bericht*, the utterances of chorus II relate to the suffering Son of God, silent to all accusations. At the trial, *Verhör vor dem hohen Rat*, the image of the stoic is forcefully represented by the singing of *Jesus schwieg still* ("Jesus remained silent"), which cuts through the turbulence of the event and closes the scene pianissimo. In *Jesus vor Pilatus* the recitative for chorus I *Antwortete er nichts* ("He answered not") merges into the stirring *Jesus antwortete nichts* for chorus II. At the words "dass sie ihn kreuzigten" ("That they crucify Him"), the scene *Jesus und die Kriegsknechte* leads directly into the *Golgatha* scene, which is immediately commented upon by chorus II with a fugue based on the central movement of the Credo, *Crucifixus etiam pro nobis*. This is stated by chorus I five times during the *Bericht*. In the first and fifth statements (to "desgleichen schmäheten ihn auch die Mörder"), the fugue subject appears in its normal form; in the second through fourth statements, it is inverted. The fugue reaches its climax with the words "gekreuzigt hatten" ("crucified") and "crucifixus est," where the two choruses are musically equal.

The musical style of this work is well suited to its text, especially the Evangelist's *Bericht*, which is set in a declamatory choral recitative style that is passion-

Ernst Pepping: *Passionsbericht des Matthäus.* Opening of the *Bericht: Verrat des Judas*

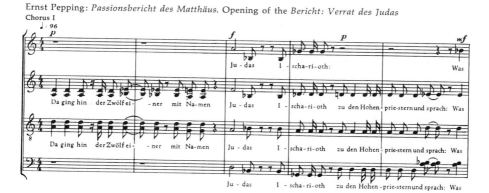

ately and impressively propelled by the dramatic momentum of the narrative. In addition, there are the expansive motet complexes that determine the texture of the three pillar movements, *Einleitung, Intermedium,* and *Schluss,* as well as of the climactic points in the *Bericht* (for example, the *Abendmahl, Gethsemane,* and *Golgatha* scenes).

In synthesizing recitative and motet principles, Pepping's *Passionsbericht* has met the challenge of the historical predecessors of the responsorial and motet Passions creatively, however heavily the work may be indebted to both types. Devotion to the reality and truth of the Gospel narrative is the source of the work's stylistic unity, which is rooted in, but at the same time transcends, the recitative style. It is based on free tonality, occasionally expanded to polytonality. Technical mastery is apparent in the way the harmonic spectrum and expressive possibilities of chromaticism are exploited for purposes of interpreting the text. In its unequivocal adherence to the Gospel Passion narrative and in its autonomous artistic form, Pepping's *Passionsbericht* is one of the towering musical testimonials to present-day Christianity.

Not until 1959 did Pepping publish his second History, *Die Weihnachtsgeschichte des Lukas* for chorus. Utilizing chapters 1 and 2 of Luke, the composer divided the Christmas story into five scenes: *Ankündigung der Geburt* (Proclamation of the Birth); *Maria bei Elisabeth; Die Geburt* (The Nativity); *Die Engel* (The Angels); and *Die Hirten* (The Shepherds). The Evangelist's story is told in the choral recitative style of the *Passionsbericht,* but in an altered form appropriate to the character of the subject matter. The passionate, agitated, often peculiarly exotic musical declamation lends the familiar story a new, vital perspective. Insertions of other scriptural texts serve structural purposes and add a deeper significance to the entire narrative. The biblical verse *Kündlich gross ist das gottselige Geheimnis* ("Great indeed, we confess, is the mystery of our religion"; I Timothy 3:16) as used in the *Eingang* points ahead to the mystery of the divine birth and of Christ's entire mission of redemption. The prophetic *Und es wird ein Reis aufgehen* ("There shall come forth a shoot"; Isaiah) indicates the character of the first scene; the five-part motet is musically related to the *Eingang* and to the tune of *Es ist ein Ros' entsprungen.* In the third scene the low male voices sing the words of the Evangelist, "The time came for her to be delivered. And she bore to her first son," and simultaneously the upper voices sing, "For when peaceful stillness compassed everything and the night in its swift course was half spent." This verse, taken from

Proverbs, is intended to reflect upon the midnight hour of the Savior's birth. It is followed (*attacca*) by a four-part motet based on the early hymn *Virga Jesse floruit*. The closing scene is based on Paul Gerhardt's seven-verse hymn *Kommt und lasst uns Christum ehren,* which evokes the lyric character of Christmas. A through-composed lied motet without cantus firmus follows, intoning *Quem pastores laudavere* in triadic sonorities. In this work, as before, the composer dispenses with the symbolic support of the chorale in order to bring to life musically the scriptural word, and to interpret contemporary man in a "distinctive (musical) form."

The Passion story has retained its enormous attraction even in the last decade, and it must be noted that the responsorial Passion for solo voices and orchestra is performed more frequently than the dramatic choral Passion (*figural Chorpassion*). Presumably this is for liturgical reasons, but perhaps it is also because of the seemingly more straightforward treatment of a powerful subject.

Rudolph Mauersberger's St. Luke Passion for double chorus (1947), which belongs to the choral category, appeared in revised form with the number of chorale settings and reflective interludes reduced. The motet-like St. Mark Passion for five-voice chorus a cappella, Op. 36/1 (1956) of J. Driessler was commissioned by the Southwest German Radio Network. Its text is taken exclusively from the Gospel (Mark 14:41c, 44c; and 15:39), abbreviated and occasionally modernized to facilitate the progress of the drama; it even dispenses with *Exordium* and *Conclusio.* The four-movement work closes (as does the St. Mark Passion of Thomas) with the words of the centurion, "Truly, this man was the Son of God!"

Kurt Fiebig adhered to the style of the responsorial Passion in his St. Mark Passion (first performance, 1952), a five-movement a cappella work that is similar to the Passion oratorio in its use of additional, nonbiblical texts and of two choruses. It opens with *Jesu Einzug in Jerusalem* (Mark 11:13), and closes with the death of Christ. The Evangelist's account and the voices of individual characters are set in monophonic, unaccompanied recitatives; the utterances of Jesus are sung by the chorus. The Passion narrative is given to the *Altarchor,* which is joined by chorus II at important junctures and in the chorale settings. In addition, reflective interludes draw upon the sacred folk song *In stiller Nacht,* the traditional *Dies irae,* and (as the concluding movement) the *Improperia.*

The majority of recent Passion compositions are of the responsorial-Passion category established by Schütz and first revived by Distler. In addition to unaccompanied monodic recitatives, there are polyphonic *turbae:* as a rule, chorale settings constitute the opening and closing movements. Among works of this sort are the St. John Passion of Heinz Sawade (first performance, 1954), in which the *turbae* are written as double canons; Eberhard Wenzel's St. Mark Passion for precentor and three-part mixed chorus (1955); and Otto Spar's St. Luke Passion for precentor and three-part mixed chorus (1956), in which the Evangelist's narrative is sung by a three-part chorus (or by a trio of soloists), the words of Jesus monophonically (bass), and the *turbae* are set in the form of choral canons. Lothar Graap's St. Luke Passion (first performance, 1955), which opens and closes with a chorale motet, is a variant of the type; the Evangelist's narrative is sung by a one- to three-part chorus, and only the utterances of Christ are presented as solo recitatives. Herbert Peter, a pupil of K. Fiebig, wrote a *Passions-musik* for mixed chorus a cappella and soloist (first performance, 1949), based upon the Gospel canticles, as well as a St. Luke Passion for three-part mixed chorus, soloist, and organ (first performance, 1956). The Passion opens and closes with a chorale motet; in contrast to the Evangelist's narrative of Christ's sufferings, told in unaccompanied recitative, are the three- to four-part *turbae*, reflective psalm motets, and chorale variations on *Da Jesus in den Garten ging;* the words of Christ are accompanied by verses from the 22nd Psalm. In keeping with the relatively modest demands of the St. Luke Passion, the organ is called upon to accompany the recitative portions and to play several chorale settings. Ulrich Baudach's *Die Passion Jesu Christi nach dem Evangelisten Johannes* for tenor, bass, and three- to five-part chorus a cappella (1957) shows the influence of Distler in its interpolation of seven chorale variations on *Jesu Kreuz, Leiden und Pein.* There is another apparent indication of this influence: Baudach has set down the recitatives in "rhythmically unfixed notation, appropriate to their narrative function, and the other solo passages in fixed rhythmic values, but by no means with the intention of committing them to a specific meter or tempo." Johannes Weyrauch used organ-accompanied recitative in his St. John Passion for three-part chorus and organ (first performance, 1958). The words of Christ are given particular prominence in settings for three-part chorus accompanied by the organ. The reflective interludes consist of three statements of the antiphon, *Kündlich gross ist das gottselige Geheimnis,* and six chorale settings for chorus. Gotthold Ludwig Richter's St. John Passion for three-part mixed chorus a cappella (1961) is a purely choral, straightforward setting.

Jan Bender's St. John Passion, Op. 11 (first performance, 1959) was also inspired by the Schütz Passions. In it the story of Christ's sufferings is preceded by a *Vorgeschichte,* with excerpts from texts leading up to the Passion drama (drawn from John 11:46 to 18:1). It utilizes two soloists in the Evangelist's role, the first (a tenor) relating the progress of events and the second (a baritone) delivering all explanatory portions of the text. A three-part chorus sings the *turbae,* the Passion hymns (sung with the congregation) closing each of the four sections, and the Old Testament prophecies cited in the Gospel narrative. The chorus also sings the motet between the *Vorgeschichte* (parts I and II) and the *Leidensgeschichte* (parts III and IV), which serves to interpret the meaning of the event. The work is scored for an orchestra which, besides woodwinds, brass, low strings, and harpsichord, incorporates a large group of percussion instruments, reminiscent of Orff's student works. The orchestra dramatizes the choral sections and plays independently in the prelude, the interlude, and a *Nachspiel zum Tod Jesu.*

Herbert Collum also departs from the a cappella ideal in his St. John Passion, which bears the somewhat pretentious subtitle *Das Leiden Christi in unsere Tage gestellt* (A contemporary View of the Sufferings of Christ). In this "symphonic

109. Johann Nepomuk David, opening of the Gospel motet No. 6, *Die zwei Blinden*, for six mixed voices (1958), autograph. Wiesbaden, Breitkopf & Härtel.

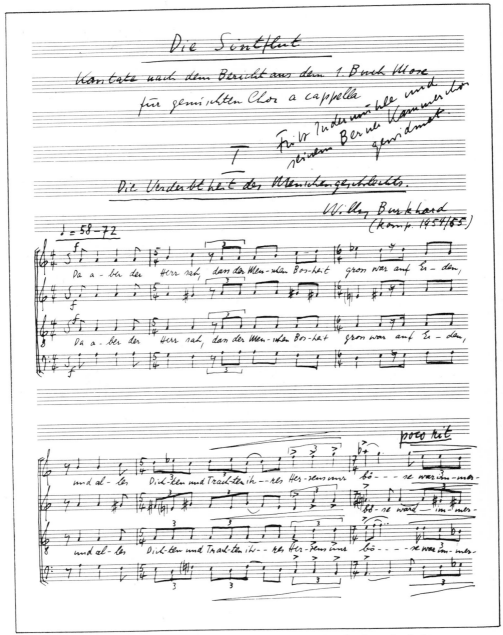

110. Willy Burkhard, opening of the cantata *Die Sintflut* for mixed chorus a cappella (1954–55), autograph. Kassel, Bärenreiter-Archiv.

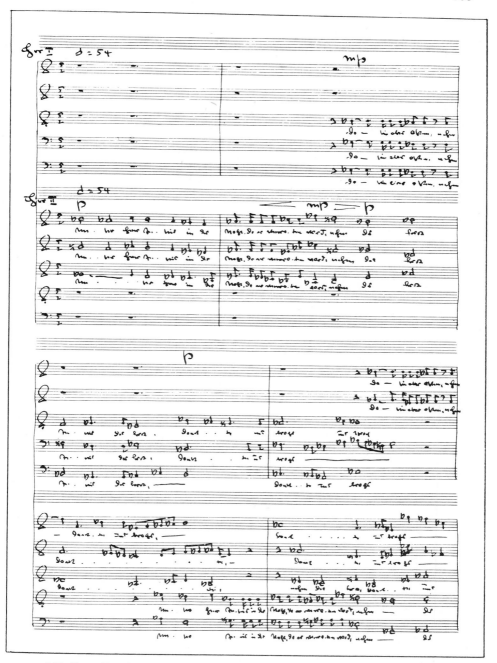

111. Ernst Pepping, *Unser Herr Jesus in der Nacht* from the *Passionsbericht des Matthäus* for four- to six-part chorus a cappella (1949–50), autograph, in the possession of the composer.

112. Hans Friedrich Micheelsen, *Die Passion* from the *Passion Jesu Christi nach dem Evangelisten Matthäus* for two- to seven-part chorus a cappella, Op. 38 (1948), autograph. Kassel, Bärenreiter-Archiv.

concerto" for tenor solo, chorus, and chamber orchestra (first performance, 1953), the Evangelist's narrative (John 18 and 19) and the utterances of the other principal characters are all sung by the solo tenor. The chamber orchestra (strings and woodwinds) accompanies him and the four reflective choruses, the texts of which show the composer's desire to underscore the immediacy of the Passion drama for today's listeners through the expressive resources of contemporary music. Because the work lasts almost two hours, it is unsuitable for the liturgy; it is, rather, a "symphonic concerto" based on the Passion narrative according to John and, despite all formal and stylistic dissimilarities, spiritually related to the ideal of the Bach Passion.

The narratives of Christmas and the Passion are by far the favorite subjects in contemporary biblical *historiae.* Next to these, only the story of the Resurrection has attracted composers to any great extent, while other biblical stories have been set to music only sporadically. Kurt Thomas again takes precedence in dealing with the Easter theme: his *Auferstehungs-Oratorium nach den Worten der Evangelisten,* for four-part chorus with instruments, Op. 24, was composed in 1934 and was published a year later.

In content, form, and instrumentation, the composition goes beyond the limits of a pure Resurrection *historia.* The designation "Oratorium" probably relates to the large three-movement design and to the complement of performers, which includes an orchestra of strings, two trombones, trumpets, and flutes in addition to chorus and organ. "In case of emergency," the brass instruments may be replaced by other instruments more readily available. The composition departs from the oratorio in dispensing with solo voices. On the other hand, the composer does reach out to the tradition of the oratorio by using chorale settings (of one or more verses) to frame the work and for meaningful insertion into the "story." Moreover, the composition is based on a purely biblical text, pieced together (presumably by the composer himself) from all four Evangelists and a chapter of Acts. Part I treats the story of the Resurrection; part II leads from the baptismal command to the Ascension, and part III deals with Pentecost according to the second chapter of Acts. The work closes with a simple setting of the chorale verse *Nun bitten wir den heiligen Geist;* according to the composer's foreword, it may be "performed at Easter, Ascension Day, or Pentecost, either individual numbers thereof or in its entirety."

Kurt Thomas: *Resurrection oratorio,* Op. 24; Part I, mm. 195–206

In this Resurrection oratorio, Thomas employs the element of recitative that is traditional in the composition of biblical narratives. Further, with the adoption of the imagery and emotional content of the scriptural text, the choral texture achieves a madrigal-like, polyphonic clarity characteristic of the composer. In addition to the graphic vocal writing, the instruments are also called upon to dramatize the text, both *colla parte* and *obbligato.*

Considering its textual basis (Scripture and chorale), its programmatic tendencies, its large musical form, and its relatively demanding performance requirements, Thomas's *Auferstehungs-Oratorium* belongs somewhere between the choir loft and the concert hall. On the other hand, Helmut Degen's *Osteroratorium,* for two- to seven-part mixed chorus a cappella (1942–43), is functional church music, but even Degen goes beyond the Gospel text by using chorales, a contemporary poem (*Der Gärtner,* by K. Müller-Osten; in several verses), and four motets based on the Scriptures (the oratorio text was written by Oskar Söhngen). Part I is an account of the Resurrection according to Mark (16:1–8) and John (20:11–18); part II focuses on the journey to Emmaus as described by Luke (24:13–25). The choral recitative sections, in one to four voice parts, are song-like in many ways; direct utterances are rendered either in the style of a song or of a simple motet. The primarily syllabic treatment of the Gospel text and the modest chorale settings, which make frequent use of unison singing, show Degen's wish to maintain a level of general accessibility; the motets, which serve for personal interpretation (principally the closing ones based on I Corinthians 15:20–21, 51–52, and 55) have a more complex polyphonic structure. G. Raphael's motet-like composi-

Helmut Degen: *Osteroratorium*; excerpt from the first part

tion *Die Auferstehung Jesu,* for four to eleven mixed voices a cappella Op. 63, No. 4 (1946), has already been mentioned in connection with the composer's motet compositions (see p. 439).

In style and in choice of media, several recent settings of the Easter story are closely related to *Gebrauchsmusik* for the church: for example, the *Ostergeschichte nach den Evangelien mit Kirchenliedern* (1945) by Max Drischner. Simple chorale settings here are connected by melodic solo recitatives with organ accompaniment; the voices of other characters may be sung by the chorus. Drischner leads the listener from Golgotha to the Resurrection, and from the Emmaus scene to the Ascension. In 1951 S. Reda augmented his set of *Evangelienmusiken,* in the series *Chormusik für das Jahr der Kirche,* with *Die Ostergeschichte als Konzert* for two high solo sopranos and four-voice mixed choir a cappella, which strictly follows Mark 16:1–8. In his foreword the composer characterizes the stylistic essence of this work:

In regard to the *concertante* treatment of the voices, the music as such assumes a more independent position in relation to the text than in my earlier Gospel compositions. Thus, important developmental material is executed on the vowel of a given word, while the remainder of the text is used to construct the opening or closing portions. In this way the actual expressive emphasis is occasionally shifted from word formations of primary expressive content [substance] to word pictures in a subordinate function [symbolism]. This sort of overlapping relationship between words and music corresponds to the spatial relationships of my formal designs, thereby intensifying the expression into the irrational.

These remarks are evidence of the persistent search, even among the younger composers, for a new relationship between text and music—for an answer to the problem of expression, which in this work has been "shifted . . . to word pictures in a subordinate function." They also refer indirectly to the difficulties performers have with intonation and rhythm in the realization of the score.

E. Wenzel's *Ostermotette,* for solo voice and mixed chorus (1952), is a concise, three-section *historia* based on the 20th chapter of John. The narrative is delivered for the most part by a four-part chorus with a richly varied coupling of voices. The character of the recitative arises from the expressive treatment of the soloists' direct utterances (Mary Magdalene: soprano; the angels: tenor and bass; Christ: bass; Thomas: tenor). The work lies somewhere between the motet and the *historia* and is an appealing example of practical, accessible church music. Felicitas Kukuck's *Osterhistorie,* for three-part mixed chorus with instruments ad lib. (1958), makes no inordinate artistic demands whatsoever. Herbert Gadsch's *Ostergeschichte,* for soprano, alto, tenor, bass, choir, and organ (first performance, 1957), is based on a combination of the four Resurrection narratives. The unaccompanied recitative of the Evangelist is in contrast with the organ-accompanied recitative of Christ, Mary, and Thomas. The *turbae* and contemplative chorale settings are sung by the chorus. Fritz Büchtger's five *historia* compositions, written since 1955, have been published only in piano reductions that offer no clear picture of the vocal-orchestral fabric. *Die Auferstehung nach Matthäus* (1955) and *Die Verklärung,* for baritone, women's voices, and strings (1956; Luke 9 and Matthew 17) make use of Emil Bock's new translation of the Bible text. *Die Himmel fahrt Christi,* for mixed chorus and orchestra (1956) is based on a new version of Acts 1, prepared by Philippine Schick. The course for the new version of the text in the History *Pfingsten* for baritone, mixed chorus, and orchestra (1957) is not given in the piano reduction. The departure in this through-composed work is its use of recitation-tone formulas in the recitatives, (always accompanied), which connect expressive elements and influence greatly the basically homophonic structure of the choral sections. In an attempt to fulfill the requirements of practical church music, the composer has allowed for four different performance possibilities in the Resurrection *historia.* The first of these —the most demanding—requires mixed chorus (with soloists ad lib.) and full orchestra, and the fourth—the simplest—four solo voices, four solo violins, viola, violoncello, double bass, and organ. The choral-orchestral History *Die Verklärung* also suggests the use of soloists (four female voices, four solo violins, viola, and violoncello) as an alternative to chorus and orchestra. At the end of the *Himmelfahrt historia,* the composer gives both of the germinal "rows" with their inversions in order to document the fact that his compositional style is based on the serial technique. This was also the case in his last History composition, the *Weihnachtsoratorium* for solo voices, mixed chorus, oboe, flute, and strings. After its premiere in 1959, W. Panofsky made the following appraisal of its serial processes: "That which . . . in . . . others . . . leads to a discrepancy between the concrete truth of the Scriptures and the abstract principle of composition becomes in his case musical elevation and absorption of the most individual sort. Büchtger subjects himself to the despotic rule of the 'rows' only to the extent that he can answer to his personal sensitivity. . . . However, this mixture radiates . . . an almost magical fascination."

SOLO CANTATAS AND CONCERTED WORKS

Apart from works by A. Mendelssohn, H. Kaminski, a few cyclic compositions by K. Thomas, and some isolated motets, the solo voice as an "instrument" has appeared up to this point only in the chorale cantatas mentioned above; it has served as a formal element only in the roles of the Evangelist and other soloists in *historia* composition. Not until the 1930s did composers gradually begin to overcome their timidity with respect to a subjective solo style. The terms "cantata" and "Geistliches Konzert," which are used interchangeably to describe solo works based on biblical texts, correspond to the practice of the historical period in which the models were produced. The new *Geistliche Konzerte* are usually patterned after those of Heinrich Schütz and his contemporaries. When sacred solos were revived (cautiously at first), composers drew upon two conspicuous sources of strength: the melodic character of the Protestant chorale and the musical recitative, which is closely associated with speech, particularly with the liturgy. Cantatas and concerted pieces fall into three principal groups according to their texts: 1) compositions based on one or more biblical verses; 2) compositions based on larger portions of a psalm, or on a single or several complete psalms; 3) compositions treating in solo form complete biblical scenes or, occasionally, even entire *historiae*.

The Swiss composer W. Burkhard has produced several works for solo voice. *Die Versuchung Jesu* (Matthew 4:1–11), which exists in an a cappella setting by G. Raphael (1934; see p. 438), was set by Burkhard in his 1936 cantata for bass (or alto) and organ (unison choir ad lib.), Op. 44. Two chorale verses by Adam Reusner (1696–1775), set to a chorale-like melody by the composer (which he labels "theme"), frame the biblical narrative. The latter, including the words of Satan, is delivered in recitative by one soloist; the replies of Jesus are made by the same soloist as a variation on the theme. Before the final chorale, the recitative sections culminate in an arioso on the closing verse, "And behold, angels came and ministered to him." The cantata follows the following form: Theme—Recitative—Variation I—Recitative—Variation II—Recitative—Variation III—Arioso—Theme. "Burkhard sees and experiences the narrative with deep inner involvement: the musical language is intensified . . . , the melodic breath is expanded; its lively tempo and its accompaniment make the development of the drama stand out in clear relief" (E. Mohr). *Christi Leidensverkündigung,* on Matthew 16:21–26, is the subject of the cantata for tenor solo, small mixed chorus, and organ, Op. 65 (1942), in which the Gospel text is presented in passionately agitated phrases by the solo tenor. The chorus sings the opening and closing chorale verses (both by G. Tersteegen, the first verse in unison, the last in two parts). In conjunction with the organ, the chorus underscores the monodic character of the solo part with imitative, lamenting vocalizations (on *ah*); it is united with the soloist at the climax of a fugato (in three parts) on the words of Jesus, "For what will it profit a man, if he gains the whole world. . . ."

For an organ dedication in 1950, the city of Thun commissioned Burkhard's Opus 84, *Und als der Tag der Pfingsten erfüllt war,* for low voice and organ with small unison chorus ad libitum. Its subject is the pouring out of the Holy Spirit upon all flesh (Acts 2). Ernst Mohr tells us that the commission "was most opportune for the composer; indeed it helped him realize a long-standing plan to set to music the story of Pentecost in the Acts of the Apostles." Once again the entire scriptural text is sung by a solo voice (Acts 2:1–21, dispensing with verses 5:9–12 and 18–20, which are not essential to the story). Again the formal organization is convincing; it contributes to a clear, graphic portrayal. The first movement, "Fantasia," based on verses 1–4, opens with a two-part introduction for organ "in the character of an improvisation." The second movement, "Recitativo," is based on verses 6–8, 13, and 14a, and the third, "Arioso," on verses 14b–17 and 21, which include a significant quote from the prophet Joel. E. Mohr rightly regards this movement as the spiritual climax of the work. Luther's hymn verse *Du heilige Brunst, süsser Trost,* in a setting with the composer's own chorale-like melody, comprises the basis for the fourth movement, designated "Chorale." In all three solo cantatas, but particularly in the cantata for Pentecost, the organ serves a largely independent function.

The *Psalmen-Kantate* for soprano solo, mixed chorus, organ, and small orchestra, Op. 90 (1952) was commissioned for the 600th-anniversary celebration of the canton of Bern's membership in the Swiss Confederation. In this three-part work the composer, taking into consideration the acoustical properties of the cathedral at Bern, looked back "to the chiseled, monumental expressive character of the Te Deum and *Isaiah*" (Mohr). Part I is a brief choral *Introitus* based on verses of the 24th Psalm (Lift up your heads, O ye gates); in part II, the chorus and solo voice join in a *maestoso* rendering of the 98th Psalm. This leads directly to part III, a closing unison "chorale" on two verses of Matthias Jorissen's rhymed transcription of the 98th Psalm (for detailed analysis see pp. 160–61 of Mohr's *Willy Burkhard;* Bibliography, section VI).

In a very special way, Burkhard's cantatas bear witness to the religious character of his creative output: permeated by a "religious strength" which is "anything but obtrusive," as E. Mohr so appropriately remarked, "his religiousness" never seems "pretentiously prophetic or extravagant, but rather restrained, serious, severe—always, however, genuine and sincere."

H.F. Micheelsen also designated his first vocal compositions for solo voice as *Solokantaten* for medium voice and organ (1937). There are three cantatas in the set; all were originally solo song settings in Micheelsen's oratorio *Ein deutsches Tedeum,* for mixed chorus, boys' choir, solo voices, and orchestra. The independent function of the organ is specifically referred to in the afterword: "By no means may the organ take on the character of an accompaniment." The second verse of the first cantata (on Psalms 104, 24, and 33) is delivered in recitative; it is followed by a *concertante* song-like hymn verse, *Ihr grünen Blätter in den Wäldern.* The work closes with the repetition of the first section combined with verse 24. The recitative and the same hymn verse recur in essentially the same form as the middle section of the later *Geistliches Konzert* for high soprano, flute, and organ, which is based on *Singet dem Herrn ein neues Lied* (Psalm 98:1a). The generic title *Geistliches Konzert* (sacred concerto) had already been used by Micheelsen in 1940 for *Was betrübst du dich, meine Seele* (Psalm 42:5) for alto or bass, solo violin, and organ, Op. 30a, from his *Sinfonia sacra, Von der Schöpfung.* This was followed in 1948 by the sacred concerto *Wenn ich mit Menschen- und mit Engelzungen redete* (I Corinthians 13) for the same combination, Op. 49.

In the foreword to Distler's three *Geistliche Konzerte* for high voice and organ or harpsichord, Op. 17 (1938), this composer, too, indicated the independence of the organ part: "Here the organ is not intended to function as a mere continuo accompaniment; rather, it is treated as an independent ensemble instrument, and . . . its dynamic relationship to the solo voice demands . . . careful consideration." As with Micheelsen, the solo part in these pieces conforms in large measure to the principles of melodic structure developed by the composer in his a cappella works. S. Reda adhered to Distler's principle in his early *Geistliches Konzert* for soprano and organ, *Tröstet, tröstet mein Volk* (1940), which combines the text from Isaiah 40:1–2 with Matthew 1:23 and Isaiah 12:5. The two sacred concertos by Gerhard Schwarz (1947 and 1949) evince greater independence. The first, *Ihr habt nicht einen knechtischen Geist empfangen,* for solo voice or unison chorus and organ, harpsichord, or piano, in three movements, deals with a text of rather large scope from Romans 8:15–23 and 31b–39. The four movements of the second *Geistliches Konzert, Ich vermahne euch aber, dass ihr euch nicht ärgert,* for solo voice and organ, harpsichord, or piano, correspond to the four verses of the text taken from the Apocrypha (II Maccabees 6:12–15). In his *Geistliches Konzert zum Advent* for high voice and keyboard instrument on *Mache dich auf, werde licht* (1956), J. H. E. Koch strove for a unique solo style; the composition, pieced together from repeated motifs, does not give the impression of containing a genuine melodic development that probes beneath the surface of the text.

In contrast to this group of solo compositions based on biblical verses is a small number of concerted pieces dealing with entire biblical scenes, written since 1932 by the Swiss composer Adolf Brunner. Their stylistic individuality grows out of a conscious involvement with historical models; every single one of these pieces presents its own solution to the problems of its respective text. In the *Geistliches Konzert* for medium voice and organ, which deals with the scene between Jesus and the adulteress (John 4:3–11), the conversational element is disregarded. The solo voice, which delivers the Evangelist's narrative and all the direct quotations (of the Pharisees and Scribes, Jesus and the woman), develops from its beginning recitative into a free-style declamation that enhances the atmosphere and spiritual significance of the scene. Independent in its own linear development, it is at the same time linked to the fundamentally linear events in the organ part, which

serves as an accompaniment but also pursues an independent course of development. In the *Geistliches Konzert* (for three voices, flute, string quintet, and organ,
with a motet for four-part chorus a cappella) devoted to the scene of Jesus and
the Samaritan woman at the well (John 4:6–26), the composer employs the
conversational principle of the *historia* by assigning the Evangelist's role to a
tenor, the role of Jesus to a bass, and that of the Samaritan woman to a soprano.
The germinal motif, from which the composition develops and which establishes
its marvelous unity, is stated in the opening bars of the instrumental introduction
and takes on its final thematic shape with the closing words of Jesus: "God is a
spirit, and those who worship Him must worship Him in spirit and truth." The
polyphonic development section of the concluding a cappella motet is based on
the final shape of the motif, an indication that the words of Jesus are the basic
thought of the entire work.

Brunner's *Geistliches Konzert* of 1939 is a choral setting of the parable of the
ten maidens (Matthew 25:1–13); although the work is for four-part chorus,
French horn, and string orchestra, "the voice and string parts may be performed
by soloists if necessary" (composer's foreword). The French horn, which fulfills
a symbolic rather than "an illustrative function, as it were," plays the first line
of the melody *Wachet auf, ruft uns die Stimme* from which the text is taken in
five of its seven entries. The vocal-instrumental organization of the score indicates
"a light, flowing . . . web of strings underlying a syllabically precise declamatory
choral setting, . . . now imitative, now alternating in *bicinium,* and now in the
manner of psalmodic recitation. . . . The whole conjures the mood of the hour
of expectancy and admonition of which the parable speaks" (O. Riemer).

Das Gespräch Jesu mit Nikodemus, set in 1937 as a Gospel motet for a cappella
chorus by E. Pepping, was also set by Brunner in the dialogue form of a *Geistliches
Konzert* for two voices, oboe, strings, and organ. Brunner avoided a realistic
dialogue structure by entrusting both the words of the Evangelist and the questions of Nicodemus to a single tenor rather than to two different soloists; the
words of Jesus are given to a single soloist (bass). With the entrance of the latter,
a reference to the *tutti* appears in the instrumental score: "If possible, the chorus
should participate in the string quartet part at those points marked *Tutti.*" Again
Brunner utilizes the recitative style in order to take advantage of the intense

Adolf Brunner: *Das Gespräch Jesu mit Nikodemus,* from the *Geistliches Konzert* for two voices, oboe,
strings, and organ

development of the dialogue, particularly between Jesus and Nicodemus, increasing the expressive possibilities of a predominantly syllabic setting through melismatic extensions.

Brunner's concerted pieces embody the ideal proposed by O. Riemer and presumably formulated by the composer himself: "The flexibility of the instruments should carry over to the chorus and, conversely, the purity of an a cappella setting should affect the instrumental style." In Brunner's *Taufkantate,* for high voice, violins, cello, and organ, "the baptismal words from Mark 10 and the chorale *Liebster Jesu, wir sind hier* are notated in supple, undulating 12/8 meter; the work ends in rhythmically elastic declamatory style with an aria based on Psalm 121 *(I will lift up mine eyes)*" (O. Riemer). The work carries the title "cantata," doubtless because of the union of heterogeneous texts and the resultant organization into several musically independent movements.

Die Versuchung Jesu (The Temptation of Jesus) is a biblical scene based on Matthew 4:1–11 that was composed in 1934 by Raphael as an a capella motet (see p. 438) and as a solo cantata by Burkhard in 1936 (see p. 471). This is also the subject of Adolf Brunner's (through-composed) *Geistliches Konzert* for four-part chorus a cappella (published 1948). The use of this generic title for an a cappella choral work presumably refers to the musical style: the flowing narrative tone of the vocal setting, in which the prevailing "declamatory style is only occasionally interrupted by long coloratura passages—for example, on the words *Gott, Geist,* and *Herrlichkeit*" (Riemer).

In contrast, W. Burkhard designated *Die Sintflut,* Op. 97 (1954–55), his last sacred vocal work, as a "cantata according to the account in Genesis" for mixed chorus a cappella. Here the generic title "cantata" seems to refer primarily to the overall form, a cycle of five a cappella motets. Using various portions of Genesis 6–9, the work deals with the history of the Flood in five motets: *The Corruption of Man, The Calling of Noah, The Outbreak of the Flood, The End of the Flood,* and *God's Covenant with Noah and the Rainbow.* Burkhard employs for the "realistic portrayal of the biblical text . . . all the resources of a cappella singing," simple note-against-note setting, "choral recitative," and imitative writing. The musical declamation is closely allied to the rhythm of speech. No image in the text is overlooked and diversified tone-painting structures appear in conjunction with pure vowel and consonant sounds (on *a, o, m*) or onomatopoeic syllables; but everything is designed to make "the event a personal experience for the listener, by the choice of compositional technique, by contrasting various kinds of settings, and by using sonorities of varying intensity" (E. Mohr). As a choral setting of an Old Testament *historia,* Burkhard's cantata *Die Sintflut* could have been included above under "Histories" or, because of its musical form, under [cyclic] motets based on the Scriptures. However, it is not typical of the vocalistic tendencies of the day, although it is a highly impressive testimony to the spiritual importance attached to the textual riches of the Bible in the stylistic development of today's choral (and soloistic) vocal repertory. Apart from works already mentioned, the generic designation "sacred concerto" has been taken up by relatively few of today's composers, among whom are Friedrich Zipp *(4 Kleine geistliche Konzerte),* Wolfgang Oehring (two concerted pieces based on chorales), and Dietrich von Baussnern.

Kurt Hessenberg's Opus 67 is also a setting of a "biblical scene": *Jesus und die Sünderin,* for mixed chorus a cappella (1956). Three cantus-firmus settings of the chorale *Wenn wir in höchsten Nöten sein* introduce, interrupt, and close the Gospel text (Luke 7:36–50). In spite of its cantata-like structure, however, the composer has refrained from using a more specific generic title. In this respect he calls to mind the new "choral" point of departure of all compositional forms based on scriptural texts. The vocal ideal in composition stems from the motet-like polyphonic treatment of biblical texts and is like a guiding star over choral and soloistic vocal works, accompanied and unaccompanied. This can be seen in the proliferation of motets, *historiae* and Passions, cantatas, and concerted pieces in liturgical forms as well as all others.

ORATORIOS

Recent developments in specific genres—motets, *historiae* and Passions, concerted pieces, and cantatas—show that using the Bible as a source of text materials has resulted in compositions other than those suitable for the service. The scope and instrumentation of many of these require concert conditions for performance in the church as well as the concert hall. This applies to all of the more extensive *historiae* and cantatas that approach the oratorio in dimensions. It also applies to long oratorios that require an evening to perform. An early example of a work having the character of an oratorio is the three-movement *Reformationskantate nach Worten der Heiligen Schrift* for three solo voices, four-part chorus, small orchestra, and organ, Op. 40 (1929) by Karl Hasse, a student of Reger. The work deals with Reformation teachings as they appear in chorales and texts from the Old and New Testaments. Although the most recent history of the oratorio cannot be covered comprehensively here, the turning back to sacred texts must be mentioned. Particularly notable examples are Arthur Honegger's *König David* (1921), Franz Schmidt's oratorio *Das Buch mit sieben Siegeln* based on Revelations (1938), Conrad Beck's *Oratorium nach Sprüchen des Angelus Silesius* (1933–35), and Frank Martin's Passion oratorio *Golgatha* (1945–48). In addition to these, several oratorios ought to be included because of their scriptural texts and their relation in spirit and style to the new Protestant church music.

Apart from the two oratorios of Kurt Thomas already referred to (see pp. 453,

467 ff.), the principal example to be cited here is Burkhard's oratorio *Das Gesicht Jesajas,* for soprano, tenor, bass, mixed chorus, organ, and orchestra, Op. 41 (1933–35), based on the composer's selections from Isaiah. Each of the seven movements closes with a hymn verse sung, in unison for the most part, to one of Burkhard's characteristic chorale-like melodies. The individuality and character of the musical organization in this oratorio, which cannot be examined in detail here, are the result of the individuality and character of the text from Isaiah. E. Mohr rightly observes in his biography (p. 40) that the work lacks "an actual 'plot,' as we think of it in the bulk of Handelian oratorios and many works of similar character in the 19th century"; on the other hand, there is "indeed the internal development that one finds in every genuine oratorio of earlier times." He also says that "Burkhard follows traditional precedents in the use of chorus, soloist, and orchestra. That which is new rests in the choice of musical resources and in the expression." The new element in Burkhard, as in Thomas and many other composers, was the use of the Lutheran scriptural text itself rather than an adaptation of biblical texts. J.H. Kohli (see Bibliography, section I) observed that "the choice and arrangement of scriptural passages and hymns alone amounts to a [personal] declaration whose power we cannot escape." Although that statement is true, we do not agree that "this oratorio's liturgical foundation cannot be doubted"; oratorio has no "foundation in the liturgy," and this would have been far from the composer's mind. What binds this work to the biblical oratorios from Carissimi to Handel is again the serious regard for biblical materials and the equally serious concern for the oratorio's task of performing "in public, the evangelistic duty of proclamation" (P. Eckhardt; see Bibliography, section II).

During and after Burkhard's time, several Swiss composers wrote cantatas and oratorios: Robert Blum wrote a two-movement cantata *Der Streiter in Christo Jesu* for soprano and chamber orchestra on texts from the letters of the Apostle Paul (1943). It deals (according to the composer) with "the attitude of the Christian toward his environment, on the one hand, and, on the other, toward his own spiritual development" (*40 Schweizer Komponisten;* see Bibliography, end of section VI). Bernhard Reichel wrote the oratorio *Emmaus* (and a second entitled *Une terre nouvelle*). Hans Studer, a pupil of Burkhard, wrote the oratorio *Die Leiden Hiobs* for soloists, chorus, and orchestra (1944–46), in addition to several cantatas and the *Drei Psalmen* mentioned earlier.

Among the composers of Protestant church music in Germany, H. F. Micheelsen was one of the most prominent to be involved with the oratorio. His works include a *Sinfonia sacra, Von der Schöpfung* (probably written before 1938), a cantata for chorus, soloists, and orchestra, Op. 30, and the oratorio *Die Weihnachtsbotschaft* for four solo voices, mixed chorus, chamber orchestra, and organ (1940). Walter Kraft's a cappella oratorio *Christus* is based on an extensive compilation from the four Gospels, with seven movements on the following themes: *The Word of God, The Kingdom of God, Miracles, Teachings, Prophecies, Passion,* and *Resurrection.* It opens with the words of John, "In the beginning was the Word," and closes with the announcement of the mission and the baptismal order, "Go therefore and make disciples of all nations." A double quartet (or small chorus) serves as the *Christuschor,* which delivers direct quotations.

113. Günter Raphael, from the *Tritychon zu Worten des Thomas-Evangeliums* for four-part chorus a cappella (1960), autograph. Kassel, Bärenreiter-Archiv.

114. Kurt Thomas, opening of the chorale motet *Ein feste Burg ist unser Gott*, Op. 14b (c. 1930), autograph, in the possession of the composer.

Juxtaposed to the double quartet, a small chorus functions as the Evangelist, or *Historicus,* who delivers the biblical narrative, while a large chorus presents the crowd scenes and reflective portions of the text. The use of three separate choruses is a unique stylistic element. The work requires two and a half hours to perform, a fact that seems to indicate the extravagance of the composer's goal: to present the entire life and teachings of Christ in a single, evening-long work. In his choral work *Die Gemeinschaft der Heiligen (Communio Sanctorum)* for soloists, choruses, winds, bells, congregation, and organ, "in the words of the Holy Scriptures of the Old and New Testaments, contrasted and superimposed in 'conversations' of Patriarchs, Prophets, Evangelists, and Apostles without regard for chronology," he attempted to deal with "the opposite poles of progress and fear in relation to the 'Communion of Saints,' presented as an eschatological event of pressing immediacy" (E. K. Rössler; see Bibliography, section II). In Kraft's words, "the 'conversations'" consist . . . of the arrangement and combination of series of verses from various books of the Bible which, in their choice, their mutual affirmation, penetration, and superimposition, often suspend normal awareness of time and space. Like medieval altar paintings, antithetical events often appear next to one another but still fit into the pattern of a larger governing order." The problems of the "libretto," merely hinted at here, indicate the problems of a work with a subject of such tremendous proportions that artistic mastery cannot be accomplished.

Comprehensive biblical librettos of an evangelistic nature also serve as the basis for an imposing series of oratorios published in the 1940s and '50s by Johannes Driessler. For the most part, his whole output of sacred works is dominated by the formal ideal of the oratorio. The first was the Christmas cantata *Denn Dein Licht kommt,* for soprano, baritone, and double choir with instruments, Op. 4 (1947), in which biblical and chorale texts are combined with a Christmas poem by Josef Weinheber. A similar affinity to the oratorio can be seen in Driessler's two large a cappella works, the *Sinfonia sacra zu Worten der Heiligen Schrift,* Op. 6 (1948), and the *Cantica nova,* Op. 13 (1949–50), an eight-voice choral work based on the Holy Scriptures requiring forty-five minutes for performance. Lina Jung characterized the content and style of the *Cantica* as follows: "The polyphonic songs encompass the entire gamut of religious feeling. In the introductory fantasia they begin with an expression of Old Testament melancholy and range from fear to hope until the exultant *Gloria in excelsis.* His opinion of the two choral works is essentially to the point: "The *Sinfonia* and *Cantica* are not actually Christian-oriented. They stem from the universal religious feeling out of which Brahms once created the *Deutsches Requiem.*" The thought content of the *Cantica* corresponds to that of the earlier oratorio *Dein Reich komme,* for soprano, tenor, and baritone soloists, five-part chorus, woodwinds, and string orchestra, Op. 11, based on the Old and New Testaments (1948–49). Here the dramatic components of Driessler's imagination and formal procedures had already clearly emerged. His introduction states: "The work represents a conscious departure from traditional form and the usual conception of the essence of the oratorio. It deals with a purely dramatic event whose principal vehicle is the chorus and the solo soprano from within the chorus. In contrast are the Prophet, speaking as an emissary of God in part I, and Christ in part II." Driessler adhered firmly to this ideal in two other oratorios that were obviously intended to form a three-part cycle with the Opus 11. In 1952 he wrote still another work based on his own selections from the Scriptures, the four-movement oratorio *De Profundis,* Op. 22, for soprano, tenor, and bass soloists, chamber chorus, large chorus, woodwinds and brass, piano, and timpani. As in the Opus 11, the solo voices are associated with specific dramatic characters. The soprano, designated as "the voice," is contrasted to "the priest" (baritone) and "the Lord" (tenor); the choruses personify "the demons" (chamber chorus) and "the people" (large chorus). The last work of the cycle is the four-movement oratorio *Der Lebendige,* for solo voices, chorus, and orchestra (consisting of woodwinds, trumpets, horns, timpani, and strings), Op. 40 (1954–56). It, too, is a setting of the composer's own selections from biblical sources. Between the Opus 22 and the Opus 40, Driessler composed two additional works in oratorio format, the *Kantate nach der Offenbarung Johannis: Darum seid getrost* for tenor solo, four-part chorus, trumpets, trombones, and organ, Op. 28, and the cantata dealing with the marriage at Cana (John 2:1–11), *Die Segnung der Freude,* for chorus and string orchestra, Op. 36, No. 2. In the latter work, Driessler used the Gospel text in conjunction with a free poetic text of Bernt von Heiseler. In the former he combined portions of Revelation with words of Christ from the Gospels and with the Apostles' Creed: the first article opens movement I, the second article movement IV, and the third article movement VII. The melody of the Lutheran confessional hymn is used symbolically each time. The whole work contains seven movements and lasts one hour. In contrast to the oratorios, in which biblical verses are all lined up together, the two cantatas show the composer's obvious concern with a greater concentration of textual and thematic material. The lack of such concentration in the larger compositions is not the least reason for their stylistic monotony, which is impossible to ignore in spite of the composer's compositional skill, and which Driessler sought to avoid primarily by exploiting the resources of sonority (his instrumentation varies from one work to the next). The factor of monotony apparently led to the recent "abbreviated version" of the successful first oratorio, *Dein Reich komme,* "which, in contrast to the original, evinces a noticeable pruning of the Old and New Testament portions of its textual nucleus" (S. Schweizer).

This situation spotlights the problem of shaping the text of an oratorio. Even the most skillful combination of unrelated biblical verses will not as a rule result in a libretto suitable for a large oratorio. A textual center is needed, about which the work can revolve—for example, a biblical story or disaster (as in Burkhard's *Isaiah* oratorio). In oratorios based on biblical texts, the composer must be conscious of his responsibility to serve the Scriptures.

Eberhard Wenzel's contributions to the genre exhibit a closer connection to specific areas of subject matter in the Bible. In his "chamber oratorio" *Emmaus,* for three soloists, chorus, and small orchestra (written before the Second World War), the text combines the Gospel narrative with appropriate chorales. The a cappella oratorio *Die Berge des Heils* (1953) articulates the message of salvation as it emanated from the various mountains of the Bible (Sermon on the Mount, Mount of Olives, Golgotha, and others).

A closing reference to several works of Herbert Peter should serve to show that younger composers other than Driessler are drawn to the oratorio. Peter's lack of restraint is demonstrated in the large forces required for performance of his Pentecost oratorio *Komm, heiliger Geist,* for tenor, bass, four- to five-part chorus, unison boys' chorus, large orchestra, and organ (first performance, 1955), to a text arranged by Kurt Tretschock. The work, in three parts, traces events from the Resurrection to the story of Pentecost. In contrast to this maiden effort, Peter's second oratorio, *Der verlorene Sohn* (first performance, 1956) shows possible signs of self-criticism on the part of the composer in his restriction of the ensemble to two four-part choruses and solo organ. A small chorus positioned at the altar relates the parable, and a larger chorus in the organ loft comments on the story with verses from the Old Testament. Both works center intellectually and spiritually around a clearly delineated biblical topic to which the commentary of the librettist and composer is bound. In its mastery of stylistic problems posed by the text, the second oratorio provides evidence of the young composer's fruitful devotion to the spirit of the liturgy and to the severity of liturgical music. Here, perhaps, one may perceive the first signs of future events defining the position of the biblical oratorio in current musical life. It needs to develop out of a clear alternative to liturgically bound music, toward its own inherent potential: to perform "in public, the evangelistic duty of proclamation" with complete freedom of artistic endeavor and with a genuine dedication to the spirit and content of the Scriptures.

ORGAN MUSIC

The new status achieved by Protestant vocal music was shared by a large body of organ literature for the Protestant church that re-entered the realm of artistic musical endeavor through the works of Reger. The development was closely connected with the "organ movement," whose beginnings may be traced to Albert Schweitzer. In 1905, in conjunction with his Bach studies, Schweitzer wrote the manifesto *Deutsche und französische Orgelbaukunst* (The German and French Art of Organ Building; published 1906). In 1909, at the Third Congress of the International Music Society in Vienna, he set forth the principles of his *Internationales Regulativ für Orgelbau* (International Standard for Organ Building). Schweitzer's organ ideal, growing out of the art of Bach and of French organ music, led him to demand that we "reject the modern factory organ with all its clever mechanical paraphernalia and return to the beautiful sound of the true organ," This led to the "organ movement," which developed after the First World War, primarily in Germany, and was based on surviving examples of the "old organ."

Hans Henny Jahnn, who had been restoring the Arp Schnitger organ at St. Jacob's Church in Hamburg since 1919, initiated, together with Gottlieb Harms, the First German Organ Conference in Hamburg (1925). The conference focused on the St. Jacob's organ in Hamburg and the small Schnitger organ at St. Jacob's in Lübeck. The German Organ Conference followed in 1926 at Freiburg; its opening paper—W. Gurlitt's *The Changing Concept of Organ Tone in the Light of Music History*—had great import for the future. The instrumental focal point at this conference was the Praetorius organ, built at Gurlitt's instigation by the master organ builder O. Walcker in the Institute of Musicology at the University of Freiburg. It had been constructed according to Michael Praetorius's own specifications in his *Organographia,* dedicated by Karl Straube on December 4, 1921, and destroyed in 1944 during the Second World War. (An endowment by Dr. M. T. Mellon of Pittsburgh made possible the reconstruction of the Praetorius organ in the new University Hall in 1954–55. Again the disposition was according to the original specifications of the *Organographia:* twenty-seven stops, two manuals, pedal, chair organ, slider, mechanical tracker action, and meantone tuning [the so-called Praetorian temperament]). In 1927, the Third German Organ Conference in Freiberg, Saxony, took its participants to the Silbermann organ in the Freiberg cathedral and to the organ in the Leipzig State Conservatory, built by Wilhelm Sauer under the aegis of Karl Straube "on inspiration from the earlier organ conferences." Prominent among the many speakers was Christhard Mahrenholz, who discussed the "Present State of the Organ Question in the Light of Organ History" and in a second paper probed the question of "The Organ and the Liturgy." Arnold Mendelssohn dealt with "The Organ in the Worship Service" in a paper that was read at the meeting by Julius Smend.

The discussions at these conferences, especially those concerning the phenomenon of the "old organ," have affected the art of organ building up to the present day. These events, and the "law of the organ," once again recognized by historians, organ builders, and composers, have also influenced the organ literature of the last four decades, which has been written more and more for the mechanical organ, either as projected or as already completed.

Many questions arising from the organ movement have still to be answered satisfactorily, as may be seen in recent writings. E. K. Rössler published a monograph in 1952 on *Klangfunktion und Registrierung* (Acoustical Function and Registration). Rössler's book, as Christhard Mahrenholz remarks in the preface, "takes as its point of departure the physical characteristics and conditioning factors of organ tone and proceeds from there to a systematic exploration of the entire realm of acoustics. It is a compendium for the benefit of organ builders, performers, and composers." In the same year H. Bornefeld published (in *Musik und Kirche* XXII) his valuable, penetrating study of *Orgelbau und neue Orgelmusik,* which was intended to be "a consideration of the changing relationship between organ building and organ composition and, wherever possible, a stimulus to practical involvement with new organ music and its acoustical problems."

Walter Supper has been president of the Society of Friends of the Organ and has edited its publications since 1952. As early as 1940 he dealt with the problem of the small organ (*Der Kleinorgelbrief,* 2nd ed., 1950). In 1958 he published his reports of the organ conferences in Stade (1954), Malmö (1955), and Hannover (1955) under the title *Orgelbewegung und Historismus* (Organ Movement and

Historicism). Hans Klotz's lecture, which is printed in the report, testifies to the lively debate still taking place.

Karl Straube achieved lasting fame as an exponent of Max Reger's organ works; in 1904 (in his edition of *Alte Meister des Orgelspiels* dedicated to "the young master Max Reger"), he had already called for "a deeper . . . involvement with the great art of the old, but eternally young, masters." In this edition Straube "as a contemporary individual . . . did not shy away from using all the expressive resources of the modern organ to achieve a musical performance appropriate to the *Affekt.*" In the foreword to his new series of *Alte Meister* (1929, 2 vols.), Straube acknowledged that a change had taken place in the style of organ composition and performance: "The challenging and fruitful purpose of our times is to clarify our understanding . . . of every style period within the framework of its own individual nature. With this knowledge . . . the desire has grown for performances in which the experience in sound comes from utilizing only such resources as the work requires. From this standpoint the attitudes reflected in the foreword . . . of the summer of 1904 . . . must be rejected." The knowledge and experience of the new organ movement was manifest in the 1929 edition with the inclusion of the "design of the disposition of the St. Jacob's organ in Hamburg," in the utilization of the "old designations *Hauptwerk, Oberwerk, Rückpositiv, Brustwerk,* and *Pedal,*" and in the omission of "markings for compensatory dynamic shadings"—all this in order "to arrive at a vital, clearly objective representation of the basic design and construction of a composition, with a minimum expenditure of resources and in a performance appropriate to the desired *Affekt.*"

Organ music devoted to the Protestant service was immediately caught up in, or at least attracted by, developments in the areas of organ building, performance, and organ composition, of which only the barest essentials are indicated by the names, dates, and facts given above. The current stylistic preference for polyphony and the rediscovered tone-ideal of the "old organ" (and that of the "new organ" oriented toward it) were beginning to merge, even though organ compositions written in the twenties were still a long way from being bound to a particular type of organ. Then in the 1930s composers of organ music produced compositions whose form and structure seem to have been inspired by specific organs. This may be inferred from the fact that registrations were usually specified for particular organs and from the corresponding prefatory explanations.

Organ compositions of the twenties should be viewed primarily in the context of the general transformation of musical style. The instrument's unique properties for the realization of polyphonic music was of great interest to composers of the younger generation. The development of this newer compositional style for organ became strikingly apparent in examples of free organ music and of cantus-firmus-based chorale settings.

Heinrich Kaminski's chorale settings, particularly his important toccata on *Wie schön leuchtet der Morgenstern* (1923), have already been mentioned (see p. 414). G. Raphael's Op. 1 (1922) is entitled *5 Chorale vorspiele;* his Op. 22, No. 1 is a partita on the chorale *Ach Gott, vom Himmel, sieh darein* (1928); No. 2, Fantasia in C minor (1928); and No. 3, Prelude and Fugue in G major (1930). Johann Nepomuk David's non-cantus-firmus works date from 1925. They include a Ricercar in C minor, a Chaconne in A minor (1927), a *Passamezzo* and Fugue in G minor (1928), a Toccata and Fugue in F minor (1928), and a *Prelude and Fugue* in D minor (1930). By 1928 he had turned to the cantus-firmus technique with two hymn settings, *Pange lingua* and *Veni creator*, and, in 1929, the *Fantasia super l'homme armé*. One of Ernst Pepping's first compositions, the 1923 *Doppelfuge* (MS), was for organ; four years later he wrote 6 *Choralvorspiele* (two of which were printed in 1932) utilizing the cantus-firmus technique (which was to characterize his later work). In 1927 W. Burkhard also began writing organ works without cantus firmi *(Triosonaten I* and *II)*, but his interest in the nature of the chorale had become apparent by 1930, when he wrote his *Variationen über Hasslersche Choralsätze (Aus tiefer Not, In dulci jubilo;* Op. 28). The organ works of Günther Ramin, organist at St. Thomas's, are noteworthy, although few in number. They include the Fantasia in C minor, Op. 4 (1924) and the Prelude, Largo, and Fugue, Op. 5 (1927); he returned to the chorale setting in the *Orgelchoral-Suite,* Op. 6 (1928). Karl Höller, son of a Bamberg organist, wrote a chorale partita on *O wie selig seid ihr doch, ihr Frommen,* Op. 1 (1929).

All of these works make use to some extent of the forms handed down in organ literature; G. Frotscher traces the development of this tradition to 1934 in his comprehensive *Geschichte des Orgelspiels und der Orgelkomposition* (2nd ed., 1959). The general development of music and the impetus provided by the "organ movement" led to a marked revival of organ music in the forties. In steadily increasing measure it was directed toward music for the church and the worship service, with the result that contemporary organ music became an essential component of contemporary church music.

The Protestant hymn became an ever more important factor in organ literature of the day. Three principal types emerged: the chorale partita, the chorale prelude, and the organ chorale. In 1932, J. N. David began publishing his *Choralwerk,* which by 1962 had grown to fourteen volumes. In 1932–33, E. Pepping wrote two chorale partitas on *Wer nur den lieben Gott lässt walten* and *Wie schön leuchtet der Morgenstern.* In 1933, H. Distler published a chorale partita on *Nun komm der Heiden Heiland,* and in 1935 another on *Wachet auf, ruft uns die Stimme* (Op. 8, Nos. 1 and 2); here, for the first time, a particular instrument (the small organ in St. Jacob's at Lübeck) had inspired a composition, necessitating detailed indications for registration and interpretation. W. Fortner's Toccata and Fugue appeared in 1930, his concerto for organ and string orchestra in 1932 (followed by the Preamble and Fugue in 1935), and his chorale partita on *An Wasserflüssen Babylon* in 1933. H. F. Micheelsen wrote *Choralmusik für Orgel* from 1933 to 1936; G. Raphael his *Zwölf Orgelchoräle,* Op. 37, in 1936; and H. Distler, the third of his *Kleine Choralbearbeitungen,* Op. 8, in 1938.

A possible parallel suggests itself between the vocal beginnings of the (German) chorale Mass and the preference for the multisectional chorale partita first encountered with Raphael (1928) and Höller (1929), then almost simultaneously with David (usually called *Kleine Partita* in his *Choralwerk),* Distler, Fortner, and Pepping. The Protestant chorale was first exploited in multisectional, cyclic organ chorales in which the structure corresponded to the several verses of the hymn. The creative minds of the time were primarily concerned with presenting the chorale in a polyphonic cantus-firmus setting, and with interpreting the text through purely musical means. Compositions written at the time were not intended primarily for the service, but rather to be heard and dignified in "church concerts" as an artistic undertaking. The deepening bond to the hymn tune and its subject matter directed the production of new organ chorale settings toward works usable within the worship service.

This circumstance was already clear in David's *Choralwerk.* Beginning in 1932 the first five volumes appeared without regard to the order of the church calendar. They were a random series of thirty-two chorale preludes, partitas, fantasias, toccatas, passacaglias, fugues, introductions, etc., based on cantus firmi. For the most part, they were eventually used in the church service. In the middle of the *Choralwerk* series (vol. VI, 1937) there appeared a "Lehrstück" for organ, consisting of an "Aria" followed by thirteen settings of the chorale *Christus, der ist mein Leben* in every conceivable canonic construction (in, for example, the second setting, double counterpoint at the sixth, and in the fourth setting a canon at the seventh). Volume VII (1939) was devoted to the positive organ and introduced a change of style in David's organ pieces, including a return to the partita in two works; the third (and last) work is a two-movement chorale and fugue on *Wie schön leuchtet der Morgenstern.* The subsequent volumes were again devoted to larger forms, quite obviously because of artistic and structural considerations: volume VIII (1941) contains a three-movement *Geistliches Konzert* for organ on *Es sungen drei Engel;* volumes IX and X (1945, 1947) and XI and XII (1952) each contain a multisectional chorale partita large in scope; volume XIII (1959–60) contains unspecified chorale settings of three hymns in six movements, in which the simultaneous use of two and even three cantus firmi is the most obvious compositional problem. In volume XIV (1962) too, David dispensed with precise indications of form: just as in the six-movement work in the thirteenth volume, the work here is a five-movement chorale fantasia, the first three movements of which are based on *Mitten wir im Leben sind;* the fourth movement is an organ chorale on the hymn *Maria durch den Dornwald ging,* and the fifth is a setting of the "Sterbelied"[1] *Wenn mein Stündlein vorhanden ist.*

The chorale partita, chorale fantasia, and chorale prelude comprise the bulk of David's chorale-based compositions; the toccata, toccata and fugue, introduction with fugue or passacaglia, chorale and fugue, small passacaglia, and *passamezzo* are each represented only once or twice in the collection.

David's compositions for organ, "which, constantly being added to, constitute the core of his creative output" (*MGG* III, 1954, 56), evince an astonishing stylistic development, with beginnings in Bach, Bruckner, and Reger. In connection with the Protestant hymn, this soon progressed toward an individual polyphonic ideal of tonally independent lines, an ideal born of strong tendencies toward a questioning constructivism. Finally, in works of the past two decades, there is an advance to the use of twelve-tone structures. The essence of David's chorale treatment is his strict adherence to the cantus firmus and his attempt to

---

1A *Sterbelied* is supposedly sung by a dying person praising death as a welcome friend who redeems us from our sinful present.

permeate the entire fabric of a piece with the substance of the chorale. This has led to a kind of serial technique in some of his later chorale settings, which the composer has acknowledged, apparently with great personal conviction.

The historical significance of H. Distler's two chorale partitas lies in the fact that their genesis is closely related to the small Schnitger organ in St. Jacob's at Lübeck.

Early masters (for example, S. Scheidt) set the example for the partita on *Nun komm, der Heiden Heiland*. The first and fourth movements of the work are toccatas featuring a pedal cantus firmus. The second movement is given over to seven variations of a chorale setting by Balthasar Resinarius. The third movement is a chaconne on the first line of the cantus firmus. In the second partita, on *Wachet auf, ruft uns die Stimme,* the outside movements, a toccata (I) and a fugue (III), enclose the central *Bicinium* (II), which adheres strictly to the cantus firmus. Distler's chorale partitas are based on an unaltered cantus firmus decorated with florid counterpoints. His percussive melodic style reflects a highly impressionistic conception of sound, but it also attests to his fancy for playfulness. H. Bornefeld, thoroughly acquainted with Distler's artistic tendencies, paid the following tribute to the organ works (*Orgelbau und neue Orgelmusik*, p. 14): "Distler's organ music is . . . 'radical' not only in one respect (i.e., stylistically) . . . but is just as 'radical' acoustically, idiomatically, liturgically, and intellectually; by this I mean [that it] penetrates to the core of the matter."

Distler made his way (in 1938) from the partitas to the liturgically functional *Kleine Choralbearbeitungen* (Op. 8, No. 3), which were followed in the same year by *30 Spielstücke* for small organ, Op. 18, No. 1, and in 1939 by the three-movement sonata for organ, Op. 18, No. 3, in strict trio style.

With Pepping, as with David, the organ was the one instrument to which he could always return to satisfy an inner creative impulse; even so, the appearance of one work after another, with and without cantus firmus, seems remarkable. His *Grosses Orgelbuch* (1939), which is in three parts following the order of the church calendar, contains 40 chorale settings (27 chorale preludes and 13 organ chorales). It was followed in 1940 by the *Kleines Orgelbuch,* which contains 18 easier chorale preludes and organ chorales.

This extensive collection is devised for performance within the worship service. Liturgical points of view establish the distinction between "chorale prelude" and "organ chorale." The length of the prelude will depend on the point at which it is used in the service. It may develop freely or be tied to a cantus firmus. Because it is often used in antiphonal performance, the organ chorale must retain the strophic form of the hymn tune, which is to be played through once from beginning to end (this does not prevent the organ chorale from serving as a chorale prelude). David met these liturgical requirements and at the same time capitalized on the distinctive quality in each of the melodies, whose forms appear "to take on new meaning," as O. Brodde has observed *(MuK):* "Form becomes the servant of the idea, of the liturgical purpose. In this way the canon becomes a sounding symbol of contemplation associated with the tranquil *de tempore* events." In 1941, Pepping wrote his toccata and fugue *Mitten wir im Leben sind,* which, like David's chorale partita *Unüberwindlich starker Held, Sankt Michael*

(1945; *Choralwerk* IX), is documentary of artistic activity in the period. Clarity is the principal stylistic feature "even in such a dramatic work as *Mitten wir im Leben sind*" (H. Bornefeld); the piece grew out of the spirit and substance of the chorale and is as imaginative as it is formally strict.

With the two *Concerti* of 1941, Pepping turned for the first time to organ compositions without cantus firmi. *Concerto I* adopts the Baroque concerto principle, most clearly evident in the first movement, the "Intrada"; this is followed by an "Aria alla Passacaglia." The "Fuge," or third movement, is a double fugue with separate developments for each of the two subjects and a closing section in which the subjects appear together. *Concerto II* opens with a solemn, festive "Praeludium," which uses an original vocal setting *(Kelterspruch* from *Der Wagen)* as its thematic point of departure. This is followed by a canzona of meditative character and a powerfully developed chaconne. These cantus-firmus-free concertos, which enjoy the freedom of the concerted style in spite of their strict formal limitations, may be contrasted to the uncommonly vital *Vier Fugen* in D major, C minor, E-flat major, and F minor (1942), the *Zwei Fugen* in C-sharp minor (1943), and the *Drei Fugen über B-A-C-H* (1943), all of which transcend the traditional conventions of fugal composition.

Only after a twelve-year interruption did Pepping return to the organ-chorale setting, first (in 1953) with three partitas on the "Sterbelieder" *Ach wie flüchtig, ach wie nichtig, Wer weiss, wie nache mir mein Ende,* and *Mit Fried und Freud ich fahr dahin.* His source for cantus firmi, *Liedweisen der Böhmischen Brüder,* supplied the material for further liturgical chorale preludes and organ chorales *(Böhmisches Orgelbuch* I and II, 1953–54). Orthodox Latin hymns served as sources for six extended cantus-firmus compositions incorporating concerted elements. The concise, straightforward *Zwölf Choralvorspiele fur Orgel manualiter* (1957) were intended to serve a wider range of liturgical functions. In the organ sonata written in the same year, the three pillars of Christian faith constitute the basis and form of the three trio-sonata movements: a pastorale on *Gelobet seist du, Jesu Christ,* an arietta on *O Haupt voll Blut und Wunden,* and a toccata on *Christ ist erstanden.* The last series of Pepping's organ works devoted to the church hymn are the *25 Orgelchoräle nach Sätzen des Spandauer Chorbuchs* (1960). Their construction is vocally oriented, following the principles of instrumental voice leading upon which the composer's entire output for organ is based. It is these principles that make his work so idiomatic for the organ, that cause him to "vary the basic features of the vocal setting to the same degree, taking advantage, however, of "the instrument's superiority to the human voice in range and ease of tone production" (E. Pepping, *Der Polyphone Satz* I, p. 23; in this connection, cf. Hans Schmidt-Bayreuth, *Musik und Kirche* XXIV, 101 ff.).

Reference already has been made (p. 447) to W. Burkhard's vocal compositions with organ. Following Opp. 18 and 28, also discussed above, are several organ works without cantus firmi, the *Orgelfantasie,* Op. 32 (1931), Prelude and Fugue in E (1932), the *Sonatine,* Op. 52 (1938), and, in 1945, the concerto for organ with string orchestra and winds, Op. 74, and a *Hymne* for organ and orchestra, Op. 75. Centrally featured in each of these concert pieces is a "chorale," written by the composer. In addition there are a few works based on old chorales: in 1931–32 the two small partitas *Wer nur den lieben Gott lässt walten* and *Grosser Gott, wir loben dich,* and the 1939 fantasy and chorale *Ein feste Burg ist unser Gott,* Op. 58. The formal design of the latter combines "elements of the Reger chorale fantasy with those of the classic organ art of the Netherlanders. . . . Apocalyptic in mood and highly improvisatory in character . . . the work seems to mirror the collective universal tragedy, flowing climactically into the last verse of Luther's hymn, reinforced with extraordinarily emotional harmonies" (E. Mohr, p. 78). The 1935 *Choraltriptychon,* Op. 91, one of Burkhard's last works, combines in part I the *Geburt Christi* with two verses of P. Gerhardt's song *Ich steh an deiner Krippe hier;* in part II, designated as the *Kreuzigung,* interpretative use is made of the chorale *O Mensch, bewein* in a line-by-line development textually under-laid. "In the *Resurrection,* Burkhard uses the power of the ancient melody *Christ lag in Todesbanden* to establish the musical atmosphere. After an improvisatory section of ambitious proportions, part III turns into a primarily unison statement of the cantus firmus; only in the closing *Halleluja* does the texture of the move-ment expand into polyphony" (E. Mohr, p. 162).

Burkhard's organ compositions do not serve primarily liturgical purposes. At most, the two small chorale partitas are functional, but the remaining chorale settings and even those works without cantus firmi owe their existence chiefly to commissions that coincided with the compositional wishes of the musician. His return to the "old chorale" and his desire to create such new chorale-like melodies as appear in several of his organ works seem to stem from the drive to express artistically his own beliefs.

Although the question of the liturgical use of freely composed organ works cannot be discussed here, it is important to mention some of the many organ concertos and sonatas that have appeared during the last decades.

H. Humpert wrote three concertos (1932, 1937, 1942), H. F. Micheelsen five (since 1940), among which the second (1943) is based on *Es sungen drei Engel.* J. Ahrens composed a Concerto in E (1943) and a *Concertino* (1944). S. Reda wrote three organ concertos (1947, 1948, 1951) as well as three chorale concertos for organ (1946–48). In 1959 Reinhard Schwarz-Schilling published a *Concerto per organo.* W. Burkhard's *Triosonaten,* Op. 18 (1927), and *Sonatine,* Op. 52 (1938), have already been mentioned. P. Hindemith wrote three sonatas for organ (I–III, 1937–40), and Ernst Krenek a sonata Op. 92 (1941). G. Raphael's *Orgel-sonate,* Op. 68, appeared in 1949, Friedrich Leinert's *Erste Orgelsonate* in 1950, K. Hessenberg's *Triosonate B,* Op. 56, in 1951. Harald Genzmer's *Orgelsonaten* I–III appeared in 1952, 1956, and 1963, S. Reda's *Sonate für Orgel* in 1960, and Max Baumann's *Sonatine für Orgel* in 1963. All of these works belong properly to the sphere of the church concert rather than the worship service, if only because of their extended scope. They obey primarily musical-artistic laws, but do not meet liturgical requirements, although an occasional movement may approach being a spiritual declaration and thus might find a place in the liturgy as an extended prelude, interlude, or postlude.

On the other hand, the eight volumes of Johannes Driessler's *20 Orgelsonaten durch das Kirchenjahr* (1954–56) were expressly intended for use in the worship service. They consist of three or four movements, each of which is based on a *de tempore* hymn. Changing with almost predictable regularity from sonata to sonata, the individual movements are designated either by type (toccata, aria, fugue, canzona, passacaglia, prelude, fantasia, partita, *bicinium,* ricercar, hymn) or by tempo indication (as in sonatas II, IV, VII, IX, XII, XV, XVIII, and XX). In contrast to other contemporary composers for organ, Driessler consciously "avoids in the score any specifications for registration, as well as for dynamics, articulation, or tempo" (foreword). The sonatas are notated throughout without bar lines. W. Bieske has objected (*Musik und Kirche* XXIV, 263) to the composer's suggestion that the individual sonata movements "be used as independent chorale preludes" because of the difficulty and the "degree of dissonance." However, the same observer does say that the sonatas, "in contrast to many other contemporary productions, evince masterful skill in handling of form and content," a judgment that presumably rests upon the work's strict contrapuntal treatment. Driessler's polyphony, in conjunction with certain stylistic mannerisms (e.g., the stereotyped use of parallel fourths), for the most part results in a rather tiring uniformity of style. Moreover, these "bold" sonatas do not seem to have found a convincing solution to the problem of creating an atonal setting for tonally based hymn tunes.

The *Choralwerk* of J. N. David is by no means the only evidence that Catholic composers have taken up the Protestant chorale. Among J. Ahren's numerous compositions for organ are four chorale partitas on *Jesu meine Freude* (1943), *Lobe den Herrn* and *Verleih uns Frieden* (1947), and the interdenominational *Christ ist erstanden* (1948, except the hymns *Pange lingua* [1936] and *Veni creator* [1947]). R. Schwarz-Schilling edited the *Canonische Choralbearbeitung "Da Jesus an dem Kreuze stund,"* which appeared in 1942, and in 1953, *Zwölf Choralvorspiele* (composed 1927–48). In addition to the above-mentioned Opus 1, K. Höller wrote, as his Opus 22, chorale variations on *Helft mir Gottes Güte preisen* and *Jesu, meine Freude* (1936).

It is not possible to discuss comprehensively at this point the enormous number of organ works written for the Protestant church from the twenties to the present. In addition to the always prominent chorale setting, the classic forms of free-composed organ composition (prelude, fantasia, toccata, chaconne, fugue, passacaglia, etc.) continue to be composed and are connected with one stylistic trend or another. The effect of an older generation of composers is still being felt.

A practical composer such as Paul Kickstat, for example, shows no trace of a style change in his *Choralvorspiele* (1933–40). These are straightforward examples of *Gebrauchsmusik* which, because of their uniform cantus-firmus treatment (only a pallid copy of Bach's), must be regarded not as compositions but as improvisations that have been written down. E. Wenzel's Toccata in D minor and *Fuga variata* contrast with his *Orgelmesse* based on hymns from the German Ordinary. In 1948 Hermann Heiss published three chorale partitas, and J. Weyrauch seven. Paul Müller-Zürich wrote a chorale fantasy, *Ach Gott, vom Himmel, sieh darein.* Freely composed organ works were also written by Walther Geiser, Johannes Engelmann (Fantasia, Passacaglia and Fugue in G minor [the latter on *B-A-C-H*], Op. 34), and Fritz Eggermann. In 1963 Fritz Werner published his Toccata and Fugue in D, Op. 32, and the partita *Christe, du bist der helle Tag,*

Op. 34. J. N. David's late organ works still to be mentioned are the cantus-firmus-based partita on *Innsbruck, ich muss dich lassen* (1955) and the Chaconne and Fugue (1962) without cantus firmus.

Of works by the generation of composers born after the turn of the century, the remainder of G. Raphael's output for organ has yet to be discussed. There are cantus-firmus compositions that draw on Finnish chorales: Op. 41, No. 1, Fantasia and Fugue; No. 2, Partita; No. 3, Passacaglia (1939); and the (also Finnish) *Sieben Choräle* (c. 1940), as well as the Toccata with Chorale *(Wachet auf, ruft uns die Stimme)* and Variations, Op. 53 (1944). A. Brunner's 1949 *Pfingstbuch über den Choral "Nun bitten wir den Heiligen Geist"* is a cycle with the following movements: 1) Preamble, 2) Chorale, 3) Partita, 4) Passacaglia, 5) Chorale (=2). Kurt Fiebig, a pupil of Schreker and for decades an expert on the organ and music of the Protestant church, wrote a series of freely composed organ works (preludes, fugues, toccatas, etc.), four chorale partitas, and approximately 50 organ chorales and chorale preludes. His contemporary, K. Hessenberg, made cantus-firmus settings of two chorale partitas on *Von Gott will ich nicht lassen* and (for positive organ) *O Welt, ich muss dich lassen,* Op. 43, "in which may be found pieces useful for liturgical performance and for *Abendmusik*" (W. Bieske). He also wrote a fantasia *Sonne der Gerechtigkeit,* Op. 66, and numerous chorale preludes for various collections. In the way of freely composed works, Hessenberg wrote Prelude and Fugue, Op. 63, No. 1, and Toccata, Fugue and Chaconne, Op. 63, No. 2 (both 1952). H. Degen wrote a Christmas fantasia on *Kommet, ihr Hirten,* as well as *Choralvorspiele,* Prelude and Fugue, and *Konzert für Orgel und Posaunenchor.*

Single chorale partitas and single (or multiple) chorale preludes were written by H. Klotz, J. Bender, W. Kraft, J. Kötschau, Gottfried Müller, Friedrich Zipp, Dieter Schmeel, Harald Heilmann, Hans Stadlmair, Hans Martin Schneidt, H. W. Zimmermann, Lothar Graap, and many others. Single organ compositions without cantus firmi have been published by S. W. Müller, Kurt Bossler (*Drei Orgelstücke,* Opp. 37, 40, and 50), F. Zipp, Jürg Baur, Ernst-Ulrich von Kameke, Manfred Kluge, Ernst Vogler, and H. W. Zimmermann, whose four *Orgelpsalmen* appeared in 1955–56. Zimmermann's foreword explains the term "organ psalm" as the "applied compositional technique of instrumental recitation, by means of which each psalm was through-composed from beginning to end and thus realized accurately on the organ, down to the very last syllable. Clearly . . . the interpretation must stem completely from the text."

The majority of organ works discussed up to this point are connected with tradition insofar as they were not conceived from the beginning with a particular type of organ in mind and their ideal realization is not dependent on a particular type of instrument. From the time of Kaminski, the development of style took place primarily on the level of compositional process. The crucial issue since the twenties and thirties has been the development of a polyphonic concept of style, and thus of works whose ideal realization lies *a priori* with "modern" instruments built along the lines of the "early mechanical organ."

On the other hand, Distler's organ works were written with one particular instrument in mind (the St. Jacob's organ in Lübeck), the first works in the recent history of organ music to be so conceived. Bornefeld and Reda reacted enthusiastically to Distler and advanced the cause of his principle both in their own works and in their respective musical spheres. (Others include E. K. Rössler, in the few works he has published to date: an *Introductio,* an *Introduktion, Rezitativ, Cantus,* and *Ricercare* on *Christe, du Lamm Gottes,* and others; in this connection compare special articles listed in the Bibliography, section V). Most of Bornefeld's works for organ are settings of chorales; the few exceptions include the *Intonationen* from the *Orgelstücke* (published 1948–49). From 1948 to 1956, Bornefeld also published eight chorale partitas for organ in his multivolume *Choralwerk* series.

The forms that Bornefeld used in these chorale settings were entirely conservative. In his Partita I, the sequence *Toccata-Fantasia-Fuge* corresponds to the three verses (Father-Son-Holy Spirit) of Luther's devotional hymn *Wir glauben all an einen Gott.* Other movements appear with titles such as *Trio, Pastorale, Ciaconna* (in II); *Toccatina, Canon, Bicinium, Ricercar* (in III); *Meditation, Canzone* (in IV); *Alla breve, Dialog, Rondo* in the strict trio setting of Partita V. Partita VI (1951–53), on *Komm, Gott Schöpfer, Heiliger Geist,* consists of a fantasia and fugue; according to the composer's foreword, it was written "for a large four-manual organ . . . that was rebuilt to include the following divisions: *Hauptwerk* (HW), *Seitenwerk* (SW), *Oberwerk* (OW), *Kronpositiv* (KP), and *Pedal* (P); . . . the *Fernwerk* (FW) had already been included in the original design of the organ (1904)." In Partita VI, Bornefeld concerned himself "quite simply with the task of subordinating the extreme tonal possibilities of the compromise organ to the serious musical meaning to be found, in the last analysis, in the nature of the instrument." The seventh chorale partita, *Christus, der ist mein Leben* (1955), is made up of the movements *Praeambel und Choral, Bicinium, Aria, Phantasie, Musette,* and *Carillon,* which correspond to the seven hymn verses. The first line of every verse in the chorale text is indicated in the score; the *Phantasie* treats verses 4 and 5. In Partitas I, IV, and V, the cantus firmus is underlaid with the hymn text. Partita VIII, on the German Te Deum *Herr Gott, dich loben wir,* consists of five untitled movements.

In addition to the large-scale chorale partitas there are two volumes of chorale preludes for church use, which Bornefeld published in 1958–60. They are arranged in *de tempore* order. The foreword states that the "concept of 'chorale prelude' should not be interpreted too narrowly" here. "In addition to a number of chorale preludes that use the substance of the chorale, there also are *intonationi,* organ chorales, variations, improvisations, postludes, and ornamentations, even arrangements, of existing compositions—my own and those of others." These works too were conceived with a particular instrument in mind: "The instructions for registration," which, however, only "provide a general indication of the actual tonal realization, are based on the disposition of the organ at the Esslingen School of Church Music." The disposition of this organ is given in the foreword. The style of the chorale preludes is characterized in W. Bieske's discussion of volume I (*Musik und Kirche* XXX, 54): "The preludes are short, sometimes too short for practical use. . . . As for content, the pieces display the ostinato rhythms so characteristic of Bornefeld and a harmony that often betrays its kinship with Stravinsky. There is a security in the writing that shows the hand of the master." The organ chorale settings, also published in 1958–60, consist of three volumes in *de tempore* order. They are meant "for chorus or soloist and organ" and are in fact organ pieces in which the cantus firmus is "to be sung." The author had in mind here the "antiphonal performance of hymns in the worship service." Bornefeld's *Begleitsätze für Orgel* (six volumes arranged according to the church calendar) were also intended for liturgical performance.

Siegfried Reda, who, like Bornefeld, began as a composer for the organ, has published a large body of organ works since about 1940 in which the juxtaposition of compositions with and without cantus firmi again seems significant. Among his cantus-firmus works are the Chorale Concertos I–III (1946–48); the chorale concerto on *O Traurigkeit, o Herzeleid* (1953), which has its origins in an organ partita of 1938; the *Triptychon* on *O Welt, ich muss dich lassen* (1951); and the Advent partita *Mit Ernst, o Menschenkinder* (1952). Reda wrote other organ pieces for liturgical performance in the more restricted sense: chorale preludes, the *Choral-Spiel-Buch* (1945–46), the *C. F.-Stücke zu den Wochenliedern der Fastenzeit* (1959), and *Vorspiele zu den Psalmliedern des EKG* (1957).

These chorale-based works bear impressive witness to Reda's use of the cantus-firmus principle. As Reda himself indicates in his foreword, the 30 chorale preludes of the earlier *Choral-Spiel-Buch* stem from the practice of improvisation; the pure organ chorale scarcely appears at all in the collection. W. Bieske has remarked (*Musik und Kirche* XXVIII, 84) about the later *Vorspiele zu den Psalmliedern:* "For the professional, Reda has worked out the elements of the chorale with great clarity. . . . For the Sunday worship service of the average congregation the pieces are essentially useless." This alludes to problems in the composer's style, which are equally evident in the larger works. The early chorale concerto *O Traurigkeit,* for example, has frequent tempo changes and performance indications ("begin excitedly," "progressively more motion," "compress," etc.) that contribute to making it a genuinely subjective piece of musical expressionism. The three three-movement chorale concertos gradually break away from this style, largely as a result of their use of strict forms such as the ricercar (in I), or canon and chaconne (in III). The third movement of the second chorale concerto is based on a theme by Distler.

Among Reda's freely composed works are three organ concertos and the *Marienbilder,* the first two movements of which bear the titles 1) *Verkündigung* and 2) *Magnificat—Im Gedanken an Igor Strawinskys Psalmensymphonie.* In the latter the *tonus peregrinus* appears in the pedal, while the evenly flowing figuration of the upper voice is reminiscent of the *Symphony of Psalms.* The remaining movements are obviously freely constructed and seek to depict their respective titles: 3) *Engelskonzert* (Concerto of Angels)—*Salve Regina;* 4) *Vesperbild— Grablegung* (Vesper Scene—Burial); 5) *Pietà.* Among the larger freely composed works are the *Praeludium, Fuge und Quadruplum* (1957) and the sonata for organ (1960). The 1957 work is based on Crüger's melody *Befiehl du deine Wege,* the first line of which is treated in the fugue. In the closing *Quadruplum,* the chorale is stated once (in the tenor). The use of the cantus firmus is not explained in the score, but has been discussed by S. Scheytt (*Musik und Kirche* XXXI, 76 f.): "It has assumed a function similar to that of the row in twelve-tone composition: it generates every note, so to speak, but is not heard as a cantus firmus." (Scheytt failed to mention the organ chorale, which is indeed present in the *Quadruplum.*)

Included in the introduction to the sonata of 1960 is the disposition of the organ built by K. Schuke in 1959 for St. Peter's at Mülheim on the Ruhr, an outline of the formal construction of the sonata, a registration setting, and a registration scheme suggested by the composer. Melodically and harmonically, the sonata is based on alternating twelve-tone rows. In homage to Anton von Webern, individual movements of the work are patterned after the various sections of sonata form: an exposition, a development in the form of a fugue, a recapitulation as a slow movement, and a finale in the form of a passacaglia. The sonata-form characteristic of thematic contrast cannot be fulfilled by the twelve-tone material since both the theme and countertheme are built from the same material. As a consequence, Reda's themes are sketchy and unclear. Formal development remains on the surface; the harmony often lapses into coincidental linear formations and is not effective as a compositional element. The composer does not seem to have fulfilled the enormous stylistic demands posed in this work.

The purpose of this chapter has been to show the fundamental importance in new Protestant organ music (as in contemporary Protestant church music) of the new search for ties with the hymn. The great number of chorale settings published in recent decades attests to the re-establishment of a spiritual center in organ music; this has become evident in freely composed organ works as well. A frequent point of departure at first was the cyclic, multi-verse chorale partita, corresponding artistically and formally to the cyclic, multi-movement vocal chorale Mass. Obviously, composers of organ music, as of vocal music, were concerned initially with purely artistic matters before they turned to musical tasks more closely connected to the worship service—the creation of chorale preludes and organ chorales. More recent freely composed organ compositions also pursue primarily artistic aims. Such traditional genres as prelude, fugue, toccata, chaconne, sonata, and concerto provided a stylistic and formal ideal of polyphony suitable to the organ. In emulating this ideal, composers have tried the most diverse procedures in order that they might be free to explore their own new ways. The diversity can in large measure be traced back to the wide variety of styles in organ literature of past eras.

In view of the abundance of these manifestations, it is hardly possible at this time to detect a unified stylistic trend. Realizations of the organ-music ideal are highly divergent. However, two principal groups of compositions emerge. In the first are works that have ties with the melodic store of the church and with the purely musical structural principle of polyphony; such works aspire to a stylistic ideal appropriate to the nature of the organ. In the other group are works of exclusively organ-oriented musicians who are concerned with the development of a genuinely "organ-like" style based on the purified sound of the "mechanical organ." A careful examination of works in this category often leads to the impression that many were written to exploit the specific tonal possibilities of particular instruments. The strong dependence of such compositions on primarily aural phenomena is evident not only in the organ dispositions and performance or registration indications often given at the front of editions, but also in the explanatory forewords that are so obviously deemed necessary and in the frequently modified notational systems. It cannot and must not be overlooked that behind this style one often finds a retrogressive, late Romantic attitude that is denied the energy of genuine polyphony.

In contrast to works whose acoustical basis lies in the "mechanical organ" are those whose spiritual essence lies in a polyphonic structure, the realization of which is in the hands of an imaginative performer skilled in the art of registration. If the compositions inspired by particular instruments seem to invert the relationship between the work and its realization—to make the form and structure of the composition dependent on an "ideal" realization upon a particular instrument— there are precedents in the great heritage of "classical" organ literature. For these new works, the modern "mechanical organ," built according to the "law of the organ" as a consequence of the "organ movement," is doubtless the ideal instrument. It gives the organist varied possibilities of registration (as in the time of Samuel Scheidt or J. S. Bach) with which he can give as vital and plastic a performance as possible, clarifying the polyphony. Only the future can judge which of the creative paths touched upon here will prove most fruitful for the organ music of these times.

Leipzig d. 10. Sept. 1918.
Dorotheenplatz 1 III

Mein lieber Dr. Gurlitt, wie sehr war ich erfreut Ihre lieben
Zeilen aus der Schweiz zu erhalten. Gott sei Dank, daß das
Schwerste überstanden ist, daß Sie wieder Ihrer Arbeit, Ihren
Freunden wiedergegeben sind, daß Sie endlich mit der Frau
vereint worden, mit der gemeinsam durchs Leben zu wandeln
Sie willens sind. Wie erstaunlich muß Ihnen dies alles vor-
gekommen sein und wie innerlich glücklich werden Sie
sein. Vielleicht, oder vielmehr wahrscheinlich werden Sie von
einem durchlebten Glücksgefühl erfüllt sein, als wir alle es
empfinden können; denn neben allem Guten und Schönen
haben Sie die eigenste Freiheit neu gewinnen dürfen
und in diesem Erleben ein Größeres empfunden, als wir
alle es jemals erfassen können. Dies allein schon wird Ihnen
eine Gewähr für Ihre Zukunft sein, denn Menschen die
so wie Sie durch Dunkel und Licht gehen mußten, die
sind gewappnet für alle Fährnisse und Glücksfälle des
Lebens. Aber im allgemeinen möchte ich Ihnen doch
wünschen, daß mehr des Glückes und des Lichtes
in Ihrem Leben sein möchte, als von den Dingen, die
auf der Schattenseite der Daseins blühen und ge-
deihen. Das Glück des gemeinsamen Lebens mit der
geliebten Frau wird Ihnen aber Kraft geben auch das
Dunkel siegreich zu überwinden, um allezeit froh-
gemut im Lichte einherzuschreiten. Und das wird

115. Letter of Karl Straube to Wilibald Gurlitt, September 10, 1918. Kassel,
Bärenreiter-Archiv.

Leipzig, 10 Sept. 1918
Dorotheenplatz 1 III

My dear Dr. Gurlitt, how glad I was to receive your letter from Switzerland. Thank God that the most difficult part is over, that you have returned to your work and to your friends, and that you finally are united with the woman with whom you wish to wander through life. How marvelous all this must have seemed to you and how inwardly happy you must be. Perhaps, or rather probably, you are filled with a richer sensation of happiness than any of us are capable of experiencing; for in addition to all that is good and beautiful, you have been able to regain the most basic of freedoms and through this experience have come to know a more complete freedom than any of us could ever comprehend. This in itself is a guarantee of your future, for those such as you who have had to walk through darkness and light are armed against all life's pitfalls and blows of fortune. In general I would like very much to wish you a life holding more happiness and light than those things that bloom and prosper on the dark side of this existence. Still, the happiness of your life together with your beloved wife will give you the strength to win out even over darkness, so that you can move about cheerfully forever in the light. That

oder so ähnlich mit Ihnen werden möge, dies ist mein Wunsch
zu Ihrer Rückkehr. –

Wie ich aus Ihrem Brief ersehe, sind Sie wieder mitten drin
in den Aufgaben des Berufes, und bemerke auch, daß Sie
während der Gefangenschaft über "musikalische Stilgeschichte"
gearbeitet haben. Von Ihren Resultaten im Durchdenken
dieses Gebietes würde ich gern manches erfahren. Vor allem
von der Kernfrage, von welchen geistigen Faktoren aus wird
der musikalische Stil entweder beeinflußt, oder vielleicht
auch geleitet und gerichtet. In der Kunst allein liegt es
nicht, es sind zwar geistige aber außermusikalische Kräfte,
die da einwirken. Selten aber sind es die gleichzeitig
lebendigen Geistesbewegungen die einer zeitgenössischen
musikalischen Kunst das ausgeprägte Zeichen aufdrücken.
So sehe ich auch nicht in der Protestantischen Kunst der
Reformationszeitalters kaum irgend etwas anderes, als ich es
nicht bei den musikalischen Meistern aus dem katholischen
Umkreis auch finden könnte. Ich kann wenigstens einen
Unterschied zwischen Joh. Walther, und Senfl und Hassler
(alle mehr oder weniger vom Lutherischen beeinflußt) einerseits und
Orlando di Lasso oder Gallus anderseits nicht finden. Erst
viel später, vielleicht bei Sweelinck und Schütz beginnend, bei
Bach sich scharf äußernd beginnt der formengebende
Einfluß des Protestantismus. Bei diesen dreien kann
wirklich von einer ausgesprochenen protestantischen
Wesensart gesprochen werden. Bei den gleichzeitig mit Luther
lebenden Musikern habe ich nichts davon spüren können.

this lot might befall you, one way or another, is what I wish upon your return.

As I see from your letter, you are hard at work again with problems of the profession, and I notice too that you did some work on the history of musical style while in the prison camp. I would like very much to know something about the results of your thinking in this area. Above all, something about the central question of which spiritual factors influence musical style or perhaps govern and direct as well. It is not intrinsic to art alone; there are indeed spiritual, but extra-musical, forces at work here. It is seldom the simultaneous, vital spiritual movements which impress the stamp of distinction upon a contemporary musical art. Thus I see hardly anything in Protestant art of the age of the Reformation that I could not also find in the musical masters of Catholic circles. At least, I can find no difference between Joh. Walter, Senfl, and Hassler (all more or less under Lutheran influence) on the one hand, and Orlando di Lasso or Gallus on the other hand. Only much later does the spiritually form-giving influence of Protestantism begin, perhaps starting with Sweelinck and Schütz and becoming sharply manifest in Bach. In regard to these three, one really can speak of a distinctly Protestant essence. I have been able to find nothing of the sort among those musicians contemporary with Luther.

Musik ist eben eine ganz späte Kunst, gewissermaßen stets ein nachgeborenes Kind und wirkt immer dann beglückend wenn sie als Nachklang erscheint. Die bildende Kunst hat dagegen in Dürers Apostelgestalten ein ausgesprochen protestantisches Kunstwerk. Dieser heroische und große Paulus ist nur möglich und denkbar während des Reformations-zeitalters. Überhaupt diese ganzen kraftstrotzenden vier Apostelfürsten mit ihrem männlichen, kriegsstarken Ausdruck sind nur möglich als Ausdruck der spezifisch germanisch-nordischen Christlichkeit eben der Protes-tantismus. Von solchem ausgeprägten Wesen zeigt die musikalische Kunst des Reformationszeitalters nichts. Mit einer Ausnahme: Luthers Choräle. Diese großen Me-lodien sind so etwas ganz anderes als die gesammte übrige Musik der Zeit daß ich allein schon aus diesem Grunde von der Autorschaft Luthers fest überzeugt bin. Philologisch kann ich es nicht nachweisen, aber für jeden geistig Wissenden kann ein Zweifel darüber nicht bestehen. – Über das ganze Gebiet Reformation – Musik ist etwas Wesentliches eigentlich überhaupt nicht geschrieben worden. Nur die landläufigen Broschüren musikbegeisterter Theologen, aber nichts tiefer fassendes und bleibend Wertvolles. Das Beste sicherlich ein Aufsatz von Kretzschmar über „Luther und die Musik" im Peterjahrbuch für 1917. Aber bei allen diesen Fragen kommt immer wieder die Kernfrage zum Durchbruch daß Kunst etwas außerhalb der Dinge und über den Dingen stehendes ist

Music simply is a very late art, to some extent always a late-born child, and it always seems to be a blessing when it appears as a reverberation. The graphic arts, however, have a decidedly Protestant work of art in Dürer's figures of the Apostles. Such a grand, heroic Paul is only possible and conceivable during the age of the Reformation; actually all four of these robust Apostle princes, with their masculine, war-like countenances, are only possible as an expression of specifically Germanic-Nordic Christendom, and only of Protestantism. The musical art of the age of the Reformation shows nothing of such distinct character with one exception: Luther's chorales. These magnificent melodies are something so completely different from all other music of the time that for this reason alone I am completely convinced of Luther's authorship. Philologically I cannot prove it, but there can be no doubt in the mind of any knowing intellectual. Actually nothing at all of substance has been written in regard to any music of the Reformation. Only ordinary pamphlets by theologians who are music enthusiasts, but nothing more thorough, comprehensive, and of lasting value. Certainly the best is an essay by Kretschmar on "Luther and music" in the *Petersjahrbuch* for 1917. But of all these questions, the central one asserts itself time and again,

Kunst lebt ihr geistiges Leben für sich allein! Deshalb auch die geringe Berührung zwischen Kunst und Krieg. Erst später, wenn das Kriegserleben entmaterialisiert zum geistigen Besitzstand geworden, erst dann wird unsere Kunst von diesen ~~Dingen~~ Erlebnissen erfaßt werden. – Von meinem persönlichen Erleben habe ich nicht viel zu sagen. Alle wichtigeren Daten kennen Sie und da wäre nichts hinzuzufügen. Ob ich ein brauchbarer, erwähnenswerter Thomaskantor sein werde, kann erst die Zukunft lehren. Was ich versuchen will, das ist eine Beeinflussung der jüngeren Generation durch die vorbachschen Meister. Vor allem ist es Heinrich Schütz, an den ich dabei denke. Von diesem Großen kann vielleicht eine starke Anregung ausgehen. Sein Schaffen – ~~p~~roblematisch im Gegensatz zu der ganz gereiften Kunst J. S. Bach's – kann vielleicht zu neuem Schaffen neuen Anstoß geben. Aber wie ich dies alles machen und erreichen soll, das weiß ich nicht! – Und nun leben Sie wohl und erholen Sie sich in der wundervollen Umgebung, in der Sie sind. Wir haben vom 15. – 22. hier eine Schweizerischer – Musikfest. Ob ich im Frühjahr in der Schweiz Orgelspielenderweise sein werde, das ist noch nicht ganz fest entschieden aber es wird davon ernstlich gesprochen. Wir denken an ein Bachfest Frühjahr 1919. Wie schön wäre es wenn Sie daran teil nehmen könnten. – Nun also endgiltig Lebe – wohl. Empfehlen Sie mich auf das Angelegentlichste Ihrer Frau Gemahlin und seien Sie herzlichst gegrüßt
von Ihrem getreuen
Karl Straube

that art is something apart from other things and above other things. Art lives a spiritual life of its own! Thus the scant contact between art and war. Not until later, when the experiences of war are no longer of material consequence and have become the property of the spirit, only then will these experiences lay hold of our art.—I have little to say in regard to my own personal experiences. You are familiar with all the more important data, and there is nothing to add. Whether I will be a useful or notable cantor at St. Thomas's Church is a question which only the future can decide. What I wish to attempt is to influence the younger generation through the pre-Bach masters. In this connection I am thinking above all of Heinrich Schütz. Perhaps a strong stimulus may emanate from this great one. His works—problematic in contrast to the completely mature art of J. S. Bach—may perhaps lend impetus to new creations. But how I shall be able to do and to achieve all this, that I do not know!—And now, may you fare well and enjoy a speedy recovery in the wonderful surroundings in which you find yourself. Here we are holding a Swiss music festival from the 15th through the 22nd. Whether I shall play organ in Switzerland in the spring has not quite been decided, but it has been discussed seriously. We are considering having a Bach festival in the spring of 1919. How splendid it would be if you could participate. —Well now, goodbye once again. Extend my kindest regards to your wife at the first opportunity, and the most heartfelt greetings to you

from your loyal
Karl Straube

116. Helmut Bornefeld, opening of the chorale motet No. 8, *Jesus Christus herrscht als König,* for four-part chorus a cappella (1953), autograph. Kassel, Bärenreiter-Archiv.

117. Hugo Distler, *Wir danken dir, Herr Jesu Christ,* chorale for three children's voices, autograph. Private collection.

118. Siegfried Reda, *Dennoch bleibe ich stets an dir* from Psalm 73 in the collection *Das Psalmbuch,* for two- to eight-part chorus a cappella (1948), autograph. Kassel, Bärenreiter-Archiv.

PART V

Church Music
in Reformed Europe

BY WALTER BLANKENBURG

Translated by Hans Heinsheimer

Switzerland and France

In the German-speaking sections of Switzerland the Reformation was introduced mainly by Huldrych Zwingli, who toward the end of 1518 came as a *Leutpriester* (people's priest) to the cathedral of Zurich. Having achieved prominence earlier, as a pupil of Erasmus of Rotterdam, because of his outstanding humanistic training, he became in the early twenties of the century more and more attracted by Luther's writings. Like Luther, he at first proceeded cautiously and conservatively with the reformation of the church at Zurich. In his treatise *De canone missae epicheiresis* (1522) he suggested a reworking of the Latin Mass canon as a transitional solution. In the same year, however, the deacons of the cathedral forbade the reading of any Mass, although it was not until April, 1525, that the Zurich City Council yielded to the urgent request to abolish the Mass. The new service order is codified in Zwingli's paper *Action oder Bruch des Nachtmals, Gedechtnis oder Danksagung Christi, wie sy uff Osteren zu Zürich angehebt wirt im jar als man zahlt 1525* (Action or Customs of Communion, Memory of and Thanksgiving to Christ As Celebrated at Easter in Zurich in the Year Counted as 1525). While it has its roots in the late medieval penitential and scriptural service after the *Manuale Curatorum* of Surgant (1506), Zwingli's service order is largely an original creation. Of basic importance—aside from the departure from old Mass formulas—is the introduction of the vernacular and of continuous reading as well as active participation by the congregation in the prayers and, finally and most important, the exclusion of all musical elements. All this signified a breach with a service tradition of fifteen centuries, an event that had important consequences for the organization of the service and particularly for church music. It can be understood only through the fact that Zwingli (like Calvin later on) interpreted the phrase "ecclesia reformata semper reformanda" in the sense of a complete break with tradition.

The high quality of Zwingli's musical education has been attested to frequently. Musically, he was clearly the most gifted of the three great Reformers. Bernhard Wyss, a contemporary chronicler, reports: "I never heard of anyone who in the art of *musica*, that is, in singing and all instruments—lutes, harps, large and small fiddles *(gigen, rabögli)*, pipes, *schwegeln* (as proficient as any Swiss), the *tromba marina*, the dulcimer, the cornet, the horn, and anything else that would be invented,—when he saw it would soon know how to handle it and who, in addition, was so erudite as he." It has been proved that he wrote the words and melody of *Herr, nun heb den Wagen selb*, the so-called *Kappelerlied*, the text of which shows the art form of the Meistersinger (for example, in the use of rhyme within individual lines), while the melody, typically for the time, is an adaptation of a secular tune, *Ich weiss mir ein Maidlein hübsch und fein*.

H. Zwingli, according to the *Nüw gsangbüchle*, Zurich, 1540

Herr, nun heb den Wa-gen selb! Schell wird su st all un-ser Fart. Das brächt Lust der Wi-der-part, die dich ver-acht so frä - -ven-lich.

The "plague song" *Hilf, Herr Gott, hilf in dieser Not* goes back to Zwingli in text, melody, and four-part setting. A melody to the versified Psalm 69 *Hilf, Gott, das Wasser gat* cannot be traced with certainty to the Zurich Reformer, but for musical reasons its authenticity cannot be doubted.

An explanation of the fact that Zwingli, despite his great musicality, did away with all music when he redesigned liturgical life in Zurich has frequently been sought in the supposition that this was merely a temporary measure, which became permanent only because of his early death. It is important to bear in mind that around 1524–25, when the Reformer decided on the new service, the Protestant church song was just beginning to emerge and had not yet been tested. In this connection a remark by Zwingli, dating from about 1525–26 and only recently rediscovered, is significant: "It is good and commendable that songs of praise be sung by all people on Sunday" (see Zwingli, Complete Edition XIII, in *Corpus Reformatorum*). A sentence from the preface of his *Action* is also important: "We do not reject other ceremonies which might be suitable and helpful for worship, such as singing and others, because we hope to make everyone bow to the Lord and to attract many people." Not less noteworthy is Zwingli's advice in *How the Monks at Rütli Should Read and Listen to Holy Scripture* (1525): every morning read four to five chapters from the Old Testament "and do this with adequate voice, not too high, not too low, in proper rhythm, not too fast and not too slow." Afterward, approximately four psalms should follow "with one voice . . . in unison" in the manner of the traditional breviary reading and, like it, alternating daily between Benedictus and Te Deum, closing with the Kyrie, Pater Noster, and a collect. The means that Zwingli recommends for the hourly prayers in the monastery is the singing of chants reduced to the *tonus rectus*. In spite of all this his ordinances for the divine service will have to be explained on the basis of his theology as well as his approach to music. His exclusion of all singing from the congregational service results from his peculiar understanding of prayer: "In your devotion you should be alone. Devotion is falsified by the participation of many" (interpretation of the forty-sixth article in his final addresses to the First Zurich Disputation, January 21, 1523). Zwingli, as it were, had the individual foremost in mind when thinking of congregational worship. Singing seemed to him like "shouting in front of the people," distracting from the *contemplatio fidei*. This is obviously related to the fact that his musical outlook was completely oriented toward the *musica reservata* ideal, with its emotional connotations (how much he was influenced by Glarean, only four years younger than he, is still to be explored); furthermore, unlike Luther, he had no real relation to the realm of the folk song, the *musica naturalis*. Congregational singing as a natural expression of life had little appeal for him because his musical thinking was undoubtedly formed by the *musica artificialis* in which he was so proficient.

The consequences of Zwingli's Reformation extended more or less to all of German-speaking Switzerland. Next to Zurich, it affected mainly Bern. The abolition of all music in the service brought about the demolition of organs (first

119. John Calvin (1509–64) in a contemporary woodcut.

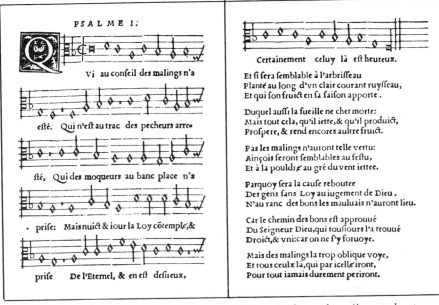

120. John Calvin, Psalm 1, *Qui au conseil* from *La forme des prières et chants ecclésiastiques,* Geneva, 1542, Jean Gerard.

121. *Confession de Foy,* Geneva, 1563, Guillaume Forest, second supplement to the *Vollständigen Liedpsalter.* Title page and Psalm 36, *Du malin le meschant.*

in the cathedral in Zurich, July 9, 1527; in Bern the organs were sold in 1528). Such radical measures were, however, too artificial to remain in effect. Of the cities of northern Switzerland, Basel, reformed by Johannes Oecolampadius and under the influence of the liturgical conditions of Strasbourg, was least touched by these developments. Contrary to Zwingli, Oecolampadius said: "Singing also helps prayer and devotion much more than do senseless ceremonies. It is a challenge to listen to God's Word and to occupy oneself with matters divine." The Basel congregation sang psalm lieder spontaneously at Easter, 1526, after the school choir had already substituted German psalms for Latin ones in 1523. The organ, too, here at least remained intact. St. Gallen, where congregational singing is attested to from 1527 on, published, under the leadership of Dominik Zili, the first Protestant hymnal in Switzerland, in 1533. How spontaneously the people were affected by congregational singing is reported in connection with a sermon by Zili on March 7, 1529, when some four thousand listeners are said to have sung Matthäus Greitter's *O Herre Gott, begnade mich* (Psalm 51), which, next to Greitter's *Es sind doch selig alle, die* (Psalm 119), was among the most celebrated hymns in southwest Germany and northern Switzerland. Both were later included in the Genevan Psalter (see there Psalm 91).

M. Greitter

Protestant church singing in northern Switzerland in the 16th century was decisively affected by the so-called Constance songbook of 1540 (see p. 133). This was the third printing of a hymnal commissioned by the city of Constance, undoubtedly first published around 1533–34 in Zurich by Christoph Froschauer, with a second printing not later than 1537. Its main compilers were the eminent poets Ambrosius Blaurer and Johannes Zwick (the name "Zwick songbook" is therefore incorrect). Zwick's *Vorred zu beschirm und erhaltung des ordentlichen Kirchengesangs* (Preface to Protect and to Maintain Orderly Church Singing) is the most important defense of singing at the service in southwest Germany during the century of the Reformation, and can rightfully be considered a counterpart to Luther's songbook prefaces. Although the Constance Reformation was advanced under the influence of Zwingli, Zwick's preface offered a challenge to Zwingli's musical views, carefully thought out and nobly formulated. It was largely because of this preface that congregational singing spread through northern Switzerland in spite of Zwingli's endeavors. Zwick's authority was still being invoked at the end of the 16th century when congregational singing was introduced in Zurich itself. The Constance songbook gained great importance in German-speaking Switzerland, first because it was published in Zurich and secondly because Ambrosius Blaurer became a parson in Switzerland after the re-Catholicization of Constance in 1548. The *Nüw gsangbüchl von vil schönen*

Psalmen und geistlichen lidern . . . (New Little Songbook with Many Beautiful Psalms and Sacred Songs . . .) contains in connection with Colossians 3:16 two principal groups of songs: versified psalms (67 songs on 55 psalms with 35 melodies) and sacred pieces and Christian songs (60 with 30 melodies). These are followed by a small group of songs based on Scripture but not designated for use in the service (23 songs with 6 melodies).

The development that gave predominance to the psalm lied had already begun in Strasbourg and Augsburg, not, however, brought about by Martin Butzer, the Strasbourg Reformer, who took a position between Luther and Zwingli. He wrote: "We use no singing or prayers in the congregation of the Lord that are not drawn from Holy Scripture" (in his brochure *Cause and Reason* . . ., which pointed the way to the reorganization of ecclesiastical matters, 1524), but neither this statement nor the preface to the Strasbourg Songbook of 1541 was a significant factor. Despite the fact that in Strasbourg, from the beginning, the rhyming psalm had greater importance than in Wittenberg (perhaps because Luther's translation of the Psalms was printed in Strasbourg), Butzer always considered the Lutheran song very important; indeed, in the most important Strasbourg songbooks—the *Enchiridion* of 1524 and the one in choirbook format of 1541—the psalm lieder do not occupy the first rank.

The earliest complete rhyming Psalters (with a rather limited number of melodies) seemed therefore to have their origins more in the private initiative of their publishers than in a liturgical trend. These are the Augsburg Psalter of Jakob Dachser (1537), on which Joachim Aberlin and Sigmund Salminger also collaborated, and the work published in 1538 by Wolff Köpphel: *Psalter. Das seindt alle Psalmen Davids mit jren Melodeie, sampt viel schönen Christlichen liedern, unnd Kyrchen übungen* . . . (These Are All the Psalms of David with Their Melodies and Many Beautiful Christian Songs and Church Exercises . . .; Köpphel was the publisher of the earliest Strasbourg songbooks, for which he also wrote his own forewords.) The Constance songbook gives complete information about the poets of individual songs. In addition to Zwick and the brothers Ambrosius and Thomas Blaurer, all important text writers of the time are represented: those from Wittenberg, led by Luther; Matthäus Greitter, Wolfgang Dachstein, and Wolfgang Capito, all of Strasbourg; the Swiss Zwingli, Jüd, and Bullinger; Jakob Dachser and Wolfgang Meuslin (Musculus) from Augsburg; but also the southwest German Anabaptist leader Ludwig Hetzer and others. Thus it presented, along with the Strasbourg songbook of 1541, a comprehensive collection, combining south and north German song material and omitting only the Bohemian Brethren. Markus Jenny has recently explored the origins of those melodies whose sources were not known. As everywhere, transcriptions of secular and of older sacred models are reflected in the Constance melodies, as E. Weissmann has established in the case of Zwick's *Auf diesen Tag bedenken wir* (first found in Strasbourg in 1537, but undoubtedly coming from Constance), which originates in the antiphon for Prime on Sundays, *Alleluia confitemini.*

The principal musical collaborators, in addition to Zwick himself, were Sixtus Dietrich, likewise a longtime resident of Constance, and Benedict Ducis (perhaps mainly for the Musculus texts), who spent his last years, from 1535 to 1544, as a country parson in the region of Ulm. The individual share of each of the various masters in the work, however, is not yet definitely established. Because the Constance songbook could already draw on complete rhyming Psalters for its versified psalms, Constance's own contribution appears mainly in its second part, which also offers important clues for the position of congregational singing in the service in the regions where this collection was distributed. Such singing had obtained a firm position as a frame for the sermon, as the heading of this section of the book expressly indicates. The contents of this section include children's songs, *de tempore* songs (only for the important church festivals), catechismal songs, and canticles based on the New Testament, as well as the German Sanctus, songs about the Holy Spirit and the Trinity, and songs for certain times of day. The greatest part of the melodic material is in mensural notation; in a few isolated cases one finds *Hufnagel* notation (the Strasbourg mixed notation is not adopted). Greitter's famous versions of the Kyrie and Gloria, undoubtedly going back to medieval models, are omitted because of the southwest German sermon services introduced in these regions. What yardstick was used to select the brief third part cannot be determined; alongside Zwingli's *Herr, nun heb den Wagen selb'* we find here, for example, a hymn from Lutheran circles, *Ich ruf zu dir, Herr Jesu Christ.*

This most influential among all the southwest German songbooks in the time of the Reformation had, during the 16th century, no fewer than seventeen printings, some of them with additions, in Switzerland. Eight more were published in Zurich up to 1608, a fact that certainly helped to introduce congregational singing eventually, even in Zwingli's city (see p. 513; of special importance in this respect was the edition brought out around 1552 by A. Blaurer's pupil Jakob Fünklin). Two more were published in Basel (1581 and 1594) and one in the Rhaeto-Romanic language, edited by Durich Chiampel, in 1562. The Constance song-book was in use almost everywhere in German-speaking Switzerland, until individual towns issued their own. Only St. Gallen (as stated above, at the instigation of the preacher Dominik Zili) and Schaffhausen had an early tradition of special material (beginning in 1533, see above; the song supplement to the Catechism of 1569, first issued as a separate publication in 1580, depends partly on Constance). St. Gallen printed its songbook in 1580 and 1588 as *Kantorei* folios, in the manner of the Strasbourg songbook of 1541. Mention should also be made of the lied Psalter (1559) of the Basel clergyman Konrad Wolffhardt, a sort of anthology which included, among other material, the psalms by Burkhard Waldis (see p. 550).

The diversified history of songbooks in German Switzerland during the 16th century shows the penetration of congregational singing into the service everywhere, despite Zwingli. Looked at as a whole, however, this was based not on a national song repertory but rather on a stock of southwest-German rhyming psalms and similar material, including Luther's sacred songs. Zwingli's own congregations were the last to take up congregational singing. In Bern its beginnings occurred in 1558, but it was not officially ordered until 1574 (a handwritten *Kantorei* folio is dated 1603; the oldest printed hymnal, of 1620, has been preserved). Finally, Zurich followed, introducing congregational singing as late as 1598 simultaneously with the publication of the first official songbook. The singing was everywhere unaccompanied and, of course, in unison, under the direction of a precentor, presumably a teacher, with a pitchpipe and a long baton. One hears little of a regularly functioning chorus, though frequently schoolchildren or (as at Zurich in 1598) students of various ages, placed throughout the church, led the singing. Perhaps a children's choir sometimes participated in the service, as seems indicated by the many children's songs in the Constance songbook, which could scarcely have been intended only for school and home use.

There is hardly a trace of polyphonic sacred singing, a style not intended for the service. The only non-monophonic songbook in northern Switzerland in the 16th century was printed, significantly, in Leipzig; it appeared in Basel in 1594 and marks the beginning of a new development. It is a lost work by Samuel Mareschall (see pp. 146 and 557). During this period, however, the organ was reinstated in the sacred service for the first time. Basel, which had rescued the organ in its cathedral, led the way; the organ was put to use again in 1561, and the organist Gregor Meyer, a friend of Glarean, was employed. His duties, it seems, were at first to play only after the noon and evening sermon, soon also after the morning service, but not during the service itself; this might indicate an early form of the custom that acquired special meaning in Reformed Holland in the 17th century. Soon, however, organ music apparently penetrated the service in alternation with verses sung by the congregation. In Bern, from 1581 on, the town pipers (cornetists and trombonists) were called in to assist at the service, perhaps also at congregational singing. This is the origin of the playing of psalms, undoubtedly in unison, from the steeple following the service.

In French-speaking Switzerland and in France, the Calvinist Reformation, which had originated in Geneva, underwent its own special development at first. Of the three Reformers, Calvin was probably the least musical. There is no evidence of his active participation in music. He had, to be sure, received a general musical education as part of his university studies: he was therefore familiar with the musical ideas and theories of the Middle Ages and the humanists as well as the musical thought of antiquity. His own attitude toward music, however, was conditioned by his strict obedience to the Word of God, that is, to the Bible. By applying certain—to him self-evident—humanistic ideas he arrived at precise rules governing singing at the service, which he undoubtedly put down himself for practical use (see below). He took the certainty of the divine origin of music from Genesis 4:21, which concerns Jubal and his lineal descent from Adam. This also meant to him that music had a duty to fulfill as a spiritual power. In spite of this basic conception, which Calvin shared with Luther (both relied in this connection mainly on St. Augustine), he was far from sympathetic to Luther's unsophisticated pleasure in the power of music. Furthermore, Luther, not so one-sidedly concerned with the psychological elements of music, kept in mind always its orderly, ontological aspect, from which attitude Calvin was prevented by his awareness of the possibility and danger of human misuse of music in the service of vanity and sensuality. This led him not to eliminate all music at the service, like Zwingli, but to omit singing at the altar, polyphony, and the use of instruments. His regard for the traditional use of music in the service as a papist aberration proved that he had no feeling at all for the developing art of sacred music. He was conscious of the significance of instruments in the Old Testament (he evaded their mention in the New Testament, Ephesians 5:19), but he considered their use in the worship service there only as a preliminary to a more perfect divine service in the New Testament, only "puerilia elementa" for which Christians no longer had any need. He was guided to this decision by the opinion that only music directly bound to a text and understandable by the congregation was justified in the service. Unison, unaccompanied congregational singing in the vernacular thus became the only form of service music. Priestly singing at the altar was abolished because as Latin song it was by its very nature unintelligible.

For Calvin the function of service music derived from the recognition of its essential nature. Because music has great power and force to move and to inflame the heart of man, it should drive him to invoke and to praise God (*J. Calvini Opera selecta* II, 15). He compared the task of music with that of a funnel *(entonnoir)*, since it should funnel the sung word into man's heart. The music's appropriateness to the text should prevent the song of the service from succumbing to the danger of sensualism. The principle of *convenable au sujet* became essential. In practice, however, it was not the treatment of individual words that was important but rather (an idea that was to have significant consequences) a style generally fitting the sacred service, which, described in such words as "poids," "majesté," "modéré," and "modeste," differed basically from the secular style, which was "léger et volage." This was a view diametrically opposed to Luther's wish that secular love songs be adapted for the service, although in practice Geneva sometimes used procedures similar to those of Wittenberg (see below). The sacred style, Calvin held, may evoke joy, to be sure, but a joy that is chaste, not sensual ("casta laetitia"). Finally, according to Calvin, the task of the service song necessitated a strong tie to the only text admissible in the service, the text of the Bible. This resulted in the exclusive use of psalms for singing, in addition to a few other biblical excerpts. That, contrary to the Anglican liturgy, no form was ever considered other than versified psalms and canticles, all in the vernacular, is undoubtedly due to an accident of history: Calvin had already become acquainted with the singing of rhyming psalms, probably in France but mainly in Basel and Strasbourg, before he began his reformative work.

Calvin's thoughts on music are to be found in many scattered remarks in his biblical commentaries and homilies, particularly in the *Epistre au lecteur* in *La forme des prières et chants ecclésiastiques* of 1542 and its enlarged edition of 1543 (reprinted in the Goudimel Psalter of 1565 and elsewhere), also in the chapter *Des chants ecclésiastiques* in *Les ordonnances ecclésiastiques* in the 1561 version and in the *Institutio Christianae Religionis* of 1559, vol. III, chap. 20, sections 31–33.

The editions of Calvinist songbooks began with the *Aulcuns pseaulmes et cantiques mys en chant,* published at Strasbourg in 1539; its editor was undoubtedly Calvin himself, at that time the pastor of congregation of French exiles in Strasbourg. This edition contained 19 versified psalms with 18 melodies and, in addition, the canticle of Simeon and the Ten Commandments, also in song form, as well as the so-called Strasbourg Credo. The poems for Psalms 25, 36, 46, 91 (listed as Psalm 90), 113, and 138 and those for the two biblical canticles and the version of the Creed are by Calvin himself. The remaining 13 psalm lieder are by Clément Marot.

In creating a rhyming Psalter, Calvin, on the eve of the Reformation, could take advantage to a certain extent of the trend emerging in France to make poems out of psalms and to sing them, and of the Protestant example of Strasbourg. At the suggestion of King Francis I, Marot, favorite poet of the French court, sent his psalm versifications even to Emperor Charles V; Catherine de' Medici, Marguerite of Navarre, Henry II, and Diane de Poitiers also used these poems sung to French melodies, which shows that such poems were at first not peculiar exclusively to reformative tendencies. It is not clear what melodies were used— that is, whether they were folk song or chanson tunes—but the latter seems more likely, since Marot's artful verse forms, created out of the spirit of humanism, had a natural relationship to the contemporary French chanson. Calvin first met Marot probably in 1531. As a consequence of this, and after he had come across Butzer's psalm commentaries, he began his psalm versifications in 1532. The publication of 30 of these, planned in 1538, was suppressed in Paris (see p. 133 f.).

The second songbook under Calvin's direct influence was *La forme des prières et chants ecclésiastiques* (Geneva, 1542), mentioned above. It was based on the Strasbourg songbook of 1539, but the number of songs had already grown to 39. While those originating with Calvin were reduced by two (Psalm 113 and the Credo), the number of those by Marot was increased from 13 to 32. As early as 1543 a new songbook (not preserved) was published, containing 50 psalm lieder, the canticle of Simeon, and the Ten Commandments lied, all put into verse by Marot, with an expanded version of Calvin's preface of 1542. Since Marot lived in Geneva from the end of 1542 on, this can only have been done at Calvin's direction: his own texts must have been removed in accordance with his personal wishes. The contents of this edition can be estimated with some likelihood by referring back from a four-part arrangement of 50 psalms by Louis Bourgeois (Lyons, 1547), since the composer speaks there only of polyphonic setting and makes no mention of original melodic creations. After Marot's death in 1544, there was a delay in the gradual versification of the whole Psalter until Theodore Beza continued the task about 1550. The first fruit of his work is the *Pseaumes octante trois de David, mis en rime françoise. A savoir quarante neuf par Clément Marot avec le Cantique de Simeon et les dix commandemens. Et trente quatre par Theodore de Beze* (Geneva, 1551). During the following years Beza finally completed the versification. The first complete Genevan Psalter (today the generally accepted name for the songbook especially authorized by Calvin in Geneva) was finished by 1562 at the latest. In addition to the previously mentioned canticles, it contained two table songs by Marot, for use before and after meals, added after 1542, while his Credo and his Lord's Prayer lied, which was temporarily introduced, were at that time eliminated. After partial Psalters had been published in 1559 and 1561, the Geneva publisher Antoine Vincent had the complete work brought out simultaneously in Geneva, Paris, Lyons, and in a number of other places by a total of fifteen printers (1562). New printings followed in succeeding years uninterruptedly; by 1565, within three years, not less than 63 recorded editions were published, undoubtedly a unique event in the history of Protestant hymnals. It shows the extraordinary enthusiasm with which the Genevan Psalter was received and undoubtedly soon introduced to every Calvinist family. There can be no doubt that behind it stood the full authority of Calvin, which made the Genevan Psalter the undisputed, official, and, for a long time, exclusive Reformed songbook in French-speaking territory (see the basic work by Pierre Pidoux, *Le psautier huguenot du XVIe siècle. Mélodies et documents,* I and II, Basel, 1962).

While the origin of the texts in the Genevan Psalter is known, that of the musical settings for the various editions remains difficult to determine. It was to be expected that Calvin would utilize Strasbourg melodies for the *Aulcuns pseaulmes* of 1539, and indeed the six psalms he put into rhyme are set to melodies found there. Four of the melodies go back to Matthäus Greitter: those for Psalms 25, 36, 90, and 138 (in the Strasbourg songbook of 1541, as in the Constance songbook of 1540, they belong to Psalm 125, Psalm 119, first part, *Es sind doch selig alle, die,* Psalm 51, *O Herre Gott, begnade mich,* and Psalm 114). Two melodies undoubtedly owe their settings to Wolfgang Dachstein—the one for Psalm 46, in Strasbourg belonging to Psalm 23, and the one for Psalm 113, the well-known second melody to Luther's *Aus tiefer Not* (Psalm 130); in the latter the contrast between the texts is remarkable. Of Strasbourg origin are also the melodies of the Credo *Je croy en Dieu,* again the work of Greitter, most likely based on an earlier model, and of the Ten Commandments lied, which may be by Dachstein. The melodies to the texts by Marot, too, were obviously created in Strasbourg especially for his artful verse forms. There is no proof that they were written by Marot himself, as is sometimes assumed. It is much more likely that Greitter and Dachstein also had a hand in these. We can assume that they, too, frequently worked from existing models, as has already been established for Marot's Psalms 51 and 114 (two Strasbourg melodies: H. Vogther's *Herr Gott, ich trau' allein auf dich* and S. Pollder's *Vater unser, wir bitten dich*). Thus, while there is still some doubt concerning melodic origins in the "Psautier primitif," on the whole it is fortunate that in Greitter and Dachstein we encounter two composers of particular artistic worth whose work can be verified. Even so, Greitter's most famous melody, *Es sind doch selig alle, die,* shows to what extent these melodies were written in Meistersinger fashion, using older models and melodic fragments (paralleling the situation in Germany at that time). Greitter's tune incorporates parts of Neidhardt von Reuenthal's *Mei hat wuniclich ent-sprossen* and of Hans Sachs's well-known *Silberweise,* sharing with the latter also the three-line *Stollen* and the repeat of the first line of the *Abgesang.*

a. M. Greitter

(M. Greitter)

b. H. Sachs: *Silberweise*, 1513 (opening of the *Abgesang*)

Vi - ta dul - ce - do bist für - war Des le - bens u - re - sprung
Et spes nos - tra, wan an dir gar Leit all un - ser Hoff - nung

c. Neidhardt von Reuenthal: *Mei hat wuniclich entsprossen*, c. 1240 (opening of the *Abgesang*)

Man siht gein der sun - ne gle - sten Niu - we bluet uf - drin - gen.
O - ben in des Wal - des e - sten Hoert man vog - lin sin - gen.

Guillaume Franc, from 1542 the first Reformed cantor at St. Peter's in Geneva, must be considered chief music editor for the Geneva publications of 1542 and 1543. Louis Bourgeois, according to recent research, did not come to Geneva until 1545, taking over Franc's position when the latter moved to Lausanne in that year. There is, however, no definite proof of Franc's editorship. Since the number of melodies in the 1547 and 1549 editions (two Lyons prints and four-part arrangements of 50 psalms by Bourgeois in 1547; see below) was the same as in 1543, Bourgeois's editorial contribution was evidently limited to the addition of 34 melodies for the newly incorporated texts by Beza in the *Pseaumes octante trois de David* (Geneva, 1551). Like his predecessor (see Paul-André Gaillard, *L. Bourgeois,* Lausanne, 1948, pp. 53, 72), Bourgeois was also very important as a teacher of psalm singing. His little theoretical work *Le droict chemin de musique* (1550) contains a *Manière de chanter les pseaumes par usage or ruse,* which uses the method of "solfier" (see the facsimile edition, Kassel, 1954). The 1551 edition set the standard for the musical character of the Genevan Psalter, to which later additions of still missing material were made to conform. Only after Beza had versified the remaining psalms around 1559–60, Pierre Dagues—apparently identical with the "Maistre Pierre" mentioned in this connection in Geneva (he was cantor at St. Peter's from 1556 on)—in all likelihood completed the melodies for the entire work, insofar as additional ones were needed (some tunes may have been used more than once: there were only 123 melodies for the 150 psalms and several canticles in the volume).

Of the Strasbourg melodies of the *Aulcuns pseaulmes* of 1539 only Greitter's famous *Es sind doch selig alle, die* found its way to Geneva in its original form; it was used for Psalms 36 and 68. Of the rest, those for Psalms 1, 2, 15, 91, 103, 114, 130, 137, and 143 were taken over more or less changed, particularly rhythmically. The 1542 Psalter also adapted the melodies for Psalms 25 and 138 and for the Ten Commandments lied, but these were later eliminated. The 12 tunes that were added to the final contents in 1542 (some at first not in their final form, however; see the facsimile prints of the 1542 and 1565 editions) were those for Psalms 4, 5, 6, 8, 9, 13, 14, 19, 22, 24, 38, and 115. Twelve additional new tunes of this edition were later dropped again. Both groups therefore seem to originate in one form or another with Franc. The 34 melodies of the 1551 edition for the poems by Beza newly published there are those for Psalms 16, 17, 20, 21, 26–31, 35, 39, 40–42, 44, 47, 73, 90, 119–127, 129, and 130–134, and must therefore be considered most likely the work of Bourgeois. However, one finds in this edition also for the first time some melodies to Marot's texts, i.e., those for Psalms 25,

43, 45, 46, 51, 101, 110, 113, and the one for the canticle of Simeon. From Bourgeois's above-mentioned collection of 50 four-part psalms (1547), 14 melodies, not yet included in the 1542 edition, return in 1552; they are those for Psalms 18, 23, 32, 33, 37, 50, 72, 79–86, 107, 118, 128, and 138, and the final one for the Ten Commandments lied. Scarcely a single one of this last group is by Bourgeois, who is identified in the title of his work of 1547 only as one who makes four-part arrangements *(vierstimmiger Setzer)*. Furthermore, the melodies for Psalms 33, 50, 72, 79, 86, and 128 can be traced to the French Strasbourg songbook of 1545. Except for the melodies for the two table songs, which appear first in Bourgeois's four-part arrangements of the 83 psalms in 1554, the remaining 40 represent all the new melodies in the complete Psalter of 1562; these are for Psalms 48, 49, 52, 54–61, 75, 80, 81, 83–85, 87–89, 92–94, 96, 97, 99, 102, 105, 106, 112, 116, 135, 136, 141, 145–150. It is therefore probable that they are chiefly the work of "Maistre Pierre." Only a painstaking comparison—not yet attempted—of the different melody groups will reveal the details of this development and the share of the individual masters in it.

Melodic creations as reflected in the Genevan Psalter can, for the most part, mean no more than it generally does in the 16th century: arranging, modifying, or sometimes transforming existing materials.

Relatively few of the models for individual tunes have so far been identified. The epoch-making theory of O. Douen that the origin of the Geneva melodies was to be sought mainly in French folk song is no longer tenable. As early as 1926, C. Haein contradicted Douen's findings in an unpublished paper, recently analyzed by H. Hasper. Both believe the roots of the Geneva melodies to be mainly in medieval church songs, thus seeing them as an outgrowth of an expressed principle of Calvin, who laid great stress on the connection with the old church. P. Pidoux, in the *Jahrbuch für Liturgik und Hymnologie* (1955, p. 113 f.) and in *Le psautier huguenot* (I, p. 10 ff.), has recently come to similar conclusions. This does not exclude the possibility that in individual cases folk and social songs also played a part in the creation of the Geneva melodies.

After all, the unofficial, so to speak, beginning of the history of Reformed church music, going back prior to the earliest official Reformed songbooks, clearly shows a connection with folk song. Furthermore, the urge to sing psalms using known tunes seems to have been in the air on the eve of the Reformation (see also the section on *Souterliedekens*, p. 565 f.). There is evidence that the Protestants at Meaux were singing sacred songs based on known folk melodies about 1524–25. The earliest printed collection is probably the *Noelz nouveaux*, published in 1533 at Neuchâtel, mainly psalm adaptations that were sung to known Christmas tunes. Also, as early as 1532 a setting of the Ten Commandments, by the French refugee Antoine Saunier, based on the chanson *Au bois de dueil* was published in Switzerland. The polyphonic chanson collections by Claudin de Sermisy (c. 1530) were used frequently. Some of his melodies are represented among the 14 Protestant songs prohibited in Toulouse in 1540 and during the following years. And as late as 1546 Eustourg de Beaulieu, a friend of Marot, published a collection of three- and four-part settings entitled *Chrestienne resjoyssance,* a large part of which consisted of secular tunes taken over, in accord with

Luther's views, with the express purpose of removing them in this way from the profane sphere. On the other hand, it is certain that Calvin aimed deliberately at a distinctive melodic style for Reformed congregational song, perceptibly different from that of folk song. Holding to this intention, he obviously could not attain his goal during his first stay in Geneva, 1536 to 1538; he was enabled to do so by the decisive suggestions he received in Strasbourg through Greitter and Dachstein (after earlier positive impressions of congregational singing in Basel).

Concerning the origin of individual tunes in the Genevan Psalter, the following may be said on the basis of the information presently (1962) available. Gregorian models and fragments were used for these psalms:

Psalm 15 *Kyrie fons bonitatis* and Introit antiphon, *Sitientes venite ad aquas*
       17 Compline hymn for Sundays, *Te lucis ante terminum*
       20 *Kyrie Cunctipotens Genitor Deus*
       31 Hymn, *A solis ortus cardine*
       32 *Cantio, Sub tuum praesidium confugimus*
       46 references to the *Leise* entitled *Laus tibi, Christe*
       51 *Kyrie Deus sempiterne*
       61 Alleluia for the Feast of the Finding of the Holy Cross
       80 Easter sequence, *Victimae paschali laudes*
       86 Sequence, *Dies irae, dies illa*
      104 Compline hymn for Pentecost, *Te lucis ante terminum*
      129 Hymn, *Iam surgit hora tertia* (by St. Ambrose), and the Compline hymn *In Nativitate Domini*
      141 Hymn, *Conditor alme siderum*

The following psalms are based on secular models:

       25 *Het was mij wel te voren gezet*
       72 *Petite camusette*
      103 *Const gaet voor cracht*
      130 *O radt van avonturen*
      138 *Une pastourelle gentille* (a Christmas song by Marot dating from 1519; the origin of the melody is not definitely established)

The extent to which some Geneva psalm tunes share certain melodic characteristics and fragments that appeared in various contexts at the turn from the 15th century to the 16th is shown, for example, by the tunes for Psalms 65 and 127. The former uses the leap of a fifth descending in the first melody line which then returns to the beginning, followed by a half tone upward, known from Ockeghem's *Mi-Mi* Mass, Hofhaimer's tenor lied *Meins Traurens ist* (which lacks the final half-tone step), and the Wittenberg melody to Luther's *Aus tiefer Not*. The second line wanders through the Ionian octave, starting with the upper tonic (compare the first two lines with the first and last lines of *Vom Himmel hoch, da komm ich her*), as do a number of German tunes of the time that seem related to Hans Sachs's *Silberweise*. However, the possibility of some completely new creations among the Geneva psalm tunes must be considered. In this connection Pidoux in his basic work (I, p. 18) calls attention to Psalms 42, 47, 72, 91, and 136. While the metric principles applicable to each individual case must always be taken into account here (see below) the consistency of the melodic construction of Psalm 42, for example, is very striking (it is the melody for *Freu dich sehr, o meine Seele—Evangelisches Kirchengesangbuch* 319—which has become part of the German sacred repertory); within the eight lines of melody there are only stepwise progressions, except in lines 5 and 7, where at the beginning of the line, each time on the same tones, there is a leap of a third (A to C), followed at the end of line 7 by an additional leap on the tones A to F. In Psalm 136 the tone-painting in the first line is surprising and can scarcely be associated with any model:

Lou - er Dieu tout hau -te - ment

The fact that most of the Geneva psalm tunes have their origin in various existing models did not, however, prevent the various melodists from following an editorial concept completely unified in its basic principles and obviously guided by Calvin himself. They developed an entirely original melody type, different from melody types of other Reform regions. Nevertheless, the characteristic traits of the Geneva tunes are to be found not in their melody but in their rhythm. It is to that element that they mainly owe their extraordinary effectiveness and widespread acceptance. In contrast to the syllable-counting rhymed poetry of the German Reformed regions, the French rhyming Psalter was clearly influenced in its creation by humanistic tendencies, through the use of rhythmic models in a manner clearly analogous to the humanistic employment of various strophic forms and fixed meters. In the French-speaking territory, the text and music of the Genevan Psalter adopted forms that did not come into general use in the German sacred song until the 17th century.

In addition to Marot's 49 psalm texts with 42 different verse forms one finds an equally large number of rhythmic models that do not necessarily fit the meter of the poems. This means that the Geneva psalm tunes were basically polymetric. However, Geneva polymeter is severely limited; in the last analysis it uses ligatures and dotted notes very sparingly and aside from the final long, rarely uses any note values other than the semibreve and the minim. It is therefore always syllabic and in addition uses only duple time. Polymeter becomes manifest only in the variety of ways in which whole and half notes succeed one another. The Geneva psalm tune, rhythmically speaking, thus takes a singular central position with respect to those tunes of the German Reformation—in part isometric, but also in part definitely polymetric—that go back to the tenors of polyphonic songs.

Basic to the rhythmic structure of the Geneva tunes were two Strasbourg models: one with a longer note at both the beginning and end of the melodic line (or two longer notes at the end for feminine endings with descending melodic progression): ♩ ♩ ♩ ♩ ♩ ♩ ♩ (see Greitter's *Es sind doch selig alle, die*); and the other with quarter notes interrupted within the line by one or more half notes —this latter clearly a special characteristic of Dachstein's melodies: ♩ ♩ ♩ ♩ ♩ ♩ ♩ ♩ | ♩ ♩ ♩ ♩ ♩ ♩ ♩ ♩ | (first and second lines of *An Wasserflüssen Babylon*). While in the Strasbourg songbook these rhythmic forms represented only one of the models possible, in Geneva all melodies were shaped after

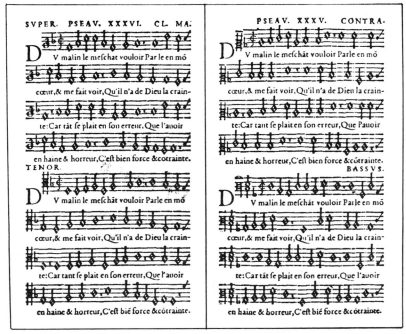

122. Claude Goudimel, four-voice setting of *Du malin le meschant,* Psalm 36, in *Les Pseaumes mis en rime françoise,* Geneva, 1565. Estate of F. Jaqui.

123. Tenor voice of the *Prière après le repas* from Pascal de L'Estocart, *150 Pseaumes de David,* Geneva, 1583, Jean de Laon.

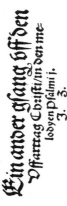

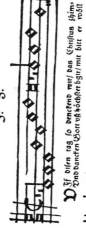

124. Johannes Zwick, opening of the lied *Auf diesen Tag bedenken wir* in the *Nüw Gsangbüchle*, Zurich, 1540, Christoffel Froschauer.

125. Foreword to Caspar Chiampell, *Ladinisches Gesangbuch*, Basel, 1562, Joachim Kündig.

126. Title page of the psalms of Ambrosius Lobwasser written on parchment in 1603 for the Bern songbook. Bern, Stadt- und Hochschulbibliothek, Codex Bernensis A 33.

127. Title page of the Lobwasser Psalter, Heidelberg, 1620, the widow J. Rosen. Stiftsbibliothek des Chorherrenstifts Klosterneuburg.

these basic patterns. The following comparison of the melodies for Psalm 15 as given in the "Psautier primitif" (Strasbourg, 1539) and in the Genevan Psalter of 1542 (this latter is, with the exception of one nonessential note in the melody, the definitive version) shows the procedure in the course of developing.

a. *Aulcuns Pseaulmes et Cantiques.* Psalm 15. Strasbourg, 1539

Qui est ce qui ha - bi - te - ra / O Seig-neur, en ton ta - ber - na - cle? Qui est ce - lui

qui monte-ra / en ton sainct mont et ÿ au - ra re - pos et pai - sible ha - bi - ta - cle?
(Cl. Marot)

b. *Genevan Psalter.* Psalm 15. Geneva, 1542

Qui est ce qui con - ver - se - ra, O Seig-neur, en ton ta - ber - na - cle? Et qui est ce - lui

qui se - ra Si heu-reux, que par grace au - ra Sur ton sainct mont seur ha - bi - ta - cle?

Based on the Strasbourg rhythmic models, the most varied possibilities of alternating half and quarter notes (in today's notation) were used in Geneva—that is, several half notes (up to three, sometimes four or even five) at the beginnings and ends of the lines, and the most differentiated, even syncopated, interruptions of quarter notes by one or two, occasionally three, half notes in the middle of the lines. This careful musical plan was immediately undertaken during the first phase of the creation of the Geneva melodic repertory; during the second phase, it was carried further by Bourgeois in a slightly exaggerated manner by applying as many rhythmic models as possible to a single melody, and in this way even changing some existing melodies; in the third phase, finally, the process was simplified again. The final editorial work on the Genevan Psalter aimed quite uniformly at: a) exclusive use of the sign ¢ ; b) a notation of semibreves and minims, aside from the final long; c) finally, the uniform notation of breathing rests (they are to be so regarded, and not as sectional indications), with the value of a semibreve, at the ends of the lines. (Exceptions to b) only in Psalms 1, 103, and 115 from the first phase of the development, which differ from the Strasbourg models by the introduction of a short appoggiatura, in the Wittenberg style, at the beginnings of two lines [in Psalm 115 only one line]; there are also a few exceptions to c)—for example, between lines 3 and 4 in Psalm 110—and in Psalm 92 two lines are always combined.) The rhythmic pattern of Psalm 42, *Ainsi qu'on oit le cerf bruire* (*Wie nach einer Wasserquelle* or *Freu dich sehr, o meine Seele*), thus appears as follows:

If the line patterns are indicated by letters, the following construction emerges: ‖: a—b :‖ c—c—a—d ‖

Each line has two sections; the first sections of all lines are similar in their rhythmic construction; finally, the rhythmic pattern of the first line returns in the penultimate line as in a rhythmic *Reprisenbar*. Other rhythmic structures have these patterns: ♩ ♩ ♩ ♩ ♩ ♩ ♩ —first line of the *Stollen* of Psalm 25; ♩ ♩ ♩ ♩ ♩ ♩ ♩ ♩ ♩ —Psalm 47 in all lines, changing Beza's twelve-line strophe form, by a musical combination of every two lines, into a six-line strophe, much to the advantage of the song, in view of Beza's many excessively short lines of only five syllables. This tune—characteristically, from the Geneva edition of 1551—is certainly a prime example for the principles applied to the melodization of the Genevan Psalter. An additional characteristic pattern is, for example ♩ ♩ ♩ ♩ ♩ ♩ ♩ —first line of Psalm 121; it occurs later again, among other instances, in all four verses of the German sacred song *Herr Jesu Christ, dich zu uns wend*.

This rhythmic schematicism of the Genevan Psalter is unquestionably rooted in a certain rationalism derived from pedagogical considerations in an attempt to find melodies suitable for the congregation. The extraordinary success of the procedure speaks for itself. Of course, the rhythmic element, because of the possibilities of its special effect, gains here a significance unequaled elsewhere in that period. The intimate interweaving of text and melody, typical for other regions of Reform song, is replaced here by a goal of rhythmic construction, i.e., by a certain measure of musical autonomy. There is no other feature in church music as typically Calvinist as this one; it is an order for artistic creation to be put to use in the organization of the congregation. Despite the great musical achievement in the melodization of the Genevan Psalter, particularly if one takes into consideration the large number of melodies created, the directed rhythmic uniformity inhibited true artistic creativeness. And yet, this is balanced to a certain degree by the wealth of beautiful melodic lines.

Melodically, the Geneva psalm tunes have their roots, in accordance with their different historical sources, in the all-embracing realm of the church modes, with a frequent tendency toward the popular major and minor. A strictly Hypodorian tune such as the following from Psalm 86 is not entirely an isolated case, although it belongs to the more unusual type:

Psalm 86. Geneva, 1551

More characteristic are certain Ionian or Hypoionian melodies, which make particular use of the fourth between dominant and tonic, as, for example, the beginning of Psalms 89 and 98 (C′–A–G–C′) and 99 (F–C–D–E–F), or between tonic and fourth degree, as in Psalm 85 (G–G–G–A–C′). They greatly stimulated later generations, as can be seen in the melodic creations of Johann Crüger (see pp. 242 and 553). One also finds more frequently the traversal of a usually Ionian or perhaps Hypomixolydian octave space between upper and lower tonic, as, for example (in addition to Greitter's *Es sind doch selig alle, die* in Psalm 36 or 68), in the melody for Psalm 32, which has a strangely remote kinship to Greitter's melody as well as to the tune for Psalm 1, and in those for Psalms 105 and 114 or 127 and 138.

While most of the Geneva psalm tunes do not present as unified a picture with respect to melody as they do with respect to rhythm, it was early observed that they were simpler and easier to grasp—a quality probably resulting from their French character, as opposed to the heavier German one, but also from their rhythmic schematicism (does this in turn perhaps show rationalistic Romanic traits?). When Cornelius Becker, whose psalm poems Heinrich Schütz set to music, spoke of "foreign French and, for ears that long for worldly delights, lovely-sounding melodies," he did not quite do justice to the Geneva psalm tunes; but this is how they impressed him when he compared them with Lutheran melodies, and there is some justification for his opinion. While it must be assumed that Calvin's demands for a melodic style with *poids* and *majesté,* but at the same time *modéré* and *modeste,* had to be fulfilled by his followers, they were undoubtedly concerned not with a solemn, slow tempo (though an inappropriate fast one was out of the question) but with melodic and particularly rhythmic simplicity. Never again, at any time or place in the history of Protestant hymnals based on Calvin's principles, would there be a treasury of poems and songs, of sheer ecumenical significance, equal to the Genevan Psalter in unity, durability, and, eventually, wide dissemination.

The significance of the fact that the Genevan Psalter achieved almost exclusive acceptance in French-speaking regions in the 16th century is best illustrated by the special traditions of psalm singing that at first were still in existence and which it displaced. Most prominent is the example of Lausanne: here, around 1552 and in 1557, were published psalm editions that were independent of Geneva (they have not been preserved). As early as 1542 the Reformer in Lausanne, Pierre Viret, remarked about psalm tunes by François Gindron used there (see Pidoux, op. cit., II, 12) that they were much easier and lovelier ("multo faciliores et suaviores") than those traditionally in use (obviously in Geneva). One may assume that these were included in the editions just mentioned. The complete Lausanne Psalter of 1565, edited by Franc, is preserved (Franc, from 1542 until his death in 1570, was cantor of the Lausanne cathedral). It is identical in its texts with the one from Geneva, but musically bears its own stamp to a large extent.

Many of the melodies have been changed, if only slightly. Twenty-one have been replaced by entirely new ones, and the 23 psalms without their own tunes have acquired melodies in Lausanne. In all this we can definitely assume decisive participation by Franc, mainly because the melodic material shows intimate acquaintance with Geneva principles. In all likelihood, however, the special Lausanne tradition of the earlier editions lived on in the melodic repertory of 1565. This would best explain the omission of several Geneva tunes. It is surprising that the Genevan Psalter did not take over the tunes present here for psalms that lacked their own melodies in Geneva.

Another special tradition was preserved in the French songbooks in Strasbourg, not least by their adherence to Calvin's texts of 1539. In this connection, mention must be made of the *Premier livre des pseaumes, cantiques et chansons spirituelles* (Geneva, 1554), mainly containing poems by G. Guéroult, while the one- and four-part arrangement is "la plus part" the work of the Geneva cantor G. de la Moeulle. The ten psalm lieder in this collection, to judge by their artistic form, were certainly meant not for use at divine services but as religious music for the home, although they are not entirely divorced from Geneva principles. This would apply even to the earliest complete Huguenot Psalter ever published with musical settings, the one edited by Ph. Jambe de Fer (Lyons, 1555), containing 49 psalms by Marot (only these have the customary melodies of 1551), and the remainder, with few exceptions, by Jean Poitevin. The character of spiritual music for the home seems even more pronounced here. The particular and often very valuable body of melody that differs from the Geneva principles has not yet been investigated. Except for the Strasbourg set, these melodies were incorporated in Pidoux's work (of the Strasbourg set Pidoux gives only those tunes that had influenced Geneva). The wealth of these melodies testifies to the extent to which psalms were sung even outside the worship service.

In his regulations for psalm singing during the service, Calvin in *La forme des prières* (1542) had stipulated only one psalm preceding the sermon. Later on, he ordered psalm singing at the beginning of the service ("après le second coup de la cloche") and before and after the sermon during morning and evening services on Sunday and the regular prayer service on Wednesday. The tables reproduced in all editions beginning with 1562 (they had predecessors in 1549 and 1552, which reflect the number of psalm lieder then existing) provide for each of the three services just mentioned a series of 25 numbers for the opening of the service and for the singing that framed the sermon (here a psalm was frequently divided for singing before and after the sermon). Sometimes two short psalms—or, conversely, half a long one—were assigned to the opening of the service. The tables state that in the three weekly main services (in addition there were regular auxiliary services) the complete Psalter was to be sung within approximately half a year. This order was so binding that the division, for service use, of most psalms into two or more sections is marked by the word "Pause" (intermission) or by asterisks or other signs (see the illustration on pp. 571–72) in countless editions of the Genevan Psalter up to the 19th century (in Holland, for example, but, significantly, only in monophonic editions; see below). In the 18th century an expression derived from this custom, "eine pausam singen," was still known in Calvinist regions of Germany. No connections with the seasons or special holidays appear in this regulation, but the gradual singing of the entire Psalter more or less in rotation is clearly discernible. This principle was not strictly carried out, however, because of the different character of the Sunday and Wednesday services. This is explained, for example, in the preface to the *Octante trois pseaumes* in the last edition of 1553, as follows: "In consideration of the fact that Wednesday is prescribed for solemn prayers, we have chosen for singing on this day those among the psalms that contain prayers and more precise requests to God, reserving those that contain acts of grace and praises of our Lord and his works for Sunday" (see Pidoux, op.cit., II, 61). Altogether 20 to 30 psalm strophes are provided for every service (for the opening psalm the number varies from 8 to 12), which means that congregational singing, depending on the length of the sermon, filled one-third to one-half of the service. There were also special occasions, such as the twenty-fifth Sunday, for whose opening alone 27 verses from Psalms 139 and 140 were stipulated. The Ten Commandments lied was sung after the sermon on the four Communion days of the year (Easter, Pentecost, first Sunday in September, and the Sunday next after

Christmas), the canticle of Simeon on the same days between the prayer of Thanksgiving and the Blessing. On ordinary Sundays the Ten Commandments lied, divided into first and second tablet, served frequently as frame for the Public Confession. During the administration of the Sacrament, Psalm 138 was sung in accordance with the earliest Geneva regulation of 1542, *La manière de célébrer la cène,* a custom probably (according to E. Encke) followed afterward too. Congregational singing during the service was supported by the school choir, singing in unison under the direction of the cantor. To what extent church and school collaborated can be seen from the generally accepted custom of inserting in editions of the Genevan Psalter solmisation syllables for all the notes (see the illustration on p. 512).

One of the most peculiar aspects of the development of Calvinistic church music in French-speaking regions is that despite the strict limitation of service music to unison unaccompanied congregational singing, it produced at the same time an amazing number of polyphonic psalm arrangements, "non pas pour induire à les chanter en l'Eglise, mais pour s'esiouir en Dieu particulièrement ès maisons" (Goudimel, 1565, see below). In this note, appearing on the back of the title page of Goudimel's work, "particulièrement" does not mean "preferably" but as much as "en son particulier"—that is, in private. There are, in fact, no records of polyphonic singing during the service in the 16th century. The numerous polyphonic settings of the Genevan Psalter can be explained, so it seems, by the great popularity its melodies rapidly achieved even beyond the denominational borders, which were at first not sharply defined. During the decades of persecution it was certainly not always declared Calvinists who made these polyphonic arrangements. Also, the numerous polyphonic editions were mostly published in Paris and Lyons. In the few, but particularly important, editions published in Geneva (see below) the place of publication, with only one exception, was not given, undoubtedly to disguise their Calvinist origin and not to impede their circulation outside of Switzerland. Bourgeois was the first to emerge with polyphonic arrangements of Genevan psalm tunes, although he did not create the most important of these settings. It was also he who introduced four-part homophonic writing to church music as a whole, in his collection *Pseaulmes cinquante . . . mis en musique . . . à quatre parties à voix de contrepoinct égal consonante au verbe* (Lyons, 1547). His purpose is indicated by the phrase "consonante au verbe"; it has its origin in certain humanistic tendencies of the French chanson composers who introduced, toward the middle of the 16th century, a new strophic, syllabic-homophonic chanson type as opposed to the old through-composed polyphonic one. These so-called *vaudevilles* or *voix de ville* are based on the principle of the tightest integration of music and text melodically as well as rhythmically, in the genuine humanistic spirit. The word-rhythm of the poem determines the musical design. The young Calvinist church music used these tendencies with great intensity for theological reasons, to project the Word of God clearly. It remains to be established whether Bourgeois's collection is not in fact the earliest homophonic collection of its time and milieu, whose strict note-against-note style of writing has its predecessors only in the humanistic ode compositions of the first third of the 16th century and in the four-part *falsobor-*

done settings developed out of *fauxbourdon* (for example, in the *turbae* of the responsorial Passion). Since these settings were intended as music for the home, it seems logical that in Bourgeois, as well as in similar collections by other composers, the cantus firmus appears in the tenor, following the tradition; there was no reason to abandon this practice. The homophonic Geneva psalm setting owes its origin therefore to an entirely different cause from that of the Lutheran cantional setting with the cantus firmus in the top voice (see p. 135 f.), which made its appearance some forty years later, although this latter undoubtedly took the Calvinist psalm settings as models for its technique of setting. The effect of Bourgeois's *Pseaulmes cinquante* must have been tremendous; he not only gained important followers with this technique (especially Claude Goudimel and Claude le Jeune) but the homophonic setting became in general the most characteristic and popular manifestation of Calvinist music. This has its explanation in Calvin's vigorous activation of congregational life, which resulted in unison and part singing of psalms in the home; for this purpose simple homophonic settings were not the only possible form, to be sure, but certainly the most popular. Nevertheless, this type of setting was perhaps not the most important aspect of Bourgeois's work; in addition to this collection there are three other collections, in part more voluminous, of psalm compositions, some of them in more elaborate settings: one with 24 four-part arrangements, also dated 1547 *(Le premier livre des pseaumes);* another dated 1555, printed, like the previous one, in Lyons, containing 83 four-part psalm settings and, as was customary, arrangements of other biblical canticles (full titles in *MGG* II, 161 and in Pidoux, op. cit., II, 35, 73); and finally a third collection of four- and six-part settings, printed in 1561 at Paris with the following revealing title: *83 Psalmes de David* "(very well suited for instruments) in four, five, and six parts, for similar or mixed voices: with the main melody in the *basse-contre*, so that those who wish to sing along with it in unison or at the octave may fit in with the other, more agile parts" (the collection also contains the other pieces of the 1555 collection and two canons). In the first collection, unfortunately the only one preserved, there are two types of setting—one that is basically homophonic although somewhat ornamented, and one with imitations line by line, frequently in pairs. The influence of the Josquin school is recognizable; but in addition there is a stronger vocal cast to the shaping of the settings and individual parts. In the motet-like settings, too, one frequently finds stretches of a decidedly declamatory nature, along with extended lines that are rich in ligatures.

a. L. Bourgeois (1547): Psalm 14

b. L. Bourgeois (1547): opening of the *Abgesang* of Psalm 91

The loss of the third collection, of 1561, seems particularly regrettable because it contained essentially instrumental settings, as is indicated by the title. Thus no complete picture of Bourgeois's compositional methods can be obtained. The possibility of instrumental execution was contemplated in the first two collections too, according to their titles ("bien convenable aux instruments"); the third one, however, reads "fort convenable. . . ."

The most influential among the polyphonic arrangers of the Genevan Psalter was Claude Goudimel, one of the most important French composers of his time. Of his numerous sacred and secular works (the former include Latin motets and Masses for the Catholic service, typifying the state of flux that still characterized denominational boundaries after 1560), his French psalm compositions undoubtedly had the greatest historical effect. Contrary to Bourgeois, he took as his point of departure the large motet form.   Goudimel published his great three- to

Cl. Goudimel (1551): Psalm 104 (melody: Geneva, 1542, G. Franc [?])

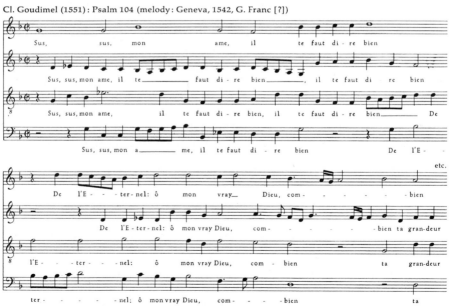

eight-part psalm motets ("mis en musique au long en forme de mottetz") gradually between 1551 and 1566. There were eight volumes, some of them reprinted several times, containing eight to ten pieces each. Because the composer was slain during the massacre begun on St. Bartholomew's Eve (1572), the work was not completed. In these motets, following the model of the contemporary French chanson in sectional form with the number of voices changing from section to section, the whole strophic text, as far as can be determined, is through-composed, with the cantus firmus employed motivically and sometimes also in strict form in the individual voices. It is a peculiarity of the history of Protestant church music that the Lutheran church never produced as large a collection of motets as did the Calvinist movement in Goudimel's more than 70 cyclic psalm-lied arrangements; moreover, from an aesthetic point of view these are among the most important creations of Protestant church music. In a second type of arrangement (published in Paris and dated 1568, according to Pidoux, but preserved only in a Geneva reprint of 1580) the cantus firmus appears mostly in the discant and is on the whole only slightly florid. Other settings show sparingly used imitations (sometimes only at the beginning of a piece); still others have two-part entrances of the two upper voices followed at a distance of two or four beats by lower voices in imitation but with independent motifs. Here, too, the setting, calculated to fit the text of one verse and always vocally conceived, remains concise:

Cl. Goudimel (1568 or 1580): Psalm 93 (melody: P. Dagues [?], Geneva, 1562)

The circulation of Goudimel's third collection, *Les pseaumes . . . mis en musique à quatre parties . . . Par les héritiers de François Jaqui* (Geneva, 1565), exceeds by far that of all other editions of the Genevan Psalter. It is frequently referred to as the Jaqui Psalter after the name of its publisher (it was published as early as 1564 in Paris, where it already had a second printing in 1565). The collection certainly owes its enormous dissemination (see p. 536 f.) not to its singular musical values but to the fact that it was the first complete Psalter in a strictly homphonic setting (only for melodies that are used repeatedly do more elaborate settings turn up on the second, third, or fourth appearance—for example, for Psalm 24; these variants are sometimes identical with those in the 1568–80 edition). That this edition was published in the Calvinist metropolis, Geneva, was of additional and decisive importance. Aside from the aforementioned editions of 1564 and 1565 (concerning these see Pidoux, op. cit., II, 141, 151), the Jaqui Psalter had already been preceded by a homophonic partial collection by Goudimel containing 83 settings under the title *Pseaumes à quatre parties . . . , dont le subject se peut chanter en taille ou en dessus,* for which only the bass part has been preserved (see *MGG* V, 586; P.A. Gaillard in *Jahrbuch für Liturgik und Hymnologie* I (1955), 123; and Pidoux, op. cit., II, 136; the latter also established that the 1580 edition mentioned above was a reprint of the one of 1568; see ibid., II, 158, 180). The Jaqui Psalter was clearly predestined for the most widespread acceptance; it was eminently suited to the aim of strict Calvinists to sing and play nothing but psalms, if possible, throughout their lives (and not at divine services only). It is interesting to compare Goudimel's settings note for note with those of Bourgeois, in which the cantus firmus is also usually in the tenor. Although Bourgeois makes ample use of sixth chords, doubling of thirds, a third in the final chord of a line, cross relations, and chord changes while the notes of the cantus firmus are sustained, and thus appears frequently to be more expressive, daring, and original, Goudimel's settings are more precise and terse within themselves, undoubtedly an essential condition for their greater popularity.

a. L. Bourgeois (1547): Psalm 6 (melody: Geneva, 1542, G. Franc[?])

b. Cl. Goudimel (1565): Psalm 105 (melody: P. Dagues [?], Geneva, 1562)

The Genevan Psalter obtained its unexampled dissemination not in unison editions but in the homophonic settings by Goudimel.

In addition to the works by Bourgeois and Goudimel, the sixth and seventh decades of the 16th century produced a whole series of other polyphonic editions of the Genevan Psalter. Next to Bourgeois and Goudimel, Philibert Jambe de Fer was the most important figure, prior to 1570, in connection with polyphonic arrangement of the Huguenot psalms. The four-part *Psalmodie de quarante et un pseaumes royaux* (Lyons, 1559) is known to be his first work of this kind. (Pidoux [op. cit., II, 87] has lately questioned the existence of the earlier psalm arrangements mentioned repeatedly in the literature, most recently in *MGG* VI, 1676.) Thirty-four of the settings, written in a lightly polyphonic style, use texts by Beza with their Geneva tunes of 1551; the rest, some of them with texts by Marot, have melodies that could possibly be by Jambe de Fer himself. Here we must mention Jambe de Fer's principle work, his *150 Pseaumes de David . . .* (Lyons, 1564), which, together with Goudimel's famous work, represents the beginning of arrangements of the complete official Genevan Psalter of 1562. The four- and five-part settings are either homophonic or only slightly polyphonic. Among the other numerous collections with psalm settings, the following are the most important: Pierre Certon, *Recueil de 31 Psaumes* (four-part, Paris, 1546) and *50 Pseaumes* (four-part, Paris, 1555), both in a somewhat loose homophonic style; Anthoine de Mornable, two volumes, one with 31 settings (his authorship of these, however, is uncertain, since this work may be identical with the 31 psalms by Certon), the other with 17 settings, all in the same style as before (Paris, 1546; concerning the connection between the works of Certon and Mornable and the importance of their cantus-firmus forms during the time prior to the final formulation of the Geneva melodies, see Pidoux, *Les Psaumes d'Anthoine de Mornable, Guillaume Morlaye et Pierre Certon* [1546, 1554, 1555], in *Annales musicologiques* V, 1957, 179 ff.); Didier Lupi Second, 30 four-part homophonic psalms, after versification by Giles Daurigny, without relation to the Geneva melodies (Lyons, 1549); Clement Janequin, a publication with 28 four-part homophonic psalms and another one with 82, also four-part and mostly homophonic psalms (Paris, 1549 and 1559); Jean Lovys, 50 five-part psalms in motet form using the first strophe only throughout and only somewhat reminiscent of the Geneva tunes (Antwerp, 1555); Jacques Arcadelt, 6 four- and five-part psalms in motet form (Paris, 1559); Michel Ferrier, 49 three-part polyphonic psalms (Lyons, 1559, and Paris, 1568); Thomas Champion, 60 psalms, four-part settings (with two five-part exceptions) in almost homophonic style (Paris, 1561). Among these early arrangers of Huguenot psalms one finds a number of composers who had only a loose connection with Calvinism if, indeed, any at all. Janequin, in those years, was a singer in the court chapel in Paris, Champion was chamber organist there, and Certon was "Maistre des enfants de la Saincte Chapelle de Paris." Goudimel and Jambe de Fer were followed in rapid succession by other masters who made additional complete arrangements of the Genevan Psalter: Richard Crassot (four-part homophonic settings, harmonized in an advanced fashion, Lyons, 1564, and Geneva, 1569), Jean Servyn (three-part, Orléans, 1565), Hugues Sureau (four-part homophonic, in part leaning heavily on Goudimel, Rouen?, 1565), and Pierre Santerre (four-part homophonic, Poitiers, 1567). Except for the three-part settings by Servyn there is throughout a tendency toward homophony, i.e., toward simple vocal settings, strictly carried out in many arrangements. (Examples from almost all the above-mentioned collections can be found in O. Douen, II, 78 ff. Several pieces each by Bourgeois, Goudimel—from the 1565 and 1568 editions —and Jambe de Fer are in *Das Psalmenbuch,* edited by H. Holliger, Basel, 1953. The series *Chants polyphoniques,* begun in 1960, edited by M. Honegger in *Les Editions Ouvrières,* Paris, offers settings from the works by Janequin, Lupi Second, and Champion mentioned above. The Jaqui Psalter was published in a facsimile edition by Bärenreiter-Verlag, Kassel, 1935.)

Indicative of the extent of psalm singing in the social life of France during the 1550s and '60s are the various arrangements of the Huguenot psalms for lute and related instruments. Among these are *Le troysieme livre contenant plusieurs duos*

128. Jan Pieterszoon Sweelinck (1562–1621) in a painting attributed to his brother, Gerrit Pieterszoon Swelinck, 1606. The Hague, Gemeente-Museum.

129. Henderick Joostsz. Speuy, *De Psalmen Davids, gestelt op het Tabulatuer van het orghel ende Clavercymmel,* Dorderecht, 1610, P. Verhaghen. Title page.

et trios . . . mis en tabulature de guiterne by Simon Gorlier (Paris, 1551) with three psalm intabulations; also the *Tiers livre de tabulature de luth, contenant vingt et un pseaulmes . . .* , based on a Lyons print of the Geneva partial Psalter of 1549, the *Second livre de cistre, contenant leas Commendemens de Dieu, six psaulmes . . .* (Paris, 1552 and 1564), and eight additional psalms with a more pronounced tendency toward homophony (c. 1567) and an intabulation of the 83 four-part psalms of Goudimel (1562) by Adrien le Roy (see R. de Morcourt, *Adrien le Roy et les pseaumes pour luth*, in *Annales musicologiques* III, 1955, 179–211, from which the following musical example is taken), then the *Quart livre de tabulature de guiterre contenant plusieurs fantasies, pseaulmes et chansons . . .* by Gregoire Brayssing (Paris, 1553), the *Premier livre des psaulmes mis en musique par maistre Pierre Certon . . . reduitz en tabulature de luth par Guillaume Morlaye* (Paris, 1554; an instructive new edition of this work with a historical preface by F. Lesure and the transcription and the musical commentary by R. de Morcourt appeared in *Editions du Centre National de la Recherche Scientifique*, Paris, 1957), and finally the *Tabulature de luth, où sont contenus plusieurs pseaulmes et chansons spirituelles* (Lyons, 1562).

The impressive number of psalm arrangements for the lute consists to a certain extent, as is indicated by the titles, merely of intabulations of vocal compositions by other masters, but some of them represent re-creations of models that are of some significance (see below, Ex. b). Certon's version of the melody, which served Morlaye as a point of departure (Certon's tunes did not find their way into the Genevan Psalter), is reproduced here for comparison. One should also note that in this piece the cantus firmus—which in Example a) was doubled in the accompaniment—appears only in the vocal line. Both pieces exhibit the high artistic level of the devotional household music of the Calvinists around the middle of the 16th century.

a. Adrien le Roy (1562): Psalm 1 [from *Annales musicologiques* III, 1955, 207 ff.] (melody: Strasbourg, 1539)

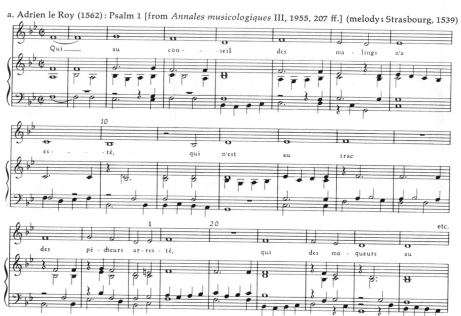

b. Guillaume Morlaÿe (1554): Psalm 6 [in a transcription by R. Morcourt]

It was certainly an immediate consequence of the public persecution of the Hugenots following the Massacre of St. Bartholomew (during the course of which Goudimel and Jambe de Fer were murdered) that soon after 1572 the publication of psalm-lied arrangements for one or several voices was abruptly reduced, indeed at first completely discontinued. Apparently, from then on both Paris and Lyons nearly ceased to function as publication centers of Reformed church music. Goudimel's work of 1568, published that year in Paris, was issued in a second edition at Geneva in 1580. Only La Rochelle maintained its position as a Calvinist outpost in France at that time, as far as Reformed publishing activities were concerned and also in other respects. The internal political conditions in France during the last decades of the 16th century, up to the Edict of Nantes (1598)— which made concessions to the Huguenots and gave them certain rights—explain why the works of Claude le Jeune were to a large extent not published until long after they had been created, some of them only after the composer's death (1600). Le Jeune, who occupied a lonely peak toward the end of the century, was the most influential and outstanding arranger of the Genevan Psalter after Goudimel. Ten of his psalms, arranged in motet form but without using Calvinist melodies, were published in Paris as early as 1564 (a second edition appeared there in 1580); after that, there was an interruption till toward the end of the century. Not until 1598 did there follow, in La Rochelle, his two- to seven-part *Dodecacorde contenant douze pseaumes . . . selon les douze modes . . .* , which made use of the Geneva psalm tunes in motet style. After this came the four- and five-part homophonic arrangements of the complete Psalter (Paris, 1601; numerous new editions in various countries and languages until far into the 17th century, the most widely disseminated polyphonic arrangement of the Huguenot Psalter after the one by Goudimel of 1565; modern edition of 15 four-part examples in the *Psalmenbuch* by H. Holliger), then three volumes containing 50 psalms each in three-part settings (Paris, 1602, 1608, and 1610) using the official melodies, and finally the two- to eight-part *Pseaumes en vers mezurez* (Paris, 1606) containing 27 psalm compositions without reference in either text or music to the Geneva psalms.

The abundance of Le Jeune's Genevan Psalter settings is matched only by the variety of forms employed. For example, along with the through-composed, sectional psalm motets in the early work of 1564 (and 1580) and in the *Dodeca-corde* there are the particularly charming three-part arrangements (mostly for two high voices and one low voice). In the *Dodecacorde,* unlike what happens in Goudimel's corresponding work, the cantus firmus is retained unchanged in long note values in one of the voices and, where possible, as a wandering cantus firmus in the various sections (for a complete reproduction of such a psalm motet see O. Douen, II, 225: here the cantus firmus wanders through the four sections from the bass through the *quinta vox* and the discant back to the bass). The three-part settings are short chorale motets, not through-composed, with or without strict cantus-firmus development but always involving a motivic imitation technique based on it (three examples from this collection, Psalms 53, 57, and 62, can be found in *Chorals de la Réforme. Un recueil de pièces vocales ... de Cl. Goudimel, Cl. le Jeune et G. Migot,* Paris, c. 1950, ed. by M. Honegger).

Cl. le Jeune (1608) : Psalm 53 [in a transcription by M. Honegger]

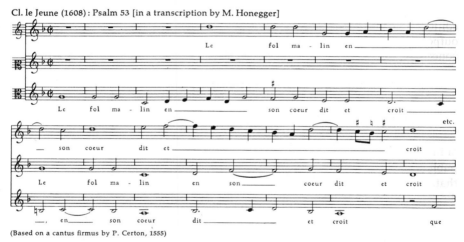

(Based on a cantus firmus by P. Certon, 1555)

Le Jeune's homophonic settings, as would be expected from their dates, show a greater harmonic variety than those of his predecessors. Cadences with a raised third at the end of a line are commonplace; open fifths no longer appear. The transformation of the church modes into the major-minor system with the intro-duction of leading tones is carried out consistently. In many of these settings, however, the cantus firmus is still in the tenor; they, too, were only meant for use outside of the service. Once again, in the complete *oeuvre* of Le Jeune, as in Bourgeois and Goudimel, the humanistic spirit in the service of Holy Scripture is particularly evident. Le Jeune was one of the chief collaborators in the humanist poet Antoine Baïf's *Académie de poésie et de musique* (1567–87), which dealt particularly with the relationship between word and tone; the expression "vers mezurez" in the title of Le Jeune's work of 1606 (see above) is a technical term of the academy of Baïf, who himself wrote a rhyming Psalter (*Les 150 pseaumes en vers ordinaires,* 1587).

Next to Le Jeune only Pascal de L'Estocart, who, like Calvin, came from Noyon in Picardy, achieved prominence; his *Cent cinquante pseaumes* was published in 1583 at Geneva. These are four- to eight-part arrangements of the Genevan Psalter in motet style. They are not through-composed, however; only the first strophe of each psalm is used, and the unaltered cantus firmus is mostly in the tenor. The work thus is to a certain extent related to the one by Goudimel of 1568 (1580); but almost all of L'Estocart's pieces are laid out more broadly, and we find in them a greater expressivity, a more varied harmonization, word repetitions to emphasize certain parts of the text, the use of madrigalisms, and, finally, the effective interchange between polyphony and homophony so typical generally of the end of the 16th century (several settings by L'Estocart exist in H. Holliger, *Psalmenbuch;* his work is also published in a facsimile edition by Bärenreiter-Verlag, Kassel, 1954).

While Calvinist polyphony naturally centered around arrangements of the Genevan Psalter in the 16th century, the *chanson spirituelle,* too, played a not unessential part, one reason for which is the outstanding importance of chanson composition in the history of French music of that period. Here, too, denominational boundaries were frequently crossed; thus texts of a Reformed nature can be found even in the voluminous chanson output by Janequin, for example. It is worthy of note, however, that it was the Reformed composers who, in collaboration with the Reformed poets, gave particular significance to the polyphonic religious song. (For the Huguenots' participation in the history of the French chanson in the 16th century, see Wolfgang Boetticher, *Orlando di Lasso und seine Zeit,* Kassel, 1958).

As early as 1533 three collections with a total of 160 religious songs, without music but with names of melodies, were published in Geneva or Neuchâtel, furnishing (according to M. Honegger) the basis for most of the later chansonniers. In addition a respectable number of collective works as well as numerous individual publications typify the quantity of religious-chanson production. In 1552 a *Premier livre de psalmes et cantiques en vulgaire françoys* (reprinted in 1556) was published in Paris, followed probably in the same year by a second volume and in 1553 by a third, containing exclusively *chansons spirituelles.* The *Premier livre des pseaumes, cantiques et chansons spirituelles, traduitz & composées bonne partie par G. Guéroult & autres nommez en leur lieu. Et mis en musique à une et à quatre parties la plus part par G. de la Moeulle dict de Genève, chantre en l'Eglise de la dicte cité* was published in 1554 at Geneva. In a *Suyte* to this volume that appeared in the same year one finds, among others, "cinq chansons spirituelles composées par cinq escoliers detenus prisonniers à Lyon pour le tesmoignage de nostre Seigneur Jesus Christ." An additional collection of religious chansons by Marot, Beza, and others, the music of which was arranged by several masters, among them Arcadelt, Certon, and Janequin, was published in 1561, also at Lyons (see *Répertoire internationale des sources musicales. Recueils imprimés XVIe–XVIIe siècles* I, Munich-Duisburg, 1960).

The most important representatives of the *chanson spirituelle* were the poet-composer Eustorg de Beaulieu and the composers Jan Caulery, Hubert Waelrant, P. Clereau (with a four-part collection of 1567), J. Servin (with two volumes of four- to eight-part chansons and an additional four-part collection, all of 1578), S. Cornet (with five-, six-, and eight-part chansons of 1584), and, most important in this respect too, Claude Goudimel, while of the Calvinist poets Guillaume Guéroult calls for special mention. To a large extent their work consisted only of refashioning secular chansons into religious ones, sometimes the text and the music, sometimes only the text. Behind the change of the "verbe lubrique en lettre spirituelle et Chrestienne" is hidden a genuine Calvinist intent. Among the new creations in this field the *chansons spirituelles* by Guéroult (Lyons, 1548; three more printings in Paris up to 1571) were the most important; their musical settings are by Didier Lupi Second. The chanson text *Suzanne un jour* from this collection was the most popular one of the century in France and achieved numerous additional musical settings. Mention must also be made of Waelrant's *Jardin musical* (Antwerp, after 1550), the *Sonets chrétiens mis en musique à quatre parties* by G. Boni (1579), the *Premier livre de sonets chrestiens . . . mis en musique en quatre parties* by A. Bertrand (1580), and *Chansons françoyses à 5, 6 et 8 parties, mises en musique* by Cornet (1581; contains among others Marot's transcription of Psalms 9 and 34, but not the Geneva tunes). The works of 1579 and 1580 clearly differ (according to W. Boetticher) in their greater simplicity from the original secular, parodied chansons. In the '70s and '80s the Reformed editors Jean Pasquier and Simon Goulart undertook systematic "purifications" of the best-known chanson texts. As a result chansons by Orlando di Lasso (among others), which had become known because of his stay at the court of Charles IX around 1571 and through Parisian publications, also became part of the Calvinist song repertory. The most important publications of the two editors are: Jean Pasquier, *Mellange d'Orlande de Lassus contenant plusieurs chansons à quatre parties desquelles la lettre profane a esté changée en spirituelle* (La Rochelle, 1575 and later), also his *Cantiques et chansons spirituelles pour chanter soubz la musique des chansons profanes d'Orlande de Lassus à 4 et 5 parties* (La Rochelle, 1578), then *Thrésor de musique d'Orlande de Lassus, prince des musiciens de nostre temps, contenant ses chansons françoises, italiennes et latines, à 4, 5 et 6 parties . . .* (1576, in all likelihood published in Geneva by Simon Goulart de Senlis, then a Calvinist parson there; significantly, the only completely preserved copy of the work, in Munich, is bound with the Jaqui Psalter by Goudimel). It is certain that Goulart edited two volumes: *Meslange des pseaumes et cantiques à trois parties recueillis de la musique d'Orlande de Lassus et autres excellents musiciens de nostre temps* (1577, probably also in Geneva). Noteworthy among other editions of this kind are the *Recueil du mellange d'Orlande de Lassus contenant plusieurs chansons tant en vers latins qu'en ryme françoyse à quatre et cinq parties* (London, 1570; the publisher of this, the earliest known source of Huguenot chanson purification, is the Calvinist émigré Thomas Vautrollier, who also published in England writings by Luther, Calvin, Beza, and others), *La fleur des chansons de deux plus excellents musiciens de nostre temps à scavoir de M. Orlande de Lassus et de M. Claude Goudimel* (four- and five-part, in two volumes, Lyons, 1574 and later), and the *Cinquante pseaumes de David avec la musique à 5 parties d'Orlande de Lassus. Vingt autres pseaumes à 5 et 6 parties pars divers excellents musiciens de nostre temps* (Heidelberg, 1597). There are also original compositions by Lasso on Genevan psalm melodies, in which a strict treatment of the tenor cantus firmus is renounced in favor of the emotional penetration of the text characteristic of that master:

O. di Lasso (1594): Psalm 130 (melody: Strasbourg, 1539)

The *Octinaires de la vanité et inconstance du monde* by Claude le Jeune are likewise religious chansons. This work, published posthumously in 1606 and comprising 36 three- and four-part pieces, is considered Le Jeune's most mature and most beautiful creation and was repeatedly reprinted until 1641. Several of the texts in it—poems by Anthoine de la Roche Chandieu—were also set to music by L'Estocart.

That the French Calvinists penetrated amazingly far into the region of the chanson, as shown by the numerous publications mentioned above, is telling proof of their spiritual strength and power in the 16th century. During the time of the persecution, the secular beginnings of the chansons, and sometimes endings too, were retained to disguise the real content of the text. At the same time, in the intensive orientation of Calvinism toward art music then taking place, a trend toward a healthy affirmation of the world is clearly visible. The following words from the epistle preceding the second volume of Goulart's *Meslange des pseaumes et cantiques* have an almost Lutheran sound: "Desiring now for my own part to see this beautiful gift of God recover its splendor without wounding honest tongues and ears, I have long wished that the excellent musicians of our age would quit those foolish and detestable texts in order to devote the beautiful gifts they have received to a subject worthy of them. . . . And as a beginning, after having published some chansons by Orlando, I have taken up these books of three-part chansons . . . so that amid the sufferings of this life, you might have some remedy to give you honest solace with your friends."

Apparently, very few biblical sections other than the Psalms were versified and set to music. Only the four-part arrangement of *Les Proverbes de Salomon* by N. Millot, after poems by A.D. du Plessis (Paris, 1567), need be mentioned here. F. Gindron had made a unison version of them earlier (Lausanne, 1556); it includes, though in incomplete form, du Plessis's versifications of Ecclesiastes.

The great period of Calvinist music in the French-speaking regions comes to an end with the turn of the century. Although external conditions improved for the Reformed church after the Edict of Nantes (1598), it, too, was affected by the general retrogression of choral music in 17th-century France. In retrospect it must be said that this period has so far remained unique in the history of Reformed church music, which never again, in any country, played so direct and valid a part in the general development of music. The embattled position in 16th-century France of the young Calvinist movement forced the development of its resources and was undoubtedly the primary reason in the history of Calvinist polyphony for the episodic character of this period, which lasted a little more than half a century. At the same time, the exclusion of all polyphony and instrumental music from the service limited the participation of Reformed church music in the subsequent general development of music; the dawn of the age of the thoroughbass—with its gradual replacement of the motet by the sacred concerto and later on the cantata, and with its increasing shift of emphasis to instrumental music—forced purist, strict Calvinism and church music to travel separate ways.

However, in the years that followed, primarily because of the extraordinary influence of the Genevan Psalter, a definite reversal of this development took place in the remaining Reformed territories of Europe. As early as the 16th century or the beginning of the 17th, the work of Marot and Beza was translated into Dutch (1566), German (see below), English (completed in 1592), Italian, and Hungarian (in the course of time, into a total of 22 languages); together with the Geneva tunes it was introduced, sooner or later officially, into all the Calvinistic regions of Europe—at times, if not quite officially, even into non-Reformed areas.

130. Jan Jacob van Eyk, *Der Fluiten Lusthof*, Amsterdam, 1646, Paulus Matthyszoon. Title page.

131. *Music-Gesellschaft ab dem Music-Saal auf der Teutschen Schul in Zürich.* Engraving by Johann Melchior Füssli, 1713.

Germany and Switzerland

In Germany, Ambrosius Lobwasser, the Lutheran law scholar of Königsberg, translated the Genevan Psalter in 1565, motivated probably as much by humanistic as by religious considerations. While he strictly preserved the original verse form, for the translation itself he used other models too, in the main probably M. Butzer's psalm translations. As far as is known at present, the Lobwasser Psalter was probably published first in 1572 at Danzig and afterward, in 1573, at Leipzig, together with the Goudimel homophonic settings of 1565 (see also p. 134).

Lobwasser was interested not only in the creation of a German rhyming Psalter but evidently also in the widespread acceptance of French melodies and their transcriptions by Goudimel. During the first decades of the Reformation the German regions under Reformed influence took their guidance from the historic development of the Strasbourg and Constance songbooks. The Bonn songbook of 1550 and later (an earlier edition was probably published in 1544; 27 editions can be traced up to 1630) achieved a position of particular influence and served in turn as a point of departure for the very important songbooks of western and southern Germany in the 16th century, among them the 1567 Reformed songbook of the Palatinate. This influence evolved from the general importance of the Cologne Reformation under the Elector and Archbishop Hermann von Wied and with the collaboration of M. Butzer. It has not yet been determined whether the latter participated in the creation of the Bonn songbook or whether it was his son-in-law, Christoph Söll.

Lobwasser's poems were not, however, the only German psalm lieder written to the Geneva tunes. In 1572 Paul Schede (Melissus) published in Heidelberg the first 50 psalms in four-part settings with a tenor cantus firmus. In 1588 Philipp (the Younger) von Winnenbergh published in Begelstein four-part psalms "auf die französischen Reimen und Art gestellt" with the melody in the top voice. In 1617 (2nd ed., 1621) there followed in Rothenburg on the Tauber *Der Lutherisch Lobwasser. Das ist der ganz Psalter Davids, auf Christum den rechten Scopum oder Zweck der Heiligen Göttlichen Schrift . . . gerichtet von Johann Wuestholtz* (the title of the unison edition with the Geneva tunes indicates that this was meant as a partial improvement of the Lobwasser texts), and even Martin Opitz, with his *Psalmen Davids nach den französischen Weisen gesetzt;* following his lead, Landgrave Ludwig of Hesse, with *Der Psalter Davids in teutsche Reime der Opitianischen Art gemäss verfasset* (Giessen, 1637); and finally the *Neun Psalmen Davids . . . auf französische Melodeyen gerichtet* by Hans von Bonneck (Glückstadt, 1639). None of these works succeeded, however, in replacing Lobwasser's rhyming Psalter or even in diminishing its circulation.

The equivalent of the Genevan Psalter on the Catholic front was the complete rhyming Psalter by Kaspar Ulenberg, published with 81 melodies of his own at Cologne in 1582. In their melodic forms, particularly in their rhythmic models, and by their frequent kinship to the Geneva tunes (three of which were even incorporated without change in the 1603 edition), the connection becomes clearly evident. Nevertheless, in spite of repeated polyphonic settings (by Orlando and Rudolf di Lasso, Sigerus Pauli, and Conrad Hagius), the Ulenberg Psalter did not attain anything like the dissemination the Genevan Psalter enjoyed in the most diversified language regions (see the new edition by J. Overath of the complete work, Düsseldorf, 1955, and his *Untersuchungen über die Melodien des Liedpsalters von Kaspar Ulenberg* [*Cologne, 1582*], Cologne, 1960: also S. Fornaçon, *Kaspar Ulenberg und Konrad von Hagen,* in *Die Musikforschung* IX, 1956, 206 ff.).

Undoubtedly the Lobwasser Psalter was first officially adopted in the Reformed Palatinate. The first Heidelberg edition was published as early as 1574. Then the Calvinist Count Johann the Elder of Nassau-Dillenburg had it printed for the territory in his spiritual jurisdiction with the unison Geneva tunes; this edition was published by Matthäus Harnisch in the Palatine town of Neustadt on the Hardt, probably first in 1583. It is likely that the first publications in Amberg in the Upper Palatinate, which then was part of the Electoral state, are from this period. In 1586 began the great number of Herborn printings (approximately 40 up to 1694) on which the Reformed songbooks of the Lower Rhine region are based. While the Neustadt prints were exclusively in unison, the Goudimel polyphonic settings appear with increasing frequency later on; this is particularly true of the Herborn prints of the 17th century. It is therefore evident that in Germany, too, the four-part Lobwasser-Goudimel Psalter had a much larger circulation than any other polyphonic psalm-lied collection, even some of the Lutheran songbooks.

The Lobwasser Psalter had been preceded in the 16th century by three polyphonic settings of a complete rhyming Psalter that owed their existence directly or indirectly to Reformed influences: the four- and five-part settings (preserved in manuscript in the Kassel *Landesbibliothek;* of the 156 settings, only 15 are five-part), made between 1555 and 1570 by the Kassel court *Kapellmeister* Johannes Heugel, of the Psalter of Burkhard Waldis (see p. 515); the *Psalter Davids* by Sigmund Hemmel (probably completed during the last years of his life between 1561 and 1564 but first published posthumously in 1569, for the court services in Stuttgart; it is documented that this collection was also in use in the monastic schools of Württemberg and at the courts of Hesse and Saxony); and, finally, the two editions, destined for the churches and schools of Strasbourg, containing four-part *Psalmen* by Daniel Wolckenstein (1577 and 1583, with 50 and 64 settings respectively). In all three collections the cantus firmus is almost exclusively in the tenor. Heugel used the melodies by Waldis, while Hemmel and Wolckenstein used south-German (Hemmel also in a few cases Wittenberg) melodic material. The part writing of Heugel and Hemmel still carries a polyphonic-figural stamp, though homophonic tendencies are evident. On the other hand, the title of Wolckenstein's second edition states explicitly: *Psalmen für Kirche und Schulen auf die gemeinen Melodien syllaben weiss zu vier Stimmen gesetzt,* which means, if one disregards the Lobwasser-Goudimel Psalter, that this is the first original German homophonic Cantionale (see p. 134).

The development in Reformed German territories after the infiltration of the Lobwasser Psalter differs in two respects from that in the cradle of Calvinism.

Hardly anywhere—and then only in passing—did the Lobwasser Psalter acquire the exclusive importance accorded the Genevan Psalter in the French-speaking regions. From this time the Reformed hymnals on every side include sections with German, sometimes even Lutheran, songs, and by no means everywhere was polyphony excluded from the service as consistently as in those regions. The Palatinate probably came closest to the Geneva model. There the Elector Friedrich III (1559–76) introduced Calvinism in all its strictness and his church regulations served as the model for all Reformed regions of Germany. Under his reign the Heidelberg Catechism was created, as, closely fashioned after Geneva, was the Palatine service order of 1563; all other Calvinist regulations in Germany depend on these to some extent. Naturally, then, in Reformed Germany too, the only form of church music at first was, in general, unison, unaccompanied congregational singing.

The Palatine Elector proceeded with particular strictness. He abolished the singing choir that had existed in Heidelberg and ordered that the "Neckar pupils" report to the precentor only to reinforce congregational singing. He himself used to sing psalms before and after meals with his wife and, in the presence of guests, even had them performed as dinner music by his military band. Still to be clarified in detail is the extent to which polyphonic versions of the Genevan Psalter were used outside the service in German Reformed territories prior to 1600. A translation of Lobwasser's poems into Latin by Andreas Speth, published at Heidelberg in 1596 in connection with the four-part Goudimel settings as "exercitium Scholasticae iuventuti matutinum et vespertinum" (see p. 145 f.), should be noted. Certainly also designed for pedagogical purposes were the verses of the Electoral court doctor Johannes Posthius, *Die Sonntags-Evangelia gesangsweise komponiert* (published posthumously at Amberg, 1608), to be sung in four parts following the Lobwasser-Goudimel Psalter. The reprint of this collection, likewise in four parts, in a songbook of Neustadt on the Hardt in 1619 does not, however, entirely preclude their use at the service, at least later on.

Conditions at the court of the Landgrave in Kassel under Moritz of Hesse were quite different at the turn of the century. This country, originally reformed under Butzer's influence, had combined within itself south-German and Lutheran elements; Landgrave Moritz first led it toward a strongly marked Reformed faith —in, however, a restricted (the so-called Lower Hessian) form, which preserved a certain independence from Calvinism, especially in matters of church music (see p. 146 ff.).

The first Kassel edition of the Lobwasser Psalter, to be used in conjunction with the previously available song repertory, was published in 1607; it was followed in 1612 by an additional songbook, containing in its first part the traditional— i.e., Wittenberg and south-German—song repertory of the unison edition of 1601 and in its second part the Lobwasser Psalter. In the 1607 Psalter, Landgrave Moritz had supplied new melodies and four-part homophonic settings (with tenor cantus firmus) for all but two of the psalms in the Genevan Psalter that did not have their own tunes, thus eliminating the settings by Goudimel; he also made four-part settings of the entire 1612 songbook. This edition in two sections subsequently attained several additional printings and remained in use throughout the 17th century. In his melodies Landgrave Moritz generally held strictly

to the guiding principles of the Geneva psalm tunes, right down to the indication
of rests; most of all, he followed the typical Geneva rhythms. Thus, his tune with
the rhythmic pattern   ♩ ♩ ♩ ♩ ♩ ♩ ♩   today used for *Gesegn uns, Herr, die
Gaben dein* (*Evangelisches Kirchengesangbuch* 374), goes back in all four lines
directly to the Geneva model (see p. 528; incidentally, this pattern also occurs
in Heinrich Schütz's Becker Psalter and in a number of other melodies originating
in Geneva). Landgrave Moritz's polyphonic settings, in accordance with the
practice of the time, owe more to functional harmony than do Goudimel's, just
as his tunes, without conflicting stylistically with their melodic sources, show no
elements of the church modes. Remarkably, the preface to the Kassel Psalter
states that the most important thing in singing is not the music but making the
words understandable; on the other hand, the title states that these settings "can
not only be sung but can also be played on all kinds of instruments," a suggestion
certainly intended to apply even to divine services. In any case, the fact that
Landgrave Moritz embraced Calvinism did not mean the end of contrapuntal
music at the court in Kassel, as is shown by the history of the court chapel. In
isolated cases Geneva tunes with Lobwasser texts were arranged polyphonically
—for example, in two versions of Psalm 95, 1–2 (two- and three-part settings
with thoroughbass) and Psalm 130 (two-part with thoroughbass). Both works,
anonymous, are preserved in the Kassel *Landesbibliothek,* which also has the
eight-part setting of Psalm 128 for double chorus by Michael Praetorius; this was
included in the second part of his *Musae Sioniae* (1607) with three additional
polychoral arrangements of Geneva melodies combined with Lobwasser texts
(Psalms 13, 42, 77, or 86). Praetorius undoubtedly received his inspiration for
these pieces from his visits to Kassel in 1605 and 1609. Altogether Praetorius left
twenty-one arrangements of Lobwasser psalms, all but one for double chorus, in
almost all instances making motivic use of Geneva melodies. Significantly, ten of
these, almost half, are contained in the section of *Musae Sioniae* dedicated to the
Palatine Elector Friedrich—the fourth part (1607). It is therefore to be assumed
that at the court of Heidelberg too contrapuntal music at the service was permissible at that time. The practice of including the congregation even in choral singing
(which, of course, required a corresponding reworking of those compositions,
with the cantus firmi shifted to the uppermost voice) was probably the result of
the stronger activation of the congregation in Reformed territories, and apparently a specialty in Kassel. Praetorius mentions it in the *Introductio pro cantore*
of his *Urania* (1613), which uses the Kassel experiences as a model. The employment of instruments during the service at the Kassel court is not an isolated case.
It is attested that the lutenist Daniel Zöllner accompanied the singing of the
Königsberg congregation, which was firmly unified under the Reform banner not
later than 1615.

In the county of Nassau-Dillenburg, with its capital and university of Herborn,
the Herborn songbook of 1618 (reprinted in 1634), arranged in four-part settings
by Bartholomäus Schümler, did not achieve much importance because of the
predominance of the Goudimel settings. There are even signs that these latter
were used in congregational singing, a case almost unique in Reformed Germany.
Of interest in the Herborn songbook is the method of setting German songs after

the Geneva models, a method also used by others (for instance, by Landgrave Moritz of Hesse).

Setting: B. Schümler (1618)

In Berlin, Johann Crüger was commissioned by the Reformed Elector Friedrich Wilhelm of Brandenburg to make a new, polyphonic arrangement of the Lobwasser Psalter, together with the customary second part containing additional Protestant songs; this resulted in his *Psalmodia sacra* of 1657–58 (see p. 242). The work shows that Reformed service music in Germany did not remain untouched by thoroughbass practices; Crüger added two to four instruments (violins or cornets) and an optional continuo part to the four-part cantional settings. Manuscript copies of some of these instrumental parts, lost in the 19th century with the exception of those for one setting (see C. von Winterfeld, *Der evangelische Kirchengesang* II, musical supplement, No. 93), were recently discovered in the Berlin State Library in the estate of von Winterfeld.

In 1663 the Schaffhausen cantor Johann Kaspar Suter brought out an edition —again in four parts—of the *Psalmodia sacra* without the accompanying instrumental parts but augmented by five-part intradas, also probably written by Crüger in continuation of the 1657–58 work. In 1700 another reprint of the chorale settings with thoroughbass was published in Berlin. How strongly the Berlin cantor was influenced by the French melodies is evident from his own work, which shows clearly melodic as well as rhythmic influences from Geneva.

Worthy of note is Crüger's repeated use of leaps of a fourth or his roving through the interval of a fourth, known to him, for example, from the Geneva tune to Psalm 118; the rhythmic reference to the French model occurs in the same connection. Of very special significance is the rhythmic formation of the first and

a. Genevan Psalter, Psalm 118 (after Psalm 66), G. Franc (?), 1543

b. Johann Crüger 1653: *Sei Lob und Ehr dem höchsten Gut*

c. Johann Crüger 1653: *Nun danket all und bringet Ehr*

third lines in Crüger's melody for *Nun danket all und bringet Ehr*, which coincides precisely with the Strasbourg rhythmic model ♩ ♩ ♩ ♩ ♩ ♩ ♩ ♩ (see p. 523) so typical of Geneva and undoubtedly dating back to Dachstein. Tunes such as *Herzliebster Jesu, was hast du verbrochen* and *Schmücke dich, o liebe Seele* also exude the spirit of the Genevan Psalter in every rhythmic and harmonic respect.

That Landgrave Moritz and Crüger were not alone in depending for their melodic material on the Genevan Psalter is shown furthermore by some of the tunes created or edited by Bartholomäus Gesius, particularly the rhythmic form of *Machs mit mir, Gott, nach deiner Güt* and of *Befiehl du deine Wege*, which takes its melodic departure from Psalm 128. Nikolaus Selnecker's *Nun lasst Gott dem Herren* and the anonymous *Herr Jesu Christ, dich zu uns wend* (see p. 529) are also fashioned after Geneva rhythmic models and, melodically, Melchior Teschner's *Valet will ich dir geben* comes from Psalm 3.

Reformed church music in Germany can hardly be called memorable or original. It played no part whatever in the history of the motet, the sacred concerto, the cantata, or the oratorio. Nevertheless, the wider dissemination in Germany of the Genevan Psalter in its monophonic or polyphonic versions, beginning in the last third of the 16th century, and its influence on the history of the hymnal in general, had a certain significance for the overall development of Protestant church music in Germany, as we have seen in connection with Moritz of Hesse, Praetorius, and Crüger. The Calvinist influence frequently reached into Lutheran regions also. Here the fact that the German nobility frequently sent its sons to France to fight in the ranks of the Huguenots, in the period between 1550 and 1618, played an essential part. Some of these soldiers were deeply impressed by the psalm singing and afterward helped to spread the Genevan Psalter in their homeland.

Several Reformed melodies were soon generally accepted by the entire German Protestant community; foremost among these are the melody for Psalm 42, particularly in connection with the text of *Freu dich sehr, o meine Seele*, and the one for Psalm 140 or the Ten Commandments, as a new tune for Paul Eber's *Wenn wir in höchsten Nöten sein*. That it was also possible to transfer a whole group of Lobwasser psalms into Lutheran songbooks was shown not only by Samuel Besler's four-part *Concentus Ecclesiastico-domesticus* (Breslau, 1618), in which several Geneva melodies were incorporated, but particularly in Weickersheim on the Tauber, a Hohenlohe territory, where Joachim Widmann incorporated nineteen Geneva tunes, in the homophonic Goudimel settings, in his four-part *Geistliche Psalmen und Lieder* of 1604, in most instances, however, exchanging tenor and discant. Among his reasons for editing this songbook he gives this one: "So that those who understand and have pleasure in music may sing in church, one this voice, another one that voice, of the commonly known chorale from this little book. Which then provides a particular charm and loveliness when all four voices may thus be heard in church and again in different places." We do not know whether Widmann's hopes were fulfilled. However, his songbook achieved a certain importance at that time and in its milieu. Johann Jeep, who succeeded him in his position and who from 1640 on spent the last years of his life as *Kapellmeister* at the Reformed court of the Count of Hanau, where he was also organist at the Reformed *Marienkirche,* in 1629 made a new edition containing 24 Geneva tunes. Still another one was edited in 1639 by Widmann's pupil Sebastian Stüx in Rothenburg on the Tauber when he was cantor there.

It is certainly due to the use of the Geneva tunes by the Reformed court congregation of Königsberg (see above) that about 1600 and after composers in East Prussia, mainly those working in Königsberg itself, employed these melodies in their works; Johannes Eccard and Heinrich Albert, for example, used them occasionally, Johann Stobäus more frequently. In Danzig, Paul Siefert, who was organist there, published in two sections *Psalmen Davids nach französischer Melodey oder Weise in Music komponiert* (the title of the second section is in Latin); section 1 (1640) contained 12 four- to five-part psalms, section 2 (1651), 28 four- to eight-part psalms and introductory symphonies, both sections with Latin and German text. The stimulus for this work is less likely to have come from neighboring Königsberg than from Siefert's apprenticeship in Amsterdam with J. P. Sweelinck. In Muskau (Lusatia) and in Bytom in Upper Silesia, Johann Georg von Schönaich had already introduced the Genevan Psalter toward the end of the 16th century; thus Bartholomäus Gesius, who was in his service for some time, came into closer contact with it, as may be seen in his melodic creations mentioned above.

Martin Jahn, while cantor of the Reformed congregation at the Piast court of Wohlau (Silesia), after 1663 wrote a four- to five-part arrangement of the Genevan Psalter which, unfortunately, is lost. Martin Hanke of Brzeg, in his *Geistliche Gesänge über die Evangelia und alle Sonn-, Hohe Fest- und Feiertage durchs ganze Jahr* (1612 and 1617), with two exceptions used Geneva tunes exclusively, altogether 67 of them, with the homophonic Goudimel settings. Martin Opitz, in addition to translating the Genevan Psalter, wrote the poems for *Die Episteln der Sonntage und führnehmsten Feste des gantzen Jahres* (altogether at least ten printings from 1624 till about 1700) also fitted to the Geneva tunes. In 1656 Johann Hildebrandt, organist in Eilenburg, published at Leipzig 50 songs in four-part settings, among them Opitz's psalms with the Geneva tunes, in addition to those by Becker with melodies by Heinrich Schütz.

Reformed church music also had a certain, if modest, share in the creation of organ music. Extreme measures against the organ were taken only in territories that had adopted the Reformed doctrine very early, as in the Palatinate, where organs were for some time completely silenced, and in East Frisia, where some organs were even dismantled (as late as 1556). Nevertheless, after 1577 the Groningen organ-builder Andreas de Mare was active in Emden. From 1577 on a certain Paul Hansen Knop, closely following the Dutch example, "on the feast days had to serve at the organ as much as possible with Christian music and other instruments suitable for it"; and a Bremen ordinance of 1594 states: "The organ is not to be used with the singing or at the service but only before nine o'clock on Sundays, when the people gather, and then again later when they leave the church." Around the same time organ arrangements of Geneva tunes make their appearance in manuscript (Berlin MS 40 115, dated 1593) as well as in print (E. N. Ammerbach), and a great number of later arrangements have been preserved in the numerous organ tablatures in the collection of Count Lynar in Lübbenau

(Spree), later in Spandau (see p. 249). The Lübbenau MS Ly B 2, dating from about 1620 to 1640, contains three anonymous sets of variations on the Geneva tunes for Psalms 23, 60, and 116, the last one possibly the work of Sweelinck. Paul Siefert, Sweelinck's pupil and, as has been documented, a composer of organ psalms, may also be represented in this manuscript as well as in the similarly anonymous Lübbenau MS Ly B 7 (about 1640) by five sets of variations on Psalms 5, 24, 66, 100, and 116. The Lübbenau MS Ly C (probably first third of the 17th century) even contains an intabulation of the complete Genevan Psalter in four-part homophonic settings; its arranger has not been identified.

That the Genevan Psalter finally reached the German-speaking regions of Switzerland also, via the long detour through Königsberg and Leipzig, is a musicological oddity, which can be explained, however, by the priority of the Lobwasser translation over any other complete German translation of the Marot-Beza poems. Despite the lateness of this event, it meant the beginning of a new phase in the development of Reformed church music in Switzerland. After this the Lobwasser Psalter gave the German-Swiss church song its character. To be sure, it did not entirely replace the "alten" (old) and "gemeinen" (commonly known) psalms, i.e., the song repertory of the past; but that repertory was, from now on, used only on holidays and at auxiliary services. In the hymnals of the 17th century, from this time on, the Lobwasser Psalter appeared as the first section; altogether, according to E. Nievergelt, 66 prints from this period can be traced. This meant that sacred polyphony had now begun to enter Reformed northern Switzerland. The first Swiss Lobwasser editions (Zurich, 1598, with all the psalms; Bern, 1606, and Basel, 1613, with 24 each) were still all unison versions. The St. Gallen songbook of 1606, however, already contained a few Goudimel arrangements. The four-part congregational songbook became more and more the rule; Zurich followed, beginning in 1636, Bern in 1676, Schaffhausen in 1680, and the Rhaeto-Romanic regions in 1683, while Basel again went its own way (see below). The Goudimel settings used were almost exclusively those of the Jaqui Psalter. They were accepted so eagerly that their use, at first limited to school and home, led gradually to four-part congregational singing, which eventually was rehearsed in special congregational singing sessions. It was a unique event in the history of Christian congregational singing and of church music, in striking contrast to the enduring difficulties faced in congregational singing by the otherwise so musically inclined German Lutheranism of the time. It has its deepest roots in the congregational structure of the Reformed communities, which allowed the individual more active participation, a development probably encouraged by Swiss democratic tendencies. With respect to its artistic importance and its unfolding, service music in Reformed German-speaking Switzerland in the 17th and 18th centuries cannot be compared with that of Lutheranism during the same period; but instead of creating a deep reaction it generated a broad reaction, positively unique, which lasted for centuries. Without it the work of H. G. Nägeli, at the beginning of the 19th century, would be inconceivable. Probably the last edition of the four-part Lobwasser Psalter was published at Zurich in 1824.

Johann Friedrich Reichardt's remarks in his *Musikalisches Kunstmagazin* of

1791 (vol. II, no. 5, p. 16) constitute a testimonial of documentary significance; under the heading Church Music in Zurich he writes: "I have never been more moved by anything than by the four-part church singing here. The whole congregation sings the psalm melodies, to which the Reformed are accustomed, in four parts from the music printed in the songbooks with the verses. Girls and boys sing the discant, adults the alto, and the older and old men the tenor and the bass. . . . Frequently when I searched among the peasants in the field or in inns for old, genuine folk songs I heard four-part psalms. He who is familiar only with our unison church singing, usually off-pitch screaming, can scarcely imagine the dignity and power of such four-part church singing by many hundreds of people of all ages." Beginning with the 17th century the enthusiasm for the Lobwasser-Goudimel Psalter was so great that older song material was also included in the songbooks in four-part settings. The most important arrangers were Jakob Altherr, who edited the 1606 and 1627 versions of the St. Gallen songbook, and Johann Ulrich Sultzberger, editor of the four Bern songbooks (1680 to 1697; see p. 562). The editorial work in Zurich was probably done by a certain W. Schwilge (in this case, too, some of the most important Lutheran hymns were rewritten after rhythmic models from the Genevan Psalter). As time went on, the Goudimel settings, in view of their use for congregational singing, underwent certain simplifications. Most important, only homophonic settings were used; in accordance with the taste of the time leading tones were inserted, little embellishments omitted, and the range of the alto part reduced. Sultzberger put all the melodies into the tenor part, including those of the seventeen Goudimel settings with discant cantus firmus. In six instances this was done by simply exchanging voices.

Basel once again went its own way. Here Samuel Mareschall published the Lobwasser Psalter based on Goudimel in 1606, a second printing in 1639 (an edition that had already been printed in Leipzig in 1594 is lost); he put the melody in the top voice throughout, and there is no question that he took as a model the German type of cantional setting by Osiander (see p. 135 f.). He explained his method thus: "I have learned through long experience that this category, in which the common voice . . . is set in the tenor, is not suitable for the type of singing practiced in our churches with the participation of the entire congregation" (preface of the 1606 edition). Mareschall's settings were therefore sung by the choir during the service at the same time the congregation was singing in unison (polyphonic congregational singing did not put down roots in Basel). Interestingly, Sultzberger justified his contrary procedure (see above) with these words: "Because the singing of a congregation is led by one man, and that is a tenor voice."

Mareschall's settings, which include songs carried over from the 16th century and retained in great numbers in the second section of the Basel songbooks, are artistically not very ambitious as a whole, but they belong to the best material of its kind in 17th-century German Switzerland. As has been mentioned, Mareschall, about 1594, had initiated the series of polyphonic songbooks in German Reformed Switzerland with a collection that was evidently not printed and has disappeared. He was also the author of a school work, created entirely in the spirit of Humanism: *Melodiae suaves et concinnae Psalmorum aliquot atque Hymnorum*

Spiritualium, collectae accompositae, in usum classis octavae et nonae Gymnasii Basiliensis, containing six four-part Latin psalms written to Horatian verse meters (see p. 146) and three hymn settings. With their rhythmic embellishments and introduction of passing tones in the subordinate voices, most of them are more appealing than those of his contemporaries. Nevertheless, they achieved only local significance. Even after Mareschall's death the Goudimel settings found no acceptance in Basel and were never published there. Instead, Johann Jakob Wolleb, Mareschall's successor as organist of the Basel cathedral, published in 1660 a revised version of his predecessor's work. Interestingly enough, only a year before that he had brought out an edition of the homophonic psalm settings by Claude le Jeune (see p. 542) with Lobwasser texts, followed in a second section by no less than 116 additional song settings, all, like those of the first section, with tenor cantus firmus. This work, considered the most important Swiss songbook of the 17th century, owed its existence to a private commission by the linen manufacturers H. and B. Gonzenbach in St. Gallen; it did not win a place of importance in the church music of Basel, but certainly did so in eastern Switzerland, particularly the Upper Engadine.

In the Engadine polyphonic religious folk singing, which was carried on into the 19th century by a special choral school, the so-called *Chant,* developed during the second half of the 17th century to a unique degree compared to the development in all other Reformed congregations of northern Switzerland. Here more than anywhere else members of the congregation, meeting regularly at services, cultivated polyphonic singing. The Gonzenbach songbook with the settings by Le Jeune, which was first circulated in the Engadine in manuscript partbooks with new text insertions, was reprinted in 1733 in Strada with the Romanic psalm texts by Lurainz Wietzel. In eastern Switzerland four-part congregational singing was practiced earlier, therefore mostly with the Le Jeune Psalter, but also—and this is almost inconceivable—sometimes even with mastery of Sweelinck's motets on rhyming psalms. The State Archives of Chur have preserved a large number of carefully written parts that give a vivid impression of the amazing activity of congregational choirs in the Engadine, particularly in the 17th and 18th centuries. Two additional 18th-century Rhaeto-Romanic songbooks are known, the *Canzuns spirituales . . . ,* published about 1764, and the *Testimoniaunza dall' amur stupenda da Gesu Cristo . . .* of 1789, both with old and new song and melody material. The earlier edition contains 37 four-part, 89 three-part, and 38 two-part settings, the later one 45 four-part, 106 three-part, and 12 two-part settings. The connection of these publications with the German songbooks of northern Switzerland in the 18th century, indicated by the prevailing three-part settings, should be investigated. Giovanni Frizzoni is named as poet of the new songs.

Along with the schools, where daily practice in psalm singing following the morning and afternoon lessons was frequently decreed, the Collegia Musica played an important part in the cultivation of psalm singing, using especially the Lobwasser-Goudimel Psalter. To a large extent the Collegia owed their formation to this, and it also provided in the beginning the basis for their activities. They were therefore frequently called *Singgesellschaften* (singing societies). The first Collegium Musicum was founded at Zurich in 1613; the most important ones to follow were St. Gallen (two different ones, 1620 and 1659), Schaffhausen (1655), Bern (1674 and 1687), and Basel (1692). There was a rule everywhere that the Collegium Musicum exercises, which took place on two weekday afternoons, sometimes more frequently, were to begin with two or three psalms and conclude with one. In addition, notwithstanding the function of the precentor, one of the main duties of a Collegium Musicum was to support congregational singing during the service. Its members were usually assigned a special location in the church, such as between the choir and the nave. In Winterthur a sort of rood-loft was especially erected for this purpose. Alternating singing between the congregation and the Collegium Musicum also took place here and there; as time passed, the Collegium even performed special song material (see below). In the beginning, the Collegia Musica consisted of no more than a dozen men, some of whom had to sing falsetto (see illustration on p. 548); at most, their number was augmented by a few boys. Their music making, though, in spite of its function at the service, was by no means limited to vocal music but encompassed, in addition to secular vocal and instrumental music, the entire abundance of (mainly) German sacred music of the age of Heinrich Schütz—that is, the period of transition from the motet to the sacred concerto. Several inventories still in existence give a vivid picture of this. The very interesting catalogues of St. Gallen (1649), Winterthur (around 1660), and Bern (1697) have been published by Karl Nef in *Die Collegia musica in der deutschen reformierten Schweiz . . .*, St. Gallen, 1897. Even if only a little of this large repertory was used for a long time thereafter in the Reformed service, it provided all the more religious music for the home, which also stimulated individual, though modest, creative efforts in German Reformed Switzerland during the 17th and 18th centuries.

First, there were the four-part settings of Johann Wilhelm Simler's *Teutsche Gedichte* by Andreas Schwilge and Kaspar Diebold (third printing, Zurich, 1663), which still have some relationship to the homophonic style of Goudimel's settings but initiate a new development by transferring the melody to the top voice and sometimes loosening the style of the setting by means of imitation; there was also the edition of Johann Crüger's *Psalmodia sacra* by Johann Kaspar Suter (Schaffhausen, 1663; see p. 553). Of special significance is the *Geistliche Seelenmusik, d.i. Geist- und Trostreiche Gesäng . . . Aus den besten Musikalischen Büchern dieser Zeit . . . samt einer kurzen Unterrichtung von der Musik und Singordnung für die christliche Gemeind und Schul* by Christian Huber (1682), published in choirbook format for four voices and containing 161 settings, a collection that took material from Johann Michael Dilherr's work of the same title, Simler's *Teutsche Gedichte*, Crüger's *Königliche Harpff*, W. C. Briegel's *Liederlust*, B. Musculus's *Cithara sacra*, D. Frederici's *Feliciae Juveniles*, and other works; it had nine printings up to 1755, each one augmented by new pieces. In 1662 Suter had already published a similar collection under the same title, which apparently was borrowed from a Nuremberg collection; its material, however, was taken from a smaller number of sources. The *Philomela* by Johannes Martinus also belongs in this category. As time passed, Pietism began to exert some influence on the contents of Huber's works: in the 1713 edition 16 songs by J. Neander were included. It is characteristic that, beginning with the 1664

STICHTELYKE
R Y M E N.
EERSTE DEEL.

Onnut' en fchadelyken Arbeyd.

(music notation)

Hou op die geyl gedicht of minne-
klachten maakt / En menig maagd'lyk hart zyn
reynigheyd ontfchaakt. Uw' zinnen is (als
rechts) om zinnen te verfraay- en: Maar wat
van zelver waft behoeft men niet te zaap- en.
2. Hou op / verweende honft / van malle Malery /
Het voedfel van qua'e luft en geilfche zotterny;
Het jong' en teere zyt bezet door onrufigfwaap- en; En

STICHTELYKE
R Y M E N,
Onderfcheyden in IV. Deelen.
Geftelt op Sleutels om te Zingen, en te Speelen
op allerhande Inftrumenten, door
JOZEPH BUTLER;
Vermeerdert met eenige nieuw gecomponeerde
Wyzen, door
M. M A T H I E U.
Geheel op Nooten.

Te A M S T E L D A M,
By KORNELIS vander SYS, Boekverkooper,
in de Beurs-ftraat, in de drie Raapen, 1727.
Met Privilegie.

132. Dirk Rafalsz Camphuysen, *Stichtelyke Rymen,* arranged by Jozeph Butler, with some new melodies added by Matthias Matthieu, Amsterdam, 1727, Kornelis van der Sys. Title page and opening of the lied *Hou op die geyl gedicht of minne-klachten maakt.*

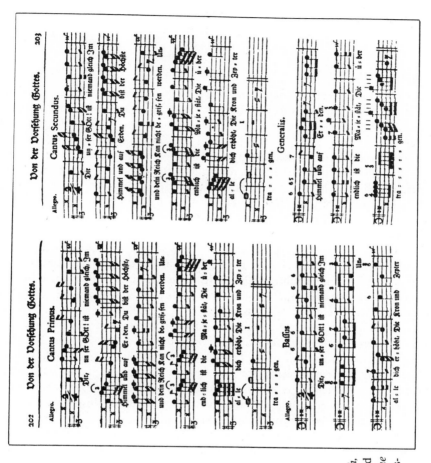

133. *Dir, unser Gott, ist niemand gleich,* three-voice lied for two sopranos, bass, and thoroughbass from J. Z. Gusto, *Auserlesene geistliche Lieder,* Zurich, 1769, Johann Kaspar Ziegler.

edition, short ritornellos for three to five string instruments were interspersed with the monophonic song tunes. They are by Rudolf Stähelin and show the connection with the early German lied. Canons were also included in later

R. Stähelin: *Geistliche Seelenmusik*, 1694. Ritornello for 2 violins, viola, and thoroughbass

editions. In the collections mentioned above the compositions of the Thuringian cantor Balthasar Musculus seem to have enjoyed the greatest popularity; through them even some lied motets—still, to be sure, homophonic—found their way into Switzerland.

Most characteristic for the development of polyphonic sacred music in northern Switzerland in the late 17th century, and the 18th, are mainly three-part works, usually for two high voices and a low one, products of the German lied-style tradition of the 17th century. They were meant principally, if perhaps not exclusively, as religious music for the home and became, in the course of time, an important entering wedge for Pietist devotional exercises.

Collections of this sort are: Johann Ulrich Sultzberger's *Dreigestimmter Zesischer Salomon* (Bern, 1674), containing, in addition to original pieces, two-part compositions by Johann Schop with a third voice added, to be performed by three male voices; the same composer's four-part *Transponiertes Psalmenbuch* (1708); Johann Ludwig Steiner's *Neues Gesangbuch . . . mit neuen und leichten, den Regeln der Composition gemässen, zu 3 und 4 Stimmen gesetzten Melodeyen und einem richtig-gezeichneten Generalbass versehen* (two parts, Zurich, 1723, and several additional printings up to 1735, a work that gave considerable space to the songs of G. Tersteegen); Johann Caspar Bachofen's distinctly Pietistic *Musikalisches Halleluja . . . mit neuen und anmutigen Melodeyen begleitet* (Zurich, 1727; contains monophonic pieces with thoroughbass, three-part pieces for two cantus and texted thoroughbass, and a number of canons; 11 printings to 1803, the fourth, of 1743, for example, containing 379 three-part pieces and 200 arias with thoroughbass); Caspar Zollikofer's *Gebät-Music* (St. Gallen, 1738, in two to five parts with thoroughbass); the *Erbauliche Musicalische Christenschatz,* with music arranged by Johann Thommen (Basel, 1745, in one to five parts with thoroughbass); an extension of H. d'Annoni's *Erbaulicher Christenschatz,* the most important Swiss poetry of that period (seven printings from 1739 to 1777) typically using Moravian and Cöthen melodies (see p. 577); Johann Schmidlin's *Singendes und spielendes Vergnügen reiner Andacht . . . zur Erweckung des inneren Christentums eingerichtet* (Zurich, 1752; in addition to many monophonic songs with thoroughbass, a number of three-part pieces; five printings up to 1792); also by Schmidlin, *Hymni oder Lobgesänge auf Gott zu drei und vier Stimmen . . . mit Generalbass* (Zurich, 1798); and Johann Z. Gusto's *Auserlesene geistliche Lieder . . . mit ganz neuen leichten Liedern versehen* with a preface by J. C. Lavater (Zurich, 1769, see illustration on p. 561). In all of these works the elimination of the absolutism of the four-part setting indicated an increasing tendency toward a solo lied style with a more distinct melodic line than was proper to a Reformed hymn. This tendency also made itself felt in monophonic thoroughbass songs by these same composers and by others. As early as in the

third printing of Chr. Huber's *Seelenmusik* the indication "Aria, voce sola" appears, a form particularly cultivated by the Basel cantors Johann Jakob Pfaff and Johann Thommen. The next step, from the aria with ritornello to the cantata,

was taken only to a very limited degree in Reformed Switzerland. To be mentioned here are the *Musikalische Stücke über das Hohe Lied Salomonis* by Joh. Jakob Pfaff, a through-composed lied in three strophes with changing distribution of the voices and with an instrumental frame, as well as the three Passion Devotions by Heinrich Kyburtz (1712), similarly organized.

Further development in the direction of the art song was made impossible by the nature of the Reformed service. Trends toward solo and concertante forms were possible at all in northern Switzerland only because of the influence of Pietist expressivity—and later of the Enlightenment—on a Reform that was already perceptibly weaker. All the works listed here cling to the same qualities of folk appeal and accessibility. They do not represent great art. No wonder that they pushed the prim Lobwasser Psalter out of its position of absolute predominance. In the preface mentioned above, Lavater spoke out against too much psalm singing and welcomed the fact that not all the psalms were included in the Bern songbook of 1766.

One can scarcely speak of a history of organ music in German Reformed Switzerland in the 16th to 18th centuries. After the organs were excluded from the service during the Reformation, or were actually destroyed, their reinstallation or rebuilding began very gradually in the second half of the 17th century; in certain localities congregational singing had been accompanied earlier—in Bern since 1581 (see p. 516)—by cornetists and trombonists (according to M. Jenny, by oboists). In 1663 the cantor H. R. Bitzius petitioned the Bern City Council, without success, to permit the rebuilding of the organ; it was not rebuilt until 1731, when a three-manual instrument with 38 stops was constructed. During the same year the accompaniment of congregational singing was introduced, following the example of other towns—for instance, Burgdorf in 1725. But the time was still not ripe in many places, among which Zurich was especially prominent. On the other hand, very remote communities such as Zerneg and Thur long preceded Bern by building organs in 1609 and 1613; this, does not mean, however, that accompanied congregational singing was introduced every-where. Basel is the only city with a continuous history of organ playing (on the preservation of the organs there during the Reformation, see p. 516). The activities of Gregor Meyer, the first Reformed organist in Basel, were followed by those of Samuel Mareschall until approximately 1641. There is a manuscript tablature by Daniel Hofer (c. 1630) with textual incipits from the Lobwasser Psalter on Geneva tunes (Basel University Library F IX 52); otherwise, Mareschall, with four manuscript tablatures (in the same place, F IX 47–50), is the only organ master of Protestant northern Switzerland in the entire epoch in question who has left any tangible product. Two of his tablatures take their departure from his Lobwasser transcriptions of 1606 and contain, respectively, 35 and 109 psalm arrangements in the manner of the 16th-century colorists with a cantus firmus that is embellished but is nevertheless kept, clearly recognizable, in the upper voice (1638 and 1640). The two additional tablature books (1639 and 1640) contain (according to G. Frotscher) mainly embellished choral songs, most of them by Lasso; the last book also includes a series "of very short 'fugues' with lively ornamentation—i.e., prelude-like pieces on the twelve tones after Italian models" (Frotscher). Such use as was made of Mareschall's psalm arrangements at the service could only have been in the form of preludes, interludes, and postludes; accompaniment for congregational singing certainly did not yet exist in Basel at that time. The names of several other organists of the Basel cathedral —Jakob Wolleb, Thomas Pfleger (until 1677), Johann Jakob Pfaff (until 1729), and Christoph Gengenbach, father and son (until 1795)—have been mentioned in other connections (see p. 557 f.); apparently none of them left any compositions for the organ. The same applies to the organists in Bern who had returned to office in 1730 (their names can be found in the *Schweizer Musikbuch*, p. 328), and to all others in Reformed northern Switzerland of the period.

The Netherlands

Protestant church music in the Netherlands is connected in its early stage with the so-called *Souterliedekens,* of which a monophonic edition (1540 and later) is attributed to the aristocrat Willem van Niewelt of Utrecht. In this region Lutheranism first found admission in the 1520s, but since all reformative attempts were subject to persecution from their beginnings, the movement of the radical Anabaptists very soon gathered momentum. The catastrophe, however, that befell them through the siege and capture of the city of Münster, the center of Anabaptism in western Germany, also brought the Netherlands Anabaptists to a violent end. From then on a renewed Reform movement developed quietly; the *Souterliedekens,* following the principle of singing rhyming psalms to well-known folk tunes, served well as a screen for this activity.

W. van Niewelt: *Souterliedekens* (1540), Psalm 65

The word "souter" came from "psouter" (psalm). The occasion for the creation of the *Souterliedekens* is not known: their origin evidently has no direct connection with the Reformation; otherwise, they would hardly have been published under an imperial imprimatur. Incidentally, they are based on the Vulgate, not on the original Hebrew text. Attempts to translate psalms into the vernacular can be traced in the Netherlands as far bask as the end of the 15th century. This phenomenon clearly paralleled corresponding events in France on the eve of the Reformation (see p. 518). Possibly the *Souterliedekens* were created, like earlier similar songs, in an endeavor by certain pre-Reform circles, or circles close to the Reformation such as the Brethren of the Common Life, to remove the amoral texts from secular songs and to join the tunes to religious poetry. The preface to the *Souterliedekens* expresses this intention in obvious accord with Martin Luther's ideas.

After 1540 the Inquisition became more and more active. It was expressly reinstated at the end of the 1550s by Philip II after Charles V had turned the countries of the Burgundian heritage, to which the Netherlands belonged, over to the Spanish crown in 1555. At the same time, in these years around and after the middle of the century, the first Calvinist refugees immigrating from France were soon able, thanks to the preceding Reform attempts, to exert a strong influence. Under the leadership of Guy de Bray of Hainaut, who, after being expelled from his homeland in 1552, spent several years in Geneva and returned in 1559, the congregations were now "quietly organized after the Geneva model" (K. Müller). In 1561 Guy de Bray completed the new creed for the Netherlands, the *Confessio belgica,* and from approximately that time on secret synods began to meet. These developments resulted inevitably, because of the authority in Geneva, in a gradual repression of the *Souterliedekens,* although they were already being used during the service. Nevertheless, 33 editions were published up to 1613, including in 1556–57 a three-part arrangement published by Clemens non Papa.

Beginning as early as 1551 two Dutch editions, containing 10 and 25 Geneva psalm lieder respectively, had been published in London by the refugee Jan Utenhove for the refugee congregation there, followed in 1557 by an additional, though not enlarged, printing at Emden; in 1566 the Complete Psalter by Utenhove was published in England. Utenhove did not always assign to individual psalms the same melodies that had received in Geneva; for example, he combined Psalm 1 with the tune of the Ten Commandments lied, and Psalms 66 and 95, which had no tunes of their own in Geneva, with that of *Ein feste Burg*. Whereas for the Dutch congregation in London the completion of the Utenhove Psalter signified a changeover from the *Souterliedekens* as early as the 1550s, the Genevan Psalter was not introduced to the motherland until 1568, when a synod accepted it in a translation by Petrus Dathenus (final permission was granted in 1578 by the Dordrecht Synod).

Unlike the practice in Geneva, several versified songs were added here: there were not only the Ten Commandments and the canticle of Simeon but also the canticles of Mary and Zachary, the Lord's Prayer, Apostles' Creed, and even Luther's *Glaubenslied* (Song of Faith) in the translation by Utenhove. Other song translations by Utenhove were also continuously used, such as his *O Gott, die onse Vater bist,* frequently sung before the sermon. These different songs (according to H. R. Benthem's *Holländischer Kirchen- und Schulen Staat* of 1698) had likewise been approved by the Dordrecht Synod of 1609; only *Christe, die du bist dagh en Licht* (Utenhove after W. Meuslin) was banned at that time. In 1612 the separate group of the "Remonstrants" (a Calvinist sect that had come into existence because of a divergent view on the doctrine of predestination) tried to reintroduce eighty-five hymns of the old church. The collection was published in 1615 under the title *Hymnische Lofzangen* but was rejected by the Synod in 1618. For approximately two hundred years the Dathenus Psalter remained in general use in the Netherlands, whose northern provinces had become officially Calvinist through the War of Independence of 1571–72 while the southern provinces were brought back to the Catholic church. Several other psalm-lieder collections that made their appearance, such as the one by Lucas d'Heere of 1565 (after Marot) or *Het boeck der Psalmen unt de Hebreische spraeke . . .* by Marnix van St. Aldegonde (1580), could not diminish the circulation of the Dathenus Psalter. Dirk I. Balfoort in *Het muziekleven in Nederland in de 17de eeuw* (Amsterdam, 1938, p. 25) lists a series of additional rhyming Psalters from the 18th century. The Dathenus Psalter was also adopted probably as early as 1667 by Holland's neighbor East Frisia and kept in use there for approximately two hundred years.

The strict Geneva Calvinist standards for church music were also applied in the Netherlands. In the services there was at first only unison psalm singing by the congregation under the direction of a leader equipped with a "pikstok," a baton. There are very few examples of polyphonic settings of the Psalter in the Netherlands. The 50 psalm compositions by Cornelis Boscoop (1562) were, like those by Clemens non Papa, arrangements (in Clemens's case in motet form) of *Souterliedekens* (a new edition of the 1568 print is in vol. 22 of *Vereenigung voor Noord-Nederlands Muziekgeschiedenis,* Leipzig, 1899). Martin David Jan's *Psalmgezang, waarin de 150 Psalmen David's gevogd met verscheiden Lofzangen zijn* (Amsterdam, 1600), according to Fétis four- to eight-part settings, has remained unknown up to now. The homophonic arrangements of the Genevan Psalter by Goudimel and Le Jeune were, however, circulated in Holland. The works of both were printed there, Le Jeune's in 1629 and 1633 at Amsterdam and 1675 at Leyden—all these, however, in French; a Dutch edition prepared by Franse van Sweelinck followed in 1665, also at Amsterdam. Goudimel's work, first published in a French edition at Delft in 1602, was printed three times in Dutch, first in 1620 at Leyden, then in 1753 at Haarlem (both editions after Dathenus), and finally in 1780 at Zoonen. While the two first printings were prompted by private initiative, the third one bears all the signs of an official songbook. Unlike Le Jeune's settings, those by Goudimel took root in certain areas of Holland in the form of four-part congregational songs. Almost the only polyphonic arrangement of the Genevan Psalter created on Dutch soil is at the same time the most famous and important of them all; it is by Jan Pieterszoon Sweelinck, published in 1604, 1613, 1614, and 1621 in four volumes (the first two in Amsterdam, the last two in Haarlem) with the original French texts. Thus the wording of the title of the fourth volume, for example, is *Livre quatriesme et conclusionnal des pseaumes de David nouvellement mis en musique à 4, 5, 6, 7, 8 parties.* From the beginning Sweelinck's work attracted great attention, not only in his homeland but also, for instance, in Switzerland (see p. 558). In Germany it was accepted most readily. As early as 1616 *Des weltberühmten Musici und Organisten zu Amsterdam vierstimmige Psalmen, aus dem I., II. und III. Teil seiner vorausgegangenen französischen Psalmen absonderlich colligiert und mit Lobwasser'schen Texten unterlegt* was published in Frankfurt on the Oder, followed by an additional selection in 1618. Sweelinck's four- to eight-part arrangements of the Genevan Psalter, some of them large-scale conceptions, are definite lied motets, only rarely leaving the cantus firmus unchanged:

J. P. Sweelinck (1621): Psalm 134 (melody: L. Bourgeois, Geneva, 1551)

Generally speaking, Sweelinck intensifies textual presentation and works out the melodies expressively in motet style in all parts, mainly in the top voice. He is a supreme master of all the devices of his time, of every possibility in the technique of imitation, the clever featuring of word (or word-group) repetitions, of emphatic exclamations, musical imagery, echo effects, and the like.

J. P. Sweelinck (1621): from Psalm 122 (melody: L. Bourgeois, Geneva, 1551)

Sweelinck's arrangement of the Genevan Psalter is not only one of the most artistic but, above all, the one reflecting the most glowing personality, a product of the passion of the Italian early Baroque. There is no trace of Calvinist sobriety and strictness. These psalm motets were, of course, not meant for the Reformed service but for music making in the home, at social functions, and perhaps occasionally in church (see below). While they owe their existence to Calvinism, they have no basic connection with it, and are a vivid testimonial to the extraordinary popularity of the Genevan Psalter outside the Reformed church. In Amsterdam a Collegium Musicum was established for the special purpose of preparing and performing Sweelinck's work.

From the beginning the activity of the Collegia Musica in the Netherlands (where they can be traced from the end of the 16th century) was apparently not as closely connected with the Calvinist service as it was in German-speaking Switzerland. The *Muziekcollege van die gereformeerde religie,* founded in 1632 at Nijmegen, was perhaps the only exception. The extent of the native religious repertory of the Collegia Musica has been difficult to ascertain, but evidently it was not very large. Other than Sweelinck's psalm motets, only one polyphonic arrangement of a rhyming Psalter from Holland is known: the *Uythbreijding over het Boek der Psalmen in verscheyde dichtmaat. Op musijk gebracht, met 1 en 2 stemmen, en 1 en 2 violen; benevens een bas continuo . . . door Remigius Schrijver* (Rotterdam, 1680–81). Details about this work have so far not come to light.

The development of Reformed church music in 17th-century Holland was otherwise essentially determined by two factors: the unparalleled flowering of small art-song forms and the struggle for the use of the organ in the service.

There appeared in the course of the 17th century numerous collections of sacred and secular songs (sometimes combinations of both), mostly monophonic and unaccompanied; they were sung in the home and in the Collegia Musica, frequently with instruments, especially lutes, playing along. The most popular sacred collection is the *Stichtelijke Rijmen om te lesen off singen* by Dirk Kamphuysen; this collection had no less than eighty, frequently enlarged, printings between 1621 (or 1624?) and 1777. Research on this is still lacking. In the 17th century, Joseph Butler, who is also the author of a two-part arrangement of the work (Amsterdam, 1652), took particular interest in "devotional rhymes" (see illustration on p. 560). Mention should also be made of the collections edited by Jan Herman Krul: *Christelijcke offerande, bestaende in gheestelijcke rijmen ende zangen* and *Den Christelijcken hoveling, misprysende 't hoofsche leven,* as well as the *Innerlykke Ziel-Tochten op't H. Avondmaal en andere vorvallente jelegentheden . . . door Hieronymus Swaerts* (Amsterdam, 1692, first printing?), which apparently were also designed for use in the service. Dirk I. Balfoort (op. cit., p. 38 ff.) mentions several additional collections of this kind, some of which have inter-denominational functions. We have an extensive collection of polyphonic music in *Het Boeck van de Zangh-Kunst,* published in seven volumes between 1630 and 1644 in Amsterdam and containing settings of a variety of sacred songs, among them some from the realm of the German hymn, by such masters as Cornelis de Leeuw, Dirkz J. Sweelinck (Jan Pieterszoon's son), and others. That these collections contain some attractive pieces is shown by the following example:

D. J. Sweelinck (1644) (melody: Ph. Nicolai, 1599)

Mention must also be made of a musical setting of van de Vondel's *'T Lof van Iubal, Eerste Vinder der Musijcke en allerley Musijck-Instrumenten Door verscheyden poeten in Duytsche en Latijnsche Vaersen gestelt* (in four to six parts with continuo) and of C. Huygens's *Pathodia sacra et profana occupati* (Paris, 1647), a collection of Latin psalms and Italian as well as French secular songs, originally with lute accompaniment, later rewritten with thoroughbass. Both works, because of their concertante style, are entirely out of the spirit of Calvinism; they do show, however, the extension of the artistic horizon of certain outstanding masters in Reformed 17th-century Holland far beyond the purist narrowness of the Calvinist service. The *Nederlandtsche Gedenck-Clanck* by Adrian Valerius (Haarlem, 1626), the well-known song collection in lute tablature that contains the so-called Netherland Thanksgiving Hymn, should also be listed here. Apparently, this all sacred music for the home grew out of the 17th-century Dutch movement of lay piety, not infrequently touched by mysticism, by which even a figure like Rembrandt was affected; detailed research, however, is still lacking.

The town pipers, who still were highly regarded in the first half of the 17th century, also participated with some frequency in church functions, although not in the service itself. Jacob van Eyck, the most outstanding player of bells and the flute in his time, was particularly famous; "he mingled the sound of his little flute with the bells of St. Jansker's in alternation." His work *Der Fluiten Lusthof beplant met Psalmen, Pavanen, Couranten, Almanden, Airs etc.* (Amsterdam, 1646 and later; new edition, Amsterdam, 1957) for soprano recorder (see illustration on p. 547), containing only unaccompanied monophonic music, is in style and content most characteristic for his time and milieu. The psalm arrangements, like most of the other pieces, are sets of variations, in which the individual verses are clearly separated by rests at the end of the line in accordance with the cantus firmus.

Of greater and more central importance was the controversy over the function of the organ in the Calvinist Netherlands. The Dordrecht Synod of 1574 had prohibited its use at divine services. This decision, however, evoked a strong counter-movement from its inception, and the demolition of instruments in Holland was carried out probably only in isolated cases. While the church remained firm in its decision, the advocates of organ playing found a successful way out. Psalm singing remained consistently unaccompanied, but organ playing broke through as a frame for the service, later also for the sermon within the service. Constantin Huygens's books, *Gebruyck of Ongebruijck van't orgel in de kercken der Vereenighde Nederlanden* (three printings, 1641, 1659, and 1660) and *Kerck-gebruyck der Psalmen* (preserved in manuscript only), were important as a program toward this goal. Only "stichtelijcke"—i.e., solemn, ceremonious pieces—not "motetten en licht-vorardige stuekens," were to be played. Since the organs were generally municipal property and the organists were paid by the cities at least in part, organists from the end of the 16th century on were also expected by the magistrates in some localities to play regularly, sometimes daily, frequently after Vespers. Sometimes solo singing and the playing of the town pipers were added. This procedure was motivated not only by fondness for organ music but also by educational considerations—specifically, the desire to draw the populace from the so-called music inns, establishments of sometimes very dubious repute. Finally, the organists had to participate at all kinds of receptions that used to take place in the churches (Calvinism does not accept the idea of a sanctuary). Thus the Netherlands, precisely because of its Reformed strictness, became at the turn of the 16th to the 17th century the cradle of the church concerto in the modern sense of the word. Widespread commercial connections resulted very soon in its setting an example for other countries, first of all for the *Abendmusiken* (evening concerts) of Lübeck and for the musical life of Hamburg. This had its inner logic. Where the Christian service has no use for art in its many forms, no function for it, art of necessity seeks ways out to attain independent development and validity. If the church refuses to be its patron, the inescapable result must be music that no longer acts as a servant in praise of the Lord and finds its own way toward absolute aesthetic values. With the origins of the church concerto in the Netherlands, Calvinism involuntarily furthered secularism and sowed the seeds for the emancipation of music from the church, more than a century before the same thing happened in Lutheran territo-

134. Title page of Johann Balthasar König, *Harmonischer Liederschatz oder allgemeines evangelisches Choralbuch,* Frankfurt on the Main, 1738. Published by the composer.

135. Conrad Friedrich Hurlebusch, embellished organ chorale on Psalm 42 from *De 150 Psalmen Davids,* Amsterdam, 1746. Published by the composer.

136. Psalm 8, with indications for rests, from *Les Pseaumes de David,* Paris, 1817, Lefevre.

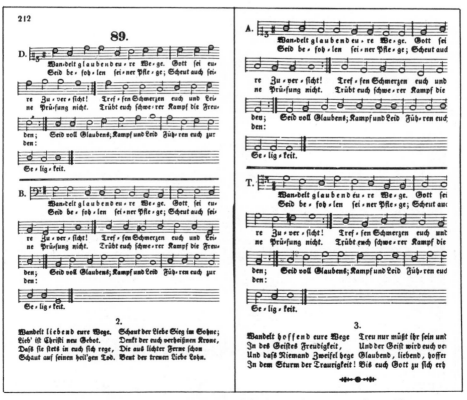

137. Four-voice setting of the lied *Wandelt glaubend eure Wege* from *Christliches Gesangbuch für den öffentlichen Gottesdienst,* Torgen bei St. Gallen, 1839, Schläpfer.

ries through the overemphasis on individual-human emotional life.

In the beginning, however, these events affected mainly performance, the composition of music hardly at all. The creative efforts of Dutch musicians were by no means up to the high artistic level and scope of organ playing in the Netherlands, as it had developed mainly in the 17th century. Almost all large churches at that time had outstanding organists on a permanent basis. Ever since then organ playing and organ building in the Netherlands have had a special reputation, which still exists, to a certain extent, at the present time. If, compared to this, the harvest of organ compositions must be considered rather meager, the widespread cultivation of improvised organ playing might serve as an explanation. Of course, in Jan Pieterszoon Sweelinck Dutch organ music produced a master of continental importance. His work, absorbing elements of Italian 16th-century organ music and English virginal music and combining both on a higher level, had an extraordinary effect, particularly in north and central Germany. However, Sweelinck's organ compositions should not be considered liturgically oriented music, any more than his psalm motets. This is clear from the prevalence of free forms—extended fantasies and toccatas—as well as from the fact that among the 24 chorale arrangements in the form of variation sets found in volume I of the Sweelinck Complete Edition (new version, Amsterdam, 1943), only three are based on melodies from the Genevan Psalter (Psalms 42, 116, and 140). Whether there are compositions of Dutch origin among the anonymous sets of variations on Geneva psalms in the Lübbenau organ tablatures has not yet been investigated, but it seems possible in a few cases. The recently discovered tablature of 1610 by the Dordrecht organist Hendrick Speuy, containing 24 psalm arrangements, is the earliest book of its kind for service use and is, besides the works of Sweelinck, also of great musical interest. In the edition of Speuy's *Psalm Preludes* prepared by Fritz Noske (Amsterdam, 1962), the arrangement of Psalm 42, which had been credited to Sweelinck, has been identified as a work by Speuy. The *Tabulatur-Boeck van Psalmen en Fantasyen . . .* by the Amsterdam organist Anthoni van Noordt (Amsterdam, 1659; new editions, Leipzig, 1896, Kassel, 1954, and Amsterdam, 1957), in which the ten psalm arrangements employ, as in Sweelinck, the form of chorale variations, is undoubtedly music for use at the service, possibly for the frame around the sermon. While van Noordt's dependence on Sweelinck is clearly recognizable, his chorale arrangements are more concise; the cantus firmus, appearing in all voices, remains, as distinguished from Sweelinck's procedure, almost always unchanged and is interrupted from time to time only by a one-measure rest between the verse lines (and not always even that):

A. van Noordt (1659): Organ variation, Psalm 116, Verse 3 (melody: P. Dagues [?], Geneva, 1562)

Another master of Dutch Calvinist organ music of this period, the organist Quirinus Gideon van Blankenburg of The Hague, is important for his *Clavicimbel- en Orgelboek der Gereformeerde psalmen en kerkzangen . . .* (1732). Van Blankenburg's collection contains a considerable number of small fugues and toccatas on chorales, with and without ornaments, doubtless exclusively for service use. Their style is closely connected with the Dutch tradition of the 17th century: there are no new formal devices; there is only, in comparison to van Noordt's pieces, a still greater tendency toward simplicity prompted by their being designed for liturgical use:

Qu. G. van Blankenburg (1732): Psalm 24 (chorale fugue for organ)

Van Blankenburg's work, printed in 1745, has the revealing title *Livre de clavecin et d'orgue pour les pseaumes et cantiques de l'église reformée avec les mêmes notes que l'assemblé chante actuellement, reduits en voix coulantes, borné en stile et hauteur, pourvu d'agrémens et enrichi par l'art.* The practice of accompanied congregational singing resulted in the publication, mainly in the 18th century, of a great number of chorale books (at first, of course, only with melody and figured bass). The most important of these is by Conrad Friedrich Hurlebusch (1696–1765) of Brunswick; it was printed three times, in 1746, 1761, and 1766, in Amsterdam. The work presents the embellished psalm tunes over a thoroughbass; because it is designed for congregational singing, the cantus firmus proceeds in equal whole notes, only the second half of each note being ornamented (see illustration on p. 571). We can infer from this that congregational singing was very slow in tempo and had lost the original rhythm of the Genevan Psalter. Another work by Hurlebusch belonging to the same category, the *Psalmenboek voor het Orgel, de vierde regel in de bas,* is preserved only in manuscript. Finally, mention should be made of Jacob Potholt's *De Muzyk van de CL Psalmen benevens de Lofzangen, naar den Nieuwsten Zangrant met Prae- en Interludiums en Bassen* (Amsterdam, 1774). In view of the great importance of the lute in 17th-century Dutch music, there must have been a considerable number of lute intabulations. However, only two works, by the Frenchman Vallet, have been preserved. Vallet was organist and carillonneur in Amsterdam beginning in 1613 and published, in 1616, 21 psalms for a single voice and lute and, in 1620, all 150 psalms in lute tablature under the title *La piété royale.* The carillon is also a factor in Reformed music in the Netherlands (the word is of French derivation from the Middle Latin *quadrilionem,* which indicates a connection with the medieval four-tone carillons). Nowhere has the carillon achieved such development and such artistic importance as in the Reformed Netherlands of the 17th century. The brothers Franz and Peter Hermony were mainly responsible for this boom: beginning in 1642 they made 47 carillons within a period of thirty-five years, the most important with more than 30 bells. Their manual (in other words, not automatic) operation was, as a rule, part of the duties of organists who, as city employees, were at the same time *Klokkenisten (beiaardier).* The carillons were sounded on certain days of the week, sometimes daily at fixed hours, and enjoyed unusual popularity, as did the players. A Utrecht ordinance of 1632 states, for example, that the bells were to be played "every Sunday and Friday one hour before noon and every Sunday one hour after noon. Item: from May to the parish fair inclusive [therefore in the summer months] one hour every evening after eating" (see Dirk A. Balfoort, op. cit., p. 64). Evidently psalm tunes were played by preference, if not, indeed, exclusively. A contemporary source describes the music as follows: "A psalm, at first somewhat fragmented, doubled on Sundays together with four or five tones forming chords with it . . . ; the bass bells should maintain the correct melody and the superius bells should ornament and embellish above it" (Balfoort, p. 65). The installation and enthusiastic use of the numerous carillons in Holland cannot be considered a typical phenomenon of Reformed church music, any more than can the flowering of Dutch organ playing in the 17th century, particularly since both had their roots in the Middle Ages. One should rather see it, apart from the general human urge to perform, as a desire for a status symbol on the part of a highly developed and prosperous middle class, a desire that prevailed even over differing Calvinist tendencies. While organ and carillon playing are by themselves of great importance, they are no doubt only marginal features of Reformed church music. It was, however, a special aspect of the development of church music in the Calvinist Netherlands in the Baroque era that marginal events had real historical significance; impulses which would decide the future originated in the carillons as well as in organ music. This strange fact is to be explained only by the relationship of Calvinism to the arts.

More Recent Music in the Reformed Church

Throughout Europe, the development of Reformed church music since the age of Pietism and Enlightenment can be characterized by an increasing relaxation of the hitherto strict Calvinist principles. A new awakening had already been set into motion around the middle of the 17th century by the work of Jodocus van Lodenstein and Jean de Labadie in the Netherlands, resulting in a stronger influx of religious songs in traditional psalm singing (see p. 568 f.). This had little effect, however, on the official divine service; mostly it concerned domestic devotions. The movement spread to the Lower Rhine region too, there laying receptive ground for Reformed hymn poetry of an individual character. Its main representatives were Joachim Neander, Friedrich Adolf Lampe, and Gerhard Tersteegen. While the theological ideas of the first two poets centered around the idea of a covenant between God and man, the poetry of Tersteegen had distinct mystical traits, with a deep longing for peace and seculsion of the soul. To this day several songs by these three poets belong to the nucleus of Protestant congregational song: Neander's *Lobe den Herren, den mächtigen König der Ehren, Wunderbarer König,* and *Der Tag is hin; mein Jesu, bei mir bleibe,* Lampe's *Mein Leben ist ein Pilgrimstand,* and Tersteegen's *Jauchzet, ihr Himmel, frohlocket, ihr Engel in Chören, Siegesfürste, Ehrenkönig, Gott ist gegenwärtig, Allgenugsam Wesen, Ich bete an die Macht der Liebe,* and many others.

These poets exerted an extraordinary influence; they made a decisive contribution within their sphere toward greatly diminishing the predominance of the psalm lied, and achieved with their songs on Reformed soil what the Freylinghausen songbook (Halle, 1704 and later) had done on the Lutheran. Frequently, however, they adopted the verse meter of the Geneva psalms, or, in isolated cases, even assigned Geneva tunes to their poems (mainly Neander); thus a certain connection with Reformed tradition was maintained. Neander's *Bundes-Lieder* (Songs of the Covenant) were soon incorporated in many songbooks, usually in their entirety, and were specifically mentioned in their titles. This was first done in the Darmstadt songbook of 1698, the most important trailblazer of Pietist song material. This development occurred without being planned by the poet. In the title of the original edition of Neander's songs (Bremen, 1680) one reads: "New settings after known and unknown melodies . . . to read and to sing during voyages, at home, or at Christian entertainments in the open air." It should be noted that the collections offer the new tunes with a figured bass, following the general trend of the time. In connection with the songs that were to be sung to existing, known melodies, preference was given to Geneva psalm tunes. Neander thought as little about congregational meetings when creating his songs as did Tersteegen, who sometimes came close to sectism; nevertheless, the songs of both writers very soon entered the general service repertory. This was also of musical significance. Among the three poets, Neander was a creator of melodies, too. His melodies, today still in general use, for *Unser Herrscher, unser König* (used for B. Schmolck's *Tut mir auf die schöne Pforte*) and *Wunderbarer König* are typical examples of the characteristics of Protestant melody construction in the second part of the 17th century. Either the contemporary solo aria style was employed, as in Neander's *Unser Herrscher, unser König*, whose original version, today no longer customary, reads as follows:

J. Neander (1680): *Unser Herrscher, unser König*

Un-ser Herr-scher,un-ser Kö-nig, un-ser al-ler höch-stes Gut! Löb-lich nah'und auch von fer-nen von der Erd'bis an die Ster-nen.
Herr-lich ist dein gro-ßer Na-me,weil er Wun-der-ta-ten tut.

Or a consistent equality of meter prevails, as it does essentially in *Wunderbarer König*. In both cases the urge for individual emotional expressivity in the spirit of Pietism found an outlet. Neander knew how to combine this with a healthy measure of folk appeal, frequently with the aid of dactylic triple meter. His most famous example of this technique is the melody to *Lobe den Herren, den mächtigen König der Ehren*, a rewriting of an older melody (see example). After Neander's death the Frankfurt *Kapellmeister* Georg Christoph Strattner provided 66 musical settings of his poems, more than Neander himself had been able to do (Neander wrote only 58 melodies of his own); Strattner's work, published in 1691 under the title *Joachimi Neandri vermehrte Glaub- und Liebesübung . . .* with melody and thoroughbass, owes so much, however, to the solo aria style that its tunes were unable to replace the more popular ones by Neander. Only recently the melody for Otto Riethmüller's *Herr, wir stehen Hand in Hand*, borrowed from Neander's *Himmel, Erde, Luft und Meer*, has found widespread acceptance; the original with Strattner's thoroughbass reads as follows:

Georg Christoph Strattner (1691): *Himmel, Erde, Luft und Meer*

A comparison between Neander's and Strattner's tunes for *Lobe den Herren* (Strattner based his version on Neander's), preceded by Neander's own model, is most instructive:

a. *Stralsunder Gesangbuch,* Part II, 1665

b. Joachim Neander, 1680

c. Georg Christoph Strattner, 1691

The Reformed regions of Germany made some additional contributions to the store of melodies, mainly in the 18th century. In addition to Neander's *Bundes-Lieder* the most influential were the *Neu aufgesetzte . . . Psalm und Choralbuch* by Johann Michael Müller of Hanau (Frankfurt, 1718; second printing, 1735) and, most important, the so-called *Cöthnischen Lieder* from Reformed Anhalt (five printings from 1736 to 1760), which carried on the pioneering task of the Pietist songbook by A. Freylinghausen (Halle, 1704 and later).

The general trends of the time were not checked even in the Calvinist service in Germany. This can be seen from the endeavor, corresponding to what happened in the Lutheran regions, to equalize the original rhythmic forms of the Geneva songs, to remove the last remnants of church modes, and to add figured-bass parts to the psalm tunes as well as other old or newly created melodies. In this connection, in addition to the chorale book by J. M. Müller just referred to, the famous *Harmonische Liederschatz* by Johann Balthasar König (Frankfurt, 1738) should be mentioned; like the Müller collection, it contains the complete Lobwasser Psalter with the Geneva tunes. At the same time the practice of accompanying congregational singing was gradually being adopted.

In Bern this happened probably at the time of the rebuilding of the organ in 1731 (other towns of northern Switzerland had undoubtedly proceeded with it previously); only a few larger localities held back until into the 19th century. Winterthur installed an organ in 1809, Wädenswil in 1829, the New Cathedral in Zurich in 1837, and the Cathedral of Our Lady there as late as 1853. In the 18th century, therefore, chorale books came into use in Reformed as well as in Lutheran regions. In addition to the two already mentioned above, two characteristic German books should be listed here: one from the Palatinate (Heidelberg, 1745), edited by J. M. Spiess under the title *Geistliche Liebes-Posaune,* in which the melodies are embellished as with C. F. Hurlebusch (see p. 574), and the other one by A. H. Pustkuchen for the Reformed congregation of the principality of Lippe-Detmold (Rinteln, 1810).

All these phenomena affected to a greater or lesser degree every Calvinist country on the European continent. In French Switzerland, however, even after new organs had been installed (in the cathedral of Lausanne in 1733, followed by Neuchâtel in 1749 and Geneva in 1756), the four-part Goudimel settings were retained and used by the organist to accompany the usual unison congregational singing. The polyphonic song literature of German-speaking Switzerland, too, must be seen as part of this general development, subject to strong Pietist influences (see p. 558 f.). In addition, during the years to follow, enlightened and philanthropic undercurrents, meeting with tendencies of democratic universal education, made themselves felt.

Two additional works by Johann Schmidlin belong in this context: *Gellerts geistliche Oden und Lieder* (Zurich, 1761) mostly for two sopranos, alto, and thoroughbass, among them several pieces in motet form (some pieces are only for two voices or even for one with thoroughbass), and *Einhundert geistliche Lieder zur Erweckung und Stärkung des . . . Christentums* (Zurich, 1764) with settings in aria style mostly of songs by G. Tersteegen. Like Schmidlin, Johann Heinrich Egli frequently came close to the motet and cantata forms, but he also emphasized small forms. His song-like settings, showing the influence of the Berlin school in their "simplicity and naturalness" (E. Refardt), surpass the work of all other masters mentioned in this connection. Two collections of religious songs (Zurich, 1779 and 1780) were followed by, among other works, *Gellerts geistliche Oden und Lieder mit Choralmelodien* (Zurich, 1789) and the same work with "easy melodies for two to four voices" (Zurich, 1791). Gellert's songs were particularly popular in northern Switzerland and still found wide acceptance in the 18th century. Jointly with Johann Jakob Walder (Egli and Walder were pupils of Schmidlin) he published the two sections of *Auserlesene geistlichen Lieder von Klopstock, Cramer, Lavater und anderen berühmten Dichtern in Musik . . .* (in two to four parts, Zurich, 1775 and 1780) and *Christliche Lieder der vaterländischen Jugend, besonders auf der Landschaft, gewidmet von Johann Caspar Lavater* (a first edition probably as early as 1775). The title of this last work (Christian Songs Dedicated by Johann Caspar Lavater to the Youth of the Fatherland, Particularly in the Country) shows clearly how, in Lavater's poetry, Christian and national-educational ideas were combined. The settings are mostly four-part simple chorale arrangements. An independent four-part collection, *Christliche*

Gesänge, is also by Walder (Zurich, 1791). Certainly all these works too were designed primarily for small combinations or for use in choral singing by the populace, scarcely for congregational singing during the service. Unlike corresponding works of the 17th century, they are not material for the Collegia Musica, once the pillars of congregational singing; these developed in the course of the 18th century, as they did all over Europe, into concert societies no longer connected with church life.

In every Reformed country the whole of the 18th century is characterized to some degree by the struggle to change the Genevan Psalter, to reduce its importance, or to eliminate it altogether. That the Psalter was old-fashioned in text and music was constantly stressed (see Lavater's remark, p. 563). Nevertheless, it was not until the age of rationalism in the second half of the century that Reformed songbooks were published systematically. The earliest one in northern Switzerland was the Zurich songbook of 1787, arranged in four-part settings by J. H. Egli; it had been prepared privately but obtained official recognition and remained in use till 1853. It included only a few scattered psalm lieder. The illustration shows to what extent the Reformed songbooks took into consideration the sentimental taste of the time. This should help to explain why polyphonic congregational singing spread at that time more rapidly than ever before, reaching its climax at the turn of the 18th to the 19th century (cf. Reichardt's quotation, p. 557). The influence of Swiss four-part congregational singing at that time was so great that attempts (which proved unsuccessful) were made to introduce it, fashioned after the Swiss model, to Württemberg. Not infrequently the members of the congregation were seated according to voice range, an indication of careful planning. This development is closely connected with the *Volkschor* (community chorus) movement, inspired by Hans Georg Nägeli (1773–1836), which had its roots in Swiss church song. Nägeli was the son of the parson Nägeli in Wetzikon (canton of Zurich), who continued there the work of his predecessor Johann Schmidlin (see pp. 562 and 578). Schmidlin cultivated unison and polyphonic singing in his congregation to a degree never before attempted anywhere, involving more or less the entire populace. Nägeli himself published in 1828–29 a *Christlisches Gesangbuch* (Reformed, of course) "for public divine services and edification in the home" in two sections of four-part settings, calling it "a new chorale work." Twenty of the twice-fifty pieces, all with original melodies, were included in the Zurich songbook of 1853 in their four-part settings and thirteen in the Swiss songbook of 1890 (see below). Only Basel was again an exception, with its songbooks containing melody and thoroughbass, as is shown by the Basel songbook of 1809. In the current Swiss songbooks only two tunes by Nägeli have been retained, of which the following is especially characteristic:

Hans Georg Nägeli,1828/29

Herr, der du mir das Le - ben / bis die - sen Tag ge - ge - ben, / dich bet ich kind - lich an. /

Ich bin viel zu ge - rin - ge / der Treu - e, die ich sin - ge / und die du heut an mir ge - tan.

Such a unique popular choral movement, originating in the Reformed service at the end of the 18th century but impinging more and more on life outside the service can be explained by two prerequisite factors. One was the increasingly active participation of the individual in Reformed congregational life; the other was the centuries-old democratic constitution of Switzerland. Both of these interacted mutually in their historic development and thus stimulated each other again and again. This typically Swiss Reformed-democratic development attained probably its most characteristic and historically important expression in polyphonic congregational and choral singing within the service as well as outside of it.

In the French-speaking regions, too, restrictions affecting church music began to be relaxed in the 18th century, although to a lesser degree than in northern Switzerland and in Germany. This applied at first only to the song material to be used for the service; polyphonic congregational singing and organ music were still completely excluded. From the end of the 17th century so-called *trompettes d'église* (reed instruments) were frequently used to lead congregational singing, mainly in the canton of Vaud (for Bern see p. 515). Beginning with the 18th century this was also, in some towns, the function of mixed choirs, organized for that purpose as *Sociétés de Chant Sacré*. In 1705 and 1708 there appeared *54 Cantiques sacrez pour les principales solennités des chrétiens* by the Geneva minister B. Pictet, to be sung to psalm tunes; twelve of them were added to the edition of the Psalter customarily used in Geneva; the congregations in France adopted them only in 1828. In the meantime the German Lutheran song repertory also found its way via Strasbourg into France and was used in various editions of the 18th and 19th centuries. The earliest was *Cantiques spirituels accommodés aux airs melodieux des originaux allemands et des psaumes de David,* 1747, brought out by L. E. Bonnen. Further editions are listed in the survey of Reformed hymnals in France in *Louange et prière* (Paris, 1938 and later, p. 636). Beginning with the middle of the century the songs of the Herrnhut Brethren, published in several French editions at that time for the benefit of the dispersed Moravians, began to influence French-speaking Calvinists.

Toward the end of the 18th century the German-speaking territories, like the Netherlands, found it possible at last to replace the 16th-century psalm translations, which for some time had been meeting with growing resistance in many places, with new, linguistically smoother versions; in the French-speaking territories a version of the Genevan Psalter, edited by Valentin Conrart, had already been generally accepted in 1679. In the Netherlands a new edition of the Genevan Psalter was introduced officially in 1773, replacing the one by Dathenus (see p. 567) with selections from various translations (the Dathenus edition was retained only in one of the Dutch provinces and in some of the Dutch congregations in America); this new edition was kept in use till 1949. The *Neue Bereimung der Psalmen* by Matthias Jorissen, minister in the Lower Rhine regions and later of several German congregations in Holland (he was a cousin of G. Tersteegen), was written in 1793 at The Hague. After its publication in 1798 it began slowly to dislodge the Lobwasser, starting from Wuppertal. The psalm translations by Jorissen are still widely used today. Beginning in 1806 an attempt, again originating from Elberfeld (Wuppertal), was made to replace the old Geneva tunes with melodies by Johann Georg Bässler (see J. Zahn, op. cit., VI, 384, No. 1050). Only the melody for Psalm 146, *Halleluja, Gott zu loben,* however, has had any recognition, mainly through the organ fantasia of that name by Max Reger.

Aside from the Reformed service orders and the special Reformed psalm lieder, there are mainly four signs of the development of church music in Reformed regions during the 19th century which also determined essentially the development of its Lutheran counterpart (cf. chap. III, *Decline and Restoration*). The first of these is the establishment of church choirs in the form of singing societies; German-speaking Switzerland led the way with its community singing movement.

The founding of the Zurich *Kirchengesangverein* (Church Singing Society) by J. P. Lange in 1846 was the decisive event. It was not, however, until 1870 that additional societies were created; some thirty of them, through the initiative of the minister Theodor Goldschmid, formed in 1893 the Federation of Swiss Church Singers, whose official organ is *Der Evangelische Kirchenchor* (since 1895). Forty years later the Federation had a membership of some three hundred choirs. A similar development took place in Germany, where the choirs of both Protestant denominations, following the 19th-century trend toward unification, in 1883 joined forces in the *Evangelischer Kirchengesangverein,* just as they combined to form state church organizations. Only two state churches, those of Lippe and East Frisia, remained exclusively Reformed.

New polyphonic compositions do not begin to appear in French-speaking regions until the opening of the 19th century; they cannot be compared, however, with the classic Calvinist settings of the 16th century. The only collection worth mentioning is the *Chants de Sion* by César Malan (Geneva, 1824), written under the influence of the movement called the Awakening; the tunes and settings of several of them with the original texts by Malan are still officially used. As far as their melodic lines and homophonic settings are concerned, Malan's compositions are simple, with distinct overtones of Romanticism in their direct expression of sentiment, as is shown by his widely known melody to *Harre, meine Seele.* In the 19th-century Netherlands, where under the influence of Abraham Kuyper the tendency toward a strict Calvinist service order remained strongest, there are even fewer traces of polyphonic music for the service.

A second sign in the musical development in both Protestant denominations in the 19th century is the far-reaching uniformity of the song repertory used by church choirs in the entire German-speaking area.

It is of some significance that the most popular collections of choral music used in and out of the church, and in Germany as well as Switzerland, originated in the Swiss *Volkschor* movement; among these were various editions of *Volksgesänge* (Songs for the People) by Benedikt Ignaz Heim, who was active in Zurich from 1852 on; beginning in 1862, 1863, and 1867 they were published for men's, mixed, and women's choruses in countless editions and arrangements (among them several by Friedrich Hegar) till far into the 20th century (for example, the 62nd [!] edition for mixed chorus for Germany in 1925). No other choral publication influenced choral music in the church between 1850 and 1910 even remotely as much as the one by Heim, which still maintains its position in many places today. Nothing, however, is more symptomatic than the fact that it shows no traces of the old Swiss Reformed tradition. Romantic composers, mainly Felix Mendelssohn-Bartholdy and Friedrich Silcher predominate, and many second- and third-rate composers are included whose pieces are of a sentimental character; not a single psalm-lied setting has been retained in the collection and there are only a few German hymn settings. The religious choral songs represented are mainly little proverb motets. Heim's collection has the sad distinction of having given church choral singing of the recent past the stamp of artistic inferiority appropriate to a shallow psychological interpretation of the service. Reformed church music has produced no composer of significance in any country during this period.

Thirdly, the development of church music in the 19th century is characterized by attempts to unify the hymnals.

In Germany, after the Eisenach church conference of the 1850s, the demand for a unified German hymnal was never stilled and the following decades saw unified hymnals of many state churches come into existence; meanwhile, in northern Switzerland official hymnals were introduced in five cantons between 1841 and 1853. In 1868 there appeared the so-called *Vierörtiges Gesangbuch* (Songbook of Four Regions) of the cantons of Glarau, Graubünden, St. Gallen (which did not join until 1871), and Thurgau, based to a large extent on the Zurich songbook of 1853; it was followed in 1886 and 1890 by the *Achtörtiges* of the state of Zurich, Bern, Basel *Stadt,* Basel *Land* (divisions of the canton of Basel), Aargau, Fribourg, Schaffhausen, and Appenzell. As distinguished from German developments, which were essentially determined by the Restoration, the trend toward unification of the hymnals in Switzerland did not bring about a noticeable return to the classic hymn of the 16th and 17th centuries; on the contrary, considerable space was assigned to devotional songs from the era of Pietism, *Empfindsamkeit,* and Romanticism. At the same time equality of meter still determined the rhythm of melodies. Developments in western Switzerland and in France ran a similar course. In France, toward the middle of the 19th century, a whole series of collections of religious folk songs were published as the result of the *Réveil* (Awakening): *Recueil de cantiques spirituels à l'usage des assemblées chrétiennes* (Basel, 1817), *Pseaumes, hymnes et cantiques spirituels* (Geneva, 1824), *Recueil de cantiques à l'usage des assemblées de prière en faveur des missions* (Lausanne, 1828 and later), *Pseaumes et cantiques publiés par la Société évangélique de Lausanne* (Lausanne, 1836 and later), *Le recueil de Lyon* (1847), *Cantiques populaires* (Paris, 1879), and others. In addition to these privately published collections, new official hymnals were brought out during the same period: in western Switzerland *Psaumes et cantiques des églises nationales de Vaud, Neuchâtel et Genève* with 63 psalms and 87 other songs (Lausanne, 1866; the revised edition of 1900 contains only 50 psalms but 213 *cantiques*) and in France *Psaumes et cantiques à l'usage des églises réformées* (Paris, 1859, with revisions in 1881 and 1894): these were published after various efforts had been made to enliven congregational (mainly psalm) singing, which dragged miserably in France too at that time. It was even suggested in 1838 that "One should ask Messrs. Rossini, Meyerbeer, and Auber whether they would not be willing to write new melodies for the psalms" (see *Musik und Gottesdienst* for 1960, p. 13).

In French Switzerland the original melodies of the Genevan Psalter, including their notation, had (unlike the texts) been retained without any change from 1560 to 1866; furthermore, the partly unison, partly four-part editions until then always contained the complete Psalms and, in addition, only the twelve *cantiques* by B. Pictet (see p. 580). This does not mean, of course, that the congregations had not long since proceeded toward *chanter en plain-chant*—that is, toward slower singing in equal meters. But the 1866 hymnal contains for the first time only a selection from the Psalms, augmented by a steadily increasing number of other songs.

A fourth general sign is manifest in the fact that neither the Reformed nor the Lutheran regions have displayed in recent times any substantial artistic achievements in organ music.

In this respect Switzerland and France probably were at the foot of the ladder, while Germany, although not in its Reformed regions, did produce Mendelssohn and Max Reger, who were so important to organ music. The Swiss organists were almost entirely under German influence, mainly that of I. C. Rinck (1770–1846), whose works are distinguished for little more than clean workmanship. But while there was hardly any creative effort in this field at that time, increasing attention was given to the training of organists in Switzerland toward the end of the century, thanks mainly to the music schools of Basel and Zurich. Guilds for Reformed organists were founded; together, until 1947, they published their own periodical, *Der Organist*. Similar events have taken place in the Netherlands, where *Het Orgel* has been the official magazine of the guild of Dutch organists since 1905, but there has been no organ composition of any consequence in the recent past. Organ playing and the construction of organs, however, have been carried on vigorously.

In one respect the history of Reformed church music in the 19th century differs basically from that of the Lutheran: it remained almost completely unaffected by the restoration movement arising from the spirit of Romanticism. There is a simple reason for this. In the Reformed church the old forms, which in Lutheran regions dissolved slowly and gradually between the 16th and 18th centuries, had already ceased to exist in the days of the Reformation. Except for the Genevan Psalter there was therefore essentially nothing to restore. But though Reformed church music produced little that was new in the 19th century, the absence of any history-making development proved to be advantageous to the present. As part of a general tendency to rejuvenate church music, quite divorced from historical considerations, the essence and purpose of church music are being thoroughly re-examined today, mainly along theological lines. Reformed and Lutheran music meet here.

It is not yet possible to see clearly the outline of future developments, but certain significant signs can already be discerned. The pattern of the Reformed order of worship of Reformation times is no longer necessarily binding. With a new awareness of the denominational individuality of the various Protestant churches, characteristic of the present situation (as opposed to the 19th-century efforts to water down differences) and reflected in a redesigning of orders of worship, there comes also a reorientation of ordinances, as in *Kirchenbuch*.

*Ordnungen für die Versammlungen der nach Gottes Wort reformierten Gemein-
den deutscher Zunge* (Ordinances for the Meetings of Congregations of the
German Tongue, Reformed in Accordance with God's Word), a kind of liturgical
source reference work, edited by E. Wolf and M. Albertz (Munich, 1941), and
in the *Kirchenbuch* published by the *Moderamen* of the Reformed Federation
(Neukirchen, 1951). For the first time in the history of the Reformed service, the
Dienstboeck voor de Nederlandes Hervormde Kerk. In Ontwerp (a draft published
by the General Synod of the Dutch Reformed Church; The Hague, 1955) does
not offer the strophic song as the only form of congregational singing but includes,
in addition, liturgical songs of Gregorian origin for responsorial pieces (such as
Amen and *Salutatio*) as well as for settings of the Ordinary. This is done mainly
in accordance with 16th century ordinances, such as the Strasbourg church orders
of 1525; beyond that, however, there are attempts at noteworthy new versions:

The *Alpirsbacher Antiphonale. Gesänge zur Messe und zum Stundengebet* (Tübingen, 1950 ff.) employs Gregorian chant exclusively. While this work has no
official character whatever, its essential purpose can be understood only through
contemporary Reformed theological ideas, particularly those of Karl Barth. The
so-called Alpirsbach movement, under the spiritual leadership of Friedrich Buchholz, questions the value of the versified psalm as opposed to the sung text of the
Bible and finds in Gregorian chant the form of service song suited to Reformed
Bible interpretation. "The Gregorian melody, providing the text—usually from
Holy Scripture—with large-scale, well-balanced, monumental, and pleasant
melodies, permits the text to govern its interpretation: the music sometimes
illustrates the text but only rarely tries to interpret it directly. This is already
evident in the fact that the chant, to a large extent, uses so-called typical melodies
which do not lend themselves to a direct interpretation of the Word" (*Vom Wesen
der Gregorianik,* Munich, 1948, p. 34 f.). Other important books by Buchholz are
Musik und Musiker in der christlichen Gemeinde, Regensburg, 1952, and *Von
Bindung und Freiheit der Musik und des Musikers in der Gemeinde,* Kassel, 1955.
A conscious connection to medieval chant is essential to the settings in the
Alpirsbach Antiphonal, while the so-called Lutheran Gregorianism of the 16th
century with its emphasis on word relationships represents a falsification of the
original Gregorian chant as well as of the purpose of music for the service.

The service in the Reformed community of Taizé in France shows that the
Alpirsbach work is not an isolated, exceptional case. Taking its departure from
pre-Reform traditions, Taizé uses the formulas for Mass and Hours, as far as this
can be done within the framework of Protestant thinking (an ancient church
tradition has even been revived in the three readings in the Mass) and with them
goes a new musical formulation, closely related to the chant but at the same time
frequently daring and entirely unconcerned with historical considerations. Unison and polyphonic sections, with or without the use of the organ, are inter-

changed; as music *sub communione* even a work for flute and organ may be used. For the Hours prayers Geneva psalm lieder are sung side by side with Lutheran hymns, the latter perhaps in settings by Johann Crüger but with the cantus firmus in the tenor. The musical creator of the order of worship is Jacques Berthier. It is too soon to pass judgment on this Reformed order and its search for an entirely new approach, since everything is still in a state of flux; but it is undoubtedly a sign of a new force when musical elements from widely different centuries are being used with considerable indifference and fused into a new unity with no apparent historical consideration. One could not imagine such a new beginning anywhere but on French soil, where 19th-century tradition continues in a positive sense as in no other European country.

The general re-evaluation of the divine service affects the problem of hymnals mainly through a renewed emphasis on the Genevan Psalter and the restitution of much of its original form. In most regions this did not mean the reintroduction of the entire 150 psalm lieder; usually only a selection was made. In Germany these tendencies did not prevent a link with the *Evangelisches Kirchengesangbuch,* already affected in the 1955 special edition for the Reformed congregations of East Germany and some dispersed congregations in the West; completely Reformed territories in West Germany and the partly Reformed Rhineland and Westphalia have not yet taken steps in this direction. The edition mentioned here contains, in addition to the psalm lieder from the *Evangelisches Kirchengesang-buch,* a special appendix of 31 psalms, mostly with text version by Jorissen; some others are by August Ebrard (1852). German-speaking Switzerland has had its common hymnal since 1952, preceded several years earlier by a trial publication. Rarely has there been such a long struggle to determine the contents of a hymnal as in the case of the new Swiss one; in the course of this a whole literature came into existence, in which even Karl Barth participated (see Barth, *Ein Friedens-vorschlag zur Gesangbuchfrage,* in *Kirchenblatt für die reformierte Schweiz* XCVIII, 1942, 338 ff.). The hymnal begins with 40 psalm lieder mostly from the Genevan Psalter with text versions by various translators. However, several psalm lieder by Luther and others have also been included. Four-part texture has been preserved in most cases; melodies conceived homophonically have been retained that way. Modern poems and music have been taken into consideration and texts mainly by A. Pötzsch, J. Klepper, A. Maurer, and R.A. Schröder have been included. Especially noteworthy are new melodies by Albert Moeschinger (born 1897 in Basel) and, above all, by Willy Burkhard.

W. Burkhard (1939): *Nun ist vorbei die finstre Nacht*

Western Switzerland acquired its new hymnal in 1937 with the *Psautier ro-mand,* Protestant France in the following year with *Louange et prière.* In the *Psautier romand* the number of psalms has grown to 89; 17 are still in the text version by Conrart while the great majority have new texts by R.L. Piachaud, some of them based on Marot and Beza. All psalms appear in the four-part Goudimel settings, but the cantus firmus is in the soprano throughout. Here, as in other Reformed regions, a backward movement toward the original Genevan Psalter is clearly traceable. The remaining 422 songs show great variety: Lutheran songs are represented, as are the *Psalmodie morave* (the songs of the Zinzendorf community of Brethren), songs from the Awakening movement of the 19th century, and many others. Among the melodists, Nägeli, Bortnjansky, and Silcher are represented. The inclusion of some liturgical pieces in the form of song fragments is striking: the last lines of *Mitten wir im Leben sind* appear as a Kyrie, the corresponding sections of *Gelobt sei Gott im höchsten Thron* and *Jesaja dem Propheten das geschah* as Halleluja and Sanctus. All the *cantiques* too are in four-part settings. Four-part congregational singing had not established itself in western Switzerland until the 19th century, and then only gradually. The *Recueil* (see p. 582) has been accepted from 1866, its date of publication, to the present. However, since approximately 1920 the congregations have been returning slowly to unison singing, owing to the increasing diffusion of organs. *Louange et prière,* too, begins with 67 Geneva psalm lieder, followed by a very diversified section, *Chorals et cantiques.* Because this hymnal addresses itself to Lutheran and Methodist congregations also, appropriate song material, mainly from the realm of English Methodism, has been included. There is also a four-part edition of the work, influenced mainly by Bach's chorale settings and not by the older, simple cantional settings.

Work on a hymnal has been in progress in the Netherlands also. The absolute predominance of the Geneva Psalms had been preserved here more than anywhere else. It was not until 1807 that they were combined with *Evangelische Gezangen,* augmented in 1866 by a *Vervolgbundel.* In 1938 the Psalms were published in new notation (reduction of note values and measure indications based on authentic rhythms), together with a new collection of *Gezangen.* Around the same time, H. Hasper undertook a new versification based on the original rhythms; it found acceptance here and there. The version now in use, *Psalmen en Gesangen voor de Nederlandse Hervormde Kerk* (1949), contains all 150 psalms and 306 other songs. In addition, various other Reformed sects, such as the "Remonstrants" (see p. 566), have their own hymnals.

The movement for a renewal of church music also had an effect on Reformed choral singing and music for the organ. The Reformed regions of Germany take a quite general interest in what is currently happening in this field. Much more than in Lutheran regions, however, pieces readily understood by the congregation are chosen for choral singing at the service; the use of polyphonic songs is therefore limited. The question of the function of the choir at the service has been asked, but no unqualified or definite answer has yet been found. In the particularly strict Calvinist congregations of the Netherlands *Gereformeerde Kerk,* as distinguished from the *Nederlandse Hervormde Kerk,* all polyphonic choral singing is still rejected as an "aesthetic horror."

Concerning participation of the choir, German-speaking Switzerland is more open-minded; the *Psalmenbuch* (Basel, 1956), prepared by H. Hollinger at the request of the Swiss *Kirchengesangsbund* and containing settings from Bourgeois to Sweelinck, shows what this region considers possible for choral singing at the service.

It is again German-speaking Switzerland that provides the largest share of contemporary church music among all Reformed regions, although so far relatively few works for service use have emerged. The following composers may be mentioned: Adolf Brunner, Willy Burkhard, Henri Gagnebin, René Matthes, Albert Moeschinger, Paul Müller-Zürich, Bernard Reichel, and Hans Studer.

While Adolf Brunner, Willy Burkhard, and Hans Studer have probably made the most important contributions in the field of vocal music for use during the service, two collections of organ music, by Burkhard and Müller-Zürich, deserve special attention. Vocal works to be mentioned are Brunner, *Fünf Motetten* (Kassel, Bärenreiter-Verlag); Burkhard, *Kleiner Psalter* (same publisher); and Studer, *Evangeliensprüche.* The most important publications of organ music for service use are Burkhard's *Kleine Partiten* on *Wer nur den lieben Gott lässt walten* and *Grosser Gott, wir loben dich,* as well as his *Präludium und Fuge in E;* Müller-Zürich, *20 Orgelchoräle* and *25 Orgelchoräle* (Bern, 1957 and 1961); and *Orgelchoräle schweizerischer Komponisten* (Bern, 1960), containing 21 preludes, interludes, and postludes by various contemporary composers. Frank Martin's oratorios *Golgatha* (1945–48) and *Mystère de la Nativité* (after 1958), his *Pseaumes* (1958), and Burkhard's *Sintflut, Das Gesicht des Jesajas,* and *Psalmenkantate* are the most important new works of sacred music from the Reformed regions of Switzerland, although they are not designed for service use. Several works by Arthur Honegger (1892–1956) show that he, too, was strongly influenced by the Genevan Psalter in spite of the fact that his creative efforts were not directed at music for the church.

Since 1920, the organ has gained increasing importance in French Switzerland as an accompanying instrument for congregational singing; in addition, organ playing before and after the service is permitted.

This development is reflected in a series, *Collection de musique d'orgue,* edited by P. Pidoux, containing organ music of the past as well as contemporary works (e.g., the *25 Préludes de Chorales* by E. Moser and L. Wieruszowski). In the area of choral singing at the service, too, things have begun to move. While so far few of the existing choirs have either a recognized service function or their own repertory (preference is given to German Lutheran material), the liturgical movement *Eglise et Liturgie* and the activities of the minister R. Paquier are the main driving forces toward an improvement of existing conditions. The *Commission de musique de l'Eglise Reformée Evangélique* is bringing out a series of music editions, *La Bible chantée,* published by Cantata Domino in Geneva; another such series, published in Lausanne, the *Collection de musique protestante,* is edited by P. Pidoux.

Two Reformed artists have made the first modern contributions to music for the service in France: Alexandre Cellier (born 1883), the composer of *Trois Chorals* [i.e., three Geneva psalm tunes] *pour grand orgue,* and G. Schott, the creator of *43 Préludes* on psalm tunes. The most important figure, however, is Georges Migot, who, having started with works in the field of the oratorio, has given increasing attention to service music during the last decade, stimulated in part by the Reformed brotherhood of Taizé. Special mention should be made of his *Liturgie pour un service oecuménique* (1958–59) and his *Cantiques,* five songs for congregational singing. These works, like the *Chants liturgiques pour le temps de Noël* (1956) by Jacques Berthier, show serious attempts toward a renewal of service music in Reformed France (see M. Honegger in *Musik und Kirche* XXXI, 1961, 19 ff.). The Reformed Netherlands has in recent times made only a few unpretentious contributions to organ music, which still receive special attention there (organists are obliged to play for up to a quarter of an hour preceding each service). Adrian Koussemacker and George Stam should be mentioned in this connection.

The rejuvenation of church music is convincingly demonstrated in Reformed territories by special attempts toward unification and the establishing of journals. The periodical *Reformierter Kirchenchor,* founded by the league of church choirs of the Protestant-Reformed church in northwestern Germany in 1949, did not succeed, however. In the Netherlands the Society for Protestant Church Music founded the periodical *Kerk en Muziek* in 1935, with G. van der Leeuw as editor; it continued until 1950. In that year *Musica sacra. Tijdschrift voor Kerkmuziek* was started under the editorship of the Lutheran Willem Mudde as a journal for all Protestant music of the country. For the last few years there has also been a school for church music, directed by Georg Stam, and a church-music department has been formed at the Conservatory of Utrecht. In addition to the periodical *Het Orgel* (see p. 583), there is the magazine *Organist en Eredienst,* which has been published since 1935. In *Musik und Gottesdienst* (edited by Edwin Nievergelt; the periodical has appeared since 1947 and has been merged with *Der Organist,* founded in 1923), the official publication of the federation of Swiss Reformed organists, German-speaking Switzerland has a magazine for its church music as vigorous as the one the Dutch have in *Musica sacra.* Since 1925 the church musicians of western Switzerland have also been united in an *Association des Organistes et Maîtres de chapelle protestants romands,* "to elevate their function and thus to serve the cause of religious music"; see the bylaws of the association in Pierre Pidoux, *Répertoire de chorals d'orgue,* Lausanne, 1941. Finally, the establishing of the *Institut für Kirchenmusik des Kantons Zürich* in 1962 is of symptomatic significance.

Music for the Reformed church, because of its active participation in the general rejuvenation of church music, is now undergoing a re-evaluation sometimes approaching a totally new beginning. One cannot yet determine where the various roads will lead or whether they will arrive at a common destination. This will depend on how the problem of the relationship between the service and music is solved. The following, somewhat resigned words by the Swiss Adolf Brunner shed light on the situation and are thought-prevoking, in both a positive and a negative sense:

> Music at the Reformed service is, as a rule, limited to organ music and congregational singing. Choral offerings are inserted only on high holy days and even then they are rarely integrated with the service. Puritan tradition and the present theological situation do not encourage increased use of music in the service, and offer little opportunity

for the development of creative forces within the church—in direct contrast to Lutheranism, which possesses and vigorously augments a remarkable repertory of contemporary church music. We are aware that where a musical liturgy once has died, it cannot be artificially restored to life. Music in the Reformed church, if we disregard the chorale as the active contribution by the congregation, has a marginal, not an essential function at the service. Everything depends on the importance given to this marginal element in sacramental life and in the promulgation of the Word. Will music retain its function as an ornamental accessory or will it be taken seriously as a means of expression which, while only serving the message, is essential for it? As we see it, music finds its proper place immediately following the sermon. Motets, cantatas, and sacred concertos have the task of illustrating and enhancing musically the Sunday Bible text. We do not believe that this will impair the central position of the preaching of the Word—as long, of course, as the music remains the servant of the text and draws inspiration from it. The "sacred concerto" in the great variety of its forms and of the forces it may employ —lovingly cultivated by Heinrich Schütz, later forgotten—is particularly suited to fulfill the function of Reformed church music as an aid to the service. [See *Musik und Gottesdienst* VIII, 1954, 56.]

Brunner has presented his thoughts in detail in *Wesen, Funktion und Ort der Musik im Gottesdienst* (Zurich, 1960). The possibilities for increased participation of music in the Reformed sermon service have recently been demonstrated in a order of worship suggested by the Zurich Commission on Liturgy, of which Brunner is a member.

One cannot do full justice to the history of Reformed church music if one looks at it from the Lutheran point of view and does not take into consideration its individuality. From the beginning its real importance, notwithstanding the polyphonic episode of the second half of the 16th century, was not in the field of contrapuntal music but in the creation of congregational songs and congregational singing. In this, Calvinism, because of its one-sidedness, has been more determined and much more successful than Lutheranism. Whether the Reformed church, however, in view of its historical experiences and because of theological consideration, directly challenged by words such as those by Adolf Brunner quoted above, should not completely reconsider the present relationship between service and music and revise it to a certain degree, is another matter. Art in all its branches is one of the gifts of the Creator, signifying—along with speech— the supreme dignity of man. It seems impossible, therefore, to renounce the ancient Christian idea that music must, for that reason, enter the service of Him who created it. The historical consequences of contrary decisions by Calvinism confirm this. Art cannot be banished from the world. If the church offers no tasks to art, art will of necessity be abandoned to secularization and the church will fail in its mission of sanctification, which it has to fulfill for and in the world and which it cannot neglect without guilt and punishment. If for no other reason than this, the Reformed church should re-examine its relationship to art. But this would also mean that the question of the relationship between the service and music—i.e., between word and music—must again be posed. Should there be no broader, more positive answer than the one the Reformed church has found so far? To be sure, there is merit in the history of a church music that was always opposed to pure aestheticism in the service, a challenge that should be preserved in the future. But the Reformed church should also remember the full significance of words recently spoken by the Calvinist theologian G. van der Leeuw: "He who praises God, sings. If he does not sing, he is not moved."

PART VI

The Music of
the Bohemian Brethren

BY WALTER BLANKENBURG

Translated by Hans Heinsheimer

The song repertory of the Bohemian-Moravian Brethren always maintained a special, outstanding position in the history of Protestant church music, largely because of its geographical origin. The Bohemian Brethren (the customary abbreviation of their name; they are also known as the *Unitas fratrum*) were a 15th-century offspring of the Hussite movement and lived from 1457 on in the remote forest regions of eastern Bohemia, west of the Habelschwerdt Mountains. In 1467 they united in a free church with strict congregational rules. Because of that and through their intensive literary and pedagogical activities they increased their influence in subsequent years and, despite persecution, attracted followers. In 1478, Hussite Waldenses, émigrés from Mark Brandenburg, settled further east in Landskron and Fulneck and founded the German branch of the *Unitas fratrum*. They were joined by the German brethren of Leitomischl. As a matter of principle, musical activities of the Bohemian Brethren were limited to singing together in the vernacular; the songs were first published in a Czech songbook in 1501, undoubtedly preceded by manuscript Cantionales.

According to early reports, this songbook was kept in the Bohemian Museum in Prague. It contained 87 songs (without tunes but with melody indications), 66 of which came from earlier songbooks or were translations of Latin songs; eleven are the work of the Brethren's Bishop Luke of Prague, four go back to Matthew of Kunwald, the first bishop of the Bohemian Brethren, and six to John of Tábor. In 1505, 1519, and 1541 additional Czech songbooks of the *Unitas fratrum* (there were also some other splinter groups) were published; only the last of these is preserved. This songbook, edited by Johannes Horn (Jan Roh in Czech), contains 481 songs and 300 melodies, and thus has a bulk surpassing by several times that of any contemporary Reformed songbook in Germany. A "smaller songbook" of 1542 is only known through contemporary reports and still another one, of 1547, was rejected by the Brethren themselves. To prevent any arbitrary action in the matter of songbooks, a commission consisting of the Brethren Jan Cerny, Jan Blahoslav, and Jiri Sturm was asked in 1555 to prepare the first "official" songbook for the *Unitas fratrum*. It was completed in manuscript by 1560, bulkier than even the one of 1541, and printed the following year in Szamotuly in Poland. It was probably mainly the work of the poet and musician Jan Blahoslav and marks the beginning of the highly developed history of the Bohemian Brethren. In addition to being a member of the Bohemian Brethren, Blahoslav was an important humanist of Reform leanings, taught along Wittenberg lines, and made use of contemporary musical treatises, particularly Ornitoparchus's *Musicae activae micrologus* (1518), in *Musica,* a publication aimed at priests, cantors, and singers, mainly with a view to training them for congregational singing. The extent of Blahoslav's participation—i.e., to what extent he undertook arrangements of existing models and to what extent he created new material—in the 1561 hymnal, for which he prepared an index, has not been clarified in detail. In his own melodies he shows, as did the German Brethren soon afterward, influences of the Genevan Psalter, whose musical formulations agreed with Blahoslav's humanistic ideals. The following tunes, in all likelihood going back to Blahoslav, using (except for the final note) only two rhythmic values in a strictly maintained rhythmic pattern (lines 1 and 3 are rhythmically identical, as are lines 2 and 4,) correspond entirely with Geneva tendencies (see p. 529).

Melody of Johann von Blahoslav (?)

O Mensch,schau an Christi Leben,welchs dir zum Fürbild ist geben; denn der wird selig gepreiset,der sich gleichförmig be-wei-set.

Another collaborator on the 1561 hymnal, Wenzel Solin, also published a small book, *Musica,* under the pseudonym of Jan Josquin, probably meant as homage to the great Netherlander. The Brethren songbook of 1561 represents the very summit of Reform songbook production, not only because of its comprehensiveness (744 songs) but even more because of its artistic quality: like various later printings, it is adorned by a great number of woodcut illuminations of initials, depicting biblical and other sacred scenes and indicating the school of Holbein the Younger. Blahoslav also included a historical essay on the past development of the songs of the Brethren. This songbook had no fewer than ten printings (a corrected edition was published as early as 1564 in Eibenschütz, Moravia); from 1577 on it was also published in folio editions for precentor and chorus, richly adorned for the Bohemian nobility, while the quarto format was for use by the congregation. In 1586 the funeral songs for use at the cemetery were published separately, and finally a small-size edition in octavo format without music was published for the poor and for use while traveling. The edition of 1564, still supervised by Blahoslav, and the one of 1576 are of special importance: they show an even higher quality of illustration than the 1561 edition. Known additional printings in the 16th century are those of 1581, 1594, and 1598. Around 1600, still another revision of the songbook was decided upon because some of the melodies were too difficult for congregational singing; a new folio edition was published in 1615 at Kraslitz, and a simple quarto edition in 1618. Since new persecutions of the Brethren set in around that time, those editions bring the development more or less to its conclusion; the only known additional prints are those of 1656 and 1753. If one surveys the entire history of the hymnals of the Czech-speaking Bohemian Brethren from the 15th century to the beginning of the 17th, one can only marvel at a unique achievement. It is even more amazing in view of the persecution of their church through many years: only during the last third of the 16th century were they temporarily allowed some measure of freedom.

The main line of Czech songbooks of the Brethren produced two branches: one in Poland with three editions, 1541 (in large format with artistic adornments), 1569, and 1589; and the German branch, which helped the song repertory of the Bohemian Brethren to attain its real significance. The latter branch had its origin in *Ein New Gesengbuchlen,* published in Jungbunzlau in 1531 and edited, according to the preface, by Michael Weisse, a native of Neisse in Upper Silesia and minister of the congregations of Brethren in Landskron (Bohemia) and Fulneck (Moravia).

Weisse's songbook, as is stated by the author himself, is based on the Czech hymnal in use at the time (therefore probably the 1519 edition) and, additionally, on an earlier, perhaps already partly German Cantionale of the Landskron congregation. Occasionally one also finds influences of Johann Walter's Wittenberg *Geistliches Gesangbüchlein* of 1524 (Weisse visited Luther repeatedly in the '20s). Apart from its content, Weisse's songbook shows its individual character in two respects, compared with Lutheran hymnals. With its 157 songs, not all of which, however, have their own tunes, it is more comprehensive than any German hymnal of the period—only the Constance songbook (1533–34 and later) and the Babst songbook of 1545 approached it—and, secondly, it shows a detailed division by titles, beginning with the seasons of the church year. Especially characteristic is the relatively large number of Passion lieder in the form of Lamentations and lied Passions, song categories that were not used by Luther and his close followers, as well as songs about the various times of day, for which, because of the intensive congregational life of the Bohemian Brethren, there was undoubtedly a special need.

The great importance of Weisse's songbook, compared to other German hymnals of the time, lies in its largely independent contents. In creating songs for the congregation, which was his only aim, Weisse proceeded basically the way Luther did, making ample use of medieval liturgical tradition. Contrary to Luther, however, he did this not directly but indirectly, by building logically on the melodic material of earlier Czech Brethren hymnals, which were themselves derived from the traditional medieval liturgy. They made more use of folk songs, however, than did the Wittenberg hymnals. In utilizing medieval sacred songs, Weisse covers much more ground than Luther; choosing from the selections he found in earlier Czech songbooks, he made arrangements of a large variety of song forms such as hymns, *Leisen,* antiphons, tropes, sequences, Lamentations, etc., while Luther followed mainly hymn and *Leise* models in order to keep his material suitable for the congregation. Weisse did not have to exercise such care: the unity and closeness of the Brethren communities created possibilities for training and practice. His historical significance rests specifically on the poetic strength of his texts and translations, not in the musical structure of his melodies. So far, only 16 songs have been identified as translations from the Czech, among them the well-known songs *Christus, der uns selig macht* and *Nun lasst uns den Leib begraben;* therefore, even if some of the song texts are new versions of Latin models, a considerable number of them still must be regarded as Weisse's original poetic work. Some of these, such as *Gottes Sohn ist kommen, O süsser Herre Jesu Christ, Christus, der uns selig macht, Gelobt sei Gott im höchsten Thron, Aus tiefer Not lasst uns zu Gott, O glaübig Herz, gebenedei, Der Tag bricht an und zeiget sich,* and *Es geht daher des Tages Schein,* are among the most important pieces in the *Evangelisches Kirchengesangbuch.* The strength of Weisse's poems, most of them easily accessible in Ph. Wackernagel's *Das deutsche Kirchenlied* I and III, and in a facsimile edition of the 1531 songbook (Kassel, 1931 and 1958), lies in their folk origins, resulting in a combination of simplicity with intensity and richness of ideas. They contain an expressive fervor along with the devotional language of prayer, both derived from congregational, rather than individual, reflection and emotion. Weisse's verses, even more than Luther's, are characterized by their

138. Hymnal of the Bohemian Brethren, in Czech, 1541 and 1561. Title pages.

syllable-counting, rhymed poetry, which takes no notice of the pleasing smoothness of verse meters in use since the days of Opitz. This should not be regarded as a primitive first step toward later methods of versification, but as an art in itself, also encountered in earlier Czech hymn poetry. It is therefore almost impossible to sing one of Weisse's texts to a strictly metered melody, as can be seen from the adaptation, customary today, of a tune by Melchior Vulpius to *Der Tag bricht an.*

Weisse, then, was no melodic inventor; rather, he selected for his songs an abundance of different models or, in the case of translated texts, took over the old melodies. He indicates the source of many tunes, mainly for religious melodies; those for which no source is given probably come mostly from folk songs. Practical hints in the chant and mensural notations facilitate identification of the melodies. After Bruno Stäblein had identified the medieval tunes (see *Die Musikforschung,* V, 1952, 138 ff.), C. Schoenbaum published a large-scale study on the origin of the melodies in Weisse's hymnal (see *Jahrbuch für Liturgik und Hymnologie,* 1957, p. 44 ff.). He offered convincing proof that most of Weisse's melodic material must already have existed in the preceding Czech songbooks of the Brethren and established the fact that while the Czech and German Brethren in Bohemia constantly made new texts for their hymnals and improved those already published, they held on very stubbornly to their melodic material. Weisse's musical procedure differed entirely from Luther's; he simply added new texts to old melodies without changing them for textual reasons, as the German Reformer did. This is clearly shown by a comparison of Weisse's *Von Adam her so lange Zeit* with Luther's *Nun komm, der Heiden Heiland* and of both tunes with their model, the hymn *Veni, redemptor gentium:*

a. Hymnal of the Bohemian Brethren, 1531, *Veni redemptor gentium* (fourth century)

Ve - ni re-demp-tor gen-ti-um, o-sten-de par - tum vir-gi-nis, mi - re - tur om-ne sae-cu-lum: Ta-lis par-tus de - cet De-um.
Von A-dam her so lan-ge Zeit war un-ser Fleisch ver-ma-le-deit. Seel und Geist bis in Tod ver-wundt, am gan-zen Menschen nichts ge-sund.

b. Erfurt, 1524

Nun komm, der Hei-den Hei-land, der Jung-frau-en Kind er-kannt, daß sich wun-der al - le Welt, Gott solch Ge-burt ihm be-stellt.

Several medieval sacred folk songs may be concealed directly or indirectly in Weisse's hymnal—for example, in the partly narrative text "Gelobt sei Gott im höchsten Thron," which appears here with the tune *Erstanden ist der heilig Christ,* or in "O süsser Herre Jesu Christ," where "aus Genaden" returns at the end of each verse; its melody is akin to *Nun bitten wir den Heiligen Geist.* (The model given by Weisse, *Jesu, salvator optime,* has not yet been identified.) Tetrachords, a typical Slav melodic element, appear in many melodies, frequently in connection with very marked rhythms, as in the following table song:

Hymnal of the Bohemian Brethren, 1531

Den Va - ter dort o - ben wol - len wir nun lo - ben, der uns als ein mil - der Gott gnä - dig - lich
ge - speist hat. Und Chri - stum sei - nen Sohn, durch wel-chen der Se - gen kommt vom al - ler - höch-sten Thron.

A three-part setting of this tune—the text is different but it is also for giving thanks after eating—can be found in the *Concentus novi* by Johann Kugelmann (1540; see vol. 2 of the special series of *Das Erbe deutscher Musik,* Kassel, 1955, p. 45). In all likelihood the tune of still another table song in the same publication (p. 42), *Gott Vater, Sohn und Heiliger Geist,* is also of Bohemian origin. The melodies for *Christus, der uns selig macht* and *Jesu Kreuz, Leiden und Pein* (*Evangelisches Kirchengesangbuch* Nos. 56 and 58) belong in this category too. Weisse's songbook achieved very rapid dissemination. In Ulm alone between 1538 and 1540 four complete, more or less revised editions were published. In 1535 and 1536, Katharina Zell published a large portion of Weisse's songs in four volumes at Strasbourg and, in 1545, eleven of his songs were included in the second part of the Babst songbook, after *Nun lasst uns den Leib begraben* (which has no melody of its own in Weisse's hymnal) had already been given its well-known Wittenberg tune for inclusion in Luther's funeral songs. Undoubtedly, Luther or one of his musical collaborators drew inspiration for the second and final melody to *Vater unser im Himmelreich* from the tune to Weisse's *Begehren wir mit Innigkeit,* unless both tunes have their origin in an earlier, common source.

Weisse's songbook was published in a new version by J. Horn (see above) at Nuremberg in 1544, with 32 new songs added, some from Horn's Czech songbook, published in 1541, and the rest probably from material left by Weisse. Among these are *Da Christus geboren war* and *Lobt Gott getrost mit Singen,* for the melody of which the tenor of the polyphonic song *Entlaubet ist der Walde* was used. A third edition followed in 1566 (it had been completed in manuscript in 1564). This is the most representative among the three 16th-century German songbooks of the Brethren; it shows evidence of its dependence on and proximity in time to the Czech songbook of 1561 or 1564. The dedication to Emperor Maximilian II and the preface, addressed to the "Reformed Protestant Christian churches of the German nation," show the intention of reaching a wide audience. Among the 343 songs of the main section, 140 are still from the first edition, 26 from those that had been added to the second edition. No less than 177 songs thus appear for the first time, approximately half of them identified as translations from the Czech songbook of 1561. The origin of these songs has not been explored in detail, nor has their wealth been utilized. *Jesu Kreuz, Leiden und Pein, Mit Freuden zart, Wohlauf, die ihr hungrig seid, Preis, Lob und Dank sei Gott dem Herren* (the two last texts by P. Herbert), *Sonne der Gerechtigkeit,* and *Die Nacht ist kommen* (P. Herbert) are songs from this rich source still being sung today. The editors of the hymnal, which has an appendix of 106 songs from Lutheran regions, were Petrus Herbert, Johannes Geletzky, and Michael Tham. Herbert is outstanding among them as a simple, popular poet of great fervor and a keen awareness of the congregation's needs. Through him also, as a consequence of his direct contacts with Calvin, the musical influence of the Geneva Psalter, combined with humanistic sentiments (see pp. 529 and 594), made itself felt in the editing of the hymnals of the Bohemian Brethren. The melody of Georg Vetter's Easter song *Mit Freuden zart* is a slight remodeling of the Geneva tune for Psalm 138 (which originated, however, in the late Middle Ages). The melody for Petrus Herbert's *Die Nacht ist kommen,* springing from humanistic soil, is entirely fashioned after Geneva rhythmic patterns. The rhythmic patterns ♩♩♩♩♩ (a) and ♩♩♩♩♩♩ (b) are used in six verse lines in the order a—b—a—b—a—b, followed by a special one for the seventh ♩♩♩♩ ○. The rhythm has been taken over exactly from the model, a tenor from *Geminae undeviginti Odarum Horatii Melodiae,* edited by Petrus Nigidius (Frankfurt on the Main, 1552). In the 1556 songbook of the Brethren the melody reads as follows (the version used today is found for the first time in the 1627 *Cantionale* of J.H. Schein):

Hymnal of the Bohemian Brethren, 1566

Die Nacht ist kom - men, drin wir ru - hen sol - len; Gott walts zu From - men nach seim

Wohl - ge - fal - len, daß wir uns le - gen in seim Gleit und Se - gen, der Ruh zu pfle - gen.

A fourth German hymnal of the Brethren, containing 377 songs and an appendix with 132 additional ones, was published in 1606 in Kraslitz. Another edition, of 1639 (printed in Lissa), is of special value because of its index with the names of the authors. It was followed in 1661 by an edition prepared by Amos Comenius and printed in Amsterdam, in three sections, augmented by a new group of songs from the Lobwasser Psalter; this group was placed at the beginning of the hymnal as "The Psalms of the Royal Prophet David," with part 2 as "Songs by Jan Huss" and part 3 as "Songs by Doctor Martin Luther." This hymnal, too, had several additional printings and thus provided a link to the re-established community of Brethren. It was the editor of the third printing, Daniel Ernst Jablonski, a grandson of Comenius, who consecrated Count Zinzendorf as bishop. A fourth printing was published in 1760 at Lissa. That the development of hymnals by the Bohemian Brethren in the 17th century lacked the intensity of 16th-century events was a natural consequence of the changed external situation of the Brethren. After they had at last gained complete freedom in 1609, they lost all the rights just granted to them in 1621 following the unfortunate outcome of the Battle of the White Hill (1620). After that time they carried on their congregational activities almost exclusively in secrecy and in hiding.

The musical history of the Bohemian Brethren is the history of their congregational singing in the vernacular and of their hymnals. In their services there was no room for contrapuntal music or for the organ or any other instrument. The fundamental statement of their earliest historian, Johann Lasitius, was obviously still true in the time of Comenius: "They have no *cantus fractus* or *peregrinus,* which the people cannot understand and which contributes nothing to churchly edification; no musical instruments nor anything else that smacks of dissipation, licentiousness, or mere ornamentation" (from chap. 13 of *Historiae de origine et rebus gestis fratrum Bohemicorum liber octavus,* edited by J. A. Comenius, Amsterdam, 1649). All the more important, then, was the practice of congregational singing and the song repertory of the Bohemian Brethren. Several pictorial representations on title pages of their hymnals show precentors with a long baton (which was, of course, only for beating time), or groups of precentors (see illustrations on p. 596). It may be assumed that antiphonal singing played an important part in the congregations of the Brethren, particularly in view of the use of the sequence form in the hymnals, but also from the illustrations. The last section of Weisse's songbook permits a glimpse at the Communion as celebrated by the Brethren: first a precentor joined by the entire congregation said a supplicational prayer, whereupon the congregation sang the verse "Amen sprech'n wir alle gleich" (or a corresponding one). This was followed by words of institution spoken by a minister, after which the congregation sang the declaration of faith *Wir glauben all und bekennen frei* as confirmation. Reference is made to songs that were apparently sung after that, during Communion. Although the Bohemian Brethren were detached from medieval tradition, an original, new order developed here from the liturgical basic principle of antiphonal procedure. To be observed in this connection is the use of song verses as responsorial pieces for the congregation, a specialty of the Bohemian Brethren that was kept alive in the renewed church of the Brethren in later times. More than anywhere else, singing in the vernacular was a fixed feature of their daily meetings in the age of the Reformation; it served liturgical (as sung Scripture and as sung prayer) and catechetical purposes at the same time. Up to thirty songs were sung, day after day, during the services.

A new chapter in the history of the *Unitas fratrum* (see p. 259) began with the establishment of the Moravian settlement in Lower Lusatia in 1722, prompted by the reawakening of remnants of the Bohemian Brethren and their emigration there. The "Renewed Church of the Brethren" took its character from Pietism and, above all, from its real founder and first bishop, Nikolaus Ludwig Count of Zinzendorf, a pupil of August Hermann Francke. It was Zinzendorf himself who in musical matters (as in others) gave the community of Brethren for the first fifty years of its existence its individual stamp through the "hours of song" that he introduced in Herrnhut and other localities, probably fashioned after the Halle practices under Francke. Some of Zinzendorf's remarks suggest that singing and the hours of song were to him the focal points of spiritual and congregational life. He felt that they were ways to a genuine expression of enthusiastic pietistic faith and therefore a measure of the spiritual condition of the congregation. He said of the songs that they were "the best method to bring God's truth to the heart and to preserve it there." Zinzendorf's first biographer, A. G. Spangenberg, writes about the hours of song:

> On Cantata Sunday (May 11, 1727) the so-called hours of song were introduced; first one took up complete songs and then continued to sing separate verses about various subjects in a touching manner. Our Count was very practiced in song and verse and so familiar with them that, without having a hymnal in hand, he not only quoted verses from many different songs on a particular subject but sang them with such continuity that one could call it a sermon in song.

Zinzendorf himself wrote to King Friedrich Wilhelm I of Prussia:

> The cantor takes up the subject of the sermons that have just been given and chooses whole and half verses from 20 or 30 songs that illustrate the subject in a clear and orderly fashion: and cantor, organist, teacher, and audience are so practiced that no one is permitted to hesitate, nobody may consult a book—something that cannot be

described unless it is seen. My ten-year-old son, when he plays the hours of song in the house, can shift imperceptibly from one melody to another so that nobody knows whether the entire hour of song had not been expressly so composed: because there is no stopping and every child joins in the singing without looking at a book, since they know the songs by heart. During public prayer hours, however, I first have a familiar song recited before [the sermon]. After it, however, if I do not find a song in the hymnal that I would like to have sung to emphasize the subject matter of my sermon to the audience and to offer it to the Savior as a prayer, I invent a new song of which I knew nothing before and which will be forgotten as soon as it has served its purpose [A. G. Spangenberg, *Leben des Grafen N. L. von Zinzendorf,* 8 parts, 1772–75].

This shows that at the hours of song, which took place daily for many years, there was, frequently for homiletic reasons, improvised singing carried out by combining verses, even half verses, chosen at random sometimes even on spontaneously invented new texts. Complete songs were customarily sung only at the Sunday sermon services.

The congregational practice of singing typical of Zinzendorf is also reflected in the history of the hymnals of the Brethren. Prior to the creation of a specific hymnal for the Moravian congregation (for which, as a matter of fact, it had no need), Zinzendorf issued four others: in 1725 the Berthelsdorf hymnal, based mainly on the one by Freylinghausen (1704 and later; only 23 songs are taken from the old songbook of the Brethren), in 1727 an excerpt from this hymnal and also a *Christkatholisches Sing- und Betbüchlein* for Catholics, and, in 1731, the Marche hymnal, aimed at sectarian circles. The first Moravian hymnal, with 972 pieces—225 by Zinzendorf himself, the remainder mostly from the above-mentioned editions—was not published until 1735. This collection has an appendix with new songs, the result of improvisations at hours of song by various members of the congregation. New editions of this in 1737 and 1741 show additional repercussions of the Moravian practice in eight and twelve appendices respectively, published gradually and bringing the total number of songs to 2201. In one of these appendices Zinzendorf calls himself "Minister and Cantor, known to the congregation." In the following years several selections from the Moravian hymnal were published till, in 1754, another typical Zinzendorf product appeared, the *Kleines Brüdergesangbuch*, containing only song fragments (3,000 of them) based on the practice of the hours of song. This hymnal, which was already out of print one year after its publication, had, after Zinzendorf's death, three additional printings up to 1772. By now, however, the desire grew to replace Zinzendorf's enthusiasm gradually with steady continuity in the singing of the Brethren. This was to be the special task of Christian Gregor.

Particular mention must be made of Zinzendorf's so-called London songbook; as an almost complete collection with 3627 songs in two volumes (published 1753 and 1754), in historical progression (beginning with antiquity), it holds a special position among the hymnals mentioned above and, as the first collection of its kind, among all publications in the history of Protestant hymnals down to the present. It served no practical purpose but was meant as an ecumenical documentation of the timeless, world-embracing significance of Christian song.

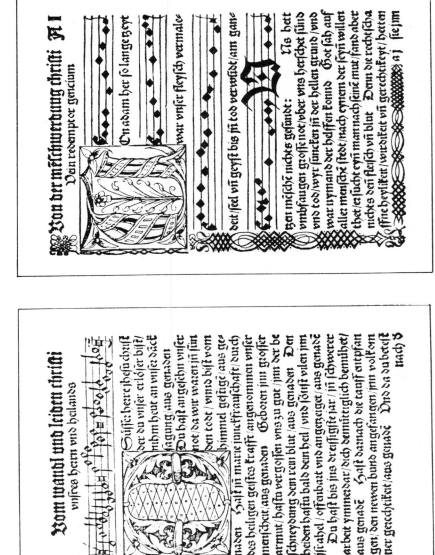

139. *Von Adam her* and *O süsser Herre Jesu Christ* from Michael Weisse's *Ein new Gesengbuchlen,* Jungbunzlau, 1531.

141. Herr Gott, dich loben wir from the Litaneyen für die Chöre in den Brüdergemeinen, Barby, 1773.

140. Christliches Gesangbuch der evangelischen Brüdergemeinen von 1735, Herrnhut, 1741. Title page.

Contrary to the old church of the Brethren, the renewed church did not limit itself to unaccompanied congregational singing. Not only organ accompaniment but polyphonic choral singing and solo singing, sometimes even by women, in response to the congregation were soon firmly established. In the 12th hymnal appendix, published in 1743, we already find text combinations of a cantata-like nature, the beginnings of the so-called *Liturgien,* of which the earliest traces can be found in 1734, according to our present knowledge. Furthermore, the origin of the modern church trombone choir goes back to the Moravians, a fact of particular importance. The introduction of music for wind instruments into Moravian congregational life, certainly prompted by a suggestion of Zinzendorf himself, was carried out by Tobias Friedrich, a native of Franconia who, from 1727 until his early death in 1736, directed the musical activities of the Brethren. The use of wind instruments is first mentioned in 1731; after that time the participation of trumpets, trombones, and horns is mentioned again and again in connection with various functions, mainly ceremonial feasts and funerals. Still unanswered is the question of whether the wind instruments joined the singing in unison or whether there were polyphonic arrangements, nor has there been a clarification of the probable connection between these trends and the trombone choirs developed during the Awakening movement in the 19th century.

The rich holdings of the Herrnhut archives, which may provide exact information on the musical practices of the Zinzendorf community of Brethren during the first decades of its existence, have not yet been explored. Nor has Zinzendorf's musical philosophy been clarified in all its aspects. His correspondence with Johann Friedrich Fasch, still uninvestigated, could reveal important information concerning his ideas on choral and instrumental music. It is known that music by composers close to the age of *Empfindsamkeit,* such as K. H. Graun, suited the Brethren particularly and was therefore used extensively.

There were no printed records of Moravian melodic material up to 1784. The hymnals contained only general indications, if anything at all, of tunes suitable for particular verse forms. In early days the Brethren obviously made liberal use of this procedure, giving preference to older, known melodies, particularly those by Freylinghausen. This soon resulted, especially because of the frequent practice of improvisation in the community, in noticeable deficiencies, which led, at first, before and after 1742, to dropping temporarily the melodic indications in the appendices in order to give them more careful consideration. The two-part *Kleines Brüdergesangbuch* of 1754 again contains an index of 242 melodic forms, enlarged in the second edition of 1761 to 575 titles.

The earliest known manuscript of Moravian melodic material is the chorale book prepared by one Johann Daniel Grimm around 1755. Actually, there must have been many previous chorale books of this kind in the Brethren community.

Christian Gregor (from 1742 on a sort of music director in Herrnhut) deserves credit for putting the songs of the Brethren into a practical order. As editor of the Brethren hymnal of 1778 he also faced the task of arranging some of the Zinzendorf texts; in the chorale book of 1784 (with melody and thoroughbass; new printings in 1799, 1820, and 1859) he gave the tunes their now generally accepted form.

The melodic repertory of the Moravians comprises three groups: 1) tunes of the Bohemian Brethren of the 16th century; 2) tunes of the Lutheran church from various periods; and 3) melodies originating from the renewed community of Brethren itself. Mention should also be made of a small, separate group of tunes by the Silesian Georg Josephi, to texts by Angelus Silesius, which Zinzendorf particularly valued (see p. 259). Gregor's chorale book contains 261 melodies while the numbers in the *Kleines Brüdergesangbuch* still run to 575; this shows that the traditional melodic material was thoroughly sifted in the course of time, probably by Gregor to a large extent. An overabundance of melodies, some of them doubtless quite disorganized, from the enthusiastic early time of the Zinzendorf community of Brethren was later reduced to a sensible amount—a unique event in the history of Protestant hymnals.

One can only speculate on the composers of the tunes. According to J. Zahn (VI, 545, No. 41), the melodies in the chorale book of 1784, except for 60 that are mentioned in the preface and marked in the musical section, are contained in the one by J. D. Grimm, a statement that needs further detailed research. Gregor was undoubtedly the composer of the new tunes of 1784 and had already participated essentially in the creation of at least the final versions of earlier melodies. Carl von Winterfeld considers that the following also played an important part in the music of the Brethren: Tobias Friedrich, who participated in the establishment of the hours of song, Johann Friedrich Franke, musical leader of the Brethren from 1739, and Ludolf Ernst Schlicht, preacher, poet, and precentor in several German and English Moravian communities.

Of the 261 tunes in the 1784 chorale book probably more than half (144) originated within the Brethren community. That the Moravian melodic style could be based on the Freylinghausen hymnal was self-evident considering the circumstances; stressing of feeling and equality of measure prevailed in it as they did widely in the hymn tunes of the end of the 17th century and of the 18th. Nevertheless, the Moravian tunes have a certain individual stamp beyond that. In contrast to the Halle melodies, dactylic measures of three beats, apparently considered too "worldly," appear infrequently and, most significantly, tunes in major keys predominate, frequently distinguished by affective leaps. It is typical that a second melody is often provided, and in major, for Phrygian and Aeolian melodies from the 16th-century hymnals of the Bohemian Brethren. C. von Winterfeld certainly did not go astray when he saw in the preference for major keys the expression of a feeling, especially characteristic of Zinzendorf and the renewed Brethren community, of absolute shelter in Christ, completely overcoming the pressures of guilt and anxiety. Few of the Moravian tunes have become generally known; among these, however, are two characteristic melodies that are still alive in many congregations. One is *Weil ich Jesu Schäflein bin,* sung frequently in many places and even used regularly at children's services, although, significantly, it was originally not a children's song at all:

Melody of Christian Gregor (?), 1784

Weil ich Je - su Schäflein bin, ü - ber mei - nen gu-ten Hir-ten, der mich lie-bet, der mich kennt und bei mei-nem Na-men nennt.
freu ich mich nur im-mer-hin der mich schön weiß zu be-wir-ten, (Henriette Luise von Hayn)

The other one is a musical setting of the so-called Pauline blessing (II Corinthians 13:14) which is still sung in quite a few congregations as a fixed part of the liturgy at the end of the service.

Melody of Christian Gregor (?), 1784

Die Gna - de un - sers Herrn Je - su Chri - sti und die Lie - be Got - tes und die Ge - mein - schaft des Heil - gen Gei - - stes sei mit uns al - len, mit uns al - len. A - men.

Gregor's hymnal remained officially in use until 1927 and thus had probably the longest life-span of any hymnal with the exception of the Genevan Psalter. In practice, however, it lost ground more and more, from 1870 on, to the *Kleines Gesangbuch des evangelischen Brüdergemeine,* an extract from the larger hymnal with some additions and improvements. In 1927, the two-hundredth anniversary of the Moravian Brethren, the hymnal now in use was completed; it is based on the *Deutsches evangelisches Gesangbuch*—in other words, it deliberately follows the general style of the hymn. Preparations for a new hymnal based on the *Evangelisches Kirchengesangbuch* were begun very recently.

The publication of the first *Liturgienbuch* (1770) also took place during the time of Gregor, although only the 1791 edition is considered his actual work. *Liturgie,* to the Moravians, meant the order for a special prayer, praise, and thanksgiving service during which litany-like songs, songs of praise in suitable arrangements, hymn verses, and so on, were sung in a rich alternation between "liturgist, chorus, brethren, sisters," and the entire congregation.

The beginnings of the *Liturgien* books date back to 1743, when Zinzendorf produced songs with texts and melodies based on the Te Deum, followed soon by corresponding litanies, which were published together with songs of several verses (after Anglican models) with the English title *Common Prayer* in 1744. These songs were designed for specific services, mainly for ceremonial feasts. Zinzendorf continued in the same direction with the *Litaneyen der Brüder-Gemeinen* (1752), the *Liturgien-Büchlein,* and the *Litaneyen-Büchlein* (1755 and 1757), including, among others, the liturgies for baptism and burial. It was not until after Zinzendorf's death that the *Liturgie* developed into a special service, similar in form to the hour of song but, unlike the hour, with a fixed order. Handwritten notes in a copy of the *Liturgische Gesänge von 1793* (the original title) in the parish archives of the Moravian community of Neuwied show how far polyphonic choral singing, completely according to contemporary taste with a preference for homophonic two-part settings rich in thirds, was incorporated in these services. Special care was given to the *Liturgien* throughout the 19th century: Gregor's edition of 1791 had new printings in 1806 and 1816; in 1823 K. B. Garve, who also participated as poet, extended the contents of the *Liturgien* book considerably, mainly by increasing the number of choral settings and of pieces for the *liturgus* (additional printings 1839, 1853, and 1864; in 1866 the addition of an appendix). The *Liturgien* books contain only texts; knowledge of their musical design awaits investigation of the archives, mainly those of Herrnhut. The last *Liturgien* books are dated 1873 and, finally, 1907. They pay particular attention to the Passion *Liturgien,* which had been published in a separate edition in 1903. In the 20th century this form of service meeting has been abandoned to such an extent that a new edition of the *Liturgien* book seems at present unlikely.

Around the middle of the 19th century a *Hilfsbüchlein für Liturgen und Organisten in den Brüdergemeinen* (auxiliary booklet for liturgists and organists in the Brethren communities) was published, with a revised edition appearing in 1891 as *Hilfsbuch . . . ;* a supplement was brought out in 1907. The book gives a comprehensive survey of the entire choral repertory used at all service functions of the Brethren during the last century, showing that the repertory always adapted itself completely to prevailing tastes. After the Graun era, during which also such composers as J. A. Hasse, J. H. Rolle, G. A. Homilius, and J. F. Reichardt were popular, Haydn, Mozart, and Beethoven, but also Bortnjansky, gained in importance. Around the middle of the century choral activities were dominated mainly by Mendelssohn. Eventually, however, the Brethren also became part of the restoration movement, greatly favoring Bach and Eccard, and later Schütz. Scarcely any composers of standing came from their own ranks. Peter Mortimer (died 1828 in Herrnhut), a younger contemporary of Gregor who also wrote many choral settings, the author of *Der Choralgesang zur Zeit der Reformation,* was also active as a composer. Christian Ignatius Latrobe, Woldemar Voullaire, and Theodor Erxleben were also quite influential; all of these composers, however, produced only unpretentious music without distinction.

Zinzendorf's original liturgical ideas, which allowed for a variety of ways for music to be sung and played, contributed much to the importance of the Moravian church in music history. The music has limited appeal only because no composer of stature has occupied himself with it. But the real significance of Herrnhut lies in the worldwide influence of its melodic repertory, a result of the music's originality in combination with the missionary activities of the Brethren. It was mainly through Herrnhut that the new *cantiques* penetrated the psalm singing of the French Calvinists, which had been nearly static for two centuries, and it was from "Herrnhuter" that John Wesley, during a crossing to America, heard in Christian songs sound entirely new to him; these would exert great influence on the song repertory of the Methodists. At least 70 Moravian hymnals in eleven languages were gradually spread around the world. In addition, there were over 40 hymnals in the native languages of all the non-European continents, published for the missionary settlements—altogether, an amazing achievement of this *ecclesiola in ecclesia,* as the Brethren community saw itself. Great art from their German homeland also traveled abroad with them sometimes, as is shown by the celebrated Bach cult of the Bethlehem Brethren community in Pennsylvania. *The Moravian Contribution to American Music* by Donald M. McCorkle, from the series *Moravian Music Foundation Publications* published there, deserves special mention.

PART VII

Protestant Church Music in Scandinavia

BY TORBEN SCHOUSBOE

Translated by Catherine Højgaard

Hymns and Liturgy

The music of the Protestant church in the Nordic countries has developed mainly within two national blocks, one consisting of Denmark, Norway, and Iceland (and, up to 1660, also the southern part of Sweden), the other of Sweden and Finland. (Scandinavia includes Denmark, Norway, and Sweden only). Norway was under Danish rule between 1380 and 1814; it was then taken over by Sweden until 1905. Up to 1809 Finland was ruled by Sweden (from 1809 to 1917 it was an autonomous state under Russia), while Iceland was part of the Danish regime until 1918 (with a free constitution granted in 1874). This account will therefore deal mainly with conditions in Denmark and Sweden.

The development of church music in the Nordic countries has followed roughly the same pattern as in Germany. The latter's influence was particularly evident in the 16th and 17th centuries, when translations of German hymns and liturgies, as well as German tunes and polyphonic works, were in general use. About 1800 the music life in Scandinavia began to take on national form.

The Reformation "officially" came to Sweden in 1527 and to Denmark in 1536. Lutheran ideas had already become known among the people through the activities of the Protestant preachers, but the political situation was equally important. Many years of civil war had brought impoverishment in their wake, and King Gustav I Vasa of Sweden and King Christian III of Denmark (a keen Protestant as the result of a visit to Worms in 1521) used the Reformation as an excuse for seizing control of the churches in order to gain control of ecclesiastic wealth. In 1536 the Roman Catholic bishops were arrested in Denmark and new superintendents ordained by Johann Bugenhagen[1] in 1537, thus interrupting the apostolic succession (the king became *summus episcopus*). The succession was maintained in Sweden by means of the consecration of Laurentius Petri by Petrus Magni[2] in 1531. However, the confiscation of church property resulted in a certain secularization which affected both liturgy and music. The clergy, heretofore in charge of Gregorian chant, yielded its role to students from the grammar schools. Though great efforts were made in both countries to continue the use of Gregorian chant (particularly in the towns: see Laurentius Petri, 1571, and Niels Jesperssøn, 1573, below), it dwindled in importance during the 17th century. The reasons for this were threefold: the interest in Latin classical literature was declining, there were language difficulties, and there was a wider use of *de tempore* hymns in the vernacular, which gradually replaced Gregorian chant. However, the first actual hymnals for congregational use did not appear until 1695 and 1699. In Denmark this development resulted in the adoption, in 1685, of a liturgy with hymns only, and that form is still in use. Combined with freedom to choose the hymns and

---

1Johann Bugenhagen (1485–1558), German Reformer active in the Hanseatic cities.
2Swedish bishop of Västerås, consecrated in Rome in 1524, died 1534.

tunes to be used in the services, this means that today Denmark is the only one of the Nordic countries without official liturgical music.

The main sources of church music in Denmark from the time of the Reformation are, for the hymns, Hans Thomissøn's *Den danske Psalmebog* (1569) and, for the Latin liturgical chants, Niels Jesperssøn's *Gradual* (1573). The appearance of these works brought to an end a protracted period of exploration, created order and lucidity in Danish church music, and at the same time laid the foundation for the liturgical song of the subsequent century. A royal decree of 1569 made it mandatory for all churches in the country to procure these books and have them chained to the chair of the parish clerk. Furthermore, Hans Thomissøn's hymnal ("and no other") was to be used in all schools.

The first Danish Protestant liturgy was published in 1528, eight years before the official advent of the Reformation, by the vicar of a church in Malmö, Claus Mortensen, who also edited the first collections of hymns (1528 ff., mostly translations from German). The Malmö Mass was modeled mainly according to German principles and contained hymns instead of the Introit, the Kyrie, the Alleluia stanzas, and the Credo, as well as hymns for use before and after the sermon, at Communion, and at the end of the service, in addition to prose texts translated from Latin. In the only copy now existing (at the Royal Library in Copenhagen) only two melodies are given, written by hand on the printed staff above the text—Johann Walter's *Aus tiefer Not* and the music to the Alleluia hymn *Gladelig vil vi Halleluja sjunge,* presumably a Danish tune adopted by Thomissøn and later taken over in Sweden (see illustration on p. 616). The Reformer Hans Tausen carried on the Malmö tradition in his hymnbooks, which were arranged according to the liturgical year and took into special consideration the hymns for the Offices (1544 lost; 1553, with 6 tunes; 1568, with 37 tunes copied from Babst, 1545). The oldest printed music in Denmark is to be found in a handbook from 1535 which replaced the Missal and contained music for the Lord's Prayer and the Words of Institution (woodcut). In an attempt after 1536 to create orderly conditions, the *Ordinatio Ecclesiastica Regnorum Daniae et Norwegiae,* complied by J. Bugenhagen and Peder Palladius (the first Protestant bishop of Zealand) and approved by Luther and Melanchthon, was authorized in 1537. The effort to preserve Gregorian tradition, undoubtedly influenced by the moderate liturgical views of Palladius, resulted in a subsequent differentiation between divine service in the towns (partly in Latin) and in the country (in Danish). A Danish translation of the ordinance was adopted in 1539 (printed in 1542) as the first authorized Danish liturgy, and contained music (woodcut notes) to the Lord's Prayer and the Words of Institution (different from the 1535 handbook); this music was included in the service book of Palladius (1556, with many subsequent editions). The handbook of 1539 by the Bishop of Lund, Frands Wormordsen, was an attempt to comply with the terms of the ordinance. It was the first to contain music for the whole Mass in Danish (hymns and Gregorian chants according to German models; the recitation melodies included were, however, according to pre-Reformation tradition, since Luther's chants for the prayers and readings were not used in the north). If Latin songs were required, reference could be made to the old Missals and Graduals. Wormordsen concluded

142. Hans Thomissøn, *Den danske Psalmebog* (The Danish Hymnal), 1569, title page. Kyrie hymn (trope) for Whitsun: text in the Malmö Mass, 1528, music in Wormordsen's handbook of 1539. Danish variant concordant with a melody form in the liturgy for use in Mecklenburg, 1540.

the Mass with the hymn based on the Ten Commandments, *Gud fader udi himmerig* (God the Father in Heaven), the oldest Danish Reformation hymn with printed music (see *MGG* VIII, 831).

Hans Thomissøn's *Den danske Psalmebog* of 1569 (the first music printed in Denmark with movable type) was the first authorized Danish hymnal (eight editions with music up to 1634, several shortened or enlarged editions without music up to 1676), containing 268 hymns with 216 unison tunes (203 different ones, mostly in mensural notation). In 1561 Thomissøn had become vicar of Vor Frue Kirke in Copenhagen, regarded as the leading church, from the liturgical point of view, from 1568 on. During his studies in Wittenberg from 1553 to 1557 and as rector of Ribe Grammar School from 1557 to 1561, he had acquired knowledge of a comprehensive musical repertory, as can be seen from the number of models used in his music editing (see Glahn). The majority of the tunes (142) is also to be found in Germany (particularly northern Germany), but as a result of his editing only 43 are exactly the same as the German originals. The remainder contain variants sometimes found in Germany (especially after 1569) but which cannot be traced back to one particular source; Thomissøn is often the oldest source of a variant. Local forms also had an influence as, according to the preface, some of the melodies were written down from traditional renderings. Thomissøn uses some Danish pre-Reformation folk tunes (see *MGG* VIII, 834)—for instance, the following morning hymn used in all the Nordic countries:

At the end of his hymnal Thomissøn gives a liturgy (hymns only) with the psalm tones according to pre-Reformation tradition as in Wormordsen's handbook (however, with subsemitonal *tubâ*). These tunes, printed for the last time in 1634, were apparently handed down from one generation to the next for the following two hundred years. Thus, Thomissøn's hymnal is a very valuable source, representing "a publishing work without compare in the whole German and Danish tradition, and the greatest achievement in the history of Danish church music" (Glahn).

With the *Gradual. En Almindelig Sangbog* (A General Songbook) of 1573 (1606, 1637) by Bishop Niels Jesperssøn, Denmark acquired liturgical music authorized to replace the Roman Catholic Graduals (Erik Abrahamsen has demonstrated that the destruction of these books and their use for bookbinding commenced in 1573, when the new Gradual was printed). Jesperssøn accomplished the aim of the ordinance to preserve part of the Gregorian repertory (cf. Lossius, *Psalmodia,* 1553, dedicated to the Danish king). His liturgy included the Introit and Alleluia in Latin for the whole of the church year and, in addition, prescribed music for the Ordinary (the Sanctus and Agnus Dei with only one tune each), the sequences, and the responsories. Jesperssøn recommended strongly the use of Latin, but suggested as an alternative some Danish hymns (in Thomissøn's version) to be used in the country "for the understanding of the common people." The Gregorian chants are shown in black square notes and the hymns in mensural notation. The Gregorian chants selected by Jesperssøn reveal in individual fashion a conflict between German and Roman Gregorian dialect.

During the years 1600–20, several Psalter paraphrases appeared with melodies according to Lobwasser. The only one of these printed is that of Th.Willumsen, *Paraphrasis Danica Psalmorum Davidis* (1600, printed 1641). Of greater significance was A. Chr. Arrebo's *K.Davids Psalter Sangviiss udsat* (King David's Psalter Arranged with Tunes; 1623, 2nd ed. 1627, with 101 tunes), which employed mainly Lutheran melodies, as did Cornelius Becker. At the end of the 16th and throughout the 17th century, many religious poems, with or without music, were published privately. In addition to the existing repertory of church music (references in H. Chr. Sthen, *En liden Vandrebog* [A Little Book for Wanderers], 1589), secular songs and dance melodies were used increasingly. A Psalter paraphrase from about 1690 by A. D. Foss contains 45 melodies with bass from Adam Krieger's now nonexistent collection of 50 tunes from 1557 (see Schiørring, p.278 ff.). The work *Aandelige Siunge-Koor* (Collection of Spiritual Songs) I–II (1674 and 1681, seven and nine melodies respectively, with thoroughbass) by the greatest orthodox Danish poet, Bishop Th. Kingo, clearly shows the influence of secular airs (J. Schop). One of these in use today, originating from J.B. Lully's *Ballet de l'Impatience* of 1661 (*Sommes nous pas trop heureux, Belle Iris,* also known as *Rofilis, mein ander Ich;* cf. Buxtehude's variations for harpsichord) is given here as an example.

The last remnants of Latin and of the Gregorian chant disappeared with *Danmarks og Norgis Kirke-Ritual* (1685). A form of service consisting only of hymns was introduced (seven hymns before and five after the focal point, the sermon). The organ accompaniment to the hymns was also codified, and the Introit replaced by a brief organ prelude and an opening prayer (there is no mention of a postlude). Replacing Thomissøn's and Jesperssøn's books, there was a new official hymnbook with the corresponding Gradual (both from 1699, published by Kingo, but compiled by a commission more conservative than he), which observed the royal edict that the traditional hymns should be retained. There was a tendency toward rhythmical uniformity of the older chorale melodies, though passing notes, embellishments, and chromatic changes were introduced simultaneously, in accordance with the taste of the period. The coming of Pietism from the south brought with it a repertory of new hymns and tunes, particularly from the Crüger and Freylinghausen collections. The most widely known were the translations and original texts by the priest H.A. Brorson, greatest of the Danish Pietist poets. Together with the hymns from Kingo's book, the new hymns and melodies were printed in *Den nye Psalmebog* of Erik Pontoppidan (1740, with 76 melodies in an appendix; 1742, with 100 melodies printed above the words). This hymnbook, which was to replace Kingo's, was the last official hymnal with printed music in Denmark. It gained but little popularity.

The 1699 hymnal, the first one actually adopted for congregational use, had won widespread acclaim. However, because of the very irregular meter and rhythm of the older hymns and the shortage of organs in the village churches, local melody traditions gradually developed. With their often lavish ornamentation, these were sometimes very different from the original tunes (particularly in Jutland, the Faroe Islands, and Norway, where Kingo's hymnal was used up to the present century). Such popular versions ("Kingo-toner") have been recorded during the past hundred years by researchers in folk music and may also be seen in the many handwritten chorale books from the 18th century.

At the request of the king, Fr.Chr. Breitendich published in 1764 his *Fuldstaendig Choral-Bog,* the first printed chorale book in Denmark, containing 196 melodies with thoroughbass. Its aim was to encourage the use of uniform melody forms, and for this purpose organ accompaniment was considered important. This chorale book contained most of the tunes from the Gradual of 1699, as well as many from the Pietist collections (Freylinghausen), but its spread was limited. The melodies contained trills and other embellishments popular at the time. The tendency toward the isometric chorale was clearly discernible, and the development was complete by the time of the chorale collections of Schiørring and Zinck, both pupils of C.Ph.E. Bach in Hamburg. For use with the rationalistic hymnbook of 1778, Schiørring published chorale melodies in various editions, notably *Kirke-Melodierne* for clavier (1781, the first four-part chorale book, intended particularly for use in the home) and *Choral-Bog* (1783, with thoroughbass notation). The tunes were edited in accordance with a careful study of older sources (particularly Eler, 1588). Schiørring's chorale book, containing for the first time in Denmark Luther's music to the German litany, became popular in South Jutland and particularly in Norway. It introduced into Danish music the isometric chorale in equal note values (half notes) and as ornamentation used only the final trill ("other ornaments do not in fact belong to the chorale"; preface, 1781). This also disappeared with H.O.C. Zinck's *Koral-Melodier* (1801 for the 1798 hymnbook), which employed the principle of equally long notes throughout and was the last Danish chorale book with thoroughbass. Out of the 130 melodies, only three are in triple time. However, some of the melodies by Zinck himself are more popular in character—the influence of J.A.P. Schulz. The four-part *Choral-Melodier* (1839) of C.E.F. Weyse is a revision of Zinck's work. Weyse's own well-known hymn tune *Den signede dag* (O day full of grace; 1826, to Grundtvig's revised version of the pre-Reformation morning hymn quoted previously) was not included in the official repertory until the publication of Berggreen's chorale book in 1853 (see example on p. 616).

The two pioneers in the development of the music of the Swedish church in the 16th century were the brothers Olaus and Laurentius Petri, the former representing the radical beginnings and the latter the more traditional continuation, also advocated by the Finnish Reformer M. Agricola.[3] Despite the fact that there was much writing and translating of hymns, Lutheran congregational song made but slow progress in Sweden and Finland. There was some hymn singing in the Offices (translations by O. Petri and M. Agricola), but the development of liturgical music was characterized by conservatism, the Gregorian chants being preserved either in Latin (MS Tunhemsboken, 1591) or in the vernacular (MS Bjuråker, c. 1541). Only after 1600 were congregational hymns used to any great extent. Three factors are evident in this development: hymnbooks with printed music were not known until the 17th century, German influence had increased (the Thirty Years' War), and in the 16th century the congregations seem to have been used to singing at least some of the Gregorian chants. It is characteristic that the liturgical manuscripts before 1600 contained mostly Gregorian chants, whereas after that date they concentrated chiefly on congregational chorales. Olaus Petri, vicar of a church in Stockholm from 1543, who had come under the influence of Luther during his studies in Wittenberg from 1516 to 1518, published the first Swedish hymnbook in 1530 (several augmented editions during subsequent years; first edition lost, only fragments of others remaining; *Swenske songer eller wisor* [Swedish Songs or Ditties; 1536] is the oldest well-preserved edition; the title *Then swenska Psalmboken* [The Swedish Hymnbook] appeared for the first time in the 1549 edition; the 1572 edition had four manuscript tunes; the first printed tunes—for the Credo in Swedish and Latin—appeared in the 1586 edition printed by A. Gutterwitz in Stockholm). Petri's Swedish liturgy (*Then Swenska Messan,* 1531), which seems to have been influenced by Luther's *Formula Missae,* although not by the *Deutsche Messe,* introduced a Protestant liturgy into Stockholm, with emphasis on the use of the Swedish language. Swedish hymns were used instead of the Introit, Gradual, and Communion chant, but were probably sung by the priest. In 1536 Luther's Credo hymn appeared in Swedish. From 1548 on, Decius's Eucharist hymn was taken

---

3Michael Agricola (1510–57), educated at Wittenberg, headmaster of a Finnish grammar school, and, from 1554 to his death, bishop of Åbo.

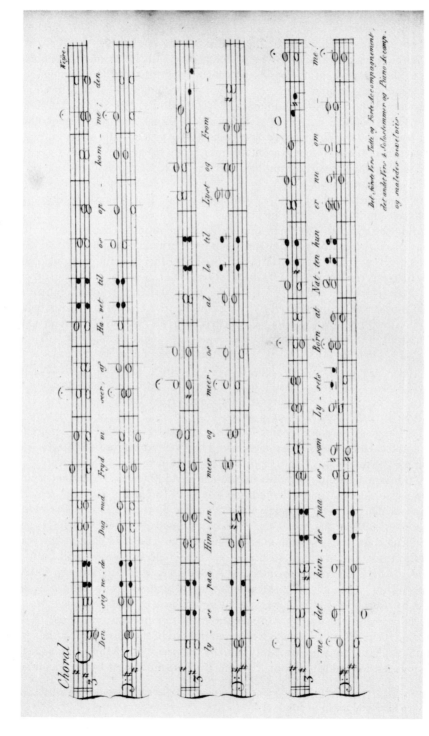

143. C. E. F. Weyse, *Den signede Dag* (O day full of grace), one of the most popular hymn tunes. First print in Grundtvig: *Danske Høitids-Psalmer til Tusindaars-Festen 1826* (Danish Festival Hymns for the Millenary Festival, 1826).

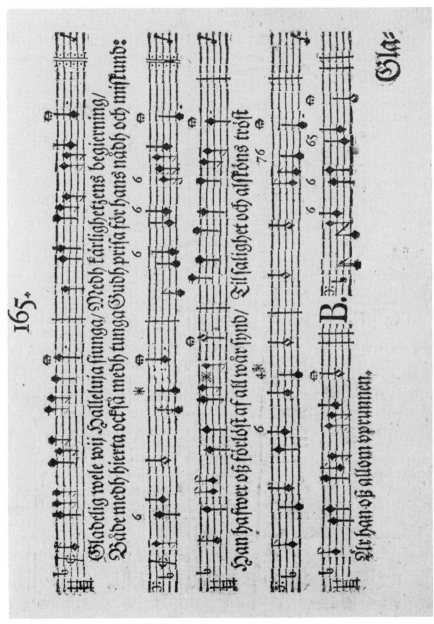

144. *Then Swenska Psalmboken* (The Swedish Hymnal), 1697. Lower half of page, with tune from the Malmö Mass of 1528.

as an alternative to the Agnus Dei; in the 1560s his Gloria hymn was introduced from Denmark and gradually replaced the Gloria in prose. The Latin Graduals seem to have been used for a long time. In *Then Swenska Messan* (1541) O. Petri had to permit the singing of the Introit and Gradual in Latin, as the choice of Swedish alternatives was too small and the difficulty in adapting the Swedish language to Gregorian chants too great. The Ordinary in Swedish was introduced for the first time with *Een lijten Songbook til at brukas j Kyrkionne* (A Little Songbook for Use in Churches; 1553, five series, with handwritten music), and has been used universally since. Archbishop Laurentius Petri was a keen admirer of the Gregorian chant, as will be seen from his treatise on recitation melodies, in the publication *Notulae de officiis* (1568), and particularly in his liturgy (1571; accepted for all dioceses in 1572), which advocated the use of Latin in the towns (Swedish hymns in the country; cf. Jesperssøn). The liturgy, however, came to be used less extensively because of the conflict aroused by King Johan III's *Nova Ordinantia Ecclesiastica* (1575) and *Liturgia suecanae ecclesiae catholicae et orthodoxae conformis* (1576; called the "Red Book," it contained most of the Roman Canon, but in the spirit of Protestantism). When these writings were discarded in 1593, after the death of the king, Petri's liturgy was reaccepted in modified form. However, in *Hand-Bok* (1614; to be used over the whole country) the Introit was omitted, a number of Swedish hymns were substituted for the Latin Gradual, and the hymn *Allenaste Gud i Himmelrik* (All glory be to God on high) took the place of the Gloria. This marked the beginning of the decline of the Gregorian chants and their substitution by congregational chorales. A remnant of the Gregorian tradition can perhaps be traced in that the hymn stanzas were sung by men and women alternately in many places in Sweden and Finland in the 16th and 17th centuries. The Gregorian chants for the Mass with Swedish text were printed in *Liber Cantus* (Uppsala, 1620), together with the chants for Matins and Vespers in Latin, but otherwise the 17th century was dominated by prints and manuscripts of Swedish hymns. The choice of tunes evidenced an increasing German influence: Danish influence was definitely weaker, probably because of the infiltration of secular tunes into Danish hymn singing. Although aria melodies had no effect on the Swedish hymn tunes, profane rhymes, on the other hand, were often sung to chorale melodies (though three of Gustav Düben's thoroughbass arias *Odae Sveticae* [1674] were later used as hymn tunes). *Then swenska Psalmboken* (1616) contained 16 printed melodies. Unison hymn tunes were also found in the private collections of H.L. Rhezelius (1619) and J.Arrhenius (1689–91), and especially in manuscripts from Kalmar (c. 1640), Mönsterås (1646), and Riddarholm (1694, with 150 melodies). The Lobwasser Psalter was represented in Sweden by C.C. Gyllenhjelm's *Schola captivitatis* (1632, with 16 melodies; more complete edition, 1650). A natural consequence of this somewhat uncertain melody tradition was the appearance of popular variants (reflected in the Rappe manuscript of 1675 by lively rhythm and melismas, and particularly characteristic in the Dalar district), to which, in 1647, Bishop Laurelius of Västerås objected, at the same time prohibiting ornamentation of hymn tunes by the organists (J. Dillner still complained of this in *Psalmodikon*, 1846).

Order and stability were created by *Then Swenska Psalmboken* (1695, edited by J. Swedberg, and the 1697 edition with music, called *Koralpsalmboken,* edited by H. Vallerius; both authorized). Marking the end of almost two hundred years of chorale development, this was the first printed tunebook for congregational use in Sweden and the most comprehensive melody source up to that time, with 254 melodies, 109 of which were Swedish variants of German tunes (31 by Crüger). The majority of the tunes had thoroughbass for simple organ accompaniment. Though Vallerius considered even measure to be the most suitable for church music, triple time was employed quite often, also in melodies where even measure was normally used. In addition to hymns, there were several Gregorian chants: the Magnificat and Benedictus in Tone 8, the Nunc Dimittis in *tonus peregrinus,* the Te Deum, hymns, and the three sequences *Laetabundus, Victimae paschali laudes* (each with Swedish stanzas inserted), and *Sancte Spiritus assit. Then Swenska Mässan* was printed with four series of Gregorian chants as an appendix to the Ordinary, though with abbreviated melismas and slight traces of modern tonality; a corresponding Finnish unison collection appeared in 1702. During the following century only new editions of the 1697 hymnbook were published. The many manuscript chorale books from the 18th century are witness to the living interest in congregational singing. The aim was to replace polymeter by isometer, and triple time by common time, and to use richer harmonies for the organ accompaniment. The melodies from the 1697 edition were retained, but were decorated with trills and ornamental notes (F. Zellbell, c. 1740; C.G. Roman, 1744) or simplified (C.G. Miklin, 1760; J. Wikmanson, c. 1785). The Pietist influence seems to have been felt less in Sweden than in Denmark, Norway, and Finland. It is characteristic that even popular collections such as *Mose och Lambsens wisor* (Ditties of Moses and the Lamb; 1717) and *Sions sånger* (Songs of Zion; 1743) refer to melodies in the official chorale book which formed the music foundation. The isometric chorale is evident in *Svensk choralbok* I–II (1820–21, to J.O. Wallin's hymnbook of 1819), edited by the German-born conductor of the Royal Chapel, J.C.F. Haeffner, who from 1808 was *director musices* at Uppsala University. Even rhythm dominates, with the half note as basic unit. The four-part organ accompaniment is conceived as suitable for four voices, in contrast to the idiomatic four-part organ accompaniment in Abbé Vogler's chorale book of 1798. There was great dissatisfaction with Haeffner's chorale book, partly because of its efforts to achieve dignity and uniformity by excluding the more lively tunes in the popular hymnal of 1697 (in opposition to Haeffner, O. Åhlström introduced popular variants in his chorale book of 1832) but also because of the great number of tunes (296), 90 of which were new (mostly German, from J.B. König and J.C. Kühnau; eight were by Haeffner himself). However, after it had been approved for use, though without absolute obligation, Haeffner's work was regarded as the actual chorale book and formed the basis of the developments during the subsequent century.

In the north, as in other places, the 19th and 20th centuries were characterized by reaction against the rigidly isometric chorale, which was not in accordance with popular musical traditions. This reaction was evident on two fronts: within church music itself and in the music of the lay religious movements. These so-called revivals used tunes which were often of doubtful quality but which, with their lively rhythm, had an appeal not found in traditional church music. It was quite usual to borrow tunes from secular folk songs. At the end of the 19th century revival tunes of poor quality from England and America supplanted the folk melodies to some extent and were even used in the church. Innumerable collections of songs and tunes appeared, one of the most popular being *Hjemlands-toner* (Tunes of the Homeland; text book 1895, four-part tunes 1896–1900, edited by H.Th. Rützebeck). In the sphere of church music a reform movement following the German pattern gradually developed. In Sweden and Norway, with their more or less authorized chorale books, the development after about 1860 was concerned especially with rhythm in connection with existing tunes, and the course was quite conservative (though in Norway, L.M. Lindeman contributed many new melodies). The ideas of the reform movement still cannot be said to have won much ground today. There was no authorized chorale book in Denmark (nor is there one today). Nationalistically flavored congregational songs with new tunes appeared about the middle of the century, thus thrusting the problem of chorale reform into the background. Beginning about 1890, Thomas Laub's work marked the start of chorale reform in Denmark, and because of the free choice of melodies, its progress was so rapid that today Denmark sets the pace in the North within that field.

The hymn writer, historian, and teacher N.F.S. Grundtvig was a central figure in Danish religious and national movements from about 1840. His imposing production of hymn texts (about 1500, some original and some adaptations of hymns from the early church and from Lutheran times) struck a new popular and national tone, causing a revolution in church song not experienced in any other Lutheran country. The new hymns were first sung by the congregation of the Vartov Church in Copenhagen, of which Grundtvig became vicar in 1839, but there was a feeling that the traditional chorale style did not correspond to the spirit of the striking metaphorical texts (particularly the hymns for Christmas, Easter, and Whitsun). To begin with, the need for new melodies was met by adopting known tunes from folk and patriotic songs. The more lively congregational singing at Vartov gripped the imagination of the leading composers, most of whom were organists, and they began to compose tunes to the new texts. A.P. Berggreen, a pupil of Weyse and one of Denmark's leading personalities within church, school, and folk music, edited a chorale book (1853; supplement, 1856) for the hymnbook of 1852 (authorized 1855), in which many of Grundtvig's hymns were included. Here the traditional chorale stood side by side with the new "religious romance." Stylistically, this resembled the Danish Romantic lied, which in turn bore traces of the influence of Danish folk tunes. In his essay *Om Menighedssangen* (On Congregational Singing, 1853), which was printed in the chorale book, Berggreen critized the Vartov group, as well as others, for employing secular tunes unsuitable for use in the church. He pointed the way to an improvement of the congregational song; by using melodies in both even and triple measure (though not changing measure); by using the old chorales and the new tunes alternately; by introducing choral music into the services (possibly alternating with the hymn singing of the congregation); and by increasing the tempo of the hymn tunes (in the first issue of the chorale book the tempo was based on m.m. $\mathsf{J} = 60$, in the fourth [1868] $\mathsf{J} = 72$, as the average when written in half notes the new melodies with notation in quarter notes and eighth notes were somewhat faster). In his own melodies Berggreen represented both the chorale type and the new religious romance. The composer Henrik Rung (founder of the Cecilian Society, 1851) charged Berggreen with lack of respect for the Weyse tradition and complained that the new melodies were unsuitable for use in church, but Rung's own chorale book (1857, enlarged 1868, issued as a supplement to Weyse's chorale book at the request of the Vartov community) was exclusively in the new style and is one of the main sources of the church music of the new era. Nevertheless, many others joined in the conflict, which can best be described as a "war by all against all,"[4] since the criteria for an actual church style could not be defined. Besides Berggreen and Rung, leading composers such as N.W. Gade (as yet quite conservative), J.P.E. Hartmann, A. Winding, and Chr. Barnekow wrote melodies in the Romantic style. Melodies by C.E.F. Weyse

(pupil of J.A.P. Schulz) were also to be found in the chorale books, the best being those composed for morning and evening songs by B.S. Ingemann (1837, 1838) for use in schools. In all fairness, it should be stated that the 1855 hymnbook, for which many of the new melodies were written, was intended to be used both in church and home. Naturally, the resulting differences in text had an influence on the tunes, and Berggreen, among others, in the preface to his chorale book emphasized the need for differentiation. Furthermore, many of the new melodies were originally intended as sacred solo songs with accompaniment, and were first published as such.

The foundation for church song in the last half of the 19th century was laid by Berggreen's chorale book, together with the chorale books of official character which Chr. Barnekow edited in 1878 and 1892 for two official hymnbook supplements. The conquest of the romance over the old chorale was quite clear in Barnekow's work. According to the preface, the choice of melodies represented

---

4Povl Hamburger, *Thomas Laub. Lans Liv og Gerning* (1942), p. 33.

the best of the congregational songs. The majority of the melodies were by composers from the 19th century, supplemented by some from the pious and religious gatherings. Quality was on the decline and continued more and more in that direction in the many subsequent hymn-tune collections, which often included melodies that were very poor. In contrast, the chorale book for the Danish congregation in Schleswig (German since 1864) by H.S. Prahl and C. Heinebuch (1895) followed the older chorale tradition in close connection with the German reform movement. The situation in Denmark was criticized by the composer Joh. Chr. Gebauer (*Om Menighedssangen,* printed posthumously in 1891) and by V. Bielefeld (publisher of a chorale book in 1900 for the hymnbook of 1899). However, it was Gebauer's pupil, the organist Thomas Laub, who with strong force and understanding advocated a reform of Danish church music and himself laid its foundation. During his travels in Italy and Germany, Laub had studied 16th-century vocal polyphony and in 1886 made the practical acquaintance of rhythmical church song in Bavaria, after having studied Winterfeld's and Tucher's works on the subject. In his book *Om Kirkesangen* (1887) he called for: 1) a return to 16th- and 17th-century style by discarding the rigid, unpopular chorale and reintroducing the rhythmical forms of the Reformation (Laub believed these to be of popular origin); 2) a sorting out of the newer melodies and the exclusion of all sentimental and artificial romances (Laub considered the simpler popular, Romantic tunes of H.Rung, for example, suitable for use in the church, but later discarded most of them); 3) harmonization of all melodies with pure triads; 4) composition of new church melodies in accordance with the tonal and formal pattern of the Reformation church song. During the years 1888–1902, Laub published chorale collections with restored church tunes, and in 1909 began to compose new melodies himself to a greater extent. The sum of his insight into church music was concentrated in practice and theory in his two main works. The first—the chorale collection *Dansk Kirkesang* (1918)—contained about 130 restored melodies from the 16th and 17th centuries, about 70 of his own compositions, and only three from the 19th century. The other, his book *Musik og Kirke* (Music and Church; 1920), which presented the developments in church music, was an extension and revision of the 1887 book, with views on true musical research that established it as a forerunner of modern Danish musicology. Ideally, according to Laub, the music should be an instrument of the text by means of regained rhythmic liveliness and flexibility. As sources for the restoration of the old melodies, Laub used Tucher's anthology (1848) and Zahn's Bavarian chorale book (1854), and he corresponded with Otto Kade regarding the harmonization problems. Laub's editing is characterized by deep insight and artistic understanding. He often makes use of free reconstruction and his changes in the original melody are seldom because of the language, stemming instead from the desire to improve (and simplify) melodic form. Triple rhythms such as ♩ ♩♩ ♩ and ♩♩♩ are typical for Laub, and he often uses changing and French Psalter rhythms. His own tunes, which bear the mark of a strong personal style, are founded on the same principles and sometimes contain characteristic Gregorian motifs—for example, as in the following melody (c. 1890) to Grundtvig's version of the Crucifixion hymn *Salve mundi salutare* by Arnulf of Louvain. Within religious

circles Laub's ideas caused a conflict on the subject of melodic principles, a conflict which occupied the minds of the next two generations and which can still be felt. It was difficult to introduce the new melodic forms since no new hymns were being written at that time, but Laub's reforms later assumed basic importance for Danish church music. Centered around the society *Dansk Kirkesang* (founded 1922), Laub's pupils continued his work, but revised his reconstructions on certain points (particularly the question of rhythm) by renewed study of their sources (for example, in the 1936 collection *130 Melodier* by J.P. Larsen, F. Viderø, and M. Wöldike, which as a supplement to Laub's work also introduced some new melodies by pupils of Laub). In connection with the authorized *Den Danske Salmebog* (The Danish Hymnbook; 1953, with the same title as Thomissøn's work), J.P. Larsen and M. Wöldike edited *Den Danske Koralbog* (1954). The aim of the work, a collection of 450 tunes, was to meet the need for melodies in the Danish church. Often several tunes were suggested for the same hymn. Tunes from the Reformation and from Crüger's period formed the foundation, and later periods (especially the 19th century) were also well represented. The chorale book shows clear evidence of Laub's ideals and 74 of Laub's own tunes are included (he wrote about 100). Newer composers represented are Carl Nielsen, Knud Jeppesen, Thorvald Aagaard, Oluf Ring, and Bernhard Christensen.

Post-Reformation church song in Norway followed the same lines as in Denmark, since the hymn and chorale books from Thomissøn to Zinck were used in both countries. In addition, the catechismal songs to old church melodies by the Norwegian Baroque poet Petter Dass were very popular. Traditions of the people developed on a local basis because of Norway's special geographical conditions and the use of different hymnbooks in individual parishes. The tunes to Kingo's hymnbook were well established (the Thomissøn tradition) and they were supplemented partially by Pietist melodies. Local versions ("Kingo-toner," compiled by L.M. Lindeman, 1848, and C. Elling, 1898 ff., among others) had changed the tunes very considerably in the course of time, and were often very different from parish to parish. There was extensive ornamentation. An account from 1857 concerning church song in outlying parishes stated that everyone sang from memory and added embellishments to the melodies on the inspiration of the moment. The parish clerk, who led the singing, did the same, and was usually distinguished only by his strong voice. The resulting slow tempo induced the organist (if there was one; not all churches had organs) to fill in with a large number of trills and interludes, very much like the dances which he, as village musician, played on festive occasions. The fermatas were drawn out until all had finished their strophes (see Sandvik). In 1838 the organist O.A. Lindeman published the first chorale book especially for Norway, containing most of Zinck's repertory and supplemented with tunes from Breitendich and Schiørring. The harmony used in the four-part arrangements was quite modern and the repetitions were harmonized differently, as was to become a Norwegian custom. The book met with strong opposition because of its use of equally long notes and simplification of the traditional song; furthermore, its authorization (1835) excluded the use of other chorale books. When, in 1857, M.B.Landstad (editor of the long-awaited *Kirkesalmebog* [Church Hymnbook] of 1861) demanded that the authorization be countermanded, a discussion arose concerning the rhythmic principles connected with a reform of church song *(Salmesangstriden),* and this lasted for the following twenty years. Reintroduction of the chorales from the Reformation in their original rhythmical forms was advocated by J.D. Behrens (1858) and O. Winter-Hjelm (in his comments on *37 ældre Salmemelodier,* 1876, the most important Norwegian essay dealing with the origin and character of the Lutheran chorale). Opposing them was the great Romanticist of Norwegian church music, the organist L.M. Lindeman (comments to *Martin Luther's åndelige Sange,* 1859), who advocated enlivening the tunes by the occasional use of dotted rhythms and replacement of fermatas by short rests. In his chorale book (two parts published in 1871; slightly revised and authorized as *Koralbog,* 1877) Lindeman worked on that principle and also added a number of his own tunes. The harmonization was in genuine Romantic style, with frequent use of weak caesuras (the last chord at the end of the line was often the sixth degree, or a sixth or seventh chord). The book became widely popular, particularly because of Lindeman's fresh and cheerful melodies, and was responsible for the regeneration of the Norwegian church song. The best known of Lindeman's tunes, and that most often sung in the North—*Kirken den er et gammelt hus* (Built on the Rock the church doth stand; lit., The church is an old house), 1840—is one of the earliest church tunes of Norwegian origin; as it is in triple time, however, it is not typical of the composer's work. All protests against Lindeman's melody editions were silenced completely (some rhythmic chorales from the 16th century were printed by request in a supplement to the chorale book, but Lindeman made slight alterations where he considered the harmony and rhythm faulty). *Koralbog for den norske kirke* (authorized in 1926, latest edition 1957) may be considered an enlarged and rhythmically revised edition of Lindeman's chorale book. The rhythmic chorale is still only sparsely represented, while many folk tunes and newly composed tunes—by J. Sletten (*Koralverk,* 1927) and others—as well as mission tunes, are included. Only since 1929 has the reform movement won acclaim through the efforts of the younger composers, particularly Per Steenberg, under influences from Denmark. Steenberg's tunes are the most significant contribution to contemporary Norwegian church song and his important *Koralbok* (published posthumously, 1949, not authorized) forms a stylistic parallel to *Den Danske Koralbog.*

At Hólar in Iceland, Bishop Gutbrandur Þorláksson printed the first Icelandic hymnal in 1589 *(Ein ny Psalma Bok)* and in 1594 *Graduale. Ein Almenneleg Messusöngs Bok* (A General Songbook for the Mass), called *Grallarinn*. These books were partly modeled after the corresponding Danish works of Thomissøn and Jesperssøn, and were used in divine service without much alteration until well into the 19th century (the 19th and last edition of *Grallarinn* appeared in 1779) as the basis for unaccompanied church song. The rationalistic, musically modern hymnbook of 1801 (with three melodies) by Magnus Stephensen was regarded as a break in tradition by those who wished to retain the old songs. Hallgrímur Pétursson's 50 passion hymns (1659, printed 1666) were of great importance for private devotions. A rich paraphrasing of the tunes developed in the congregations through the centuries. Often the tunes were sung as *Tvisöngur*—i.e., as two-part organum in slow tempo—with combinations of parallel movement (in fifths) and contrary movement (with primes, octaves, and thirds, but not fourths) in which the *vox organalis* (*bassus,* as solo voice) ran alternately as upper and lower voice to the *vox principalis* (tenor). The *Tvisöngur* tradition was popular and was retained in some places right up to the beginning of the present century. The Danish Weyse tradition was introduced into Iceland by Pétur Guðjonsson, who used a handwritten chorale book by Weyse in his position as first organist at the cathedral in Reykjavík, where he was employed in 1840. Guðjonsson edited a hymnbook with unison tunes in 1861, and his three-part chorale book (revised by Berggreen) was printed posthumously in 1878. The Weyse tradition was continued with the first four-part chorale book (1884, supplement 1886) by Jónas Helgason, and in the still valid *Sálmasöngsbók* (Chorale Book; 1936) by Sigfús Einarsson and Páll Isólfsson, which includes many older Icelandic folk tunes.

About 1860 a movement began in Sweden toward reform of the church's tunes. The many chorale books that appeared during the subsequent fifty years were, for the most part, Haeffner editions. Some were conservative (Josephson, 1877; Rendahl, 1899; Hjort, 1906; Nodermann and Wulff, 1911). In others, efforts were made to give the melodies a livelier form, either by employing rhythmic versions from the hymnbook of 1697 (Södling, 1878); by imitating Lindeman (Sandström, 1877) or Zahn (Humbla, 1885; Lagergrén, 1886); by using rhythmically free execution without bar lines (Anjou and Törnwall, 1882); or employing the Aristoxenian rhythmical theory (Norén and Morén, 1891–94). The society *Kyrkosångens Vänner* (founded 1889) made a considerable contribution in their desire to reinclude the melody forms from the 1697 hymnal, taking into account Zahn's research (*Svensk Koralbok i reviderad rytmisk form* [Swedish Chorale Book in Rhythmically Revised Form], 1901, 1904). The use of so many chorale books gradually resulted in a great lack of uniformity in church song, and it became evident that there was a need for an authorized chorale book to be used throughout the whole country to the exclusion of all others. The provisional edition of 1921 (proposed in 1917) was built on the Haeffner tradition, but the reform tendency could be seen in the use of triple time, dotted rhythms, and sometimes changing measure. Furthermore, it included Swedish melodies, particularly from the 19th century, as well as a number of mission songs. However, in *Den svenska Koralboken* I–II (authorized 1939, published in connection with the new hymnbook of 1937), the reform tendencies were no longer evident. There were no dotted rhythms and the more rigid Haeffner rhythms dominated (though some melodies were in triple time). Many folk tunes were included, but even the newly composed tunes followed the traditional pattern. The Haeffner tradition could be sensed also in the harmonization, which was in major-minor tonality, even in the modal melodies, though dominated by pure triads. Corresponding Finnish chorale books were printed in 1903 and 1944, both showing a strong national profile with their inclusion of Finnish sacred songs. By the use of *alternatim* practice— i.e., distributing the stanzas of the hymns between the congregation with organ and the choir—restored chorales have also found their way into Swedish hymn singing, as manifested by such publications as *Koralmusik* (1957 ff., edited by H. Göransson).

As the result of inter-Nordic teamwork, *Nordisk Koralbok* was published in 1960. In this an attempt is made to co-ordinate the many individual melodic interpretations of the basic Lutheran tunes which had developed in the course of time in the different countries, and to adjust them to their original forms. Thus this chorale book is a preliminary milestone in northern reform efforts and its aim is to form the basis of future melodic revisions. Such revision has already been carried out in a 1963 supplement to the Swedish chorale book, in which can also be seen a tendency toward the freer instrumental accompaniment long attempted in many parts of Sweden and Denmark, following the principles of H. Bornefeld's *Begleitsätze.*

The decline in liturgical understanding on the part of Pietism and rationalism has been felt in various ways in the Nordic countries. The liturgy of the Danish-Norwegian ritual (1685) concentrated on the hymns, but by 1798 the *de tempore*[5] principle of the hymnbooks had already been discarded in Denmark, and the practice of substituting hymns for the Kyrie, Gloria, and Credo gradually fell into disuse. In Norway, where Kingo's and Guldberg's hymnbooks (1699 and 1778) were in use for a long time, the *de tempore* arrangement and the Kyrie hymns were retained. The recitation melodies were gradually changed under the influence of modern tonality, with emphasis on a more melodious style. J.Wiberg's *Messe-Melodier* (Recitation Melodies; Copenhagen, 1832), which became very popular, have only one recitation melody common for all the readings, with *tuba* a diminished fourth below the tonic. According to the preface, these tunes represent the best of oral tradition and are perhaps actually built up on reminiscences from the pre-Reformation melodies for the liturgy. Wiberg's recitation melodies formed the basis of the first Norwegian liturgy (1870, by L.M. Lindeman) and were also used in Iceland. In some places the desire for a richer musical recitation at the festivals led to composition of new melodies (J.P.E. Hartmann, *Jule-Collect* [Collect for Christmas], 1853; A.P. Berggreen, *Antiphonale,* 1867). The notable *Liturgiske Melodier* (1889) by Prahl and Heinebuch, based on 16th-century sources and, on the basis of common practice, making use of psalmody in the Introit, for example, was intended for use in South Jutland and was not used in Denmark. Th. Laub's reform of the hymn tunes brought him only tentatively in

5The *de tempore* principle operated in the arrangement of hymns according to the Sundays of the ecclesiastical year rather than by subject matter.

touch with liturgical song, but his use of Gregorian motifs (Eucharist liturgy, 1918; Te Deum, Litany, etc., 1922 for choir) showed the way. The efforts of Laub's pupils are in the direction of a reintroduction of the chanted prose sentences of the Ordinary, and attempts are being made to adjust the classical liturgical tones to the Danish texts (J.P. Larsen, *Messetoner* [Recitation Tones], 1935, and music to the liturgy proposed by the society *Dansk Kirkesang*, 1943). A corresponding Norwegian work has been carried out in the authorized *Liturgisk Musik for den norske Kirke* (1920) and *Graduale* (1925) by O.M. Sandvik, the latter work employing part of Luther's music for the German Mass, with organ accompaniments by P. Steenberg to the recitations (according to Swedish custom).

In Sweden the Kyrie, Sanctus, and Agnus Dei were retained in their original prose form, but the declining interest in the Swedish Mass tradition was revealed in Haeffner's *Svenska Mässan* (The Swedish Mass) of 1817 (his 1799 version was edited by Åhlström in 1818), which had only one series of liturgical music (instead of the four or five series used from the late 16th to the early 18th centuries), and whose four-part arrangements revealed but poor knowledge of the Gregorian chant. (The Gregorian tradition in Finland was definitely discontinued with the *Suomalainen Messu* [Finnish Mass] of A. Ehrström, 1837). Further simplification and abbreviation of the melodies occurred in the liturgies of Törnwall (1863) and Humbla (1875), and new recitation melodies were composed by C.L. Lindberg (1858) to take the place of the old "monotonous" forms. The work *Musiken till Svenska Mässan* (1897) marked the beginning of a restoration of liturgical music, based on a strong Swedish interest in choral music and the choral services at Vespers popular since the 1890s (with Schoeberlein's and Max Herold's works as models). Choir singing has a primary place in the abundant selection of classical and newly composed music for the Ordinary, while simpler forms are intended for unison song with organ accompaniment. A number of Gregorian melodies from Swedish and foreign sources are used, but with modern harmonization and rhythm. This applies also to the many newly composed, pseudo-Gregorian Introit chants and antiphons in *Missale* (1914) and *Vesperale* (1915), particularly those by J. Morén. The revised *Vesperale* (1925) shows a better understanding of the Gregorian tones. The corresponding Psalter is the first more comprehensive and discerning effort to reintroduce Gregorian psalmody into Swedish divine services. The music in *Den Svenska Mässboken* I–II (authorized 1942 and 1944) is strongly influenced by Gregorian tones, though it embraces a number of newer compositions, including some from the 1897 Mass. Primarily, 16th-century Swedish sources are used for the Gregorian chants. The Introit is in either Gregorian form or the form of a chorale (arrangement of a hymn tune "à la gregoriana"). As in earlier liturgies, the songs (also the recitation tones) are harmonized, though here as free organ arrangements following the harmonic principles of the 1939 chorale book. Similarly, the Gregorian tradition is revived in the Finnish *Messu-sävelmistö* (Compositions for the Mass, 1951). During the past fifty years or so, efforts to promote the use of Gregorian chant in the vernacular for the canonical hours have been gaining ground. Knut Peters and Arthur Adell published *Det svenska Antifonalet* I–II (1949 and 1959), based on

Swedish Reformation practice and sources, in addition to Roman chant books; leading in the work today is Ragnar Holte, chairman of the Laurentius Petri Society (founded 1941). Similar work has been done in Denmark by Gunnar Pedersen and especially by Dag Monrad Møller, E. Rosenkilde Larsen, and Finn Viderø, who founded the society *Dansk Tidegærd* in 1965. Viderø's adaptations of Gregorian melodies to Danish texts are based on thorough studies of Gregorian style (*Det Danske Antifonale* I–II, 1971 and 1974).

Polyphonic Church Music

In the 16th and 17th centuries polyphonic church music in the Nordic countries was completely dependent on foreign compositions and musicians, especially those from Germany. The Chapels Royal in Copenhagen and Stockholm were the most important musical centers, around which the development quite naturally concentrated. An impression of the repertory of the Chapel Royal in Copenhagen can be gained from two sets of partbooks from 1541 and 1556 (The Royal Library, Gl. Kgl. Saml., 1872–73), which contain more than 300 religious and secular compositions, mostly for five and six voices, primarily by composers from Germany and the Netherlands. For the most part, only the beginnings of the texts, principally German and Latin, are cited (in the 1541 collection the bass part has the whole text in some cases). Among the composers of religious works were Josquin, Nicolas Gombert, Ludwig Senfl, Johann Walter, Adrianus Petit Coclico, the court conductor Georgius Preston (eighteen works), and court organist David Abell (four works). The musical repertory of the grammar schools also came from Germany. At the end of the 16th century, works by Josquin, Lasso, Meiland, Gallus, and others were included in Swedish school libraries, in accordance with Bishop Laurentius Petri's conservative attitude toward music and his insistence that the pupils be instructed in polyphonic music. On the other hand, there appear to have been no representatives of the German chorale motets. The well-known Finnish collection *Piae Cantiones ecclesiasticae et scholasticae,* edited in 1582 by Theodor Petri (Rwtha), contained 74 Latin religious and secular songs (eight in two parts, two in three parts, and two in four parts), some of which are undoubtedly of Nordic (Finnish?) origin. At the beginning of the 17th century, music in the Venetian style was brought into northern regions (G. Gabrieli, Hassler, Scandellus, M. Praetorius, Schein, Eccard, and others), and Cantionales by Raselius, Gesius, Vulpius, Bodenschatz, and Melchior Franck (not Osiander). Characteristically, quite a few sources substituted new Swedish texts for the non-Latin. Later in the century, Scheidt's *Tabulaturbuch* found its way north, and compositions by Hammerschmidt became especially popular (Norlind). The repertory of the Danish grammar schools developed in the same way. About 1650 the Copenhagen School obtained *Geistliche Konzerte,* dialogues, and motets by Hammerschmidt, Vierdank, Schein, and Rosenmüller, as well as Crüger's *Geistliche Kirchenmelodien* and other collections. The purchase of musical instruments, for use partly in church services, was a big item in the school accounts. The activities in Copenhagen of the conductors Heinrich Schütz and Caspar Förster and the organist Chr. Geist bear witness to the strong German influence.

Before 1800 the national contribution to church music in Denmark was small. Bordering on polyphonic music is a St. John Passion resembling Walter's chorale Passion, with traditional roles and *turba* choirs (an unusual element is the singing of the words from Matthew 27:46 on different tonal levels). This Passion was sung at Evensong on Good Friday in Roskilde Cathedral until 1736, when it was prohibited and a sermon was substituted. The manuscript (from 1673, now in Rigsarkivet, Copenhagen) shows that inserts in concertato style, mostly to hymn texts and often with viol accompaniment, were used frequently. The organ accompanied the recitations all the way through. The Passion was published in 1946 *(Roskilde Passionen)* for practical use. A similar Swedish Passion, apparently drawn from Danish and German sources, and found in ten 17th-century Swedish manuscripts, has also been published (*Monumenta Musicae Svecicae* III). A unique and distinguished collection is *Pratum spirituale* by Mogens Pedersøn, printed in five partbooks by H.Waldkirch, Copenhagen, in 1620 (new edition by Knud Jeppesen in *Dania Sonans* I, 1933). Pedersøn was a pupil of M. Borchgrevinck and G. Gabrieli, and from 1618 to 1623 was deputy conductor of the Chapel Royal. His collection contains 37 five-part works: arrangements of 29 Danish hymns and two Latin sequences (the Easter sequence is for three to six voices in varying combinations), with melodies from Thomissøn; a fragment of a Latin Mass consisting of the Kyrie, Gloria, abbreviated Credo, and Sanctus with Hosanna; three Latin motets; and *Responsoria Danica* and *Responsoria Latina*. Stylistically, Pedersøn approaches the Italian-influenced Germans Eccard and Hassler. Tonally, he represents a transitional stage between church modes and modern tonality, but he shows a strong inclination toward the new harmonization in his emphasis on the dominant-tonic relationship and his frequent use of leading tones. The three Latin motets display an imposing command of the polyphonic technique. The hymn arrangements are mostly in cantional style, though with emphasis on independent polyphonic lines (particularly beautiful in No. 2, *Alleniste Gud* [All glory be to God on high], and No. 12, Kyrie *Om Pintzdag* [On Whit Sunday], with the cantus firmus in Tenor II). The collection was probably intended primarily for the Chapel Royal, but, according to the preface, could also serve the practical needs of school choirs. The order of the settings shows the liturgical function of the collection: first come the songs pertaining to Christmas, Easter, and Whitsun, arranged in groups, each beginning with a Kyrie hymn; next follow hymns not connected with any particular religious festival; Latin compositions come at the end. With three exceptions, all the verses (or, at any rate, the most important) are arranged with careful consideration for metrical variety, thus emphasizing the practical aim of the collection. Thirty-nine Latin motets by the organist Thomas Schattenberg were published in 1620 as *Jubilus S. Bernhardi . . . Cantiones sacrae . . . 4 voc. Canticum Canticorum Salomonis,* in Hebrew, Latin, and Danish, by L.P. Thura (1640), contains 31 Lutheran melodies in four-part arrangements by D. Scheidemann, H. Praetorius, S. Calvisius, and the Danish composers Peder Stub (ten works) and Jacob Ørn (one work). Little remains of the church music by the Danish organists Joh. Schröder (J.Ph. Krieger's teacher) and Joh. Lorenz, Jr., whose *Abendmusiken* were famous ("Organista ipse nulli in Europa secundus"—from a diary by H. Jacobaei, 1672). During his period as organist in Elsinore (1660–67), Buxtehude composed the cantata *Aperite mihi portas justitiae.*

The few Swedish contributions to the church music of the 17th century are mainly connected with the activities of the Chapel Royal, and particularly those of Sweelinck's pupil Andreas Düben and his son, Gustav Düben. Both were court conductors, as well as organists for the musically influential German community in Stockholm. The German church concert style dominated (dialogue, motet, cantata). A favorite form was the simplified chorale cantata, with a sinfonia as an introduction and with ritornellos between the stanzas. The earliest existing motet with original Swedish text is *Fader wår* (Our Father) for solo voices, five-part choir, and orchestra (1654) by the opera conductor Vincenzo Albrici. A few works by A. Düben, by O. Rudbeck, vice-chancellor of the University of Uppsala, and by the violinist P. Verdier have been handed down. Gustav Düben's music tends toward the conventional, but his chief work *Surrexit pastor bonus* (1664, for four voices, two viols, and continuo) shows a more individual structure. The funeral cantata *O flyktig fröjd* (O passing delight, 1685), by the organist Ludert Dijkmann, is the first purely Swedish work in more mature cantata style. G. Düben's greatest contribution was the so-called Düben collection of more than 1500 works by leading German and Italian composers of the time, including Chr. Ritter and Chr. Geist, who worked for some time in Stockholm. The Düben collection is famous as the main source of Buxtehude's cantatas.

The greatest Swedish composer of the 18th century was the court conductor J.H. Roman (called the father of Swedish music), who was much influenced by Handel. Roman never served as an organist, and his church music was primarily intended for the religious festivals held in the court. He was the first to use the Swedish language to any great extent in polyphonic music, partly in his own works and partly in arrangements of foreign church music. The authenticity of the manuscripts of Roman's church music, most of which is not printed, is as yet not quite clarified (see *MGG*). In addition to his Swedish Te Deum and *Missa brevis* (concert Mass, 1752?), some of his nearly 100 compositions with texts from the Psalter (or paraphrases thereof) were written for solo voices, choir, and orchestra (e.g., Psalm 100), while the majority were intended for solo voices with continuo or, in exceptional instances, string orchestra. Little Swedish church music by other composers remains to be mentioned: A.N.v. Höpken, *Jule* [Christmas] *Pastorale,* 1751; F. Zellbell, Jr.; J.C.F. Haeffner, who was influenced by Gluck and was composer (in 1809, with text by S. Ödmann) of the first Swedish oratorio, *Försonaren på Golgatha* (The Redeemer at Golgotha), as well as cantatas for special occasions; Per Frigel, who wrote (in 1815, with text by S. Ödmann) the oratorio *Försonaren på Oljoberget* (The Redeemer at the Mount of Olives); and the foreigners J.M. Kraus and Abbé Vogler (the latter's hymn *Hosianna* has been sung in Finnish churches on the first Sunday in Advent since 1807). In Denmark, J.A. Scheibe was a pioneer in the use of the Danish language in polyphonic music (the Passion *Den døende Jesus,* 1762, and cantatas with own text). In the small number of Danish church works by J.E. Hartmann, H.O.C. Zinck, S. Wedel, J.A.P. Schulz, and F.L.A. Kunzen, the main emphasis is on the cantata form, although Schulz also composed motets with or without chorale stanzas. An outward sign of the secularization of church music was its place in the official concert life, particularly as organized by Roman in Stockholm (1731) and Scheibe in Copenhagen (1744). Here a lively interest developed in the performance of church music, especially oratorios and Passions, by Handel, Pergolesi, and other German and Italian composers, whose influence on domestic music was strong. Little is known about the repertory at divine services, but interest in it seems to have been on the decline.

However, the congregation of Moravian Brethren at Christiansfeld (South Jutland), founded in 1772, apparently used music extensively in its services, mostly in connection with the Communion on festive days. Recent investigation of the Christiansfeld repertory from 1772 to 1880 has shown a music collection of about 1600 items, some of which are movements from one and the same composition but listed separately. Among the 79 composers mentioned by name are Chr. Gregor (106 works), J.L. Freydt (67), J.Chr. Geisler (67), G. Fr. Hellström (organist at Christiansfeld, 46), J.H. Rolle (24), J. Haydn (18), and K.H. Graun (7). The scoring is often for four-part choir, strings, and continuo (winds ad libitum), and the texture is mostly homophonic, if necessary obtained by arrangement in order to guarantee the comprehensibility of the text (see Reventlow).

The most general form for church music in Denmark in the 19th century was the cantata for church festivals and other special occasions. The cantatas of the court composer and organist C.E.F. Weyse were of great significance (ten for Christmas, Easter, and Whitsun, besides a number of cantatas for other occasions —for example, at the university); they were composed for solo voices, choir, and orchestra, and show the influence of Handel and Mozart. Weyse's cantatas were very popular—particularly *Den ambrosianske Lovsang* (The Ambrosian Anthem, 1826)—and were often performed at musical devotions in connection with services. They included a few chorale inserts and recitatives, but in general homophonic choral movements alternated with melodically well-formed ensembles and arias. Among the prominent composers of cantatas later in the century were J.P.E. Hartmann (of special beauty are his works *Quando corpus morietur*, 1850, *David's 115. Psalme*, 1871, and *Hellig tre Kongers Kvad* [Song of the Three Kings], 1894) and Hans Matthison-Hansen, best known for his organ works. During the last half of the century an increasing interest developed in the simple choral hymn (J.P.E. Hartmann, A.P. Berggreen, Otto Malling), probably due to the influence of the Cecilian Society. N.W. Gade wrote four chorale preludes for the organ, while Godfred Matthison-Hansen and the French-influenced O. Malling wrote organ fantasies on chorale motifs. The change in taste, of which Th. Laub's reform work was an expression, and which resulted in the revival of works and styles from the 16th and 17th centuries, is being felt in the 20th century. This is due to a great extent to the work of Mogens Wöldike, as organist and conductor of the Copenhagen Boys' Choir and as leader of the society *Dansk Kirkesang*. Typical of this new era is a concentration on relatively short compositions for liturgical use. While N.O. Raasted, a pupil of Straube, tends toward the Leipzig School, Laub's ideals are clearly evident in the few church works of Carl Nielsen and the many organ and choir compositions by P.S. Rung-Keller, Knud Jeppesen, Svend-Ove Møller, Finn Viderø, Bjørn Hjelmborg, and Bernhard Christensen. Newer European influences (Bartók, Stravinsky) can be sensed in the works of the younger composers, represented by Vagn Holmboe's expansive a cappella motets, Leif Thybo's motets and St. Mark Passion (1964), and the

Roman Catholic composers Leif Kayser and Bernhard Lewkovitch.

Swedish church music in the 19th century was mainly characterized by a simple form of choral hymn, strongly influenced by the male choir tradition so popular in the country. In addition to the capital, the university town of Uppsala, with its inspired *director musices* and representative of the Leipzig School, J. A. Josephson, was a center for the cultivation of church music in concert form. As early as the 1830s, A. Mankell had advocated a moderate Cecilianism, holding church concerts at which works of Palestrina, Lasso, Eccard, Bach, Handel, and Mozart were performed. As a result of the interest in choir singing and the efforts to raise the standard of church music, a number of anthologies were published in the middle of the century—for example, by A. Mankell (1841, 1865), J. P. Cronhamn *(Musica Sacra,* 1854, 1867), and J. A. Josephson (1867 ff.). These included short compositions dating from the 16th to 19th centuries, as well as many works by recent Swedish composers. Josephson's anthologies ("for home, school, and church") became popular, but the inclusion of many works by lesser composers of the 18th and 19th centuries was an expression of the "hopeless confusion of styles and groping attempts in various directions" prevailing in the middle of the 19th century (Moberg). A master of contrapuntal technique and a keen champion of Cecilianism was the organist B. V. Hallberg, who composed two Masses, a Requiem, and a number of cantatas. *Stycken ur Davids Psalter,* for solo and choir with piano (1861–66), by the amateur composer and politician G. Wennerberg (influenced by Handel) won great acclaim; he also wrote three oratorios with Bible text and chorale inserts. The work of the great national Romanticist J. A. Söderman, *Andelige sånger* (Spiritual Songs) for choir and organ (1872), bore traces of the influence of Liszt's mysticism. Swedish organists allied themselves to the French late Romantic style, and Josephson's Classico-Romantic ideals formed the background for the society *Kyrkosångens Vänner,* a leading factor in the church reform movement around the turn of the century. Important choral anthologies, such as *Hymnarium* (1914, with 392 pieces, about 200 by Swedish composers) and *Musica Sacra* I–II (1916), include not only many works from the classical period of church music—up to c. 1650—but also several works from the "period of decay." The 20th-century reform movement, the organization of choral societies (*Sveriges Kyrkosångsförbund,* 1925, comprising about 900 choirs), and the need growing out of regularly held church choir festivals (1927 ff.) have produced a great amount of new church music of all kinds. Among the prominent composers in the national Romantic style are Otto Olsson, K. I. Wideen, O. F. Lindberg, and H. Alfvén; D. Wikander, G. D. Olson, and A. Runbäck use a newer, more polyphonic style. The modern linear, Baroque-inspired mode of writing is represented by Hilding Rosenberg's pupils Sven-Erik Bäck and I. Lidholm, as well as by O. G. Thyrestam, T. Sörensen, T. Nilsson, and V. Söderholm.

In Norway and Finland the influence of folk music, particularly religious folk tunes, has been felt in the music of the church since the rise of the national style in the late 19th century. National Romanticism in Norway is represented by L. M. Lindeman, C. Cappelen, and J. Haarklou, and in Finland by I. Krohn, H. Klemetti, A. Maasalo, and (with newer traits) by J. Sundberg, S. Carlsson, and

T. Kuusisto. The works of P. Steenberg, A. Sandvold, and L. Nielsen in Norway, and S. Salonen and T. Stenius in Finland, display the trend of the reform movement toward an objective style in church music. In Norway new tendencies toward neoclassicism appear in the music of R. Karlsen, K. Nystedt, and E. Hovland, while the intensely expressive motets of F. Valen, in his personal, atonal style, are unique.

PART VIII

Protestant Music in America

BY ROBERT STEVENSON

EARLY CONTACTS WITH THE ABORIGINES

In the spring of 1564 three shiploads of Huguenots under the command of René de Laudonnière settled ten miles down St. John's River from what is now Jacksonville, Florida. Their principal recreation consisted in singing Marot psalms. The sturdy Calvinist tunes to which these were sung caught the immediate fancy of the surrounding Florida Indians, who came from far and near to enjoy the Huguenots' music. Before long, the natives were singing the same tunes, learned by rote. After the Spaniards massacred the encroaching French colonists, the Indians for many years continued to sing snatches of these vigorous Huguenot tunes as "code words" to determine whether any stragglers along the seacoast were friendly French or sullen Spanish.

Nicolas Le Challeux's *Brief Discours et histoire d'un voyage de quelques François en la Floride,* published at Geneva in 1579 as an appendix to Girolamo Benzoni's *Histoire nouvelle du Nouveau monde,* specifies the very tunes that were used as signals—those for Psalms 128 and 130. He writes that the Florida Indians "yet retain such happy memories that when someone lands on their shore, the most endearing greeting that they know how to offer is *Du fons de ma pensée* [Psalm 130] or *Bienheureux est quiconques* [Psalm 128], which they say as if to ask the watchword, are you French or not?" Le Challeux continues that the Indians do so because "the French, while there, taught them how to pray and how to sing certain psalms, which they heard so frequently that they still retain two or three words of those psalms."

Both Psalms 128 and 130 had been published *à 4* in Louis Bourgeois's *Pseaulmes cinquante, de David* (Lyons, 1547), with the congregational melody confided to the tenor. A comparison of the Huguenot tune for Psalm 128, as taught the Florida Indians in 1564 and 1565, with the tune as it was published in a pioneer Germantown psalmbook of 1753, shows how remarkably faithful to their primitive tunes the Calvinists in America remained after two centuries. The Bourgeois version (this became definitive throughout the French-speaking Calvinist world with its republication at Geneva in *Pseaumes octante trois de David,* 1551, and *Octante trois pseaumes,* 1554) differs from that printed in 1753, 1763, and 1772 by Christopher Saur for the Pennsylvania Reformed Churches in only such small details as the addition of leading-tone accidentals and some note-value adjustments at phrase endings.

Octante trois pseavmes de David (Geneva: Jean Crespin, 1554)

Der CXXVIII. 128. Psalm, from *Neu-vermehrt und vollstaᵉndiges Gesang-Buch Worinnen sowohl die Psalmen Davids* (Germantown: Christopher Saur, 1753)

Saur's 1753 psalmbook heads the long list of Calvinist musical publications in America with German text. The first American Psalter with English text to include this same *Bienheureux est quiconques* tune saw light at New York only fourteen years later in a 479-page collection sponsored by the Reformed Dutch Church. Francis Hopkinson (1737–91), the famous signer of the Declaration of Independence, was, however, forced to fit a different psalm text to the old tune. Finding that the English iambic Psalm 128 in the Tate and Brady New Version (1696) did not match the trochaic Geneva tune, he wedded the tune to verse of similar sentiment (Psalm 112) in 7.6.7.6. D. meter. As a result the historic tune survives almost unscathed in *The Psalms of David . . . Translated from the Dutch. For the Use of the Reformed Protestant Dutch Church of the City of New-York* (New York, 1767). Hopkinson's tact in finding alternate psalms to mate with traditional tunes—which might otherwise have died spinsters' deaths—won such approval that he could write Benjamin Franklin a letter of December 13, 1765, rejoicing that: "I have finished the Translation of the Psalms of David, to the great Satisfaction of the Dutch Congregation at New York & they have paid me £145 their Currency."

The Psalms of David (New York: James Parker, 1767)

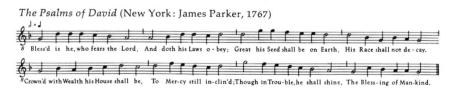

The longevity of the *Bienheureux est quiconques* tune, first brought to North America in 1564, can be matched by the success of that other tune taught the Florida tribesmen by pioneer Huguenots—*Du fons de ma pensée.* Taken over into Henry Ainsworth's *The Book of Psalmes: Englished both in Prose and Metre*

(Amsterdam, 1612) as the proper tune for no less than nine different psalms (Nos. 7, 10, 14, 16, 74, 83, 90, 116, 143), the Ainsworth version of the *Du fons* tune differs from its French prototype in only a single insignificant trait. Where Ainsworth repeats a note before the final of a phrase, the French version combines the repeated notes.

The Book of Psalmes (Amsterdam: Giles Thorp, 1612)

The Psalter of Ainsworth, in use at Plymouth until 1692, guarantees the currency of the *Du fons de ma pensée* tune among the Pilgrims. This same tune had also been printed in at least fifteen Sternhold and Hopkins Psalters before 1600, and was again to be repeated as the proper tune for Psalm 130 in Thomas Ravenscroft's *The Whole Booke of Psalmes . . . Composed into 4. parts* (1621). Because of the early vogue of the Ravenscroft Psalter among Massachusetts Bay colonists, his version certifies that the psalm-singing Bostonians knew the *Du fons de ma pensée* tune with a much richer overlay of accidentals than did the Knickerbockers for whom Francis Hopkinson compiled *The Psalms of David* in 1767.

The Whole Booke of Psalmes (London: Stationers' Company, 1621)

The text in Ravenscroft's *Whole Booke* conforms with the one sung after 1640 by Anglicans throughout the American colonies—the so-called Old Version, i.e., the Sternhold and Hopkins version. This was used in California as early as 1579. Sir Francis Drake's chaplain, Francis Fletcher, recounts the enthusiasm of the California Indians for the psalm singing of Drake's men on June 26, 1579:

Our generall with his company in the presence of those strangers fell to prayers. . . . In the time of which prayers, singing of psalms, and reading of certain chapters in the Bible, they sate very attentively; and observing the end of every pause, with one voyce still cryed, oh, greatly rejoycing in our exercises. Yea, they took such pleasure in our singing of psalmes, that whensoever they resorted to us, their first request was commonly this *Gnaah,* by which they intended that we should sing.

" 'Gnaah' was an imitative word, representing the nasal tone in which, we have been told, the Puritans sang," or so, at least, thought Otto Kinkeldey, the dean of American musicologists. However, Percy Scholes countered by observing that "such tone was evidently not a Puritan characteristic since Drake and his men were certainly not, as a body, Puritans."

On whichever side justice may lie, the Puritans can at least take credit for the first Protestant metrical Psalter in an Indian tongue. That same fondness for Calvinist psalm tunes which left *Du fons de ma pensée* and *Bienheureux est quiconques* so deeply etched in the memories of the Florida Indians, with whom Laudonnière's Huguenot group came into contact in 1564, had a similar effect in the Massachusetts Bay colony. The pioneer minister at Cambridge records this fondness in a tract published in 1648. Psalm singing was therefore one of the first habits that the Massachusetts natives picked up from the English.

The Narragansetts of Rhode Island even preserved a "tradition" (first put in print in 1845) that before the Pilgrims landed they had already heard Calvinist psalms. In *Indian Melodies* composed by Thomas Commuck, "a Narragansett Indian," and harmonized by the famous Thomas Hastings (New York, 1845), Commuck inserts one *Old Indian Hymn* at page 63 with the following footnote:

The Narragansett Indians have a tradition, that the following tune was heard in the air by them, and other tribes bordering on the Atlantic coast, many years before the arrival of the whites in America, and that on first visiting a church in Plymouth Colony, after the settlement of that place by the whites, the same tune was sung while performing divine service, and the Indians knew it as well as the whites. The tune is therefore preserved among them to this day, and is sung to the words here set.

Long before Commuck, this tune had obviously blossomed with the kind of thick passing-note foliage recommended by the author of *A New and Easie Method . . . applied to the promoting of Psalmody* (London, 1686, p. 101). Whether or not it was taught to the 17th-century Narragansetts in anything like the form notated by Commuck, the 1845 version deserves insertion here (see example below). The rest of Commuck's collection consists of "original tunes" by a "son of the forest," as he calls himself. Edward MacDowell based the third movement of his *Indian Suite,* Op. 48, on Commuck's tune for a Charles Wesley hymn, and quoted Commuck's *Old Indian Hymn* in its entirety in the fifth of his *Woodland Sketches,* Op. 51, *From an Indian Lodge.*

Thomas Commuck: *Old Indian Hymn.* C. M. (Double), from *Indian Melodies* (New York: G. Lane and C. B. Tippett, 1845)

Missionary work amongst the Indians was "a principal end of our coming hither," vouched John Endecott (c. 1589–1665; first Massachusetts Bay governor) in his letter of August 27 to the president of the "Corporation established in Parliament for Promoting the Gospel among the Heathen in *New-England.*" Earlier in the month he had visited a settlement of "praying Indians" thirty-eight miles away. John Eliot (1604–90), their evangelizer, had already finished metrical translations of several psalms into their language (later he undertook the complete Psalter) and of the first books of both Old and New Testaments (the whole Bible was printed in their tongue at Cambridge in 1663). When Endecott arrived, one Indian began expounding two kingdom-of-heaven similitudes (Matthew 13:44–46). This lasted half an hour. About one hundred of his tribesmen and women listened attentively. Next, Eliot discoursed three-quarters of an hour in the Massachusetts Bay tongue.

> After all there was a *Psalme* sung in the *Indian* tongue, and *Indian* meeter, but to an English tune, read by one of themselves, that the rest might follow, and he read it very distinctly without missing a word as we could judge, and the rest sang chearefully, and prettie tuneablie.

Such concrete evidence strongly suggests that the missionaries in Massachusetts found "Calvinist" music no less popular with the Indians there than Motolinía and Sahagún in Mexico, Gerónimo de Oré in Peru, and Nobrega in Brazil had been finding "Catholic" music to be with the indigenes farther south. For an outline of such a tune as Endecott would have heard the Natick Indians singing "chearefully and prettie tuneablie" in early August of 1651, Psalm 1 is shown here in the example below, the English text being the Sternhold and Hopkins translation (with the tune to which the arriving Puritans sang it), and the Indian text being Eliot's *Wame Ketoohomae uketoohomaongash David* metrical version in *Up-Bookum Psalmes.*

In the firm conviction that nothing was so good for the Indians to learn as Calvinist psalm tunes, Dutch as well as English missionaries made it their first business to teach their converts psalms "upon our Notes." So much is certified in a lengthy letter written from Albany in 1694 by a pioneer Dutch missionary who signs himself Godefridus Dellius (published the same year at Boston in Matthew Mayhew's *A Brief Narrative of The Success which the Gospel hath had, among the Indians*). Although wars with the Indians blighted missionary labors toward the close of the century, especially when Christianized Indians in New England were expected to side with the colonists, still Cotton Mather could boast in 1705, in *A Letter; About the Present State of Christianity, among the Christianized Indians of New-England* (Boston), of their "Excellent Singing of Psalms, with most ravishing Melody." In 1721 he harped again on the same theme in his *India Christiana* (Boston) when he called the Indians converted by Eliot "Notable Singers" of the metrical psalms in their own language and claimed that among the approximately thirty-eight New England congregations ministered to by some twenty-five Indian "teachers" in his own day, psalm singing was frequently better than in "our English Assemblies."

NEW ENGLAND PURITANISM, 1620–1720

The non-Separatist Puritans who began settling in and around Boston a decade after Plymouth was founded by the Pilgrim forefathers (the Pilgrims were Separatists from the Church of England) took second place to no other colonists "in wealth, station, education or capacity." Nonetheless, they rejected the tunes in the Pilgrim Psalter, preferring Ravenscroft's plainness to "the difficulty of *Ainsworths* tunes." This difficulty had not so much to do with range as with length (eighty or more notes for Psalms 20, 67, 84, 113, 136; 37, 49, 119, 139; 49, 78, 80, 91, 94). Moreover, Ainsworth used too many meters. The compilers of the so-called Bay Psalm Book, after laboring a quadrennium, produced a Psalter in 1640 that incorporates only six kinds of meter. Ainsworth resorted to no less than fifteen.

Of course, Ainsworth himself professed to have chosen the "easiest tunes of the French and Dutch psalmes." Daily converse with the Dutch doubtless taught the Pilgrims the fifteen tunes that had never before appeared in any English Psalter. If he took only the "easiest," then such a tune as the following for Psalm 95 accounts for opposition to Ainsworth's novelties among the Massachusetts Bay Puritans who had never lived on the continent.

Praising the vocal skill of the Pilgrims before their leaving Leyden, one trustworthy witness reports:

> Wee refreshed our selves after our teares, with singing of Psalmes, making joyfull melody in our hearts, as well as with voice, *there being many of the Congregation very expert in Musick;* and indeed it was the sweetest melody that ever mine eares heard.

And many "very expert in Musick" would indeed have been required if the whole Pilgrim band grasped the rhythm of such a syncopated passage as measures 8–9, or cleanly negotiated the skips that outline a downward minor seventh in measure 6.

Psalm XCV from *The Book of Psalmes* (Amsterdam: Giles Thorp, 1612)

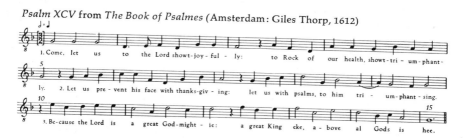

When in 1640 the Massachusetts Bay Puritans rejected the excessively long tunes, the multiplicity of metrical patterns, the extensive borrowing from Continental sources, and the jaunty rhythms to which Ainsworth's 1612 Psalter committed the Plymouth and Salem congregations, they merely conformed with a trend that before 1700 reduced the number of tunes "in general use" throughout the English-speaking world to scarcely more than a dozen. Salem congregation itself dropped Ainsworth—after a vote taken in church meeting on May 4, 1667 —for almost identical reasons. The first was "the difficulty of the tunes, and that we could not sing them so well as formerly." The same story repeated itself at Plymouth. On May 17, 1685,

> the Elders stayed the chh after the publick worship was ended & moved to sing Psal: 130: in another Translation, because in Mr Ainsworths Translation which wee sang, the tune was soe difficult few could follow it, the chh readily consented thereunto.

Seven years later the knell sounded once again. John Cotton, Plymouth pastor from 1669 to 1697—son of that erudite patriarch of Boston John Cotton (1584–1652), who had published the Magna Charta of Puritan music in New England, *Singing of Psalmes A Gospel-Ordinance* (1647)—had grown up singing his father's Bay Psalm Book and naturally favored it. This preference can be condoned all the more easily when one recalls that not only Psalm 23 but others in the Bay collection had been translated by the elder Cotton. On June 19, 1692 (*Plymouth Church Records* I, 277), "after the Evening worship, the Pastour stayed the church & propounded . . . That seeing many of the Psalmes in Mr Ainsworths Translation which wee now sung had such difficult tunes as none in the church could sett," they therefore find a way to bring in another version, with easier tunes. The following August 7, "at the conclusion of the sacrament, the Pastor called upon the church to express their Judgments as to the Proposall made about the Psalmes June 19: & put to vote, whether they did consent, that when the Tunes were difficult in our Translation, wee should sing the Psalmes now in use in the neighbour-churches in the Bay." After "two brethren vocally exprest their approbation . . . by a silentiall vote the whole church consented it should be soe, not one opposing" (*Records* I, 278).

The contents of the so-called Bay Psalm Book did not change so utterly in fifty-odd re-editions as those of another famous American bibliographical deceiver, the Little and Smith *Easy Instructor,* in thirty-four re-editions; but the psalmbook adopted at Salem in 1667 and at Plymouth in 1692 does differ from the 1640 edition. Because only the first edition can at present fetch $151,000 a copy in open market, specialists in Americana often disregard the 1651 edition, published after "a little more of Art was employ'd upon" the psalms by Henry Dunster, the president of Harvard who was forced to resign in 1654 because he could no longer accept infant baptism as scriptural. Just as the New England translations cannot be judged without comparing the original editions (facsimiles of the 1640 imprint are conveniently accessible), so also the variety of the tunes cannot be known without consulting original imprints. To show what melodies were recommended by the 1640 compilers, Irving Lowens listed all forty-eight of the Ravenscroft psalm tunes that are mentioned in "An Admonition to the Reader" at fol Ll3v of the first edition. However, Ravenscroft (a copy of whose 1621 *Whole Booke* John Endecott brought over) and Richard Allison (a copy of whose 1599 *Psalmes of David* William Brewster owned in 1643) had by 1698 fallen so much behind the times that all thirteen psalm tunes in the 1698 Bay Psalm Book are copied from either the seventh (1674) or eighth (1679) edition of John Playford's *Brief Introduction to the Skill of Musick.*

Samuel Sewall (1652–1730), whose diary gives the fullest picture of everyday New England life in his period, owned the 1679 edition of Playford. A key figure in Boston cultural life throughout his long life, his services to music included twenty-four years (1694–1718) as precentor (director of congregational singing) in the Old South Church. Long before he succeeded Captain Jacob Eliot (1632–93) in this coveted office, he began recording his musical experiences. Three typical entries during 1687 and 1688 will illustrate:

August 25, 1687: Benjamin Eliot [youngest son of the "Apostle to the Indians" and co-translator of the Bay Psalm Book, John Eliot] would sing with me, which did; he read three or more staves of the Seventy first Psalm, 9 verses, his Father and Jno Eliot singing with us; Mr. Benjamin would in some notes be very extravagant. Would have sung again before I came away.

October 17, 1688: The 132. Psal. sung from the 13th v. to the end. . . . Mr. [John] Eliot ordain'd [Nehemiah Walker]. . . . After Dinner sung Zech'^{s} Song from 76th v. to the end, and the Song of Simeon [Benedictus and Nunc Dimittis].

October 23, 1688. Heard Mr. Bayly preach from Numb. 33. 8, 9. Sung the prayer of Jonah.

Numerous similar diary entries attest the genuine popularity of public as well as private singing throughout the last decade of Captain Jacob Eliot's precentorship. As if the 150 psalms were not enough matter for singing, the other Old and New Testament passages versified in 1651 were also in constant demand. Such "very extravagant notes" as Benjamin Eliot introduced—though later in New England history regarded as abusive—gave fancy its needed room to roam in the heyday of psalm singing.

Captain Eliot fell "sick from Muddy-River" and died, aged sixty-one, on August 16, 1693, whereupon Sewall wrote: "We shall hardly get another such sweet Singer as we have lost—he was one of the most Serviceable Men in Boston." A quarter century later when Sewall himself, at sixty-six, resigned the precentorship, he had to admit that his own "enfeebled" voice had long since lost the luster which had endeared the captain's voice to everyone in Boston.

Pitching the tune properly and keeping the congregation on the same tune throughout an entire psalm proved to be Sewall's knottiest problems. The singer in the gallery whom he selected as his best-qualified successor was none other than the tallow-chandler Josiah Franklin, whose son Benjamin, then sixteen years old, was one day to write a string quartet and to render enough other musical services for an entry in *Grove's Dictionary*. Baptized in Old South Church, Benjamin thus enjoyed the twin advantages of Sewall's early influence and of his father's. Nor did he forget his father when years later he reminisced in *The European Magazine and London Review* XXIII (January, 1793), p.20:

> [My father's] voice was sonorous and agreeable; so that when he sung a psalm or hymn, with the accompaniment of his violin, with which he sometimes amused himself in an evening, after the labours of the day were finished, it was truly delightful to hear him.

The tunes mentioned in Sewall's diary tend to be those that gave Sewall trouble on one occasion or another. However, the sheer number mentioned by name gives some clue to their variety: *High Dutch* (= *85th Psalm* in Tufts and Walter), *Litchfield*, *Low Dutch* (= *Canterbury* in Playford, Tufts, and Walter), *Martyrs, Oxford, Psalm 72, Psalm 119, St. David's, Westminster, Windsor*, and *York. High Dutch*, thus newly baptized in Ravenscroft's *Whole Booke* of 1621 (pp. 196, 226), proves to be none other than the ancient Lutheran chorale *Vater unser im Himmelreich*, printed by Valentin Schumann in 1539, adapted to Marot's *Enfans qui le Seigneur servez* (Psalm 113) in *Pseaumes de David, mis en rime* (Strasbourg, 1553), and the subject of at least seven of Bach's chorale preludes (BWV 636, 682, 683, 737, 760, 761, 762). It was into this 8.8.8.8.8.8. *Vater unser* tune that Sewall inadvertently fell at the close of the Friday service on December 28, 1705, when he intended the common-meter *Windsor* instead. Twice printed nameless as early as 1591, *Windsor* awaited christening in Ravenscroft's classic 1621 *Whole Booke. Westminster*—one of the sixteen tunes composed by Orlando Gibbons for George Wither's *The Hymnes and Songs of the Church* (1623)—reappears identically in three collections: Playford's *Whole Book of Psalms* (1677), Tufts's *Introduction*, 5th. ed. (1726), and Walter's *Grounds* (1721, 1723). It still remains current today in *The Hymnal 1940* (No. 573).

Litchfield (Playford, *Brief Introduction*, 8th ed., p. 71), the tune that confused Sewall on October 25, 1691, joins *High Dutch* and *Windsor* in being another minor melody. Evidence both external and internal confirms its more recent origin. When first printed (*Brief Introduction*, 1654), it was categorized by Playford as a "New Tune." Liberal use of large leaps distinguishes not only *Litchfield* but also *St. David's* and *York*, the tunes that by twice painfully unhorsing Sewall in February of 1718 made him resign the precentorship, after twenty-four years in the office. *St. David's*, listed in Ravenscroft's 1621 *Whole Booke* as a "Welch

Tune," begins with fifths in every line but one; for every scale step there are 1.6 skips in this vigorous tune. *York* (first printed in the Scots *CL.Psalmes of David* (Edinburgh, 1615) receives as its more appropriate name in all Scottish tunebooks *The Stilt.* The thirteen skips in this splendid major triadic tune (Ravenscroft changed its name from *The Stilt* to *York*) contrast with only eight scale steps.

Such numerous wide skips outlining chords leave open arteries for the many "extravagant notes" with which enthusiastic improvisers such as Benjamin Eliot liked to embolize their psalmody. True, the chords are only implied when the whole congregation stays together on the tune. But with individual singers lagging or running ahead, the harmony becomes explicit. When this happened, Puritans who had so long denied themselves the delights of harmony (because of Calvin's interdict) could at last enjoy the forbidden fruit of common chords with clear conscience.

"REGULAR SINGING," 1720–75

As early as 1721 the twin tendencies to treat the psalm tunes as mere melody types that, like a *maqam,* could be embellished at will, and to transform the psalmody into "song tunes" of ever more rustic flavor, had so aroused two enterprising Harvard graduates that they published almost simultaneously the first two music tutors printed in English America. Aiding John Tufts and Thomas Walter in the campaign for musical literacy, there simultaneously sprang up a battalion of pamphleteers whose trenchant prose still continues to be widely quoted in histories of American music. The profoundest of these was Cotton Mather, the saltiest, Thomas Symmes. Both shared the new-found zeal for "regular singing"—that is, by note and according to musical rules.

Cotton Mather (1663–1728), the "most celebrated of all American Puritans," encouraged singing schools, published *The Accomplished Singer,* and wrote letters ventilating the controversy. In one to Thomas Hollis, London nephew of the benefactor who endowed the first Divinity chair at Harvard, Mather wrote on November 5, 1723:

> A mighty Spirit came Lately upon abundance of our people, to Reform their singing which was degenerated in our Assemblies to an Irregularity, which made a Jar in the ears of the more curious and skilful singers. Our ministers generally encouraged the people, to accomplish themselves for a Regular singing, and a more beautiful Psalmody.

Earlier his own Second Church had alarmed him, and on March 13, 1721, he had asked himself, "Should not something be done towards mending the *Singing* in our Congregation?" A singing school then in progress offered the most obvious means, and on March 16 he preached "in the School-House to the young Musicians, from Rev. 14. 3.—no man could learn that Song." Samuel Sewall, whose musical enthusiasm remained keen despite his having resigned the precentorship, wrote of the occasion: "House was full, and the Singing extraordinarily Excellent, such as has hardly been heard before in Boston. Sung four tunes out of Tate and Brady." Even with this impetus, however, Mather feared that the lessons were not coming home to his own congregation. On June 5, 1721, he confided to his diary: "I must of Necessity do something, that the Exercise of *Singing* the sacred *Psalms* in the Flock, may be made more beautiful."

Within the next three years, sophisticated Boston—now a city of twelve thousand with eleven churches, two grammar schools, two writing schools, and three thousand houses—responded so well to treatment prescribed by the musical uplifters that by 1724 Mather could consider the battle won in the city. Only country yokels still held out. A letter of his dated April 22, 1724, expresses the sort of biting contempt for "a Little Crue at a Town Ten miles from the City of Boston" that was to be frequently voiced by later 18th-century writers, under similar provocation. The hinterland pocket of resistance to which Mather refers was so "sett upon their old Howling in the public Psalmody, that being rebuked for the Disturbance they made, by the more Numerous Regular Singers, they declared They would be for the Ch. of E. and would form a Little Assembly for that purpose."

Thomas Symmes (1678–1725), whose sermon *The Reasonableness of Regular Singing* (1720) vouched for the printing of Harvard College musical theses as early as the 1650s, viewed the intervening decades from 1660 to 1720 as an era of continuous decline. This sermon, first delivered in his own rural Bradford (thirty-five miles north of Boston), brought him numerous invitations to repeat it elsewhere. Both the 1720 sermon and the 1723 dialogue *Utile dulci* reveal his favorite musical theorist to have been the polymath Johann Heinrich Alsted (1588–1638). Alsted, the encyclopedist whom Calvinists revered as a latter-day Isidore of Seville, enjoyed universal renown in his own century. In proof of its continuing popularity, Alsted's *Templum musicum* was as late as 1664 still regarded by a London publisher as a sufficiently important work to be published in an English translation. Symmes—Harvard valedictorian in 1698—knew the original Latin, if his quoting Alsted's *De musica* on the title page of *Utile dulci* is sufficient evidence. But when he adapts Alsted's account of the Guidonian syllables (*Utile dulci*, p. 36 = *Templum musicum*, pp. 35–36), or when on Alsted's authority he classifies music as a "special arithmetick" (p. 14 = p. 2), he carefully scales down the text to the capacity of the Bradford rural community of sixty families to whom he ministered from 1708 to 1725, and who knew a mere five tunes when he first moved there from Boxford (*Utile dulci*, p. 25). Some of his flock were so misinformed as to imagine that King David himself composed *St. David's* psalm tune (p. 37). Others removed their hats religiously on hearing merely the textless tune of this or that psalm. Such reverence borders on superstition, argues Symmes.

Symmes's unusual doubling as preacher and precentor enabled him not only to introduce such new tunes as *Isle of Wight, 24th Psalm = Bella, Brunswick,* and *Standish* (first published in 1700) but also to take the lead in abolishing the ubiquitous country custom of "lining out" the psalms—that is, of reading each line before it was sung. One admirer of his courage wrote:

He thought it was high time that our common Custom of Reading the Line in Singing, should be laid aside, not only because of its very much interrupting the Melody and sometimes the Sense, but because the Reason of it now ceases, which was for the help of such as could not read, or want of plenty of Psalm-Books; both of which may now be sufficiently remedied.

As the most suitable means of teaching congregations to read the tunes as well as the words in a book like the 1698 Bay Psalm Book (earliest extant with a tune supplement), Symmes advocated singing schools, to meet "Two or Three Evenings in the Week" from five or six to eight o'clock. Ministers should take the lead in establishing such singing schools. When the people learned to sing by note they would no longer interpolate ornaments so lengthy as to triple the number of notes in the original tune.

The way in which so hoary a common tune as *Southwell* (printed 1591; in Tufts, 1726, p. 4; in Walter, 1721, p. 30) was being embellished—by English as well as New England country singers c. 1686—can best be understood from the example below, which pairs (I) the unvarnished traditional tune with (II) a contemporary transcript of the ornamenting notes that country singers delighted in adding. The editor of *A New and Easie Method* prints first the unvarnished tune, then the embellished, with this observation: "The Notes of the foregoing *Tune* are usually broken or divided, and they are better so sung, as is here prick'd." It was against such "breakings" and "divisions" that Symmes, Tufts, Walter, and their abettors inveighed from 1720 to 1760.

I. John Tufts: *An Introduction To the Singing of Psalm-Tunes*, 1744, and Thomas Walter, *The Grounds and Rules of Musick Explained*, 1721
II. *A New and Easie Method To Learn to Sing by Book*, 1686

A quick survey of the editions of Tufts's *Introduction* shows "20 Psalm Tunes, with Directions how to Sing them" in the *editio princeps* (announced January 2–9, 1721), 28 tunes in the second (April 24–May 1, 1721), and 18 (later amplified to 34) in the third (January 21–28, 1723). Only in the third did he begin providing basses to the trebles. The "Fifth Edition (with several excellent Tunes never before publish'd here)," announced October 17–24, 1726, contains "a Collection of Thirty Seven Tunes in Three Parts" that was to serve as model for the numerous later editions (those of 1738 and 1744 are in the Library of Congress). Tufts's letter notation, using only *mi-fa-sol-la* syllables, caught on so quickly that in this very same year another "Collection of Psalm Tunes in Three Parts . . . with Letters instead of Notes" was announced at Boston.

Psalm 100 New, which now rates as a likely candidate for the honor of being the sole original New England contribution to Tufts's 1726 edition, eventually garnered sufficient popularity in Boston for Beniamin Mecom in 1760 to insert

145. From John Tufts's *An Introduction To the Singing of Psalm-Tunes, In a plain & easy Method.* Library of Congress copy, tenth edition, 1738.

it on page 17 of "Walter's Singing Book . . . With eight tunes more than usual." Illustrating how loosely the term "anthem" was used in Boston in 1760, Mecom now calls it "Anthem to 100." Is it coincidence that the same page shows the much more correctly written *Warwick Tune,* on which *Psalm 100 New* indeed seems to have been modeled? Only one other "new tune" was picked up from the fifth edition of Tufts (1726) by Walter's 1760 editor—*Portsmouth* (Mecom, p. 18), which, however, merely echoes *Psalm 113* (Tufts) = *Psalm 115* (Walter, 1721).

Mecom's 1760 edition and Thomas Johnston's of 1764 bring Walter's reign to a close. The fifth edition still includes *Vater unser im himmelreich,* but no longer the historic *Lasst uns erfreuen* (1526) that had been included in every New England collection of psalm tunes from Ainsworth, through the ninth edition of the Bay Psalm Book (1698), to Tufts. So far as changes between 1721 and 1746 in *The Grounds and Rules* are concerned, Walter can be held responsible for only those in the second edition (1723), published two years before his premature death of tuberculosis. What had started as Dorian music—*Penitential Hymn* (first English printing, 1562)—appears with one flat in his 1721 *Grounds,* but with two flats in the 1723 edition. The notes on an Italian augmented sixth chord crop up in the 1723 G-minor harmonization (p.10) as a result of the added signature flat.

"Mr. *Walter's* Sermon on Regular Singing," *The sweet Psalmist of Israel* (Boston, 1722), molded the future of New England psalmody hardly less forcefully than did his *Grounds and Rules*. Later called "the most beautiful composition among the sermons which have been handed down to us from our fathers, this was a sermon "Preach'd at the Lecture held in Boston, by the Society for promoting Regular & Good Singing And for Reforming the Depravations and Debasements our Psalmody labours under, In order to introduce the proper and true Old Way of Singing." One purpose was to convince the opinion makers of Boston Congregationalism that three-part vocal harmonizations such as he had published the year before in *Grounds* ought to be sung in public worship. His method was simple: he "proved" that David's psalms were sung thus in biblical times. Whereas John Tufts in his 1721 *Introduction* (and in successive issues to 1726) dared publish only the tune, Walter began at once in 1721 with all three parts: cantus, medius, bassus. In his sermon, he explains his reasons:

> The *Music* of the Temple, as it was under the Management and Direction of our *Sweet Psalmist* of Israel, was a *Chorus of Parts*. The Singers and the Players upon Instruments, were divided into THREE Sets or Quires. One for the Bass, another for the *Medius* or inner Parts; the third for the *Trebles* or *Altus's*. Mr. *Ford* in his Preface to his Exposition on the *Psalms,* has done to my Hand, what I might have attempted; even to prove that *Music in Parts* (in spight of popular Ignorance) is as Ancient as the Times of holy *David.*

Walter continues by approving this translation of I Chronicles 15:21: "To lead with lyres, according to the Sheminith." His interpretation of Psalm 6:1 *(Lhal hassheminith)* reads: "To a grave and low Symphony: that is, to a *Bass* Note and Key." Jeduthun "had the regulation of the *lower Parts.*" Heman "was the Master and Moderator of the *Altus* or highest Part," and *"Asaph* therefore was the Master of the Medius or middle Quire."

The upward surge of New England psalmody from 1714 to 1769 can best be seen in: 1) the mushrooming of singing schools (taught by such masters as James Ivers, John Waghorne, Skiner Russell, Moses Deshon, Jacob Buckman, and John Barry); 2) the rise of choral concerts; 3) the enlargement of the choristers' repertory. Already in the dedication of his 1722 sermon to Governor Paul Dudley, Walter commends "the Reverend Mr. *Brown* of *Reading"* for having addressed "a *Singing Lecture* there." Five years later, Timothy Woodbridge printed in New London a sermon preached at a "Singing Lecture." This neutral name covered the public exhibitions offered by choirs at the singing-school graduations, for which, as a rule, the numbers were picked from tunebooks peddled by the singing master who ran the school. The three factors—the singing schools, the graduation concerts, and the selection of repertory from the singing master's personally sold books—made possible the career of the first famous American composer of church music, William Billings. Resting on the same foundation were the careers of numerous contemporaries and successors, who were to publish between 1770 and 1800 no less than twenty-six tunebooks containing music composed exclusively by American natives—Samuel Babcock (*The Middlesex Harmony*, 1795), Supply Belcher (1751–1836), Daniel Belknap (1771–1815), Jacob French (*The New American Melody*, 1789; *The Psalmodist's Companion*, 1793), Oliver Holden (1765–1844), Samuel Holyoke (1762–1820), Solomon Howe (1750–1835), Jacob Kimball (1761–1826), and Merit Woodruff (1780–99).

What the singing schools did from 1720 onward in making possible church-music composition throughout New England was repeated in Pennsylvania (James Lyon's *Urania*, 1761, and the publications of Andrew Adgate's Uranian Academy, 1785–88). In Virginia, where William Byrd of Westover mentions the movement as early as 1710, the Tidewater gentry not only accepted singing by note as proper for psalmody but also took up four-part singing of psalms as an accepted social diversion. By 1775 only the backwoods Scotch-Irish clung to such old customs as having "the Clerk raise the tune . . . with a deep-strained Gutteral, from the last Word of the Reading." A Presbyterian missionary from New Jersey who toured the Staunton region in 1775 "was agreeably entertained and surprized to hear an Irish Congregation singing universally without the Roll & Whine," but soon found the reason—a singing school begun shortly before his arrival. He mentions the son of John Trimble, a Princeton graduate, as teacher. After attending the young lad's singing school, the missionary confided to his diary: "It is beautiful, to behold the Progress of Civilization."

PENNSYLVANIA GERMANS

Although the Quakers were no great friends of music, William Penn's "Holy Experiment" turned the colony (of which Charles II made him proprietor in 1681) into a haven for religious perfectionists from Germany and Holland, many of whom were musicians. Their numbers included Johannes Kelpius (1673–1708), Johann Conrad Beissel (1690–1768), and a dynasty of Moravians stretching from Jeremias Dencke (1725–95) to Johann Friedrich Peter (1746–1813), whose careers trace a constantly rising musical trajectory.

What seems to be the earliest musical manuscript compiled in the colony was the work of Kelpius, an Altdorf University graduate distinguished for his mastery of Hebrew, Greek, Latin, and English. Translated from German the title of the manuscript reads: "The Lamenting Voice of the Hidden Love at the time when She Lay in Misery & forsaken" (MS Ac. 189, Historical Society of Pennsylvania). All ten melodies scattered through the seventy leaves of this manuscript breathe the middle Baroque, and indeed four melodies with basses come from a hymn-book printed at Nuremberg in 1684, only a decade before Kelpius and his disciples reached Pennsylvania (Christian Knorr von Rosenroth's *Neuer Helicon*, Nos. 56, 34, 18, and 30 = Kelpius, fols. 1 [35], 9, 21 [57], and 66). Three other melodies (fols. 63, 17 [56c], and 30) show affinities with German sources dated 1690, 1693, and "before" 1718. Still another waited until 1708 for its first printing in J. A. Freylinghausen's *Geistreiches Gesangbuch* (p. 515 [No. 333] = Kelpius, fol. 56b). Those two melodies (fols. 56a, 68) that have not yet been traced

146. Page from Conrad Beissel, *Das Gesaeng der einsamen Turtel-Taube.*
Library of Congress, Washington, D.C.

obviously belong to the same era. The rich harmonies designated in the seven melodies with basses, and the warm modulations implied by the three without, prove how responsive Kelpius must have been to all the more recent trends in German Pietist hymnody. Even if he was no composer himself, the filling up of the middle parts with chords suitable for keyboard without pedals (fol. 21 [57]) shows musical intelligence beyond the capacity of any contemporary musician in the English colonies. The errors that sometimes intrude can be debited to the copyist of the extant manuscript, who was not Kelpius but was possibly his disciple Dr. Christopher Witt (c. 1675–1765), who translated all of the perfervid poetry into English. Even so, the literacy of the transcript far outruns anything by Sister Anastasia, copyist of hundreds of Beissel's original hymns.

Conrad Beissel, whose musical career earns its most sympathetic recent treatment at Thomas Mann's hands in *Doktor Faustus,* was orphaned by the death of both father and mother before he was nine. Learning his father's trade of baking, he was apprenticed to a master baker who played the violin, and learned fiddling as well. According to a contemporary report, Beissel "had the opportunity to display his bright disposition at weddings, at which, when exhausted with playing the violin, he would betake himself to dancing." After sojourns in Mannheim and Heidelberg, he emigrated to Germantown by way of Boston in 1720. When baking proved to be of little avail in Pennsylvania, he studied weaving with Peter Becker, a German Baptist missionary. In 1721 he moved inland to what is now Lancaster County, and on November 12, 1724, accepted Becker's baptism by immersion. Four years later he published a tract urging seventh-day observance, and in 1732 gathered a band pledged to follow him in a life of celibacy at Ephrata, sixty-five miles from Philadelphia.

During the first decade, this perfectionist group sang both Pietist hymns and traditional chorales such as *Ein feste Burg.* In 1743 the afflatus seized Beissel and during the next quarter century he composed "thousands of pieces"—hymns, whole chapters of the Old Testament, and two entire settings of the Song of Songs. Before his death, his many musical outpourings were transcribed with loving care into a series of copybooks called by Hans T. David the "most beautiful illuminated MSS executed in Colonial America."

The general character of this music, which is much less varied in style than its quantity might suggest, finds apt characterization in a letter written by the "Assistant Minister of Christ's Church, Philadelphia," Jacob Duché (1737–98), to the Lord Bishop of B—l, October 2, 1771. First published as Letter V in *Observations on a Variety of Subjects, Literary, Moral and Religious* (Philadelphia, 1774) Duché's account gives a picture of Ephrata three years after Beissel's death. Although Duché found that "their society seems to be upon the decline, not exceeding one hundred members" at the time of his visit, he could not sufficiently extol their singing. He reserves a description for the close of his letter:

I shall at present remark but one thing more with respect to the *Dunkers,* and that is, the peculiarity of their *music.* Upon an hint given by my friend, the sisters invited us into their chapel, and, seating themselves in order, began to sing one of their devout hymns. The music had little or no air or melody; but consisted of simple, long notes, combined in the richest harmony. The counter, treble, tenor and bass were all sung by women, with sweet, shrill and small voices; but with a truth and exactness in the time and intonation that was admirable. It is impossible to describe to your Lordship my feelings upon this occasion. The performers sat with their heads reclined, their countenances solemn and dejected, their faces pale and emaciated from their manner of living, their clothing exceeding white and quite picturesque, and their music such as thrilled to the very soul.—I almost began to think myself in the world of spirits, and that the objects before me were ethereal.

Beissel's restricting his first singing school to women owed something to chance. Since his knowledge of violin did not qualify him to conduct or compose, he engaged "ein Meister des Singens" named Ludwig Blum to instruct some Sisters who showed musical aptitude. Blum was let go after a while for disloyalty to Beissel, but not before one or two of the Sisters had siphoned off what they could understand and had taught it all to Beissel. He thereupon began rehearsing them four hours nightly. Arrayed in "white habits, they made such a singular procession that people of quality frequently visited the school." His exacting discipline eventually wore everyone out, and only the devoted Sister Anastasia saved his singing school. With the addition of two bass parts, his entire choir in its heyday reached twenty-five (fifteen women, ten men). Many of their best effects depended on a skillful antiphony such as is required in the *Die Braut des Lamms* (printed on pp. 140–43 of *Das Gesaᵉng der einsamen und verlassenen Turtel-Taube Nemlich der Christlichen Kirche,* Ephrata, 1747) by the rubrics "Erster Chor," "Zweyter Chor," "Der Mittel-Chor," and "Drey Vers werden mit dem folgenden Lied Chor-weiss gesungen."

Better to give a foretaste of heavenly harmony, Beissel on principle excluded all strong-beat dissonances, not allowing even suspensions. To show how reduced a role he wished passing-note dissonances to play, he enjoined his copyists to transcribe them as small-note graces resembling plicas in the beautiful but extremely mannered Ephrata manuscripts. Just as the Renaissance humanist insisted on favoring accented syllables with longer time values, so also Beissel wished to wed all accented German syllables to lengthier triadic ("master") notes.

With all his megalomania, he was not completely insensitive to the monotony of so much consonance, great quantities of it moving in forbidden parallels and most of it eschewing minor chords. Throughout the 375 hymns copied by Sisters Anastasia and Iphigenia in New York Public Library MS *KD 1747, a tunebook that is the counterpart of the 1747 *Turtel-Taube,* he seeks variety by changing keys schematically from hymn to hymn. His circle of keys includes all majors from three sharps to three flats. The infrequent minors inhabit narrower bounds, since sharp signatures are for them interdicted. To move from one key to another as lithely as possible proves a problem to Beissel, one which he attempts to solve with some not altogether clear instructions in the *Turtel-Taube* preface, *Vorrede uᵉber die Sing-Arbeit.* To a modern analyst, his naïvetés presage the similar innocence of harmonic "rules" noticeable in the early works of William Billings,

Daniel Read, and other New England worthies. Moreover, by propagating his effusions through a singing school and flattering himself into thinking them worth preservation, Beissel keeps company with the New England group active from 1770 to 1800. His insistence on unrelieved consonance also jibes with New England practices.

On the other hand, by persistent use of the six-four chord, by making women the foundation of his choral group, by counting consonances downward from the top voice rather than upward from the bottom, by treating the men as only more or less incidental appurtenances, by assigning much wider melodies to the women's upper voices (middle C to high B), and by requiring the men to sing such ungainly skips as ninths and sevenths, he contrasts with the New Englanders who flourished a generation later. A considerably more devious personality than any of the New Englanders, he knew how to infuse *Sehnsucht* alien to their thinking. The following G-minor hymn serves as a specimen (the text deals with Christ's wounds). Certainly no New Englander would have so prominently displayed the augmented chord as does Beissel in *Wo geh ich hin* (New York Public Library, MS *KD 1747, No. 410 = *Turtel-Taube*, p. 324), or would have conceived sequences of hymns as sets of variations (*KD 1747, Nos. 344, 352, 389 = pp. 305, 308, and 320 in *Turtel-Taube*), however primitively the variations are worked out. Of course, the very system prescribed by Beissel inflicts upon him turns of phrase repeated from one hymn to another (a scale step down followed by the drop of a fourth is a typical melodic mannerism). Other mannerisms include numerous phrases beginning with eighth-note upbeats and eighth-note anticipations of final chords. Although he uses nothing but cut-time signature, he casts all but his most joyous hymns in rhythms free enough to please even a Dom Mocquereau.

Ich werde aufs Neue

When Benjamin Franklin labeled the Ephrata manuscript given by Peter Miller a "curiosity," he might equally well have been describing Beissel's music itself. But some compositions entitle the Moravian school of sacred composers centered at Bethlehem in the latter part of the 18th century to first-class honors in any history of Protestant music in America: those of Jeremias Dencke, who arrived in nearby Bethlehem in 1760; of Johann Friedrich Peter, who came a decade later; of Georg Gottfried Müller (1762–1821), who reached America in 1784; of Johannes Herbst (1734–1812), who began at Lancaster in 1786 and at Lititz in 1791; of John Antes (1741–1811), who though born in Fredericktown (Pennsylvania) spent his adult life abroad; and of Jacob Van Vleck (1751–1831), who was the second American-born Moravian composer of consequence. Memorabilia of the Moravian heritage include: 1) organs built by such workmen as Johann Gottlieb Klemm, who installed an organ at Bethlehem as early as 1746 and then plied his trade there from 1757 to 1762, and David Tanneberger (Tannenberg), who after sixteen years in America, in 1765 set up an organ shop at the Moravian settlement of Lititz that eventually won him renown as the best organ builder in the English colonies; 2) *de rigueur* instrumental accompaniment for all choral singing; 3) a healthy tradition not only of voluntary choir singers but of voluntary string and other instrumental players, meeting for regular rehearsals in anticipation of church services; 4) an avid interest in new sacred music, especially the compositions of local Moravians; 5) perfect integration into worship services of even the most "artistic" concerted music (such as anthems and arias with continuo, strings, and winds); 6) intriguing extensions of such practices as polyglot singing (imported from Herrnhut) to include singing in as many as thirteen languages; 7) foundation of a Collegium Musicum at Bethlehem in 1744 (others at Lititz, c. 1765, and Salem, c. 1786) that before the end of the century became a playing group capable of performing "the chamber music and the orchestral music of the Grauns, the Hasses, the Haydns, the Stamitzes, the Bachs who were the great figures of the period," according to Irving Lowens.

J. F. Peter, already rated in Gilbert Chase's *America's Music* (1955) as "the chief member of the group," in his first American year composed a delightful solo with strings and organ, *Leite mich in Deiner Wahrheit* (July 13, 1770). But the ingenuous part writing cannot be compared with such harmonic niceties as the ingenious German augmented sixth chords reserved for "es sey vor Ihm stille" in his moving *Der Herr ist in Seinem heiligen Tempel* (November 13, 1786), belonging to his North Carolina decade. Even in the mass of music that he chose to copy, he made a clear advance on American soil. His growth responded to suggestions read out of the various masters' works that he was constantly transcribing. This copying habit, acquired while he was still in school in Germany (between 1767 and 1770 he transcribed numerous symphonies and chamber works by C. F. Abel, J. C. F. Bach ["Bückeburg"], Stamitz, and Haydn), persisted through life, culminating in the parts for the first American performance of Haydn's *Creation* at Bethlehem in 1811. Nor was he averse to copying and recopying his own compositions, in the process improving them. In this way he resembles the prolific Herbst, who likewise in his last years completely rewrote several early anthems, at the same time turning them into truly "exceptional" works.

Peter's *Unto us a Child is born* in the improved final version (David ed., No. 5) vies worthily with Handel's *Messiah* chorus, many characteristics of which it self-consciously appropriates. The larger conceptions of Peter's later years not only exploit more instruments (two flutes, two horns, bassoon added to strings and organ in *Unto us*) but also *cori spezzati*. The brilliant antiphonal play in *Lobet den Herrn*—and for that matter the antiphony of paired voices in *Unto us*—provides especially welcome relief to choral writing from which fugues are excluded. So far as form is concerned, the anthems commence with the concise instrumental statement of a subject that is at once repeated by voices with instruments. Following a sharpward thrust, Peter places the initial subject in the dominant, next pleasantly involving himself in altered chords. He thence returns to the tonic, restating material gleaned from the first bars. He rounds out the anthem with a brief instrumental epilogue to frame what may best be thought of as a monogenic concept. In length his anthems compare with a four-stanza hymn. Never ostentatious or "learned," they exploit only the resources at Peter's immediate command, even compensating for the men drawn off to play instruments by doubling the tenor part an octave higher in second soprano.

Because Peter knows so well how to wring dry the expressive possibilities of even a single German word ("stille" in *Der Herr ist in Seinem heiligen Tempel*), adaptation of his German anthems to English texts poses all the problems deplored by Christian I. Latrobe in the preface to *Anthems for One, Two or more Voices performed in the Church of the United Brethren* (London, 1811). Still another roadblock prevents easy present-day access to Peter's and Herbst's anthems: the obtaining, at least in a church, of a proper instrumental cadre. The famous trombone choir (treble, alto, tenor, bass) that announced "weddings, christenings, pageants, funerals, church and community affairs," with different music cuing the age and sex of those for whom the announcement was being made, does not enter his accompaniments. But *Da werdet Ihr singen* for double chorus does bespeak horns, clarinets, flutes in pairs, bassoon, and organ. To these he adds a second bassoon and two trumpets in *Singet Ihr Himmel*.

NATIVE-BORN COMPOSERS IN THE MIDDLE ATLANTIC COLONIES

Who was the first native American composer? O. G. Sonneck, answering this query, wrote:

As our knowledge stands today, it was not the tanner and psalmodist William Billings of Boston (1746–1800). Though public and historians have worshipped this eccentric but remarkable man, whose crude utterances contain a spark of genius, as the Father of American Composers for well nigh a century, the title belongs to either James Lyon of Newark, N. J. (1735–1794), or Francis Hopkinson (1737–1791).

147. A setting of Psalm 23 from *Francis Hopkinson His Book,* (above), and the same piece as printed in James Lyon, *Urania* (1761). Library of Congress, Washington, D.C.

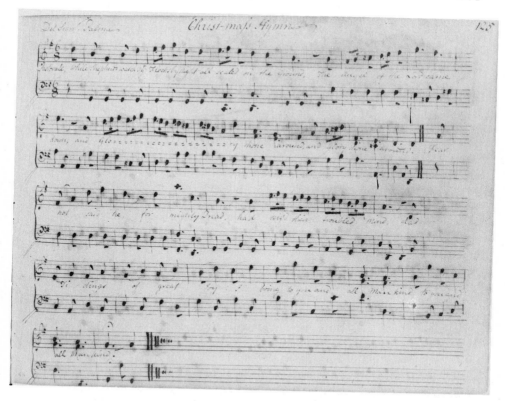

148. A Christmas song from *Francis Hopkinson His Book*, (above), and the same song as printed in James Lyon, *Urania* (1761). Library of Congress, Washington, D.C.

Despite having chosen for the text of his first dated composition, *An Anthem from the 114th Psalm* (1760), three verses from the prose of the Authorized Version (Psalm 114: 5–7), the youthful Hopkinson trips as delicately over the trembling earth in his maiden anthem as does Dr. Arne on similar prompting. This anthem, for two sopranos, bass, and continuo (in addition to text, the bass line carries figures), appears on pages 180–81 in a large, oblong manuscript book compiled by Hopkinson while a student at the newly founded College (later University) of Pennsylvania. The first entry in the manuscript points to a teacher who arrived in Philadelphia in the 1750s and gave his first public concert January 20, 1757 —Giovanni Palma. Enamored of vocal display, Palma shows his mettle with thirty-nine notes for "da" in the second line of his *Di render mi la calma* (p. 1 of Hopkinson's manuscript). "Glo-"ry in Nahum Tate's *While Shepherds watch'd y^r Flocks by Night* (Palma's first Anglican composition is in both the Hopkinson manuscript [Library of Congress, ML96.H83, p. 125] and Lyon's *Urania* [pp. 192–94]) revels in runs of no less than sixteen notes. With Palma's example to guide him, Hopkinson assigns thirty-two notes to "trem-"ble.

In his "Anthem from the 114th Psalm," just as in his famous song *My days have been so wondrous free,* Hopkinson adopts three emphatic quarter notes moving stepwise to the tonic as the characteristic tag ending for nearly every phrase. His Tate-Brady 23rd Psalm (MS, p. 179) exploits the same cadential descending three-note figure (here made even more emphatic because it is in half notes). This 23rd Psalm in retorted cut meter obviously enjoyed the most immediate popularity of all of Hopkinson's work. James Lyon, the Princeton graduate (B.A. 1759, M.A. 1762) who made musical history with *Urania, or A Choice Collection of Psalm-Tunes, Anthems, and Hymns, From the most approv'd Authors, with some Entirely New; in Two, Three, and Four, Parts* (1761) includes it as one of the "entirely new" works in *Urania.* He makes only a few minor changes, such as dispensing with the instrumental epilogue, adding a fourth voice ("counter") to Hopkinson's three, and suppressing any hint of a figured bass.

Lyon addressed his collection "To the Clergy of every Denomination in *America.*" Consequently, he had to forgo figured bass, and also such instrumental interludes as he was advantageously to insert under the title of "symphonies" in the first, second, and fourth choruses of the incidental music for the "Commencement, held in Nassau-Hall, New-Jersey, September 29th, 1762" (*The Military Glory of Great Britain,* Philadelphia, 1762). Hopkinson had never tried appealing to "every denomination." When he published his 23rd Psalm anew in *A Collection of Psalm Tunes with a few Anthems and Hymns Some of them Entirely New for the Use of the United Churches of Christ Church and S.Peter's Church in Philadelphia,* 1763, he therefore felt free to figure the bass and to revert to his original three voices. The figured bass implies keyboard accompaniment, which was available, at least in St. Peter's, from 1763 (the year in which Philip Feyring erected an outstanding organ). The Nonconformist ministers to whom the young Presbyterian minister-to-be James Lyon principally addressed himself did not begin approving of church organs until much later.

When Lyon announced *Urania* in the Philadelphia press (May 22, 1760), he called it the "first Attempt of any kind to spread the Art of Psalmody in its Perfection, thro' our American Colonies." Certainly, Lyon was the first to emphasize boldly the "entirely new" compositions: three psalm tunes, two anthems, and a hymn tune. To this band of six novelties he might also have added *Jehovah reigns*, "An Anthem taken out of the 97th Psalm," by William Tuckey (1708–81), appointed clerk at Trinity Church, New York, in 1753. Tuckey, the first to conduct a reasonably complete *Messiah* in America (January 16, 1770), roams through five keys, changes meter five times, and shifts frequently from solo voices and duets to full chorus. Lyon's most ambitious contribution to *Urania*, "Two Celebrated Verses by Sternhold & Hopkins," veers from duet to full chorus, exploits the antiphony of answering voices, includes some vocal flourishes that would tax any singer's virtuosity, and divides into sections to be sung at contrasting speeds. On the other hand, the Lyon of *Urania* betrays himself an American (in contrast with Tuckey, whose excellent organ at Trinity, New York, could always be relied on to keep the pitch up) by modulating no further afield than the dominant. In his "Anthem taken from the 150th Psalm," Lyon proves himself similarly reluctant to modulate, except from A to E.

Tuckey's Tate-Brady *Jehovah reigns* (lacks verses 9–11), Lyon's *The Lord descended from Above* ("Two Celebrated Verses by Sternhold and Hopkins"; Psalm 18: 9–10), and Lyon's Tate-Brady *Let the shrill trumpets* ("An Anthem taken from the 150th Psalm"; verses 3–4) continued to be choral *pièces de résistance* for a generation. On May 4, 1786, Andrew Adgate conducted all three at "the Reformed Church, in Race Street" (Philadelphia). A chorus of 230 singers accompanied by 50 instrumentalists drew an audience of one thousand. A reviewer in the *Pennsylvania Packet*, May 30, called them "the *celebrated* anthems." The next year Adgate revived another Lyon anthem—*Friendship*, to Isaac Watts's lyrics. More ambitious harmonically than Lyon's anthems to Sternhold-Hopkins and Tate-Brady texts, *Friendship* first reached print in John Stickney's *Gentleman and Lady's Musical Companion* (1774), probably because it had not been composed by 1760. In the same 1774 collection Stickney reprinted Lyon's *Let the shrill trumpets*.

As late as Elias Mann's *Massachusetts Collection of Sacred Harmony* (1807), Lyon's *Friendship* continued in sufficient demand for Mann to include it. In the preface to this same book, Mann lambasted fuging tunes and excoriated the erratic bounciness of the Billings school. Andrew Law (1749–1821), another frequent opponent of the fuging company, did not disdain to include Lyon's Psalm 19 in *The Rudiments of Music*. Some of the qualities that gave Lyon so enduring a cachet can easily be listed: 1) he never constructs an imitative point involving text conflict; 2) for textural relief he prefers antiphony; 3) his vocal writing includes brilliant shakes and runs, but always in musical illustration of scriptural words such as "fly," "rode," "trumpets," "harps," "organs." Like that of most early Americans, his part writing will strike a Victorian as execrable. However, as a mitigating attraction, the individual parts can be quite grateful. This is particularly true of such an anthem as "Two Celebrated Verses by Sternhold and Hopkins" published in *Urania* and reprinted at Philadelphia as late as

1808 in Nathan Chapin and Joseph L. Dickerson's *The Musical Instructor,* but with the title *Anthem. From Psalm 18,* and now in shape notes.

In 1774 Philip Fithian met Lyon in Cohansie, New Jersey. On April 22 "that great master of music, Mr. Lyon . . . sung at my request, & sing with his usual softness & accuracy." On April 23 Fithian spent the morning copying "some of Mr. Lyon Tunes" and the afternoon and evening visiting with him:

> He sings with great accuracy I sung with him many of his tunes (*he is about publishing a new Book of Tunes which are to be chiefly of his own composition*) & had much conversation on music, he is vastly fond of music & musical genius's We spent the Evening with great satisfaction to me.

THE SOUTH BEFORE 1800

Virginia, the oldest colony, remained a wholly agricultural economy throughout the 169 years from the founding of Jamestown to the Declaration of Independence. Jefferson in his *Notes on Virginia,* written in 1782–83, recorded that even Williamsburg (capital, 1700–80) had never exceeded 1800 inhabitants and that Norfolk, the largest place, never rose above 6000. Nevertheless, Virginia gentlemen visited London and discussed the relative merits of Cuzzoni, Faustina, and Senesino in *The Virginia Gazette* (November 6, 1736), and congratulated Handel on making £1500 from a single night's oratorio performance (July 28, 1738). That slaves as well as masters played the violin appears from such notices as: "a likely young Negroe Man . . . plays very well on the Violin" (December 5, 1745) and "a Negro Man, named Harry . . . plays upon the Fiddle" (March 27, 1746). Important collections of secular music reached Virginia, including works (in 1755) by Handel, Hasse, Purcell, Rameau, and their less celebrated English contemporaries, and (in 1775–76) by such composers as Stamitz, Richter, Gasparini, and Vivaldi ("cuckoo concertos").

As early as 1710, William Byrd II recorded the birth of the singing-school movement in Virginia. On the afternoon of December 15, 1710, he "went with two colonels to hear the people sing Psalms and there the singing master gave me two books, one for me and one for my wife." Next afternoon he had a quarrel with his wife "about learning to sing Psalms, in which she was wholly in the wrong, even in the opinion of Mrs. Dunn, who was a witness of it." The day before Christmas he went to church, "where we began to give in to the new way of singing Psalms." On January 25, 1711, "my two boys, Bannister and G-r-l, began to learn to sing Psalms," presumably by the new book method imparted by the singing master.

Philip Pelham became organist of Bruton Parish Church in November, 1755, and in 1774 the singing of four-part hymns and anthems was an accepted diversion in a country house: such are the next landmarks in the history of sacred music in Virginia. Philip Fithian vouches for the latter in his diary entry for Monday, June 27, 1774:

Evening at Coffee the Colonel [Councillor Robert Carter of Nomini Hall, downstream from Mount Vernon in Westmoreland County] shew'd me a book of vocal Musick which he had just imported; it is a collection of psalm-Tunes, Hymns & Anthems set in four parts for the Voice; He seems much taken with it & says we must learn & perform some of them in their several parts with our voices and with instruments.

But it was South Carolina with populous Charleston—the largest city south of Philadelphia in 1775—that took the lead in importing organs and organists, in installing expensive rings of bells, in attracting printers such as Lewis Timothy, who published John Wesley's first hymnbook in 1737, and in developing before the close of the century a "school" of church composers. The original church edifices of St.Philip's and St.Michael's (the senior Anglican parishes) date from 1682 to 1690 and from 1751 to 1763; it was in these two that the early musical life of South Carolina found richest expression.

The organist of St.Philip's from 1737 to 1750 was Charles Theodore Pachelbell (1690–1750), son of Johann Pachelbel. Born at Nuremberg, Charles Theodore composed a *Magnificat à 8 Voci con Continuo ex C* before leaving Europe for Boston at about the age of forty. From 1733 to 1735 he served as organist of Trinity Church, Newport, Rhode Island, where he played the new English instrument donated by the metaphysician George Berkeley. After exhibiting himself as a harpsichordist in two New York City concerts (January 21 and March 9, 1736), he relinquished the North in favor of Charleston. In 1737—the year that Wesley gave his first hymnbook to the press at Charleston—Pachelbell at last felt securely enough placed to marry; he also gave his first public concert in South Carolina. Twelve years later he began to suffer from "lameness in his hands" and thought for a time of abandoning the organ bench in favor of a singing master's livelihood. However, death intervened in September, 1750. His will itemizes "Sundry books of Musick, paper and Crow Quills, 1 small spinnet, and 1 Clairchard" (clavichord), valued at £21 in a total estate of £579.14.9.

This sum was slightly in excess of the amount St. Michael's paid in 1768 (£528) for the two-manual Johann Snetzler organ that by virtue of its size took second place in America only to the organ by the same maker in the Trinity Church, New York (that instrument was imported in 1764 and destroyed by fire in 1776). From 1782 to 1803 St. Michael's had for its rector Dr. Henry Purcell (1742–1802), himself an amateur composer, who encouraged the congregation to sing original hymn and psalm tunes by the St. Michael's organists Peter Valton (c. 1740–84) and Jervis Henry Stevens (1750–1828); these rank among the earliest sacred compositions produced in the South and are invariably "genteel" music. As an example of the Reverend Dr. Purcell's own muse, his setting of Psalm 89 is extracted from the Eckhard MS, which it enters as No. 25 with the title *Hereford*. The figures for the harmony are his; he places these between the two outer parts in the manuscript. The Long Meter text was printed in *A Selection of Psalms with Occasional Hymns* (Charleston, 1792) after the rectors of St. Philip's and St. Michael's found that the prayer book adopted by the Protestant Episcopal church in 1789 had expunged the musical supplement, reduced the number of hymns from 51 to 27, and had rejected all the condensed psalms of the "proposed" (never adopted) prayer book of 1786.

Henry Purcell: *Hereford*

SINGING-SCHOOL MASTERS IN THE NEW REPUBLIC

In contrast with Charleston, where such "correct" English composers as Boyce, Nares, and Kelway were the idols of church musicians in the 1780s, New England during the same decade basked in rays shed by Britishers who moved outside the cathedral orbit. The favorites of the New Englanders included: 1) Aaron Williams, whose *The Universal Psalmodist* (London, 1764) was "calculated to promote and improve the most excellent Part of Social Worship, and thereby render it both useful and delightful in all Country Choirs"; 2) Joseph Stephenson, the third edition of whose *Church Harmony Sacred to Devotion* had appeared as early as 1760 with a fuging tune, *Thru all the changing scenes* (Psalm 34), that was to be reprinted frequently in New England, beginning with Daniel Bayley's *The American Harmony: or Universal Psalmodist* (Newburyport, 1769)—thereby setting the fashion for a huge American output in the fuging-tune vein before 1810; and 3) William Tans'ur, whose *The Royal Melody Compleat* had by 1740 already given him the reputation of being one of the "best Authors . . . of the present Age."

It is especially easy to document Tans'ur's early influence on William Billings, whose debut publication, *The New-England Psalm-Singer: or, American Chorister* (Boston, 1770), begins with an introduction adapted from Tans'ur's *New Introduction to the Grounds of Musick* and in whose *Singing Master's Assistant* (Boston, 1778) the glossary is copied from Tans'ur. Even more crucially, Tans'ur's influence can be detected in Billings's musical praxis. Tans'ur in *A New Musical Grammar* (London, 1746, p. 119) decreed that "two *Fifths,* or two *Eighths* (and no more) may be taken together in *Three,* or more *Parts* (when it cannot be well avoided) rather than spoil the Air." Billings, whose "greatest asset was his unerring feeling for melody," embraced Tans'ur's dictum with such wholehearted abandon that scarcely one of his 257 psalm tunes or 45 anthems lacks parallel octaves and/or parallel fifths. Two typical passages from *The Royal Melody Compleat . . . The Third Edition* (London, 1764)—page 240, last four bars of *O praise the Lord of Heaven,* and page 246, third bar, on the word "peace"—show how freely Tans'ur, when composing, availed himself of the license he had granted as a theorist, a license that Billings and his New England confrères later turned into law.

Among other New England style traits from 1780 to 1805, one of the more noticeable is the lack of suspensions. This again is a hallmark of the Tans'ur repertory as well. The "country" composers in both England and New England seem to have missed the formal training in counterpoint needed by those who wished to write "4th species" involving several parts. Even if they could have done so, the hearty, bluff tread of their typical product left no room for enervating suspensions, colorful chromaticisms, subtle modulations, and the like. Charles II, who came to the throne in 1660, liked church music to which he could tap his foot; the rustic subjects of his kingdom a century later can scarcely be blamed for having had no better taste.

> Examination of the native music makes it quite apparent that the basic elements of the peculiar idiom in which it is written are derived from British sacred choral music of the previous one or two generations. . . . Aside from its archaic aspect, American music may be recognized by two general features. In the first place it seems more closely allied with folk music. For instance, there is a greater use of the natural minor scale, especially in gapped varieties, and much more irregularity of phrase. All American music has a strong rhythmic pulse, a characteristic only occasionally to be sensed in the earlier English music. In the second place, American music displays a far greater number of what to the musician's eye seem to be harmonic ineptitudes.

These were Allen P. Britton's conclusions in *The Musical Idiom in Early American Tunebooks,* a summary written after examining the "more than 130 tune-

149. Frontispiece from William Billings, *The New-England Psalm-Singer* (1770).

books (collections of unaccompanied three- and four-part choral music for use in churches) . . . published in the United States by the close of the year 1800" (*Journal of the American Musicological Society* III/3, Fall, 1950, p. 286). Twenty-six of the 130 tunebooks studied by Britton contain contemporary music by American composers and sixteen "are devoted to the compositions of single composers."

William Billings, the earliest and most prolific of the singing masters to publish original compositions exclusively, issued his first collection when he was only twenty-four. However, he soon discovered that many of the pieces were "never worth my printing" and returned eight years later with his second publication, *The Singing Master's Assistant,* in the preface to which he wrote: "Therefore in order to make you ample amends for my former intrusion, I have selected and corrected some of the Tunes which were most approved of in that book, and have added several new pieces which I think to be very good ones." *Lebanon* is a sample of a tune from 1770 "corrected" in 1778 (reprinted in the emended form the next year). The corrected form adjusts the prosody, doubles note values but under a retorted signature moving the 1778 half note at the gait of the 1770 quarter note, and limns a bolder harmonic outline involving three cross-relationships (flatted vs. sharped leading tone). Even in so short an exercise as a psalm tune, Billings thus shows the self-consciousness of an artist rather than a mere artisan.

William Billings: *Lebanon.* C.M.
a. Original version

b. Corrected version

Another psalm tune (but of diametrically opposed sentiment) "improved" in his 1778 *SMA (Singing Master's Assistant)* is the delightful Christmas carol to the folkish melody *Boston (NEPS [New-England Psalm-Singer],* p. 23= *SMA,* p. 2). *Africa* (14=4), *America* (1=5), *Amherst* (48=7), *Brookfield* (7=4), *Dorchester* (78=9), *Marblehead* (71=14), *New Hingham* (59=15), and *Pumpily* (60=24) exemplify the same trend toward "self-improvement" —sometimes in the principal melody itself (always confided to the tenor), occasionally in the bass, but most often in the two upper voices, and in the third phrase.

His willingness to change time signatures when revising his pieces *(Amherst, Dorchester, Pumpily)* should prepare us for his skill as a writer of variations. J. Murray Barbour draws attention to the meter change in the middle of another delightful Christmas carol, *Shiloh.* Upon shifting from 4/4 to 6/4 Billings contrives a "clever variant of the first melody" (tenor). On a larger scale, he devised the anthem *Lamentation over Boston (By the rivers of Watertown),* published in *The Singing Master's Assistant,* pages 33–38, as a "chaconne."

William Billings: *Boston.* C.M.
a. Original version

b. Corrected version

Me - thinks I see a Heav'n - ly host, Of An - gels on the wing; Me - thinks I hear their chear - ful notes So mer - ri - ly they sing Let all your fears be ban - ish'd hence, Glad ti - dings we pro - claim, For theres a Sav - iour born to - day, And Je - sus is his name.

Billings, whose favorite poets were Isaac Watts (1674–1748; revealed to be an Arian in his later writings) and James Relly (c. 1722–78; Universalist), set his own poetry at least three times—in *Chester,* his patriotic hymn given a fresh lease on life by William Schuman (*New England Triptych,* Bryn Mawr, 1957, pp. 31–47), in *Boston,* and in *Shiloh.* Even better than in his verse, his literary penchant shows

William Billings: *Shiloh*

FIRST SHEPHERD Me - thinks I hear a heav'n - ly host of An - gels on the wing me -
Lay down your crooks, and quit your flocks to Beth - le - hem re - pair; And

thinks I hear their chear-full notes So mer - ri - ly they sing, so mer - ri - ly they sing.
let your wand' - ring steps be squar'd By yon - der shin - ing Star. by yon - der shin - ing Star.

FIRST ANGEL Let all your fears be ban - ish'd hence Glad ti - dings we pro - claim For
Seek not in Courts or Pal - a - ces Nor Roy - al cur - tains draw; But

Glad ti - dings
Nor Roy - al

there's a Sav - ior born to - day And Je - sus is his name, and Je - sus is his name.
search the Sta - ble, see your God Ex - tend - ed on the straw, ex - tend - ed on the straw.

born to - day
see your God

to advantage in his lively prefaces. His *Dialogue, between Master and Scholar,* in *The Continental Harmony* (Boston, 1794), contains the famous encomium of fuges that has been quoted to prove him fonder of the fuging tune than of any other variety of music. Although recent research denies Billings the honor of having published more fuging tunes than such less famous men as Samuel Holyoke, Daniel Read, Stephen Jenks, and Jacob French, at least he still retains his laurels as the first American to publish specimens of the genre.

The vicissitudes of the fuging tune can best be understood by showing in their original form and in their later transformations two tunes by composers—Edson and Read—whose fuges far outdistanced any of Billings's in the public favor. *Lenox* (1782), the *succès fou* of Lewis Edson (1748–1820), appears here first in its primitive state, then in the revised form published by the famous composer of *Toplady (Rock of Ages),* Thomas Hastings (1784–1872). Not shown, but easily accessible, is the still staider version considered appropriate for *The Army and Navy Hymnal* (New York, 1920, No. 82) and *The Methodist Hymnal* (1935, No. 211).

Lewis Edson: *Lenox*

Ye tribes of A - dam join, With heav'n and earth and seas, And of - fer notes di -

b. Arrangement by Thomas Hastings

Read's *Russia,* because it is in minor, has proved less attractive to denominational hymnbook editors. Isaac B. Woodbury (1819–58), who made a "purified" arrangement of *Russia* for *The Dulcimer* (1850), started life as a blacksmith, just as Billings began as a tanner, Daniel Read (1757–1836) a comb maker, and Oliver Holden (1765–1844) a carpenter. But Woodbury visited Europe and, like Lowell Mason (1792–1872), William B. Bradbury (1816–68), and George F. Root (1820–95), came back a "scientific" musician. He therefore footnotes his arrangement of *Russia* (shown with Read's original in the example below) thus:

We insert a few of these Continental tunes at the earnest request of many old and venerated people, who in their younger years were wont to perform them in the house of God with perhaps *as much devotion and religious effect* as more modern choirs now sing the music of the day. The Melodies and Bases have always been retained, when consistent with the rules of counterpoint, and in order to do this several licenses have been taken in the arrangements.

Daniel Read: *Russia*

b. Arrangement by I. B. Woodbury

THE HALF CENTURY PRECEDING THE CIVIL WAR

Disdained even in its own time by such college-bred composers as Andrew Law (1749–1821; honorary M.A., Yale, 1786) and Samuel Holyoke (1762–1820; A.B., Harvard, 1789), the fuging tune with its dispersed harmony lost ground steadily in New England after Billings's death. European professors of "scientific" music such as the Danish Hans Gram (1754–1804) and the English Dr. George K. Jackson (1745–1822) so deprecated the native school that by the time Elias Mann's *The Massachusetts Collection of Sacred Harmony* (Boston, 1807) appeared —with the famous preface warning against "those wild fugues, and rapid and confused movements, which have so long been the disgrace of congregational psalmody"—*Lenox, Sherburne, Russia,* and *Northfield* were no longer welcome on the soil that gave them birth. In their place, sedate pieces by Dr. Samuel Arnold (1740–1802), William Selby (1738–98; organist at King's Chapel, Boston, from 1777), and other "correct" composers now enjoyed seats of honor. James Hewitt (1770–1827), organist at Trinity Church, Boston, from 1812 to 1816, included nothing by Billings, Holden, French, Ingalls, Edson, Read, or any of their tribe in his *Harmonia Sacra* (Boston, 1812)—instead advertising the collection quite rightly on the title page as "selected and adapted from the works of Handel, Luther, Ravenscroft, J. Clark, Drs. Croft, Arnold, Howard, Boyce, &c. &c. with which are interspersed a number of new tunes composed expressly for this work" by himself.

Anthem collections published in New England around the time of the War of 1812 show the same curious "anti-American" trend. *A Volume of Sacred Musick containing Thirty Anthems selected from the works of Handel, Purcel* [sic], *Croft and other eminent European authors* (Newburyport, 1814) ranges as widely as Elizabethan literature for William Byrd's *Bow thine ear,* but includes nothing from the compiler's compatriots—unless William Selby, who emigrated to New England around 1771, qualifies as an American. John Hubbard (1759–1810), the Dartmouth College professor who selected the anthems, provided in this predominantly a cappella collection a set of anthems suitable for so "refined" a group as the Harvard University choir; still, there must have been enough less cultivated buyers to make commercial publication profitable. Other New England collections shared in the same trend: for instance, the *Old Colony Collection,* vol. I (1818), included Mozart's *O Isis und Osiris* arranged as a four-voice anthem *(Almighty God, when round thy shrine),* and vol. II (1819) the Kyrie and Gloria of the Mass once attributed to Mozart, K. Anh. 233 (Köchel-Einstein, *Chronologisch-thematisches Verzeichnis,* 3rd ed., Ann Arbor, 1947, pp. 875–76, 1047), adapted to English text. The *Old Colony Collection,* vol. II, included also two lengthy choruses from *Christus am Ölberge,* Beethoven's Op. 85, the more popular of the two choruses proving to be *Hallelujah to the Father,* or *Welten singen Dank und Ehre,* final piece in the oratorio.

With all these "better music" influences at work, Lowell Mason found a ready-made public waiting for such tunes as the six he ascribes to Beethoven in his "epoch-making" *Boston Handel and Haydn Society Collection of Church Music* (Boston, 1822). Taking his cue from William Gardiner (1770–1853), the British stocking manufacturer whose *Sacred Melodies* (1812–15) contained numerous adaptations of the Viennese classicists, Mason included the following traceable Beethoven excerpts: *Vienna* (28 = Andante Scherzoso of Violin Sonata, Op. 23), *Weston* (48 = Adagio of Trio for clarinet, cello, and piano, Op. 11), *Ganges* (186 = *Romanza* for violin, Op. 40), and *Havre* (207 = Adagio of Piano Sonata, Op. 2, No. 1). An even larger number of selections flowed from the pen of the formidable czar of Boston good taste, Dr. George H. Jackson, whose favorable recommendation induced the Handel and Haydn Society to publish this 320-page collection made by a mere bank clerk working in Savannah, Georgia. Between 1822 and 1858, twenty-two editions appeared, netting Mason a profit from this one collection alone estimated at from $10,000 to $30,000. Dr. Jackson died, however, in 1822, and from the ten selections tactfully included in the first edition his representation slips in the next decade to nothing, while Mason from a mere three lines at page iv of the 1822 preface moves up to the title page as sole editor.

Mason learned the precepts of correct German harmony from C. F. Abel, an immigrant whose settlement at Savannah was as fortunate for the young bank clerk as, somewhat later, Hermann Kotzchmar's settling in Portland was advantageous for the young John Knowles Paine (1839–1906). It was Abel who set Mason on the track he was to follow throughout his long teaching and composing career, that of always turning to German treatises and German musical practice for the only true and "scientific" models. Mason's enormously successful *Manual of the Boston Academy of Music* (Boston, 1834; 8th ed. New York, 1861)—which, according to the preface, boasted an approach to music instruction "essentially different" from any other known in America—claimed to derive from the "system of Pestalozzi," but was in reality a mere annotated translation of G. F. Kübler's *Anleitung zum Gesang-Unterrichte in Schulen*, published at Stuttgart in 1826. The same Kübler's name appears on the title page of *The Boston Academy's Collection of Church Music . . . with many beautiful pieces, tunes and anthems selected from the Masses and other works of Haydn, Mozart, Beethoven, Pergolesi, Righini, Cherubini, Romberg, Winter, Weber, Nägeli, Kübler, and other distinguished composers arranged and adapted to English words expressly for this work* (Boston, 1835; 11 later editions).

Of course, no one denies that this essentially pro-German collection does make a few polite bows to the early American repertory as well, bows completely lacking in Mason's maiden publication of 1822. For instance, Billings (pp. 105, 130), Holden (128), Law (91), and Read (49, 92) each enjoy at least token representation. But with the harmonies retailored in Mason's shop, Billings's *Lebanon* now dons the harmonic habits of a polite chorale in Mendelssohn's *St. Paul* (1836). Similarly, Read's *Windham*, when newly decked out with a different time signature and with numerous added accidentals, speaks in as proper a German textbook accent as do any of the hymns of J. G. Nägeli (1768–1836) in the same collection (pp. 45, 70, 135).

Read was himself still alive (but died the next year, 1836) when Mason published the first edition of the *Boston Academy's Collection*. Not only he but also Supply Belcher, the "Handel of Maine" (1751–1836), Timothy Swan, whose *China* was the "most unscientific tune" ever penned (1758–1842), Oliver Holden, and Stephen Jenks (1772–1856) thus shared the misfortune of much outlasting their glory. What was their reaction to Mason, his new "scientific" music, his wholehearted endorsement of organs and choirs, his distrust of the casual singing school, and his obeisance to Germans? Read's opinions survive in a letter written when he was seventy-one. He acknowledges the harmonic sins of his youth, and to correct his errors has studied J. L. d'Alembert, A. F. C. Kollmann (1756–1829), and other theorists. After "carefully examining the system of harmony exhibited in Handel's *Messiah*, Haydn's *Creation* and other similar works," and after having tried the "allowed and forbidden" progressions, his "ideas on the subject of music have been considerably altered"—so much so that his own unpublished *Musica Ecclesia,* finished in 1832, repudiates everything in his long bygone past that is now recognized as distinctively Read.

Mason headed a bandwagon that proved to be irresistible in his own epoch, and a century later the force of his personality was not spent. No American has ever written so many hymn tunes that have endured. Fifteen lyrics in *The Hymnal* (Presbyterian Board of Publication, 1935) join his tunes; he was the composer or arranger of nine tunes in *The Hymnal 1940;* and *The Methodist Hymnal* (1935) depended upon him more than on any other composer. What particularly strikes a student is Mason's ability to keep turning out "hit" hymn tunes throughout the entire span of his creative activity. Of the seven representative tunes chosen by Seth Bingham for chorale-prelude elaborations (*Seven Preludes or Postludes on Lowell Mason Hymns,* New York, 1945), *Wesley (Hail to the Brightness)* was published in *Cantica Laudis,* 1850; *Boylston (Blest be the tie that binds)* in *The Choir; or Union Collection of Church Music,* 1832; *Missionary Hymn (From Greenland's icy mountains)* in *The Boston Handel and Haydn Society Collection,* 7th ed., 1829; *Watchman (Watchman, tell us of the night)* in the same collection, 1830 ed.; *Laban (A Charge to keep I have)* in 1830; *Henley (We would see Jesus)* in *The Hallelujah,* 1854; and *Work Song = Diligence (Work for the Night is coming)* in *The Song-Garden,* 1864. His *Hamburg (When I survey the wondrous cross)* was published in 1825, *Olivet (My faith looks up to thee)* in 1834, but *Bethany (Nearer my God to Thee)* not until 1859 in *The Sabbath Hymn and Tune Book.*

Mason preached these requisites for a good congregational tune: simplicity of intervals and rhythm; range not exceeding an octave or ninth, with D as the preferable upper limit and nothing ever above E. J. S. Bach's chorale harmonies he considered utterly unsuited to congregational hymnals: "Congregations might as well undertake to sing Beethoven's Mass No. 2, as these chorals, with all sorts of complicated and difficult harmony parts." When introducing unfamiliar German chorales to his American public, Mason therefore leaned on harmonizations by the discreet Conrad Kocher (1786–1872), not Bach. Even in so ambitious a book as his *Carmina Sacra* he kept "the harmony as simple as possible" because "the knowledge and taste of the public cannot be forced."

He justified his fifth large miscellany of church music—the 350-page *Carmina Sacra*—with the motto "Excelsior." "Every well organized choir, if kept up with interest, must have a constant succession of new music; without this there will be no advancement," he claimed in his preface. Fortunately for him, no copyright laws prevented his carrying as much European grist as he pleased, thus keeping his American mills active continuously. But once having adapted a foreign tune, he could prove extremely jealous of property rights in his own country. A group of three rather chilly letters to his rising rival, William B. Bradbury (1816–68), dated July 1, August 20, and October 10, 1861, culminate in the warning that "this property extends both to music and to words or poetry." He also claimed property rights in the lengthy pedagogical introductions that were a prime buying attraction of such works as the *Carmina Sacra*—teaching how to sing, defining 276 musical terms, and explaining the principles of chant. His *Carmina Sacra* alone, after going through thirteen editions in the 1840s and '50s, sold half a million copies. The income, plus that from such prior successes as the *Handel and Haydn Society Collection* (1822), *The Choir; or Union Collection* (1832), and *Modern Psalmist* (1839), brought him eventually to such affluence that he could purchase the estate of Silver Spring at South Orange, New Jersey, gather the finest private musical library in America of his day, have the best musical helpers in the country, and indulge in such acts of largesse as underwriting Alexander Wheelock Thayer's third and final trip to Europe.

By virtue of the spell cast over northern church music for at least a half century, Mason and Hastings give their name to the 1825–75 epoch. However, when Boston and New York became too refined to sing the native American repertory any longer, other sections of the country fell heir to it and built upon it. The stigmata of all the more characteristic tunebooks circulating in the South and West in the forepart of the 19th century were the shape notes introduced in William Little and William Smith's *The Easy Instructor* (1801). In their new invention the "four singing syllables" (four were considered sufficient) each take a different shape: "*Fa* is a triangle, *Mi* a diamond, *La* an oblong square, and *Sol* the usual form [circle]." The advertisement appearing in the August 22, 1801, *Philadelphia Repository and Weekly Register* continued: "It is evident that their different characters, indicating at sight the names of the notes, will greatly aid the student of Sacred Harmony."

Less than a year after Little and Smith's 1801 *Easy Instructor* was advertised, Andrew Law—who had pioneered with such other innovations as placing the "tune" in the top part instead of the tenor (1793), making the half note the basic unit of all time signatures and reducing the number of moods—patented his markedly similar "New Plan of Printing Music." This called for "four kinds of characters" to "denote the four singing syllables; and the learner will immediately learn the notes with great facility." Like Little and Smith, Law reserved the round note for *sol,* interchanging, however, their triangle and square, and dispensing with the five-line staff. The Little and Smith, Law, and other schemes toward simplifying music notation introduced by such 18th-century precursors as John Tufts and Benjamin Dearborn (*A Scheme for Reducing the Science of Music to a More Simple State,* Portsmouth, N. H., 1785) all had one object: making written music "so simple as scarcely to perplex the youngest child who can read." These printing innovations require attention in a history of American church music because the announced purpose was always to bring sacred song to the common folk and the earliest books always contained sacred texts exclusively.

Hastings—whose name is today kept alive with his three tunes, *Ortonville* (1837, *Majestic sweetness sits enthroned*), *Toplady* (1830, *Rock of Ages*), and *Zion* (1830, *Guide me, O thou great Jehovah*)—voiced the sentiment of the entire "better music" battalion when he labeled the most successful and enduring of these notation reforms, the Little and Smith shape system, as no more than "dunce notes." If so, they were exactly the teaching aid needed by Ananias Davisson and the Chapins when they moved west and south.

From the start, these "dunce-note" publications specialized in the early American repertory. For instance, Little and Smith's *Easy Instructor* (New York, 1802; no less than 27 re-editions, 1805–31) pitted only five European tunes against a hundred by "unscientific" Americans. Of the 156 tunes in John Wyeth's frequently reprinted *Repository of Sacred Music* (Harrisburg, 1810; at least eight later editions, 1811–34) nearly half are plagiarized from the *Easy Instructor*'s American list. The slightly later *Repository of Sacred Music, Part Second,* published by Wyeth (1770–1858) at Harrisburg in 1813 and reissued in 1820, contains a group of thirteen new items by Elkanah Kelsay Dare (1782–1826), a Methodist minister active in Delaware who also wrote on music, and of seven by [Lucius] Chapin (1760–1842), a Yankee singing master who worked forty years in Kentucky; these were to be constantly copied by later compilers of southern tunebooks.

The Repository of Sacred Music, Part Second not only served as quarry for later compilers but also was one of the earliest collections to emphasize melodies of folkish cast. Lowens tells us that many of the folk hymns first printed in *Part Second* are now to be found in modern anthologies of American folk hymnody such as George Pullen Jackson's *White Spirituals in the Southern Uplands* (1933), *Spiritual Folk Songs of Early America* (1937), *Down-East Spirituals* (1943), and Annabel Morris Buchanan's *Folk Hymns of America* (1938). Even the melodies ascribed to such named composers as Chapin in *Part Second—Ninety-Third* (24 = Ananias Davisson's *Kentucky Harmony*, 26 = William Walker's *Southern Harmony* [1847 ed.], 7), *Rockbridge* (95 = 16 = 257), and *Vernon* (21 = *SH*, 34), for instance—bear folkish trademarks. When a folkish five-note tune such as *Glasgow* appears in *Part Second,* 1813 (42) labeled as a "new" composition by Dare and, with a different harmonization, in *Kentucky Harmony,* 1815–6 (45) as a "new" piece by Davisson, the obvious explanation is that both worked with an already existing folkish melody. Similarly, Chapin's *Unitia* (*Part Second,* 97) is in all likelihood his harmonization of an already existing melody. The willingness of these singing masters to cull the folk repertory assures their collections an appeal more lasting than that of the modish Mason manuals.

Who all these western frontiersmen were has also begun to be investigated recently. For example, Ananias Davisson, too obscure for mention in the long list of tunesmiths prepared by W. S. Pratt and C. N. Boyd for the American Supplement to *Grove's Dictionary* (New York, 1920, pp. 386–91), has yielded to George Pullen Jackson's research: Davisson (1780–1857) grew up a staunch Presbyterian like the Chapins, with one of whom—"a teacher of the first eminence" who had been "teaching for fifteen years"—he seems to have studied after 1794. When Davisson reached Tennessee, the *Knoxville Register* for May 26, 1818, carried his typical announcement of a new edition ready to sell (*Kentucky Harmony,* 2nd ed.), his general invitation to "all young people taught by [Capt. R.] Monday to spend Saturday, June 20 singing," and his special invitation to Archibald Rhea, a precentor of the First Presbyterian Church who had previously taught at Lebanon, five miles away, to attend. The very homeliness of the beginnings along the frontier guaranteed that the music would stay close to the people. Just as Little and Smith had disdained such enervating comforts as accidentals, so also Davisson and his frontier ilk "never were stopt by the interposition of an accidental flat, sharp, or natural, either to sink half a tone, raise half a tone, or make any primitive restoration." Bare fourths and fifths, unalloyed diatonicism (often with modal flavor), abounding "prohibited" consecutives, a repertory favoring the old Yankee tunes (especially fuges), an invincible fondness for the shape notes invented by Little and Smith—these were the characteristics of the music system carried west and south by the Chapins, Davisson, and their followers.

Gilbert Chase in *America's Music* summarizes George Pullen Jackson's remarks on such later "fasola folk" as James P. Carrell (1787–1854), who with David L. Clayton issued *The Virginia Harmony* (Winchester, Va., 1831 [Library of Congress M2117.C61 V5 1831]); William Walker (1809–75), whose *Southern Harmony* sold 600,000 copies (four editions published 1835–54 [Library of Congress M2117.W18 S5 1847]); and William Hauser (1812–80), whose last publication, *The Olive Leaf* (Wadley, Jefferson Co., Ga., 1878), bridges the gap between revival and Gospel song. The musical examples in chapter X of Chase's standard text sketch the profile of the rural music. At its most characteristic, the "air" of any given hymn sounds as if it should have been collected by Cecil J. Sharp and edited by Maud Karpeles.

Charles Seeger, who studied the part writing indigenous to the southern fasola books (*Contrapuntal Style in the Three-Voice Shape-Note Hymns,* in *The Musical Quarterly* XXVI/4, October, 1940, pp. 483–93), borrows *Wondrous Love* from John McCurry's *The Social Harp* (Philadelphia, 1868) for John A. and Alan Lomax's *Folk Song U. S. A.* (New York, 1947, pp. 348–49). This same folk hymn appears in Hauser's *The Olive Leaf* (p. 371), and may serve as an earnest of that immense repertory of folk melody recorded for posterity in 19th-century southern shape-note books.

NEGRO SPIRITUALS: ORIGIN AND PRESENT-DAY SIGNIFICANCE

In his epochal *Spiritual Folk-Songs of America,* George Pullen Jackson divided the repertory of the rural books for whites into: 1) religious ballads, with *Poor Wayfaring Stranger* as one of 51 examples; 2) folk hymns, with *Holy Manna* and *Pisgah* as two examples among 98; 3) revival "spiritual songs," with *Roll, Jordan, Roll* and *Old-time Religion* as two well-known examples among 101. The third type, "the *spiritual songs,* rather than the *hymns* or the *ballads,*" came into full bloom with the millenial surge of the 1840s; it was this type "which appealed subsequently most deeply to the Negroes and has reappeared most often among their religious songs," according to Jackson, who in *White and Negro Spirituals* (1943) documented his assertion with 114 parallels, extending to even such famed spirituals as *Down by the riverside, Go down, Moses, Go tell it on the mountain, Roll, Jordan, Sin-Sick Soul,* and *Were you there.* Convinced by the wealth of evidence, Jackson summarized thus: "The Negroes' spirituals were, up to com-

paratively recent times, adopted from the stock of tunes and texts which originated in the white man's revivals." Since this revival music stemmed from a
known folk tradition, "we may conclude then, and with a high degree of certainty,
that the Afro-American has been a potent factor in the carrying on of the
Celtic-English-American's folk songs."

How the slaves came to learn the white man's repertory has been documented
with gratifying fullness in Dena J. Epstein's *Slave Music in the United States
before 1860; A Survey of Sources,* in *Notes of the Music Library Association*
(XX/2–3, Spring and Summer, 1963, pp. 195–212 and 377–90). Such early white
missionaries among them as the Presbyterian Samuel Davies wrote from Hanover, Virginia, to a friend in London as early as the spring of 1755: "The Books
I principally want for them are, *Watts's Psalms and Hymns,* and *Bibles.* . . . I
am the rather importunate for a good Number of these, as I cannot but observe,
that the *Negroes,* above all the Human Species that I ever knew, have an Ear for
Musick, and a kind of extatic delight in *Psalmody;* and there are no books they
learn so soon, or take so much Pleasure in." Three years later he wrote (August
26, 1758): "I can hardly express the pleasure it affords me to turn to that part
of the gallery where they sit, and see so many of them with their Psalm or Hymn
Books, turning to the part then sung, and assisting their fellows, who are beginners, to find the place; and then all breaking out in a torrent of sacred harmony,
enough to bear away the whole congregation to heaven."

However, psalm- and hymnbooks were perennially in such short supply that
many southern churches as late as the 1840s still resorted to "lining out" the
hymns. "The minister reads a line, and the congregation sing it; then he reads
the next, and so on. The slaves (to whose accommodation the galleries are
frequently devoted) are so accustomed to this way of singing that they seem to
think the tune incomplete without the intervention of *spoken* lines." So wrote a
correspondent in *The Musical Gazette* (I/12, Boston, July 6, 1846, p. 91), continuing with an anecdote of a lone Negro who alternately spoke and sang. "Many
of the slave melodies are well known at the north . . . many of them sing all
common psalm tunes with accuracy, and in addition there are verses evidently
original."

Dwight's Journal of Music (X/7, November 15, 1856, pp. 51–52), reprints an
article entitled *Songs of the Blacks* from a New York weekly, *The Evangelist,*
which had carried it unsigned the previous month. Like much later descriptions
of Negro activity, this article loses critical value because the author prefers to
indulge in racial theorizing. Nonetheless, the author does record their participation in camp meetings. "As hundreds assemble at a camp meeting in the woods,
and join the chorus of such a [Watts] hymn as 'When I can read my title clear,/To
mansions in the sky,' the unimpassioned hearer is almost lifted from his feet by
the volume and majesty of the sound." This open-air singing reflects the fact that
"the Negro is a natural musician" who "will learn to play on an instrument more
quickly than a white man."

So far as style of singing is concerned, a Russian traveler who visited a Philadelphia Negro Methodist church published in 1815 a not very sympathetic account
of the "loud, shrill" unison wail of the congregation responding to the lined-out

psalms, and of the twenty minutes taken up after the sermon by the men and women (seated separately on right and left) singing psalm stanzas alternately. Part singing was unknown in this church, nor does polyphony seem to have been used farther south. Certainly it was not used in Georgia, on the authority of the antislavery English actress Frances Anne (Fanny) Kemble, who wrote in her *Journal of a Residence on a Georgian Plantation in 1838–1839* (London, 1863, pp. 140 and 159): "The whole congregation uplifted their voices in a hymn, the first high wailing notes of which—sung all in unison," and "They all sing in unison, having never, it appears, attempted or heard anything like part-singing." Though agreeing that Negro tunes were "often plaintive and pretty," she claimed that "almost always" they were plagiarized from "white men's" tunes (p. 160). Both she and her son-in-law who visited he same plantation after the Civil War agreed that "their voices have a peculiar quality, and their intonations and delicate variations cannot be reproduced on paper."

Although some Negro secular songs were printed before the war and others were transcribed in manuscript collections (*Notes* XX/2, 209–11; XX/3, 390), the first and still one of the most importatn collections with religious texts, *Slave Songs of the United States* (New York, 1867), appeared in the early Reconstruction period. W. F. Allen, C. P. Ware, and Lucy McKim Garrison cooperated in issuing this *Lyra Africana,* as they dubbed their compilation. "The greater part of the music here presented has been taken down by the editors from the lips of the colored people themselves"; of the 136 songs, all without harmony because "the Negroes have no part-singing," the first 43 were collected "by Mr. Charles P. Ware, chiefly at Coffin's Point, St. Helena Island," but new materials from Virginia and South Carolina enlarged the original corpus threefold. "The songs from Virginia are the most wild and strange." The editors cite the piece shown in the following example.

O'er the crossing from *Slave Songs of the United States,* 1867

The offbeat pattern in this hymn, collected by Capt. James S. Rogers, matches similar characteristically Negroid rhythmic patterns in *The Lonesome Valley* (No. 7), *The Graveyard* (No. 21), *I saw the beam in my sister's eye* (No. 23), *Gwine follow* (No. 25), and some dozen other songs in the 115-page anthology. "The preference for off-beats is of African origin," writes Hans Nathan in *Early Banjo Tunes and American Syncopation,* in *The Musical Quarterly* (XLII/4, October, 1956, p. 467), invoking Richard A. Waterman's authority (*"Hot" Rhythm in*

Negro Music). Nathan cites parts of *I saw the beam* and *O'er the crossing.*

Five years after *Slave Songs,* Biglow & Main in New York issued the first collection of *Jubilee Songs: as sung by the Jubilee Singers of Fisk University.* Theodore F. Seward (1835–1902)—aligned with the Lowell Mason–George F. Root–William B. Bradbury musical axis, sometime supervisor of music at Orange, New Jersey, and prominent editor—claimed in the preface to have "taken down [the melodies] from the singing of the band, during repeated interviews for the purpose." In his "technical analysis" he wrote: "The first peculiarity that strikes the singer is in the rhythm." The following, culled from *The Rocks and the Mountains,* struck Seward especially:

Since mere authenticity had never been the announced goal of the touring Jubilee Singers, but rather fund raising for Fisk, Seward hastened to assure the polite public of "the quickness with which they have received impressions and adopted improvements from the cultivated music they have heard." "By the severe discipline to which the Jubilee Singers have been subjected in the school-room, they have been educated out of the peculiarities of the Negro dialect," proudly boasted E.M. Cravath, Field Secretary of the American Missionary Association (sponsoring agency for the tour). "They have also received considerable musical instruction and have become familiar with much of our best sacred and classical music, and this has modified their manner of execution."

The enormous success of the group inspired the Reverend Theodore L. Cuyler (1822–1909), pastor of Lafayette Avenue Presbyterian Church in Brooklyn and one of America's most renowned preachers, to write a letter to the *New York Tribune,* duly reprinted in *Jubilee Songs:* "I never saw a cultivated Brooklyn assemblage so moved and melted under the magnetism of music before. The wild melodies of these emancipated slaves touched the fount of tears, and grey-haired men wept like little children. In the program last evening were not only the well-known slave songs 'Go down, Moses,' 'Roll, Jordan, roll,' and 'Turn back Pharaoh's army,' but a fresh collection of the most weird and plaintive hymns sung in the plantation cabins in the dark days of bondage. One young negress . . . sang a wild yet most delicious melody, 'I'll hear the trumpet sound in the morning,' which was the very embodiment of African heart-music."

I'll hear the trumpet sound in the morning (included, of course, in the very collection that the Reverend Theo. L. Cuyler's newspaper puff was designed to advertise) joined *Steal away* and *Swing low, sweet chariot* to make a collection of twenty-four *Jubilee Songs,* none of which had ever before reached print—or at least so claimed the American Missionary Association ("Neither the words or the music have ever before been published, or even reduced to written form"). The tune for *I'll hear the trumpet* originated "near Atlanta," according to John W. Work (1871–1925) when "a slave was sold from his wife and it seemed that he would really die of a broken heart." James Weldon Johnson corroborates the "Negro" origin of this tune when he calls it "the Negro's piercing lyrical cry."

If so, B. F. White plagiarized it when he published the same tune under the title *The Morning Trumpet* in *The Sacred Harp, A Collection of Psalm and Hymn*

Tunes . . . together with nearly one hundred pieces never before published (Philadelphia, 1844), crediting himself with its confection. No doubt White was himself a Georgian (residing at Hamilton, Harris County, when he and E. J. King published *The Sacred Harp*). Because so many of the *Jubilee Songs* of the "Cabin and Plantation Songs as sung by Hampton Students arranged by Thomas P. Fenner in charge of the musical department at Hampton" in *Hampton and its Students* (New York, 1875), and of *Revival Hymns and Plantation Melodies* (Cincinnati, 1882), bear affinities with tunes already published in southern white collections, the Fisk *Jubilee* "unpublished" 1872 version of the "very embodiment of African heart-music" is here shown for comparison with B. F. White's version of the same tune published at Philadelphia twenty-eight years earlier. "The only essential changes that the Negro singers have made in the earlier white camp-meeting melody are their raising the seventh and injecting a sharped sixth," claims Jackson, who adds that even the accidentals may well have been intended in the B. F. White original. "The hymn is a typical campmeeting type, with its 'Shout O Glory!' refrain and trumpet burden added to John Leland's text," says Annabel Morris Buchanan in discussing its origins (*Folk Hymns of America*, New York, 1938).

B. F. White: *The Morning Trumpet*

O when shall I see Je - sus, And reign with Him a - bove, And shall hear the trum-pet sound in that morn-ing.
And from the flow-ing foun-tain, Drink ev - er-last-ing love, And shall hear the trum-pet sound in that morn-ing.

Chorus

Shout, O glo - ry! for I shall mount a-bove the skies, When I hear the trum-pet sound in that morn - ing.

Jubilee Songs (New York: Biglow & Main, 1872)

You may bu - ry me in the East, You may bu - ry me in the West; But I'll hear the trum-pet sound In that morn - ing.
[stanzas 2-5 follow.]

In that morn - ing, my Lord, How I long to go, For to hear the trum-pet sound, In that morn - ing.

Apart from the moot questions of white cognates for certain Negro spirituals and the first publication dates for various favorites, the double meaning of many famous ones such as *Steal away* (Steal away North) has been argued heatedly by the polemicists. The Moses of *Go down, Moses* has been identified as Harriet Tubman (1821?–1913), herself a fugitive slave who became the leader of the Underground Railroad. The role of spirituals, regardless of how much veiled meaning is read into the texts, still looms large enough for Harold Courlander to devote a chapter to "Anthems and Spirituals as Oral Literature" in *Negro Folk Music, U. S. A.* and to transcribe twenty-four songs with religious text against only nineteen with secular text when showing the 1963 reader what elements are still most vital and alive in the present-day Negro milieu.

Hymnbook editors, who continue to shrink from other types of rural expression, make an exception for spirituals, if "properly" harmonized. *The Pilgrim Hymnal*, 1958, edited musically by Hugh Porter (1897–1960), head of the Union

Theological Seminary School of Sacred Music in New York from 1945 to 1960, includes seven Negro spirituals (against nine tunes by Mason, five by Bradbury, and eleven by John Bacchus Dykes). *Were you there, Lord, I want to be a Christian,* and *Go tell it* are the pentatonic melodies among the seven spirituals in this hymnal for the Congregational church. As if entrée into the genteel company of an official hymnal were insufficient, Negro spirituals have also been saluted by such dignified art composers as Daniel Gregory Mason, who based his String Quartet in G minor, Op. 19 (G. Schirmer for S. P. A. M., 1930) on spirituals—for example, *Deep River*—and Leo Sowerby, who dedicated a prelude on *Were you there* to Vernon de Tar (H. W. Gray, 1956).

DIVERGING CURRENTS, 1850–1960

By 1850 the American denominations had already so drawn their social lines that some ministered to the wealthy and elite in big cities while others served the common folk on farms and frontiers. Speaking of one "elite" denomination in a course of historical lectures given at Berlin in 1854, Philip Schaff claimed that the Protestant Episcopal church had addressed itself "heretofore almost exclusively to the higher classes of society, and had rather discouraged the poor man from joining it." With such a constituency, the music published for use in Episcopalian churches at mid-century sounded quite a different note from that prevailing in publications for frontier churches, or even for middle-class urban churches.

Typical of the successful city church musicians was Henry Wilson (1828–78). His European studies (1854–55) resulted from a chance encounter with Alexander Wheelock Thayer, who, having read of an Episcopal church organist in Greenfield (Massachusetts) capable of "taking Jullien's 'Prima Donna Waltz' and in a flash arranging it as a hymn 'A charge to keep I have' for the choir to sing the next Sunday, told a stranger on the train 'that is the sort of man I should like to know.' " As the anecdote runs, the stranger replied, "I am the man," whereupon Thayer suggested that Wilson accompany him to Europe. Upon returning home, Wilson accepted in 1855 the position of organist at Christ Church, Hartford, Connecticut, occupying it for the next twenty-two years. His *Christ Church Collection of Sacred Music* (New York, 1861) dons regal attire with forty (of the sixty-five) psalms, hymns, and canticles borrowed from such purple composers as "Mendelssohn, Mozart, Rossini, Schumann, & others." His "others" include Handel, Haydn, Weber, Marschner, Thalberg, Herz, and Hérold—but no Americans except himself.

"Elevated" as were Wilson's musical intentions, a higher level yet was sought in the 203-page *Cathedral Chants: including the Gregorian Tones. Adapted to the Canticles, and Occasional Services, of the Protestant Episcopal Church . . . By S. Parkman Tuckerman, Mus. Doc.,* published at Boston by Oliver Ditson in 1858. Dr. Tuckerman (1819–90), successively organist in New York City of Trinity Chapel (1855) and in Boston of St. Paul's Church (1863), must surely be the first American editor who so reveled in his own Lambeth degree (1853) as to have added "Mus. Doc." after the names of every doctor from William Crotch to

Edward Hodges (1796–1867) who gained admittance to his select book. He proves also to be the morning star of that large group of American church composers whose lights have shown at their brightest in prize contests, by including at pages 191–203 his own Te Deum, "written in competition for a prize of One Hundred dollars offered by the last General Convention of the Protestant Episcopal Church." Further to forestall the future, when nothing is so important as length, he prefaces his Te Deum with the astute promise that "the time of performance should not exceed seven minutes."

Wilson and Tuckerman appealed about 1860 to a metropolitan seaboard sector of the American public; and—if Philip Schaff was right—offended the masses by their "exclusiveness and pedantry." The generality, even in New York, preferred the music at the Broadway Tabernacle, where Bradbury spoke their language not only in his hymns—*Just as I am* (1849), *Sweet hour of prayer* (1860), *He leadeth me* (1864)—but also in lengthier works such as the cantata *Esther, the Beautiful Queen* and the anthem *And it shall come to pass in the last days* ("sung at the closing services of the Broadway Tabernacle Church on April 26, 1857"). At its weakest in such a maudlin effusion as *The Blind Orphan Girl*—a solo to melodeon accompaniment overlaid with many a *rallentando con espressione,* harmonized with barbershop chords, and concluding with an operatic flourish on "I'm blind, O! . . . I'm blind," Bradbury was but echoing the Bellini bravura of the *Norma* adaptations being simultaneously sung in nearby silk-stocking Incarnation Church.

American hymnody in the last hundred years keeps pace with the denominations themselves. The activist, mission-minded denominations, from Mormons to Methodists, have sponsored official hymnals with a hard core of dignified hymns for polite city congregations surrounded by the juicy fruit of *Blessed assurance* (a longtime favorite in Billy Graham campaigns), *I need Thee every hour* (one of Mrs. Mary Baker Eddy's three favorite hymns, which must never be omitted from Christian Science hymnals), and other like-minded "songs of salvation." Side by side with the official denominational hymnal, the same activist denominations have allowed a dense orchard of Sunday School and "auxiliary" hymnbooks to grow up, fruited with hymn tunes by such Gospel composers as B. D. Ackley, E. O. Excell, W. G. Fischer, Charles H. Gabriel, Phoebe Palmer Knapp, B. B. McKinney, G. C. Stebbins, John R. Sweney, and Will L. Thompson. The composers of the popular tunes in the Sunday School type of books have often been as innocent of any academic training as Dan Emmett. Bricklayer, shoe salesman, or plumber, these composers have found formal musical instruction no more useful than Moody and Sunday found Hebrew and Greek.

Even in Britain, Gospel hymnody has not lacked its advocates. After the mammoth Moody-Sankey campaign of 1875, Lord Shaftesbury claimed that had American evangelists done "nothing more than teach the people to sing such hymns as 'Hold the Fort, For I Am Coming' [Philip P. Bliss, 1838–76] they would have conferred an inestimable blessing on Great Britain." Cliff Barrows and George Beverly Shea did not find that American Gospel songs had lost any of their mass appeal when Graham conducted his London campaign in 1954. But Eric Routley, in *The Music of Christian Hymnody: A Study of the development of the hymn tune* (1957), has qualms concerning the "inestimable blessing" bestowed by this class of American tune: "At best this music is honestly flamboyant and redolent of the buoyancy of the civilization that created New York and Pittsburgh and Chicago; at its worst it is flabby and futile." Horatio W. Parker (1863–1919) and Winfred Douglas (1867–1944) did something to rescue America from "the slough of sentimental music-hall sloppiness and campfire heartiness" into which it fell after the Civil War. But "American taste has proved itself hard to rescue," Routley adds. Even so adept a master of the popular idiom as Stephen Collins Foster could not write anything with religious words that equaled his *Camptown Races, My Old Kentucky Home,* and *Old Folks at Home.* Foster's twenty Sunday School songs divided between Horace Waters's *Golden Harp* and *Athenaeum Collection* (1863) never approach anywhere the vitality of *Old Black Joe* (1860) or *Beautiful Dreamer* (1864). For his hymn *The pure, the bright, the beautiful* he chose two stanzas by so eminent an author as Charles Dickens (*The Athenaeum Collection,* pp. 212–13). However, he failed to rise above routine level, whether setting Dickens's poetry or his own.

Since hymn tunes are pre-eminently the food of the common man, their importance in church history exceeds that of all other musical types in a nation as democratic as America. But during the last half of the 19th century, city churches began nearly everywhere to depend also on ensembles of paid soloists for their more pretentious Sunday fare. The mixed quartet in a side gallery or above the pulpit became the norm in such churches, even in the newly settled West. As early as 1856, when the *San Francisco Bulletin* published a series of articles on local church music, the reporter thought it odd that "The First Presbyterian Church has a choir of ten instead of the fashionable quartet so much in vogue in other churches." In Episcopalian churches throughout the West—whether at Virginia City in boom days or in Los Angeles at the predecessor of the present cathedral —the taste in the 1870s and 1880s was just as much for the quartet as in the East, where Dudley Buck (1839–1909) reigned as king of church music.

Describing the music in the leading Episcopalian church, a reporter for the *Los Angeles Express* wrote in the issue of March 22, 1875, that the "air of the prayer in the opera of *Zampa*" provided a "delicious conclusion to very interesting services." The two female soloists were Miss Florida Nichols, with a soprano voice "which would attract attention in any choir," and Miss Belle Mallard, whose "notes are fresh as a bird's." For such singers as these, Dudley Buck composed scores of highly successful anthems, many of which still "deservedly remain upon our choir programs," according to Peter Lutkin, who praises him above every composer of his generation. Even though "most of his music was intended for the quartette choir, it was a marked advance on anything which had preceded it." Lutkin attributes Buck's weaker moments to his "too frequent cadences giving something of a patchwork effect," and his "oversentimental" approach to the historic texts of the Bible and the liturgy. Buck—born in the same year as his fellow New Englander John Knowles Paine, educated in Germany as was Paine, honored by Theodore Thomas with Exposition commissions at Philadelphia in 1876 and again at Chicago in 1893 (as was Paine, also)—"stood more nearly for a distinctive style of American Church music than any other composer." In Lutkin's opinion, Buck's approach to an American style sufficiently condones his faults.

Buck turned his hand to any text, Latin or English, with the same facility and tuneful zest. His *Ave Maria* and *Requiem aeternam*—quartet choruses in *The Legend of Don Munio* (a cantata published by Oliver Ditson in 1874 as Buck's Op. 62)—bow just as low to *Vierhebigkeit* and round off the musical cliché just as smoothly as does the choral finale from the same cantata in praise of the Protestant Jehovah, *In thankful hymns ascending.*

Besides Buck, several other New England composers wrote cantatas and oratorios that were printed by Oliver Ditson in the 1870s. Eugene Thayer, born at Mendon, Massachusetts, in 1838, and one of the first native-born Americans to win a Mus. Doc. degree at Oxford University, returned to Boston to take up an organist's career; in 1872 Ditson brought out Thayer's *Festival Cantata.* Two years later, the same firm followed with John Knowles Paine's 174-page oratorio *St. Peter* (given its premiere at Portland, Maine, on June 3, 1873). This was Paine's first large work performed in this country. A smaller choral work, his sacred ode for four men's voices and orchestra, *Domine salvum fac,* had been sung at the inauguration of Thomas Hill as president of Harvard University on March 4, 1864; it was repeated for the inauguration of Charles Eliot, October 19, 1869. Abroad, he had garnered praise in the German press with a Mass in D, which he directed at Berlin in 1867. However, it was *St. Peter* that established him as the "first American who has shown the genius and the culture necessary for writing music in the grand style," to repeat John Fiske's encomium. W. S. B. Mathews, discussing "American Oratorio" in *The Nation* (XVI, No. 398, February 13, 1873, pp. 116–17), added his accolade. Buck is the only composer who comes near Paine, if one may believe *The Nation,* and *St. Peter* "is without doubt the most important musical work yet produced in this country."

Oliver Ditson's other large sacred publications continued with Buck's 46th Psalm in 1872 and the *Redemption Hymn* and *The Blind King* by James Cutler Dunn Parker (1828–1916; no relation to Horatio W.), issued in 1877 and 1883. J. C. D. Parker, for twenty-seven years organist at Trinity Church, Boston, wrote also a *St. John* cantata (1890). *The Life of Man,* his farewell choral work (introduced to Boston by the Handel and Haydn Society at an Easter concert, 1895), had a powerful Resurrection scene, in the opinion of Louis Elson, and showed "masterly canonic writing in the portrayal of the seven churches of Asia." So evanescent are such triumphs, however, that few students of American music would today recognize a *Doppelmeister* problem.

A Parker so much more eminent rose in the 1890s as to overshadow not only his Harvard-trained namesake but all American sacred composers of his century. *Hora Novissima,* Horatio Parker's first large choral work (Op. 30), breathed the spirit of the times when he chose Latin for his language. Even Mrs. H. H. A. Beach was in February of 1892 making her Boston debut as a composer with a Mass in E-flat, Op. 5, performed by the Handel and Haydn Society under Carl Zerrahn. Two months later Parker finished scoring *Hora Novissima,* which he had started to compose in the spring of the previous year. His daughter alludes

150. Page from autograph of Horatio Parker, *Hora Novissima* (1892). Library of Congress, Washington, D.C.

to his many personal griefs in the year that he wrote this important oratorio, based on thirty-five six-line stanzas from Bernard of Cluny's *De contemptu mundi*. The poem had been a favorite of his father, Charles Edward Parker, who died in the year Horatio was working at *Hora Novissima*. So also did Mary, Horatio's younger sister, and his only son. From these griefs he turned to the oratorio that more than any work has kept his name alive. First performed by the Church Choral Society of New York under Richard Henry Warren on May 2, 1893, it made an ever more profound impression at the Handel and Haydn Society premiere in 1894 and the Cincinnati Festival performance under Theodore Thomas in the same year. Before its premiere at the Three Choirs Festival in Worcester (1899) it had already been acclaimed in the English press as a work worthy of comparison with the best that Europe was producing.

The resurgence of the Mass, whether set by Roy Harris, Lou Harrison, Roger Sessions, or Randall Thompson, is interestingly paralleled in modern America by the use to which such lights as Samuel Barber, Aaron Copland, Ross Lee Finney, Lukas Foss, Howard Hanson, Alan Hovhaness, Norman Dello Joio, Normand Lockwood, Peter Mennin, Vincent Persichetti, and Leo Sowerby have put numerous other classic religious texts. These range from the creation poem in Genesis, psalms in both scriptural prose and rough-hewn Bay Psalmbook meter, selections from such other books of the Bible as Isaiah, Ecclesiastes, and the Gospel of St. Luke, to John Chrysostom's Greek liturgy and selected prayers from Kierkegaard. Our established American composers of the present, unlike MacDowell and Charles T. Griffes, have almost to a man made some sort of "religious" gesture. Curiously, the gestures of even the most avant-garde have been bows to the traditionally accepted masterpieces of religious prose and poetry.

When, for instance, Copland composed his a cappella masterpiece *In the Beginning,* he hewed as closely to Scripture as did Handel in *Messiah.* Thompson, in his sequence of sacred choruses for unaccompanied mixed voices, *The Peaceable Kingdom,* invoked the painter-preacher Edward Hicks (1780–1849) as his patron, but confined himself textually to passages from Isaiah. When for a brief interlude he did consent to stray from Scripture in one scene of *The Nativity according to Saint Luke* (composed for the bicentennial of the dedication of Christ Church, Cambridge, 1961), he chose a poem by Richard Rowlands (1565–1630?) rather than by a contemporary. Leo Sowerby (1895–1968), the most professionally church-oriented of composers, chose texts from Revelation for *The Throne of God* (1956–57) or from St. Francis for the Alice Ditson commission, *The Canticle of the Sun* (Carnegie Hall, April 16, 1945). Both *Christ Reborn* and *Forsaken of Man* with texts "arranged" by Edward Borgers culminate in Scripture. Sowerby's *The Vision of Sir Launfal* (1928) came nearer to our time, but no nearer than James Russell Lowell.

In 1958 Sowerby—after surveying the American scene from the organ bench of the Episcopalian cathedral in Chicago—awarded merit ribbons to these native-born composers of church music: Seth Bingham, Everett Titcomb, Philip James, Joseph W. Clokey, Randall Thompson, Normand Lockwood, Richard Purvis, Robert Elmore, Searle Wright, and Robert Crandell. Mark Siebert, who published a lengthy White List of anthems by contemporary composers in *Notes of the Music Library Association* (2nd series, XV/1, December, 1957, p. 159), largely endorsed Sowerby's choices (he added a half dozen names not in Sowerby's list).

To summarize what was happening in American church music in the 1950s: famous contemporary American composers continued to pour out a steady stream of first-class services, psalms, anthems, and odes invoking the name of God. Their difficulty often precluded use outside such privileged environments as heavily endowed metropolitan churches or college and university chapels. The hymnals of the larger denominations, except such religious bodies as flourish principally in the South, grew more and more "respectable" musically with each new edition. To ensure propriety in these official hymnals, the few older American compositions had to undergo extensive cosmetic surgery. Paradoxically, the early American hymn tunes rejected by editors of "respectable" humnals became the chief cornerstones of important secular works by such "respectable" composers as Copland, Cowell, Ives, Schuman, and Thomson.

The "hot Gospel" denominations continued to depend on numerous late 19th-century salvation songs of the P.P. Bliss and Charles H. Gabriel variety. Even Billy Graham, the most successful of modern revivalists, surrounded himself with performers rather than composers able to match the appeal of Bliss, Sankey, or Gabriel. As a result, anything distinctively American continued to mean (so far as the broad masses were concerned) such Gospel hymns popularized before the First World War as *Blessed Assurance* and *The Old Rugged Cross.* The music for the most popular "new" song, featured in the Graham campaigns of the 1950s —*How Great Thou Art*—was an arrangement (copyright 1955) of the traditional Swedish folk melody *O Store Gud.*

PART IX

Church Music in England from the Reformation to the Present Day

BY WATKINS SHAW

PRELIMINARY NOTES

The following section deals with the church music of the principal indigenous religious bodies of England and Wales that are not in communion with Rome. With reference to the Church of England (and to the church in Wales, part of the Anglican Communion) it is well now to speak thus rather than to use the term "Protestant." Though this appellation was proudly held in the years following the Reformation (when it was refused to such as the Anabaptists), there are many in these churches who today—whether rightly or wrongly is not to the point—would repudiate it now that it has acquired other overtones. This being so, its use might be taken to exclude these churches, and it is therefore avoided.

The nonepiscopal churches, known first as "dissenting" and later as "Nonconformist," are now generally called "Free Churches."

As to Ireland, the whole of which (including what is now the Republic of Eire) was part of the United Kingdom up to 1937, neither the Church of Ireland (within the Anglican Communion) nor the Free Churches have developed on any independent lines in church music from their brethren in England.

Scotland, politically united with England and Wales in 1707, has had an independent religious history. In 1560 Presbyterianism established itself as the national religion, and so remains to this day as the Church of Scotland. As befitted its Calvinist origin, this sternly rejected all forms of instrumental music down to the later 19th century, and permitted only the unaccompanied congregational singing of metrical psalms and paraphrases of Scripture to the old psalm tunes. This, then, until very recent years, has been the nature of Scottish church music since the Reformation. Lately it has admitted a wider range of hymns and tunes and in some churches an anthem after the English fashion will be sung. Organs are generally found. Information about Scottish psalmody (whose origins, like English psalmody, are in Geneva) may be found in:

Begg, James, *The Use of organs . . . indefensible,* Glasgow and London, 1866.

Farmer, H. G., *A History of Music in Scotland,* London, 1947.

Johnson, David, *Music and Society in lowland Scotland in the 18th Century,* London, 1972.

Moffatt, James, and Patrick, Millar, *Handbook to the Church Hymnary,* Rev. ed., London, n.d.

Patrick, Millar, *Four Centuries of Scottish Psalmody,* London, 1949.

Ritchie, W., *The Organ Question,* Edinburgh, 1856.

My discussion is limited to settings of the liturgy designed for use within services, to anthems, and to metrical psalm and hymn tunes. On the one hand I have excluded (though a distinctive product) the "Anglican Chant," and on the

693

other cantatas and liturgical settings not designed for use in services. Though religious, a work like Vaughan Williams's *Hodie* is not "church music," as Bach's Passion according to St. Matthew unquestionably is.

HISTORICAL BACKGROUND

The Reformation in England was an act of state. At every point touching jurisdiction, organization, discipline, formularies, and liturgy, matters proceeded from the authority of the Sovereign, Council, and Parliament. Much of this far-reaching revolution would have been carried through, doctrinal changes or no. In this respect the English Reformation differs from Lutheran, Zwinglian, and Calvinist movements: for, in those, belief (admittedly related to political factors) was the primary driving force which cleared new paths in institutions and church government, while in England institutional and juridical reform preceded liturgical and doctrinal. It followed that continental and Scottish changes were more radical, less conservative of old habits and traditions, and this was important in its musical consequences.

We may conveniently regard the period 1531–75 as decisive for the English Reformation. From 1531, the year in which Henry VIII exacted the submission of the clergy until the Act of Uniformity in the first year of Elizabeth I and that sovereign's Royal Injunctions, there is a period of ebb and flow and intermingled cross-currents. Thence, from 1559 to the end of the episcopate of Archbishop Matthew Parker in 1575 there is a period of steadfast consolidation. Yet even the success of the Elizabethan Settlement in avoiding disruption of national unity at a perilous time of English history could not cloak the well-defined existence within the same church of a conservative "High Church" party on the one hand and a radical "Puritan" party of Calvinistic derivation on the other. There could be no permanent marriage between the medieval constitution of the Elizabethan church, together with its liturgy (however designedly comprehensive that might be) and the Calvinistic theology prevalent among a large number of its ministers, some of them in high places. In the 17th century these differences became acute and took on political affiliation with "Cavalier" and "Roundhead." The comprehensive ideal broke down in 1662, and separately organized dissenting churches developed musical traditions distinct from those of the Church of England and in accordance with their characteristic positions.

During the reign of Henry VIII two institutional upheavals closely affected music and musicians. Between 1536 and 1540 every monastery was compelled to surrender to the crown. In 1545 an act (confirmed by a further act of Edward VI in 1547) was passed affecting all secular (i.e., nonmonastic) clergy organized into colleges. These two "Chantries Acts" thus added the collegiate churches to the loss of the monasteries. Standards in both were variable, though some few were (or had been) high; yet to the extent to which monasteries and collegiate churches had maintained music in the Daily Offices and in the Masses of the Virgin Mary and had educated choristers in their schools, their abolition reduced the number of foundations dedicated to the musical services of the church.

However, something, at least, was saved. The thirteen cathedrals[1] organized as collegiate churches were suffered to survive; so also St. George's Chapel in Windsor Castle and the college foundations of Oxford and Cambridge, Eton and Winchester. To take the place of the monastic bodies which had formerly served eight other cathedrals,[2] Henry VIII established deans and chapters and the personnel needful to maintain choral services; and, further, he created new cathedrals with similar provision out of six former monasteries.[3] Queen Elizabeth I founded a collegiate church at Westminster (Westminster Abbey) and in her reign and that of her successor, James VI & I, similar churches were revived at Manchester, Southwell, and Ripon. Thus continuity was assured to some thirty regularly constituted and endowed choral foundations, and so, by a slender thread, the medieval tradition of the musical observance of the Daily Offices was secured to the Church of England. This degree of institutional continuity has been of incalculable importance. In spite of efforts to dislodge it, and the bitter dislike of the extreme reforming party, it fortunately survived the doctrinal and liturgical changes shortly to follow. Its survival may have been by a hairbreadth, and there is some likelihood that at a crucial moment only the intervention of Queen Elizabeth saved it; yet survive it did, to become a part of a national inheritance at once religious and artistic. "The choral services, as rendered daily in the English Cathedrals," said Fellowes, "are unique in the world of modern music; nothing quite like them exists on the Continent of Europe."

During the last ten years of Henry's reign there was an increasing use of the English language in the services; this followed naturally from the setting up of a Bible in English in all parish churches in 1538. In 1544 a notable further step was taken by the official issue of a "Letanie with suffrages to be said or songe in . . . processyons," the work of Thomas Cranmer and to all intents and purposes the Litany in the present Book of Common Prayer. At the same time there was a growing practice of drawing on vernacular forms of prayers, canticles, and psalms as set forth in the. Primers (books of private devotions). But in matters of doctrine King Henry was strongly conservative; only after the accession of Edward VI in 1547 did the party of reform grow strong in official circles, leading to the promulgation of a definitive English service book, the first Book of Common Prayer, authorized to take exclusive effect not later than Whitsun, June 9, 1549.

To deal with the doctrinal issues reflected in the Prayer Book is beyond our present scope. Archbishop Cranmer, the principal author and translator, to whom chiefly we owe its majestic, expressive, and august language so frequently set to music from that time to this, had already reached a tolerably advanced reforming position. Yet there is no harsh iconoclasm or intransigence in his liturgical work. As Sir Maurice Powicke has expressed it: "In 1549 Cranmer and

1St. Paul's (London), York, Salisbury, Lincoln, Chichester, Exeter, Wells, Hereford, Lichfield, St. David's, and (though poorly equipped for music) Llandaff, Bangor, and St. Asaph.
2Canterbury, Carlisle, Durham, Norwich, Ely, Rochester, Winchester, and Worcester.
3Chester, Peterborough, Bristol, Gloucester, and Christ Church (Oxford); also, for a period of ten years only, Westminster.

his colleagues carefully refrained from making the ritual and prayers of the Church capable of expressing only, and nothing more than, his increasingly definite standpoint in regard to the Eucharist. He was more than a theologian learned in all the liturgies of the past, he was a priest who for thirty years had . . . used words and prayed prayers which had become part of his spiritual life." Broadly speaking, the Prayer Book of 1549 determined the liturgy, and thereby the music, of the Church of England from that day to this. Numerous differences were introduced in the second Prayer Book of Edward VI in 1552, marking the furthest Zwinglian influence to be officially approved by Parliament. Hardly had it become effective when the young king died, whereupon his sister Mary restored the unreformed Latin rite. But the Prayer Book of Elizabeth I (1559) largely reintroduced the second Edwardian book, carefully modified to avoid the more extreme position of 1552 without completely reverting to 1549. From this time there have been no changes in the Prayer Book affecting music, except a slight alteration, made in 1662,[4] to the responses before the psalms at Morning and Evening Prayer; since the later part of the 19th century, however, composers have frequently set the English versions of *Benedictus qui venit* and Agnus Dei in the Communion service, though these were not found in Prayer Books between those of 1549 and 1928.

When discussing church music in England it is necessary to draw a clear distinction between parish church worship on the one hand and the worship of the choral foundations (cathedrals, collegiate churches, and college chapels with endowed choirs) on the other. For something like two hundred years, though the people's music of the parish church was not without its impact on cathedrals, cathedral music had no relation to the parish church, nor was any such intended. When, from the 18th century, its influence began to affect parish churches somewhat, and from the 19th century overwhelmingly, the results were of questionable value for the most part. One need not deny the richness of congregational melody that is one of the treasures of English religious life to assert that the loftiest achievements of English church music of the past four centuries belong to the realm of cathedral music, and with this we shall be very largely concerned in the present survey.

To grasp the true nature of English cathedral music one must have some appreciation of its scale. The large size of most cathedrals may be superficially misleading here. For though the building may be vast, the portion used for choir services—a small three-sided chamber within the great edifice, set apart by stone screens and woodwork—has a remarkable intimacy.[5] Even in a huge church like Lincoln Cathedral or Westminster Abbey this is marked, while at Norwich, Ripon, or St. David's one has, within the choir, the scale of a college chapel as at Magdalen College, Oxford. This, then, is music performed in a small setting,

4The Prayer Book of Charles II, 1662 (see below, p. 708), is still law in England and Wales. A proposed revision, rejected by Parliament in 1928, gradually came into use when desired, on the authority of the bishops. Further permissive alternatives are at present undergoing experimental use.
5The fact that in some cathedrals this has been destroyed by misconceived alterations, though deplorable, is beside the point.

and also by small forces. For though such choirs are smaller now, as regards men's voices, than in Elizabethan or Jacobean (even Georgian) days, cathedral choirs have never been large. Sixteen men, clerical and lay, with eight boys represented a typical constitution; ten boys and twenty-four men, clerical and lay, as at Canterbury and Winchester Cathedrals, represented a large choir, while at Ripon Collegiate Church (now the Cathedral) seven men and six boys were constituted as the choir under James I. Moreover, this handful of men and boys was accompanied, for two hundred years after the Reformation, by a small sweet-toned organ very different from the rolling giants of today. The seating arrangements preserved the medieval division of the choir into two equally balanced halves, one sitting on the south, or dean's side *(decani)*, the other on the north, or precentor's side *(cantoris)*, so making possible a responsive element with a certain spatial characteristic of which English cathedral composers have made full use.

The music thus performed was in no sense intended for an audience or to edify a congregation. The dean and canons together with the men and boys of the choir were constituted to be a worshiping community, meeting in choir daily to give prayer and praise to God. Thus the composer of cathedral music no more addressed himself to a body of auditors than did a composer of chamber music in the late 18th century. It is true that during the 18th and 19th centuries a small class of auditors began to frequent the cathedral service and a class of music developed which expressly encouraged admirers of particular men and boy solo singers; but this was not true to type and has fortunately not proved durable. By this self-contained intimacy, then, we may account for a characteristic quality in English cathedral music. Certainly it is sharply differentiated from, for example, the Lutheran church cantata, sung publicly from a church gallery, not in the intimacy of an enclosed choir.

THE ENGLISH REFORMATION AND MUSIC

Religious reformers who took their cue from Calvin rather than from Luther were not disposed to look kindly on music or any other artistic adjunct of worship, and this influence was strong in England. They objected to organs and disliked choir music, with its polyphony and repeated words ("reports and repeats," in the terminology of the day). Some would have abolished choirs or harmonized singing altogether; others were prepared to admit music to the cathedral service provided the words were made clear. In practice this meant applying the principle of one note to a syllable whether the music was in unison or not, and, if harmonized, keeping the same note duration in every voice part. An oft-quoted letter of Cranmer's to Henry VIII (1544), using the phrase "But in my opinion, the song that should be made thereunto would not be full of notes, but, as near as may be, for every syllable a note," is generally cited as the classic statement of the English reforming position concerning music. But, read in its context, Cranmer's remark refers to what he considers well-established practice, "as be in the matins and evensong . . . and in the mass," not to any new principle.

In any event, this was but an opinion, not, as has sometimes been made to appear, an authoritative direction. Surer statements of the position may be found in the Royal Injunctions for Lincoln Cathedral, 1548, which enjoin that anthems must be set to "a plain and distinct note for every syllable one," and in the Injunctions issued to his cathedral in 1552 by Holgate, Archbishop of York, which rule that there must "be none other note sung or used in the said church at any service there to be had, saving square note plain [i.e., unharmonized music] so that every syllable may be plainly and distinctly pronounced, and without any reports or repeats which may induce any obscureness to the hearers" (who Holgate supposed the listeners would be one cannot imagine). The archbishop also silenced the organ in York Minster. In Elizabeth's reign an official view was uncompromisingly expressed in the *Second Book of Homilies* (1563), which says that "piping, singing, chanting and playing upon the organs" are things "which displeased God so sore, and filthily defiled his holy house." About the same time objections to cathedral music were expressed in John Field's "Admonition to the Parliament" when he termed cathedrals "the dens of all loitering lubbers, where . . . squeaking choristers, organ players . . . live in great idleness." As in other matters, however, Elizabeth was not prepared to allow this question of music to be pushed to extremes. John Bosewell in book 3 of his *Works of Armory* (1572) stated that "If it were not the Queen's majesty did favour that excellent Science [music], singing men and choristers might go a-begging." And item 49 of the Royal Injunctions dated 1569 reads as follows:

> And that there be a modest and distinct song as used in all parts of the Common Prayers in the Church, that the same may be as plainly understood as if it were read without singing. And yet, nevertheless, for the comforting of such that delight in music, it may be permitted, that in the beginning, or in the end of Common Prayers, either at morning or evening, there may be sung an hymn, or such-like song to the praise of Almighty God, in the best sort of melody and music that may be conveniently devised, having respect that the sentence of the hymn may be understood and perceived.

Under cover of this authority, the singing of metrical psalms became possible; and no doubt it was also held to cover the cathedral anthem, for which no place was allotted in the Edwardian and Elizabethan Prayer Books.

Fortunately for our artistic heritage, although musicians took some steps to conform to the desire for plainness and distinctness in the early years of the English Reformation, no compulsion was exerted on them, and, as the years went by, though doubtless local and personal influences differed, ample opportunities were afforded for the fullest employment of their skill. This was markedly so in the Chapel Royal of Elizabeth and her two successors, and also more generally under the High Church revival in the reign of Charles I (1625–49), greatly to the offense of sterner Puritans like Peter Smart, who so bitterly objected to the amount and style of music introduced into Durham Cathedral, of which he was a canon.

The most thoroughgoing application of reforming principles to music was the complete setting of the 1549 Prayer Book by John Marbeck (Merbecke) (c. 1510–c. 1585), entitled *The Book of Common Prayer Noted* (i.e., set to music). In this publication the melodies, designed for unison singing without accompaniment, are largely simplifications and adaptations of familiar plainsong; it has been shown by R.R. Terry that only *Gloria in excelsis,* the Creed, the Offertory Sentences, and the Post-Communion (all from the Communion service) are by Marbeck himself, Te Deum, for example, being a condensed form of the Ambrosian melody. The result departs greatly from plainsong by maintaining the principle of one note only to each syllable and also by using leaps. For his purpose Marbeck devised something like a mensural notation, which he described thus: a "strene note" or breve ▉; a "square note" or semibreve ■; a "pycke" [i.e., a note shaped like the head of a pike] or minim ◆; a "prick" or dot, adding to a "square note" half its value; a "close," the last note of a verse ▉. It must be remembered that he was catering to singers in whom the habits of singing the Latin quantities were firmly engrained, and who would run into trouble with a word which, though very close in appearance to the Latin, had a slightly different stress in English. To this extent one may agree with H.C. Colles in praising Marbeck for "a first essay in accommodating the prose rhythms of the language to a free musical rhythm." But Marbeck went further. In his own melody to the Creed, the combination of tonic and agogic accent is clearly intentional in the following phrases:

by whom all things were made   or   and was made man

Three phrases involving the word "father" are also instructive when placed side by side:

right hand of the fa - ther   from the fa - ther and the son

with the fa - ther and the son

Here Marbeck is surely on the very border of mensural music.

The issue of the Second Prayer Book of Edward VI set Marbeck's work at naught, and he made no attempt to revise it. It was put on the shelf to await revival in the second half of the 19th century at the hands of that party in the church with which Marbeck, the staunch Protestant, would have had least sympathy. Since that time its application—a commendable one, let it be said—has been in the form of a people's music, a congregational setting of the Holy Communion, with organ accompaniment. But for Marbeck it was Protestant choir music, for cathedral use, notwithstanding C. Henry Phillips's assertion to the contrary.

CONGREGATIONAL PSALMODY

For the earliest congregational music we must turn to metrical psalm tunes. By the time Edward VI died, Thomas Sternhold and John Hopkins had rendered 44 psalms into English rhyming verse. During Mary's reign these were transferred to Geneva upon the migration thither of many English Protestants. There, in 1556, appeared *One and fiftie Psalms of David in Englishe metre* with accompanying melodies. This, and a further Genevan publication of 1558, lies directly behind the publication in England by John Day, early in the reign of Elizabeth I (1562), of *The Whole Book of Psalmes, collected into English metre,* together with 65 tunes. This appeared under cover of the Royal Injunctions of 1559 already mentioned. The tunes were such as did not rely on harmony and were readily learned by heart and sung in unison. As there were no organs in parish churches—save in exceptional instances—the tunes were pitched by the parish clerk, who was expected to have some rudimentary skill in music and who, for the benefit of the illiterate majority, would sing each line of the metrical psalm in turn for repetition by the congregation. For the rest, parish church services were spoken, the clerk making the responses to the minister and reading aloud alternate verses of the prose psalms; these became known as the "reading psalms," in distinction to the metrical psalms, which were sung congregationally.

In 1563 Day published a version of his earlier book with the tunes harmonized in four parts, placing the tune in the tenor. Devout amateurs may have used Day's partbooks at home; but as metrical psalms were also used in cathedrals it was doubtless there that they were used in services. Metrical psalm singing grew further in popularity along with sermons, which began to be preached as independent items after Morning Prayer in cathedrals, and wherever else adequately equipped clergy could be found, preceded and followed by a metrical psalm.

Of later metrical Psalters (all with harmonized tenor tunes) up to the Civil War (1640), the most famous and influential were two collections by William Daman (1591), East's (or Este's) Psalter (1st ed., 1592), and Ravenscroft's (1621); the second of Daman's two books was exceptional in placing the tune in the treble, not the tenor (or, very occasionally, the alto). The harmonized settings in these collections varied from fairly plain note-against-note style to something akin to an anthem style with imitation, even canon, between the voices. Daman wrote his own settings; the Psalters of Day, East, and Ravenscroft draw on the work of numerous composers. As to the tunes themselves, those found in the earliest Genevan Psalter must have been English in origin: but the contact made there led to considerable French influence (Old 100th and Old 122nd) as well as a little Lutheran (Old 112th). Back in England, the "church tunes" (as the psalm melodies came to be called) appear to have been influenced in composition by the musical phraseology of Tye's *Actes of the Apostles,* a series of settings for domestic use of a doggerel translation of Scripture made by Tye himself: both *Winchester Old* and *Windsor Tunes* are cited as examples.

Of the early "church tunes" still in common use, Old 44th and Old 127th are survivors of the Genevan Psalter of 1556; Old 25th, Old 112th, Old 120th, and Old 127th of the 1558 publication; Old 81st and (derived from the French Genevan Psalter of 1551) Old 100th are from Day's Psalter; *London* (or *Southwell*) and *Windsor* from Daman, 1591; *Winchester Old* from East, 1592; and Old 104th and *Bristol* from Ravenscroft, 1621.

Two other sets of tunes have influenced modern hymnology but achieved no currency (for reasons other than musical) in their own day. The first consists of the harmonized tenor tunes, including the famous canon written by Thomas Tallis for a Psalter projected by Archbishop Parker (1567); the second consists of fourteen tunes (treble and bass only) written by Orlando Gibbons for George Withers's *Hymns and Songs of the Church,* 1623. Both sets have greater rhythmic subtlety than the "church tunes" generally current in their day. Whether at that time they could ever have become truly congregational does not affect their value today. Thomas Tomkins also wrote some psalm tunes, but these remain little known. None of these sets of tunes was conceived independently of the harmony.

CATHEDRAL MUSIC FROM THE REFORMATION

TO THE LONG PARLIAMENT

Nothing more was done on Marbeck's lines and the future of English cathedral music lay entirely in the harmonized style. In discussing this one must speak not only of what came to be called "anthems" but also of "services." By "service" is meant a musical setting of the canticles prescribed at Morning Prayer—Venite, Te Deum (or *Benedicite*), Benedictus (or *Jubilate*)—and Evening Prayer—Magnificat (or *Cantate Domino*), Nunc Dimittis (or *Deus Misereatur*)—as well as Kyrie, Credo, Sanctus, and Gloria in excelsis in the Communion service. One may thus speak of a "morning service," and "evening service," and a "Communion service"; or, if all are furnished, a "complete service." It has been the convention at all periods to write each movement of a service in the same key, and to name it as thus: "Purcell in B-flat." Only early composers set Venite (e.g., Byrd, but not Purcell). In the early part of the 17th century the practice was gradually to omit it. In the Communion service from the time of Elizabeth I onward, few composers set any more than Kyrie and Credo (Blow is one exception) until the later 19th century.

Our first well defined period runs from the first English Litany (1544) to the suspension of the Prayer Book by the Long Parliament (1644), a century throughout which the style remained polyphonic, little touched, even at the end, by monody and the basso continuo. For convenience we may consider first the works of composers up to the end of the 16th century, or the death of Elizabeth I (1603).

There were some tentative essays in the form of the English service during the years immediately before the first English Prayer Book. Among these, the Complete Service in the Dorian mode by Thomas Tallis (c. 1505–85) stands out as the earliest artistic achievement for the English rite. Written almost strictly on the note-against-note principle and devoid of verbal repetition, this is the classic model of a style which, born of reforming ideals, was to persist in English cathedral music up to the time of Goss and S. S. Wesley and which is known as the "short" service. Apart from some passages sung by the full choir, the short verbal clauses are treated responsively by *decani* and *cantoris,* which unite, of course, for the Gloria. This is the regular treatment in short-service style throughout its history, although, curiously enough, Tallis does not adopt it for the Evening Canticles. This short quotation shows his general style and the slight degree in which he departs from the complete austerity of the note-against-note principle. In an early Elizabethan short service in A minor by Richard Farrant

(d. 1580) more variety is obtained by differently disposed groups of voices, sometimes more, sometimes less than the basic four. This attractive work, though in general spirit a specimen of the short service, permits itself some few touches of imitation and occasionally repeats a clause of the words; perhaps one may coin the expression "relaxed short service" style. Other short services written before the end of the century include those by Thomas Morley (c. 1558–?1603) and Nathaniel Patrick (d. 1595). But the finest short service not only of this period but of all time is that by William Byrd (1543–1623). He invests the limited principle with beauty of phrase and sensitivity to syllabic values of rare genius and with felicitious expansion of the four-part texture, notably in the Communion Service.

Tallis himself wrote another service, of which only Te Deum survives (in five parts). This is composed in an extended imitative manner uninhibited by reforming principles; like his Short Service, this also dates from the 1540s. Another fine and elaborate service is that for men's voices by John Shepherd (d. ?1563), his so-called First Service; this makes effective use not only of the response between *decani* and *cantoris* but also of their overlapping. But, as with the short-service style, so with the imitative polyphonic style it is Byrd who provides the noblest example, one which in sweep of phrase and richness of polyphony (not to speak of expressive power) was never to be surpassed in this style. Well does this service deserve its appellation of "Great."[6] It is written for double choir of five voices each, and obviously must have been composed for some fine choir, doubtless the Chapel Royal.

Byrd wrote two other services, both confined to the Evening Canticles. No. 3 is generally in short-service form, but because, with considerable individuality, he wrote it in triple time it was known to contemporaries by the quaintly attractive title "Mr. Bird's Three Minims." His Second Service introduced a solo voice with organ accompaniment; that is to say, it is a "verse" service, "verse" being the name then used for solo passages in church music. In all probability this is the first to be cast into such a style. Byrd alternates his solo and choral passages, and the organ accompaniment is polyphonic in texture.

Morley also made important contributions to service literature. Apart from two Evening Services in the short form there is a beautiful complete service in verse form on more elaborate lines than Byrd's, employing not only a single solo voice line but solo ensembles of two, three, and four voices with organ. This short passage illustrates the combined texture of solo voices with organ.

Anthem literature during the second half of the 16th century reveals Christopher Tye (d. c. 1573) as the important early figure beside Tallis and Richard Farrant, who have already been mentioned. The principle underlying the short service was not without a certain impact on early anthems. A beautiful application of it is found in Richard Farrant's *Hide not thou thy face*. The famous anonymous anthem *Lord, for thy tender mercies sake* maintains a similar style until the words "that we may walk," when it breaks into a slightly polyphonic

---

6 I feel bound to say (though the matter cannot be argued here) that I do not accept the view found in standard works that "Great" defines a *category* of services of which Byrd's is but one. It seems to me simply a well-deserved description of this supreme essay by Byrd. Only one other service is so named (once), Tomkins's third, no doubt to distinguish it similarly; but it is different in resource from Byrd's

texture. For the most part it is an equilibrium of this kind which is to be observed in anthems by Tallis (e.g., *If ye love me,* or *Hear the voice and prayer*) and in other early works such as *O Lord, the maker of all thing* by William Mundy (d. c. 1591). On the other hand, even early in Elizabeth's reign, anthems of purely polyphonic style were common. Tye, who is known to have been a convinced Protestant, wrote a powerful and extended setting of *I will exalt thee.* Yet, freely polyphonic though it is, each separate voice part adheres largely to the principle of one note to a syllable, even though the voices are generally singing different syllables simultaneously. This is true also of his *Praise the Lord, ye children* and Tallis's *O God, be merciful.*

In considering Byrd, as with Tallis, one can only take the measure of his stature by reviewing his Latin music. He continued to compose, and, what is more, to publish this in the reigns of Elizabeth I and James I, although it could have no part in the cathedral music of his day,[7] and remains outside our present survey. While his "Great" Service may fittingly be placed beside his settings of the Mass, his English anthems cannot compare with his Latin pieces either in quality or quantity. They are good, but not superb. The famous six-part *Sing joyfully* does not represent him at his best, and the well-known *Prevent us, O Lord* is on a small scale. These, like all those by Tallis, Tye, and Farrant, are "full" anthems. But Byrd wrote some five anthems including solo passages with organ accompaniment —for example, *Thou God, that guid'st both heaven and earth* and *Hear my prayer.* As with the verse service, it is likely that Byrd was here breaking new ground in post-Reformation English music. However that may be, there are good grounds for thinking that the early verse anthem arose as an extension of the training of Chapel Royal choristers to sing solos outside their normal chapel duties.

In Morley's extremely accomplished art there are but few English anthems. His verse anthem *Out of the deep,* with bass soloist, follows Byrd's model in the simple alternation of solo and chorus. Its reserved beauty deserves a short quotation:

7Two short specimens, one by Tallis, one by Byrd, were adapted as English anthems during Byrd's lifetime as *I call and cry (O sacrum convivium)* and *Bow thine ear (Civitas sancti tui)*. These are from publications of *Cantiones Sacrae;* it is unthinkable that any of Byrd's *Gradualia* could have been turned into English anthems at that period.

Morley's work is the link between that of Byrd (who, though he lived till 1623, reached back to early Elizabethan days) and the early 17th century. In this period three figures are outstanding: Thomas Tomkins (1573–1656), Thomas Weelkes (c. 1575–1623), and Orlando Gibbons (1583–1625), all of them, like Byrd and Morley, many-sided in their achievements in secular ensemble music, keyboard and consort music. To them may be added Batten and Hooper, whose work lies exclusively in the ecclesiastical field. Gibbons's fame has never been dimmed, though for long it rested on a restricted knowledge of his work. Tomkins has lately come more into his own; even so, an appraisal of his work awaits the publication of his complete church music in modern score, now in progress. Since this chapter was written, Weelkes's collected anthems have been published. With these men, younger contemporaries of Shakespeare, we reached for the first time a generation of composers not concerned with the Latin rite.

It was a time of much activity in writing services, but "Gibbons in F" is the only one continuously in use ever since then. This is a Complete Service in highly relaxed short-service style, abounding in points of imitation and rhythmic independence in part writing, yet (with one exception) each voice part sings the words of the text once only. In addition there is a Second Service by Gibbons, Morning and Evening, in verse form. Weelkes and Tomkins between them wrote seventeen services of one kind and another, though by no means all of them have survived intact. There appear to have been ten services by Weelkes, six of them in verse form. Of this extensive amount of music, however, only the Morning Canticles from his Short Service survive in complete text; and this is the more tantalizing since, even from incomplete text, it is obvious that he addressed himself to this branch of composition with a versatility hardly rivaled. The Evening Canticles of the Short Service have been readily reconstructed; more intricate reconstructural work has also been successfully carried out on the Magnificat and Nunc Dimittis from both the full service for five voices and the full service for seven voices. Of the verse services the Magnificat and Nunc Dimittis of that entitled "For Trebles" has been reconstructed, and so also the Magnificat and Nunc Dimittis designated "in medio chori." It is clear that Weelkes sought to create variety, when setting the same text time and again, by resourceful disposition of voice groups and the deployment of "verse" and "full" passages. In the service "For Trebles" the full choir is in five parts; the verses are mainly for two trebles, though at one point they are joined by two basses, and there are solo passages for tenor and second treble.

Five of Tomkins's seven services are complete. The First and Second are short services, but this style here includes not only an alternation between the two sides of the choir but ensembles of solo voices, though not such as to involve an independent organ bass as in a true verse service. The Fourth and Fifth services are of that class, the latter giving prominence to a bass soloist, with other verses for varied ensembles. Tomkins's Third Service (designated "Great" in one of its sources) is basically for five-part choir, expanding occasionally to six and seven, with frequent dovetailing of *decani* and *cantoris,* and using verse ensembles of varying composition. These, however, are not woven into a texture involving an independent organ part. Verbal phrases are freely repeated.

Adrian Batten (d. 1637) was a voluminous composer of services in both short and verse styles, and one of his incomplete compositions is styled his "Long" Service. Among the five services by Edmund Hooper (c. 1553–1621), one is a highly elaborate Evening Service in verse form.

From Byrd's time there had always been a recognized practice (though not by any means regularly observed, and sometimes only tenuous in application) of creating unity between movements of a service by using a recurrent opening phrase, or "headpiece," and, less frequently, a "tailpiece" also. This feature meant little to Gibbons, but Tomkins acknowledged it—as, for instance, in Jubilate, Kyrie, Magnificat, and Nunc Dimittis of the Second Service. Its application by Weelkes is of great interest, and he also achieved an unusual degree of integration by the use of thematic relation within some of his movements. Clearly, too, he designed some of his anthems to be associated with certain of his services, since they contain certain musical phrases in common.

It is clear that though the Short Service (with some elaboration) continued in commission, no doubt for everyday purposes and especially for provincial use, a group of composers either based in London or combining a Chapel Royal post with work in the provinces was stimulated to enlarge the possibilities of the verse service so that this, rather than the extended purely vocal polyphonic type in the line of Byrd's "Great" Service (of which Tomkins's Third Service is a fairly isolated example surviving complete), became the larger form. Its possibilities were obviously richer—the contrast in tonal level; the skill of the individual voice; the organ with its independent bass and treble parts; the multiple variety of possible ensembles. There can be no doubt that this branch of composition, as cultivated by these masters, represents a distinctive English contribution to the music of the period.

Turning from services to anthems, one should mention the numerous religious pieces found in madrigal and other printed publications of vocal part music of this time—for example, Byrd's *Psalmes, Sonets and Songs* of 1558 and *Psalmes, Songs and Sonnets* of 1611. Other instances in point are Sir William Leighton's *Teares or Lamentacions of a Sorrowfull Soule* (1614), an anthology by various composers, and the *Sacred Hymnes . . . for Voyces and Vyols* (1615) by John Amner (d. 1641). Generally speaking, however, these must not be classed or judged as cathedral music as strictly understood by their composers, though Amner's *O ye little flock,* a work with viol accompaniment, appears to have had some currency as cathedral music with its accompaniment for organ (cf. Tenbury MS 791). In the field of the anthem proper, 42 of Tomkins's (rather less than half) are verse anthems, or, as they are called in his published *Musica Deo Sacra* (1668), "Songs to the Organ"; of some 40 anthems by Weelkes (not by any means all of them complete) 23 are verse anthems; and of Gibbons's 29 complete extant anthems, 17 are verse anthems. Ten of those have viol parts, representing an exceptional resource available in the Chapel Royal. There used to be a tendency to give faint praise to verse anthems of this period in general, and Gibbons's in particular, as "pioneer work," but such criticism cannot stand. There is nothing unsure or experimental about *This is the record of John* or *See, see, the Word is incarnate,* while the grave, moving beauty of solo voice and polyphony of viols in *Behold, thou hast made my days* is among the most memorable things in music.

There is in all of Gibbons's work a quality of warmth of response to his text that readily appeals. In his full anthems he is among the few English church composers who can be really jubilant—in *Hosanna to the Son of David* (six parts) or the superb *O clap your hands* with its second part, *God is gone up* (eight parts). Conversely, *O Lord, in thy wrath* (six parts) shows his somber power, and the small full anthem *Almighty and everlasting God* is a well known favorite.

Tomkins showed great confidence in handling a large number of parts, culminating in the twelve-part anthem *O praise the Lord, all ye heathen*. Against this resplendent piece we should place the five-part *Then David mourned* to grasp something of his expressive range and power. His numerous verse anthems, such as *My shepherd is the living Lord*, like those of Gibbons, are the work of a master of that medium. Batten, a copious writer of anthems both full and verse, is accomplished rather than distinguished, but his five-part setting of *Hear my prayer, O God* strikes a note of lingering romantic loveliness. It is only since this chapter was first written that Weelkes's complete anthems have become available for study; until then not one of his verse anthems had achieved print. The full anthems range from very simple examples to elaborate works of complex polyphony, among which the brilliance of *Gloria in excelsis. Sing my soul to God* may be singled out. When writing verses, Weelkes tended to treat his voices less soloistically than Gibbons, and more as a lighter sonority in full texture. As compared with each other, Gibbons has wonderful plasticity of phrase, Tomkins rather more surprises in his texture. It will be interesting now to fill out the picture of the early 17th century by extending the field of comparison to Weelkes.

Two tiny examples of the short full anthem, *Let thy merciful ears, O Lord* and *O Lord, increase my faith,* formerly attributed respectively to Weelkes and Gibbons, have recently been shown to be by Mudd (dates uncertain) and Henry Loosemore (d. 1670). This interestingly illustrates how the leading composers were surrounded and supported by a school of well-equipped musicians. There has been no other period in the history of English cathedral music corresponding to the fifty years before the Civil War, when there was so remarkable a concentration of talent, with Byrd as its father, brilliant in technique, strong in imagination, fertile in output, and working in many other branches of music. The younger men were content without a sharp division between a *prima* and a *seconda pratica,* working in a style evolving without conscious break from half a century before their own maturity, handling English words with consummate art, creating a line and texture of rarely failing beauty, and not seldom touching some of the heights of religious art on a relatively miniature scale. Their achievement defies adequate treatment in summary form.

THE LATE 17TH CENTURY (1660–c. 1700)

After Charles II returned to his kingdoms in 1660 and the Church of England, complete with liturgy and choral foundations, was restored with him, a slightly revised form of the Elizabethan/Jacobean Prayer Book was promulgated in 1662. The revisions have no practical bearing on music; but for the first time official cognizance was taken of the anthem at Morning and Evening Prayer by a rubric following the third Collect: *In Quires and Places where they sing* [i.e., in choral foundations] *here followeth the Anthem.*

Meanwhile, fragments of the old repertory were sought out and copied anew into choirbooks, with the result that a not insubstantial number of pre-Civil War anthems and services were brought back into regular use. In this way the style of great figures like Byrd and Gibbons (as well as much by smaller men) exerted an influence on composers such as Blow and Purcell. Composition, too, was resumed. The 1660s, however, were an era of changed taste, not to be contented with a revival of the old style or with newer essays derived from it. The influence of the king himself in the Chapel Royal provided a strong stimulus, and he introduced, after the manner of the French court, a small string ensemble, more lively in tone than the old-fashioned viols, and better adapted to the well-marked rhythm—especially triple-time rhythm—which he had admired abroad during his exile. Meanwhile, the tide of a more fundamental change reached English church music, dramatic monody and the basso continuo, though here again no doubt the king's taste hastened what conservative musicians would have resisted. Much earlier—as, for example, the melisma to the word "am" in Gibbons's *This is the record of John*—there was evident awareness of newer elements of style, and there are some signs of change in the work of William Child (1606–97) and Matthew Locke (1630–77); but it was Pelham Humfrey (1647–74) who, early noticed by the king for his boyhood talents and sent to France and Italy for wider experience, delineated with remarkable insight the characteristics of a new type of anthem. He extended the principle of declamation supported by a basso continuo to a form of multiple recitative, and he made the fullest use of the fine adult solo voices (countertenor, tenor, and bass) available without stint in the Chapel Royal. His anthems are built up in short sections, each dealing with a clause of the text and firmly marked off, and they invariably conclude with a passage for full choir, generally held in reserve for that purpose. His declamation is in common time and sometimes its successive phrases are distributed among more than one solo voice. Triple time is freely used for solo work of more melodious character and for homophonic ensembles. Solo declamation may merge into arioso, multiple declamation into an ensemble lightly touched with imitation. The first vocal section of the Humfreian anthem is nearly always for a group of solo male voices in which phrases are passed from one voice to another, at first with only slight overlapping but leading eventually to a texture for the combined ensemble. In the successive sections of his anthems Humfrey uses to good advantage the contrast—which also implies a change of tempo—between common and triple time, a feature of style he no doubt learned from France.

In by far the greater number of his sixteen extant anthems he used the royal string ensemble partly to provide ritornellos between (rather than as an accompaniment to) the vocal sections, as well as to furnish an instrumental introduction, or "symphony." This consisted of a movement in common time of moderate tempo, frequently followed by a quick movement, nearly always with two related strains, in triple time; neither of these movements is imitative. The ritornellos, by rounding off certain sections, do much to offset what otherwise might seem the short-winded effect of a string of short vocal sections. A degree of unity is obtained by the frequent practice of repeating the opening symphony at some point in the middle of the anthem.

Of textural beauty as such there is singularly little in Humfrey's music, which is justified by its treatment of the words it deals with. When writing for instruments, without prose rhythms to guide him, his triple-time movements tend to adopt stereotyped dactyl patterns. On the other hand, his solo vocal writing reveals, not only in point of pitch and rhythm but also of phrase length, a fine sensitivity to the language he set. The following example is chosen in illustration of this. Both his solos and ensembles disclose abundant and original

powers of picturesque and emotional expression. He was less successful with jubilant than with pathetic texts, though *Rejoice in the Lord, O ye righteous* is an attractively extrovert work which is an exception to this. *By the waters of Babylon* is a particularly notable work. The pathos of the opening words (finely declaimed by a bass solo), the confrontation of the Israelites by the Babylonians (chorus) with the taunt "Sing us one of the songs of Sion," the longing for Jerusalem, the bitterness of the concluding words (chorus)—to all of these Humfrey's dramatic and expressive instinct responds easily and directly. Yet, in some ways this anthem is atypical of its composer's convention. Instead of a self-sufficient instrumental movement to open with, there is a brief prelude passing without a break into the first vocal section (a method later much used by John Blow); the first substantial vocal section is for solo voice, not solo group; and, because of the nature of his text, not only does Humfrey give more work to the chorus than usual, but he employs a concertante relationship of chorus and solo voices not otherwise exploited in his anthems.

That Humfrey's music represents no form of compromise with, or derivation from, the earlier English styles is because it was written exclusively for the Chapel Royal, where the king's taste, availability of string instruments, and the resources of fine solo voices gave his methods and aptitude unreserved scope. At an uncertain juncture his work was dynamic enough to prove decisive. Both Blow and Purcell continued to move in a direction first clearly pointed by Humfrey, so clearly, in fact, that they were free to look back from time to time without danger of losing the way.

Surveying the English anthem as it left the hands of Purcell (1659–95) and Blow (1649–1708), one can discern more than one category. There was the "verse" anthem as developed from Humfrey's type, whether with or without the string orchestra. Humfrey's output includes only rare examples of the verse anthem without orchestra, and it is readily possible to suppose that these merely happen to have come down to us without their string passages (copies of the anthems with strings often exist in this truncated form). Verse anthems with organ only figure quite extensively in the work of Blow and Purcell, but they do not differ in character from such anthems with strings as developed by them but shorn of their instrumental movements. Some, like Purcell's *O Lord, who can tell how oft he offendeth,* still retain vestigial traces of postulated instrumental passages; and it would be no difficult matter to supply instrumental movements to build up, for example, his *Thy word is a lantern* into a "symphony" anthem without tampering with any of the voice parts.

Starting with essays closely in line with Humfrey's work, these composers developed the verse anthem in scope, style, and expression. A freer, confident use of florid, melismatic phrases imparts a wider sweep to their dramatic, declamatory style, and their rhythmic vocabulary is wider than what was available to Humfrey, while they both possessed a highly developed melodic sense. They gradually learned to adopt a phraseology whose contours, braced by a clearly implied progression of underlying harmonies, link them to the latest phase of the Baroque style. So, in these anthems, they could draw on their own extension of the purely Humfreian type; or there might be found rotund, florid melody of a Handelian type, or verse ensembles and choruses in the new contrapuntal style. Added to these was some concertante-wise use of verse ensembles in conjunction with full choir and even orchestra. Orchestral symphonies and ritornellos acquire more intrinsic interest and organization. There is no standard pattern for these at all, but several examples show the influence of French models later than those known to Humfrey, particularly in the imitative style of the second (quick) movement, when two-movement form was used. The practice of repeating part of the opening symphony, or some ritornello, in the course of the anthem is maintained, but essays are also found in other methods of achieving closer relation between voices and orchestra and of unity within an anthem.

Unlike Humfrey, both Blow and Purcell were interested also in more traditional technique, and this gave a new lease of life, albeit in characteristic manner, to the polyphonic anthem. Hence their work illustrates both a *prima* and a *seconda prattica.* Sharply opposed to the verse anthem is a very small group of full anthems, polyphonic in texture, but characteristic of their period in harmonic content. Closely related to this is another relatively small group of anthems, described as "full with verse." These contain no solos, and the verse passages are wholly for an ensemble of voices. This type does not depend on the basso continuo technique and is derived from the polyphonic idiom. Apart from the lighter sonority of the verse ensembles (which may be for a reduced number of voices), these do not differ in essence from the full anthem. It is therefore unnecessary to maintain the rather artificial distinction which the terminology appears to draw, and full anthems and "full with verse" anthems may be treated as one class. In this group of works Blow and Purcell demonstrated their understanding of the method whereby the harmony was ruled by the intervals created by a combination of melodies. But their resulting harmony was both darkly colored and highly spiced; and they added new elements to the verse ensembles by employing, at times, a triple-time homophonic treatment and also by deploying the voices in contrasted high and low groups.

Purcell's output of anthems comprises some seventy known items, written for the most part within a period of twelve years, 1677–88. Of the verse anthems with organ accompaniment, the well-known *Thy word is a lantern* is a straightforward but not notably distinguished example. The less celebrated *Let my tears run down* draws on altogether deeper powers of expression, with its five-part verse ensembles, and fine solo declamation. Purcell developed a very personal form of solo declamatory writing, remarkable examples for solo bass being found in the "symphony" anthems *It is a good thing to give thanks* and *Awake, awake, put on thy strength. My beloved spake* (another "symphony" anthem) far surpassed, in gaiety and charm, any other work of its class written in Purcell's lifetime, and the harmonies and tonality of the famous passage about the voice of the turtle are unforgettable. For broad and massive effect, using six voice parts both "full" and "verse," *Praise the Lord, O my soul, and all that is within me* extends the scope of this type of anthem, with bolder handling of vocal masses and string orchestra, and a searching turn of solo phrase. *O sing unto the Lord* is distinctive in point

of style, more formal than the typical English verse anthem of its day. Knowing it is by Purcell, one can readily see his hand; but without that knowledge one would not so readily recognize it. The section *Tell it out among the heathen,* to name no other, is Handelian rather than Humfreian, and its use of the strings breathes the air of the late Baroque. Something of a corresponding change in manner in an anthem with organ can be seen between *Be merciful* and *O give thanks unto the Lord,* which is Purcell's latest anthem proper (1693).

His full anthems do not exhibit within their range any such change in style as that between, say, *My beloved spake* and *O sing unto the Lord* among the verse anthems. One notes, however, that Purcell limited himself to somber and prayerful psalm texts in this class of his work. Supreme in the controlled yet passionate intensity of their expression are two short works, *Remember not, Lord, our offences* (five parts), and *Hear my prayer, O Lord* (eight parts), though the latter is no more than the torso of an unfinished work. Both exemplify the handling of part writing which is so characteristic of Purcell in this style, notably an assured diatonic dissonance arising from the clash of polyphonic parts.

Blow, in his longer career, produced some ninety anthems, of which nearly one-third are verse anthems with orchestra and about one-fifth full anthems, with just less than one-half verse anthems with organ. The closer comparison lies between his full anthems and Purcell's. Blow's *Save me, O God* is akin to Purcell's

O God, thou art my God, and the magnificently somber *O Lord God of my salvation* may be placed beside *Hear my prayer, O Lord.* This was a class of work which he cultivated more than Purcell did, and he composed a group of fourteen anthems (probably in his later years) which appear to form a set and are technically less demanding than those mentioned. These are the descendants of the short full anthems of before the Civil War. It is clear that Blow fully understood the part played by rhythmic independence between the parts in this style.

In the case of verse anthems, especially with orchestra, the great variety of layout makes parallels with Purcell more difficult to point. In its extended melodic character, Blow's *I beheld, and lo! a great multitude* has little direct kinship with Humfrey or Purcell. A beautiful and unusual anthem is *The Lord is my shepherd,* from which comes the lovely tune used by Arthur Bliss as the basis of his *Meditations on a Theme by John Blow.* The anthem is marked by a particularly intimate relationship between the opening symphony and ensuing vocal movements. The symphony of this anthem has the full two-movement structure of Humfrey, but Blow (not because of any weakness in writing instrumental music but evidently because he found it fitting so to do) was fond of beginning his anthems with a few preludial bars only, leading without a break into the first verse, in which the first violin was then likely to concertize. In this kind of work a moderately substantial symphony would come later. An example is *I said in the cutting off of my days,* an impressive work of interesting design and displaying in the opening a happy relationship of material between voice and orchestra. The final "Hallelujah," so prone to conventionality, is here raised to an unusually energetic level by means of vigorously overlapping phrases from the orchestral violins.

Like Gibbons's anthems with viols, the orchestral anthems of Blow and Purcell, written for the special circumstances of the Chapel Royal of Charles II and James II, form a self-enclosed episode in the history of English church music. They had no regular successors, for their raison d'être disappeared in 1688 with the accession of William III, after which this kind of music ceased to be required for the Chapel Royal, and England's national forms of the sacred concerto came to an end. Such of the symphony anthems as survived in general use did so either shorn of their orchestral passages, or with brief phrases adapted from them for organ. This certainly damages them greatly; but it was not the result of impertinence on the part of later editors, for Blow himself wrote out organ adaptations of some of his own and Purcell's orchestral anthems, including *O sing unto the Lord.* But from this time anthems with orchestra have been composed only to mark special, festive, or ceremonial occasions. Among the earliest of this class is Blow's *I was glad,* written for the opening of St. Paul's Cathedral, London (1697). In this work Blow, who now includes a trumpet in his orchestra, does not follow the style of his Chapel Royal anthems, and, in spite of some rather stiffly florid solo writing, draws close to a Handelian breadth.

Connected with such a school of anthem composition one might well expect to find the development of the service with solos, ensembles, and instrumental accompaniment on the same lines as the musical setting of the Roman Mass or (in Lutheran Germany) Magnificat developed. But this was not so. Except for out-of-the-ordinary settings of Te Deum and Jubilate shortly to be mentioned, the

English service was carried on either in short-service or "full with verse" style. For some reason unconnected with music, the alternatives to Magnificat and Nunc Dimittis—that is, Psalms 98 and 67—were frequently set at this period. Purcell's extensive essay, the Morning, Communion, and Evening Service in B-flat (including all alternative canticles) is an interesting and ambitious work apparently from his early years, but it can hardly be said to glow with expressive vitality. The *Benedicite* may be singled out for its effective "terraced" treatment of the full choir, each side of the choir, and two verse ensembles for two trebles and alto, and alto, tenor, and bass respectively. Purcell wrote only one other service, a setting of Magnificat and Nunc Dimittis in G minor; but Blow was indefatigable in this branch of composition. He wrote four settings in the direct "short service" line of succession, using alternate sides of the choir but no "verses." These are sound works of which little need be said. His more elaborate "full with verse" services are not untouched by the short-service principle, but they contain rather irritating stretches of somewhat jaunty passages in triple rhythm. Yet his setting of Magnificat and Nunc Dimittis from the Service in G is one of his finest works, firmly in the polyphonic tradition yet exceedingly individual in manner and expression and using for verse ensemble a quartet—treble, alto, tenor, bass. Blow and Purcell, in setting the Gloria, both appear to have been moved by some impulse to enshrine these words in canons of various kinds—three in one, four in two, and so on.

Some other categories of sacred music by these composers lie outside the scope of this essay. Blow and Purcell contributed large-scale ceremonial anthems for the coronation of James II (1685)—*God spake sometime in visions* and *My heart is inditing* respectively. But these are hardly church music in the usual sense. Both composers, having at their disposal a magnificent choir, disposed variously constituted verse ensembles amidst sumptuous passages for eight-part chorus richly introduced and interlaced by orchestral symphony, ritornellos, and accompaniments in a unique adaptation of the "full with verse" style. Similarly, their settings of Te Deum and Jubilate, written in 1694 (Purcell) and 1695 (Blow), with string orchestra and trumpets, were composed for special events organized by a society in honor of St. Cecilia's Day. These are the first of their kind in English sacred music; throughout the 18th century Purcell's settings remained in favor, both in London and the provinces, for large-scale festal services, and they formed something of a pattern for Handel's "Utrecht" Te Deum and Jubilate. Yet again, both Blow and Purcell wrote a little sacred music to Latin words, including two notably fine items, Blow's *Salvator mundi* and Purcell's *Jehovah, quam multi sunt hostes mei;* the precise reason for this Latin music is doubtful, but one could not regard it as intended for the Anglican rite. Lastly, there were sacred songs for domestic use; fine examples to words by Donne (*And art thou grieved* and *Hymn to God the Father)* were composed respectively by Blow and Humfrey, and the famous *Evening Hymn* by Purcell to words by Bishop Ken.

Of the lesser composers surrounding Blow and Purcell, Michael Wise (d. 1687) carried the new verse-anthem style outside London, and left some twenty works of individual distinction. Brought up, like Blow and Purcell, as a Chapel Royal choirboy, his adult career lay in the provinces. None of his church music therefore includes passages for strings. Nor, unlike Blow and Purcell, was he interested in polyphony, and an anthem such as *Christ rising again,* in the "full with verse" style, is largely homophonic. In verse-anthem form he cultivated a style of expressive melodic beauty. His verse ensembles make considerable use of boys' voices, alone or in combination with the men, and he knew well how to use them both melodiously and affectively, as may be seen in the treble solo *Is it nothing to you?* from *The ways of Zion do mourn.* That his work possessed elegance rather than rugged power is illustrated by the high praise which Burney (no great admirer of English music of this period) gave to this anthem in his *History.* A celebrated piece attributed to Wise is *Thy beauty, O Israel,* but this is, in fact, an expansion and redistribution by Henry Aldrich (1647–1710) of his anthem *How are the mighty fallen.*

CATHEDRAL MUSIC FROM QUEEN ANNE

TO THE EARLY VICTORIAN ERA

The substantial amount of cathedral music written by William Croft (1678–1727) clearly marks the beginning of the 18th-century repertory. For some twenty years before Blow's death in 1708 the practice of using a string orchestra in the Chapel Royal had fallen into disuse, and Croft's extended verse anthems (except those written for occasions of national thanksgiving) rely on organ accompaniment. A favorite device of his was to preface some section of an anthem by a statement on the organ of a loud bass phrase softly harmonized by the right hand, this proving to be the bass of the opening phrase of the voice, for example:

Solos and duets are freely used in his anthems, but though he continues the practice of giving prominence to an alto-tenor-bass trio, this was a less regular procedure than formerly, and pure declamation is rare. To end an anthem there is a marked tendency toward what became fairly standard throughout the century, a fugally imitative short chorus.

Croft's handling of the contemporary idiom is generally stiff, as illustrated by the organ bass just quoted. He published the greater part of his church music in score in two handsome, engraved folio volumes entitled *Musica Sacra* (1724), containing a preface arguing in favor of publication in score (then a novelty). These dignified volumes may have done something to invest his music with an importance beyond what it is entitled to. He certainly carried the late 17th-century verse anthem forward into a new era and style; but he is a competent rather than an inspired craftsman.

It is significant that his finest verse anthem, *Praise the Lord O my soul, O Lord my God,* retains rather more kinship with Purcell than most others. One cannot help feeling that Croft, for purposes of his Church Music, was a man to whom the idiom of the early 1700s was artificial, whether he realized it or not. It is in certain full anthems that his expression and power go deepest. Some of these are merely in the conventional imitative style of early 18th-century counterpoint, like *God is gone up with a merry noise;* on the other hand, the penitential texts "O Lord, rebuke me not" and "Hear my prayer" bring forth splendid, somber works (for six and eight voices respectively), worthy inheritors of the mantle of Blow and Purcell in that same vein. His setting of the Sentences sung at the Burial of the Dead, nearly all note-against-note, is an almost flawless work of the highest artistry, and deservedly a classic; but it is the work of a mind steeped in an old tradition. His other contribution to liturgical music, a Morning Service in A, is a workaday example of the short-service style.

The truly important figure in English cathedral music of the 18th century is Maurice Greene (1696–1755). For the substance of this branch of his art—for he wrote some not insignificant secular music also, as well as an oratorio, *Deborah and Barak*—one may turn to his *Forty Select Anthems in Score* (2 volumes, 1743), issued by Handel's publisher, Walsh. In turning over these pages it is hard to understand how earlier writers—Bumpus, Walker, Fellowes—have combined to place Greene on a lower level than Croft. Maintaining the same clear distinction between verse and full anthems, Greene's follow Croft's plan; but in beauty of expression they far outstrip them. Greene had a genuine vein of pure melody which he could blend with ensemble verse treatment derived from Humfrey. His characteristic 18th-century counterpoint is more supple in phraseology and surer in technique than Croft's.

Good examples of his solo melodies may be seen in *The sun shall be no more* and *The gentiles shall come,* both from the splendid verse anthem *Arise, shine; I laid me down and slept,* a melody both lovely and serene, comes from *Lord, how are they increased;* and there are numerous others, of which the opening of *Acquaint thyself with God* may be quoted. Moreover, he can use the chorus

imaginatively in a verse anthem, as shown in *Like as smoke vanisheth* from *Let God arise*. Greene's achievements in the verse anthem give a distinction to English church music of the first half of the 18th century which no other composer can match. Anthems containing aria-like solos are today out of fashion in cathedral use, and Greene's work has tended to be dismissed, perhaps on this account, as "secular," a criticism which is not to the point unless Handel's *But thou didst not leave his soul in hell* is also criticized on that ground. Again, he has been under fire as an imitator of Handel; conversely, Handel's influence has been held to have stifled the native genius of such a man as Greene. The first point is irrelevant as a basis of criticism; the second is wide of the mark. Handel or no Handel, Greene would have written in the current idiom shared by all European composers, though he may have done better for the greater man's example, while as for design and resource, the line of evolution connecting him to Croft, Purcell, and Humfrey is firm and clear.

In Greene's full anthems there is an additional element of nobility. They are the work of a man in whom the spirit of his early 17th-century predecessors was thoroughly alive. But, unlike Croft, he was not obliged to have recourse to archaism to achieve his finest pages. A work of grave beauty, worthy to be set beside Gibbons's *Behold, thou hast made my days but a span long,* is *Lord, let me know mine end.* Nevertheless, it is of its own day and age, even though it would be hard to point to any passage of Handel that would match it in manner. Its reliance on an organ bass entirely independent of the vocal bass is an original and important feature, furnishing an obbligato background of solemn power. *Lord, how long wilt thou be angry* is another notable work in the full style, and one must not forget *O clap your hands together,* where Greene successfully essays a note of jubilation.

Greene was organist of St. Paul's Cathedral and Master of the King's Music. His successor in the latter post, William Boyce (1710–79), was organist of the Chapel Royal. He too left a good deal of church music behind him, but, as his real gifts lay elsewhere, only a few anthems keep his reputation alive in this sphere. In his extended works in the verse-anthem form—for example, *O sing unto the Lord a new song*—he follows Greene's methods in producing a miniature cantata with separate short movements each with its own style, tempo marking, and characteristic *Affekt.* This is, of course, the eventual outcome of the rapid succession of brief sections, less independent and differentiated, of the Humfreian anthem. There is one work by Boyce that is strikingly close to Humfrey in method and spirit, though in the smoother idiom of his time: *I have surely built thee an house.* The declamation of this anthem has been deservedly praised; and even the organ octave passage, which looks so curious on paper as it punctuates the Lord's words to Solomon, is found to give an effect of solemn awe when properly played in a resonant building. *Turn thee unto me* is a good work, with a spacious opening for five-part chorus, followed by a duet in which the words "The sorrows of my heart are enlarged" are set "with a justice of feeling for their measure which Handel could not touch" (H.C. Colles). Curiously, the final chorus is the one spot above all others where Boyce's church music incontrovertibly declares a completely Handelian style. His most individual work is *O where shall wisdom be found?* Apart from a rather dry trio in the middle, this owes but little to earlier or contemporary models—a notable and very distinctive piece. There are also some full anthems of Boyce—for example, *By the waters of Babylon* or *Save me, O God.* While these are works of good quality, they fall short of the achievements of Greene in this form.

Croft, Greene, and Boyce all held central positions in London, and between them they account for practically the total achievement of English church music of note during their lives, though one should mention *Ascribe unto the Lord* by John Travers (1703–58) and Jonathan Battishill (1738–1801; gave up composing about 1770), who in the midst of much else was responsible for the last splendid manifestation of the glories of the full anthem in *Call to remembrance* and, especially, *O Lord, look down from heaven,* an accomplished work of powerful expression and rare beauty.

It was the anthem that chiefly occupied them. Besides Croft's Service already mentioned, Boyce contributed two hard-wearing but undistinguished Morning Services in the short style in C and A respectively, and Travers wrote a similar Morning and Evening Service in F. Greene essayed a large-scale Service for five voices in C, deliberately written in an older style that may be described as a sober, 18th-century version of Purcell in B-flat; it is the work of an excellent craftsman, and the Glorias, especially that to Nunc Dimittis, are fine bits of work. But in the field of service composition, prolific though the additional contributions of provincial musicians were, the 18th century was undistinguished. It is perhaps here that the respectable sobriety of 18th-century Anglicanism is reflected in its music.

After Boyce there was a decline in cathedral music generally. What to Greene had been the *stile moderno* of the late Baroque now in itself was old-fashioned, like Handel's music; but there was no English Haydn to admire Handel yet write a *Nelson Mass.* Instead, John Stafford Smith (1750–1836) took refuge in distressingly meretricious work, only surpassed by the feeble theatricalism of John ("Christmas") Beckwith of Norwich Cathedral (1750–1809), while the jejune invention of William Jackson of Exeter (1730–1803) in his short Service in F probably plumbed the depths in this class of cathedral music.

Thus, of composers junior to Boyce, only Battishill had written even a small quantity of church music of any significance before the century closed with his death and that of Samuel Arnold (1740–1802), a musician memorable only (in composing church music, that is) for his setting of the Evening Service in A as a companion to Boyce's Short Morning Service in that key. A considerable gap ensured, bridged only by the prolific but unmemorable output of John Clarke (in later life, Clarke-Whitfeld; 1770–1836); the not very effective contribution of Thomas Attwood (1765–1838), Mozart's English pupil; and the agreeably mellifluous but not very memorable work of Joseph Pring (1776–1842). Only toward the end of their lives did work of more significance, and in a changed style, begin to appear from a new generation, headed by John Goss (1800–80).

For a long time the role of the organ had been growing in importance. It had, of course, been necessary in the "verse" style of composition; but although it was regularly used in the "full" style it merely reinforced the vocal harmonies. This was the usage maintained by Croft. But Greene treated the organ part independently, as we have seen in *Lord, let me know mine end,* even though he left it to be "realized" from the basso continuo; likewise, Battishill's two fine full anthems use sustained "pedal" points, to say nothing of the showy effects indulged in by Beckwith. From Goss's time the obbligato written-out organ part becomes a regular feature. It should be recalled that pedal organs were only just beginning to make headway in England in the 1830s, and that for long afterward these were generally of short compass, precluding the performance of Bach's organ works. The organ on which S. S. Wesley played at the end of his life in Gloucester Cathedral had only a short pedal board and one pedal stop.

Goss, who had some little contact with the theater in his earlier career, was a prolific writer of anthems, most of them dating from after 1850. The longer specimens include a type of recitative born of Mendelssohn out of Handel, but nothing that could be described as aria. Occasionally there is a rather weak attempt at the dramatic *(The lions do lack and suffer hunger* in *O taste and see),* and, rarely, a lapse into sentimentality, but generally his style is equable, lying on the surface of things. When his music is not simply chordal in style, its texture is not too elaborate, not too learned, to attain ready popularity, and whatever it may lack it has the merit of sounding well for voices—for example, the eight-part *Lift up thine eyes.* Such real artistic success as he achieved was in quite miniature pieces, like *I heard a voice from heaven, O Saviour of the world,* and *God so loved the world,* 19th-century successors of the "little gems" of the Jacobean period. Goss wrote an acceptable Service in E which, along with that in F by S. S. Wesley, is the latest noteworthy appearance of the "short service" style in English cathedral music. One very original contribution which he made to hymnology is his well-known tune to *Praise my soul the king of heaven,* composed in two versions, one in unison with varied organ accompaniment to each verse, at that time (1869) a novel procedure, the other in the customary four-part harmony. Modern hymnals usually provide a conflation of the two versions.

Rather younger than Goss was Samuel Sebastian Wesley (1810–76), illegitimate son of Samuel, himself the son of Charles Wesley (the hymn writer) and composer of fitful genius, as well as a pioneer in the English appreciation of J. S. Bach. Not that there is much of Bach's influence in the music of S. S. Wesley. In fact, individuality is a marked feature of his music. He is the first composer of note in English cathedral music after Adrian Batten to be a specialist in it and to have essayed no composition worth mentioning outside it. For the most part he eschewed 18th-century contrapuntal technique (which by his day lingered only in academic composition) and he was very little influenced by history, not even by Handel. In the main, he also successfully avoided the unhappy influence of Mendelssohn which fell so heavily on English composers in general.

Today he is chiefly remembered by his beautiful shorter anthems, among which *Wash me thoroughly* is an admirable characteristic example of his style, while *Cast me not away* is exceptional in not requiring organ accompaniment. But his real gifts are found in a series of extended anthems, now judged too long for general use, such as *O Lord, thou art my God* (probably his masterpiece), *The Wilderness, Ascribe unto the Lord,* and *Let us lift up our heart.* One of their most prominent features is Wesley's fine solo recitative manner. In its noble breadth this has some affinity with Purcell, though in no sense does it consciously revive or imitate him. The celebrated Morning, Communion, and Evening Service in E breaks new ground in this class of composition: it is on a large scale with organ accompaniment, and, save in its sectional construction, has no kinship with anything that had gone before.

A marked element in Wesley's musical thought is a love of harmonies as such in their emotional sonority; for though his part writing is always beautifully contrived, counterpoint is not the predominant element in his work. Allied to this is his exploitation of key relationships; he does not shrink from reaching A-sharp major, or slipping from A-flat major to E minor, or quitting the chord of C-sharp major as D-flat major. His harmonies show a characteristic fondness not so much for the degree of chromaticism that has sometimes been remarked (amounting to not much more than the chord of the diminished seventh), but for diatonic suspensions and accented passing notes creating things like chords of the ninth. His delight in harmonic sonority is revealed in his love of simple, long-sustained chord progressions, quite commonplace in themselves, at moments of climax.

His work, then, has richness and color as well as resourceful inventiveness and expression. But his organ parts are undistinguished, even when they are not simply doubling the voices. When he essays independence of the choir the result can be deplorable, as in the Creed of the E-major Service; when accompanying a solo or unison passage the texture of his favorite harmonies provides a clotted style disastrously imitated by many an aspiring young organist since. One important factor in his music must be firmly stressed: it was born of the buildings in which it was to be heard. Greene's anthems (and most of Purcell's) would lose very little, if anything, sung in a small concert room, a Wren church, or a broadcasting studio. But S. S. Wesley is often seeking, by means of a chamber choir supported by the richest sonority his organ could achieve, to ally his music to the resonance of a loftily arched Gothic cathedral and so flood the building with romantically pervading sound. So far as a short extract may do so, the following example gives some idea of his style:

His contribution to English cathedral music is original, extensive, and important. Yet, as Ernest Walker said in an exceedingly perceptive comment: "No doubt his music does not appeal to all alike, and it is perhaps with a somewhat conscious effort that some, not in sympathy with its composer's temperament, have to realize that it is worth taking on its own terms." It would have been well, therefore, had it been left to him to make this contribution once and for all. He occupied ground that would not stand too much working. Admittedly he formed no school, and his great anthems had no real successors (except Parry's *Hear my*

words); but the more superficial effects of the Service in E were not without imitators, as likewise some of his harmonic characteristics, which unhappily proved fatally attractive to the second-rate.

On a smaller scale and with a lower level of achievement stands Thomas Attwood Walmisley (1814–56), who nevertheless contributed one work of permanent and influential value, his Service in D minor. Walmisley's music as a whole leans a good deal on the influence of Mendelssohn, but this particular service (only one among many that he wrote), consisting of the Evening Canticles alone, is remarkable in its quality and conviction. The organ is here handled with new freedom and great assuredness. This in turn led to new resource in the relation between organ and voices, and laid the basis of what was to become a long-established style. The service is one of the select group of compositions universally known to every English church musician.

PARISH CHURCH AND NONCONFORMIST MUSIC, 1660–1860

At this point we must retrace our steps to pick up the history of music for parish church and Nonconformist chapel. In parish churches the basic musical element of worship after the Restoration, as before the Commonwealth, was the metrical psalm. In 1671 John Playford placed himself in the succession of Day, Este, and Ravenscroft by issuing *Psalms and Hymns in solemn musick of four parts on the Common Tunes to the Psalms in Metre used in Parish Churches*. A few years later he produced *The Whole Book of Psalms* (1677), in which the harmonies were in three parts only and the tune placed in the treble. He explained that in doing this "with the Bass under it" he believed that "since so many of our Churches are lately furnished with Organs, it will be useful for the Organist."

Following the Restoration there was indeed a discernible spread of organs to parish churches. Nevertheless, in relation to the number of such churches in town and country throughout the land, the organ still remained uncommon until after

1850. Yet the existence of organs in certain leading parish churches increased the number of professional musicians working in church music outside the choral foundations. Around them there gathered "bands" of singers who assembled in the organ lofts (situated at the west end of the church) to lead the singing of the metrical psalms. Publications appeared to show the parish organist how the psalm tunes were "given out," with florid interludes between lines; and other books giving harmonized versions of the well-known psalm tunes, supplemented by an ever increasing number of new ones, began to stream from the press from the time of Playford's *Supplement to the New Version*[8] (1700) up to the first part of the 19th century. These stimulated the formation of choirs, and John Chetham, of Skipton, Yorkshire, urged that "Societies of such may be formed in every parish" (*Book of Psalmody,* 3rd ed., 1724).

But bands of singers were not confined to church with organs. During the second half of the 18th century they arose throughout the length and breadth of the country, in villages as well as towns, performing in west galleries erected for this express purpose. The adult members of such choirs were exclusively male, but children of either sex were allowed to sing treble. Groups of instrumentalists began to be formed to accompany these singers. The "village church band" was a more typical feature of later 18th-century and early 19th-century parish church music than an organ. A good deal of evidence about these bands has been gathered from the counties of Dorset, Norfolk, Oxford, and Sussex, and these, no doubt are typical. In its humblest and most rudimentary form the instrumental accompaniment was furnished by a bassoon or a cello alone. The most popular melody instrument was the clarinet. Four nearby villages in Dorset had bands which survived well into the later 19th century; one of them, Winterborne St. Martin, in 1820 had a band consisting of two first clarinets, two second clarinets, oboe, and cello.

Such amateur activity in music connected with parish churches, especially country parishes, was a significant social force in English life, embracing not only performance but also, in a humble way, composition. It is part and parcel of our picture of the 18th-century parish church, with its three-decker pulpit, sermons preached not in surplice but in gown and hood, its box pews and ample squire's pew. It was familiar to Thomas Hardy from his Dorset boyhood, and in the preface to the 1896 edition of *Under the Greenwood Tree,* he says: "From half a dozen to ten full-grown players, in addition to the numerous more or less grown-up singers, were officially occupied with the Sunday routine and concerned in trying their best to make it an artistic outcome of the combined musical taste of the congregation."

Valuable though such an activity certainly was as a social force, the charm of Hardy's account has possibly caused us to idealize too much the conception of humble rural amateurs producing homely music for the glory of God. The reality was by no means ideal, for two reasons. In the first place the west-gallery singers

8The "New Version" was the name given to the version of the psalms in meter composed by Tate and Brady (1696), which thence ran parallel with the "Old Version" associated with the names of Sternhold and Hopkins.

and players arrogated to themselves exclusively the music of the service just as firmly as the surpliced choirs, seated in the chancel, which eventually displaced them. As Hardy himself causes Mr. Penny to say in *Under the Greenwood Tree* (part 1, chap. 6): " 'Tis the gallery have got to sing, all the world knows. . . . Why, souls, what's the use o' the ancients spending scores of punds to build galleries if people down in the lowest depths of the church sing like that at a moment's notice." Secondly, as to standard of performance, roughness appears to have gone hand in hand with enthusiasm. Chetham, in the book already quoted, complains of "such a wretched Mixture of Noise and Confusion as ought never to be heard in a Christian Congregation," and Riley *(Parochial Music Corrected)* repeats this complaint in 1762.

The music available was at first confined to the psalm tunes of pre-Commonwealth days. But from the early years of the 18th century a new repertory of tunes began to appear, which may be dated from 1701 with the issue of Henry Playford's *Divine Companion*. The strength of the 17th-century tunes is replaced by a new gracefulness, triple time being freely used. Fine examples are *Hanover* and *St. Matthew*, from the *Supplement to the New Version* (1708) and attributed to William Croft. The new style of melody is well illustrated by a tune not in triple time, the so-called *St. Magnus* of Jeremiah Clarke (Playford's *Divine Companion*, 3rd ed., 1709). These men were cultivated professional musicians and were followed in something of the same vein by William Boyce and William Hayes. But durable contribution came from less likely sources throughout this period—for example, William Jones, clergyman and F.R.S., 1726–1800 *(St. Stephen's* or *Nayland* or *Newington)*, and William Knapp, parish clerk of Poole, Dorset, d. 1768 *(Wareham, 1738)*. Early in the century a tendency to florid melody appeared—for example, in the well known *Easter Hymn (Lyra Davidica, 1708);* often its results are trivial or amusing, but sometimes they are fine, as in *University* (or *Hall)* from *Psalm and Hymn Tunes* edited by John Randall, 1794. The developing egotism of choirs led many local composers away from the tune apt for congregational singing to something verging on a primitive chorus with instrumental interludes. It is evident that the dividing line between such pieces as these

and what may be called "easy popular anthems" in similar vein was only a thin one, and indeed certain books of psalmody included anthems. Knapp's *New Church Melody* (1753) is an album of such things. Usually they are poor and uninteresting. James Nares, successively organist of York Minster and the Chapel Royal, expressed himself thus: "Having often been an auditor in country churches, where what they called Anthems were sung in parts, I own I have been usually mortified by the performance, although at the same time I pitied the performers; who had against them not only their own inexperience, but the badness of the music." As a result Nares composed three anthems for country churches which "require only a Bassoon or other Bass Accompaniment," but unfortunately they are uninteresting.

A less praiseworthy effort to improve the quality of music sung in parish churches attempted to imitate cathedral use. Thus John Arnold, who echoed Chetham's wish to encourage parish churches "as much as may be to imitate their Mother Churches the Cathedrals," printed thirty-five anthems in his *Compleat Psalmodist* (1741), including such cathedral classics as Tallis's *I call and cry,* Byrd's *Bow thine ear,* and Purcell's *O give thanks.* The same tendency is found in Langdon's *Divine Harmony* (1774); he also included a popular feature, namely, well known extracts from Handel which were already is use by parish choirs, and even adaptations of *Verdant Meadows* and the minuet from *Berenice.* This blurring of the boundaries between cathedral and parish choir music led to the widespread adoption and popularity of Jackson's Te Deum in F, which obtained a remarkable hold on parish choirs.

It is in the course of the 18th century that one can first discern a corpus of music distinctively associated with the dissenting bodies. At the end of the 17th century, when, following the Act of Uniformity in 1662, the Presbyterians, Baptists, and Independents (Congregationalists) were formally separated from the Church of England, there was widespread conscientious objection among them not only to instrumental music in church but also even to the unaccompanied singing of metrical psalm tunes and to the old tunes representing the Genevan tradition of the Reformation. But among the Independents the literary work of Isaac Watts (1674–1748), a father of true hymnody in England (as distinct from psalmody), exercised a liberating influence by encouraging singing; and in 1707 the Presbyterian Meeting in Eastcheap, London, instituted a "Friday Lecture" with the furtherance of hymn singing as one of its aims. Thus, little by little objections gave way. But it was the Methodist movement which, from the 1740s, swept English Nonconformity into the flood tide of popular hymnody. John Wesley demanded cheerful music, sung at a good pace; and the hymns by which he, and still more his brother Charles, enriched English religious life called for tunes in a far wider variety of meters than hitherto. For a collection of twenty-four *Hymns on the Great Festivals and other occasions* (1746), all by Charles Wesley, the services of J. F. Lampe (1703–51), Saxon-born musician and a convert to Methodism, were employed as a composer. One or two of his tunes survive in several modern hymnals, but shorn of their characteristic ornaments and with a somewhat altered bass. Of three tunes written by Handel for the Wesleys, only one, *Gopsal,* eventually achieved a tardy popularity. From a later Methodist collection *(Select Hymns with Tunes Annexed),* in its second edition of 1765, comes the original of the famous *Helmsley,* printed as an unharmonized melody whose florid outlines are smoothed down in modern hymnbooks.

One of the most celebrated of 18th-century Nonconformist hymn tunes is *Miles Lane,* by William Shrubsole (1760–1806), organist of the Countess of Huntingdon's chapel, Spa Fields, London. Its original three-part harmony, tune in the tenor, serves as a typical reminder that the modern concept of a hymn tune as consisting either of four voice parts or a melody with organ accompaniment was not then standard. In open-air evangelism unharmonized melodies like *Helmsley* were used; in chapels, just as in Anglican west galleries, three-part harmony was quite common, while the practice of placing the tune in the tenor long survived.

The Countess of Huntingdon's movement was outside Methodist control. During John Wesley's lifetime only three of his chapels possessed organs. Suspicion against organs lingered long, and as late as 1805 the Methodist Conference resolved: "Let no instruments of music be introduced into the singers' seats, except a bass-viol [cf. the use of the bassoon in west galleries], should the principal singer require it." In the same way choir music in the form of anthems was for a long time officially discouraged in Methodism, though the enthusiasm of choirs could not be wholly restrained from indulging in it. The style of anthem is illustrated by the amusing naïveté of the highly popular setting by Edward Harwood (1707–87) of Pope's "Vital spark of heavenly flame," which, though it was also admired in Anglican west galleries, kept its long hold on Methodist choirs from about 1789 to the early years of the present century.

It is clear that Methodism brought an extrovert, unashamed cheerfulness into hymn music. But as the 18th century ran its course any distinctive denominational boundaries within the repertory tended to break down. For example, *Warrington* (1784) by Ralph Harrison, a Presbyterian minister, has all the gusto which might be associated with Methodism, while *New Sabbath,* familiar to Thomas Hardy from Stinsford Parish Church, Dorset, was to be heard in Nonconformist chapels also. However, the life of this class of music was to be longer in Nonconformist circles than in the Church of England after the appearance of *Hymns Ancient and Modern* in 1861.

Nevertheless, as the 18th century gave way to the 19th, Nonconformity developed a type of hymn music which was never shared by the established church. These pieces depend for their effect on full-throated four-part harmony. They are, of course, related to the "fuging" tunes of the Anglican west gallery; but Methodist singing had always been congregational in the real sense. Therefore, in considering these tunes, slight in texture, limited in harmonic resource, and with melodies entirely dependent on the harmony, account must be taken of the undeniably thrilling effect when sung by an entire chapel congregation of men and women *all singing in parts.* Jarman's *Lyngham* (or *Nativity,* 1821) exhibits the simple fuging easily picked up and memorized by a congregation; likewise the conclusion of *Diadem* by Ellor (1838), still popular as an alternative to *Miles Lane* for *All hail the power of Jesu's name.* A notable writer of this class of tune was Thomas Clark (1775–1859), onetime leader of the "psalmody" at the Wesleyan Chapel in Canterbury, best known by his *Cranbrook.* Another of his tunes, *Calcutta,* clearly shows that bold treatment of the congregation as a choral body which by the time of his death represented a characteristic development of this branch of people's music. In Wales, where Nonconformity was very strong, hymn singing made a particular appeal, and the composition of the "harmonic" type of hymn tune was prolific among minor musicians associated with local chapels. Most of these, however, circulated exclusively within Wales. The most famous and widely used Welsh-composed tune, *Aberystwyth,* appeared a little later than the period now under review, in 1879. It was the work of Joseph Parry (1841–1903), a Welsh musician of national distinction.

THE LATER VICTORIAN ERA AND ONWARD (c. 1860–1960)

Long before Goss and S. S. Wesley died, parish church choirs of men and boys dressed in surplices and seated in chancels had begun to oust the charity children and west-gallery choirs. This was a direct influence of the Cambridge "Ecclesiological" movement, which, in its efforts to revive what it chose to regard as correct practice, laid stress on chancels and saw in the provision of cathedral-like choirs a useful purpose to which they could be put. The later part of the 19th century, an era of expanding urban population, was a time of great church-building activity. These new churches, unlike others (e.g., those of Wren) built since the Middle Ages, were all equipped with chancels, following "ecclesiological" precept. Thus surpliced parish choirs rapidly grew in number, and with them was established a pseudo-cathedral type of choral service (on Sundays only).

This created a new need which, though satisfied at first to draw on the shorter works of Goss and earlier composers, gradually widened to demand works of superficial effectiveness and immediate appeal. A sharp deterioration in quality followed, accompanied by greatly increased output from amateurs, from small musicians of no talent, and from facile professional pens. All this was deeply affected by the prevailing sentimentalism of later Victorian religion. The result was a flow of bombastic or sugary imitations of feeble continental models, an art well insulated from invigorating influences and with its sights kept down. At the same time, Nonconformity began bit by bit to relax its distinctive traditions and to use much Anglican music drawn from the worst period of its history. Furthermore, as cathedrals began to rouse themselves from a period of lethargy and indifference (for S. S. Wesley's activity had not been typical and was much resented), this was the music taken up and endlessly reproduced, even by the better sort of musician like John Stainer (1840–1901), who should have had greater self-restraint. The wide propagation of this deplorable work was helped by two factors in themselves beneficent, the cheap octavo editions initiated by the house of Novello and the spread of musical literacy resulting from Curwen's Tonic Sol-fa movement, an educational by-product of Nonconformity.

In this climate the famous *Hymns Ancient and Modern* first appeared (1861). One must not be blind to the many undoubted beneficial influences this had on English hymnody in other ways; here it is only to our purpose to observe that while on the one hand it despised such characteristic "west gallery" tunes as *Sarah* and *New Sabbath,* which now lived on in Nonconformist use, it began the cultivation of a sentimental type of hymn tune, not unlike a brief part song. In this class of work the leading figure was John Bacchus Dykes (1823–76), whose weaker and better sides are respectively typified by his tunes *Calm* and *Dominus regit me.*

The chief redeeming figure of the late Victorian period was Charles Villiers Stanford (1852–1924), a composer of Irish birth who worked in England. Unlike other church composers of the period, Stanford was an all-round, fully equipped professional composer and he brought a fresher mind to bear on the writing of cathedral music than anyone since Humfrey. His Complete Service in B-flat (1879), while carrying on Walmisley's method in the relation of choir and organ, achieved a unity as yet completely novel in service writing, whereby some motif was woven into, or repeated in, the music set to the various clauses of the canticles and liturgical texts. This device, obvious enough today, has perhaps been overemphasized in critical appraisal of Stanford; nevertheless, he was the first to apply it and so to divert the service from the disjointed clause-by-clause construction hitherto used. Some of the motifs used in this service—that is to say, in Te Deum, Credo, and *Gloria in excelsis*—were derived from the Gregorian Intonations associated with these texts, and Stanford also employed a version of the "Dresden" Amen in all movements ending with that word. It was not only the method but the healthy invention and technical handling that immediately placed this service in a class apart from its contemporaries. An Evening Service in A major was originally written with orchestral accompaniment for festival use (1880), but it secured permanent hold in an organ version to which a Morning and Communion Service was added in 1895. In this, as well as in his Complete Service in G (1904), unifying motifs are again used. The Evening Canticles of the Service in G are interestingly conceived. In Fellowes's words, in writing Magnificat, "Stanford had the idea in his mind that, in accordance with Jewish custom at the period, the Blessed Virgin might have been little more than a child at the time of the birth of Christ; so he pictured her with a spinning-wheel happily singing *Magnificat.* It is consequently scored for treble-solo with choral and organ accompaniment with a spinning-wheel obbligato for a flute-stop. The *Nunc Dimittis,* as the song of Simeon, is set as a baritone solo with choral and organ accompaniment." His latest Complete Service is that in C (1909), a glorious piece of confident power. All these need good choirs and have an organ part essential to both texture and design. By contrast a simpler Service in F may be sung without organ.

Stanford's anthems are not numerous, and, except for *The Lord is my shepherd,* a colorful and picturesque setting, are relatively unimportant. But he wrote six pieces for unaccompanied choir. Very effective and accomplished in themselves, they also inaugurated a type of cathedral anthem[9] to which the name "motet" is now generally given. Three are in Latin (by this date such pieces are no longer necessarily Roman in their connotation), three in English.

In the church, present-day liturgical taste tends not to look kindly on Stanford's Communion Services. Among musicians it is hardly possible to discuss him without emotional reactions. On the one hand, he needs to be saved from his friends; on the other hand, there are many who would dismiss him as a mere technician, out of date even at the moment of composition ("Mendelssohn, on a really good day, might have risen to *Beati quorum via.* Not a paragraph . . . shows any trace of the kind of dissent that Berlioz, who died in 1869, wrote into every bar of his music"). These would point to the daily round of cathedral services as the reason why his church music has not followed his symphonies into oblivion. But this is not a just appraisal. Conservative he was indeed; but he was also a composer whose individual successes needed a small canvas to contain them (for example, the song *The Faery Lough* or the part song *The Blue Bird*). Church music was on this scale, and Stanford's obstinately survives in spite of his critics because it says something which would not otherwise have been said in this particular field. In that he had too many imitators, he shares the disability of Mendelssohn.

Charles Wood (1866–1926) wrote a little early church music and then in the later part of his life cultivated it with great assiduity. In all, for example, there are about twenty settings of Magnificat and Nunc Dimittis, possibly a record, if as such it has any worth. He handled unaccompanied voices with skill and effect; at least five of his motets (of which *Hail, gladdening light* is the best known) are

9The notable unaccompanied setting of *In exitu Israel* and some other Latin works by Samuel Wesley (1766–1837) were almost certainly not designed for English cathedral use.

for double choir. The influence of polyphony was stronger on him than on Stanford, but another, altogether unusual, influence was that of the old metrical psalm tunes, which he used as the basis of several anthems, for example, *O thou the sweetest source*. Three of his four Communion Services are unaccompanied, a new feature in this department. That which he headed "mainly in the Phrygian mode," a sort of neopolyphonic "short service" of simple character, has proved of real worth. The best of them is an impressive setting in C minor. His Communion Services (he actually calls two of them Masses) romantically evoke something of what was conceived to be the liturgical spirit of the polyphonic period. Some of his Morning Services are for men's voices, again a novelty, one for double choir. In his Evening Services—for example, that in F for double choir—the metrical psalm tunes are used as a basis; and there is one eccentric essay in which he goes further by marrying his music based on psalm tunes to the Sternhold and Hopkins rhyming metrical version of Magnificat and Nunc Dimittis. It should be remarked that the music Wood builds on these sturdy melodies, whether in anthem or service, is never of their severe character, but always flowing and expressive.

Following Stanford (and even he began as a college organist at Trinity, Cambridge), few all-round composers have troubled to write music for English cathedral or parish church (or Nonconformist chapel, for that matter). In these circumstances the repertory has been renewed by a group of men of high ideals, admirable taste, and excellent technical skill, none of whom, one imagines, would wish to be ranked higher than as a first-rate craftsman, proud of the quality of his work and its suitability for the job. Beginning with E. C. Bairstow (1874–1946), they have been open to influences that have kept the pool of cathedral music from stagnation. In Bairstow, that influence was Brahms; later influences have been Elizabethan and Jacobean polyphony and a degree of modalism; diatonic dissonance well rooted in the key system, not chromaticism, has been a feature of their style. Following Bairstow, the names of Harold Darke (b. 1888), W. H. Harris (b. 1883), Heathcote Statham (b. 1889), and Herbert Sumsion (b. 1899) stand high in repute in this group.

Outside it, Vaughan Williams (1872–1958) composed practically no church music in the narrow sense. There is hardly anything that can be called an anthem, while his only service, a Complete Service in D minor, was written for a school (Christ's Hospital) and includes, in addition to choir and organ, a part in unison for congregation. In response to an invitation to compose for the choir of King's College, Cambridge, in 1946, he wrote: "The atmosphere of smugness has so settled on those canticles that it seems almost impossible to lift the pall and get at the essence." Notwithstanding such a view, Herbert Howells (b. 1892) has made an outstanding contribution to service composition when at the height of his powers. A few words cannot give an adequate idea of the numerous essays in this form by means of which he has broken through the hard outer crust of long usage and sought to interpret the almost too familiar text of the canticles (especially the Evening Canticles) by considering their expression afresh from several different points of view. Howells is fond of allotting the opening words of Magnificat to treble voices. These two extracts reveal something of his diverse interpretations:

He has evolved for himself a very personal style, by no means simple, which, without echoing the past, does not reject it. It does not break with tonality, though it is modern in tone and always intensely expressive. The following quotation illustrates his combination of choral and organ texture:

Benjamin Britten (b. 1913) has written a little for the English church, including a Service in C and a beautiful anthem, a setting of George Herbert's *Praised be the God of Love,* entitled *Antiphon,* composed for the centenary of St. Michael's College, Tenbury Wells. A welcome sign now is that occasionally a young composer, such as Kenneth Leighton (b. 1929), holding no official post as a church organist, will make a contribution to cathedral music.

As for parish church music since the Victorian era, a new note in hymnody (both in original composition and in what it revived from the past) was struck by *The English Hymnal* in 1906; this was edited by Vaughan Williams and contains two or three fine tunes by him. Its influence was limited by its distinctively High Church tone (though Vaughan Williams had nothing to do with that). After the First World War an effort to clear away Victorian sentimentality in public worship was associated with Martin Shaw[10] (1875–1958), who sought improvement mainly by the introduction of unison music, broadly diatonic and sometimes touched with modalism. But this tended to make progress only among those who were self-consciously determined to improve. Nevertheless, the movement helped to bring about a change of attitude. The nondenominational hymnbook *Songs of Praise* (1925, enlarged 1931), which Shaw edited with Vaughan Williams, did something to propagate its smaller forms (e.g., Shaw's own *Little Cornard*) and also gave currency to some things found in *The English Hymnal*. It has influenced considerably more recent books issued by the various Free Churches (as the Nonconformist bodies are now known).

But as to other music, both Free Churches and Anglican parish churches—which today stand on more or less common ground where the anthem is concerned—are now provided with a flow of talented, derivative, and ephemeral music of more or less easy character of which nothing more need be said. This also applies to a category of "special music," used to some extent in parish churches and to a liberal degree by the Free Churches, in the form of short cantatas for solos, chorus, and organ shortly before Christmas and at Passiontide or even Harvest Festivals. Few churches have the skill, and not many have the taste, to rise to Britten's *Rejoice in the Lamb*, composed for just these resources.

As the non-Roman churches move forward not only to contemporary architecture and ecclesiastical art but possibly to a new liturgy, neither the work of men of talent nor desperate attempts to make use of "pop" music will be sufficient to address that challenging situation with the church music it will require. We must discover a latter-day Tye or Tallis, on whom a William Byrd and Orlando Gibbons may build.

10No relation whatever to the present writer.

Bibliography

The following bibliography contains selected writings chosen by the authors of each chapter. It attempts to be nothing more than a restricted selection—a first introduction; were it more, the lists would grow to ridiculous lengths. Long titles are often given in abbreviated form; for missing details, the reader should consult the conprehensive bibliographies in *MGG*.

The classification by subject will help the user to orient himself. It is not an ideal classification, nor could it be made ideal, because most of the writings listed cover many subjects, categories, works, persons, etc.; furthermore, many writings are not restricted to church music and would, ideally, have to be listed under several headings. The titles are arranged alphabetically by author, except for the section "Monographs on Individuals," which is a guide to writings about individuals (rather than categories, works, etc.), and is therefore arranged alphabetically by subject. Since there are no monographs in the strict sense for many of the people mentioned in the text, titles of other sorts have often had to be listed in that section.

Musical editions have been excluded. The great quantity of titles is impossible to canvass, and no bibliographical tool exists that would permit one to survey the mass of editions of older music with confidence. For information about editions, the reader should consult the comprehensive lists in *MGG*.

I: General History, Church History, and Theology

Addleshaw G. W. O., and F. Etchells. *The Architectural Setting of Anglican Worship.* London, 1948.

Albrecht, Johann Lorenz. *Abhandlung über die Frage: Ob die Musik bey dem Gottesdienste der Christen zu dulden oder nicht? . . . .* Berlin, 1764.

Altenburg, Bruno. "Die Mystik im lutherischen Pietismus." *Jahrbuch für brandenburgische Kirchengeschichte* XXVI (1931 f.).

Althaus, Paul. *Zur Charakteristik der evangelischen Gebetsliteratur.* Leipzig, 1914.

Andreas, Willy. *Deutschland vor der Reformation. Eine Zeitenwende.* Stuttgart and Berlin, 1932; 5th ed., 1948.

Beck, Theodor. "Neuordnung der Erneuerung des reformierten Gottesdienstes?" *Musik und Gottesdienst* XVI (1962), 127 ff.

Becker, B. *Die christliche Volksunterweisung als Bindeglied zwischen der Reformation und dem Pietismus.* 1891.

Benz, E., and H. Renkewitz. *Zinzendorf-Gedenkbuch.* Stuttgart, 1951.

Bezold, Friedrich von. "Staat und Gesellschaft des Reformations-Zeitalters." *Kultur der Gegenwart* II/ 5 (1908), 1.

Boehmer, Heinrich. *Ignatius von Loyola.* Ed. by H. Leube. Leipzig, 1941.

Brandi, Karl. *Deutsche Geschichte im Zeitalter der Reformation und Gegenreformation.* 2nd ed. Göttingen, 1942.

Brickenstein, H. A. "Sketch of the Early History of Lititz, 1742–75." *Transactions of the Moravian Historical Society* II (1886).

Cellier, A., M.-L. Girod, M. Honegger, *et al. Protestantisme et musique.* Paris, 1950.

Davies, Horton. *The Worship of English Puritans.* London, 1948.

Dietz, Otto. *Die liturgische Bewegung der Gegenwart im Lichte der Theologie Luthers.* Göttingen, 1932.

Droysen, Gustav. *Geschichte der Gegenreformation.* Berlin, 1893.

[Duché, Jacob]. *Observations on a Variety of Subjects, Literary, Moral and Religious.* Philadelphia, 1774.

Ehrensperger, Alfred. "Was erwartet die Gemeinde von der musikalischen Neuordnung des reformierten Gottesdienstes?" *Musik und Gottesdienst* XVI (1962), 81 ff.

Felt, Joseph B. *Annals of Salem* I, 497–505. 2nd ed. Salem, 1845.

Fendt, Leonhard. *Der lutherische Gottesdienst des 16. Jahrhunderts.* Munich, 1923.

Fithian, Philip V. *Journal and Letters 1767–1774.* Princeton, 1900.

———. *Journal, 1775–1776.* Ed. by Robert G. Albion and L. Dodson. Princeton, 1934.

Goetz, Walter, Paul Joachimsen, Erich Marcks, and Wilhelm Mommsen. "Das Zeitalter der religiösen Umwälzung." *Propyläen-Weltgeschichte* V (1930).

Gosslau, Werner. *Die religiöse Haltung in der Reformationsmusik, nachgewiesen an den "Newen Deudschen Geistlichen Gesengen" des Georg Rau 1544.* Erlanger Beiträge zur Musikwissenschaft, I. Kassel, 1933.

Gothein, Eberhard. "Staat und Gesellschaft im Zeitalter der Gegenreformation." *Kultur der Gegenwart* II/ 5 (1908), 1.

Graff, Paul. *Geschichte der Auflösung der alten gottesdienstlichen Formen in der evangelischen Kirche Deutschlands.* 2 vols. Göttingen, 1921; 2nd ed., 1937 and 1939.

Grünberg, Paul. *J. Philipp Spener.* 3 vols. Göttingen, 1893–1906.

Günther, H. R. "Psychologie des deutschen Pietismus." *Deutsche Vierteljahrsschrift für Literaturwissenschaft und Geistesgeschichte* IV (1951).

Hark, J. Max, trans. *Chronicon Ephratense; A History of the Community of Seventh Day Baptists.* Lancaster, Pennsylvania, 1889.

Hartung, Fritz. *Deutsche Geschichte im Zeitalter der Reformation, der Gegenreformation und des Dreissigjährigen Krieges.* Berlin, 1951.

Hering, C. W. *Geschichte der kirchlichen Unionsversuche.* 2 vols. 1836–38.

Heussi, Karl. *Kompendium der Kirchengeschichte.* 10th ed. Tübingen, 1949.

Holl, Karl. *Die Bedeutung der grossen Kriege für das religiöse und kirchliche Leben.* Tübingen, 1917.

———. "Luther." *Gesammelte Aufsätze zur Kirchengeschichte* I. Tübingen, 1923.

Jannasch, W. *Geschichte des lutherischen Gottesdienstes in Lübeck 1522–1633.* Gotha, 1928.

Joachimsen, Paul. *Die Reformation als Epoche der deutschen Geschichte.* Ed. by O. Schottenloher. Munich, 1951.

Markus, Jenny. "Musik und Gottesdienst nach dem Neuen Testament." *Musik und Gottesdienst* III (1949), 97 ff.

Koepp, W. *Johann Arnd.* Berlin, 1912.

Kohli, Hans Joachim. "Versuch einer theologischen Deutung von Burkhards Oratorium 'Das Gesicht Jesajas.' " *Musik und Kirche* XXII (1952), 144 ff.

Leeuw, G. van der. "Einige Betrachtungen zum Gottesdienst in der reformierten Kirche der Niederlande." *Musik und Gottesdienst* II (1948), 66 ff.

———. *Vom Heiligen in der Kunst.* Trans. from the original Dutch ed., *Wegen en Grenzen,* by A. Piper. Gütersloh, 1957.

———. and H. P. Bernet Kempers. *Beknopte Geschiedenis van het Kerklied.* 2nd ed. Groningen, 1948.

Leube, Hans. *Die Reformideen in der deutschen lutherischen Kirche zur Zeit der Orthodoxie.* Leipzig, 1924.

———. *Calvinismus und Luthertum.* 1928.

Levering, Joseph M. *A History of Bethlehem, Pennsylvania 1741–1892.* Bethlehem, 1903.

Liliencron, Rochus von. *Liturgisch-musikalische Geschichte der evangelischen Gottesdienste von 1523–1700.* Schleswig, 1893.

Lindström, Martin. *Philipp Nicolais Verständnis des Christentums.* Gütersloh, 1939.

Lortz, Johannes. *Die Reformation in Deutschland.* 2 vols. 3rd ed. Freiburg/Br., 1948.

Mahrholz, Werner. *Deutsches Selbstbekenntnis. Ein Beitrag zur Geschichte der Selbstbiographie von der Mystik bis zum Pietismus.* Berlin, 1919.

———. *Der deutsche Pietismus. Eine Auswahl von Zeugnissen.* Berlin, 1921.

Mather, Cotton. "Diary. 1709–1724." *Massachusetts Historical Society Collections.* Series 7, VIII (Boston, 1912).

Müller, Karl. *Kirchengeschichte II/2.* Berlin, 1919.

Die Musik in Geschichte und Gegenwart. Allgemeine Enzyklopädie der Musik. Ed. by Friedrich Blume. 14 vols. Kassel and Basel, 1949 ff.

"Plymouth [Mass.] Church Records 1620–1859. Part I." *Publications of The Colonial Society of Massachusetts* XXII (Boston, 1920).

Powicke, F. M. *The Reformation in England.* London, n.d.

Procter, F., and W. H. Frere. *A New History of the Book of Common Prayer.* London, 1905, 1961.

Rambach, Aug. Jak. *Ueber das Bedürfniss einer verbesserten Einrichtung des Gottesdienstes in den protestantischen Kirchen, mit besonderer Hinsicht auf Hamburg.* Hamburg, 1815.

Die Religion in Geschichte und Gegenwart. 6 vols. 2nd ed. Tübingen, 1927–32; rev. edition, ed. by K. Galling. Tübingen, 1957 ff.

Rice, John H., ed. "Attempts to Evangelize the Negroe-slaves in Virginia and Carolina." *The Evangelical and Literary Magazine* IV (Richmond, Va., October, 1821), 538–50.

Rietschel, G. *Lehrbuch der Liturgik.* Ed. and rev. by P. Graff. 2 vols. 2nd ed. Göttingen, 1951 f.

Ritschl, A. *Geschichte des Pietismus.* 3 vols. 1884–86.

Ritter, Gerhard. *Luther. Gestalt und Symbol.* Munich, 1925; 5th ed., 1949.

———. *Weltwirkung der Reformation.* Munich, 1941; 2nd ed., 1950.

Roth, E. *Die Geschichte der Gottesdienste der Siebenbürger Sachsen.* Göttingen, 1954.

Sachse, Julius Friedrich. *The German Pietists of Provincial Pennsylvania 1694–1708.* Philadelphia, 1895.

Schleiff, Arnold. *Die Selbstkritik der lutherischen Kirchen im 17. Jahrhundert.* Berlin, 1937.

Schlink, Edmund. *Zum theologischen Problem der Musik.* 2nd ed. Tübingen, 1950.

Schmidt, Eberhard. *Der Gottesdienst am Kurfürstlichen Hofe zu Dresden.* Göttingen, 1961.

Schmidt, Friedrich. "Das Musikleben der bürgerlichen Gesellschaft Leipzigs im Vormärz (1815–1848)." *Musikalisches Magazin* XLVII (Langensalza, 1912).

Schottenloher, Karl. *Bibliographie zur deutschen Geschichte im Zeitalter der Glaubensspaltung 1517 bis 1585.* 6 vols. 2nd ed. Stuttgart, 1956–58.

Schweizer, Julius. "Vom Antworten der Gemeinde im Gottesdienst Zwinglis." *Musik und Gottesdienst* VIII, 161 ff.

————. *Reformierte Abendmahlsgestaltung in der Schau Zwinglis.* Basel, n.d.

Sehling, Emil. *Die evangelischen Kirchenordnungen des 16. Jahrhunderts* I–VI/1. Leipzig, 1902–55.

Sewall, Samuel. "Diary 1624–1729." *Collections of the Massachusetts Historical Society.* Series 5, V–VII (Boston, 1878–82).

Seybolt, Robert, F. *The Private Schools of Colonial Boston.* Cambridge, Mass., 1935.

Smend, Julius. *Der evangelische Gottesdienst. Eine Liturgik nach evangelischen Grundsätzen in vierzehn Abhandlungen.* Göttingen, 1904.

————. *Vorträge und Aufsätze zur Liturgik, Hymnologie und Kirchenmusik (aus den Jahren 1918–1925).* Gütersloh, 1925.

Spazier, Karl. *Freymüthige Gedanken über die Gottesverehrungen der Protestanten.* Gotha, 1788.

Stahl, Herbert, and A. H. Francke. "Der Einfluss Luthers. . . ." *Forschungen zur Kirchen- und Geistesgeschichte* XVI (Stuttgart, 1939).

Stählin, Rudolf. "Die Geschichte des christlichen Gottesdienstes von der Urkirche bis zur Gegenwart." Section F: "Die liturgische Erneuerung im 19. u. 20. Jahrhundert." *Leiturgia* I (1954).

Strich, Fritz. "Renaissance und Reformation." *Deutsche Vierteljahresschrift für Literaturwissenschaft und Geistesgeschichte* I (1923).

Tappolet, Walter. *Das Wort Gottes und die Antwort der Gemeinde.* Kassel, 1956.

Tholuck, A. *Das kirchliche Leben des 17. Jahrhunderts.* 1861–62.

Troeltsch, Ernst. "Renaissance und Reformation." *Historische Zeitschrift* (1913), 110.

————. "Leibniz und die Anfänge des Pietismus." *Gesammelte Schriften, IV: Aufsätze zur Geistesgeschichte und Religionssoziologie.* Tübingen, 1925.

Vajta, Vilmos. *Die Theologie des Gottesdienstes bei Luther.* Göttingen, 1952.

Wallau, R. H. *Die Musik in ihrer Gottesbeziehung. Zur theologischen Deutung der Musik.* Gütersloh, 1948.

Washington, Joseph R., Jr. *Black Religion: The Negro and Christianity in the United States.* Boston, 1964.

Weber, Otto. *Versammelte Gemeinde. Beiträge zum Gespräch über Kirche und Gottesdienst.* Neukirchen, 1949.

Wendland, W. "Erbauungsliteratur." *Die Religion in Geschichte und Gegenwart* II, 217–21. 2nd ed. Tübingen, 1928.

Wernle, Paul. *Der schweizerische Protestantismus im XVIII. Jahrhundert* I. Tübingen, 1923.

Wertenbaker, Thomas J. *The Golden Age of Colonial Culture.* New York, 1949.

————. *The Old South. The Founding of American Civilization.* New York, 1942.

White, J. F. *The Cambridge Movement.* Cambridge, 1962.

Williams, George W. *St. Michael's, Charleston, 1751–1951.* Columbia, South Carolina, 1951.

Zeller, Winfried. "Lutherische Lebenszeugen." *Evangelisches und orthodoxes Christentum.* Ed. by E. Benz and L. A. Zander. Hamburg, 1952.

————. *Der Protestantismus des 17. Jahrhunderts.* Bremen, 1962.

————. and K. Utz. "Theologie und Kirchenmusik." *Musik und Kirche* XXIV (1954), 1 ff.

II: Music History and Church History

Aber, Adolf. *Die Pflege der Musik unter den Wettinern.* . . . Leipzig, 1921.

Abert, Hermann. *Gesammelten Schriften.* Ed. by F. Blume. Halle, 1929.

Abrahamsen, Erik. *Liturgisk Musik i den danske Kirke efter Reformationen.* Copenhagen, 1919.

Adams, Charles G. "Some Aspects of Black Worship." *Journal of Church Music* XV/2 (February, 1973).

Adrio, Adam. "Die Komposition des Ordinarium Missae in der evangelischen Kirchenmusik der Gegenwart. Ein Überblick." In the *Blume Festschrift,* 22–29. Kassel, 1963.

Alberti, C. E. R. *Die Musik in Kirche und Schule. Ein Beitrag zur christlichen Erziehungswissenschaft.* Marienwerder, 1843.

Allwardt, Anton P. "Sacred Music in New York, 1800–1850." D.S.M. dissertation, Union Theological Seminary, 1950.

Altmann, W. *Die musikalische Noth in der Kirche des XIX. Jahrhunderts und die Mittel zu deren Abhülfe.* . . . Erfurt and Leipzig, 1853.

Ameln, Konrad, Christhard Mahrenholz, and Karl Ferdinand Müller, eds. *Jahrbuch für Liturgik und Hymnologie.* Kassel, 1955 ff.

Ameln, Konrad, Christhard Mahrenholz, and Wilhelm Thomas, assisted by Carl Gerhardt, eds. *Handbuch der deutschen evangelischen Kirchenmusik.* Göttingen, I/1 (1941), I/2 (1942), II/1 (1935).

Andrews, Edward D. *The Gift to be Simple. Songs, Dances and Rituals of the American Shakers.* New York, 1940.

_____. "Shaker Songs." *Musical Quarterly* XXIII (1937), 491–508.

Anthes, Friedrich C. *Die Tonkunst im evangelischen Cultus, nebst einer gedrängten Geschichte der Kirchlichen Musik. Ein Handbuch für Geistliche, Organisten, Vorsänger und Lehrer . . . Von der Herzoglisch Nassauischen Regierung zur Anschaffung für die ev. Landeskirchen empfohlen.* Wiesbaden, 1846.

Armstrong, Thomas. *Church Music Today.* Church Music Society Occasional Papers, No. 17. London, 1946.

Arnold, John. *Church Music Reformed.* London, 1765.

Arrington, Elwyn Golden. "Nationalism and American Music, 1790–1815." Ph. D. dissertation, University of Texas, 1969.

Ayars, Christine M. *Contributions to the Art of Music in America by the Music Industries of Boston, 1640–1936.* New York, 1937.

Bachmann, Franz. *Grundlagen und Grundfragen zur Evangelischen Kirchenmusik.* Gütersloh, 1899.

Balfoort, Dirk Jacobus. *Het muziekleven in Nederland in de 17de en 18de eeuw.* Amsterdam, 1938.

Balthasar, Karl. *Grundsätze und Richtlinien für den musikalischen Teil des evangelischen Gottesdienstes.* Kirchenmusikalisches Archiv, XXI. Bremen, 1913.

Barrett, Philip. "The Tractarians and Church Music." *Musical Times* CXIII (1971), 301, 398.

Barth, Hermann. *Geschichte der geistlichen Musik.* Hamburg, 1903.

Bartlett, Joseph. *Music as an Auxiliary to Religion.* Boston, 1841.

Beck, Dorothea. "Krise und Verfall der protestantischen Kirchenmusik im 18. Jahrhundert." Dissertation, Halle-Wittenberg, 1951 (1953).

[Becker, E. E., F. Flöring, and J. Plath]. *50 Jahre Ev. Kirchengesangverein für Deutschland 1883 bis 1933.* Ed. by the Board of Directors of the Central Committee. Essen, 1933.

Bergt, August. *Briefwechsel eines alten und jungen Schulmeisters über allerhand Musikalisches. Nach des Verfassers Tode als ein durch seine reichhaltige Beispielsammlung nothwendiges und nützliches Handbuch für junge Cantoren, Organisten und Musikstudirende herausgegeben und mit einer Lebensbeschreibung des Verstorbenen begleiter von M. C. G. Hering.* Zittau and Leipzig, 1838.

Bieske, Werner. "Neue Kirchenmusik und Gemeinde." *Musik und Kirche* XXI (1951), 267–77.

Blankenburg, Walter. "Der mehrstimmige Gesang und die konzertierende Musik im evangelischen Gottesdienst." *Leiturgia* IV (1959).

Bloch, Dieter. "Geschichte der Kirchen-, Schul- und Stadtmusik in Neustadt an der Aisch bis zum Beginn des 20. Jahrhunderts." Dissertation, Erlangen, 1956.

Blum, Beula Blanche. "Solmization in Nineteenth-Century American Sight-Singing Instruction." Ph.D. dissertation, University of Michigan, 1968.

Blume, Friedrich. *Einleitung zu Geistliche Musik am Hofe des Landgrafen Moritz.* Kassel, 1931.

———. *Das Monodische Prinzip in der protestantischen Kirchenmusik.* Leipzig, 1925.

———. "Das Problem der Kirchenmusik in unserer Zeit." *Musik und Kirche* XXX (1960), 129–37.

Bopp, August. *Das Musikleben in der Freien Reichsstadt Biberach unter besonderer Berücksichtigung der Tätigkeit Justin Heinrich Knechts.* Kassel, 1930.

Boyd, M. C. *Elizabethan Music and Musical Criticism.* Philadelphia, 1973 repr. of 1962 ed.

Brandon, George. "A Plea for Early American Tunes." *The Hymn* XVIII/2 (April, 1967).

Braun, Werner. "Musikgeschichte der Stadt Freyburg (Unstrut)." *Wissenschaftliche Zeitschrift der Martin-Luther-Universität Halle-Wittenberg 1960* IX/4, 477–500.

Britton, Allen P. "A Bibliography of Early Sacred American Music." *Musurgia.* Series A, VIII (1951).

———. "Theoretical Introductions to American Tune-Books to 1800." Ph.D. dissertation, University of Michigan, 1949.

———, and Irving Lowens. "Unlocated Titles in Early Sacred American Music." *Notes* XI (1953).

Broder, Nathan. "Out of Our Own Heritage . . . Music of the American Moravians." *High Fidelity* X/6 (1960).

Brown, David, Walter Collins, and Peter le Huray. "Introduction." *Musica Britannica* XXIII. London, 1966.

Bruinsma, Henry A. "Calvinistische Musik." *MGG* II (1952), 666 ff.

Brunner, Adolf. *Wesen, Funktion und Ort der Musik im Gottesdienst.* Zurich, 1960.

Bumpus, John S. *A History of English Cathedral Music 1549–1889.* 2 vols. London, 1908; reprint 1973, with Introduction by Watkins Shaw.

Burney, Charles. *A General History of Music.* 4 vols. London, 1776–89.

Butze, Robert. "Der Kunstgesang im Gottesdienst." *I. Denkschrift des Kirchenchor-Verbandes der evangluth. Landeskirche Sachsens.* . . . Rötha, 1892.

Chandler, Grace Muriel. "A Study of the 1618 and 1644 Editions of Henry Ainsworth's Psaltor." S.M.M. thesis, Union Theological Seminary, 1951.

The Choral Foundations of the Church of England. Church Music Society Occasional Papers, No. 8. London, 1924.

Colles, H. C. *Voice and Verse.* London, 1928.

Cook, Harold. "Shaker Music. A Manifestation of American Folk Culture." Ph.D. dissertation, Western Reserve University, 1947.

Courtois, Daniel. *La Musique sacrée dans l'église réformée de France. Ce qu'elle a été. Ce qu'elle est. Ce qu'elle devrait être.* Paris, 1888.

Covey, Cyclone. "Did Puritanism or the Frontier Cause the Decline of Colonial Music." *Journal of Research in Music Education* VI (1958).

———. "Puritanism and Music in Colonial America." *William and Mary Quarterly* VIII/3 (1951), 378–88; addendum, IX/1 (1952), 129–33.

Dahlenberg, William J. "Music in the Culture of Miami: 1920–1966." Ed.D. dissertation, Florida State University, 1967.

Daniel, Ralph T. *The Anthem in New England before 1800.* Ph.D. dissertation, Harvard University, 1955.

_____. "English Models for the First American Anthems." *Journal of the American Musicological Society* XII (1959).

_____. and Peter le Huray. *The Sources of English Church Music 1549–1660.* London, 1972.

Dannreuther, Edward. *The Romantic Period.* London, 1905.

David, Hans T. "Background for Bethlehem. Moravian Music in Pennsylvania." *Magazine of Art* XXXII (1939).

_____. "Ephrata and Bethlehem in Pennsylvania. A Comparison." *Papers Read by Members of the American Musicological Society, 1941* (1946).

_____. "Musical Life in the Pennsylvania Settlements of the Unitas Fratrum." *Transactions of the Moravian Historical Society* XIII (1942).

Davidson, James Robert. "A Dictonary of Protestant Church Music." D.M.A. dissertation, Southern Baptist Theological Seminary, 1970.

Dearnley, Christopher. *English Church Music 1650–1750 in Royal Chapel, Cathedral, and Parish Church.* London, 1970.

Dennison, Peter. "Introduction." *Musica Britannica* XXXIV–XXXV. London, 1972.

Detlefsen, Hans Peter. *Musikgeschichte der Stadt Flensburg bis zum Jahre 1850.* Schriften des Landesinstituts für Musikforschung Kiel, II. Kassel and Basel, 1961.

Dickson, W. E. *Fifty Years of Church Music.* Ely, 1894.

Dietrich, Fritz. "Kirchenmusik und Kirchenstil." *Musik und Kirche* II (1930), 204–09.

Döring, Johann Friedrich Samuel. *Etwas zur Berichtigung des Urtheils über die musikalischen Singechöre auf den gelehrten protestantischen Schulen Deutschlands. Eine Fortsetzung des vor 10 Jahren angefangenen Versuchs. . . .* Görlitz, 1806.

Doughty, Lloyd Gavin. "The History and Development of Music in the United Presbyterian Church in the United States of America." Ph.D. dissertation, University of Iowa, 1966.

Douglas, Winfred. *Church Music in History and Practice.* With additional material by Leonard Ellinwood. London, 1963.

Downey, James Cecil. "Revivalism, The Gospel Songs and Social Reform." *Ethnomusicology* IX/2 (1965).

_____. "The Music of American Revivalism." Ph.D. dissertation, Tulane University, 1968.

Eckhardt, Paul. "Musikalische Einführung in Burkhards Oratorium 'Das Gesicht Jesajas.' " *Musik und Kirche* XXII (1952), 148 ff.

Edwards, George T. *Music and Musicians of Maine.* Portland, 1928.

Ehmann, Wilhelm. *Tibilustrium. Das geistliche Blasen. Formen und Reformen.* Kassel and Basel, 1950.

_____. "Das Schicksal der deutschen Reformationsmusik in der Geschichte der musikalischen Praxis und Forschung." *Monatsschrift für Gottesdienst und kirchliche Kunst* XL (1935), 18 ff.

_____. "Der Thibaut-Behaghel-Kreis. Ein Beitrag zur Geschichte der musikalischen Restauration im 19. Jahrhundert." *Archiv für Musikforschung* III (1938), 428 ff., and IV (1939), 21 ff.

Ellerbe, Marion Fred. "The Music Missionary of the Southern Baptist Convention: His Preparation and his Work." Studies in Musical Arts No. 7. D.M.A. dissertation, Catholic University of America, 1970.

Ellington, Charles Linwood. "The Sacred Harp Tradition of the South: Its Origin and Evolution." Ph.D. dissertation, Florida State University, 1969.

Ellinwood, Leonard. *The History of American Church Music.* New York, 1953.

———. "Introduction." *Early English Church Music* XII–XIII. London, 1971.

Elson, Louis C. *The History of American Music.* New York, 1925.

Engel, Carl. "Views and Reviews [Ephrata music]." *Musical Quarterly* XIV (1928).

Engelbrecht, Christiane. *Die Kasseler Hofkapelle im 17. Jahrhundert und ihre anonymen Musikhandschriften aus der Kasseler Landesbibliothek.* Kassel, 1958.

———. "Die Psalmvertonung im 20. Jahrhundert. Eine Überschau." In the *Oskar Söhngen Festschrift.* Witten and Berlin, 1960.

Engelke, Bernhard. "Musikgeschichte von Magdeburg." *Geschichtsblätter für Stadt und Land Magdeburg* XLVIII–L (1913–15).

Epstein, Peter. *Der Schulchor vom 16. Jahrhundert bis zur Gegenwart.* Leipzig, 1929.

Erzleben, Th. "Kirchenmusik der Brüderkirche" I. 1919 (Ms. in the Herrnhuter Archiv).

Eyck, E. J. van. *Der Fluyten Lust-Hof (Amsterdam 1646), naar de oorsprongelijke uitgave verzorgd door H. Vellekoop.* 3 vols. Amsterdam, 1957.

Fallet, J. *La Vie musicale au pays de Neuchâtel.* Strasbourg, 1936.

Farlee, Lloyd W. "A History of the Church Music of the Amana Society, The Community of True Inspiration." Ph.D. dissertation, University of Iowa, 1966.

Feder, Georg. "Das barocke Wort-Ton-Verhältnis und seine Umgestaltung in den klassizistischen Bach-Bearbeitungen." *Kongress-Bericht Hamburg.* 1956.

———. "Kantate. D. Die protestantische Kirchenkantate." *MGG* VII (1958), 581 ff.

———. "Oratorium. D. Das Oratorium in Deutschland bis J. Haydn." *MGG* X (1962), 136 ff.

Fellowes, E. H. *English Cathedral Music.* London, 1941; 5th ed., rev. by J. A. Westrup, 1969.

Fiedler, Samuel Christlieb. *Zufällige Gedanken über den wahren Werth und moralischen Nuzzen einer harmonischen und zweckmässigen Kirchenmusik.* Friedrichstadt, 1790.

Fink, G. W. "Ueber Cantate und Oratorium im Allgemeinen." *Allgemeine musikalische Zeitung* XXIX (1827), 625–32, 641–49.

Finney, Theodore M. "The Collegium Musicum at Lititz, Pennsylvania, during the Eighteenth Century." *Papers Read by Members of the American Musicological Society . . . 1937.*

Fisher, Miles Mark. *Negro Slave Songs in the United States.* Ithaca, N.Y.,1953.

Fisher, William A. *Notes on Music in Old Boston.* Boston, 1918.

Fortner, Wolfgang. "Geistliche Musik heute." *Musik und Kirche* XXVII (1957), 9–14.

Foss, Julius. "Det Kgl. Cantoris Stemmebøger A.D. 1541." *Aarbog for Musik 1923* (Copenhagen, 1924), 24–40; cf. M. van Crevel, "Adrianus Petit Coclico," 337 f.

Foster, Miles Birkett. *Anthems and Anthem Composers.* London, 1901.

Frankenberger, Heinrich. *Anleitung zur Instrumentirung zunächst für Kantoren, Schullehrer und Alle, denen die Aufführung von Kirchenmusiken auf dem Lande obliegt, auch für Seminaristen und zur Selbstbelehrung verfasst.* Langensalza, 1854.

Frantz, K. W. "Singechöre, eine nützliche Anstalt." *Allgemeine musikalische Zeitung* (1802), 69 ff.

Fuller-Maitland, J. A. *English Music in the Nineteenth Century.* London, 1902.

Galpin, F. W. "The Village Church Band." *The Musical News* V/123–24 (July 8 and 15, 1893).

Gardner, George, and S. H. Nicholson. *Manual of English Church Music.* London and New York, 1923.

Gebhardt, Friedrich. "Die musikalischen Grundlagen zu Luthers deutscher Messe." *Luther-Jahrbuch* X (1928).

Geering, Arnold. "Die Vokalmusik in der Schweiz zur Zeit der Reformation." *Schweizerisches Jahrbuch für Musikwissenschaft* I (1933).

————. "Geschichte der Musik in der Schweiz von der Reformation bis zur Romantik." *Schweizer Musikbuch* (Zurich, 1939), 54 ff.

Gerguson, Robert Edward. "A History of Music in Vicksburg, Mississippi." Ed.D. dissertation, University of Michigan, 1970.

Gerson, Robert A. *Music in Philadelphia.* Philadelphia, 1940.

Gipson, Gerald L. "The Church and Jazz." *The Hymn* XXI/4 (October, 1970).

Glahn, Henrik, ed. *Dansk Kirkesangs aarsskrift.* 1940 ff.

Gleichmann, J. A. "Werth der Kirchenmusik." *Allgemeine musikalische Zeitung* XXXIII (1831).

Goldman, Richard F. "Arias, Anthems and Chorales of the American Moravians" [record review]. *Musical Quarterly* XLVI (1960), 547–48.

Gould, Nathaniel. *Church Music in America.* Boston, 1853.

Grider, Rufus. *Historical Notes on Music in Bethlehem, Pennsylvania.* Philadelphia, 1873; reprinted in *Moravian Music Foundation Publications* IV (1957).

Grusnick, Bruno. "Die Dübensammlung. Ein Versuch ihrer chronologischen Ordnung." *Svensk tidskrift för musikforskning* XLVI (1964), 27 ff., and XLVIII (1967), 63 ff.

Güttler, Hermann. *Königsbergs Musikkultur im 18. Jahrhundert.* Kassel, n.d.

Hagen, S. A. E. "Københavns Skoles Regnskab 1646–1653." *Musikhistorisk Arkiv* I (1931), 101–16.

Hall, Harry Hobart. "The Moravian Wind Ensemble: Distinctive Chapter in America's Music." Ph.D. dissertation, George Peabody College for Teachers, 1967.

Hall, Paul M. "The *Musical Million:* A Study and Analysis of the Periodical Promoting Music Reading Through Shape-Notes in North America from 1870 to 1914." Studies in Musical Arts No. 5. D.M.A. dissertation, Catholic University of America, 1970.

Hampel, Norbert. "Deutschsprachige protestantische Kirchenmusik Schlesiens bis zum Einbruch der Monodie." Dissertation, Breslau, 1937.

Handschin, Jacques. "Die Anfänge des Kirchengesangs in der Schweiz." *Aufsätze und Bibliographie* (Bern, 1957), 188 ff.

Hartmann, Fritz. "Evangelische Kirchenmusikpflege in Greiffenberg." *Zeitschrift für Musikwissenschaft* XIV (1932), 465–71.

Hasper, H. *Een reformatorisch Kerkboek.* Leeuwarden, 1941.

————. *Het boek der psalmen.* 1949.

Hastings, Thomas. *Dissertation on Musical Taste.* Albany, N. Y., 1822.

Häuser, Johann Ernst. *Geschichte des christlichen, insbesondere des evangelischen Kirchengesanges und der Kirchenmusik von Entstehung des Christenthums an, bis auf unsere Zeit. Nebst Andeutungen und Vorschlägen zur Verbesserung des musikalischen Theiles des evangelischen Cultus. Ein historisch-ästhetischer Versuch,* 239–410. Quedlinburg and Leipzig, 1894.

Hawkins, John. *A General History of the Science and Practice of Music.* 5 vols. London, 1776.

Heilbut, Tony [Anthony Otto]. *The Gospel Sound: Good News and Bad Times.* New York, 1971.

Held, Karl. "Das Kreuzkantorat zu Dresden. Nach archivalischen Quellen bearbeitet." *Vierteljahrsschrift für Musikwissenschaft* X (1894), 239–410.

Hellerström, A. O. T. *Liturgik.* Stockholm, 1932; 3rd ed., 1954.

Herold, Max. *Alt-Nürnberg in seinen Gottesdiensten.* Gütersloh, 1890.

Herold, Wilhelm. *Unsere Kirchenkonzerte und die gottesdienstlichen Aufgaben der Kirchenchöre.* Erweiterter Sonderdruck aus Siona, Monatsschrift für Liturgie und Kirchenmusik, XL. Gütersloh, 1916.

Heydt, Johann Daniel v. d. *Geschichte der evangelischen Kirchenmusik in Deutschland.* Berlin, 1926.

[Hiller, Johann Adam]. "Ueber die Kirchengesänge." *Wöchenliche Nachrichten und Anmerkungen die Musik betreffend* I (1767), 237-43.

———. *Ueber Alt und Neu in der Musik. Nebst Anmerkungen zu Händels grossem Te Deum, und einem andern von Jomelli.* . . . Leipzig, 1787.

———. "Kirchenmusik." *Berlinische Musikalische Zeitung* II (1806); a modified version of the foreword Hiller wrote for his first volume of sacred-music texts for the Thomaskirche in Leipzig (1789–90).

———. *Vorworte zu den Fortsetzungen der geistlichen Musiktexte.* . . . 1789–1792.

———. *Beyträge zu wahrer Kirchenmusik, von Johann Adolf Hasse und Johann Adam Hiller.* 2nd rev. ed. Leipzig, 1791.

———. *[Foreword to] Allgemeines Choral-Melodienbuch für Kirchen und Schulen . . . in vier Stimmen gesetzt.* . . . Leipzig, [1793].

Hjortsvang, Carl T. "Scandinavian Contributions to American Sacred Music." D.S.M. dissertation, Union Theological Seminary, 1951.

Hodges, Edward. *An Essay on the Cultivation of Church Music.* New York, 1841.

Hoffmann, Ernst Theodor Amadeus. "Alte und neue Kirchenmusik (1814)." *Musikalische Novellen und Aufsätze* . . . II, 108–42. Ed. by E. Istel Regensburg, 1919.

Hoffmann, Hans. *Vom Wesen der zeitgenössischen Kirchenmusik.* Kassel and Basel, 1949.

Hoffmann-Erbrecht, Lothar. "Die Chorbücher der Stadtkirche zur Pirna." *Acta musicologica* XXVII (1955).

Hohenemser, Richard. *Einflüsse hatte die Wiederbelebung der älteren Musik im 19. Jahrhundert auf die deutschen Komponisten?* Breitkopf & Härtels Sammlung musikwissenschaftlicher Arbeiten von deutschen Hochschulen, IV. Leipzig, 1900.

Hohmann, Rupert K. "The Church Music of the Old Order Amish of the United States." Ph.D. dissertation, Northwestern University, 1959.

Hood, George. *A History of Music in New England. With Biographical Sketches of Reformers and Psalmists.* Boston, 1846.

Hooper, William L. *Church Music in Transition.* Nashville, 1963.

Howe, M. A. DeWolfe. "Venite in Bethlehem." *Musical Quarterly* XXVIII (1942), 174–85.

Hutchings, Arthur. *Church Music in the Nineteenth Century.* London, 1967.

Isler, Ernst. "Die evangelische Kirche der deutschen Schweiz und die Musik." *Schweizer Musikbuch,* 324 ff. Ed. by W. Schuh. Zurich, 1939.

Jackson, George Pullen. "The Strange Music of the Old Order Amish." *Musical Quarterly* XXXI (1945).

Jackson, James Leonard. "Music Practices among Churches of Christ in the United States, 1970." D.Mus. Ed. dissertation, University of Oklahoma, 1970.

Jansonnius, R. B. *Geschiedenis van het Kerk-gesang bij de Hervormden Nederland.* 2 vols. Arnheim, 1860 f.

Johnson, Frances Hall. *Musical Memories of Hartford.* Hartford, 1931.

Johnson, H. Earle. *Musical Interludes in Boston, 1795–1830.* New York, 1943.

Jones, William. *The Nature and Excellence of Music.* London, 1797.

Kaminski, Heinrich. "Einiges über 'alte und neue Musik,' über Sinn und Wesen des Kunstwerks." *Programmheft Musikkollegium Winterthur* (Nov. 26, 1926).

————. "Über polyphone Musik." *Musica* I (1947), 82 f.

Katterfeld, Julius. *Die Musik als Förderungsmittel der religiösen Erbauung. Eine Würdigung des Standpunkts der kirchlichen Musik und einiger damit verwandten Fächer in den Herzogthümern Schleswig und Holstein.* Schleswig, 1845.

Keene, James Allen. "A History of Music Education in Vermont 1770–1900." Ph.D. dissertation, University of Michigan, 1969.

"Kerkmuziek." *Handboek voor den Eredienst in de Nederlandsche Hervormde Kerk.* Rotterdam, 1934.

Kessler, Fr. *Der musikalische Kirchendienst. Ein Wort für Alle, denen die Beförderung des Cultus am Herzen liegt; insonderheit für Organisten und Prediger.* Iserlohn, 1832 (Foreword, 1830).

Kocher, Conrad. *Die Tonkunst in der Kirche oder Ideen zu einem allgemeinen, vierstimmigen Choral- und einem Figural-Gesang für einen kleineren Chor, nebst Ansichten über den Zweck der Kunst im Allgemeinen.* Stuttgart, 1823; cf. the review by W. Ch. Müller in *Cäcilia* II (Mainz, 1825), 141–55.

Köstlin, Heinrich Adolf. "Kirchenmusik." *Realencyklopädie für protestantische Theologie und Kirche* X, 443–58. 3rd ed. 1901.

Kraft, Günther. *Die Thüringische Musikkultur.* 2 vols. Würzburg, 1940–41.

Krause, Emil. "Zur Pflege der religiösen Vokalmusik im 19. Jahrhundert bis auf die Gegenwart." *Musikalisches Magazin* XV (Langensalza, 1912).

Krause, Georg. *Geschichte des musikalischen Lebens in der evangelischen Kirche Westfalens von der Reformation bis zur Gegenwart.* Kassel, 1932.

Kretzschmar, Hermann. *Führer durch den Konzertsaal.* Section II, Part I: *Kirchliche Werke.* 3rd ed. Leipzig, 1905

————. *Ueber den musikalischen Theil unserer Agende.* Leipzig, 1894.

Kümmerle, Salomon. *Enzyklopädie der ev. Kirchenmusik.* 4 vols. 1888–95.

Lansemann, Richard. *Die Heiligentage, besonders die Marien-, Apostel- und Engeltage in der Reformationszeit,* I (no others appeared). Göttingen, 1939.

LaRue, Jan. "English Music Papers in the Moravian Archives of North Carolina." *Monthly Musical Record* LXXXIX/995 (Sept.–Oct., 1959).

Laub, Thomas. *Musik og Kirke.* Copenhagen, 1920; 2nd ed., 1937.

Launer, G. J. "Vom Leben und Wirken des reformierten Kirchenchors." *Der Kirchenchor* X (1950), 34 ff.

Lawson, Charles Truman. "Musical Life in the Unitas Fratrum Mission at Springplace, Georgia, 1800–1936," Ph.D. dissertation, Florida State University, 1970.

Lehmann, Arnold Otto. "The Music of the Lutheran Church, Synodical Conference, Chiefly the Areas of Missouri, Illinois, Wisconsin and neighboring states, 1839–1941." Ph.D. dissertation, Western Reserve, 1967.

le Huray, Peter. "The English Anthem 1580–1640." *Proceedings of the Royal Musical Association* LXXXVI (1959–60), 1 ff.

————. *Music and the Reformation in England 1549–1660.* London, 1967.

Leichtentritt, Hugo. *Geschichte der Motette.* Leipzig, 1908.

Leupold, Ulrich. " 'Wortgebundenheit' und 'Liturgischer Stil' in der zeitgenössischen Kirchenmusik. Theologische Gedanken zum Fest der deutschen Kirchenmusik." *Musik und Kirche* IX (1937), 243–47.

————. *Die liturgischen Gesänge der evangelischen Kirche im Zeitalter der Aufklärung und der Romantik.* Kassel, 1933.

Lightwood, J. T. *Methodist Music in the Eighteenth Century.* London, 1927.

Liliencron, Rochus von. "Die horazischen Metren in deutschen Kompositionen des 16. Jahrhunderts." *Vierteljahrsschrift für Musikwissenschaft* III (1887).

————. *Chorordnung für die Sonn- und Festtage des evangelischen Kirchenjahres.* Güters-loh, 1900; cf. F. M. Rendtorff, in *Sammelbände der Internationalen Musikgesellschaft* II (1900–01), 308–29.

————. "Ueber den Chorgesang in der evangelischen Kirche." *Deutsche Zeit- und Streit-Fragen* IX (Berlin, 1880).

————. "Die Zukunft des evangelischen Chorgesanges." *Jahrbuch Peters* (1895).

Linscome, Sanford Abel. "A History of Musical Development in Denver, Colorado, 1858–1908." D.M.A. dissertation, University of Texas, 1970.

Lobe, Johann Christian. "Ein Wort über die Fuge in der Kirche." *Allgemeine musikalische Zeitung* XXXIII (1831).

[————]. "Die Kirchenmusik." *Musikalische Briefe. Wahrheit über Tonkunst und Tonkünstler. Von einem Wohlbekannten.* Leipzig, 1852.

Loessel, Earl O. "The Use of Character Notes and Other Unorthodox Notations in Teaching the Reading of Music in Northern States During the Nineteenth Century." Ed.D. dissertation, University of Michigan, 1959.

Long, Kenneth. *The Music of the English Church.* London, 1972.

Lowens, Irving. "Moravian Music—Neglected American Heritage." *Musical America* LXXVIII (Feb., 1958).

Lucas, G. W. *Remarks on the Musical Conventions in Boston, &c.* Northampton, 1844.

Lutkin, Peter C. *Music in the Church.* Milwaukee, 1910.

MacArthur, Donald. "Old Village Church Music." *Musical Times* LXIV (1923), 264.

McCorkle, Donald M. "The Collegium Musicum Salem. Its Music, Musicians, and Importance." *North Carolina Historical Review* XXXIII (1956).

————. "The Moravian Contribution to American Music." *Notes* XIII (1956).

————. "Moravian Music in Salem." Ph.D. dissertation, Indiana University, 1958.

————. "Musical Instruments of the Moravians in North Carolina." *American-German Review* XXI (1955).

Macdermott, K. H. *Old Church Gallery Minstrels.* London, 1948.

McDonald, Dean Earl. "An Analysis of the Attitudes of Worship of Roman Catholics Toward the Music of the Renewed Liturgy." Ph.D. dissertation, University of Denver, 1969.

Mackerness, E. D. *A Social History of English Music.* London, 1964.

McKinnon, James William. "The Church Fathers and Musical Instruments." Ph.D. dissertation, Columbia University, 1965.

Mahan, Katherine Hines. "History of Music in Columbus, Georgia, 1828–1928." Ph.D. dissertation, Florida State University, 1967.

Mahrenholz, Christhard. Various essays on the history of Protestant church music, liturgy, etc., in *Musicologica et Liturgica.* Kassel, 1960.

Mangler, Joyce E. "Early Music in Rhode Island Churches." *Rhode Island History* XVII (1958).

Marrocco, William T., and Harold Gleason, eds. *Music in America: An Anthology from the Landing of the Pilgrims to the Close of the Civil War.* New York, 1964; reprint, 1974.

Martius, Christian Ernst. *Dass eine wohleingerichtete Kirchenmusik Gott wohlgefällig, angenehm und nützlich sey, und was zu einer guten Ausführung derselben erforderlich* . . . . Plauen, 1762.

Mason, Lowell. "Letter to the Editor." *Musical Magazine* III/63 (June 5, 1841), 170–71.

————. *Musical Letters from Abroad.* New York, 1854.

————. *Song in Worship.* Boston, 1878.

Mason, William. *Essays on English Church Music.* York, 1795.

Mathews, W. S. B. *A Hundred Years of Music in America.* Chicago, 1889.

Mauer, Joseph A. "Moravian Church Music—1457–1957." *American Guild of Organists Quarterly* II (1957).

———. "The Moravian Trombone Choir (Bicentennial of Bethlehem's Historic Music Ensemble)." *Historical Review of Berks County* (Oct.–Dec., 1954).

Maurer, Maurer. "Music in Wachovia." *William and Mary Quarterly* VIII (1951), 214–27.

Maust, Earl Marion. "The History and Development of Music in Mennonite Controlled Liberal Arts Colleges in the United States." Ed.D. dissertation, George Peabody College for Teachers, 1968.

Mendelssohn, Arnold. *Gott, Welt, und Kunst.* Notes ed. by W. Ewald. Leipzig, 1949.

Menke, Werner. "75 Jahre Hannoverscher Schlosskirchenchor (Domchor) in Hannover." *Zeitschrift für evang. Kirchenmusik* X (1932), 136 ff.

Mergner, [Friedrich]. "Gibt es eine evangelische Kirchenmusik und wodurch charakterisiert sich dieselbe?" *Der dritte deutsch-evangelische Kirchengesang-Vereinstag zu Halle . . . 1884.* Stuttgart, 1885.

Metcalf, Frank J. *American Writers and Compilers of Sacred Music.* New York, 1925.

Michaelis, C. F. "Einige Bemerkungen über die Kirchenkantate und das Oratorium." *Allgemeine musikalische Zeitung* VII (1804–05), 461–68, 493–500.

———. "Ueber den Charakter der Kirchenmusik." *Berlinische Musikalische Zeitung* II (1806).

Migot, Georges. "La Musique et le Protestantism en France." *Protestantisme et musique.* Paris, 1950.

Milo, D. W. L. *Zangers en Spellieden. Bijdrage tot de ontwikkeling van een calvinistische Kerk-muziek.* Goes, 1946.

Moberg, Carl-Allan. *Kyrkomusikens Historia.* Stockholm, 1932.

Moleck, Fred. J. "Nineteenth Century Musical Activity at St. Vincent Archabbey, Latrobe, Pennsylvania." Ph.D. dissertation, University of Pittsburgh, 1970.

Molnar, John W. "A Collection of Music in Colonial Virginia. The Ogle Inventory." *Musical Quarterly* XLIV (1963).

Morris, R. O. *Contrapuntal Technique in the Sixteenth Century.* London, 1922; see especially Chapter VIII.

Morse, Edward S. *Olden-Time Music. A Compilation from Newspapers and Books.* Boston, 1888.

Moser, Hans Joachim. *Die ev. Kirchenmusik in Deutschland.* Berlin, 1954.

———. *Geschichte der deutschen Musik.* 3 vols. 5th ed. 1930.

———. *Die mehrstimmige Vertonung des Evangeliums* I (no others appeared). Berlin, 1931.

———. *Die Musik im frühevangelischen Österreich.* Kassel, 1954.

———. *Musik in Zeit und Raum. Ausgewählte Abhandlungen.* Berlin, 1960.

Müller, Karl Ferdinand, and Walter Blankenburg. *Leiturgia. Handbuch des evangelischen Gottesdienstes.* 5 vols. Kassel, 1954 ff.

Müller-Blattau, Joseph. "Zur Musikübung und Musikauffassung der Goethezeit." *Euphorion* XXXI (1930), 427–54; an extract of this appeared as "Die Idee der 'Wahren Kirchenmusik' " in *Musik und Kirche* II (1930), 155–60, 199–204.

Nauenburg, Gustav. *Ideen zu einer Reform der christlichen Kirchenmusik mit besonderer Beziehung auf die neuesten kirchlichen Verhältnisse. Ein Wort zur Beherzigung für alle Verehrer des öffentlichen Gottesdienstes.* Halle, 1845.

Naumann, Emil. *Über Einführung des Psalmengesanges in die evangelische Kirche.* Berlin, 1856.

Nedden, Otto zur. "Zur Frühgeschichte der protestantischen Kirchenmusik in Württemberg." *Zeitschrift für Musikwissenschaft* XIII (1930–31).

Nederlandsch Muziekleven 1600–1800. s'-Gravenhage, 1936.

Nef, Karl. *Die collegia musica in der deutschen reformierten Schweiz . . . Mit einer Einleitung über den reformierten Kirchengesang. . . .* St. Gall, 1897.

Nelle, Wilhelm. "Zur Geschichte des gottesdienstlich-musikalischen Lebens unserer Kirche im letzten Menschenalter." *Kirchliches Jahrbuch f. d. ev. Landeskirchen Deutschlands* XLV (1918).

Neve, Paul Edmund. "The contributions of the Lutheran College Choirs to Music in America." S.M.D. dissertation, Union Theological Seminary, 1967.

Nicholson, Sydney H. *Quires and Places Where They Sing.* London, 1932.

Norlind, Tobias. *Från Tyska Kyrkans glansdagar.* 3 vols. Stockholm, 1944–45.

———. "Musiken i Västerås under 1600-talet." *Kult och Konst* (1907), 97–110.

———. "Vor 1700 gedruckte Musikalien in den Schwedischen Bibliotheken." *Sammelbände der Internationalen Musikgesellschaft* IX (1907–08), 196 ff.

Norton, M. D. Herter. "Haydn in America (before 1820)." *Musical Quarterly* XVIII (1932).

Oehlmann, Werner. "Gottesvorstellung und Gottesgegenwart in der modernen Musik, in Gestalt und Glaube." In the *O. Söhngen Festschrift*. Witten and Berlin, 1960.

Oesterley, Hermann. *Handbuch der Musikalischen Liturgik in der deutschen evangelischen Kirche.* Göttingen, 1863.

Olson, Ivan. "Music and Germans in Nineteenth Century Richmond." *Journal of Research in Music Education* XIV/1 (Spring, 1966).

Paige, Paul Eric. "Musical Organizations in Boston: 1830–1850." Ph.D. dissertation, Boston University, 1967.

Pennsylvania Society of the Colonial Dames of America. *Church Music and Musical Life in Pennsylvania in the Eighteenth Century.* 3 vols. Philadelphia, 1926–47.

Perkins, Charles C., and John S. Dwight. *History of the Handel and Haydn Society of Boston, Massachusetts.* Boston, 1883–93.

Phillips, C. Henry. *The Singing Church.* London, 1945.

Pichierri, Louis. *Music in New Hampshire, 1623–1800.* New York, 1960.

Pidoux, Pierre. "Lied. C. Kirchenlied. 3. Schweiz b. Die welschen Kantone." *MGG* VIII (1960), 816 ff.

———. "Notes sur quelques éditions de psaumes de Claude Goudimel." *Revue de Musicologie* (1958), 184 ff.

———. "Les Psaumes d'Antoine de Mornable, Guillaume Morlaye et Pierre Certon (1546, 1554, 1555). Etude comparative." *Annales musicologiques* V (1957), 179 ff.

———. *Le Psautier Huguenot.* 2 vols. Basel, 1962.

———. "Reformierte Kirchenmusik in Frankreich seit der Reformation." *Musik und Gottesdienst* IV (1950), 9 ff.

———. "Über die Herkunft der Melodien des Hugenotten-Psalters." *Jahrbuch für Liturgik und Hymnologie* I (1955), 113 f.

Pitroff, Karl. "Aus vier Jahrhunderten evangelischer Kirchenmusik in Augsburg." *Zeitschrift für evang. Kirchenmusik* IV (1931).

Pratt, Waldo S. *The Music of the Pilgrims.* Boston, 1921.

Preussner, Eberhard. *Die bürgerliche Musikkultur. Ein Beitrag zur deutschen Musikgeschichte des 18. Jahrhunderts.* 2nd ed. Kassel and Basel, 1950.

Prümers, Adolf. "Über das Kantorenwesen." *Musikalisches Magazin* LVI (Langensalza, 1913).

Pugh, Donald Wagner. "Music in Frontier Houston, 1836–1876." D.M.A. dissertation, University of Texas, 1970.

Purdy, William E. "Music in Mormon Culture, 1830–1876." Ph.D. dissertation, Northwestern University, 1960.

Quinn, Eugene F. "A Survey of the Principles and Practices of Contemporary American Non-Liturgical Church Music." D.C.M. dissertation, Southern Baptist Theological Seminary, 1963.

Rabich, Ernst. *Der evangelische Kirchenmusikstil.* Langensalza, 1909.

Rainbow, Bernarr. *The Choral Revival in the Anglican Church.* London, 1969.

Rau, Albert G., and Hans T. David. *A Catalogue of Music by American Moravians 1742–1842. From the Archives of the Moravian Church at Bethlehem, Pennsylvania.* Bethlehem, 1938.

Rauschning, Hermann. *Geschichte der Musik u. Musikpflege in Danzig.* Danzig, 1931.

Rautenstrauch, Johannes. *Luther und die Pflege der kirchlichen Musik in Sachsen.* Leipzig, 1907.

Ravenzwaaij, G. van. *Het Kerkkoor in den Eredienst der Nederlandsche Hervormde Kerk.* Goes, 1947.

Reichardt, Johann Friedrich. *Briefe eines aufmerksamen reisenden die Musik betreffend. An seine Freude beschrieben. . . .* 2 vols. Vol. I: Frankfurt and Leipzig, 1774; Vol. II: Frankfurt and Breslau, 1776.

————. *Musikalisches Kunstmagazin.* 2 vols. Berlin, 1782, 1791.

Reimann, Hannes. *Die Einführung des Kirchengesangs in der Zürcher Kirche nach der Reformation.* Zurich, 1959.

Reventlow, Sybille. "Det musikalske repertoire i Brødremenigheden i Christiansfeld fra 1972 til ca. 1880." Thesis, Århus Universitet, 1973.

Rice, William Gorham. *Carillon Music and Singing Towers.* New York, 1925.

Riehl, Wilhelm Heinrich. "Protestantische Kirchenmusik." *Religiöse Studien eines Weltkindes,* 341–59. 2nd ed. Stuttgart, 1894.

Riggenbach, Chr. Johann. *Der Kirchengesang in Basel seit der Reformation.* Basel, 1870.

Riley, William. *Parochial Music Corrected.* London, 1762.

Ritter, Frédéric L. *Music in America.* New York, 1890.

Rohleder, F[riedrich] T[raugott]. *Vermischte Aufsätze zur Beförderung wahrer Kirchenmusik.* Löwenberg, 1833.

Rollberg, Fritz. "Aus der Geschichte der ländlichern Kirchenchöre in Westthüringen." *Zeitschrift für evang. Kirchenmusik* IX (1931).

Rose, Bernard. "Introduction." *Early English Church Music* V. London, 1965.

Rosewall, Richard Byron. "Singing Schools of Pennsylvania, 1800–1900." Ph.D. dissertation, University of Minnesota, 1969.

Rössler, Ernst Karl. "Zeitgenössische Kirchenmusik und christliche Gemeinde." *Musik und Kirche* XXVII (1957), 14–22.

Routley, Erik. *Twentieth Century Church Music.* London, 1964.

Sachse, Julius F. *The Music of the Ephrata Cloister; also Conrad Beissel's Treatise on Music.* Lancaster, Pennsylvania, 1902.

Saemann, Carl Heinrich. *Der Kirchengesang unserer Zeit.* Königsberg, 1834.

Sandberger, Adolf. "Lasso und die geistigen Strömungen seiner Zeit." *Schriften der Bayer. Akademie d. Wissenschaften.* Munich, 1926.

————. "Zu Lassos Kompositionen mit deutschem Text." *Ges. Aufsätze* I. Munich, 1921.

Sander, Hans-Adolf. *Beiträge zur Geschichte des lutherischen Gottesdienstes und der Kirchenmusik in Breslau.* Breslau, 1937.

Sass, Johannes. "Die kirchenmusikalischen Ämter und Einrichtungen an den drei evangelischen Haupt- und Pfarrkirchen der Stadt Breslau. Ein Beitrag zur Musikgeschichte der schlesischen Provinzialhauptstadt von der Reformation bis zur Mitte des 19. Jahrhunderts." Dissertation, Breslau, 1922 (typescript; a short extract is printed).

Schauer, J. K. *Geschichte der biblisch-kirchlichen Dicht- und Tonkunst und ihrer Werke.* Jena, 1850.

Schering, Arnold. "Evangelische Kirchenmusik." *Handbuch der Musikgeschichte.* Ed. by G. Adler. 2nd ed. Berlin, 1930.

————. *Geschichte des Oratoriums.* Leipzig, 1911.

————. *J. S. Bach und das Musikleben Leipzigs im 18. Jahrhundert.* Der Musikgeschichte Leipzigs, III: 1723–1800. Leipzig, 1941.

————. *Musikgeschichte Leipzigs.* II–III. Leipzig, 1926, 1941.

————. "Volk und Kirchenmusik." *Blätter für Haus- und Kirchenmusik* V (1901), 17–19.

Scheytt, Siegfried. "Musik im Getto, Soziologischer Kommentar zur modernen evangelischen Kirchenmusik." *Musik und Kirche* XXX (1960), 107–13.

Schild, Emilie. *Geschichte der protestantischen Messen-komposition im 17. und 18. Jahrhundert.* Dissertation, Giessen, 1934; published, Wuppertal and Elberfeld, 1934.

Schipke, Max. "Geschichte des Akademischen Instituts für Kirchenmusik in Berlin." In the *Festschrift* prepared by the Institute for its 100th anniversary, 5–40. Berlin and Charlottenburg, 1922.

Schletter, Hans Michael. *Übersichtliche Darstellung der Geschichte der kirchlichen Dichtung und geistlichen Musik.* Nördlingen, 1866.

Schlimbach, G. Ch. F. "Ideen und Vorschläge zur Verbesserung des Kirchenmusikwesens." *Berlinische Musikalische Zeitung* I (1805).

Schneider, Charles. *La Crise de la musique culturelle dans les Églises réformées.* Neuchâtel and Paris, 1932.

————. *L'Évolution musicale de l'Église Réformée de 1900 à nos jours.* Neuchâtel and Paris, 1952.

Schoeberlein, Ludwig. *Die Musik im Cultus der evangelischen Kirche.* Heidelberg, 1881.

————. *Über den liturgischen Ausbau des Gemeindegottesdienstes in der deutschen evangelischen Kirche.* Gotha, 1859.

Scholes, Percy A. *The Puritans and Music in England and New England.* London, 1934.

Schönian, Hans Georg. "Das kirchenmusikalische Aufbauwerk." In the *Oskar Söhngen Festschrift* 162–68. Witten and Berlin, 1960.

Schulze, Willi. *Die mehrstimmige Messe im frühprotestantischen Gottesdienst.* Kieler Beiträge zur Musikwissenschaft, VIII. Wolfenbüttel, 1940.

Schünemann, Georg. *Geschichte der deutschen Schulmusik.* 2nd ed. Leipzig, 1931.

Scott, Ruth H. "Music Among the Moravians. Bethlehem, Pennsylvania, 1741–1816." M.M. thesis, University of Rochester, 1938.

Seccombe, Joseph. *An Essay to Excite a Further Inquiry into the Ancient Matter and Manner of Sacred Singing.* Boston, 1741.

Senft, Willy. *Brüdersang. Eine geschichtliche Studie zur Fünfhundertjahrfeier der Brüderunität.* Hamburg, 1957.

Serauky, Walter. *Musikgeschichte der Stadt Halle.* 2 vols. Halle, 1939–43.

Shaw, Watkins. *Eighteenth-Century Cathedral Music.* Church Music Society Occasional Paper, No. 21. London, 1953.

Simon, Richard G. "The Propriety of the Study of Sacred Music in the Public Schools of Greeley, Colorado: A Community Survey." Ed.D. dissertation, Colorado State College, 1968.

Smend, Julius. *Die evangelische deutsche Messe bis zu Luthers deutscher Messe.* Göttingen, 1896.

Socher, Otto. *700 Jahre Dresdner Kreuzchor.* Dresden, 1937.

Söhngen, Oskar. *Die Erneuerungskräfte der Kirchenmusik unserer Tage.* Berlin, 1949.

————. "Grundsätzliche Überlegungen zum Problem der gottesdienstlichen Musik." *Musik und Kirche* XXX (1960), 179–86.

————. "Kirchenmusik und Theologie." In the *Max Schneider Festschrift.* Leipzig, 1955.

————. *Das kirchenmusikalische Amt in der Evangelischen Kirche der altpreussischen Union. Die wichtigsten geltenden Verordnungen und Erlasse auf dem Gebiete der Kirchenmusik. Mit Erläuterungen herausgegeben.* . . . Berlin, 1950.

————. "Theologische Grundlagen der Musik." *Leiturgia* IV (1961), 19 ff.

————. *Vor der Revision der preuss. Agende.* Gütersloh, 1952.

————. *Die Wiedergeburt der Kirchenmusik. Wandlungen und Entscheidungen.* Kassel and Basel, 1953.

Sørensen, Søren. *Kirkens Liturgi.* Copenhagen, 1952; 2nd ed., 1969.

Spitta, Friedrich. *Über Chorgesang im evangelischen Gottesdienste.* Strasbourg, 1889.

————. "Neuere Bewegungen auf dem Gebiete der evangelischen Kirchenmusik." *Jahrbuch Peters* VIII (1901), 15–27.

————. "Der Sologesang im Gottesdienste." *Monatsschrift für Gottesdienst und kirchliche Kunst* VI (1901), 302–07.

Spitta, Philipp. "Musikalische Seelenmessen." *Zur Musik. 16 Aufsätze,* 431 ff. Berlin, 1892.

————. "Die Wiederbelebung protestantischer Kirchenmusik auf geschichtlicher Grundlage (1882)." *Zur Musik. 16 Aufsätze,* 29–58. Berlin, 1892.

Stahl, Wilhelm. *Geschichtliche Entwicklung der evangelischen Kirchenmusik.* Leipzig, 1903; 3rd rev. ed., Berlin and Schöneberg, 1936.

Stansbury, George William. "The Music of the Billy Graham Crusades, 1947–1970: An Analysis and Evaluation." D.M.A. dissertation, Southern Baptist Theological Seminary, 1971.

Starling, Leonard Bryan, Jr. "A Survey and Analysis of the Protestant Chapel Music Program of the Armed Forces of the United States." D.M.A. dissertation, Southern Baptist Theological Seminary, 1970.

Statham, Heathcote. *Restoration Church Music.* Church Music Society Occasional Paper, No. 19. London, 1949.

Stearns, Charles. *A Sermon Preached at Exhibition of Sacred Musick.* Boston, 1792.

Stein, Fritz. *Geschichte des Musikwesens in Heidelberg bis zum Ende des 18. Jahrhunderts.* Heidelberg, 1921.

[Steinberg, Christian Gottl.]. *Betrachtungen über die Kirchen-Music und heiligen Gesänge derer Rechtgläubigen und ihren Nutzen.* Breslau and Leipzig, 1766.

Stevens, Denis. *Tudor Church Music.* London, 1961.

Stevenson, Robert M. *Patterns of Protestant Church Music.* 2nd ed. Durham, N. C., 1957.

Stoffel, Alex Franz. "An Analysis of Liturgical Response by Confirmed Members of the American Lutheran Church." Ed.D. dissertation, Colorado State College, 1969.

Stoutamire, Albert L. *A History of Music in Richmond, Virginia, from 1742 to 1865.* Ed.D. dissertation, Florida State University, 1960.

Symmes, Thomas. *The Reasonableness of Regular Singing, or, Singing by Note.* Boston, 1720.

————. *Utile Dulci., or A Joco-Serious Dialogue Concerning Regular Singing.* Boston, 1723.

Tell, Werner. *Kleine Geschichte der deutschen evangelischen Kirchenmusik, Liturgik und Hymnologie.* Rev. by Georg Eberhard Jahn. Berlin, 1962.

[Thibaut, Anton Friedrich Justus]. *Über Reinheit der Tonkunst.* 2nd enlarged ed. Heidelberg, 1826.

Thomascick, J. C. F. "Der Kirchengesang als Gegenstand der Pflege von Seiten der Geistlichern." *Preussisches Provinzial-Kirchenblatt* IV (1842), 153–82, 249–61.

Thompson, Edward. "Introduction." *Early English Church Music* VII. London, 1967.

Tortolano, William. "The Mass and the Twentieth Century Composer." D.S.M. dissertation, University of Montreal, 1964.

Trautner, F. W. *Zur Geschichte der evangelischen Liturgie und Kirchenmusik in Nördlingen.* Nördlingen, 1913.

[Triest]. "Über die Ausbildung der Tonkunst in Deutschland im 18. Jahrhundert." *Allgemeine musikalische Zeitung* III (1801).

Tweed, Myron Leland. "The Function of Music within the United Missionary Communion." D.M.A. dissertation, University of Southern California, 1970.

Van Camp, Leonard. "The Formation of A Cappella Choirs at Northwestern University, St. Olaf College, and Westminster Choir College." *Journal of Research in Music Education* XVIII/4 (Winter, 1965).

Vincent, William. *Considerations on Parochial Music.* London, 1790.

Vötterle, Karl. "Die Funktion des Musikverlegers im Baume der Kirche." *Musik und Kirche* XXI (1951), 241–43.

Walker, Ernest. *A History of Music in England.* Rev. and enlarged by J. A. Westrup. London, 1952.

Walter, Thomas. *The Grounds and Rules of Musick.* Boston, 1721.

———. *The sweet Psalmist of Israel. A Sermon Preach'd at the Lecture held in Boston, by the Society for promoting Regular & Good Singing.* Boston, 1722.

Weber, Gustav. *Geschichte des Kirchengesangs in der deutschen reformierten Schweiz seit der Reformation. Mit einer Beschreibung der Kirchengesangbücher des 16. Jahrhunderts.* Zurich, 1876.

Weimar, Georg Peter. "Eine kleine Nachricht von der Einrichtung der Kirchenmusic in dem thüringischen erfurthischen Dorfe Stotternheim." *Cramers Magazin der Musik* II (1784), 354–59.

———. "Von dem Zustande der Musik in Erfurt." *Cramers Magazin der Musik* II (1784), 392–417.

Werner, Arno. *Freie Musikgemeinschaften alter Zeit im mitteldeutschen Raum.* Schriftenreihe des Händelhauses in Halle. Wolfenbüttel and Berlin, 1940.

———. *Geschichte der Kantorei-Gesellschaften im Gebiete des ehem. Kurfürstentums Sachsen.* Leipzig, 1902.

———. *Städtische und fürstliche Musikpflege in Weissenfels.* Leipzig, 1911.

———. *Städtische und fürstliche Musikpflege in Zeitz.* Leipzig, 1922.

———. *Vier Jahrhunderte im Dienste der Kirchenmusik. Geschichte des Amtes und Standes der evangelischen Kantoren, Organisten und Stadtpfeifer seit der Reformation.* Leipzig, 1933.

———. "Zur Musikgeschichte von Delitzsch." *Archiv für Musikwissenschaft* I (1918–19).

Wesley, S. S. *A Few Words on Cathedral Music.* With an introduction by F. B. Westbrook and a historical note by G. W. Spink. London, n.d.

Whitehill, Walter M. "Communication" [on early Harvard graduates' musical encounters]. *William and Mary Quarterly.* Series 3, IX (1952), 134–36.

Widmann, B. "Die Kompositionen der Psalmen von Statius Olthoff." *Vierteljahrsschrift für Musikwissenschaft* V (1889).

Widmann, Joachim. "Kirchenmusik und säkulare Musik." *Musik und Kirche* XXXI (1961), 209–18.

Wilhite, Charles Stanford. "Eucharistic Music for the Anglican Church in England and the United States at Mid-Twentieth Century (1950–1965)—A Stylistic Study and Historical Introduction." Ph.D. dissertation, University of Iowa, 1968.

Williams, George W. "Charleston Church Music 1562–1833." *Journal of the American Musicological Society* VII (1954).

Winterfeld, Carl von. *Der ev. Kirchengesang.* 3 vols. Berlin, 1843–47.

———. *Zur Geschichte heiliger Tonkunst.* Vol. I: *Kirchengesang der Brüdergemeine,* 215 ff., Leipzig, 1850; Vol. II: *Der Kirchengesang der englischen Brüdergemeine im 19. Jahrhundert,* 77 ff., Leipzig, 1852.

Wolf, Edward C. "Lutheran Church Music in America during the Eighteenth and Early Nineteenth Centuries." Ph.D. dissertation, University of Illinois, 1960.

Wörner, Karl Heinrich. *Musik der Gegenwart.* Mainz, 1949.

———. *Neue Musik in der Entscheidung.* Mainz, 1954.

Wright, Louis B., and Marion Tinling, eds. *The Secret Diary of William Byrd of Westover 1709–1712.* Richmond, 1941.

Wulstan, David. "Introduction." *Early English Church Music* III. London, 1964.

Wustmann, Rudolf. *Musikgeschichte Leipzigs* I. Leipzig, 1909.

Zenck, Hermann. "Grundformen deutscher Musikanschauung." *Numerus und Affectus. Studien zur Musikgeschichte.* Ed. by W. Gerstenberg. Musikwissenschaftliche Arbeiten, XVI. Kassel, 1959.

Zimmermann, Heinz Werner. "Kirchentonalität und Bewusstseinsspaltung." *Musik und Kirche* XXIV (1954), 112–13.

———. "Kirchentonalität und Kirchensprache." *Musik und Kirche* XXIV (1954), 59–65.

———. "Was ist neue Musik? Zur Kritik der Kriterien." In the *Oskar Söhngen Festschrift,* 197–212. Witten and Berlin, 1960.

III: Chorales, Hymns, Religious Songs; Hymn Books

Acquoy, J. G. R. "De psalmwijzen der Nederlandsche Hervormde Kerk en hare herziening." *Archiv f. Ndl. Kerkgeschiedenis* VI (s'-Gravenhage, 1892).

Adell, Arthur. *Gregorianik I.* Lund, 1963.

Ameln, Konrad. "Kirchenlied und Kirchenmusik in der deutschen reformierten Schweiz im Jahrhundert der Reformation. Ein Literaturbericht." *Jahrbuch für Liturgik und Hymnologie* VI (1961), 150 ff.

Anderson, John. *Vindiciae cantus dominici.* Philadelphia, 1800.

Arnold, John. *The Compleat Psalmodist.* 5th ed. London, 1761.

Aulcuns Pseaumes et Cantiques mys en chant. Strasbourg, 1539; new eds. by Delétra, Genf, 1919, and by R. R. Terry, London, 1932.

Balslev, C. F. *Den lutherske Kirkesang i Danmark.* Copenhagen, 1934.

Bauer, E. *Das Choralbuch der Brüdergemeine von 1784.* Gnadau, 1867.

Bäumker, Wilhelm. *Das katholische deutsche Kirchenlied von den frühesten Zeiten bis gegen Ende des 17. Jahrhunderts.* 4 vols. Freiburg, 1883–1911.

Bernet Kempers, Karl Philip. "Lied. C. Das Kirchenlied. 5. Niederlande." *MGG* VIII (1960), 823 ff.

———. "Meerstemmig Psalmgezang in de Kerk onzer Vaderen." *Pro Regno pro Sanctuario.* Nijkerk, n.d.

Bertheau, M. *Vierhundert Jahre Kirchenlied.* Hamburg, 1924.

Biber, Walter. *Das Problem der Melodieformel in der einstimmigen Musik des Mittelalters, dargestellt und entwickelt am Luther-Choral.* Bern, 1951.

Blankenburg, Walter. "Böhmische Brüder." *MGG* II (1952), 36 ff.

———. "Gemeindegesang. B. Evangelischer Gemeindegesang." *MGG* IV (1955) 1649 ff.

———. *Geschichte der Melodien des evangelischen Kirchengesangbuchs.* Göttingen, 1957.

———. "Der gottesdienstliche Liedgesang der Gemeinde." *Leiturgia* IV (1959).

———. *Kirchenlied- und Volksweise.* Gütersloh, 1953.

———. "Kritische Fragen zu den Versuchen mit neuen religiösen Liedern." *Musik und Kirche* XXXIV (1964), 135–40.

———. "Zur Frage nach der Herkunft der Weisen des Gesangbuchs der Böhmischen Brüder." *Musik und Kirche* XXI (1951), 67 ff.

———. "Zur Verbreitung des Genfer Liedpsalters in Mitteleuropa . . . ." *Jahrbuch für Liturgik und Hymnologie* IX (1964).

Blindow, Martin. *Die Choralbegleitung des 18. Jhs. in der evangelischen Kirche Deutschlands.* Cologne and Regensburg, 1957.

Bohlin, Folke. "Haeffner och mässmusiken." *Kyrkohistorisk årsskrift* LXIX (1969), 174–202.

———. "Liturgisk sång i svenska kyrkan 1697–1897." Dissertation, Lund, 1970.

Bonhôte, Jean-Marc. "Neuchâtel—La Collection de Psautiers de la Bibliothèque de la Ville." *Jahrbuch für Liturgik und Hymnologie* VII (1962), 182 ff.

Bordier, Jules. *Le Chansonnier huguenot du XVIe siècle.* 2 vols. Paris, 1870.

Bork, Gerhard. *Die Melodien des Bonner Gesangbuches in seinen Ausgaben zwischen 1550 und 1630.* Beiträge zur rheinischen Musikgeschichte, IX. Cologne, 1955.

Bourgeois, Louis. *37 Psalmen in vierstemmige Bewerking van Lois Bourgeois uit 1547.* Ed. by K. Ph. Bernet Kempers. Delft, 1937.

Bovet, F. *Histoire du psautier des Eglises réformées.* Neuchâtel, 1872.

Brandon, George. "Some Classic Tunes in Lowell Mason Collections." *The Hymn* XVIII/3 (July, 1967).

Burdet, J. *Histoire du Chant Choral dans le Canton de Vaud.* Lausanne, 1946.

Burger, Erich. "Deutsche Kirchenmelodien in Schweden." *Kyrkohistorisk årsskrift* XXXII (1932), 105–271.

Burkhardt, K. "Der altreformierte Kirchengesang in der Grafschaft Limburg." *Heimatblätter für Hohenlimburg und Umgebung* XVIII/5, 65 ff.

Cauchie, Maurice. "Les Psaumes de Jannequin." *The Lüttich Congress Report*, 86 ff. 1930.

Cellier, Alexandre. "La Valeur musicale des Psaumes de la Réforme française." *Protestantisme et musique.* Paris, 1950.

Cheek, Curtis Leo. "The Singing School and Shaped-Note Tradition Residuals in Twentieth-Century American Hymnody." D.M.A. dissertation, University of Southern California, 1968.

Chetham, John. *A Book of Psalmody.* London, 1718.

Choralbuch der evangelischen Brüdergemeine. Ed. by the Board of Directors of the Brüderunität in Herrnhut and Bad Boll. Berlin, 1960.

Cordier, Leopold. *Der deutsche evangelische Liedpsalter. Ein vergessenes evangelisches Liedgut.* Giessen, 1929.

Crouse, David Lee. "The Work of Allen D. Carden and Associates in the Shape-Note Tune-Books, *The Missouri Harmony, Western Harmony* and *United States Harmony.*" D.M.A. dissertation, Southern Baptist Theological Seminary, 1972.

Dearmer, Percy. *Songs of Praise Discussed.* London, 1933.

Devoluy, P. *Le Psautier huguenot.* Paris, 1928.

Dibelius, Franz. "Zur Geschichte der lutherischen Gesangbücher Sachsens." *Beiträge zur Sächs. Kirchengeschichte* I (1882).

Dietz, Philipp. *Die Restauration des evangelischen Kirchenliedes. Eine Zusammenstellung der hauptsächlichsten literarischen Erscheinungen auf hymnologischem Gebiete. . . .* Marburg, 1903.

Downey, James Cecil. "The Gospel Hymn, 1875–1930." M.A. thesis, University of Southern Mississippi, 1963.

Duyse, Florimond van, *Het oude nederlandsche lied. Wereldlijke en geestelijke liederen uit vroegeren tijd. Teksten en melodieën.* 4 vols. s'-Gravenhage, 1903–08.

Ellinwood, Leonard. "John Wesley's First Hymnal Was Never Officially Condemned." *The Hymn* XII/2 (April, 1961).

Encke, Elisabeth. "Das Psalmlied in den frühen reformierten Liturgien." *Musik und Gottesdienst* X, 10 ff.

Engelke, Hans. "A Study of Ornaments in American Tune-Books, 1760–1800." Ph.D. dissertation, University of Southern California, 1960.

Enschedé, J. W. *Opmerkingen over de Psalmmelodieën.* Utrecht, 1899.

Eskew, Harry. "Shape-note Hymnody in the Shenandoah Valley, 1816–1860." Ph.D. dissertation, Tulane University, 1966.

――――. "Changing Trends in Today's Hymnody." *The Hymn* XVII/1 (January, 1966).

――――. "A Cultural Understanding of Hymnody." *The Hymn* XXIII/3 (July, 1972).

Farlee, Lloyd W. "Hymn-Singing at Amana." *The Hymn* XXI/2 (April, 1970).

Fellowes, E. H. "Appendix." *Tudor Church Music.* London, 1948.

Finney, Theodore M. "The Third Edition of Tufts' *Introduction to the Art of Singing Psalm-Tunes.*" *Journal of Research in Music Education* XIV/3 (Fall, 1966).

Fischer, A., and W. Tümpel. *Das deutsche evangelische Kirchenlied des 17. Jahrhunderts.* 6 vols. Gütersloh, 1904–16.

Foote, Henry W. *Recent American Hymnody.* New York, 1952.

――――. *Three Centuries of American Hymnody.* Cambridge, Mass., 1940.

Fornaçon, Siegfried. "Johann Crüger und der Genfer Psalter." *Jahrbuch für Liturgik und Hymnologie* I (1955), 115 ff.

――――. "Lobe den Herren, den mächtigen König der Ehren." *Jahrbuch für Liturgik und Hymnologie* II (1956), 130 ff.

――――. "Das neue Gesangbuch der Reformierten in Ostdeutschland." *Musik und Gottesdienst* VIII, 52 ff.

Frage (kurtze) und bestendige Antwort, ob die Psalmen von H. Laubwasser aus dem Frantzösischen in Teutsche Sprache versetzet in Lutherischen und Bäbstlichen Kirchen zu singen unzulässig sey. Hanau, 1608.

Frost, Maurice. *English & Scottish Psalm & Hymn Tunes c. 1543–1677.* London, 1953.

――――. *Historical Companion to Hymns Ancient and Modern.* London, 1962.

Gabriel, Paul. *Das deutsche evangelische Kirchenlied von Martin Luther bis zur Gegenwart.* 2nd ed. Berlin, 1951.

――――. *Geschichte des Kirchenliedes.* Göttingen, 1957.

Garside, Charles. "Calvin's Preface to the Psalter." *Musical Quarterly* XXXVII (1951), 566 ff.

Gastoué, Amédée. *La Cantique populaire en France.* Lyon, 1924.

Gerber, Rudolf. "Zu Luthers Liedweisen." In the *Max Schneider Festschrift.* Halle and Eisleben, 1935.

Gerhard, Carl. *Die Torgauer Walter-Handschriften. Eine Studie zur Quellenkunde der Musikgeschichte der Reformationszeit.* Musikwissenschaftliche Arbeiten, IV. Kassel, 1949.

Gérold, Théodore. "Clément Marot, les psaumes avec leurs mélodies." *Bibliotheca Romanica* (1919), 252 ff.

———. *Les Plus Anciennes Mélodies de l'église protestante de Strasbourg et leurs auteurs.* Paris, 1928.

Glahn, Henrik. "Lied. C. Das Kirchenlied, Dänemark." *MGG* VIII (1960), 829 ff.

———. *Melodistudier til den Lutherske salmesangs historie fra 1524 til ca. 1600.* 2 vols. Copenhagen, 1954.

———. "Salmemelodien i dansk tradition." *Salmen som lovsang og litteratur,* 191–234. Ed. Th. Borup Jensen and K. E. Bugge. Copenhagen, 1972.

Goldschmid, Theodor. *Schweizerische Gesangbücher früherer Zeiten.* Zurich, 1917.

Goudimel, Claude. "150 Psaumes (1580)." *Maîtres Musiciens de la Renaissance française.* Ed. by H. Expert. Vols. 2, 4 and 6. Paris, 1894–97.

Greenlaw, Kenneth Gould. "Traditions of Protestant Hymnody and the Use of Music in the Methodist and Baptist Churches of Mexico." D.M.A. dissertation, University of Southern California, 1967.

Hach, H. Theodore. "[Review of] *The Massachusetts Collection of Psalmody.*" *Musical Magazine; or, Repository* III/61–62 (May 8 and 22, 1841), 139–43, 153–59.

Haein, Emmanuel. "Le Problème du Chant Choral dans les Eglises Réformées et le Trésor liturgique de la Cantilène huguenote." Dissertation, Montpellier, 1926.

Halaski, Karl. "Zum Psalmengesang der Reformierten." *Monatsschrift für Pastoraltheologie* XLIII (1954), 332 ff.

Hallersleben, Rolf, and Kurt Schulz. *Der Psalter. Begleitbuch. Neu gesetzt.* Moers, 1953.

Handbuch zum Evangelischen Kirchengesangbuch. Ed. by Chr. Mahrenholz and O. Söhngen. See especially Vol. II/1: T. W. Lueken, *Lebensbilder der Liederdichter u. Melodisten;* Vol. II/2: Paul Gabriel, *Geschichte des Kirchenliedes,* and Walter Blankenburg, *Geschichte der Melodien des Evangelischen Kirchengesangbuches,* Göttingen, 1957; and the special volume: Johannes Kulp, *Die Lieder unserer Kirche,* rev. and ed. by A. Büchner and S. Fornaçon, Göttingen, 1958.

Hennig, Kurt. *Die geistliche Kontrafaktur im Jahrhundert der Reformation.* Halle, 1909.

Hess, Albert G. "Observations on The Lamenting Voice of the Hidden Love." *Journal of the American Musicological Society* V (1952).

Heydt, Daniel von der. *Niederländische Psalmdichtung im 16. Jahrhundert.* Utrecht, 1890.

Higginson, J. Vincent. "Notes on Lowell Mason's Hymn Tunes." *The Hymn* XVIII/2 (April, 1967).

———. "Adventures in American Hymnody." *The Hymn* XXIII/2 (April, 1972).

Hoberg, Martin. "Eine verfolgte Kirche schmückt ihr Gesangbuch." *Kunst und Kirche* XV (1938), 11 ff.

Holliger, Hans. "Vorwort." *Das Psalmenbuch.* Kassel, 1953.

———. "Zur Pausenfrage in den Hugenottenpsalmen." *Musik und Gottesdienst* VIII (1954), 108 ff., and X (1956), 70 ff.

Honegger, Marc. "La Chanson spirituelle populaire huguenote." *Jahrbuch für Liturgik und Hymnologie* VIII (1963), 129 ff.

———. "Le Choral protestant." *Protestantisme et musique.* Paris, 1950.

Hollweg, Walter. "Das Gesangbuch für niederländischen Flüchtlinge in Emden vom Jahre 1574 und seine Auswirkungen auf den Kirchengesang der reformierten Gemeinden Ostfrieslands." *Friesisches Jahrbuch* (1961), 39 ff.

———. *Geschichte der evangelischen Gesangbücher vom Niederrhein im 16.–18. Jahrhundert.* Gütersloh, 1923.

———. "Quellen zur Hymnologie—Emden." *Jahrbuch für Liturgik und Hymnologie* VII (1962), 181 f.

Horn, Dorothy. "A Study of the Folk Hymns of Southeastern America." Ph.D. dissertation, University of Rochester, 1952.

Hubert, Friedrich. *Die Strassburger liturgischen Ordnungen im Zeitalter der Reformation nebst einer Bibliographie der Strassburger Gesangbücher.* Göttingen, 1900.

Huygens, Constantinus. *Gebruyck of ongebruyck van t'Orgel in de kercken der Verenighde Nederlanden.* Leiden, 1641; Rotterdam, 1937.

————. "Kerck-gebruyck der Psalmen." Ed. by W. Moll. *Studien en Bijdragen op het gebied der historische theologie* III (1876).

————. *Pathodia sacra et profana unae voci basso continuo comitante.* Ed. by F. Noske. Amsterdam and Kassel, 1957.

Hymns Ancient and Modern . . . Historical Edition. London, 1909.

Iperen, Josua van. *Kerkelijka Historia van het Psalmgezang* I. Amsterdam, 1777.

Jackson, George P. "Buckwheat Notes." *Musical Quarterly* XIX (1933).

————. "Early American Religious Folk Songs." *Proceedings of the Music Teachers National Association* XXIX (1934), 74–79.

————. *The Story of the Sacred Harp, 1844–1944.* Nashville, 1944.

————. *White and Negro Spirituals. Their Life Span and Kinship.* New York, 1943.

————. *White Spirituals in the Southern Uplands.* Chapel Hill, N.C., 1933.

Jahr, Hannelore. *Studien zur Überlieferungsgeschichte der Confession de foi von 1559.* Neukirchen, 1964.

Jahrbuch für Liturgik und Hymnologie. Ed. by K. Ameln, Chr. Mahrenholz, and K. F. Müller. I– (1955 ff.).

Johnson, Axie Allen. "Choral Settings of the Magnificat by Selected Twentieth Century American Composers." D.M.A. dissertation, University of Southern California, 1968.

Jenny, Markus. "Die beiden bedeutendsten deutsch-schweizerischen Kirchengesangbücher des 17. Jahrhunderts." *Jahrbuch für Liturgik und Hymnologie* I (1955), 63 ff.

————. "Das erste offizielle Zürcher Gesangbuch von 1598." *Jahrbuch für Liturgik und Hymnologie* VII (1962), 123 ff.

————. "Die ev. Kirchenmusik in der bernischen Landeskirche." *Musik und Gottesdienst* IX, 129 ff.

————. "Das ev. Lied der Berner Kirche im 16. Jahrhundert." *Musik und Gottesdienst* V, 98 ff.

————. *Geschichte des deutsch-schweizerischen evangelischen Gesangbuches im 16. Jahrhundert.* Kassel, 1962.

————. "Lied. C. Das Kirchenlied. Schweiz. Die deutschen Kantone." *MGG* VIII (1960), 810 ff.

————. "Zur Geschichte des ev. Gesangbuchs in Basel im 16. und 17. Jahrhundert." *Stultifera navis, Mitteilungsblatt der Schweizer Bibliophilen-Gesellschaft, Festgabe Emanuel Stickelberger zum 70. Geburtstag.* Basel, 1954.

Jung, Hildegard. "Das geistliche Sololied im 19. Jahrhundert. Ein Beitrag zur Geschichte des deutschen Kunstliedes." Dissertation, Cologne, 1950.

Kade, Richard. "Das erste Dresdner Gesangbuch 1593." *Dresdner Geschichtsblätter* III (1894).

Kist, Florens Cornelius. *De Toestand van het protestantiche Kerkgezang in Nederland.* Utrecht, 1840.

Kling, Henri. "The French Hugenot Psalters." *Rivista Musicale Italiana* VI (1900), 496 ff.

Koch, Eduard Emil. *Geschichte des Kirchenlieds.* 8 vols. 3rd ed. 1860–71.

Kretzschmar, Hermann. *Geschichte des neueren deutschen Liedes* I. Leipzig, 1912.

Krohn, Ilmari. "Den lutherski koral i Finnland." In the *O.M. Sandvik Festschrift*, 122–47. Oslo, 1945.

Krüger, Eduard. "Die Wiederbelebung des evangelischen Kirchengesanges." *Allgemeine musikalische Zeitung* XLVIII (1846), 569–75, 585–90.

Kulp, Johannes. "Das älteste Gesangbuch der Böhmischen Brüder." *Monatsschrift für Pastoraltheologie* XLIII (1954), 177 ff.

Lagerkrantz, Ingeborg. *Lutherska Kyrkovisor i finländska musikhandskrifter från 1500– och 1600–talen*. 2 vols. Helsinki, 1948, 1954.

Langdon, Richard. *Divine Harmony*. London, 1774.

Larsen, Jens Peter. "Koralbøger og Koralbogsproblemer siden Laubs 'Dansk Kirkesang.' " *Dansk Kirkesangs aarsskrift* (1971–72), 76–103.

Lárusson, Magnús M. "Den islandske kirkemusiks udvikling." *Organist-Bladet* XIX (1953), 49–65.

Lenselink, S. J. *De Nederlandse Psalmberijmingen van de Souterliedekens tot Dathenus*. Assen, 1959.

Lesure, François. "Chanson." *MGG* II (1952), 1065 ff.

———. *Musicians and Poets of the French Renaissance*. New York, 1955.

Lightwood, J. T. *The Music of the Methodist Hymn Book*. London, 1935.

Lindsley, Charles Edward. "Early Nineteenth-Century Collections of Sacred Choral Music, 1800–1810. Part I: A Historical Survey of Tune-Book Production to 1810; Part II: An Annotated Bibliography of Tune-Books, 1800–1810." Ph.D. dissertation, University of Iowa, 1968.

Lowens, Irving. "The Bay Psalm Book in 17th-Century New England." *Journal of the American Musicological Society* VIII (1955).

———. "The Origins of the American Fuging Tune." *Journal of the American Musicological Society* VI (1953).

———, and Allen P. Britton. "Daniel Bayley's 'The American Harmony.' " *Papers of the Bibliographical Society of America* XLIX (1955), 340–54.

———. "*The Easy Instructor* (1798–1831). A History and Bibliography of the First Shape Note Tune Book." *Journal of Research in Music Education* I (1953), 30–55.

McCutchen, Robert G. *Hymn Tune Names. Their Sources and Significance*. New York, 1957.

Macdougall, Hamilton C. *Early New England Psalmody*. Brattleboro, 1940.

Mahrenholz, Christhard. *Das Evangelische Kirchengesangbuch. Ein Bericht über seine Vorgeschichte, sein Werden und die Grundsätze seiner Gestaltung*. Kassel and Basel, 1950.

———. "Gesangbuch." *MGG* IV (1955), 1876 ff.

Malling, Anders. *Dansk Salme Historie*. 7 vols. Copenhagen, 1962 ff.

Maresch, Johannes. "Die Bedeutung des Goudimel'schen Hugenottenpsalters von 1565 für die protestantische Kirchenmusik." *Musik und Kirche* X (1938), 89 ff.

Mason, John Russell. *American Hymnology. A Bibliography*. New York, 1933.

"Les Mélodies de nos cantiques." Foreword to *Psaumes et Cantiques (Recueil Laufer)*. Lausanne, 1927.

Metcalf, Frank J. *American Psalmody. Or, Titles of Books, Containing Tunes Printed in America from 1721 to 1820*. New York, 1917.

———. " 'The Easy Instructor.' A Bibliographical Study." *Musical Quarterly* XXIII (1937), 89–97.

Monastier, L. "Les Psautiers suisses du 19e siècle." *Le Lien* III–IV (Lausanne, 1928).

Monastier-Schroeder, L. "La Musique des Psaumes huguenots." *Bibl. Universelle,* 85 ff. Lausanne, 1924.

Morlaye, Guillaume. *Psaumes de Pierre Certon réduits pour chant et luth 1554.* Historical introduction by François Lesure; transcriptions and commentary by Richard de Morcourt. Paris, 1957.

Moser, Hans Joachim. *Die Melodien der Lutherlieder.* Welt des Gesangbuchs, IV. Leipzig and Hamburg, 1935.

Müller, Günther. *Deutsche Dichtung von der Renaissance bis zum Ausgang des Barock.* Potsdam, 1927.

————. *Geschichte des deutschen Liedes vom Barock bis zur Gegenwart.* Munich, 1925.

Müller, Joseph Th. "Bohemian Brethren's Hymnody." *Dictionary of Hymnology.* Ed. by J. Julian. London, 1925.

————. *Geschichte der Böhmischen Brüder.* 3 vols. Herrnhut, 1922, 1931.

————. *Hymnologisches Handbuch zum Gesangbuch der Brüdergemeine.* Herrnhut, 1916.

Natorp, Bernhard Christoph Ludwig. *Ueber den Gesang in den Kirchen der Protestanten. Ein Beytrag zu den Vorarbeiten der Synoden für die Veredlung der Liturgie.* Essen and Duisburg, 1817.

Nelle, Wilhelm. *Geschichte des deutschen ev. Kirchenliedes.* 2nd ed. Hamburg, 1909; 3rd ed., ed. by K. Nelle, Leipzig and Hamburg, 1928.

Nelson, Edward W. "Problems of Compiling a Hymnal for Spanish Speaking Evangelical Churches." Ed.D. dissertation, New Orleans Baptist Theological Seminary, 1972.

Nicholson, Sydney Hugo. *The Parish Psalter.* London, 1928.

Nievergelt, Erwin. "Die Musik in der Gestalt des ev. Gottesdienstes." *Musik und Gottesdienst* X, 2 ff.

————. *Die Tonsätze der deutsch-schweizerisch-reformierten Kirchengesangbücher im 17. Jahrhundert.* Zurich, 1944.

Nitz, Donald. "The Norfolk Musical Society 1814–1820: An Episode in the History of Choral Music in New England." *Journal of Research in Music Education* XVI/4 (Winter, 1968).

Noordt, Anthoni van. *Tabulatur-Boek van Psalmen en Fantasyen.* Amsterdam, 1659; new edition, ed. by M. Seiffert, Leipzig, 1896.

Overath, Johannes. *Untersuchungen über die Melodien des Liedpsalters von Kaspar Ulenberg (Köln, 1782).* Cologne, 1960.

Paulstich, D. *Der Kirchengesang in den Hessen-Casselischen Landesteilen seit der Kirchenreformation.* Kassel, n.d.

Pearce, C. W. "Sacred Folk-Song of the West Gallery Period." *Proceedings of the Musical Association* XLVIII (1921–22).

Pedersen, Gunnar. "Dansk Kirkesang og den liturgiske udvikling." *Dansk Kirkesangs årsskrift* (1971–72), 53–75.

Perrin, Phil D. "Systems of Scale Notation in Nineteenth-Century American Tune Books." *Journal of Research in Music Education* XVIII/3 (Fall, 1970).

Petrich, Hermann. *Unser geistliches Volkslied. Geschichte und Würdigung lieber alter Lieder.* Gütersloh, 1920.

————. *Unser Gesangbuch. Seine Vergangenheit, Gegenwart und Zukunft. Ein Jubiläums-Notschrei.* 2nd ed. Gütersloh, 1924.

Phelps, Austin, E. A. Park, and D. L. Furber. *Hymns and Choirs.* Andover, 1860.

Phillips, C. S. *Hymnody, Past and Present.* London and New York, 1937.

Pierce, Edwin H. " 'Gospel Hymns' and Their Tunes." *Musical Quarterly* XXVI (1940), 355–64.

————. "The Rise and Fall of the 'Fugue-Tune' in America." *Musical Quarterly* XVI (1930).

Poincenot, Ph. *Essai sur l'origine des cantiques français.* Paris, 1908.

Poppen, Hermann. *Das erste Kurpfälzische Gesangbuch und seine Singweisen.* Lahr, 1938.

Pratt, Waldo Selden. *The Music of the French Psalter of 1562.* New York, 1939.

Rapp, Robert Maurice. "Stylistic Characteristics of the Short Sacred Choral Composition in the U.S.A., 1945–1960." Ph.D. dissertation, University of Wisconsin, 1970.

Reindell, Walter. *Das de tempore-Lied des ersten Halbjahrhunderts der reformatorischen Kirche.* Musik und Schrifttum, I. Würzburg, 1942.

————. "Das Elberfelder evangelische Gesangbuch." *Beiträge zur Musikgeschichte der Stadt Wuppertal.* Cologne, 1954.

Reusch, Fritz. "Die Reichslieder, auch 'Englische Lieder' genannt." *Musik und Kirche* II (1930), 262–69.

Riggenbach, Chr. Johann. "Die französischen Psalmmelodien." *Monatshefte für Musikgeschichte* II (1870).

Rimbault, Lucien. "Le Psautier huguenot, lien universel d'amitié entre les peuples." *Bericht über den Internationalen Kongress für Kirchenmusik in Bern,* 52 ff. Bern, 1953.

Röbbelen, I. *Theologie und Frömmigkeit im deutschen ev.-luth. Gesangbuch des 17. und frühen 18. Jahrhunderts.* Göttingen, 1957.

Rogal, Samuel. "Noted Hymn Writers of New York State." *The Hymn* XXIII/2 (April, 1972).

————. "The Gospel Hymns of Stephen Collins Foster." *The Hymn* XXI/1 (January, 1970).

————. "A Sampling of American Temperance Song-Books (1845–1964)." *The Hymn* XXI/4 (October, 1970).

Rokseth, Y. "Les Premiers Chants de l'église calviniste." *Revue de Musicologie* XXXVI (1954), 7 ff.

Rössler, Ernst Karl, and Walter Kraft. "Die Gemeinschaft der Heiligen." *Musik und Kirche* XXIX (1959), 103 ff.

Sandvik, O. M. *Norsk koralhistorie.* Oslo, 1930.

Scheurleer, Daniel François. *De Souterliedekens. Bijdrage tot de geschiedenis de oudste nederlandsche psalm berijming.* Leiden, 1898.

Schild, Emilie. "Das gesungene Wort Gottes und die Musik in der Kirche." *Kirchenbuch. Ordnungen für die Versammlungen der nach Gottes Wort reformierten Gemeinden deutscher Zunge.* Ed. by E. Wolf and M. Albertz. Munich, 1941.

Schiørring, Nils. *Det 16. og 17. århundredes verdslige danske visesang.* 2 vols. Copenhagen, 1950.

Schlisske, Otto. *Handbuch der Lutherlieder.* Göttingen, 1948.

Schoenbaum, Camillo. "Hymnologische Forschung in der Tschechoslowakei. Ein Literaturbericht." *Jahrbuch für Liturgik und Hymnologie* V (1960), 157 ff.

————. "Die Weisen des Gesangbuchs der Böhmischen Brüder von 1531." *Jahrbuch für Liturgik und Hymnologie* III (1957), 44 ff.

Schrems, Theobald. *Die Geschichte des gregorianischen Gesangs in den protestantischen Gottesdiensten.* Veröffentlichungen der gregorianischen Akademie zu Freiburg/Schweiz, XV. Freiburg/Schweiz, 1930.

Seeger, Charles. "Contrapuntal Style in the Three-Voice Shape-Note Hymns." *Musical Quarterly* XXVI (1940).

Simoneaux, Michel Saville. "An Evaluation of the *Baptist Hymnal* (1956) in comparison with Five Hymnals previously popular among Southern Baptists from

1904 until 1956." Ed.D. dissertation, New Orleans Baptist Theological Seminary, 1969.

Sims, John N. "The Hymnody of the Camp-Meeting Tradition." D.S.M. dissertation, Union Theological Seminary, 1960.

Smith, Carlton Y. "Lutheran Hymnody in the United States Before 1850." Ph.D. dissertation, University of Southern California, 1956.

Sørensen, Søren. "Allgemeines über den dänischen protestantischen Kirchengesang." *Kieler Schriften zur Musikwissenschaft* XVI (Kassel, 1965), 11–21.

Stäblein, Bruno. "Die mittelalterlichen liturgischen Weisen im Gesangbuch der Böhmischen Brüder von 1531." *Musikforschung* V (1952), 138 ff.

Stevenson, Robert. "John Marbeck's 'Noted Book' of 1550." *Musical Quarterly* XXXVII (1951), 220 ff.

Sturm, Paul. *Das evangelische Gesangbuch der Aufklärung.* Barmen, 1923.

Tappolet, Walter. "Das neue Gesangbuch der welschen Schweiz." *Volkslied und Hausmusik.* Kassel, 1937.

Teuber, Ulrich. "Notes sur la rédaction musicale du psautier génevois (1542–1562)." *Annales Musicologiques* IV (1956), 113 ff.

————. "Richard Crassots psalter paa kungl. Musikaliska Akademien." Paper read at the second Nordic Musicological Congress, Stockholm and Upsala, 1954 (in Ms.).

Teuscher, Hans. *Christ ist erstanden. Stilkritische Studie über die mehrstimmigen Bearbeitungen der Weise von den Anfängen bis 1600.* Königsberger Studien zur Musikwissenschaft, II. Kassel, 1930.

Thuner, O. E. *Dansk Salme-Leksikon.* Copenhagen, 1930; supplement, 1934.

"Untersuchungen zu den Aulcuns Pseaumes et Cantiques mys en chant à Strasbourg 1539." Parts I and III by Pierre Pidoux, part II by Markus Jenny. *Jahrbuch für Liturgik und Hymnologie* II (1956), 107 ff., and III (1957), 126 ff.

Van Burkalow, Anastasia. "Expanding Horizons: Two Hundred Years of American Methodist Hymnody." *The Hymn* XVII/3 (July, 1966).

Viderø, Finn. "Om gregoriansk sang på dansk." *Gregoriansk sang på dansk*, 25–34. Copenhagen, 1968; also in *Dansk Musiktidsskrift* (1964), 229 ff.

Wackernagel, Philipp. *Bibliographie zur Geschichte des deutschen Kirchenliedes im 16. Jahrhundert.* Frankfurt a. M., 1855; reprint, Hildesheim, 1961.

————. *Das deutsche Kirchenlied von der ältesten Zeit bis zum Anfang des 17. Jahrhunderts.* 5 vols. Leipzig, 1864–77.

————. *Lieder der niederländischen Reformierten aus der Zeit der Verfolgung im 16. Jahrhundert.* Frankfurt a. M., 1867.

Warrington, James. *Short Titles of Books Relating to or Illustrating the History and Practice of Psalmody in the United States 1620–1820.* Philadelphia, 1898.

Westphal, J. *Das ev. Kirchenlied.* 5th ed. 1918.

Wetzstein, O. *Das deutsche Kirchenlied im 16.–18. Jahrhundert.* 1888.

Whitinger, Julius Edward. "Hymnody of the Early American Indian Missions." Studies in Music, No. 46. Ph.D. dissertation, Catholic University, 1971.

Whitley, W. T. *Congregational Hymn Singing.* London, 1933.

Widding, Severin. *Dansk Messe-, Tide- og Salmesang 1528–1573.* 2 vols. Copenhagen, 1933.

Wieder, Fr. Casparus. *De Schriftnurlijke liedekens. De liederen der Nederlandsche Hervormden tot op het jaar 1566. Inhoudsbeschryving en bibliographie. Academisch Proesschrift.* 's-Gravenhage, 1900.

Wieruszowski, Lilli. "Früheste und 'Klassische' Hugenotten-Psalm-Bearbeitung." *Musik und Gottesdienst* VI (1952), 135 ff.

_____. "Die Genfer Psalmen des neuen Gesangbuches." *Musik und Gottesdienst* VIII (1954), 41 ff., 73 ff.

Wilkes, William. *Borrowed Music in Mormon Hymnals.* Ph.D. dissertation, University of Southern California, 1957.

Winterfeld, Carl von. *Über Herstellung des Gemeine- und Chorgesanges in der evangelischen Kirche. Geschichtliches und Vorschläge.* Leipzig, 1848.

Wiora, Walter. "Die Melodien der Souterliedekens und ihre deutschen Parallelen." In the report of the 5th *International Musicological Society Congress,* Utrecht, 1952. Amsterdam, 1953.

Wolkan, Rudolf. *Das deutsche Kirchenlied der Böhmischen Brüder im 16. Jahrhundert.* Prague, 1891.

_____. "Der Kirchengesang der Böhmischen Brüder." *Protestantische Realenzyklopädie.* 3rd ed. X, 426 ff.

Work, John W. "The Negro Spiritual." *Addresses at the International Hymnological Conference, September 10–11, 1961, New York City. Papers of the Hymn Society* XXIV (1962).

Zahn, Johannes. *Die Melodien der deutschen evangelischen Kirchenlieder.* 6 vols. Gütersloh, 1888–93.

Zelle, Friedrich. *Das älteste lutherische Hausgesangbuch 1524.* Göttingen, 1903.

_____. *Das erste evangelische Choralbuch.* Berlin, 1903.

Zimmermann, Heinz Werner. "Neue Musik und neues Kirchenlied." *Musik und Kirche* XXXIII (1963), 54.

Zindel, O. *Les Psautiers de l'Eglise Réformée française de Francfort.* Lausanne, 1933.

Facsimile Reprints of Early Hymnbooks and Other Printed Works

Etlich Christlich lider Lobgesang vnd Psalm (Achtliederbuch). Nuremberg, 1523–24; Kassel, 1957.

Enchiridion Oder eyn Handbuchlein. Erfurt: M. Maler, 1524; Erfurt, 1848.

Eyn Enchiridion oder Handbüchlein. Erfurt: J. Loersfelt, 1524; Kassel, 1929.

Etliche Christliche Gesenge vnd Psalmen/wilche vor bey dem Enchiridion nicht gewest synd. Erfurt: J. Loersfelt, 1525; Weimar, 1952.

Teutsch Kirchen ampt mit lobgsengen. Strasbourg, 1525; Erfurt, 1848; also in H. Hasper, *Calvijns Beginsel voor den Zang in den Eredienst,* 234 ff., 's-Gravenhage, 1955.

Eyn gesang Buchleyn. Zwickau, 1525; Zwickau, 1935, and Berlin, 1960.

Martin Luther. *Deudsche Messe.* Nuremberg, 1526; Kassel, 1934.

Die zwei ältesten Königsberger Gesangbücher von 1527. Kassel, 1933.

Thet cristelighe messze embedhe paa dansche. Malmö, 1528; in *Danske messebøger fra reformationstiden,* Copengahen, 1959.

Enchiridion geistlicher gesenge. Leipzig: M. Blum, 1528–29; Leipzig, 1914.

Ein New Geseng buchlen. Jungbunzlau: Böhm. Brüder, 1531; Kassel, 1931; 2nd ed., 1957.

Geistliche lieder auffs new gebessert. Wittenberg: J. Klug, 1533; Kassel, 1954.

Een handbog. Malmö 1535. In *Danske messebøger fra reformationstiden,* Copenhagen, 1959.

Johann Walter. *Lob und preis der löblichen Kunst Musica.* Wittenberg, 1538; Kassel, 1938

Een gantske nyttelig . . . handbog. Malmö: F. Wormordsen, 1539; in *Danske messebøger fra reformationstiden,* Copenhagen, 1959.

Aulcuns pseaulmes et cantiques mys en chant à Strasburg 1539. Genf, 1919; also in H. Hasper, *Calvijns Beginsel voor den Zang in den Eredienst,* 456 ff., 's-Gravenhage, 1955.

Nüw gsangbüchle. Zurich, 1540; Zurich, 1946.

Gesangbuch [large ed.]. Strasbourg: J. Waldmüller, 1541; Stuttgart, 1953.

La forme des prières et chantz ecclésiastiques. Geneva, 1542; Kassel and Basel, 1959.

Geystliche Lieder. Leipzig: V. Babst, 1545; Kassel, 1929.

John Marbeck, *The Book of Common Prayer Noted.* 1550; ed. by J. Eric Hunt, London, 1939.

En Ny Psalmebog. Copenhagen: Hans Tausen, 1553; Copenhagen, 1944.

Johann Walter, *Ein newes Christlichs Lied.* Wittenberg, 1561; Kassel, 1933.

Les pseaumes mis en rime françoise . . . mis en musique à quatre parties par Claude Goudimel. Geneva, 1565; Kassel, 1935.

Den danske Psalmebog . . . Aff Hans Thomissøn. Copenhagen, 1569; Copenhagen, 1933; new facs. ed., Copenhagen, 1968, with an appendix by Erik Dal: "Hans Thomissøns salmebog 1569–1676."

Cent cinquante pseaumes de David . . . mis en musique à quatre, cinq, six, sept et huit parties par Paschal de l'Estocart. Geneva, 1583; Kassel, 1954.

The Bay Psalm Book Being a Facsimile Reprint. 1640; ed. by Wilberforce Eames, New York, 1903.

Thomas Kingo, *Graduale.* Odense, 1699; Odense, 1967.

Fuldstaendig Choral-Bog . . . af Friderich Christian Breitendich. . . . Copenhagen, 1764; Copenhagen, 1970 (ed. H. Glahn).

Gradual. En Almindelig Sandbog . . . Ved Niels Jesperssøn. Copenhagen, 1773; Copenhagen, 1935.

William Billings, *The Continental Harmony.* 1794; ed. by Hans Nathan, Cambridge, Mass., 1961.

IV: Historia and Passion

Abraham, Gerald. "Passion Music in the 15th and 16th Centuries." *Monthly Musical Record* LXXXIII (1953), 208–11, 235–41.

Adams, H. "Passion Music Before 1724." *Music and Letters* VII (1926).

Adrio, Adam. "Die Matthäuspassion von J. G. Kühnhausen." In the *A. Schering Festschrift.* Berlin, 1937.

Birke, Joachim. "Die Passionsmusiken von Thomas Selle. Beiträge zur Geschichte der Passion im 17. Jahrhundert." Dissertation, Hamburg, 1957.

――――. "Eine unbekannte anonyme Matthäuspassion aus der 2. Hälfte des 17. Jahrhunderts." *Archiv für Musikwissenschaft* XV (1958).

Blankenburg, Walter. "Die Aufführungen von Passionen und Passionskantaten in . . . Gotha." In the *Blume Festschrift.* 1963.

――――. "Die deutsche Liedpassion." *Musik und Kirche* IX (1938).

――――. "Historia." *MGG* VI (1957), 465–89.

――――. "Passion. C. (Protest. Passion)." *MGG* X (1962), 911–33.

――――. "Zu den Johannes-Passionen von Ludwig Daser (1578) und Leonhard Lechner (1593)." In *Musa-Mens-Musici-Im Gedenken an Walther Vetter,* 63–66. Leipzig, 1969.

Braun, Werner. *Die mitteldeutsche Choralpassion im 18. Jahrhundert.* Berlin, 1960.

――――. "Zur Passionspflege in Delitzsch. . . ." *Archiv für Musikwissenschaft* X (1953).

Eggebrecht, Hans Heinrich. "Die Matthäuspassion von M. Vulpius." *Musikforschung* III (1950).

Epstein, Peter. "Ein unbekanntes Passions-Oratorium von Chr. Flor." *Bach-Jahrbuch* XXVII (1930).

――――. "Zur Geschichte der deutschen Choralpassion." *Jahrbuch Peters* XXXVI (1929).

Fischer, Kurt von. "Ambrosius Beber, Markuspassion." *Musikforschung* XII (1959).

_____. "Passion. B. (Mehrstimmige und katholische Passion)." *MGG* X (1962), 898–911.

_____. "Zur Geschichte der Passionskomposition . . . in Italien." *Archiv für Musikwissenschaft* XI (1954).

Gerber, Rudolf. "Die deutsche Passion von Luther bis Bach." *Luther-Jahrbuch* XIII (1931).

_____. *Das Passions-Rezitativ bei Heinrich Schütz und seine stilgeschichtlichen Grundlagen.* Gütersloh, 1929.

Hammermüller, Joseph. "Passionen i Roskilde Domkirke." *Aarbog for Musik 1924* (Copenhagen, 1926), 50–59.

Handschin, Jacques. "Das Weihnachtsmysterium als musikgeschichtliche Quelle." *Acta Musicologica* VII (1935).

Hörner, Hans. *G. Ph. Telemanns Passionsmusiken.* Leipzig, 1933.

Jung, Lina. "Johannes Driessler." *Schweizerische Musikzeitung* XCI (1951), 150 ff.

Kade, Otto. *Die ältere Passionskomposition.* Gütersloh, 1893.

Kent, Ralph M. "A Study of Oratorios and Sacred Cantatas Composed in America before 1900." Ph.D. dissertation, University of Iowa, 1954.

Kitzig, B. "C. H. Brauns Passionskantate Der Tod Jesu." *Monatsschrift für Gottesdienst und kirchliche Kunst* XXXV (1930).

Knoke, K. *Die Passion Christi von Thomas Mancinus.* Göttingen, 1897.

Lott, Walter. "Zur Geschichte der Passionskomposition von 1650–1800." *Archiv für Musikwissenschaft* III (1921).

_____. "Zur Geschichte der Passionsmusiken auf Danziger Boden." *Archiv für Musikwissenschaft* VII (1925).

Mathews, W. S. B. "American Oratorios" [J. K. Paine's "St. Peter" and Dudley Buck's "46th Psalm"]. *The Nation* XVI/398 (Feb. 13, 1873), 116–17.

Matthäus, Wolfgang. "Die Evangelienhistorie von Johann Walter bis Heinrich Schütz mit Ausschluss der Passion." Dissertation, Frankfurt, 1943.

Moser, Hans Joachim. "Aus der Frühgeschichte der Generalbasspassion." *Jahrbuch Peters* (1920); reprinted in *Musik in Zeit und Raum,* Berlin, 1960.

Osthoff, Helmuth. "Die Historien R. Michaels." In *Festschrift Arnold Schering zum sechzigen Geburtstag.* Berlin, 1937.

_____. "R. Michaels Weihnachtshistorie." *Musik und Kirche* IX (1937).

Richter, B. F. "Gottesdienstliche Passionsaufführungen in Leipzig." *Monatsschrift für Gottesdienst und kirchliche Kunst* IX (1904).

_____. "Zur Geschichte der Passionsaufführungen in Leipzig." *Bach-Jahrbuch* VIII (1911).

Römhild, Hans. "Die Matthäuspassion von Johann Theodor Römhild." *Musikforschung* IX (1956).

Schmidt, Günther. "Grundsätzliche Bemerkungen zur Geschichte der Passionshistorie." *Archiv für Musikwissenschaft* XVII (1960).

_____. "Zur Quellenlage der Passionen J. Meilands." *Jahrbuch für Liturgik und Hymnologie* III (1957).

Schmitz, Franz Arnold. "Die Bedeutung Oberitaliens in der Geschichte der Passionskomposition." *Oberitalienische Figuralpassionen.* Mainz, 1955.

Schneider, Max. "Zum Weihnachts-Oratorium von H. Schütz." In the *Th. Kroyer Festschrift.* Regensburg, 1933.

Spitta, Friedrich. *Die Passion nach den vier Evangelisten von Heinrich Schütz.* Leipzig, 1886.

————. "Die Passionen von Heinrich Schütz und ihre Wiederbelebung." *Jahrbuch Peters* XIII (1906).

————. *Die Passionsmusiken von Johann Sebastian Bach und Heinrich Schütz.* Leipzig, 1893.

Stäblein, Bruno. "Passion. A. (Einstimmige lat. Passion)." *MGG* X (1962), 886–98.

Wallon, S. "Un Manuscrit d'Ambrosius Beber à la Bibliothèque du Conservatoire de Paris." *Revue de Musicologie* XXXVI (1953).

V: Organ Music

Beasley, William Joseph. "The Organ in America, as portrayed in Dwight's *Journal of Music.*" Ph.D. dissertation, University of Southern California, 1970.

Bleyle, Carl Otto. "George Andreas Sorge's Influence on David Tannenberg and Organ Building in America During the Eighteenth Century." Ph.D. dissertation, University of Michigan, 1969.

Bornefeld, Helmut. "Orgelmusik heute." *Musik und Kirche* XXXI (1961), 55–65.

Boston, Noel, and L. G. Langwill. *Church and Chamber Barrel Organs.* Edinburgh, 1967.

Bruinsma, Henry A. "The Organ Controversy in the Netherlands Reformation to 1640." *Journal of the American Musicological Society* VII (1954).

Buck, Dudley. *Choir Accompaniment.* New York, 1888.

Dean, Talmadge W. "The Organ in Eighteenth-Century Colonial America." Ph.D. dissertation, University of Southern California, 1960.

Dietrich, Fritz. "Bachs Orgelchoral und seine geschichtlichen Wurzeln." *Bach-Jahrbuch* XXVI (1929).

————. *Geschichte des deutschen Orgelchorals im 17. Jahrhundert.* Kassel, 1932.

Fellerer, Karl Gustav. *Beiträge zur Choralbegleitung und Choralverarbeitung in der Orgelmusik des ausgehenden 18. und beginnenden 19. Jahrhunderts.* Sammlung musikwissenschaftlicher Abhandlungen, VI. Strasbourg, 1932.

————. *Orgel und Orgelmusik. Ihre Geschichte.* Augsburg, 1929.

————. *Studien zur Orgelmusik des ausgehenden 18. und frühen 19. Jahrhunderts. Ein Beitrag zur Geschichte der Orgelmusik.* Münsterische Beiträge zur Musikwissenschaft, III. Kassel, 1932.

Freudenberg, Carl Gottlieb. *Aus dem Leben eines alten Organisten.* Ed. posthumously from the author's unpublished papers by W. Viol. 2nd ed. Leipzig, 1872.

Frotscher, Gotthold. *Geschichte des Orgelspiels und der Orgelkomposition.* 2 vols. 2nd ed. Berlin, 1959.

Girod, Marie-Louise. "L'Orgue et le Protestantisme." *Protestantisme et musique.* Paris, 1950.

Gurlitt, Wilibald. "Die Wandlungen des Klangideals der Orgel." *Bericht über die Freiburger Tagung für deutsche Orgelkunst.* Augsburg, 1926.

Hasse, Karl. "Die geistlichen und religiösen Grundlagen der Orgelmusik seit Bach." *Bericht über die dritte Tagung für deutsche Orgelkunst in Freiberg i. Sa.,* 46–57. Kassel, 1928.

Hieronymus, Bess Estelle. "Organ Music in the Worship Service of American Synagogues in the Twentieth Century." D.M.A. dissertation, University of Texas, 1969.

Hilfsbuch für Liturgen und Organisten in den Brüdergemeinen. Ed. by Th. Erzleben. Gnadau, 1865; 2nd ed., 1892; supplement, 1907.

Hombraeus, Bengt. "Reise nach Hohenzell (E. K. Rössler)." *Musik und Kirche* XXIX (1959), 282 f.

Kelletat, Herbert. *Zur Geschichte der deutschen Orgelmusik in der Frühklassik.* Königsberger Studien zur Musikwissenschaft, XV. Kassel, 1933.

Kessler, Franz. "Neue Bestrebungen auf dem Gebiet des Orgelchorals." Dissertation, Mainz, 1949.

Kist, Florens Cornelius. *Het Kerkelijke Orgel-Gebruik, bijzonder in Nederland. Archief von Kerkelijde Geschiedenis.* Leiden, 1840; new ed. by A. P. Oosterhof and E. J. Penning (Orgelbouwkundige Bijdragen, Series A, Vol. II), Leeuwarden, 1938.

Kittel, Johann Christian. *Der angehende praktische Organist oder Anweisung zum zweckmässigen Gebrauch der Orgel bei Gottesverehrungen in Beispielen.* Part I, 2nd ed., Erfurt, 1808; Part II, 1803; Part III, 1808.

Kittler, Guenter. *Geschichte des protestantischen Orgelchorals.* Greifswald, 1931.

Klotz, Hans. "Die kirchliche Orgelkunst." *Leiturgia* IV (1961), 759 ff.

_____. *Über die Orgelkunst der Gotik, der Renaissance und des Barock.* Kassel, 1934.

Mahrenholz, Christhard. *Der gegenwärtige Stand der Orgelfrage im Lichte der Orgelgeschichte. Bericht über die 3. Tagung für deutsche Orgelkunst in Freiberg (Sa.).* Kassel, 1928.

_____. "Versch. Aufsätze zur Orgelfrage." *Musicologica et Liturgica.* Kassel, 1960.

Müller, Johannes. "Die Choralbearbeitung von Bach bis zur Choralfantasie Regers in Gedrängter Form." *Schweizerische Musikzeitung* LXII (1922), 272 f., 288 f., 300 f., 330, 338 f.

Müller, Wilhelm Adolph. *Die Orgel, ihre Einrichtung und Beschaffenheit sowohl, als das zweckmässige Spiel derselben. Ein unentbehrliches Handbuch für Cantoren, Organisten, Schullehrer und andere Freunde des Orgelspiels.* 2nd ed. Meissen, 1823.

Het Orgel. Nederlandse Organisten Vereniging 1890 bis 1960. Kollum, 1960.

"Orgel, Orgelmusik, Orgelspiel." *MGG* X (1962), 228–396.

Petzold, Joachim. *Die gedruckten vierstimmigen Choralbücher für die Orgel der deutschen evangelischen Kirche (1785–1933).* Halle, 1935.

Pirro, André. "L'Art des organistes." *Encyclopédie de la musique.* . . . Ed. by A. Lavignac. II, 2 ff.

Reimann, Margarete. "Pasticcios und Parodien in norddeutschen Klaviertabulaturen." *Musikforschung* VIII (1955).

Riedel, Friedrich Wilhelm. *Quellenkundliche Beiträge zur Geschichte der Musik für Tasteninstrumente in der 2. Hälfte des 17. Jahrhunderts.* Kassel, 1960.

Rietschel, G. *Die Aufgabe der Orgel im Gottesdienst bis in das 18. Jahrhundert.* Leipzig, 1892.

Ritter, August Gottfried. *Rhythmischer Choralgesang und Orgelspiel . . . 33stes Werk.* Erfurt and Leipzig, 1857.

_____. *Zur Geschichte des Orgelspiels, vornehmlich des deutschen, im 14. bis zum Anfang des 18. Jahrhunderts.* Leipzig, 1884.

Scheide, August. *Zur Geschichte des Choralvorspiels.* Hildburghausen, 1930.

Schierning, Lydia. *Die Überlieferung der deutschen Orgel- und Klaviermusik aus der 1. Hälfte des 17. Jahrhunderts.* Kassel, 1961.

Schink, Fritz. *Festschrift zur Feier des 55jährigen Bestehens des Berliner Organisten-Vereins und seines 25jährigen Jubiläums als "Verein Berliner Organisten und Kirchenchor-Dirigenten." Als Manuskript gedruckt.* . . . Berlin, 1928.

Seiffert, Max. *Geschichte der Klaviermusik.* Leipzig, 1899.

Sietz, Reinhold. "Die Orgelkompositionen des Schülerkreises um Johann Sebastian Bach." *Bach-Jahrbuch* (1935), 33–96.

Sonnenkalb, Johann Friedrich Wilhelm. *Kurtze Entscheidung der Frage: Wie sollen die Praeludia eines Organisten bey dem Gottesdienste beschaffen seyn? Oder: Welches sind die Kennzeichen eines in seinen Amts-Verrichtungen verständigen Organisten?.* Torgau, 1756.

Stevens, Denis. *The Mulliner Book: A Commentary.* London, 1952.

Teichfischer, Paul. *Die Entwicklung des Choralvorspiels unter besonderer Berücksichtigung Joh. Seb. Bachs und der Meister der neuesten Zeit.* Langensalza, 1913.

Trötschel, Heinrich R. "Die Permanenz der Orgelbewegung." *Musik und Kirche* XXVII (1957), 123–35.

Türk, Daniel Gottlob. *Von den wichtigsten Pflichten eines Organisten. Ein Beytrag zur Verbesserung der musikalischen Liturgie.* Halle, 1787; a later edition (Halle, 1838) bears the subtitle *Neu bearbeitet und mit zeitgemässen Zusätzen herausgegeben von Dr. Naue.*

Valentin, Erich. *Die Entwicklung der Toccata im 17. und 18. Jahrhundert.* Munich, 1930.

Vardell, Charles G. *Organs in the Wilderness.* Winston-Salem, North Carolina, 1944.

Vente, Maarten Albert. "Überblick über die seit 1931 erschienene Literatur zur Geschichte des niederländischen Orgelbaus." *Acta Musicologica* XXX (1958), 26 ff.

Viderö, Finn. "Zu E. K. Rösslers 'Klangfunktion und Registrierung.' " *Musik und Kirche* XXII (1952), 245 ff.

Voge, Richard. "Zur Interpretation der Orgelwerke von E. K. Rössler." *Musik und Kirche* XXIX (1959), 278 ff.

Vollhardt, Reinhard. *Geschichte der Cantoren und Organisten von den Städten im Königreich Sachsen.* Berlin, 1899.

Wagner, Hans-Joachim. "Die Orgelmusik in Thüringen in der Zeit zwischen 1830 und 1860. Ein Beitrag zur Geschichte der Orgelmusik des 19. Jahrhunderts. Dissertation, Berlin, 1937.

Williams, George W. "Eighteenth-Century Organists of St. Michael's, Charleston." *South Carolina Historical Magazine* LIII (1952).

Zimmer, Friedrich. *Der Verfall des Kantoren- und Organistenamtes in der evangelischen Landeskirche Preussens. Seine Ursachen und Vorschläge zur Besserung.* Quedlinburg, 1885.

VI: Monographs on Individuals

Abeille, Johann Christian Ludwig (and other Swabian composers)

Haering, Kurt. "Fünf Schwäbische Liederkomponisten des 18. Jahrhunderts: Abeille, Dieter, Eidenbenz, Schwegler und Christmann." Dissertation, Tübingen, 1925.

Agricola, Johann Friedrich

Wucherpfennig, Hermann. "Johann Friedrich Agricola (Sein Leben und seine Werke)." Dissertation, Berlin, 1922.

Ahle, Johann Rudolph and Johann Georg

Brinkmann, E. "Neue Forschungen zum Leben der grossen Mühlhäuser Musiker." In the *Armin Tille Festschrift.* Weimar, 1930.

Wolf, Johannes. "Johann Rudolph Ahle." *Sammelbände der Internationalen Musikgesellschaft* II (1900–01), 393–400.

Aichinger, Gregor

Aichinger, Chr. *Die Aichinger.* 1909.

Kroyer, Theodor. "Introduction." *Denkmäler der Tonkunst in Bayern* X/1 (1909).

Altenburg, Michael

Meinecke, Ludwig. "Michael Altenburg." *Sammelbände der Internationalen Musikgesell-schaft* V (1903–04), 1–45.

Amon, Blasius

Huigens, Caecilianus. "Blasius Amon." *Studien zur Musikwissenschaft* XVIII (1931), 3–22; also in *Denkmäler der Tonkunst in Österreich* XXXVIII/1.

Antes, John

McCorkle, Donald M. "John Antes, 'American Dilettante.' " *Musical Quarterly* XLII (1956).

Bach, family

Geiringer, Karl. *The Bach Family.* London, 1954.

Bach, Carl Philipp Emanuel

Busch, Gudrun. *C. Ph. E. Bach und seine Lieder.* Kölner Beiträge zur Musikforschung, XII. Regensburg, 1957.

Miesner, Heinrich. "Philipp Emanual Bach in Hamburg. Beiträge zu seiner Biographie und zur Musikgeschichte seiner Zeit." Dissertation, Berlin, 1929.

Bach, Johann Cristoph

Fischer, Martin. *Die organistische Improvisation im 17. Jahrhundert, dargestellt an den Vierundvierzig Chorälen zum Präambulieren von J. Christoph Bach.* Kassel, 1929.

Bach, Johann Christoph Friedrich

Schünemann, Geog. "Johann Christoph Friedrich Bach." *Bach-Jahrbuch* (1914), 45 ff.

Bach, Johann Sebastian

For the older literature, see the bibliographies by M. Schneider in the *Bach-Jahrbuch,* 1905 and 1910, and the supplements by A. Landau and G. Frotscher in the *Bach-Jahrbuch,* 1918 and 1930. A comprehensive summary of the entire Bach literature to 1950 is give in *MGG* I (1949–51), 1043 ff. The following bibliography can give only a brief survey of the most important writings since 1950 that deal with sources and chronology, the sacred vocal works, and the organ music. For a critical description of the most recent Bach literature, see W. Blankenburg, "Theologische und geistesgeschichtliche Probleme der gegenwärtigen Bachforschung," in *Theolog. Literaturzeitung 1953,* No. 7, 391 ff., and the same author's "Zehn Jahre Bachforschung," in *Theolog. Rundschau,* new series, XXIX (1963), 335 ff. In addition, the state of research on works printed in the new *Bach-Ausgabe* is reported in the *Kritische Berichte* volumes.

Blankenburg, Walter. "Das Parodieverfahren im Weihnachts-Oratorium." *Musik und Kirche* XXXII (1962), 245 ff.

Dadelsen, Georg von. *Beiträge zur Chronologie der Werke Bachs.* Trossingen, 1958.

———. *Bemerkungen zur Handschrift Bachs.* Trossingen, 1957.

———. "Friedrich Smends Ausgabe der H-Moll-Messe." *Musik und Kirche* XXX (1960).

———. "Originale Daten auf den Handschriften Bachs." In *Hans Albrecht in memoriam,* 116 ff. Kassel, 1962.

———. "Eine unbekannte Messenbearbeitung Bachs." In the *K. G. Fellerer Festschrift,* 88 ff. Regensburg, 1962.

———. "Zum Problem der H-Moll-Messe." In the program book of the thirty-fifth Bach Festival in Stuttgart (1958), 77 ff.

Dürr, Alfred. "Bach's Magnificat." *Music Review* XV (1954), 182 ff.

———. "Der Eingangssatz zum Himmelfahrts-Oratorium." In *Hans Albrecht in memoriam,* 121 ff. Kassel, 1962.

———. " 'Ich bin ein Pilgrim auf der Welt.' " *Musikforschung* XI (1958), 422 ff.

———. "Wieviele Kantatenjahrgänge hat Bach komponiert?" *Musikforschung* XIV (1961), 192 ff.

———. "Zur Chronologie der Leipziger Vokalwerke Bachs." *Bach-Jahrbuch* (1957), 5 ff.

Emery, Walter. "The Compass of Bach's Organs as Evidence of the Dates of his Works." *The Organ* XXXII (1952), 92 ff.

———. "A Note on the History of Bach's Canonic Variations." *Musical Times* CIV (1963), 32 f.

———. *Notes on Bach's Organ Works.* London, 1952.

Feder, Georg. "Bachs Werke in ihren Bearbeitungen 1750–1950. I. Die Vokalwerke." Dissertation, Kiel, 1955.

———. "Bemerkungen über einige Bach zugeschriebene Werke." *Musikforschung* XI (1958), 76 ff.

Foch, Gustav. *Der junge Bach in Lüneburg.* Hamburg, 1950.

Geck, Martin. "Bachs Weihnachts-Magnificat und sein Traditionszusammenhang." *Musik und Kirche* XXXI (1961), 257 ff.

Gudewill, Kurt. "Über Formen und Texte der Kirchenkantaten Bachs." In the *F. Blume Festschrift,* 162 ff. Kassel, 1963.

Hudson, Frederick, and Alfred Dürr. "An Investigation into the Authenticity of Bach's 'Kleine Magnificat.' " *Music and Letters* XXXVI (1955), 233 ff.

Irtenkauf, Wolfgang. "Bachs Magnificat und seine Verbindung zu Weihnachten." *Musik und Kirche* XXVI (1956), 257 ff.

Kilian, Dietrich. "Bachs Praeludium und Fuge D-Moll BWV 539, ein Arrangement aus dem 19. Jh.?" *Musikforschung* XIV (1961), 323 ff.

———. "Studie über Bachs Fantasie und Fuge C-Moll BWV 562." In the *Hans Albrecht in memoriam,* 127 ff. Kassel, 1962.

Mendel, Arthur. "More on the Weimar Origin of Bach's 'O Mensch, bewein dein Sünde gross.' " *Journal of the American Musicological Society* XVII (1964), 203 ff.

———. "Recent Developments in Bach Chronology." *Musical Quarterly* XLVI (1960), 283 ff.

———. "Traces of the Pre-History of Bach's St. John and St. Matthew Passions." In the *O. E. Deutsch Festschrift,* 31 ff. Kassel, 1963.

Mies, Paul. *Die geistlichen Kantaten Bachs und der Hörer von heute.* 2 vols. Wiesbaden, 1959–60.

Neumann, Werner. "Eine verschollene Ratswechselkantate." *Bach-Jahrbuch* (1961), 52 ff.

———. *Handbuch der Kantaten J. S. Bachs.* 2nd ed. Leipzig, 1953.

———. *J. S. Bach. Sämtliche Kantatentexte.* Leipzig, 1956.

Riedel, Friedrich Wilhelm. "A. Fuchs als Sammler Bachscher Werke." *Bach-Jahrbuch* (1960), 83 ff.

Ruhnke, M. "Moritz Hauptmann und die Wiederbelebung der Musik J. S. Bachs." In the *F. Blume Festschrift.* Kassel, 1963.

Sailer, Bill. "Bach in Bethlehem. Amerika und die protestantische Kirchenmusik." *Musik und Kirche* XX (1950), 71 ff.

Scheide, William Hurd. "Bachs Sammlung von Kantaten J. Ludwig Bachs." *Bach-Jahrbuch* (1961 and 1962).

———. "Ist Mizlers Bericht über Bachs Kantaten Korrekt?" *Musikforschung* XIV (1961), 60 ff.

———. "Nochmals Mizlers Kantatenbericht." *Musikforschung* XIV (1961), 433 ff.

Schmieder, W. *Them.-syst. Verzeichnis der Werke J. S. Bachs.* Leipzig, 1950.

Schulze, Hans Joachim. "Zur Identifizierung der anonymen Messe BWV Anh. 4." *Musikforschung* XIV (1961), 328 f.

Siegele, Ulrich. "Bemerkungen zu Bachs Motetten." *Bach-Jahrbuch* (1962), 33 ff.

Stockmann, Bernhard. "Bach im Urteil Carl v. Winterfelds." *Musikforschung* XIII (1960), 417–26.

Werthemann, H. *Die Bedeutung der alttestamentlichen Historien in Bachs Kantaten.* Tübingen, 1960.

Whittaker, William Gillies. *The Cantatas of Bach.* 2 vols. London, 1959.

Bach, Wilhelm Friedemann

Falck, Martin. *Wilhelm Friedemann Bach. Sein Leben und seine Werke mit thematischem Verzeichnis seiner Kompositionen und zwei Bildern.* Dissertation, Leipzig, 1912; published, Leipzig, 1913.

Beaulieu, Eustorg de

Becker, Georges. *Eustorg de Beaulieu, poète et musicien. Notice biographique et bibliographique publiée avec la musique de deux chansons.* Paris, 1880.

Beissel, Johann Conrad

Blakely, Lloyd G. "Johann Conrad Beissel and Music of the Ephrata Cloister." *Journal of Research in Music Education* XV/2 (Summer, 1967).

Briner, Andres. "Wahrheit und Dichtung um J. C. Beissel. Studie um eine Gestalt in Thomas Manns 'Dr. Faustus.' " *Schweizerische Musikzeitung* XCVIII (1958).

Mann, Thomas. *Doctor Faustus.* New York, 1948.

Belcher, Supply

Owen, Earl McLain, Jr. "The Life and Music of Supply Belcher (1751–1836), 'Handel of Maine.' " D.M.A. dissertation, Southern Baptist Theological Seminary, 1969.

Berggreen, Andreas Peter

Skou, C. *Andreas Peter Berggreen. Et Mindeskrift.* Copenhagen, 1895.

Berner, Friedrich Wilhelm

Eschenbach, Wolfram. "Friedrich Wilhelm Berner (1780 bis 1827). Ein Beitrag zur Breslauer Musikgeschichte." Dissertation, Breslau, 1935.

Bernhard, Christoph

Ilgner, Gerhard. *Matthias Weckmann.* Dissertation, Kiel, 1939; published, Wolfenbüttel, 1939.

Krüger, Liselotte. *Die Hamburger Musikorganisation im 17. Jahrhundert.* Strasbourg, 1933.

Rauschning, Hermann. *Geschichte der Musik . . . in Danzig.* Danzig, 1931.

Besler, Samuel

Hampel, Norbert. "Deutschsprachige prot. Kirchenmusik Schlesiens." Dissertation, Breslau, 1937.

Starke, Robert. "Samuel Besler." *Monatshefte für Musikgeschichte* XXXI (1899).

Billings, Nathaniel

Link, Eugene P. "The Republican Harmony (1795) of Nathaniel Billings." *Journal of Research in Music Education* XVIII/4 (Winter, 1970).

Billings, William

Barbour, J. Murray. *The Church Music of William Billings.* East Lansing, Mich., 1960.
Garrett, Allen. "The Works of William Billings." Ph.D. dissertation, University of North Carolina, 1952.
Lindstrom, Carl E. "William Billings and His Times." *Musical Quarterly* XXV (1939).
Morin, Raymond. "William Billings. Pioneer in American Music." *New England Quarterly* XIV (1941), 25–33.

Blahoslav, Jan

Hostinský, Otokar. *Jan Blahoslav a Jan Josquin.* Prague, 1896.
Quotika, Rudolf. "Die Musica des Jan Blahoslav 1569." *International Musicological Society Congress. Bamberg, 1953,* 128 ff. Kassel, 1954.

Blow, John

Shaw, Watkins. *John Blow* (in preparation).

Bodenschatz, Erhard

Riemer, Otto. *Erhard Bodenschatz und sein Florilegium Portense.* Leipzig, 1928.

Böhm, Georg

Böhme, Erdmann W. "Georg Böhm." In the *M. Seiffert Festschrift* (typescript, 1948).
Waldschmidt, C. L. "Georg Boehm." Dissertation, Northwestern University, 1963.
Wolgast, Johannes. "Georg Böhm." Dissertation, Berlin, 1924.

Bourgeoys, Loys

Gaillard, Paul-André. "Loys Bourgeoys." *MGG* II (1952), 161 f.
———. *Loys Bourgeoys, sa vie, son oeuvre comme pédagogue et compositeur.* Lausanne, 1948.
———. "Le Matériel melodique employé par Loys Bourgeoys dans son Premier Livre des Pseaulmes Lyon 1547." *Schweizerische Musikzeitung* XCII (1952).
———. "Petite Étude comparée du 'note contre note' de Loys Bourgeoys (1547)." *International Musicological Society Congress. Basel, 1949,* 115 ff. Basel. 1949.

Boyce, William

Shaw, Watkins. "William Boyce." *Musical Times* CI (1960), 479.

Brahms, Johannes

Gerber, Rudolf. "Das 'Deutsche Requiem' als Dokument Brahmsscher Frömmigkeit." *Musikleben* II (1949).
Henried, Robert. "Brahms und das Christentum." *Musica* III (1949).
Köser, Werner. "Johannes Brahms in seinen geistlichen Chorwerken a cappella." Dissertation, Hamburg, 1950.
Spitta, Friedrich. "Brahms und Herzogenberg in ihrem Verhältnis zur evangelischen Kirchenmusik." *Monatsschrift für Gottesdienst und kirchliche Kunst* XII (1907), 36–45.

Briegel, Wolfgang Carl

Hirschmann, Karl Friedrich. "Wolfgang Carl Briegel." Dissertation, Marburg, 1934.
Noack, Elisabeth. *Wolfgang Carl Briegel.* Berlin, 1963.

Bristow, George Frederick

Rogers, Delmer D. "Nineteenth Century Music in New York City as Reflected in the Career of George Frederick Bristow." Ph.D. dissertation, University of Michigan, 1967.

Brooks, Phillips

Higginson, J. Vincent. "Phillips Brooks and Sunday School Music." *The Hymn* XIX/2 (April, 1968).

Bruhns, Nikolaus

Kölsch, Heinz. *Nikolaus Bruhns.* Dissertation, Kiel, 1938; published, Kassel, 1958.

Buck, Dudley

Dudley Buck. A Complete Bibliography of his Works. New York, 1910.
Gallo, William K. "The Life and Church Music of Dudley Buck (1839–1909)." Ph.D. dissertation, Catholic University, 1968.

Burck, Joachim a

Birtner, Herbert. "Ein Beitrag zur Geschichte der protestant. Musik im 16. Jahrhundert." *Zeitschrift für Musikwissenschaft* X (1927–28), 457–94.
————. "Joachim a Burck als Motettenkomponist." Dissertation, Leipzig, 1924.

Burkhard, Willy

Mohr, Ernst. *Willy Burkhard. Leben und Werk.* Zurich, 1957.

Burleigh, Harry T.

Murray, Charlotte W. "The Story of Harry T. Burleigh." *The Hymn* XVII/4 (October, 1966).

Buttstett, Franz Vollrath

Kern, Hans. *Franz Vollrath Buttstett (1735–1814). Eine Studie zur Musik des Spätbarock.* Würzburg, 1939.

Buttstett, Johann Heinrich

Blume, Friedrich. "Buttstett." *MGG* II (1952), 533 ff.
Schild, Emilie. *Geschichte der prot. Messenkomposition im 17.–18. Jahrhundert.* Wuppertal and Elberfeld, 1934.

Buxtehude, Dietrich

Blume, Friedrich. "Das Kantatenwerk Dietrich Buxtehudes." *Jahrbuch Peters* (1940), 10 ff.
Geck, Martin. *Die Vokalmusik Dietrich Buxtehudes und der frühe Pietismus.* Kieler Schriften zur Musikwissenschaft, XV. Kassel, 1964.
————. "Das Vokalwerk Buxtehudes in quellenkritischer Sicht." *Musikforschung* XIV

(1961), 393 ff. See also the Maxton–Geck debate in the same journal, XV–XVI (1962–63).

Grusnick, Bruno. "Dietrich Buxtehude." *Musik und Kirche* VII (1935), 22 ff., 58 ff.

————. "Zur Chronologie von Dietrich Buxtehudes Vokalwerken." *Musikforschung* X (1957), 75–84.

Hedar, J. *Dietrich Buxtehudes Orgelwerke.* Stockholm and Frankfurt, 1951.

Hennings, Johann. "Neues über Franz Tunder und Dietrich Buxtehude." *Deutsche Musikkultur* VI (1942), 157 ff.

Karstädt, Georg. *Die "extraordinären Abendmusiken" D. Buxtehudes.* Lübeck, 1962.

————. "Das Textbuch zum Templum honoris." *Musikforschung* X (1957), 506 ff.

Kilian, Dietrich. "Das Vokalwerk Dietrich Buxtehudes." Dissertation, Berlin, 1956.

Maxton, Willy. "Mitteilungen über eine vollständige Abendmusik." *Zeitschrift für Musikwissenschaft* X (1927–28), 387 ff.

Moser, H. J. *D. Buxtehude.* Berlin, 1957.

Pirro, André. *Dietrich Buxtehude.* Paris, 1913.

Sørensen, Søren. *Diderich Buxtehudes vokale Kirkemusik.* 2 vols. Copenhagen, 1958.

————. "Monteverdi–Förster–Buxtehude." *Dansk Aarbog for Musikforskning* III (1963).

Stahl, Wilhelm. *D. Buxtehude.* Kassel, 1937.

————. "Franz Tunder und Dietrich Buxtehude." *Archiv für Musikwissenschaft* VIII (1926), 1 ff.

————. "Die Lübecker Abendmusiken im 17.–18. Jh." *Zeitschrift des Vereins für lübeckische Geschichte* XXIX (1938), 1 ff.

Byrd, William

Andrews, Herbert Kennedy. *The Technique of Byrd's Vocal Polyphony.* London, 1966.

Buck, P. C., *et al.* "William Byrd." *Tudor Church Music* II, xi. London, 1922.

Fellowes, E. H. *William Byrd.* 2nd ed. London, 1948.

Palmer, William. "Byrd and Amen." *Music and Letters* XXXIV (1953), 140 ff.

Westrup, J. A. "William Byrd (1543–1623)." *Music and Letters* XXIV (1943), 125 ff.

Calvin, John

Blankenburg, Walter. "Calvin." *MGG* II (1952), 653–66.

Büsser, Fritz. "Calvin und die Kirchenmusik." *Musik und Gottesdienst* III (1949), 97 ff.

Geering, Arnold. "Calvin und die Musik." *Calvin-Studien.* Ed. by J. Moltmann. Neukirchen, 1960.

Schild, Emilie. "Calvins Vermächtnis an die evangelische Kirchenmusik." *Musik und Kirche* XIV (1942), 36 ff.

Tappolet, Willy. "Genf." *MGG* IV (1955), 1741 ff.

Capricornus, Samuel Friedrich

Buchner, Hans. "Samuel Friedrich Capricornus." Dissertation, Munich, 1922.

Caulery, Jean

Becker, Georges. *Jean Caulery et ses chansons spirituelles. Notice biographique et bibliographique publiée avec la musique de deux chansons.* Paris, 1880.

Certon, Pierre

Lesure, François. "Pierre Certon." *MGG* II (1952), 974 ff.

Chapin, family

Hamm, Charles. "The Chapins and Sacred Music in the South and West." *Journal of Research in Music Education* VIII (1960), 91–98.

Scholten, James William. "The Chapins: A Study of Men and Sacred Music West of the Alleghenies, 1795–1842." Ed.D. dissertation, University of Michigan, 1972.

Coclico, Adrianus Petit

Crevel, Markus van. *Adrianus Petit Coclico. Leben und Beziehungen eines nach Deutschland emigrierten Josquin-Schülers.* The Hague, 1940.

Crassot, Richard

Gaillard, Paul-André. "Richard Crassot." *MGG* II (1952), 1768 f.

Croft, William

Carpenter, Adrian. "William Croft's Church Music." *Musical Times* CXII (1971), 175.

Crüger, Johann

Blankenburg, Walter. "Johann Crüger." *MGG* II (1952), 1799 ff.

Fischer-Krückeberg, Elisabeth. "Johann Crüger und das Kirchenlied." *Monatsschrift für Gottesdienst und kirchliche Kunst* XXXIV (1929), 310 ff.

_____. "Johann Crügers Choralbearbeitungen." *Zeitschrift für Musikwissenschaft* XIV (1931), 248 ff.

_____. "Johann Crügers Praxis pietatis melica." *Jahrbuch für Brandenburgische Kirchengeschichte* XXVI (1931), 27 ff.

_____. "Zur Geschichte des reformierten Gesangbuchs . . . Johann Crüger." *Jahrbuch für Brandenburgische Kirchengeschichte* XXV (1930), 156 ff.

Dagues, Pierre

Fornaçon, Siegfried. "Pierre Dagues." *Musik und Gottesdienst* XII (1958), 79 ff.

Gaillard, Paul-André. "Pierre Dagues." *MGG* II (1952), 1858 f.

Dahle, John

Hoyem, Nell Marie. "John Dahle: A Positive Influence in the Development of Church Music in the American Mid-West 1876–1931." Ph.D. dissertation, University of Minnesota, 1967.

Daser, Ludwig

Kellogg, King. "Die Messen von Ludwig Daser." Dissertation, Munich, 1935.

Marquardt, Hans. "Die Stuttgarter Chorbücher." Dissertation, Tübingen, 1934.

Davisson, Ananias

Harley, Rachel Augusta Brett. "Ananias Davisson: Southern Tune-Book Compiler (1780–1857)." Ph.D. dissertation, University of Michigan, 1972.

Dedekind, Constantin Christian

Stege, Fritz. "Constantin Christian Dedekind." Dissertation, Berlin, 1922.

_____. "Constantin Christian Dedekind." *Zeitschrift für Musikwissenschaft* VIII (1925–26), 476 ff.

Demantius, Christoph

Kade, Reinhard. "Chr. Demant." *Vierteljahrsschrift für Musikwissenschaft* VI (1890), 469–552.

Dett, Robert Nathaniel

McBrier, Vivian Flagg. "The Life and Works of Robert Nathaniel Dett." Studies in Music No. 32. Ph.D. dissertation, Catholic University of America, 1967.

Wilson, J. Harrison. "A Study and Performance of *The Ordering of Moses* by Robert Nathaniel Dett." D.M.A. dissertation, University of Southern California, 1971.

Dickinson, Clarence

Rogal, Samuel. "Clarence Dickinson Dies at 96." *The Hymn* XX/4 (October, 1969).

Dietrich, Sixt

Zenck, Hermann. *Sixt Dietrich.* Leipzig, 1928; reprinted in *Erbe Deutscher Musik, Reichsdenkmale* XXIII, Leipzig, 1942.

Distler, Hugo

Rauchhaupt, Ursula von. "Die vokale Kirchenmusik Hugo Distlers. Die liturgische Praxis an St. Jakobi in Lübeck von 1930–1937 und Distlers Kompositionsstil in ihrem wechselseitigen Verhältnis, dargestellt an ausgewählten Beispielen." Dissertation, Hamburg, 1960.

———. *Die vokale Kirchenmusik Hugo Distlers. Eine Studie zum Thema "Musik und Gottesdienst."* Gütersloh, 1963.

Doles, Johann Friedrich

Banning, Helmut. "Johann Friedrich Doles. Leben und Werke." Dissertation, Berlin, 1939.

Blume, Friedrich. "Doles." *MGG* III (1954), 627 ff.

Dressler, Gallus

Luther, Wilhelm Martin. *Gallus Dressler.* Dissertation, Göttingen, 1936; published, Kassel, 1941.

Düben, family

Lindberg, Folke. "Düben." *MGG* III (1954), 865.

Ducis, Benedict

Bartha, Dénes. *Benedict Ducis und Appenzeller.* Wolfenbüttel, 1930.

Borren, Charles van den. "Benedictus de Opitiis." *Musica Sacra* XXXIV (1927).

Dulichius, Philipp

Kittler, Günther. "Philipp Dulichius." *Monatsblätter der Gesellschaft für pommersche Geschichte* . . . LI (1937), 1–7.

Schwartz, Rudolf. "Ein pommerscher Lassus." *Monatsschrift für Gottesdienst und kirchliche Kunst* I (1896), 50 ff., and V (1901), 117.

———. "Introduction." *Denkmäler Deutscher Tonkunst* XXXI (1907) and XLI (1911).

Eccard, Johann

Brinkmann, E. "Neue Forschungen zum Leben der grossen Mühlhäuser Musiker." In the *Armin Tille Festschrift* 190–97. Weimar, 1930.

Winterfeld, Carl von. *Der ev. Kirchengesang.* 3 vols. Leipzig, 1843–47.

————. *Zur Geschichte heiliger Tonkunst.* Leipzig, 1850.

Eckhard, Jacob

Williams, George W. "Jacob Eckhard and His Choirmaster's Book." *Journal of the American Musicological Society* VII (1954).

Elsbeth, Thomas

Grimm, Heinrich. *Meister der Renaissancemusik an der Viadrina.* Frankfurt/Oder, 1942.

Hampel, Norbert. "Deutschsprachige prot. Kirchenmusik Schlesiens." Dissertation, Breslau, 1937.

Erlebach, Philipp Heinrich

Baselt, B. "Die Musikaliensammlung der Schwarzburg-Rudolstädtischen Hofkapelle." *Traditionen und Aufgabe der Hallischen Musikwissenschaft.* 1963.

————. "Der Rudolstädter Hofkapellmeister Philipp Heinrich Erlebach." Dissertation, Halle, 1963.

Kinkeldey, Otto. "Introduction." *Denkmäler Deutscher Tonkunst* XLVI–XLVII (1914).

l'Estocart, Pascal de

Lesure, François. "Pascal de l'Estocart." *MGG* III (1954), 1577 ff.

Fabricius, Werner

Günther, Siegfried. *Die geistliche Konzertmusik von Thomas Selle.* Giessen, 1935.

Fasch, Johann Friedrich

Engelke, Bernhard. "Johann Friedrich Fasch." Dissertation, Leipzig, 1908.

————. "Johann Friedrich Fasch." *Sammelbände der Internationalen Musikgesellschaft* X (1908–09), 263–83.

Schünemann, Georg. *Die Singakademie zu Berlin.* Regensburg, 1941.

Figulus, Wolfgang

Brennecke, Wilfried. "Zwei Beiträge zum mehrstimmigen Weihnachtslied des 16. Jh., II, Das Weihnachtsliederbuch des C. Freundt." *Musikforschung* VI (1953), 313 ff.

Clemen, O. "Ein Buch aus dem Besitz des Wolfgang Figulus." *Zeitschrift für Musikwissenschaft* XI (1929), 441 ff.

Eitner, Robert. "Wolfgang Figulus." *Monatshefte für Musikgeschichte* IX (1877), 126 ff.

Flor, Christian

Epstein, Peter. "Ein unbekanntes Passions-Oratorium von Chr. Flor." *Bach-Jahrbuch* (1930), 56–99.

Schulz, Walther. "Studien über das . . . Kirchenlied des 17. Jh." Dissertation, Breslau, 1934.

Wolffheim, Werner. "Die Möllersche Handschrift." *Bach-Jahrbuch* (1912), 56 ff.

Forchhammer, Theophil

Schmidt, Peter. *Theophil Forchhammer, ein unbekannter Meister des 19. Jahrhunderts. Beitrag zur Geschichte der liturgischen Orgelmusik.* Kiel, 1937.

Förster, Kaspar, father and son

Rauschning, Hermann. *Geschichte der Musik . . . in Danzig.* Danzig, 1931.
Schering, Arnold. *Geschichte des Oratoriums,* 158–61. Leipzig, 1911.
Sørensen, Søren. "Monteverdi–Förster–Buxtehude." *Dansk Aarbog for Musikforskning* III (1963).
Wolffheim, Werner. "Gedenksäule Kaspar Försters." *Archiv für Musikwissenschaft* II (1920), 289–92.

Förtsch, Johann Philipp

Kümmerling, Harald. "Johann Philipp Förtsch als Kantatenkomponist." Dissertation, Halle, 1956.
Stahl, Wilhelm. *Musikgeschichte Lübecks* II. Kassel, 1952.
Weidemann, Carla. *Leben und Wirken des J. Ph. Förtsch.* Kassel, 1955.

Foster, Stephen Collins

Atkins, Charles L. "The Hymns of Stephen Collins Foster." *The Hymn* XII/2 (April, 1961).

Franc, Guillaume

Fornaçon, Siegfried. "Guillaume Franc." *Musik und Gottesdienst* VIII (1953), 105 ff.
Gaillard, Paul-André. "Guillaume Franc." *MGG* IV (1954), 619 f.

Franck, Johann Wolfgang

Klages, Richard. "Johann Wolfgang Franck, Lebensgeschichte und geistliche Kompositionen." Dissertation, Hamburg, 1937.
Schmidt, Günther. *Die Musik am Hofe der Markgrafen von Brandenburg-Ansbach.* Dissertation, Munich, 1953; published, Kassel, 1956.
Schultze, K. E. "Johann Wolfgang Franck und die Ahnen seiner Kinder." *Musikforschung* XIII (1960), 173–78.
Werner, Arno. "Johann Wolfgang Francks Flucht aus Ansbach." *Sammelbände der Internationalen Musikgesellschaft* XV (1913–14).
Zelle, Friedrich. *Johann Wolfgang Franck.* Berlin, 1889.

Francke, August Hermann

Blankenburg, Walter. "A. H. Francke." *MGG* IV (1954), 683 ff.
Förster, Th. "August Hermann Francke." *Realenzyklopädie für Theologie und Kirche* VI, 150 ff.
Leube, A. "August Hermann Francke." *Die Religion in Geschichte und Gegenwart.* 2nd ed. II, 651 ff.
Serauky, Walter. *Musikgeschichte der Stadt Halle* II/1. Halle, 1939.
Sommer, F. *August Hermann Francke und seine Stiftungen.* Halle, 1927.

Freundt, Cornelius

Brennecke, Wilfried. "Zwei Beiträge zum mehrstimmigen Weihnachtslied des 16. Jahrhunderts." *Musikforschung* V (1952), 166 ff., and VI (1953), 313 ff.
Göhler, Georg. "Cornelius Freundt." Dissertation, Leipzig, 1896.

Friderici, Daniel

Ruhnke, Martin. *Joachim Burmeister.* Dissertation, Kiel, 1954; published, Kassel, 1955.
Voll, Wolfgang. *Daniel Friderici.* Dissertation, Rostock, 1933; published, Kassel, 1936.

Funcke, Friedrich

Fock, Gustav. *Der junge Bach in Lüneburg.* Hamburg, 1950.
Junghans, W. *J. S. Bach als Schüler . . . in Lüneburg.* Lüneburg, 1870.
Kümmerle, Salomon. *Enzyklopädie der ev. Kirchenmusik* I. Gütersloh, 1888.

Gerhardt, Paul

Aullen, E. *Quellen und Stil der Lieder P. Gerhardts.* Bern, 1912.
Nelle, Wilhelm. "Paul Gerhardt und J. S. Bach." *Bach-Jahrbuch* (1907), 11 ff.
————. *Paul Gerhardts Lieder und Gedichte.* Hamburg, 1907.
Petrich, H. *Paul Gerhardt.* 3rd ed. Berlin, 1914.
Spitta, Friedrich. "Paul Gerhardts Lieder u. d. Musik." *Monatsschrift für Gottesdienst und kirchliche Kunst* XII (1907), 84 ff.
Zeller, Winfried. "P. Gerhardt." *Musik und Kirche* XXVII (1957), 161 ff.

Gerstenbüttel, Joachim

Krüger, Liselotte. *Die Hamburgische Musikorganisation im 17. Jahrhundert.* Strasbourg and Zurich, 1933.

Gesius, Bartholomäus

Blumenthal, Paul. *Der Kantor Bartholomäus Gesius.* Frankfurt/Oder, 1926.
Grimm, Heinrich. *Meister der Renaissancemusik an der Viadrina.* Berlin, 1942.
Schönherr, Friedrich Wilhelm. "Bartholomäus Gesius." Dissertation, Leipzig, 1920.

Geuck, Valentin

Gutbier, Ewald. "Valentin Geuck und Landgraf Moritz als Verfasser einer Musiklehre." *Hessisches Jahrbuch für Landesgeschichte* X (1960), 212–28.

Gibbons, Orlando

Armstrong, Thomas. *Orlando Gibbons.* The Heritage of Music, III. London, 1951.
Buck, P. C., *et al.* "Orlando Gibbons." *Tudor Church Music* IV, xi. London, 1925.
Colles, H. C. "A Master of Song." *Essays and Lectures.* London, 1945.
Fellowes, E. H. *Orlando Gibbons.* London, 1951; repr., 1970.
Palmer, William. "Gibbons's Verse Anthems." *Music and Letters* XXXV (1954), 107.

Glaser, Johann Wendelin

Treiber, Richard. "Kantor Johann Wendelin Glaser (1713 bis 1783) und die Wertheimer Kirchenmusik im 18. Jahrhundert." *Jahrbuch des Historischen Vereins "Alt-Wertheim"* (1936), 39–57, and (1937), 37–76.

Goudimel, Claude

Becker, Georges. "Goudimel et son oeuvre." *Bulletin de la société d'histoire du protestantisme français* XXXIV (1885), 337 ff.
Gaillard, Paul-André. "Claude Goudimel." *MGG* V (1956), 584 ff.
————. "Zum Werkverzeichnis Claude Goudimels." *Jahrbuch für Liturgik und Hymnologie* I (1955), 123.

Lesure, François. "Claude Goudimel." *Musica Disciplina* 1948, 225 ff.

Trillat, Ennemond. *Claude Goudimel, le Psautier huguenot et le Saint-Barthélemy lyonnais.* Lyon, 1949.

Graupner, Christoph

Nagel, Wilibald. "Das Leben Christoph Graupners." *Sammelbände der Internationalen Musikgesellschaft* X (1908–09).

Noack, Friedrich. "Bachs und Graupners Kompositionen zur Bewerbung um das Thomaskantorat in Leipzig." *Bach-Jahrbuch* X (1913).

———. *Christoph Graupners Kirchenmusiken.* Leipzig, 1916.

———. "J. S. Bach und Chr. Graupner. 'Mein Herze schwimmt im Blut.' " *Archiv für Musikwissenschaft* II (1919–20).

Greene, Maurice

Graves, Richard. "The Forty Anthems of Maurice Greene." *Musical Times* XCI (1950), 24.

Walker, Ernest. "The Bodleian Manuscripts of Maurice Greene." *Musical Antiquary* I (1909–10), 149, 203.

Greitter, Matthäus (Matthias)

Fornaçon, Siegfried. "Matthias Greitter." *Die Hugenottenkirche.* Berlin, 1954.

Grimm, Heinrich

Lorenzen, Hermann. "Der Kantor Heinrich Grimm." Dissertation, Hamburg, 1940.

Riemer, Otto. "Heinrich Grimm, ein mitteldeutscher Musiker." In the *A. Schering Festschrift,* 180 ff. Berlin, 1937.

Guéroult, Guillaume

Becker, Georges. *Guillaume Guéroult et ses chansons spirituelles. Notice biographique et bibliographique publiée avec la musique de deux chansons.* Paris, 1880.

Gumpelzhaimer, Adam

Mayr, Otto. *Adam Gumpelzhaimer.* Dissertation, Munich, 1907; published, Augsburg, 1908. "Introduction," *Denkmäler der Tonkunst in Bayern* X/2 (1909).

Wessely, Othmar. "J. Entzenmüller, der Lehrer Adam Gumpelzhaimers." *Musikforschung* VII (1954), 65 f.

Haeffner, Johann Christian Friedrich

Engländer, Richard. "Haeffner." *MGG* V (1956), 1224 f.

Hainlein, Paul

Seiffert, Max. "Introduction." *Denkmäler der Tonkunst in Bayern* VI/1 (1905).

Zirnbauer, H. "L. F. Behaim." *Mitteilungen des Vereins für die Geschichte der Stadt Nürnberg* L (1960), 330–51.

Haman, Johann Georg

Müller-Blattau, Josef. *Haman und Herder in ihren Beziehungen zur Musik. Mit einem Anhang ungedruckter Kantatendichtungen und Liedmelodien aus Herders Nachlass.* Schriften der Kgl. Deutschen Gesellschaft zu Königsberg i. Pr., VI. Königsberg i. Pr., 1931.

Hammerschmidt, Andreas

Leichtentritt, Hugo. "Introduction." *Denkmäler Deutscher Tonkunst* XL (1910).
Schmidt, A. W. "Introduction." *Denkmäler der Tonkunst in Österreich* VIII/1 (1901).
Schünemann, Georg. "Beiträge zur Biographie Andreas Hammerschmidts." *Sammelbände der Internationalen Musikgesellschaft* XII (1910–11), 207 ff.

Hanff, Nikolaus

Holm, Theodora. "Neue Daten zur Lebensgeschichte Nikolaus Hanffs." *Musikforschung* VII (1954), 455 ff.
Schilling, Hans. "Tobias Ennicelius, Friedrich Meister, Nikolaus Hanff." Dissertation, Kiel, 1934.

Hardy, Thomas

Grew, Eva Mary. "Thomas Hardy as Musician." *Music and Letters* XXI (1940), 120 ff.
Hardy, Florence E. *The Early Life of Thomas Hardy.* London, 1928.

Harnisch, Otto Siegfried

Hiekel, Hans Otto. "Otto Siegfried Harnisch." Dissertation, Hamburg, 1956.

Hartmann, Johann Peter Emilius

Hove, Richard. *J. P. E. Hartmann.* Copenhagen, 1934.

Hasse, Johann Adolf

Müller, Walther. "Johann Adolf Hasse als Kirchenkomponist. Ein Beitrag zur Geschichte der neapolitanischen Kirchenmusik." Dissertation, Leipzig, 1910.

Hasse, Peter and Nikolaus

Hennings, Johann. "Das Musikergeschlecht der Hasse." *Musikforschung* II (1949), 50 ff.
Reimann, Margarete. "Pasticcios und Parodien." *Musikforschung* VIII (1955), 265 ff.
Stahl, Wilhelm. *Musikgeschichte Lübecks* II. Kassel, 1952.

Hassler, Hans Leo and his brothers

Bäuerle, Hermann. "Hasslers Messen." *Musica Sacra* LXVI (1936).
Sandberger, Adolf. "Bemerkungen zur Biographie Hans Leo Hasslers und seiner Brüder." *Denkmäler der Tonkunst in Bayern* V/1 (1904).
Schmid, Ernst Fritz. "Hans Leo Hassler und seine Brüder." *Zeitschrift des historischen Vereins für Schwaben* LIV (1941), 61–212.

Hastings, Thomas

Scanlon, Mary B. "Thomas Hastings." *Musical Quarterly* XXXII (1946), 265–77.

Helmbold, Ludwig

Birtner, Herbert. "Ein Beitrag zur Geschichte der protestant. Musik im 16. Jahrhundert." *Zeitschrift für Musikwissenschaft* X (1927–28), 457–94.

Thilo, W. *Ludwig Helmbold nach Leben und Dichten.* Berlin, 1851.

Hemmel, Sigmund

Uebele, Gerhard. "Anfänge der prot. Kirchenmusik in Württemberg und Sigmund Hemmels Psalter." *Württemberg Blätter für Kirchenmusik* (1934), 142 ff.

Henrici, Christian Friedrich (Picander)

Flossmann, Paul. "Picander." Dissertation, Leipzig, 1899.

Smend, Friedrich. "Neue Bachfunde." *Archiv für Musikwissenschaft* VII (1942), 3 ff.

Tagliavini, Luigi Ferdinando. *Studi sui testi delle cantate sacre di J. S. Bach.* Padua and Kassel, 1956.

Hensel, Walther

Vötterle, Karl. "Walther Hensel und die evangelische Kirchenmusik." *Musik und Kirche* XXVII (1957), 102 ff.

Herbst, Andreas

Epstein, Peter. "Die Frankfurter Kapellmusik zur Zeit Johann Andreas Herbsts." *Archiv für Musikwissenschaft* VI (1924), 85–102.

———. "Johann Andreas Herbsts geistliche Kompositionen." *Kongressbericht Leipzig 1925–26,* 368 ff.

———. *Kirchliche Musikhandschriften der Stadtbibliothek Frankfurt.* Frankfurt, 1926.

———. "Das Musikwesen der Stadt Frankfurt/M. z. Z. des Johann Andreas Herbst." Dissertation, Breslau, 1923.

Herbst, John

Falconer, Joan Ormsby. "Bishop John Herbst (1735–1812), an American Moravian Musician, Collector, and Composer." Ph.D. dissertation, Columbia University, 1969.

Herder, Johann Gottfried

Günther, Hans. "Johann Gottfried Herders Stellung zur Musik." Dissertation, Leipzig, 1903.

Hoffmann, Karl. "Herder und die evangelische Kirchenmusik." *Musik und Kirche* VII (1935), 121–27.

Ingen, Ferdinand van. "Herders kirchenmusikalische Anschauungen." *Musik und Kirche* XXXIII (1963), 193 ff.

Müller-Blattau, Josef. *Haman und Herder in ihren Beziehungen zur Musik. Mit einem Anhang ungedruckter Kantatendichtungen und Liedmelodien aus Herders Nachlass.* Schriften der Kgl. Deutschen Gesellschaft zu Königsberg i. Pr., VI. Königsberg i. Pr., 1931.

Schünemann, Georg. "Reichardts Briefwechsel mit Herder." In the *Max Schneider Festschrift.* Halle, 1935.

Wiora, Walter. "Herders Ideen zur Geschichte der Musik." *Im Geiste Herders,* 73 ff. Ed. by E. Keyser. Kitzingen, 1953.

Herzogenberg, Heinrich von

Altmann, Wilhelm. "Heinrich von Herzogenberg. Sein Leben und Schaffen." *Die Musik* II/19 (1903), 28–47.

Spitta, Friedrich. "Heinrich von Herzogenberg." *Monatsschrift für Gottesdienst und kirchliche Kunst* V (1900), 113–20.

————. "Heinrich von Herzogenbergs Bedeutung für die evangelische Kirchenmusik." *Jahrbuch Peters* XXVI (1919), 34–55.

Heugel, Johann

Knierim, Julius. "Die Heugel-Handschriften der Kasseler Landesbibliothek." Dissertation, Berlin, 1943.

Nagel, Wilibald. "Johann Heugel." *Sammelbände der Internationalen Musikgesellschaft* VII (1905–06).

Hewitt, James

Wayne, John Waldorf. "James Hewitt: His Life and Works." Ph.D. dissertation, Indiana University, 1969.

Hewitt, John Hill

Huggins, Coy Elliott. "John Hill Hewitt: Bard of the Confederacy." Ph.D. dissertation, Florida State University, 1964.

Holden, Oliver

McCormick, David W. "Oliver Holden, Composer and Anthologist." D.S.M. dissertation, Union Theological Seminary, 1963.

————. "Oliver Holden 1765–1844." *The Hymn* XIV/3 (July, 1963).

Holyoke, Samuel

Willhide, J. Lawrence. "Samuel Holyoke, American Music-Educator." Ph.D. dissertation, University of Southern California, 1954.

Hopkinson, Francis

Sonneck, O. G. *Francis Hopkinson, the First American Poet-Composer (1737–1791) and James Lyon, Patriot, Preacher, Psalmodist (1735–1794). Two Studies in Early American Music.* Washington, 1905.

Humfrey, Pelham

Dennison, Peter. "The Church Music of Pelham Humfrey." *Proceedings of the Royal Musical Association* XCVIII (1971–72), 65.

Huygens, Constantijn

Noske, Frits. "Constantin Huygens." *MGG* VI (1957), 582 ff.

————. "Rondom het orgeltractaat van Constantijn Huygens." *Tijdschrift voor Muziekwetenschap* XVII (1956), 1 ff.

Jeep, Johann

Brennecke, Wilfried. "Das Hohenlohesche Gesangbuch von 1629 und J. Jeep." *Jahrbuch für Liturgik und Hymnologie* IV (1958–59), 41–72.

Giesecke, G. "Johann Jeep." *Zeitschrift der Gesellschaft für niedersächsische Kirchengeschichte* XLI (1936), 256–61.

Jorissen, Matthias

Henn, Friedrich August. *Matthias Jorissen. Der deutsche Psalmist in Leben und Werk.* Leipzig, 1955.

Kaminski, Heinrich

Samson, Ingrid. "Das Vokalschaffen von Heinrich Kaminski mit Ausnahme der Opern." Dissertation, Frankfurt/M., 1956.

Stein, Fritz. "Heinrich Kaminskis Chorwerke." *Musikpflege* I (1930–31), 477.

Keiser, Reinhard

Petzold, Richard. *Die Kirchenkompositionen und weltlichen Kantaten Reinhard Keisers.* Düsseldorf, 1935.

Kelley, Edgar Stillman

King, Maurice R. "Edgar Stillman Kelley: American Composer, Teacher, and Author." Ph.D. dissertation, Florida State University, 1970.

Kelpius, John

Williams, H. Francis. "John Kelpius, Pietist." *New World* III/10 (June, 1894).

Kimball, Jacob, Jr.

Wilcox, Glenn. "Jacob Kimball, Jr. (1761–1826). His Life and Works." Ph.D. dissertation, University of Southern California, 1957.

Kindermann, Erasmus

Samuel, H. E. "The Cantata in Nuremberg during the 17th Century." Dissertation, Cornell University, 1958.

Kittel, Johann Christian

Dreetz, Albert. *Johann Christian Kittel, der letzte Bach-Schüler.* Leipzig, 1932.

Klein, Bernhard

Koch, Carl. "Bernhard Klein (1793–1832). Sein Leben und seine Werke. Ein Beitrag zur Musikgeschichte, im besonderen Berlins." Dissertation, Rostock, Leipzig, 1902.

Knecht, Justinus Heinrich

Kauffmann, Ernst Friedrich. *Justinus Heinrich Knecht, ein schwäbischer Tonsetzer des 18. Jahrhunderts.* Tübingen, 1892.

Knöfel, Johann

Scholz, W. "Zu Johann Knöfel." *Archiv für Musikwissenschaft* VII (1942), 228 f.

Knüpfer, Sebastian

Schering, Arnold. *Musikgeschichte Leipzigs* II. Leipzig, 1926; and "Introduction," *Denkmäler Deutscher Tonkunst* LVIII–LIX (1918).

Serauky, Walter. *Musikgeschichte der Stadt Halle* II/1, and supplements. Halle, 1939–40.

Köler, David

Eismann, Georg. "David Köler." Dissertation, Erlangen, 1942.

———. *David Köler*. Berlin, 1956.

Krieger, Adam

Osthoff, Helmuth. *Adam Krieger*. Leipzig, 1929.

———. "Neue Quellen zu Adam Krieger." *Archiv für Musikforschung* VII (1942), 71 ff.

Krieger, Johann Philipp

Samuel, H. E. *The Cantata in Nuremberg during the 17th Century*. Dissertation, Cornell University, 1958.

Seiffert, Max. "Introduction." *Denkmäler Deutscher Tonkunst* LIII–LIV (1916).

Kuhnau, Johann

Münnich, Rudolf. "Kuhnaus Leben." *Sammelbände der Internationalen Musikgesellschaft* III (1901–02), 473 ff.

Schering, Arnold. *Musikgeschichte Leipzigs* II. Leipzig, 1918.

———. "Über die Kirchenkantaten vorbachscher Kantoren." *Bach-Jahrbuch* IX (1912), 86 ff.; and "Introduction," *Denkmäler Deutscher Tonkunst* LVIII–LIX (1918).

Kühnhausen, Johann Georg

Adrio, Adam. "Die Matthäuspassion von Johann Georg Kühnhausen." In the *A. Schering Festschrift*. Berlin, 1937.

Lange, Gregor

Hampel, Norbert. "Deutschsprachige prot. Kirchenmusik Schlesiens." Dissertation, Breslau, 1930.

Law, Andrew

Crawford, Richard, and H. Wiley Hitchcock. "The Papers of Andrew Law in the William L. Clements Library." *University Library Bulletin* LXVIII (Ann Arbor, 1961).

Lowens, Irving. "Andrew Law and the Pirates." *Journal of the American Musicological Society* XIII (1960), 206–23.

———. "Copyright and Andrew Law." *Papers of the Bibliographical Society of America* LIII (1959), 150–59.

Lassus, Roland de

Bötticher, Wolfgang. *Aus Orlando di Lassos Wirkungskreis*. Kassel, 1963.

———. *Orlando di Lasso und seine Zeit, 1532–1594*, 2 vols. Kassel, 1958 f.

Winterfeld, Carl von. "Das Verhältnis des Orlandus Lassus zu den Psalm-Melodien der französischen Singweisen. . . ." *Zur Geschichte heiliger Tonkunst* II, 54 ff. Leipzig, 1852.

Laub, Thomas

Hamburger, Povl. *Bibliografisk Fortegnelse over Th. Laubs litteraere og musikalske Arbejder.* Copenhagen, 1932.

————. *Thomas Laub. Hans Liv og Gerning.* Copenhagen, 1942.

Jensen, Jørgen I. "Musikalsk isolation og gudstjenstligt faellesskab i Thomas Laubs to tidlige skrifter." *Dansk Kirkesangs aarsskrift* (1971–72), 34–52.

Lechner, Leonhard

Ameln, Konrad. "Herkunft und Datierung der Handschrift Mus. fol. 15. . . ." *Musikforschung* VI (1953), 156–58.

————. "L. Lechner." *Lebensbilder aus Schwaben und Franken* VII, 70 ff. Stuttgart, 1960.

————. "Leonhard Lechner." *Musik und Kirche* XXVI (1956), 223–31.

————. *Leonhard Lechner.* Lüdenscheid, 1957.

Schreiber, Max. "Leonhard Lechner Athesinus." Dissertation, Munich, 1932.

Le Jeune, Claude

Walker, D.-P., and François Lesure. *"Claude le Jeune and 'Musique mesurée.'"* *Musica Disiplina* III (1949), 151 ff.

Le Maistre, Matthäus

Kade, Otto. *Matthäus Le Maistre.* Mainz, 1862.

Lindeman, Ole Andreas

Hernes, Asbjörn. *Ole Andreas Lindeman og has tid.* Oslo, 1956.

Loewe, Carl

Anton, Karl. *Beiträge zur Biographie Carl Loewes mit besonderer Berücksichtigung seiner Oratorien und Ideen zu einer volkstümlichen Ausgestaltung der protestantischen Kirchenmusik. . . .* Halle, 1912.

Hirschberg, Leopold. "Carl Loewe als Kirchenkomponist." *Die Musik* IV/2 (1904–05), 383–406.

Loewe, Carl. *Selbstbiographie.* Ed. by C. H. Bitter. Berlin, 1870

Louis, Jean

Gaillard, Paul-André. "Essai sur le rapport des sources mélodiques des Psaulmes cinquantes de Jean Louis (Anvers, 1555) et de Souterliedekens (Anvers, 1540)." *International Musicological Society congress. Utrecht, 1952.* Amsterdam, 1953.

Lübeck, Vincent

Rubardt, Paul. "Vincent Lübeck." Dissertation, Leipzig, 1920.

————. "Vincent Lübeck." *Archiv für Musikwissenschaft* VI (1924), 450 ff.

Luther, Martin

Abert, Hermann. "Luther und die Musik." *Gesammelte Schriften und Vorträge.* Ed. by F. Blume. Halle, 1929.

Blankenburg, Walter. "Luther." *MGG* VIII (1960), 1334 ff.

Honemeyer, Karl. "Luthers Musikanschauung. Studien zur Frage ihrer geschichtlichen Grundlagen." Dissertation, Munich, 1941.

Mahrenholz, Christhard. *Luther und die Kirchenmusik.* Kassel, 1937; also in *Musicologica et Liturgica. Gesammelte Aufsätze,* ed. by K. F. Müller, Kassel, 1960.

Preuss, Hans. *Martin Luther, der Künstler.* Gütersloh, 1931.

Wetzel, Christoph. "Die theologische Bedeutung der Musik im Leben und Denken Martin Luthers." Dissertation, Munich, 1954.

Lyon, James

Sonneck, O. G. *Francis Hopkinson, the First American Poet-Composer (1737–1791) and James Lyon, Patriot, Preacher, Psalmodist (1735–1794). Two Studies in Early American Music.* Washington, 1905.

Mancinus, Thomas

Flechsig, W. "Thomas Mancinus." *Jahrbuch des Braunschweig. Geschichtsvereins.* New series, IV (1932), and Wolfenbüttel, 1933.

Ruhnke, Martin. *Beiträge zu einer Geschichte der deutschen Hofmusikkollegien im 16. Jahrundert.* Berlin, 1963.

Mareschall, Samuel

Kendall, William Raymond. "The Life and Works of Samuel Mareschall." *Musical Quarterly* XXX (1944).

_____. "Samuel Mareschall. His Life and Works (1554–1640)." Dissertation, Cornell University, 1940.

Linden, Albert van der. "La Légende d'un Psautier perdu de Samu ' Mareschall." *Hommage à Ch. van den Borren.* Antwerpen, 1945.

Marot, Clément

Douen, Orentin. *Clément Marot et le Psautier Huguenot.* 2 vols. Paris, 1878–79.

Mason, Lowell

Ellis, Howard. "Lowell Mason and the Manual of the Boston Academy of Music." *Journal of Research in Music Education* III (1955), 3–10.

Mason, Daniel Gregory. "A Glimpse of Lowell Mason From an Old Bundle of Letters." *New Music Review and Church Music Review* XXVI/302 (1927), 49–52.

_____. "Some Unpublished Journals of Dr. Lowell Mason." *New Music Review and Church Music Review* IX/108 (1910), 577–81, and X/110 (1911), 62–67.

Mason, Henry L. *Hymn Tunes of Lowell Mason. A Bibliography.* Cambridge, Mass., 1944.

_____. *Lowell Mason. An Appreciation of His Life and Work.* New York, 1941.

Pemberton, Carol Ann. "Lowell Mason: His Life and Work." Ph.D. dissertation, University of Minnesota, 1971.

Rich, Arthur L. *Lowell Mason.* Chapel Hill, 1946.

Thayer, Alexander W. "Lowell Mason." *Dwight's Journal of Music* XXXIX/1007 (Nov. 22, 1879), 186–87, and 1008 (Dec. 6, 1879), 195–96.

Mattheson, Johann

Becker, Heinz. "Johann Matthesons handschriftliche Einzeichnungen. . . ." *Musikforschung* V (1952), 346–50.

Braun, Werner. "Johann Mattheson und die Aufklärung." Dissertation, Halle, 1952.

Cannon, B. C. *Johann Mattheson.* New Haven, 1947.

Meiland, Jakob

Oppel, Reinhard. *Jakob Meiland.* Pfungstadt, 1911.

Schmidt, Günther. *Die Musik am Hofe der Markgrafen von Brandenburg-Ansbach.* Kassel, 1956.

Meister, Johann Friedrich

Schilling, Hans. "Tobias Ennicelius, Friedrich Meister, Nikolaus Hanff." Dissertation, Kiel, 1934.

Mendelssohn, Arnold

Hering, Hermann. "Arnold Mendelssohn. Die Grundlagen seines Schaffens und seine Werke." Dissertation, Marburg, 1929.

Mendelssohn-Bartholdy, Felix

Werner, Rudolf. "Felix Mendelssohn-Bartholdy als Kirchenmusiker." Dissertation, Frankfurt a. M., 1930.

Merbecke, John

Colles, H. C. "John Merbecke." *Essays and Lectures,* 125 ff. London, 1945.

Terry, R. R. "John Merbecke." *Proceedings of the Musical Association* XLV (1918–19).

Merkel, Gustav

Janssen, Paul. *Gustav Merkel, kgl. sächs. Hoforganist. Ein Bild seines Lebens und Wirkens.* Leipzig, 1886.

Meyer, Gregor

Fornaçon, Siegfried. "Gregor Meyer." *Musik und Gottesdienst* X (1956), 65 ff.

Michael, Rogier and Tobias

Federhofer, Hellmut. "Jugendjahre und Lehrer Rogier Michaels." *Archiv für Musikwissenschaft* X (1953), 221–32.

Frank, Johannes. "Die Introituskompositionen von Rogier Michael." Dissertation, Giessen, 1937.

Kade, R. "Der Dresdner Kapellmeister Rogier Michael." *Vierteljahrsschrift für Musikwissenschaft* V (1889), 272–89.

Osthoff, Helmuth. "Die Historien Roger Michaels." In the *A. Schering Festschrift,* 166–79. Berlin, 1937.

Moritz, Landgraf von Hessen

Birtner, Herbert. "Heinrich Schütz und Landgraf Moritz von Hessen." *Hessenland* VII–VIII (1935).

Engelbrecht, Christiane. *Die Kasseler Hofkapelle im 17. Jahrhundert.* Kassel, 1958.

Müntzer, Thomas

Thomas Müntzer. Sein Leben und seine Schriften. Edited with an introduction by O. H. Brandt. Berlin, 1932

Natorp, Bernhard Christoph Ludwig

Knab, Hans. *Bernh. Chr. Ludwig Natorp. Ein Beitrag zur Geschichte der Schulmusik in der ersten Hälfte des 19. Jahrhunderts.* Münsterische Beiträge zur Musikwissenschaft, IV. Kassel, 1933.

Neander, Joachim

Iken, J. F. *Joachim Neander. Sein Leben und seine Lieder.* 1880.
Nelle, Wilhelm. *Joachim Neander.* Hamburg, n.d.
Noack, Elisabeth. "Georg Christoph Strattner." Dissertation, Berlin, 1921.
Vormbaum, K. *Joachim Neanders Leben und Lieder.* 1860.

Neithardt, Heinrich August

Thomas, Max. "Heinrich August Neithardt." Dissertation, Berlin, 1959.

Nettleton, Asahel

Birney, George H., Jr. "The Life and Letters of Asahel Nettleton, 1763–1844." Ph.D. dissertation, Hartford Theological Seminary, 1943.

Neumeister, Erdmann

Brausch, P. "Die Kantate." Dissertation, Heidelberg, 1921.
Dürr, Alfred. *Studien über die frühen Kantaten Bachs.* Leipzig, 1951.
Schering, Arnold. *Musikgeschichte Leipzigs* II–III. Leipzig, 1926–41.
Seiffert, Max. "Introduction." *Denkmäler Deutscher Tonkunst* LIII–LIV (1916).
Tagliavini, Luigi Ferdinando. *Studi sui testi delle cantate sacre di J. S. Bach.* Padua and Kassel, 1956.

Nicolai, Philipp

Blankenburg, Walter. "Die Kirchenliedweisen von Philipp Nicolai." *Musik und Kirche* XXVI (1956), 172–76.
———. "Neue Forschungen über Philipp Nicolai." *Jahrbuch für Liturgik und Hymnologie* IV (1958–59), 152 f.

Nielsen, Carl

Meyer, Torben, and Frede Schandorf Petersen. *Carl Nielsen. Kunstneren og Mennesket.* 2 vols. Copenhagen, 1947–48.
Schousboe, Torben. "Barn af huset? Nogle tanker og problemer omkring et utrykt forord til Carl Nielsens 'Salmer og Aandelige Sange.' " *Dansk Kirkesangs aarsskrift* (1969–70), 75–91.

Nopitsch, Christoph Friedrich Wilhelm

Mlynarczyk, Johannes. "Christoph Friedrich Wilhelm Nopitsch, ein Nördlinger Kantatenmeister (1758 bis 1824)." Dissertation, Leipzig, 1928.

Olthof, Statius

Schwartz, Rudolf. "Magister Statius Olthof." *Vierteljahrsschrift für Musikwissenschaft* X (1894), 231 ff.
Widmann, B. "Die Kompositionen der Psalmen von Statius Olthof." *Vierteljahrsschrift für Musikwissenschaft* V (1889), 290–321.

Otto, Georg

Grössel, Heinrich. *Georgius Otto.* Dissertation, Leipzig, 1933; published, Kassel, 1935.

Otto, Stephan

Müller, E. "Musikgeschichte von Freiberg." *Mitt. des Freiberger Altertumsvereins* LXVIII (1939).

Schünemann, Georg. "Die Bewerber um das Freiberger Kantorat." *Archiv für Musikwissenschaft* I (1918).

Pachelbell, Charles Theodore

Redway, Virginia L. "Charles Theodore Pachelbell, Musical Emigrant." *Journal of the American Musicological Society* V (1952).

Pachelbel, Johann

Eggebrecht, Hans Heinrich. "Johann Pachelbel als Vokalkomponist." *Archiv für Musikwissenschaft* XI (1954), 120–45.

Moser, Hans Joachim. "Johann Pachelbel." *Musik und Kirche* XXIII (1953), 82–90.

Nolte, E. V. "The Magnificat Fugues of Johann Pachelbel." *Journal of the American Musicological Society* IX (1956), 19–24.

Seiffert, Max. "Introduction." *Denkmäler der Tonkunst in Bayern* IV/1 (1903), and VI/1 (1905).

———. "Pachelbels 'Musik. Sterbensgedanken.' " *Sammelbände der Internationalen Musikgesellschaft* V (1903–04), 476 ff.

Päminger, Leonhard

Roth, Ilse. *Leonhard Päminger.* Munich, 1935.

Paine, John Knowles

Huxford, John Calvin. "John Knowles Paine: His Life and Works." Ph.D. dissertation, Florida State University, 1968.

Parker, Horatio

Kearns, William Kay. "Horatio Parker 1863–1919: A Study of His Life and Music." Ph.D. dissertation, University of Illinois, 1965.

Semler, Isabel P., and Pierson Underwood. *Horatio Parker.* New York, 1942.

Parry, Sir Charles Hubert Hastings

Fuller-Maitland, J. A. *The Music of Parry and Stanford.* Cambridge, 1934.

Pedersøn, Mogens

Jeppesen, Knud. "Preface." *Dania Sonans* I. Copenhagen, 1933.

Pepping, Ernst

Adrio, Adam. "Ernst Pepping." *Jahrbuch 1954,* for the 110th *Niederheinischen Musikfest* in Düsseldorf.

Dürr, Alfred. "Gedanken zum Kirchenmusik-Schaffen Ernst Peppings." *Musik und Kirche* XXXI (1961), 145–72.

Manicke, Dietrich. "Gesetz und Freiheit. Gedanken zum Schaffen Ernst Peppings." *Kirchenmusik heute.* Ed. by H. Böhm. Berlin, 1959.

Schmidt-Bayreuth, Hans. "Untersuchungen zum Orgelchoral Ernst Peppings." *Musik und Kirche* XXIV (1954), 101–08.

Witte, Gerd. "Gleichnisse geistiger Ordnung (zu Ernst Peppings neuen Bicinien)." *Zeitschrift für Hausmusik* XVIII (1954), 120–23.

————. "Zu Ernst Peppings Psalmbicinien." *Musik und Kirche* XXV (1955), 58–62.

Pfleger, Augustin

Nausch, Annemarie. *Augustin Pfleger.* Dissertation, Kiel, 1942; published, Kassel, 1955.

Stein, Fritz. "Ein unbekannter Evangelien-Jahrgang von Augustin Pfleger." In the *M. Schneider Festschrift.* Halle, 1935.

Pinkham, Daniel

Johnson, Marlowe Wayne. "The Choral Writing of Daniel Pinkham." Ph.D. dissertation, University of Iowa, 1968.

Playford, John

Temperley, Nicholas. "John Playford and the Metrical Psalms." *Journal of the American Musicological Society* XXV/3 (Fall, 1972).

Pohle, David

Engelbrecht, Christiane. *Die Kasseler Hofkapelle im 17. Jahrhundert.* Kassel, 1958.

Serauky, Walter. *Musikgeschichte der Stadt Halle* II/1. Halle, 1935.

Polschitz, Christoph Garent von

Quoika, Rudolf. "Christoph Garent von Polschitz und seine Zeit. Ein Kapitel aus der böhmischen Musikgeschichte der Renaissance." *Musikforschung* VII (1954), 414 ff.

Praetorius, Hieronymus and Jakob

Eitner, Robert. "Jacob Praetorius und seine Familie." *Monatshefte für Musikgeschichte* III (1871), 65–80.

Friederich, Bruno. "Der Vokalstil des Hieronymus Praetorius." Dissertation, Hamburg, 1932.

Hoffmann-Erbrecht, Lothar. "Das Opus Musicum des Jacob Praetorius." *Acta Musicologica* XXVIII (1956), 96–121.

Praetorius, Michael

Blume, Friedrich. "Das Werk des Michael Praetorius." *Zeitschrift für Musikwissenschaft* XVII (1935), 321–31, 482–502; both writings are also published in F. Blume, *Syntagma musicologicum,* 229–74, Kassel, 1963.

Forchert, Arno. *Das Spätwerk des Michael Praetorius.* Berlin, 1959.

Gurlitt, Wilibald. *Michael Praetorius.* Leipzig, 1915.

Ruhnke, Martin. *Beiträge zu einer Geschichte der deutschen Hofmusikkollegien im 16. Jh.* Berlin, 1963.

Purcell, Henry

Arundell, Dennis. *Henry Purcell.* London, 1927.

Holland, A. K. *Henry Purcell.* London, 1932.

Quervain, Fritz de. *Der Chorstil Henry Purcells.* Bern and Leipzig, 1935.

Westrup, J. A. *Henry Purcell.* London, 1937.

Zimmerman, Franklin B. *The Anthems of Henry Purcell.* 1971.

Raphael, Günter

Mezger, Manfred. "Günter Raphaels Kirchenmusik." *Musik und Kirche* XXIII (1953), 150–53.

Riemer, Otto. "Prophetische Musik. Zur geistlichen Chormusik Günter Raphaels." *Musica* I (1947), 280–86.

———. "Ein Weg der Treue. Geistliche Chormusik von Günter Raphael." *Musik und Kirche* XIX (1949), 19–22.

Rapp, George

Wetzel, Richard Dean. "The Music of George Rapp's Harmony Society: 1805–1906." Ph.D. dissertation, University of Pittsburgh, 1970.

Raselius, Andreas

Roselius, Ludwig. "Introduction." *Denkmäler der Tonkunst in Bayern* XXIX–XXX (1931).

Read, Daniel

Lowens, Irving. "Daniel Read's World. The Letters of an Early American Composer." *Notes* IX (1952), 233–48.

Reger, Max

Hasse, Karl. "Max Reger und die deutsche Orgelkunst." *Bericht über die Freiburger Tagung für deutsche Orgelkunst . . . 1926*, 122–29. Augsburg, 1926.

Holle, Hugo. *Regers Chorwerke. Max Reger. Eine Sammlung von Studien aus dem Kreise seiner persönlichen Schüler.* Ed. by R. Würz. Munich, 1922.

Huesgen, Rudolf. *Der junge Max Reger und seine Orgelwerke.* Dissertation, Freiburg i. Br., 1932; published, Schramberg, 1935.

Kalkoff, Artur. *Das Orgelschaffen Max Regers im Lichte der deutschen Orgelerneuerungsbewegung.* Kassel and Basel, 1950.

Keller, Hermann. "Reger und die Orgel." *Max Reger. Eine Sammlung von Studien aus dem Kreise seiner persönlichen Schüler* IV. Ed. by R. Würz. Munich, 1923.

Rahner, Hugo Ernst. *Max Regers Choralfantasien für die Orgel. Eine Studie über Grundlagen und Werden des Regerschen Orgelstils.* Heidelberger Studien zur Musikwissenschaft. Ed. by H. Besseler. Kassel, 1936.

Schmidt, Hans. "Untersuchungen zur choralbezogenen Orgelmusik seit Max Reger." Dissertation, Erlangen, 1951.

Walter, Rudolf. "Max Regers Choralvorspiele." *Kirchenmusikalisches Jahrbuch* XL (1956), 127–38.

———. "Max Regers Choralvorspiele für Orgel." Dissertation, Mainz, 1949.

———. "Max Regers Choralvorspiele op. 67 und 79b in ihrem Verhältnis zu J. S. Bach und den vorbachschen Meistern." *Kirchenmusikalisches Jahrbuch* XXXVII (1953), 103–14.

Reichardt, Johann Friedrich

Kahl, Willi. "Johann Friedrich Reichardt und die Idee der 'wahren Kirchenmusik.' " *COV Zeitschrift für Kirchenmusik* LXXI (1951), 64–67.

Salmen, Walter. *Johann Friedrich Reichardt.* Freiburg i. Br. and Zurich, 1963.

Schletterer, Hans Michael. *Johann Friedrich Reichardt. Sein Leben und seine musikalische Tätigkeit.* Augsburg, 1865.

Schünemann, Georg. "Reichardts Briefwechsel mit Herder." In the *Max Schneider Festschrift.* Halle, 1935.

Reincken, Johann Adam

Riedel, Friedrich Wilhelm. *Quellenkundliche Beiträge zur Geschichte der Musik für Tasteninstrumente.* Kassel, 1960.
Stahl, Wilhelm. "Zur Biographie Johann Adam Reinckens." *Archiv für Musikwissenschaft* III (1920–21), 232 ff.

Rinck, Christian Heinrich

Donat, Friedrich-Wilhelm. "Christian Heinrich Rinck und die Orgelmusik seiner Zeit." Dissertation, Heidelberg, 1931.

Rist, Johann

Krabbe, Wilhelm. "Johann Rist." Dissertation, Berlin, 1910.
Lueken, W. "Johann Rist." *Handbuch zum ev. Kirchengesangbuch* II/1. Göttingen, 1957.
Schulz, Walther. "Studien über das deutsche protestantische monodische Kirchenlied." Dissertation, Breslau, 1934.

Ritter, August Gottfried

Schmidt, Peter. "August Gottfried Ritters Erfurter Jahre." *Musikforschung* XIII (1960), 427–40.

Ritter, Christian

Buchmayer, Richard. "Christian Ritter." In the *H. Riemann Festschrift,* 354 ff. Leipzig, 1909.
Norlind, Tobias. "Zur Biographie Christian Ritters." *Sammelbände der Internationalen Musikgesellschaft* XII (1910–11), 94 ff.
Serauky, Walter. *Musikgeschichte der Stadt Halle* II/1. Halle, 1939.

Rolle, Johann Heinrich

Kaestner, Rudolf. *Johann Heinrich Rolle. Untersuchungen zu Leben und Werk.* Kassel, 1932.
Valentin, Erich. "Johann Heinrich Rolle. Ein mitteldeutscher Musiker des 18. Jahrhunderts." *Jahrbuch der Historischen Kommissionen für die Provinz Sachsen und für Anhalt* IX (1933), 109–60.

Roman, Johan Helmich

Bengtsson, Ingmar. "Roman." *MGG* XI (1963), 770 ff.
Vretblad, P. *Johan Helmich Roman 1694–1758.* Svenska musikens fader, I–II. Stockholm, 1914.

Romberg, Andreas

Stephenson, Kurt. *Andreas Romberg. Ein Beitrag zur hamburgischen Musikgeschichte.* Veröffentlichungen des Vereins für Hamburgische Geschichte, XI. Hamburg, 1938.

Römhild, Theodor

Paulke, Karl. "Johann Theodor Römhild." *Archiv für Musikwissenschaft* I (1918–19), 1956.

Römhild, Hans. "Die Matthäuspassion von Johann Theodor Römhild." *Musikforschung* IX (1956).

Root, George F.

Root, George F. *The Story of a Musical Life*. Cincinnati, 1891.

Rosenmüller, Johann

Hamel, Fred. "Form- und Stilprinzipien in der Vokalmusik Johann Rosenmüllers." Dissertation, Giessen, 1930.

_____. *Die Psalmkompositionen Johann Rosenmüllers*. Strasbourg and Zurich, 1933.

Horneffer, August. "Johann Rosenmüller." Dissertation, Berlin, 1898.

Schering, Arnold. *Musikgeschichte Leipzigs* II. Leipzig, 1936.

Rubert, Martin

Engel, Hans. "Gemeinschaftsmusik in Stralsund." *Musik in Pommern* IV (1936), 209 ff.

Krüger, Liselotte. *Die Hamburgische Musikorganisation im 17. Jahrhundert*. Dissertation, Heidelberg, 1930; published, Strasbourg, 1933.

Müller, Willibert. "Musikgeschichte Stralsunds bis zum Jahre 1650." Dissertation, Freiburg, 1924.

_____. "Stralsunds literarisch-musikalische Reformarbeit." *Baltische Studien* XXX/1 (1928).

Rung, Henrik

Thrane, Carl. *Caeciliaforeningen og dens stifter*. Copenhagen, 1901.

Rust, Friedrich Wilhelm

Czach, Rudolf. "Friedrich Wilhelm Rust." Dissertation, Berlin, 1927.

Sailer, Leonhard

Schanzlin, Hans Peter. "Die Cantiones sacrae von Leonhard Sailer." *Musik und Gottesdienst* IX, 109 ff.

Savage, William

Farmer, H. G. "A Forgotten Composer of Anthems. William Savage (1720–89)." *Music and Letters* XVII (1936), 188.

Scandello, Antonio

Gurlitt, Wilibald. "Johann Walther und die Musik der Reformationszeit." *Luther-Jahrbuch* (1933).

Kade, Otto. "Archivalische Studien über Antonius Scandellus." *Monatshefte für Musikgeschichte* IX (1877).

Kade, Reinhard. "Antonius Scandellus." *Sammelbände der Internationalen Musikgesellschaft* XV (1913–14).

Schadaeus, Abraham

Riemer, Otto. *Erhard Bodenschatz*. Dissertation, Halle, 1927; published, Leipzig, 1928.

Schaffner, Caspar

Kieffer, Elizabeth C. "Three Caspar Schaffners." *Papers of the Lancaster County Historical Society* XLII (1938), 181–200.

Scheibe, Johann Adolph

Eggebrecht, Hans Heinrich. "Scheibe gegen Bach—im Notenbeispiel." *Das Musikleben* V (1952), 106–08.

Scheidemann, David and Heinrich

Breig, Werner. "Die Orgelwerke von Heinrich Scheidemann." Dissertation, Erlangen, 1962.
_____. "Der Umfang des choralgebundenen Orgelwerks von J. P. Sweelinck." *Archiv für Musikwissenschaft* XVII (1960), 258 ff.
Reimann, Margarete. "Pasticcios und Parodien." *Musikforschung* VIII (1955), 265 ff.

Scheidt, Samuel and Gottfried

Adrio, Adam. "Zu Samuel Scheidts Vokalmusik." *Musik und Kirche* XXIV (1954).
Gessner, E. "Samuel Scheidts geistliche Konzerte." Dissertation, Berlin, 1961.
Mahrenholz, Christhard. "Aufgabe und Bedeutung der Tabulatura nova." *Musica* VIII (1954), 88 ff.
_____. "Der 3. Band von Samuel Scheidts Tabulatura nova." *Musikforschung* I (1948), 32 ff.
_____. *Samuel Scheidt.* Leipzig, 1924.
_____. "Samuel Scheidt und die Orgel." *Musik und Kirche* XXV (1955), 38 ff.
Serauky, Walter. *Musikgeschichte der Stadt Halle* II/1. Halle, 1939.
_____. *Samuel Scheidt in Seinen Briefen.* Halle, 1937.
Werner, Arno. "Samuel und Gottfried Scheidt." *Sammelbände der Internationalen Musikgesellschaft* I (1899–1900), 401 ff., and XIII (1911–12), 297 ff.

Schein, J. Hermann

Gurlitt, Wilibald. "Ein Autorenprivileg für J. H. Schein." In the *K. G. Fellerer Festschrift,* 200–04. Regensburg, 1962.
Hueck, Irmgard. "Die künstlerische Entwicklung J. H. Scheins." Dissertation, Freiburg, 1943.
Prüfer, Arthur. *Johann Hermann Schein.* Leipzig, 1895.
_____. "Scheins Cymbalum Sionium." In the *R. von Liliencron Festschrift.* Leipzig, 1910.
Reckziegel, W. "Das Kantional von J. H. Schein." Dissertation, Berlin, 1963.

Schelle, Johann

Graupner, Friedrich. "Das Werk des Thomaskantors Johann Schelle." Dissertation, Berlin, 1929.
Schering, Arnold. "Introduction." *Denkmäler Deutscher Tonkunst* LVIII–LIX (1918).
_____. *Musikgeschichte Leipzigs* II. Leipzig, 1936.
_____. "Über die Kirchenkantaten vorbachischer Thomaskantoren." *Bach-Jahrbuch* IX (1912), 86 ff.

Schildt, Melchior

Schierning, Lydia. *Die Überlieferung der deutschen Orgel- und Klaviermusik.* Kassel, 1961.
Werner, Theodor Wilhelm. "Archivalische Nachrichten . . . Familie Schildt." In the *Th. Kroyer Festschrift,* 130 ff. Regensburg, 1933.
_____. "Melchior Schildts Testament." *Archiv für Musikforschung* II (1937), 77 ff.

————. "Melchior Schildt und seine Familie." *Archiv für Musikwissenschaft* II (1919–20), 356 ff.

Schop, Johann

Krüger, Liselotte. *Die Hamburgische Musikorganisation im 17. Jahrhundert.* Strasbourg, 1933.

Stephenson, Kurt. "Johannes Schop." Dissertation, Halle, 1924.

Schröter, Leonhart

Hofmann, Gertrud. "Die freien Kompositionen Leonhart Schröters." *Zeitschrift für Musikwissenschaft* XVI (1934), 344–51.

————. "Leonhart Schröter." Dissertation, Freiburg, 1932.

Schütz, Heinrich

Birtner, Herbert. "Heinrich Schütz im Schrifttum der neueren Zeit." *Deutsche Musikkultur* I (1936–37), 51–56, 116–21.

Bittinger, W., ed. *Schütz-Werke-Verzeichnis.* Kassel, 1960.

Blume, Friedrich. "Heinrich Schütz in den geistigen Strömungen seiner Zeit." *Musik und Kirche* II (1930), 245–54.

Gurlitt, Wilibald. *Heinrich Schütz.* Die grossen Deutschen, V. 2nd ed. 1957.

Moser, Hans Joachim. "Fortschritte der Schützkenntnis in den letzten zwanzig Jahren." In the *Festschrift in honor of H. Schütz,* 83 ff. Weimar, 1954.

————. *H. Schütz.* 2nd ed. Kassel, 1954.

————. "Heinrich Schütz, Lehrer, Prediger und Prophet." *Bekenntnis zu Schütz.* Kassel, 1954; also printed in *Musik in Zeit und Raum,* Berlin, 1960.

————. "Neues über H. Schütz." *Acta Musicologica* VII (1935), 146–52.

————. "Schütz und das evangelische Kirchenlied." *Jahrbuch der Staatl. Akademie für Kirchen- und Schulmusik* III (1929–30); also printed in *Musik in Zeit und Raum,* Berlin, 1960.

————. "Zwischen Schütz und Bach." *Wissenschaftl. Zeitschrift der Universität Leipzig* IV (1954–55); also printed in *Musik in Zeit und Raum,* Berlin, 1960.

Müller von Asow, Erich Hermann. *Heinrich Schütz. Gesammelte Briefe und Schriften.* Regensburg, 1931.

Schuh, Willi. "Das neuere Schütz-Schrifttum." *Das musikal. Schrifttum.* Kassel, 1929.

Schrade, Leo. *Das musikalische Werk von Heinrich Schütz in der protestantischen Liturgie.* Basel, 1961.

Smend, Julius. "Heinrich Schütz und die ev. Gemeinde." *Vorträge und Aufsätze zur Liturgik.* Gütersloh, 1925.

Spitta, Philipp. "Heinrich Schütz' Leben und Werke." *Musikgesch. Aufsätze,* 3–60. Berlin, 1894.

Schweitzer, Albert

Quoika, Rudolf. *Albert Schweitzers Begegnung mit der Orgel.* Berlin and Darmstadt, 1954.

Schwemmer, Heinrich

Samuel, H. E. "The Cantata in Nuremberg during the 17th Century." Dissertation, Cornell University, 1958.

Seiffert, Max. "Introduction." *Denkmäler der Tonkunst in Bayern* VI/1 (1905).

Schwenkfelder, family

Kriebel, Howard W. *The Schwenkfelders in Pennsylvania.* Lancaster, 1904.

Selle, Thomas

Birke, Joachim. "Die Passionsmusiken von Thomas Selle." Dissertation, Hamburg, 1957.
Günther, Siegfried. "Die geistliche Konzertmusik von Thomas Selle." Dissertation, Giessen, 1935.
Krüger, Liselotte. *Die Hamburgische Musikorganisation im 17. Jahrhundert.* Strasbourg, 1933.

Sermisy, Claudin de

Fornaçon, Siegfried. "Claudin de Sermisy." *Musik und Gottesdienst* IX (1954), 4 ff.

Shaw, Martin

Dunlop, Colin. "Martin Shaw." *English Church Music* XXI (1959), 12.

Shaw, Oliver

Thompson, J. William. "Oliver Shaw, 1779–1848: Forgotten Master." *The Hymn* XI/3 (July, 1960).
Williams, Thomas. *A Discourse on the Life and Death of Oliver Shaw.* Boston, 1851.

Siefert, Paul

Feicht, Hieronim. "Musikalische Beziehungen. . . ." *Festschrift der Akademie,* 121 ff. Graz, 1963.
Rauschning, Hermann. *Musikgeschichte Danzigs.* Danzig, 1931.
Riedel, Friedrich Wilhelm. *Quellenkundliche Beiträge zur Geschichte der Musik für Tasteninstrumente.* Kassel, 1960.
Schierning, Lydia. *Die Überlieferung der deutschen Orgel- und Klaviermusik.* Kassel, 1961.
Seiffert, Max. "Paul Siefert." *Vierteljahrsschrift für Musikwissenschaft* VII (1891), 397 ff.

Smith, William

Buttrey, John. "William Smith of Durham." *Music and Letters* XLIII (1962), 248.

Sowerby, Leo

Hinds, Wayne B. "Leo Sowerby, A Biography and Descriptive Listing of Anthems." Ed.D. dissertation, George Peabody College for Teachers, 1972.
Tuthill, Burnet C. "Leo Sowerby." *Musical Quarterly* XXIV (1938).

Speuy, Hendrick

Curtis, Alan. "Hendrick Speuy and the Earliest Printed Dutch Keyboard Music." *Tijdschrift van de Vereniging voor Nederlandsche Muziekgeschiedenis* XIX (1963), 143 ff.

Staden, Johann and Sigmund Gottlieb

Druener, Hans. "Sigmund Theophil Staden." Dissertation, Bonn, 1946.
Kahl, Willi. "Das Nürnberger historische Konzert." *Archiv für Musikwissenschaft* XIV (1957), 281 ff.
Schmitz, Eugen. "Introduction." *Denkmäler der Tonkunst in Bayern* VII (1906), and VIII (1907).

Stanford, Charles Villiers

"Charles Villiers Stanford (by some of his pupils)." *Music and Letters* V (1924), 193–207.
Fuller-Maitland, J. A. *The Music of Parry and Stanford.* Cambridge, 1934.
Greene, Harry Plunket. *Charles Villiers Stanford.* London, 1935.

Steigleder, Ulrich

Emsheimer, Ernst. *Johann Ulrich Steigleder.* Dissertation, Freiburg, 1927; published, Kassel, 1928.
Hirtler, Franz. "Neuaufgefundene Orgelstücke von Ulrich Steigleder." *Archiv für Musikforschung* II (1937).

Steuerlein, Johann

Kraft, Günther. "Johann Steuerlein." *Zeitschrift für Musikwissenschaft* XIII (1931), 425 ff.
————. *Johann Steuerlein.* Die thüringische Musikkultur, II. Jena, 1939.

Stobaeus, Johann

Haase, Hans. "Eine wichtige Quelle für Johann Stobaeus." In the *F. Blume Festschrift,* 176 ff. Kassel, 1963.

Stoltzer, Thomas

Hampe, Karl-Ludwig. "Die deutschen Psalmen des Thomas Stoltzer." Dissertation, Posen, 1943.
Hoffmann-Erbrecht, Lothar. *Thomas Stoltzer.* Frankfurt, 1961.
————. "Thomas Stoltzers Octo tonorum melodiae." *Archiv für Musikwissenschaft* XIV (1957), 16 ff.

Stölzel, Johann Gottlieb

Fett, Armin. "Musikgeschichte der Stadt Gotha . . . bis zum Tode Gottfried Heinrich Stölzels." Dissertation, Freiburg, 1951.

Straube, Karl

Straube, Karl. *Briefe eines Thomaskantors.* Ed. by W. Gurlitt and H.-O. Hudemann. Stuttgart, 1952.

Strunck, Delphin and Nikolaus Adam

Berend, Fritz. "Nikolaus Adam Strunck." Dissertation, Munich, 1913.
Riedel, Friedrich Wilhelm. *Quellenkundliche Beiträge zur Geschichte der Musik für Tasteninstrumente.* Kassel, 1960.
Schierning, Lydia. *Die Überlieferung der deutschen Orgel- und Klaviermusik.* Kassel, 1961.

Sweelinck, Jan Pieterszoon

Breig, Werner. "Der Umfang des choralgebundenen Orgelwerks von J. P. Sweelinck." *Archiv für Musikwissenschaft* XVII (1960).
Gerdes, Gisela. "Die Choralvariationen J. P. Sweelincks und seiner Schüler." Dissertation, Freiburg, 1956.
Sigtenhorst Meyer, Bernhard van den. *Jan P. Sweelinck en zijn instrumentale muziek.* 2nd ed. The Hague, 1946.

Symmes, Thomas

A Particular Plain and Brief Memorative Account Of the Reverend Mr. Thomas Symmes. Boston, 1726.

Tag, Christian Gotthilf

Vieweg, Heinz Joachim. "Christian Gotthilf Tag (1735 bis 1811) als Meister der nach-bachischen Kantate." Dissertation, Leipzig, 1933.

Tallis, Thomas

Doe, Paul. *Tallis.* London, 1969.

Ellinwood, Leonard. "Tallis's Tunes and Tudor Psalmody." *Musica Disciplina* III–IV (1948), 189.

Tanneberger, David

Beck, Paul E. "David Tanneberger, Organ Builder." *Papers Read Before the Lancaster County Historical Society* XXX (1926).

Telemann, Georg Philipp

Hörner, Hans. "Georg Philipp Telemanns Passionsmusiken." Dissertation, Kiel, 1933.

Meissner, Richard. *Georg Philipp Telemanns Frankfurter Kirchenkantaten.* Dissertation, Frankfurt, 1925; published, Frankfurt, 1929.

Menke, Werner. *Das Vokalwerk Georg Philipp Telemanns.* Dissertation, Erlangen, 1941; published, Kassel, 1942.

Rhea, Cl. H. "The Sacred Oratorios of G. Ph. Telemann." 2 vols. Dissertation, Florida State University, 1958.

Ruhnke, M. "Telemann im Schatten Bachs?" In *H. Albrecht in memoriam,* 134 ff. Kassel, 1962.

Schneider, Max. "Introduction." *Denkmäler Deutscher Tonkunst* XXVIII (1907).

Valentin, Erich. *Georg Philipp Telemann.* Burg, 1931; reprint, Kassel, 1952.

Tersteegen, Gerhard

Tersteegen, Gerhard. *Eine Auswahl aus seinen Schriften.* Ed. by W. Nigg. Basel, 1948.

Theile, Johann

Mackey, E. J. "The Sacred Works of J. Theile." Ph.D. dissertation, University of Michigan, 1968.

Maxton, Willi. "Johann Theile." Dissertation, Tübingen, 1926.

————. "Verzeichnis der erhaltenen Werke des Johann Theile." In the *Festschrift in honor of H. Schütz,* 89 ff. Weimar, 1954.

Schild, Emilie. *Geschichte der protestantischen Messenkomposition im 17. und 18. Jahrhundert.* Wuppertal-Elberfeld, 1934.

Zelle, Friedrich. *Johann Theile und Nikolaus Adam Strunck.* Berlin, 1891.

Thomas, Kurt

Stein, Fritz. "Kurt Thomas." *Zeitschrift für Musik* (1931).

Tomkins, Thomas

Buck, P. C., *et al.* "Thomas Tomkins." *Tudor Church Music* VIII, xi. London, 1928.

Gill, Louis A. "The Anthems of Thomas Tomkins. An Introduction." *Musica Disciplina* XI (1957), 153.

Rose, Bernard. "Thomas Tomkins." *Proceedings of the Royal Musical Association* LXXXII (1955–56).

Stevens, Denis. *Thomas Tomkins.* London, 1957.

Tufts, John

Lowens, Irving. "John Tufts' *Introduction to the Singing of Psalm-Tunes* (1721–1744). The First American Music Textbook." *Journal of Research in Music Education* II (1954), 89–102.

——. "A Plain Introduction to Singing Psalm-Tunes." In the facsimile of John Tufts' *An Introduction to the Singing of Psalm-Tunes.* 5th ed. Philadelphia, 1954.

Poladian, Sirvart. "Rev. John Tufts and Three-part Psalmody in America." *Journal of the American Musicological Society* IV (1951), 276–77.

Tunder, Franz

Hennings, J. "Neues über Franz Tunder und Dietrich Buxtehude." *Deutsche Musikkultur* VI (1942), 157 ff.

Riedel, Friedrich Wilhelm. *Quellenkundliche Beiträge zur Geschichte der Musik für Tasteninstrumente.* Kassel, 1960.

Schierning, Lydia. *Die Überlieferung der deutschen Orgel- und Klaviermusik.* Kassel, 1961.

Stahl, Wilhelm. "Franz Tunder und Dietrich Buxtehude." *Archiv für Musikwissenschaft* VIII (1926), 1 ff.

——. *Musikgeschichte Lübecks* II. Kassel, 1952.

Türk, Daniel Gottlob

Hedler, Gretchen Emilie. "Daniel Gottlob Türk (1750 bis 1813)." Dissertation, Leipzig, 1936.

Serauky, Walter. "Daniel Gottlob Türk. Sein Weg vom Kantatenschöpfer zum Begründer einer Händeltradition." *Daniel Gottlob Türk, der Begründer der Hallischen Händeltradition.* Schriftenreihe des Händelhauses in Halle, IV. Wolfenbüttel and Berlin, 1938.

Tye, Christopher

Langdon, John. "Tye and his church music." *Musical Times* CXIII (1972), 1011.

Vaughan, James D.

Fleming, Jo Lee. "James D. Vaughan, Music Publisher, Lawrenceburg, Tennessee, 1912–1964." S.M.D. dissertation, Union Theological Seminary, 1972.

Vierdanck, Johann

Müller, Willibert. "Musikgeschichte Stralsunds." Dissertation, Freiburg, 1953.

Weiss, Gerhard. "Johann Vierdanck." Dissertation, Marburg, 1956.

Vierling, Johann Gottfried

Paulke, Karl. "Johann Gottfried Vierling (1750–1813)." *Archiv für Musikwissenschaft* IV (1922), 439–55.

Vulpius, Melchior

Eggebrecht, Hans Heinrich. "Die Kirchenweisen von Melchior Vulpius." *Musik und Kirche* XXIII (1953), 52 ff.

_____. "Die Matthäuspassion von Melchior Vulpius." *Musikforschung* III (1950), 143 ff.

_____. "Melchior Vulpius." Dissertation, Jena, 1949.

_____. "Melchior Vulpius." In the *M. Schneider Festschrift.* Leipzig, 1955.

_____. "Melchior Vulpius." *Musik und Kirche* XX (1950), 158 ff.

Waelrant, Hubert

Becker, Georges. *Hubert Waelrant et ses Pseaumes. Notice biographique et bibliographique publiée avec la musique de deux chansons.* Paris, 1881.

Walmisley, Thomas Attwood

Shaw, Watkins. "Thomas Attwood Walmisley." *English Church Music* XVI, 2 ff.

Walter, Johannes

Gurlitt, Wilibald. "Johannes Walter und die Musik der Reformationszeit." *Luther-Jahrbuch* XV (1933).

Walter, Thomas

Jones, Matt B. *Bibliographical Notes on Thomas Walter's "Grounds and Rules of Musick Explained."* Worcester, Mass., 1933.

Walther, Johann Gottfried

Brodde, Otto. *Johann Gottfried Walther.* Dissertation, Münster, 1935; published, Kassel, 1937.

Jauernig, Reinhold. "J. S. Bach in Weimar." *J. S. Bach in Thüringen,* 49 ff., and especially 78 ff. Weimar, 1950.

Jerger, Wilhelm Franz. "Ein unbekannter Brief Johann Gottfried Walthers an Heinrich Bokemeyer." *Musikforschung* VII (1954), 205 ff.

Schünemann, Georg. "Johann Gottfried Walther und Heinrich Bokemeyer." *Bach-Jahrbuch* (1933).

Seiffert, Max. "Introduction." *Denkmäler Deutscher Tonkunst* XXVI–XXVII (1906).

Senn, Kurt Wolfgang. "Über die musikalischen Beziehungen zwischen J. G. Walther und J. S. Bach." *Musik und Kirche* XXXIV (1964), 8 ff.

Wecker, Kaspar

Samuel, H. E. "The Cantata in Nuremberg during the 17th Century." Dissertation, Cornell University, 1958.

Seiffert, Max. "Introduction." *Denkmäler der Tonkunst in Bayern* VI/1 (1905).

Weckmann, Matthias

Ilgner, Gerhard. *Matthias Weckmann.* Dissertation, Kiel, 1939; published, Wolfenbüttel, 1939.

Riedel, Friedrich Wilhelm. *Quellenkundliche Beiträge zur Geschichte der Musik für Tasteninstrumente.* Kassel, 1960.

Schierning, Lydia. *Die Überlieferung der deutschen Klavier- und Orgelmusik.* Kassel, 1961.

Seiffert, Max. "Matthias Weckmann und das Collegium Musicum in Hamburg." *Sammelbände der Internationalen Musikgesellschaft* II (1900).

Weelkes, Thomas

Brown, David. "The Anthems of Thomas Weelkes." *Proceedings of the Royal Musical Association* XVI (1964–65), 61.

Weisse, Michael

Fornaçon, Siegfried. "Michael Weisse." *Jahrbuch für Schlesische Kirche und Kirchengeschichte,* new series XXXIII (1954), 35 ff.
Lehmann, Emil. *Michael Weisse.* Landskron, 1922.

Wesley, Samuel Sebastian

Colles, H. C. "Samuel Sebastian Wesley." *Essays and Lectures,* 131 ff. London, 1945.
Routley, Erik. *The Musical Wesleys.* London, 1969.
Spink, Gerald W. "Samuel Sebastian Wesley." *Musical Times* LXXVIII (1937), 44, 149, 239, 345, 432, 536.

Weyse, C. E. F.

Berggreen, A. P. *C. E. F. Weyse's Biographie.* Copenhagen, 1876.

Williamson, John Finley

Wehr, David A. "John Finley Williamson (1887–1964): His Life and Contribution to Choral Music." Ph.D. dissertation, University of Miami, 1971.

Wise, Michael

Smith, Michael J. "The Church Music of Michael Wise." *Musical Times* CXIV (1973), 69.

Wolf, Ernst Wilhelm

Brockt, Johannes. "Ernst Wilhelm Wolf (Leben und Werke). Ein Beitrag zur Musikgeschichte des 18. Jahrhunderts." Dissertation, Breslau, 1927.

Wood, Charles

"Charles Wood" [obituary]. *Music and Letters* VII (1926), 393.

Woodbury, Isaac B.

Higginson, J. Vincent. "Isaac B. Woodbury (1819–1858)." *The Hymn* XX/3 (July, 1969).

Wyeth, John

Lowens, Irving. "John Wyeth's *Repository of Sacred Music, Part Second.* A Northern Precursor of Southern Folk Hymnody." *Journal of the Americal Musicological Society* V (1952).

Zachow, Friedrich Wilhelm

Seiffert, Max. "Introduction." *Denkmäler Deutscher Tonkunst* XXI–XXII (1905).
Thomas, Günter. *Friedrich Wilhelm Zachow.* Dissertation, Cologne, 1962; published, Regensburg, 1964.

Zangius, Nikolaus

Grimm, Heinrich. *Meister der Renaissancemusik an der Viadrina.* Frankfurt/Oder, 1941.

Zelter, Carl Friedrich

Schünemann, Georg. *Carl Friedrich Zelter, der Begründer der Preussischen Musikpflege.* Berlin, 1932.

Zinzendorf, Nikolaus Graf v.

Blank, Fritz. *Zinzendorf und die Einheit der Kinder Gottes.* Basel, 1950.
"Geistliche Singpraxis bei Zinzendorf." *Musik und Gottesdienst* IV (1950), 139 f.
Marx, Rudolf. *Zinzendorf und seine Lieder.* Leipzig, n.d.
Uttendörfer, O. *Zinzendorfs Gedanken über den Gottesdienst.* Herrnhut, 1931.

Zwart, Jan

Kreft, A. J. *Feike Asma u. z., Jan Zwart, 1877–1937. Een profeet op de orgelbank.* Kralingse Veer, 1957.

Zwingli, Huldrych

Cherbuliez, Antoine-Elisée. "Zwingli, Zwick und der Kirchengesang." *Zwingliana* IV (1926), 353 ff.

Index